1945

By the same author

The Imperfect Peasant Economy: The Loire Country 1800–1914

At the Heart of a Tiger: Clemenceau and His World 1841–1929

1815: The Roads to Waterloo

1918: War and Peace

1945

The War That Never Ended

GREGOR DALLAS

Yale University Press
New Haven and London

First published in the United States in 2005 by Yale University Press.
First published in Great Britain in 2005 by John Murray (Publishers).

Thanks are given to the following for permission to reproduce copyrighted material: extracts
from Field Marshal Lord Alanbrooke, *War Diaries, 1939–1945* (Weidenfeld & Nicolson)
reproduced by permission of David Higham Associates Ltd; quotations from 'La Sauterelle'
from Robert Desnos, *Chantefables et Chantefleurs* © Editions Gründ, Paris; quotations from
'A Legend', 'You Who Wronged', 'Songs of Adrian Zeilinski' and 'Songs of the End of the
World' from Czesław Miłosz, *Collected Poems, 1931–2001* (Allen Lane, The Penguin Press,
2001). Copyright © Czesław Miłosz Royalties Inc., 1988, 1991, 1995, 2001.

Printed in the United States of America.

Library of Congress Control Number: 2005926051

ISBN-13: 978-0-300-10980-1 (cloth : alk. paper)
ISBN-10: 0-300-10980-6 (cloth : alk. paper)

A catalogue record for this book is available from the British Library.

The paper in this book meets the guidelines for permanence and durability of the Committee
on Production Guidelines for Book Longevity of the Council
on Library Resources.

10 9 8 7 6 5 4 3 2 1

In memory of my friend, Bob White
US fighter pilot, Italy, 1943–5

Contents

𐓟

SEASONS

Paris and Warsaw in summer

London and Washington in autumn

Berlin and Moscow in winter

PEOPLE

People without cities

Endings

EUROPE, EUROPE

CONTENTS

Illustrations

ᕗ

ARMIES AND DIPLOMATS

1. A soldier carries a child through bombed Caen, Normandy
2. The Battle of Kursk, aerial view
3. The Battle of Kursk, ground view
4. British soldiers landing in Normandy
5. Americans snowbound in the Ardennes
6. An American parachutist prepares to jump
7. Building a pontoon bridge across the Rhine
8. The Quebec Conference, 1944
9. The Moscow Conference, 1944
10. The Yalta Conference, 1945
11. The Potsdam Conference, 1945
12. De Gaulle and Churchill
13. Hitler and Goebbels

CITIES

14. The Liberation of Paris: snipers fire on Parisians
15. The Place de l'Opéra just before Liberation
16. After the Liberation: a French citizen carries away a German signpost
17. VE-Day in Paris, 1945
18. The 'Liberation' of Warsaw: the ruined city under snow
19. The 'Liberation' of Warsaw: an abandoned monastery
20. Paddington Station, London: the evacuation of mothers and children, 1944
21. A V-2 bombing at Farringdon, March 1945
22. VE-Day, Piccadilly, London, 8 May 1945
23. Bonfire on VE-Day, Croydon, south London
24. Wartime Washington: 'tempos' beside Memorial Pond, the Mall
25. US fast-food stall
26. Berlin: concertgoers return home through rubble and snow
27. Moscow: VE-Day, 9 May 1945

PEOPLE

28. A Russian soldier seizes a bicycle from a German woman, Berlin
29. German prisoners of war marched eastwards, through the centre of Moscow
30. German prisoners of war assaulted by French civilians near Caen
31. German prisoners of war marched westwards along an autobahn near Frankfurt
32. German prisoners of war marched through an English street
33. The German surrender to Montgomery, Lüneburg Heath
34. A soldier returns home to Frankfurt
35. German civilians search a bombed factory for fuel
36. Handout of potatoes in Berlin, summer 1945
37. Teenagers consult message boards for missing persons, Normandy, July 1944
38. British Nissen huts for the homeless, Berlin, summer 1946
39. An overcrowded train with refugees, post-war Germany
40. A German boy finds a mouldy loaf of bread in a rubbish dump, autumn 1945

The author and publisher would like to thank the following for permission to reproduce illustrations: Plates 1, 7, 8 and 33, © Bettman/CORBIS; 2, 3, 27 and 29, Novosti (London); 4, 12 and 37, Rex Features/Roger-Viollet; 5, Vaccaro; 6, © Robert Capa R/Magnum Photos; 9, 14, 28, 30, 31, 34 and 36, akg-images, London; 10 and 35, Associated Press; 11 and 26, Bildarchiv Preußischer Kulturbesitz; 13, Ullstein Bild; 15, 16, 17, 18 and 19, BDIC, Paris; 20, 21, 22, 23 and 32, Hulton Archive; 24, US National Archives, photo BDIC, Paris; 25, Time Life/Getty Images; 38, © Hulton-Deutsch Collection/CORBIS; 39, SV-Bilderdienst; 40, Illustrated London News Picture Library.

Every effort has been made to clear permissions. If permission has not been granted please contact the publisher who will include a credit in subsequent printings and editions.

Preface

꙰

The first vague awareness I had of a thing called the 'Second World War' must have been on the day I was born, in July 1948. A post-war polio epidemic was then at its height in London and that was the day I got it; the result is I have two partially paralysed legs. I often jokingly referred to myself as the 'last of the war disabled'. But even as an infant I knew it was not the case. London's hospitals in the late 1940s and early '50s were crammed with children born after the war with diseases directly arising from the war. The artisan who made my orthopaedic boots was a Viennese Jew who had come to London because of a Nazi mass murder programme (I knew about that before I was two); he was a quiet-spoken, cultivated man with manual talents you would never find today; heaven knows what he had been through. Many of the hospital personnel had strange, unpronounceable names; they were also 'Displaced Persons' – the lucky ones – of this 'Second World War'. My frequent trips to and from hospital took me across devastated wastelands in the heart of what my Edwardian parents proudly called 'the greatest city in the world'; I can remember very clearly the rough grasslands of Battersea and the gaping holes of destruction in the City. There was the sight of the poor, plenty of poor in the streets, which astonished a boy up from privileged rural Sussex. War rationing of essentials was at its height in 1948 (not 1945) and ended in England only in 1954.

Poverty, disease, rationing, refugee camps – these, much more than my legs, served as reminders that the Second World War was 'the war that never ended'. Perhaps all books are basically autobiographical: it is interesting to note how historians build up subjects, sometimes obsessively so, which are obviously by-products of some feature of their childhood or youth. Jules Michelet, the French historian, was born in the heartland of the French Revolution, eastern Paris, in 1799; interest in the past, he wrote, begins with a curiosity in what happened just before one's birth. Victor Hugo was born in 1802, the son of one of Napoleon's generals. 'Ce siècle avait deux ans' ('This century was two years old') began one of his most famous poems: Hugo could never stop looking at what happened before he was born. Walter Scott, the inventor of the historical novel, was not born in a year of particular note – 1772 – but in infancy he did catch polio, though the disease had not yet been given that name. He came from peaceful, civilized Edinburgh but became fascinated with the violence, which had ceased not so long before, in the neighbouring Scottish Highlands. In nearly every novel he wrote, the leading character, often an Englishman, crosses a frontier of time and of place: Scott put historical events in their physical setting, a detailed physical setting.

My own condition is probably what led me eventually, after exploring other fields of the past, to examine the moment wars have turned to peace, not just in England but right across Europe. What was it like in the different cities of Europe when the Napoleonic wars ended? I followed Lord Castlereagh, the British Foreign Secretary, in his carriage across Europe in the years 1814–15. How did the face of nineteenth-century civilization change at the instant the whole of Central Europe collapsed in the autumn of 1918? I took the route of the German plenipotentiaries from Berlin across the Western Front to a point near Paris, where they sued for peace in November that year; then I followed the process on through the diplomats in Paris, to the Armistice crowds of London, of Washington, the chaos and violence of a revolution in Berlin, then on to Moscow devastated by the Bolsheviks.

And naturally, and autobiographically, I came to ask: what actually happened to Europe in 1945?

In my books on peace there is always a hinge to the story, the moment the peace broke out. There is always a branching out from that moment and from that place. These last three books, combined, cover two and a half centuries of the history of Europe, with North America included. Yet I am by taste and by training a local historian; it is the detail that interests me – like those bomb craters in Battersea. But it is the fitting of the bits and pieces of real life and real places into the enormous puzzle that fascinates me. Peace is fragile. Undoubtedly, the noblest activity of man is the construction of peace; after all the barbarisms, a few brave people somehow manage to make us civilized again. It happened just before I was born.

I must admit that, despite my personal experience and commitment (indeed, in some deep psychological sense because of it), I was daunted at the prospect of writing a book about the Second World War, especially its ending. There was no formal peace settlement, no peace conference, no key treaties. The war legally only came to an end with a series of accords and treaties in 1990, culminating in the Conference on Security and Co-operation in Europe when thirty-two European countries, along with the United States and the disintegrating Soviet Union, signed in November of that year a declaration in Paris that they were 'no longer adversaries'. The press of the time proclaimed that the three-day summit 'interred the Cold War for ever'; but by formally recognizing a united Germany, its frontier with Poland on the Oder–Neisse line and drastically reducing conventional armaments right across Europe, this was also the finale of the Second World War, its 'peace conference'. The British Prime Minister, Margaret Thatcher, who wore black at the occasion, flew back to London and promptly lost her job. But at least she had the satisfaction of having concluded an accord that her predecessor, Winston Churchill, would have dearly loved to have signed, within the context of a general Peace Conference, in 1945. As it happened, within a year the Soviet Union ceased to exist and Europe – Western, Central and Eastern – sprang back into life.

But that was a long way off. Back in 1945, only the movement of huge industrial armies and the way they halted that May determined the shape of Europe at the close of the Second World War. The diplomacy, the politics, and a post-war culture, slowly emerged in the years that followed, but in a most unnatural environment.

Very few works have examined that transition from war to peace in a systematic manner – the majority of books available to date end abruptly with the defeat of the Nazis. Or there is that other kind of book which, after a superficial survey of the events of the war, plunges into 'The Origins of the Cold War'. Yet the two topics are inseparable. Though the transition of 1945 happened sixty years ago, it is still not truly history. Even in this year, 2004, lawyers are still flying from one national capital to another in an attempt to exact reparations from those responsible for the war crimes of 1939–45. Nobody, however, seems to be flying around seeking reparation for the mass crimes committed immediately afterwards – though millions were their victims. We Westerners have some difficulty telling the truth about the events that revolved around 1945; we have a vested interest in keeping this sensitive subject divided into separate lockers, with academically armed guardians standing over them. Each historian clings to his own autobiographical version. Each nation holds tight to its national myth.

Polemic is not my style. Yet every section, paragraph, every sentence even, written in this book can be developed into the subject of bitter current debate – that is not history, it is journalism, sometimes good but usually bad. There is barely a political party in Europe which does not owe its origin to the closing months of the Second World War. Though our Continent carries within it the history of millennia, the strongest national myths of today were created at the end of the war: the victors, the losers, the resisters, the collaborators, the heroes, the poltroons, the people who did nothing at all. Most of the myths are nonsense and very narrow-minded. An example: who during the sixtieth anniversary cele- brations of D-Day and the Liberation of Paris between June and August 2004 heard a word mentioned in our media that, during the same months, the city of Warsaw was being wiped off the map? There was only one national television service in Europe which covered the subject – the Polish. By late August, even the Olympic Games dominated them.

Paradoxically in 1945, while national myths were being created, the organization of Europe into nation states virtually collapsed. Tens of millions in Europe, like my talented cobbler on the corner of Baker Street, found they belonged to no nation state at all.

Daunting indeed the subject was. Whole towers of libraries are filled today with books on the Second World War, the Cold War, the Western Front, the Eastern Front; there are multi-volume works on major and minor politicians and generals; one specialist on the subject of 'German resistance to the Nazis' – not, one would have thought, the most import- ant phenomenon of the war – has said that no human being in a lifetime could read every work that has been written about it.

But I already had behind me works on the transition from war to peace in 1815 and 1918. And I had this childhood myth that I wanted to get out of me – the cause of all the books I had written to date. I had no choice: 1945 was the book I had to write.

I have organized the book along the same lines as my previous two studies. The style remains visual; the events are always placed in their geographic setting. I begin with a brief vertical descent from the sky, to the roofs, to the apartments, to the streets, and on to the underground life of Berlin on 30 April 1945, the day Hitler shot himself; the same day the Red Army took the Reichstag. These few pages are the pivot of the whole book. From there I open out horizontally to give a picture of the entire war, with the emphasis of course on how it ended. I have divided the book into three major sections: 'Armies', 'Seasons', 'People'. I conclude with a smaller section entitled, as in my previous two books, 'Europe, Europe', which carries the story on several decades, looking at it from different angles.

The movement of the armies, I have noted, was all-important because there was no political settlement at the end of the Second World War. It was the military movements of 1944–5 that determined life in Europe for the next two generations. Keep a particular eye on the weekend of 19–20

August 1944: everything happened then. It is one of those great unsung events of history. Army movements right across Europe were determined that weekend; there was a sea change in the relationship between the Allies. From a historical point of view, the weekend of 18–19 August was more important than D-Day: this was the moment that would determine the shape of post-war Europe.

The reader may also find it useful to take note of the contrast in European army movements since 1815. At the end of the Napoleonic wars, the Allies outmanoeuvred Napoleon as they moved down the funnelling, narrowing northern plain of Europe westwards into France; the westward movement of the Russians into Central Europe became a problem which nearly broke out into a separate war with the other Allies (or 'United Nations' as they called themselves) in October 1814 – Poland was sacrificed to Russia to avoid it. The First World War was unique in that the whole northern plain across France was turned into a single battle-line, a fortress, and the war became a European siege. Germany turned the Western Front into a war of movement in early 1918, but only by overextending her limited forces in useless offensives that merely spread out on the plain ('like the white of an egg,' said Clemenceau); in 1918 her backbone was broken when pushed up against the then impenetrable Ardennes of Belgium and she was forced to sue for peace. But the war did not end in 1918: the fragments of Germany's western armies marched eastwards: they were still fighting in Poland in 1920. Half of Europe, in fact, was still at war when the Peace Conference met in Paris in 1919. This significant fact is often forgotten. It could be argued that in Russia some form of civil war continued right through the inter-war years.

The Second World War contains parallels with the end of the Napoleonic wars in that there is a Russian front moving westwards again into Central Europe. But on this occasion the northern plain once again forms the front: the Russian front was the main front of the war. The major fact to watch is how the movements created civilian margins on either side of the armies, civilians drawn into the war and facing conflicting loyalties. From here were born the myths of collaboration and resistance. One of the principal questions the reader wants to ask is: were the Western and Eastern Fronts of 1944–5 really fighting as allies? That is where we have a continuing problem with the truth, even sixty years after the war's end. I myself am convinced that this is the reason why historians have kept the subject divided: quite simply, they don't want to know of the horrors that happened on the other side of Europe – it was the British and Americans who won the war, that is the history they write, and we'll leave the matter there: we're bored with Poland.

The second, longer section, 'Seasons', corresponds closely in style and conception to my previous books: history is given its place and time; the experience of the capital cities is described in detail, from the spring of 1944 to the cruel winter of 1944–5, by which time most Westerners had imagined that the war would be over – after all, didn't the First War end in autumn? The armies move into the background of the story; the civilians move to the fore.

The cities have been selected largely with the purpose of contrasting life on either side of the battlefronts. The obvious starting point is the contrast between the Liberation of Paris – which marked for many an illusionary end to the war – and the total destruction of Warsaw. Many of the post-war international institutions were formulated in the summer and autumn of 1944, in the United States, not Europe, at a time when a large part of the Continent was still occupied by the Nazis. This pre-peace institutional construction was again another new departure, and had a major impact on post-war relations within and beyond Europe. We shall contrast, here, life between London and Washington in a season when everyone expects the war to be soon over. Finally there is the disappointment of winter, as the armies return with a vengeance. The cities compared are Berlin and Moscow. In which of these cities was life more 'totalitarian'?

As one enters the winter of 1944–5 the war, in its final phase, turns more barbaric than ever, the armies more chaotic, and the life of civilians in several parts of Europe unbearable, unrecognizable. The direction of life is lost, the orientation of civilization has disappeared. The focus inevitably shifts from the traditional notion of cities – the centres of European civilization – to a new huge assembly of suffering people who belong to no cities, who have no hope, no notion where they are going. The 'end of the war' is no longer an issue. Because this is the most human aspect of war, its most disgusting, and most distant from peace and civilization, I have called this last part of the book 'People' – 'People without cities' and 'Endings', which for too many meant simply death. But it was out of this that the new Europe was born, the Europe that our press and politicians argue about so much today. It is at this moment that the concept of a Europe of nation states completely broke down. Were those nation states ever re-formed? It has to be admitted that Europe's 'nation states' after the war were never quite the same as they had been before: here is one of the central issues of 'Europe, Europe'. We enter, at this point, contemporary events where the story and the debates have yet to be concluded. But we must remember its tragic beginning, in the winter of 1944–5.

★

My thanks must go to many people without whom I would never have been able to finish this book. First of all is my gratitude to hundreds of researchers and authors I have never met, but whose work has made this attempt at a synthesis possible. Some of their work I have read late in the writing. I particularly regret not being able to acknowledge in my notes Norman Davies's *Rising '44: The Battle for Warsaw* (London: Macmillan, 2004); it supplants all other accounts of the event, but appeared when most of this book, particularly the sections on Poland, had been written. I thank my faithful agent Caroline Dawnay, who first introduced me to my editor at John Murray, Grant McIntyre, when I began work on the end of the First World War and who has not only guided me so ably through these last two books but also become a good friend in the process. His assistant, Caroline Westmore, has worked closely, kindly and industriously with me over every step of the production of my version of the Second World War – which I had promised, somewhat ambitiously, to research and write in two years; in fact it took me four. I am also grateful for the work undertaken by the new team at John Murray, notably Roland Philipps, Matt Richell and Sam Evans. Cecilia Mackay helped with illustrations. Douglas Matthews prepared the index. I must have driven Howard Davies, my copy-editor, to the limits of his patience with my long comments and answers. There is only one word to describe his detailed, sensitive work on the text: exquisite. Antony Wood has helped me transcribe Russian expressions, names and places in a systematic, consistent manner. Jean-Claude Famulicki, Curator of the Musée de l'Histoire Contemporaine at the Invalides in Paris, has been my guide on Poland. I have picked at his detailed knowledge of both the country and its history over many an hour. Nigel Jones in England has let me use him as a sounding board for several of my thoughts on the Second World War; long e-mails zip across the Channel, sometimes on a daily basis. We do not always agree but Nigel Jones is one of the most energetic and imaginative of the independent historians still around – unfortunately, an increasingly rare species today. His friendship flatters me. My magnificent wife, Christine, has given me total support through the writing of four major books now; they would certainly never have been completed without her; and she, like no one else, knows their cost.

I dedicate this book to the memory of Bob White, a long-time friend during the years I lived in Princeton, New Jersey. During the war he flew over sixty missions into enemy territory from Italy. 'If you want to know what it was like,' he told me, 'read Joseph Heller's *Catch Twenty-Two.*' Naturally I did, and I discovered Bob White in it. The stories Bob told were harrowing. I remember in particular the way he described the British pilots who often flew with him. 'My cockpit is on fire and I am now going down,' he would sometimes hear over his cockpit radio. One unforgettable evening that would mark my whole approach to history, Bob said he was not going to talk about war, but about the day peace broke out. The friends in his squadron had just entered Venice; the buildings were untouched by war, the people were smiling. To celebrate, he and his comrades drove north to the airport and, one by one, took off into the afternoon sun, then flew in formation down the east coast of Italy; there was no firing of guns, no flak, no sparks flying – just the quiet drone of the engines and the sight of the coast, the blue Apennines in the evening and, beyond them, all Europe preparing for its first night at peace. 'It was magic,' Bob said to me quietly. For a moment we looked at each other in silence; I had discovered the book I had to write.

The story I tell here is a tragic one, more tragic I think than the First World War, if that is imaginable. But what I referred to briefly at the beginning of this preface, the start of my own life in the post-war years, was not tragic. I always for some reason received a smile from those nurses and doctors with strange-sounding names, even from my cobbler. My father had the smile of God. From them all, it was always the same, intense, beautiful smile, and I have carried it with me through my life. Simply call it the post-war smile. Bob White, as he spoke, had the same kind of smile. In dedicating this book to him I hope to show in some impossible way that smile to millions, the tens of millions who in the Second World War suffered and died in Europe, and never had the chance to see it.

GD
Anet
Eure-et-Loir
2000–4

Maps

High ground
National frontiers

UNITED KINGDOM OF
GREAT BRITAIN
AND
NORTHERN
IRELAND

NORWAY

SWEDEN

Oslo

Sto

*North
Sea*

DENMARK

Copenhagen

Hamburg

Berlin

London

NETHERLANDS

BELGIUM

LUX

GERMANY

Prague

CZEC

Brest

WESTERN FRONT
JULY 1944

Paris

Munich

Vien

*Atlantic
Ocean*

FRENCH DEMARCATION LINE

SWITZER-
LAND

AUSTRIA
Klagenfurt

FRANCE

River Po

Trieste

Marseilles

Adriatic

SPAIN

ITALY

Madrid

CORSICA

Rome

SARDINIA

M e d i t e r r a n e a n

A F R I C A

MALT

EUROPE BEFORE THE SECOND WORLD WAR

FINLAND

Helsinki

Leningrad

ESTONIA

Riga

LATVIA

LITHUANIA

EAST RUSSIA

Minsk

EASTERN FRONT

LAND

Lvov

JULY 1944

AKIA

dapest

RY

ROMANIA

lgrade

Bucharest

VIA

BULGARIA

BANIA

GREECE

Salonica

Athens

EASTERN FRONT JUNE 1943

Moscow

UNION OF
SOVIET
SOCIALIST
REPUBLICS

Kursk

Kiev

Odessa

Sea of Azov

Black Sea

Istanbul

TURKEY

High ground
National frontiers
Western & Eastern
Fronts, 8 May 1945
Iron Curtain

NORWAY

SWEDEN

Oslo

Stoc

North

N.IRELAND

UNITED
KINGDOM

DENMARK

Copenhagen

IRELAND

Sea

Hamburg

Berlin

London

NETHERLANDS

BELGIUM

GERMANY

Prague

CZEC

Brest

Paris

Munich

AUSTRIA

Atlantic
Ocean

FRANCE

SWITZER-
LAND

Klagenfurt

Geneva

River Po

Trieste

Marseilles

Adriatic

SPAIN

ITALY

Madrid

CORSICA

Rome

SARDINIA

Mediterranean

AFRICA

MALT

EUROPE AFTER THE WAR

FINLAND

Helsinki

Leningrad

Riga

Minsk

ND

Warsaw

Kiev

Lvov

AKIA

dapest

RY

ROMANIA

grade

Bucharest

LAVIA

BULGARIA

Istanbul

ABANIA

Salonica

GREECE

Athens

Moscow

UNION OF SOVIET
SOCIALIST
REPUBLICS

Kursk

Sea
of
Azov

Black Sea

TURKEY

1945

One flag, one shot

Berlin, Monday, 30 April 1945

♈

Contrary to legend, a red flag was probably not flying from the roof of the Reichstag on the day Adolf Hitler shot himself. But the order had certainly been issued.

The old Bolshevik practice of 1917 – the bearing of red banners into battle – had only been revived two weeks earlier when the assault on Berlin was launched westwards from the River Oder. The Communist slogans, on the other hand, were by now a habit. They came straight from Stalin's mouth, repetitive, always hammering home the same curse-word, 'Fascist'. Men repeated them like lyrics of a well-known song: 'Under the blows of the Red Army the Fascist Bloc is shattered', 'the Hitler-Fascists are in retreat', 'the heroic efforts of the Red Army and the Soviet People have cleared our Land of the German Fascist Invaders', 'the end of Fascist Germany is at hand'.[1]

It was the banners and slogans that drove two and a half million exhausted soldiers into Berlin. Imagine, they were told, the red flag unfurling above the Reichstag. Imagine it swaying there, what's more, on the First of May, 1945 – the jubilee of the Revolution. Red flags were flown from the tanks, the slogans written on their sides: 'Moscow to Berlin', 'Fifty kilometres to the Den of the Fascist Beast'.

In his headquarters behind the Oder, Marshal Georgi Zhukov kept a large model of Berlin, with wooden miniatures of government buildings, bridges, railway stations, airports, all set in their precise locations. His principal objectives were flagged and numbered. The Ministry of Foreign Affairs, for example, was 108; the New Reich Chancellery was 106. His first objective was Number 105, the Reichstag.

'Who is going to be the first to reach the Reichstag?' he had asked his officers on the eve of the offensive. On 30 April, with the battle raging in central Berlin, still no one knew.[2]

Two days earlier, however, the order had gone down the line of V. I. Kutzetsov's Third Shock Army, which had been battering its way through the city's northern working-class districts, to Major General S. N. Perevertkin's 79th Rifle Corps: 'The Corps will assault the River

Spree, occupy the Reichstag, raise there the flag of victory and then unite with our troops proceeding from the south.'

That day Perevertkin had taken the district of Moabit; his forward troops were assembling in a customs yard that looked across the stone-built Moltke Bridge, strewn with barbed wire and other obstacles, swept by German machine-gun fire – and just five hundred yards from the Reichstag. 'This present order had for us a special meaning,' Perevertkin later wrote. 'We saw in it the end of this arduous and bloody war.'[3]

Hitler's Third Reich was by now reduced to ten square miles; it took on the form of a crudely crushed lemon, an ellipse some nine miles long and, in parts, not even a mile wide. It followed almost exactly the old east–west line – stretching from the Spandau fortress in the west to a bridge that lay at the far end of the Unter den Linden – around which the Prussian capital had been built. But not much was left now of 'the sandpit of the Holy Roman Empire', as the place had been rudely nick-named in the eighteenth century. Not much of it, either, resembled Marshal Zhukov's fabulous model. Many of the streets were unrecognizable. The armies followed the waterways, like Roman legions in a primeval forest; only this was First World War fighting, across trenches, barbed wire and rubble; yard by bloody yard. Country campaigning had entered a metrop-olis the size of Greater London.

The Moltke Bridge was taken in a bloody local battle, in rain, that lasted through the night of 28/29 April. Supporting Soviet artillery was brought under rocket attack from a German battery located on Potsdamer Platz. The heavy Soviet tanks sent in to push aside the southern barri-cade were shelled by heavy anti-aircraft guns at the top of the Zoo flak-tower in the Tiergarten; all that was left of the tanks was a high pile of metal wreckage blocking the whole bridge: Soviet infantry were sent in – led, according to Perevertkin, by 'Communists and Komsomols'. The Germans blew the bridge with mines; but the explosives proved insufficient for this massive stone structure: by early morning, the 29th, the Russians were fighting at the foot of Gestapo Headquarters, 'Himmler's House', on the north-western corner of Königsplatz. The Reichstag was on the other side of the square: three hundred yards away.[4]

Aerial reconnaissance had revealed the existence of a huge pit filled with water on the north side of Königsplatz. It had been dug a year earlier to divert the Spree as part of a grand architectural scheme for a new Berlin, fit for a Nazi world Reich. Now it was an anti-tank ditch. The cutting for a U-bahn tunnel was used to extend the defence across the middle of the square; this was also filled with water. The whole area was mined. The Reichstag's doors and windows had been bricked up, save the cellar windows which had been converted into virtually impervious gun embrasures. Machine-guns had been placed higher up in the building. Perevertkin's men would have to push south into the Kroll Opera House to stand any chance of taking the Reichstag. Fighting for this objective took another day. By the morning of the 30th the front line lay at the edge of the tank ditch: two hundred yards from the Reichstag.

Perevertkin had, the previous day, brought his headquarters up to 'Himmler's House'. Towering up before his eyes was 'the great grey building of the Reichstag'.

It was the image that obsessed all Russians. As the largest building in the city centre it represented for them the Kremlin of Berlin. But it represented nothing for the Nazis; it had been a burnt-out shell since February 1933, one month after they had seized power – Nazis were not interested in this parliamentary building. Today, the elite of the Nazi Party lived fifty feet underground, beneath the garden of the Old Chancellery, a further five hundred yards south of the Reichstag; the Russians were unaware of Hitler's Bunker.[5]

'Into the den of the Fascist Beast,' they proclaimed, adopting Stalin's slogan. Yet Russians, paradoxically, continued to gaze upwards.

'The flag, where is the flag? Do you see it?' asked Perevertkin desperately on the afternoon of the 30th. Russians were approaching the Reichstag from north, south, east and west. Perevertkin's 79th Rifle Corps was competing with Vasili Chuikov's Eighth Guards Army advancing into the Tiergarten that day; N. I. Berzarin's Fifth Shock Army was pushing up from the Belle-Allianz Platz, while a tank army – the Third Guards – was uncoiling terror up the Kurfürstendamm. Early in the afternoon two groups of fighter pilots flew in low and, at minimum speed, managed to drop several six-yard-wide red silk panels inscribed with the word '*Pobeda*' (or 'Victory') on the bent girders that were all that remained of the Reichstag's 'dome'. Perhaps that was why Zhukov reported in an order issued later in the day that 'Units of the Third Shock Army . . . having broken the resistance of the enemy, have captured the Reichstag and hoisted our Soviet Flag on it today, 30 April 1945, at 1425 hours.' The news was flashed to Moscow and around the world within instants. A few brave war correspondents and photographers crept in to the heart of the battle, but they saw no flag flying from the Reichstag.

Major General V. M. Shatilov, who commanded a front-line rifle division on Königsplatz, became demented: 'Somehow you have to hoist a flag or pennant, even on the columns at the main entrance. Somehow!' he yelled at his exhausted men.[6]

Three waves of assault were launched – Somme-like – across the open asphalt surface of the square; the first was repelled in a counter-attack by SS guards and a unit of German sailors who had been flown in from Rostock,[7] while the second was shattered under fire from the heavy artillery guns on the top of the Zoo flak-tower. In the meantime, Perevertkin was reinforcing himself at the former Gestapo headquarters with tanks, self-propelled guns, heavy artillery and rocket launchers, the dreaded 'Stalin organs': some 90 barrels in all. Amazingly, the grey granite of the nineteenth-century Reichstag stood impervious to all this. But it was enough to give the troops a foothold on the far side of the tank ditch.

At 6 p.m. a third assault was launched. The infantry were led by their regimental and battalion standards. The most important flag of them all was the 150th Rifle Division's 'Red Banner No. 5', with an extra-large hammer-and-sickle emblem, and escorted by hand-picked members of the Communist Party and Komsomols. Some of the soldiers managed to clamber up the front staircase of the Reichstag and, by firing two light mortars horizontally at point-blank range, blasted a small hole in the bricked-up wall of the main entrance; the fighting now spread gradually through the building – down corridors and up stairwells – in total darkness.

'Our corps' red banner journeyed slowly from one floor to another,' wrote Perevertkin. 'And as the sun began to sink, lighting up the horizon with its red rays, two of our soldiers hoisted the Flag of Victory over the burnt-out dome of the Reichstag.'[8]

The researches of the military historian, Tony Le Tissier, suggest this was not entirely true. The fighting in the Reichstag continued long after sunset. In the darkness the soldiers fanned out in every direction. At last, two sergeants of the special banner party, M. V. Yegorov and M. V. Kantaria, groped their way to the back of the building where they fell upon a stairway: it led up to the roof. There they found a statue, shoved their flag in a convenient hole, and retreated. It was 'seventy minutes before dawn',[9] and the start of the May Day celebrations in Moscow.

But Yegorov and Kantaria (conveniently for Stalin, a Russian and a Georgian) were not the first to plant a red flag on the roof. Captain V. N. Makov's gunners had attached their flag to the Goddess of Victory above the front of the building 'some two or three hours before the official party'. And a third party, Sergei E. Sorokin's reconnaissance platoon, are recorded as having put up a flag somewhere on the roof 'ten minutes later'.

So, considering the long April sunsets that occur in these northern latitudes, it is just possible, juggling with the hours, to imagine the last red rays of the sun, as it set below cloud on 30 April 1945, catching in outline a small red flag fluttering above the Reichstag.[10]

★

A cold westerly wind was blowing and the skies had been overcast most of the day.[11] Did anyone in Berlin notice?

An anonymous woman diarist queuing for water in a nearby south-eastern suburb remarked that the sky was 'hidden by a black wall of smoke'. The centre of the city seemed to be 'smoking and steaming'. Later in the day, surrounded by the howling of the Stalin organs, she caught a glance of a 'sky overcast with blood-red clouds'. 'Because the smoke and haze diffuses the light,' a war correspondent wrote, 'it looks as if the very clouds are on fire.' The sky, said another, was like a burning carpet being beaten above their heads. As a result of trenches, rubble and other obstacles in the streets the Russians in some quarters, like Alexanderplatz or the approaches to the Tiergarten, were having to blast their way through houses and walls. 'Split branches of trees, stone and dust whirl about,' wrote Paul David, employed at the Swedish embassy on the Reichstag battlefront of Königsplatz. 'The sky is no longer to be seen. It reeks of dynamite.' Night and day lost their distinction. A 'greyish-pink glow', was the way the anonymous diarist had described the sky that morning.[12]

The artillery and rockets scribbled fiery traces in the glimmer of cloud. It was on the morning of the 30th that Chuikov's Eighth Guards Army began its final assault on the Landwehr Canal and the Tiergarten. He had brought up heavy artillery and rows of Stalin organs to the very banks of the canal; from the heights of Viktoria Park he fired 250-mm mortars straight into the Anhalt railway station, hardly a mile away. The Germans responded with their own heavy mortars that they had lined up along the length of the Unter den Linden. The anti-aircraft guns on the Zoo tower were lowered to roof level. 'Artillery shells sped over us in a high curve,' wrote the anonymous diarist.[13] Rockets, yowling and screeching, threaded their way in batches through the sky's low vapours, leaving long white trails behind them; they sounded, said one witness, like huge blocks of steel grinding together;[14] they gave off a smell of petrol.

All sense of time vanished. The few diarists who recorded these events, in cellars or in the shambles of their apartments, often got their dates wrong. 'I figure that that day was Sunday. But Sunday is such a civilian word, meaningless at the moment.' How much longer could it last? Where was the front? When would peace be made? 'In the week-long debates that we used to have in January, February and March,' wrote the journalist Margret Boveri, now in a kind of 'no man's land' to the west of the Tiergarten, 'we were even then asking: how long will it last? Several then thought that the workers, whether Communist or not, would rise up and bring things to an end within three days.' 'I suddenly realize how degraded we are, deprived of all rights – prey, dirt,' recorded the anonymous diarist.

'Anxious questions: Where is the front? When will peace be made?' 'We are wading in filth, deep filth. Each minute of life has to be paid for dearly. A storm is raging through us . . .'[15]

Conquering Russians might have looked upwards to the skies. But surviving Berliners, degraded and filthy, looked down at their ruin.

There were rooftops to look down from. Buildings still stood in the centre. If any of the soldiers who had been to the top of the Reichstag had taken a glimpse, they would have seen roofs and chimneys, even if most were damaged by bombardment. The dense agglomeration of massive old buildings, apartment blocks and monuments had struck Marshal Ivan S. Konev on 24 April after the First Ukrainian Front had stormed the Teltow Canal and taken the heights of Lankwitz. Konev, seeing the immense metropolis, was appalled at how poorly prepared the Russian armies were; no tank army was going to be able to enter this. The huge Soviet columns of tanks were halted at Berlin's periphery. The city would have to be entered by small infantry detachments; the artillery was dragged in by lorries, tractors, horses, and even dog carts. Tanks went in individually. 'That last nut was hard to crack!' exclaimed Chuikov on the 30th.[16] Though the heavy guns cut out great swathes of rubble, next to these were houses, erect and inhabited.[17]

Berlin siege life started under the roofs, in lofts. Most Russians were unaware of the existence of lofts; their peasant homes had been built without them. Once the front had passed they were the safest place to be. Servants had been housed in lofts. During school holidays, children used to play there, under the sun-warmed timbers. Now they were places for hiding, as long as relatives or friends supplied water and food. When the Allied armies arrived in July, the city's few remaining virgins emerged from Berlin's lofts.[18]

Berliners looked down. Beneath the lofts were the apartments. Margret Boveri had refused to descend to the stinking cellars and shelters, whatever the risk to her life; she wanted to clean up her beautiful home by the Lietzensee. There were holes in the wall that looked straight down on to the street; she filled up her shattered window-panes with cardboard and paper; for the 'nights of bombardment' she would protect her bed with a piano – on which she would play Bach fugues as the shelling continued. She wrote in her diary of her yearning for cleanliness and culture. She worried about her linen. 'What I have here is black,' she recorded on 30 April, 'and my winter linen is at Frau Becker's laundry.' She made her own candles. When not outside with her two water pails (which she would dip into the filthy lake nearby) she would attempt to clean up the rubble and dust in her rooms, though frequently interrupted by the clatter of falling bricks and beams. She noticed that, in contrast to Anglo-American aerial bombing, her vases and other small valuables remained standing under Russian shelling.[19]

Boveri was not alone in her obsession with cleanliness. The anonymous diarist writes how, on the 27th, the day the Russians arrived in her district, she and a widow next door climbed upstairs: 'We started dusting her apartment, wiping, sweeping and scrubbing with our next-to-last bucket of water.' She realized that the activity was not exactly rational. They did it, she thought, 'to escape once more from the future into the tangible past'.[20]

Most adult Berliners were women. No accurate record exists of Berlin's population at the time of the siege and sacking in April–May 1945, but it has been estimated that the total number had dropped from 4.3 million in 1939 to around 2.7 – of which roughly 2 million were women. It was a city exposed to the dangers of rape. Most rape took place in the apartments.

Both the anonymous diarist and Boveri appear to have developed a certain contempt for German men. They were no longer heroes, they were no longer protectors; they were dirty; and most of them, anyway, were by now either sick or dead.

And what had been their purpose? German men, remarks the diarist, 'ought to feel even dirtier than we sullied women'. Boveri notes that she had never met a man whom she could respect. And the Russians? Refugees from the east had been spreading fearful reports. Goebbels's propaganda machine encouraged them. The Russians themselves didn't provide much in the way of comfort. 'Soldiers of the Red Army,' the propagandist Ilia Ehrenburg wrote in one of his pamphlets, 'German women are yours!' Yes, but then Russians were, thought Berliners, 'only men' and perhaps with a little feminine guile they could be manipulated like men.[21]

Those apartments! Not only the howl of the Stalin organs and the whipping of machine-guns could be heard from their broken windows on 30 April 1945. With the odd lull in the firing a strain of music might come from some room. The diaries describe a distant performance of accordions, the faint tones of a harmonica, or the scratchy rhythms carried by the wind from a hand-wound gramophone; Soviet soldiers took a peculiar liking to the foxtrot. Not everyone in the Red Army was fighting.

Historians have spoken of the Russians entering Berlin in two waves: first, the elite combatants who showed a gallant respect for civilians, and then the rabble. Perhaps. But it was not so evident to the residents,[22] who had difficulty enough distinguishing the officers from the men; the red stars on their caps seemed to mean nothing. With holes in the walls, the wind whistling through the windows and the doors battered in, most apartments in Berlin were open to intruders. One soon got accustomed – after the appearance of the first Russian lorry in the streets – to the comings and goings of the 'regulars', who would turn up every morning and evening, cut up oily herring with their knives on the table, place the pieces with their hands on soggy black bread, share it with anybody, and pour vodka into glasses from their mess tins; and the 'strange male folk', bristling with weapons, rows of watches strapped to their hairy arms, who could appear at any time of the day or night.

Was it on the night of the 28th? 'The one who got hold of me was an older man with grey stubble on his face,' wrote the anonymous diarist. He threw an armchair against the door, pushed her on to the bed and ripped apart her underwear; having got his way, 'the man above me' forced her jaws apart adroitly with his fingers, then 'slowly let his spittle dribble into my mouth'. 'Paralysis. Not disgust, just utter coldness . . . I find myself gliding and sinking deep down through the pillows, through the floor. So that's what it's like – sinking through the floor.'[23]

Down and down. From the lofts, to the apartments, to what remained of the streets and the squares: the country invaded the town, the whole metropolis was transformed into a grim farmyard. It reeked of horse dung. Cockerels could be heard crowing. Cows were heard mooing. Streets, within days, were turned into rural bivouacs, the Russian soldiers sitting in circles around their fires. Women passing by with their water pails noted how former shops now served as stables; horses stood by the counters, their heads occasionally protruding from the open windows.

Two weeks earlier observers of the Red Army columns, advancing from the Oder, got an idea of what was coming to Berlin. 'Behind the tank spearheads rolls on a vast horde largely mounted on horses,' noted General Hasso von Manteuffel, whose Third Panzer Army was attempting to stem the tide in the north. One of five hundred Frenchmen who had been deported to the factories of Oranienburg, north of Berlin, witnessed a brief skirmish with SS troops and then watched in astonishment as Mongolian cavaliers arrived and tied up their horses. 'In the midst of the horses,' he recorded in his diary on 21 April, 'I saw three camels!' Nearby were parked covered 'light chariots'; through the gaps in their slatted woodwork he noticed food supplies, artillery shells and 'aged men and women gathered, I suppose, in tribes'. There were also cannon; 'many cannon, lacking front axles, were dragged painfully by horses.'[24]

In the streets of Berlin these long supply columns were described by Margret Boveri on 3 May — the freckled cows, mares with their foals, horses running freely, and a cacophony of clanging chains, neighing and mooing.[25]

The tanks came first. They smashed up the feeble defences like matchwood, blew up the overturned buses and trams at point-blank range, and demolished walls that got in their way. Hitler Youth of fifteen and sixteen waited in their pits with rifles that had no ammunition; their uniforms were too large, their helmets didn't fit; the most effective weapons they carried were *Panzerfauste*, bazooka-like tank destroyers. But some shrewd engineer in Chuikov's army had come up with an answer to this: bedsprings tied to the front of the tanks; the deadly bombs simply bounced off, often back into the defenders' pits.

Most battles in history are described by men; women described the Battle of Berlin. It made no sense to them. It seemed chaotic and frequently quite ridiculous. 'Today I am more than ever convinced that the major part of war, at least in a city battle, proceeds without plan or aim,' wrote Boveri in 'no man's land' on 27 April. She found both the German commander and his troops in front of her house 'extremely nervous'. 'Both sides shoot. The soldiers run away from where the shooting comes. Then they come back. There is no obvious purpose to this kind of struggle.' She returned to cleaning up the shambles in her home. The Russians appeared to be even more confused. They could be seen, on the 29th, on the north side of the river, running backwards and forwards less than ten minutes' walk from two bridges of the Ringbahn. Didn't they have a map of the town?[26]

As for the German soldiers, they looked so tired and filthy. 'We will never wash until the end of the war,' one of them told Boveri. 'What's going on?' cried women from their doorsteps. 'Where are you off to?' The men never answered. They came from fragments of the Wehrmacht, the Volkssturm, the Hitler Youth. They, too, were provincials who couldn't tell east from west.

Boveri found one of them wandering lost in the park; he asked her the way to the Charlottenburg Opera House where his battalion was supposed to be collecting. Getting lost like this could be fatal: marauding gangs of SS men were on the lookout for 'deserters', which many were not. 'The city railway tunnel is blocked. People standing in front of it said that at the other end a soldier in underpants is hanging, a sign saying "Traitor" dangling from his neck.'[27]

There was worse to be seen in the epicentre of the fighting — by the Reichstag and the neighbouring eastern corner of the Tiergarten.

One officer of the Müncheberg Division sent off a report after spending the night of the 30th by the Zoo's aquarium. The area was a mass of craters, steaming with vapour and the stench of bodies. Shells had blown holes in Moltkestrasse, exposing parts of the U-bahn tunnel to the air – 'columns of fire leapt forth.' Piles of up-ended, burnt-out cars filled the avenue leading from the Brandenburg Gate down the Linden to the fire-gutted royal Schloss at the end.[28]

Yet, even here there were trees in blossom; a scent of lilac and hawthorn came in waves from the ownerless gardens. After all, it was spring.

Down, and further down, lay Berlin's underground world 'whispering and trembling'. Six months of incessant aerial bombardment had driven life into the depths and crevices of the city. Urban life had given way to subterranean social fragments, each one of them isolated from the other. That was the most striking thing about Berlin's new degraded existence: it had begun to resemble the front-line experience of the First World War; the terrible reversal of cosmology was seen here; the living survived below ground, the dead lay on top.

Tens of thousands of dead. What did Berliners do with their dead? Those who ventured outside, for water and food, saw bodies carted around in wheelbarrows. Corpses were covered with a scratch of earth in what open land was available, in parks and back gardens. Makeshift coffins were fabricated from broom cupboards, suitcases or cardboard boxes for the children.

The public 'bunkers' had been prepared in Berlin since the first British raids of 1941. Nearly every square had one; the cellars of major buildings, such as railway stations, were reinforced; as in London, the underground railways were also used – only they had the serious defect of having been built, as in New York and Paris, out of trenches which followed the streets and which were then covered with thick concrete slabs. Berlin's authorities thought the slabs would provide sufficient protection from bombs and shells; they did not.

In fact, the most effective bunkers proved to be Berlin's six flak-towers. The most important were at Humboldthain, Friedrichshain and – largest of them all – at the Zoo, a few hundred yards from the Reichstag. The towers were not mere gun posts. They served as military garrisons, warehouses for art treasures, hospitals and massive air-raid shelters. Strange as it sounds, tens of thousands of Berliners sought protection from bombers and artillery by clambering into tall anti-aircraft gun towers. But the fact remains that existence inside them was the equivalent of being underground; their reinforced concrete walls were more than eight feet thick and what apertures existed were shuttered by 4-inch steel plates. Night and day lost their meaning.

Life underground was indescribably awful. This explains why many Berliners, like Margret Boveri, preferred to risk death in their shattered apartments rather than descend into these infernal pits. Maurice Georges, a French worker who had discovered that he could wander at ease around the city, entered one huge bunker under Friedrichsplatz during an air alert in March. At least fifty identical babies' prams were lined up at the entry; he wondered how anyone could tell one from the other. There was panic among those still outside as the first bombs fell. 'Finally we were stuffed into the maw of the monster. Then its heavy armed door closed on us.'[29]

Another Frenchman, Dr Pagès, working at a prisoner-of-war hospital at Neukölln when the Russians entered the district on 27 April, described what the cellars under Hermannplatz were like at that moment. The kerosene lamps had all gone out and there were virtually no candles left. The sick and wounded were laid side by side on stretchers, on straw or directly on the concrete floor. The numbers increased every minute as the German wounded were brought in.[30]

One of the ugliest bunkers lay under the Anhalter station. The largest hall was lit by a single lamp hanging from the ceiling; people crowded every square foot of floor space and stairway. There was a strong stench of urine and excrement; the toilets were unusable because of the lack of water. The upper floor was reserved for the sick and wounded, who screamed day and night. Worse was the squalling of infants: no milk was available.[31]

It was always an uncomfortable moment when the Russians broke into the cellars and bunkers. They used electric torches or kerosene lamps to light up the faces of the 'silent ones', or 'niemtsy', as they called the residents. In the bunker by the Gedächtniskirke they forced the women, at rifle point, to strip, and then led them out.[32]

Most cellars and bunkers emptied once the districts were occupied; Berlin's troglodytes gradually emerged into the rubble of their streets, destitute, hungry, hollow-eyed, with white rags tied around their arms in sign of submission. Soviet historians claimed that in the working-class suburbs of Wedding and Moabit people welcomed the Russians by hanging red flags out of their windows – fabricated, added cynics, by able seamstresses from old Nazi banners.[33] The majority of inhabitants would have been glad to have the flags as bed covers.

They could at least be grateful they had not escaped to the Zoo flaktower for protection. There were, according to some sources, over 30,000 inside it at the time of the storming of the Reichstag. The heavy Russian bombardment drove many insane. The building was as crowded as the cellars of the Anhalter station, with men, women and children sitting and standing on the staircases, landings and every floor. The presence of the hospital made the stink overpowering; 'perspiration, smelly clothes, babies' nappies, all mixed with the smell of disinfectant'. Suicides weren't noticed; two old ladies had sat down in a corner, taken poison, and there they remained for days, side by side, jammed in an upright position by the crowd. Young boys sold cyanide pills they carried in baskets. 'Last night [the 30th],' reported the officer of the Müncheberg Division, 'on the upper storey, and despite the uninterrupted roar of heavy artillery, officers and men of the police celebrated their *adieux* to life. Men and women lay this morning intertwined in the staircases.'[34]

Another series of reinforced concrete tunnels and bunkers lay under the central administrative district between Vossstrasse, Wilhelmsstrasse and Hermann-Göring Strasse. No Russians knew of this, and very few Berliners were let into the secret. But around a thousand people were lodged there – ministers, SS guards, secretaries, doctors with a hospital under the Reich Chancellery, and, beneath the bombed-out gardens of the Old Chancellery, the Führer himself.

When General Karl Weidling, Berlin's commander, first visited the Führer on 23 April he discovered what he called an 'underground city'. Colonel General Gotthard Heinrici, responsible for Army Group 'Vistula' outside Berlin, has described how, on 5 April, he stepped into 'an un-believable underworld' beneath the garden, where he found the Führer's quarters 'relatively spacious'.[35]

A maze of underground passages provided access to the Führerbunker. Under interrogation in 1945, Erich Kempka, Hitler's personal chauffeur, spoke of walking down, on the afternoon of 30 April, a long tunnel from his office on Hermann-Göring Strasse through to the Chancellery cellars and thence into the Führerbunker. Ludwig Stumpfegger, Hitler's surgeon, regularly used another tunnel from his underground Chancellery clinic. Hitler's personnel lived in a world of crypts, concrete holes and dungeons. Main access to the Führerbunker was through the so-called 'Kannenberg-alley', named after Hitler's butler, Artur Kannenberg. It was found at the back of the New Chancellery, which stood on Vossstrasse. This is presum-ably what Weidling was referring to when he spoke of 'proceeding along a subterranean tunnel, then through a kitchen and dining room, and finally down a staircase and into the Führer's personal quarters'.[36]

The Führerbunker itself, holy of holies, was the lower floor of a two-storey bomb shelter initially built in 1936 and then extended in the winter of 1944–5, while Hitler was in his 'Eagle's Eyrie' in Bad Nauheim attending to the Ardennes offensive. The plasterers had not managed to finish their work, which is why the walls, painted light beige and battleship grey, 'sweated'. A main corridor went down the middle of each floor, and metal doors opened on to rooms on each side. The combination of low ceilings, doors and no windows gave one the impression, said Heinrici, of entering 'the passageway in a small liner'.[37]

Each end could be closed off by huge steel airtight and watertight bulkheads. The north end led to the Kannenberg-alley; the south end served as an emergency exit, with a narrow concrete staircase leading up to the Chancellery garden. There was nothing much left of the garden now. The trees had been uprooted by bombs and shells, the statuary had been smashed, great black holes gaped in the walls where once there were windows, large craters marked the spots where the tea pavilion and botanical greenhouse had stood; the whole scene resembled a First World War battlefield.

Members of the German General Staff who attended the Führer's two daily military conferences would be ushered into the lower corridor of the Bunker. It was brightly lit by the domed lights protruding from the ceiling and had a luxurious look with its floor covered with an oriental carpet, the edges folded under at each side, and the upholstered chairs lining the walls, on which hung haunting landscapes by the early nineteenth-century architect, Karl Friedrich Schinkel. But bombardment above did bring down some of the loose plaster, creating a dusty, hazy atmosphere; and bunker aesthetics were not served by the tangle of cables laid down the middle of the corridor. They led to an engine room, where two throbbing diesel motors brought air, power and life to the whole shelter. The corridor itself had been divided into a waiting room and conference chamber. Almost opposite the engine room lay the Führer's private suite.

Its antechamber and small living room had steel doors, airtight and watertight – and thus sound-tight. Hitler kept his favourite portrait in this living room, Anton Graff's *Frederick the Great*. There was a white vase on the coffee table regularly replenished with tulips and daffodils, to remind the Führer that it was the month of April. Beyond the table stood a narrow sofa, upholstered in blue and white.

'The captain also goes down with his ship,' said Hitler to Dr Goebbels on the afternoon of the 27th. It did seem by then that they were going down. Yet even at this late date, they didn't regard the plunge as inevitable.

The inmates of the Bunker had pinned their hopes on relief from

General Walther Wenck's new Twelfth Army; but its forward guard had only got as far as Potsdam, and as Hitler had remarked during the morning's conference, 'I'm not in Potsdam but in Potsdamer Platz.' In their doomed cubicle old Nazis, particularly Hitler, spent hours reminiscing about past glories, their legends, and their future renaissance; if the reality of night and day had disappeared from the consciousness of most Berliners, here in the Bunker the residents had also lost touch with the absolute certainty of their doom. They lived in a never-never land, in 'the myth'.

Vice-Admiral Erich Voss, liaison officer for the navy, greatly appreciated Hitler's nautical cliché; he, like Heinrici, imagined himself in a boat. 'It's just like the command-bridge of a ship,' he said. 'We are all bound to our duty. We don't want to get away. We belong together. It's only a matter of every one of us standing firm.' The Nazis would go down together.[38]

But, historically, the communal myth had been more one of burial than drowning. It was the first distortion that the Nazis had made of the idea of a German Reich. '*Das Reich*' meant 'reach', and it was the idea of the horizontal 'reach' of the Emperor across Germany's little sovereign states and principalities that had dominated the thought of the Habsburgs and their Holy Roman Empire. The Weimar Republic of the 1920s had adopted this idea of the 'Reich' into its constitution.[39]

The Nazis, on the other hand, transformed the idea of the Reich; they made it vertical and monolithic, a stone post extending upwards and downwards – an authoritarian Reich emanating from one source only, '*der Führer*'. They changed the sense of German history. Rejecting recent memories of the Austrian Habsburgs, the Nazis resurrected the old saga of Frederick Barbarossa not dying (as a matter of fact, he drowned) but sleeping beneath his holy mountain of the Kyffhäuser in Thuringia until the rebirth of his medieval 'Reich' of conquering Christian knights.

That was the myth Hitler sought to create in his death: that of a modern Barbarossa sleeping beneath the ruins of Berlin until his vertical Reich rose from the ashes, was born again. Nazis, like the Red Army, looked upwards.

Glorification of the underground life did not require revival of a twelfth-century legend; it had been honoured and exalted by many a German of Hitler's generation through a more recent event: the First World War. 'There were many pleasant hours even in the line,' recalled Ernst Jünger in his popular 1920 memoirs of the trench war. 'I often sat at the table of my little dugout, whose roughly planked walls, hung with weapons, had a look of the Wild West, and enjoyed a pleasant feeling of being comfortably tucked away . . . Around us in heaped-up mounds of earth lay the bodies of fallen comrades . . . And yet all of us felt a strong attachment to our sector and had almost grown to be a part of it.' 'We stand in the memory of the dead who are holy to us, and we believe ourselves entrusted with the true and spiritual welfare of our people,' Jünger wrote in his conclusion. 'So long as the blade of a sword strikes a spark in the night may it be said: Germany lives and Germany shall never go under!'[40] The outbreak of the First World War 'began the greatest and most unforgettable time of my earthly existence', wrote Hitler in 1924. 'I was a soldier then.'[41] Here, in the making, was the modern legend of Barbarossa.

In Germany, the experience of the First World War did not give rise to a literature of 'disillusionment' and pacifism; what spread through Germany in the 1920s and '30s was the cult of the soldier. Hundreds of thousands on either side of the Rhine might have wept over Erich Remarque's *All Quiet on the Western Front*; but in the West those tears were prompted by the futility of war, while in Germany they were shed on account of the sacrifice. Europe was not united in her mourning. In Germany, the soldiers' lives were not lost for nothing; through their blood sacrifice, they had marked the beginning of 'the myth'. The victors of the West could cater to the luxury of pacifism. Germany, the loser, could not. Germany had been betrayed by the 'fools of 1918'.

'For us the war cannot be lost,' Hitler's comrades-at-arms in the List Regiment remembered him endlessly repeating between 1914 and 1918. 'They wanted to capitulate,' chaffed Hitler in 1924; 'miserable and degenerate criminals!'; the Kaiser's abdication and armistice of November 1918 was 'the greatest villainy of the century'. From the moment he grabbed power Hitler promised Germans that there would never be another 1918. He tore up the Versailles Treaty, he went to war. He engaged Europe in an even greater bloodletting to compensate for the betrayal of the sacrifices he had witnessed at Ypres, the Somme and the Second Battle of the Marne.

'I have striven from the beginning', he told commanders in the 'Eagle's Eyrie' in December 1944, 'to conduct the war wherever possible offensively' with the idea that the enemy 'whatever he does can never reckon with capitulation, never, never'. 'A 9 November in the German Reich will never repeat itself,' he promised on the radio on 1 January 1945. Though he damned his Army General Staff for not living up to 'the General Staff of the first World War', in the last written message he sent out to the world – at midnight, on 29 April 1945 – he complimented the navy, which 'by its high morale has wiped out the disgrace of 1918'.[42]

How was the war to end if Nazi Germany, faced so obviously with superior enemy might, refused to capitulate? Hitler's answer was simple: 'the myth' dictated that the war would never end. This was the guiding theme of Goebbels's Radio Werewolf, which had opened up on the airwaves on 1 April, All Fools' Day. If the worst came to the worst, Barbarossa would lie sleeping beneath the city's rubble.

Duly enough, the worst came to the worst. Treachery replaced loyalty. All of Germany's losses in the East, explained the Führer, were to be traced to treachery; the Allied landings in Normandy and their subsequent advance were also the result of betrayal – the Western Command had to be replaced twice in two months; Field Marshal Erwin Rommel was compelled to take cyanide. Anglo-American forces raced across the northern plain. Soviet tanks turned up on Wilhelmsplatz. 'I will fight as long as I have a single soldier,' Hitler told the chief of operational staff on 21 April. 'When the last soldier deserts me I shall shoot myself.'[43]

Soldiers were lost and Nazi strength dissipated not because of enemy force, but because of betrayal. Reichsmarshal Hermann Göring was arrested for high treason. And then came the hardest blow: Himmler, '*der treue Heinrich*', was reported to be negotiating with the enemy. It was 'the most shameful betrayal in human history'.[44] Hitler had his own brother-in-law, and Himmler's liaison officer, shot, and then set about preparing his will. He had chosen death voluntarily, he dictated with a glassy film in his blue-grey eyes, 'in order to escape the shame of overthrow or capitulation'. He ordered his body burnt in the place where he had done most of his work, the Reich Chancellery, 'during the course of my twelve years' service to my people'.[45]

No war leader spent so much time – two, and sometimes three, military conferences a day – personally directing the war. No war leader had been so little in touch with his people. Since his invasion of Russia in July 1941 he had spent most of his time underground, in the bunker at Rastenburg, in the bunker of Bad Nauheim, and finally in the bunker of the Reich Chancellery. The number of public addresses rapidly declined from nine in 1940, seven in 1941 and five in 1942; the last two in his life were delivered in Berlin in 1943. He seldom spoke on the radio and, by 1944, was hardly even seen in the newsreels. He never visited the bombed quarters of his cities. He was rarely seen on the front. When his special train passed troop transports, he ordered his valet to pull down the blinds. He worked, as his architect and Armaments Minister, Albert Speer, put it, an 'artist's hours', rising only at midday or even one in the afternoon and attending military conferences which, as the enemy fronts closed in, lasted until the early hours of the morning. Hitler's 'day' always concluded with tea and cream buns, over which he made his interminable soliloquies that secretaries and flunkeys were obliged to attend; they would file off to bed after dawn.

'Nothing can wear me down,' he told his exhausted commanders as they set out on Germany's last great offensive on 1 January 1945.[46] But Hitler was by then a human wreck – or a 'walking corpse' as Heinrici described him in late March. He is known to have had a heart problem, and was probably suffering from Parkinson's disease. But the main cause of his poor health was an untenable lifestyle, which Hitler managed to keep going with doses of amphetamines, sedatives and 'Dr Koester's Anti-Gas Pills' – a cocktail of strychnine and belladonna.

One must picture the Führer fifty feet underground in his map room, coloured crayons shaking in his hands, as he moves imaginary brigades and regiments along roads that in truth are blocked towards cities which have been obliterated. He mumbles his commands; he screams treachery; he falls 'like a sack into the armchair, not uttering a word'. Are there moments of depression and despair? 'Nothing can wear me down.' But where in fact is his army? And who are the people that he serves?

In the corridor outside his private suite six men stand silently waiting, SS Adjutant Otto Günsche by the door, his feet apart, a pistol clasped to his chest. Upstairs Dr Goebbels's five young daughters are sitting down for lunch. Suddenly one of the men, Heinz Linge, Hitler's personal servant, loses his nerve; he runs up the flight of stairs of the nearby emergency exit, out into the bombed garden, and then runs all the way down again. The others simply watch these antics 'in amazement'.[47] The muffled sounds of bombardment above mix with the drone of the diesels in the engine room.

General Perevertkin had just launched his second offensive against the Reichstag to plant a flag high in the skies of Berlin. In the streets and the squares machine-guns, bazookas and rockets were firing.

But only one person, behind sealed doors, heard the pistol shot that destroyed Adolf Hitler: his wife of a day, Eva Braun. 'The moment you hear a shot,' Professor Werner Haase, the resident doctor, told her early that morning, 'simply bite quickly into your capsule.'[48]

Jazz, it seems, was played over the loudspeakers of the Reich Chancellery canteen after Hitler died. Grand Admiral Dönitz might have chosen Bruckner's Seventh Symphony and a selection of Wagner's operas to announce the next evening, on Radio Hamburg, the death of the Führer 'at the head of his troops'. But few Berliners heard this; most radios in those days had to be plugged into the mains – in Berlin there was no electricity.

On 2 May the anonymous diarist noticed a rosy-cheeked Russian playing an accordion on the street below. '*Gitler kaputt, Goebbels kaputt, Stalin goot!*' he shouted up at her, then laughed, yelled a curse, and banged a comrade on his shoulder. Margret Boveri continued the chores of Sisyphus in her ruined apartment; she heard rumours that there were Russians in her staircase.

On 20 May, 10,000 Berliners gathered in the former Reichssportfeld Stadium to watch a football match, where only three weeks before one of the last battles of the Second World War had been fought. The death of Hitler did not end the life and history of the *Reichshauptstadt*, 'sandpit of the Holy Roman Empire'.[49]

On the First of May, the 'workers' international festival', Stalin issued from the Kremlin his order of the day. He announced that the Great Patriotic War was coming to a victorious end, that in short order Poland, Hungary, the major part of Czechoslovakia, and a large part of Austria as well as the Austrian capital, Vienna, had been 'liberated'. The flag of victory had been planted in Berlin. The World War launched by the German imperialists was near its end.

'The Fascist Beast, mortally wounded, is in its death throes,' he said; 'all that remains to be done is to kill it.'[50]

Stalin did not indicate that day that Hitler was already dead. And, most significantly, he never would.

Armies

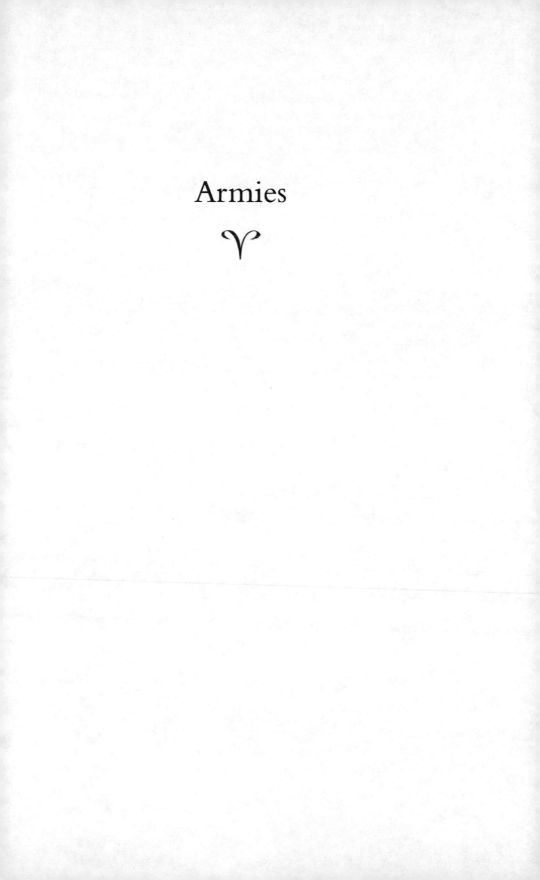

Beginnings

ϒ

'*Paris. Paris outragé, Paris brisé, Paris martyrisé, mais Paris libéré!*' The whole world heard that line. One black-and-white newsreel camera purred as General Charles de Gaulle, President of the Provisional Government of the French Republic, pronounced it in a poorly lit hall on the first floor of Paris's Hôtel de Ville on the evening of 25 August 1944. It was the day Paris was liberated.

'Paris. Paris abused, Paris broken, Paris martyred, but Paris . . .' – his body sways slightly – 'liberated!' De Gaulle's hands move up and down like a minstrel strumming his lyre. 'Liberated by itself, liberated by its people, with the help of the armies of France, with the help and support of the whole of France, that is to say of the France which fights, that is to say of the real France, of eternal France.' He lifts his head and closes his eyes, as in prayer; de Gaulle is singing his sacred solo of history.

Motionless in the audience around him are some very serious male faces. Are they happy? De Gaulle, towering above them, sings on without appearing to notice them. Beside him stands a rather stout, older looking man; this is Georges Bidault, coordinator of the French resistance movements. '. . . *mais Paris libéré, libéré par lui-même, libéré par son peuple avec le concours des armées de la France* . . .' Bidault's face, at this point, assumes a very definite grimace.

Behind de Gaulle stands a pretty young woman, her dark hair pushed up and back in the style of the day; she wears a small black-rimmed hat and a necklace of pearls that are possibly false. '*Paris* . . .': she is smiling. '*Paris martyrisé* . . .': she bites her lower lip. '. . . *mais Paris libéré*': she smiles again. '. . . *libéré par son peuple* . . .': stealthily she raises her right hand to wipe away the tears from her eyes; as she turns her head you can see her two huge round earrings that are almost certainly home-made.[1]

'De Gaulle is not what one would call an orator,' wrote the editor of *Combat* the next day. 'Many of those who have followed him did not like his way of speaking.'[2]

The Communist newspaper, *L'Humanité*, barely reported the speech. It limited itself to de Gaulle's call for national unity in a short paragraph next to an article about the raising of flags in the city; at ten o'clock that morning the tricolour had replaced the swastika at the top of the Eiffel Tower. The following day's edition included a photograph of the red flag being raised above the Soviet embassy on Rue de Grenelle, and an editorial comment on the 'profound convergence, once more, between the country and its Communist Party'.[3]

Unlike in the Soviet Union, the word 'Fascist' had disappeared from the French Communist Party's vocabulary. The emphasis now was on the formation of a 'National Front' to drive out and defeat the 'Hitlerian Beast' with all haste, and to chastise 'traitors' at home.

1 Heartlands in the West

Paris liberated by itself? And with the help of all France? When General de Gaulle took off in a small biplane from martyred France to London on 17 June 1940 he was already convinced that Hitler could be beaten.

He seemed, however, hardly the choice for a national war leader. Outside a handful of politicians, generals and well-briefed journalists, he was virtually unknown in his own country. He had been Under-Secretary of State for War and National Defence for less than a fortnight in a government that had just resigned; he had been a general *à titre temporaire* for a little over three weeks, though, up to the moment he landed in London, he continued to call himself a colonel.

De Gaulle's confidence in an eventual victory lay in his view that Hitler's invasion of Poland in 1939 and of France in May 1940 was the start of a 'world war'. Hitler would not win this 'world war', thought de Gaulle, whereas France in the end could gain, for 'the world was there, able to give us fresh weapons, and later, powerful aid'. What de Gaulle reproached most bitterly in the capitulators of Vichy was their blind provincial understanding of the conflict. They were the men of yesterday. They couldn't understand how technology had speeded up movement and communication. Pétain, for instance, could see no further than the frontiers of France; 'in the vision of the old marshal, the world character of the conflict, the potential of the overseas territories, the ideological consequences of Hitler's victory barely entered into account.' What frightened de Gaulle most was not that Hitler would one day govern the world, but that the eventual victory of his opponents would not include France; that France would merely be a *motte de terre*, a 'patch of land', over which triumphant Allied armies would pass.[4]

De Gaulle's conviction that Hitler could not win a 'world war' lay partly in the way he read maps; he never limited his vision to their frames. Officers of the 4th Armoured Division would remember how, outside a war-torn Laon in May 1940, Colonel de Gaulle would open up his campaign maps (in one of the few French operations that actually retrieved territory from the invading Germans) and then start his conference with the words: 'Prenez donc une mappemonde.' For de Gaulle, all maps were maps of the world.[5]

Winston Churchill, the new Prime Minister in a desperate London, also worked with maps – as can be seen in the wonderful maps that illustrate his war memoirs. Like de Gaulle, Churchill always looked beyond the map's frame; and because of that he too concluded that Hitler, in the end, would probably not win his war.

Thus, from the very beginning of the conflict there was a fundamental accord in the way the two men, one a prime minister, the other a colonel, perceived the pattern of forces in the world. Each was determined that his own country would play its part in the eventual victory; each was a defiant opponent of negotiation with the enemy, however bleak the immediate turn of events. Though their relationship proved stormy, 'we were' – as de Gaulle put it a quarter of a century later – 'accrochés', 'hitched'. Charles de Gaulle, said Churchill, was 'l'homme du destin'.[6]

One curious fact confirmed their tie at an early point in their acquaintance. Both made the most famous speeches in their lives on the same day, in London on 18 June 1940. It was, strangely enough, the 125th anniversary of the Battle of Waterloo.

De Gaulle, on the BBC that night, applied what he had learnt from his mappemonde: 'Car la France n'est pas seule! Elle n'est pas seule! Elle n'est pas seule!' She would form a bloc with the British Empire, which holds the seas; she would use the boundless industrial resources of the United States. 'This war is not limited to the unhappy land of our country. This war is not decided by the Battle of France. This war is a world war.' He made his first call that night for a 'French resistance'.[7]

Churchill had addressed the Commons that afternoon and he repeated his celebrated conclusion over the radio one hour before de Gaulle addressed France.[8] Churchill's decision to fight on was likewise based on a mappemonde. In casting up the 'dread balance sheet', he said, 'I see great reasons for vigilance and exertion, but none whatever for panic or fear.' In contrast to de Gaulle, however, his purpose was not to appeal for resistance after a battle lost; his was a call for readiness in a battle about to be waged. 'What General Weygand called the Battle of France is over,' said Churchill. 'I expect that the Battle of Britain is about to begin. Upon this battle depends the survival of Christian civilization . . . The whole fury and might of the enemy must very soon be turned on us.' The tone of Churchill's appeal is familiar to everybody: 'Let us therefore brace ourselves to our duties, and so bear ourselves that, if the British Empire and its Commonwealth last for a thousand years, men will still say: "This was their finest hour." '[9]

The decision to continue the war against Hitler was thus made in London. The appeals had been launched. De Gaulle and Churchill breathed confidence. But in June 1940 their success was far from certain.[10]

The Russians had no plan for the defeat of Germany for Stalin was, at that time, the ally of Hitler. The French had no plan because the government had capitulated. The British Chiefs of Staff, on the other hand, did have a plan. They presented it to the Cabinet on 25 May,[11] at the very moment that they were drawing up their project for the evacuation of the British Expeditionary Force, now trapped by fast-moving German Panzers on the French–Belgian frontier. The idea was to combine aerial bombardment of Germany and German-controlled Europe with a naval blockade so tight that popular uprisings would occur all over the Continent. Britain would further weaken German authority through small operations in 'subsidiary' theatres that would overextend her forces.

It was the sort of plan Pitt the Younger might have drafted against French hegemony in the 1790s – if Pitt had had an air force. But such British plans of bombardment from the coast and tiny expeditions to the enemy's distant outposts had never proved very effective in the past. Napoleon had been defeated by huge coalition armies outside Paris and Brussels in 1814 and 1815, not by peripheral operations. Germany's Imperial Army was smashed in 1918 when it was backed up against the Ardennes on the Belgian border, not by the 'sideshow' campaigns in Turkey and the Balkans.

Britain's peripheral operations ran counter to an old military principle: that wars cannot be finally won without the use of land armies at the enemy's centre – the centre in this case being a great northern plain stretching across peninsular Europe from France through to Russia.

The Americans, who in 1940 were not yet involved in the war, were the first to grasp the significance of this – ironically, perhaps, for Americans were averse to geopolitics. They placed priority on ideals – on freedom of the seas, world peace, collective security, liberty and democracy. They were wary when talk in international conferences turned to peninsulas, isthmuses, sea chambers and islands; this was the language of European warmongers and colonialists. Establish the principles first, said the American delegates at the Paris Peace Conference in 1919, and only then take out the maps.[12]

It is an irony wrapped in paradox. One of the reasons why there were so many military plans produced by the American General Staff in the 1930s was that they had no geographic focus. They worked to a more abstract theory of probabilities: the United States faced a number of possible enemies; which one, or which combination, would it be? They had their plans divided up accordingly in cardboard files designed in every colour of the rainbow, along with various blends. The Orange and Red plan, for example, prepared for a war against Japan and Britain – in the world of probability theory it was a possibility.[13]

But then came the plan that would seal the fate of Adolf Hitler. It was not an American product, but an import. And it was not an import from just anywhere; it had been brought in from the enemy's very centre, Nazi Germany.

The man who carried the idea to America was Albert C. Wedemeyer. Born in Ohio in 1897 of German parentage, he graduated from West Point just in time to miss the First World War and to serve, instead, in China and the Pacific. In 1934 he entered the prestigious Command and General Staff School at Fort Leavenworth. During these two decades of peace Wedemeyer had found the time to read many works of history and economics; he also discovered the books of the famous British geographer, Sir Halford Mackinder. In a short summary on the course and effects of the First World War, Sir Halford had mused on the possibilities of a second great war. This included a comparison of Europe and the Far East of Asia, a subject that was particularly dear to Wedemeyer. Japan, he said, was the Britain of Asia; China, with almost as many provinces as Europe had states, was the Continent. But there was one major difference between the Far East and Europe, explained Mackinder; the Far East did not have a Mediterranean which 'peninsulates and sub-peninsulates Europe, whereas China is a compact, almost circular land in the massive side of Asia'.[14] It was this that made Europe so strategically important in the future of the world: it was a land of ports, of trading, of fighting states that spread their influence outwards.

But Mackinder took into account the development of new technologies, particularly air power. The maritime inventions and discoveries four centuries old had made Europeans 'free of the ocean'; the development of aircraft would make 'us and our children . . . free of the air'. This would lead Mackinder to develop a 'heartland theory' which envisaged the possibility – frightening for a Briton – of the maritime powers, which had through shipping been able to carry their arms and wealth around the 'world island' of Europe–Asia–Africa, being outflanked by continental powers, which moved with railways, motor vehicles and aeroplanes.[15]

Wedemeyer graduated from Fort Leavenworth with high honours in 1936 and, as his reward, won a two-year scholarship to the German Kriegsakademie in Berlin. There, to his amazement, he discovered that Mackinder's geopolitics were all the rage.

The most influential lecturer there was Dr Karl Haushofer, a man well versed in Nazi ideology. Haushofer had, like Wedemeyer, read widely in history and economics; he could quote the ancient philosophers, speak freely of Hannibal and Scipio, of medieval empires and of the Han dynasty in China. To this he added the concept of 'living space', '*Lebensraum*', a notion that had been incorporated into Hitler's *Mein Kampf*, although Haushofer claimed only that in each culture, primitive, historical and contemporary, there was 'a multiplicity of possible living-spaces and of ways of imagining space'.[16] Indeed, Haushofer reads like a modern-day ecologist compared to Hitler. Nevertheless, it is clear where the combination of 'heartland theory' (and its formulation of land power outflanking sea power) with 'living space' would eventually drive Germany's armies: into the eastern base of the European peninsula, Russia, in the summer of 1941.

For the American Wedemeyer the problem was obviously different: how would America outflank this expanding, technologically advanced continental power under Hitler? Perhaps, as American war planning had indicated, Japan would be an enemy of America too. But Wedemeyer's reading taught him to place priority on Europe, not Asia. Heartland theory taught him that peripheral operations would not win a war with the Nazis. On his return to the United States in 1938, Captain Wedemeyer composed a long report on German military thought and organization.

It landed on the desk of General George C. Marshall who, at the time, ran the 'War Plans Division' of the still chaotic American Department of War. Marshall, a man who terrorized his subordinates, was impressed with both the clarity and breadth of Wedemeyer's thinking and asked him in for a chat. Captain Wedemeyer, only forty-one at the time, from that day on found himself at the centre of American war thinking.

Rainbow plans proliferated. What became America's 'Victory Program' in September 1941 was the product of despair over Britain's revised version of Pitt's eighteenth-century strategy. Hitler's apparently unstoppable continental armies were now advancing towards the Russian Caucasus. Japan had in the meantime signed a Neutrality Pact with her former Soviet foe to the north and a Tripartite Pact (the previous year) with Germany and Italy. Negotiations with Vichy France led to Japan's occupation of Indochina. The signs were clear: Japan was preparing to move south. Could the Axis powers meet her in the Indian Ocean? That would hand them control of the 'world island', the Eurasian continent.[17] After the Atlantic Conference of August, where Britain presented her scattergram of global operations, including reinforcements in Singapore, the defence of Egypt, seizure of Atlantic islands and the occupation of North Africa, the US Army staff went into a fury. Britain was just 'groping for panaceas', they said. Wedemeyer recommended that Britain import some of India's 390 million people to England to make up for her labour shortages.[18] At the same time the American staff had to admit that their own potential military contribution to the struggle against Hitler did not look particularly imposing. The American military build-up had progressed since 1939 – when the US Army of 190,000 men ranked nineteenth in the world armed forces, just behind Portugal's – to around 600,000 men in the summer of 1941, roughly equivalent to the combined armies of Belgium and Holland before their surrender in May 1940.

The 'Victory Program' itself consisted of several plans, of which Wedemeyer's project was only one.[19] And yet, conceived at a time when the United States possessed no military might, when France had collapsed, when Britain faced a series of disasters, when Stalin's Soviet Russia seemed the only power capable of resisting Germany, this was the project that eventually breached the walls of the Nazi citadel of Europe.

Wedemeyer used his maps. He defined the Nazi 'heartland'. He sought out the closest possible foothold where America and her Allies could land a force of such overwhelming strength as to break Germany's 'will to combat'. The maps provided his answer. The foothold would be in northern France, on the plain that led directly to the heartland. First, the Western Allies would have to achieve mastery of the Atlantic and mastery of the air. Wedemeyer calculated the force required. Traditional doctrine demanded a 2-to-1 troop ratio for an attacker. Wedemeyer insisted on a ratio of almost 3 to 1, which would require a US Army alone of 8.8 million men, with over 5 million transported to European ports.[20] There was no time to lose, 'otherwise, we will be confronted in the not distant future by a Germany strongly entrenched economically, supported by newly acquired sources of vital supplies and industries . . . and in a position of hegemony in Europe'.[21] In Haushofer's terms, Germany would have become an impenetrable continental military empire. Wedemeyer estimated that by mid-1943 at the latest, with the Soviet Union 'substantially impotent', the critical deadline would have been reached.

The great Allied invasion of northern France occurred on 6 June 1944, D-Day. General Albert Wedemeyer was by then on his way to China.

2 Their saddest hour

Churchill's defiant appeal of 18 June 1940 had included an important reference to the last great war and the events of 1918. 'We repeatedly asked ourselves the question "How are we going to win?"' recalled Churchill, 'and no one was able to answer it with much precision, until at the end, quite suddenly, quite unexpectedly, our terrible foe collapsed before us, and we were so glutted with victory that in our folly we threw it away.'[22] Churchill was a historian and his assessment was pretty accurate.

Since the seventeenth century the French had developed a habit of referring to Great Britain as 'Perfidious Albion'. For much of the time the term was used simply as a propaganda instrument against what the French perceived as their hereditary enemy; this was most obvious during Napoleon's desperate recruiting campaign of 1813, when the term first became widespread. But in the 1920s and '30s 'Perfidious Albion' described well the attitude among Britain's governing classes; they tore up treaties, they failed to honour their guarantees, they turned their backs on their friends. It is one of the saddest periods of British history.

Britain was governed by arrogant men, who misunderstood the nature of the world in which they were living. They were prepared to defend the outer borders of the Sudan, India and Burma as a matter of 'national interest'; while on the question of Czech and Polish frontiers they were utterly indifferent. They often spoke of moral and social progress on the planet, but they would not use maps; they could not use maps. Unfortunately, after 1918 those maps had become essential.

Britain's retreat from international treaties and alliances began at the Paris Peace Conference of 1919. She readily adopted the language of that settlement's greatest enemies, Germany and Soviet Russia – the two expansionist continental powers of Europe. Germany put out the word that the treaty she had signed at Versailles in June 1919 was 'punitive'. Yet Germany, in fact, lost little territory; the initial financial reparations required of her were less than what was demanded of her after 1945, and, anyway, Germany would never pay; and it was hardly surprising that the Allies should set a low limit on German militarization, having been invaded, without warning, by seven industrially equipped armies in 1914. Bolshevik Russia described the Paris peace settlement as 'acquisitive' and 'imperialist'. Yet it was a doctrine of 'permanent revolution', inciting 'armed insurrection' against existing governments and their takeover by Communist parties answerable to Moscow, that first demonstrated the acquisitive nature of the Leninist regime and its successors over the greater part of the century. Britain, appalled at the scale of her sacrifices in the recent war, was prepared to speak to her enemies on a narrow, unilateral basis. 'Unjust', 'punitive', 'iniquitous Versailles' – hadn't the discussions been in Paris? – would have to be revised.[23]

There was ample range for revision under the terms of the series of treaties the Allies had signed with their former enemies in 1919 and 1920. The peacemakers at Paris were perfectly aware of the need – much of Central and Eastern Europe was still at war during these years. One of the great problems had been the new state of Poland. France, with her own land frontier with Germany, wanted a military guarantee for Poland; Britain, confident in the security of her seas, was wary of granting it. 'Would we make war for Danzig?' asked the Prime Minister, Lloyd George, during deliberations in April 1919.[24]

The key to the whole peace settlement was not, however, the specific definition of Europe's eastern frontiers; it was the maintenance of the western alliance that had won the war and was alone capable of enforcing the peace settlement, in its original terms or revised. The United States, which had always only considered itself an 'associate', not an 'ally', pulled out when the Senate failed to ratify the Treaty of Versailles with Germany in the autumn of 1919; whereupon Britain refused to honour her part of the guarantee. Throughout the 1920s and 1930s – in the very face of the Nazi threat – there existed no western military alliance. At Locarno in 1925 Britain did offer France a guarantee to the limited extent that Germany was willing to recognize her existing western frontiers with France and Belgium. But Germany refused to recognize her eastern frontiers. Thus Locarno, hailed at the time by cartoonists as the moment when civilization stepped 'into the light', in fact undermined the whole peace settlement of 1919, first, by duplicating an agreement on western frontiers that had already been written into the Treaty of Versailles and, second, by opening up the possibility of German expansion eastwards.

Britain's guarantee to France looked very flimsy. France built a wall – the Maginot Line – across her vulnerable plain; but only in the most mountainous part, because Belgium did not want to find herself on the wrong side of the wall. So Belgium herself continued the line along her eastern frontier with Germany, using small iron and concrete obstacles that delighted German armies would eventually transport to the beaches of the Atlantic and English Channel once France had been occupied: Wedemeyer's invading force would have to cross them.

Britain's guarantee at Locarno was nullified when Hitler's troops marched into the demilitarized Rhineland one Sunday morning early in March

1936. The British Secretary of War assured the German ambassador in London that the British people 'did not care "two hoots" about the Germans reoccupying their own territory'.[25] But the demilitarization of the Rhineland had been a condition set at both Versailles and Locarno. Ignoring both treaties, Britain opened bilateral talks with Nazi officials for an agreement on new upper limits to Germany's air and naval forces. In the meantime, Germany built the Westwall in the Rhineland, or what the Allies would later call the Siegfried Line, another obstacle that Wedemeyer's invading force would have to surmount.

France's defences were paralysed. It is true, as Colonel de Gaulle pointed out at the time, that the French armed forces were commanded by old men who did not appear to know that tanks now moved at 40 mph or that heavy artillery transported by horse and trains had been replaced by twin-engined dive-bombers. But this was more an effect than a cause. What had reduced France to military immobility behind her frontier fortress was Britain's mad diplomacy. Like the military strategy that she would develop during the war, Britain had tripped along case by case, crisis by crisis, theatre by theatre, on a bilateral basis. In neither diplomacy nor strategy was this a valid method. The picture of a changing world was lost.

When Hitler, in March 1938, annexed Austria before the cheering crowds of Vienna, barely a ripple was heard in the foreign offices of Paris and London. There was panic later that year when Hitler invented a region he called the 'Sudetenland' on the hills of Czechoslovakia and demanded that it too be annexed to the new German Reich. Lord Halifax reminded the French that the Locarno agreement only applied to French frontiers. Lord Runciman flew to Prague and told the democratically elected government there to prepare for their country's dismemberment. The Italian dictator Mussolini saved the world from war by initiating an accord on the division of Czechoslovakia which the British and French swallowed at Munich – the Czechs were left in an ante-room. In March 1939 Hitler's troops entered Prague.

British public opinion, till then as keen on appeasement as their Prime Minister, swung round: they wanted action. Neville Chamberlain's government performed a volte-face. What the smaller states had been demanding of Western Europe for twenty years at last came about. What the Paris Peace Conference had attempted to achieve in 1919 was belatedly recognized in London. Chamberlain rained down Britain's unilateral guarantees on to every corner of the Continent, including Poland and Romania. That was a sorry error: it drove Stalin straight into Hitler's arms, for Stalin would never accept a Western guarantee of Poland and Romania.

With the signing of the Nazi-Soviet Pact in August 1939 war was inevitable. Britain was obliged to go to war over Danzig.

Churchill well describes the unhappy scene at Tours on 13 June 1940 – the bomb craters, the refugees, the sullen faces of French officialdom, the 'dripping and sunlit garden' of the prefecture – where he solemnly declared to the French Prime Minister, Paul Reynaud, that he was 'not in a position to release France from her obligation' and allow her to seek a separate peace with Germany. 'Our war aim remained the total defeat of Hitler, and we felt that we could still bring this about.'[26] But how far back did that 'obligation' go? To Paris in 1919? To Locarno in 1925? Many Frenchmen would have dearly loved that to have been so. In fact, the 'obligation' had been cobbled together by Chamberlain and Reynaud on 28 March 1940, six weeks prior to the German invasion of France.

3 Heartlands in the East

That war began in the mind of one man in the summer of 1919. The peace treaty between Germany and the Allies had just been signed at Versailles. Adolf Hitler had joined the 'Information Department' of the army forces that had crushed a Soviet Republic in Munich and he had made a discovery: 'I could speak!'[27] In the autumn and winter he was haranguing the crowds in Munich's beer halls on such subjects, he relates in *Mein Kampf*, as 'War Guilt' ('which at that time nobody bothered about') and the 'Peace Treaties'. 'Nearly everything was taken up that seemed agitationally expedient or ideologically necessary,' noted Hitler.[28]

Indeed, his ideology developed with the crowd in a kind of spiralling exchange, like a Baptist minister with his congregation. Hitler wanted the truth told, and no secrets kept. He contrasted the 'manly forthrightness' of the speaker on the tavern table with the 'cowardly swindlers' who worked in the 'darkness of silence'. 'A man who knows a thing, who is aware of a given danger, and sees the possibility of a remedy with his own eyes,' said Hitler, 'has the duty and obligation, by God, not to work "silently", but to stand up before the whole public against the evil and for its cure.'[29] A recurring theme in Hitler's speech was the need for interchange between the 'inner' and the 'outer': between the 'inner' thought and the 'outer' expression, the 'inner' vision of the inarticulate crowds and the 'outer' words of the orator on the table; the 'inner' unity of the national will and its 'outer' freedom.

This would determine his approach to foreign policy. 'Without the recovery of our external freedom,' he wrote, or rather dictated, in 1924, 'any internal reform, even in the most favourable case, means only the increase of our productivity as a colony.' A reformed Germany would have to decide on her own frontiers.[30]

That meant war. His whole policy – racial, social, educational, health – revolved around this one thing: war, its preparation and its execution. 'He who rests – rusts,' was the cosy little phrase he shared with his followers; 'victory lies eternally and exclusively in attack.' His party did not propose reform or revolution, it called for 'victory'. Some historians, in their study of the Nazi treatment of minorities, make a distinction between the Nazis during the years of peace and the Nazis at war. This is a misconception. The Nazis were never at peace. Hitler had been openly calling for war since the beginning of his speaking career, in 1919. 'What could have been done with this peace treaty of Versailles?!' 'Give us arms again!' 'Lord make us free!' Hitler mocked those who simply wanted a restoration of Germany's frontiers of 1914 – 'entirely suited to our bourgeois society', he scoffed; these old frontiers were neither sufficient for 'people of German nationality', nor did they correspond to 'geomilitary expediency'. Yet 'even the restoration of the frontiers of 1914 could be achieved only by blood.' So there had to be war, for Hitler was not going to stop at the frontiers of 1914.[31]

Germany, Hitler acknowledged, was not yet a continental power, so in order to go to war she would need allies. There was nothing equivocal about the meaning of an alliance with Hitler. 'An alliance', he announced, 'whose aim does not embrace a plan for war is senseless and worthless. Alliances are concluded only for struggle.'[32]

But this time it would be Germany that would pick both the time and the place of the struggle. How badly war had been executed in 1914! 'The guilt of the German government was that in order to preserve peace it always missed the favourable hours for striking, became entangled in the alliance for the preservation of world peace, and thus finally became the victim of a world coalition.'[33] Germany had ended up fighting the impossible war, the war on two fronts. This, Hitler was determined to avoid. Each campaign would be an isolated affair, prosecuted with the speed of lightning. Alliance with the left, and strike at the right. Alliance with the right, and strike at the left. But never strike, like those fools of 1914, in all directions at the same time.

This was not only the policy Hitler followed at the outbreak of war, it was also what drove him in the years leading up to the war – for Hitler was always at war.

How lucky it was that the Weimar Republic had set the precedent. Germany at peace? Germany was never at peace. Germany never accepted the peace. During the 'week of mourning' in May 1919, when the terms of the Treaty of Versailles were published, the German press howled about the system of 'slavery' imposed by 'Entente' imperialists. The popular slogan that the treaty was 'Unacceptable! Unfulfillable! Unbearable!' had been composed by the German delegation at Versailles. Germany's policy, Hitler's policy, of the isolated strike, combined with a decoy of alliance, began that May.[34] The main characteristic of German foreign policy over the next twenty years would be its continuity.

German Supreme Command had moved east. By May 1919 its head-quarters were in Kolberg. It was involved in battles in the Baltic states and in Poland; German forces were still fighting a war in Silesia in 1921. Rearmament was achieved by an agreement dating from that same year between members of the 'Eastern Department' of the German Foreign Ministry and Soviet Russia (under the guise of 'prisoner-exchange offices'). In the meantime, Germany sought a pact with the Western Powers to secure her Rhineland frontiers (Versailles, on this matter, was apparently not sufficient).

The whole complex issue of reparations had a political dimension in Germany that was poorly understood in Britain. For the officials of the British Foreign Office and Treasury it was a mere problem of accounting that had developed when the United States had refused, in the aftermath of the war, to cover or even to discuss Allied war debts. For the Germans, it opened the road to the 'revision' of Versailles. In 1922 the accountants of London proposed an economic 'Consortium' that would sort out Europe's money problems; Germany jumped at the opportunity and, when all Europe assembled in Genoa in April of that year, signed a treaty in the neighbouring town of Rapallo with Soviet Russia that opened the way to a mutual revision of Europe's eastern frontiers and, through Soviet good graces, the rearmament of Germany. The origin of the Nazi–Soviet Pact lay here.

The widening window of opportunity in the East required increased security in the West. This Germany achieved at Locarno in 1925. Germany recognized her Rhineland frontier, the Allied occupation forces were with-drawn and the Inter-Allied Military Control Commission was eventually abolished. Nothing was said on Germany's eastern frontiers. All this was the achievement of the Weimar Republic. The Versailles Treaty lay in tatters.

Hitler, the revivalist beer-hall preacher with his eyes and ears open to his congregation of militants, seized the momentum and pushed it to an extreme that the Republic would never have dared. 'The future of a move-ment is conditioned by the fanaticism, yes the intolerance, with which its adherents uphold it,' was the rule Hitler imposed on his disciples.[35] He denounced restrictions on German armament – by the mid-1920s there had been effectively none. He rejected the demilitarization of the Rhineland – manifestly, neither Britain nor France had the will to enforce it. The peaceful and tolerant democracies of Western Europe were utterly confounded by the fanatics of Germany.

As long as Hitler directed it, the war followed the same process as the peace: a friendly decoy here, an isolated attack there. Hitler had world ambitions; but he had hoped to avoid a world war. As both Churchill and de Gaulle foresaw in June 1940, world war and a dispersal of Germany's forces across several fronts would be an early sign that Hitler was losing his war. The way Hitler proceeded was, first, to make sure he had the allies he needed – alliances concluded 'only for struggle' – and then to attack their common enemy. Why wait? Hitler arranged the 'incidents' that started his war with Poland in September 1939; he got some inmates of his concentration camps dressed up in Polish uniforms and had them shot on the German side of the border.[36] His pretext was at hand. A nice, brutal, short, localized war was his ideal. Once completed, he would rearrange his alliances to strike at another common enemy in another ruthless little war. And eventually he would get where he wanted: to the heartland, Russia.

Professor Karl Haushofer claimed at the Nuremberg trial – just before he and his wife committed suicide – that Hitler had never quite grasped the subtleties of his 'living space' theory.[37] Hitler didn't worry about the subtleties. That occupation and settlement of the steppes of Russia would be the aim of the next German war was stated plainly enough in the pages of *Mein Kampf*.[38]

A. J. P. Taylor, in his famous, stimulating essay on *The Origins of the Second World War*, was right to stress that it was the incompetence of the Western democracies, and in particular the British Foreign Office, which led Hitler to his war; but to suggest that Hitler had no project is a distortion of the story.[39] Taylor, here, confused the immediate opportunism of alliances and foreign policy with Hitler's ultimate, unchanging aim, the conquest of Russia. No one, including Hitler, could predict who Hitler's allies would be, or where he would strike first. But Hitler always knew where he would ultimately be heading. The fact that for hundreds of thousands of German migrants and would-be migrants over the preceding two centuries 'living space' had been in the plains of North America and not the steppes of Russia did not bother Hitler; we must 'stop the endless German movement to the south and west', he proclaimed, and pursue a programme of one Reich, one blood by pushing eastwards. How this would be achieved was a matter of political ability and manoeuvre.

A reading of *Mein Kampf* would suggest that his first alliance would be with Britain, and that his first strike would be against France, the greatest military power in the world in the 1920s. An attack on France would offer 'the rear cover for an enlargement of our people's living space in Europe'.[40] But by the mid-1930s the experience of the Rhineland had taught Hitler that there was nothing to fear from French power; it had become entirely dependent on the serviceable appeasers of London: so Hitler, in order to cover his western rear, would first strike against both a weak France *and* Britain. Hitler's attitude towards France by the late 1930s was one of contempt. Britain was the main challenge to his rear, not France.

He made a 'Pact of Steel' in May 1939 with Italy, which was designed to attack British interests in the Mediterranean (though Mussolini was still dreaming of the years of peace ahead of him). He tried to make a pact with the Japanese whom he wanted to move southwards against British interests in the Pacific and the Indian Ocean – the idea, to which Albert Wedemeyer was a witness at the Kriegsakademie in Berlin, of an en-circlement of the 'world island', with German continental power stretching eastwards into Russia and reaching down into the oil rich Near East, was taking on a more concrete form. But the silly Japanese understood nothing about heartlands and world islands; they did not want an alliance against Britain and insisted instead on making war with the Russians on the borders of Manchuria: their military force was concentrated in the north and did not yet look southwards. So Hitler had to settle for second best, an alliance with the Russians first to knock out Britain.

There was the small matter of Poland. The obstinate Poles did not accept Hitler's offers, between October 1938 and March 1939, of subservience to the Reich so they had to be destroyed before they could become a distraction to his plans for Britain and France. Stalin proved very helpful here; by October 1939 they were able to divide up the spoils. So, in fact, were the British and the French; though they declared war on Germany they let Hitler launch his first war of extermination eastwards without making a move.

The movement of Hitler's armies in the spring of 1940 demonstrated his contempt for France and the principal object of his concern, Britain. Norway, which he occupied in April, was hardly a stepping stone to Paris; it was a major threat to Britain. So was the defeat of Holland and Belgium, which surrendered respectively on 15 and 28 May. Inasmuch as the recently formed western military alliance had a plan, it was modelled on the German invasion of Belgium in 1914; they were expecting another version of the famous Schlieffen Plan which had aimed at encircling French forces by moving round Paris and entrapping them from the west. But Hitler didn't worry about the French forces. He sent his main thrust north-west, through the 'impenetrable' Ardennes and up into the Channel ports. From there they could aim at Britain. Paris was occupied by a German infantry division on 14 June almost as an afterthought.

Hitler's war on Western Europe was not a war of extermination. It was more a military exercise designed as a preparation of the western rear for his next push eastwards. Spared the main thrust of the attack, many Frenchmen, after the initial shock of defeat and during the first weeks of occupation, thought German soldiers 'decent'. It was the *temps des autruches*, the 'time of ostriches'.[41]

But things did go wrong. In the first place, during the Norwegian operations Germany's newest heavy cruiser, the *Blücher*, was sunk along with ten destroyers – Hitler was left with no effective surface fleet with which to invade Britain. Then, he lost a significant portion of his air force during the Battle of France, particularly over the beaches of Dunkirk. An even larger part of his air fleet was demolished in the subsequent Battle of Britain. By autumn 1940 he had to limit his attacks to night-time bombing – hardly an alternative to an invasion that could only take place in daylight.

Hitler did not despair. Britain had been expelled from the Continent. His attention, even before the Battle of Britain, had turned to the main matter of concern, the war with Russia. Once Russia had been defeated Britain would be first paralysed and then defeated as Germany shifted her armaments industry from weapons for the army to the manufacture of a greater air force and navy. Maybe the United States would be drawn in at this stage. It was not an eventuality that worried Hitler much; the United States obviously had no army, navy or air force worth speaking of. By the time the Americans got around to arming themselves Hitler would be master of his continental heartland.

The whole process, so conveniently prepared by the foreign policy of the Weimar Republic in the 1920s, thus depended on Germany avoiding a 'world war'; on the concentration of her armies and resources on one front at a time, on local wars, on well-calculated alliances and relations with neighbours. Hitler's system completely undermined the effectiveness of Britain's naval blockade; Germans, in the first years of the war, were better fed and better clothed than any other belligerent. It destroyed the effectiveness of bombardment, for Germans could swiftly rebuild what British bombers destroyed in their long and perilous missions. Britain set up, in the summer of 1940, a Special Operations Executive (SOE) designed to 'set Europe ablaze' with revolt; ineffective blockade and bombardment ensured there would be no such revolt. Hitler's system worked, just as long as there was no 'world war'.

The alliances fell into place, all under Hitler's initiative. Once the war in Western Europe had started, the Italians and the Japanese were quick to respond. Mussolini declared war on France and Britain on 10 June as France crumbled and Britain evacuated her troops for a second time. On the day Hitler invaded the Netherlands, 10 May, Japan at last moved south, sending her new Fourth Fleet in readiness to seize the Dutch East Indies; within a month she had settled her frontier dispute in Manchuria and drafted a neutrality treaty with Hitler's ally, the Soviet Union; in July she got a new prime minister, Konoe Fuminaro, who set up a one-party regime and ordered the army and navy to prepare for war with the Netherlands (that is, the Dutch government-in-exile), the British and the United States. Japan never quite grasped Hitler's idea of limiting oneself to one enemy at a time.

4 The Pact and the periphery

The Soviet Union understood Hitler's strategy only too well, though Stalin could never bring himself to believe that his country could seriously be regarded by the Germans as an enemy, an object for conquest and settlement. It made no sense to him. Stalin had studied the historical science of Marx and Lenin, not *Mein Kampf*, and this science laid down the law that capitalism, in its final stages, developed into imperialism; Germany, under the National Socialists, was a monopoly capitalist power that, having thrown other capitalists off the Continent, would pursue other capitalists in their empires. During the 'Second Imperialist War', as capitalists fought capitalists in the West, a new Communist era would be born in Eastern Europe on the base of an expanding Soviet Union. That was Stalin's purpose when he signed the Nazi-Soviet Pact in August 1939 and a peace campaign was begun by obedient Communist parties throughout the world: this war was an affair of capitalists and Western imperialists. In the latter, Nazi Germany and Soviet Russia had a common enemy. Why would Germany want to invade Russia? She could have everything she asked for without a fight – weapons, food, all the products of Asia (rubber, tin, tungsten) carried by train across Siberia.

The Nazi-Soviet Pact opened up fantastic perspectives for Stalin: new western frontiers with Germany, peace with Japan, improved relations with Fascist Italy: together they would all march south against the empires of the Western imperialists. Germany and Italy would partition Africa, Russia would have the outlets into the Indian Ocean and the Mediterranean that the Tsars had only dreamed of, Japan would occupy South-East Asia. This was the substance of the talks between the German and Russian foreign ministers, Ribbentrop and Molotov, in Berlin in October 1940 as they negotiated the Soviet Union's entry into the Tripartite Pact. Ribbentrop even presented Molotov with a draft treaty, though he knew full well it would lead nowhere: Hitler's generals were planning next year's invasion of Russia.

On 25 November 1940 Moscow sent a revised protocol of the proposed treaty to Berlin. Why didn't Berlin answer? Hitler's allies, Italy and Japan, were very keen on the new deal with the Soviets, and would remain so until the end of the war. Mussolini thought he could reach an agreement over the Balkans. The Japanese, relieved at the idea of having peace in their rear, were so impatient with German stalling that, in the end, they signed a separate Neutrality Pact with the Soviets in April 1941; it remained in force until 1945 and it meant that Japan would never be bombed from Russian air bases.

Stalin never understood the purpose of the Balkan wars in the winter and spring of 1940–1; he thought Hitler was moving against British interests, not preparing his right flank against Russia. He complained about German armaments to Finland, but failed entirely to see this as a move-ment on the German left flank; instead, the Red Army occupied the whole of Lithuania and paid Germany for the portion that had been promised Hitler in 1939 – at the equivalent US dollar price that Americans had paid for the purchase of Alaska back in 1867.

Stalin, in fact, never abandoned the great dream of the Nazi-Soviet Pact, even after the Nazi invasion of 22 June 1941, the anniversary of Napoleon's invasion in 1812. Stalin would teach Hitler an old Russian lesson as the 'Second Imperialist War' was transformed into the 'Great Patriotic War'; but he had a fascination for Hitler, just as the mystic Tsar Alexander had a fascination for Napoleon: he would teach his *frère-ennemi* a lesson, and then make an offer for peace.

The Battle of Stalingrad, in the winter of 1942–3, is often considered the great turning-point of the Second World War – the 'stern lesson in history', as the Russian papers proclaimed at the time[42] – but there was nothing to indicate, after the surrender of the German Sixth Army, exactly where that war was turning. Stalin received the greatest shock of his life when the Germans took Kharkov the following March and established a line on the Donets, 150 miles east of the Dnieper. By that time the Germans had captured, since the invasion, 3.9 million Soviet soldiers, of whom 2.8 million were already dead (at least a quarter of a million had been shot, the rest had starved).

In the spring and early summer of 1943, Stalin's representatives in Stockholm attempted to negotiate a revived Pact; it failed because Hitler insisted on holding on to the Ukraine, which he would lose, anyway, the next winter. The summer of 1943 was the real turning-point of the war. Hadn't Hitler yet learnt his lesson? Gradually the idea dawned on the Soviet dictator that he could do without Hitler. As the Soviet armies rolled forward, Stalin could nourish the dream of imposing on Europe a novel kind of Nazi–Soviet Pact – one minus the Nazis.

The long jagged Eastern Front, devouring lives by the million, set the general pattern of fighting elsewhere. It played the part of the Western Front in the First World War, though, if the parallel is to be pursued, this was the Western Front of 1918, the 'war of movement', during which Ludendorff pressed offensive after offensive to his right and to his left, without ever managing to establish a point of strategic strength. Hitler had the same problem in Russia; those isolated strikes of his led nowhere. Yet there was this major difference between the two wars: in the First World War German military command gave the orders and political authority followed; in the Second World War German political authority gave the orders, and it was the military command that followed. There would be no ambiguity about German political responsibility at the end of the Second War.

Insofar as the situation on the Eastern Front was to determine the rest of the war, Hitler still held the initiative in 1943. But he was no longer fighting on a single front; he no longer faced an isolated enemy. At the moment that Stalingrad fell, Hitler was building up his forces – including a large proportion of his air force and almost all of his bombers – for not simply a holding operation, but an offensive in Tunisia. During his critical summer offensive on Kursk, German troops were being poured into Italy. At the same time, the numbers game in the naval battle of the Atlantic was turning against him. The Japanese, drawn into a war of attrition at Guadalcanal in the South Pacific, were not responding to his pleas to move into the Indian Ocean. Hitler was fighting a 'world war', the war he could not win.

His carefully calculated shift in armaments production in preparation for an air and naval war against Britain and the United States following the defeat of Russia had been thrown askew. Confident of annihilating Russia within a few weeks he had ordered the reorientation in war manufacture in the week prior to his invasion in June 1941, but he had already reversed this decision by September. By 1943, as a result of Allied bombing campaigns, half of Germany's artillery was pointing into the skies and 45 per cent of Germany's fighters had been brought west. The Battle of the Atlantic demanded an increase in submarine production at the expense of thousands of needed tanks. German manufacturers could not keep up with the series of conflicting orders; in June 1944, as Allied troops poured into Normandy, they delivered four battleship engines, with no ships to put them in.[43] As a result of Hitler's drawn-out war in the east, the initiative moved west.

On the ground, the contrast between British peripheral strategy and the American desire to strike at Hitler's Europe in her heartland was never as great as it appeared in theory. Britain had been thrown off the Continent three times in 1940 and America, for a long time thereafter, had no means of re-entering it. All the Allies – British, Americans, the Free French, the Poles, all the governments-in-exile – were obliged to fight a war on the peripheries of the 'world island'.

From 1940 to 1943 the two main peripheral theatres for the Allies were, first, in North Africa and the Near East, which denied Germany oil resources and access to the Indian Ocean, and, second, in the South Pacific. Though 14,000 miles from Europe the Battle of the Coral Seas and the subsequent fighting in the Solomons, the Bismarck Archipelago and New Guinea (almost wholly conducted by the Americans) contributed to the Allied cause in Europe by preventing Japan from moving westwards and joining the Axis powers in the Indian Ocean, as Hitler was so keen for them to do. Thus, far from being a diversion, action in the Pacific fell into line with the Allied policy of 'Europe First'; the victory in the Pacific, it was thought, was years off, while a victory in Europe would have an immediate impact on Japan's fighting power.

The German capture of the British garrison of 33,000 men at Tobruk, Libya, in June 1942 had the effect of concentrating Allied minds on the significance of the peripheral war. The command in North Africa was changed (General, later Field Marshal, Sir Harold Alexander became Commander-in-Chief, and General Bernard Montgomery took command of the British Eighth Army). American Sherman tanks and combat troops were committed to North Africa for the first time; they were joined by the Free French and the Poles.

After Montgomery's dramatic victory at El Alamein in October 1942 over the German Afrika Corps of General Erwin Rommel – who was, not for the last time, away on leave at the critical opening moments of the offensive – the peripheral war gained momentum. Over the next year the Americans themselves were obliged to follow the main lines of British strategy on German-controlled peninsular Europe: blockade, bombing and the encouragement of revolt.

Blockade had little effect on Germany. Unlike Japan, Germany had plenty of neighbours who were willing or forced to supply her needs. The thousand-bomber raids of 1942, on the other hand, began to divert German weapons and disperse her manufactures – which she could ill afford during the second year of war on the Eastern Front. As for the encouragement of internal rebellion, the Western Allies soon discovered that they were working in competition with Stalin's Soviet Union.

Among the foes of Hitler's Reich, the Soviet Union was at all times the great exception. Her war was not peripheral; she bore the brunt of the fighting in Europe's heartland. But was the Soviet Union an ally of the West? 'We rejoiced to have this mighty nation in the battle with us,' wrote Churchill. Yet Churchill himself remarked on the coldness, the 'hectoring and reproaches', that were felt by every Westerner who had to deal with the Kremlin.[44] Britain and America shared their secrets with Russia; Russia shared none. The Western Allies delivered goods and armaments; but Stalin, unlike with his former German ally, never granted credit; he did not even provide air protection at the main northern port of Murmansk. Stalin never opened serious negotiations with the West, as he had – and would continue to do – with his earlier German ally. An Anglo-Soviet agreement not to make a separate peace or armistice without mutual consent was signed, at Stalin's request, on 12 July 1941; but that agreement never calmed the well-founded fears of the Allies, confirmed by their reading of Japanese diplomatic telegrams, that Stalin was always ready for a separate peace.

Almost a year passed before Stalin signed, on 26 May 1942, a formal alliance with Britain and the United States; unlike the Nazi-Soviet Pact, however, it contained no territorial provisions. Stalin refused to attend all alliance summits until the summer of 1942, and even then no meeting took place until the following November, more than seventeen months after Hitler's invasion. Again, through their ability to break the Japanese diplomatic code, the American and British governments were aware of Soviet peace offers to Hitler in 1943; indeed, Stalin recalled his ambassadors from London and Washington that June for consultations. Britain and America feared Stalin was about to change sides once more.

Even as Hitler's empire was crumbling, the shadow of the Nazi Soviet Pact lay over the 'alliance' of the Western Powers with Stalin.

5 Partisans

By all accounts of the war, 1943 was the turning point. But the view provided by historians is usually military. An understanding of what was to emerge as the post-war world requires a wider lens. Something changed in Western and Soviet efforts 'to set Europe ablaze' with rebellion. The post-war mythologies about Nazi 'resisters' and Nazi 'collaborators' began to take shape now, in a way often crude and manichean. Western efforts tended to reflect the style of their military campaigns; they were peripheral, isolated operations. Soviet efforts, on the other hand, sought at first to retrieve and then expand a Soviet state system in lands lost during the initial Nazi offensive of 1941; like its campaigns, Soviet-inspired resistance was continental in nature, its networks answerable to a single state authority, Moscow. There was no such authority in the West. London might have set up the SOE in the summer of 1940 to encourage rebellion in occupied Europe; but rebellion was its only ambition, and it soon found itself competing with other agencies among the various governments-in-exile in London as well as with agencies of its own government and armed forces. Resistance in Eastern Europe had an authoritarian model standing behind it; resistance in Western Europe showed a marked tendency to slip into anarchy.

There was also a whole historical ideology sustaining resistance in the East, while the idea of resistance in the West was vague, revolving around an old-fashioned theme, 'liberty'. In Stalin's view of the global historical process the Nazi state, a state monopoly of capitalism, was more compatible with the Communist state – more historically evolved – than the anarchic liberal capitalism of the West. The Nazi-Soviet Pact was not, thus, just a quirk of circumstances but a perfectly natural development that aligned one state system at the withering end of capitalism with another, now entering the new age of Communism, the future of the world. Germany might be expected to become the stepping stone of the Communist system westwards (as the writings of Lenin had already foreseen): Hitler's revolution set the stage. Liberal capitalist Britain and France declared war on state-capitalist Germany: 'Let them wear themselves out on each other,' Stalin told Molotov on 7 September 1939.[45] When Hitler launched his war of extermination eastwards in June 1941, Stalin was so shocked he withdrew to his dacha at Kuntsevo for almost a fortnight; but he didn't abandon his vision of history. Western Communists spoke of the Nazi-Soviet Pact as a 'tactical parenthesis' and promptly forgot it: not Stalin. So, he would have to fight his colossal neighbour on the European plains, this system just a few steps behind in the historical process; but that in no way contradicted his own hopes of expansion, and he was always ready for another accord. The battle required soldiers; Stalin had no difficulty in finding them. It also required people who were ready to lay down their lives for the history Stalin believed in, for the lands he had been forced to abandon, for the lands into which his system was eventually expected to expand. These were the 'Partisans' – fighting comrades in the Nazi-occupied territories who prepared the ground not only for soldiers, but also for the future Soviet state system.

As with the armies, there was a geography that defined the place of Communist Partisans. On the Eastern Front they lay beyond the battle zones on the German side of the line. They could not hide in the open plains of the southern Ukraine, and in the Crimean peninsula and the northern Caucasus German forces were able to hunt them down. Their terrain lay in the forests and swamps of the northern Ukraine, in Belorussia and those parts of the Russian Soviet Socialist Republic that the Germans had taken over. They grew up among former Soviet petty officials, the men of the tractor stations, the collective farms, the army officers who had escaped the great manoeuvres of German encirclement; they recruited the stragglers, terrified to be caught in the German net, in which they knew they would be either shot or starved. They armed themselves with the weapons Germans had abandoned. As the tide of the war turned, Germans no longer had the means to police them with the Security Divisions, which now had to be sent to the front. Whole areas were thus brought back to Soviet rule – with its newspapers, its intelligence service, its people's courts, its methods of punishment – long before the Red Army reappeared. By early 1944 Partisans were in a position to blow the roads, smash the rails, destroy the telegraph poles, harass enemy reinforcements and, in general, prepare the ground for the armies of Aleksandr Vasilevsky, Georgi Zhukov, Konstantin Rokossovsky and Ivan Konev on their bitter way westward, on to Warsaw.

The Partisans were thus both spearheads for the armies and the vanguards of post-war government. Resistance organizations in the West performed a similar task. But it would be wrong to portray the resistance movements as simply marginal forces in front of the advancing armies and the precursors of governments of liberation once the armies had passed. In the first place, Western-inspired resistance was not limited to the West, while Communist-inspired resistance was not confined to the East. More importantly, beneath all movements of resistance to – as well as collaboration with – the Nazi empire lay an age-old history of national identities, ethnic rivalries and regional disputes that defined the very character of Europe.

These pasts, some dating back centuries, 'folded over one another like tectonic plates' as one historian has put it recently.[46] Though the cry went up for a new world as the armies marched forward to liberate one city after another, the truth was that it was an old world the inhabitants would have to face. Europe was criss-crossed by frontiers that just would not go away. Thus, the enormous variation in the forms of resistance.

Once Russia was invaded, the Partisan movement spread south-east into the Balkans. But Tito's organized army was a force unique to Yugoslavia; ethnic, religious and national rivalries in this old frontier area of the Ottoman Empire threw it into a civil war with Croatian 'Ustasha' and Serb 'Chetniks', whose violence shocked even the German SS; over ten per cent of Yugoslavia's population would die, in less than five years, of war-related deaths. Greece was a peninsula that relied on overseas trade, so when Germany turned it into a part of 'Fortress Europe' nearly a quarter of a million people, during the first winter of occupation, died of starvation: Greece was so exhausted by the experience of occupation that the main resistance movement, EAM, with its armed units, ELAS, both run by Partisans, barely showed its head until after the Germans had withdrawn, when it plunged into a civil war with Greek monarchists. Britain's SOE was behind the assassination of Reinhard Heydrich, Deputy Protector of Bohemia and Moravia, in May 1942. Hitler's brutal reprisal – 1,300 Czechs were rounded up and executed, and the village of Lidice (whose name was discovered on one of the arrested SOE agents) was destroyed – in this case seemed to work, for no large-scale resistance movement developed among the Czechs. It was quite the opposite in neighbouring Slovakia, a puppet state of the Reich since 1939, where the army, aided by Partisans, in autumn 1944 led one of the largest national uprisings in all Europe; it was savagely repressed.

In the West there would never develop anything comparable to the underground armies and state systems that were to be found in the East. Denmark was taken over so quickly by the Germans that it did not have time to develop a resistance; until August 1943 she was left to govern herself, but with the military emergency proclaimed that month organized opposition grew. Sweden maintained a policy of collaborative 'neutrality' with Germany until she was sure the Reich was going to collapse. Finland was an uncertain ally. Norway was famous for its Quisling; the country was the last battlefield of the war – Germans were still busy executing their own troops in the area after the formal surrender of 8 May 1945. Belgium, it must be said, had one of the gentler experiences of the war, though, out of spite, the Louvain library was burnt down again, as it had been during the First World War. Luxembourg, like Belgium, was tempted to follow the French model and sign an armistice with the Germans in 1940, but Hitler wasn't interested. By the time these two small countries had organized their resistance, the Allied armies had crossed their borders. Is it surprising that the Netherlands, the 'Low Lands by the Sea', the land of the stadtholders, the Arminians, the Remonstrants and Contra-Remonstrants, should have produced one of the largest resistance networks in Western Europe? The Netherlands had been a friend to Germany both during and after the First World War. Germany returned the compliment by stripping this agricultural country of its food reserves. The Netherlands was, like Greece, a seaborne nation; like Greece, she starved.

Nowhere did resistance organizations absorb the majority of inhabitants. Everywhere they bore the legacy of their country's past. They would become, after the war, the subject of legends and the flag of many governments. In no place would they have existed without the presence of the advancing armies, just beyond, just the other side of that sea, that mountain, the lake, the river; resistance of every political complexion and colour grew in the knowledge that 'they were coming'.

In the late spring of 1944, as the Eastern armies gathered forces for the move towards Warsaw, the armies that had recently landed in Normandy looked down the Route Nationale 13 to Paris. Warsaw and Paris: it was here that the first rumours spread in occupied Europe that this terrible war might be over before Christmas.

6 Coincidental deaths

In the month that Stalin withdrew his ambassadors from London and Washington, Jean Moulin, leader of the French National Resistance Council, was arrested by the Gestapo in Lyons (21 June 1943) and General Stefan Grot-Rowecki, Commander-in-Chief of the Polish Home Army, was arrested by the Gestapo in Warsaw (30 June). Four days later General Władysław Sikorski, Prime Minister of the Polish Government in London, was killed in an air crash off Gibraltar. Moulin's disappearance was a near disaster for de Gaulle's provisional government, which was just beginning to take form (as a 'French Committee of National Liberation') in Algiers that month. The loss of Sikorski and Grot-Rowecki proved to be catastrophic for Poland. Who benefited? Nazi Germany was obviously not in mourning. But nor was Stalin. Nobody linked these events at the time, nor have they since. But in the years after the war Western governments – more experienced in the secret ways of the Soviet Union – became suspicious of coincidences like these.

The exact circumstances of Jean Moulin's arrest and death remain one of the most controversial mysteries of recent French history, and will probably never be solved. On evidence left in the 'testament' of his arresting officer, Klaus Barbie, Moulin, shortly after his arrest, threw himself headlong down a stairwell at Gestapo headquarters in Lyons but failed to kill himself. It was, apparently, a recommended technique for maintaining silence under Nazi custody. Pierre Brossolette, who ran the Coordinating Committee of the northern French resistance, ended his life by throwing himself from a balcony after his arrest in Paris the following November. At any rate, German interrogators learned nothing from Moulin. He was transported to Paris. There, at least three French prisoners were asked to identify him, but his head wounds were so severe that this proved virtually impossible. 'How do you expect me to recognize a man in such a state?' said General Delestraint, commander of the French Secret Army, who had been seized at a secret rendezvous point on 9 June. The formal death certificate, delivered by a Gestapo officer to Moulin's mother in May 1944, stated that Moulin had died in Metz, on the German frontier, at 2 a.m. on 8 July 1943.[47]

Who betrayed Jean Moulin? It was a burning question in post-war France. The left blamed René Hardy, deputy to Henri Frenay's conservative southern resistance movement, Combat. The right suspected Raymond Aubrac, a Communist and the main military organizer of the leftward-leaning Libération-Sud. Both men were arrested at Caluire and both of them made the most miraculous escapes – Aubrac's story being made into a self-serving film in 1995.[48] But it is possible that neither man was guilty. Moulin, who held the first meeting of the centralizing National Resistance Council in Paris only three weeks before his arrest, had plenty of enemies on the left and the right. Between April and May 1943, as Moulin pursued his delicate task in occupied France of uniting all the resistance movements, a campaign of denigration was launched against him by leaders of different networks and movements. They complained that he was secretive (it was, sure enough, one of his natural traits), out of touch, and that he behaved like a colonial officer towards 'native chieftains'. Frenay complained that the French Resistance was being bureaucratized by the desk wallahs of London. In London Colonel Passy, head of the Gaullist intelligence agency, the BCRA, and Pierre Brossolette presented a sneering report which claimed that his centralized communications system put in danger the entire Secret Army. Moulin responded to the attacks in kind. During a Paris meeting with Brossolette in April he suddenly stood up, turned his back on Brossolette, dropped his trousers and, waving his bare bottom, screamed, 'Now you can see my opinion of you.' It was a sad scene for two brave men who would both be dead within months.[49]

As Passy and Brossolette's report put it, Moulin certainly did have some bizarre friends who might have been 'indoctrinating him'. Most of them centred around what came to be known as *la bande de Cot*, named after Pierre Cot, who had been the Aviation Minister of France's left-wing Popular Front government of 1936–8.[50] With the war, Cot moved to New York and his close associate, André Labarthe, migrated to London. Both Cot and Labarthe worked for the NKVD, the Soviet intelligence agency and forerunner of the KGB, and were in regular contact with Moscow.[51] In Paris, several of Cot's old friends used to meet regularly at the café, Les Deux Magots, in Saint-Germain-des-Prés – a small fact that would prove to be of some cultural significance in post-war France.

There is no documentary evidence that Moulin was ever a Communist, but his sympathy for many Party members, especially in Paris, cannot be doubted. However, once he had established contact with de Gaulle in London and began work, on de Gaulle's behalf, on the National Resistance Council, that sympathy turned sour. He deliberately kept his distance from Labarthe when in London. He overruled Communist delegates to the Council and – like the good provincial French prefect he was – refused them funding by his control of the budget. This was not simply an act of disloyalty to old friends, a distressing change of heart; it was mortal.

In the two weeks that preceded Moulin's arrest, the Gestapo broke seven resistance networks in France, three of them controlled by the French London-based BCRA, two of them by the British SOE, and two by the Vichy armistice army (such an anti-Nazi resistance existed). No resistance organization linked with the Communists was touched. In the years immediately after the war the French Communist Party claimed to be the party of the '*75,000 fusillés*' ('shot'), which was quite an achievement for a party that had only 10,000 members in 1940. As a matter of fact the Germans did execute a large number of French resisters: around 40,000 of them between June 1940 and July 1944. Many of them died following the wave of arrests that began in the spring of 1943; and the vast majority of them were not Communists.

The Poles called the last day of June and first days of July 1943 the 'Black Week'. Rumours were only just beginning to spread in Warsaw about the arrest of the legendary and mysterious 'General Grot', head of the Home Army, when news of Sikorski's death was triumphantly announced on German loudspeakers. Youngsters of the Small Sabotage – an underground Boy Scout movement – almost immediately began scribbling on the walls,

'The Country with Sikorski'. Everyone knew of 'Grot'; he signed all the communiqués which appeared in the underground newspapers. As for Sikorski, his name was sacred, his 'orders were sacrosanct', he represented Poland at home, Poland abroad; he was the hope of Polish freedom.[52]

Not many in Warsaw would have known 'Grot's' real name, Stefan Rowecki, or his background. He was a professional soldier who, like de Gaulle, had risen to the rank of colonel and, again like de Gaulle, had commanded a motorized army unit at the time his country was invaded. He was an excellent organizer and, once more like de Gaulle, was not interested in party politics. The grandson of a leader of the Polish insurrection against Russia in 1863, he had fought – like many leaders of the Polish Underground – in Józef Piłsudski's Legions in the First World War, as well as in the Soviet-Polish War of 1920 (a campaign in which de Gaulle had also played a small part). But Colonel Rowecki had thereafter kept his distance from Piłsudski and his *Sanacja* regime – a dictatorship of generals. His one concern was 'my country', its straw-thatched cottages, the small fields, the wooden churches in which the brightly coloured kerchiefs of the women mingled with the black caps of the men. Like de Gaulle, he was convinced Hitler was going to lose his war. Unlike de Gaulle, he recognized the threat from a second giant to the east, the Soviet Union, and he developed, under the German occupation, a 'doctrine of two enemies'. Grot-Rowecki worked for a post-war world where a sovereign Poland would have earned her place on Europe's northern plain, and would not be dismissed as *'une motte de terre'*.[53]

When, early on Wednesday morning, 30 June, SS Untersturmführer Erich Merten turned up at his door with a posse of Gestapo men, he could not have been too surprised. In Warsaw, wrote Jan Nowak, who spent his time commuting between wartime London and the occupied Polish capital, 'pure chance decided between life and death'.[54] The cycle of reprisals and counter-reprisals was reaching unprecedented heights at that moment; the Germans had shot five hundred men and twenty-five women in Pawiak gaol – 'prisoners in Pawiak were overcome with nausea from the putrid smell of burning flesh' – so underground commandos gunned down an SS captain and two German lieutenants in the dance hall of the Adria Hotel. Now Poles were boycotting Germany's desperate campaign for 'voluntary labour' in the Reich.[55] Grot-Rowecki was dragged off to a prison outside Berlin and later transferred to the Oranienburg concentration camp, where he was executed on the personal orders of Himmler in early August 1944, at the outbreak of the Warsaw Rising.

Sikorski's death was all the more sudden for being unexpected. He had flown out from London to review the Polish II Corps, made up of about

200,000 deportees who had been released by Stalin, during the brief thaw in Russian-Polish relations in 1941, from his prison camps in Siberia and Central Asia; from Tashkent, they had crossed Persia, and were now stationed in the Middle East, under British command. Diplomatic relations between Russia and Sikorski's government in London were broken at the end of April 1943, shortly after the Germans announced and produced film of their discovery of a mass grave of around 4,000 Polish officers in Katyn Forest, outside Smolensk. Stalin used the occasion to grind down the authority of the London government along with that of the Home Army and Underground State in Poland that was answerable to it: he accused the London Poles of cooperating with the Nazis (which he was, in the meantime, attempting to do himself), and began building up a new Communist Polish force under the command of the Red Army. Many in the British and American press thought that the London Poles, when they demanded that the International Red Cross investigate the report of the massacre, were playing to Goebbels's propaganda. But, sure enough, it was Stalin who had ordered the shooting of the 4,404 Polish officers at Katyn (the instructions were confirmed in a meeting of the Politburo on 5 March 1940) as he had ordered the shooting of 3,896 at Kharkov and 6,287 at Kalinin (modern Tver) – these facts were, however, gradually revealed only after 1990. Another 15,000 Polish soldiers appear to have been deliberately drowned in the White Sea.[56]

London and Washington were desperately trying to keep Stalin in the Western camp. Napoleon had once referred to Poland as the 'key to the vault', the capstone, of Europe; so it was proving to be in the alliance system against Hitler. On 16 June Roosevelt sent a sealed message to Sikorski in Beirut urging him to discourage extremist talk about their recent experience of Soviet hospitality; Sikorski explained to the troops on review that he followed a policy of 'seeking and maintaining an honourable agreement with the Soviet Union'. He then headed back to London for further negotiations with his Western Allies over Poland's place in the post-war world.

He got no further than Gibraltar. There, on Sunday evening, 4 July, the pilot of the Lancaster bomber carrying Sikorski, his daughter, and leading figures of the Polish General Staff, lost control immediately after take-off and the aircraft tumbled into the sea. The sodden bodies of Sikorski and his chief of staff were recovered the next day and were carried, in solemn procession, to the Roman Catholic Cathedral of St Mary the Crowned.[57]

'The consequences of this tragedy', wrote Jan Nowak, looking back over thirty years, 'went beyond the loss of an outstanding leader. General

Sikorski held both political and military power. After his death, that power was split.'[58]

'The Poles', Anthony Eden, the British Foreign Secretary, reported in July, 'are being very difficult about their aspirations.'[59]

7 Coincidental battles: continent and periphery

Resistance to the Nazis in occupied Europe was always just one step ahead of the armies. The movement of the armies determined the size of its membership, the complexity of its organization and the intensity of its violence. Jean Moulin himself, as a prefect in Chartres, was a public advocate of collaboration with the enemy in 1940. The Poles had no such choice; they could either submit to lawless terror, or resist. Even here, however, it was the approach of Hitler's enemies that set the tone and the scale of underground activity.

In 1943 Hitler's war became the world war he had so wanted to avoid. He lost the initiative. The two major military events of that year were the failure of the German armies to close the southern Russian salient around Kursk and the landing of the Allied armies in Italy, their first foothold in Europe. Both occurred almost simultaneously, in early July. The same year, western German cities were exposed to massive bombardment.

The German offensive towards Kursk began on Sunday, 4 July – the day Sikorski died – with a huge air attack on what were taken to be Russian airfields inside the salient; many of them however were made up of dummy planes and hangars lovingly prepared by Major Lukyanov of Russia's Second Air Army. German ground forces moved forward early the next morning against what turned out to be the heaviest Russian defences they had met to date; all spring, the Russians had been receiving daily reports from 'Lucy' (Rudolf Rossler), a top-level Soviet agent inside OKW, the German Army High Command. Within twelve hours the fight for Kursk had been transformed into a 'great glowing furnace'; by the following weekend it had become the largest tank battle in history: on the steppe south of Prokhorovka, studded with small plots, gardens, and the cornfields about them; under skies of rolling storm clouds; in winds, lightning and a scudding rain, well over a thousand tanks fought in groups and in individual actions. The 'slaughter at Prokhorovka', which left the ground strewn with burnt-out tanks, lorries and tens of thousands of dead, was completed in eighteen hours. Hitler called off the entire operation on Tuesday, 13 July.[60]

The Allied invasion of Sicily had begun that weekend. The bombing preliminaries, involving night attacks by Wellingtons and daylight raids by Flying Fortresses, had lasted over a month. Naval bombardment had reduced the tiny but strategic island of Pantellaria, sixty miles south of Sicily, to rubble – more bombs were dropped on its thirty square miles than on all targets in Tunisia, Sicily, Sardinia and Italy in April. On 11 June it was occupied in an operation that lasted twenty minutes and cost the Allies two wounded soldiers. Smiling Italian prisoners of war were photographed by reporters. General George Marshall, Chief of Staff of the United States Army, warned in a speech delivered in Columbus, Ohio, on 21 June, against 'hasty conclusions or impromptu conceptions regarding the utilization of air power or any special weapons in the conduct of this war'; then promptly added, 'This is a most critical summer, both for us and in the history of the world . . . We have seized the initiative, the most vital factor in war.'[61] Deception operations were mounted to give the Germans the impression that the main landings were to take place in Sardinia or in Greece. One of them relied on the pro-Axis sympathies of Franco's Spain; forged papers were floated ashore on a Spanish beach upon the body of a 'naval officer', who was in fact a civilian who had died of pneumonia, the 'Man Who Never Was'. The combined Anglo-American assault on Sicily was only partly successful; it led to the capture of many more smiling Italians, while the Germans were pushed off to the mainland, where they prepared for another fight. Alan Moorehead, one of the most famous newspaper correspondents of the Second World War, described his lazy July days with some British soldiers who made their home in the pinnacled village of Taormina overlooking the Straits of Messina and the mainland beyond. There was the owner, an Italian architect, and his bulbous and blooming Latin wife; there was the cook, Sofia (or was it Sophia?) – 'Yes, yes, yes. Onions in the soup. Of course'; and there was the 'gap between them [the Italians] and the enemy'.[62]

In many parts of Europe, that 'gap' between and around the warring armies was most frequently filled by the Resistance. That 'gap' set the conditions that led to the disappearance of Jean Moulin, Grot-Rowecki and Sikorski.

In the two months that preceded Kursk and the Italian invasion there had been a lull in military activity. There had been no major actions on the Eastern Front. The Allies had cleared North Africa of Italian and German forces by early May. Bad weather even postponed bombardment of the German Rhineland and the Ruhr. The most notable action of the time was Russia's escalating 'Partisan war', which would exercise an influence on resistance networks, Communist and non-Communist alike, throughout Europe – networks that were burgeoning with new recruits trying to escape the German levy of slave labour, itself a product of earlier military losses.

The Partisan war, fought in the western borderlands of Russia at the time under German occupation, was hardly a minor affair. In the weekend of 12–13 June, for example, a German source reported that 1,600 Partisans had been killed or captured in the forests and swamps of the Bryansk region and '118 villages and forest camps' taken.[63] In all likelihood a large number of the 'SS and police troops' involved in the operation were not German: a civil war was raging between pro-Soviet and anti-Soviet bands and battalions equipped with machine-guns, artillery, tanks and even aircraft. They were fighting with words, too – wicked words and slogans that spread across frontiers, some directed from Berlin and Moscow, others invented on the spot.

The propaganda was vicious because it was competing for the allegiance of these heavily armed bands. They could be Nazi 'collaborators' one month and Communist 'partisans' the next, and both sides were infiltrated with agents and double agents, who themselves became confused about who they were fighting for. By 1943 the Germans, despite their death-dealing scorn for the Slav *Untermensch*, were running a huge campaign to gain the loyalty of the occupied districts, recruit former Soviet citizens for military service, and encourage defection from the Red Army. The Soviets countered with a 're-defection' campaign that promised a new world after the war: the churches would be revived, the nations that made up the Soviet Union would become separate republics, the Communist Party would be transformed into a people's party. Stalin himself was portrayed as a temporary expedient, the necessary leader who would prosecute the war and then retire. But it was 'the people's' war, 'the people' under arms, and 'the people' who would create the new world. This message passed through all the Partisan networks of Europe.

The Comintern, which united the Communist parties of the world, was formally abolished. The idea of 'liberation committees' – which went back to the Russian Civil War of 1919 – was revived. For every area liberated by the Red Army, there would be a committee in waiting, ready to take over the administration.

In the Russian borderlands the 're-defection' campaign was proving, by late spring and early summer 1943, to be an enormous success. The armed bands were beginning to appreciate which way the wind was blowing. Tens of thousands switched sides. Gill-Rodionov's '1st Russian SS National Regiment', operating out of Mogilev, negotiated with the Belorussian Staff of the Partisan Movement for over a month, and in mid-August – having shot the Germans amongst them and handed over two of their commanders for execution – became the '1st Anti-Fascist Brigade'.

But there were some 'defector-collaborators' who put no faith in Partisans and their liberation committees. The most notorious was General Andrei Vlasov, a high-ranking Soviet commander until he was captured on the Volkhov front south of Leningrad in May 1942. Vlasov was carted off to Berlin, where he converted to a new cause. It was Vlasov who was, to a large extent, responsible for the German propaganda campaign in the Russian borderlands, beginning with the Smolensk Manifesto of early 1943. He also ran the anti-Partisan forces in the area, of which the powerful Kaminsky Brigade was the most famous, and murderous. Stalin said at the time that Vlasov was 'at the very least a large obstacle on the road to victory over the German Fascists'.[64]

The Communist project was to kill him.

Grot-Rowecki, in the months preceding his arrest by the Gestapo, had been warning London about the spread of Communist support in Poland. The propaganda, he said, was beginning to have an effect, particularly among the 'less politically conscious elements' of Poland's unhappy population. The Communists had never been very popular in the country, for understandable reasons: the Russian Bolsheviks, with their military invasion of 1921 (in which Stalin had played a major role), had nearly throttled Poland at its birth; in the late 1930s Stalin had liquidated the Polish Communist Party during his purges; then after signing the Nazi-Soviet Pact he invaded the country for a second time – in the two years of Soviet rule east of the Bug, he had managed to kill more Poles (half a million of them) than even the Nazis had achieved in the same period. 'Stalin's trains', which deported over one and a half million men, women and children, would never be forgotten.

A new Polish Communist Party, the PPR (or 'Polish Workers' Party'), was set up in 1942. It was coordinated with the 'Partisans' in Russia, and specialized in sabotage and assassination – an activity that had its attractions in occupied Poland. Yet, in early 1943, it is estimated that the Party had only 8,000 members, well below the 400,000 in the Home Army and its affiliates. Nevertheless, Grot-Rowecki was right: 1943 was the year Communist support in Poland began to grow. As in the Russian borderlands, the Polish Communists promised a future free from 'Fascism' and economic exploitation; they spoke of setting up a 'democratic' and 'anti-Fascist national front'. In language that was remarkably similar to the Partisan slogans around Bryansk, they continually repeated, 'The Red Army is doing its job – we must do ours.' The Red Army was never far from the thoughts of the Partisans.[65]

But for Poles, if they thought at all about the army that they had, they concentrated even more on the army that was gone. Around 200,000 Poles managed to escape their country before the Nazi-Soviet pincers closed the frontiers in late September 1939. Unlike France, which sat comfortably ensconced between two seas on the western end of peninsular Europe, Poland offered no easy route of exit; the sea to the north was under the control of both enemies, while the roads south led overland across countries that had not traditionally been friendly. Many did, however, escape through Lithuania and then westwards via the Baltic; Romania, which at that time had a common frontier with Poland, provided a major route; and some tens of thousands got out through Hungary.

The Germans referred to these exiled Poles as 'Sikorski's tourists'. As Hitler and his allies extended tentacles into the 'world island', Sikorski's tourists joined hands in the peripheral operations of the opposition. They fought alongside the British at Narvik, in Norway, in April 1940. They contributed to the defence of France in May and June. Between 17,000 and 18,000 then escaped to Britain – 15 per cent of the enemy aircraft destroyed in the Battle of Britain were shot down by Polish pilots. Britain, in her wisdom, sent most of these refugee soldiers north to man Scotland's coastal defences. With the help of the Americans they bought their own guns, their own tanks, and formed, under the command of Stanisław Maczek, the 1st Polish Armoured Division: it would be one of the grandest fighting units on the Normandy front.[66]

Another hundred thousand-odd Poles, both soldiers and civilians, made their way across Persia after being released by Stalin, without food rations, in the summer of 1942 – as the fight for North Africa got under way. They formed the Polish II Corps and joined the campaigns of the British Eighth Army at Tobruk, Anzio, Rome, Sangro and the Gothic Line.

Would the Poles accompany the Western armies to Poland? Poles inside Poland hoped they would.

7 Terror in Poland

Once the pincers had closed, Poland, isolated from all outside help, was transformed into one vast camp of terror, destruction and extermination. And so it lasted for over five long years.

'The fact of being a Pole was a deadly sin in itself,' recalled one resistance leader. Poland was divided. The western provinces were incorporated into the Reich, the eastern provinces into the Soviet Union, while the rest was known as the 'General–Gouvernement' – the name 'Poland' was wiped off the map. The General–Gouvernement was extended south and east into Galicia after Hitler's invasion of Russia. The population was classified into four separate races, *Reichsdeutsch* (Germans born within the former frontiers of the Reich), *Volksdeutsch* (those who could demonstrate German ancestry in their blood), *Nichtdeutsch* (the Poles) and *Juden* (the Jews). Then they were segregated and the programme of terror was installed. Of the 18 million Nazi victims in Europe, 11 million of them died in Poland. Many had been transported to Poland to die.[67]

There is no doubt about it, the Jews fared worst. The purpose of the sterilization experiments that were conducted on them was not for their benefit, for all Jews were to be murdered; sterilization was to be applied to the Slavs.

The terror developed in waves.[68] The months that preceded Sikorski's death and the Kursk battle was one of the worst, up to that date. Late April and May 1943 saw the total destruction of the Warsaw Ghetto. Meanwhile, in the Zamość region over 100,000 Polish peasants were evicted from 300 villages in a pilot programme of the project *Generalplan Ost*, designed to replace all Slavs between the Oder and the Dnieper with German settlers, in accordance with the gospel of *Mein Kampf*.

Back in 1515, when the Republic of Venice decided to segregate all Jews behind a high wall guarded by ten watchmen on the site of a former canon foundry known as the *ghetto nuovo*, they gave a new word to the world; but the Venetian *ghetto* was full of treasures, there was no lack of gaiety among the people, there were schools, and a grand culture developed.[69] The Warsaw Ghetto was built by the Nazis as one collecting centre for Jews from all over Poland – similar ghettos were constructed at Łódź and Wilno. Its sole purpose was their extermination, though the official reason given was that Jews were the carriers of typhus.

Located in the western half of the Old Town, the Warsaw Ghetto only vaguely corresponded to the Jewish district before the war; when the Jews, in October 1940, were ordered to move into it, around 113,000 other Poles were forced to move out. The high red-brick wall had started going up in May; by November 1940 its ten gates, heavily guarded by German security forces with specially trained attacker dogs, were closed. In March 1941, 460,000 Jews had been squeezed into an area of narrow streets and old buildings that had a total of only 140,000 rooms. Around 83,000 died of hunger and sickness in the next eighteen months.

The programme of deportation for mass murder at Treblinka and

Auschwitz began in earnest in July 1942: the Jews were collected in a square by the branch railway at Stawki with the promise, in the first days, of three kilogrammes of bread and one kilogramme of jam for each person who 'volunteered' for 'labour'. Adam Czerniakow, head of the German-organized Jewish Council and 'mayor' of the Ghetto, committed suicide at the end of that month – a clear signal to the population as to what was happening. 'Three p.m.,' he wrote in his last desperate note. 'So far, three thousand ready to go. By four p.m., according to orders, there must be nine thousand. I am helpless; sorrow and pity fill my heart. I cannot stand it any longer. My end will show everybody what must be done.' He then took cyanide.

By September over 300,000 Jews of the Ghetto had been transported to their deaths. Poles living in the neighbourhood could hear their cries. The district court of Leszno was housed in a building on Ogrodowa Street with windows that overlooked the collecting point. The Jews could be seen half-running, jostling each other, as German guards drove them on with whips, shouting, '*Los! Los! Aber schnell!*'

'Don't die with a Torah in your hand,' read posters rapidly stuck up on the walls; 'die with weapons in your hand!' They started appearing in early September 1942, placed there by a 'Jewish Battle Organization' which was collecting guns supplied through the city's sewer tunnels by the 'Council for Assistance to Jews' (RPZ), a branch of the Home Army. By then the Ghetto had been reduced to 100,000. People moved around the streets like skeletons, 'scarecrows with sunken, glassy eyes'. The 'dying lay on the ground or leaned against the buildings'. The dead were covered with newspapers, and collection of the bodies was organized twice daily by the Jewish street-cleaning department.

The Ghetto Rising began early Monday morning, 19 April 1943. Using heavy artillery at point-blank range, the German SS and Police, under the command of SS Brigadeführer Jürgen Stroop, destroyed one house after another. On Thursday the Luftwaffe joined in, dropping incendiary bombs which created great cumulus clouds turning from amber to deep red; that entire section of the city was enveloped in grey and black smoke, the glow visible from every part of Warsaw. Typed posters began to appear on walls outside the Ghetto the next day reading, 'We, the prisoners of the Ghetto, send you brotherly heartfelt greetings . . . The Fight is being waged for Your Freedom and Ours! For Your and Our Honour and Dignity – Human, Social, National!'

Cinder and burnt paper covered the streets of the most distant suburbs. Heinkel bombers roared across the sky. In the second week of the fighting the cinemas showed film of the pile of Polish officers' bodies uncovered by the Germans in Katyn Forest; it was as if the denunciation of one crime could detract from the other going on under the very eyes of Varsovians. In the fourth week the slaughter was given a finishing touch: Stroop's soldiers dynamited the few ruins still standing. A whisper went round the rest of Warsaw, 'It will be our turn next.'[70]

For many, their turn had already arrived. Since 1939, the Nazi programme had been neither to integrate nor to marginalize Poland; it was to destroy it and, in particular, to eradicate all purveyors of culture, of learning, of political, military and moral leadership. Like the Jews, the 'Polish intelligentsia' was to be wiped out, the 'intelligentsia' being officially defined as 'priests, teachers (including university lecturers), doctors, dentists, veterinary surgeons, officers, executives, businessmen, landowners, writers, journalists, plus all the people who have received a higher or secondary education'. Hans Frank, Hitler's former lawyer who had been named Governor of the General-Gouvernement in September 1939, wrote in his diary, 'All the representatives of the Polish intelligentsia must be killed. It sounds cruel, but it is the right of life.'[71]

Frank ruled from Wawel Castle, a grand palace on a high hill in Cracow. Cracow had been a city contested for centuries between Czechs, Poles and Austrians; it could never be considered the capital of Poland – which is why the Germans chose to place their administration there.

Warsaw was to be turned into *ein neue deutsche Stadt*, a provincial German town. The executions were carried out in the surrounding Palmiry and Kampinos forests, in the prisons, in the Parliament Gardens and, after May 1943, behind the walls of the flattened Jewish Ghetto. The winter of 1942–3 – which coincided with the siege of Stalingrad – saw the first public executions by hanging. Between October 1942 and October 1943, 11,000 residents of Warsaw alone (not counting, of course, the Jewish holocaust) were executed and 13,000 were transported to concentration camps. After that, the 'law' of *lapanka*, or 'seizure of hostages', was introduced; its victims were publicly tormented and killed in the streets.

In Poland people were killed for no reason at all – for being out after curfew, for possessing a radio, for selling white bread, or simply for being present when the guards or the troops passed by. But it was the 'intelligentsia' who were targeted. There are no reliable statistics on how many teachers, how many dentists, how many vets, how many businessmen, writers and journalists were liquidated – all one can say is, a lot. Several bishops lost their lives, and over three thousand priests were executed.

Karol Wojtyła, who would later become Pope John Paul II, saved his life working with enslaved stone-breakers in a quarry.

Though small resistance units existed from the very beginning of the occupation, organized resistance to these atrocities was slow to develop; like resistance elsewhere, it was related to the movement of Allied armies. It is often observed that the Polish resistance failed to take action against the slaughter of the Jews; it is rarely noticed that the Polish resistance did not, until 1943, take action against the evacuation, the train deportations or the mass executions of other Poles either.[72] Only after the military tide turned against Hitler, did such resistance develop on a significant scale. Posters began to appear on street walls, the anchor sign of Fighting Poland was painted on signposts and street bollards. Communist Partisans accused non-Communists of *attentisme*, of waiting; non-Communists charged Communists with manoeuvring for a *coup d'état* on that inevitable day when the Nazis left Poland.

It was during this wave of civil violence in 1943, accompanied by accusations and counter-accusations, that General Sikorski died.

9 Choice in France

Across the great European plain, on the other side of the Reich, lay occupied France. This area also was influenced by the turn of the fighting on the Eastern Front and by the vicious propaganda campaigns that developed in the Russian borderlands. And among the Nazi victims, the Jews again fared worst.

In France, the fate of the Jews was linked to the general incidence of terror in a way that found no parallel in the rest of Nazi-occupied Europe. This was because France faced a choice, a harrowing choice, that the Nazis offered no other part of Europe. There were members of the governments of Belgium and Luxembourg who would have dearly loved to have signed an armistice with the German invader; but Belgium and Luxembourg were eventually to be incorporated into the German Reich and so there would be no armistice. On the other hand, Hitler never decided what he wanted to do with France. France lay to the rear of his principal project, the German settlement of the Slav lands in the East. Since the diplomatic fiascos of the 1930s she was no longer considered Germany's major enemy in the West, which was Britain; once defeated, France provided a buffer and, during the first year of western hostilities, was even regarded as a 'bridge' to Britain. But nothing more.

'Can we absorb them with advantage?' wondered Hitler aloud in front of Admiral Raeder; 'do they belong by blood to our race?' Better to leave the mongrels alone. Goebbels proposed that they be 'put on ice': 'The longer one leaves them hanging in the air the readier they will be to submit.' On 18 June 1940, as Churchill and de Gaulle broadcast appeals from London to their respective peoples, Hitler was in Munich persuading Mussolini, who entered the war a week earlier, not to demand too much of France at this moment; in particular, he said, it was in the Axis interest that the French fleet not fall into British hands, 'quite apart from the unpleasant administrative responsibility which the occupying powers would have to assume'. Let the dogs administer themselves. By late 1940 German occupying forces in France numbered around 30,000; Hitler was preparing for his big push east.[73]

So France faced the bitter choice: she could exile her government and join the peripheral operations that the British and later the Americans would develop outside Europe, as the Poles had done; or she could sign an armistice with Germany.

The route of resistance was followed by some, most famously under de Gaulle's leadership, and many of the French who joined it would find themselves fighting side by side with the Poles in Africa, in Italy, and in Normandy. The last prime minister of the Third Republic, Paul Reynaud, was an advocate of this, but he lost to those in his government, under the influence of General Weygand and Marshal Pétain, who wanted to sign an armistice. Pétain, on 13 June, had argued in Reynaud's Cabinet that to form a government in exile would be to abandon the country to the invaders; he himself would stay 'among the French people to share their sorrow and their miseries'.[74]

Article 3 of the Armistice – which the official French delegation signed on 22 June 1940 in the same forest clearing outside Compiègne and in the same wagon–lit where the German delegation had signed the Armistice of 11 November 1918 – stated that the French government retained full administrative responsibilities 'on condition that it conforms to the regulations of the German military authorities and collaborates with these authorities in a correct manner'. 'It is in a spirit of honour,' said Pétain, the new 'Head of State', on the radio in October after shaking hands with the Führer, 'and in order to preserve the unity of France – a unity which has lasted ten centuries – within the New European Order which is being built, that I today embark on the path of collaboration.'[75]

The Armistice of 1918 had led to an international peace conference and a series of peace treaties. That is clearly what the French party of collaboration was expecting after the Armistice of 1940, but they were living – as de Gaulle pointed out at the time – under their own parochial

Franco-French illusions: the Armistice of 1940 was not the beginning of any peace process, it was the start of a process of world war. At the heart of 'collaboration' lay not a new, peaceful European order, but a police operation carried out for and on behalf of German Nazis, a police operation that would rob France of 50 per cent of her iron ore, 99 per cent of her cement, 92 per cent of her lorries, 76 per cent of her locomotives, a massive amount of her agricultural produce and over 50 per cent of her non-agricultural production; it would send, by the end of 1943, 646,421 French men and women to labour in Germany; and it deported almost 76,000 Jews to their deaths.[76]

The ink had barely dried on the armistice document when the effect of Pétain's choice of collaboration over continued military resistance became painfully clear. Most of the 1.5 French prisoners of war interned in German camps were captured after the cessation of hostilities. Alsace and Lorraine were annexed by the Reich, though no mention of this was made in the Armistice. The two north-eastern departments of Nord and Pas-de-Calais were incorporated into the military administration set up in Brussels. In the last two months of 1942 Pétain's France lost what remained of her army, her fleet, her empire and, most galling of all, the 'independence' of the southern Unoccupied Zone: on 11 November – of all days – Hitler sent his troops across the demarcation line. The Armistice was a dead letter.

Pétain and his administrators had seriously misunderstood the mood of the French. There had, understandably, been panic in the wake of the military defeat. But the French were not pacifists. Marcel Déat, a former pacifist socialist who would found a tiny pro-Nazi party in Paris during the war, repeated Lloyd George's old question in an article he published in May 1939: '*Mourir pour Dantzig?*', 'Die for Danzig?' he asked. Déat, like Lloyd George in 1919, imagined that Westerners would reply 'No'; but in an opinion poll taken in France in July of that year, 76 per cent of those polled answered with a resounding 'Yes' (only 17 per cent said 'No', and only 7 per cent abstained).[77]

There was much disgust felt among troops for not advancing into Germany at the time of the 'phoney war', as can be confirmed in Sartre's diaries of the time, *Les Carnets de la drôle de guerre*. In the six-week campaign of May and June 1940 the French did die: 90,000 of them, along with 200,000 wounded – or almost as many as in the gruelling 300-day Battle of Verdun in 1916. There may have been some sense of relief when the fighting stopped and German troops, acting 'correctly' according to orders from Berlin, handed out food and treats they had pilfered in Belgium and eastern France; there was some anger with the British after they bombarded the French fleet at Mers el Kebir; but, as countless local studies show, opinion was broadly pro-British and anti-German by the time the nights got longer and the weather started turning cold.[78]

Pétain's regime was not prepared for all seasons.

Every student of the French Third Republic has learnt how the republican victory of the 1870s was assured by the painful building up of local government; Pétain's regime lost all sympathy because it destroyed it. The democratically elected *conseils généraux* of the local departments were replaced by appointed *commissions administratives*, elected mayors were replaced by appointed ones; the number of bureaucrats and technocrats, who invented the most extraordinary plans for a 'National Revolution', expanded: but the state had lost contact with the population.

There was a Peasant Charter, an Artisan Charter and a Workers' Charter, all of which were designed to 'integrate' France's famously individualistic, fragmented society into a bloated state bureaucracy: but the state no longer related to peasants, artisans and workers. So the technocrats turned to allocating raw materials, controlled by the Germans; to planning the economy, guided by the Germans; and to policing, under the eye of the Germans. They lost the support of the old political parties, the support of the Church, and most significantly the support of the young. Already, by the summer of 1941, leading figures of the 'National Revolution' were admitting that it was not working; many of the technocrats involved would subsequently become leaders of the French Resistance, where they would again plot out their projects for a new world.

Contrary to legend, Pétain's regime never renounced the Republic: the Marshal's bust frequently stood beside Marianne's in the local *mairies*; the brass bands would follow up a '*Maréchal, nous voilà!*' with the march of the *Marseillaise*; the tricolour flag was never torn down. But by 1943 it had renounced the people, who were cut off and isolated.

It continued to proclaim its 'choice' for peace and to defend the principle of French 'sovereignty'. Most symbolic of this 'choice' of 'sovereignty', by the French authorities and not the German, was their designation of Vichy as their new capital. Vichy was a small watering resort in a lowland area of the Massif Central. It could be compared to the choice of Cracow, in the foothills of the Carpathians, as a capital for Poland; only in this case the Germans, at the time of the Armistice, had invited the government back to Paris where, presumably, it would be easier to control.

But Pétain's government insisted on Vichy, which was in the Unoccupied Zone, and — the deciding factor — had 'over 15,000 hotel rooms'. Its nineteenth-century pavilions and castles, designed in a fabulous mixture of Flemish Renaissance, faux Gothique, Swiss, Italianate and Spanish styles, should have helped to relieve boredom and avoid thoughts of war. But they didn't. Vichy, being at the bottom of a valley, trapped the winter fog and summer haze, creating a 'colonial mugginess'. The bureaucrats worked in their hotel rooms, storing their files in bathtubs and bidets; they typed memos and reports on the edge of their double beds. Meetings took place in staircases. The streets were empty: life in Vichy took place in endless corridors where technocrats, with hairbrush moustaches and folders under their arms, tacked back and forth. A few uniformed Germans would appear now and then. Well-dressed women sidled from room to room. Members of the Resistance, spies and counter-spies found an ideal hiding-place in this labyrinthine world, right in the heart of affairs.

There were cheats, extortionists, thieves and murderers here – Simenon had Maigret sniffing around the dark, creaking, carpeted passages. Vichy was not comfortable. 'We would go out to dinner, three or four of us, and then we would come back to the hotel, and at that point the only thing on our minds was to pile on the jackets, because we were very, very cold,' recalled one senior aide who had worked at the Hôtel des Célestins (the Ministry of the Interior). 'The meals were not particularly tasty,' said another. By 1943 most functionaries had belatedly taken up Hitler's invitation and were working in the ministry buildings in Paris.

But the name tag stayed, as did the ministers. It had been on 10 July 1940 that the French members of parliament had assembled at Vichy in the art-nouveau Grand Casino and voted the Third Republic out of existence, handing full powers to Pétain; that is why people would refer to France's wartime administration as the 'casino government' and the regime simply as 'Vichy' – it rhymed softly and smoothly with 'Nazi'.[79]

10 The French connection: terror and extermination

Poland, to the east of the Reich, was subjected from the very beginning to Hitler's continental system of extermination and settlement; France, to the west, in a wide isthmus, had no significant role to play and it was this that offered her a 'choice' between collaboration and resistance. Paradoxically, surrounded by seas and so close to Britain, she was in a much better position to resist than Poland, which was never offered the choice. But many in her governing circles chose collaboration because they thought that by this they could wipe out the humiliation of defeat. And, absurdly, the more the Nazi vice tightened on her, the more her collaborating administrators 'negotiated'.

In Poland, there was no direct link between the extermination of the Jews and the haphazard, though increasingly violent, acts of terror perpetrated on the rest of the population. In France there was. That link was forged by France's 'negotiators'. It was a French connection that had a particularly pernicious effect on the whole war.

Chief among the negotiators was Pétain's Deputy Prime Minister in 1940, the feline conjuror of impossible contracts and accords, Pierre Laval – the only politician, it was said in his day, whose name spelled the same whether one moved from Left to Right or Right to Left. Laval was sacked in December 1940, when one of his own plots misfired (as they often did), but he was back as Prime Minister in April 1942, thanks in large part to German support. Laval was Hitler's man, as German correspondence between Berlin and Paris confirmed on several occasions.[80] But he was neither a Nazi nor a Fascist; he was a lawyer. He was born just a few miles south of Vichy, in a small town of the Auvergne, Châteldon. A 'member of a true peasant family', he boasted (in fact his father made his living as the local innkeeper, butcher and postman), he was able to buy the town château in the 1930s. Paris, however, was his base. He had made his name there as a defender of trade unionists and got himself elected as deputy mayor of the poor working-class suburb of Aubervilliers, which earned him the enmity of the Communists who considered the outskirts of Paris their fiefdom. In the Chamber of Deputies during the First World War he had been a pacifist Socialist and, in 1919, out of consideration for German sensibilities, he voted against the Versailles Treaty. But his subsequent squabbles with the Communists pushed him to the right. That didn't make him inconsistent. Laval was loyal to his clients – of which he had, in Paris, a good number. And he remained faithful to one idea: peace, and especially peace with Germany. 'Regimes follow one another and revolutions take place, but geography remains unchanged,' he wrote shortly before his execution for high treason. 'We will be neighbours of Germany for ever.'[81]

Laval's clientelism brought him success and riches as a politician: between 1925 and 1935 he was eleven times minister and four times Prime Minister; in the critical early 1930s he controlled foreign policy. But, though peace was his goal, he proved to be no good as a diplomat. Negotiations with the German Chancellor Heinrich Brüning in 1931 did nothing to improve Franco-German relations; his apparent endorsement in 1935 of Mussolini's plans to invade Ethiopia caused an uproar in Britain as well as in France and was a major reason for the development of the Italo-German Axis; the Franco-Soviet Pact which he signed that same year was stillborn. A background like this hardly recommended him to the job of 'negotiating' a compromise peace with the Nazis after the Armistice.

But Hitler was not looking for diplomats; on his western flank all he wanted was a cheap occupation that paid dividends. In Poland, the Germans went to the expense of doing their own dirty work since they were preparing their launching pad into Russia. In France – of marginal significance to the Nazi Eastern enterprise – it would be the French who would have to do it.

Laval, thanks to his contacts in Paris, was the first member of the Vichy government to visit Paris: on 19 July 1940. 'Vichy' was only nine days old. Through a network of able-minded technocrats, who during the 1930s had been building cultural and economic bridges with Germany in the sincere belief that these provided the way to peace, Laval established a working relationship with Otto Abetz. Abetz, an artist, a Francophile and an early Nazi ideologue, had no official position at the time; but for years he had acted in Paris as an agent for Ribbentrop, Hitler's Foreign Minister. Conversations began. In August, Abetz was named German ambassador. Laval spoke of the end of the age of *revanche*, the beginning of the age of reconciliation, the opening of a 'beautiful Franco-German collaboration in British Africa'.[82]

Laval was making the same mistake as Stalin, as Mussolini, as the Japanese. They were all preparing for the great march south, against Anglo-Saxon imperialism. But Hitler was a continental, and he was heading east. The common interest between occupied France and expanding Germany was an illusion. Laval's politics of 'collaboration' were flawed from the start.

It was worse than that. In making himself '*l'homme nécessaire*' in Vichy diplomacy, he offered himself up as Hitler's vassal; he became an instrument of Nazi terror. More, he accomplished something that not even the Nazis had worked out at the time: through his 'negotiations', he managed to link the elimination of the Jews to terror.

Laval was not an extreme man, he was a sincere advocate of peace, he was a man who cultivated friendship, he was certainly no murderer; but it was he who forged the link, the French connection between terror and extermination.

It was the Nazis who planned the eradication of the Jews. It was the Nazis also who established the principle of 'collective responsibility' of the population for acts of resistance. This was the case throughout occupied Europe. Indeed, given a cold statistical comparison between France and Poland, it is tempting to say that France got off lightly. The official estimate of 'racial deportees' from France has been set at 120,000,[83] of whom 3,000 survived; the German nominative lists of 79 convoys to Poland give an exact total of 75,721 – or about 12 per cent of French Jews and 41 per cent of foreign Jews living in France. Poland lost about one third of her population during the war, though the Nazis were not entirely responsible for this; of the 3.35 million Jews living in Poland in 1939, only 369,000 survived.

The Nazis, however, did not have the same plans in Western Europe as they did in the East. Their limited Western aim of a cheap, defensive occupation made them mildly sensitive to public opinion, something that was of no concern in their Eastern operations. In Poland, the extermination of the Jews and 'collective responsibility' for acts of sabotage or the assassination of Germans were entirely separate matters: when the Germans wanted to shoot or hang a few hundred hostages they simply went into the streets and rounded up whomever they found; they were indifferent to the public reaction. They could not do this in the West. They could not even deport Jews at will. In the Netherlands they started arresting Jews in January 1941; by February they had a national strike on their hands. It was a costly experience that they wanted to avoid in France. The small army of occupation, in particular, did not want to expose itself to the odium of police work. The commander of the German military headquarters in Paris, Luftwaffe General Otto von Stülpnagel, warned Berlin that mass shootings would increase popular resentment of his army; he recommended the deportation of 'great masses of Communists and Jews' as a more effective intimidatory response to French acts of sabotage and assassination.[84]

Without a police force? Contrary to the terms of the Armistice, Germany did in 1940 secretly install its own security police force, the Reichssicherheitshauptamt (RSHA), on Avenue Foch – a landscaped alley of luxury houses and flats between the Arc de Triomphe and the Bois de Boulogne. But in mid-1942, when it was giving orders to the military staff in the nearby Hôtel Majestic, it still had only around 2,400 German police (including drivers and telephone operators) directly under its command – hopelessly insufficient for a mass deportation programme.

Laval was aware, in 1940, of the German shortage and he realized that this gave him a critical point of leverage on the occupying authorities: French policing in the two major zones, Occupied and Unoccupied, would make him 'l'homme nécessaire': Laval would play the role of Fouché in the 'National Revolution' of 1940.

Ironically, things did not get moving until 1941 when Germany invaded Russia and the French Communists – perfectly happy with the politics of 'anti-imperial' collaboration up to then – started bombing trains and shooting German officers. This was the only year Laval was out of office: Vichy's Prime Minister in 1941 was Admiral François Darlan, who had spent his life in the ministries of Paris and never so much as set foot on a boat. But one naval passion did run in his blood: Anglophobia, the shame of Trafalgar. He was very much taken with the idea of a joint march southwards, Germans and Frenchmen together, *bras-dessus, bras-dessous*, into the African heart of the British Empire. He developed a whole geopolitical plan on this basis (thus ensuring France an 'honourable – if not important – role in the future Europe'), barely noticing that Hitler's troops were now pouring into Russia. Like all who governed at Vichy, his views were ultimately provincial.

Pétain did catch sight of the Communist campaign – it threatened his 'National Revolution'. On 12 August he interrupted a performance of *Boris Godounov* in Vichy's Casino to warn that an 'ill wind' was blowing across France. In a tone reminiscent of King Louis XVI addressing the States-General, he announced that 'Authority no longer comes from below; it is only what I propose or delegate.' He then outlined twelve emergency measures designed, like those of a mad king, to change the direction of the wind, including the setting up of special courts, *Sections Spéciales*, that would apply summary justice to 'terrorists'.

Thus, when nine days later a German naval cadet was gunned down in a Paris métro station, Pierre Pucheu, Pétain's new Interior Minister, was immediately able to assure the German authorities that six persons had been picked and would be 'executed in an exemplary fashion by decapitation by guillotine in a public square in Paris'.[85] The first man to be guillotined was, significantly, an immigrant Jew, though the sentence was carried out behind prison walls, for even Vichy 'authority' had to be careful about opinion 'from below'.

In 1941, before the SS had even formulated the 'Final Solution', Jews in France were already paying a heavy price for 'terrorism'. SS-Obersturmführer Theodor Dannecker, the twenty-nine-year-old Nazi fanatic charged with the Jewish Affairs Section of the RSHA in Paris (after following a crash course on mass murder in Poland), had demanded that year the arrest of Jews, against the advice of his own senior officers. Vichy complied, using its own police force.

The French authorities set to work in May, more than a month before the Russian invasion, with a call on foreigners in Paris to renew residence permits in their local police station; 3,747 Polish, Czech and Austrian Jews never returned home. Between 20 and 23 August, as the Communist attacks began, French police, this time under German command, arrested 4,230 Jews and shipped them out to the brand new French-run concentration camp in an unfinished housing estate at Drancy, next to Le Bourget airport – two hundred French lawyers were among those taken. On 12 December, 560 German police arrested 743 prominent French Jews, including the brother of the former premier, Léon Blum: no complaint from Vichy was forthcoming.

Executions of groups of 'hostages' in batches of fifty or a hundred were by now taking place in prisons and behind walls, and were then announced by poster; most of the victims were Jews picked from camps like Drancy.

On 20 January 1942 senior SS officials met in Wannsee, a pretty suburb with trees and lakes on the west side of Berlin, to lay down plans for the 'Final Solution'. It is most unlikely that any administrator in Vichy was aware of this; what worried Vichy was the 'sovereignty' of its police force – they did not want to hand power to the Germans. So when Germany started her programme of deportation from Paris to Auschwitz on 27 March, the French rail company, the SNCF, laid on a train of third-class carriages; French police both manned the train and guarded the rails to the German border. No French official asked where it was going. There were 1,112 men aboard, mostly Jews and over half of the total French. Theodor Dannecker rode in triumph in a comfortable compartment at the back.

In the meantime Admiral Darlan, pursuing his provincial illusions, got word from Ambassador Abetz that Hitler was prepared to sign a pact with the French. The great moment had come, he announced to his Cabinet: 'It is peace with the Reich and war with the others.' Effectively, Vichy had burnt its bridges. But there would be no pact. Abetz did not have the ear of his Führer. Germany eventually did reply in late February 1942 to Abetz's wild rumour through a counsellor at the embassy; he brought word that Hitler no longer trusted Darlan and demanded the return of *l'homme nécessaire*, Laval.

Pierre Laval was reappointed Prime Minister (in point of fact, 'Head of Government') on 18 April. It meant a return of the lawyer's clientelist practice and an expansion at both national and local level of technocratic 'experts'. The most brilliant of them was the young and enchanting René Bousquet, *le fonctionnaire remarquable*, who became chief of police.[86] Hitler's troops were now racing across southern Russia to the Caucasus; Britain at Tobruk suffered her most serious defeat to date; Japan, locked for the previous six months in a war of attrition with the Americans at Guadalcanal, did eventually manage to send a small fleet westwards into the Indian Ocean: the 'world island' might, after all, become German. 'I desire the victory of Germany,' Laval boldly announced on the radio on 22 June, 'for without it, Bolshevism would tomorrow install itself everywhere.'[87]

There had been some debate among the experts about the word 'desire'; Laval had used 'believe' in his initial draft. Three years later, that change would convict him: Vichy's commitment to Nazi Germany, by June 1942, was total.

That was the month preparations were made between French and German police authorities for the biggest sweep of Jews in the entire period of Nazi occupation. For the Germans it was part of a much larger, European-wide plan to slaughter all Jews. For the French it was a matter of preserving 'police sovereignty'; after the war, the French officials involved would always deny knowledge that the deported were being sent to their deaths – and, given both the German policy of *Nacht und Nebel* ('night and fog') and the narrowness of the French administrative mind at the time, it is quite conceivable. Be that as it may, Laval's experts were so anguished about their evidently declining sovereignty that, in their eagerness to please, they were ready to 'negotiate' the rounding up of more Jews than was actually being demanded of them. One of the first things Bousquet asked his opposite number, Karl Oberg, the SS chief for France, was whether foreign Jews in the southern Unoccupied Zone could be included in the deportations; this delicious thought had not yet crossed Oberg's nasty mind ('he was rather distant,' thought an ordnance officer at German military headquarters, 'a man from a modest social background').[88] It was Laval who added Jewish children to the list, on the 'humanitarian' grounds that families should not be split up – in the event, children would be shipped off for slaughter in separate cattle trains.

The French wavered at the last minute. Dannecker started demanding that almost half of the Jews arrested in Paris be naturalized French. This was a serious error, for it infringed on French 'authority'. Bousquet threatened not to evacuate 10,000 Jews from the Unoccupied Zone. The Germans became desperate. Adolf Eichmann, head of the SS Jewish Section, flew in from Berlin.

It was a huge relief for the undermanned SS authorities in Paris when on 4 July Dannecker received, through Bousquet, a formal go-ahead from Vichy: 'Bousquet declared that, at the recent Cabinet meeting, Marshal Pétain, the Head of State, together with Pierre Laval agreed to the deportation, as a first step, of all stateless Jews from the Occupied and Unoccupied Zones.' Dannecker and his black-uniformed colleagues would soon make it clear that the next step – or the 'last phase' as they put it – would 'also include Jews of French nationality'.[89]

11 Raffle is a game of chance

Nazis were deporting Jews the moment they entered Poland in 1939. There are even cases in Germany that pre-date the war. But the programme of mass transportation of entire city quarters only got under way in the month of July 1942, at the very time Hitler's armies were scoring their greatest successes in Russia and in North Africa – the murder of Jews was the Nazi way of celebrating victory. In the Netherlands, the Gestapo removed Jews from their homes, assembled them in the Zentralhalle für Jüdischen Auswanderungen and then transported them to Westerbork. In Belgium, cohorts of the SS surrounded quarters known to be inhabited by Jews, they invaded the houses and questioned the inhabitants about the presence of Jews; men, women, children, the old and the sick were dragged from their beds. That was the month residents of Warsaw could observe from Ogrodowa Street teams of Jews being led to the trains with the help of horsewhips.

What was terrible about France was that, in most cases, it was the French police and gendarmes who carried out the job: in France, the Nazis were too worried about public opinion to do the work themselves; they didn't have the men. The French would call the round-ups 'rafles' – a medieval term that is related to our own word 'raffle', a game of chance played with dice: the winner hauls in all the stakes. In July 1942 rafles were conducted by the French police in Rennes, Bordeaux, Tours and Dijon. In Rouen, Châlons, Nantes, Saint-Malo and La Baule the task was performed by the German Feldgendarmerie. Vichy contributed the largest number of her foreign Jews in the Unoccupied Zone during the month of August. Most famous of all, however, was the French haul in Paris.

The Paris Prefecture of Police had initially scheduled the two-day round-up, 'Operation Spring Wind', for the start of the week, early Monday morning, 13 July. Around 9,000 police – the equivalent of a small division – were instructed to assemble at four in the morning, form into équipes d'arrestation (they used the term 'agents capteurs' among themselves) and arrest in their homes the 27,391 Jews whose names had been drawn up out of a list carefully prepared during the early days of occupation. Around fifty buses had been laid on. 'When you have a contingent sufficient to fill your bus,' ran the Prefecture's circular, 'you will direct (a) to the camp at Drancy the individuals without children under sixteen, (b) to the Vélodrome d'Hiver the others.'[90] The Vel' d'Hiv' was a huge sports stadium in the 15e arrondissement. But then some official remembered that Tuesday was Bastille Day: with all of Paris in the streets, they risked a riot. So the round-up was postponed to Thursday, the 16th.

The Jews remembered it as 'Black Thursday', '*der Finsterer Donerztig*' in Yiddish. There was, during the two days of the operation, an intense heat-wave, interrupted on Friday afternoon by a violent storm. The *agents capteurs*, made up of one or two uniformed police with their flowing capes and a policeman in civilian clothes, moved in before dawn. At this stage the witnesses (most of them children who later escaped) are almost unanimous: the police were polite, if cold. Some carried the children in their arms to the waiting bus or police van. They had been instructed to 'proceed with the greatest speed possible, without useless words, and without commentary'. A bang at the door at dawn. A child opens. 'You've got five minutes to pack up your bags. You're coming with us!' Mother rushes around; though it is so hot, warm clothes might be useful; the silver cutlery. '*Dépêchez-vous, Madame, nous sommes pressés!*' You know that my children are French? '*Allons, Madame, ne nous compliquez pas la tâche et tout se passera bien.*' Hélène Zytnicki's mother had heard the rumours the night before – 'in the streets, the Jews spoke of nothing else' – and had decided to spend the night with her children in the neighbours' place upstairs; but Madame Zytnicki used to take tea before going to bed, so descended with her children and slept in her own flat: the knock sounded before dawn. '*Pressez-vous, préparez quelque chose, vous devez nous suivre.*' One last look at the childhood home. 'Turn the gas off, switch off the electricity meter. Are there animals in the house?'[91]

Around 7,000 people, 4,000 of them children, were assembled in the Vel' d'Hiv' for seven days. The delay was presumably caused by the fact that Adolf Eichmann had not yet given the green light for the deportation of children; incredibly, the Nazis had not prepared for the gassing of French children. 'It was there,' said Rosette Schalit of the Vel' d'Hiv', 'before Auschwitz, that the dehumanization, the denial of humanity, began.' The brown cycle track looked – from the high stand upon which she, her Polish parents and two brothers were seated – like 'wooden paving stones'. From some of the balconies bundles of clothes fell, turning, to the ground; 'it was only later that I knew that these bundles of falling clothes were in reality women killing themselves with children in their arms.' There were two toilets, which were soon blocked. There was one water outlet. There was no food. 'I will always remember', recalled a doctor, 'this old grandmother, immobile on a folding seat, her hands holding her knees, which were covered with a beautifully embroidered apron. One could not get a word out of her, in whatever language. It was a haunting image and a living personification of silent pain and crushing fate.' A hot sun beat down on a huge blue glass dome, creating a ghostly half light. It was, recorded Joseph Weismann, who had been snatched from his home in Montmartre, 'like a film in black and white because I saw only white faces and an amphitheatre where all was black'. A loudspeaker called out names. Hélène Zytnicki remembered 'stink, heat and projectors'.[92]

Eichmann's permission was finally granted on 20 July. The detainees were first transferred in cattle trucks to two French camps near Orléans, at Pithiviers and Beaune-la-Rolande, where the men were immediately separated from the women; when the moment of deportation arrived, the children were separated from the mothers in a scene of violence and horror. Most were carried to the French waiting-station at Drancy and, thence, to the death camps within the General-Gouvernement (Poland).

Unbelievable though it seems today, French officials probably did not know the destination. Raymond Aron, who in London was in a place better informed than anywhere in France, wrote of the mass murder of Jews: 'I did not imagine it, and because I could not imagine it, I did not know.' Georges Wellers, a Jewish doctor at Drancy for two years before himself being deported, said he did not believe in the extermination programme even when he arrived at the gates of Auschwitz; 'one had to be mad to believe it.' If such was the case for one of the greatest philosophers of the time and a witness of the Holocaust, one begins to grasp what was going on inside the provincial brains of Vichy.[93] Be that as it may, the *rafle* of July 1942 quickly proved to be a public relations disaster for Vichy of a kind few regimes in history have suffered. On 22 July there was an assembly of cardinals and bishops in Paris which condemned the action; by August, every Christian denomination in France had distanced itself from Vichy – Pétain and his government had just lost their main pillar of support.[94] In its daily French-speaking programme, *Les Français parlent aux Français*, the BBC began broadcasting news on 3 August of an 'ignoble pogrom' and of sinister 'concentration camps' at Drancy, Compiègne and the Vélodrome d'Hiver. The clandestine press in Paris was full of the news. But most disastrous for Vichy was the indication by early autumn that Hitler's armies were showing signs of weakening. Could it be that Laval had staked his bets on the wrong side?

With a few exceptions, the prisoners of the Vel' d'Hiv' would never know of the reports and the sympathy their suffering was generating beyond their cells and wagons. Most survivors' accounts speak of the indifference, the 'heavy atmosphere' in the streets. Anna Radochitzki, who lived with her family not far from the Bastille, was forced to walk with ten other families, carrying their cases, the yellow stars on their chests, down Rue de la Roquette towards Place Voltaire: 'People saw us pass, surrounded by French police. They knew us well, for this was our quarter, but they didn't react. I felt a kind of apathy.' Lazare Pytkowicz, in the same quarter, remembered how, as the Jewish families were collected in the courtyard of their apartment home, the neighbours just looked from their windows 'with a reproving look at the police'. As Sarah Lichtstein's bus descended Rue de Belleville 'I noticed one of my schoolmates . . . She didn't see me, we were too packed in. People looked at the bus passing with a distressed air.' Hélène Zytnicki's bus descended Rue Laumière so early in the morning that the street was almost empty; but there were people in the windows – 'some made signs with their hands, others wept as they saw us depart.' 'The French population', wrote Dannecker's aide Heinz Röthke in a report dated 18 July, 'has expressed, in repeated instances, much pity for the Jews arrested.'[95]

In the same report, Röthke noted that many Jews had been success-fully hidden as a result of warnings from the French police. Indeed, what did that cold and silent expression at the moment of arrest, the '*regard crispé*', that look of a 'dead fish' in the policeman's eye, mean? The survivors are virtually unanimous: at the time of arrest the police were polite and never violent.[96] The gendarmes, who were run by the War Department, were vicious with the panicking crowds at the Vel' d'Hiv'; the violence of the guards in the French camps would become famous. But the French police? Understandably, few of them would talk about the experience after the war; while great armies fought in every corner of the planet, while heroes were being made in the Pacific, North Africa and the Ukraine, they were landed with the job of arresting 30,000 unarmed immigrants. Many were provincials – a large contingent from Brittany – and several were former POWs who had volunteered for service in the French police force in order to get repatriated; they had been the defenders of France in 1940.

Inspector Louis Petitjean, a rare witness on the policemen's side, had been assigned to pick up Madame Fuhrmann of 1, Passage Saint-Sébastien in the 11e arrondissement. He and his uniformed colleague, who 'did not seem to enjoy this kind of operation very much', clambered up the stairs and found a young woman with a small boy of around seven clinging to her skirts – they were already dressed ('They must have been alerted by the screams of the other Jews'). 'Maman, they are going to deport us!' cried the child. The inspector asked the mother to trust him, to follow him without making a fuss, and assured her that he would do all he could to save them. The mother looked in his eyes and said, 'I believe you and I will follow you.' Thus, at seven o'clock in the morning, Madame

Fuhrmann and her son were taken to a school playground and, from there, transported by bus to the Vel' d'Hiv'. 'As for me,' said the inspector, 'I took leave of my *gardien de la paix*, delivered my report and returned home shattered. What a trauma it was!'[97]

Several survivors say they saw policemen weeping.[98] That summer's morning, 16 July, Annie Kriegel, whose family came from Eastern Europe, was returning to her home on Rue de Turenne, in the Marais, when she ran into a policeman. He was carrying a suitcase in each hand and crying: 'I distinctly remember those tears running down a rugged, rather reddish face because you would agree that it is rare to see a policeman cry in public.' He was followed by children and old people, carrying little bundles. At the crossroads she heard screams 'rising to heaven' – the kind of screams 'you hear in hospital delivery rooms'. She was confused. She was fifteen years old. She sat down on a park bench lost in silence. 'It was on that bench that I left my childhood.'[99]

Annie Kriegel joined a small Communist resistance group of immigrant workers, the MOI (or Main d'Oeuvre Immigrée). It is a signal fact that many of the Jews who escaped the *rafle* in Paris of July 1942 owed their lives to the Communists. Of the 28,000 due to be arrested, 'only' 13,000 were taken, three quarters of them women and children. At the time, the German SS blamed this serious shortfall on the French police. 'An important number of foreign Jews had advance warning of the round-ups and were able to hide,' Röthke despondently noted in his report of 18 July, adding: 'The clerical staff of the French police seem, in several cases, to have informed people of the planned round-ups.'[100] This was perfectly true. Women working as telephone operators and secretaries in police headquarters were particularly active. Jews were forbidden bicycles, radios and telephones; but the French administration was so inefficient that few controls had been carried out. And there were the famous *pneus*, messages written out on small blue paper slips and distributed through an urban network of pneumatic tubes – a mechanical version of fax and e-mail today.

But the Communists were very active too. Triumphant Nazism was having its effect in France, especially in the Paris region. Following the order from Moscow, in July 1941, to launch an armed struggle, French Communists had set up action groups such as MOI or the Bataillons de la Jeunesse, and had restructured earlier secret cells, like the Organisations Spéciales (OS). There is much debate over the degree to which Moscow controlled these tiny bands – probably not much, though there was an attempt by the veteran Communist organizer, Charles Tillon, to centralize them. In July 1942, as Hitler advanced towards the Caucasus, they called for a national insurrection – not an easy task for a few hundred partisans armed with pistols; by the end of August German and French police had virtually wiped them out.

So this was the situation of the French Communists in Paris at the time of the *grande rafle*: a handful of desperate young militants in the process of being decimated. Their suffering became swiftly identified with the general plight of the Jews. With rumours of an imminent round-up spreading through the poorer, eastern quarters of Paris, they formed the 'Fonds de solidarité' – or 'Solidarité' in short – that was designed both to warn Jews and bring them into their resistance groups. They printed tracts which they slid under doors or slipped into the hands of surprised pedestrians. '*Faites passer!*', 'Pass it on!', was handwritten in block capitals at the foot of the page. One of the pieces, *Notre Voix*, was written in both Yiddish and French. 'Several days before 16 July, many rumours of an imminent round-up were circulated by the Jewish resistance,' remembered one survivor. 'On the eve of the *rafle*, we received a telephone call from the widow of one of my father's colleagues,' said a German Jew. 'On the eve of the *rafle* of 16 July, a schoolfriend told me that they were now talking about the arrest of women and children on the following day and that she was going into hiding,' recorded a Polish Jew. She continued, 'My mother did not want to believe it.' It was unheard of. The round-up of Jews had started in 1941 – but never of women and children. Women and children were more isolated from networks of information. 'Around the middle of July, there may have been rumours circulating in the quartiers about a *rafle*, but we, we knew nothing,' recorded another Polish Jew, who was twelve at the time. The men went into hiding, if they hadn't already been arrested; it was the women and children who were taken on Thursday, 16 July.[101]

> Saute, saute, sauterelle,
> Car c'est aujourd'hui jeudi.
> . . .
> Saute, saute, sauterelle,
> A travers tout le quartier.[*]

The surrealist poet Robert Desnos got away thanks to his Communist connections. He was arrested in 1944 and died the next spring in the concentration camp of Terezin, Czechoslovakia.

---

[*] 'Hop, hop, grasshopper / For today is Thursday. / Hop, hop, grasshopper, / Across the whole quarter.' Robert Desnos, *Chantefables et Chantefleurs* (Paris: Gründ, 2003) – put so delicately to music by the Polish composer, Witold Lutosławski.

In Poland, which had already witnessed two years of Soviet occupation, there were those who held on to the incredible hope of being liberated by the Western armies. In France, where Communists were equated with nothing more than strike activity and the Spanish Civil War, there were those who thought that the liberating hand was that of the Soviets. In France, in 1942, the Communists saved lives. Raffle is a game of chance.

12 Frenchmen and Poles, Poles and Frenchmen

Poland provided the German armies with their main avenue to Russia, from which Hitler planned to dominate the Eurasian 'world island'. France was a launching pad and a defensive fortress against Britain, the maritime power which, since the 1930s, seemed the greatest threat to the rear of Hitler's Eastern project. Neither Poland nor France were of essential importance to Hitler; they provided, rather, a means to his end. But, as the fortunes of war turned, as the initiative moved away from Hitler, as the isolated campaigns of Blitzkrieg were transformed into total war, both Poland and France became determining points in the struggle; their fate would, to a great extent, decide the form Europe would take once the war was done.

Resistance to the Nazis in occupied Europe lay one step ahead – and only one step ahead – of the Allied armies. The British policy of 'setting Europe ablaze' by aiding internal revolt was consistent with the late eighteenth-century Pittite policy of small maritime operations launched against a continental enemy. But it did not contribute much, in military terms, to the war against Hitler; the Nazis were masters of continental forces that were inconceivable at the time of Napoleon. Effective resistance to the Nazis first developed in the forested areas around the central battlefront of the war, Russia. This 'Partisan war' was directed from Moscow, not London. Its vicious propaganda would become part of the language of resistance throughout Europe, including groups that were not Communist.

In France, as in Poland, one only began to speak of 'Partisans' in 1943, as Germany went on the defensive and the war became total. Recruits to the Communist cause increased with the mass deportation of French workers to Germany and the exponential growth of Nazi terror in Poland. As the Communist Partisans rose in number, life became difficult for other independent resistance groups. July 1943 was the month Moulin and Sikorski died.

★

There is a simple way of tracing the evolution of Communist thinking during the war: through the pages – often typewritten – of the clandestine French journal, *L'Humanité, organe central du Parti Communiste Français*. By early 1943 its columns were dominated by a campaign for the 'combat' or the 'mass struggle against deportations'. This no longer concerned Jews (though their deportation to death camps continued into the very last days of the occupation) but the voluntary and later conscripted departure of workers for Germany. Vichy and the 'Boches', warned *L'Humanité* on 20 January 1943 (during the last agonizing fortnight of Stalingrad), were conducting a *rafle* of Frenchmen to 'send them to Germany as *work fodder*, and perhaps as *cannon fodder*' so as to make up for German losses in Russia.[102] 'DO NOT LEAVE FOR GERMANY,' the paper repeated over the following months. In France, unlike in Poland, that choice actually existed. In several industrial centres of the country there were strikes and demonstrations – 'preparations for the national insurrection', as *L'Humanité* put it early the following year.

The deportation of French workers arose from another of Laval's 'negotiated' deals with German extortionists, in this case under the direction of Gauleiter Fritz Sauckel, the Reich's Commissar-General for Labour. It was a real bargain: Laval managed to haggle out an exchange rate of one prisoner of war returned to France for three French workers deported to Germany. French workers were asked to volunteer for this patriotic scheme; amazingly, 40,000 workers did turn up in August 1942 – out of the 250,000 Sauckel demanded. Laval was forced to introduce the Service du Travail Obligatoire (STO),* which did more to alienate the French population from his collaborationist regime than any other action taken to date. Thousands of young men fled to the countryside, where some were recruited into the Maquis. By the first quarter of 1943, 251,000 workers had been shipped to Germany; Sauckel demanded another 250,000, and by August he was demanding yet another 500,000. But after April 1943 only 37,000 left for Germany.

As of 1943 a '*déporté*' in France was a worker, not a Jew. This was because, in the first place, the reaction to the first deportation of Jews caused enough consternation among Vichy authorities and the under-policed Germans for the number of Jewish deportations to fall off in the last months of 1942. But, secondly, every family was directly affected by the STO; it became a national obsession. A perverse result was that the suffering of the Jews was forgotten – it even disappeared from Communist propaganda – and the memory of it would not be revived in France until more than twenty years after the war was ended.

---

* The law was promulgated in September 1942 and came into effect in February 1943.

Whatever popular following Vichy had had, it was gone by 1943. 'The circle of those who stick to Germany and wish for a German victory has become very small indeed,' remarked the German military commander in Paris in January of that year.[103] In the same month Laval created the Milice, a paramilitary organization designed to protect his regime (its oath was 'I swear to fight against democracy, against Gaullist insurrection and against Jewish leprosy'). The Milice was never a mass movement.

Independent resistance movements, particularly strong in southern France, were now faced with a burgeoning number of Communist groups whose front organizations always kept their distance, despite much talk of 'unity'. As the prospect of an Allied invasion increased, the special, separate identity of the French Communists became ever more evident.

By early 1944 L'Humanité was publishing articles on Poland. The Red Army was closing in on her frontiers. So it would be a Soviet liberation of Poland? A model for post-war Europe?

What L'Humanité provided was, at any rate, a model of ideas and slogans that would be adopted in post-war Communist Europe; here was the prototype. First came the act of denial: 'After the liberation by the Red Army of the region of Smolensk, where the forest of Katyn is to be found,' the paper reported on 1 February 1944, 'the Soviet government named a commission of inquiry charged with shedding light on the massacres.' Over 4,000 Polish officers had been shot there on Stalin's orders in April 1940. Never mind: the commission has reported that 'the prisoners were killed in the autumn of 1941, as documents found on their bodies prove.' The 'Boches' had been in the region since July.

Second, an affirmation: the Poles loved the Soviets. They had already been won over to the idea of re-attachment to the Soviet Union. 'During the occupation, in 1939, of one part of its territory by the Red Army,' explained L'Humanité, 'a plebiscite organized in the regions under Soviet administration completely confirmed this sympathy.'[104]

Third, the denunciation of alternatives to Communist power. 'There has been, since the beginning of the war, a Polish government in London. This government only represents itself.'

Fourth, the declaration of intent: the article on Poland's love affair with the Soviet Union appeared in a number under the slogan 'Long live the French Republic in the Soviet European Union'. Moscow, it was reported, had just accorded 'autonomy' to the Soviet Republics. It was a 'historical fact' – as all such announcements in Communist literature were – that 'has significance well beyond a simple internal reorganization of the USSR'. It provided 'for French Communists a great hope. At the moment of victory France must constitute a Communist government which will enthusiastically adhere to the Union of Peoples liberated from Nazi slavery and pre-war capitalism.' The massing of workers will not be enough. 'All militants in occupied France must redouble their activity and their proselytism . . . The great day of peace must also be that of the final elimination [*écrasement*] of bourgeois stupidity . . . Long live the Red Army! Long live the French Republic of Soviets!'[105]

So there it is in black and white: the intention of the French Communists was to take over France at the moment of Liberation. Long live the Red Army! Would it liberate France? That thought oddly mirrored the attitude of the Poles who supported London and hoped the Western Allies would free them from their horror.

The desire for a Liberation from both Nazis and pre-war institutions was in fact widespread. In France, all resistance movements were opposed to the reinstatement of the former Republic. The same was true in Poland. But whereas the French resistance groups saw a party system of government as the source of all evil, it was a party system that politically active Poles sought above all.

Frenchmen and Poles wanted to be free of their past. Historians have long been aware of the presence of concentration camps on French soil during the last year of the Third Republic; they have for decades been writing about the existence of anti-Semitic groups and of the advocates of Hitler and Mussolini during the 1930s. It is upon such continuities that the notion of a home-grown 'Vichy syndrome' has been constructed – the idea that France was not simply a victim of the invading Nazis. Even during the war there was a certain consciousness of this, which is why many French wanted a clean break at the 'Liberation'. Less well known are the continuities that could be found in Poland; pre-war Poland was not a democratic regime, anti-Semitism was rife, and terrorism, particularly in the form of 'rural pacification', was widespread. Such continuities are often made the object of polemic and accusation, but – to put it bluntly – they seem to be the way history operates.

Did the Russian Revolution begin in 1917? Was Nazi ideology really just a product of the First World War? Was the French Revolution only started with the fall of the Bastille? Was Charles I responsible for the religious rifts of the English Civil War?

The Polish slogan '*sanacja*', which gave rise to the name of the pre-war regime, means 'return to health' – as if the perpetrators of the 1926 military *coup d'état* were themselves aware of some kind of continuity. This was certainly the case with Marshal Józef Piłsudski, the Polish dictator. He was hardly, as the Communists made him out to be, the devil incarnate.[106] He had an impressive knowledge of Polish history, Polish culture, and could wax poetic over the ancient Polish countryside. But he turned vicious after Ukrainian separatists assassinated one of his aides in 1931. This led to the repression of several minorities in Poland, not just the Ukrainians. Piłsudski died in 1935; his increasingly unattractive regime survived until the Nazi and Soviet invasions of 1939.

The parliamentary parties had been silenced. The main opposition revolved around the Swiss home, in Morges on Lac Léman, of the great pianist and composer, Ignacy Paderewski. Practically every major figure of the wartime London government-in-exile came from, or had been in contact with, this 'Morges Front'. That was another curious element of continuity; its members, long before the outbreak of war, had already constituted a kind of government-in-exile. They hated Piłsudski's *Sanacja* regime and they did everything in their power, even at the height of the war, even when one would have thought the Underground Army needed a little support, to prevent the military forces of Poland from ever seizing political power again.

It was thus the greatest of ironies that the new and growing Polish Communist Party (the PPR) should in 1943–4 argue that the London government was simply another *Sanacja* regime in waiting. They even put out word that leaders of the London-supported Polish Underground were secretly collaborating with the Nazis – a slanderous charge at a time when Warsaw was experiencing the worst phase of terror since the suppression of the Ghetto Rising. Street executions were being performed daily. Between October 1943 and February 1944, between 270 and 300 Warsaw residents were shot or hanged in public every week,[107] a fact that puts the Nazi atrocities in France in perspective. In the five years of German occupation, Warsaw alone lost 40,000 inhabitants shot or killed, and between 150,000 and 160,000 deported for labour – figures that exclude, of course, the murder of the Jews and the victims of the Warsaw Rising of 1944. The armed branch of the Communist Party, the People's Army (*Armia Ludowa* or AL), became active in the autumn of 1943; it bombed cafés and dance halls frequented by Germans; it fired on German troops as they marched down the open streets and avenues.

'Chaos', Jan Nowak noted, 'gave a minority a chance.'[108] And, in contrast to France, Communists in the Polish resistance were only a minority: while the Home Army (*Armia Krajowa* or AK) in late 1943 numbered around 400,000, making it the largest resistance organization in Europe, the People's Army had certainly no more than 10,000. But it was the Polish Communists, like their French comrades, who called loudest for 'national insurrection' and denounced the Home Army, the London-supported 'Delegacy' (the executive branch in Warsaw of the Underground State) and the London government for criminal *attentisme*, or 'waiting'. Their tracts were broadcast on Radio Moscow and Kosciusko Radio, which was also based in Moscow.

In fact, both the London Poles and the Home Army had planned a national 'Rising' from the very beginning of the war. 'The main mission of large parts of the Underground is to train and prepare for the Rising,' for the 'rebirth of the nation', wrote Julian Kulski in July 1941.[109] The initial idea was to synchronize the Rising with the Anglo-American invasion of the Continent and even encourage a Western intervention in Poland itself. Such a rising would necessarily involve surviving parts of the Polish army. The predicament the London Poles faced was to build up that army and yet ensure that, at the time of the Rising, it would not take over Poland – not impose another *Sanacja* regime. The advance of the Red Army towards Poland in 1943, coinciding with growing Nazi terror within, turned the problem into a full-scale dilemma: the Rising would be against whom? the Nazi oppressor? the Soviet oppressor? both at the same time? Sikorski, who combined in himself both military and political authority, had the stature to resolve this. His successors did not.

Sikorski's solution to the menace of a pre-war *Sanacja* regime being re-established had been to appoint a civilian representative of London in Warsaw, known as the 'Delegate', and to build up a small clandestine parliament in the occupied capital in which the major political parties of the pre-war era would be present.

The life expectancy of the Delegate in Warsaw was short; the first three were killed in swift succession between 1942 and 1943; the last, J. S. Jankowski, would be the witness of Poland's 'Liberation'. The task of organizing the parliamentary assembly was, for reasons easy enough to imagine, complicated and was only effectively realized in early 1944 in the form of the Council of National Unity (the RJN). Long before that time, however, the various branches of an Underground State – including schools, universities, social services and law courts – were operating both in the General-Gouvernement and in the former western Polish provinces now annexed to the Reich. The Home Army was answerable to the civilian authorities.

Sikorski was killed before he could begin to unravel the problems created by the discovery of the Katyn massacre and the immediate break in diplomatic relations, ordered by Stalin, between the London government-in-exile and the Soviet Union. After their one meeting, back in 1941, Stalin had expressed his admiration for Sikorski – a deadly compliment, which may have been the cause of his death.

Sikorski had two successors in London. Stanisław Mikołajczyk, 'a small, squat, bald, typical peasant type', became the new Prime Minister. General Kazimierz Sosnkowski, a chain-smoking nobleman who 'looked like a hetman of an earlier century', became Commander-in-Chief of the Polish armed forces.[110] The two men had nothing in common.

There had already been trouble between Sikorski's London government and the Home Army in Warsaw under the command of Grot-Rowecki over the question of 'replacement administration' (administracja zastępcza). Who would take over local administrations at the moment the Germans retreated, the Home Army or the representatives of the State? De Gaulle would face a similar problem in France. Grot had wanted it to be the Army and had created a Military Bureaux Administration in preparation for the transition; Sikorski had forced them to be merged with the existing underground civilian departments. But it was not a neat operation, and many key areas, like the post, railways and military industries, remained under the control of the Army – itself an underground institution.

After the disappearance of both Sikorski and Grot matters got worse. Communist intransigence made them worse than worse. Sosnkowski wanted the Home Army to prepare itself for a new underground war against the Soviets, if this proved necessary. Mikołajczyk was ready to negotiate with Stalin. The new commander of the Home Army, General Tadeusz Bór-Komorowski, wanted to show the Soviets what a valuable ally his troops, behind German lines, could be and he intended to bring them into the open (rather than continue to hide) once the Red Army arrived. Sosnkowski warned this would be suicide.

Mikołajczyk's negotiations with the Russians were like Laval's negotiations with the Germans: they were not negotiations at all. Stalin held all the stakes. Every time Mikołajczyk thought he had made an advance, Stalin changed the rules. Well-meaning British intervention, by both Churchill and his Foreign Secretary, Anthony Eden, only aggravated the situation.

Ostensibly, the sticking point was territory. Stalin had discovered that Lord Curzon, Lloyd George's Foreign Secretary after the First World War, had proposed to his own government in late 1919 a Polish boundary that roughly followed ethnic frontiers. Put forward by his civil servants, the 'Curzon Line' had no legal basis whatsoever; it had never been discussed at the Paris Peace Conference and it had nothing to do with the frontier ultimately drawn up by warring Poles and Bolsheviks in 1921. But, with the exception of its northern outline, it corresponded approximately – and quite by chance – to the border Molotov and Ribbentrop had scrawled across Poland when they revised the Nazi–Soviet Pact late in September 1939. So Stalin informed his British 'ally' in February 1943 that he wanted the 'Curzon Line', knowing full well that what he was really demanding was a return to the Pact – without Germany this time (though Stalin's alliance system was very much in balance at that moment). He broke off relations with Poland two months later and, within a further three months, Sikorski was dead. 'No Polish government abroad would be able to discuss the question of the reduction of Polish territory,' Mikołajczyk warned Eden in September.[111]

For the Poles – both the London government and the Home Army – territorial concessions would gain nothing if Stalin's real intention, as they suspected, was to impose a Communist puppet government. For the British, such concessions were the means to an accord with their indispensable Russian ally. They set off to the Teheran Conference with that in mind. There, Eden did point out to Stalin that the 'Curzon Line' looked strangely like the 'Ribbentrop–Molotov Line'. Stalin was unmoved. Churchill proposed that Poland get equal compensation in the west – an area made up of East Prussia and frontiers extending to the Oder. Stalin agreed. The British, quite unintentionally, had just locked themselves into the logic of the Pact, which meant two things: massive population movements and a large number of deaths.

Stalin's armies marched on. In January 1944 they crossed Poland's pre-war frontier. Rumours seeped through to London that there were signs of cooperation in the Volhynia district between the Red Army and the Home Army; so perhaps Bór-Komorowski was right and the Home Army could 'come into the open'. The British urged further 'negotiation', without divulging the agreement they had made at Teheran. Stalin simply added a new condition: he demanded a change in the composition of the London government.

He already had his own Polish army in Russia, under the command of General Zygmunt Berling and made up of the Polish deportees he had not either murdered or dispatched to North Africa. He had just set up in Moscow the kernel of a Communist puppet government, a 'National Council', which would be transformed into a 'Committee of National Liberation' the instant the Red Army crossed the 'Curzon Line'. Now he worked on dividing the London Poles.

What the Communists in Poland had called 'Sanacja', Stalin called 'Fascist'. The message was passed on through the American ambassador in Moscow, Averell Harriman. Molotov told him that the Russians wanted 'a new government of "honest" men, untainted by Fascism and well disposed to the Soviet Union'.[112] It was only in June, two weeks after the Allied landings in Normandy, that the Soviet ambassador explained to Mikołajczyk exactly what Stalin's conditions for diplomatic relations were: the dismissal of Sosnkowski along with that of the President of the Polish Republic (Władysław Rackiewicz), the Minister of National Defence (Marian Kukiel) and the Minister of Information (Stanisław Kot); the acceptance of the 'Curzon Line'; and a condemnation by the new government of its predecessor's 'mistake in the Katyn affair'.[113]

Sosnkowski was put on the defensive. Miko/lajczyk feared mutiny in his army. Bór and his underground officers in Warsaw worked on a revised version of the 'Rising'. They code-named the operation 'Burza' – 'Tempest'.

Movements

♈

1 French Tempest

The Western Allies had been stirring up a tempest of their own – from the air. Two elements of British anti-Nazi strategy had failed entirely, the blockade and the encouragement of rebellion. The American plan for an invasion of the heartland had been delayed by the submarine war in the Atlantic and setbacks in the North African campaign. For Westerners, the war on the land was still essentially a peripheral campaign. The landings in Italy hardly proved to be an invasion of the Continent; their main significance was the provision of air bases.

The only alternative was bombing. In January 1943, at Casablanca, Britain and the US had agreed to the principle of a Combined Bomber Offensive that would aim at the 'progressive destruction and dislocation of the German military, industrial and economic system and the under-mining of the morale of the German people' – a nicely vague objective that left the initiative to the Allied Bomber commanders. That was just as well; in the age of free-falling bombs released by bombers with no fighter escort the commanders needed all the leeway they could get. By the pivotal month of June, as the Allies prepared to set foot in Italy and Hitler manoeuvred for his fatal tank offensive at Kursk, the task of the bombardment of Germany had been divided: the Americans flew in daylight on 'precision bombing' missions directed at industrial plants; the British came in under cover of night to hit the surrounding area. By autumn they were flying in different directions. The Americans, still without escort, kept up pressure on the industrial regions; the British launched a series of raids against the enemy's capital designed, as Air Chief Marshal Arthur Harris put it to his crews late that November, to 'burn his black heart out'.[1]

This was barely six months before D-Day. In the aerodromes of England every chill afternoon, the Lancasters rumbled down the runways and lifted out into the fading winter light for Germany. Berlin suffered its most devastating air attack of the war on the night of 22/23 November 1943.

But the forces became dispersed. The weaker Stirlings and Halifaxes were pulled out. The losses were enormous. The RAF had its worst night over Nuremberg on 30/31 March 1944 when it lost 12 per cent of the force sent. Enemy night fighters had worked their way into the bomber stream and demonstrated the still formidable power of Göring's Luftwaffe.

Those planning the landing in northern France developed an almost irrational fear of it. The Normandy beaches were only eighty miles from the English coast, so well within the range of Allied fighters. None the less, it was decided in Teheran in December 1943 that 'the whole of available airpower in the United Kingdom, tactical and strategical, will be employed in a concentrated effort to create the conditions essential to assault.'[2] It took a lot to persuade Bomber Command to abandon their air war on Germany. In late March, there was still no sign that they had. By then, they had brought into service a new long-range fighter, the P-51 Mustang – built, symbolically, on an American frame and powered by a British engine – that was shooting the Luftwaffe out of Germany's skies.

The RAF attacks on Berlin petered out. The USAAF daylight raids, escorted with Mustangs, on Schweinfurt, Brunswick, Gotha, Augsburg, Leipzig and other industrial centres picked up. The shift from the air war on Germany back to tactical bombing, aimed at disrupting war production and communications in aid of the Allied invasion, began around September 1943 with a series of missions targeting occupied France. Civilian casualties in this case were obviously not the aim. In February, over Limoges, Group Captain Leonard Cheshire developed a technique of low-level bombing designed to improve accuracy and warn civilians of what was coming. By March the RAF was, as much as it was able, using its Mosquitoes like German Stukas to dive-bomb French targets.

Thus, gradually, Allied air forces shifted their focus from Germany to the preparation of the great landing in Normandy. Only on 17 April 1944 did Allied Supreme Command issue the directive to provide all possible air support to the Allied armies in order to 'assist them in establishing themselves in the lodgement area'.

Two days earlier, the German news agencies started forecasting an imminent Anglo-American 'invasion of Europe'. The *National Zeitung* in Berlin predicted a landing for today, tomorrow, or in several months – and called the event 'D-Day'.

The collaborationist press in Paris picked up the news. The whole matter, it was reported in *Aujourd'hui*, rested on 'weather conditions' and the element of surprise. 'Interest is concentrated less on the Eastern Front than on the West,' noted *Les Nouveaux Temps*.[3]

2 Pétain's plebiscite

There were a few well-known figures in Britain, like Lord Salisbury, the Bishop of Chichester or Arthur Harris's own chaplain, John Collins, who spoke up against the area bombing of Germany. The chairman of the Society for the Preservation of Historic Buildings recommended that the staff of RAF Bomber Command should include an art historian and, amazingly, the Air Ministry took the proposal seriously. A list of historic towns was made up, and Harris was told not to attack them without first obtaining permission from the Ministry. Though this would do little for the turrets and medieval walls of Augsburg, the crooked, half-timbered houses of Leipzig or the baroque treasures of Dresden, it was this that saved Florence and Rome from the storm of Allied bombs. And so it was for Paris.

There was a phenomenon that the bombers called 'creep back'. Their bombs tended, in the course of a raid, to 'creep back' from the aiming point. It meant that, as in a hurricane, one of the safest points was in the centre, at the city church or cathedral – nearly always a marker for the bombers, but not targeted. Inhabitants got to know this in the year of the whirlwind, 1944.

On Easter Sunday and Monday attacks were launched on Lille, Le Havre and the industrial belt and railway marshalling yards on the north side of Paris. 'Red Easter' was what the Parisian collaborationist press called it. Three days later a new wave of bombardment swept through Rouen and northern Paris again. Several thousand were left homeless. One bomb went off on the steps of the Sacré Coeur. '*Les gangsters de l'air sur Paris,*' cried the collaborationists, 'Montmartre and the northern suburb of Paris have suffered from the most violent Anglo-American terrorist bombardment since 1940.' Pétain and Laval went on the radio. 'My thoughts never leave you,' quavered the old man; he had just celebrated his eighty-eighth birthday: 'your pain is mine.' It was the typical Pétainist line. But this time something new happened: Pétain visited Paris.

Pétain's visit to Paris on 26 April received huge press coverage at the time. Historians have frequently commented on it since, comparing Parisian enthusiasm for the Marshal with the celebration of their liberation only four months later. It was filmed.[4]

Look at those crowds. Are they celebrating? Pétain had come to Paris to attend at Notre Dame Cathedral, as the official newsreel distributed two days later put it, 'a religious ceremony for the memory of the latest victims of bombardment'. So the occasion was not even formally designed for jubilation – state ceremonies in Pétain's France rarely were. He is welcomed on his arrival by a small contingent of the Garde Municipale and a few civilians who give a Fascist salute. The lawn behind them is neatly mown and empty. Fernand de Brinon, Pétain's representative in Paris, is seen shaking the hand of a Nazi dignitary on the square in front of the cathedral and Pétain then enters a sombre aisle to the sound of a tolling bell.

In a pamphlet published to commemorate the event, Philippe Henriot, the Secretary of State for Information and Propaganda, announced that with Pétain's visit to Paris 'the plebiscite has been held.'[5] 'Messieurs Roosevelt, Cordel Hull [sic] and Churchill want to know what the people of France think,' he commented. 'They have only to look at Paris, to listen to Paris on this day.' No doubt he was thinking of that December day in 1918 when, at a victory parade held in Metz, an embarrassed Georges Clemenceau kissed Raymond Poincaré on the cheek and Pétain, the victor of Verdun, received his marshal's baton. 'The plebiscite has been held!' exclaimed all the French newspapers – meaning that they weren't expecting a formal plebiscite to be conducted in Alsace under the aegis of the League of Nations; the enthusiasm of the crowds was enough.

There was no such enthusiasm in Paris on 26 April 1944. The Marshal's visit had been kept a secret, says the news announcer, 'but the news spread like a fuse of gunpowder'. There is a shot of a mourning woman in a headscarf – it was cut from later versions of the film. The camera is invariably kept low to hide the thinness of the crowds. Perhaps half a dozen people cry 'Vive Pétain! Vive Pétain!' Some gloomy faces are seen singing a strained version of the Marseillaise, out of tune. As Pétain's black car moves up the Rue de Rivoli, there is a shot of a building with people standing on the balconies cheering; but every building on the Avenue de l'Opéra is empty. And there is a telling scene as the car turns before the opera house, for the camera has to move up: the well-behaved crowd is only two rows deep; the streets behind them are empty.

The newsreel also includes a speech made by Marshal Pétain 'on the balcony' of the Hôtel de Ville. There is no balcony to the neo-Gothic Hôtel de Ville. A wooden one, draped in purple velvet that appears black in the film, was erected specially for the occasion. 'I cannot address each one of you individually,' says Pétain in a speech that corresponds in no way to the texts published in the press the next day. 'There are too many of you.' The crowd is indeed substantial, divided by empty straight corridors, like fire breaks in a forest.

Nowhere in print was the Marshal's final phrase to the Parisians recorded: 'Alors, à bientôt j'espère!'*

* 'Well, see you soon I hope!'

3 Pétain's heir

General Charles de Gaulle had what the French call a *trogne*: a kind of involuntary mask frequently encountered in military men. It made him look stiff at public appearances or during formal meetings and interviews. Even in private, there were few who managed to uncover his inner soul, the secret chamber which made him the man he was. André Malraux described long philosophical conversations he had supposedly had with his master – but they were largely a product of that novelist's vivid imagination. Claude Mauriac, another writer, came closer to capturing the words the General used, showing to the world his hidden fits of anger, his barbed tongue and many of his personal idiosyncrasies. Was that genuinely the way he was? 'To each one his de Gaulle,' asserted Alain Peyrefitte who, as spokesman for the Elysée Palace through the 1960s, probably got to know him better than most. 'He was different with each new person he met.' Peyrefitte made notes of his conversations day by day and published them in two hefty volumes twenty-four years after his subject's death; they read like a long play. 'The General laughs,' he records in one typical aside. 'But he remains impenetrable.' The very fact that he laughed was apparently thought worth noting.[6]

De Gaulle's aloofness was particularly unsettling for people willing to risk their lives in the struggle against the Nazi occupation. André Dewavrin, who adopted the pseudonym 'Colonel Passy' when he joined the Free French in London, described his first encounter with de Gaulle at St Stephen's House, in July 1940, as 'glacial'. 'His immense form unbent and rose' from his desk and he barked out a series of brief questions, 'clear, incisive and somewhat brutal'. Having answered to apparent satisfaction Passy was told, 'Good. You will be head of the Deuxième and Troisième Bureaux of my General Staff. *Au revoir. A bientôt.*'[7] Passy thus became head of the intelligence section of de Gaulle's Free French, though he had no qualifications for the job. Resistance leaders who made the hazardous voyage to London had a similar experience. De Gaulle would rise three quarters of the way to the ceiling, give his orders and dismiss them. Christian Pineau, who had a dangerous job as leader of the Paris movement Libération-Nord, was invited to join the General at a chair by his fireplace and, without as much as an introduction, was commanded, 'Now tell me about France.'[8]

What every resistance leader discovered was that de Gaulle had not the slightest interest about life in occupied France or in the organization of their networks; invariably, after telling him 'about France', they would be given a long and bitter speech about the unreliability of the General's Anglo-Saxon allies. 'France' for de Gaulle was something other than the direct experience of occupation. In fact, it was something wider and grander.

'All my life, I have retained a certain idea of France,' announces de Gaulle in the famous opening passage of his war memoirs. It has frequently been compared to the 'overture' of Marcel Proust's *A la recherche du temps perdu*. There is the timelessness of the first sentence, set to the deliberate slow rhythm of the words: *'Toute ma vie, je me suis fait une certaine idée de la France,'* writes the General; *'Longtemps, je me suis couché de bonne heure,'* begins Proust. *'Je me suis'* – they both begin with a mysterious, repetitive 'I' (notably absent from Churchill's initial world-embracing sentence: 'After the end of the World War of 1914 there was a deep conviction and almost universal hope that peace would reign in the world'). In Proust, 'I' becomes 'he'; in de Gaulle, 'I' becomes France. Both are grown men evoking childhood – *puer senilis*, the 'boy of old age' as one critic has put it – and one is tempted to regard these pages as nostalgic. But they are not. There is ritual and myth in them: de Gaulle muses on the destiny of the princess in fairy tales and the Madonna in frescoes; Proust thinks back to a magic lantern reflecting images on the bedroom curtains. But something is seriously wrong. The childhood remembered is not bliss. In Proust the problem is insomnia provoked by the refusal of the boy's mother to come to his room and embrace him; in de Gaulle it is the recollection of French weakness – the British at Fashoda,* the Dreyfus Affair, social and religious discord, and the despair of his mother when she recalled her own parents' tears in 1870: 'Bazaine has surrendered!' 'France cannot be France without grandeur' encapsulated the 'certain idea' the General held of his country. But in de Gaulle's memory of his childhood, France was not so grand: it was like 'maman' who had refused to give him a kiss.[9]

His own physical grandeur and a strict Jesuit education had naturally fashioned him for the part of an exiled monarch who, out of place in his surroundings, never stopped thinking about his distant, idealized kingdom.

---

* In 1898 a small French expeditionary force attempted to settle at the abandoned Arab fort of Fashoda on the Upper Nile, thus cutting the British off from their route south to East Africa and the Cape. General Kitchener, who had been at war with the Mahdi, sailed with a small fleet of gunboats down to Fashoda and, in a most diplomatic manner, persuaded the Frenchmen to leave. The 'retreat from Fashoda' became a great scandal in the Paris press. The government even talked of war, but found it had other more pressing problems, such as the Dreyfus Affair, to sort out.

He was 6 foot 5 inches tall. This made him awkward, even shy. 'We people are never quite at ease,' he told Louis Joxe, who would one day be his Minister of Education, 'I mean – giants. The chairs are always too small, the tables too low, the impression one makes too strong.' It was rumoured that his English landlord had thrown him out of his wartime home in Reading because he had broken the bathtub when he got into it. At the military college of Saint-Cyr he had been known as 'the Great Asparagus' (he had a small forehead) and was made to lie down to gauge the width of the courtyard in 'melon-kilometres', that is, the length of his body.[10]

Happiness was never a goal in de Gaulle's life. He took solitude as his lot, he cultivated few friends and, instead, applied his immense intelligence and Jesuit-trained memory to a grander cause: that is how the mysterious 'I' became 'France'. 'You are not France! I do not recognize you as France!' exclaimed the earthly Churchill. 'Why then do you treat with me?' asked the General from on high. Churchill remained silent.[11] For de Gaulle, recognition was a desire that arose from a profound pain in his soul. To relieve it, he waged psychological war on the world.

The real French world, occupied by the German army, got to know de Gaulle as a disembodied voice on the jammed airwaves of the BBC. The power of his physical presence only became known after the Allied invasion of June 1944. It quickly achieved fame.

De Gaulle is often described as a Northerner. In fact he was a Parisian, and a western Parisian at that, with little practical knowledge – besides family holidays, army exercises and war – of anything beyond the city and its suburbs. De Gaulle's 'certain idea of France' was symbolized in the overture of his war memoirs by 'the night descending on Notre Dame, the majesty of an evening in Versailles, the Arc de Triomphe in the sun, the flags of the conquered quivering under the arches of the Invalides'.[12] His family was descended from a mixture of bourgeois, the lesser *noblesse de robe* and clerks; they were not rich. Opportunities for the career of their second son were thus limited, in the main, to the civil service or the army. De Gaulle, with his 'certain idea', of course picked the army.

Paris at the turn of the last century was still a city of provincial immigrants, who kept their local identity. Both his parents were Northerners, though his father, Henri, spent most of his life, like Charles, in Paris. His mother was from Lille, and it was a tradition for the daughters of Lille to return to their birthplace to give birth. So Charles de Gaulle was born in Lille in 1890. This had a double significance in his life. In the first place, he remained faithful to the strict Catholic upbringing of the bourgeoisie of the North. Secondly, Lille was a city on the great northern plain of

Europe whose history was marked by the passage of armies. When de Gaulle deplored 'our weaknesses and our errors' he invariably had in the back of his mind the vulnerable zone in French defences that the flat lands of his birthplace represented.

De Gaulle's peculiar personality – his identification with France (which dated back at least as far as his adolescence), his awkwardness, his loftiness and his determination to mark out his own way   caused him problems in the army. After his first year of military service, in 1910, he received only the rank of corporal when most of his officer-cadet contemporaries became sergeants. He left Saint-Cyr in 1912 as a second lieutenant, which was hardly exceptional. His performance under fire was extraordinarily courageous and his comrades remembered him with respect – but not love. As a captain in Paris in the 1920s he became a history professor at Saint-Cyr. His lectures, delivered after the ostentatious removal of white gloves from his musical hands, were brilliant little treatises on military theory. But his colleagues distrusted him; it was at Saint-Cyr that he developed a reputation for conceit and insolence. This became the cause of much grumbling and gaffawing among senior officers after he entered the Ecole Supérieure de Guerre, on the Champ de Mars. As a result he graduated in 1925 with the grade of '*bien*', not '*très bien*'. For de Gaulle, it was an insult.

One man supported him, and acted as his patron, friend and defender against the hostility of the military hierarchy. Like de Gaulle he was a rebel, and a Northerner – from the Pas-de-Calais, the son of a Picardian peasant. Their relationship dated back to de Gaulle's assignment, in 1913, as second lieutenant to a regiment in Arras, halfway between Lille and Paris. 'I served my apprenticeship as an officer in the 33rd Infantry Regiment at Arras,' de Gaulle tersely noted on the third page of his memoirs. 'My first colonel, Pétain, showed me what was meant by the gift and the art of leadership.'[13]

Philippe Pétain was de Gaulle's mentor, and de Gaulle was Pétain's own designated successor in his personal staff on the Boulevard des Invalides. In the 1920s de Gaulle was a frequent guest at the Marshal's home on Place Latour-Maubourg; de Gaulle's first-born son was christened Philippe. In 1926, the hero of Verdun took de Gaulle on a trip to the battlefield. 'I want to cover the front', Pétain told a friend before leaving, 'with the most intelligent officer of the French army, to know what he would have done opposite me if he had been the Crown Prince'[14] – in fourteen years they would be facing each other across the Channel.

Pétain imposed his 'successor' on the hostile staff at the Ecole Supérieure de Guerre: he asked de Gaulle to give a series of lectures on military leadership, which was quite a challenge for a captain, graded '*bien*', in an auditorium filled with generals. De Gaulle spoke of character and prestige, quoting without a glance at his notes from Plato, Lucretius, Scharnhorst, Goethe and Bergson. 'Distance is indispensable,' he said, staring into the Marshal's blue eyes. 'There is something in the nature of religious faith about the confidence that men place in another man.'[15] The book that grew out of this, *Le Fil de l'épée* (or *The Edge of the Sword*), was dedicated to Pétain: 'Nothing indicates better than your own Glory the virtues of Action derived under the Light of Thought.'[16]

Pétain was an original thinker. Defying the military dogma of his day, Pétain before the First World War, like de Gaulle before the Second, propounded a heresy. He argued that modern technological war would be won not by grandly designed offensives, but by the concentration of firepower. Guns kill, he said with insight. There was no point therefore in charging straight into them. Pétain was a man of the defensive, a man of forts, the man of static 1916; not the war of movement of 1918. He raged, just like de Gaulle, against the mediocrity of high command, and never felt a part of it. Even as Marshal of France in the 1920s he sought out the rebels, the military theorists of unconventional thought. He cultivated them in the personal staff he housed at 4 bis, Boulevard des Invalides. That is where de Gaulle had his office. Before he was forty de Gaulle was at the heart of French military planning for the next war.

De Gaulle was a writer. Pétain was not. 'I would put more trust in the production of a life of Pétain by Turenne than of a life of Turenne by Pétain,' Georges Clemenceau told Marguerite Baldensperger, when she engaged the Marshal to write a biography of the great seventeenth-century French commander; the biography never appeared.[17] In addition to supplying ideas, the purpose of Pétain's personal staff was to act, as they said of themselves, as his '*porte-plume*', his 'pen-holders'. Pétain's procedure for composing a work, whether an article or a book, never varied: first he would select a suitable officer, outline for him the general theme, and then tell him to get on with the job; periodically there would be a review of the work in progress. This infallible method – always popular among men of power – won Pétain a chair at the Académie Française in 1929. De Gaulle was brought into Pétain's team as an 'editorial officer' in 1925, and was involved in two grand projects, one on the lessons to be learnt from the Great War as a basis of army reform, the other aiming to portray the soldier throughout history. De Gaulle, typically, worked diligently on both, without breathing a word to anyone. Pétain became worried about the lack of progress reports. In January 1929 he passed the task of writing 'The Soldier' to a certain Colonel Audet, just as de Gaulle was called up for an assignment in the 'Levant' (as the Middle East was then known). De Gaulle's reaction was sharp. 'A book is a man,' he wrote to Audet, as if playing on the Proustian 'I'. 'This man up to now has been me.' He even reprimanded the Marshal himself, 'author' of the book: 'I agree whole-heartedly to seeing you sign the work alone, [but] I cannot abandon what I have put into it myself.' Pétain, always moderate in tone, replied that he would be willing 'to continue your collaboration'. But this was the beginning of the end.[18]

In fact, such 'collaboration' had never existed. In ideas, the two men were leagues apart. Both had, perhaps, their hearts in the North. But Pétain's eyes were drawn to the forts that had sprung up on the plains since the seventeenth century, his war was one of guns, walls and entrench-ments. De Gaulle always had a wider view; he looked to the horizons, he knew the depth of the plain: his war was built on movement. Pétain had the foresight, before 1914, to appreciate the firepower of steel cannon. De Gaulle understood, before 1940, the full significance of tanks.

Pétain's two projects of the 1920s, on army reform and 'The Soldier', became de Gaulle's two books of the 1930s, Vers l'armée de métier and La France et son armée. By the time the second was published in 1938 French staff officers were calling him 'Colonel Motor'; it was not meant to be a compliment.

On 11 July 1941 the war had brought de Gaulle back to the Levant. He was having dinner that night in Damascus with General Georges Catroux, the only colonial governor to come over to de Gaulle at the time of his appeal in June 1940. There were several younger officers of the Free French at the table. 'Pétain was a great man,' admitted de Gaulle in front of them all: 'he died in 1925.'[19]

Why 1925? This was the year Pétain rescued de Gaulle from a humble post he had been assigned in Mainz after the average grade he had received at the Ecole Supérieure de Guerre. Pétain had saved his career. De Gaulle considered his protector dead as of that moment? De Gaulle's ideas about an army in movement were already developing, it is true. But it was not this that underlay his harsh judgement. Pétain did something in late 1925 which proved to his junior colleague that he had no vision of 'France' beyond her physical frontiers. Pétain, under pressure from the Prime Minister, Aristide Briand, had set off to Morocco to suppress a revolt and, in particular, end the career of one of the grandest colonial governors France had ever known, Marshal Louis Lyautey. Lyautey had been following a moderate diplomatic policy that encouraged Morocco to be Morocco and not just a French colony. Pétain took over Lyautey's command, and Lyautey lost his standing in the French army. As the new commander, Pétain simply followed the orders of his provincial political masters. He returned with blood on his hands, having destroyed the great Lyautey.

For de Gaulle the event showed two things. First, the unjustified contempt high command within France held for commanders overseas. Second, Pétain's failure of nerve. He was quite obviously no longer his own man; he had capitulated and given way to repression.

This would be de Gaulle's understanding of Vichy: defeatist, repressive and with limited horizons.

4 Le Quatorze Juillet

By the end of 1942 the war had overborne all limits; frontiers, moral as well as territorial, disappeared: Hitler's war of isolated offensives had degenerated into a conflict fought on every front. The traditional boundary between soldier and civilian had faded; the annihilation of whole races began. Old military ideas had to be abandoned. The initial British, Pittite strategy of blockade, bombing and incitement to rebellion had proved obsolete; the debate between American and British staffs over the invasion of Europe's heartland had become academic – the Western armies, American and British, had to fight their war on the periphery. If resistance did develop inside Nazi-dominated Europe its chief inspiration came from Moscow, not London. On Russia's western borderlands the whirlwind of violence intensified: from that spring the Partisan movements spread in eddies right across the Continent.

In all this, France seemed to play only a minor role. A backwater in Hitler's scheme of things, she was of no importance either to the Soviet Union. Nor did France appear, after June 1940, to be of central concern to the British or the Americans. Ultimately she was designed to provide a slab of territory for a landing and an invasion into the heartland of the enemy. But many military minds, especially in Britain, were beginning to think that even this could be avoided, either by bombing alone or by an advance through Italy.

After the fall of France, it was the French Empire which suddenly became strategically important in the Allied peripheral war. One can understand why de Gaulle in the Levant in 1941 should be so scornful of Pétain's attitude towards the colonies. For de Gaulle, the French Empire had become 'France'; the mother country had been occupied and betrayed by Pétain's team; the colonies were the only cards the General had left to play. And

he had not so many of these. De Gaulle's loyal General Catroux abandoned Indochina (which the Vichy authorities then handed over, without
a shot being fired, to the Japanese) and was named commander of the
Free French forces in the Near East. The other governors remained loyal
to Vichy. It is easy to understand why: French colonial administrators had
always hated the British; like de Gaulle, they had never forgotten Fashoda.
French Equatorial Africa provided one notable exception.

Before the First World War it had been a German colony. The French
administrators did not want the land to become German again and, in
August 1940, they rose in revolt and declared for de Gaulle. Within three
months de Gaulle had thousands of square miles of territory under his
control and armed forces of 17,500. Thus, in the rainforests of Africa,
across the deserts of the Sahara and onward to the Allied forces gathering
in North Africa, de Gaulle's march on Paris began. De Gaulle had a territorial base that he could call 'France' and could press forward a war of
movement such as he had always advocated. But the change in Equatorial
Africa's allegiance turned out to be even more significant than either he
or his Allies had first imagined. In 1941, the Americans instituted a line
of air supplies, the 'Takoradi route', that crossed the Atlantic and stopped
in Nigeria and Fort Lamy in Chad, on their way to the main North
African forces supply centre of Khartoum in the Sudan. Without that
route the war in North Africa would have been unsustainable, the peripheral war would have collapsed, the invasion of the Continent could not
have occurred. In the slow transition, between 1942 and 1944, from peripheral war to invasion, 'France', with its capital in Brazzaville and London,
and later in Algiers, played a pivotal role. This point was not lost on the
General.

All armed forces opposed to Hitler which had escaped from occupied
Europe, and which did not want to disappear into Soviet camps and the
Red Army, were obliged to follow the African route. Among them, the
most important were the Poles.

De Gaulle had established a special relationship with the Poles. He had
spent more than half of the First World War as a prisoner in Germany,
after a bayonet had been thrust in his thigh at Verdun in March 1916.
Prison might have saved his life, but it was not very good for his career.
He had missed virtually the whole of the Verdun campaign, the offensives
and new defence strategy of 1917, and the advance of 1918. Pétain's whole
defence strategy, which moulded military opinion in France for the next
two decades, was based on that experience. For many Eastern Europeans,
however, the fighting did not end with the Armistice of 1918; the years

1918–22 were marked by countless small wars of movement. De Gaulle was a witness to this. In May 1919 he had been sent out to Poland as an adviser to 'Haller's Army'. It was a chance to gain the experience he had missed as a prisoner of war. With his eye for the northern plain, what he saw were the manoeuvres of Piłsudski's armies against Lenin's Bolshevik forces. De Gaulle was in Warsaw, its streets decorated with French as well as Polish flags, when in August 1920 the Red Army, just on the other side of the River Vistula, was routed by a brilliant Polish flanking attack. '*Ah! la belle manoeuvre que nous avons vue là!*' wrote de Gaulle three months later.[20] De Gaulle became France's advocate of movement.

He developed a passion – a word not easily applied to de Gaulle – for Poland: he loved Warsaw, and the working people of its two poor suburbs, Wola and Praga, whose national enthusiasm proved so much stronger than the social ideology of Lenin's armies on the eastern side of the river; and his sentiments for the beautiful Countess Strumilla, in whose salon his barely disguised figure prowled, were probably not so innocent. De Gaulle's marriage to Mademoiselle Yvonne Vendroux of Calais was arranged by his family immediately upon his return to France.

Poland would always hold a special corner in de Gaulle's heart. Gaston Palewski, a Pole who had been on Lyautey's staff in Morocco, left a bomber squadron in 1940 to become, in London, the director of Free French political affairs and de Gaulle's private secretary – he would remain a powerful Gaullist organizer until his death, in 1984. Most significant of all was the coincidence of Poland's struggle for existence with that of France; as de Gaulle completed his long wartime march on Paris, the Nazis destroyed Wola and another Red Army stood on the eastern side of the Vistula, at the suburban borders of Praga.

'Action in war essentially assumes the character of contingency,' said de Gaulle, philosophically, on opening his series of lectures in 1927.[21] There is no rule to war, no law of necessity. The choices are determined by the prevailing circumstances. Poland had no choice: she was occupied and terrorized. France did: she could have continued her fight in her colonies; Vichy's authorities, instead, signed an armistice with the enemy. De Gaulle rightly saw what a disastrous course this would take.

His main concern was the existence of France as a nation. This led him to concentrate on a post-war plan for his country, a post-war plan conceived in wartime. It was pressing. France's shape and status in the post-war world had to be determined before the Western peripheral war against Germany was transformed into a continental invasion. By then it would be too late.

The case of Italy would prove this. There are parallels between Fascist Italy and Vichy France. Their foreign policy was guided by collaboration with Nazi Germany; their domestic policy failed because they never managed to establish an effective local administration to execute it. Most Frenchmen were not Vichyites. Most Italians were not Fascists. Many would have agreed with the exiled Socialist leader, Pietro Nenni, who wrote in his diary on 10 June 1940, the day Mussolini declared war from the balcony of the Palazzo Venezia, 'This is a war without any reason, for no real Italian interest is at stake; it is without excuse . . . and it is without honour.'[22]

Under the Fascists, hundreds of thousands of Italians were drafted into labour service in Germany, just as the French were under Vichy. The Jews, less numerous and to begin with more secure under Mussolini than they were under Pétain, were in the end rounded up and sent to their deaths. Resistance movements developed in Italy, as they did in France; and in northern Italy, by the end of 1943, they were dominated by the Partisans, as indeed they were in France. There are parallels even between Marshal Pietro Badoglio, who took over the Italian government when the Fascist Grand Council ousted Mussolini late in July 1943, and Marshal Pétain: they were both military heroes of the First World War, both spoke of themselves as standing above vulgar 'politics', guiding and nurturing their countries through their dark hour – and both negotiated simultaneously with Nazis and Western Allies as the end of the war approached. Both would set up governments far from the national capital: Pétain in Vichy, Badoglio in Brindisi, a coastal town on the heel of Italy. The Italian crowds cheered the Allies when their tanks and armoured cars eventually rumbled down their streets, in the same way as the French: '*Viva gli Inglesi! Viva gli Americani!*' they cried, throwing flowers at the liberating troops.

But the Italians did not have a de Gaulle. Badoglio had no authority. The Americans signed an armistice with Badoglio, just as they were willing to do with Pétain, because he was regarded as the only legitimate representative of government available. Later, there would be democratic elections. In the meantime the Allies would both occupy and administer the liberated territories. In Charlottesville, Virginia, the Americans had prepared their 'sixty-day marvels', administrative officials who would be brought in to do the job. They were collectively known under the acronym AMGOT, Allied Military Government for Occupied Territories.

First the territories had to be occupied. Italy is one of the forgotten campaigns of the Second World War. The landings were isolated rehearsals for the major invasion of 1944. The advance up the peninsula was slow and soon lost any military objective. The armies were polyglot, made up of Moroccans and Frenchmen, British and Americans, Indians and New Zealanders, and of course the Poles. Mountain ranges had to be crossed, routes were blocked by chasms and gorges, bridges were blown; it degenerated into a sapper's war, an uncomfortable war. Civilians were dragged into it. Men ploughed fields while the mortars fell. Peasant women, with bundles on their heads, passed back and forth on the bombarded roads. When a child was killed there would be anguished screams over the implacable will of God. No government official was there to hear them. There was no food, no rationing. Young AMGOT officers were overwhelmed by the situation. They spoke no Italian, they did not know the history of the region, and they had no idea whom to turn to; they fell prey to the black market and rampant local corruption, mere spokes of an evil wheel. AMGOT was a 'vast Tammany Hall', according to Harold Macmillan, the UK High Commissioner in Italy, 'designed to give good jobs to people strong in the New York Italian community – make them all colonels. They didn't care tuppence about what the Italians really needed.'[23] '*Pane! biscotti! sigarette!*' chanted hysterical rows of hungry children.

Alan Moorehead, the British war reporter, saw Naples in the autumn of 1943. It was the first great city of Europe to fall into Allied hands; Naples was 'the peace behind the war'. Moorehead remarked: 'It was not the war, it was the aftermath of the war that destroyed Italy.' In Naples, after the Allied armies passed, he witnessed 'the moral collapse of a people. They had no pride any more, or any dignity. The animal struggle for existence governed everything. Food. That was the only thing that mattered.'[24]

The Americans and the British had no specific post-war plans. This was particularly the case of the Americans, who were playing an increasing part in the war effort. They wanted to win it, they wanted it over. They were not going to worry now about what might happen after it. Roosevelt's guiding principle was to deal with each political situation as it arose. If this meant shaking hands with the odd Nazi or Nazi collaborator, it was of no concern to the American President; the Allied armies were going to advance and occupy; elections and politics would come later. The Allied armed forces were prepared to take over French territory in any part of the world to prevent its use by the Axis powers, Roosevelt declared as the British started their operations in the French colony of Madagascar; 'the good people of France will readily understand.' The good Free French were not consulted. After 'Operation Torch', when the Allies seized Algeria, Roosevelt explained to de Gaulle's two representatives in Washington that the United States was henceforth the 'occupying power'. Four months later he told Anthony Eden, the British Foreign Secretary, that the 'smaller powers should have nothing more dangerous than rifles'. The Big Three – Britain, the United States and Russia – 'should police Europe in general'. In connection with Western police work, Roosevelt spoke of 'a new state called "Wallonia" [which] would include the Walloon parts of Belgium with Luxembourg, Alsace-Lorraine and part of Northern France'.[25]

Britain also had first to win the war. This was no time to question her powerful ally. Churchill was always ready to cover Washington, to save the face of the President and his advisers, even when their statements were preposterous. Thus, his greatest fits of anger against de Gaulle invariably coincided with his trips to America.

De Gaulle was not in a position to wait. In need of a post-war plan, he had to force a commitment from the United States and Britain before the Allies landed in France, shook hands with whatever compromised authority remained in the country and then instituted AMGOT, 'the peace behind the war'. He started early. On 19 June 1940, the day after his first appeal on the radio, he was back at the microphone identifying '*moi, général de Gaulle, soldat et chef français*' with 'France': 'In the name of France I officially declare . . .' The register of his supporters at Carlton Place was at that time very short. The British were still negotiating with Pétain, and would continue to do so until the autumn. The campaign for legitimacy had opened; the fight for recognition was on. 'France' had shifted to the colonies. 'It is not tolerable that the panic at Bordeaux should cross the sea. Soldiers of France, wherever you are, stand up!' 'France' would join the armies at the periphery, where the real war against Hitler had begun. And 'France' was going to win it.[26]

De Gaulle, at an early stage of the war, won the support of the Allied press. This in turn troubled Roosevelt, who right up to the time of the Liberation of Paris in 1944 was at heart an ally of Vichy, thinking always that at any moment Vichy would switch sides and become a convenient client state of the Americans. On several occasions, the situation required Churchill's intervention to prevent Roosevelt's hostility towards de Gaulle from becoming totally destructive.

On one date in particular, every year, de Gaulle laid down his challenge: *le Quatorze Juillet*.

Bastille Day may seem an odd choice for a conservative Catholic general. In fact, unlike his parents, de Gaulle was as committed to the French Revolution as he was to Joan of Arc; he saw it as part of the vast historical continuity implicit in his 'certain idea of France'. High in his roll of honour stood the republican and revolutionary General Lazare Hoche. In

Le Fil de l'épée the Revolution was depicted as one of the most glorious chapters of French history, along with the first decades of the Third Republic, Clemenceau's Republic. What he could not abide was the feeble Third Republic of the inter-war years; he did not want post-war France to resemble it.

The celebration of Bastille Day had not been outlawed by the Vichy authorities. But they had attempted to raise the springtime sap in the people with alternative festivals: Joan of Arc's feast day on 11 May and – a complete innovation – Mother's Day on the last Sunday of May.

No one in France felt like celebrating on 14 July 1940. But in London it was an occasion for de Gaulle. A few hundred French sailors with red poppies in their caps, airmen in blue, soldiers with rifles and fixed bayonets and crewmen of French tanks with their padded helmets assembled before the Cenotaph in Whitehall. Two steel-helmeted trumpeters sounded a call and General de Gaulle marched out to lay at the foot of the British war memorial a wreath, marked '*Les Français Libres*'. De Gaulle returned to the ranks and sharply ordered, '*Salut aux Morts!*' Then the assembly marched over to Grosvenor Gardens, to the statue of Marshal Foch, Commander-in-Chief of the Allied Armies in 1918. As they marched, Londoners began to gather. By the time the Frenchmen reached the statue, the crowd was thousands-strong. '*Vive de Gaulle!*' they cried out in French, '*Vive la France!*' They sang a halting version of the *Marseillaise*. French films were shown in the cinemas that night. Churchill sent a telegram to de Gaulle that was printed in all the newspapers. 'I look forward with confidence', he wrote, 'to a time not far distant when July 14 will once again be celebrated as a day of rejoicing by a free and victorious France.'[27]

It took two years for the forces of the Free French, under General Philippe de Hauteclocq, better known as Leclerc, to make their way through French Equatorial Africa and over the Sahara to join the Allied armies in North Africa. While Leclerc was conducting operations against the Italians in the desert oases of southern Libya, General Marie Pierre Koenig gathered a motley array of colonials, mostly members of the Foreign Legion, into a light infantry division under the auspices of the British Eighth Army. They were ready just in time for Rommel's eastward offensive in late May 1942 and conducted a spectacular holding action at Bir Hakeim. In late June both the British and the American presses were filled with the news; it added some tonic to the announcement of the British disaster at Tobruk.

What the French accomplished on foot from Equatorial Africa corresponded roughly to the roundabout path the Americans were taking by air: they carried in their aircraft tanks and munitions to the British in

Egypt along a line that also went through Equatorial Africa. Early in June 1940 Roosevelt established the famous Takoradi air route, an assemblage of airfields that linked the US suppliers to Latin America and from there across the South Atlantic to the British Gold Coast (today Ghana), to Khartoum in the Sudan and, from there, finally to Egypt. The early switch in allegiance of French Equatorial Africa to de Gaulle (the area had little desire to become again the German colony it had been before the First World War) and Leclerc's armed takeover of the Sahara made the Takoradi route secure; Fort Lamy became one of the major chain ports in the route. Montgomery's march eastwards from Egypt to Tunisia and Algeria would have been impossible without it. Such was the only way of attaining the Nazi-occupied Continent: through the jungles of Central Africa. America's first gound combat in the war was with the landings on the Algerian coast, following Montgomery's advance westwards across North Africa towards Tunisia. After months of gruelling struggle – some of the battlefields resembling Ypres and the Somme – the Allies were at last able to disembark at Sicily in July 1943. The war for Western Europe finally began the moment the Soviets defeated the Germans in the huge tank battle at Kursk. July 1943 was the turning point of the war: a nice time to bring out the flags and celebrate Bastille Day.

This by now was developing into a major Gaullist festival, much to the displeasure of Vichy – and the irritation of Vichy's friends in Washington. In London Bastille Day 1942 had been celebrated once more before the statue of Marshal Foch. De Gaulle had laid a wreath of white lilies, joined with blue delphiniums and red carnations. His language had become a good deal more radical. He no longer spoke on the radio of 'honour and patrie', it was now 'Liberty, Fraternity, Equality' (a subtle turn of the usual phrase); he saluted the Republic, and claimed that France was going through the 'greatest revolution in her history'. That Bastille Day de Gaulle announced a change in the name of his soldiers: the 'Free French' became the 'Fighting French'.[28]

There were, following de Gaulle's appeal, small demonstrations inside France. In Paris the *Marseillaise* was sung, which even the Germans permitted. '*Aux armes, citoyens,*' was not their favourite line. But that year they and the Vichy authorities were concentrating on the Jews; it was the season of the *Grande Rafle*.

The most astonishing celebration of Bastille Day was in New York. The period between 4 July and 14 July was declared by Mayor Fiorello La Guardia to be 'Free French Week'. Wendell Willkie, who had been the Republican presidential candidate in 1940, came over to Freedom House, where a large tricolour flag with the Cross of Lorraine was flying outside, and said that both the war and the peace would be won 'with the aid of France'. 'Whatever may be the cautious and dubious diplomacy of the government,' he added, 'we, the people, repudiate the Laval and Vichy collaborationists.' A spokesman for the US State Department published a wooden article in the *New York Times* arguing that diplomatic relations with Vichy were 'valued as a means of keeping in contact with the French people'.[29]

Roosevelt and the State Department declared war on the press. Churchill stood behind the President. The Allied armies invaded Algeria: the peripheral war was closing in on Europe. In Algeria, the Americans pressed forward their candidate to unite the French 'factions', the former Prime Minister of Vichy France, Admiral Darlan. He was murdered on Christmas Eve. The Americans came up with another Pétain loyalist, General Henri Giraud. But they made the colossal error of inviting Giraud to tour the United States in the month of July 1943. At the same time de Gaulle toured North Africa.

The tour came to a close on Bastille Day in the Place du Forum in Algiers. 'Let us lift up our heads,' he declared, throwing his arms in the air (the Gaullist method of oratory was developing), 'let us close our ranks in the spirit of brotherhood, let us all march together, through the struggle and the victory, towards our new destiny!'[30]

French victory. French destiny. It was all symbolic, of course. And de Gaulle was the master of symbols.

5 Legitimacy: de Gaulle and the Communists

As the peripheral war turned into invasion, the issue of French legitimacy came to a head. It would turn out to be one of the major factors shaping post-war Europe, though few thought so at the time. For Hitler, France was unimportant after 1940; Stalin had other parts of the world on his mind; for the Anglo-American commanders France was a mere stepping-stone into the enemy heartland.

Two virtually simultaneous events in mid-1943 had given legitimacy to de Gaulle, though the Americans and the British still refused to recognize it: the setting up of the National Council of Resistance (the CNR) under the presidency of Jean Moulin, which proved that de Gaulle had won the respect, if not the support, of the interior resistance movements; and the creation in Algiers of the French Committee of National Liberation (the CFLN), which was, to all intents and purposes, a French provisional government. However, after the arrest and death of Moulin, de Gaulle faced a serious rival inside France, the French Communist Party (the PCF).

The increase in Communist influence in France after June 1943 was nothing short of sensational. A major point of leverage had been exerted through the trade unions, dominated, despite Vichy, by the General Confederation of Labour (the CGT) which was, in turn, largely controlled by the Communists. The Vichy programme of conscripted labour and 'deportations' – as the clandestine Communist press insisted, not incorrectly, on calling forced labour in Germany – magnified the trend. There was a wave of strikes in the summer and autumn of 1943 contesting conditions and control by the legal, Vichyite unions. Secretaries of the legal unions were occasionally murdered by 'unknowns' after being denounced in the clandestine press as 'traitors'. In Paris there was a wave of sabotage actions. At the same time the Communists started setting up their own 'replacement administrations' – *organisations populaires* – that were designed to take over local affairs at the moment of Liberation. This was the purpose of the Departmental Liberation Committees that were supposed to represent all movements but, by autumn, had been turned into little soviets. The CNR itself fell under Communist influence. The PCF did everything to prevent a representative of de Gaulle's Délégation Générale from succeeding to Moulin's position; eventually, with the help of the other movements, still jealous of their independence, they nominated Georges Bidault. Bidault was not a Communist, but he was a member of the Communist National Front, so was susceptible to pressure.

By early 1944 the Communists had total control of the paramilitary forces of the resistance movements. This was achieved by the fusion, in December 1943, of the various armed groups into the French Forces of the Interior (the FFI). The military commission responsible for this was dissolved and a new one set up in its place, COMAC (or 'Comité d'action'), a veritable general staff of the resistance army. Two of the three members of COMAC were Communists. It was a typical Communist manoeuvre. By the spring of 1944, as the moment of Allied invasion approached, the Communists aimed to reconstitute the entire French army around the FFI and the Communist Partisans.[31]

This was not idle talk. The non-Communist resistance in Poland awaited the Western Allies to liberate them; the Communists in France stood ready for a Soviet liberation. It seems fantastic today. But in the winter of 1943–4 there was nothing ridiculous about the prospect of the Red Army arriving at the gates of Paris. Western advance through Italy was obviously slow. Even if the Anglo-American armies did land in northern France, would they hold on? Would the Americans want to hold on? Nothing in their history or in their current political behaviour suggested much of a commitment.

The Comintern might have been officially dissolved on 15 May 1943, but the basic message of Communist propaganda in France was laid down in Moscow. Its chief apostles were the French Communist General Secretary, Maurice Thorez, a leading Communist parliamentary deputy, André Marty, and the Italian Communist, Palmiro Togliatti.

On 6 November 1943, with preparations under way for the first summit between Stalin and his Western 'allies', the Soviet leader made a speech that would set the tone of Communist propaganda throughout Nazi-occupied Europe; it would also colour the canvas of the post-war world. Here was the grammar and vocabulary of an international language that would be spoken by the apostles. The war, said Stalin, had two aims: first, 'to free the people of Europe from the yoke of the Fascist invader'; and second, 'to grant to the peoples of Europe the full right and full freedom to decide for themselves the organization of their States'.[32]

In later years, as the Cold War developed, Communist watchers would learn to study and interpret the language of official Soviet statements. During the war years, in contrast, Westerners were naive; they did not know what Stalin was implying. Communist language at that time depended on the degree of certainty of Soviet army success. By late 1943 the Communists were confident that Soviet armies would overrun a large part of Eastern Europe, and even Germany. Here, the enemy was defined as 'Fascist' – one could easily slip the odd 'bourgeois democrat' in here, and hang him. But in France? Perhaps the Western armies would advance. Perhaps the 'bourgeois' General Charles de Gaulle would succeed. The future of France was uncertain. So the French Communists never pronounced in the clandestine press the word 'Fascist'. They had to make sure they were on the side of 'History', and in late 1943 and early 1944 they could not see exactly which way events would turn. The same would apply to the people's 'freedom to decide for themselves the organization of their States'. Where the Soviet armies were the masters this 'freedom' would be decided by 'popular committees' under the command of the local Communist Party. But in France? For the moment it would have to remain a game of double 'legitimacies' – between de Gaulle and the Communists – until it was decided which way History was blowing.

History was always on the side of Communism. That was its great attraction. But sometimes the goalposts had to be moved, the lines on the field altered; this was what was known as 'praxis'. 'Praxis', the practice of

adjusting policy to fit events, corrected the errors of theory. Every generation of the twentieth century saw a host of disillusioned idealists break
from the Party. But every generation also threw up swarms of new young
recruits eager for the historical certainties the Party presented.[33]

'In the struggle for national liberation', observed the French Communist
trade union journal *Vie Ouvrière* in April 1943, 'the working class must
provide the example of union and action.'[34] Behind this 'working class'
was the Party, behind the Party was Stalin.

By late 1943 the Party had complete control of the trade union press
in France. It also controlled most of the clandestine press along with the
political tracts which began showering the streets at that time. It has been
estimated that between November 1943 and April 1944 the unions in Paris
had multiplied their printing capacity by seven times. Two members of
the 'popular committee' for the Paris builders' union had walled up a
section of their apartment on Rue Neuve Popincourt where they kept
the archives of the CGT, powerful printing machines and a number of
typewriters. From places like this spread a new kind of propaganda.

While Communists in Eastern Europe occupied themselves with the 'war
against Fascism', those of France concentrated on the 'struggle against
anti-Communism'.

'Anti-Communism' is usually associated with American rednecks and
McCarthyites of the 1950s, who were themselves the caricatures of
Communist propaganda. But the word first became current in France in
1943–4 – and it was a slur invented by the Communists. It was aimed not
at the Nazis or at the administrators of Vichy; its victims were Socialists,
who competed for the control of the unions. The campaign had a lot of
success: 'traitors' were eliminated; clandestine general assemblies developed
into blood feuds. The working-class 'example of union and action' first
meant unity behind the Party. 'There are still here and there', noted a
columnist menacingly in *Vie Ouvrière* just one week after Moulin's arrest,
'some men who haven't learnt anything and who still indulge in the little
game of anti-Communism in the unions.'[35]

In classical Leninist strategy, union of the working class would encourage
action of the 'masses', 'general strike', 'insurrection' and finally 'takeover'
of the powers that be. That, in the Communist view, was the predestined
order of events. But in France there was a distinct possibility that the
Gaullists would get there first. So the Communists developed a system of
'alliance', which foresaw a neat division of power: 'outside France' the
struggle against 'Hitlerism' (never 'Fascism', by now an Eastern European
term designed to be turned by the Soviets against the 'bourgeoisie') would

be left to Allied 'bourgeois' forces; on the 'soil of the *patrie*', however, the duty of struggle fell to the Communists.

In invoking the *patrie*, the Communists were making up for lost time – the period of the Nazi-Soviet Pact of 1939–41. At that time their struggle had been with the Western 'imperialist bandits', and most particularly their Socialist apologists. 'The Blums [Léon Blum, the Socialist leader] and the Jouhaux [Léon Jouhaux, the non-Communist trade unionist] bustle about exhorting soldiers and workers to make the supreme sacrifice and denouncing "German imperialism",' ran an article in *L'Humanité* just as the German armies broke through Western lines in May 1940. 'While fulminating against German imperialism they try to clear the names of their own masters, the Franco-English imperialists.'[36] But the goalposts were successfully shifted, the lines on the field redrawn. By 1943 all Communists were patriots, while the Socialists had been transformed into anti-Communist traitors and collaborators.

It was too dangerous to say as much of the 'bourgeois' Gaullists. The Communists had to be ready to follow through their historical sequence of 'general strike', 'national insurrection', 'rupture' with the bourgeois allies, and 'takeover'. But how far they would proceed along that line would depend on the balance of the Western and Soviet armies.

Moreover, there was a problem developing around the term 'working class'. The French working classes had been considerably weakened by four years of occupation; by the spring of 1944 almost a million Frenchmen had been shipped off to Germany to work, while another 700,000 had been requisitioned into operations like the building of the Atlantic Wall. Factories and workshops had been emptied, particularly in the Paris region. The great Renault works in the western suburb of Boulogne-Billancourt, with 30,000 workers, had been the spearhead of the Communist-led strike movements of 1936; when the Allies landed in Normandy in June 1944 only 3,000 of them were left. The building industry, railways, the post office and the printing presses of Paris all witnessed the same decline.

Such realities were not, however, enough to dissuade the French Communist Party from their historical project, from preparing for a national insurrection and eventual rupture with the 'bourgeois' resistance to 'Hitlerism'; after all, if the Soviet armies did arrive in Paris, they wouldn't need a 'working class'.

Their seedbed was bureaucracy, local and national, not the working class. This itself had its basis in the historical theory of certainties, that of 'dual power' first developed by Marx in his observations on the Paris

Commune of 1871 and perfected into an ideology by Lenin. 'Dual power' became 'many local powers' when the Bolsheviks put theory into praxis in 1917; henceforth the basic historic model for Communists throughout the world derived from the competition which had developed in Petrograd that year between Kerensky's Provisional Government and the Soviet Executive. In this context, it is remarkable how early the Communist press in France started speaking of de Gaulle's French Committee of National Liberation as 'the real Provisional Government'. Would it be followed by France's 'October Revolution'?

'Dual power' was applied to the letter by the French Communists: every time the Committee in Algiers, supported by a Consultative Assembly, passed a decree or made a statement on the administrative machinery to be put in place in France after the Liberation, the Communists replied in kind, setting up their own regional and national committees, as if they were a second 'Provisional Government'. It was the same with the unions where, if workers dared to establish independent representation, the Communists would organize a parallel 'popular committee'. It was the same with the French resistance armed forces – the Communists had their own army, the FTP (Francs-Tireurs et Partisans) or simply 'Partisans'.

At the height of the war, as the Allied armies approached and violence grew, the central concern of the Communists was always bureaucratic. A page of French Communist history during the Second World War resembles an overturned pot of alphabet soup: MOI, the FN, the CMN, the CCR, COMAC, the FFI, the FTP, the CPL, UDs, CDLs . . .

By early 1944 it was curiously the Communist parallel administrations inside France that always came out on top. The fate of Combat, a major independent resistance movement in southern France set up by Henri Frenay in 1941, is suggestive of how this happened. In 1943–4 the Communist press was full of the attacks and acts of sabotage committed by the Partisans; it rarely mentioned the operations of other resistance movements. Readers exposed to this sort of propaganda could well believe L'Humanité when it commented on 12 November 1943 that the FTP 'are, as it were, the only ones to fight'. Frenay left for Algiers at about that time to participate in the Consultative Assembly. His successor, Claude Bourdet, managed to maintain a balance between his forces and those of the Communists. Bourdet was arrested by the Germans on 24 March 1944. The organization was immediately placed under the control of a central committee dominated by the Communist Marcel Degliame-Fouché and his aide Pascal Copeau. Copeau explained in May 1944 that an 'executive in the Southern Zone' was needed so that 'the Resistance be a totally independent affair'. Frenay, a champion of independence, had not foreseen this. In the months prior to D-Day, history accelerated in favour of the Communists, to the detriment of everyone else.[37]

Copeau's text also noted that de Gaulle was only a representative of the 'Resistance à l'extérieure', implying that he had no legitimacy whatever within France. Yet the Communists, by now, were members of de Gaulle's Committee. It was typical of Communist 'dual power' strategy: in Algiers they played the role of government ministers; in France they prepared for 'national insurrection'.

While the French Communists manoeuvred, in their ambivalent way, into the French Committee of National Liberation in Algiers – 'the central power', as de Gaulle emphasized – the General continued his struggle for Anglo-American recognition. Roosevelt's policy was to treat all French territory as occupied until after the war was won, at which time the French would be permitted to hold an election. Churchill's policy was always, as he told Roosevelt in July 1943, 'to keep in step with you'.

But de Gaulle in the war years was popular in defiant Britain, and the British government could not afford to ignore this. Moreover, American high-handedness in Africa, and later in Italy, irked British sensibilities. There thus crept into British policy towards de Gaulle's Committee an ambivalence comparable to that of the Communists.

Britain, of course, had no desire to take over France. But, unlike the Americans, she had an intense interest in the shape of post-war Europe. The critical figure in Britain's own ambivalent approach towards de Gaulle and his Committee was a junior member of Churchill's government, the publisher Harold Macmillan. Macmillan acted as a foil to Roosevelt and Churchill, and was much appreciated by Churchill for that. It was Macmillan who constantly mollified Churchill's rages with de Gaulle; 'Perhaps you are right,' Churchill would repeat, 'perhaps you are right.' Shortly after his arrival in Algiers, on 5 June 1943, de Gaulle wrote to Macmillan to say 'how much I appreciated' Macmillan's actions and to express 'to what point your sympathy is precious to me, which permits me also to call it our friendship'.[38] A rare declaration, indeed. De Gaulle's driving will-power was behind the creation of the Committee in Algiers, but it was Macmillan who made it possible.

In December 1942 Churchill had nominated Macmillan as Minister Resident to represent the British government at Allied Force Headquarters, then in Algiers. 'What sort of Minister are you?' asked the Allied Commander Dwight D. Eisenhower sourly when Macmillan stepped into his office. 'I am not a diplomatic Minister,' answered Macmillan; 'I am something worse.'[39] Thus began another important friendship.

Robert Murphy, who represented the US State Department in Algiers, took an instant liking to him, calling him a man of 'excellent common sense'. Macmillan in his baggy trousers and rimless spectacles, 'almost the American popular image of an English gentleman' – though his mother was, happily for his American friends, born in Indiana – had found two men who could be usefully employed to counter the anti-Gaullist policy of Roosevelt and Cordell Hull. And counter it he did, at every stage of the tale. When, shortly after the Casablanca Conference Roosevelt, deviously, signed a memorandum stating that both the United States and Britain had agreed that the 'French fighting against Germany' should be reunited under one authority, that of General Giraud, Macmillan scotched the project at once by sending a copy to London, which repudiated it with anger.

That spring Roosevelt sent the brilliant French businessman, Jean Monnet – the future 'father of Europe' – to Algiers, because he knew Monnet did not like de Gaulle. Macmillan again used his powers of persuasion, and within a month Monnet was arguing the need for a French 'provisional government' and the importance of having de Gaulle in it. Macmillan personally drafted the invitation to de Gaulle to come to Algiers: Macmillan, in the face of Anglo-American opposition, was Charles de Gaulle's kingmaker.

Why did he do it? He explained himself privately to de Gaulle shortly after the General's arrival. It all went back to the First World War. Whenever Macmillan spoke of 'the war' – and he lived into the 1980s – he was referring not to the Second World War, but to the First, the 'Great War'. He had been wounded on French soil on three occasions, he told de Gaulle, who himself had been wounded twice; 'I had lost many of my best and dearest friends . . . We formed an affection for France which had never been broken.' Then he looked into the future. De Gaulle, in another rare moment of his life, listened. In a post-war Europe great wealth would pass away; property 'would be regarded as a trust, for the general benefit'; there would be a transformation of one society to another 'without revolution or disturbance'; and it would depend 'in my country, as in his, on whether men of progressive opinions could work together'.[40] So an experience of war and an almost messianic vision of the future: Macmillan and de Gaulle had this in common. It was something frequently discovered among men who had survived the combat of the First World War.

A few days later both de Gaulle and Macmillan were invited to have lunch with King George VI, who was visiting his troops just before the Italian campaign got under way. The meal was a great success. Macmillan declared that he was going to inspect the Roman ruins in the coastal town of Tipasa that afternoon; de Gaulle asked if he could accompany him. So the two drove off together, strolled through the ruins and discussed 'every conceivable subject – politics, religion, philosophy, the Classics, history (ancient and modern) and so on'. They walked down to the sea, and Macmillan stripped naked and went for a swim. De Gaulle meanwhile sat on a rock in a dignified manner, 'with his military cap, his uniform and belt'. Macmillan never forgot that scene 'with this strange – attractive and yet impossible – character'.[41]

Macmillan's politics were as English as his looks. He saw de Gaulle as a man of the 'left', known as 'Ramrod' at Allied Force Headquarters because he had 'all the rigidity of a poker without its occasional warmth'. He regarded Giraud as a man of the 'right', an 'old-fashioned, but charming colonel, who would grace the Turf Club'. He couldn't under-stand de Gaulle's insistence on a 'purge' of the Vichyites in the French administration in Africa. Nor did he quite pick up the point about the Russian diplomatic presence in Algeria. Macmillan thought Aleksandr Bogomolov or 'Bogo', the Soviet ambassador (no less) to de Gaulle's Committee, dressed appallingly and had an uproarious laugh. He found that Andrei Vyshinsky, Soviet representative to the Advisory Council for Italy, looked 'exactly like Mr Pickwick'. Though he knew Vyshinsky had been the chief prosecutor in the Soviet purges of the 1930s, he could not bring himself to believe that this round and charming man was dangerous.

The peripheral war was being transformed into an invasion. Eisenhower left for Britain. Macmillan left for Italy. Vyshinsky disappeared with a swarm of advisers into the survival politics of Naples and its surround-ings; Togliatti, the Italian Communist, was brought in from Moscow to join them. The French Communists manoeuvred for posts in de Gaulle's Committee; and de Gaulle made indications that they would be welcomed.

Macmillan had been instrumental in gaining a *de facto* recognition of the Committee by the Americans. On 26 August 1943 Roosevelt signed the mealy-mouthed document, acknowledging the Committee as 'the body qualified to ensure the conduct of the French effort in the war' but noting that its desires to administer French interests would be 'reserved for consid-eration in each case as it arises'. 'This statement', it grotesquely concluded, 'does not constitute recognition of a government of France or of the French Empire by the Government of the United States.' By then twenty-six states, including all of the European governments-in-exile, had extended full diplomatic recognition to de Gaulle. Most notable was the Soviet statement acknowledging the Committee as 'the sole representative of all French interests of the French Republic' and 'the sole representative of all French patriots in the struggle against Hitlerism'. Over the next two months de Gaulle repeated that France must stand by Russia.

Bogo, in his demonstrative manner, treated de Gaulle as a Head of State. Up until the eve of D-Day, when the scandal of the delayed recognition erupted in a bitter House of Commons debate, the Americans refused and the British did not dare to advance further than the statement of 26 August. The French Communists trumpeted out a fanfare of propaganda. *L'Humanité* celebrated the New Year of 1944 with a declaration that 'the Communists support with all their forces the CFLN in its patriotic actions.' The Committee was 'the true government of the Republic'. Its opponents were 'traitors' – a term which designated their fate.[42]

The Communists, being a parallel state like the Soviet Executive of 1917, laid down their conditions for membership in de Gaulle's 'provisional government' (a title that the Committee, in fact, only assumed on 3 June 1944). First they wanted their own programme to be adopted: implementation of a maximum war effort against Hitlerism, including the arming of 'French patriots' inside France; the 'chastisement of traitors'; a social and democratic policy to 'galvanize popular energies for the war'; a policy to unite all the French through the 'satisfaction of the legitimate demands of the masses'; and a reinforcement of the 'independence of France' within the Allied bloc.[43] Second, they wanted to nominate their own members.

Such an approach did not impress de Gaulle; in November 1943 he broke off negotiations. But the propaganda campaign continued inside France. And de Gaulle realized that, if he was legitimately to claim that he represented the forces of resistance within France, he had to have the support of the Communists, which by now dominated them. By early 1944 the accusation of 'anti-Communism' was enough to brand someone a 'Vichyite traitor'. A purge of traitors was already implicit in the Communist programme of November 1943. Linked to this was the theme of *attentisme*: the Vichyite traitors and bourgeois 'men of the Trusts', like the Comité des Forges, who had supposedly sold out France to the Hitlerites, were simply playing a waiting game, thus delaying the great patriotic war that was going to save France.

De Gaulle could not afford to ignore this. Anglo-American support might have helped him to stand up to the pressure, but that recognition was not forthcoming. At the moment he broke off negotiations with the Communists in November, de Gaulle, wanting to dampen Communist criticism in France, arrested some of the leading Vichyite administrators in North Africa. Roosevelt was incensed. He demanded that Eisenhower immediately order their release. Macmillan successfully blocked this. But, in confirmation of his English ideas of politics and his failure to appreciate the real nature of the Soviet menace, he ascribed the whole business of French purges to a matter of national honour. 'The liberation of France would be by British and American armies,' he wrote. 'But the fact that they [the French] could do so little to achieve it added to the burden of bitterness and shame. The one thing they could do at once was to set about a series of State trials.'[44]

National honour was an ingredient, but no more than that. For de Gaulle, the purge was the political price to pay for the support of France's internal resistance forces. For the French Communists it was a way of gauging their own legitimacy. If they were all-powerful – which basically required the presence of Soviet armies in France – they could turn it into the Leninist model of civil war and purge France of all 'class enemies'. If their influence depended on an alliance with de Gaulle – a necessity if the Western Allies occupied France first – a purge provided the best means of controlling him, for no resistance movement in 1944 would support de Gaulle without the promise of a purge. The balance of the armies advancing against Hitler would determine how far along the line of 'popular logic' – from mobilization of the 'masses', through 'general strike', to 'national insurrection', 'rupture' and 'takeover' – they would be able to go.

In this context, the propaganda campaign in the winter of 1943–4 against 'anti-Communism', '*attentisme*', and for the purge of all 'traitors' and the union of 'patriots' against 'Hitlerism' became critical: these weapons of words could be turned in any direction. If the Soviet armies advanced quicker than expected, they could be used against de Gaulle's '*attentiste*' Committee. If the Western Allies made an early landing they would be employed, in contrast, to support de Gaulle.

As it happened, none of the armies made any serious advance in the first half of 1944.

Two leading Vichyites who had defected to Algiers in spring 1943 with a promise of safe conduct by General Giraud were the civil servant Maurice Couve de Murville and Darlan's former Minister of Interior, Pierre Pucheu. Couve de Murville went on to become one of de Gaulle's foreign ministers and, briefly, prime minister. Pucheu was executed.

Pucheu's fate was closely linked to the ongoing manoeuvres between de Gaulle and the French Communists. As Minister of Interior he had played a central role in the Vichy negotiations over hostage shooting. The Communists argued that he was responsible for selecting lists of Communists to be shot in October and November 1941; this was never proved – Pucheu claimed, at his brief military trial, that he reduced the number executed. In the 1930s Pucheu had been an international sales director for the French steel industry and belonged to a group of financial counsellors and economic experts who were precursors of the post-war French 'technocrat'. He had also been for two years a member of Jacques Doriot's Parti Populaire Français (the PPF), which was about as close as anyone could get to being a Fascist in France at that time. Significantly, in its violent campaign against Pucheu in the early months of 1944, the French Communist Party did not call Pucheu a 'Fascist'; he was an '*homme de Trust*', one of those rich 'bourgeois' who had sold out French interests to the enemy. Thus the Communists signalled that they were keeping their options open regarding the future of class warfare, as well as that of the 'bourgeois' resistance. They were also proving what great patriots they were.

All the same, it was becoming increasingly clear that the Western Allies would soon be arriving on the soil of the *patrie*. On 18 March de Gaulle announced that his 'Government' would include all French forces fighting for the country's liberation. At dawn, 20 March, Pucheu was shot – de Gaulle was reported that day to have appeared, as he announced the news, with 'his eyes hollow from lack of sleep'.[45] On 4 April three Communists entered de Gaulle's Committee.

The campaign in the clandestine Communist press against 'anti-Communism' and '*attentisme*' did not, however, stop there. The call for a 'national insurrection' was stepped up. So, too, was the appeal for Anglo-American recognition of the Committee as the real government of France, after 'the example of the USSR'. Ten days after D-Day, with rumours spreading that a non-Communist resistance was preparing an uprising in Warsaw, *L'Humanité* professed itself to be baffled at the attitude of the Western Allies, 'a position rendered even less comprehensible by their recognition of the Polish émigré government in London which, itself, represents nothing in Poland'.[46] There is no clearer statement of what the intentions of the Communists were for the summer of 1944.

6 Legitimacy: Poland and the Communists

Occupied Poland, on the other side of the Reich, was the mirror image of occupied France. She had no de Gaulle to speak for the nation – General Sikorski had been killed in an 'accident'. She had no Macmillan who could diplomatically counter the worst abuses of the main liberating power – the Soviet Union in the case of Poland; de Gaulle might have had some difficulties with the United States, but they were nothing compared with what Poland faced with Stalin's Russia. The Communists played a part in the Polish resistance to the Nazis and, as in France, they organized their own parallel underground armed forces and administration in preparation for events. But – a crucial feature of the comparison – the Communists did not dominate the Resistance as they did in France. On the contrary, they were very much in the minority; four years earlier Poles had already had their first practical lesson on the meaning of Communist 'liberation'.

In the fifth spring of the war the forces that would determine the special fate of the national capital, Warsaw, began to take a definite shape. Foremost among them was the movement of the armies.

The winter had been peculiarly mild. Unlike Stalingrad, the winter campaign of 1943–4 was not fought across frozen tracts of snow. The grey, wet fogs of autumn refused to yield. Soviet and German soldiers struggled under leaden skies over a morass of mud and slime; a wide expanse of marsh and squelching country pathways – rather than an ocean and a sea channel – marked the eastern boundaries of 'Fortress Europe'. The Red Army, with its wide-tracked tanks and American trucks, was a good deal better equipped to meet the challenge than the horse-drawn divisions from Germany. One infamous area, to the north of the Crimean peninsula, was the Sivash lagoons, where battalions of men disappeared into a wasteland of salt lakes and stagnant marshes; or the appalling Korsun salient to which the southern forces of Germany held on so desperately in January and February 1944 in the hope of renewed eastern conquest. The last battles around Leningrad were waged those same months, following the greatest artillery show in history, in a zone where the ice on the fresh-water rivers broke under the weight of armies and the marshes of Volkhov failed to freeze. Starving Leningrad was liberated in sleet, not snow.

By May 1944 the 2,000-mile German-Soviet front formed a kind of drunken 'S' in reverse. The German Army Group Centre in Belorussia and based in Minsk bulged eastwards into the Soviet lines; to the south, where the Soviet armies had had a huge, unexpected success, the line protruded westwards to the very frontiers of Romania, Hungary and Czechoslovakia. German commanders in the field recognized that the situation here in the south was virtually untenable.

At Stalingrad, Germany had lost one army. During the winter campaign of 1943–4 four had been crushed and a fifth annihilated in the Crimea. For the summer, Germany expected a Soviet offensive from the south through the Ukraine into Poland; it was a line of march which armies had followed for centuries. Like the Western Allies in their preparations for D-Day, the Soviets encouraged Germans in their delusion with an immense deception campaign. But what Stalin and his generals were concentrating on was the northern bulge in the hummocks, woodlands, small rivers and bogs of Belorussia – Napoleon's line of retreat to Wilno and Warsaw.

In the first week of April the Soviet General Staff received notification from the Western Allies that they would launch their cross-Channel invasion around the 'R date', 31 May. Stalin had promised a major offensive to coincide, but, typical of the way in which the 'Grand Alliance' worked, he told neither the Americans nor the British where.

One of the advantages for Stalin of an offensive upon the Belorussian 'balcony' was that it could be coordinated with the intensifying Partisan war. The small bands of 1942–3 had, by early 1944, been organized into regular brigades, some of them numbering several thousand. In the area around Pskov, near the Estonian frontier, there were about 35,000 men in action, fighting the German garrisons, blowing up railway lines, and liberating small towns and villages which they held on to until the Red Army arrived. South of Polotsk, 140,000 Partisans lived in the forests and swamps of Ushachi, Lepel and Senno, from where they launched punitive raids on the German Third Panzer and Fourth Army. In the spring of 1944 the Germans responded with a ruthless *Bandenkrieg*, executed by SS units with the help of the infamous 'Kaminsky Brigade', made up of Russian defectors to the German side; they cut a great swathe of burning villages and massacre through central Belorussia to improve 'communications' for the forward Third Panzer. This only spread the Partisans further afield.

They began a civil war in the north-western Ukraine. Ukrainian nationalist guerrilla armies formed to oppose them; the Partisans then turned on the Germans in a bloodbath reminiscent of the civil war that was born out of the German retreat of 1918–19. Ukrainians had been among the minorities most severely repressed by the Polish *Sanacja* regime in the 1930s. So, not surprisingly, when the first Soviet Partisan units crossed the 1939 Polish frontiers from the Ukraine in late winter 1944 – with instructions to 'act independently according to the existing conditions and the conscience of Soviet citizens' – they brought civil war with them: a civil war in an area already subject to Nazi terror.

The enormous success of Stalin's armies in the south-western Ukraine had opened up the prospect of a Soviet liberation of Romania, the first country beyond Soviet frontiers to be offered such a service since the annexations of the Nazi-Soviet Pact.

Marshal Ion Antonescu, who had lived uncomfortably in Hitler's Europe, negotiated with the Western Allies through General Maitland 'Jumbo' Wilson, the British Commander-in-Chief in the Middle East, and with the Soviets through his minister in Stockholm; on 22 March he flew off to the Berghoff, Hitler's Alpine palace (now in blackout and covered with camouflage netting), to negotiate a withdrawal of his troops from the beleaguered Crimea: Antonescu failed in every one of these missions. Like all the minor tyrants of Europe, his future would be determined by the movement of the armies.

Meanwhile the Soviet Union swiftly organized a parallel Romanian administration and army in preparation for their takeover. In Cairo, under the aegis of a pro-Soviet British civil service, a 'Democratic Bloc' was set up — which was as democratic as the 'National Front' of France. Within the Soviet Union the 'Tudor Vladimirescu Division' was constituted out of indoctrinated Romanian prisoners of war.

Petru Dumitriu, in his epic novel, *Incognito*, described the humiliating process by which a soldier of Antonescu's forces was turned into a soldier of Communism. There was the outside authority: 'At every new delirious impulse from on high, you were shattered inwardly, you yielded one more time.' There was the denial: 'It is my family that is bourgeois, not me.' There was the history: 'For the poor individual, what has happened is awful. But from the perspective of the history of class struggle, it is only a detail.' There was the moral: 'The Soviet army is the army of the most advanced country in the world, and its soldiers respect proletarian morality, which is the most noble morality.' And there was the new legitimacy: 'Why do I die, Lieutenant?' 'For Socialism.' 'For the working class.' 'For humanity.' It was 'comfortable', admits Dumitriu, to yield to the justifications offered by Marxism. 'But I', he recants, 'distrusted comfort, there was something inelegant about it, it smacked of defeat.'[47]

The Soviet objective, declared Stalin in his May Day Order of 1944, was to clear Soviet soil of remaining German troops, and to lift 'the Fascist yoke' from Poland, Czechoslovakia and other 'fraternal' Slav nations.[48]

With the approach of Soviet troops to international frontiers, the Partisan campaigns were integrated into the plans of the Red Army and given a new direction. In January 1944 the General Staff of the Partisan Movement in Moscow was abolished and, in its place, local *oblast* committees and regional staffs were set up to take charge of operations in the field; the aim of Partisan activities was now not so much the re-establishment of the powers of state in former areas of the Soviet Union as the control of neighbouring nations.

In Poland, Stalin was faced with the largest resistance movement in

Nazi-occupied Europe, and it was not Communist. 'The Communist Underground was weak,' wrote the poet and essayist Czesław Miłosz who, as a resident of Warsaw at this time, knew what he was talking about. 'The hopes of the masses were turned to the West, and the "Underground State" was dependent upon the Government-in-Exile' in London.[49] Only in January 1944, with the reorganization of the Partisan movement, did Stalin hasten to organize parallel systems of civil and military administration in Poland – as had existed in France for virtually a year. A 'National Homeland Council' (the KRN) was formally set up by the tiny Warsaw-based Polish Workers' Party (the PPR) on 1 January. It was presided over by Bolesław Bierut and Władisław Gomułka, who had both escaped Stalin's first purge of Polish Communists in the 1930s, and felt safer living in Nazi-controlled Warsaw than in Moscow. But the 'National Homeland Council' was controlled, and its policy statements were dictated, by the Moscow-based Union of Polish Patriots (the ZPP) and the Central Bureau of Polish Communists (the CBKP). When the hugely popular, non-Communist Polish Home Army under Bór-Komorowski started to set in motion its independent plan for the Rising in Warsaw, most Communist leaders pulled out of the capital and crossed the line to territory controlled by the Red Army, leaving only the skeleton of a Party behind.[50]

Of course, the Polish Communists, like the French, had their own army of the interior, the so-called 'People's Army' (the AL), made up of Partisan detachments operating within Poland. But this was only put in place in January 1944 – again, much later than the parallel 'Francs-Tireurs et Partisans' (the FTP) inside France. In March the 1st Polish Corps of the Red Army, under Brigadier General Berling, was transformed into the First Polish Army; it was made up largely of 're-educated' Poles deported to Russia during the period of the Nazi-Soviet Pact. Simultaneously, Soviet Partisans began to weave their way from the war-torn Ukraine into south-eastern Poland.

6 Legitimacy in Nazi Warsaw

Nazi terror reached new heights for the non-Jewish population of Warsaw in the winter of 1943–4. People were seized at random in the streets and executed on the spot; between October and February some 270 to 300 men and women were publicly hanged or shot each week – the kind of atrocities the French commemorate in Tulle and Oradour were, in Warsaw, a part of daily life. 'On my way to Leszno Church today,' Julian Kulski, a young soldier of the Home Army, recorded on 11 February 1944, 'I saw a crowd of people standing in front of the Wall. They were gazing at something above the Wall, on the Ghetto side of it. As I got closer, I could see for myself – hanged from the upper-storey balconies of what had been an apartment house were the bodies of twenty-two of our Freedom Fighters.' Kulski, at any rate, took them for Freedom Fighters.[51]

But not every hour saw terror, not every street lived in horror. Warsaw in early 1944, with its dense traffic of carts, bicycles, home-made rickshaws and overcrowded streetcars, had a misleadingly calm, even banal look. The Ghetto, it is true, had been reduced to a greyish-pink expanse of rubble already overgrown with weeds and blue buddleia, but you could not see it because of the high wall. Immediately beside it was the clamour of craftsmen and poor people whom the war had pressed into the Old Town. There were more restaurants and cafés open here than before the war – serving bean soup was one of the few means of earning a zloty. Orphaned children begged at every street corner. The damage inflicted on buildings by the aerial and artillery bombardments of 1939 had deliberately not been repaired by the German authorities; the Castle had been destroyed, the Cathedral of St John and the Church of Bernardynów had been wiped off the map, several streets had disappeared, the Town Hall, the Ministry of Foreign Affairs and the building of the Chief of Staff had been seriously damaged; the Prudential building still loomed over the Centre City; electricity, plumbing and telephones were, most of the time, out of operation.

Warsaw had never been rich. De Gaulle in 1920 had developed an affection for Wola, on the west side of the city, and Praga, to the east, not out of any kind of picturesque quality in their streets but because the inhabitants had proved such enthusiastic nationalists: they had stood up to Lenin's armies. Wola was only given municipal status in the 1930s; many of its houses were built of wood and several of its streets were unpaved. As for Praga, isolated on the other side of the Vistula, it had always been grim.

Warsaw did not have a profound sense of its roots. Miłosz wrote of the founding of Warsaw:

> Nobody knows the beginning of the city.
> Slushy ruts, a call at the ferry,
> Resin torches, a fisherman leaning on a spear,
> And fish pots and mists of the shallows.[52]

Nobody cared about the beginnings of Warsaw. What fired the imagination of Varsovians was the way in which, following the First World War, the city had suddenly been transformed from a troublesome provincial town in 'western Russia' into the capital of a new independent nation. It led to a cultural revolution. There may have been poverty, there may have been high rates of unemployment, but popular theatres were opened, poets recited their works on stage; concerts were performed, music was composed, songs were written, and newspapers sprang into life. There was something very literary about Warsaw. Then the immigrants poured in, looking for work. By 1939, Warsaw had, within twenty years, almost doubled its population from 758,000 to 1,407,800 – including its 380,600 Jews.

Nobody knows how many Jews lived in Warsaw in early 1944. Most had been either murdered or deported. Under the Nazis the idea of legitimacy was pushed to one side: no citizen of Warsaw had the protection of civil law; between November 1939 and July 1944, 35,000–40,000 Poles had been killed while a much larger number had been transported to concentration and labour camps. The total population in the spring of 1944 probably stood at around 900,000; the streets were so crowded only because there were fewer of them.

Were the walls actually greyer? It seemed so to the inhabitants. All social, political and cultural life had been driven 'underground'. Miłosz has described how, alongside the 'Underground State', there existed an 'underground press' and an 'underground theatre'. Unlike Parisians, Varsovians had no choice but to live 'underground'. Nothing was open or public. That is what made the city look greyer than before the war.

Miłosz depicts this graphically in his story of an 'underground' nativity play, *Pastoralka*, performed illegally just before Christmas 1942 in a nunnery on the north side of Praga. Crossing the Centre City on a jam-packed tram he noted the grey appearance of the streets under occupation in the 'greyness of a wet winter'. He must have been descending Jerusalem Avenue, a straight and wide thoroughfare that led past the Central Station to Poniatowski Bridge. It was lined with high nineteenth-century apartment buildings, with big gateways opening into the courtyards of the tenements. On the east side towered the sixteen-storey Prudential building, Warsaw's only skyscraper. During the Rising of 1944 Varsovians referred to this long, central artery simply as 'the Avenue': it became a sinister place.

Miłosz's Christmas trip to the other side of the river took on the dimensions of an epic voyage to unknown territory, save that all seemed featureless, grey – until the moment he entered the chapel, where the play was to be performed. There was an audience of around a hundred people sitting on low benches. The actresses were prostitutes who had been brought in from the streets. The 'Mother of God' was dressed in blue and sang with a tiny, mouse-like voice. Old merry carols were sung with joy. The performers danced in 'crazy leaps and turns'. In the 'drab colourlessness of the occupied city' Miłosz discovered in the Christmas of 1942 what true theatre was: the 'creation of magic space'.[53]

Miłosz's work explains the dilemma which was Warsaw's in 1944; indeed, it pries into its very roots. As no understanding of the Liberation of Paris can be complete without a consideration of the grand speeches and writings of Charles de Gaulle – they reveal the myths behind it, the enthusiasms, and most importantly the legitimacy of the political authority which was established immediately following it – no inkling of what occurred in Warsaw that same August can be attained without, first, lifting the screen of politics; one is obliged to turn to a poet.

On the surface can be seen the mirror image: Poland was the reverse of France. There was an immense resistance movement, the Communists were insignificant, the government-in-exile in London was the source of the resistance's claim to legitimacy, not Moscow; the country was almost certainly going to be liberated by the Red Army, yet the hopes of the population lay in the Western Allies somehow arriving first. The recently organized Council of National Unity (RJN), corresponded to the French Committee of National Liberation established in Algiers – only this Council was operating inside Warsaw at the height of the Nazi terror.

There was no de Gaulle; Sikorski was dead. For their aspirations to post-war legitimacy the people of Poland had to rely on formal statements from London or declarations issued in the occupied capital. On 15 March the Council of National Unity published – a word with a special sense in Warsaw – a manifesto, *What the Nation Is Fighting For* (*O co walczy naród*). Like similar manifestos issued by the French Gaullists, it reflected the pressure being exercised at the time by the extreme left, and particularly by the Communists. It included promises of a future planned economy and the nationalization of various economic sectors, such as transportation, banking, utilities and forests. As a counter to the threat posed by the Soviet armies it also proposed the creation of a federation of the states of 'Central and South Europe'.[54]

That was the politics of the underground world in Warsaw. But it was not the way Varsovians lived. 'You summon me to assist in the struggle against armies of the most varied moral laws,' wrote Miłosz in Warsaw in the autumn of 1942 to his closest friend, Jerzy Andrzejewski. 'Doubt', he said, 'is a noble thing.' So was he wavering? Andrzejewski wavered all the time. Before the war he wrote for the Catholics; during the first part of the occupation he called for brave acts of resistance; as war neared its climax he opposed the resistance for its 'unreality'; after the war he became a Marxist and a Communist; when the Communists, in the 1970s, lost all credibility, he became a spokesman for the democratic opposition. He wanted to be a 'moral authority'. That was not Miłosz's aim. Confronted with the most appalling conditions – 'For five and a half years we lived in a dimension completely different from that which any literature or experience could have led us to know. What we beheld surpassed the most daring and the most macabre imagination' – there was one thing to which Miłosz remained constant, his poetry.[55]

The German philosopher and sociologist Theodor Adorno remarked famously that after the Holocaust poetry was impossible. Miłosz claimed the exact opposite: the only form of truth left was in poetry. In a novel he wrote on the Warsaw Rising, a black notebook is discovered in a wrecked aeroplane. On its last page is written: 'You can only express things properly by details. When you've observed a detail, you must discover the detail of the detail.'[56] That is the guiding principle of Miłosz's poetry. In one of his best known poems, 'You Who Wronged', he writes:

> Do not feel safe. The poet remembers.
> You can kill one, but another is born.
> The words are written down, the deed, the date.[57]

That is typical Miłosz: the simple words, the deed, the date. No point in analysing it. No elaboration.

> I will not find a real rose,
> Real moth, real stone, round and shiny;
> For me, always, there will be this earth: tiny.[58]

This was written in Warsaw in the winter of 1943–4.

When Miłosz expresses doubt to Andrzejewski about joining the struggle against 'armies equipped with swastikas, hammers and sickles, portable shrines, banners' he puts it this way: 'Just as human sight is capable of taking in only one side of an apple, human speech cannot encompass any phenomenon in its total roundness.' Why do so many tens of thousands die? Why are so many apparently willing to die? That may be said to be the ultimate question of political legitimacy – like Dumitriu's private, 'Why do I die, Lieutenant?' Miłosz implies that no complete answer is possible.

But there is a truth. In his letter to Andrzejewski, Miłosz expresses his astonishment at the plasticity of human nature, a feature which he also describes in the actors performing the wartime nativity play – 'every man is the home of many personalities that dwell within him potentially.' In Nazi-occupied Warsaw all morality seemed abolished, all law; even the ceremonies of death were laid aside: the ritual was gone; whole peoples were being exterminated like the 'extermination of bedbugs or flies'. 'Who knows,' speculates Miłosz, 'perhaps this is the path to absolute indifference, including indifference to one's own death.' But he refuses to believe it. He stops just before this ultimate absurdity. Man's plasticity is not limitless. There is a kernel of ethical intuition inside every man that you just cannot stamp out. Miłosz quotes Machiavelli's observation that a ruler cannot appeal exclusively to man's lowest impulse; he has to be seen as a human benefactor. Even the Nazis appealed to chivalry, the Communists called for sacrifice. The lie was in the generalization that justified the destruction of an enemy race or an enemy class. The truth was in the detail, and the detail of the detail: the words, the deed, the date.[59]

Miłosz at times would refer to the source of his poetry as his 'inner castle', at times – as in his letter to Andrzejewski – as his *daimonion*, common sense, his moral kernel. A poet, he thought, must be a man of his times, of his place, an observer of the facts, and humble. 'On the day the world ends,' he wrote in Warsaw in 1944,

> Women walk through the fields under their umbrellas,
> A drunkard grows sleepy at the edge of a lawn,
> Vegetable pedlars shout in the street
> . . .
> And those who expected lightning and thunder
> Are disappointed.[60]

7 Invasion

Caen, ten miles from the Normandy beaches, was the sort of small town – with its white stone churches and gabled, half-timbered houses – that had made Flaubert's heart leap. Monday, 5 June 1944, had been like most other days that spring. It poured with rain until the evening, when the clouds gradually dispersed. Then, at dusk, and about as regular as the weather, in came the English bombers.

Caen thought itself lucky. So far not much damage had been done; during the last months the inhabitants had watched the lightning glow set off by the Pathfinders over neighbouring towns such as Franceville and

Sallenelles; the pale violet flickering looked like distant firework displays. That night, as usual, the sirens wailed and German ack-ack guns pounded upwards, making zebra patterns in the black sky. People went to bed to try and get a little sleep.

A few already knew that this was going to be a night not like the others. In a flat not far from the Abbey of Saint-Etienne, a small group of French resisters tuned into the BBC at 9.15 p.m. and picked up the message, '*Blessent mon coeur d'une langueur monotone*':[61] so the D-Day invasion was to be expected in the next forty-eight hours. Field Marshal von Rundstedt's headquarters at Saint-Germain-en-Laye, outside Paris, also understood the meaning of the message and sent out an alert.

The French resistance in Caen probably did not number more than a few dozen at that time; it managed to publish one clandestine newspaper. With its network of roads and railways, Normandy was not the kind of country in which a large underground organization could operate effectively.

When one of the resisters, Madame L. Corbusson, got home to pack and head with her three children for her cellar she noticed, peeping through the curtains of her window, that German soldiers, armed and wearing steel helmets, were in a flap. She saw a young Frenchman being arrested. Many innocent men were arrested that night: none of them would be seen again.

At two o'clock in the morning the whole of Caen was awoken by a series of hollow booms, of a kind which no one had ever heard before. It came from the coast. The ground shook; the walls vibrated. Thousands came into the streets. To the north, towards the sea, they observed a huge, burning red glow; it was not the rising sun, but the effect of naval gunnery. The bakers' shops were besieged. Bakers, half dressed, were forced to serve bread. It seemed like the beginning of Armageddon.

The morning was dominated by the sound of German tanks rolling over the cobbles. Columns of soldiers in field grey funnelled into the Rue de Géole, the Rue du Vagneux, the Rue des Chanoines which all led north. The first soldiers in khaki were seen at 9.30 a.m.; they were driven in German lorries to a square where they were assembled: prisoners of war. The Germans were smiling. Had the Allies been thrown back into the sea?

The droning of Allied aircraft above never stopped. Shortly before midday they showered the town with leaflets warning that the Caen railway station, the electrical depot and other buildings of strategic importance were about to be bombed. The first attack came at one o'clock in the afternoon. It lasted ten minutes. The worst hit area was around William the Conqueror's castle; the shopping centres of Monoprix and the Nouvelles Galeries were burnt down. Major fires broke out in a dozen other parts of the city. People recalled the continual sound, like hail, of stone falling on the pavements.

A second shorter bombing raid occurred at 4.30 p.m. 'Not even the most pessimistic could have imagined the horrors we witnessed,' wrote the Mother Superior of the Bon Sauveur convent. Just after Vespers three large buildings of its mental home were hit; nuns and patients were buried beneath the debris. A roar of firestorms began.

Between two and three the next morning waves of Lancasters and Halifaxes passed overhead; a blinding flash heralded the series of detonations, one more deafening than the other. Houses seemed to lift themselves from the ground. Through the doors and windows torn open one could see dazzling fire and sniff the reek of explosive. It was the small details that stuck in minds: a perpetual cascade of tiles, glass and shattered porcelain.

There were few places to hide in Caen. There was no underground railway, and not many tunnels. Those who could get out of the city walked south – the war would catch up with them later. Between eight and ten thousand discovered a haven in the underground stone quarries about eight miles from Caen, on either side of the River Orne. Practically nobody was aware of their existence until that June, yet they had supplied the stone of Caen as well as many of southern England's great monuments, including the Tower of London and Westminster Abbey. In the quarries of Fleury wound mile upon mile of galleries and caverns; some of the grottos were over fifty feet high. Lighting was provided by huge lamps that had been found in nearby factories. Families built their underground homes out of stone, of which there was plenty. There was no shortage of meat, for this was dairy country. But precious little else, besides straw for the stone beds, was on offer.

For those who could not leave Caen – and after a month of bombardment by bombs and shells about 10,000 remained out of an initial population of 55,000 – two major centres of refuge existed, the great Abbey of Saint-Etienne and the aptly named Bon Sauveur convent. An ancient Norman rhyme warned 'When Saint-Etienne falls down / Then falls the English crown.'[62] Somebody must have got the message through to Bomber Command, and kept the secret from Hitler, for Saint-Etienne remained standing throughout the Battle of Normandy. William the Conqueror's tomb lay underneath the altar, from where old Monsignor des Hameaux said mass every day, come bomb, come shell. He lived in the vestry. Every corner of the abbey was piled high with baggage. Many had come with their mattresses. The nave was laid out in one vast field of straw. The confessionals were used as coat cupboards. The altars of the side chapels were used as kitchen tables. Some of these chapels served as special dormitories. The Chapel of Saint-Etienne, for example, was reserved for tram drivers, while the Chapel of the Sacré-Coeur was put aside for high civil servants – the most chic territory within the abbey. Priests slept in the choir. Every man was assigned his *corvée*, his task, and those who refused were deprived of food.

The nuns of Caen were among the bravest of the town's inhabitants. They worked day and night, even under intense bombardment, in the convent as if they were trained nurses and doctors. They had to deal with the most appalling casualties. One teenage girl was brought in with the orbits of her eyes hanging down her face and her nose blown off; yet miraculously she was saved, and managed to smile. A 'town within a town', with many large buildings and halls, this was the mother convent of the order. The two other branches in Normandy were, ironically enough, situated exactly on the flanks of the Allied attack on D-Day: one on the east side of the Orne, where the British airborne division launched their attack; during the battle for Caen it was wiped off the map. The other was at the foot of the Contentin peninsula, just behind the village of Sainte-Mère-Eglise, where the American parachutists landed; it was seriously damaged during the desperate struggle of 6 June.

But there were even greater ironies to the story. No Norman had ever forgotten that nine hundred years earlier his province had invaded and conquered England. Duke William had been born in the great medieval fortress still overlooking Falaise, 32 miles from the coast, down the straight road from Caen. As the first Norman king of England he was buried in Caen. The beginning and the end – or, as it was in 1944, the end and the beginning. Sixty-five days after the first bombardment of Caen, the Battle of Normandy concluded outside Falaise.

The opening of a new front in northern France, as Wedemeyer had predicted back in 1941, had a radical effect on the course of the war and the plans for what would follow. Except to a few fanatics, it became clear that the Nazi order was going to collapse. Equally obvious, it would not be solely the Communists who replaced it. The debate over what constituted legitimate post-war authority in Europe intensified in 1944.

It would all be determined by the movement of the armies. In June and July Russia's forces manoeuvred into a position that would take them towards Warsaw; the main roads from the Western Allied 'lodgement area' led to Paris. The Americans and the British had committed themselves to an invasion of North-Western Europe at the Casablanca Conference in January 1943. At Quebec that summer they had agreed – the British reluctantly – on their point of landing, the beaches of Normandy in the Bay of the Seine. No Allied commander was going to repeat the mistake of Dieppe and attempt a landing at a major port; lessons had also been learnt from the 1943 amphibious operations in Italy: the land had to be flat.

The Americans came into France to the right of the British because, quite naturally, they had collected their forces in south-western England, and not the south-east. Theoretically it might have been better if the Americans, with their unending reserves of manpower, tanks and aircraft, had landed to the left of the British forces, already at their limits, because it was obvious that no German commander was going to let Allied armies take the straight Route Nationale 13 from Caen to Paris: there was bound to be fighting around Caen. But the logistics of such a switch proved impracticable. For the remainder of the war, the Americans would remain on the right flank of the British. Such simple military facts would exert an influence on the entire post-war settlement of Europe.

The initial invasion project – developed in 1943 by a largely American team, chaired by a British general – was smaller than the one executed. It was British command, exercised by doubts, who pushed in early 1944 for an expansion of both the numbers and the area involved. They would never consider the plan large enough. 'The invasion is a day older. I am not very happy about it,' confided General Sir Alan Brooke, Chief of Imperial General Staff, to his diary on 7 June. 'I do wish to heaven that we were landing on a wider front.'[63]

It was the Americans, and particularly Eisenhower, who insisted on shifting the bulk of the air forces involved in the strategic bombing of Germany to tactical bombing in support of the land operations in France. In December 1943 Arthur Harris was still arguing that, with increased production of Lancasters, Germany could be defeated by spring from the air alone. Then, eight weeks after the landing he insisted on a return of the strategic air forces to the bombing of Germany. Undoubtedly, the huge damage inflicted on French transport networks was of critical importance to the success of the invasion; but some residents of Caen thought it a trifle overdone.[64]

Since April the German press had been giving notice of an impending Allied landing, which they even called 'D-Day'. Hitler had rightly predicted that it would be in Normandy, but his marshals and generals – duped by the build-up in Kent of the wooden tanks and planes of the American 'First Army Group' commanded by the flamboyant General George S. Patton, the group's sole soldier – were convinced the main attack would be across the Straits of Dover. German command, a cat's cradle answering to many authorities, was divided between a forward strategy and a policy of deep reserves, in the end they compromised, holding their armoured divisions back, while assigning their worst foot divisions to the coast – many of these troops had been recruited from the crowd of defectors that had sprung up in the Russian borderlands. But, whatever their differences, all German commanders agreed that the invasion would be launched at high tide: it came in on the ebb. And they knew it would be on a sunny day: it followed two days of rain and winds of force five.

Ninety per cent of Germany's armed forces moved by rail, horse or foot. Allied tactical bombing ensured they would travel largely by foot.

'I am quite positive we must give the order,' announced a strained Eisenhower to his senior commanders on Sunday evening, 4 June. 'I don't like it, but there it is.' They had already delayed the invasion twice during that wet weekend. But now weather forecasters were predicting a slight break in the spell of bad weather. Eisenhower gave the order to sail the next day; operations would begin on Monday evening: 'I don't see how we can do anything else.'[65] For the people of southern England, who looked up from their gardens and fields on Monday evening and Tuesday, it seemed as if the whole world was on the move.

The soldiers had been living in camps, separate and solitary places, the perimeters of which were marked with posters: 'Do not loiter. Civilians must not talk to army personnel.' With every day and every hour they felt increasingly cut off from daily life. They were aware that they were part of a great plan but, not knowing what exactly it was, felt they were just a part of a machine, a number.

There was no singing on the boats that crossed the Channel. Doug Halloway of the 49th West Riding Division (the Polar Bears) found himself on a ship crammed from top to bottom with equipment, mainly vehicles and guns; sleeping quarters were confined to amidships; 'the floor was covered with palliasses with no space between them, and above was about the same amount of hammocks.'[66] Each sickening lurch brought up a heap of yesterday's bully beef and cabbage. 'I think', said Ronald McKinlay of the RN Commandos, 'one of the main reasons why Normandy was a great success was that the soldiers would much rather have fought thousands of Germans than go back into those boats.'[67] On some American ships swing music was repeated throughout the night; it was still playing over the loudspeakers as the troops went into action.

France, for those who saw it, appeared from the vantage point of the ships 'toy-like and unreal'. On the horizon were ugly little seaside villas, green copses, straggling farmyards, a windmill on a hill – until one noticed that a battle was going on and that all those toy landmarks were mere silhouettes of what had been destroyed.[68]

Over the next two and a half months Normandy was the focus of the world. Bomber crews would look down in amazement upon the Channel now converted into a vast, living conveyor belt of ships and minesweepers sailing back and forth; like stanchions, destroyers and corvettes were moored on either side of the sea lane, their guns scanning horizons for enemy boats and aircraft. The beaches formed a mere prolongation of the sea, and the land behind it a mere extension of the beaches: a great flat expanse, the plain of Europe.

On the afternoon of D-Day, when the first Allied infantry broke through General Richter's thin grey line of defence at Bernières, they found themselves advancing into deserted country. Rommel's forward strategy had left few Germans here. The French had either been killed in the bombardments or were hiding in their cellars; the small number who did emerge were astonished to discover that the Allied troops in front of them spoke fluent French: they were French Canadians, many of whose ancestors had emigrated from Normandy. The Canadians marched on to within three miles of the outskirts of Caen. But there they stopped for about two months: the biggest battle outside Russia was about to begin.

Lieutenant General Crocker of British I Corps had ordered that, before the end of D-Day, Caen must be 'captured or effectively masked'. Those last two words could mean many things. In the initial invasion plan Caen was to act merely as a decoy, absorbing Germany's main armoured divisions, while the Americans, on the right flank of the invasion, were to swing up into the Contentin peninsula to seize the port of Cherbourg and then down west, along the flat coastal corridor, through Upper Brittany to the Loire and east towards Paris, eventually rejoining the British to the north in a 'long hook'. But the British decoy at Caen, like Joseph Bonaparte's attack on Hougoumont at Waterloo, was transformed into a major battle, and the battle fostered the stubborn will to win.[69]

The Americans eventually took Cherbourg at the end of June, but around Saint-Lô they ran into difficulties advancing south. The British became totally absorbed in their battle for Caen.

The major reason for the stalemate was that beyond the coastal plain lay hills, and beyond the hills, in the south-east of Normandy – acting as one of the gateways to Paris – was an area of high crags and ridges, *la Suisse normande*, 'Norman Switzerland'. Parts of the coastal plain itself were covered with copses and hedgerows; the villages were connected by sunken roads. In south-western England the same kind of landscape was known to the natives as 'bosky country'; in France they called it the 'bocage': ideal terrain for a defender, a nightmare for an invader.

8 Monty

Is it true that Montgomery was mad? The generals in Eisenhower's English headquarters began to wonder about the character of this British field commander in Normandy; Churchill, always impatient for a spectacular success, did too. Such chatter did not perturb Montgomery. 'I understand there are people who often think I am slightly mad,' he had told his officers two years earlier on taking over command of the British Eighth Army, beleaguered in the North African desert. 'In fact, if I am slightly mad, [there are] a large number of people I could name who are raving lunatics!!' Montgomery looked mad. His grey-blue eyes would stare straight at an interlocutor like those 'of a horse with blinkers on'; his chin, it has been remarked, came up to about the level of the decorations on his predecessor's chest – the majestic General Sir Claude Auchinleck. But it was Auchinleck who was preparing for a retreat into Palestine and the Sudan, not 'Monty'. In three weeks General Bernard Law Montgomery – 'a stringy, bird-like little man', remarked one of his soldiers on receiving one of his many unannounced 'visitations' – turned a polyglot defeatist force of the British Empire and Commonwealth into an army that could beat Rommel out of Africa; that required a grain of madness.[70]

The delinquent son of the Bishop of Van Diemen's Land, he was treated at school at St Paul's in London as a Tasmanian savage, though actually he was born on the south bank of the Thames. At twenty he was sent down from Sandhurst for pyromania. His senior colleagues at the first staff college where he taught considered him 'a bloody menace'. When he got to Poona, in India, he developed a reputation as an 'upstart', then returned to England to become 'that damned pipsqueak'. He was loathed by Etonians and Harrovians, by the dons of Oxford and Cambridge, by the lords of the land, and the lords of the army, of the Admiralty and, most especially, of the Royal Air Force. The Americans hated him, with the important exception of Eisenhower, who had an eye for talent. Churchill was appalled by him and was the main obstacle to his promotion to battlefield command. It was almost too late when Churchill registered: 'If he is disagreeable to those about him, he is also disagreeable to the enemy.'[71]

After that, there was no turning back. Montgomery was Britain's most enthusiastic supporter of the initial American plan for an invasion of northern France. He instilled that enthusiasm in his conscript troops. Montgomery would jump up on a jeep in front of a loudspeaker and tell them to gather round. 'We have been fighting the Germans a long time now' – they called it 'Monty parlance' and it was repetitive – 'a very long time . . . a good deal too long. I expect like me you are beginning to get a bit tired of it . . . beginning to feel it's about time we finished the thing off. And we can do it. We can do it. No doubt about that. No doubt about that whatever. The well-trained British soldier will beat the German every time.'

Monty parlance went with Monty thought, Monty tactics, and a Monty strategy. 'I don't know why they call it the Second Front. I myself have been fighting the Germans on a number of fronts, and I expect a good few of you have too. They should call it Front Number Six or Front Number Seven. As long as they don't want us to fight on Front Number Thirteen.'[72]

Monty tactics were single-tracked: forward planning, no static front, flexibility, 'smack it about', but no 'footling around', 'fluid fighting'. The troops must have 'the light of battle in their eyes. They must look forward to a good fight. They must be full of "binge".'[73]

That was the way Montgomery talked. But also the way he thought. He thought with his troops. He knew they were conscripts. He knew that, faced with a well-trained and indoctrinated enemy, there would always be a temptation to dig a hole and wait for the storm to pass. His soldiers had to feel overwhelming force behind them: overwhelming. Hence the bombing. 'That's the stuff to give 'em!' the troops yelled as they prepared to advance on German positions around Caen. 'We howled in unison,' recollected one of them, 'the smoke and dust billowing up till the sky was black with man-made clouds.'[74]

9 Norman stalemate

Montgomery landed in Normandy on 8 June and set up his headquarters in the village of Creully on the main road between Bayeux, now in British hands, and Caen, ruined and German. He frequently visited the troops – wearing 'image order': a faded bush jacket, turtleneck sweater, corduroy trousers and a black beret. Or he would be seen consulting his commanders. An important channel of communication between the troops and command was a team of around forty young 'gallopers', or liaison officers. No one could really tell exactly where the 'front' was. There were chaotic scenes as army units poured in from the coast; every field was turned into an ammunition dump.

The truth was that the 'lodgement area' for the Allies in Normandy was narrower, and more crowded, than had been initially planned; it was about ten miles deep, and would remain so for about two months. To the west, the Americans had, according to plan, cut across the Cotentin peninsula and the American VII Corps, under General J. Lawton Collins, had eventually taken Cherbourg on 26 June. But the Germans had destroyed the port facilities; they were not operable for almost three months. In the meantime, General Omar Bradley's First American Army suffered around 40,000 casualties in the deadly La Haye-du-Puits corridor, outside Saint-Lô. Hitler's strategy of containment looked as if it were working.

British casualties were also mounting. They had had a light time of it during the first ten days after D-Day but, as the German Panzer divisions were drawn into battle around Caen (according to plan), the ratio of loss mounted from 2:1 to 3:1 by early July: that is, three dead British infantrymen for every dead German. And Britain was reaching her limit; she did not have the means of replacing her infantry. In *bocage* country tanks were useless, sitting ducks, without infantry.

Montgomery was receiving daily 'eggs' from 'Ultra', Britain's device at Bletchley Park for decrypting Germany's most secret military signals; it was one of the greatest feats of intelligence in military history. Only outside El Alamein in the summer of 1942 was so much information gathered on the enemy in such a small area. So Montgomery knew exactly what was in front of him. Always concerned about the rate of casualties in his conscript army, he became cautious.

Just to the south of Caen lay the two high ridges of Verrières and Bourguebus, tempting targets for any Norman army that wanted to move eastwards, for they dominated not only the main road to Lisieux and Paris, but also the route to Falaise in 'Norman Switzerland'. Even a feint to capture those ridges would pull in the main reserves of German armour. Yet, as June turned to July, Panzer divisions gradually slipped west. As American movement ground to a halt outside Saint-Lô, pressure grew within Eisenhower's command in London, and particularly in the press, to seize Caen and attempt a breakout at Verrières and Bourguebus. Monty tactics, anyway, never recognized a static front.

He tried a double encirclement of the city, then a great 'right hook' across the Rivers Odon and Orne, and after these failed he launched a direct assault on Caen itself from the north. His forces clambered through the rubble as far as the water barriers of the Odon and Orne; the Germans still held Verrières and Bourguebus.

Montgomery always argued for a 'clarity of aim' that should be printed in the mind of every soldier. But no soldier came out of the Caen campaign with a clear narrative of what had happened. It was more like a hundred or a thousand small separate engagements: one tank ramming another, a friend blown up by a mine, an artillery barrage, a night in a ditch, bombing, traffic jams, dead bloated cows, blueflies, mosquitoes. The Canadians' struggle for Carpiquet airport, held by 150 teenagers of the Hitler Youth, became a legend in fanatical fighting. The grand operation – the great 'right hook' – that Montgomery's staff formally called 'Epsom' was known among the soldiers as 'the Odon', or (because of the presence of the 15th Scottish Division) as the 'Scottish Corridor'; and later, 'Death Valley'. Infantry advanced in mists reminiscent of the First World War – as were the battle outposts and honeycomb of machine-gun nests the Germans had prepared on the banks of the Odon.

This stalemate in Normandy turned attention once more to the Eastern Front. The advance of the Red Army raised hopes again for Europe's Communists everywhere.

10 Eastern response

The Russian answer to D-Day was very different from the campaign in Normandy. In the first place, no 'allies' were consulted; indeed, there were only five people in the world who knew the full outline of the plan that spring, including Stalin; he signed the approval on 26 May 1944 in his dacha on the Dmitrovsk highway just three weeks before it was due to be put into effect. The Germans were convinced that the main thrust of the attack would come from the south-east, up from the Ukraine towards Lwów and on to the Vistula and Warsaw: the old battlefields of 1914, the route of the Bolshevik armies during the Russian civil war and the war with Poland after the Armistice of 1918. They were wrong. They would be trapped and butchered on Napoleon's route of retreat in 1812, across Belorussia. One of the worst scenes of destruction would be witnessed in late June 1944 as German forces attempted to save themselves on the banks of the Berezina – a river proverbial in French for 'catastrophe'.

Stalin himself picked the name of his early summer offensive, 'Bagration'. Prince Piotr Bagration was the hero who had fallen mortally wounded at the Battle of Borodino in 1812. National heroism was undoubtedly what Stalin wanted to inspire in Russia in 1944. But his 'allies' might also have taken the name as a warning; Bagration's seductive young widow, Katarina Bagration, the 'Russian siren', was the single most destructive force at the post-war Congress of Vienna of 1814–15.

Belorussia in the Second World War was the heartland of the Partisan war. Partisans were to play a crucial role in the coming campaign there. Not so in Normandy. A lot of literature and romantic films have been produced on the military contribution of French Partisans to France's liberation: British Lysanders land silently by moonlight on secret airfields, the SOE parachutes in arms and munitions, colour codes lead to the sabotaging of rails and communications at the moment of the invasion. But, because of the terrain, most militarily active Partisans were in the hills, forests and plateaux of the South of France and their operations were not coordinated with the army movements. The largest and most famous operations – Glières in March 1944, Mont Mouchet in May and June, and the Vercors in June and July – are remembered because they were disasters.

In Belorussia, the Partisans had been incorporated into the re-formed, locally commanded Red Army at the beginning of the year and were, from that date, considered a part of combined operations. On the night of 19 June Soviet Partisan brigades set off 10,000 demolition charges tearing up the rail links west of Minsk to the front-line defences of the German Army Group Centre. The next night, and for the following three short summer nights, 40,000 explosions destroyed junctions, sidings and tracks; yet this did not raise German suspicions. The four Soviet Front army groups – the 1st Baltic, the 3rd, 2nd and 1st Belorussian – moved forward in phases staggered over forty-eight hours, starting on the morning of 22 June. It took well over a day before the Germans recognized that they were facing a major offensive. Infantry, artillery, aircraft, tanks and the terrifying Katyusha rockets were gradually brought up. 'We mustn't let go of the Fascists,' declared Marshal Vasilevsky, who coordinated the 1st Baltic and 3rd Belorussian Fronts before Vitebsk.[75] German command, holding a conference in Minsk on the morning of 25 June, dismissed the incursions as 'reconnaissance' and 'holding attacks'. By the same afternoon four divisions were hopelessly trapped in the Vitebsk 'bog'.

Montgomery's forces at Caen were staring into German defences on the Orne at the moment the whole of German Army Group Centre was annihilated in Belorussia. Within ten days of the first Partisan demolitions, 130,000 German troops had been killed, 66,000 were taken prisoner, 900 tanks had been destroyed along with thousands of motor transports. 'Hitler's fireman', Field Marshal Walter Model, a lean, ideologically pure Nazi with a reputation in southern Russia as a mender of fronts, was sent in. But not even Model could prevent the fall of Minsk on 3 July. By now a 250-mile gap had been torn in the German defences and all that remained of Army Group Centre were eight scattered divisions.

It was a further left punch that would determine the fate of Poland and Warsaw. The 1st Belorussian Front had been separated into two flanks by the Polesian swampland well to the rear of the main campaign. The Front was commanded by Konstantin Rokossovsky – he would be promoted to marshal that July. Often considered Stalin's most humane commander, he was certainly one of the bravest. In the military purges of 1937–8 he defended himself against charges of spying, conspiracy and 'crimes against the people' by proving to his bewildered prosecutor that his 'fellow conspirator' had died seventeen years earlier 'in the cause of the Revolution'. Rokossovsky escaped death by a hair's breadth on the grounds that 'the dead cannot give evidence.' As a commander during the war he would often take his own initiative, contradicting Stalin to his face. He spoke Russian with a Polish accent. And here is a mystery. His Soviet biographer claims he was born to a railway official in Velikie Luki, became a stonecutter and soon was 'drawn into the struggle for the liberation of the working classes and the Polish nation'. But there is some evidence that he was the son of a landowner and was born near Warsaw. His service to the Tsar during the First World War was suppressed by Rokossovsky himself (or 'Rokosowski' as the British press sometimes liked to call him). An elegant, impressive cavalryman, he bore every trait of an aristocrat.[76]

Within Rokossovsky's front was Berling's First Polish Army. In June, the important Eighth Guards Army had been secretly transferred north by train from the Dniester to join Rokossovsky's southern flank; it was commanded by Vasili Chuikov, a peasant from Tula province. Rokossovsky and Chuikov had first collaborated at Stalingrad. Together they prepared a huge encirclement scheme, the right flank of the 1st Belorussian Front cutting off the Germans at Brest-Litovsk and the left clearing Lublin; after that they would head along the 'Warsaw axis' to the River Vistula. Not only would Soviet armed forces be advancing beyond their own frontiers, they would be beyond the 'Curzon Line' and crossing the initial demarcation line of the Nazi-Soviet Pact of August 1939.

So Stalin was redrawing the map. Or was he?

Rokossovsky's left flank was now the most powerful section in the Red Army. Outside Kovel, tanks, troops and guns were manoeuvred into positions under the cover of night; track and tyre marks were carefully swept; radio communication was forbidden and all radio equipment was sealed. The invasion of Poland opened at dawn on 17 July with a barrage of 170,000 shells; then the armies moved forward in the same staggered fashion that had so confused German defenders during the initial offensive. It was the same story all over again.

Rokossovsky's line of advance lay across marsh, peat bogs, woodlands, small rivers and tiny lakes; the roads themselves were barely passable because of heavy rains – tanks struggled along, lorries slipped to the side. the traffic jams rivalled those in Normandy. Chuikov's Eighth Guards took Lublin in two days of fighting, on 23–24 July. To complete the encirclement the right flank would then close on German forces still fighting in the area of Brest-Litovsk while the left would curve up through Dęblin and onward up the Vistula to Praga, the eastern suburb of Warsaw, thus cutting off the German line of retreat.

Rokossovsky's forces were now reaching old demarcation lines. Strange things began to happen. Normal Russian strategy, judging from campaigns over the last year, would have involved 'jumping', that is, taking bridgeheads on the next river, the Vistula. When Chuikov's Eighth Guards arrived at the Vistula they received no such order. Brest-Litovsk fell on 27 July. Chuikov, in the meantime, was getting confused instructions: 'halt the advance', 'consolidate positions', 'resume the advance', 'concentrate', 'do not become dispersed.'[77]

On the 29th he reached Magnuszew, about twenty miles south of Warsaw. He decided to conduct his own reconnaissance. In the village of Wilga, just to the north, he ran into a crowd of Poles in holiday mood; they were taking the air on the river banks and enjoying accordion music. He raised his binoculars and studied the opposite bank: no sign of Germans. But he needed permission from Rokossovsky to cross. Rokossovsky made him wait three days.

The encirclement was never completed. The Second Tank Army moved up to Otwock and Radzymin, within a dozen miles of Warsaw, where they came to a halt. A few tank units stumbled on what looked like a formidable array of German armour around Praga, itself bristling with defences, and they withdrew.

For the rest of his life, Rokossovsky would always say that further advance was impossible. To have attempted to seize Warsaw, he claimed, 'with its strong defences and substantial enemy garrison [would have] overstretched our logistics'.[78] Poland was thus divided between two warring titans, Nazi and Soviet. The sectors they controlled were not very different from those they had agreed on in the Pact of 23 August 1939, with Ribbentrop's red line running down the east bank of the Vistula, through the suburbs of Warsaw.

Seasons

Paris and Warsaw in summer

♈

1 Waning 'Tempest'

Lublin, which lay south-east of Warsaw, almost exactly halfway between the Rivers Bug and Vistula, had been taken on the afternoon of 23 July. The leading Russian column, consisting of one tank and two jeeps, entered an eerie landscape of broken houses and rubble; nothing stirred, no shots, no sign of life in the open windows. A brigade of the Polish Home Army, which had been cooperating with the Russians in the suburban battle, made the same discovery. 'Liberated' Lublin was lifeless, empty.

On the same day in Moscow Stalin wrote a note to Churchill announcing that in order to solve 'the practical problem of administration on Polish territory' he had asked the self-proclaimed Polish Committee of National Liberation (the PKWN) to fly out from Moscow to Lublin and establish 'their own administration'. This would avoid, explained Stalin, Russian interference in 'Poland's internal affairs'. 'The so-called underground organizations led by the Polish Government in London', he added, 'have turned out to be ephemeral and lacking in influence.' Stalin would not refuse to meet Stanisław Mikołajczyk of the London 'Polish Committee' ('I cannot consider it a Polish Government') − Churchill had been urging such an encounter for months. 'It would be better, however, if he were to approach the Polish National Committee, who are favourably disposed towards him.'[1] In other words, Stalin was asking the Polish Prime Minister to pay homage to a puppet Soviet government set up in empty Lublin.

About three miles to the south of Lublin, at Majdanek, Russian troops stumbled upon something that no Allied army had ever seen before, a Nazi extermination camp. Over 300,000 people had been murdered here. Photographs were taken of the ovens, the piles of bodies, the stacks of shoes and clothes, the bales of human hair. Throughout August and September they appeared in the world press. But what eyes saw, the minds did not register. Nobody was prepared for it. The world was getting ready for the end of the war. It was watching the advance of the armies on the west and east side of Europe. It saw the celebrations of victory, it heard the cheers of liberation. It was convinced that this year, 1944, would be the last year of war. The world was not yet conscious of the complications that would follow.

One of the first acts of the Polish Committee of National Liberation was to order the arrest of the Polish soldiers of the Home Army in the area of Lublin. In the summer of 1944 Majdanek was transformed into a detention camp for thousands of Polish soldiers who had fought for the freedom of their country.[2] This was another post-war phenomenon that the world was not yet prepared to see.

As far as Western opinion was concerned, warned Jan Nowak in a Warsaw meeting of the Home Army's commanders on Saturday, 29 July, 'TEMPEST will be, literally, a tempest in a teacup.'[3] Nowak, who had the dangerous job of acting as courier between London and Warsaw, was the only person in that private apartment who knew what he was talking about. General Bór-Komorowski, field commander of the Home Army, presided. Nowak's chief worry was that, with the opening of the new Western Front in Normandy, Polish affairs would be of mere peripheral interest to the Western Allies, even if the Russian Front moved right through Warsaw. General Bór was more concerned with the welfare of his own troops. He had conceived his own version of a national Rising – which he called 'Burza' or 'Tempest' – because of the weakness he perceived in the exiled and divided London government following Sikorski's death. Indeed, by spring, all the major initiatives in the non-Communist Polish resistance were being taken by the Home Army command in Warsaw – exactly what the London government, afraid of a post-war Sanacja regime, wanted to avoid. Bór's initial idea was to use 'Tempest' as a substitute for diplomatic relations with Moscow, which had been broken off the previous year when the Poles had the effrontery to suggest that it was the Soviets who had massacred 4,000 Polish officers at Katyn and not the Nazis. In the original 'Tempest' plan the Home Army and all Poland's underground institutions would stay put; they would coordinate actions with the advancing Red Army and open their gates to them as Polish 'hosts', the legitimate representatives of the Polish government-in-exile. Poland, partner in the war against Hitler, would thus remain Poland.

Lublin and neighbouring Majdanek were the last in a series of reverses encountered by 'Operation Tempest'. At Wołyń, Wilno, Białystok, Lwów and many other points in Poland's eastern borderlands the Red Army welcomed the aid they received from units of the Home Army. But they were never invited to proceed with Soviet troops. Once behind the lines, agents of Stalin's secret service, the NKVD, moved in. The Poles were

then presented with a stark choice: either they could be forcibly incorporated into Berling's Polish Army, under Soviet command, or they could
be arrested. Many were given no choice at all: they were deported or
shot.

In order to avoid civilian casualties, the main campaign of 'Tempest'
was to take place outside the major cities, and particularly outside Warsaw.
Valuable arms caches were therefore removed from Warsaw, which, like
Paris in 1940, would be declared an 'open city'. Faced with both Nazi
and Soviet opposition, Bór was still doubting the feasibility of a Warsaw
Rising in the second week of July as Rokossovsky's armies were advancing
on the Vistula. But, confronted with appalling reports coming in from
eastern Poland, he changed his mind sometime between 20 and 25 July –
probably on the 21st. Warsaw would make a stand. Warsaw would eliminate the Nazi garrison in their midst and receive Rokossovsky's troops as
their guests. Warsaw, as the Chief of Operations, General Okulicki, put
it, would 'stir the consciousness of the world'.[4]

The atmosphere in Warsaw and its surroundings was electric. Nowak
noticed this on a train journey to the city on Wednesday, 26 July. He had
not been in Poland for eight months. He had been parachuted into western
Poland by the RAF on a flight from Brindisi, Italy, where he had had one
final conversation with Poland's Commander-in-Chief, General
Sosnkowski, who was still clinging to the hope that the Polish II Corps
in the British Eighth Army would somehow clamber over the Alps and,
with the help of the Western Allies, free Poland from the west. Cooperation
with the Red Army, he thought, was 'collective suicide'.

It was a brilliant, sunny day and people in Nowak's carriage were talking
to each other without constraint. What a contrast to the previous
September! They talked about the approaching front – one old woman
boarded the train at Radom and said that Cossacks on horseback had been
sighted on the west side of the Vistula. They talked about the flight of
the Germans. Every now and again the train would stop at a level crossing
to let long lines of German lorries loaded with German civilians with
their furniture and other belongings pass by: they were leaving all right.
The crisis was approaching. There was even a reported assassination attempt
on Hitler the previous week by officers of his own army. The war would
soon be over.

The train did not reach Warsaw's Central Station until after nine that
evening. Since the curfew was in force, the passengers had to spend the
night in the station. Outside they could hear tanks rumbling along
Jerusalem Avenue. From where they were, they probably could not detect

the direction of the traffic; but if they had known those tanks were heading eastwards to the Vistula they would have had cause for worry.

Varsovians had been watching the emaciated crowds of troops and civilians – Hungarians along with Germans, Ukrainians and the multitude that had defected to the German side in the borderlands – retreating through their city for more than two weeks now. They came on foot, on bicycles, on peasant carts, driving sheep, cows and dogs in front of them. The older generation were reminded of similar scenes in 1918. 'They were no longer soldiers but moving human tatters: exhausted, horrified, inert . . .' A 'heavenly sight'![5] When Nowak eventually got to the northern suburb of Żoliborz the morning after his arrival by train he looked out on to a tiny side street and saw columns of retreating troops passing by: 'their uniforms were unbuttoned, their rifles and helmets hung limply, their faces were dirty and sweaty.'[6] There were several Soviet air raids. Witnesses like Nowak and Anna Bogusławska, a resident of the Centre City who kept a detailed diary, speak of hearing the distant boom of artillery on Friday, 28 July.

The mood of the population was like a tinderbox, as if one match lit anywhere would set the whole people ablaze. German terror did not let up. On the day Nowak arrived in Warsaw several dozen Polish prisoners in Pawiak gaol were led out to the rubble of the Jewish Ghetto and shot – the sort of atrocity described in detail in the history of occupied France but passed over in silence in the history of Poland. Four days later, on Sunday morning, 1,400 men and 410 women and children were shipped off to concentration camps. But what Nowak noted that Friday, on taking a tram to the Centre City, suggested something more grim in preparation. Right in front of him marching down Jerusalem Avenue in the direction of Praga was a full armoured German column. 'They were proceeding in exemplary order, fresh, clean, and rested.' Suddenly he grasped why the retreating troops were being sent down the side streets, as in Żoliborz: German traffic was two-way: the Germans were reinforcing their positions to the east of Warsaw.[7]

Ludwig Leist, the German Stadthauptmann of Warsaw, had ordered the evacuation of German administrators to be stopped on Wednesday, 26 July; at the same time he began strengthening police and SS forces in the city. All the major German buildings and strong points – like the Gestapo Headquarters on Szucha Avenue, the Belweder Palace, the City Hall, the stations, and the university – were surrounded by barbed-wire entanglements and gun barrels could be seen poking out of the concrete bunkers.

The next day, in the evening, police with loudspeakers announced an order from Ludwig Fischer, the District Governor, requiring all men between the ages of seventeen and sixty-five to report at collecting points at eight the following morning, Friday, for trench digging and other work connected with the fortification of the city. Very few turned up. In the Old Town only seventy people volunteered for work, and many of them were physically handicapped. But for the commanders of the Home Army this was taken as a warning; the Germans were taking preliminary measures to decimate their forces. Colonel Antoni Monter-Chruściel, the Home Army's Warsaw District Commander, ordered a total mobilization in preparation for the Rising.

Throughout the steaming hot day men and women dressed in anoraks and thick sweaters (to hide their arms) could be seen mounting trams and buses to make their way to their rallying points. Later in the afternoon, General Bór, convinced that the Russian army was not about to break into the city, ordered everybody to return home, it caused an administrative and popular confusion that would never, in the two months of the Rising, be sorted out. But what everybody noticed at the time was that there was no German reaction to this brazen attempt at mobilization. Nor was any further call made from Fischer for fortification work.

2 Warsaw's Rising

During the weekend there were two further significant developments not unlike those which characterized resistance behaviour in Paris just prior to its liberation: the growing intensity of Communist propaganda, and the degree of local control in the decision to fight.

For the last six months the Communist propaganda of the small Polish Workers' Party – aided by Partisans who had sneaked in from the borderlands, along with the whole apparatus of the Soviet regime – had been spreading accusations of increasing acrimony and rancour. The themes were the same as in France: rival resistance groups (in the case of Poland, the vast majority) were defeatist, unwilling to fight the Germans, and were perversely 'anti-Communist', even 'anti-Soviet'. The Home Army was condemned for waiting idly while innocent Polish workers were being massacred; the Communists called for a 'national insurrection'. Polish Communist propaganda followed the same line of historical stages as in France – from strikes, to insurrection, to rupture with 'bourgeois' authority, to the final takeover[8] – only the Polish Communists knew that, with the Soviet army behind them, they had a good chance of success. By the last week of July, most of the Polish Communist leaders, like Bierut and Gomułka, had left for their empty new national capital, Lublin. But that did not diminish the propaganda. On the contrary, it became ever more intense.

In the last week of July Radio Moscow and the Polish-speaking Radio Kościuszko made repeated calls for insurrection. Few of these could have been heard, because Varsovians did not have radios: the crime of possession of a radio was punishable by instant execution. Even during the Rising, so few radios were available that they had to be linked up to loudspeakers in corridors and streets. But the word spread. It made the commanders of the Home Army jittery; they feared that the Communists would act first. On Saturday, 29 July, the Commander of the Polish People's Army plastered the walls with notices proclaiming that the commanders of the Home Army had fled the city and that he himself was assuming command of all units.

Radio Moscow broadcast the same day: 'Poles, the time of liberation is at hand! Poles to arms! There is not a moment to lose!' And Sunday: 'People of Warsaw! To arms! Let the whole population stand up as a wall around the National Council of the Homeland, around the Warsaw Underground Army. Attack the Germans . . . Help the Red Army in its crossing of the Vistula.'[9] To ensure the message got across, it was printed on thousands of leaflets and dropped by Soviet aircraft over the city that Sunday evening. The distant sound of artillery could still be heard.

The Poles were far more disoriented by this kind of propaganda than the French, because they had lost their leader; their de Gaulle was dead. The London government-in-exile was divided and had lost its authority. Even more serious was the waning of civilian authority inside the Underground State. By July 1944 all major decisions were being made by the Polish Home Army, including the most significant of them all, the commencement of the Warsaw Rising.

That decision was made in a hurry on Monday evening, 31 July, at a meeting of the Home Army commanders chaired by General Bór. It was precipitated by Colonel Monter, who came rushing in to announce that Russian tanks had been sighted in Praga, the east bank suburb. Bór himself chose the 'W-Hour': 5 p.m. the following evening, Tuesday, 1 August, during rush hour, the purpose being to create the greatest surprise. It did, especially among civilians – whole families would be separated as a result of the timing. Since it took three hours for the detailed orders to be prepared, they were not ready until eight o'clock, Monday evening, by which time it was curfew. The couriers had to wait until Tuesday morning to deliver them. Many of the major Polish leaders, both military and civilian, learned of the orders by pure chance; Korboński, Head of Civilian

Resistance, was informed by his wife. Jankowski, Government Delegate and Deputy Prime Minister, held an emergency meeting with three of his ministers just four hours before the deadline.

Was Jankowski even involved in the decision? The remaining evidence is contradictory. Adam Bien, the only permanent civilian representative to Home Army command, said the order was simply 'communicated'. But Colonel Pluta-Czachowski, present at the Monday evening commanders' meeting, claims that Jankowski definitely gave his approval. What is certain is that, only three hours earlier, Jankowski – 'a man of middle height, balding, wearing glasses . . . a strong personality, a determined individual, very resolute'[10] – was telling deputies of the Underground Polish Parliament (the RJN) that an outbreak of the Rising was 'not foreseen within the next five days'.[11]

As a result of the haste, Poland's Delegacy in Warsaw was split. Jankowski joined the Home Army headquarters in the western suburb of Wola – from which they soon had to flee to the Old Town by the river. He made no public statement for ten days. Bien and several aides remained in the Centre City, and it was here that a civilian administration was organized during the Rising. It is one of those minor epic stories of the Second World War that has rarely been told. The Home Army itself organized – at least on paper – a 'Civilian Commissary', which Stanisław Ziemba of the Polish press agency PAT called 'their kind of *Sanacja* coup' against the pre-war opposition.[12] At the moment of their direst crisis, Poles could not escape their history.

The first hint most people got that something unusual was going on that Tuesday, 1 August, was at 11 a.m. when the air-raid sirens started wailing. But there was no drone of engines. It was a parched summer's day, no sign of a plane in the sky. The factory hooters started screaming, as if possessed by the devil – the sign of the all-clear. Then silence.

Everyone was disoriented, but nobody seemed to think it of great significance. 'Don't run around on the streets today, Maggie,' said Mike Bogusławski to his sister at lunchtime. 'Don't run around on the streets yourself,' she joked back. She made the mistake of crossing 'the Avenue' that afternoon; it was only by luck that she managed to return.

When the first shots went off, people were making their way home from work. Machine-guns started chattering, rifles popped, the hand grenades made a 'deafening, drawn-out sound'. 'Everyone expected something undefinable, unknown,' wrote Kazimierz Szymczak, who was in Żoliborz, 'but not that which broke out, the Rising.' 'I refused to believe this was the Rising,' recalled Anna Bogusławska, who lived just north of Jerusalem

Avenue. But the chattering of the guns and the exploding of grenades went on, even after dusk. Nowak was also in the Centre City; his flat overlooked a courtyard, so he could only hear the commotion until a neighbouring *Volksdeutscher* was arrested and he was able to reach a window looking down on the street. Pedestrians were running into the doorways for shelter. There was a banging of window shutters. Insurgents poured out of the courtyards, wearing an odd array of uniforms, mostly German; the only way one could tell they were Polish was by their white-and-red armbands marked 'WP' (*Wojsko Polskie*, 'Polish Forces'), some bearing an eagle.

Holes were knocked in cellar walls that night as pedestrians went underground – one of the major features of city battlefields in the Second World War. Countless numbers were isolated from their families. The streets were empty, silent, scattered with debris; then there would be the chatter of guns again, or 'deafening, drawn-out' explosions.

There was a loud shouting at midnight. 'Polish men and women!' yelled the voices, 'the Rising has begun. All out into the streets! Build the barricades!' The same slogans were painted on Warsaw's nineteenth-century walls. There was a rush of feet on the staircases; people poured into the streets. Old and young, women and children broke up paving stones with axes and shovels; they carried furniture, barrels and buckets. Material was stripped from the courtyards. The barricades were decorated with Polish flags and, on top of several, could be seen portraits of Adolf Hitler for the Germans to shoot at. 'People feel an odd mix of euphoria and rage at their new-found liberty to think and talk freely. They are literally gasping at the fact that we are finally free,' wrote one Pole in his diary. Ensign Garbaty from Section Kiliński, who had had a lung removed because of tuberculosis, clambered up the sixteen floors of the Prudential building and planted on the roof a huge white-and-red flag that could be seen for days flying over Warsaw. Garbaty himself had to be carried down after his exploit.

At two o'clock, Wednesday morning, it started to rain. Water and mud splashed and squelched as the paving stones were hauled away. 'All class differences had disappeared,' wrote Nowak describing that crowd of builders. 'Truly, we are all one big family,' thought Anna Bogusławska.

In the Market Square of the Old Town – now completely under insurgent control – they built a bonfire out of furniture, bits of wood; one writer's son even contributed his father's books. The fire would be a sign to the Russians at Praga that Warsaw had been liberated. By three in the morning the rain had extinguished the flames to a damp ember.

Colonel Monter declared to his commanders in the Centre City on

Friday, 4 August, that the Polish forces 'had had success, not complete, but partial. The Rising had achieved its goal: two thirds of the city was in our hands.' But the major strong points were still surrounded by barbed wire, trenches and concrete defences; the three bridges across the Vistula were firmly under German control; all the main arteries, including 'the Avenue', were exposed to constant enemy fire; and down the main rail track swept regularly an armoured train firing its deadly load to either side. That Friday the skies cleared and the Stuka bombers came in, diving in groups of three.

Nowak, the courier, was sent out west to Wola to report to the Home Army headquarters in Kammler's factory. He clambered through cellars, courtyards and gaps in the walls of houses. When he eventually got to Wola he found the city's main street 'empty and dead'. He passed burning houses. He came across groups of refugees, with bundles on their backs. Reaching the factory, he was obliged to speak to one of Bór's aide-de-camps, the General was too busy. The windows of his office overlooked a 'grim view of the ruined buildings of the Ghetto stretching as far as the Powązki Cemetery'. Headquarters were transferred the next day to the Old Town, by which time Wola had been virtually wiped off the map.

The German authorities in Warsaw, despite all the signs, had been surprised by the outbreak of the Rising. The task of the counter-offensive was taken over personally by Heinrich Himmler, the head of the SS and, since the assassination attempt of 20 July, the closest of Hitler's collaborators. Where he could, he avoided using the army, drawing most of his forces from SS divisions and regiments, as well as a motley collection of defectors from the borderlands – starved Soviet prisoners, the Russian National Liberation Army, Hungarians, Ukrainians, and an 'anti-Partisan' brigade of reprieved criminals – who would have no qualms in killing Poles. The ancient ethnic hatreds of Eastern Europe were applied in the repression of Warsaw.

What Nowak had stumbled upon in Wola was Himmler's first counter-offensive. Inhabitants were systematically hunted out of their homes by soldiers using dogs, and then lined up on the pavements outside to be machine-gunned or otherwise shot. Their houses were burnt down; those who escaped were thrown back into the flames – even women and children. Hospitals were selected for special treatment. Patients were led down into the courtyards for machine-gunning; those who could not leave their beds were killed by the flamethrowers. Civilians were forced to march in front of tanks as human shields. Men, women and children were roped on to their steel hulls before the tanks were moved into action. No building was left standing. About 40,000 people are estimated to have been killed in Wola between 1 and 5 August.

The Centre City and the Old Town filled with refugees. 'You don't really know the meaning of war,' one thin teenage girl told Anna Bogusławska. Anna was working in a children's canteen, which doubled as a hospital.

On Sunday, 6 August, she and several colleagues went out on to the roof: 'The sky glowed brightly in the directions of Narutowicz Square, Ochota and Wola. Nearer, too, in several parts of the town you could see great nests of fire. The air was saturated with smoke making breathing difficult.'

Is 'Dantesque' the word? Warsaw's slide into hell had only just begun.[13]

3 Military 'yo-yo'

Throughout Europe there developed, in the first weeks of summer 1944, an expectation that the war would be over within a few months. France awaited her Liberation; Poland prepared her Rising; in Britain and America the serious business of planning the economic and political post-war world began; Stalin prepared his own scheme for a world without Hitler; popular morale within Germany itself reached an all-time low; and the German High Command began to feel that their hour of doom was approaching, and secretly embarked on their own private project. This was one of the most important contrasts between the end of the First World War and the end of the Second. In 1918 practically nobody expected the war to be finished that year; but it was. In 1944 many imagined this would be the last year of the war; it was not. It would have a profound influence on the style of peace that followed.

The other major difference was, of course, the advance of Russia into Central Europe. In a geopolitical sense, the concluding period of the war, 1944–5, bore a closer resemblance to 1814–15 than 1918 – when, after the signing of the Armistice, the violence of the war was carried east-wards, through Germany, across Poland and into Russia.

A major reason for the prolongation of the war was a military yo-yo effect between the Eastern and Western Fronts in Europe that nobody had foreseen. When the West advanced, the East stalled; similarly, accelerated movement in the East often coincided with slowdown in the West. Obviously, this was to the advantage of the defender, Germany.

Russia's greatest gains, resulting from Operation Bagration, were made in the month of July, their most notable feature being Rokossovsky's left-flank wheel into Poland: it corresponded to a total stalemate in Normandy. In August, the Russian advance slowed down and fell into retreat, in Normandy, the Americans launched a powerful right-flank wheel into Brittany and the Loire Country, which totally altered the military situation in France.

But this 'yo yo effect' was not solely the product of military forces. Political forces were exerting an influence, too.

On Wednesday, 9 August, as the Warsaw Rising entered its second terrible week, Stalin in Moscow had a conversation with the Polish Prime Minister, Mikołajczyk, in which he outlined his version of the military situation in Poland. Mikołajczyk had flown out to Moscow from London on 26 July at Churchill's insistence. The immediate result of the journey was to encourage General Bór and his commanders in Warsaw to launch their Rising, thinking this would strengthen Mikołajczyk's negotiating position – a serious miscalculation. Stalin had no intention of negotiating at all. Mikołajczyk was kept waiting for several days before his first interview and was then persuaded to speak to representatives of Stalin's puppet Lublin Committee. Their main demand was that both the Home Army and the London government be dissolved. The chairman of the Committee had apparently visited Warsaw, reporting that 'it was quite quiet there until 4 August. They misled you in London.'

Stalin's lecture on the military situation began with the observation that the struggle going on in Warsaw was 'unreal'. Perhaps that might not have been the case if the Soviet armies were approaching Warsaw, but 'unfortunately this is not the case. I had reckoned on our army occupying Warsaw on 6 August but we failed to do so.' Now, several German armoured divisions were attacking the Red Army. By 8 August five of them had barred the way to Warsaw, and three were 'still posted round Praga'. There was not much use of an 'air lift', commented Stalin; all that could provide was 'a certain quantity of rifles and machine-guns, but we cannot parachute cannon'. However, he concluded, 'so far as we are concerned we shall try to do everything possible to help Warsaw.' This final remark was reported to Downing Street; Churchill the next day sent Stalin a message of thanks – his last friendly comment to the Russian leader over the developing disaster in Warsaw.[14]

The Red Army was under attack. Field Marshal Model, 'Hitler's firefighter', had gathered together twelve divisions retreating from Belorussia, and moved in fresh forces from Western Europe and the Balkans, including two Panzer divisions. From the north he began breaking into weak points of Rokossovsky's flank between Praga and Siedlce, about sixty miles to the east of Warsaw. By the second week of August Siedlce had become the centre of the Soviet defensive front. Bór, in Warsaw, had demanded on 1 August an 'immediate attack from outside'. Tragically, the Red Army 'outside' was retreating eastwards.

In his memoirs Rokossovsky claims his plans were to move on Praga after learning, only on 2 August, of the Rising; he even describes climbing a factory chimney outside Praga and looking out over Warsaw: 'a pall of smoke hung over the city, houses were burning amid the flashes of bombs and shells.'[15] He wanted the insurgents to take the bridges over the Vistula while his forces, spearheaded by Chuikov's Second Tank Army, would strike at the Germans in their rear.

But the situation between Praga and Siedlce was deteriorating. To the south of Warsaw a major fight was developing around Chuikov's bridge-head across the Vistula. Chuikov, however, was still expanding his hold when, on 3 August, he was suddenly ordered by Stavka, the Russian supreme command, to swing three divisions north and go on the defensive. Chuikov was reportedly stunned at the news.

The purpose of Stavka's transfer was to counter Model's attacks by crossing the River Narew, well to the north of Warsaw. It was the first sign of a developing Soviet strategy that would concentrate their attacks north towards the Baltic and south into the Carpathians. Soviet military movements would follow these two flanking lines, north and south, for the remainder of 1944.

Surely, thought the insurgents in Warsaw, the Red Army is going to have to cross our embattled city out of military necessity; Warsaw is on the road to Berlin. But Stalin was not interested in the road to Berlin. First he wanted to re-establish the gains he had made and expected out of the Nazi-Soviet Pact of 1939, an empire stretching from the Baltic to the Adriatic. The advance into Germany had been deliberately stalled.

In late July, as Rokossovsky's left flank pushed towards the Vistula, America's right flank in Normandy was gathering a force which easily outweighed that available to Montgomery in his sluggish battlefields around Caen. Basically that had been the plan since 1943. But the fight for the heights behind Caen had become a costly 'battle within a battle', while the projected American wheeling turn south through Brittany and east towards Paris along the Loire was now more than a month behind schedule. So far, Hitler's forces had successfully contained the Allied bridgehead.

On 25 July rank upon rank of American Flying Fortresses dropped a carpet of bombs that turned the area between Saint-Lô and Périers into

a moonscape. The German line of defence was devastated, and no immediate reserves were available. American armoured divisions were brought
up to the line and, behind a barrage created by another bombing raid,
slowly advanced south-westwards. Breakthrough was eventually achieved
on 30 July when the coastal town of Avranches was seized. It was just at
this moment that the Soviet advance on the Vistula stalled – and final
plans for the Warsaw Rising were laid.

With the breakthrough, the American forces were divided into two
armies. Bradley now became commander of the two-army group,
Lieutenant General Courtney Hodges succeeded him as commander of
the American First Army, and a new Third Army, largely made up of fresh
divisions pouring into the bridgehead, was placed under the command of
General George Smith Patton.

As with Montgomery, there was a grain of folly in Patton, though he
was no marginal in social origin: he came from one of the richest families in America, went to the right schools, was a hero in the First World
War, and married into fortune. He treated military life as a kind of glam-
orous hobby, dressing himself up according to his own code while regarding
the hierarchy of rank with contempt. He could go too far. He had been
dismissed from battlefield command in 1943, during the Sicilian campaign,
after slapping and cursing at soldiers under shell shock. But as Eisenhower
recognized at the time, he had 'an extraordinary and ruthless driving
power'.[16] Patton was the indispensable man of the offensive, the man who
thought he could finish the war in 1944.

A student of Harvard Business School, Patton had organized an exceptionally efficient staff system – which explains how, within three days of
the breakthrough, he had managed to pass seven divisions through the
new Avranches corridor into Brittany, his front troops already eighty miles
along the roads leading west to Brest. Rennes was seized on 4 August.
Mortain, in the hills on the east side of the Avranches corridor, had been
taken the day before: it would surely now be impossible for the Germans
to close it. Bradley made a change in plan: forget Brittany, he ordered,
and turn east. Germany's forces in France, concentrated on the containment of the bridgehead, could be encircled and trapped. Montgomery
confirmed Bradley in his general order of 4 August: 'Everyone must now
go all out day and night. The broad strategy of the Allied armies is to
swing the right flank round towards Paris, and force the enemy back against
the Seine.'[17]

4 Emigrant armies

Among the reinforcements pouring into Normandy at that time were two emigrant units, the Poles and the French. The 1st Polish Armoured Division, under the command of Major General Stanisław Maczek, crossed the English Channel on Monday, 31 July, the day General Bór ordered the Warsaw Rising. It was made up of the remnants of a force that, having retreated from southern Poland in September 1939 through Hungary to France, having then defended the frontiers of France in May 1940 and retreated via Algeria and Morocco to Britain, had managed to piece together – through a manipulation of the American Lend-Lease programme – a tank formation, while posted on the coast of Scotland. In Normandy they came under Montgomery and joined the First Canadian Army on 7 August when, in 'Operation Totalize', it finally blasted its way through German defences south of Caen and scrambled towards Falaise.

General Leclerc's 2nd Tank Division – *la Deuxième Division Blindée* or *Deuxième DB*, after which many a street and avenue in France has been named – crossed the Channel on Tuesday, 1 August, the day the Warsaw Rising broke out. Leclerc's troops were made up of the Gaullist forces he gathered while crossing the desert from Equatorial Africa to Tunisia, joined to those Koenig pulled together in Syria to win his small victory at Bir Hakeim in June 1942. In Normandy it was placed under Patton's command in the new American Third Army and was at the head of his troops as they probed eastwards and then northwards for a point where they might join with Montgomery's forces as they started to move south.

Nothing illustrates more graphically the turning of the peripheral war against Nazi Germany into the continental war of 1944 than the return of these two armoured divisions to Europe's great northern plain. And there is something satisfying in the thought that, during that August, as Warsaw burned, Poles and Frenchmen were at the head of the Western armies manoeuvring – if chaotically – into the positions that would defeat the German occupation forces in France and liberate Paris.

Hitler's decision to launch a counter-offensive on Mortain and the Avranches corridor was made in his East Prussian headquarters on the same day, Wednesday, 2 August, as he put Himmler in charge of the operation to destroy Warsaw. German authorities had long been expecting the Polish Rising but, when it happened, they were taken by surprise. Faithful Himmler rushed to Hitler with the news. 'Mein Führer,' he said, 'the moment is unfavourable, from a historical point of view; however, it is a blessing what the Poles are doing.' Hitler's headquarters would, over the next nine months, become increasingly obsessed with the 'historical point of view'. 'In five or six weeks it will all be behind us,' continued the SS leader. 'Then Warsaw will have been extinguished, the capital, the head, the intelligence of 16–17 million Poles, the *Volk* which has blocked our way east for seven hundred years . . . Then the Polish historical problem will no longer be a matter of consideration for our children and for all our descendants, yes, even for ourselves.' It was Himmler who then gave the order that Warsaw should be totally destroyed: 'every block of houses is to be burnt down and blown up, so no units can dig in any more.' Having gathered together various SS units along with foreign formations drawn from all over Hitler's empire, he gave field command to SS-Obergruppenführer Erich von dem Bach-Zelewski, who had learnt his murderous trade killing Jews in Russia.[18]

Hitler's simultaneous order to open 'Operation Lüttich' (or 'Liège') against the American corridor into Brittany was, in Churchillian vein, 'to close the ring in southern Normandy'. So, while Model pressed on Russian supply lines between Praga and Siedlce and Bach-Zelewski wiped out the capital of 16–17 million Poles, German forces in France were supposed to plug the leak in Lower Normandy and return the Allies to their tiny bridgehead. Early August was to be the historic moment for the Third Reich.

It was, but not in Hitler's sense. Rommel had been seriously wounded a fortnight earlier and his field command was taken over by Field Marshal Günther von Kluge, who was also now Supreme Commander West, with his headquarters in Saint-Germain-en-Laye, just outside Paris. Kluge, in preparation for the counter-offensive, gave orders to transfer his armoured divisions around Caen westwards. Every order – general and local – was picked up by Britain's decrypting service 'Ultra' and passed on to local American commanders, who prepared a welcome around Mortain. Allied air attacks were launched against German airfields as far as Paris, thus assuring the Germans no cover from the skies. On the first day of their counter-offensive, 7 August, the Germans lost sixty tanks. The next day they were in full retreat. A second offensive never materialized. By 11 August, 'Lüttich' was dead. 'The attack failed', commented Hitler, with a harshness in his voice, 'because Field Marshal von Kluge wanted it to fail.'[19]

The major part of the German Seventh Army and the Fifth Panzer, as well as reinforcements from the Pas-de-Calais and the Bay of Biscay, had been pushed westwards to Mortain. Patton's Third Army, to the south, was moving eastwards through the Loire Country. The transfer of German armour westwards enabled the Canadians to break through the southern line at Caen on 7 August and then strike down the difficult route to 'Swiss Normandy'. The Germans to their west were thus caught in the 'Falaise Pocket'.

By Friday, 4 August, Warsaw's insurgents had lost the initiative. Bach-Zelewski launched an attack on the south-western suburb of Ochota on 6 August; in the night surviving inhabitants could hear the singing of drunken Ukrainians mixed with the screams of their captives. The Rising was over for Ochota by the 12th. Bach-Zelewski began to concentrate his forces on the Old Town.

Civilian morale here plummeted. Colonel Karol Wachnowski-Ziemski, commanding the Home Army in the district, reported that same day to the Polish Government Delegate that 'hunger, terrible hygienic conditions, no organization at all, nor outside help' were causing a spirit of 'defeatism' and 'even in places antagonism towards the Army'.[20]

On 8 August Colonel Monter, Warsaw's District Commander, sent out an appeal to Rokossovsky for 'speedy relief'. 'We are fighting a strenuous battle,' wrote Monter in a message transmitted to Moscow. 'The Germans, to ensure channels of retreat for their troops, are burning the town and exterminating its population.' Monter received no answer.[21]

After the collapse of Hitler's counter-offensive at Mortain, there was some confusion in Western Allied Headquarters about what to do next. Montgomery was aware that advancing his own forces south towards Falaise could cut off the enemy to the west, but it took him a while to realize that Hitler had shifted the major part of his armoured strength westwards to the American sector. So he stuck to his 'broad strategy' of swinging Patton's 'right flank round towards Paris' and cutting the enemy off at the Seine – a 'long hook' that would envelop German forces escaping eastwards. Eisenhower came over to Normandy to establish advance headquarters on the Continent on 7 August. The next morning, at the moment of the German move on Mortain, he wrote to Marshall that the enemy's counter-attacks 'make it appear that we have a good chance to encircle and destroy a lot of his forces'.[22] This is the first hint that a 'short hook' was being contemplated around Falaise. But its terms are extremely vague.

To the south of Normandy Patton was racing eastwards. 'Forget this goddamned business of worrying about our flanks,' Patton told his Third Army. By the third week of August he was at Dreux and Chartres, and was directing a new XII Corps on to Orléans – he was within fifty miles of Paris. Patton's idea was to let the isolated enemy forces behind him 'wither on the vine'. There was just one small problem with the strategy: some of those forces were not dead grapes.

Montgomery complained that Patton was leaving behind him 'a scene of intense military confusion'. Meanwhile Eisenhower and Bradley were pressing Montgomery to push his Canadians and Poles onwards through Falaise and link up with the Americans to the south, thus closing the pocket on the German forces in the west. 'It is difficult to say what enemy are inside the ring,' Montgomery confessed to Bradley on 14 August; but all the Allied commanders were by now aware that something momentous was about to happen.[23]

The American forces directly to the south of Falaise were thinly spread and were in no position, as Patton had jokingly commented, to drive 'the British back into the sea for another Dunkirk'. All that Patton had left there was a provisional corps, borrowed temporarily from the American First Army, and Leclerc's *Deuxième DB*, stationed to the west of Argentan in the village of Écouché.

The men of the *Deuxième DB* – many of whom had trekked across French Equatorial Africa and the Sahara to liberate France – were not all that interested in joining up with Montgomery's forces, let alone driving them into the sea; they were looking over their right shoulders at Patton's own spearhead, within a day's jump of the national capital. Leclerc had had a gentleman's agreement with Eisenhower, dating back to North African days, that the *Deuxième DB* would be the first to enter Paris. By the second week of August he was beginning to have his doubts about American gentlemen. So he began secretly storing extra petrol and food supplies for the 130-mile trip to Paris; his men were determined to make it whether the Americans liked it or not. On 15 August, some of the troops started to move east; Gerow, the American corps commander, directed them to 'get the hell back where they belonged'. On the 16th Leclerc was ordered to take the village of Trun, to the north, within the German gap. Leclerc simply refused.[24]

So it was not clear at all, at this moment, how a 'short hook' around the main German forces in France was going to work. Furthermore, Patton's move on to Chartres and Orléans made nonsense of Montgomery's 'long hook' northward along the banks of the Seine. Patton's main achievement up to this point was political rather than military. He had created excitement inside Paris, particularly within the Communist-dominated resistance movements. the Americans were coming.

They were. But the Germans had not yet been checked. Restless Paris could be turned into another Warsaw. An ominous sign came on 15 August

– the same day American and French forces landed in the south of France – when Hitler replaced his Western commander, von Kluge, with his 'fireman' from the East, Field Marshal Walter Model, the very man who had halted Rokossovsky's advance on the Polish capital.

Model's first task was to keep open the German escape route, south of Falaise. He moved in II Panzer Corps, which had escaped early from the 'pocket' to a camp behind Vimoutiers, for the purpose. 'My aim: to withdraw to the Seine,' he announced at a swiftly organized conference on Friday morning, 18 August. 'To achieve this: keep open the pass between Argentan and Trun.' He turned his thin face to the Corps commander: 'It is you, with your tanks, who will hold the gate open.'[25]

The 'pass' was now about eight miles wide. The entire German Seventh Army and Fifth Panzer Army lay behind it. Two old, narrow stone bridges across the River Dives, at Saint-Lambert and Chambois, provided their only means of escape.

The Americans had reason to be unhappy with the French. Montgomery was none too pleased with the Poles either. 'So far the Poles have not displayed that dash we expected, and have been sticky,' he reported to Brooke, the Chief of Imperial General Staff, two days after 'Totalize' had been launched. They were still on their 'starting line'. Montgomery ordered the commander of the Canadian army to give them 'a kick up the fork'.[26]

But the fire inside the French and the Poles was being seriously underestimated by their militarily more powerful allies.

What developed over the following weekend around the villages of Trun, Saint-Lambert and Chambois – within five miles of each other – may be regarded as the last great battle in European history, in the sense of a military manoeuvre taking place within a finite space of hills, streams, walls, a medieval castle and forest cover. But unlike Blenheim, Austerlitz or Waterloo, this was not a mere clash of armies but of whole army corps and army groups equipped with tanks, artillery and machine-guns. Never before or since has there been such a concentration of fire. At one moment, during the fighting at Chambois, exhausted American and German troops were sleeping in neighbouring rooms of the same ruined building; in one kitchen, converted into an operating theatre, German doctors worked side by side with Polish doctors on wounded Germans and Poles.[27]

To the west side of the three villages lies the Forêt de Gouffern, which separates them from the town of Argentan, which by the 18th was held tenuously by the French and the Americans. It was to this woodland that the Germans fled when under fire. On the east side rises Mount Ormel – what the locals call the Mount Everest of Normandy, though it is more of a ridge than a mountain. Just beyond the crest is the source of a stream called, unbelievably, La Vie. The first hamlet it crosses is called, more amazingly, Survie. But the real aim of the trapped German armies was fifteen miles further down that stream, at Vimoutiers, the capital of Camembert cheese and a door on the road to the Seine and Paris. Indeed, cross the barrier of Mount Ormel, and you are on the approaches to Paris.

The Allied purpose was to close the gate. By dawn on Saturday, 19 August 1944, Poles, Canadians, Scotsmen, Germans, Americans and Frenchmen were converging on this tiny area of Normandy. It would be a Battle of the Nations which was to determine the final phase of the war and the shape of the peace to come.

That Saturday – in Paris and in Normandy – was a heavy, humid summer's day. The cloud cover hindered Allied bomber support, which is what turned the struggle into a horrifying, conventional ground battle.

5 Maczuga

Despite his earlier reservations, Montgomery gave Maczek's 1st Polish Armoured Division the job of closing the Falaise Pocket. The order had gone out on Thursday afternoon just after they had won, in a gruelling fight, a hill four miles south of Falaise. They had not had a rest since their advance from Caen ten days earlier, were covered in white dust and, worse, had only half of their allocation in ammunition and petrol. 'Mission impossible!' exclaimed Lieutenant Colonel Stanisłas Koszutski, commander of the 2nd Polish Armoured Regiment. He wiped his eyes. 'What can they be thinking of? Chambois? Eleven miles from here? Four miles inside the front line!' But the order was plain: 'Take the region of Chambois. And establish contact with the Americans. Extremely urgent.'

Koszutski's regiment had been designated as the spearhead. He decided to form his unit in two simple columns, without patrols, without any sign of combat formation, and to advance through the night, in silence. In the darkness, they lost their way: their French guide mistook 'Chambois' for 'Les Champeaux', which lay halfway along the road to Vimoutiers; two identical trigonometrical points, both marked as 'Point 262', added to the confusion. German soldiers were queuing up with their horse-drawn wagons and lorries along the same road to make their escape; at one point a German traffic-controller held up the line to let the Poles through – Koszutski was sure the man had recognized their British uniforms and, terrified, hoped nobody else would notice. The full tank regiment, along with a battalion of infantry, passed through in silence.

Friday was sunny, an ideal day for bombing and rockets. Thanks to Koszutski's ruse Maczek's Polish division managed to get to the outskirts of Chambois. The Canadians moved forward, though the village of Trun remained in the hands of the Germans. That night Maczek decided to divide his force into two; half of them would concentrate on the taking of Chambois while the other half – including Koszutski's tank regiment – would climb the heights of Mount Ormel.

The fighting in Chambois that Saturday was amongst the ugliest ever witnessed in the war. Roads were blocked by wounded and dead horses, men lying in agony, burning tanks, exploding munitions. 'In all my life', remembered Captain L. E. Waters of the 359th American Infantry Regiment (which was approaching from the south), 'I have never seen so many horse harnesses.' In the afternoon the Poles noticed a full battalion of infantry advancing on them; the Poles readied machine-guns, then noticed through their sights that the troops were all waving white hand-kerchiefs. One tall 'enemy' soldier raced across the field, lifted the small Polish commander up in his arms and screamed in English, 'Buddy! I sure am glad to see you folks around here!'

The Americans had contacted the Poles. Was the Pocket now closed as Captain Waters claimed? A thin piece of string had been wound around it. The Allies had not yet taken into account Model's II SS Panzer Corps driving in from the east.

'Immediate advance on "Maczuga"! I repeat: immediate!' Koszutski had ordered his tank regiment at dawn that Saturday. The engines were strained to breaking point as they climbed up the hillside road. 'Maczuga' was Polish for 'mace'; Maczek, when studying the map the previous evening, had remarked that the Mount Ormel ridge resembled a caveman's mace, with two bulbous heads; the Poles struck for the extreme northern one, Hill 262.

From the heights, through the morning haze, they could see what looked like the whole Norman *bocage*, and two German armies in flight. 'It's a swarm of ants!' cried a lookout. The artillery and guns of their Churchill tanks pounded and pounded.

No reserves came through, and the 1,800 men on the top of Hill 262 were already short of food, water and ammunition; they had no petrol, so there could be no retreat. On Saturday night there was relative silence in the area, save for the roll of wagons and tanks which could be heard in the distance. Before dawn on Sunday the enemy assault began, from the west, from the north, from the east.

'I no longer understand anything,' commented Second Lieutenant Tadeusz Krzyżaniak. 'Where are we? Where are they? In fact I know very well. THEY are in front of us, WE behind. At the same time, THEY are behind us, WE in front. Then it's the opposite. Everywhere explosions, and everywhere blood: the blood of horses, the blood of others, and my blood.'

The spearhead of the German attack from outside the Pocket was launched by the 2nd SS Division, 'Das Reich', which had already made a name for itself in the press by its murderous rampage of a journey from Toulouse to Normandy in early June; among other atrocities it had committed was the killing of all the inhabitants of Oradour-sur-Glâne – a common enough phenomenon for Poles, but it had shocked the French.

Six miles to the south of 'Maczuga', the 12e Chasseurs d'Afrique, which Leclerc had recruited in North Africa, manoeuvred a way from Villebadin to Fel and, from there, around the right flank of the Americans, in an attempt to make contact with the Poles on the heights. But the Germans were already in control of the southern hill of 'Maczuga' and firing their deadly artillery into the Poles. The Americans were fully engaged in a fight inside Chambois. Four miles directly to the west of 'Maczuga', on a hill overlooking the village of Saint-Lambert, the Canadians kept up a permanent barrage of fire.

Up the western slopes, so steep that they had to cling on to the branches of bushes, the Germans launched wave upon desperate wave of infantry attack. In one sector a column of men waving white handkerchiefs appeared; but they were not Americans. They started falling. 'Who is shooting?' wondered the Poles. The fire came from the SS Panzer behind them.

Koszutski received a serious wound in the chest from shrapnel.

The following night there fell a calm, more frightening than the preceding night. The Poles had no food, little water and only a few hours of ammunition left. German prisoners of war, unguarded, dug graves for their dead comrades. Fires could be seen burning in the distance. 'The battlefield', noted the French Canadian observer attached to the Poles, Captain Pierre Sevigny, had 'all the aspects of a nightmare'. No one slept.

In his tank, Sevigny played with the buttons on his radio. He heard a German report on the 'total encirclement of a whole Polish division in the Falaise region'. Strauss waltzes were being performed in London – he could hear the voices and the laughter of the dancers. The theatres were filled in Canada. There was notably no report on Warsaw: contrary to popular belief, no one in the West knew what was going on in Warsaw, save for a brief early statement from the BBC that there had been a 'Rising'.

At 10 p.m. it poured with rain. Koszutski, 'suffering terribly', called his officers into the makeshift hospital at the Manoir de Boisjos, where he lay. 'Gentlemen,' he said, 'all is lost, I do not believe the Canadians can come to our aid. We have no more than one hundred and ten fit men. No food. Very little ammunition . . . Fight, all the same! To surrender to the SS is useless, you know that. I thank you: you have fought well. Good luck, gentlemen. Tonight we die for Poland and for civilization!'

The German suicide attacks began early Monday morning, 21 August. Neither the Germans nor the Poles had ammunition; it became a hand-to-hand fight with bayonets and knives.

Sevigny was asleep on his feet when he felt his signaller shaking him. '*Mon capitaine! Hep! Eh . . . oh . . . mon capitaine!*' he burbled incoherently. '*Mon capitaine! J'entends nos blindés!*' – 'I can hear our tanks!' They were the tanks of the Canadian Grenadier Guards. 'We laughed, we cried, we embraced each other,' recalled Sevigny.

Lucien Meyer, a French Canadian, noted the sort of detail that caught Miłosz's attention in Warsaw. 'From one moment to the next, a pastoral silence followed the hell of explosions.' All he could hear was the sound of tracked vehicles; there was the smell of fires, the smoke, the stink of death. And 'the birds sang, as if they had never stopped singing while the bullets whistled and shells flew around.'

The Poles had closed the Falaise Pocket. The Poles had opened the gate to Paris.[28]

6 Sartre's Paris

On Saturday morning, 19 August, just as Koszutski's tank regiment climbed up the side of 'Maczuga', an insurrection broke out in Paris. Not many people noticed it at the time. Simone de Beauvoir looked out of her hotel window on the corner of Rue de Seine and Boulevard Saint-Germain and noticed a swastika flag still flying over the Senate. Then two cyclists came by and shouted, 'The Prefecture has been taken!' Sartre went over to the Comédie Française, which for him was the centre of French resistance to the Nazis, while de Beauvoir joined her friends, Michel and Zette Leiris, who had a flat overlooking the Seine. Sure enough, on the other side, there was a huge tricolour flag flying from the top of the Prefecture. So the insurrection in Paris began with the police, the same police who had, not so light-heartedly, been rounding up Jews in 1942.[29]

'Nowadays, if you don't proclaim that Paris liberated herself, you are taken for an enemy of the people,' Sartre remarked one year after the dramatic events that followed. Yet, he went on, 'it seems obvious that the city would not even have considered an uprising if the Allies had not been quite close.'[30]

Sartre, the idol of the young after the Liberation, the king of philosophy in the post-war years, a man whose name competed with pop stars, is in many ways comparable to Miłosz, the Polish poet whose name remained virtually unknown over the next few decades. Both men were witnesses of an uprising in their cities in August 1944. Sartre became famous as the philosopher of liberty and choice; Miłosz was the poet who would argue that poetry was the only possible form of expression left when a man was faced with no choice. Paris was liberated. Warsaw was annihilated.

Sartre did not know Warsaw, and only on rare occasions in his post-Liberation literature did he refer to it. Miłosz had lived in Paris before the war. He returned after it to discover every street, every shop and monument still standing: 'Paris had been barely touched by the wing of every cyclone – a fact that made me angry.' At the Soviet embassy he saw 'Leftist luminaries of French literature and art' gather around a Soviet diplomat and bow at every word he pronounced – 'polite little boys in front of their teacher'. Miłosz developed the greatest contempt for Sartre and his popular 'existentialist movement'; Sartre's philosophy, he thought, 'makes man foreign to Nature'.[31]

Modes of thought being what they are, the tide has today shifted in favour of Miłosz and against Sartre. Sartre, it is true, became an apologist for some of the most tyrannical regimes of the twentieth century – the Soviet Union, Maoist China and Castro's Cuba. His political route shows some similarities with that of Miłosz's philosopher friend, Jerzy Andrzejewski. But the route itself is of interest, because so many were to follow it as a result of the war and their experience of liberation – and a liberation it certainly was. Sartre was an acute observer of the Liberation, he lived through it, and his world fame was a product of it.

The literature of Sartre and his lifelong partner, Simone de Beauvoir, contains some of the best descriptions of what life was like in Paris under the German occupation: the queues in front of the baker's shop, the early closing of the métro, the curfew, the darkness, the sound of soldiers' boots on the cobbles; the red and yellow *Avis* which listed the names of 'terrorists' executed or warned about 'collusion' with the enemy, the crowds at the Palais-Royal trying to get a view of the list of prisoners of war in Germany, the defiant 'V' daubed on walls, the German '*Viktoria*' sign placarded high on the Chamber of Deputies and over the metal arches of the Eiffel Tower; the emptiness of the streets, the silence, the lack of petrol, the infrequent buses – fuelled with '*gazogène*'. 'One walked between walls of stone,' wrote Sartre. 'The horror seemed outside in things.' 'Our solitude was total.' 'Paris was populated by absences' – a very Sartrean phrase.[32]

And with Sartre, of course, there were the cafés. A rivalry developed between the Flore and the Deux Magots, neighbouring cafés by the Eglise Saint-Germain-des-Prés. Sartre's café was the Flore, where he would arrive at opening time at his table in the back, order an *ersatz* coffee, and sit there all day working on his manuscripts. De Beauvoir describes the circle of friends and 'family' that developed in Sartre's café – characters such as the young Spanish Jew, Bourla. 'What I need to do', said the doomed Bourla, 'is to develop my confidence in emptiness' – a very Sartrean thought.[33]

Sartre developed a cult of the young. He had a horror of ageing. It is what made his thinking appear so modern, though in time he would become a prisoner of his perpetual need to please radical youth. 'I am, I exist, at this moment, in this place, me.' Sartre had no time for the past, for nostalgic thoughts and memories; he wrote for the here and now.

Typically, then, he took a series of notes as the Liberation was happening. They were published the following week as a series of seven articles in *Combat*, edited by his friend Albert Camus. With the exception of a few quotations, they have never appeared in print since.[34]

They are made up of a number of disjointed scenes that he himself saw from his hotel window (Sartre preferred hotels to anything permanent that might suggest a 'home'), from the roadside, and during his walks across the Seine to join his actor friends in the 'resistance' at the Comédie Française. He obviously has no idea of the state of the military front or, indeed, of anything else that is going on outside Paris. Indeed, like most inhabitants, he does not even know what is happening inside Paris itself. He just notes what is in front of his own eyes.

'It begins as a festival and even today' – Sartre is writing on Tuesday, 22 August – 'Boulevard Saint-Germain, deserted and swept now and again by the fire of machine-guns, retains an air of tragic solemnity.' Festivals are not always filled with fun; a funeral, after all, is a festival. The atmosphere outside made him think of 'those old Sundays, those Sundays during the peace when crowds pressed into fairs, or sporting events, and then, all of a sudden, an accident occurred'. The faces of women in their white dresses would suddenly turn pale as they stared at the bloodied body lying under the sun. Yes, that is what it was, a festival: 'three bloody Sundays in a row'.

He knew nothing about Warsaw. He was unaware of the battle outside Falaise. But he had read details, like most Parisians, about the village massacre at Oradour, and this haunted him during the Liberation. Many rumours were being put about. The Senate was about to be blown up (in fact, the charges had been laid), the Hôtel de Ville was on fire, the Germans had installed a huge cannon at Longchamps that was going to be fired on Paris (indeed, the siege gun of Sebastopol was on its way, but had been held up at Soissons because of Allied bombing).

But 'who would want to stay alone in his room while Paris fights for her liberty?' It *was* like a festival. People even dressed up in their Sunday best to go out on the streets and watch the Liberation – which is why, when the Allies eventually arrived, they were surprised at how chic Parisians were after four years of German occupation. The colours of the clothes were so bright that Sartre was reminded of 'Spanish crowds';* their taste for blood made him think of bullfighting. On the fourth day of the insurrection he was, for example, at the Leirises' flat. Everybody in the quarter – save the Germans – knew that armed men of the FFI were hiding in the stairs of the station of Place Saint-Michel. People at their windows waited for a 'bull' – a 'Boche' tank or lorry – to drive to its brute fate, 'death in the afternoon'. Along roared a first lorry. 'The Parisians, leaning on their balconies, knew that all they had to do was make a gesture . . . to save these men from death, but they did not WANT to.' There was a sound of explosions, a screeching of brakes: the lorry made a quick U-turn and got away. A second bull came running down the boulevard. This time the FFI got it in its tyres; it was immobilized. One German soldier jumped out and threw a grenade; it failed to explode; a Frenchman picked it up and threw it in the Seine. Then a whole army of resisters appeared from the station stairways, firing their machine-guns. The onlookers disappeared from their balconies and waited for the shooting to stop. After five minutes there was silence. Heads began to appear again at the balconies; when they saw the Germans dead on the pavement, they broke into applause.

Scenes like this were frequent. Sartre was walking from Rue Montorgueil to Les Halles when, in an empty street, he came across another lorry turned over on its back 'like a crab'. There was blood on the cobbles. Within minutes the area was swarming with an inquisitive crowd.

Accompanying this morbid kind of festival was a general anxiety, a feeling that catastrophe was just around the corner. Would Paris become a large-scale Oradour? Would the city be turned into rubble? Were they all facing death?

Members of the Resistance all at once became visible, though presumably they had been living in Paris for some time – the myth of 'the

---

* Sartre had visited many places in Europe, but not Spain, where 'dressing up' actually meant wearing black.

Resistance' became a reality. The Germans, who had been constantly present, disappeared. Already, on Saturday evening, the 19th, rumours were spreading. Sartre looked out of his hotel window on Sunday morning and noticed that the swastika flag had disappeared from the Senate's high mast; but 'they' were still there. The idea that the enemy had become invisible terrified.

Sartre being Sartre, he could not prevent himself from developing a theory, even in his jotted notes, about the Liberation. The facts seemed to fit in well with his general philosophy about human existence and choice that he had put together while serving in the French army in 1939, during his ten months as a prisoner of war in Germany, and during a year in which he had cycled around France pursuing his own plan of resistance to the Nazis. In 1943 this vast but highly readable work was published as *Being and Nothingness* (*L'Être et le néant*).

In his notes on the Liberation, Sartre combines the festival sense of hope (the Allies will be in the city by next Saturday or Sunday) with the *angst* of complete annihilation (the presentiment of Oradour being repeated on a grand scale) to define what he calls that particular week's 'spirit of insurrection'. There is no reference in Sartre's notes to the cause of the insurrection – like the Allied military advance from Normandy, or the German withdrawal – or even any reflection on its possible consequences. The emphasis is purely on the choice that Parisians made during that week to be part of the great event: 'Who', asks Sartre, 'would want to stay alone in his room while Paris fights for her liberty?' The streets may empty for a moment as the odd gunfight went on; but within minutes they would fill up again with crowds dressed in their colourful Sunday best. 'The people are transformed,' wrote Sartre. 'Their little cosy dreams . . . are dead.'

A greater antithesis to the thinking of Miłosz is hard to imagine. In Sartre the 'Spanish crowd' develops an anxious collective consciousness of liberty. In Miłosz a swallow flies above the smoke of destruction, a butterfly warms its wings on a broken brick.

7 The greatest urban catastrophe of mankind

Nobody thinks of Saturday, 19 August 1944, as one of the key moments of the Second World War. But everything happened during that weekend and the days which immediately followed. It was the instant of a great turning.

The Poles climbed the hill of 'Maczuga' and opened the last battle of

A British soldier carries a young girl through the rubble of Caen – the 'Anvil', as it was known – the devastated point on the east side of the Normandy landings, where the Western Allied armies swung into France

Left: An aerial view of the Battle of Kursk in Central Russia, 4–13 July 1943 – the greatest tank battle ever and turning point of the war. Soviet negotiations with the Nazis at Stockholm were broken off and dialogue was cautiously begun with the West

Below left: A ground view shows the intensity of the fighting. Throughout Europe the Soviet-directed Partisan war took off at this period. Many leading figures of Western resistance movements mysteriously disappeared and the movements became dominated by the Communists

Below: British landings in Normandy, June 1944. Hereafter the British always remained on the left of the Americans: an arrangement that affected the political shape of post-war Europe, especially when the Americans separated from the British in August and headed for Central, rather than Northern Europe

Left: Americans snowbound in the Ardennes, December 1944–January 1945. The separation of American and British forces at Normandy gave the Germans the opportunity to counter-attack in December. Isolated from their command, many American units in the area came temporarily under British command again

Right: The Rhine crossing into Germany was delayed by at least four months. Here an American parachutist prepares for the jump over the Rhine in March 1945

Below: American troops, under fire, build a pontoon bridge across the central Rhine. Once in southern Germany, the Americans under their commander Eisenhower abandoned Berlin to the Red Army

At the Second Quebec Conference of September 1944 relations between the American and British Allies were tense. Churchill was preoccupied with the Communist menace and the state of British finances, Roosevelt with the forthcoming presidential elections. Admiral Leahy, former ambassador to Vichy, is seated to Roosevelt's right

Stalin shares a joke with Churchill at the Moscow Conference of October 1944. The Conference is best known for the 'percentages agreement', which divided the Balkans into spheres of influence – a first attempt to limit Soviet expansion

he Yalta Conference, February 1945 – often compared to the great peace conferences that
ided earlier European wars – decided very little that had not been determined by earlier
onferences or the movement of armies. Here the ailing Roosevelt confers with Churchill

ill less was achieved at the Potsdam Conference of July 1945. Here the new British Prime
linister, Attlee, is seated second from the left. To his right is his Foreign Secretary, Bevin.
resident Truman is seated next to Molotov, in deep discussion with Marshal Stalin to his
ft. Opposite Truman is the American delegation and between Admiral Leahy and the
oviet delegation is young Alger Hiss of the US State Department

A victorious Churchill and de Gaulle, as awkward as ever, are greeted by Parisians on Armistice Day (11 November) 1944. De Gaulle offered Churchill a Franco-British Pact to counter an over-powerful America, which had supported Vichy. Churchill declined

The speaker and the myth-maker: at the 'Wolf's Lair', East Prussia, a shaken Hitler converses with Goebbels five days after the Bomb Plot of 20 July 1944

Normandy. The insurrection in Paris broke out. De Gaulle flew to France to assert his political authority. General Bradley of the American 12th Army Group came to Montgomery's headquarters 'for conference on plan after the Seine' and announced a radical change in American strategy: instead of joining the dwindling British 21st Army Group north on the plain and driving on to Belgium and the Ruhr, Montgomery was told that 'Ike wants to split the force and send half of it eastward to Nancy.' Thus it would be an independent American force that would first cross into southern Germany – a plan not dissimilar to Pershing's failed project of a pure American victory in late 1918, which was superseded by the Armistice of November. The main problem of the American plan was that it not only split Allied forces, but it would also take the Americans over some rugged country – hardly a formula for a quick end to the war. But after 19 August political considerations in military movements started to come to the fore. The post-war world was taking shape.

During that same weekend, the language of the Kremlin began to change. In an exchange of letters with the Polish Prime Minister Mikołajczyk, Stalin had dissociated himself from the 'reckless Warsaw adventure' and 'disclaimed responsibility'. By Tuesday, 22 August, Stalin was referring to the Warsaw insurgents as 'power-seeking criminals'. Roosevelt was careful not to commit himself either way on the Warsaw Rising, explaining that it would not be 'advantageous to the long-range general war prospect'. Churchill, down in Italy developing his own post-war plans, wrote to Eden in London expressing serious concern over Stalin's new attitude and complaining that the Russians had only to fly 100 miles to parachute supplies into Warsaw but were doing nothing; the Allies meanwhile were flying 700 miles from their bases in Italy and were not even permitted to land in Russian-held airports behind the Polish capital.

The Western press were full of reports on the defeat and retreat of 'von Kluge's army' from Normandy without realizing that von Kluge no longer existed. After his dismissal by Hitler he held a brief farewell ceremony at La Roche Guyon and then headed by car back to Germany. On that fatal Saturday, 19 August, not far from Metz, between Clermont-en-Argonne and Dombasle, the car and its escort stopped for a lunch break. Von Kluge's serving officer laid out a table beneath the shade of a bush. He left the field marshal to have his meal alone. When the time came to go he returned and thought von Kluge, looking crisp and stiff, was having a siesta. As he approached he let out a yell; a broken glass phial of cyanide lying on the green grass told the story.

★

No news was coming out of Warsaw. Worse, Warsaw was receiving no news from the outside world. Districts lived in complete ignorance of what was going on just a few streets away. Jan Nowak tells how Krucza Street and Moniuszki Street – separated from each other by the terrifying 'Avenue', down which constant German fire was directed from the Central Railway Station and the Poniatowski Bridge – communicated with each other via short-wave radio through London. The hunger for news has always been one of the greatest torments of a city under siege; it kills hope in the future. 'I go to Pieracki Street to listen to the radio more rarely nowadays,' wrote Anna Bogusławska on Sunday, 20 August, 'because often there is such a cannonade in the early evening that I don't want to run around the streets unless it's strictly necessary.' A week later she was despairing, 'In vain the press declares that this moment is the test of the world's conscience. The world's conscience is silent. It's deaf and insensitive.'[35]

Radios were rare. Transmitters were rarer still because of the lack of suitable components. Insurgent loudspeakers kept repeating a patriotic song, 'Z dymem pożarów' ('With the smoke of fires'), which did nothing to improve morale. Nowak records that it took a week to put together Warsaw's first Home Army radio, known as 'Błyskawica', or 'Lightning'. 'By comparison with most radio stations, Lightning was a buzzing bee. Its power was only a hundred watts, but we hoped that the BBC's most powerful advance monitoring receivers would pick up our voices.' There was no echo: 'we were speaking only to the walls before us.'[36]

Stories of enthusiastic emigrant Polish soldiers marching on to the hill of 'Maczuga', roused by news of the fighting in Warsaw, are false; there was no news from Warsaw.

It seems to have been only in the third week of August, at about the time the insurrection in Paris was beginning, that a British pilot, Flying Officer John Ward, who was being kept under cover in Warsaw, made contact with London through 'Lightning'. Ward started sending dispatches in Morse to well-placed individuals in London whose names were supplied by Nowak. By the end of the month, Ward's reports were being reproduced in the British press. By the first week of September, over five weeks after the outbreak of the Rising, and a fortnight after the Liberation of Paris, the British public were developing an awareness of the horror that was Warsaw.

Nobody inside Warsaw knew what was happening. Command posts were separated. The Underground civilian authorities, which had been so laboriously built up to act as a counter to a military Sanacja-type regime, were fragmented into uncoordinated block and housing committees.

Żoliborz, the well-to-do suburb on the north side of Warsaw, became the independent *Republika Żoliborska* ('Republic of Żoliborz') out of necessity, not from any inborn sense of autonomy. Rumours of German barbarism spread from district to district chiefly through the refugees who now crowded the Old Town and the Centre City. The fear of German atrocities, not patriotic enthusiasm or a Sartrean choice of liberty, was the chief motive for continuing the fight in these two quarters.

On that critical Saturday, 19 August, Bach-Zelewski launched his first major ground attack on the Old Town. Up until that time, civilian life in the Old Town had been, if not comfortable, at least sustainable. Refugees coming in from devastated Wola and Ochota noticed people in the streets who were still smiling; shops, bakers, restaurants and chemists were open; there was a market in the main square; Polish flags hung out of the windows, along with portraits of the great leaders. Children played on the roundabouts and swings. Remarkably, Orthodox Jews could be seen in the crowds, often carrying huge sacks of dried potatoes. On 9 August the Germans started bombing the Old Town; civilian morale swiftly plummeted. The electricity was cut off. People started leaving their homes for cellars and shelters, lit by candles and acetylene lamps. In the hot August atmosphere, tempers soon frayed. The Home Army took a lot of the blame.

On Sunday afternoon, 13 August, a booby-trapped German tank blew up in the middle of a crowd of curious onlookers; over four hundred people were killed. (Nothing of this sort was ever recorded in Paris.) 'That moment, said the writer Jan Dobraczyński, seemed 'to presage defeat in the Old Town. From that day there was a considerable increase in the number of victims. More and more graves appeared in the courtyards and on the grass . . . We all feel like a lion in a trap.'[37]

The trap closed the following Saturday, the 19th. 'Today, at the very moment I am writing,' reported the Government Delegate, 'there are virtually no civilians on the streets.' On Wednesday, Professor Dzwonkowski took the occasion of a lull in artillery firing to leave his shelter: 'I walked out on the street; nothing but ruins, houses are burning. I went out from the corner of Freta, Nowomiejska and the Market Place, to the narrow streets of the Old Town behind Podwale – everything is one large pile of corridorless rubble, heaps of debris fill the street, burnt and bombed out houses, even the silhouette of buildings has been destroyed – only the odd chimney sticks out and one or two bricks.'[38]

General Bór and his staff, the Government Delegate and what was left of the Polish Parliament (the RJN) escaped through the sewers to the

Centre City in the early hours of Saturday morning, 26 August (the day of de Gaulle's formal entry into Paris). The reputation of the Home Army had sunk to an all-time low by this time. 'The rats have left with the sinking ship,' was the kind of comment one heard in civilian shelters once the news was out. The fighters that remained were ordered to hold out to the end. When Lieutenant Janusz had both legs blown off by German grenades he was carried into a civilian shelter. The women and children scowled. One officer ordered his soldiers to be careful not to stain the sheets; somebody was heard to say, 'It doesn't matter, the blood of a Polish soldier is like wine.' Janusz died within a few hours.[39]

Among workers and small shopkeepers there was still the faint hope that the Russians would soon arrive with a 'real army'. But they never did. There was a desperate effort to get permits to descend into the sewers, the only route of escape. But the soldiers always got priority, creating another source of tension. The Germans had thrown reels of barbed wire into the sewers, which caused festering wounds for those who attempted to wade through the filthy waters. It could take as much as twelve hours in the sewers to cover a distance that could be walked in fifteen minutes above ground; and there was always the terror of getting lost, or of falling. The Germans also attempted flooding the sewers and periodically tossed in the odd hand grenade that would resound through the pitch-black, reeking wet tunnels. Some women got through, with children. 'You've not had any hard times here,' one escaped soldier told Anna Bogusławska on 29 August. 'This is probably the softest district in the whole of Warsaw; you don't really know what hunger is.'[40]

But she was soon to find out. On 31 August, Monter, with his head-quarters in the Centre City, ordered troops remaining in the Old Town to evacuate through the sewers, leaving the injured and civilians behind. The district finally surrendered on 2 September in a state, described by one witness, of something like apathy; 'we did not see any significant cases of revolt, or any kind of demonstration that would have been justified in the situation.' Between 50,000 and 60,000 people filed out across the rubble to the German lines, from where they were marched off to the transit camp of Pruszków.

Pockets of resistance held out for another month. Desperate appeals continued to be sent out to London by radio. The Soviets finally opened their airports to Allied aircraft, flying in from Italy, on 9 September, but this did little to help what remained of Warsaw. Czerniakow fell on 23 September, Mokotw on the 26th, Żoliborz on the 30th. In the Centre City two isolated pockets on either side of 'the Avenue' were completely surrounded by Bach-Zelewski's forces. 'Warsaw no longer has any hope

of defence,' General Bór radioed to London. 'I have decided to start negotiations.' He was being urged on by Jankowski, the Deputy Prime Minister
and Government Delegate, who believed the fighting should be ended in
order to save the 'biological substance of the nation'. Contact was made
with the Germans. Bach-Zelewski agreed to recognize combat status for
the insurgents who surrendered.

Silence descended on Warsaw on 1 October. One witness spoke of many
crying, but of others 'happy that the moment has come when they can
look at the sun'. A woman noticed other women digging graves while a
lively waltz was being played. Barter had begun again in the open. People
walked around carrying onions. Few wanted to leave. But on 2 October,
under rain, the Germans began the evacuation. 'There were only narrow
paths, slippery from rain,' wrote Maria Gleysztor. 'People pushed from
behind, and everyone was in a hurry . . . A long trail of many thousands
of people, dragging bundles, knapsacks and cases with them.'[41] By 8
October the entire city had been evacuated. Hitler ordered Warsaw 'razed
without trace'; demolition squads dynamited what remained.

No reliable estimate can be made of the number of lives lost during
the Warsaw Rising. Only one fact is certain: of Poland's capital of 1.3
million in 1939, there was not a soul left, or a building standing by
November 1944. Among the survivors, most were shipped by cattle train
to Pruszków and from there either to the concentration and extermination camps within the 'General Gouvernement', or to slave labour within
Germany – there was a serious need for slave labour in the last six months
of Hitler's Third Reich.

No city, including Stalingrad, Dresden, Berlin and Hiroshima, has ever
faced as great a catastrophe as Warsaw in the summer and autumn of 1944.

8 Assumption Day

Thanks to 'Lightning', the Home Army radio transmitter, and the broadcasts of Flying Officer John Ward, the first details of the horror that was
Warsaw started seeping into Western government and military minds during
the week of 21 August, as the insurrection in Paris gained in intensity.

Many historians today play down the significance of Paris's insurrection. They will tell you the Germans were simply performing a small
holding manocuvre as they retreated eastwards, that Hitler was bluffing
when he ordered the destruction of the French capital, and that the French
Communists – the main driving force of the street violence – never really

intended to take over the city. In terms of body counts and destruction, Paris's insurrection was indeed small when compared to Warsaw; 901 members of the FFI were killed in the week of the Liberation, and another 582 civilians lost their lives; 2,000 Frenchmen were wounded; the German casualties were around 3,200; only one building, the Grand Palais on the Champs Elysées, was seriously damaged.

But casualties of nearly 7,000 is quite a large number for a city to suffer within a week, even for Paris, which had a total population of around three and a half million. It is not the body count which is at issue anyway. Current cynicism about Paris's insurrection revolves around a somewhat obsessive interest in political mythmaking: the ruling argument is that the post-war French state was, in late summer 1944, creating the 'myth' that would sustain its own legitimacy and power in the years to come. Confronted with both Communist and American hostility, the newly installed French state certainly faced, over the following months, an uphill struggle to establish its legitimacy.

The main problem, however, with the 'mythmaking' view of history is that it is written from the angle of hindsight; it ignores the three facts that dominated the place and the moment – Paris in late August 1944. The first, as always, was the military situation. The German High Command had not yet abandoned its 'forward strategy' in France; this gave Paris a special role after the closing of the Falaise Pocket. The second fact to consider is the unrelenting determination of Hitler to murder, maim and destroy; those who took his orders for 'bluff' were always proved wrong. Thirdly, the idea that the French Communists had no serious intention of taking over power in Paris – an idea put about by the Communists themselves in the months and years that followed the Liberation – overlooks the Communists' own long-term plans, published over the previous eighteen months, for the future of France. Why should anybody disbelieve them?

Unlike Warsaw – which had no choice – both the occupiers and the occupied in Paris were confronted with agonizing decisions regarding their future: Paris, in the last ten days of August 1944, was truly a world of harrowing, Sartrean choice: a place of the present, the option, the act.

For the destruction of Warsaw, Hitler had bypassed the regular army and, on 2 August, had handed over the task to Himmler's SS. For Paris, on the other hand, he relied on the army to carry out his orders. The reason for this was that, whereas the Russian military advance had evidently reached a stalemate in early August, Western Allied movement had suddenly accelerated. Up until August Hitler's two daily conferences in the 'Wolf's

Lair' at Rastenburg had started with reports on the state of the nearby Eastern Front; now it was the maps of France which were examined first. Paris was the focal point of a whole military manoeuvre that Warsaw had expected, but failed, to be.

Karl Oberg, the SS chief in France, would doubtless have been delighted to have had the chance to massacre and destroy Paris. But, unfortunately, the entire SS and occupying German police forces were, on Himmler's instructions, withdrawn from the city before the occasion presented itself. Since D-Day, when an observant street stroller like Jean Galtier-Boissière would note how the passers-by all 'reflected a quiet joy', there had been visible signs of German movement. 'A column of German tanks rolls down Boulevard Saint-Michel,' he recorded on 2 July. 'Standing on their turrets, with their headphones on, the tank drivers head for the firing line, watching, as they clench their teeth, Parisian couples on café terraces sipping peacefully at their aperitifs. In the other direction there is an interminable convoy of ambulances returning from the front. Every day it is like that.' In the first week of August the journalist Alfred Fabre-Luce – whose curious ideas would land him first in a Gestapo gaol and then in a Gaullist prison – was struck by the 'strange spectacle' of 'these tanks, charging along in their retreat, blowing high the light skirts of women cyclists so that they balloon above their heads . . . On the café terraces, elegant ladies watch the cars of wounded Germans with a smile of satisfaction, as they dip into their strawberry ice cream. On the quay, a bathing girl lifts her arm and waves at a column of American prisoners.' But he adds, 'with the approach of Assumption Day the town tightens up.'[42]

Assumption Day, 15 August, was one of the great holy days of France. Louis XIII had popularized this day of rest in the early seventeenth century: it was the day given over to celebrating the Virgin Mary and the Sovereign of France. Napoleon I was born on 15 August and made it the first day of his regime. No one worked on 15 August. In 1944 it fell on a Tuesday. That meant a long weekend of idleness and reflection on a France which went back further than the Bastille, an old France, sovereign France.

On that day Hitler ordered all military staff and non-combatant services, including the Gestapo and the security forces of the SS (the SD), to withdraw eastwards. Even the army command posts were pulled back; Supreme Command West, which had its base at Saint-Germain-en-Laye, withdrew to Verzy, near Rheims; the command of Army Group B, now under the orders of Field Marshal Model, headed for the huge underground centre of Margival, near Soissons, which had been constructed in 1940 as Hitler's headquarters for the direction of the invasion of England.

Having spent a day in a siding under a torrid sun, the last train of deportees pulled out of the Gare de Pantin around midnight, 15/16 August. 'There was no longer room even for our own sweat,' recalled one of the few survivors of the 2,453 men and women transported to Ravensbrück and Buchenwald that day. As the wheels began to turn the prisoners, mostly Jews, could be heard singing the *Marseillaise*. To prevent the departure, the FFI had torn up seventy-five metres of rail outside Nanteuil-Sarcy. The train was backed into a tunnel; several prisoners were asphyxiated by the smoke of the locomotive. A wife of one of the prisoners had followed the train for nearly forty miles by bicycle. When the prisoners were transferred under guard to another cattle train, she was allowed to walk by the side of her husband, the Communist leader, Pierre Lefaucheux. 'After this trip, Marie-Hélène,' he said as he clambered aboard the cattle wagon, 'I promise you I will never again discuss the price of a wagon-lit!' Less than three hundred would return to France. Pierre Lefaucheux was not among them.[43]

'You could feel that everything was at an end,' wrote Robert Brassillach, perhaps the most famous of Paris's collaborationist authors – six months later he ended his thirty-four years of life in front of a firing squad at Fort de Montrouge. 'You could measure the catastrophe inch by inch, and yet the weather was marvellous, the women were delicious, and you caught your breath at the most magical sights – the Seine, the Louvre, Notre Dame – the whole while wondering whatever would become of it all.'[44] From dawn until dusk on Wednesday, 16 August, the roads of Paris were jammed with German lorries and automobiles evacuating civilian personnel and all of Oberg's police. The hotels were emptied – of their curtains, telephones, radios, bathtubs and bidets. 'Around each building little crowds formed,' wrote Fabre-Luce. 'A double joy burst out on their faces: the Germans were off, and they had managed to make a last good deal with them': the Germans were giving away bicycles, furniture and food. What the Germans could not either carry with them or hand over to the French they burnt: the sky was black with smoke.

In Paris, the Nazi Party had yielded authority to the German army – another contrast to Warsaw. In Paris itself there were about 16,000 troops left. There was also, to the north, the whole of the Fifteenth Army, two Panzer divisions were being moved down from Denmark, and at least 100,000 troops had escaped from the Falaise Pocket, including a unit of the 2nd SS Division, 'Das Reich', which set itself up in the Château de Vincennes, on the east side of town, where it continued its murderous ways.

But the German army in France was famously insubordinate; the command chain was chaotic, initiative lay with local commanders. Hitler was right when he suspected Paris as a major centre of the plot against his life on 20 July. Paris was a place of terrible choices.

9 Von Choltitz's choice

The former military governor of France, General Karl von Stülpnagel, had been hopelessly implicated in the plot, arresting on the afternoon of 20 July the entire SS in the Paris region, including Karl Oberg. The first thing Stülpnagel heard after the news that the Führer had miraculously survived was an order to return to Berlin. He released his SS prisoners and held a grim drinks party for their leaders in his residence. Early the next morning he boarded his black Horch and drove to the old battle-field of Verdun. By the banks of a canal, where he had seen action in 1916, he shot himself in the head; but all he succeeded in doing was to blind himself. He was dragged out of the water and his gruesome journey to Berlin continued. There he was thrown into Plötzenzee prison where, on 30 August, he was hanged on a thin cord, thus assuring death by strangulation.

Stülpnagel's arrest would lead to a change in the German command structure in France that was even more complicated than the one preceding it. It would eventually lead to Model's command of Army Group B, stationed in the bunkers at Margival; and, in what the Germans called 'Greater Paris', to the nomination on 3 August of General Dietrich von Choltitz as military commander. Von Choltitz's nomination was made within twenty-four hours of Hitler's decision to put Himmler in charge of destroying Warsaw.

There was one person who had hopes that the change in command in Paris would improve a situation that was beginning to look like a powder box. That was the Swedish Consul General, Raoul Nordling. Nordling and von Choltitz would prove to be the two key players in the last two weeks of the German occupation of Paris. But this was hardly what Nordling imagined when he first caught sight of von Choltitz as his 'grand limousine' rolled into the courtyard of the German embassy on the day of his arrival, 7 August: 'The car stopped and a general in a magnificent uniform stepped out; he was wearing a monocle and his chest was covered with decorations. He was a most corpulent man, strong-looking with wide shoulders, extremely stiff in manner, imposing, and what seemed to me a terribly Prussian appearance. The expression on his face was hard, his lips tight, his gestures frigid. I kept myself modestly to one side, watching this character and thinking to myself that it would not be easy to deal with him.'[45] But deal he did. Raoul Nordling and Dietrich von Choltitz together saved Paris.

Neither could be considered angels. Nordling had spent most of his life in Paris, and insisted throughout the insurrection that he was acting as a 'citizen of Paris' rather than as the Swedish Consul. His father was a Swede, and also Consul at Paris, while his mother was from the Auvergne. This could be seen in his face: at the age of sixty-two his thinning blond hair and forehead were certainly that of a Swede, but from his eyes down to his round jowls he looked every bit the good-living Auvergnat that he fundamentally was. It used to amuse that other well-known Auvergnat, Vichy's Prime Minister, Pierre Laval, whom he slightly resembled. 'The cross between Swede and Auvergnat has excellent results,' Laval typically quipped with the Consul. 'I have a bitch dog that, on its mother's side, comes from the Auvergne and, on the father's side, is from Spitzberg. There's no better beast.' Nordling nodded at the compliment, but reminded Laval that Spitzberg was not in Sweden. 'It's all the same thing,' responded the Prime Minister; 'they're both in the North.' As with all officials from Vichy, the world beyond France was a foreign planet.[46]

Not unlike Laval, Nordling's appreciation of politics was based on the numerous personal contacts he had established in Paris since he had first come to work in his father's consulate in 1905. Abstract ideologies such as Nazism or Communism never entered his friendly head. This war was a matter of conflict between major powers; his little country was neutral and his job was, through his contacts, to attempt to bring these countries together, whatever their differences. For at least twelve months he had been trying to 'spare the Allies and Europe the great landing on the Continent'. Laval thoroughly approved. 'I still maintain the best relations with the Anglo-Saxons,' Laval boasted at a reception in January 1944 – and it is true that the Americans kept all doors open regarding Vichy.

Nordling claimed that his dealings with the Germans were 'solely official' and were principally limited to 'protecting Swedish interests, almost always industrial relations'.[47] Now Nordling was a rich man not because of his diplomatic salary but rather because his family firm, SKF, manufactured steel ball-bearings – not an innocent trade in time of war; in fact, Nordling's firm kept Germany's military machine running. On 31 December 1943 the RAF bombed one of his factories, in the Parisian suburb of Ivry.

It was this event which brought Nordling into contact with de Gaulle's French Committee of National Liberation in Algiers: Pierre Lebrun, a Gaullist unionist, came to warn him of the bombing a day before it occurred. Lebrun opened up to Nordling the whole Gaullist network in Paris. Until August, Nordling refused to meet de Gaulle's General Delegate, Alexandre Parodi, out of fear of being unduly compromised. But on Wednesday, 16 August, as the German civilians and police were being evacuated, they had their first encounter in front of the Café de la Paix, like 'theatrical conspirators'. 'Parodi wore a soft hat with its rim covering his face. I myself was a bit worried and must have looked like a man who carried a terrible secret.' They first passed each other on the pedestrian crossing on the boulevard, then swept by each other on the pavement opposite and, on their final crossing, shook hands. The deal was struck in a back street: the Gaullists had found a man who could speak directly to the highest German authority in Paris, von Choltitz.[48]

'Sweden is the only country which can open the way to peace,' Otto Abetz, the German ambassador to Paris, had told Nordling the previous March. After D-Day it became a matter of saving the capital.

General von Choltitz, the new military commander of the city, was hardly the kind of man one would expect to do this, which is precisely why Hitler had picked him. Neutrality was not something von Choltitz respected – he had been the first German officer to land in neutral Holland on 10 May 1940. Destroying cities was one of his specialities – he had personally given the order to firebomb Rotterdam, and it was under his command that the siege of Sebastopol was brought to a fearsome end in July 1942. He did this with the biggest gun of the war, 'Karl', which fired shells of 2,200 kilos up to a distance of six kilometres – 'Karl', in August 1944, was on its way to Paris. For two years he had commanded rear areas during Germany's long retreat across Russia and had applied to the letter the Reich's 'scorched earth' policy. He had no qualms about the shooting of prisoners and defended the massacre of some 200 captives in Caen in June 1944; they were, as he later explained to Nordling, simply 'bandits' and 'freeshooters' whom the Germans could not afford to leave behind when the Allied bombing started.

Nor was von Choltitz under any illusion about what was being demanded of him in his new job at Paris. Four days before his arrival in the capital he had had a face-to-face encounter with the Führer in his 'Wolf's Lair'. He had noted in an exercise book both Hitler's instructions and the five-point summary subsequently given to him by General Alfred Jodl, Chief of Army Supreme Command. Hitler's policy was that his western forces should make a stand *before* the Seine and that Paris – the loss of which would, in Hitler's view, be psychologically catastrophic for the morale of both the army and the population back home – should be converted into a front-line city. As commander he would have all the prerogatives of a fortress under siege. Terror would be exercised on German 'shirkers', and all attempts at revolt by the civilian population would have to be repressed 'without pity'.

Planning for the destruction of Paris, in the case of German retreat, went back to the ill-fated 1942 Canadian raid on Dieppe, which had raised an alert in occupied France. By late spring 1944 the Germans had developed a two-phased plan eliminating, first, all gas, water and electricity supplies, and then sabotaging major industrial installations. By the time von Choltitz had set himself up at his command post in the Hôtel Meurice, on the Rue de Rivoli, the plan had been extended to include all forty-two bridges across the Seine, and many of the major buildings of the capital. The rumours that spread through the population after the insurrection broke out were not unfounded. Several hundred oxygen bottles – at a pressure of 180 atmospheres – had been placed in the cellars of the Invalides; two tons of explosive were planted behind the pillars of the Chambre des Députés; the German labour force Organisation Todt was using pneumatic drills to prepare chambers under the Senate for seven tons of cheddite; five tons of explosive were carefully laid out under Gabriel's eighteenth-century Ministry of the Marine on Place de la Concorde; and mines were attached to the south-east leg of the Eiffel Tower. Four experts in demolition, under the command of Captain Werner Ebernach, were housed on the fourth floor of Hôtel Meurice. But their full report on plans was still not ready when General Jodl called for the third time from Rastenburg on Sunday, 20 August, to ask why nothing had yet been blown up.

In his memoirs, von Choltitz explains that he had no fear of death, but that he began having nightmares of his own body hanging over the ruins of Paris.[49] Doubt had been placed in his mind. Neither in Russia nor on the Western Front had he ever exercised such executive authority as he now had in Paris; up to this time he had merely carried out orders. Now he was alone. The instructions he was receiving seemed contradictory. When Field Marshal Model visited him in Paris on 17 August he coldly concluded his interview, before mounting his black limousine, with the words: 'What took forty minutes at Kovel will take forty hours at Paris. But the town will be razed.'[50] And yet, throughout the following week, once the Falaise Pocket had been closed, Model conducted an extraordinary operation every night, using pontoon bridges and ferries that carried the major part of his forces across the Seine well to the north of Paris. This completely flouted the instructions von Choltitz had heard from Hitler's own mouth.

More influential than Model's actions in the north – of which there was little knowledge in Paris because communications between Hôtel Meurice and the bunkers of Margival were poor – was the behaviour of the Swedish Consul General: Nordling was a man who listened. Forty years of training in the palaces, salons and restaurants of Paris had made him something of a professional confidant. Laval had appreciated this. So now did von Choltitz.

Nordling's first contact with von Choltitz was in a thirty-minute conversation on Wednesday, 16 August – the same day he had shaken hands outside the Café de la Paix with de Gaulle's General Delegate, Alexandre Parodi. Nordling had come to the Hôtel Meurice to make an appeal for the political prisoners whom the Germans still held in various Paris prisons; he wanted them placed under the authority of the French Red Cross. Without giving his direct approval, von Choltitz indicated how this could be achieved. Nordling did not succeed in stopping the last deportation train to Germany, but he did manage to free the 3,893 French men and women detained at Fresnes, at the Fort de Romainville, Drancy, Compiègne, and the smaller gaols inside the city; it was no mean success. Before the last 1,482 Jews left Drancy on 17 August for freedom they ripped off their yellow stars; the ground of the camp, according to Nordling's nephew, Edouard Fiévet, looked 'like a carpet of dead leaves'.[51]

Nordling's second meeting with von Choltitz was on Saturday afternoon, 19 August, the day the insurrection broke out.

Nordling had spent the morning at the Prefecture of Police, having received, the evening before, an urgent call from Vichy's Prefect of Police, Amédée Bussières. When he arrived at around 11 a.m. he was surprised to discover the place swarming with armed civilians (in fact, non-uniformed policemen) and was introduced to a new Gaullist Prefect, Charles Luizet. 'You can have a talk with Monsieur Bussières without any difficulty if you want to, Monsieur Nordling,' Luizet said with a grin; Bussières was under armed guard. Nordling said he had no interest in a deposed prefect: 'However, if you need any help, don't hesitate to call me because I am the senior member of the consular corps in town.' Thus contact with the Gaullists was confirmed. Nordling's next point of call was Hôtel Meurice.

As he left the Prefecture he noticed a remarkable sight: a huge tricolour flying at the top of the building. Rue de Rivoli was empty. The odd shot could be heard. There was a huge barricade across the street, level with Joan of Arc's statue. But in the Tuileries garden mothers were walking with their children and there were pleasure boats sailing on the Seine. 'During the following week I would often witness such contrasts,' said

Nordling, confirming the picture Sartre was to publish in *Combat* a fortnight later.

Von Choltitz was in a restless mood, his short, round figure pacing up and down the parquet flooring; at one moment he would be perfectly jovial (though 'his sense of humour was, one could say, a little Germanic'); then he would sink into the blackest of tempers, yelling obscenities: he would look out of the window at the Tuileries garden and the Seine, bathed in sun – it was one of the best views of the city. Freeing those prisoners was a terrible mistake! 'They were just a gang of riffraff. Everybody talks all the time of the "Resistance" or the "Forces Françaises de l'Intérieure" as if they were organized and disciplined troops, as if they had any real authority. But they are nothing but freeshooters firing on my men. If it continues I promise you I will take tough action. I will order that Paris be defended and will destroy the city before evacuating it.'

'It's not riffraff you are dealing with,' replied Nordling. He started defending de Gaulle – behind de Gaulle was the Resistance, and behind the Resistance was the French people. In fact, said Nordling, it was a 'civil war'; a civil war of the French people against the government of Vichy.

'It's not a civil war,' interjected von Choltitz. 'It's us they are shooting at! Just look over there!' He pointed at a few German soldiers with rifles prowling through the Tuileries. 'Is that what you call an insurrection against Vichy?' He became unpleasantly silent. A young woman came cycling down the Rue de Rivoli, completely indifferent to the battle going on about her; her dress billowed slightly. 'Well, you can't shoot at her,' von Choltitz suddenly chuckled. 'Ah,' he sighed, 'Paris is a beautiful city.'

'Paris', he would later say to Nordling, pointing out the Louvre, under assault by an SS unit, 'is like a pretty woman; when she gives you a smack, you don't smack back.' Paris was a woman: he was hardly the first man to say it. But von Choltitz still had these nightmares.

'I was at Stalingrad, you know,' continued von Choltitz that Saturday afternoon. 'And from that time onwards I have done nothing but manoeuvre to escape encirclement by the enemy: retreat on retreat, defeat upon defeat. And here I am in marvellous Paris. What do you think is going to happen now?'

'And what if we could find a modus vivendi?' According to Nordling, it was von Choltitz who asked the question. Others have argued that the whole initiative came from Nordling. Historically it does not matter. What matters is that together, that Saturday afternoon, von Choltitz and Nordling were looking out of that window; and Nordling had contacts.[52]

10 Prelude to an insurrection

The Poles had just reached the summit of 'Maczuga'. Leclerc's 12e Chasseurs d'Afrique began their manoeuvre to the south of Chambois to make contact with them. But on the following stormy Sunday night – as Koszutski summoned his officers for his last appeal, 'Tonight we die for Poland!', and Captain Sevigny in his tank tuned into British waltzes – Leclerc, totally ignoring his American superiors, ordered an even bigger operation: Lieutenant Colonel Jacques de Guillebon was instructed to gather seventeen tanks, a dozen machine-gun carriers and two infantry sections and drive straight to Paris. To make sure the Americans knew nothing, he 'kidnapped' the two liaison officers, Rifkind and Hoye. Pointing his walking stick in the dark at their tent he told Captain Alain de Boissieu, 'Take them off for a little tour of the region.' By wet Wednesday morning, 23 August, the whole of Leclerc's *Deuxième DB*, in two motorized columns, each fifteen miles long, was sending up clouds of blue diesel exhaust on the road to Paris.

On Saturday, 19 August, General de Gaulle was flying from Algiers to northern France. The original plan had been to travel in an American Flying Fortress, which could carry more than enough fuel for the trip; but the Americans managed to supply a B-17 with its landing gear in such a state of disrepair that 'several days' delay' were required. 'You think this is done out of the kindness of their hearts,' de Gaulle remarked to his aide-de-camp and decided to take the French-owned Lodestar Lockheed, 'France'; it had two extra fuel tanks attached to its wings for the purpose of the trip, and only just managed to take off. De Gaulle sat in the back, chain-smoking: he hated flying.

Over the south coast of England, 'France' was supposed to be met by an RAF escort. But nothing turned up. 'Head for France,' ordered the General. The plane had only thirty minutes of fuel left for the Channel crossing. The sea, a thousand feet below, was choppy. It was de Gaulle himself who recognized out of a starboard window the coast east of Cherbourg. They landed in the little airfield of Maupertuis, near Saint-Lô, with about two minutes of fuel left. De Gaulle, president of the newly declared 'Provisional Government of the French Republic' (GPRF), was met by three people, the commander of the FFI, General Koenig, the French Commissaire de la République for Normandy and an American military representative. He had to borrow a razor to shave and was then driven in an old Celtaquatre lorry *à gazogène* to Eisenhower's headquarters outside Granville.

Both Eisenhower and de Gaulle learned of the Paris insurrection that morning. Eisenhower was intransigent: he did not want to march on Paris. De Gaulle insisted that there was a real danger that the Communists would take over the city and the whole rising could end in disaster. It would take two separate missions from Paris itself to change Eisenhower's mind. But by Wednesday, 23 August, he had ordered the American 4th Infantry Division to cross the Seine at Melun and join Leclerc by attacking Paris from the south-east.

In the meantime, de Gaulle had gone on another of his grand speaking tours, throwing his arms in the air like the film star he now was: Cherbourg, Coutances, Avranches, Fougères, Rennes. Anthony Eden, the British Foreign Secretary, was astonished at the effect. 'The morale of the French population is incredibly good,' he reported back to London in his unassuming way, 'I myself am surprised at all this.'[53] But after Tuesday night, the 22nd, which was spent at Laval, de Gaulle simply disappeared. Where was he?

Naturally, the French Communist Party had not planned on a Gaullist takeover of the Paris insurrection. Parallel authorities under their control had, by spring 1944, been set up within the Resistance, in the clandestine armed forces, in the unions and, most particularly, the press. The Communists kept driving home the theme that if de Gaulle's French Committee of National Liberation represented resistance in the exterior, it was they, the Communists, who were the legitimate force of resistance within the *patrie*. They kept to their historical plans for strike and 'national insurrection'. This would be their policy for France's 'Liberation' – thus following exactly the same policy as their Communist colleagues in Poland.

But they soon encountered a problem. In 1943 it remained entirely conceivable that the Red Army would 'liberate' France. By early 1944 the Western Allies were clearly going to do the job. This affected the interpretation of 'National Insurrection' – which the Communists began to forecast with capital letters. Unlike Polish Communists, they could not prepare for an early rupture with 'bourgeois' parties. So the French Communists abstained from the word 'Fascist' (used in Poland indiscriminately against *all* class enemies, whether Nazi or bourgeois). French Communists were obliged to concentrate on the Nazis as their enemies while maintaining, for the moment, an alliance with the Western capitalists, including de Gaulle. Hence, French Communists defined their enemy as 'Hitlerite'.

Another serious problem had developed in their historical scheme. As a result of the deportation of labour, the working classes were weak, and this undermined projects for the 'mass movement' and the 'general strike'.

But what really caught them unawares (the Communists had only been admitted into the French National Committee one month earlier) was de Gaulle's decree on 21 April in Algiers, setting up his own system of local government. It included a full list of departmental prefects (for whom the 'Committees of Liberation', the CDLs, would perform only a consultative role) and regional Commissaires de la République, all answerable to a General Delegation representing de Gaulle in person. As for municipal councils, until local elections were held, they would be made up of the same members as sat in France before the war, in 1939. Adding insult to injury, shortly before D-Day de Gaulle named General Koenig, the hero of Bir Hakeim, commander-in-chief of the French Forces of the Interior – so even Communist control of the interior armed forces was thrown into doubt. Simultaneously, the French Committee of National Liberation became the 'Provisional Government of *the French Republic*' – as if Vichy were merely an illegal hiatus in the regime of a Republic that went back to 1871. That had not been the Communist purpose in fighting the war. Clearly there was going to be trouble.

The riposte came from the Communist-controlled clandestine press. From April onwards *L'Humanité* and *Vie Ouvrière* drove home the theme that no 'provisional government' was a genuine government until it had achieved 'national union'. And this meant the support of the worker organizations, such as the CGT, which, as André Marty had grandiloquently claimed on 11 April, represented '*97 pour cent des fusillés*'.[54] The Communists founded a new paramilitary group of *milices patriotiques* that answered to their own 'Central Committee', an authority that would be in direct competition with the National Resistance Council (where the Communists already had a controlling vote).

Calls for preparation of the 'National Insurrection' followed immediately after D-Day. On announcement of the landings, *L'Humanité* published a list of actions in which 'all Frenchmen must participate': sabotage of the factories, destruction of the mines, 'mass protest actions' that would lay the ground for the 'National Insurrection'. 'More than ever, *attentisme* is dishonourable and cowardly . . . To kill one of Darnand's[*] *miliciens* is to kill a Boche soldier, and one must kill as many as possible as quickly as possible.' The 'working class' gradually found itself second on the agenda. Action was made in the name of the *Patrie* more than in

---

[*] Joseph Darnand, a Socialist in the early 1930s, later a failed leader of France's minuscule extreme-right, was Vichy's 'Secretary-General for the Maintenance of Order'.

the name of the working class. As *L'Humanité* put it on 16 June, patriotic struggle now cleared the country of 'the great treason of 1940 which delivered the *Patrie* to the Hitlerian invader' – wise strategy for the Communists: the louder one shouted the quicker past sins might be forgotten.[55]

But the 'mass movement' never got going. In most of France, cities were liberated because the Germans withdrew and the Allies moved in. There were, however, some significant exceptions, though these were not exactly cheerful inducements to insurrection. On 19 August, for example, a 'general strike' was proclaimed in Limoges. The Maquis – resistance members who had named themselves after the wild heathlands of the south – surrounded the town and its chief, Colonel Guingouin, persuaded the Germans to surrender. For the next four months – long after the Germans had departed – Guingouin became a kind of local warlord and the area was subjected to guerrilla warfare and summary executions of 'traitors'. On 24 August, an 'insurrection' broke out in the Lyons suburb of Villeurbanne. After two days of vicious fighting the Germans regained control of the ruins. Another insurrection broke out in the factory suburb of Oullins, with exactly the same result. On 28 August a 'general strike' was declared: in the fighting, which continued until the arrival of the Allies on 3 September, every bridge in Lyons was destroyed with the exception of two.

The largest insurrection outside Paris was undoubtedly in Marseilles. In late May a general strike 'for bread' was initiated by local Communists; the movement spread through the whole surrounding region. It suddenly came to an end, not because of German action, but because the Allies – as a preliminary to their southern landings of 15 August – conducted a devastating bombardment of the city. On 17 August the local CGT had another go at a general strike. The Germans brought in heavy artillery and tanks. A Communist 'Committee of Liberty' installed itself. Finally, a French unit of the invading Allied force entered the city – to discover that the Germans had demolished the industrial infrastructure, and most importantly the port. But because of the insurrection the Communists had succeeded in getting what they sought: the major administrative posts of the city. Raymond Aubrac, one of the men suspected of betraying Jean Moulin to the Gestapo in June 1943, became Marseilles' Commissaire de la République. He ruled the region like a latter-day Fouché, installing a reign of terror that lasted until he was removed from office in late January 1945.

★

Two days after the Allied landing in Normandy, on 8 June 1944, the Paris Committee of Liberation (the CPL) set up a command system to direct all insurrectional armies in the Paris region. The Paris Committee was dominated by the Communists and presided over by a Communist, André Tollet, who spent a large part of his time denouncing Socialist 'traitors'. On the same day as the 'army' reform, Tollet's Committee attacked the whole principle of de Gaulle's *rouage de fonctionnaires* ('bureaucratic network') and demanded that the (Communist-dominated) National Council of Resistance become the 'official mouthpiece of the provisional government'. Through July and early August a bitter war of words developed between Tollet's Committee and de Gaulle's General Delegation over the issue.[56]

During the war, the *Quatorze Juillet* had been de Gaulle's day. In 1944, the Communists of Paris decided it would be theirs. 'The 14th of July 1944', announced *L'Humanité*, 'must be a day of the people's struggle towards National Insurrection, which is inseparable from National Liberation . . . *En avant pour un 14 juillet de combat!*'[57] A number of marches were organized involving, according to the Communists' estimate, '100,000 workers'. One of the leaders was shot by a policeman. This was to be followed by a 'strike of solidarity' in various suburbs. The movement gradually petered out.

Not to be deterred, the Communists then prepared for the next historical stage of Paris's insurrection, the 'general strike'.[58] It was to start with a train drivers' strike.

Now, most of the main railway lines around Paris in August 1944 had been destroyed by Allied bombers. Besides deportees (who in the case of the last cattle-train load had, we have seen, been forced to walk several kilometres at gunpoint), very few people travelled by train that August in northern France, including the German army. Not even goods supplies came in – which was beginning to cause problems.

On Thursday, 10 August, Charles Tillon, Communist leader of the Communist Francs-Tireurs et Partisans launched an order for a general strike. The order was officially addressed to two other distinguished Communists of the Paris region, André Tollet and a spiky little Breton called Colonel Henri Rol-Tanguy, commander of the FFI-Ile-de-France.

Thursday, 10 August, was the eve of the 'long weekend': Assumption Day was on Tuesday, 15 August. No Parisian works during a long weekend, even during war (indeed, especially during war). The few train drivers who did turn up to sit in their immobile trains were sent off on holiday. Thus began the Communists' 'general strike'. Among the bathers in the Seine observed by Sartre and Nordling were the 'strikers'. In the meantime, during the horse-racing at Longchamps that Sunday, people said they could hear the distant thunder of cannon.*

11 The policemen's role

Diving off the barges of the Seine into the 'great swimming pool' were also a number of Paris policemen. They had reasons for being idle. Von Choltitz that Sunday had ordered their disarmament and had managed to seize over 5,000 weapons. There had been no opposition at all – undoubtedly because most of the police stations, like the railway stations, were empty.

These police had fought as soldiers for their country in 1940, and had arrested Jews in 1942. They were not heroes. But they were bitter over the humiliating situation in which Vichy had placed them. Proclamations like that of the Communist slogan, 'the great treason of 1940 which delivered the *Patrie* to the Hitlerian invader', had a special meaning for the Paris police. So did Gaullist statements that they would be at the heart of a legitimate 'government force'. Despite their appalling past – and in many ways because of it – there was no more patriotic group in Paris than the police. So when the police went on strike on Assumption Day, 15 August, it was clear that something very serious was about to happen.

There were three resistance groups operating inside the Paris police force: one was Communist, the 'Front National'; another was Socialist, 'Police et Patrie'; a third was Gaullist, 'Honneur de la Police'. The Front National dominated the other two and took the initiative in the call for a strike.

The lack of police in the streets, along with the withdrawal of the German civilian authorities and police forces, encouraged some rash actions by the various splinter groups of the Resistance that existed in Paris at the time. Eight German soldiers were killed in the working-class suburb of Aubervilliers on Assumption Day. Taking advantage perhaps of the holy day, a group of 'Jeunes Chrétiens Combattants' joined with a group of 'Jeunes Communistes Combattants' in an arms-carrying mission. They started out at dawn in a truck at Porte Maillot and five minutes later were surrounded by German troops; when arrested, they were heard repeating the Lord's Prayer. They were found the next morning by the Cascade in

---

* What were these 'cannon'? The sound of the fighting around Falaise over 100 miles away? More likely it was Allied bombing of bridgepoints on the Seine – hardly the sign of an Allied approach to Paris. There was little fighting at this time around the thinly spread spearheads of Patton's Third Army, still over fifty miles from Paris.

the Bois de Boulogne, their thirty-five mutilated bodies torn apart by the grenades the Germans had thrown at them.

In the meantime Colonel Rol-Tanguy began frantically organizing the Communist 'Mobilisation Générale'. Posters were printed that were to be plastered all over Paris on Saturday, 19 August. On Friday afternoon the Paris Committee of Liberation met under André Tollet's chairmanship in a shack behind a vegetable plot in Le Petit Clamart. They decided to go ahead with their plan for a general insurrection. It was agreed that this could cause massive destruction and loss of life as the Germans retaliated; but, once started, nothing could stop the fighting: the Communists would seize all the main administrative posts and the Gaullists would be faced with a fait accompli. Henri IV, head of the Protestant League, had declared in January 1593 that 'Paris vaut bien une messe' ('Paris is worth a mass'). On Sunday, 20 August 1944, Colonel Rol declared, in front of the National Council of Resistance, the new Communist version: 'Paris vaut bien 200 000 morts' ('Paris is worth 200,000 dead').

There was just one little problem to the plan hatched in the shack at Le Petit Clamart. The Communists might have controlled Tollet's Committee, but of its five members only four were Communist. In one corner of the room sat the silent Professor Léo Hammon; Hammon was a Gaullist. He immediately passed on the Communist plan to Alexandre Parodi, de Gaulle's General Delegate. Parodi and Jacques Chaban-Delmas, de Gaulle's young military representative, decided to launch their own insurrection through their own police network, 'Honneur et Patrie'. They had one advantage over the Communists: for reasons of security, the Communists were dependent on a complicated system of message delivery; Gaullist messages were swifter and direct.

Colonel Rol had set up headquarters underneath Place Denfert-Rochereau in cellars of the Paris Department of Water and Sewers. Right next to the catacombs, it was connected also to medieval stone quarries, nineteenth-century sewers and the whole métro system. Moreover, the department had its own telephone network, entirely independent of the Paris system of the PTT, and was thus free from German interference. Rol could telephone every official building in Paris at a moment's notice.

He thus set out on his bicycle early on that historic Saturday morning, 19 August, for the centre of town fully confident that the Communist 'great insurrection' was about to begin. But as he rolled down an empty Boulevard Saint-Michel he got the shock of his life. Flying from the top of the Prefecture of Police was a huge tricolour flag: the Gaullists had got there first.

12 The Château de Rambouillet

The Château de Rambouillet, thirty miles south-west of Paris, was a famous place for farewells. François Ier, taken ill in the late winter of 1547, decided that this was where he was going to die, which he did a month later in the tallest and oldest of the château's four towers. It was at Rambouillet in March 1814 that Marie-Louise, the Empress, met her father, Kaiser Franz of Austria, and promised to join him in Vienna, thus separating herself from her husband. Napoleon himself spent an unhappy night at Rambouillet after the Battle of Waterloo; he reminisced all evening over dinner and, early the next morning, set off for La Rochelle and St Helena. Charles X abdicated his throne there in 1830. Marie Antoinette spent the last tranquil years of her marriage to Louis XVI at Rambouillet; she hated the place, calling it 'La Crapaudière' ('Toad Hall') – the King had built a large fancy milk parlour for her amusement. In the late nineteenth century it became the official country residence of the Presidents of the Republic, for Rambouillet was less than an hour's drive from Paris.

It was pouring with rain when the first of Leclerc's two columns arrived there for a night's stop after driving the hundred miles from Ecouché on Wednesday, 23 August 1944. In the park and the surrounding woodland areas they set up tents; a strong scent of soldiers' cooking pervaded the town. They had passed through the cathedral town of Chartres at around midday; the Germans had destroyed all its beautiful old bridges and had evacuated all the surrounding houses, many of which lay in ruins. Tomorrow Paris! Some would not live to see it.

At the best restaurant in town, Le Grand Veneur, only rations were served. Journalists from around the world had gathered there. Making himself noticed was 'Captain' Ernest Hemingway – he would promote himself to 'General' on entering Paris. But that evening not even Hemingway was the star of the show. Lieutenant Sam Brightman, an American intelligence officer, had just ordered beans and Ration K when his waitress suddenly stared out of the window and stuttered, 'De Gaulle . . . De Gaulle . . . It's de Gaulle.'[59]

Nobody could fail to notice de Gaulle, even if he was just passing by on the street. He would not have made a very good spy: he could hardly remain in hiding for long. It was not just his height; there were those odd flourishes with his arms, the unexpected bursts of energy, the sudden poke of a finger, the broadening of the shoulders. And his head was so narrow, as British high civil servants – who played with his hat while the General was in conference with Churchill – would confirm. Even when motionless, which he often was, others could feel the volcano inside.

Though neither the British nor the American authorities could locate him that Wednesday, he had not made much of a secret of his presence to the population. At La Ferté-Bernard, Nogent-le-Rotrou and at Chartres the flags came out. '*Vive de Gaulle!*' shouted the people from the pavements and the windows.[60]

De Gaulle did not want to be seen to abuse his residence in the château. While he waited for Leclerc, he took out a copy of Molière's *Le Bourgeois gentilhomme* from the château's library to read, smoking incessantly. Outside, rain continued to patter.

Leclerc outlined his plan. Initially the project had been to approach Paris through Saint-Cyr and Versailles; but de Guillebon's forward units had already come upon some heavy enemy opposition in the area that day. So Leclerc moved his main objectives eastwards, dividing his division into three separate columns. Lieutenant Colonel Pierre de Langlade was to cross the Pont de Sèvres, enter Paris through the Porte de Saint-Cloud and head for the Arc de Triomphe. Meanwhile, the two major lines of attack would be launched by Colonel Dio towards the Porte d'Orléans and on to the Ecole Militaire and the Eiffel Tower; and by Colonel Pierre Billote through the Porte de Gentilly or the Porte d'Italie passing the Panthéon and on to the Prefecture of Police and von Choltitz's headquarters by the Tuileries – the same route Napoleon had followed during his 1815 campaign of the Hundred Days. This infuriated the Americans who had wanted to send their 4th Infantry Division along the same route. Now they had to move even further eastwards, for it had been agreed with Eisenhower in Algeria that the French would enter Paris first – whenever that late moment would be decided by Allied command. But the Second World War, if made up essentially of military movement, was no longer determined by the strategic decisions of army commanders: international politics were becoming increasingly significant.

Telephone lines to Paris were, amazingly, still open. French troops, for example, could call up from a local café and tell parents, wives and lovers that they were on their way – several, in fact, would be killed on that last day, as their families waited. But information on the fast-moving political developments was scant. To make a scoop Charlie Collingwood of the American station, CBS, had recorded a false report on the 'liberation of Paris'; New York, San Francisco, Mexico City and London were celebrating the event forty-eight hours before it occurred

– much to the surprise of embattled Parisians, who picked up the news from the BBC.[*]

Two telegrams sent by de Gaulle to his government in Algiers – one from Rennes at 11 p.m. on Monday, 21 August, and a second from Chartres at 1 p.m., Wednesday, 23 August[61] – suggest what limited information de Gaulle had on the situation in Paris. 'The French police have disappeared,' he notes, and 'the Vichy administration is impotent.' The population has begun 'to pillage food stocks and shops'. 'The Germans continue to hold the points that interest them.' He seems only to have learnt about an attempted ceasefire on Tuesday, forty-eight hours after it had been declared – he did not approve of it. His main concern was the confusion in the Allied armies after 'the major part of their forces have lost time in the region of Falaise–Argentan': de Gaulle showed no interest in the closing of the Falaise Pocket – any more, it must be said, than have most historians of the Liberation of Paris. Yet the two events were closely linked.

Concerning the politics of Liberation, on the other hand, de Gaulle showed his true genius. 'France', de Gaulle told a young FFI commander while at Rambouillet, 'is a country which continues, not a country which begins.'[62] That was typical of de Gaulle and his concern for 'legitimacy'. But it was also Talleyrand writing 131 years earlier, at the close of the Napoleonic wars. De Gaulle undoubtedly knew the passage: 'A legitimate government,' Talleyrand had written in 1813, 'whether it is monarchical or republican, hereditary or elective, aristocratic or democratic, is always the one whose existence, form and mode of action are consolidated and consecrated by a long succession of years, and I would even say by prescription of the centuries.'[63]

So it could be republican, hereditary or democratic, as long as it was consolidated by 'a long succession of years'. France for de Gaulle was Joan of Arc, the Revolution and the 'heroic' period of the Third Republic, 'Clemenceau's Republic'; de Gaulle found nothing contradictory in this, just as long as it was 'authentic', as Sartre might have said. But Sartre lived for the moment; de Gaulle epitomized Talleyrand's long succession of years.

If France had a 'tradition of revolution', she had also established, over the years, customs for resolving them, of recreating 'legitimate' government. Talleyrand himself had recalled what remained of the Senate to declare Louis XVIII king in 1814. Ledru-Rollin had declared the Second Republic from a window of the Hôtel de Ville by popular acclamation

[*] Almost exactly the same comic episode had happened in 1918. Much to the embarrassment of President Woodrow Wilson, New York and Washington celebrated the Armistice in the week before it was signed.

in 1848. Jules Ferry, temporary head of government, had united the mayors of Paris's arrondissements to inaugurate the Third Republic, and then announced it by popular acclamation, like Ledru-Rollin, from the same window of the Hôtel de Ville in 1870. Thus 'legitimacy' had come to embody several things – popular acclamation, the recalling of a parliamentary chamber – and particular places had begun to exert an importance: Paris had come to have priority over the provinces, and in Paris one building in particular had primary significance, the Hôtel de Ville.

De Gaulle claimed in his memoirs, written ten years after the event, that he had restrained the forces of so-called 'popular' government which, within France, had been progressively eliminating competitors in order to establish the 'dictatorship of the proletariat'. Obviously he was referring to the Communists. At the time, it certainly looked as if the Communists were preparing for a takeover. As Claude Bourdet of Henri Frenay's southern movement 'Combat' – totally marginalized by the Communists – put it, the Communists had not advanced 'to the banks of the Rubicon in order to go fishing'.

But de Gaulle in his memoirs was making out his opposition to Communism to be more cut-and-dried than it was; in the summer of 1944 he was not beyond appealing to 'popular' forces himself. Just before leaving Algiers, he had outlined a 'Directive to Resisters' which, for all its vehemence, sounded like a statement from Tollet's Paris Committee: he recommended 'initiating strikes', 'taking hostages' and 'preventing the enemy from retreating with personnel and *matériel*' – though 'once the Allied forces have arrived' people should 'immediately return to work and re-establish order'. He was totally opposed to any kind of ceasefire between resisters and the Germans, even though it would be a policy actively pursued for several days by his own Delegation in Paris; de Gaulle in this case supported the Communists. Moreover, de Gaulle had his ambassador in Moscow, Roger Garreau, who kept up a constant dialogue with the General Secretary of the French Communist Party, Maurice Thorez.

'Listen to Maurice Thorez speak on Radio Moscow every Thursday at 8 p.m.,' announced *L'Humanité* in every issue – an exhortation that often sounds as if it came from General de Gaulle himself. His ambiguous relationship with the Communists, *frères ennemis* in summer 1944, would remain a mark of his long political career. It was, indeed, one of the most durable features of post-war French party politics, one of the great *non-dits* of history.[64]

The basic reason for the loveless match was that in the summer of 1944 de Gaulle was confronting other competing claims for 'legitimacy' – those of Vichy France. By August 1944 this central question of legitimacy involved a contest between three different parties: the Gaullists, who had already set up France's Provisional Government in Algiers and were now moving fast into metropolitan France; the Communists, who controlled virtually the whole of the interior Resistance; and, against all expectation, the men of Vichy who were looking belatedly for a way of changing sides. The Vichyites had a few cards to play, the most important of all being the American government. There was, for instance, Admiral Leahy, Roosevelt's chief foreign policy adviser, who still regarded Vichy as the legal government of France.

The result was some complicated manoeuvring in the ten days that preceded the insurrection of 19 August. The first move was played by Laval and the Vichyites on 10 August: they hoped they could set up a parliamentary mechanism in Paris that would preserve their authority while the Germans retreated and the Americans advanced. The second move was that of the Gaullists who, in the early hours of 19 August, jumped the gun on the Communists by leading an insurrection of their own. Once they had all the local government offices under control they wanted the insurrection to stop, and there they would sit until the Allies arrived. However, to stop the insurrection there would have to be a ceasefire with the enemy, the remaining German local authorities. Why not simply ignore Hitler, argued de Gaulle's representatives, recognize reality and peacefully negotiate a local surrender with the Allies? Nordling, the Swedish Consul General, acted as mediator and the 'ceasefire' was declared on Sunday, 20 August. The third contestants in the game, the Communist Resistance, had nothing to win by it. They continued the fight with the 'Hitlerites' on Sunday, and on Monday, 21 August, carried their insurrection one step further with the so-called 'Day of the Barricades'.

Paris was in another world from Warsaw. In Paris it was conceivable that the Communists could be outmanoeuvred. For the Home Army in Warsaw this looked less and less likely. In Paris German authorities could be found who would consider handing Paris over to the approaching Western armies; no German authority in Warsaw would for a second think of handing Warsaw over to the Red Army. Finally, the citizens of Paris did have their own authorities – some of them not very attractive – while in Warsaw even underground civilian authority had virtually ceased to exist by late August 1944. Parisians had a choice, and the room for manoeuvre; Varsovians simply faced annihilation. That, in a nutshell, was the great difference that would develop between the 'Eastern' and 'Western' blocs of Europe – the two great post-war entities that did not even exist before the Second World War.

The first of the manoeuvres was, then, that of the Vichyites. The men of Vichy could not look beyond a national frontier, but they knew their French history. First among them was Pétain who, incredibly, revived his old project of making de Gaulle his 'heir'. The idea can be traced back to Admiral Gabriel Auphan, who had been Darlan's *chef de cabinet*. Darlan had left for North Africa in November 1942 with the idea of setting up a separate Pétainist regime under the protection of the Americans, one which would exclude de Gaulle; that Christmas Eve he was assassinated for his pains. Auphan had also wanted to exclude de Gaulle from Allied sponsor-ship; in the same November, 1942, he started pressing Pétain himself to leave for Algeria; but the old hero of Verdun suffered from incontinence – there was no question of putting him on a plane. By 1943, following Hitler's takeover of the Unoccupied Zone, Pétain was under constant German surveillance. That November, fearing for his own life, he devised a project for his succession: the parliamentary chambers of 1940 would be reconvoked and a temporary executive, a 'college', of seven leading person-alities would designate Pétain's heir. There was an element of Talleyrand in Pétain. After the Allied invasion of Normandy it became clear who the heir would be: de Gaulle. 'I had never wanted to shoot de Gaulle,' confided Pétain to Admiral Auphan on 11 August and sent him off to Clermont-Ferrand with the mission of contacting his former subordinate. 'I am ready to efface myself,' he remarked obscurely in his appeal to de Gaulle. What did he mean? That he was going to resign? Or – more like Pétain – play ceremonial president until the chance of intrigue with the Americans arose? 'Let us not break with legality, let us not shatter legitimacy,' he went on. 'Let us avoid a revolution.' De Gaulle never replied. On Sunday, 20 August, the Germans ordered Pétain to leave Vichy for Germany.[65]

Laval did not limit himself to words. His own attempt at a new 'legit-imacy' imitated both Talleyrand in 1814 and Jules Ferry in 1870. After a desperate effort to get Pétain to take refuge in Eisenhower's headquarters, he arrived on 10 August in Paris where, in an assembly of the arrondisse-ment mayors, he formally recalled the old Parliament of 1940. Not surpris-ingly, the few deputies in town remained as silent as oysters. So Laval, before dawn the next morning, drove to Nancy to obtain the release of Edouard Herriot; the Nazis had locked up this prestigious former President of the Chamber in a lunatic asylum. Herriot did accompany Laval in his car back to Paris, but he refused to go along with Laval's plan. The Nazi collaborationists in Paris would never let Laval become head of an Allied-sponsored government. Nor would Hitler. He had Herriot immediately arrested and carted off to a prison in Potsdam (where he was eventually released by the Red Army in April 1945).

The atmosphere in the Hôtel Matignon, the Prime Minister's official residence in Rue de Varenne, is well conveyed in Nordling's memoirs, which record the last meeting in Paris of the Vichy government on the night of 15 August: 'The building was plunged in darkness as if devoid of all life. I met a few ushers groping around in the corridors with the aid of candles. I had an electric torch. After a while I bumped into Laval in an antechamber; he also had a torch. He led me to his office where an oil lamp flickered.' Two nights later, again using his electric torch, Laval descended the great stairway to the courtyard where his black Hotchkiss, escorted by Germans, waited to take him east to Belfort. Before boarding he embraced his daughter, Josée, for a long while. The car started moving off, then stopped. Laval jumped out. 'You again,' said Josée. He took his daughter in his arms once more, then left. The next time she saw him, one year later, he was on trial in Paris for his life.[66]

De Gaulle commented on Laval's last claim to legitimacy: 'He had, in the cataclysm, developed a feeling for the misfortune of his country but had also seized the occasion to grab the reins of power. He then used his vast abilities to deal with whoever came along . . . Laval had played. He had lost.'[67]

In the Château de Rambouillet late on Wednesday evening, 23 August, after listening to Leclerc's plan of attack, a curious team turned up in de Gaulle's office. It was led by Rolf Nordling, brother of the Swedish Consul who now lay in a hospital having suffered a heart attack. There was Alexandre de Saint-Phalle, who was Parodi's financial consultant; Jean Laurent of the Bank of Indochina, whom de Gaulle remembered as a *chef de cabinet* during his brief tenure in the War Ministry in June 1940; and then there was Baron Poch-Pastor, who nobody to this day has managed entirely to fathom out. He was an Austrian, he worked as an aide-de-camp for von Choltitz, he was certainly employed by the Abwehr, German military intelligence in Paris; but it is quite possible that he acted as a double agent.

The mission had been initiated by Raoul Nordling when von Choltitz, a glass of whisky in his hand, started screaming at him that the 'ceasefire' had failed. Von Choltitz threatened to blow up all Paris. Nordling had suggested gently that there was an alternative (the sort of word one could never use in Warsaw): the French Resistance was a chaotic mixture of different parties and factions; only one man could create order out of it, General Charles de Gaulle. Why not put a small party together to cross the lines and fetch de Gaulle? Von Choltitz refused to give his formal approval, but Nordling by now knew how his mind wavered. He went back to his consulate to organize his team. It was at this moment that he fell on his couch in agony; he made an appeal to his brother. Rolf Nordling and his four* strange colleagues set off from Paris on Tuesday afternoon.

Only a historian can travel in the opposite direction from Rolf Nordling's team, from the Château de Rambouillet on the Western Front back to Paris. But in that trip of thirty miles could be noticed an increase in the will to compromise. Rambouillet was in the world of battle; the place was governed by a spirit of absolutes. Paris was a more extraordinary place. An insurrection was going on, at times murderous. But there was popular festival in the streets. And, most remarkably, enemies were talking to one another.

During the insurrection, Gaullists and Communists were daggers drawn over who commanded what and how to deal with von Choltitz's Germans. But an accord between them had been drawn up immediately after Charles Tillon, on the eve of the long weekend, had launched his order for a 'general strike'. Alexandre Parodi outlined its terms in a telegram he sent to Algiers on Friday, 11 August – interestingly enough, the same day de Gaulle composed his snarling, populist 'Directive to Resisters'.

Parodi's terms read like the sort of agreement on 'zones of influence' which Churchill and Stalin would draw up three months later, an accord between distrustful foreign powers; only here, the subject at issue was not nations, continents and peninsulas, but streets and buildings in a town, the capital of France.

'The governmental sector, liberated by force,' read Parodi's document, 'will be directly under the orders of the government' – that is the prefects and state councillors nominated by de Gaulle. 'The non-governmental sector shall be liberated by the Forces Françaises de l'Intérieur [FFI], and put at the disposal of the Paris Committee of Liberation' – that is, the Communists. The forces designated for the 'liberation of the capital' were defined with mathematical precision: Garde Républicaine and Gendarmerie (Gaullist) – three quarters; Milices Patriotiques and FFI (Communist directed): one quarter. 'Mixed detachments' were to be organized for the takeover of buildings of 'symbolic character'. The Prefecture of Police was to be taken over by the 'police themselves' and 'elements of the Resistance'.[68]

---

* 'Bobby' Bender, who was definitely a German double agent and played a vital role in Raoul Nordling's political circle at Paris, was one of the team. He is not mentioned in de Gaulle's memoirs. Before eventually finding de Gaulle at Rambouillet, the group had visited General Bradley's headquarters. It was as a result of this visit that Bradley, on Wednesday, the 23rd, ordered the American 4th Infantry Division to join Leclerc in the advance on Paris.

Of course, come Saturday, 19 August, there was a chaotic, and sometimes vicious, race for power. But agreements had been formally drawn up before the insurrection had begun: in absolute contrast to Warsaw.

The ceasefire that officially began that night showed the same kind of mixture of compromise and anarchy. Nordling swears that the initiative came from a telephone call he received that Saturday evening from the Gaullist-controlled Prefecture of Police. The Gaullists have maintained ever since that the negotiated ceasefire was a product of Nordling's mind. Whatever the case, Parisians on Sunday afternoon were exposed to the extraordinary sight of lorries in which unarmed German soldiers stood next to Frenchmen wearing tricolour armbands proclaiming on loudspeakers that 'the Provisional Government of the French Republic and the National Council of the Resistance asks you to suspend your fire against the occupier until his evacuation of Paris'[69] – a scene unimaginable in Warsaw. In fact more people were killed in gunfights that Sunday than on Saturday; the Communists never accepted the ceasefire. In the Prefecture that afternoon there was an angry debate during a formal session of the National Committee of Resistance (now chaired by the history professor, Georges Bidault). The Gaullist Alexandre de Saint-Phalle accused the Communists of wanting to cover their hands 'with the blood of millions of innocent Parisians'. It was then that Colonel Rol riposted that '*Paris vaut bien 200 000 morts!*'

The barricades went up. A new free press came out on Monday morning, universally calling for the 'Battle of Paris' to continue. *L'Humanité* repeated Colonel Rol's new slogan, which was now plastered all over the walls of Paris: '*A chacun son Boche!*'[*]

Perhaps the Gaullists in Paris had secretly initiated the ceasefire. They had every reason to do so. After the seizure of the Prefecture they started installing their men at the ministries and in other public buildings. The young FFI officer, Yvon Morandet, after getting lost on his bicycle in the side streets of the 7e arrondissement, eventually found his way on Monday afternoon to the Hôtel Matignon. He knocked on the high green gates, which were opened by one of Laval's black-uniformed guards. He asked to see the commander. Another black-uniformed officer stepped forward and Morandet fearlessly declared, 'In the name of the Provisional Government of the French Republic I take possession of this building.' The commander politely bowed and then took him round the sights of the palace, including Laval's bathroom.[70]

---

[*] Meaning roughly that each Parisian should pick a German to shoot, which, given the numbers involved, would not have been an easy task.

On Tuesday afternoon the first Conseil des Ministres, made up of General Secretaries whom de Gaulle had previously named, took place in Matignon. Gaullist behaviour inside Paris is thus easily explained. If the takeover was that easy then, effectively, why fight?

De Gaulle had only got news of the ceasefire on Monday, while he was on his speaking tour. It made on him a 'disagreeable impression', as he later put it himself. How could he make good the claim that Paris was liberating herself? How could he clear the name of that crucial 'governmental force', the police of Paris? How could he explain the silence of the elites? How, in a word, could he establish in the eyes of the Allies and enemy the legitimacy of French sovereignty without a fight? De Gaulle was more than ever pressed to send Leclerc's force into Paris – even, as he put it in a plea to Eisenhower that day, 'if it does lead to a few combats and some destruction inside the town'.[71]

Inside Paris the Gaullists had suffered a serious setback. On Sunday afternoon, during the ceasefire, German troops arrested both Parodi and his assistant, Emile Laffon, their car filled with machine-guns and rifles. The delighted German officer of military justice at Saint-Cloud asked von Choltitz if he should have these 'ministers of de Gaulle's government' immediately shot. Instead, von Choltitz ordered that they be brought round to the Hôtel Meurice. There, in front of Nordling, direct negotiations for a prolongation of the 'ceasefire' between de Gaulle's chief representative in Paris and the German commander were undertaken. Parodi and his assistant were promptly released.

'You are a lucky man!' remarked de Gaulle on Wednesday night as he bid farewell to Leclerc. He then sent a note to Charles Luizet, his Prefect of Police in Paris. 'Tomorrow is going to be decisive in the way that we want. When I arrive I will go immediately to "the centre". We'll organize the rest with Quartus [one of Parodi's many pseudonyms] and with you.'[72]

In fact, de Gaulle did not leave the Château de Rambouillet until three o'clock, Friday afternoon. Leclerc on Thursday had run into trouble.

What did de Gaulle mean by 'the centre'? The Hôtel de Ville, where the regimes of the past had been proclaimed? The Prefecture of Police, controlled by his own 'governmental force'? Hôtel Matignon, where the Council of Ministers had already been organized? None of these. De Gaulle was referring to the Ministry of War on Rue Saint-Dominique.

The Ministry of War? That inconspicuous place? He explained his choice to Louis Joxe, another history professor who was a member of his Provisional Government. Well, said de Gaulle, there is a tendency to forget that the war hasn't finished yet. But more significantly, 'The Ministry of War, it's Clemenceau.'[73]

This was de Gaulle's singular claim to legitimacy, the great continuity consecrated by the succession of years: it lay between his own solitary march from Bordeaux to London, to Brazzaville, to Algiers, to the Château de Rambouillet and to Paris – and the defiance in the last year of the First World War of the old French Prime Minister, Georges Clemenceau.

13 National sovereignty and King Charles

Eisenhower believed that the cause of Leclerc's delay was that his troops were celebrating too much with the French crowds that accompanied them. The thought also crossed Montgomery's mind. On the slow progress of the *Deuxième DB* he wrote, in true Monty style: 'they received such a tumultuous welcome from the population that most of the men became very drunk and nothing happened for the rest of the day.' On Friday, 25 August, he cabled Brooke, inappropriately in Italy at the time, suggesting that 'no celebrations are held in LONDON'.[74]

It was a wicked remark, though it should be put in the context of the isolation in which Montgomery found himself during this critical week when politics, throughout Europe, overtook military considerations. Montgomery had lost telephone contact with his own American subordinates.

The reason why Leclerc made slow progress on that grey, misty Thursday, 24 August, was that the Germans were putting up stiff resistance. Most of the huge anti-aircraft guns in the city had been transferred to the southern suburbs to meet the attack. At Toussus-le-Noble, south of Versailles, one column of Leclerc's tanks and half-tracks was blown apart in a few seconds. There was severe fighting in the village of Savigny-sur-Orge. Men who had travelled all the way from Equatorial Africa were losing their lives only ten miles from Paris. It was at Savigny, on a route descending a steep hill, that the first of Leclerc's soldiers noticed through the smoke something rising into the sky that 'hit us like an electric current': the Eiffel Tower. It was like arriving before the walls of Jericho.

But some of those walls were tough to penetrate. A major battle developed outside the prison of Fresnes; the prison had been emptied of French inmates and the German military defaulters who remained were ordered to man the great guns now put at their disposal. Leclerc's main line of attack was thus halted. One can only imagine what would have happened if the municipal council of Paris had not, in the month the Treaty of

Versailles was signed, May 1919, ordered the demolition of the fortified walls around Paris. In the wisdom of the day it was thought, after the experience of the First World War, that fortifications served nothing. The Second World War had proved otherwise. In the case of Paris, Hitler would have undoubtedly had his way and the city would have been defended, by the enemy, to the last man. As de Gaulle had put it to Leclerc the night before, 'You are a lucky man!'

But Leclerc on Thursday evening was getting desperate.

Among his forces was a red-bearded captain of the Régiment du Marche du Tchad, who had never seen France before August. But like many colonials, he was more French than the French; and if he could not be described as more patriotic than de Gaulle, he was at least his equal. He drove an American jeep that he called – its name was written in large capitals on the windscreen – 'Mort aux cons' ('Death to cunts'). 'What are you doing here?' demanded his commander, General Leclerc, when he noticed Captain Dronne at the back of the line struggling around Fresnes. Dronne murmured that, against his will, he had been ordered to retreat. 'Dronne, you know well that you should never obey absurd orders!' Pointing his stick towards the front he shouted, 'You clear off straight for Paris, the heart of Paris. Don't bother about the Germans. You just go straight through, that's all. Tell the Parisians to hold on. We'll be there tomorrow.'[75]

Dronne put together a small detachment of three tanks and half a dozen half-tracks and just drove. He entered Paris by the Porte d'Italie, which he found unguarded, descended the Avenue d'Italie with tanks and half-tracks roaring behind him, reached the quays, passed the cathedral of Notre Dame and, at precisely 9.23 p.m., 24 August, parked his jeep outside the Hôtel de Ville. Inside he found Georges Bidault. There was a growling of tank engines outside. Windows on the quaysides were thrown open; telephones started ringing throughout the city. Within half an hour every bell of every church in Paris was pealing.

At the Hôtel Meurice, von Choltitz, who was having a miserable staff dinner party at the time, returned to his office and telephoned Model's underground headquarters at Margival. Model's chief of staff, Lieutenant General Hans Speidel, who had not seen the light of day in more than a week, answered. 'Good evening, Speidel,' said von Choltitz, 'I have a surprise for you.' He held his receiver to the window. 'Do you hear?' 'Yes,' replied Speidel just as coldly, 'that is the sound of bells, is it not?' Von Choltitz asked Speidel to protect his wife and children, who lived in Baden-Baden, then bid him adieu.[76]

Von Choltitz was taken prisoner the following morning after a short skirmish outside his hotel. Nordling, who had recovered from his heart attack, played a final role as broker. '*Sprechen Sie deutsch?*' asked the first haggard-looking Frenchman to burst into the General's office. 'Probably better than you do,' answered von Choltitz. He was escorted to the Prefecture where, in a billiard room, a typed-up surrender document was presented to him by General Leclerc. While von Choltitz signed his name, Colonel Rol, the Communist leader, came into the room and insisted that he sign too. There was a fairly heated argument between Leclerc and several other Communists present; but Rol eventually signed – above Leclerc's name.

'I shall leave Rambouillet at 1500 hours,' telegrammed de Gaulle to Leclerc's personal secretary at 1.45 p.m. that same Friday. 'First destination: Gare Montparnasse, where I count on meeting you. My itinerary will be: Porte d'Orléans, Avenue d'Orléans, Avenue du Maine, Rue du Départ, Hall de la Gare Montparnasse. Please inform General Leclerc.'[77] So there had been a slight change in plan since Wednesday night. Gare Montparnasse was where Leclerc had set up his command post. 'A railway station!' exclaimed de Gaulle one week later; he did not think it the best stage of entry, right by the departure platform. 'What an idea! Well, we've seen everything.'[78]

Huge crowds turned out to welcome de Gaulle, stretching all the way from the Porte d'Orléans to the Hôtel de Ville, for that is where everyone was expecting de Gaulle to be heading. Georges Bidault with his National Council of Resistance and Tollet's Paris Committee of Liberation were eagerly awaiting him there. The Hôtel de Ville was traditionally the place where the Republic was declared before the cheering people of Paris.

But de Gaulle turned off the road at the Avenue du Maine and headed for the railway station. Photographs, only published fifty years later, show de Gaulle with a pair of spectacles seated at a wooden table inspecting the surrender document. He points at the foot of the page where there is this signature, 'Rol'. Leclerc, with a serious look on his face, is attempting to explain. Then there is a photograph of de Gaulle standing before Rol himself, who is still wearing his black beret. According to de Gaulle's memoirs he was congratulating both men.

He did not, however, then go to the Hôtel de Ville; he headed for 'the centre', the Ministry of War. There he was astonished to find everything as he had left it in June 1940 when he had served briefly as Under-Secretary of State – it was one of those signs of continuity that de Gaulle liked so much. Parodi came in and pleaded for him to go to the Hôtel de Ville. De Gaulle did leave, but not for the Hôtel de Ville: he drove over to the Prefecture of Police where he inspected his '*force gouvernementale*', noting their 'joy and pride'.

Thus the centre of government was established in the war ministry and the legitimacy of the police force recognized. Only then, almost at night-fall, did he go on foot to the Hôtel de Ville.

Georges Bidault and André Tollet were waiting for him at the foot of the stairs. A group of resisters, tears pouring down their cheeks, presented arms. There was a huge crowd in the square, not neatly divided up as it had been for Pétain's day in Paris. There could be no doubt about their enthusiasm. But Bidault found the General cold.

In the *salon* of the first floor, de Gaulle made his speech: '*Paris. Paris outragé, Paris brisé, Paris martyrisé, mais Paris*' — and there is a slight move in his body — '*libéré!*' Bidault's face gradually formed a grimace.

When the speech was finished, Bidault asked de Gaulle, 'General, we ask you here, in the name of the French Resistance, solemnly to proclaim the Republic before the assembled people.' 'But the Republic has never ceased to exist,' replied de Gaulle. He then listed all the institutions that had kept it going: Free France, Fighting France, the French Committee of National Liberation — not a word on the National Council of Resistance. 'I myself am the President of the Government of the Republic. Why should I now proclaim it?' He went over to the window and raised his arms. Cheers roared out from below. That, claimed de Gaulle, was the proof.

There was still fighting going on. Strong points like the Senate and the Ecole Militaire did not surrender until that evening. There was shooting from rooftops. De Gaulle himself had to avoid a small battle around the Eglise Saint-Sulpice when he first headed to the Ministry of War. He returned there that night.

For de Gaulle Paris would not be liberated until he made a formal entry at the Arc de Triomphe. He had outlined the plan to Parodi.

Traditionally, the kings of France had entered from the north at the Porte Saint-Denis, thus following the route that Saint Denis is supposed to have walked, with his decapitated head under his arm, in AD 250. This was the route that Louis XVIII had taken on the two occasions of his restoration, in 1814 and 1815. It was the route of sainthood and Parisian legitimacy, quite distinct from the one to the west which the usurper, Napoleon I, designated for his new empress in 1810: through the Barrière de l'Etoile (future site of the Arc de Triomphe) and down the Champs Elysées. The first king to take this western route was Louis XVIII's ultra-royalist brother, Charles X, at the time of his accession in 1824. He rode in on horseback, say contemporary reports, to the acclaim 'of every class of the people'.[79]

King Charles? De Gaulle was a defender of the Republic. Napoleon? He was not one of de Gaulle's heroes. De Gaulle had a great literary and dramatic sense; it has been argued that his model was Victor Hugo, defender of Republican liberties, whose catafalque was carried in 1885, before a seething crowd, to the Panthéon. 'From the Etoile to the Panthéon, Victor Hugo, escorted by all, advanced,' wrote Maurice Barrès in a passage de Gaulle could probably cite by heart. 'From the pride of France he went to the heart of France.' Charles Péguy, another of de Gaulle's literary heroes, similarly describes this route. But de Gaulle was heading not for the Panthéon, but Notre Dame Cathedral – exactly the route of King Charles.[80]

There was probably no more memorable day in the history of Paris than de Gaulle's entry on that sunny Saturday afternoon, 26 August 1944. The people were ecstatic. The newsreels show men and women, hands to their faces with emotion. Witnesses, sixty years after the event, tell the story with tears welling up in their eyes. The only comparable occasions were the entry of Henri IV, at the end of the Wars of Religion in March 1594, and Armistice Day 1918, when celebrations lasted over a week.

At the Arc de Triomphe de Gaulle shook hands with members of his government, Bidault's Council, Tollet's Committee and Leclerc's staff; he saluted the Regiment of Chad as they passed, standing in their vehicles and staring at the arch 'as if a dream were being realized'. De Gaulle then lit the flame to the Unknown Warrior, which had been extinguished for four years. Then the procession began.

There was some shooting. At the Rue de Rivoli the crowds had to fling themselves to the ground as somebody began firing from the roof of the Hôtel Meurice. But the worst case occurred in the Cathedral. De Gaulle was just about to enter the west door when a machine-gun started firing from one of the towers. Then, as one contemporary newspaper report described it, 'within the interior of the Cathedral, hidden in the gallery and the rood-loft, other assassins started firing on the pious assembly.' A manhunt was pursued through the high galleries of the cathedral as members of the congregation sang the Magnificat and a choir of nuns sang 'Ave Maria'. Two men, according to this report, were arrested; but their identity has never to this day been revealed. De Gaulle entered after the shooting had ended. The thanksgiving service began.[81]

Newsreel shows the gun fight outside the Cathedral. The crowd is in panic, while de Gaulle stands majestically alone with a cigarette in his hand. The footage was played repeatedly in German cinemas throughout that autumn to demonstrate what chaos Allied 'liberation' brought to ordinary citizens.

But the panic was momentary. Paris in late August was *en fête*. As de Gaulle was to remind the Americans, 'The plebiscite has been held.' That phrase, too, had its traditions.

14 East is East, and West is . . .

According to Sartre and several other witnesses, on the streets of Paris that late August one could often hear people singing 'Madelon'. The song was about a barmaid, and many versions of it had been invented since it was first composed in 1913 by a man called Bach – some of them gross. It had a merry, marching swing. It was the song the soldiers sang on their way to Verdun in 1916. Many of the Allies were singing it in 1918. It became the song of the Armistice, as popular as the *Marseillaise*. 'Madelon' was revived in the summer of 1944.

But another song began to spread at the time of the Liberation. It is about a girl called 'Marjolaine' and it, too, had a merry marching rhythm. Its lyrics, however, are haunting. No woman in France is called 'Marjolaine'; it is a *herbe de cuisine* that softly rhymes with 'Madelon'. As the song develops one asks oneself, does Marjolaine exist or is she just a dream?

The song begins with an unknown young man, *un inconnu*, playing a guitar on a foggy street and singing a song, which his two companions repeat. The song *they* sing is about this dreamlike Marjolaine: '*Marjolaine, ma si jolie, Marjolaine . . .*' Spring is flowering; I was a soldier but today I have returned to you. You said you would wait; I had promised to return. I left as a child; but I am now a man. '*Marjolaine, ma si jolie, Marjolaine . . .*' I did not lie. I was a soldier then; today, I'm back.

Back to what? Everything has changed. 'Nothing is the same, and in the streets / Apart from the sky I can recognize nothing.'

An *inconnu*, with his guitar, disappears into the fog. He and his companions; they have gone carrying away with them this song . . . And it ends with just the merry marching tune playing, '*Marjolaine, ma si jolie, Marjolaine . . .*', without the words.

Paris was saved. But many Parisians knew that in northern and western France there were cities with streets and neighbourhoods, even whole townships, where 'apart from the sky' nothing was recognizable: Caen, Cherbourg, Alençon, Brest and later, within a fortnight of Paris's Liberation, Le Havre. And so it would go on that autumn, eastwards. For many the war ended with nothing, nothing but the sky. There were no words for that sort of thing.

★

'Marjolaine' brought home the contrast – of which most Parisians were only too conscious – between their city and the devastation to the north, on the coastal plain. But in August 1944 there had grown up another even wider disparity in ruin and war experience, of which hardly anyone at the time was aware: between 'Eastern' and 'Western' Europe. The frontier between the two followed no historical tradition and it was a total contradiction of natural geography. Yet the difference was there all right; it could be neatly summed up in the contrast between the 'Western' philosophy of Jean-Paul Sartre and the 'Eastern' poetry of Czesław Miłosz.

On 24 August 1945, at the first anniversary of Paris's Liberation, Sartre published a piece in the review *Clarté*. He spoke characteristically of choice, of ceremony and of history, and compared 1944 with the revolutionary upheaval of 1789. Many did that. What was more important about the article – and it was again typical of the younger Sartre – was his return to his 1944 theme of festivity, a terrifying kind of festivity but one that was at the base, Sartre argued, of human freedom.

Looking back one year, he said that that 'festive air has not left the city'; the streets were 'still decked out in their Sunday best'. What exactly was being celebrated? he asked himself: 'I realize that it is mankind and its powers.'

'Mankind and its powers' was of intense interest to Sartre. In August 1945, as Paris celebrated its anniversary, two atomic bombs were dropped on Japan. Sartre regarded the atomic bomb as 'the negation of mankind'. Not only did it provide the means of destroying all mankind, it also rendered void the main qualities of mankind – courage, patience, intelligence, initiative. The forces of the Liberation were entirely different, claimed Sartre; they were a fundamentally *human* struggle against the blind forces of a German machine. Here was the spirit of Liberation – a very French idea, casting resisters as men in revolutionary Phrygian bonnets: they had been, in that August of 1944, 'intoxicated as they felt the freedom and the lightness of their own movements'. They 'exercised freedom for themselves and for every French person'.

What a disaster it would be, thought Sartre, if that spirit of festival in the Liberation were lost. The significance of the French struggle was not in its power of destruction, which was negligible compared to the armies in Normandy, but in the power of choice it offered. And that had been the point of the French experience throughout the war: every man and woman there had been faced, since June 1940, with a terrible choice. The Liberation brought it to a climax; it was a positive affirmation of human, as opposed to mechanical, power.[82]

★

Czesław Miłosz remembered the news of the atomic bombing of Japan. Unlike Sartre he did not think this spelled the beginning of a new inhuman era; that had already begun in 1939. Miłosz had witnessed the 'Apocalypse' with his own eyes: it had been achieved with ordinary guns and bombs. In Miłosz's corner of Europe 'apocalypse was routine'. The bombing of Hiroshima and Nagasaki taught him nothing new. There was no anguishing question of choice in his poetry and essays: just remember, write it down, the deed, the date. And yet, he was as much concerned about the human qualities of life, as opposed to mechanical armed power, as Sartre. He was as much the individualist as was Sartre at this date.

Miłosz was in Cracow when the bombs went off in Japan. He was working on a film – 'anxious', he said, 'to preserve in a concrete form the vision of things newly seen' – about a modern Robinson Crusoe. The original Robinson Crusoe had been trapped 'on a scrap of land not yet touched by the power of mind capable of transforming matter'. Miłosz's Crusoe, on the other hand, was trapped 'as a result of the use of the power of mind over matter for suicidal aims'.*

This 'power of the mind' troubled Miłosz. In the twentieth century it had become too self-centred. Philosophy had come to focus solely on the mind. Far from making man more human, it had led him to become self-obsessive and to take himself for a god. The result was the two ideological poisons of the century, Nazism and Communism. The Nazis bowed down to the god of human will; the Communists to their icon of human history. Both were inhumane.

This 'power of the mind' was also at the origin of the problem Miłosz had with 'the renaissance in France of German philosophy, particularly that of Hegel via Sartre'. One needed to be more modest, use one's eyes, preserve the concrete in the vision of things. Choice and freedom were hardly the issue for Miłosz. Just observe, said Miłosz, and record the details, the deed, the date; be a poet, not a philosopher.

In Paris, Sartre could talk about terrible festival and the power of men to liberate themselves. In Poland, Miłosz could not.

Three months before Hiroshima, Miłosz, accompanied by his philosopher friend, Jerzy Andrzejewski, who was by now an active Communist, revisited Warsaw. The war in Europe was just coming to a conclusion. 'We spent several hours in a once familiar part of the city,' he recalled.

---

* The Communist censors completely changed Miłosz's film script, which they thought 'asocial'. In place of a Polish 'Robinson Crusoe' they substituted a Soviet parachutist, hero of the Communist cause, who carried his great historical message to the surviving people of Warsaw. After this experience, Miłosz – again in contrast to Sartre – thought there was no future in cinema as a medium of art.

'Now we could not recognize it. We scaled a slope of red bricks and entered upon a fantastic moon-world. There was total silence.'[83]

In the month of August 1944 the experience of 'Eastern' and 'Western' Europe separated. The contrast between Paris and Warsaw is the most radical example; but it was a pattern repeated elsewhere. The division between 'Eastern' and 'Western' Europe had no historical roots – for most of what was becoming 'Eastern' had been 'Central Europe' before the war. Nor was the issue geographical: Warsaw lay on the same northern European plain as Paris.

Was the slope of red bricks in Warsaw any different from the corner where *un inconnu* sang to 'Marjolaine' and where only the sky was recognizable? Yes it was, and the difference lay in the way the armies moved. That movement, of course, went back to the outbreak of the war in 1939. But it was the anti-German forces that were taking the initiative now. And in the month of August 1944 this initiative suddenly turned political. Post-war Europe – unhistorical and blind to geography – was just beginning to appear.

London and Washington in autumn

1 London's 'doodlebugs'

During the three summer months that separated the D–Day landings from the Liberation of Paris there was heard, day and night, over southern England a grating and sinister growl of pilotless German planes; when their engines stopped they fell to the ground, causing immense destruction. Most of them were aimed at London, which is why the government authorities called the attacks and the counter-measures taken with AA guns and fighter aircraft the 'Battle of London'. But the term never caught on. Every child of 1940 would be able to recount the story of the 'Battle of Britain'. Every generation after the war knew the meaning of the German word *Blitz*. But by the winter of 1944–5, the expression the 'Battle of London' had already disappeared from folk memory. What people remembered was the weapon that was the cause of all the devastation: the 'flying bomb', the 'buzz bomb', the 'bumble bomb', the 'doodlebug'.

London, spreading out its suburban tentacles into Surrey, Kent, Essex and other counties to the north and west, offered a huge and tempting target to Hitler once the war had turned total.[1] Since 1942 substantial progress had been made on what would become known in the Führer's circle as the 'wonder' weapons: unleashed in vast numbers on the British capital they would turn the course of the war by their destructiveness and their effect on morale.

British intelligence was slow to penetrate the secret of Germany's wonder weapons; Lord Cherwell, Churchill's scientific adviser, thought it was all German bluff; the intelligence services were confused by the existence in Germany of not one, but several competing programmes. The first definite signal the British got was from a recorded conversation about rockets between two German generals taken prisoner in Tunisia on 22 March 1943 – their room had been bugged. Further prisoner interrogations and aerial reconnaissance unfolded a fuller picture.

Development of the German army's liquid fuel rocket, initially called the A-4 and designed at first to drop poison gas on London, was decisively checked by the RAF night bombing, in August 1943, of the Peenemünde experimental station on the Baltic. The programme was maintained, but huge investments both in labour and money were then poured into the development of alternative *Vergeltungswaffe*, or 'retaliation weapons' (the term itself indicating which way the war was turning). The Luftwaffe rushed through its project of a pilotless plane propelled by jet and launched by catapult from ramps – the *Vergeltungswaffe-1*, or V-1. These were the 'doodlebugs' that began to rumble over England one week after the Normandy landings. The army's rocket, now equipped with a one-ton explosive warhead, was not ready for firing until September; it thus became the V-2. The army also began work on a huge gun, with a barrel 150 yards long and a shell propelled by several powder charges as it passed through it: a modified version of the V-3, with two barrels of only 50 yards long, went into service in December 1944 and was fired not at London, as originally planned, but at Luxembourg. The German army did have one other wonder weapon up its sleeve, a four-stage solid-fuelled rocket, the V-4 or *Rheinbote* ('Rhine Messenger'). All fifty of them, launched on Antwerp in December 1944 and January 1945, missed their target: total casualties amounted to a crowded chicken coop, one dog and two wounded cows.[2]

Londoners were calling the V-1 the 'doodlebug' within hours of the first attack, at dawn on 13 June. The origins of the word remain obscure. A 'doodlesack' is slang for a bagpipe, and the idea that the missile's 'disagreeable splutter, like an aerial motor bicycle in bad running order',[3] could be related to the 'tootle' of a cheap bagpipe does not seem wholly out of place. Dr N. E. Odel of Clare College, Cambridge, wrote to *The Times* on 9 October to remind readers that a 'doodle-bug' was the word Canadian and American miners had been using for a magnetic prospecting instrument for the last twenty years – and that this colloquial term had been used by iron-ore prospectors in Sweden since the seventeenth century.

It was hardly a term of endearment. On the day Paris was liberated, 24 August, waves of doodlebugs roared across the Channel towards London. The experience of V-1s was terrifying, and Hitler was not entirely wrong in thinking that they could have a highly damaging effect on civilian morale. 'It is curious how many people are angry at Churchill,' remarked the American journalist, Richard Brown Baker, in his diary after the Prime Minister had spoken in the Commons, on 2 August, about the damage done. 'We seem to have forgotten the war in France and Italy, and are too occupied with this war on London,' commented another diarist.[4]

Nothing in London could be compared to the destruction of Warsaw or even to the movement of the armies around Paris and the subsequent euphoria of the Liberation. Jan Nowak, the Polish courier, had been shocked during his visit to London in early 1944 by British attitudes towards his country, and particularly the posturing of London's press. Poland, he noted, got a bad press 'from the right end of the spectrum, *The Times* and the popular conservative press of the Beaverbrook group, to the left, such periodicals as the *New Statesman* and the *Tribune*. The *Times* articles [were] most dangerous because of the influence the paper had on the political elite.' One day in early spring he was invited to the editorial lunch, which was held in the *Times* offices every Thursday. Sitting next to the editor, Robert Barrington-Ward, he had an opportunity to ask him about the articles by Professor E. H. Carr that proposed a division of Europe which would place Poland under Soviet control. 'You Poles', responded Barrington-Ward with a soothing smile, 'remind us of the Irish. You possess too long a historical memory . . . Russia is undergoing a tremendous revolution. For the moment there is no reason to disbelieve Stalin when he assures us that he wants a strong and independent Poland. You will see, my friend, that your fears are groundless.' In August and September, as Warsaw was being wiped clean from the map, there appeared in *The Times* a few articles, two or three paragraphs long, about the 'Rising'. True, information from Warsaw was difficult to acquire; but this was nevertheless surprising for such a well-informed newspaper as *The Times*. On 1 September readers were treated to a huge two-column article on 'Life in Lublin To-Day: Tasks for the New Polish Committee', written by 'Our Moscow Correspondent'. A monument, reported the correspondent, was being inaugurated as 'a reminder of Russian blood being spilt for Poland's freedom'; 'Every one with whom I talked . . . expressed profound longings for a united Poland'; and 'It is reported that the entire Home Army organization is submitting to General Żymierski's authority after hearing what kind of army he commands' – Żymierski's army was a part of the Red Army. *The Times* devoted half a column to the surrender, on 2 October, of Warsaw to the Nazis and printed with an illustration, two pages further on, a charity appeal for 'Russia Still Bleeds' – Russia did, but not for Poland.[5]

London, if it had a poor understanding of the disaster overtaking the eastern half of Europe, showed more curiosity in Paris. There were long reports in London's press on the Liberation, on de Gaulle, and much sympathy shown for the 'Resistance', always spelt with a capital 'R'. There was even, after Calais had been taken by the Canadians, a celebration of the 'Liberation of Dover' on the weekend of 30 September–1 October with the mayor's formal announcement on the public loudspeakers that four years of continuous German shelling on 'Hellfire Corner' (Dover, Folkestone, Deal and Ramsgate) had come to an end. As in Paris, the women put on their brightest dresses, people danced and sang in the streets; tradesmen's vans, lorries and children's perambulators carried the Union Jack, which also hung from every cinema, shop, pub and private home. Nothing like that was seen in London.

The doodlebugs continued to wail in. During the Blitz, German bombers had attacked at night. Doodlebugs, on the other hand, came in waves – sometimes every hour, day and night. It was impossible to sleep. Until August there was no warning, and even when klaxons were introduced they merely gave one time to run for a cupboard, a nearby stairwell or – which could be disastrous – simply to stand and watch. Because they landed at an angle the surface damage they caused was much greater than standard bombs of equivalent explosive power. Whole rows of houses could be wiped out; by mid-September it had been calculated that each V-1 crashing in the London area wrecked ten homes and damaged nearly 500 others in some degree.[6] On impact there would be a blinding flash, followed by a tall, sooty plume of smoke. A number of witnesses near where the bombs went off spoke of a curved ripple or a 'line' that rapidly 'expanded to about the size of a rainbow'; scientists of the day could not decide whether this was due to condensation of the humid London air or a mirage effect.[7]

There was a marked tendency for the bombs to fall short of London's centre. Thus Croydon was the worst hit area, followed by Wandsworth, then Lewisham and Woolwich. Residents in a swath of territory across Sussex and Kent – so called 'Bomb Alley' – also suffered serious casualties. Part of this was due to a malfunctioning of the missiles, part to their destruction by British fighters and anti-aircraft guns, and part to the 'Deceptionists' among the British Secret Service who employed German double agents in Britain to send out deliberately misleading information about the targets hit.[8]

Nonetheless, it was London that suffered most. By early September, 2,340 flying bombs had hit the city and its suburbs; around 5,500 people had been killed. V-1s and V-2s destroyed 30,000 houses in the area and damaged another 1.25 million. In material terms this was not on the same scale as the Blitz, but it lasted longer, it came without warning, and the mood of Londoners was different. As one resident told the diarist Richard Brown Baker, in 1940 everybody had set their teeth and fatalistically gone about their tasks. 'Now people are annoyed and scary. They feel the war is so close to being won that they want to live to enjoy the peace.' 'It has been a bad summer,' wrote Cyril Connolly in his literary magazine *Horizon*. London was 'more dirty, more unsociable, more plague-stricken than ever'.[9] For strategic reasons, the press never revealed exactly the zones hit; Londoners began to resent this concealment of their ordeal. The V-1, noted General 'Pug' Ismay, Churchill's personal representative to the Chiefs of Staff, had 'a greater effect on public morale than the authentic blitz had done'.[10]

London's morale rose and fell in waves. June and July had been the worst months. The Weekly Home Intelligence Report noted an increase in wild rumours and a general mood of fear and despondency; only three weeks after the D-Day landings, Herbert Morrison, the Home Secretary, presented the Cabinet with the grimmest assessment of public morale to date. Churchill, of course, remained defiant in Parliament and out. On 6 July he proposed to the Chiefs of Staff the destruction of a hundred German towns by bombing along with the use of mustard gas: 'It may be several weeks or even months before I shall ask you to drench Germany with poison gas,' he added, but 'if we do it, let us do it 100 per cent.' The generals did not think it a very good idea.[11]

At any rate, the proportion of flying bombs destroyed grew rapidly over time. The V-1s were low flyers, so nearly two thousand barrage balloons were set up around London – not very encouraging for those who lived under them, but they saved the city centre. Further south a mobile 'gun belt' was constructed, utilizing 35 miles of railway line and 22,500 sleepers collected from 20 different railway depots. Six hundred guns were in action and over 59,000 gunners were employed. Every two miles, between Maidstone and East Grinstead, powerful searchlights beamed into the night sky. By August, half the fighters of the RAF were flying on mission over the North Sea and the Channel in the hunt for 'doodlebugs'. Of the total 6,725 V-1s fired on London, only a third got through to their target. By the first week of September most of the launching sites had been overrun by Montgomery's 21st Army Group.[12]

So the feeling in London by early September was that the war was about to end. It was not the defiant spirit of 1940, or the festive mood of Paris, but an exhausted expression of relief. On 7 September Duncan Sandys, Churchill's son-in-law, who as Minister of Supply chaired the Flying Bomb Counter-Measures Committee, announced in a press conference: 'Except possibly for a few last shots the Battle of London is over.' However, when he came to the matter of German rockets he admitted, 'I am a little chary of talking about the V-2, [though] we do know quite a lot about it.' Germany's answer was delivered the next morning at dawn with a thunderclap heard all over London, followed almost immediately

by a second explosion. Two large craters were blown open in Chiswick
and Epping, on the western and eastern sides of London. The government announced that the noise was due to 'exploding gas mains'; the press
remained totally silent. Several such explosions occurred during the weeks
that followed. A Home Guard asked an American GI, who was building
a fence around one of the craters, whether the cause had been a rocket.
'No, man,' replied the GI, 'that's no rocket; it's one of those flying gas
mains.' Churchill finally admitted in the Commons on 10 November that
Britain had been under German rocket attack for the last two months.
He also explained why the rocket dealt less damage than the 'doodlebug':
the rocket's explosive nose would bury itself deep in the ground, destroying
everything directly above it; but the neighbouring houses remained
standing.[13]

The last V-2 launched on the British Isles was fired on 27 March 1945.
The last V-1 fell two days later.

A hint of what life was like in London during its long and stressful transition from war to peace can be acquired by a visit to the city's railway
stations in the first fortnight of September 1944. Many people in London
could still remember the significance of railway stations during the First
World War: the railways – and ferry – were the only link with the Western
Front. The stations were filled with men in khaki; it was there that wives
and mistresses said a last farewell. London's terminuses were where the
convoys of wounded came in, the platforms lined with stretcher cases, the
ambulances outside queuing up in place of taxis. It was there that London
received its first shocks of the First World War – and nobody old enough
to remember those scenes ever forgot them.

The scene in railway stations during the Second World War bore some
resemblance to the First. There were plenty of men in khaki – though
rather more Americans than there had been a quarter of a century earlier.
There were many farewells. The trains looked much the same, letting out
great clouds of steam as they approached and left the platforms. The great
difference was the presence of huge crowds of children.

'I've never seen anything like it,' commented one old railway porter.
Rumour had got through to the evacuees' 'reception areas' in the Home
Counties, in the North and in the West Country that the war for London
was over. Duncan Sandys's report was partly to blame. 'Yesterday', reported
The Times on 14 September, 'Paddington Station looked like a pram and
bicycle emporium. Perspiring porters tried to sort out claimed articles as
the owners came forward. Some of the perambulators were readily identified, but others, mainly of the fold-up type, required a sometimes

prolonged scrutiny of labels.' Mothers had stood in the crammed corridors of trains, with children in their arms, all the way from Manchester.
Prams, cots, trunks and cases piled up around the left luggage offices and
in the waiting rooms; each train disgorged hundreds of children under
the age of five, toddlers, babes in arms. The mothers had wanted to come
home. The 'reception areas' were glad to be rid of them. Who was going
to pay attention to the government notices printed in newspapers and
posted on pillars and walls? 'Stay away until you are told to come back.
If you come back now no one but you is responsible for anything that
may happen to you – or to your children.' Churchill himself had announced
in July that those not directly contributing to the war effort would serve
their country best by getting out of London; British railway companies
had laid on special trains to help the exodus: by August nearly a million
and a half people had left the city. 'Do not be influenced by one or two
quieter nights,' pleaded poor Mr Morrison. Nobody took heed. By mid-
September the evacuees were pouring back.

The problem London now faced was not so much flying bombs and
rockets; it was the number of houses which had already been destroyed.
The mothers had returned with their children; but many had no homes
to go to, or they had to put up with the damp, dark, draughty remains
of what had been home. Ernest Bevin, the Minister of Labour, began a
programme that brought in 45,000 construction workers from counties as
far away as Northumberland; many of them had to sleep in camps set up
in Wembley Stadium. The production of Morrison and Anderson shelters was intensified to improve security within existing homes; whilst for
the homeless new wooden and metal prefabricated houses were put up in
the devastated quarters of central and eastern London. It was a race against
time. With autumn came the cold – harbinger of one of the severest
winters of the century. Talk between neighbours no longer turned around
the defeat of Hitler; London's concern was coal for the fires, food for the
children, health, jobs, social security.

On 13 September the National Executive Committee of the Labour
Party met to discuss plans for the next General Election – the last one
had been in November 1935. Clement Attlee, the party's leader, pledged
to go to the country 'on a full Socialist policy' and hinted – though he
refused to promise – that 'the right time to end the present Government'
would be 'immediately at the end of hostilities with Germany'.[14] The
feeling in London was that it could happen within a matter of weeks.
But, as with the V-2, nobody in the press was ready to admit what everyone
knew: Britain's heated post-war electoral campaign had just been launched
by Labour.

2 Washington's 'gobbledegook'

Unlike anywhere in Europe, national and local elections in the United States chimed with the regularity of a clock. Their dates were as simple to learn as the two times table. War or the death of the President made no difference. Representatives to the Congress in Washington were elected for a term of two years, Senators for six. The President was elected every four years. Election day was always the first Tuesday of November. National party conventions had developed by the 1820s and, over the next century and a half, gradually moved forward from the month of May to the month of August. There would always be a 'pre-convention campaign', which would begin around the month of January of election year, and a 'national campaign' which would start up after the conventions had nominated their presidential candidates. After Election Day there would be several months' wait before the President-elect was inaugurated. Traditionally, the President was always inaugurated on 4 March. When Franklin D. Roosevelt became President in March 1933 he persuaded Congress to introduce a constitutional amendment: 'The terms of the President and Vice-President shall end at noon on the 20th day of January.' Henceforth Inauguration Day would always fall in the depths of Washington's winter.

Thus in 1944 America's 'pre-convention campaign' began, as usual, in January and lasted until July. The 'national campaign' picked up in August and September – as Paris was liberated and Warsaw destroyed. The election would be held on the first Tuesday of November, and the President-elect was due to be sworn in on 20 January 1945. Most Americans, in August and September 1944, were sure that the European war would be over by then. Their year-long campaign therefore came to be dominated by the issue of what kind of peace would follow it.

No national capital in Europe resembled Washington, DC. Berlin, the Kaiser's *Residenzstadt*, founded on the sandy wastes of central Prussia for no economic purpose save fishing, came closest. But Berlin was not planned, like Washington. Congress had voted in 1790 to establish a 'Federal City' somewhere on the Potomac, and left the honour to George Washington to choose the site; he picked ten square miles of woodland and malarial swamp to the west of his home at Mount Vernon, where the Anacostia flowed into the Potomac. Major Pierre Charles L'Enfant, a Frenchman attracted to the American cause, drew up the plan, was dismissed for his pains and died in poverty. The idea was to create a governing community in accordance with the mechanical principles of the Constitution, a balance of power between the legislative, executive and judicial authorities. There would be no one focus of activity, no central place of assembly – the capital would be dependent on interaction with outlying society (hence the names of states for the main avenues). The Capitol was set up on the highest hill; the starling-infested Supreme Court (by the 1930s electrical devices had been installed to get rid of the birds) was deliberately set aside from the avenues; the executive mansion (painted white after the British burnt it in 1814) was placed on a piece of flatland equidistant, one mile and a half, from the other two. The wide-ranging avenues, extending outwards, were, as L'Enfant had originally put it, to instill a sense of 'grand and far-distant points of view'. There were no walls and no military protection was foreseen for the capital of the United States of America.[15]

The main government buildings were, in the spirit of L'Enfant's century, Greco-Roman temples. White columns, plinths, architraves and friezes mixed with the green of the wood and marshlands. The practical demands of the nineteenth century had placed the tracks of the Baltimore and Potomac Railroad across the Mall between Capitol Hill and the red sand-stone castle of the Smithsonian Institution; another great obstacle blocking L'Enfant's vistas was the Gothic railroad depot, which prevented a view of the Mall. L'Enfant had made no allowance for the growth of the Executive Departments – little states unto themselves – which had to be placed near the White House, and as distant as possible from Congress. The two most important obstructed the view from the executive palace up the outward-bound Pennsylvania and New York Avenues. On the east side was the heavy stone block of the Treasury; it had gone up during the federal banking debates of General Jackson's presidency. On the west side was the State Department, America's ministry of foreign affairs and generally considered the ugliest building in Washington. It was built ten years after the Civil War, 'in a style of architecture', wrote the bureaucrat and reporter, W. M. Kiplinger, in 1942, 'based upon the idea that the more pillars could be piled atop of other pillars the better the effect'.[16] Childs' restaurant lay nearby, on Pennsylvania Avenue, where, for 40 cents, State Department employees enjoyed pot roast, mashed potatoes and string beans in compartmented blue platters.

Jonathan Daniels, son of Woodrow Wilson's Secretary of the Navy, had been called to work on a top secret mission within the State Department in 1943. He was not, he bragged, disturbed by the rats which 'came out of the holes with the heat pipes'. But a lot of people complained about the halls with their floors of shiny black and white squares of marble, so slippery that diplomatic callers skidded, and often fell, before being introduced to the top brass who worked upstairs. The Secretary of State, Mr

Cordell Hull, whose angular head with a shock of white hair itself had a semblance of Greco-Roman marble, worked in Room No. 208, part of an extensive suite in the southern wing of the building. Hull, a lawyer and senator from Tennessee, had entered this office on 4 March 1933, the day Roosevelt was inaugurated. On the walls hung eleven maps of a world he was determined to liberate according to his own American plan. In one corner stood the desk on which John Quincy Adams had drafted the Monroe Doctrine, designed to keep Europeans from interfering in the New World.[17]

The Secretary of State was traditionally a close political adviser to the President, who lived just the other side of Executive Avenue. Woodrow Wilson during the First World War had, it is true, ignored his Secretary of State and developed his notion of 'internationalism' with Colonel House, who had no government position at all; but this was exceptional. Roosevelt's brand of 'internationalism' grew out of the ideas of Cordell Hull. Roosevelt, unlike Wilson, was a team man, and his team lay in the Executive Departments that surrounded the White House – and blocked L'Enfant's 'grand and far-distant points of view'. Several times each week the Secretary of State would cross the narrow street to the White House. Cordell Hull, who for many years had been chairman of the Democratic National Committee, was one of the keys to Roosevelt's successive electoral victories. This made nonsense of the Department of State's old saying, 'there shall be no domestic politics in foreign affairs'; every time Hull crossed that street, American domestic politics became part of the world's affairs.

It was a tendency reinforced by the situation at the Treasury, just to the east of the White House. Henry Morgenthau, Jr., the Secretary, had been an apple-grower in Dutchess County, upstate New York, and a neighbour of Roosevelt, whom he worshipped; they had even developed together a scheme for making squash a cash crop, and founded a company called 'Squashco' – it was not very successful. Naturally, Morgenthau had wanted to be Secretary of Agriculture, but the farm people did not want him. So in 1934 he became Secretary of the Treasury. He turned out to be more conservative than 'the boss'. In 1938, as the Depression took a second dip and stock prices plummeted, he had opposed Roosevelt's plan to increase government spending by $3 billion, telling the President that such a deficit 'frightens me but will also frighten the country'.[18] It did, and the Republican gains in the congressional elections that year brought the New Deal almost to a halt.

All the same, Morgenthau never wholly mastered the intricacies of government finance and budgeting. For that he relied on the brilliant

Harry Dexter White, who had got a temporary job at the Treasury in 1934 and, in that critical year for the New Deal, 1938, was named Morgenthau's Director of Monetary Research. White had been born 'Weit' in Boston to Lithuanian Jews who had escaped the Tsarist pogroms. He had served in the US Army in the First World War, had married a Russian, and then studied economics at Columbia, Stanford and Harvard. In 1934 he was preparing to leave for Moscow to study Stalin's innovative system of state planning but, persuaded by one of his former professors, took his own thoughts on planning to Washington instead. Harry Dexter White introduces an interesting twist to the story of how the Second World War ended.[19]

It was not the New Deal that transformed America but the war, and nowhere was this more true than in the nation's capital. The United States not only had to build up its armed forces from scratch, it also had to construct a federal bureaucracy; no world war could be fought and won without it. Hitler and his Nazi colleagues quite reasonably assumed that America was incapable of responding to the challenge: America's military show at the end of the First World War had not been very impressive.[20] When Göring was warned of American potential in autumn 1940 he shrugged, 'What does the United States amount to anyway?' The answer, in autumn 1940, was not much. On learning of the Japanese attack on Pearl Harbor a little over a year later, Hitler jubilantly exclaimed, 'There's no way we can lose the war now', and declared war on Roosevelt's America backed, as he said in his speech to the Reichstag, by the 'entire satanic insidiousness' of the Jews. How could this racial mish-mash of Americans succeed in mobilizing before Hitler and his Japanese allies had control of the entire Eurasian continent, the 'world island'?[21]

Between 1940 and 1945 Washington's population almost doubled. In 1930 it had been a relatively small town of 621,000, considered more southern than northern, even though linked economically by road and rail to the north-eastern urban constellation of Baltimore, Philadelphia, New York and Boston. In summertime the wealthy who remained in town wore white linen suits and panama hats; the middle classes rocked on their chairs behind the screened porches; the blacks, who made up about a third of the population, still lived behind the stone houses that fronted the streets in the 'alleys', which had been reserved in pre-Civil War days for slaves and horse carriages. The 1930s had brought in the New Dealers; but only after September 1939, when Roosevelt declared a 'limited national emergency', did the real rampage begin. A War Resources Board was set up, then the war agencies, then the Office of Production Management, run as well as it could be by William Knudsen, who had directed General Motors, and Sidney Hillman, the president of the Amalgamated Clothing Workers Union – 'Why is it that you don't want a single, responsible head?' Roosevelt was asked at a press conference. 'I have a single responsible head. His name is Knudsen and Hillman,' replied the President. So the press called the leaders 'Mr Knudsen–Hillman'; he was a schizophrenic.[22] Why did one have to bring in so many new people? asked congressmen. Why not draw on the Agricultural Department, the Commerce Department, or Labor Department? Because the federal bureaucracy was simply not large enough to deal with the enormity of this war. Roosevelt, who had once called himself 'Dr New Deal', had become 'Dr Win-the-War' – and the new doctor, unlike the old, was forced to turn to businessmen to run the new war agencies. Thus were born, in November 1941, the 'dollar-a-year men' – industrialists and corporate lawyers who volunteered their services for one dollar a year: the belief at the time was that the new bureaucracy would only be a temporary affair. 'They range', wrote Kiplinger in 1942, with tongue in cheek, 'from $1-a-year men who can afford it, to $1-a-year men who cannot afford it, and a multitude of others who take whatever jobs are offered at whatever pay is offered.'[23] Direction of a war agency gave a man prestige in America's national capital.

Others just came for the jobs. Since the beginning of 1940, 5,000 new federal workers had been swarming into Washington every month; 70,000 arrived in the first year after Pearl Harbor. The more they came, the more they were wanted. The age of the New Deal was over. By the end of 1941 the population of Washington was well over a million. Unemployment disappeared. Applicants on the register of the District Employment Center fell from 62,000 in September 1939 to 27,000 in December 1940. Over the next four and a half years all able-bodied, mentally competent adults found jobs. Washington had become boomtown.[24]

With all the accompanying problems. The dollar-a-year men may have been familiar with business, but they did not know how to deal with Congress; nor could they handle a government budget. A senator from Missouri earned a reputation for honesty after setting up a committee to investigate waste and corruption; his name, most appropriately, was Harry Truman. The greenery of Washington began to disappear: the trees on the avenues were cut down to provide more space for the increase in traffic; barracks-like wood and stucco 'tempos' were erected on either side of the reflecting pool between the Washington Monument and the Lincoln Memorial. The handsome houses up Massachusetts and New Hampshire Avenues now accommodated six people to a bedroom. Many newcomers were surprised to discover that 'an efficiency', a small room with kitchenette and bath in the closet, cost as much to rent as a house in their home town. Harry Truman found a small hotel room, while his wife and children remained back in Independence. Roosevelt himself had a hand in designing the cubicles in the residence halls reserved for 'white government girls'. Race relations deteriorated. The anti-racist organization, the NAACP, and the New Negro Alliance called for 50,000 blacks to demonstrate against job discrimination in front of Congress and the White House in July 1941. 'What will they think in Berlin?' asked government officials. The demonstration was avoided after two hurried conferences at the White House were organized and the President issued an Executive Order on Fair Employment Practices – it was the first presidential order protecting blacks since Lincoln's Emancipation Proclamation in 1863.

The erection of the Pentagon, for the army, deprived many blacks of their homes; Jonathan Daniels thought it looked 'like an old-fashioned fort magnified to mastodonic proportions'.[25] Roosevelt had wanted no windows, but the Californian architect, George Edwin Bergstrom, pointed out that if the place were bombed the glass would be blown out, thus saving the concrete complex from collapsing. A National Airport was opened. And a new National Gallery, with a black marble floor in the Rotunda surrounded by green marble columns, reminded Washingtonians that they were fighting this war for civilization.

To that might be added Washington's new language. The thousands of new office and shop workers in town suddenly became 'personnel'. They worked under novel rules which demanded 'tooling up', 'getting out production', and 'stockpiling' – according to the 'priorities' and 'quotas' set. Their desks, their chairs, their paper and, in the case of the soldiers, even their clothes were 'government issue'; but it was only in 1944 that word spread that the soldiers were 'GIs'. When the chairman of the Chesapeake and Potomac's telephone system explained that its near collapse was due to 'maladjustments co-extensive with problem areas', Maury Maverick of Texas, head of one of the war agencies, decided the time had come to give the language itself a name; he called it 'gobbledygook'.[26]

Washington's wartime revolution hatched pride and hatreds of a kind not known in Europe. They were like the mix of State Department marble with Childs' restaurant cardboard or the hovels that neighboured the Capitol, the proximity of rich and poor, the Memorial next to the 'tempos', the elegant beside the vulgar: they astonished. The down-to-earth W. M. Kiplinger would say that Washington was 'not a diamond sitting on a piece of velvet', but rather a 'collection of tools or implements'. Yet even his heart swelled when he wrote that Washington was 'the control center of the United Nations', as the Allies against Hitler formally called themselves (as, indeed, did the Allies against Napoleon). 'Washington', he confirmed, 'is called capital of the nation, but it is really more than that – it is the capital of a World in the Making.' Jonathan Daniels rated Washington's politicians the 'damnedest set of men on earth – and . . . together they make the greatest government in the world'. World history seemed to be moving in one direction. Not an eye blinked, not a throat chuckled, there was not a simper of ridicule in the Senate when Kenneth Wherry of Nebraska declared his plan for post-war aid to China: 'Shanghai can be raised up and up until it's just like Kansas City.' This, after all, was America's manifest destiny.[27]

Such a singular, linear progress of history seemed evident in the way the population grew, with one generation replacing another with increasing speed. The New Dealers called the descendants of Washington's first residents the 'Cave Dwellers' because, hidden in their grand houses out in the Kalorama neighbourhood, nobody ever saw them. With the 'gold rush' of the Second World War every new group became suspicious of the ones that had arrived just before. 'Old-timers in Washington know how the Indians felt when the hunters and trappers came to their forests,' noted a reporter for the *New York Times* in 1943, 'how the cattlemen felt when the settlers staked claims upon their range.'[28] There was not much love lost between the New Dealers of the 1930s and the 'dollar-a-year men' of the early 1940s. The former were deeply suspicious of these 'robber barons' still on the payroll of private industry. The latter dismissed the former as college professors, social engineers, Communists and fellow-travellers.

The more Washington became the 'control center of the United Nations', the more the domestic struggle on the Potomac turned vicious and ideological. It crept into the Executive Departments surrounding the White House, it influenced the minds of Cordell Hull, Henry Morgenthau and that son of a Lithuanian immigrant, Harry Dexter White. It had even crossed the thoughts of the President as he contemplated running for a fourth term in office.

3 America first?

They were fighting united against Nazism, though some among them called it Fascism. Whatever the term, the Allies, east and west, were convinced throughout most of the war that they were the forces of good engaged in a battle with a universal evil. Only in 1944 did London, Washington and Moscow show an awareness that they were not in fact fighting the same war. It happened quite suddenly. In the week Paris was liberated – with the American presidential elections under way and what was beginning to look like a general election campaign in Britain – American and British forces in northern France separated. That was the week Stalin damned the leaders of the Warsaw Rising as 'power-seeking criminals'. The Red Army had halted at the Vistula and was now reclaiming, to north and south, the territories Stalin had sought within the Nazi-Soviet Pact; the main Russian military campaign in late August 1944 was directed towards the Balkans, in Romania.

The separation of the British and Canadian 21st Army Group from the American 12th Army Group in northern France occurred quite suddenly on that forgotten Saturday, 19 August. While Koszutski's Polish Armoured Regiment clambered up the side of 'Maczuga', south of Falaise, and the insurgency in Paris took hold, General Bradley, commander of the American Army Group, paid a flying visit to Montgomery's headquarters in an apple orchard outside Condé-sur-Noireau. Montgomery was still nominally commander of all the Allied ground forces in northern France. But that morning he got the shock of his life. Bradley, before an assembly that included British, Canadian and American field commanders, informed him that 'Ike [Eisenhower] wants to split the force and send half of it eastward to Nancy.'[29] Eisenhower had been commander of the Supreme Headquarters the Allied Expeditionary Force (SHAEF) since January, when it had been agreed, in London, that he would eventually take over ground forces when the US 12th Army Group had become 'operational'. Quite obviously it had been so for some time. But Eisenhower, always the diplomat, had been wary of taking over from Montgomery, who was prickly and as houseproud as ever. It was only a fortnight earlier that Eisenhower had moved his headquarters out of England to Granville, in western Normandy.

Eisenhower's formal decision – made on Monday, 21 August – to take over and split the two army groups was clearly politically motivated. Montgomery had already started to express concern about 'political currents' after Bradley's visit on Saturday. But it was Eisenhower himself, when he came to lunch in Montgomery's caravan the following Wednesday (Leclerc's *Deuxième DB* was marching on Paris at that moment), who brought up the matter of 'public opinion in the States'. 'I asked him why public opinion should make him want to take military decisions which are definitely unsound,' noted Montgomery in a letter to London three days later. 'He said that I must understand that it was election year in America; he said he could take no action which was calculated to sway public opinion against the President and possibly lose him the election.'[30]

In early summer, while the national party conventions nominated their presidential candidates, a vicious press campaign developed in America over the way the war was being run in France. It was aimed at Montgomery, stalled at Caen; it glorified Patton, racing across the Loire Country. Gossip spread that Montgomery was about to be sacked. Eisenhower, to the shame of America, was portrayed as a mere figurehead. The *Washington Times Herald* complained of 'British dominance of the Expeditionary Forces' – taunting the British lion was an old sport in American electoral years. General George Marshall wrote to Eisenhower on 17 August saying that he and the Secretary of War, Henry L. Stimson, 'and apparently all Americans' were 'strongly of the opinion that the time has come for you to assume direct command'. The press campaign, he added, 'could become an important factor in the coming Congressional Elections'.[31]

Before Bradley's visit to Montgomery on 19 August there was little in the military manoeuvres to suggest that the Americans and the British were going to separate. Bradley had stopped Patton's eastward advance in the area of Orléans and Châteaudun for an 'administrative pause', the operation to close the Falaise Pocket was under way and there was everything to suggest that, after this 'short hook' behind the German armies trapped in Normandy, a 'long hook' would be attempted, the Americans moving north up the Seine to join the British, thus cutting off those who had escaped. Furthermore, there remained the German Fifteenth Army, which covered the Channel ports and was throwing V-1s in the direction of London.

None of the authorities in London, political or military, suspected that the most important Allied strategic decision since 'Overlord' was about to be made in northern France: Churchill had left for Italy on 10 August to inspect what remained of Alexander's armies in Italy and discuss the deteriorating situation in the Balkans; Brooke, the CIGS, flew off to join him on Saturday morning, 19 August – 'I entirely agree with your plan,' he briefly cabled Montgomery before jumping on his plane. Brooke's worries in August, his diaries show, were about the Po valley and Burma. Leigh-Mallory, the Air Chief Marshal, stopped taking day-to-day notes on the French battle on 15 August and turned his attention to the Far East, where he would shortly become Allied Air Commander-in-Chief. Clement Attlee kept the Cabinet running, listened to his Labour colleagues' plans for the future of Britain, and comforted Londoners under the rain of the 'doodlebug'. Nor did the British Chiefs of Staff show any concern about the army movements just across the Channel. Their short notes to Montgomery, and a one-day visit by General Sir Archibald Nye, indicated that they, like Brooke, simply 'agreed'.

Montgomery was isolated when he faced the American decision. His American 'subordinate' commanders never answered the telephone. Montgomery's plan, once the Falaise operation was completed, was to combine the major part of the Allied armies in a 'solid mass of some 40 divisions', clear out and cut German communications with the Pas-de-Calais, march north of the Ardennes, establish a substantial air force in Belgium, and cross the Rhine into the Ruhr, the industrial heartland of Germany. Until his visit of 19 August, Bradley appeared to agree fully with the strategy. But what Montgomery did not know was the effect Eisenhower exerted on him in a meeting of American commanders on Friday, the 18th. Nor did the extent of the change sink in even after the visit. In one of his last directives to the Allied forces, he announced that same Saturday that the 'beginning of the end of the war' was within sight: 'We must hurl ourselves on the enemy while he is still reeling from the blow. Let us finish off the business in record time.'[32]

The military chiefs in London and Washington, their governments, and indeed the whole Western world thought that the war was going to be over in months, if not weeks. Eisenhower thought so too – which is why he came to the opposite conclusion from Montgomery. Montgomery's 21st Army Group, he announced on taking control of the armies in France on 1 September, 'did not need that much strength to destroy the Germans on his front'. Far better, thought Eisenhower, for the Americans, during this election year, to affirm their independence and strike eastwards 'towards METZ and the SAAR' – into that picturesque, craggy Rhineland which the tourists so like, along the same route that Pershing's American First, and then Second, Army had been planning to take in the American victory campaign of 1919. It was during preparations for the 1919 campaign, which never took place, that General George Patton developed his interest in French tanks.[*]

Montgomery did not get much support from home, save the odd 'I agree'. Nor did he have the divisions to back up his argument with Eisenhower. Shortly after Falaise he had to break up one division to reinforce the others; in addition, one infantry brigade was disbanded, along with two armoured brigades. By the time Paris was liberated, the American and British armies were going in separate directions. Bradley had set the tone of American command at a press conference he held at his headquarters on Monday, 21 August. The American 12th Army Group, made up of Patton's Third Army and Hodge's First, would take the 'direct route

---

[*] All military equipment – guns, tanks, aircraft – employed by the Americans during their First World War campaign was supplied by the French.

to Metz and the German border; the British, including the Canadians and the Poles, would follow 'the rocket coast', as the Americans dismissively called the north coast of France, the launching area of V-1s and V-2s. Basically, what was required of the British was a cleaning up job, while the Americans would 'violate the German border as quickly as possible'. The Germans, confirmed Bradley, were in 'a complete tailspin'.[33]

Patton's Third Army continued onwards without as much as a skirmish. On 27 August he captured a huge German petrol depot, which permitted him to move all the faster. Then on 10 September he arrived before Vauban's old fortress of Metz, and there he came to a halt. He managed to establish bridgeheads across the Meuse to the north and south. But there was no major movement (except backwards) on Patton's line until late winter, 1945.

Hodge's First Army, further north, did manage to cross the Meuse. It ran into Aachen on 10 September. And there it stopped. German resistance and supply shortages forced it to turn right, towards Patton's army – exactly the opposite move to that advocated by Montgomery since August. It was fatal for the British 21st Army Group, which had taken Amiens on 1 September, Brussels on the 3rd and Antwerp on the 4th: their whole right flank was exposed. The separation of the two Western Allies at the foot of Belgium's little Switzerland, the Ardennes, offered the Germans a golden opportunity, a classical Napoleonic stab between the forces: Hitler's winter Waterloo.

But, first, there was autumn at Arnhem. Montgomery never gave up his idea of a northern thrust, a swift 'left hook', into the Ruhr and beyond. After the seizure of Antwerp he was even speaking of reaching Berlin within two or three weeks. But though Belgium and Holland were flat, they had their obstacles, well known to soldiers of the myriad armies that had encountered them over the previous thousand years. The chief barrier was water, water in many forms. Doug Halloway, a gun artificer who had come over to Normandy with the Duke of Wellington's Regiment in June, spent the first part of September alone driving his unreliable hundred-weight Carrier as fast as he could to catch up with his comrades, miles ahead. 'The enemy retreated as we moved forward to his next line of defence, a river or a ditch.' One day he ran into a group of Polish tanks, which had been clearing a wood of Germans. 'It wasn't much good digging a trench here,' recorded Halloway, 'as it was water about two feet down.' 'Our Captain', he went on, 'would appear and start crawling about on his hands and knees among the cabbages with his map board doing a recce as if he knew where Jerry was.'[34] So it was for many of Montgomery's troops that autumn – crawling among the cabbages, with no protection from the fire of an invisible enemy, in a country of rivers, canals, wide estuaries, constantly liable to flooding and with deep drainage ditches on each side of the roads.

Montgomery made the monumental error of ignoring the movements of the German Fifteenth Army to his left, though Ultra signals from Bletchley Park were constantly reminding him of the danger. He stopped at Antwerp for a three-day rest, and failed to take the important Albert Canal just to the north, nor did he clear the sixty-five miles of the Scheldt estuary which – just as it had 350 years earlier when the United Provinces were in revolt against Spain – flowed north-east to the sea. In the second week of September the German Fifteenth Army, virtually all that remained of Hitler's forces in France, could have been hopelessly trapped on the coast. Field Marshal von Rundstedt was reinstated as Commander-in-Chief West; the efficient Model remained commander of 'Army Group B' – which by now meant the Fifteenth Army plus new forces of old men and fanatic teenagers combed out of the Reich. Model had two new Panzer armies coming in from the east, while, after the capture of Antwerp, he managed to get some 100,000 men across the mouth of the estuary to Walcheren Island – where Pitt had lost an army in the 1790s and the Duke of Wellington received a damp baptism of fire. The Germans had not forgotten their history; Montgomery, isolated and angry, had.

In response to his plan, on 9 September, for 'Operation Market-Garden' Eisenhower of course cabled, 'I agree.'[35] He always did. But Eisenhower, far from reinforcing Montgomery's right flank, insisted on a 'broadening' of the front 'between the Saar and the Ruhr' – he wanted everything in one month. Montgomery thought Eisenhower 'completely out of touch'. But he went ahead, all the same. 'Market' was the drop of paratroopers on the north bank of the Rhine at Arnhem, 'Garden' was the 45-mile advance the land forces were supposed to cover in two days to join them; they both got going on 17 September. The skies were filled with white parachutes; the ground troops advanced ten miles in three days. The new Panzers prepared a reception at Arnhem, though Model escaped 'through the eye of a needle' from his headquarters in the Taffelberg Hotel at Oosterbeek. Montgomery had pushed himself into an impossible salient, a 'bridge too far'. The casualties were appalling. Of the 11,000 landed on the north bank only around 3,000 were successfully withdrawn; the rest were either killed or made prisoner. The Poles had once again acted as a spearhead, an airborne brigade being landed near Nijmegen to form a link between the land forces and the paratroopers at Arnhem. They received, however, no thanks from Montgomery: 'I do not want this Bde here again,' he informed Brooke on 17 October, 'and possibly you may like to send it to join other Poles in Italy.'[36] The Nijmegen bridgehead was only ready for exploitation in March 1945; much of starving Holland was still under German control in April.[37]

Life on the stagnating front of the Lowlands, autumn turning into one of the coldest winters of the century, was recorded in the journal of Peter White, a twenty-four-year-old lieutenant in the King's Own Scottish Borderers, the 'Jocks'. Londoners started receiving the V-2 rockets in September, White saw them being fired: 'In the daytime, to our north, the sky sometimes displayed a thin vertical vapour trail which rose from a slow start with unbelievable acceleration until within seconds it had passed straight up out of sight. At night, a star-like light replaced the vapour trail to indicate the rocket's course.' 'Weasels' and 'Buffaloes' paddled the Jocks across waterways and sodden marshes, flags hung out in the ruined villages, the barrel organs played, 'Tiffys' (Typhoons) wheeled over-head like vultures over the killing grounds while, two miles from the forward positions, civilians went around as if the front were 'miles away'. Checkpoints were instituted.

White's descriptions of the approach to the front – 'the now familiar quickening of the pulse, and reaction of the stomach, crept upon us' – puts one in mind of Edmund Blunden on his way to the Somme, with this difference: 'The village we had arrived at was Vught,' site of a German concentration camp. New inmates – 'Dutch Quislings and German civil-ians bombed out from Aachen' – were being stripped and sprayed with DDT powder as a protection against lice. There were gas chambers and other rooms where the Germans had steamed their prisoners to death. Vivisection chambers, gibbets and three crematoria, one of them mobile, were on display.

The front was on the River Maas. Night ruled day. Those on 'stag' (watch) peered into the inky floodwaters towards the enemy until morning's colour; 'between us flowed the broad placid Maas, reflecting the radiant dawn sky like a shimmering sheet of mother-of-pearl.' Besides night and day, and the creep of the season, the scene barely changed before December.[38]

4 'Nazidom' and Just William

The military 'yo-yo' effect between the Russian and Western Fronts continued through early autumn. There was one week in late August when the Russian movement in South-Eastern Europe began to accelerate; so with the Eastern Front in movement it was the turn of the Western Front to slow down. While there was stagnation in Holland, the Rhineland and Lorraine, the Red Army ran over the whole of Romania and from there advanced across Bulgaria. The entire Aegean, including Greece and Yugoslavia, looked as if it were going to fall into Soviet hands, which had been Stalin's goal under the initial Nazi–Soviet Pact; only now he did not even need the Nazis. In mid-September, when the Western armies had completely stalled, a Russian offensive was launched on the Baltic states. The Red Army had difficulty reaching the Baltic Sea, and instead drove the German forces out of Estonia and a large part of Latvia. On 9 October Russian forces did eventually reach the port of Klaipeda, or Memel, thus isolating the German Sixteenth and Eighteenth armies. As in the First World War, these marooned German armies would hold on doggedly to Courland – because of its strategic value on the Baltic – until the end of hostilities.

But even Soviet movements were slowing down by late autumn. One major factor was geographic. Most of the Russo-German war had been fought on the wide continental base of Europe, in the plains of Russia and the Ukraine. As they advanced westwards they entered the narrowing funnel of the European peninsula; thus the front, likewise, became narrower. With the exception of Hungary, the European plain was now limited to a great northern swath that stretched uninterrupted down to the Pyrenees. But the Russians insisted on going south-eastwards into hilly and mountainous country. For political reasons, they refused to advance across the northern plain of Poland, and preferred to set up camp in Praga, Warsaw's eastern suburb, while the Nazis completed the job of wiping out the city. Even in Hungary, where the Russians were eventually heading, they were more circumscribed by hills than the British and Canadian forces in Holland. In the meantime, on the Western Front the Allies were strung along a line on an even narrower part of the European funnel. Yet, the Americans had managed, by separating from the British in southern Normandy, to avoid the plain and head into the hilly and mountainous parts of Lorraine, Alsace and the Rhineland – old hunting country for the 'doughboys' of 1918–19. The huge, deserted Ardennes lay between them and the British and Canadians, isolated on the narrowest part of the European plain, Belgium and the Netherlands. The advantage of this absurd situation – why on earth didn't the Eastern and Western forces head straight across the plains to Berlin? – obviously lay with the defender, the Germans.

In early autumn Finland and Romania switched sides and began a war on Germany. Admiral Horthy made the same attempt for Hungary, but Hitler took him prisoner and a *coup d'état* was orchestrated by the Nazis in Budapest in mid-October. With a new puppet regime installed under the certified lunatic Ferencz Szálasi and his Hungarian Arrow Cross movement, the last remaining Jews of Central Europe – about half a million of them – were shipped off to Poland for murder in the normal appalling Nazi manner. Hitler managed to establish a relatively stable front in Hungary, but he could not prevent the Red Army from entering the Hungarian plains in October. By late November Budapest was surrounded. Some of the most vicious fighting of the war occurred in this area.

In late August and September the Japanese began a diplomatic campaign to persuade Germany to make peace with the Soviet Union – all picked up by Western Allied radio decrypters. Less obstinate now concerning the Japanese pleas for a Soviet peace, in late 1944 Hitler decided to listen to them. On 4 December, as he prepared to separate British and American forces by a Waterloo-style offensive in the Ardennes, he told Szálasi that he was prepared to do everything possible 'to reach an understanding with the Soviet Union'.[39] Unfortunately for Hitler, Stalin had realized by this time that he could get everything he wanted from his new Western 'allies'.

Hitler still had his eyes on the Ukraine – he would never abandon this dream. But by late August he had realized that a strategic withdrawal from South-Eastern Europe, one of the launching pads of his attack on Russia in 1941, would be necessary. The withdrawal from Greece and Yugoslavia was conducted slowly, in stages, through the month of October. In the process, of course, the Jews of the area were carried off for extinction in Poland. Athens was thus evacuated by German forces on 13 October, Salonica on the 31st.

The Russian advance into and the German withdrawal from South-Eastern Europe had a significant impact on relations between the two major Western Allies, the United States and Britain, and it did this in many subtle ways, rarely noticed at the time and almost never discussed since.

Both countries were entering a pre-electoral campaign. Britain would abandon hers because of the setback in Holland; the United States, bound to the electoral time clock, would hold elections on the first Tuesday of November. Both Britain and the United States were oddities in the war. In the first place, nowhere in Europe outside Britain (and, in fact, occupied Denmark) was there any question of an election in 1944; even the liberated areas were too absorbed with the re-establishment of some form of state authority to worry about elections: there were acts of revenge, purges, gangland briberies, anarchy and criminality, yes, but civilized talk of elections was hardly of the moment. Secondly, there was no vicious conflict of loyalties between 'resisters' and 'collaborators' in Britain; nor did the question of resistance to Nazi authority – always just one step ahead of the moving armies – ever arise. As a result, the reasons invoked in Britain for fighting Germany took on a certain kind of abstractness that was not to be found on the Continent.

Most of the troops, of course, would be able to explain without difficulty why they were fighting – there was no 'disillusionment' among British soldiers as there had been during, and particularly after, the First World War; Peter White, for example, would simply have to mention the concentration camp he visited at Vught. Churchill's wartime speeches gave reasons for the fight, speeches that filled households between 1940 and 1945. The enemy was 'Na-azidom', which he pronounced with a long 'a' in the old, Edwardian English way. Thus: 'there can never be a friendship between the British and the Nazi power, that power which spurns Christian ethics, which cheers its onward course by a barbarous paganism.' Great sacrifices and exertions were demanded from all 'if the name of England is not to fail'. Churchill made the name of the 'Na-azis' and 'Na-azidom' so evil that no loyal resident of those ancient royal isles could possibly yield to it: 'If this long island story of ours is to end at last, let it end only when each one of us lies choking in his own blood,' he said in May 1940.

It is interesting to note that the aim of the war of Churchillian England was the defeat of 'Nazidom', not 'Fascism'. In the 1930s Churchill's quarrel with the governments of MacDonald, Baldwin and Chamberlain was over their craven attitude towards the 'odious conditions' in Germany – not the Japanese in Manchuria, Mussolini in Abyssinia or the civil war in Spain, which he regarded as peripheral to the main German issue. The Focus Group, which formed around Churchill in 1936 and included some prominent Labour Party members, became the 'Anti-Nazi Council' and not the 'Anti-Fascist Council'. During the Russian invasion of Finland in December 1939 Churchill expressed his fears that the smaller states of Europe would be 'divided between the barbarisms of Nazidom and Bolshevism'; and even when Hitler invaded Russia he was careful to take note, during his BBC broadcast on the day of the attack, that 'no one has been a more consistent opponent of Communism for the past twenty-five years' than himself, but that 'any man or state who fights against Nazidom will have our aid.'

Only in private with his ally and friend, President Roosevelt, would Churchill raise the word 'Fascism'. In a long appeal for American aid in the Atlantic, for instance, Churchill spoke on 8 December 1940 of the 'defeat of the Nazi and Fascist tyranny' as a 'matter of high consequence to the people of the United States and to the Western Hemisphere'.[40] Churchill, as always, was picking his words for his audience: in the United

States the terms 'Fascist' and 'Communist' had been incorporated into the domestic tribal mud-slinging between New Dealers and their opponents – so graphically illustrated in the story of the growth of Washington, DC. 'Fascist' could be applied equally to the 'Cave Dwellers' of the Kalorama neighbourhood of West Washington and the 'dollar-a-year men' brought in to run the war agencies; 'Communist' was a neat slur used by 'Cave Dwellers' to describe anything from the President down to local trade union bosses. Historians expend great effort fitting regional tensions into great world systems, but sometimes one is closer to human truth when one fits world systems into the reality of local political tussles.

Under the threat of bombs and German invasion, most British people were convinced that Churchill's struggle against 'Nazidom' was justified. But, with the passage of the war years, with London looking increasingly grubby – more and more areas were strewn with rubble, whilst ugly brick 'surface shelters', which provided no more protection than the walls of a house, were crumbling – the list of reasons for the fight lengthened. Women who made those exhausting train trips out into the provinces and back to fetch their children, after standing for hours on end in railway carriage corridors, began to wonder why nobody had thought of how to transport luggage across town – you could not carry a trunk on to a bus. Why were the railings in London's green squares going up again in 1944? They had all been torn down in 1940 purportedly for scrap metal and the squares were thus opened to the public. Who owned these squares? There was the problem of health. There was the problem of food. And, above all, there was a terrible shortage of housing. When the Labour Party published in September 1944, in the midst of all the electoral talk, a manifesto called *From a People's War to a People's Peace* they hit the central nerve of wartime Britain.

'The new democratic world order', it read, 'will not come by hopes alone. It must be built through unremitting struggle and international Labour and Socialist unity.' This is what would destroy for all time the 'forces responsible for the rise of Hitlerism'. 'Peace without prosperity for the great mass of wage and salary workers', it went on, 'would be both a sham and a danger.'[41] So was Britain turning Socialist?

The short answer is probably not. The leading proponent of planning for a post-war Britain, Sir William Beveridge, was not even a member of the Labour Party; he eventually got himself elected to Parliament in a by-election in September 1944, at the age of sixty-five, as a Liberal from Berwick. 'Every citizen of this country', he told his constituents, 'needs as conditions of a happy and useful life after the war . . . freedom from want and fear of want; freedom from idleness and fear of idleness enforced by unemployment; freedom from war and fear of war. In regard to each of these three problems it is obvious to me that the action required is essentially Liberal.' He said much the same in his maiden speech delivered on 3 November to a crammed House of Commons – there were notably fewer people present when Churchill had presented his report on his visit to Moscow one week earlier.[42]

Beveridge, in his baggy tweeds, was the kind of hero Britain produced in the age of Bovril, half-cooked bacon fat, Cadbury's Milk Tray chocolates and girls with bobbed hair. He became famous as a permanent feature on the BBC's *Brains Trust*, which had borrowed its name from Roosevelt's circle of advisers and was broadcast over the wireless every Sunday afternoon. The programmes started in early 1941 but the popularity of their debates only caught on in the year of the 'hinge', 1942, as Britain began defeating 'Nazidom'. Everybody, including the overseas armed forces, tuned in. Beveridge with the zoologist Julian Huxley, the conductor Malcolm Sargent, the retired naval officer Commander A. B. Campbell, and the philosopher Professor Cyril Joad discussed such critical war questions as 'Why can you tickle other people but you can't tickle yourself?', 'Why do children's ears stick out?' or 'How does a fly land on the ceiling?' 'I would not deny that the Brains Trust is a very dismal thing,' wrote Orwell in his column of the *Tribune* on the week of D-Day; but he had to admit it was 'genuinely popular'.[43]

Beveridge was as humourless as he was confident in his own powers of persuasion. Nigel Nicolson, son of Harold, the famous diplomat, parliamentarian and diarist, tells how one day he encountered on a train to Cambridge an 'elderly man' explaining to a companion a recent report he had drafted on social services. 'His self-laudation continued for half an hour,' recounted Nicolson, 'and what was remarkable about it was his anxiety to impress not only his friend, but me, a total stranger, giving sidelong glances in my direction as he completed each boastful point or anecdote. His name, of course, was Sir William Beveridge.'[44]

He had the manners of an evangelist, which is basically what he was. His father had been a judge in the Indian Civil Service, his grandfather a Congregationalist bookseller; his maternal grandfather had been a businessman and Unitarian. As a pupil at Charterhouse he had studied Classics and Hebrew before going up to Balliol College, Oxford, for further drilling in Classics and the Christian ethic. He had become director of the London School of Economics in 1922 and was appointed master of University College in 1937.

The first politician to exploit Beveridge's talents for civil service reports had been Churchill – back in 1908 when Churchill was a reforming

President of the Board of Trade. In the early years of the Second World War Beveridge prepared reports on coal mining, manpower and rationing. Most politicians were dismayed by his arrogance, particularly Ernest Bevin, Minister of Labour, who in 1941 pushed him out into an Interdepartmental Committee on Social Insurance and Allied Services, where he thought Beveridge could do no harm. Beveridge produced a White Paper. It was published in December 1942, six weeks after El Alamein, and became an instant bestseller; the public queued up at shops of His Majesty's Stationery Office to acquire copies of what everybody called the 'Beveridge Report' – it was the founding document of the British welfare state.

Many of the British at the end of the First World War would have liked to have returned to the certainties of a pre-1914 world, a world 'very brilliant' as Churchill had called it. But as the Second World War drew to a close nobody in Britain wanted a return to a pre-1939 world. On the fifth anniversary of the outbreak of the war, a Sunday, 3 September 1944, as electoral fever grew, there was a national 'day of prayer'. Church bells rang across the country and in every place of worship of every denomination people gathered to give thanks that the dark days of 1940 were gone and that the end of the war was in sight. Special services were broadcast on the BBC throughout the day. Dr William Temple, the Archbishop of Canterbury, in his morning sermon said, 'We look forward to victory as something within our grasp, and beyond victory to the use that should be made of it. We are concerned with the spirit in which we shall enter upon the new era. For it must be a new era; otherwise we shall have failed.'[45]

Within two months Dr Temple was dead. But in the short two and a half years of his primacy he had done almost as much as Sir William to galvanize spirits for what he called a 'Christian Socialism' that would build 'Jerusalem in England's green and pleasant land'. Three weeks after the 'day of prayer' Temple – a Balliol man like Beveridge – had introduced the latest work of one of his church assemblies, *The Church and the Planning of Britain*, its main emphasis on housing and the 'restoration of natural ways of living' for the bombed people of London and other major cities. It coincided with the appearance of both the new Labour Manifesto and Beveridge's new Social Insurance Plan – a plan likely to cost, *The Times* noted, '£650,000,000 in the first year, rising to £831,000,000 in 1975'. It was a 'comprehensive scheme of social insurance which will include the entire population' – coverage 'from cradle to grave' as Churchill had put it in a broadcast in 1943.[46]

In London, the argument over social reform never got as vicious as it had in boom-town Washington. Sir William Beveridge and Archbishop

Temple were hardly cast for the roles of a British Harry Hopkins or an FDR. Besides, the main political proponents of reform were members of Churchill's Coalition Government. But Churchill had something to worry about as electoral passions picked up in the last autumn of the war. In evangelizing Britain, where even the most radical reformers spoke in terms of seventeenth-century Levellers, the Communists – as vote-getters – counted for nothing (Harry Pollitt, General Secretary of the Party, had made repeated unsuccessful attempts to establish an electoral alliance with Labour). There was, however, growing opposition to the Coalition. It came in the form of a new party, the Common Wealth, whose eloquent leader, Sir Richard Acland, argued that choices in social, industrial and economic action had to be based on principles that were 'morally the most righteous'.[47] Its posters consisted merely of the three words 'Is it expedient?' crossed out and replaced by 'Is it right?' In two recent by-elections, the Common Wealth had won two 'safe' Conservative seats. 'Anglican priests', remarked Orwell, 'are much to the fore in the movement though the Catholics seem to be opposing it.'[48] Ethical, Beveridge-style politics had a following. There were lessons in that for Labour, committed since 13 September to fighting the next General Election alone 'with a full Socialist policy'.

But autumn's expected elections never happened. The armies had ground to a halt. There was very little awareness of what had occurred at Arnhem; the press presented the campaign as a great success. But when Churchill proposed in the House, on 31 October, the motion for 'the prolongation of the life of this Parliament for another year' it was clear that the victory parades, and the election, were no longer in season. London was set for a cold winter.

5 The Beasts of England

George Orwell had been working on a project about farm animals. He had always been interested in the countryside; the green meadows, the hedgerows and most especially the animals were, for Orwell, what made England. Sartre in Paris hated what he called the 'chloroform' of the countryside. Miłosz in Warsaw thought that the worst thing about Communism was the war it made on the rural landscape. Orwell was closer to Miłosz. He had, indeed, Miłosz's taste for detail. Writing at the end of July 1944, for example, he evokes the nineteenth-century Notebooks of Samuel Butler which 'have worn well' because Butler 'never lost the power to use his eyes and to be pleased by small things'.[49] It was the detail that gave Miłosz hope; it was the detail, albeit not rural, that saved Sartre. As in Miłosz, there was an element of something lost in Orwell's descriptions of the countryside, even though by 1944 he was stressing how much the war had contributed to a revival of English agriculture. As Orwell's wartime London grew shabbier and more rickety, so did the surrounding countryside change its face – 'the once green meadows having changed into cornfields, and in the remotest places one cannot get away from the roar of aeroplanes'.[50] England, dominated by London and other urban sprawls, had long since abandoned the more pleasant features of the old countryside. Orwell disliked intensely the spread of the signposts 'Trespassers will be prosecuted'; he regretted the loss of old English flower names; he regarded pheasants as a foreign pest that were driving gamekeepers to wipe out stoats, weasels, hedgehogs, jays, owls, kestrels and sparrow-hawks – the real animals of England. And Orwell detested the 'animal cult', as manifested in the spread of dog cemeteries, miniature stretchers for cats, animal bomb shelters and an annual 'Animal Day' which had begun at the time of the Dunkirk evacuation. He considered the cult an urban phenomenon, one that was responsible for the decline in the birth rate; women had, over their lifetime, more dogs than babies.

Animals were frequently present in Orwell's fiction and journalism. He was born Eric Blair in 1903 in India, where his father worked for the Civil Service. He dropped out of Eton and joined the Indian Imperial Police Force in Burma; it was this experience, according to his own account, that made him an 'anti-imperialist'. Two events, in particular, made a mark on him. One was the hanging of a Hindu, 'a puny wisp of a man', one rainy morning. As Orwell and other guards were marching with the prisoner to the gallows a large woolly dog appeared from nowhere, made a dash for the prisoner and tried to lick his face. The superintendent was furious. But the dog stayed out of reach, it 'danced and gambolled', taking everything as a game. At the moment the man was hanged the dog ran to the gallows, 'stopped short, barked, and then retreated into a corner of the yard'.[51] One can recognize this dog in the animal book Orwell completed in 1944. Equally significant in Orwell's experience was his shooting of an elephant that had run wild in a bazaar. 'A white man mustn't be frightened in front of "natives".' Orwell took his shot. The elephant 'neither stirred nor fell, but every line of his body had altered. He looked suddenly stricken, shrunken, immensely old.' The terrible thing was how long it took for the elephant to die, despite several shots. 'I often wondered', remarked Orwell, 'whether any of the others grasped that I had done it [shooting the elephant] solely to avoid looking a fool.'[52] In Orwell's writings, such fear was a key to the political atrocities of his day.

Orwell himself claimed that his wartime animal project was inspired by a scene he witnessed as an 'anti Fascist' during the Spanish Civil War. Unlike most British and American volunteers at the time, Orwell did not join the Communist International Brigades; as, briefly, a member of the Independent Labour Party he enlisted instead in a contingent under command of the POUM, a Catalonian movement that had social roots in the syndico-anar-chism of the local artisans: the POUM was liquidated by the Soviet-run Spanish Communist Party, based in Madrid, during the terrible 'May Days' of 1937 — and Orwell was a witness. Few people of the British left were willing to believe this. The total cynicism Orwell encountered back in England led him to wonder whether a true history of his times would ever be possible. What kind of records would the future historian have to go upon? Winners of a war seemed now capable of suppressing whole areas of truth. Orwell was still arguing in 1944 that this capacity to suppress the truth was even more frightening than the atrocities of war itself.[53] Miłosz had said the same about contemporary Poland.

Orwell was living, shortly after his return from Spain, on a farm in Hampshire — where he kept a village shop and a goat — when he spied a little boy of around ten whipping a huge carthorse every time it attempted to turn off the narrow path they were driving up. If animals only became aware of their strength, thought Orwell, men would not be able to exploit them. 'I proceeded to analyse Marx's theory from the animals' point of view,' recorded Orwell. 'The true struggle is between animals and humans.'[54]

'I am writing a little squib which might amuse you when it comes out,' Orwell wrote to a Russian correspondent in London in February 1944, 'but it is so not OK politically that I don't feel certain in advance that anyone will publish it.'[55] All through the following spring and summer — past D-Day, the Warsaw Rising and the Liberation of Paris — Orwell attempted and failed to find a publisher for his Animal Farm. Orwell's home was V-bombed; life in London got less and less tolerable; the dreams of a 'New Jerusalem' spread. Victor Gollancz, Orwell's original publisher, turned it down because it was critical of the Soviet Union; T. S. Eliot (to whom Orwell had sent a crumpled manuscript retrieved from the rubble of his home) rejected it for Faber & Faber; André Deutsch turned it down twice; Jonathan Cape used their contacts with the Ministry of Information to pass it over — 'highly ill-advised to publish at the present time,' wrote Peter Smollett, head of the Russian Department, and now proven to have been in the pay of the Soviet NKGB.[56] Eventually in late August it was accepted by Fredric Warburg of Secker & Warburg, but publication was delayed for another twelve months.

All revolutions begin with a dream; even Sir William Beveridge had a dream. The Revolution on Orwell's *Animal Farm* was, famously, started by the pigs, who outlawed humanity and set up a new dream society, governed by the pigs themselves. 'Four legs good, two legs bad,' bleat the sheep in unison. But actually it is the pigs who govern from the last human farmer's manor house. Not even under the farmer had there been such fear, torture and violence. 'Of course I intended [*Animal Farm*] primarily as a satire on the Russian revolution,' Orwell wrote to a carping American critic. 'But I did mean . . . that *that kind* of revolution (violent conspiratorial revolution, led by unconsciously power-hungry people) can only lead to a change of masters.'[57]

After witnessing one particularly violent scene of butchery, Clover, the old mare, looks sadly down from a knoll overlooking the farm; tears well from her eyes: surely all the violence and hard work had not been the aim when they originally sought to overthrow the human race? But the pigs' argument is incontrovertible. 'Surely, comrades,' they ask, 'you do not want [the humans] back.'

Eventually one of the human farmers invades Animal Farm, and in the course of combating him a deal is struck with the owner of another farm. The animals of the farm are shocked to discover one day that the pigs are walking on their hind legs. 'Four legs good, two legs *better!*' bleat the sheep. Operating under the rubric, 'All Animals are Equal, But Some Animals are More Equal than Others', the lower animals, as the tale ends, begin to notice an extraordinary thing: the faces of the men are melting into the faces of the pigs, the faces of the pigs into the men. 'It was impossible to say which was which' – did the men become pigs? or the pigs men? Orwell wrote this last scene shortly after the Teheran Conference of November 1943 between the 'Big Three', Stalin, Roosevelt and Churchill.[58]

On completing the book, Orwell, significantly, set about writing an article about that central word of the Soviet state: 'Fascism'. If Churchill never spoke of 'Fascism' except when corresponding with Roosevelt, Sartre seldom referred to 'Fascism' until after the Liberation of Paris. The same was true of French Communists. 'Fascism' was more a word that came to the lips of Eastern and Central Europeans. But the poet Miłosz and his comrades of the Polish Home Army never used the term; rather, 'Fascism' was a crime they stood accused of after the Red Army swept into their country.

'What is Fascism?' asked Orwell in his article, written in late March 1944 – the month he completed *Animal Farm*. He wondered if it was a useful term since the 'major Fascist states' – he was thinking principally of Italy and Germany – 'differ from one another a good deal in structure and ideology'. As for the way the term was bandied around in Britain, 'Fascism' he thought had lost the 'last vestige of meaning': there was no political party or set of people 'which has not been denounced as Fascist during the past ten years'. Orwell drew up a list of the bodies of people labelled 'Fascist' since the rise of Hitler in 1933; it included the Conservative Party, the Labour Party, Catholics, pacifists, supporters of the war, Trotskyists and even Communists. In conversation, Orwell noted, the word was even more widely used than in print.

So did it mean anything to say that one was fighting a war 'against the Fascists'? Curiously, Orwell thought it did. As he limply explained in his article, beneath all the mess 'there does lie a kind of buried meaning': Fascism meant 'something cruel, unscrupulous, arrogant, obscurantist, anti-liberal and anti-working-class'. Except for a few 'Fascist sympathizers', said Orwell, 'almost any English person would accept "bully" as a synonym of "Fascist".' In the sixty years since Orwell wrote this article our libraries have been filled with books explaining the 'kind of buried meaning' and developing a theory of Fascism.[59]

As is so frequently the case with 'isms' and 'doms', exploration of the local use of the word 'Fascism' reveals much more than the universal, general theoretical approach. During the war, the word was much more widespread in Britain and the United States – which never had the lines of military combat drawn across their soil – than on the western Continent (Orwell himself admitted that continental Europeans had, 'since the rise of Fascism', developed a literature much closer to the facts of the struggle than the English – 'English disapproval of the *Nazi* outrages', he said, typically mixing his terms, 'has been an unreal thing').[60] In Britain and America, one's attitude to 'Fascism' was what defined one politically. Roosevelt's New Dealers were always attacking the 'Fascists' at home and abroad. In Britain, employment of the term against political enemies put one in the camp of the left, the Socialists. 'I would never be led up the garden path in the name of Capitalist democracy,' wrote Orwell on his return from Spain.[61] This was true. To the end of his life Orwell was a defender of 'Socialist democracy'. That is why he found the word 'Fascist', though 'deprived of the last vestige of meaning', useful.

Why had the word become so widespread in Britain and America? It obviously did not have much to do with Mussolini, Franco and Hitler; it had everything to do with the Soviet Union. The blackshirted *arditi*, formed out of the ranks of demobilizing Italy in spring 1919 and the first to carry the ancient Roman magistrates' emblem of power (the *fasces*, a bundle of rods bound up with an axe), were not a focus of interest in Britain and

America. Nor was Mussolini's party. Why should Britain or America be concerned with peripheral Spain? The civil war that broke out there in 1936 grew out of a military insurrection born of a conflict over the Catholic Church, property, monarchists and reforming republicans that went back over a century – the 'Phalange' of Primo de Rivera was actually losing influence; the military leader who emerged on the 'Nationalist' side, General Francisco Franco, was the most uncharismatic of all of Europe's dictators in the 1930s. What had raised passions throughout Europe's parties on the left was not the complexities of poor Spain's conflict, it was Moscow's new 'Popular Front' policy, buoyed up by the slogans of 'anti-Fascism'.[62] Moscow set the tone of international debate, defined international discussion, simplified the divisions – much in the way Orwell's pigs stopped argument with their appeal, the sheep bleating behind them, for loyalty and obedience: 'One false step, and our enemies will be upon us.'

The Bulgarian Communist, Georgi Dimitrov, who had managed to put Göring to shame at the time of the Reichstag Fire trials, had set the new Popular Front anti-Fascist line as General Secretary of the Comintern in Moscow in July 1935. At the VII Comintern Congress, Dimitrov, drawing on Lenin's gospel of *Imperialism: Last Stage of Capitalism*, laid down the theory that 'Fascism' was the product of class fragmentation. Fascism in power, he stated, was 'the open terrorist dictatorship of the most reactionary, the most chauvinist, the most imperialist elements of financial capitalism'. Among the Fascists he included Mussolini of Italy and Piłsudski of Poland; but above them all stood Hitler. The real centre of defence against the Fascists was the Soviet Union, bastion of the world proletariat.[63]

The war separated most of Europe's left-wing parties from the great 'anti-Fascist' struggles of the 1930s. Western occupied Europe, where Communists had to live with the Nazi-Soviet Pact for two years, abandoned the term for the duration of the war. The Soviet Union, following the Nazi invasion of 1941, returned to the term with a vengeance, imposing it on its expanding Eastern European empire. In Britain and the United States, with no military lines and no military resistance to 'Hitlerism', the dilemma never presented itself to Communists and fellow-travellers. So they had no trouble with continuing with the 'anti-Fascist' cry of the 1930s. Orwell, himself a Socialist, never abandoned it, though he was fully aware how irrational it was.

Exceptionally, however, for a man of the left Orwell had abandoned his faith in the 'bastion of the world proletariat', the Soviet Union. In the place of the Soviet Union, Orwell put 'England'. Orwell was a patriot of the left.

'In "enlightened" circles,' he wrote just before D Day, 'to express pro British sentiments needs considerable moral courage.'[64] English intellectuals were hostile to their own country: one could criticize Churchill and lampoon his wartime government; but Stalin and the Soviet Union were sacrosanct. A voluntary form of censorship had developed among publishers and newspaper editors that simply forbade negative comments about Stalin. Orwell described in an introduction ('Freedom of the Press') to *Animal Farm*, which did not appear until 1972, the 'cowardly desire' that had developed within a British intelligentsia 'whose patriotism is directed towards the USSR rather than towards Britain'. Even if *Animal Farm* were published, he was convinced the press would dismiss it as a 'dull, silly book', one that 'oughtn't to have been published'.[65]

What Orwell sought was English-bred Socialism, one that welled up from the English 'masses', that corresponded to the English sense of fair play, one that was not imposed by power-hungry bullies like the Soviet Communists. It was something that England (he distrusted the Welsh and the Scots) could contribute to the world: the revolution, after the war, which everyone sought. Orwell was delighted with the Beveridge Report. But Orwell wanted more, much more: a totally planned economy, nationalization of the land, mines, railways, banks and the major industries; limitation of incomes along with a minimum wage; and a British Empire transformed into a 'federation of Socialist states'. There could be no return to the laissez-faire 'free-for-all'. There would be no return, Orwell was convinced, because Socialism was superior to Capitalism.

But he saw two troubling signs in the autumn of 1944. One was Poland. Orwell was virtually the only person writing in London's press who showed sympathy for the men behind the Warsaw Rising. Why should Poland's London government be classified as 'émigré' and not Poland's Communists in Moscow? If the London government was to blame for the Rising then surely some people in Warsaw must be listening to it, no? Why was Moscow and not London considered 'representative'? Orwell was worried that this lopsided view in favour of Moscow was having an effect on British foreign policy. Worse, it was undermining the beneficial influence which the 'English revolution', he hoped, would have on the rest of the world. The 'English revolution' would establish a true Europe of Soviets, that is, a Europe of independent Socialist sovereign state councils – a 'Europe of councils' as German Socialist idealists had called it in 1919.

The second problem Orwell was beginning to sense that autumn was over the strength of the 'English revolution'. The natural levelling effect of war seemed to be wearing off. There were those little details: men and women were wearing hats again, wealthy men were wearing trousers with turn-ups (forbidden during the rationing of 1940), the railings were going up in London's squares. Then there was the appalling prospect that the 'Tories' might actually win the next General Election with the claim that they were the 'party that won the war'. But the most worrying matter for Orwell was that 'Englishness' seemed to be on the wane. People were not reading the right books. The archetypal English legend for Orwell was Jack the Giant Killer – it illustrated the strength of the small man standing up to the big; it was reflected in foreign policy by England's traditional pursuit in Europe of a 'balance of power'. But now people were reading the horrible 'action' novels of James Hadley Chase, 'pure Fascism', in which sadistic heroes sided with the strongest, the biggest bullies; or they were buying up American 'pulp magazines', which carried the same message. The basic myth now was Jack the Dwarf Killer 'which teaches, either overtly or implicitly, that one should side with the big man against the little man'. 'Most of what is now written about foreign policy is simply an embroidery on this theme,' added an anxious Orwell. The English were losing their human face; the men were turning into pigs, and the pigs into men.[66]

6 The flying premier

At the time of Churchill's visit to Moscow in October 1944 a dinner was held in the Bolshoi Theatre. The guests were dressed to the nines in their uniforms, coats and ribbons, but the mood was playful. Marshal Stalin heard somebody in the British party refer to the Big Three as the 'Holy Trinity'. 'If that is so,' quipped Stalin, 'Churchill must be the Holy Ghost; he flies around so much.'[67] Stalin could be like that at a dinner table: funny and right on the mark. In the 'Grand Alliance' between Britain, America and Russia Churchill, at sixty-nine, played the role of a flying Holy Ghost – his inspiring words were heard throughout the globe and he seemed to be everywhere at once.

He had always been a traveller, which is what gave him such a broad vision of politics. No other war leader knew so much geography or had so daunting a grasp of historical time; de Gaulle came the closest. For British travelling statesmen one must go back to the end of the Napoleonic wars to find a parallel – to Lord Castlereagh voyaging in his coach and absorbing the different landscapes and customs of Europe's peoples; or to his diplomatic partner the Duke of Wellington, who combined travelling, soldiering and high politics, rather like Churchill. But Castlereagh and Wellington were Irishmen who became English: they were always seeking a centre, whether in London or on the Continent. Churchill was an Englishman who went in the opposite direction – perpetually reaching for the periphery. He was not an Orwellian Englishman, even if both he and Orwell were products of the Empire. Orwell dug his roots into London, his identity in the surrounding countryside. Churchill had no roots at all. He may have considered himself an aristocrat, but he was an aristocrat of a very marginal kind – he had no land and no money, and his closest friends were described by many of the high-born of the day as 'louche', not aristocratic. He belonged to no region of England. Blenheim Palace, built in honour of his eighteenth-century forebear, the first Duke of Marlborough, was certainly not his home; he was born there on the last day of November 1874 by accident of an American mother who suffered a sharp fall while walking with shooters on a hunt: an appropriate start for her premature son's life. Lord Randolph's short-lived household in London was hardly a home. Nor was Harrow. It was his nurse from one of the Medway Towns, Mrs Elizabeth Everest, 'My darling Old Woom', who made Kent his favourite county; she was one of the reasons why, at the age of forty-eight, and twenty-seven years after her death, he buried funds he did not have into the purchase of Chartwell, just inside Kent and only 24 miles from Westminster. Westminster was his home, Whitehall and Parliament – the walk across Horse Guards Parade, the corridors of Barry's riverside palace, Downing Street, the Hotel Metropole and the Hotel Victoria on Northumberland Avenue, by Trafalgar Square. He even married Clementine Hozier (who had spent her childhood shuttling between Seaford, Sussex, and Dieppe) at St Margaret's, Westminster. Churchill's London was political London. From this central point he looked out upon and travelled the world. Between 1940 and 1943 Churchill had covered over 110,000 miles, had spent thirty-three days at sea and fourteen days in the air. In the first half of 1944 his travelling slowed down somewhat; but most of the summer and autumn was spent overseas.

His critics among the American Chiefs of Staff and within the US State Department were convinced his 'peripheral' strategy during the war was derived from a desire to vindicate his personal responsibility, as First Lord of the Admiralty, for the Dardanelles expedition that had ended so disastrously in 1915. They suspected that some evil British 'imperial' motive was behind it. Churchill definitely sought exoneration for what he considered had been a grand plan, a great flanking movement, an alternative to 'barbed-wire chewing' on the Western Front, which had been botched by poor coordination between the armed services. He was demoted to the

Duchy of Lancaster and eventually resigned from the government over the issue on 11 November 1915; then spent, himself, five and a half months on the Western Front. Churchill's argument was that his peripheral strategy – moving round to the base of peninsular Europe – could save lives. He took the same position as Prime Minister during the Second World War.

An imperial motive was there, too. But here the matter was much more complicated, and vaster, than officials in Washington imagined. After visiting Pope Pius XII in the Vatican on 23 August – the week of Paris's Liberation – Churchill, according to his physician, Lord Moran, opened his eyes wide and 'declaimed a fine passage from Macaulay's essay on Ranke's *History of the Papacy*'.[68] As a schoolboy in Harrow he had won a prize (though he remained in the bottom form) for reciting by heart 1,200 lines of Macaulay's *Lays of Ancient Rome*. Italy, the Adriatic, Greece, the Aegean and Asia Minor were, for an Englishman educated in the Victorian age, at the heart of an ancient civilization; it was something worth saving.

Churchill's London followed the thread of Britain's merchant and royal navies outward across the Mediterranean and round the 'world island' to Asia. He had been a free trader from the beginning of his career. He 'crossed the floor' – changed political parties – twice, but he never abandoned his outgoing principle: 'our harbours' are as 'nature made them', they are not obstructed 'with fiscal stake nets and tariff mud bars'.[69] He had been a soldier and reporter on the frontiers of the Empire, always following the sound of the cannon – even as, while Home Secretary, he had made the trip from Whitehall to East London personally to assist in the 'Siege of Sidney Street'. Churchill's political London stretched to America, to which he had first travelled in 1895. 'If time is given, nothing can stand against Great Britain and the United States together,' he had said in a secret Commons session in a desperate May of 1917. 'But a long time will be needed – a time measured not by months but by years.'[70] Churchill was as surprised as Lloyd George and the Americans when the war was ended, one year later, by the British army in France.

Outward, around the flanks, round continents, free trade with all the nations, and a strong Atlantic bond: that was the view from Churchill's London. After the evacuation of France in 1940, Churchill, against the opinion of his Chiefs of Staff, began building his forces in Egypt and fostering US relations. The advisers in Washington wanted forces aimed directly at the heartland of Germany; London showed a preference for thrusts at the periphery. There was bitter argument between the two. There were grim setbacks. Churchill used a metaphor that was dear to Sartre; he likened the progress of the war to a bullfight, as he saw it – first were the preliminaries with picadors and banderillas, then D-Day, the matador entering at the crucial moment to make the kill, waiting till the bull's head was down. As Churchill prepared himself for his eighth summit with Roosevelt, 'Octagon', he could speak of a 'path of dazzling victory'. 'I must express my admiration to you', wrote the Prime Minister, 'not only for the valour but for the astonishing mobility and manoeuvring power of the great armies trained in the United States.' The letter was posted from Naples on 29 August at the moment British and American forces separated. By autumn there were at least two matadors in the ring and the bull, its head bowed, was angry.[71]

7 Travelling the Gulf Stream

The weather in London in early September had been grey and drizzly, the mood was strained because of the bombing. But there was a feeling that the war was nearly over and that elections were not far off. Anxiety was expressed about exports lost during the six years of war, the debts to America and the millions of men about to be demobilized; yet there was the promise of social security from the cradle to the grave and a health service for everyone – 'And I John saw the holy city, new Jerusalem, coming down from God out of heaven . . .'[72]

Churchill's special train pulled out of Addison Road station on Monday morning, 5 September, heading for the port of Greenock in Scotland, where the *Queen Mary* was waiting to take him to America. The train stopped once, just outside London, because the Prime Minister had forgotten his spectacles, and a second time at Carlisle where the telephone was plugged in to the stationmaster's office and the news came through from Downing Street that Germany had just capitulated. The whole team prepared to turn round for London again for work on armistice terms and the peace treaty. But it was a false alert and the train carried on for Greenock, where it arrived just after seven o'clock in the evening.[73]

Roosevelt and Churchill had promised each other to keep the numbers down for their conference in Quebec. Yet the party accompanying the Prime Minister filled the huge main dining room and took up more cabins than could be found on the main deck. Four thousand servicemen accompanied them, most of them American and many of them wounded. Churchill asked Roosevelt to grant the men extra leave for the time spent waiting for the departure at Greenock; the request was granted. Jock Colville, who worked in Churchill's private office, was talking to an American pilot who thought it was terrific that the US Government should pay tribute to the British by naming the ship after one of their queens.

'But it's a British ship,' explained Colville. The pilot gaped. 'No, no,' he answered. 'It's the biggest and fastest in the world.' Colville had to persuade the pilot to lean over the side carefully and look at the flag flying at the stern. 'How could our Government have let themselves be out-smarted like that?' gulped the pilot.[74] The attitude was widespread in America. As the British visitors discovered that autumn, the American newspapers gave the impression that the only people fighting Hitler were the Americans. George Orwell was the one person in the British press who had the courage to draw attention to anti-British feeling among the Americans.[75]

Churchill was only too well aware of the problem, though he had a tendency – unfortunate for Britain's future, if understandable at the time – to limit his attention to the military issues. 'This visit of mine to the President is the most necessary one that I have ever made since the very beginning,' he had told his wife in a long letter written in Naples on 17 August. What upset him was the apparent American failure to appreciate both the military effort (equal in size to the Americans') and sacrifice (far greater) Britain had made in the Allied cause. 'We have three armies in the field,' he went on to explain to his wife. 'The first is fighting under American Command in France, the second under General Alexander is relegated to a secondary and frustrated situation by the United States' insistence on this landing on the Riviera. The third on the Burmese frontier is fighting in the most unhealthy country in the world under the worst possible conditions to guard the American air line over the Himalayas into their very over-rated China. Thus two-thirds of our forces are being mis-employed for American convenience, and the other third is under American Command.'[76] What he should have said was that he and his Chiefs of Staff had abandoned Montgomery and the British army in France to American command and had set off – at the very moment the split between the two armies occurred – for Italy. It seemed as if Churchill, following his old Mediterranean instincts, was determined to build up a purely British force in Italy that would be able to counter not only the weight Russia was applying in the direction of the Balkans but also the American takeover in North-Western Europe. Thus Churchill aggravated the nature of the Western Allied military separation, giving it a European dimension rather than one limited to the northern plain.

Brooke, the CIGS, was worried, though he had himself contributed to Montgomery's isolation. After a dinner aboard ship he, the Air Chief and the First Sea Lord climbed the liner's bridge to watch their departure from Greenock and the descent down the Clyde. 'I am not looking forward to this journey and conference,' he noted in his diary that night.[77] They descended the Irish Sea and within twenty-four hours, churning ahead at

28 knots (the one cruiser in escort had difficulty keeping up), the *Queen Mary* entered the Gulf Stream.

Woodrow Wilson, when he had travelled to Europe as American President, enjoyed the Gulf Stream, the ocean current that flowed eastwards from the Caribbean and made the coasts of France, Britain and Scandinavia green; the warmth gave him more energy and the whole ship's company, as a result, cheered up. But that had been in the winter of 1918–19. In September 1944 the Gulf Stream had the opposite effect on Winston Churchill and the passengers of the *Queen Mary* on their way to America.

Brooke said it was like living in a Turkish bath, with the temperature between 75° and 80° Fahrenheit. It was, recorded Colville, 'very hot, very sticky and cloudy like at the Equator'. The Prime Minister was 'definitely not his brightest and best'; he spent a considerable amount of time in his cabin reading the novels of Anthony Trollope. His spirits were 'desperately flat'. At the daily military staff conferences he was invariably in 'a most unpleasant mood'. 'Some of us had a tough passage,' Ismay noted sourly. 'It was a ghastly time from which I have carried away the bitterest memories,' recollected Brooke.[78]

Churchill had been suffering from recurrent bouts of pneumonia, most recently on his return flight from Italy. To get his temperature down he was taking a sulphonamide, 'masses of M & B' (May and Baker) as he put it to Roosevelt 'in these days of glory'. He had also been prescribed malaria tablets for his Italian trip and was ordered by his doctors to continue taking them for four more weeks thereafter – they upset some people considerably. Those close to Churchill got seriously worried about his state of health. His wife, who was travelling with him, sent him a cheering note on 7 September: 'Darling – How are you this morning? What a rousing news Bulletin this morning! Calais, Boulogne, Dunkirk, Le Havre more & more closely invested – 19,000 Prisoners to the poor unnoticed British! Is the Moselle the frontier between France & Germany? because if so we are in the Reich.' Two days later Lord Moran confided to Colville that he did not give Churchill 'a long life and he thinks that when he goes it will be either a stroke or the heart trouble . . . May he at least live to see victory, complete and absolute . . . Perhaps it would be as well that he should escape the aftermath.' The war premier, who as a young man had expected an early death like his father, was to survive two decades of post-war Britain.[79]

The transatlantic voyage was one of the rare occasions when he peered into the glass darkly and spoke of both the next election and the prospect for Britain after the defeat of Nazidom. Churchill painted a wintry picture.

At dinner one night he said that 'old England was in for dark days ahead, that he no longer felt he had a "message" to deliver, and all that he could now do was to finish the war, to get the soldiers home and to see that they had houses to which to return. But materially and financially the prospects were bleak and "the idea that you can vote yourself into prosperity is one of the most ludicrous that ever was entertained".' Besides housing, Churchill's ideas for national social coverage did not extend much beyond 'milk for the babies'. His entire welfare philosophy consisted of the vague belief that 'we did not enter this war for any gain, but neither did we propose to lose anything through it.' To ensure that Britain lost nothing through it was the purpose of his trip to America.[80]

Churchill was well aware that British finances were going to have to be 'one of the main subjects' of the conference. Financial delegations of all members of the 'United Nations' – the Allies, including the Soviet Union – had gathered together at Bretton Woods, a luxurious retreat in the White Mountains of New Hampshire, in the two months following the Normandy landings to reach an agreement governing international currency exchange and, by implication, trade policy in the post-war world. The agreement, an attempt to restore a system of multilateral payments that had been the basis of trade expansion in the nineteenth century, was signed in the 'Gold Room' of the Mount Washington Hotel late in July; but still, in September, it had not been ratified by the British Parliament – nor would it be for another year. The debate in Britain was bitter. Bank of England officials called the scheme of fixing the exchange rates of all currencies to the dollar, itself the only currency convertible to gold, a 'swindle', the 'greatest blow to Britain next to the war', or, as a *Times* review was to put it in October, a system that would 'maintain, if not reinforce, the United States position [of preponderance] to the detriment of the weaker nations'.[81] Churchill knew all this; it was one of the issues that had made him so gloomy. But he would not let it distract him from his main concern: finishing the war as well and as soon as possible. He had brought along as his main economic adviser, not an economist, but one of his 'louche' friends, Frederick Lindemann, now Lord Cherwell, an Oxford physics professor, who doubled as Churchill's adviser on the secret Anglo-American atom bomb project. Colville was not the only one to think that Churchill 'has not yet given his mind to the complicated problems connected with finance . . . Lord Cherwell is in despair.'[82]

Churchill was not going to be diverted by the electoral passions of the month either. He thought the main Labour figures would attempt to stay with the government until a year or so after the defeat of Germany, though it was possible that the rank and file of the party would not allow this.

After the year had passed the Opposition would then attempt to profit from the 'inevitable disillusionment at the non-appearance of an immediate millennium'. Labour would undoubtedly try to sling mud, but he and his Conservative colleagues had a 'full armoury of mud to sling back'. He would not regret the departure of any of the Labour members of the current government who, apart from his Minister of Labour, Ernest Bevin, 'were mediocrities'. Churchill had little more to say on the matter. Perhaps there would be an early election. Perhaps Parliament would be taken over by a great left-wing majority. Then, 'let it be so,' said Churchill: 'What is good enough for the English people, is good enough for me.'[83]

His reticence was to a great extent due to a realization – several weeks before his generals or public opinion in the United States and Britain – that the war was not going to be finished in 1944. He thought the Chiefs of Staff were too optimistic in their estimates. 'At the present time', he minuted Ismay on 8 September, 'we are at a virtual standstill.'[84] He appreciated the yo-yo effect: the Red Army was advancing fast into Romania and Bulgaria. But Hitler, he thought, would still be fighting on 1 January 1945 and the war could go on until spring or summer.

This would affect not only the British electoral date but also Britain's finances. How great would be the gap between the defeat of Germany and the defeat of Japan? Marathon negotiations with US Treasury officials had produced 'Stage I' and 'Stage II' extensions of Lend-Lease – the American war loans financing Britain's military effort and her dramatic loss of exports; but they were not designed to support a new welfare state, too. 'Stage I' took the loans up to Germany's defeat; 'Stage II' up to Japan's. But what then? As at the close of the First World War, American officials were silent on this point. Thus, from a purely financial point of view, it was in Britain's interest that the lapse of time between the German defeat and the Japanese lasted as long as possible. It was no mere coincidence that Britain's chief economic adviser aboard the *Queen Mary* was also privy to the development of the atom bomb.

'We received 2 minutes from the PM today which show clearly that he is a sick man,' wrote Brooke in his diary on 9 September. As CIGS, Brooke was solely concerned with military affairs. Churchill's arguments, he went on, 'are again centred on one point – Istria. We have come for one purpose only – to secure landing craft [from the Americans] for an operation against Istria!'[85] Istria was a peninsula at the north end of the Adriatic, just inside the Yugoslav border, though contested since the end of the First World War by Italy. Istria, technically speaking, was not a part of the Balkans, though it was definitely a part of the American

'Balkan bogey', as Ismay called it: Washington's suspicions of British 'imperial' intentions in Italy.

The Balkans, properly speaking, were certainly a part of Churchill's concern, most particularly Greece, birthplace of Western democracy and a possible bulwark against Russian-led Communism. Churchill was already expressing anxiety about this in September 1943, after a series of curious coincidences (like the deaths of Jean Moulin and Sikorski), after Kursk and the growth of the Partisan war in Belorussia, and before he set off for the summit with Stalin and Roosevelt in Teheran. He stated the problem even more clearly at an Imperial Conference in London the following spring, shortly before D-Day: he asked the Foreign Office to prepare a paper setting forth 'the brute issues between us and the Soviet Government which are developing in Italy, in Romania, in Bulgaria, in Yugoslavia and, above all, in Greece'. At the same time he told Eden, the Foreign Secretary, 'We are approaching a showdown with the Russians about their Communist intrigues in Italy, Yugoslavia and Greece.' On 31 May he broached the subject with Roosevelt and got a brusque response from Cordell Hull's State Department that they were opposed to 'establishing any postwar spheres of influence'.[86]

What drove Churchill to despair – and it was the reason he was in Italy during that crucial period in August as the American and British armies separated in France – was the depletion of Alexander's armies in Italy to serve in northern France, which made sense, and to join a new landing in the South of France, which did not. Why liberate southern France now? As events turned out, the area was delivered to three months of civil war and summary executions carried out by the French Communists. If reinforcements had to be sent into France, then why not land them in Brittany and strengthen the successful military advance on the northern plain. Most particularly – and close to Churchill's civilized heart – why not help instead of hinder Alexander's push north in Italy? Not only would this serve a similar purpose as the invasion of southern France, it also opened the possibility of getting Western troops to Vienna and even Prague before the Russians. Churchill had a point.

While in Italy, noting how weak the Italian front had become, he developed with his generals the idea of an amphibious operation on the Istrian peninsula. He faced three obstacles. In the first place, he did not have the landing craft; they would be needed for an operation on Rangoon, southern Burma, before the monsoon began in March, and the transfer over such a distance would take time. Secondly, there was the barrier of the misleadingly named 'Ljubljana Gap' which separated Istria from the Hungarian plain and Vienna: it was only a 'gap' in the sense that this formidable range of hills did not reach the heights of the Alps to the north or the Dinaric Alps to the south; but no army would have enjoyed crossing it. Thirdly, an obstacle of which few were aware at the time, was the extent to which misplaced 'patriotism' ('towards the USSR rather than towards Britain,' as Orwell had put it) had gone in the high civil service – several well-placed British functionaries were working for Soviet interests and not Britain's.

This was disastrously the case in Cairo, where southern European governments-in-exile (from the Nazis) were based and where many major Mediterranean strategic decisions were made. The British were the cause of their own problems here. In 1942 they had placed at the top of the Yugoslav section of SOE Cairo a most charming specialist in Balkan affairs. Like many civil servants in Cairo, James Klugmann turned out to be a Soviet agent.[87] All the reports briefing Allied military and political leaders were doctored in favour of Tito's Partisans and against Mihailović's royalist Chetniks, who were said to be working for the Germans (it was, in fact, Tito who was negotiating a truce with the Germans to keep the non-Communist Allies out of the region).[88] Churchill, under the influence of Klugmann's mendacious reports, pulled out all support for Mihailović and sent arms and agents, including his own son Randolph, to Tito. The week Churchill sailed for America the Royal Air Force and Tito's Partisans launched 'Operation Ratweek' designed to cut road and rail routes through Yugoslavia. Meanwhile the Red Army was on the Danube pushing south-east. 'I have asked Tito to make every effort to move his forces north-wards [towards Istria],' Churchill told his Chiefs of Staff, 'instead of using our weapons against his own countrymen.'[89]

Montgomery, in the meantime, had been promoted to Field Marshal; but he was left to decide on his own how best to deploy his army group in the lowlands of Belgium and Holland, with little support from the Americans.

A German submarine was reported to be lurking in the Gulf Stream on Saturday, 9 September; the *Queen Mary* veered northwards and 'there was a sudden fall of about 20 degrees in temperature, accompanied by clear skies and a fresh breeze.'[90] But no wind would blow away the difficulty facing Britain's dispersed armies, or the country's financial debt.

On Sunday, after lunch, the ship entered the port of Halifax, in Nova Scotia. The troops on board cheered, a band of Royal Canadian Mounties pounded out 'God Save the King' and 'O Canada'. Churchill was met by the British High Commissioner, Malcolm MacDonald, and accompanied to a train where, standing on the rear observation platform, Churchill made a little speech. 'This is not the first time we have been here in the war,' he said, recalling a summit he had had with Roosevelt one year earlier, 'but we have never been here before when the skies were brighter.' The crowd was ecstatic. Churchill liked that sort of thing, and was in excellent humour during the twenty-hour trip to Quebec.

His plan was to hold a formal reception on Roosevelt's arrival at the spot, below Quebec's cliffs, where General Wolfe had launched the battle that had turned the French out of Canada in 1759. But the President, forewarned of the schedule, made sure his special train, the *Ferdinand Magellan*, got there first; Roosevelt was seated in a car on the tarmac when Churchill's train pulled into Wolfe's Cove. 'I'm glad to see you,' roared out the President proudly, as the Prime Minister stepped up to the car. 'Look,' continued Roosevelt, waving his hand at his wife, 'Eleanor's here.' Churchill boomed out, 'Hello there.' Ismay said it was more like a happy family reunion than the beginning of a state summit. Eleanor recorded the same day: 'There is something boyish about the PM. Perhaps that is what makes him such a wonderful war leader.'[91]

8 The Knickerbocker president

On the same Sunday that Churchill landed in Nova Scotia, the National Weather Bureau in Washington received a report of a hurricane developing south-east of Puerto Rico. There was nothing unusual about this. It was the beginning of the standard hurricane month in the Caribbean, as cool autumnal air from continental America drove a wedge under the hot and sticky atmosphere of the Gulf Stream. Winds whirled upwards to over 100 mph, clouds spiralled to 40,000 or 50,000 feet. Such systems (hurricanes did not have names in those days) would normally move north-eastwards, losing their strength in the Atlantic and then drop bucketloads of rain in England and the northern plain of Europe. But during the night something freakish happened; the system turned west and headed, at a stately speed of 10 mph, towards the coast of Florida. On Tuesday night it changed direction again, rolling northwards at 30, 40, then 50 mph. 'It now appears certain that the Bahama Islands will escape full hurricane winds,' read the advisory bulletin of 9 p.m. By Wednesday morning it was clear that the storm was going to hit the coast somewhere between New Jersey and Long Island. There was a sudden shiver in the most populated corner of North America: no one there had forgotten the great hurricane of September 1938.

Heavy rains began falling on New York City on Thursday afternoon,

14 September. Many of the subways were closed. Seas rolled into the flat beaches of southern Long Island. Half a dozen communities on the New Jersey shore were evacuated. The wooden cottages of Manasquan Beach, Bay Head and Mantoloking were battened down with wire and rope. Because of the fear of German U-boats, ships had not been sending radio signals; instead, to get a bearing on the storm, the Army and Navy had been ordering aircraft out over the Atlantic. 'It was just like going up in an elevator,' reported Colonel Lloyd B. Woods, who flew a Douglas Havoc into the centre of the hurricane, just off Chesapeake Bay; 'it was like a giant upright funnel.'[92]

It slammed into the New Jersey coast and New York at around nine o'clock that night. The Gothic gables and the gingerbread decor of Cape May's ocean houses were torn apart. Trees were toppled, power lines snapped. The famous steel pier of Atlantic City was broken apart by mountainous waves and the boardwalks ripped up. Gusts of over 100 mph were recorded blowing up Broadway at the corner of Wall Street. Cornices crashed down from towering buildings. Brooklyn and Queens were plunged into darkness. Mrs Frank 'Sis' Norris, the proprietress of Ocean Beach Inn on Fire Island, had been through all this in 1938. She offered her inn as a haven to the several hundred persons trapped on the beach. One of the residents had landed a 22-pound striped bass while surf-casting. A fish-fry was organized. Then the electricity cut off and the jukebox went dead. In the blackness, Mrs Norris arranged a 'community sing'.

The Connecticut State War Council cancelled the night shift in the factories of Hartford. The war industries of Boston, central and western Massachusetts were likewise closed. Cape Cod was cut off from the rest of the world. As dawn came on Friday people emerged to inspect the damage, the rows of felled trees, the roofs torn up, the flooding. Some of the new electoral posters were scattered about the streets. On one of them, Uncle Sam was pointing at a portrait of the President: 'I want YOU, FDR,' read the caption. 'Stay and finish the job.'

The presidential campaign of 1944 got into full swing during the week of the hurricane. Roosevelt was in Quebec discussing the end of the war and the future of the world with Churchill. The Republican Governor of New York, the forty-two-year-old Thomas E. Dewey, was touring the corn belt of the Midwest in his bid for the presidency; he had to leave the handling of the hurricane crisis to Acting Governor Joe R. Hanley. 'By the time I've finished my campaign the Democrats will know they've been in a fight,' proclaimed Dewey from his platform in Billings, Montana. Roosevelt's popularity had slipped sharply in the week of the Liberation of Paris; in seven days his support had gone down, according to the polls, from a 55 per cent rating to 49 per cent. Dewey had picked up four points, to 44 per cent. This was almost entirely due to Dewey's charisma, which stood out brightly against the ageing Roosevelt. There was, as the pollsters remarked, 'a tendency to shy away from the Democrats with the end of the war and a feeling that the liberation of Paris brought the end near'.[93] The New Deal had lost its glamour by the late 1930s; only the war had saved Roosevelt. Though the US was probably no further right by late 1944, Roosevelt clearly was in for a fight.

Dewey made an appeal to Polish-American voters by declaring 1 September, the sixth anniversary of Hitler's invasion of Poland, 'Tribute to Poland Day'; Ambassador Jan Ciechanowski came to New York and opened an exhibition on 'Poland's Underground State' in the Rockefeller Center. But as electoral passions mounted, Poland slipped from the attention of Americans. Warsaw came into the news at the time of the hurricane – but that was Warsaw in upper-state New York from where Thomas J. Curran, candidate for the Senate, denounced 'New Deal extravagance' and the 'failure of boondoggling projects'. In Columbus, Ohio, Governor John W. Bricker, Dewey's running mate, went further: the New Deal, he said, 'has adopted the basic doctrines of Nazism and Fascism'. The November election was 'as important a date to the future of America as V-day will be to the future of the world'.[94] In democratic America world ideology was rammed unbefittingly into local bottles – as the arguments that had raged in Washington over the last decade demonstrated so well.

The national leader, Roosevelt, was in large measure responsible for this. By birth, he was in many ways a more genuine aristocrat than Churchill, if one considers, not wholly incorrectly, the early settler families of the Eastern Seaboard as a home-grown American aristocracy. The Roosevelts were one of the 'Knickerbocker' families – New York's equivalent of the 'Cave Dwellers' in Washington. They were of Dutch and English stock. 'Our society was a little "set", with its private catch-words, observances and amusements,' wrote Edith Wharton, one of Roosevelt's famous cousins. Their wealth came from commerce and real estate; they shunned industry and finance; they held New York's 'plutocrats' in contempt. One morning at breakfast Franklin's mother announced they had received a dinner invitation from Mrs Cornelius Vanderbilt. 'Sally, we cannot accept,' said Franklin's father – who thought Mrs Vanderbilt lovely and her husband delightful. 'If we accept we shall have to have them to our house.' Churchills were linked with the Vanderbilts; Roosevelts were not. It was that disdain for the moneymakers that drove many of Europe's high-born aristocrats into the left of politics; so it was for the Roosevelts.[95]

Franklin Roosevelt went to all the right schools – Groton, Harvard, Columbia Law. He had a quick grasp of facts, and a charm that could win over most people (including de Gaulle on two personal encounters). His manner of speech was conversational – it was Roosevelt who introduced the radio 'fireside chat' – not oratorial like Churchill. A man of broad ideals, he was not a writer and lacked Churchill's flair for history and geography. He collected books, but probably did not read them.

The guide of his life was his cousin, President Theodore Roosevelt. Though separated by a generation, they went to the same schools; both served in the New York State Legislature and were appointed Assistant Secretary of the Navy in Washington; both were elected Governors of New York. They both fathered six children. Franklin married Theodore's niece Eleanor; it was President Teddy Roosevelt who gave the bride away in an elegant New York brownstone house on St Patrick's Day, 1905. 'Well, Franklin, there's nothing like keeping the name in the family!' noted the President at the end of the ceremony.[96]

FDR – he was 'Franklin' to no one but his cousin, his mother and his wife – cast his first vote in a presidential election in 1900 for the Republican McKinley–Roosevelt ticket. McKinley was assassinated the following year and Cousin Teddy moved into the White House. The President, though a Republican, was no conservative; he made his reputation as a 'trust-buster', breaking up the big financial corporations that ran America – trust-busting was second nature to a 'Knickerbocker' Roosevelt. Theodore Roosevelt moved left. Franklin Roosevelt moved left. For ten years, and for the only time in her history, America had a three-party system: Democrats, Republicans and the Roosevelts. But Franklin Roosevelt continued moving left. In the 1912 presidential election FDR gave his support to the Democratic candidate, the idealistic professor from Princeton, Woodrow Wilson. The Roosevelts were split between the Oyster Bay branch (Cousin Teddy) and the Hyde Park branch (FDR). FDR was awarded the post of Assistant Secretary of the Navy by Wilson, who got into the White House on the divided vote – one needed a name like Roosevelt to become a civilian boss of the Navy at the age of thirty-one. Cousin Teddy struggled like a bull-moose in the wilderness until his sudden death from exhaustion in January 1919.

FDR would remain loyal to Wilsonian ideals – the social programmes, the 'internationalism', the Points, Principles and Particulars of 1918[*] – until the end of his own life. But in one very important sense he remained

---

[*] Between January and September 1918 Wilson laid out his war aims in the form of Fourteen Points, Four Principles and Five Particulars. As the French Prime Minister, Georges Clemenceau, commented at the time, 'Even the Lord Almighty limited himself to Ten.'

a Roosevelt: as Assistant Secretary of the Navy his sympathies lay with Cousin Teddy's campaign to join the Allies in their war against expansionist Germany and not maintain the United States in an unreal, isolationist 'neutrality'. If anything the addition of this element to FDR's foreign policy pushed him yet further to the left because it would lead him to develop, in an ephemeral, Wilsonian fashion, sympathy for the Soviet Union.

The word 'Fascism' frequently came to Roosevelt's lips. As in the case of Orwell's England, the term owed more to Moscow's Popular Front of 1934 than to either Mussolini, Franco or Hitler. In 1938, the year the New Deal ran out of steam, Roosevelt told an audience in Gainesville, Georgia, how strongly he disagreed with an opinion expressed by the British economist, John Maynard Keynes, that businessmen were no more immoral than politicians. 'Today,' said Roosevelt, sounding as much a Knickerbocker as a Marxist, 'national progress and national prosperity are being held back chiefly because of selfishness on the part of a few.' His criticism of the 'plutocrats' could have been drawn straight out of *Pravda*. The 'plutocrats' opposed to progress believed 'that the feudal system is still the best system'. To which Roosevelt added this important historical point: 'There is little difference between the feudal system and the Fascist system. If you believe in the one, you lean on the other.'[97]

W. M. Kiplinger explained Roosevelt's vision of the post-war world in his guide to Washington, written in early 1942. 'If the planned economy of war works reasonably well,' he argued, 'it undoubtedly will be changed over and adapted for peace.'[98] Victory would bring the defeat of the plutocrats, the break-up of their international trusts and cartels, and end the feudal anachronisms of the Fascist system; world peace would be established in collaboration with the Soviet Union.

While on holiday in 1921 at the family's summer home of Campobello, in New Brunswick, Roosevelt had been struck down, at the age of thirty-nine, by a disease still popularly known as 'infantile paralysis', polio. Polio baffled the doctors. Polio epidemics were a recent phenomenon, they followed no pattern, they appeared without warning. The disease struck the richest countries in the world, and the richest classes in those countries – it seemed like God's revenge on the wealthy for the social inequity evident in all other diseases. It had been around for far longer than one thought; it was probably polio that crippled Walter Scott; and the Prince de Talleyrand, France's great statesman at the Congress of Vienna, was almost undoubtedly a victim of polio. Polio was spread by the great epidemic of 1916. But only after the war did it start attacking adults –

Roosevelt was one of the first victims of this new version of polio. It would add to the awe Americans and Europeans felt for the wartime President: for the Second World War gave polio a second boost and it became one of the great pests of the post-war world. Roosevelt was a model of courage for all those who had polio.

Roosevelt was paralysed from the hips down. But he was most discreet about this handicap. Anyone who attempted to photograph Roosevelt in a wheelchair, or being carried or pushed, was liable to have his camera snatched from him by a Secret Service man and his film exposed. In the Roosevelt Library at Hyde Park there are 35,000 photographs of the President, and only two of him in a wheelchair; no newsreels show him being carried or pushed. At public meetings he was seated before the public entered; a suite was designed at the Statler in Washington so that no one could notice his transfer; the White House was refurbished; his special train departed from the basement of the Treasury.

Polio could well have destroyed his political career, for Americans liked their president to be athletic. Instead, polio pushed him along a singular, determined line; he became the saviour of the destitute during the Great Depression, the hope of the nation during the war. Polio did not change Roosevelt's personality, it confirmed it: it made him even more ambitious. The victory in his personal struggle convinced him of his indispensability; the need to hide his physical handicap made him the greater dissimulator. It made him secretive. The small circle around him, his 'Brains Trust', knew that his friendly, hearty talk was only a front. De Gaulle made the unusual mistake of relaxing his guard when he received a 'Hallo, Charles!' from the President in Casablanca, but was quick to lose his illusions; Churchill always believed Roosevelt 'a friend' and was permanently deceived. Many of Roosevelt's closest acquaintances at the White House wrote, after his death, what 'life was like at the centre'. But none of them were at the centre, for Roosevelt, unlike Churchill, confided in no one. He would never let them know the whole picture. Sam Rosenman, one of Roosevelt's speech-writers (a job unknown to Churchill), claimed that Roosevelt was the 'only person who knew everything about a project'. Anna, his daughter, told a friend in 1944, 'He doesn't know any man and no man knows him.'[99]

In 1944 Roosevelt had a major secret to keep. On 18 August his running mate, Harry Truman, came round to the White House for a meeting, only their second during that electoral year. Tea was served and, according to Truman, in pouring the cream into his cup Roosevelt's hands were shaking so much 'that he got more cream in the saucer than he did in the cup'. Truman's impression was that physically Roosevelt was 'just going to pieces'.[100]

A hand tremor is one of the side effects of polio, and is hardly serious. But Roosevelt's thin, wan appearance suggested something else. At Bethesda, the main military hospital in the Washington area, Dr Howard G. Bruen, a leading specialist in cardiovascular disease, had inexplicably left his post in April. In San Diego on 21 July, on his way out to visit the Pacific fleet, Roosevelt delivered his acceptance speech as presidential candidate for a fourth term. By all accounts, his performance was poor. The photographs, however, were worse. His withered legs were plainly visible beneath the small table from where he spoke; his elongated face was turned down as he read, thus making it look thin. Behind him was the profile of a man whom Dr Ross Golden of Columbia Presbyterian Hospital instantly recognized. 'Did you notice?' he asked his X-ray assistant after seeing the photograph in *Life* magazine. 'That man is Dr Bruen, a cardiologist.' Rumour spread through several major hospitals in America that the President had a heart problem.[101]

He did. But J. Edgar Hoover of the FBI was not going to let the truth out. His agents were sent into the hospitals concerned and some very muscular methods were used to ensure that the news was not carried beyond their own green corridors.[102]

Roosevelt had suffered a serious heart attack on 28 March 1944. From that day on he was rarely able to work over four hours a day. He frequently rose from his bed after 11 a.m. (Churchill did too, but he had already put in a morning's work) and was back in bed before 6 p.m. His main diet was rice and scrambled egg. Roosevelt was absent from the White House for 175 days in the year 1944; not, like Churchill, because he was travelling, but because he was resting, often at Bernard Baruch's 23,000-acre estate in South Carolina, in the polio clinic at Warm Springs in Georgia or, less frequently, on his own estate at Hyde Park. Sprawling, discordant, tumultuous Washington had no active President in the White House in the last year of the Second World War.

9 In his absence

This is not to say that Washington had no policy. London simply sought to survive the war; Washington had a distinct set of war aims, defined at root by Roosevelt's peculiar version of Wilsonism: a revised League of Nations, a break-up of the plutocrats' international (and 'Fascist') cartels, money reform, trade reform, and a partnership with the Soviet Union – all imposed, rather than negotiated, by American economic power. The policy was already in place with the passing of the Lend-Lease Act in

1941, but with the resident of the White House largely absent the initiative had moved, by 1944, across to the two neighbouring buildings, the State Department and the Treasury. The future of Europe lay largely in their hands. America's post-war policy and the institutions it created for the world were born out of the actions of Cordell Hull's State Department and its rival, Henry Morgenthau's Treasury.

As had been the case with Wilson during the First World War, the territorial issues of Europe had been of no concern to Roosevelt since the outset of hostilities: set up sound international institutions first, Roosevelt seemed to say, and the territorial problems will settle themselves. At Stalin's insistence, however, a broad outline had been agreed upon at Teheran in November 1943: the Soviet Union would be granted the frontiers of 1941 (that is, those gained by the Nazi-Soviet Pact); Poland, by way of compensation, would have its western border with Germany shifted to the Oder–Neisse line (thereby abolishing Prussia); and Germany would be partitioned by the occupants. Up to the end of the war there was frequent talk of an 'Armistice' with Germany followed by a general 'Treaty', in conformity with the old European way of settling wars; but where exactly the Western Allies met up with the Red Army was a matter of indifference to Roosevelt. In particular, he did not want ticklish problems like Poland or Italy, which could upset the ethnic vote at home, discussed before the presidential elections.

Letters Roosevelt wrote in response to Churchill's lively, sprawling epistles, were brief – and were in many cases written by his new Chief of Staff, Admiral William Leahy, Roosevelt's former ambassador to Vichy France. Robert Murphy, who as American resident in Algiers had engineered America's disastrous Darlan scheme to keep the Vichy regime alive, was now America's chief civilian counsellor to the Allied armies on the occupation of Germany. Churchill, misguided by British Soviet agents in Cairo, did manage to persuade the Americans to cease all support to General Mihailović in Yugoslavia. Leahy, signing as the President's proxy, confirmed this on 3 September. 'The mission of OSS [America's equivalent of SOE] is my mistake. I did not check with my previous action of last April 8th. I am directing Donovan[*] to withdraw his mission' – so Mihailović was doomed, eventually executed on Tito's order in 1946. Another brief missive, drafted by Leahy on 5 September, seemed to indicate a solution to the Warsaw dilemma: 'I am informed by my office of

---

[*] General 'Wild Bill' Donovan, head of OSS, was not much concerned about Communist infiltration of his organization. 'I'd put Stalin on the OSS payroll if I thought it would help us defeat Hitler,' he boasted. Soviet agents at OSS headquarters in Washington, it is said, 'were probably well into double figures'.

Military Intelligence that the fighting Poles have departed from Warsaw and that the Germans are now in full control. The problem of relief for the Poles in Warsaw has therefore unfortunately been solved by delay and by German action and there now appears to be nothing we can do to assist them.' Roosevelt had never and would never get involved in diplomatic discussions concerning Central and Eastern Europe; he thus succeeded in keeping Poland out of the electoral campaign, though the desperate fight in Warsaw was to continue until October.[103]

It was America's electoral timetable, not the war's progress, which pushed Roosevelt's administration to lay the foundations of three of the most important international institutions of the post-war world: the International Monetary Fund, the World Bank and the United Nations. Roosevelt's team was determined to prove that they were 'internationalists' while their opponents were 'isolationists' – though Dewey would deny this to the end. Never, in the history of war and peace, had an international order been established in such a manner.

Nor had economics ever played such an essential role in the manner in which the principal post-war institutions were established. Adolf Berle, now Assistant Secretary of State, had got an inkling of this development when, as a young American delegate to the Paris Peace Conference in 1919, he had noted the swarm of what he called 'economic men' occupying the main hotels in the French capital – 'they are the hosts of minor retainers, gold-plated secretaries swaggering in splendid and unused uniforms'.[104] They were chiefly American and served as reminders to Europeans that in 1919 the gross national product of the United States had just overtaken that of the whole of Europe combined. Europe in 1919 still retained the military power – an imbalance which largely explained the difficulties of maintaining the peace during the inter-war years. During the Second World War, most of Europe was occupied by Nazi Germany, so that, besides Britain, there were no Western Allies to represent Europe.

Britain's successful resistance to the Nazis had the effect of reinforcing her imperial ties on the 'periphery' of the 'world island', as Sir Halford Mackinder had called the Eurasian continent: in economic terms this meant a reinforcement of the 'sterling area' as a single, but dispersed financial bloc – something that Joseph Chamberlain and his imperialist followers in 1900 could only have dreamed of. A curious alliance developed in Britain during the war years between imperialists, so unexpectedly strengthened, and left-wing dreamers of the social 'New Jerusalem'; both of them thought the future of British finance, and welfare, lay in imperial preferences, exchange control and the general defence of sterling.

For the Americans, particularly in Roosevelt's administration, the sterling area was an obstacle to the expansion of US trade in dollars. 'The United States is a coming nation and England is a going one,' said Henry Dexter White who, given his influence by the 1940s, should have been called Assistant Secretary of the Treasury but in fact remained Morgenthau's Director of Monetary Research until 1945. White, like Roosevelt, thought that the future of the world lay in a partnership with that other planned economy, sister in an international New Deal, the Soviet Union. Britain lay in the way of the march of history, not the Soviet Union.

When Churchill made his famous appeal for American financial aid in 1940 – 'Give us the tools and we will finish the job' – high officials in Washington immediately realized what this meant: an opportunity to smash the sterling area. It was the source of one of the greatest misunderstandings of the Second World War. The British spoke of a developing 'special relationship'; the Americans pursued their aim of undermining sterling.

At the end of the First World War Britain was able to counter American financial and trade demands by forming a front with her European allies, particularly France – this had proved to be especially effective, for example, in the negotiations over food commodities. A central figure in these negotiations had been the young Cambridge economist John Maynard Keynes, whose best-selling pamphlet, *The Economic Consequences of the Peace* (1919), deliberately omitted all the difficulties he had been having with the United States in order to blame, unfairly, the problems of the peace on the 'Carthaginian' peacemakers at Paris and the harsh conditions they imposed.

In the early 1940s, older and less healthy, he again represented the British Treasury and he was once more confronted with an aggressive America. But he had only a shadow of Europe to turn to, the London governments-in-exile; they were united in a 'European Advisory Commission' (which Gladwyn Jebb of the Foreign Office – the creator of many post-war European institutions – claimed was 'first advocated by me' at the time of the Teheran summit in November 1943).[105] The EAC met on several occasions in the last two years of the war to deliberate on the economic negotiations Keynes was undertaking with America and also to prepare the 'armistice terms' with Germany. It supported Keynes, but its powerless members complained that they were not sufficiently consulted.

The Second World War, by artificially reinforcing the sterling area, gave Churchill's Britain delusions of independent world power, bolstered by the 'special relationship', which in fact she did not have. Keynes's own negotiating position was influenced by this; most remarkably, in complete contrast to the Americans, Russia received no attention at all in his plans.

What Keynes ultimately sought was an economic *Pax Anglo-Saxonica*; what the officials in the American Treasury were after was an American–Soviet condominium, an 'international New Deal'.

The text of the Lend–Lease Act of 1941 had been prepared by officials of both the Treasury and the State Department. Section 3(b) authorized aid to Britain on 'terms and conditions' designed to 'benefit' the United States, by 'payment or repayment in kind on property or any other direct or indirect benefit which the President deems satisfactory'. For the US Treasury this meant the sale of Britain's overseas assets and a lowering of Britain's gold and dollar reserves. Article VII, the centrepiece of the treaty, was similar to Woodrow Wilson's 'free trade' clause in his Fourteen Points: 'the terms . . . shall be such as not to burden commerce between the two countries . . . they shall provide against discrimination in either the United States of America or the United Kingdom against the importation of any produce originating in the other country.' What Cordell Hull's State Department sought was the abolition of Britain's currency exchange controls and the dismantling of Britain's 'imperial preference' system. Keynes and his colleagues called the State Department's agenda behind Article VII 'Hullism' – it contained no guarantee that the United States would not, in subtle ways, erect tariff barriers of her own, while at the same time signalling the end of the sterling area.[106]

Lend–Lease, which enabled increasingly impoverished Britain to stay in the war, turned around trade systems and currency exchange; it denoted not merely a shift in the balance of power across the Atlantic, but also a change in the way wars were won and ended. In the Napoleonic wars Britain had financed her coalition partners (the 'United Nations') through direct subsidies that were not expected to be paid back. In the First World War she had extended credit to her European Allies; but to cover this Britain, in her turn, had become increasingly reliant on American credit – Keynes had tried, in vain, to get the Americans to extend credit directly to the European Allies but the United States, which insisted on being an 'associate' and not an 'ally', refused. In the Second World War, there were no European Allies for they had been knocked out by the Nazis; and it was Britain herself that was in desperate need of American credit.

Britain's subsidy system during the Napoleonic wars had kept economics in the background of the final peace conference; the Congress of Vienna (1814–15) was essentially a political settlement. The tangled network of war credits and debts during the First World War (for which Keynes himself was to a great extent responsible) created a tension at the Paris Peace Conference (1919–20) between political affairs and economic matters that, though complex, was by no means insoluble: it was the statesmen of the

1920s and '30s who blocked the solution, not the peacemakers at Paris. In the Second World War, the financial dependence of Britain, without European Allies, on the United States expelled politics from the developing plans for a peace settlement. Thus, it was the discussion of monetary matters which led to the creation of the World Organization (later 'United Nations'), not the other way round. Both the monetary agreement and the accord for a World Organization were achieved within the frontiers of the United States; they followed an American electoral timetable, not the war: and here lies one of the principal reasons why the Second World War, in contrast to all preceding major European wars, was not concluded by an international peace conference. Indeed, no politically agreed peace was ever established in Europe as a whole.

Trade and money would establish the peace. But until late in 1943, just months before the D-Day landings, neither London nor Washington could decide whether the process should start with trade or with money. Hull's State Department kept pressing for a trade agreement, but neither the British Treasury nor the Foreign Office could accept the terms of Hull's agenda. The solution was found by two men working, independently and unknown to each other, on plans inside the Treasury in London and inside the Treasury at Washington: a trade agreement, they both admitted, was most unlikely; so start with a monetary accord – this will bring the nations together and from that you will be able to build up world trade and prosperity.

Keynes was an old English Liberal. He had a quasi-religious belief in the corporate freedoms of the old universities, in the general benefit of elitist culture, in the superiority of art over industry and finance. He was nostalgic for a Victorian world of free trade and stable currencies. But he was also the greatest economist of the inter-war years; he knew there was no going back. He had opposed the return to the gold standard in the 1920s because it forced downward adjustment on the small debtor countries, the countries that were least likely to force their exports on the rest of the world by a relative lowering of their prices; the cumulative effect of this was, as he had predicted, a decline in the flow of trade. Keynes's plan introduced modern 'banking principles' into world trade: gold reserves were dead, he argued, like medieval coins; instead he advocated a new international Clearing Union in which each member country would have access to an account, with overdraft facilities, held in a new international money, 'bancor'. 'Bancor' would be created by the monetary authorities and not tied to gold. Thus the Credit Union would possess the power of credit creation and provide a motor to trade development.[107]

Keynes's plan was a precursor to monetary supply doctrines which govern world trade today. His idea of an international bank opened the way for discussions between the London and Washington Treasuries in late 1942, which the trade disagreements had prevented. But Keynes's notion of a created 'bancor' was too unorthodox and 'inflationary' for the Americans; it was White's plan that became the basis of the new international currency project, and pivot for the whole network of post-war international institutions.

White was not a liberal. He thought little of Europe; his main concern was how the Great Ally, the Soviet Union, would fit in. Keynes had nothing to say on the Soviet Union; his principal worry was finding a place for Britain. But White, an energetic planner and organizer, sought to make the alliance between an America of the New Deal and the Soviet New World Order an economic reality. His own staff, selected and vetted during his five years as Director of Monetary Research, easily outgunned his boss, Henry Morgenthau; and he pushed the elderly Cordell Hull into retreat. By 1944, with the President so frequently absent, high civil servants of the State Department worried that White was not only appropriating the economic policy of the nation but also advancing dangerously into their own fiefdom of foreign policy. White's chairmanship of several inter-departmental committees from spring 1942 seemed to set him on the steps to coronation. Henry Wallace, Roosevelt's Vice-President during his third term of office, said that if the President had died during that time he would have made Henry White his Secretary of the Treasury and Laurence Duggan – another friend of the Soviet Union who had come under the influence of Alger Hiss in the State Department – his Secretary of State.[108] But it was Harry Truman who was nominated vice-presidential candidate in August 1944, when the Democrats found they needed the centre vote; Roosevelt did not die until the following April.

White's plan involved the setting up of two institutions, an International Stabilization Fund designed to prevent disruption of the monetary and credit system between participating members, and a Bank of Reconstruction and Development that would supply relief and reconstruction capital. White's plan even included, like Keynes's, an international currency called 'unitas' that would be based, in contrast to Keynes's system of credit creation, on receipts for gold deposits. Faced with the opposition of both the State Department and New York bankers, 'unitas' quickly disappeared from the plan and the Bank was pushed into the background.

Many economic technicians around Keynes were elated to discover the similarities between Keynes's plan and White's. 'The Americans offer us

. . . what we could never have asked of them in the negotiations,'
exclaimed Roy Harrod, a member of Churchill's Statistical Branch and
a man very close to Keynes.[109] Keynes himself was less enthusiastic: he
rightly saw that White sought to revive the gold standard, by pegging
the dollar to gold and all other currencies to the dollar, that freedom to
change the exchange rate would be lost; and that this was no solution
to Britain's dire balance of payments deficit. What he did not know was
that White was deliberately aggravating the trade balance problem through
a mechanical control by the US Treasury (and therefore by White and
his colleagues) of British currency reserves as stipulated in the terms of
Lend-Lease. Nor did Keynes realize that the purpose of the revived gold
standard was to attach the Soviet Union to the system and support it
through a separate Lend-Lease agreement.

The secret White never revealed to Keynes was his role, as interdepartmental chairman, in keeping British reserves in gold and dollars within the
range of $600 million and $1 billion. This was done with the help of a
close colleague of White's, Lauchlin Currie, who was chief administrator
of the Foreign Economic Administration (the FEA), the organization that
ran Lend-Lease. They achieved this by extending American requirements
for free deliveries from Britain and by reducing the supply of American
goods, which was possible under the terms of the Lend-Lease agreement.
Thus White and Currie could be sure that Britain by the end of the war
would be facing a hugely adverse balance of payments deficit – even before
Beveridge's campaign for a 'New Jerusalem' got fully under way.

Jacob Viner, the economics professor who had first introduced White
into Morgenthau's Treasury, complained from a position he held in the
State Department that neither Keynes's nor White's plans took into account
the difficult 'transition' that countries would face as war turned to peace.
Within months of the reopening of financial negotiations between Britain
and the United States, 'transition' became the name of the game – an
extension of Lend-Lease beyond 'Stage I' (total world war with Germany
and Japan), to 'Stage II' (semi-war with Japan), to 'Stage III' (world peace).
The State Department began hinting to British officials that at 'Stage II'
Lend-Lease would be converted into a straight loan, with interest. This
gave Harry White a golden opportunity to extend his influence.

White wanted an international treaty for his Fund, if possible approved
by Congress, ready to hand to Roosevelt at the outset of the presidential
campaign in August 1944. He had written to Keynes to this effect on 19
November 1943, asking that they be prepared for an international conference to take place in Washington between March and April 1944 so that
the treaty could go before Congress in May. There were delays – due to

D–Day and British insistence on a bilateral accord before the conference – so that the conference did not take place until July, a hot and sticky month in the District of Columbia. Keynes, who was not in the best of health, pleaded with White not to 'take us to Washington in July, which should surely be a most unfriendly act'. So the great international encounter on world money took place in a north-eastern mountain resort, Bretton Woods.[110]

There were more nations represented at the Bretton Woods conference in July 1944 than at the Paris Peace Conference of 1919. Many of these nations, of course, were but shadows of themselves – among them, France, whose Provisional Government under de Gaulle had still not been recognized by either the Americans or the British. Pierre Mendès-France, the Socialist parliamentarian and adept economist, who would later be Prime Minister, was the country's chief delegate. With the Western Allies stalled under heavy German resistance, and Warsaw preparing its Rising, one might have expected other things than money to be on the minds of world leaders. But the determining factor was not the progress of the war; it was the American election.

The conference lasted less than a month. The hustle of the 730 delegates and their clerical staffs was reminiscent of Paris in 1919, or Vienna in 1814–15; the concluding agreement was called the 'Final Act', just as it had been at Vienna. Harry White played a role similar to that of Friedrich Gentz at Vienna, or Maurice Hankey at Paris. Except that White dominated the proceedings. He ran the daily journal, which reported on the conference's progress; he spoke at the daily press conferences; he manipulated the lawyers who added to the growing 'Articles of Agreement'; the principal accords were made in his private offices; he chaired the most important of the three Commissions, that of the Fund – Morgenthau chaired the third, while Keynes was put in charge of the Commission of the Bank. The Bank was not at that time of any importance; Keynes's chairmanship of this Commission kept him out of mischief (or 'bamboozlement', as the Americans regularly denominated it).

The Final Act, as it was presented to forty-four nations at a banquet on Saturday evening, 19 July, was wholly American, wholly White. Keynes achieved just three things: he prolonged the 'transition' phase for Britain; he assured a degree of freedom for changes in sterling exchange rates; and he changed the name of White's 'International Stabilization Fund' to the 'International Monetary Fund', the 'IMF' – and so it remains to this day.

One of the problems solved was the number of dollars made available to each country as their 'quotas' within the Fund. White's assistant in the

Treasury worked out the amounts allocated, though how he calculated this was never made public. Russia was angry because she did not get as much as Britain; France was furious at getting less than China. Morgenthau boasted that he was Secretary of the Treasury because 'I can add and subtract.' The final distribution of quotas was announced on 14 July. The largest five quotas were held by the USA, Britain, the Soviet Union, China and France, who over the next nine months would secure their seats as permanent members of the United Nations Security Council.

This was the link between the monetary agreement and the new version of the League of Nations. Cordell Hull was eager to make his gift, too, to the President's campaign, so immediately after the presentation of the IMF's 'Final Act', the State Department organized a new international conference at a complex on the west side of Washington, Dumbarton Oaks. Hull, another sick man, was not nearly as accomplished a showman as White; one British official with a long memory complained that working with Hull was like dealing with Prime Minister William Gladstone in his old age. And the Russians proved hard to accommodate: they demanded a right of veto in voting on the Security Council.

Time was pressing – not because of Arnhem, or the Russian advance into the Balkans, but because there were barely four weeks left to the presidential campaign. 'Tentative Proposals' of the 'World Organization' were therefore published in Washington on 9 October. They were virtually identical to the final 'Charter of the United Nations Organization' presented to the nations assembled in San Francisco the following April, as Berlin fell. The only Article left completely unresolved was in Chapter VI, on 'Voting': 'The question of voting procedure in the Security Council', it read, 'is still under consideration.'[111]

Roosevelt was thus armed to lead his campaign against the 'isolationist' Republicans. Governor Dewey, on the day the UN proposals were published, announced that he was 'going as far as the Administration, and would be willing in certain respects to go farther'. He hinted that it was the Democrats who were being isolationist, reminding them: 'What we are doing is not writing an American programme, but one that will be agreed to by other nations, whose points of view also have to be considered.'[112]

While the conference at Dumbarton Oaks was under way, Morgenthau and White took a plane to London, ostensibly to discuss their plans for imposing an American printed currency on the liberated areas of France (standard practice for zones under AMGOT). But this was a hopeless task; de Gaulle had beaten them to it. Their real purpose was to involve the

US Treasury in the coming negotiations on 'Stage II' of Lend-Lease while Hull was busy at his conference – 'Dumbunny Oaks' as his enemies called it.

Besides the control White and Currie were exerting on British reserves, there were other secrets kept from both British and American governments. Currie was a Soviet agent. So was White.

Roosevelt was, or at least should have been, aware of the fact. In 1938 Whittaker Chambers, a courier for the Soviet intelligence network in the United States, left the Communist Party at the height of Stalin's purges. The following year, on 2 September, shortly after the signing of the Nazi-Soviet Pact and one day after Hitler's invasion of Poland, he gave a list of names of Soviet agents working in Washington, including those of Currie and White, to Adolf Berle, the Assistant Secretary of State who also worked as Roosevelt's security adviser. Berle drafted a memorandum, but Roosevelt completely ignored it: during the 1930s his government had frequently been labelled by his opponents as 'Communist', and he treated such charges as absurd. The FBI finally laid hands on the report in 1943; but it took Edgar Hoover over a year to move in on what proved – with the publication in the late 1990s of the VENONA transcripts of messages to Moscow along with the Mitrokhin Archive, painfully copied by a KGB employee (under threat of his life) from Soviet secret documents – to be a vast wartime network of Soviet espionage throughout the Western world.[113]

White was considered such an important spy for the Russians that the Soviet secret service, the NKGB (as it was known at the time), insisted on maintaining contact with him even when he travelled. Though he deserves as much notoriety as the Cambridge Five – Anthony Blunt, Guy Burgess, John Cairncross, Donald Maclean and Kim Philby – economics remains an obscure subject for most historians; it is much easier, and more romantic, to write about the betrayal of state secrets of high diplomacy, military planning and atomic bombs, than the world organization of currencies and finance. Yet it was the latter that laid the base of the post-war order.

Immediately after the Bretton Woods Conference, on 31 July, White had a conversation in his own Washington flat with a Soviet 'illegal resident', Vasili Zubilin. He told him about the Lend-Lease negotiations he was expecting to hold with the British, the plans he had for the 'technique of control over Germany while reparations are being paid', the trade policy he was going to pursue 'by means of bilateral agreements with individual states', and the trip he was about to make to Normandy and England (he noted his fear that Britain's reserves were growing and would have to be reduced by charges on the 'use of amphibians'). More particularly, in the area of foreign policy (over which he now clearly thought he had significant control), he confirmed what Roosevelt had already agreed informally with Stalin during the Teheran Conference of November 1943: that the Soviet Union's 1941 frontiers, which included annexations made under the terms of the Nazi-Soviet Pact, would be acceptable to the United States. Finland had lost the sympathy of Americans, he said. Seizure of the 'Baltic Countries' would not arouse American protest. And, most ominously on this day that the Rising was ordered in Warsaw, 'there will be achieved a compromise agreement to exclude from the Polish Government the most hostile elements' – hostile, that is, to the Soviet Union.

White also expressed fears about encroachments by the FBI. According to the encrypted message sent to Moscow, White himself 'did not think about his personal security but a compromise would lead to a political scandal and the discredit of all supporters of the New Deal'. Henceforth, he would have to be cautious: a few meetings in friends' houses, and 'conversations lasting up to half an hour while driving in his automobile'.[114]

Soviet agents in the United States acted under similar motives as the misplaced 'patriots' in Britain, inspired by the fight against 'Fascism' (even when they knew of the Stalinist Terror and the Nazi-Soviet Pact), the myth of the 'first worker-peasant state', a vision of the human race freed from exploitation by capitalists, the defence of the ideals of the left against the onslaught of 'reaction', the hatred of new men for the old which so characterized Washington in the early 1940s. But what was special about the American pro-Soviet networks was their complexity – as sprawling and as labyrinthine as the new American bureaucracy itself.

In the 1930s Stalin, like Hitler, did not consider the United States important. The centre of Western capitalist and imperialist power, he thought, lay in Britain, and it was to Britain that he sent his 'Great Illegals', the NKVD's illegal residents, the Soviet organizers of spy rings. The United States was left to the 'Fourth Department', a branch of military espionage and forerunner of the wartime GRU, which had nothing like the importance of the NKVD. The 'Great Illegals' were liquidated during Stalin's purges of 1937–8, as part of his war on foreigners and foreign residents. But 'illegal residents' returned to Britain once Hitler had invaded Russia. The ideologically faithful 'patriots' were waiting for them. The spy rings of Britain – like Whitehall, the civil service and the old university corporations – followed hierarchical lines.

There was nothing of the kind in the United States. In the first place, the Soviet 'illegals' had to be introduced during wartime; there would be vicious competition between them. Secondly, the home-grown spy rings, defenders of the New Deal and of the Soviet planned system, were not as willing as Britain's misplaced 'patriots' to recognize Soviet illegal residents as their superiors; they wanted control of their own rings.

Such, for example, was the case of the Victor Perlo group, which recruited mainly within the growing War Production Board (WPB). The same was true of a major group organized around Nathan Gregory Silvermaster, born in the Ukraine, educated at the University of California at Berkeley, from where he got his doctorate in economics. Under Roosevelt's New Deal, Silvermaster worked as a statistician for the Farm Security Administration, around which he recruited his ring. He did this by advancing his adherents selectively up the ranks of government bureaucracy, a feat that was rendered possible by the cooperation of Lauchlin Currie, adviser to the President, and Harry Dexter White of the Treasury, the most important members of Silvermaster's group.

Silvermaster's Soviet controller was Jacob Golos. The 'courier' between Washington and Golos in New York was Elizabeth Bentley, a graduate of Vassar College, a Soviet spy as of 1938, and Golos's lover. Golos died suddenly on Thanksgiving Day 1943. Bentley fought for control of the Silvermaster group, refusing even to recognize the authority of the Soviet 'legal resident', linked with the Soviet embassy, Ishak Akhmerov. Such anarchy in the ranks of spies made it easy for the FBI to penetrate. Careless acts were performed. Elizabeth Bentley herself, like Whittaker Chambers in 1938, eventually 'defected'.

If anarchy was the chief mark of American Soviet spies, fervour for an American planned economy was their chief characteristic – a determination, as Julian Wadleigh, Soviet spy within the State Department, put it, 'to help stem the Fascist tide'.[115] It was an intrinsic part of American bureaucracy and politics. Communist sympathizers and fellow-travellers were as American as apple pie.

10 An American-Soviet house

Harry White, doctor of economy, had a most successful trip to England in 1944. It confirmed the magic charm he held over Henry Morgenthau, while at the same time increasing significantly his influence on London's Treasury and, through that, on Churchill's War Cabinet.

Both White and Morgenthau were Jews who, understandably, did not have much love for Germany. While flying to London, White showed

Morgenthau a plan the rival State Department had just produced for replacing 'German economic self-sufficiency for war' with 'an economy which can be integrated into an interdependent world economy'. It had been developed in coordination with the US Chiefs of Staff and it fitted in well with the 'free trade' ideology of 'Hullism'; it also, more surprisingly, tallied with a British interdepartmental paper, composed under Keynes's guidance in 1943, on post-war German 'reparations' – a subject dear to Keynes. The British plan, like that of the State Department, was to demilitarize and 'normalize' Germany's economy, returning it to the international world of trade.

Morgenthau was predictably furious at the State Department plan; 'a nice WPB job,' he called it. He told White to develop an alternative scheme. White, of course, already had one. He had discussed it in his Washington flat with the Soviet 'illegal', Zubilin – 'the technique of control over Germany while reparations are being paid'.[116]

White's plan was placed before a group of representatives from the American embassy, brought down to a rural retreat in Hampshire on 12 August. It was radical. Morgenthau made the presentation. The best way to destroy Germany's capacity for future wars, he argued, was to destroy all her industry and to divide the country into small administrative areas that would be converted to agricultural production. An important point, given the interest the US Treasury had in the 'Stage II' Lend-Lease talks, was that the plan offered Britain a chance to take over Germany's eliminated exports. One American official pointed out that Germany's huge population could not survive on agriculture alone; the surplus population, replied Morgenthau, could be shipped off to North Africa (Americans were still convinced that they, and not the French, administered the area). Another expressed concern that the proposal would 'replace a German hegemony on the Continent by a Russian one'. That was precisely what White was seeking: a New Deal, Soviet-planned, world condominium.[117]

The British Chancellor of the Exchequer was Sir John Anderson, a pompous civil servant who had, however, been admitted into Churchill's War Cabinet. Morgenthau made a great effort to cultivate Anderson; when Anderson, briefed by Keynes, revealed that his country was on the point of bankruptcy, Morgenthau said he thought he could arrange a generous deal on Stage II, provided, that is, the British did not lobby the friends they had been cultivating in the State Department, like Edward Stettinius or Dean Acheson. So Anderson placed the future of Britain's finances in the hands of Henry Morgenthau and, thus, those of Harry White.

Morgenthau and White's English visit strengthened the link between a number of post-war issues. Bretton Woods had posited the creation of a 'World Organization' (later the 'United Nations Organization') on the basis of a monetary agreement, with the hope that this agreement would extend into trade. The major trading problem of 1944 was between an artificially reinforced sterling area and an expanding dollar area. Linked to this were the developing negotiations over Stage II of Lend-Lease – which implied that Britain would seek a major role in the defeat of Japan after Germany's collapse. The United States showed little concern about Soviet advances into Europe; where the Western and Eastern armies met was a matter of complete indifference to the Americans – they expected to pull out their own forces soon after the war was ended. Churchill's government, on the other hand, was beginning to get worried; this was what lay behind their concern over the Italian campaign and Istria – a hope that Alexander's Eighth Army could be in Vienna and even Prague before the Russians.

The presence of many Soviet agents in high places in the British and American administrations had a distorting effect on policy – more so in the United States, where the President, because of his politics, had never taken the Communist menace seriously and had been, since March, critically ill. It is remarkable to note that American and British spying within the Soviet Union was virtually non-existent during the war years.

But by the autumn of 1944, as the American election campaign gathered pace, many Soviet agents in the United States were beginning to worry that their groups could be uncovered. No one was more concerned than Harry White – though he had assured Vasili Zubilin that he and his wife were 'ready to make any self-sacrifice' for the Soviet cause[118] – all the more since just at that moment he was developing his radical plan for post-war Germany, to the benefit of the Soviet Union and with the support, because of Lend-Lease, of Great Britain.

11 The pastoralization of Germany

One could hardly imagine a finer setting for a wartime summit. The view from the ramparts of Quebec's Citadel across the St Lawrence seaway, the Île d'Orléans and the hills beyond created a sense of being on the top of the world. The Union Jack, Royal Standard and Stars and Stripes fluttered at the mastheads. A soft, northern sun shone into the interior courtyard as the cars of Roosevelt and Churchill entered shortly before noon on Monday, 11 September.

Churchill was by now in sparkling spirits; he spent that afternoon with his Chiefs of Staff balancing the merits of a springtime attack on Rangoon,

Burma, against the need for a stab at Istria, Hitler's Adriatic 'armpit'. Churchill's main target was the armpit.

Roosevelt was grey and silent. General Ismay had not seen him since December. 'He seemed to have shrunk,' recollected the general; 'his coat sagged over his broad shoulders, and his collar looked several sizes too large.' Observant Clementine was quick to realize that he worked no more than four hours a day. The Canadian Prime Minister, W. L. Mackenzie King, confided in his diary how thin the President looked: 'It seemed to me that he had failed very much since I last saw him.' Admiral Cunningham, the First Sea Lord, thought he 'looked very frail and hardly to be taking in what was going on'. Churchill used the same phrase in private; 'very frail,' he remarked to Colville after taking his bath on Tuesday night.[119]

In fact, Churchill became extremely worried. On Thursday, after dinner in the Citadel, Roosevelt showed what Colville simply termed 'a shockingly bad film' – 'the PM walked out halfway through.' It was a sentimental colour film on the life of Woodrow Wilson, dwelling on the devastating stroke Wilson suffered while campaigning for the League of Nations in autumn 1919; Wilson failed in his campaign and was dead within five years. Churchill missed what Roosevelt exclaimed at the film's end: 'By God, that's not going to happen to me!'[*] But he saw enough footage to be frightened by the parallel. On Saturday, the last day of the conference, Churchill asked one of Roosevelt's doctors, Admiral Ross McIntire, to come to his room and then demanded a confidential statement on the President's condition. McIntire said that a June check-up had shown he had had a gall bladder attack while resting at Baruch's South Carolina estate, that he was tired, but that there was nothing organically wrong. 'With all my heart I hope so,' replied Churchill. 'We cannot have anything happen to this man. His usefulness to the world is paramount during these troubled times.'[120]

'What an ineffectual method of conveying human thought correspondence is,' said Churchill that same day at a press conference – 'telegraphed with all its rapidity, all the facilities of our – of modern intercommunication.' There were hoots of laughter in the crowd of journalists. 'They are simply dead, blank walls compared to personal – personal contacts.'[121]

Churchill believed in the value of summits: put well-meaning heads of state together and they will solve their differences. Churchill was more like Metternich than appeasing Chamberlain, to whom he is sometimes misleadingly compared. If Metternich had had his way, he would have

---

[*] Is this a defiant answer to George IV's famous last words, 'My God, this is death!'?

transferred a few of the leading statesmen of the Congress of Vienna to the nice little suburb of Baden, where, over a game of whist, they would have been able to solve the great problems of the day, create a 'Europe without distances', as Metternich called it. Metternich even spoke with Napoleon; but he understood the danger Napoleon represented. Chamberlain spoke with Hitler; but he did not understand Hitler. Churchill spoke with Stalin; but he knew Stalin's system had its prototype in Hell.

The structure of the conferences that developed in wartime America, with their plenary sessions, commissions and committees, had its ancestry in the Congress of Vienna. It showed even closer parentage with the Paris Peace Conference of 1919, which itself grew out of the Supreme War Council organized by the Allies during the First World War. There was an obvious parallel between the Big Four of Paris in 1919 and the Big Three of the Second World War. What had been drawn up at Dumbarton Oaks, and became the Charter of the United Nations Organization, had its origins in the work of the Phillimore Committee and General Jan Smuts, who had drafted the constitutional clauses of the League of Nations long before Woodrow Wilson took an interest in them. There was frequent reference during Second World War conferences, even at Quebec, to a future 'Armistice' with Germany to be followed by a 'Peace Conference'. The European Advisory Commission in London had even drawn up preliminary terms of an 'Armistice'. Roosevelt, like Wilson, had refused to commit himself to any details, while Cordell Hull's State Department remained opposed to 'secret treaties' and planned 'spheres of influence', which it considered the evil of European peacetime planning. The United States was now strong enough to impose its own terms.

But terms it began to seek. Harry Hopkins, Roosevelt's closest adviser during the New Deal years but now sick and falling out of favour, warned the British embassy in Washington in August that Roosevelt might 'be ready to take wider decisions than anyone at present expected'. On 2 September Lord Halifax, the ambassador, informed London that a Cabinet Committee on Germany had been set up; the Reich, as had been agreed at the 1943 Teheran summit, would be partitioned by the occupying powers and the industrial Ruhr Valley would be turned into an international zone; Morgenthau, reported Halifax, was working on a plan that would prevent the kind of hyperinflation that had struck Germany when the French reoccupied the Ruhr in 1923.[122]

Nobody in London was fully aware of Roosevelt's incapacity. Nor had they grasped the ferocious competition that had developed between the State Department and the Treasury, which, like two sovereign nations on Pennsylvania and New York Avenues, had by 1944 their own rival foreign policies. During the election campaign, with Governor Dewey already on the stump in the Midwest, government officials in Washington wanted to keep the public eye out of 'politics' at Quebec and emphasized that the summit dealt purely with 'military strategy'. This was also Churchill's view. In particular, as he put it in his memoirs, 'I wanted . . . to harmonize and grip the many plans and projects which were now before us. In Europe, "Overlord" was not only launched, but triumphant. How, when, and where could we strike at Japan, and assure for Britain an honourable share in the final victory there?' 'At 11.30 we had a Plenary meeting, which consisted of a long statement by the PM giving his views as to how the war should be run,' recorded the exasperated General Brooke in his diary on Wednesday, 13 September. 'According to him we had two main object-ives, first an advance on Vienna, secondly the capture of Singapore!'[123]

But Churchill knew, through the British embassy, that something polit-ical was in the offing and, with talk about 'Stage II' of Lend-Lease devel-oping, had realized the linkage between the Japanese war and Britain's economic future. What did the Americans have in mind for Europe? He had his moments, as during his Gulf Stream voyage, of despair. He was expecting some discussion on the future of Germany, but had not yet had time to go over the briefs on the 'vexed Zones of Occupation'. Colville proposed to read them aloud as he took his bath on Tuesday evening. 'This bizarre procedure was accepted,' recorded Colville, 'but the diffi-culties were accentuated by his inclination to submerge himself entirely from time to time and thus become deaf to certain passages.'[124]

The split of the British and American armies on their approach to the Rhine was never discussed – Montgomery was left to face this problem entirely alone. The last horrifying phase of the Warsaw Rising was not mentioned – Warsaw was the forgotten orphan of the conference, as it was of the press.

Churchill, however, was deeply worried about Russia. That same Tuesday he received a telegraph from Eden that Bulgaria was already discussing armistice terms with the Soviet government; the Soviet 'pres-ence in the Balkans is bound to produce strong political reactions'. Churchill answered that there was 'a general feeling among the Staffs that we ought to have a showdown with the bear pretty soon': these were 'profound matters' and he ordered Eden to fly out immediately to Quebec. At the same time he informed Roosevelt that Eden would be 'here on Thursday or Friday'. 'Glad Anthony is coming,' came the reply from the President. 'I will get Cordell or Stettinius here on Friday. Morgenthau gets here Thursday at noon.' But neither Cordell Hull nor Edward Stettinius of the State Department ever turned up. Hull was still running his conference at Dumbarton Oaks; it was the Treasury that had the upper hand in Washington politics at this moment. On Wednesday afternoon, much earlier than expected, the two leading figures of the Treasury joined the summit conference, Henry Morgenthau and his Director of Monetary Research, Harry Dexter White.[125]

The first plenary session was just concluding. Churchill had dominated the meeting. But Roosevelt made some final remarks that seemed to come out of the blue. 'There are certain groups in the United States, and no doubt similar groups exist in Great Britain,' he said reproachfully, 'who evince a kindly attitude towards the Germans.' No doubt, Roosevelt was thinking of many German-Americans in the Midwest, where Dewey was busy campaigning. 'Such sentiments would never be tolerated in Great Britain,' responded Churchill, unaware that a major American policy decision was about to be announced. 'The British people would demand a tough policy.'[126]

That evening in the Citadel there was a banquet, with seating arrangements that placed Morgenthau next to Roosevelt, Lord Cherwell next to Churchill and Harry Dexter White on the same table – seating that represented a remarkable break in protocol. Morgenthau began the evening by describing the radical plan White had been working on since his July discussion with Vasili Zubilin. Morgenthau had only got through a few sentences when Churchill began fidgeting and muttering. When he got to the end, the Treasury Secretary received a 'verbal lashing' such as he had never received in his life. Churchill said the plan – the 'Morgenthau Plan' as it has gone down in history – was 'unnatural, un-Christian and unnecessary'. 'I'm all for disarming Germany, but we ought not to prevent her living decently,' said Churchill, who could remember the way the German 'indemnities' issue had developed during the 'Coupon Election' of November 1918. 'There are bonds between the working classes of all countries and the English people will not stand for the policy you are advocating. I agree with Burke, You cannot indict a whole nation.' There was the memory of the 'War Guilt' clause in the Versailles Treaty. And, at that moment, it was still thought that Germany could be beaten within months, perhaps weeks: a British general election would swiftly follow.

Roosevelt remained disconcertingly silent, finally breaking the tension with a little joke. Morgenthau did not sleep well that night.[127]

The next morning, Thursday, Cherwell had a long discussion with Morgenthau and then came back to Churchill in the early afternoon to explain the linkage of the plan to Britain's economic future.

Churchill's concern that morning had been to get the Americans to accept a major role for the British fleet in operations against Japan following the defeat of Germany. The American naval chief, Admiral Ernest King, 'lost his temper entirely' – his daughter had said he was 'the most even-tempered man in the Navy; he is always in a rage' – but Roosevelt simply accepted the British proposal, and that was the end of the argument. A story circulated that Admiral King went into a swoon; but this was an exaggeration. 'A very successful meeting,' concluded Brooke in his diary that day.

The link with Britain's finances was established in the afternoon when Churchill met with Roosevelt to discuss 'Stage II', the continuation of Lend-Lease during what was then calculated to be the eighteen-month period between Germany's defeat and the surrender of Japan. Churchill, according to the minutes, asked for 'food, shipping etc. from the United States to cover our reasonable needs'. Roosevelt 'indicated assent'. Churchill then asked that the United States not attach conditions to supplies deliv-ered to Britain which, according to the minutes, 'would jeopardize the recovery of her export trade'. Roosevelt replied, as usual briefly, that Churchill's proposal 'would be proper'. Neither of these answers were formalized in writing. Churchill's frustration is indicated by his wondering aloud, at one stage in the conversations, whether he ought to stand up on his hind legs, like Roosevelt's Scotch terrier, Fala, and beg.

Yet he had won his greatest prize, the honour of having the British navy participate in Pacific operations. And before he went to bed at two o'clock the following morning, he told Colville of the financial advan-tages the Americans had promised the British. 'Beyond the dreams of avarice,' remarked Colville. 'Beyond the dreams of justice,' growled back Churchill.[128]

It was probably the accord on the navy, along with his conversations with Roosevelt on Lend-Lease, which finally changed Churchill's mind on the plan Morgenthau had presented on Wednesday night. Moreover, all day Thursday the Prime Minister's old friend Cherwell had been badg-ering him on the financial advantages the plan represented for Britain's export trade. Eden had arrived late in the afternoon, after a seventeen-hour flight across the Atlantic. He was joined by another Foreign Office official, Sir Alexander Cadogan, who had flown up from Washington, where he was attending Hull's conference at Dumbarton Oaks. 'The future of my people is at stake,' said Churchill in presenting Eden the plan, 'and when I have to choose between my people and the German people, I am going to choose my people.' Morgenthau, who thought he had won Eden's support during his London trip in August, was shocked to discover Eden's outright hostility. Eden told Churchill that he would never get the support of London's War Cabinet, let alone Parliament. But Churchill was now determined to agree some version of the plan with the Americans. An accord was reached on Friday, 15 September.[129]

White's initial plan had gone through four successive drafts, each one more radical than the last. By the end of the first week of September the plan envisaged turning the Ruhr into a 'ghostland'. The industrial region of the Saar was to be destroyed, as were all war-related manufactures throughout Germany. All machinery and factory materials were to be turned over to the Russians. The advantages offered to the begging dog, Britain, were to be in terms of an expanded export business (one which, so White had made clear to the Russians, he intended to control).[130]

On Thursday, 14 September, while Churchill was winning a place for the Royal Navy in the Japanese war, Morgenthau, White and Cherwell worked on a short version of the plan. It was presented to Churchill on Friday morning. Churchill did not like it at all. He dictated his own version, which was considerably milder than the plan White had intended. Although it is Churchill's version that is usually quoted in history texts, it was White's version that continued to dominate thinking in the US Treasury Department. The differences were capital. In particular, the short version rejected by Churchill stated that 'Russia and the remaining Allies' should take from the Ruhr and the Saar the machinery 'they wanted'; Churchill's version spoke of the machinery 'they needed'. The rejected version spoke of the closing down of the Ruhr and Saar regions as being merely 'a part of a program for the transformation of Germany into a dominantly agricultural economy'; Churchill's version referred to the elimination of the 'war-making industries' in the Saar and the Ruhr as being 'one step in the direction of converting Germany into a country primarily agricultural and pastoral in character'. The word 'pastoral' appears to have been picked up by the Prime Minister from Morgenthau during his visit to London and, at Quebec, introduced into this resounding Churchillian phrase. Most significantly, Churchill and Roosevelt initialled the text; they did not sign it. An initialled text is not a legal document.[131]

That evening the British and the Americans decided on which zones of Germany they would occupy. The Americans had wanted to occupy the north-west of the country because, they argued, they did not want to have to cross French territory – de Gaulle's territory – in order to reach the sea. But it was by now quite obvious that the American armies were heading for the south of Germany. The British offered the Americans free access to the northern ports of Bremen and Bremerhaven; at the same

NOROOSEVELT AND THE STATE DEPARTMENT

time they insisted that American command of their armies would cease once the German surrender had been signed. Thus, responsibility for the 'pastoralization' of Germany – the elimination of the Ruhr's 'war-making industries' – would fall largely into the hands of an independent British army. That was no meagre success of British diplomacy. And it was no small chance for post-war Germany.[132]

12 Roosevelt and the State Department, Churchill and Metternich

The accord on the Anglo-American occupation of Germany – how much of the eastern part of the country would be left to Russia was still un-decided – brought the Quebec Conference to a close. It was during that weekend that the 1st Airborne Division, made up of British and Polish paratroopers, took off for their ill-fated expedition to Arnhem. By the end of the following week it became clear that the war with Germany would not be over before Christmas, and that there would be no British general election until 1945.

The American election campaign, on the other hand, gathered steam. Dewey's tour of the Midwest, where so many Germans had migrated (much preferring the American 'Corn Belt' to Hitler's programme of settle-ment in the Russian steppes), had demonstrated growing support for the Republicans. But worse for the Democrats was the fight that developed in Washington over the 'Morgenthau Plan'. A vicious war of words broke out for the control of Roosevelt's government.

On the last day of the Quebec Conference Hull, still preoccupied with the Dumbarton Oaks meeting, had received a report from the President on the plans for Germany and the verbal agreements made with the British over the extension of Lend-Lease. He thought the German plan would be impossible to execute over the long term and was furious that better trade terms had not been negotiated with Britain.

But it was the Republican Secretary of War, Henry Stimson, who launched the first salvo against Morgenthau's project. In a long memorandum to the President dated 15 September he criticized the Treasury Secretary for pursuing a policy that went against the principles of the Atlantic Charter of 1941 and the President's own stated commitment to 'freedom from want and freedom from fear'. In his diary he described Morgenthau's 'Carthaginian views' as 'Semitism gone wild with vengeance'.[133]

Roosevelt remained on his estate at Hyde Park, exhausted by conver-sations he had had with Churchill, some of which had lasted until one in the morning. Morgenthau and White were back in Washington on 19 September. Morgenthau drafted a long memorandum defending his German policy as 'especially humane' and an effective way of preventing the outbreak of World War III; he forwarded these thoughts to Hull and Stimson on Wednesday, 20 September.

On Thursday, the hum over the 'Morgenthau Plan' began in the press. By the weekend, it had become a central theme of the presidential campaign, and of the war between the departments in Washington.

The man responsible for the press leak was Drew Pearson, a *Washington Post* columnist who had a reputation for stirring up divisions in bureaucratic boomtown with his astounding knowledge of State Department secrets. The story was picked up by the *New York Times* on Friday, the 22nd. On Saturday the *Wall Street Journal* reported on plans for a 'starvation economy' in Germany; the Washington *Evening Star* spoke in terms of a 'Carthaginian peace'; New York's *Daily News* noted that the plan 'would make Russia the strongest power in Europe'. The *New York Times*, in its gargantuan Sunday edition, provided the details of how Germany was to be divided into small rural administrative units with a total population of 40 to 50 million west of the Oder forced 'to live off an essentially agricultural economy'. 'The complete defeat of Germany is now in sight,' reported an accompanying article. 'Reformation of the German people must be one of the major preoccupations of the Allies.' *Time* magazine the following week headlined its story 'Sterilize all Germany!'[134]

Roosevelt was back in Washington on Saturday, 23 September, to launch his presidential campaign with a speech to the Teamsters Union. His speechwriter, Sam Rosenman, came to his bedroom with his final draft and found the President leaning on Dr McIntire's arm; 'he was literally trying to walk again!' noted Rosenman in his diary. The speech in fact went well. But Roosevelt was already backing off from the 'Morgenthau Plan' – and, at the same time, retreating from his financial promises to Britain.

On 29 September he made public a letter he had sent to the Foreign Economic Administration, which ran Lend-Lease. Lend-Lease 'should be continued in the amounts necessary', ran the statement, 'to enable the combined strength of all the United Nations to defeat our common enemies'. But, it went on, 'you should continue to take every reasonable measure to see to it that no unnecessary surpluses develop out of procurement' – in other words control on Britain's dollar and gold reserves would be as stringent as ever. In his press conference he denied the reports of conflict between the Treasury, the State and War Departments; 'every story is basically untrue in its basic facts,' he stated. 'The President's letter to the FEA seemed to puzzle some officials who have been working on the German plans,' noted the reporter for the *New York Times*.[135]

One of the most puzzled officials of them all, the Republican Secretary of War, Stimson, had lunch with Roosevelt on 3 October. Roosevelt's daughter, Anna, and her husband, Major Boettiger, were there. Stimson found the President absent-minded and his faith in his old friend, Morgenthau, shaken. 'Henry has pulled a boner on me,' remarked Roosevelt. 'I never intended to transform Germany into an agricultural country.' A shift in the balance of power was developing in Washington, away from the Morgenthau–White axis towards a Hull–Stimson alliance.[136]

At that same moment, in the Willard Hotel opposite the Treasury, Keynes was meeting British officials to discuss the opening of negotiations for Stage II of Lend-Lease. Keynes had arrived in Washington the day before to represent London's Treasury on a 'Joint Committee', set up almost as an afterthought at Quebec and supposedly chaired by Morgenthau, and he had gone straight over to the Treasury to talk out matters with Morgenthau and White. To his dismay, neither of them showed the slightest interest in Stage II of Lend-Lease; they were totally absorbed in their 'mad' plan to de-industrialize Germany. Keynes asked whether the British would have to supply the bread to the bread lines that would obviously develop in the de-industrialized British zone. White assured him that the US Treasury would pay for it, just so long as it was on 'a very low level of subsistence'. 'How I am to keep a straight face', reported Keynes back to London, 'I cannot imagine.'[137]

Keynes's position in the negotiations had been weakened by Churchill's demand that Lord Cherwell, against his will, also represent Britain on the Joint Committee. Cherwell thought a five-minute chat alone with Morgenthau would solve all the problems. But, as Keynes told the British officials in the Willard Hotel, this was a total illusion: Morgenthau obviously no longer had the power to deliver; White's brilliant career was on the way down. Not only would this affect the future of Lend-Lease; unknown to Keynes, it would also considerably diminish the influence of Soviet sympathizers and fellow-travellers working in the offices of the US federal government. The implications for both post-war British finances and post-war American politics were enormous.

Keynes's task of negotiating Stage II during the last weeks of an American presidential election was not much easier than that of the generals on the Rhine. He faced battalions of American lawyers, academics and journalists; Morgenthau was absent for half of the time; 'any argument or indeed more than a dozen simple sentences were always out of place';

participants were continually rushing out to the telephone. Yet Britain did in fact gain more in Lend-Lease than she was asking for (about $7 billion-worth of goods delivered). The catch was that nothing was signed. Furthermore, while Keynes was busy negotiating, Lord Cherwell was touring America to coordinate the Anglo-American combined effort to build an atom bomb. All of Keynes's persuasive force on behalf of 'British requirements for the first year of Stage II' would be brought to naught by the historical fact that 'Stage II' – between VE-Day and VJ-Day – would last only three months.[138]

During the week that news of the 'Morgenthau Plan' broke in America, Churchill was once more on the *Queen Mary* travelling the hot and cloudy Gulf Stream. As the ship approached Europe, all radio contact was broken off on account of the threat of U-boats. But Churchill was 'in the best of humours', playing bezique with his staff until the early hours of the morning, dictating a major policy statement for the House of Commons and worrying about the Balkans once more. The old Churchill was returning, the Churchill of an old Europe, a Churchill increasingly aware of Britain's limits, but keen to play a game of power wherever and whenever he could. Nine thousand American troops were also on board.

Churchill's position was not unlike that of Metternich's at the close of the Napoleonic wars. Both men were presiding over declining powers. Both were at the centre of the international summit conferences that brought the peace. Both were caught between giants, pursuing their own gigantic interests. Both Metternich and Churchill were convinced of their charm and of the merits of personal contacts between leaders. '*Lavieren, Ausweichen und Schmeicheln*' – 'hedging, evasion and flattery' – Metternich once described his negotiating technique as the smallest of the Great Powers. On first sight, this hardly seems to fit Churchill: no other war leader in the 1940s spoke more directly than Churchill and the personalities of Churchill and Metternich could not be more different. Yet, both were marginal aristocrats, and both represented waning power. Did Churchill 'hedge'? Sometimes he had to. Did he 'evade'? In summit encounters there can be no doubt about it. Did he 'flatter'? He flattered his two more powerful colleagues, Roosevelt and Stalin, to such a degree that, in reading the dialogues that took place between them, one can barely imagine a major issue separating them. He adopted their language, he even used their mannerisms. 'I agree,' he would say with a slight nod of the head, 'I agree.'

As his ship approached Europe, the serious economic problems which faced his country drifted once more into the background; territorial and strategic matters surged to the forefront. The Balkans became again his centre of interest and his one great wish was to reach Vienna before the Russians. Greece, he was convinced, could be kept out of Russian control. An increasing worry was, as it had been for Metternich in 1814, Poland.

The *Queen Mary* docked at Greenock in mist and rain late Tuesday evening, 26 September. In London a large crowd gathered next morning at Euston Station to greet the Premier, who smiled and gave a V-sign. Within two hours he was in his seat at the House of Commons where, in answer to Prime Minister's Questions, he spoke of the 'heroism and tenacity of the Polish Home Army and the population of Warsaw'.[139]

The next day, 27 September, he telegraphed Stalin that 'on the agreement of our three nations, Britain, United States of America, and USSR, stand the hopes of the world.' A meeting of the three leaders, he thought, was essential. Roosevelt had his elections. But, concluded Churchill, 'I will gladly come to Moscow in October if I can get away from here.'[140]

On Thursday, 28 September, he spoke for over two hours in the Commons – one hour before lunch on the military situation in the world, and one hour afterwards on foreign policy. The first half hour went well, but then his voice became husky, and many MPs walked out for lunch early; the foreign policy portion of his speech was not universally acclaimed: he sounded, according to the Conservative MP Harold Nicolson, 'tired and bored'.[141] Yet it was at this moment that the key message was delivered. 'I cannot conceive that it is not possible to make a good solution whereby Russia gets the security which she is entitled to have,' he said, and 'the Polish nation have restored to them that national sovereignty and independence, for which . . . they have never ceased to strive.' Metternich had understood, in 1814, that this was the central, irreconcilable riddle of Europe. Churchill must have been aware of the same problem in the autumn of 1944. 'We recognize our special responsibilities towards Poland,' he stated – Britain had declared war on Nazi Germany over Poland's independence – and then he contradicted himself: 'The future of Europe, perhaps for several generations, depends upon the cordial, trustful and comprehending association of the British Empire, the United States and Soviet Russia.' In no manner could one have it both ways. Somebody was going to be deceived. Lines would have to be drawn somewhere.[142]

The following day, Friday, the Polish government in London – under considerable pressure from Churchill and Eden – forced the retirement of their Commander-in-Chief, General Sosnkowski, as Stalin had been demanding since spring. They named as his successor General Bór-Komorowski, commander of the Home Army and leader of the Warsaw Rising. The last Polish stronghold in Warsaw collapsed that weekend.

Bór-Komorowski surrendered himself, his 'army', and the entire population of the city to the Nazis on Monday.

On Sunday Churchill received Stalin's formal invitation to Moscow. 'The Russians and I are delighted that you have decided to come here,' telegraphed Britain's Moscow ambassador on Monday. Churchill was in Northolt that day inspecting the aircraft which would fly him to Moscow via Naples and Cairo the following Saturday, 7 October. On Thursday he made a brief statement in the House of Commons: 'In the battle for Warsaw terrible damage has been inflicted upon that noble city [it was wiped off the map], and its heroic population has undergone sufferings and privations unsurpassed even among the miseries of this war.' Though Churchill announced that 'the epic of Warsaw will not be forgotten', the British press, in its desire not to offend its Soviet 'ally', was notably discreet in its reporting of the annihilation of Warsaw. So was the American. And so have been many historians since.[143]

Roosevelt telegraphed Churchill on Wednesday, 4 October – one day after his lunch with Stimson. 'I wish you every success in your visit with U.J. ['Uncle Joe', as Stalin was known between the two leaders],' he said in a first draft. 'Regarding Dumbarton,' he added, 'I cherish a hope that you will find some means of reaching an agreement between the three great powers.' This draft was vetoed by the State Department, conscious of its new power in Washington; it thought, correctly, that it reflected an American indifference to the outcome of the talks. The new draft was three times as long and contained a definition of the US ambassador's role in Moscow 'to stand by and to participate as my observer'. 'I could not permit anyone to commit me in advance,' added the new draft. And: 'Like you, I attach the greatest importance to the continued unity of our three countries.' The telegram contained no reference to the Balkans, and no reference to Warsaw. It was Churchill who would have to draw the lines.[144]

A second area of silence in Britain was the 'Morgenthau Plan', which was becoming one of the major campaign issues in the United States: the American public did not like it, so the British remained mum. Churchill made no reference to it at all in his Commons speeches; the little said about it in the British press was confined to reports on the US elections. Britain was clearly not committed to the 'Morgenthau Plan'.

Silence also surrounded Montgomery and the separation of the British and American armies in the week Paris was liberated. Even more astonishing was the silence in the diaries of the CIGS, General Brooke: they show him wholly concerned, like the Prime Minister, with the situation in Italy and the Balkans. Churchill's first reaction to the news of Arnhem was: 'I like the situation on the western front.'[145] Brooke, just before leaving for Moscow with the Prime Minister, flew off for one day's conference with Eisenhower's SHAEF, now installed (like the Supreme War Council of the First World War) in the Hôtel Trianon at Versailles. He was enchanted by the way Eisenhower chaired the large meeting and put complete trust in Britain's representatives to SHAEF. Montgomery, who was there, considered them navvies of the Americans; Montgomery had to fight his battles alone.

Before his Versailles trip, Brooke had advised Churchill and the British Chiefs of Staff to delay the operation on Rangoon until November 1945 so that the depleted forces in Italy could be sure to move in on Istria – and onwards, it was hoped, to Vienna. Churchill and the COS agreed. 'It is *very* disappointing,' recorded Brooke on the delay of the Rangoon attack, 'but I think the correct decision.'[146]

Churchill's York airliner took off from Northolt shortly before midnight on Saturday, 7 October. 'I am glad to say that it is possible to travel from London to Moscow without at any point touching the Gulf Stream,' remarked Churchill just before his departure.[147]

Behind him, in the dark, lay a London pockmarked by bombing. One third of the City's 460 acres had been flattened; a wide band of ancient buildings, old Company halls, museums and churches, running northwards from the Thames to Cripplegate, lay in ruins. The eastern boroughs of Stepney, Poplar and Bethnal Green, and the northern boroughs of Holborn, Finsbury and Shoreditch had lost 19 per cent of their built-up area. Those were only the worst hit areas. The 'flying gas mains' – still not officially identified by either the government or the press as German V-2s, but recognized as such by every inhabitant of London – became an increasing threat in the week of Churchill's departure. Yet there can be no doubt that Churchill had instilled in the people of London a sense of pride and courage. Sir William Beveridge had given them hope. His White Paper on Social Insurance, promising the expenditure of £650 million in the first year alone of comprehensive benefits, was published on 26 September – the week negotiations began in Washington on Stage II of Lend-Lease, and one week before Warsaw fell.[148]

13 Hurricane season

Hurricane season in America, born in the Gulf Stream, started early in the autumn of 1944 and ended late. A peculiar feature was the way the storms turned north, whirling up the waters of the Atlantic seaboard and dumping them on the urban constellation of the north-east. One such tropical storm hit the New Jersey shore on Friday, 20 October, and then passed over Long Island to New England where it petered out on Saturday evening. Gusts up to 50 mph were recorded in parts of New York City; two and a half inches of rain dashed against the buildings and flooded the streets on Saturday morning. That was the day picked by Roosevelt's supporters to demonstrate their candidate's healthy vigour.

Dewey clocked up over 20,000 miles by the time the campaign came to an end; Roosevelt confined his 'stomp' of New York, Philadelphia, Chicago and Boston to the last three weekends. Rumours that he was a tired, uninspired old man had spread immediately after his poorly delivered acceptance speech in San Diego in late July. He had made matters worse on his return from his tour of the Pacific when, in the harbour of Bremerton, in Washington State, he presented what was designed as a 'homey report' on his trip. He was standing on the leaning deck of a destroyer, in wind, wearing leg braces he had not used in months – they did not fit. The text he had dictated himself because none of his speechwriters was available. But most humiliating of all, he suffered, right in the middle of his speech, an attack of angina: he was in agony. The crowd was made up mostly of naval yard labourers who had just got off work. They stood glumly silent. Bravely, Roosevelt continued speaking for over half an hour.

When Roosevelt addressed the International Brotherhood of Teamsters, Chauffeurs and Warehousemen on 23 September in Washington DC his doctors expected the worst. They categorically refused to let him stand. 'It's the kind of speech which depends almost entirely on delivery, no matter how good the writing,' said Sam Rosenman, who had written the speech. The delivery was in fact superb.[149]

As the campaign picked up, Roosevelt found himself in his element. Nobody could sound better than FDR on the radio or in front of a crowd when he was confident. His high blood pressure declined. His colour returned. Governor Dewey attacked Roosevelt on the 'Morgenthau Plan' – 'just what the Nazis needed; it is as good as ten fresh German divisions'. Dewey was not far wrong; but Roosevelt simply denied its existence, thus winning much support from the State Department. Dewey claimed that Communists were seizing control of the Federal Government. There was more of an element of truth in this, too; but Roosevelt found the charge easy to ridicule. On 6 October, as Churchill was preparing for his trip to Moscow, Roosevelt stated over the radio that his opponents were 'dragging red herrings across the trail of this national election. Labor baiters and bigots and some politicians use the word Communism and apply it to any social legislation and to views of foreign born citizens with whom they disagree.' He accused the Republicans of building up 'bogies of dictatorship, although they know that free elections would always protect the nation'.[150] Communism, during the election of 1944, became an issue of national hatreds; the 'red spectre' was going to divide the country for well over a decade. But Dewey, for all his campaigning in cattle country and around the great coal mines, could not beat Roosevelt's powerful rhetoric once it got moving.

There remained the issue of his health. It was for this reason Roosevelt took on New York, on 21 October, in the tail-end of a hurricane.

Roosevelt's special train pulled into Pennsylvania Station at six o'clock in the morning. The *Ferdinand Magellan*, the President's private railcar, was a fantastic machine, built by the Association of American Railroads and sold to the White House for one dollar. It had two lifts to pick up Roosevelt's wheelchair and contained an office, a lounge, a bedroom and a galley. There were twelve inches of reinforced concrete underneath the floor to serve as protection in case a bomb went off on the roadbed as it rolled along, never at more than 30 mph; the windows were bulletproof. In Washington it was kept on a secret siding underneath the Bureau of Engraving and Printing, where the Treasury printed green dollars; when Roosevelt travelled it was usually parked in the cellar of the building in which he was speaking so that the President could be rolled out of town without any reporters noticing. But in New York he insisted on getting into a huge convertible green Packard, its canvas top down, so that he was exposed to the diluvian rains.

Roosevelt smiled and waved at the crowds, which Mayor La Guardia's Police Department estimated at over three million − greater than those at King George VI's visit in 1938. Other estimates spoke of one million. In Ebbets Field, a baseball stadium, he discarded his naval cloak and − sensational news as reported in the *New York Times* − 'stood on his feet for five minutes' in a downpour. His speech, delivered over loudspeakers before a crowd of 10,000, was short and grand, an endorsement of Senator Robert Wagner. Roosevelt said, 'He deserves well of mankind.' So did Roosevelt.

The green Packard, accompanied by a retinue of secret servicemen, proceeded down Seventh Avenue to Twenty-third Street, where the International Ladies Garment Workers Union, headed by David Dubinsky, was waiting to greet him. When he arrived, Dubinsky stepped forward to the car, accompanied by 'three pretty girls', and presented Roosevelt with flowers. 'I wish you the best of luck,' said Dubinsky.

Despite the rain, the crowds here were huge. Placards could be seen reading 'Hail our Commander in Chief', 'First in our hearts, Roosevelt', 'It's a date: 'Till 48 with Roosevelt'.

Sitting beside him was his estranged wife, Eleanor. At Washington Square he stopped off for lunch at Eleanor's apartment, which he had never before seen in his life, quaffed three glasses of bourbon – 'the only occasion on which I knew him to have more than a couple of drinks,' remarked his speechwriter Grace Tully – and slept until his speech that evening before the Foreign Policy Association in the ballroom of the Waldorf-Astoria. The *Ferdinand Magellan* was waiting beneath in a railway siding to take him directly to his estate at Hyde Park.[151]

The speech, a product of teamwork, laid the outline of United States foreign policy at the end of the Second World War. Roosevelt delivered it brilliantly, though sitting.

The State Department clearly now had the upper hand. Cordell Hull was mentioned several times; the name Morgenthau had disappeared into oblivion. The 'Morgenthau Plan' was rejected, even though no direct reference was made to it: 'We and our Allies are entirely agreed that we shall not bargain with the Nazi conspirators, or leave them a shred of control. [But] we bring no charge against the German race . . . The German people are not going to be enslaved.' Roosevelt said he would not 'be false to the very foundations of my religious and political convictions' – a swipe at Dewey's charges of encouragement within the Administration of Communist 'pagan religion' – and claimed that his main aim was to create 'strong brothers in the family of mankind, the family of the children of God'. It could have been Wilson speaking.

Roosevelt spoke of the importance of maintaining good relations with the Russian Soviets. He recalled a classroom that Eleanor ('a certain lady who sits at a table in front of me') had visited in 1933; on the wall 'there was a map of the world with a great big white space upon it', the Soviet Union; Roosevelt claimed to have filled in the 'white space'.

In 1919, he stated, the United States 'had failed to organize the kind of world in which future generations could live with freedom'. The twin objectives of this war, he said, were 'defense of our country' and 'perpetuation of our American ideals'. The latter goal would be achieved by the organization of the 'Council of the League of Nations of the United Nations' which 'must have the power to act quickly and decisively to keep the peace by force, if necessary'. This was the first time the world organization planned at Dumbarton Oaks was referred to publicly as the 'United Nations'. Roosevelt did not invent the term, which had been introduced by Churchill in reference to the forces allied against Nazidom at the time the Atlantic Charter was signed in summer 1941; Churchill, no minor historian, drew the term from the coalition forces united against Napoleon. But Roosevelt now applied the name of the Alliance to the post-war world organization, created under the guidance of the State Department in Washington. Roosevelt placed at the centre of the 'United Nations' the four world powers: the United States, the Soviet Union, China and Britain. Churchill did not consider Chiang Kai-shek's China a world power. Roosevelt's main doubt, in contrast, concerned Britain.[152]

Roosevelt won his fourth term as President. As the campaign reached its climax, Dewey became increasingly vocal about how Roosevelt 'very softly disavowed Communism'. 'Everyone knows', he stated in his closing speech in Boston Gardens, 'that Communism is for State ownership of all property.' Roosevelt, he claimed, 'wages war against the American enterprise system'.[153]

In collegial votes, counted by state, Roosevelt won an easy majority over Dewey (432 over 99). But Roosevelt's popular vote (53 per cent over 45 per cent) was the smallest of his four presidential victories. Dewey, so much more subtle than earlier 'red baiters', had exposed a major issue that would not go away: America's domestic debate over Communism had only just begun.

14 Moscow: hot and cold

Roosevelt may have very softly disavowed Communism; on Poland he was totally silent, right through the catastrophe that was Warsaw. Churchill, on the other hand, openly declared that the main aim of his trip to Moscow was to solve 'the Polish problem'. There was a lot of the old European in the way he went about this. He flattered Stalin. He attempted first to draw a line where, despite ongoing civil wars, massacre and genocide, matters were simpler: not across Poland, but across the Balkans. Only after this line was established did he turn to Poland.

The American government would later be very critical of Churchill's actions in Moscow. But the Americans had not even begun to approach the problem. Their criticism was like that of a book reviewer who had never written a book.

The State Department made it clear in advance that it wanted no lines drawn without the presence of the President in a meeting of the Three. In addition to its drafting of the telegraph to Churchill of 4 October, it persuaded Roosevelt to send a note to Stalin, dated 5 October, stating that 'I am convinced that the three of us, and only the three of us, can find the solution of the questions still unresolved.' Stalin replied on the day Churchill arrived in Moscow: 'I am somewhat embarrassed by your message of October 5. I had supposed that Mr Churchill was coming to Moscow in accordance with agreement reached with you at Quebec.' Harriman was equally embarrassed. 'There is one subject on which I had hoped a definite understanding with Stalin might be reached by the Prime Minister, namely the Polish situation.' But the American government remained as silent on Poland as it did on the Balkans – even though, on 4 October, the British had landed a force on the Peloponnese with the clear intention of imposing a non-Communist government in Athens. 'The clock was ticking,' Harriman later recollected, 'and I felt the opportunity slipping away.'[154]

Churchill, the weakest of the Three, knew that some sort of agreement on who would control which parts of Europe after the collapse of Germany was necessary while they still had a common enemy. The Americans seemed to think that, after their own withdrawal, there would be no contest over what they left behind; or, as the worried American official in London had said in August over Harry White's plans for Germany, there seemed a deliberate policy to 'replace a German hegemony on the Continent by a Russian one'. Churchill was determined to avoid that.

When Churchill arrived in Moscow on Monday afternoon, 9 October, he had not properly rested in over sixty hours. He had, however, a most effective system of relaxation: like Napoleon after a battle, he would soak himself in a bath. Whatever the occasion, a bath for Churchill was always a necessity. Thus, in January 1916, soldiers of the 6th Royal Scots Fusiliers noted that their new commander on the Western Front, Colonel Churchill, turned up with luggage well over regulation weight, including a long tub and a boiler for heating the bath water. He frequently took a bath before speaking in the House of Commons; one cause for his poor delivery on 28 September was that he had remained in his tub in Downing Street until only ten minutes before he was due to begin his speech. A small item that drew Churchill to his new Soviet ally was his admiration of Russian plumbing; on his first visit to Moscow, in the disastrous summer of 1942, he found to his amazement that 'hot and cold turned on at once through a single spout, mingled to exactly the temperature one desired.' 'In a modest way I have adopted this system at home,' he noted in his war memoirs.[155]

On his visit of October 1944, Churchill arrived earlier than expected at his dacha (Molotov's residence), twenty-three miles outside Moscow, despite the fact that his plane had first landed at the wrong airport and had to be diverted. The luggage had not yet arrived. 'Never mind,' said Churchill; 'I will have a bath.' Russian plumbing did not prove so magical on this occasion. Five minutes later the Prime Minister's detective came rushing down the stairs. 'The bath is filling with cold water,' he exclaimed. The tap, marked with sticking plaster 'Hot', was gushing out cold. After trying the other tap Churchill had lost all hope of having a decent warm bath. It was an inauspicious beginning to one of the most famous diplomatic encounters in the Second World War.[156]

A brief dinner was prepared at the dacha. Then Churchill and Eden, accompanied by the British ambassador, Sir Archibald Clark Kerr, drove to the embassy in Moscow and, from there, to the Kremlin. The American ambassador, Harriman, was notably absent. It was already ten o'clock in the evening when Churchill presented a signed photograph to Marshal Stalin. Both men were in ebullient mood.[157]

Churchill, testing the water, came straight to his central concern, the 'most tiresome question – Poland'. His worry was not so much the frontier; the 'Curzon Line' (which so closely corresponded to the line of the Nazi-Soviet Pact) had been more or less agreed at Teheran between Roosevelt and Stalin.[158] The problem was who was going to control the new Poland, between the 'Curzon Line' and the Oder. 'At present,' he said to Stalin, 'each [of us] has a game-cock in his hand.' Stalin made his first joke of the evening, saying it was difficult to do without cocks, 'they gave the morning signal.'

Churchill said that at the 'armistice table' there would be no problem about Poland's frontiers: both Britain and the United States endorsed what had been said at Teheran. General Sosnkowski had objected, but he had just been sacked, and as for the new Commander-in-Chief, General Bór, 'the Germans were looking after him,' said Churchill.

Churchill by now had Stalin's total attention. So, the difficulty in Poland was less frontiers than the content of the post-war government: London or Lublin? Churchill said he currently had Mikołajczyk and his Foreign Minister 'tied up in an aircraft and it would take only thirty-six hours to Moscow'. Would they be able to speak to the Lublin Poles? Stalin assured Churchill that they would, so Churchill immediately sent a telegraph off to Mikołajczyk ordering that he and his colleagues either come to Moscow now or forfeit the support of the British government. Mikołajczyk boarded a plane the following day.

'The difficulty about the Poles', said Churchill, 'was that they had unwise political leaders. Where there were two Poles there was one quarrel.' Stalin's second joke of the evening: 'Where there was one Pole he would begin to quarrel with himself through sheer boredom.'

The Polish problem was thereupon postponed until the arrival of the London Poles. Churchill had humoured Stalin at the expense of the Poles, not unlike the manner in which he used to humour Roosevelt at the expense of de Gaulle. This was the old European in operation again; a weaker power manoeuvring around his more powerful partners. Churchill, in fact, had no intention of abandoning Central and Eastern Europe to Stalin, just as he had no intention of dropping de Gaulle. What he sought in the autumn of 1944 was room for an increasingly impoverished Britain to manoeuvre among the powers that be.

Stalin came round to the 'embarrassment' he had felt at Roosevelt's last telegraph. He told Churchill that he thought Roosevelt seemed 'to demand too many rights for the USA, leaving too little for the Soviet Union and Great Britain'. It was at this point that Churchill produced his 'naughty document'. It focused on the Balkans.

Churchill wrote down on a half sheet of paper:

Romania	
Russia	90%
The others	10%
Greece	
Great Britain	90%
(in accord with USA)	
Russia	10%
Yugoslavia	50–50%
Hungary	50–50%
Bulgaria	
Russia	75%
The others	25%

What Churchill would call in 1946 the 'Iron Curtain', separating the Communist bloc from the democratic bloc in Europe, was in formation here. Churchill had used the Polish dilemma as a preliminary and then traced in outline the division across the Balkans. But it cannot be said that Churchill invented the 'Iron Curtain'. The division was created by the movement of the armies against Hitler. Churchill, as the weakest of the Big Three, was retrieving as much as he could. His armies in Italy and on the Rhine had come to a standstill. Stalin's armies were in Romania and Bulgaria, they had joined hands with Tito's Partisans in Yugoslavia, and they were now moving, in alliance with a Russian controlled Romania, on Hungary: two nights later there was an awesome fireworks display over the Kremlin to celebrate the capture of Cluj, not far from the Hungarian frontier. The Americans had committed themselves to nothing.

According to Churchill's war memoirs, there followed a long silence with the half sheet of paper lying on the table separating the two war leaders. According to British minutes kept by Major A. H. Birse – later censored by the Foreign Office – the conversation turned to Bulgaria, where, said Churchill, Britain had to be 'a little more than a spectator'. As for Turkey, Stalin told Churchill he had no interest, save access to the Straits, which Churchill assured him he would have. Greece, Stalin admitted, fell within a British zone.

As for Germany, Stalin and Molotov showed great interest that evening in the 'Morgenthau Plan'. Stalin, in particular, wanted Germany 'split up' and 'her heavy industry . . . reduced to a minimum'. Churchill warned that 'the President and Mr Morgenthau were not very happy about [the plan's] reception' – and then got himself out of a tight corner by bringing up the subject of 'war criminals', a subject on which he had already outlined his ideas in a letter to Roosevelt; he had even mentioned his thoughts in his recent speeches in the House of Commons.

Churchill wanted local Nazi criminals tried in the countries where they had committed their deeds, while 'major' criminals, leading members of the regime (about fifty to a hundred persons), should be shot within one hour of their capture by the invading armies.[159] On his first evening with Stalin, Churchill said that 'Great Britain would not agree to mass execution of Germans, because one day British public opinion would cry out. But it was necessary to kill as many as possible in the field. The others should be made to work to repair the damage done to other countries.' It was Stalin who insisted, later in the Moscow Conference, on having a trial for the 'major criminals'; thus began the process that led to Nuremberg. Stalin had always had a great respect for public trials.[160]

Until the arrival of the Poles on Thursday night, 12 October, the conference focused on a haggling over the 'percentage agreement' in the Balkans. Churchill, Stalin, Eden and Molotov were very busy. Most of the other participants at the conference found they had nothing to do. General Brooke spent most of his time visiting what remained of the monasteries in the Moscow area. 'There is some fable about some hunters going out to shoot a bear, who on the eve of the shoot became so busy arguing about the sale of the skin and the sharing of the proceeds, that they forgot to shoot the bear!' he wrote in his diary on 12 October; Brooke's concern was that the war against Germany had not yet been concluded.[161]

Harriman who, as instructed by Roosevelt (or, rather, the State Department), attended some of the meetings between Churchill and Stalin got an inkling of what was going on, but no more. 'On the matter of the Balkans, Churchill and Eden will try to work out some sort of spheres of influence with the Russians,' Harriman warned Roosevelt on 10 October – 'the British to have a free hand in Greece and the Russians in Rumania and perhaps other countries. The British will attempt to retrieve a position of equal influence in Yugoslavia.' Roosevelt, in the midst of his campaign, showed not the slightest interest. The State Department stuck to a policy of no wicked European 'spheres of influence'.[162]

It was as if the war, obviously nearing a close, would somehow magically solve itself. The Americans would commit themselves to nothing, save those matters like money and the 'World Organization' which could be entirely managed on their own territory. The Soviets were building, with their armies, as extensive a territorial empire as they thought possible. There were no European powers left in the game, save Britain, which was losing her strength, and France, just re-emerging from Nazi occupation. Europe carried such little weight that a European-style peace conference would prove impossible; everything on the 'old Continent' would be determined by force of arms, the position of armies, and wartime agreements between Allies who would not long remain friends.

In the fabulous pre-revolutionary Spiridonovka Palace on Friday afternoon, 13 October, the conference between the British, the Russians and the London Poles was opened. Two issues had to be confronted: what would be the frontiers of an independent post-war Poland? and what would be the composition of its government? The two were closely related. The Stalinist technique, which simply used diplomacy for his own expansionist ends, was to establish by agreement a Soviet frontier as far west as possible, and then impose its own puppet government on its neighbour further west. The London Poles, with the experience of the Nazi-Soviet Pact behind them, were fully aware of this. Churchill, and most especially his civil servants, still thought in terms of gentlemanly European diplomacy: a line was a line.

Mikołajczyk, however, was more concerned about the independence of Poland than the drawing of lines. He thus began by observing that his government had been formally recognized by Britain and the United States, the Lublin Poles were recognized by the Soviet Union; he proposed a new government representing both parties. Stalin introduced the issue of frontiers: he would only talk about government composition after the 'Curzon Line' (which was also the Nazi-Soviet Pact line) was recognized by the London Poles. Churchill supported Stalin on account of Soviet 'sacrifices' and 'efforts towards liberating Poland' – a comment not easy for Mikołajczyk to accept just eleven days after Bór's surrender of Warsaw. Churchill did add that Poland would be compensated to the west by the acquisition of German territory up to the Oder – only this was not to be mentioned publicly since the land was still in the hands of the Nazis.

Mikołajczyk told Stalin that no one would respect him if he ceded 40 per cent of Polish territory and five million Poles to the Soviet Union. Stalin appealed for the rights of Ukrainians (many of whom had in fact allied with the Germans against the Soviets). Churchill made what he considered a reasonable Western European appeal, saying 'a sword hung over our heads' and asking the Poles 'for a great gesture in the interest of European peace'. He looked at Mikołajczyk straight in the eyes and said, 'I hope that you will not hold against me these unpleasant but frank words which I have spoken with the best of intentions.' 'I have already heard so many unpleasant things in the course of this war', replied the brave Polish leader, 'that one more will not throw me off balance.'

Churchill came up with a compromise over the question of the frontier: accept the 'Curzon Line' as a *de facto* frontier now, while reserving the right for discussion at the 'Peace Conference'. Stalin categorically refused Churchill's proposal, making the point that the frontier had to be accepted now because the Soviet Union had a different social system; 'we have collective farms.'

It was a critical point: a 'collective-farm' state was not going to be drawn into a 'peace conference'. The United States had shown no intention of holding a 'peace conference' either. Quebec, supported by the planks of Bretton Woods and Dumbarton Oaks, had provided the materials for the coffin of a European-style peace conference; Moscow drove in the nails. After October 1944 it was clear there was going to be no peace conference after the Second World War: the new Europe would be constructed strictly along Soviet-American lines.

Churchill, according to the minutes of the Spiridonovka Palace meeting, made 'a gesture of disappointment and helplessness' on hearing Stalin's words. But he stubbornly insisted on his idea of a *de facto* agreement on the Curzon Line, along with a later 'Peace Conference'. Stalin stubbornly resisted.[163]

Churchill left with Eden and the British ambassador for a town house reserved for them by the Soviets. After dinner they returned to the Spiridonovka Palace to meet the Lublin Poles. It was a chilling experience.

Bolesław Bierut, who headed the Lublin delegation, said: 'We are here to demand on behalf of Poland that Lwów shall belong to Russia.' Edward Osobka-Morawski joined him in listing 'grievances' against Mikołajczyk's émigré committee in London. Churchill, in a letter to Attlee, described them as 'inverted Quislings', who were 'only an expression of Soviet will'.[164]

But Churchill stubbornly persisted with his *de facto* 'Curzon Line'. There were some ugly scenes between him and Mikołajczyk that weekend, similar in style to his earlier wrangles with de Gaulle. There was, traditionally, among the British, not much sympathy for the Poles. At Paris in 1919, Lloyd George had shamed himself by comparing the Poles disparagingly with the Irish – the troublemakers of Europe. Churchill, a more generous man, relied on Macaulay's histories: he referred repeatedly to Poland's eighteenth-century 'Liberum Veto' – the aristocratic parliamentary check on the king, the arbitrary use of which had shattered Polish independence. 'Unless you accept the frontier,' said Churchill, 'you are out of business for ever. The Russians will sweep through your country and your people will be liquidated. You are on the verge of annihilation.' Mikołajczyk wondered aloud, 'Should I sign a death sentence against myself?' Oliver Harvey, high civil servant, deemed 'the PM so right and the Poles so foolish – like Bourbons expecting everything to come back to them'. History must record that it was Harvey, dictating to people he was supposed to be protecting, who behaved most like an old Bourbon.[165]

The weekend ended with Churchill in bed with a fever. But a little M & B did the trick. The following week the Prime Minister was again in battle with Mikołajczyk, though he did attempt, unsuccessfully, to get Stalin to grant the Poles Lwów – a city which had bitter memories for both men. Stalin defended the rights of his loyal Ukrainians. Finally Eden, in a quiet conversation with Mikołajczyk in the British embassy, managed to get 'Curzon' accepted as a 'demarcation line', which is exactly what it was in October 1944: Stalin's armies had, since July, barely advanced beyond it.

There were more firework displays over the Kremlin – for the taking of Riga, the entry of the Red Army into Czechoslovakia, the capture of frontier posts in Hungary. But the front remained static in Poland as the residents of Warsaw were shipped off to Nazi camps. Hitler arrested the Hungarian leader Admiral Horthy; the deportation and murder of Hungarian Jews accelerated.

Churchill expressed doubts to Stalin that the British could get to Vienna before the spring of 1945; but during the same week in Moscow, Churchill received news from General Maitland Wilson that the Germans had evacuated Athens and that the British had sent in specially trained squads, the 'Jellicoe patrols', to secure the city 'in which democracy was born'

Churchill and Stalin took the occasion to discuss the future of Germany. The Soviets had shown a keen interest in the 'Morgenthau Plan', at the same time as American voters were repudiating it. Churchill, mindful of the Polish dilemma, admitted the principle of vast population movements so that ethnic groups could be fitted into agreed frontiers rather than the reverse. One issue discussed in this connection was the fate of the 11,000 Soviet ex-prisoners of war who had already fallen into Western Allied hands; some of them had been forced to fight for Germany, said Stalin, while others did so voluntarily. Churchill remarked that it would be impossible for British authorities to separate the two, and there, unresolved, the matter rested.

In front of Stalin, Churchill proved an enthusiastic supporter of the 'Morgenthau Plan', though this had hardly been the case when he was in London. The old Prussian military caste, he told Stalin, should be isolated, and Allied military control should be established in the Ruhr and the Saar. Stalin took a lively interest in the proposal of 'getting the machine tools required by the Ukraine and other ravaged regions'.[166] Thus the 'Morgenthau Plan', with Churchill's apparent encouragement, shifted from the United States to the Soviet Union, where it would remain Stalin's pet project for Germany.

The division of the Balkans, the doubts expressed over the legitimacy of the London Poles, the whole westward shift of Poland's frontiers, the approved mass movement of populations, and the agreed de-industrialization of Germany may not stand as grand achievements for Churchill in Moscow. But the fact remains that he was the only Western leader at the time to realize that a serious problem was developing with the Soviet 'ally'. Churchill has been accused of practising the same 'appeasement' policy with Communist Russia as Chamberlain did with Nazi Germany. But there is this crucial difference: Chamberlain could have stopped Germany in her tracks and drawn a line; Churchill could not stop the advance of Russia, but he did attempt to draw a line. That was the parallel with Metternich's diplomacy, exactly one hundred and thirty years before.

Churchill's charm certainly worked on Stalin. For the first time during the war, Stalin made a public appearance outside the Kremlin, standing by Churchill's side in the Bolshoi Theatre. It was the biggest gala festival Muscovites had seen in years. There was a continual banter of humour between the two men. Referring back to his anti-Bolshevik policy of 1919, Churchill said to Stalin, 'I'm glad now that I did not kill you. I hope you are glad that you did not kill me?' 'Readily,' replied Stalin, then quoting a Russian proverb, 'A man's eyes should be torn out if he can only see the past.'[167]

As Churchill's plane took off for London, Stalin stood in the rain, waving a white handkerchief.

15 The Eleventh of November

Paris and Warsaw are the two symbols of the closing months of the Second World War: Paris was liberated, Warsaw was annihilated. Washington and London are the symbols of democratic defiance: Washington became richer, London poorer. One of the great paradoxes of the war is that Washington gave no open support to the democratic government of Warsaw and refused to recognize the democratic government of Paris. London followed Washington's example.

Or, to put it more precisely, Churchill played to Roosevelt's ill humour whenever he was in the American President's presence; and by autumn a sick Roosevelt was under the influence of Cordell Hull, who loathed de Gaulle. But unlike the President, Churchill did not remain silent. In London, he argued with Mikołajczyk and quarrelled with de Gaulle. Churchill excused himself to Mikołajczyk for his 'frank words', when in Moscow; at the same time, he started to press Roosevelt for recognition of de Gaulle's Provisional Government.

The situation had become absurd. Since September Britain had an ambassador, Duff Cooper, accredited to an unrecognized government. The United States had just recognized Bonomi's new government in Italy. As the *Franc-Tireur* put it on 2 October, the next new government the United States and Britain will recognize will probably be Romania, then Bulgaria, then Hungary; after the defeat of Berlin and Tokyo their new governments will be recognized; then the Papuans, the Hottentots and the Lapps – 'after which, who knows, we French may at last get a look in'.[168] Furthermore, the House of Commons and the British press were getting restless; de Gaulle was still popular in Britain.

'I have been reflecting about the question of recognition of the French Provisional Government,' Churchill wrote to the President from Moscow the day after his conference in the Spiridonovka Palace. 'I think events have now moved to a point where we could take a decision.' It took five days, and some drawn-out discussions with Cordell Hull, for Roosevelt to answer on this point. Eventually he wrote, 'I think that until the French set up a real zone of the interior that we should make no move towards recognizing them as a provisional government.'[169] Roosevelt pointed out that recognition would oblige them to offer France a seat on the European Advisory Commission in London, and this Hull did not want. He had managed to keep the French out of the 'World Organization' conference at Dumbarton Oaks, even though France (through Pierre Mendès-France) had been very active at Bretton Woods.

But Cordell Hull did not have the American press or American opinion behind him. Most particularly, he did not have the support of New York which had been enraptured by a speech made by de Gaulle in English at the side of Mayor La Guardia the previous July. La Guardia was a good friend of de Gaulle's. And Roosevelt, in October, needed the votes of La Guardia's New York.

On Saturday morning, 21 October, at six in the morning – the same day Roosevelt made his campaign tour of New York – Sir Alexander Cadogan was woken by a telephone call from the American embassy in Paris announcing that they had just been instructed by the State Department to 'prepare' for French recognition. There was panic in London. The British were not going to allow the Americans to recognize de Gaulle's government first! British recognition was rushed through on Sunday. Moscow was informed. The Soviet Union and the United States recognized de Gaulle on Monday. On Tuesday journalists and photographers rushed to the War Ministry in the Rue Saint-Dominique, where de Gaulle's government still sat, to get the great man's response. Can you give us your impressions of all these recognitions? asked one reporter. De Gaulle answered with one sentence, 'I can tell you the Government is satisfied that people wish to call it by its name.'[170]

Churchill let it be known that he wanted to be invited to the first Armistice Day celebrations in the French capital since the Liberation. De Gaulle, incensed at his exclusion from the European Advisory Commission, the Dumbarton Oaks Conference, Quebec, Moscow, and at the lack of *matériel* for his rapidly growing armed forces, spread word that the British Prime Minister was not going to be invited. The American formula of recognition, 'transferring powers' from Eisenhower to the Provisional Government as though France were a zone of American occupation, had not been very diplomatic either. De Gaulle informed the ministries, the General Staff and the Prefecture of the Seine by circular: 'If Monsieur Churchill passes through Paris, no approach, nor demonstration, nor presence of any kind may be made on the French side without my agreement. Please make it clear to all that I attach the utmost importance to this.'[171] Churchill still insisted on an Armistice Day visit to the French capital 'to see General Eisenhower'.

He arrived on 10 November with his wife, his daughter and his Foreign Secretary, Anthony Eden: Charles de Gaulle was waiting for them at Orly airport. He accompanied them to the Quai d'Orsay where the entire first floor was put at their disposal. The organization and service, recalled Churchill, was 'sumptuous'. And what a delight: the bathtub was in gold. Churchill later learned it had been installed during the German occupation for Hermann Göring; Eden's bathtub was only in silver.

On the eleventh hour of the eleventh day of the eleventh month General de Gaulle turned up at the Churchill party's apartment to accompany them to the Arc de Triomphe and celebrate the Armistice of 1918.

Paris's Armistice Day of 1944 was a second Liberation. The sky was a brilliant blue, the weather bitterly cold. All along their way to the Arc de Triomphe, and down the Champs Elysées, huddled on pavements, balconies and rooftops were crowds waving tricolours and Union Jacks, and shouting, '*Churcheel! Churcheel!*' 'Never have I heard such a sustained roar of cheering,' wrote General Ismay several years later, who, by then, had seen a demonstration or two. 'Winston . . . had a wonderful reception and the Paris crowd went quite mad over him,' wrote General Brooke on the day.[172] Churchill and de Gaulle together laid a wreath on the tomb of the Unknown Warrior; then de Gaulle relit the perpetual flame. They marched together several hundred yards down the Champs Elysées to a stand that had been hastily erected the night before; there was quite a scramble among the officials to get on to it because none of the seats had been marked. The police were helpless. '*La foule déborde!*' cried out some general. But Churchill was careful to remark to de Gaulle how well ordered Paris appeared after her Liberation.

The two leaders boarded a black Citroën and drove down to the Rondpoint des Champs Elysées where, under the bare chestnut trees, stood a bronze statue to Georges Clemenceau.* Churchill laid a wreath at his feet – many of Churchill's wartime speeches, and even the title of his last volume of war memoirs, were inspired by Clemenceau's defiant words of 1917–18. A military band struck up Paulus's 'Père la Victoire', dedicated to Clemenceau – de Gaulle remembered an evening at Chequers in summer 1940 when Churchill had sung the entire song and then said, 'We shall march together, hand in hand, down the Champs Elysées.' As the band pounded away, de Gaulle turned to Churchill and said in his French English, '*For you.*'

Lunch was given at the Ministry of War – it will be remembered that

---

* Today, a striding de Gaulle stands opposite Clemenceau (who should be wearing a woollen cap, not a soldier's helmet). At the other end of the Avenue Winston Churchill, stands a bronze Churchill – a better likeness than at Westminster.

de Gaulle had, at the moment of the Liberation, set up his government at the Ministry of War with the statement, '*Le Ministère de la Guerre, c'est Clemenceau!*' At the end of the meal de Gaulle stood up and proposed a toast to his guest: 'Hitler used to say in the old days that he was building for a thousand years. I cannot say what will remain of his system in a thousand years. But I do know that France, which has some experience of blood, sweat and tears, will not have forgotten in a thousand years what was accomplished in this war through blood, sweat and tears by the noble people the Right Honourable Mr Winston Churchill is leading to the heights of one of the greatest glories in this world . . . Gentlemen, we raise our glasses in honour of Mr Winston Churchill, Prime Minister of Great Britain.' Mr Winston Churchill was by now in tears.[173]

Churchill had been Minister of Munitions when he met the French premier, Clemenceau, in his Ministry of War in March 1918, just at the moment when the first of Ludendorff's spring offensives broke out. Churchill arrived in the morning and, instead of being ceremoniously received in the Prime Minister's office, was driven by Clemenceau and his chauffeur straight to the front. A few days later he witnessed Clemenceau standing on the tribune of the Chamber of Deputies declaring, without notes: 'We shall fight them before Paris, we shall fight them in Paris, we shall fight them behind Paris; but we shall never surrender.'

On the night of 12 November 1944 Churchill joined de Gaulle on his special train; it headed straight for the front. General de Lattre de Tassigny had been amassing a sizeable force of volunteers over the last three months; by spring 1945 he was expecting to be in command of eight new divisions in addition to his existing eight – the problem, as de Gaulle complained the day before, was that the Allies were stalling on the delivery of equipment. De Lattre's French First Army was manoeuvring in the Vosges for the capture of Alsace. Brooke, on being presented with the plan, remarked in his diary that 'it is an example of the American doctrine of attacking all along the line . . . another case of Eisenhower's complete inability to run the land battle as well as acting as Supreme Commander.' Patton's static American Third Army was just to the north and 'is attacking in an impossible country'.[174]

The train emerged into a hilly country covered in whiteness. It was snowing.

Clemenceau's France of 1918 had been bound to Britain by an alliance (the Americans had been only 'associates'). On the train, de Gaulle proposed to Churchill – after some prompting from Churchill – a special Anglo-French alliance. 'Should England and France agree and act together on tomorrow's settlements, they will wield enough power to prevent anything being done which they themselves have not accepted or decided,' said de Gaulle, revealing a new European policy. 'Our two countries will follow us. America and Russia, hampered by their rivalry, will be unable to counter it.' Many other states would follow France and Britain, because the world has 'an instinctive fear of giants'.

Churchill refused the offer. 'It is better', said Churchill, 'to persuade the stronger than to go against them. That is what I am trying to do.' The Americans had immense resources, though they did not always use them to the best advantage: 'I am trying to enlighten them.' As for Russia, it was a starving 'great beast' which 'must be kept from devouring everything': 'I am trying to restrain Stalin, who has a large appetite, but is not devoid of common sense.'[175]

De Gaulle did not think this was a sound method. But on the train he kept his thoughts to himself. Never again would de Gaulle, during his long post-war years as President of the French Republic, offer Britain such a privileged position in his vision of Europe.

The train came to a halt in a driving snowstorm. Churchill, de Gaulle and several generals were carried by car for about sixty miles to a place called Maîche, where de Lattre had his advanced headquarters. From there they were hoping to observe the launch of the battle that would liberate Alsace. But the storm was so intense that they could not see a thing; there was already a foot of snow on the ground. The battle was called off. Churchill's own car suffered two punctured tyres and got stuck in a rut at the side of the road. 'The PM', recorded Brooke, 'was very cold and miserable looking.'[176]

Berlin and Moscow in winter

1 Hitler's Waterloo

In the early hours of Saturday morning, 16 December, a young American soldier from Company K, 110th Infantry, had the unenviable job of keeping watch on top of a concrete water tower at Hosingen, just inside Germany, about a mile east of the Belgian border. The German front line was three miles further east behind highlands known as the Schnee Eifel. The area had been taken by Hodges' US First Army in September and, typically, there had been no movement on the front since. The Americans called the road running through Hosingen the 'Skyline Drive' because it put a lot of troops in mind of a route that ran near the top of the Blue Ridge Mountains in Virginia.

There had been a heavy rainstorm in Holland the previous Tuesday, 12 December; the whole area south of Arnhem was now under water. On the Schnee Eifel the storm had turned into a blizzard. Towards the end of the week temperatures had risen again, which only made conditions worse for the soldiers: their feet sank into mud, the snow clung to their clothes, which became sodden. Then at night temperatures dropped to well below freezing; the soldiers took cover in small depressions in the land that they called 'sugar bowls'. The late morning light was accompanied by dense fog, which lifted briefly at midday and returned with the approach of darkness three hours later. On top of his water tower the sentry on duty that grim Saturday morning could find little to screen him from the raw wind.

Split seconds before 5.30 a.m. he noticed a peculiar phenomenon: there appeared, on the German side of the front, countless flickering pinpoints of light. He telephoned his company commander. Soldiers on outpost duty in neighbouring villages to the north, at Roth, Weckerath and Krewinkel, saw the same flutter and flashes of light – but were quicker to realize what was going on. In an instant there was a roar of explosions, great fir trees were split, branches came crashing to the ground: most terrifying was the screech of rockets – *Nebelwerfer* or 'Screaming Meemies' –

fired from multi-barrelled German launchers. The ground, said one witness, 'shook like a bowl of Jell-O'.[1]

The bombardment did not last an hour. The moment it was over, rows and rows of searchlights on the German side were switched on. They were pointed into the misty pre-dawn skies, creating, as it was technically known, 'artificial moonlight' – all the more effective as it was reflected in a landscape of snow. Penetration began in the northern sector of the offensive. At dawn, American defenders of the Schnee Eifel could make out German paratroopers in white camouflaged smocks equipped with sub-machine guns and automatic pistols ('burp guns' the Americans called them because of the sound they made). Behind them followed the roar of tank engines.

The defenders had the temporary advantage of their 'sugar bowls'. From among the German dead was retrieved their order of the day: 'Soldiers of the Western Front!!! Your great hour has arrived. Huge armies have gone on the offensive against the Anglo-Americans. I do not have to tell you anything more than that. You feel it yourself. WE GAMBLE ON EVERYTHING! You carry with you the holy obligation to give your all to achieve things beyond human reckoning for our Fatherland and our Führer!' It was signed by Field Marshal von Rundstedt.[2]

In the town of Bastogne, about thirty miles to the south-west, Major General Troy H. Middleton had set up headquarters of American VIII Corps. Telephone communications with front lines were poor. This was particularly the case of his line with General Alan Jones's 106th Division at Saint-Vith, just behind the Schnee Eifel. But Middleton did receive a call that night. When he put down the receiver, he turned to one of his staff and said, 'I just talked to Jones. I told him to pull his regiments off the Schnee Eifel.' But it was already too late. As the VIII Corps intelligence officer noted in his report that same night, 'The enemy is capable of pinching off the Schnee Eifel area . . . at any time.'[3]

Most Europeans referred to the bloody encounter that followed as the Battle of the Ardennes. The Americans named it 'the Bulge', after the German salient as it appeared on the maps they saw in the press.[4] It would drag on until the end of January 1945, delaying the end of the war by several months and exacerbating existing tensions between the British and the Americans, most particularly in the press. It was Hitler's Waterloo, the battle that the Allies, who had already outlined their terms for Europe's peace, did not expect. Its most durable effect was the advantage it gave the Soviet Union: as a result of army movements around the western 'Bulge', Stalin's Communist empire would stretch across the whole eastern half of Europe.

★

The Ardennes of southern Belgium and Luxembourg meant more to Europeans than Americans. The Supreme Allied Commander of 1918, Marshal Ferdinand Foch, called the Ardennes 'an almost impenetrable massif'; his generals thought it a death trap. Emperor Napoleon III's army had been destroyed when the first Moltke, the great Moltke, cornered it against the Ardennes at Sedan in September 1870. Kaiser Wilhelm's armies were shattered when British, French and American forces pushed them up against the Ardennes in the autumn of 1918. If there was no military opposition, it was ideal country from which to launch a surprise attack: one of the main armies in the first German offensive of August 1914 passed through the same zone, the so-called 'Losheim Gap', just north of the Schnee Eifel, as Rundstedt's spearhead in December 1944; General Erwin Rommel's Panzers advanced along exactly the same road in the attack that defeated France and isolated Britain in May 1940. That was Hitler's plan in late 1944. 'Here,' he exclaimed, stamping a finger on the desolate area outlined on his map: 'out of the Ardennes, with the objective, Antwerp!'

American eyes had been drawn to the Lorraine, further south – on the map this appeared the most direct route to Germany. So thought General Pershing in the autumn of 1918 when he had set up an American Second Army designed to storm eastwards from Metz and win the war in 1919; Clemenceau believed that one of the reasons the Americans refused to ratify the Treaty of Versailles was because they had been robbed of their victory. Patton, a veteran of America's foreshortened campaign of 1918, was determined this time to lead the Allied armies to an American victory – which is no doubt why, since September 1944, his Third Army had been struggling to obtain a breakthrough at Metz.

General Eisenhower was both land commander of the Allied forces in North-Western Europe and supreme commander. Supreme Headquarters of the Allied Expeditionary Forces (SHAEF) were now based in Versailles, at the same Trianon Palace Hotel where the Germans had been presented with the Versailles Treaty. Eisenhower had a similar opinion of the Ardennes as Foch; it was an impenetrable massif.

It had been the most forested region of Roman Gaul, the westernmost part of a highland system that stretched north-eastwards into lands where the Romans dared not set foot – the Eifel mountains, the Westerwald and the Herz mountains, which petered out in Saxony: the southern wall of Europe's great plain. Patton's southern line of attack would have to penetrate all that if it was ever to reach Berlin. In the Ardennes there were scattered hamlets and clusters of farmhouses with barns attached, built beside narrow cobbled streets; the inevitable Café de la Poste was where rumours passed; the dung heaps lay beyond the farmhouses for spreading on the fields that ran up to the forest line. The Ardennes was known for its seasoned hams. The streams cut great ravines through the region; the most famous was the River Meuse, whose high banks formed cliffs.

When the British and American forces separated in the third week of August, Montgomery's 21st Army Group kept to the plain. Montgomery may have failed at Arnhem, but his troops stood poised to take the Ruhr, heartland of Germany's war machine; this should have been the aim of all Allied armies, so Montgomery had argued since the end of the Normandy campaign. But the Americans were drawn, by their own First World War mythology, southwards. Bradley's American 12th Army Group was itself forced to split when confronted with the Ardennes. Hodges' American First Army circuited the northern side of the massif where it was joined by General William H. Simpson's new American Ninth Army. For two months they battered in what was left of Charlemagne's old capital, Aachen (or Aix-la-Chapelle), in the hope of breaking a way through to Cologne, key to the southern side of the Ruhr. But one could tell where Bradley's preferences lay: he had set up Army Group Headquarters in Luxembourg city on the southern side of the Ardennes, where he was much closer to Patton's Third Army and its struggle at Metz. 'At present there are 17 American divisions south of the Ardennes, and 18 north of the Ardennes,' wrote a frustrated Montgomery to General Brooke in London on 18 November; there was, he went on, no 'system or plan for switching strength'.[5] Nor, after Rundstedt broke into the Ardennes, was there any system of communication.

When Eisenhower, in Versailles, finally realized – four days after the initial attack – how serious was the situation, he telephoned Montgomery in his dreary headquarters of Zonhoven, southern Holland, and offered him command of Bradley's two isolated northern armies. Montgomery took advantage of the fact that the telephone line was very poor. He shouted into the receiver, 'I can't hear you properly. I shall take command straight away' – and hung up.[6]

A fuming General Omar Bradley was left Army Group Commander of just one army: Patton's, stuck down in Metz. This touchy matter was kept a military secret and was not revealed to the press until January. Many American historians to this day remain silent on the fact that a major part of American forces in the 'Bulge' were under the command of British Field Marshal Montgomery (he had received his baton in September).

Simpson kept Ninth Army Headquarters in Maastricht, on the Maas (as the Flemish called the Meuse), not far from Montgomery's own forward Dutch headquarters. The Field Marshal's system of communication was very old-fashioned, but it worked; he used his young Liaison Officers, LOs, 'Monty's gallopers', to go out into the field and see what was happening – every night he sent a situation report to Brooke in London, the only such regular report made by the Western Allies during the whole course of the battle.

Hodges' First Army Headquarters were right in the middle of the Ardennes, at the famous watering resort of Spa. Hindenburg and Ludendorff had kept German Supreme Command here, in the Hôtel Britannique – they lived, with the Kaiser as their neighbour, in the villas above the town. Hodges and his senior staff resided in the same villas; formal headquarters were in the same Hôtel Britannique. But like Hindenburg and Ludendorff they had little communication with the outside world, nor did the outside world know much about them. When two of Montgomery's LOs arrived in Spa early in the morning of 19 December, they were surprised to find no American Army MPs in town. They went straight to the Hôtel Britannique – 'literally', recorded one of the LOs, 'not one single person there except a German woman'. Breakfast was laid out, a Christmas tree decorated the dining room, telephones were in all the offices, 'papers were all over the place'. 'Germans in the town', he went on, 'said that they had gone suddenly and quickly down the road at 3 a.m.'[7]

Hodges had just fled across the Meuse. The Americans were in a rout: no news was coming out of the main American headquarters; nothing from Bradley in Luxembourg; nothing from Eisenhower in Versailles.

'Pardon my French, Lev,' gasped Bradley to his chief of staff, General 'Lev' Allen, 'but where the hell has the son of a bitch gotten all this strength?'[8] Bradley had been in Versailles and had only returned to his Luxembourg headquarters twenty-four hours after the German offensive had begun. The power of the attack astonished all Western commanders.

Hitler's German Reich and occupied territories had, by early December 1944, been reduced to its core. The Russians had made inroads into East Prussia. The Germans had invaded 'neutral' Finland and in their with-drawal towards Norway were conducting one of the most brutal scorched earth policies of the war; Germans would continue shooting and hanging their own men in Norway after the surrender was signed in Berlin on 8 May 1945. Half of Poland, including Warsaw, remained under Nazi control, more thanks to Soviet politics than to German strength in the area. Romania and Bulgaria had switched sides. General Kesselring held on to a small part of northern Italy. France had been cleared, save a few ports. Western Allied forces had advanced to the Westwall, or the 'Siegfried

Line', guarding the Reich's western frontier; at Aachen the Americans had even gone beyond it. Surely this was the end. Surely the United Nations would soon begin its work of peace, the IMF set about the reform of the world's currencies, and the West sit down with the East and finally settle their spheres of influence.

The great drama was Hungary. The defection of both Romania and Bulgaria to the Soviet camp had given the Hungarian Regent, Admiral Horthy, ideas; his delegation to Moscow arrived the very week Churchill and the Poles were in town. Molotov dictated to them the normal harsh terms and it was agreed that Horthy would announce on the radio his armistice with the Soviet Union on Sunday afternoon, 15 October.

But the great new forces Hitler was building up for his offensive in the west – particularly his new aircraft – depended on Hungarian-Austrian oilfields for four fifths of their fuel needs. Hitler had already prepared his *coup*. Otto Skorzeny (the hero who had rescued Mussolini from his mountain-top prison in 1943) was put in charge of a special SS unit, including SS-Obergruppenführer von dem Bach-Zelewski (who had just completed his duties in Warsaw), to take over the Citadel of Budapest, where Horthy's government resided. Hitler had his own government in waiting, Ferencz Szálasi's fanatical, pro-Nazi Arrow Cross. The operation went into effect late Sunday morning and, shortly after Horthy announced his Soviet 'armistice', Szálasi came on the radio to proclaim the Nazi takeover.

Up to the day he shot himself Hitler had a peculiar obsession, perhaps related to his Austrian origins, that the way to defeat the Soviet enemy was by a thrust south-eastwards – formerly into the Ukraine, now into Hungary, and later into Bohemia – which would somehow split up the Red Army; he was still ordering elite units in this direction in April 1945.

'Well done, Skorzeny!' exclaimed Hitler when the tall blond Austrian SS officer entered the Führer's study at the 'Wolf's Lair' in Rastenburg. Hitler pinned on his lapel the German Cross in Gold and then entered into a long monologue on how he was going to save the Reich: an attack on the Ardennes and the seizure of Antwerp. 'One of the most important tasks in this offensive will be entrusted to you and the units under your command,' said Hitler. Skorzeny was to form a special brigade that would precede the attacking Panzer armies and seize the bridges over the Meuse. To ease their task of infiltration they were to wear American uniforms and drive American vehicles.[9]

Even Himmler, 'loyal Heinrich', admitted that the scheme was idiotic. Skorzeny was worried that his men, in wearing American uniforms, were violating international law and would be shot on the spot if captured; he was told that such *ruses de guerre* were permitted, provided they did not fight: they could wear their German uniforms underneath and strip down if they saw any Americans approaching! Finding the American uniforms was not easy; the first consignment turned out to be British, and the second had huge prisoner-of-war triangles painted on them. Of the ten armoured cars supplied, six were British, and they all broke down. So too did the two American tanks Skorzeny managed to get hold of. In the end, he decided to paint his twelve Panthers in American camouflage – at night, at a distance, it was possible for Americans to make a mistake of identity.

A circular had been prepared for local commanders to capture American uniforms and equipment and screen troops who spoke English, in the 'American dialect'. The circular, of course, found its way into American hands. Rumours spread on both sides. Sightings were made among troops of the US Ninth Army of 'American soldiers' wearing dark glasses in winter and accompanied by 'girls' whose thick male shins were covered in silk stockings – no Belgian woman in 1944 wore silk. One rumour, which had its origin in the training camp of Grafenwöhr, near Nuremberg, was that a special assassination squad was being prepared for Eisenhower. There was no such squad: but it explains why General Eisenhower remained locked up in the Trianon Palace Hotel, in Versailles, during most of the Ardennes battle. Bradley shut himself up in his hotel in Luxembourg city. Not much news came out of either headquarters.

Skorzeny's undermanned brigade never got as far as the Meuse. One of their number is supposed to have posed as an American military policeman and misdirected part of an American infantry division. A few were captured by the Americans; sixteen were shot, three were acquitted.[10]

History, it is famously said, never repeats itself. In the first place, there is the factor of geography: events located in a different physical setting cannot repeat themselves. Secondly, the unending march of technology makes duplication difficult: a war fought with Wellington's six-pounders will not be the same as one prosecuted with Hitler's tanks and aircraft. The scale of events, of casualties, of suffering, is of a different order. There are historians today who have called the Napoleonic wars, and even the eighteenth-century Seven Years War, the 'First World War'; but no one could consider these the same as Hitler's world war. And yet, if technology and scale are cumulative, the human element involved is arguably constant. Lessons of morality are not passed easily from one generation to the next. The quest for power has never been abandoned. As that grand European literary critic, George Steiner, has pointed out, there is not a story whose original cannot be traced to the ancient Greeks or the Bible.

The scale, the technology employed, his propaganda machine and ideology set Hitler apart from all precursors. But it cannot be claimed that he and his war were unique. There are some uncanny parallels between Hitler's last months and Napoleon's desperate 'Hundred Days' of spring 1815. The basic shape of the peace in Europe had already been decided – in the case of Napoleon's campaign, in Vienna in 1814; in the case of Hitler, during the wartime Allied peace conferences, particularly those held in America. Napoleon was faced with declining domestic morale; so was Hitler. Napoleon became increasingly dependent on a party of fanatical supporters; so did Hitler. Napoleon could not rely on the loyalty of his officer corps; nor could Hitler. All of Napoleon's leading government officials were seeking a way out of the war with the dictator's main enemies; so were Hitler's – with the important exception of Goebbels.

But the most striking parallel between Napoleon's end and Hitler's is in the plans each concocted to win the impossible victory. Napoleon planned to defeat what seemed to him an untenable coalition by driving his last remaining reserves between them – with the help of batteries of cannon; his final assaults were suicidal strikes because, failing to divide his enemies, he had left himself no political alternative but to go on. Similarly, Hitler placed his hopes in a thrust between quarrelling allies – with the help of new 'miracle weapons'. He had left himself no political alternative. Wellington was criticized for holding his troops back at Waterloo; but his idea, which proved correct, was to let Napoleon overextend himself and then attack. The parallel must have crossed Montgomery's mind, when he placed four full British divisions on the west bank of the Meuse even before assuming command of the American armies on the north side of the Ardennes. Hitler's route to Antwerp was thus sealed within two days of his offensive, before either Eisenhower or Bradley realized what was happening. Montgomery refused to drive his divisions into the Ardennes because, like Wellington, he was holding them for another offensive – in Montgomery's case, on the Ruhr.

The commander of British XXX Corps, Lieutenant General Brian Horrocks, clearly saw the parallel. On 27 December he even recommended that the defenders of the Meuse let Manteuffel's Fifth Panzer Army through and penetrate as far as a southern suburb of Brussels: Waterloo! Horrocks, wrote a witness in his diary that day, 'would let the Germans over the river and then win the final battle of the war on the field of Waterloo'.[11]

Born of the French Revolution, Napoleon presented himself as the modern man who had come to suppress the forces of 'feudalism'. Hitler's political career was moulded by the events of 1918; he was 'the man who did not capitulate'. The plan that developed in his mind between July and

September 1944, when Germany lost over a million men and was reduced to the core of the Reich, was classic Hitler, the Hitler of *Mein Kampf*: concentrate on one thrust, a *Schwerpunkt*. On the Eastern Front Germany could afford to be flexible; in the West, she could not. Thirty new and refitted divisions added to the Eastern Front would not make much difference; driven through a weak enemy point on the Western Front it could change the course of the war. Hitler chose the Ardennes in August, but needed the bad weather of autumn to prevent the Allies from exploiting their superior air power.

Dr Goebbels, now Reich Plenipotentiary for the Total War Effort, understood Hitler like no other. On 20 September he sent Hitler a memorandum on future war plans, which he considered of such capital importance that he copied it into his diary. It could have been taken straight out of *Mein Kampf*. Germany, noted Goebbels, had never won a two-front war. One would have to aim, as on 30 January 1933 when Hitler seized the Chancellorship, at a 'limited victory' – not the whole programme realized at once, or 'the victory we had dreamed of in 1941', but still 'the greatest victory in German history': make some arrangement with the Soviets, suggested Goebbels; the Anglo-Americans would be unable to continue their war indefinitely.[12]

Earlier in the month the Japanese ambassador, Baron Oshima Hiroshi, had suggested to Hitler exactly the same idea. In the company of Foreign Minister von Ribbentrop, he visited Hitler in his East Prussian bunker to urge him to make an accord with the Soviets. Hitler emphasized the importance of his new weapons and then spoke of a 'large-scale offensive' he was planning in the West. He seems to have ignored Goebbels's plan.

There is, however, evidence that as autumn wore on he did consider some form of accommodation with the Soviet Union. He discussed the matter, for example, when the new Hungarian Nazi dictator, Szálasi, visited him in Berlin on 4 December. But Szálasi himself had stalled the Russian advance in the south-east. From the Carpathians up to the Baltic, with the exception of bitter fighting, to and fro, in East Prussia itself, the front had been stable since September.

So Hitler did not need an agreement with the Soviets. Nor, for that matter, was Stalin much interested in his old ties with Hitler: his conferences with Roosevelt and Churchill, along with the mass of information provided by his network of 'illegals' and spies in Britain and America, suggested that he was going to get all he demanded from the West. For Hitler, the most pressing matter was to launch and complete a successful attack on the Western Allies before the Russians began their winter offensive, which the Germans expected in mid-January. By that time, the new divisions could be transferred east – the classic Hitler manoeuvre that avoided a two-front war.

The generals were not at all keen on Hitler's planned offensive, not even the cold, humourless General Alfred Jodl, head of the operations staff of OKW (High Command of the Armed Forces), who was considered one of the Führer's closest collaborators. Jodl and his staff had been instructed to prepare plans in September – 'out of the Ardennes, with the objective Antwerp,' said Hitler. Not one of the five alternative plans presented by Jodl in early October mentioned Antwerp as an objective, and only one of them followed Hitler's course through the Ardennes.

But the plan which Hitler eventually accepted on 21 October corresponded exactly to the operation he had demanded. It was called '*Wacht am Rhein*' ('Watch on the Rhine') after a cheerful First World War song. Just before the offensive began in December Jodl admitted he was 'filled with doubt'.[13]

The field commanders were only informed of the plan at the end of October. They worked frenziedly on an alternative, less ambitious operation, which they named '*Herbstnebel*' ('Autumn Mist') – which already had a ring of 1918 about it. Their idea – not too different from Jodl's initial projects – was to form a pincer movement along the line of the Meuse and surround the American First and Ninth Armies. But the trapping of ten, fifteen or even thirty US divisions was not enough to satisfy Hitler's political needs: he had to get through to Antwerp and split the Western Allies in two. Even the most loyal of his SS generals could not understand the significance of their Führer's desperate project.

Hitler eventually accepted the generals' name for the operation, 'Autumn Mist'; he accepted the delays imposed by the difficulties of collecting thirty divisions in the Eifel mountains – until winter was almost upon them. But he refused to alter his plan. He left the 'Wolf's Lair' for the last time on 20 November, spent three weeks in Berlin, and on 10 December headed west for the 'Eagle's Eyrie', beneath the woods of the Taunus Hills, near Bad Nauheim, not far from the Rhine. 'I have striven from the beginning to conduct the war wherever possible offensively,' he told the field commanders.

SS Obergruppenführer Sepp Dietrich – beer-hall companion of Hilter in Munich, street-fighter in Berlin, leading participant in the Night of the Long Knives, mass-murderer in Russia, and hated by most of the generals – was one of the few at the briefing who told Hitler that 'Autumn Mist' would not work: 'Cross a river, capture Brussels, and then go on and take

Antwerp! And all this in the worst time of the year through the Ardennes, where the snow is waist deep! . . . Where it doesn't get light until eight and it's dark again at four, and with re-formed divisions made up chiefly of raw, untried recruits! And at Christmas!'[14]

Sepp Dietrich commanded the newly formed Sixth Panzer Army (Hitler sometimes called it the 'Sixth SS Panzer Army', but it only took on this title in the last weeks of the war). With four SS Panzer divisions it was supposed to form the iron lance of the offensive, leading the less trust-worthy regular army units on to Antwerp and victory. According to Jodl's plan they were supposed to reach the great chasm that formed the River Meuse by the second or third day; on learning this, Dietrich caustically remarked that 'Jodl had waged war only on maps' – which was not entirely true: he had been a Bavarian artillery officer during the First World War. Montgomery's British XXX Corps was already in place on the other side of the Meuse with the bridgeheads in British hands.

Dietrich's forces never saw them. His route out of Monschau took him through the Hautes Fagnes, the 'High Marshes'. Dietrich, interrogated in 1945 by American officers, told how one of his leading Panzer divisions had only 100 litres of fuel per tank; 'we thought this would be good for 50–60 km, but, in the swampy terrain, low gear had to be used quite a bit, and the fuel didn't last.' The route planned did not permit the troops to follow and they had to search, in the mist, for roads by which to get through. Division boundaries and army boundaries got muddled up. By Christmas Day they were completely stalled only a dozen miles from where they had started. By that time the skies had cleared and the Allies were launching devastating air attacks. 'The whole attack was a big mistake,' Dietrich repeated during his interrogation. 'To use those two armies at that time of year was the biggest mistake they made in the War . . . Very poor weather, the roads were bad, it was a poor time of the year for tank movement.'[15]

Joachim Peiper's SS-Panzergrenadiers, which had spent long months of destruction and murder in Russia, captured on 17 December around two hundred American infantry in a village just south of Malmédy, inside the Losheim Gap. A hundred of them were herded into a field and machine-gunned; 86 died while several escaped to tell their tale to the commander of the American First Army still in Spa, General Hodges. His aide, William C. Sylvan, noted in his diary: 'There is absolutely no question as to its proof – immediate publicity is being given to the story.'[16] The slaughter was small by comparison to the atrocities still being committed in Eastern and Central Europe, but the Malmédy massacre was – amazingly – the first reported in detail in the American press. It was Malmédy, not

Auschwitz or Warsaw, that began the popular outcry in America for a trial of Nazi war criminals.[17]

To Hitler's mortification, General Hasso von Manteuffel's Fifth Panzer Army of regulars to Dietrich's south became the iron lance, bypassing Spa, laying siege to the American 101st Airborne Division in Bastogne, and moving on to within a few miles of the Meuse, at Dinant. A small tank battle between the British and the Germans took place here on Christmas Eve; two German Tigers were knocked out. But the problem for the Germans now was a spell of clear weather.

In answering a written questionnaire prepared by the Americans after their capture in 1945, Jodl and his chief, Field Marshal Wilhelm Keitel, reported that the Allied bombing of 24–25 December was more significant in its effect on rear transport facilities – 'especially at the middle Rhine Zone, Koblenz–Mainz–Frankfurt' – than on the actual attacking units. These 'crushing air attacks', they reported, 'had grave consequences'.[18] There was no fuel left. Von Manteuffel's Panzers, in bypassing the main towns, also failed to uncover the fuel depots the Americans had liberally scattered around the country; one huge depot of 3,300,000 gallons in Hodges' abandoned headquarters at Spa was still full to the brim when the Americans eventually returned in January.

After the New Year, temperatures fell below freezing; there was a blizzard on 4 January and visibility was reduced to zero.

Down in Luxembourg, with the news only dribbling through, Bradley attempted to keep crowds of reporters satisfied. Famous baseball players turned up to remind the troops that America was behind them.

But it was a tall, slim German lady who won the hearts of the soldiers. At Diekirch, just one day before the offensive, Marlene Dietrich sang to them in a hoarse, almost spoken voice, in German, '*Wie heisst Lili Marlene, Wie heisst Lili Marlene . . .*' Nobody ever forgot it. 'Lili Marlene' became, and remained, the song of the 'Bulge'.

Patton had abandoned his frontal assaults on German positions in Lorraine on 19 December and turned all his forces round ninety degrees northwards. Bradley was predicting to his reporters that Patton would be in Bastogne within a matter of hours. The Third Army advanced abreast over a front almost thirty miles wide across a slippery, rugged terrain against the opposition of the entrenched German Seventh Army.

On Christmas Day – ten days after the beginning of the offensive – Bradley at last made the long journey around the periphery of the salient to visit the new commander of the two northern American armies, Montgomery. On his arrival Bradley was not offered so much as a biscuit; Montgomery was at his cocksure worst. 'Bradley is trying hard to get to Bastogne,' Montgomery wrote to Brooke that night. 'He may possibly get to that place, but he admits himself that he is not strong enough to get any further.'

Patton eventually broke through the southern front on the day after Christmas and his tanks rolled into Bastogne at dusk. Bradley began making snide remarks about Montgomery's 'stagnating conservatism of tactics'.[19] Why didn't the British commander attack from the north? Because Montgomery had no intention of committing himself to the death trap of the Ardennes; he was saving his forces for the Ruhr – and, after that, Berlin. Montgomery would have left the 'Bulge' behind him.

Never before in their history had the Americans been involved in such a huge battle. By the time they had cleared the 'Bulge', on 30 January 1945, they had lost 100,000 men, 18,000 of them dead, most of the rest prisoners; they stood on the same frontiers as they had in December. Never had the Western press been so involved in the course of a battle, though it was not too precise about the details; the most significant feature in their stories was the war of words that developed between the Americans and the British. Ironically, its origin was not even over the 'Bulge', but the coincident British presence, that December, in Greece. In the American press this was adduced as proof of Britain's old 'imperialist' ambitions. For Churchill, who spent Christmas Day in Athens, it was a signal to Stalin that the line, agreed in October, was being drawn. Washington remained apparently unconcerned about Soviet progress in Eastern Europe.

What brought the 'Bulge' to the forefront in the newspapers was not so much the loss of territory on the Western Front, as the issue of Allied command. The quarrel between Bradley and Montgomery soon became a vicious press campaign over who ought to direct the Western armies. The Americans demanded Americans; the British, led by the *Daily Mail*, retorted that 'Monty' should be Deputy Commander of the Allied Expeditionary Forces.

On New Year's Day Patton gave a ranting press conference – 'We can lick the Germans any place'; 'Bastogne is . . . as important as the Battle of Gettysburg.' On 5 January SHAEF at last made the official announcement that command of the American First and Ninth Armies had been transferred from Bradley to Montgomery, because of a breakdown in communications – which hardly pleased Bradley. On 6 January Montgomery read a press statement which, if hardly as bombastic as Patton's, soon ruffled feathers. Army commanders had not yet mastered the art of mass media management. But they were quick learners: they would demonstrate their new talents a few months later to the post-war world.[20]

Had Hitler achieved his purpose, and split the Western Alliance? His greatest feat was to ensure for his countrymen that Anglo-American forces would not be the first to arrive in the capital of the Reich.

More immediately important, Hitler's losses in the Ardennes proved irreversible. In the 'Eagle's Eyrie' he told the field commanders, two days after Patton relieved Bastogne, that on this battle in the Ardennes depended 'the existence of the substance of the German people'. An enemy victory would 'bolshevize Europe'. There would be no November 1918. 'I have never in my life recognized the term capitulation.'[21]

The Soviets, in a welcome response to Allied difficulties, advanced their planned offensive in the direction of the German capital by one week. On Friday, 12 January, they at last broke out across their lines on the Vistula – where they had held their positions since the outbreak of the Warsaw Rising – advanced through the rubble of Warsaw and on to western Poland. There were no Varsovians to greet them.

Four days later Hitler returned to Berlin, never to leave it again.

Sepp Dietrich – no relation to the singer – told his interrogators later in 1945 how his prize army was evacuated from the Ardennes. 'These orders came through about the end of January,' he said. 'We marched back over the Rhine on foot in twelve days. Because we were waiting for more petrol, the tanks moved very slowly to conserve fuel and many vehicles were towed by tractors.' They gradually made their way across Germany to what Hitler considered the most strategic point remaining of his empire, Hungary. 'We left the Rhineland area by train between 5 February and 17 February, and the main body arrived in Hungary on 1–2 March 1945. One corps attacked on 4 March, and by 6 March, we launched an army attack on Lake Balaton.' This would prove to be the last major assault launched by the Third Reich.[22]

2 A Gaullist mirror

At New Year, however, Hitler had managed to deliver a surprise parting shot. On 31 December 1944, at 11 p.m., he ordered an attack on General Jacob L. Devers' overstretched American 6th Army Group in Alsace. With New Year's Day he gained several miles of snow and, in launching a simultaneous air offensive against the major airfields of northern France, managed to wipe out what remained of his own Luftwaffe, thereby assuring the

Western Allies air superiority over Germany for the last four months of the war. Like the 'Bulge', fighting in Alsace would last most of January, again delaying the Allied advance into Germany.

Hitler's 'Operation North Wind' also introduced on to the world stage a phenomenon that was to baffle pundits of post-war European diplomacy for several decades: the French Gaullist movement. Spurning the alliance that liberated the country, it presented itself as a conservative movement while developing a highly ambivalent relationship with the Communists – one in which it always seemed ready to cooperate with the Soviet Union. The Gaullist movement became, as de Gaulle himself described it, the politics of the 'third way'.

De Gaulle's 'third way' would act as an imperfect mirror, in a western corner of Europe, of the critical situation developing on the east side of the Reich. The movement is interesting for this reason.

Intelligence signals from Bletchley Park had been coming through since Christmas indicating German preparations for an attack on Alsace. Leclerc's *Deuxième DB* had eventually liberated the province on 22 November, with his old companion, Colonel Dio, leading a column of tanks into Strasbourg the next morning – thus fulfilling a pledge that brave French unit had made in the African desert in 1941. The celebrations which followed the liberation of Strasbourg were like those of Paris. But, unlike Paris, Strasbourg could not forget the ongoing war. De Gaulle had paid a visit to the city at Christmas time as it anxiously watched developments in the Ardennes. There was no doubt in its citizens' minds that a return of the Nazis and Gauleiter Wagner's Gestapo would mean a massacre of the worst kind. In November, Hitler gave Heinrich Himmler personal responsibility for the policing and administration of reconquered Alsace – there was an ugly scent of Poland in Hitler's 'North Wind'.

Upper Alsace was, at the time, under the control of General Jean de Lattre de Tassigny's French First Army, which had formed the right flank of the American invasion of the Riviera in mid-August. On 28 December de Lattre had received an order from Devers to prepare for a withdrawal to the Vosges mountains; since the order was in English, de Lattre did not take much notice of it. De Gaulle was only informed of the planned withdrawal once Hitler's attack began. He threatened to pull all French forces out of the Western Alliance.

'General Eisenhower', wrote de Gaulle in his war memoirs, 'played his role well, in a manner both loyal and methodical . . . For my own part, I was determined not to complicate his task . . . But, beyond the common interest of winning the battle which was everyone's concern, there was the French national interest. And that was my business.' Faced with Eisenhower's plan to withdraw from Alsace – perfectly understandable from a military point of view when the forces of the American General Patch and the French General de Lattre found themselves faced with Panther tanks that could outgun them and, for the first time in history, enemy jet aircraft flying faster than any other plane in the air – de Gaulle argued that he had no option but to break the Alliance. The Americans, de Gaulle claimed, were acting unilaterally, without any consideration of coalition politics. 'If the French government undertook to entrust its forces to the command of a foreign commander,' he explained in his memoirs, 'it was on the strict condition that they be employed in conformity with the interests of that country. Were this not the case, the government had a duty to resume control of them. This is what I decided to do.'[23]

That was the Proustian de Gaulle, remembering things past. The actual confrontation between the French and the Americans on 2 January 1945 was rather more brutal. In the morning de Gaulle had received, through the new French military governor at Strasbourg, formal notice of Eisenhower's order to pull out of the province; Eisenhower's SHAEF, ensconced in the Trianon Palace Hotel at Versailles, had maintained its customary silence. De Gaulle instructed his chief of staff, General Alphonse Juin, to go over to Versailles and inform the Americans that France intended to pull out of the Alliance. Juin had a short encounter with Eisenhower's chief of staff, General Walter Bedell Smith (pronounced 'Beedel').

'General de Gaulle', announced Juin, 'has ordered de Lattre to take full account of the defence of Strasbourg.' 'In that case, which is a matter of pure and simple disobedience,' announced Bedell Smith in return, 'the French First Army will no longer be supplied with a single bullet or a single litre of gasoline.' 'Very well,' retorted Juin. 'General de Gaulle will henceforth forbid all American forces usage of French railways and other forms of French transport.' The discussion ended there.

De Gaulle immediately cabled Roosevelt and Churchill, informing them that, at the very least, the French would fight for Strasbourg. Roosevelt, through his recently installed ambassador to Paris, Jefferson Caffery, replied that this was purely a military matter (not exactly the line followed by President Woodrow Wilson and General Pershing when presented, in 1918, with orders from Allied Supreme Command seated in the same Trianon Palace Hotel). De Gaulle, who knew his history, argued that the Americans were ignoring all precedents of coalition warfare.

He cabled, at the same time, the British Prime Minister. Churchill, typically, boarded a plane the next morning. There was a howling wind.

After a bumpy ride he arrived in the afternoon at Versailles, where he found Eisenhower and de Gaulle already in conference. Eisenhower presented the same argument as his chief of staff – not a bullet, not a litre of gasoline. De Gaulle had the same riposte – no transportation for the Americans. The atmosphere, however, was cordial: that was Eisenhower's greatest talent.

Accounts of the exchange differ. But it seems Churchill remained largely silent. According to de Gaulle's memoirs he did at one point intervene and say, 'All my life I have known the place Alsace has held in the hearts of Frenchmen. I therefore believe, like General de Gaulle, that this fact has to be taken into account.' The remark has the authentic sound of Churchill. At any rate, Eisenhower immediately rescinded his order.

The formal conference was followed by the service of warm tea. Eisenhower, amiable as ever, explained how difficult was his task of command, involving so many governments, the jealousies of armies, navies and air forces – he was having, he noted, some difficulty with Field Marshal Montgomery. 'Glory will be the reward,' replied de Gaulle. 'You will conquer.' The two men stood up and shook hands.

With the order to withdraw rescinded, Himmler never got the opportunity to turn Alsace into another Poland.[24]

The matter went deeper than a mere quarrel between statesmen and generals. Policy lines were being set right across Europe. These in turn were being determined by the movement of armies; in the absence of inter-allied political discussion – as in 1815 and in 1918 – they could rely on nothing else. In brief, European policy lines were now solely the product of military movements.

But two critical margins of manoeuvre followed these lines: one just before the arrival of the armies, the other just after. Because of the geography of peninsular Europe, these margins were much wider at the base, in Eastern Europe, than they were at the terminal end of the funnel, in the West. Resistance to the Nazi occupier was only effective within the margin that preceded the arrival of the armies – the mythology of resistance, which became the base of most political formations in Europe after the war, has to take this fact into account. The armies passed. Behind them lay a second margin, a political vacuum and, in the case of Eastern Europe, a historical desert – the records were either destroyed or distorted. Orwell's concern that a history could never be written of the twentieth century, particularly of the Second World War – and most especially the end of the Second World War – should be the anguish of everyone. Much of what happened within the first margin, before the arrival of the armies, has been documented and told. It is within the second margin, after the armies had moved by, that one finds the great silence.

Even in the case of France, which has been studied and debated – obsessively, one might say – more than any other country in Europe, there remains many a question mark over what exactly happened after the armies had passed. France was a backwater in Hitler's empire. He accorded it no importance, save that of a defence against the British Empire and, much later, the Americans. This gave the French a degree of choice, a terrible kind of choice, that existed nowhere else in Hitler's Europe. There was less hostage shooting, there were fewer deportations, and there was less dire poverty – that is, physical starvation – than elsewhere within Nazidom.

The case of the second margin – behind the armies, after the Normandy landings – is fairly clear-cut in northern France. The Gaullists took over the administration; the provincial towns and villages of Brittany, Normandy, the Loire Country and eastwards to Champagne and Lorraine, were often run by the same notables who had been there during the occupation, but they all deferred to de Gaulle's new Provisional Government. It is in southern France, after the passage of the 'liberating' armies, where questions still remain to this day: they will probably never be answered.

There are, as Mark Twain might have put it, the statistics, and then there are the statistics. There are also the politics. The left minimizes the number of summary executions at the end of the war; the right maximizes. For a long time a national figure of 100,000 summary executions was repeated by historians for the whole period 1942 to 1945. In 1981 the Institut d'Histoire du Temps Présent estimated the total to be under 10,000 ('of which 1,459 of these executions, at least, took place after the Liberation'). The higher figure has its origins in an article published in the *American Mercury* in April 1946 by an American reporter, Donald B. Robinson, who had acted as a liaison officer for the American Seventh Army after the liberation of Marseilles in August 1944. The low figure, based on a twelve-year inquiry made department by department, is almost certainly an underestimate. No figures, for example, are provided for six French departments, amongst which three (Lot-et-Garonne, Hérault and Les Landes) are known to have witnessed horrors. The department of Ariège saw, in the 1980s, the estimated number of summary executions following the Liberation rise from zero to 76. Part of the difficulty is due to the problem of defining 'summary execution', or *épuration sauvage*; for there existed 'courts martial', 'popular justice' and 'revolutionary justice' which, according to local 'officials', provided the basis of legitimacy for the new social Republic. De Gaulle, in the third volume of his war memoirs, published in 1959, stated that 'among the French who, by murder or by denunciation, caused the death of combatants of the Resistance, there were killed, without regular trial, 19,842, of whom 6,675 died during combat with the Maquis before the Liberation, and the rest afterwards, in the course of reprisals.' What is the source of figures so precise?[25]

The armies that landed on the French Riviera on 15 August moved swiftly up the Rhône valley. One of the reasons for this was that Hitler had decided to withdraw all his troops save those in certain key areas, especially the major ports, where they were supposed to fight to the last man. There was thus no national political authority in the areas left behind by these armies. De Gaulle had officially installed, throughout France, departmental prefects and regional Commissaires de la République. But after the armies had gone, these exercised very little authority. The Communist leader of the Vaucluse, for example, declared in the presence of the Commissaire that it was the Communist-dominated Comité de Libération (CDL) that 'represented the people, and all authority was in the hands of the Resistance, and the Prefect was there only to execute orders'. The same situation existed in Languedoc. In Nice the Communist CDL simply took over control of the municipal government and, on 2 September, the Prefect was expelled from the town.[26]

The word 'Fascist' crept back into French politics once the armies had passed. Answering an internal questionnaire of the FFI as to why nine *miliciens* were shot before a large crowd in the Roman arena of Nîmes shortly after the town's liberation, the presiding FFI officer answered: 'In response to the reaction of Fascist elements in [the department of] the Gard who wanted to spread trouble.' And who were the judges in this 'court martial'? 'The people of France and the victims of Fascism.' Even de Gaulle began to use the term. Hitler's political doctrine was, according to de Gaulle, made up of a mixture of 'Fascism and racism'.[27]

'Purification' was the order of the day in the Limousin after the Germans withdrew, leaving the region to the charge of the FTP leader, 'Colonel' Georges Guingouin (he was later elected Communist mayor of Limoges). Many of his 'patriots' were veterans of the International Brigades during the Spanish Civil War, and were not even French. But they killed parish priests, doctors, lawyers, wine-growers and mayors; women were stripped and tortured, and their heads shaven. Marseilles suffered some of the worst of the post-Liberation violence, under the guidance of the Commissaire de la République himself, the Communist Raymond Aubrac. He set up his own private security unit, the Forces Républicaines de Sécurité (FRS)* which liquidated 'traitors', arrested 'suspects', and stripped and humiliated

---

* Ancestor of today's CRS.

women. Within the first two weeks of liberation, 3,000 arrests were recorded in Marseilles, Aix-en-Provence and Arles. Among Aubrac's torturers was 'Major Coco', who worked in Aubrac's prefecture. Jean-Elie Nevière, one of the victims, observed that 'the prison in the cellars of the prefecture closely resembled the cellars of the Hôtel California which the Gestapo of Marseilles had vacated only a few days earlier. The same methods of torture were used in both places.' Nevière knew what he was talking about, for the Gestapo had been his prison hosts in February 1944.[28]

During the Nazi occupation of France, hostages had been shot, civilians had been deported, and some villages had been either wiped out or decimated as the occupying troops withdrew. With the approach of the Allied armies the resistance grew. As the armies passed there was a 'settling of scores'. But it was all on such a small scale compared to what happened as the Soviet armies moved westwards across Eastern Europe. The case of France is of interest because of the detail that has survived – inaccurate and fragmentary as these details will undoubtedly remain. The problem of Eastern Europe, in the margins that preceded and followed its armies, is that those empty spaces are huge. Is a history of the end of the war there even possible?

The dilemma that de Gaulle faced after the Liberation was how to plug the gaps left by the movement of armies. It was the dilemma of all formerly occupied Europe. But the peculiar problem for France was that to some outsiders, particularly the British and the Americans, she did not seem to have suffered enough. 'In arriving in Paris, many English and Americans are astonished to find us less skinny than they expected,' wrote Sartre, the philosopher of the Liberation. He took to task the *Daily Express* which started putting about the idea that, compared to the English, the French had not come out of the last four years too badly. An Englishman, replied Sartre, had nothing to envy in the French. There was an 'abyss' between them that no words could fill: how could one begin to explain what occupation meant to a people who had remained free? 'The English and the French have not a single memory in common,' he wrote; 'everything that London lived out in pride, Paris lived through in despair and shame.'[29]

De Gaulle summarized the problem well in the two key chapters of his memoirs describing France's transition from war to peace. Entitled 'Rank' and 'Order', the first concerned the establishing of France's place in world decisions of peace; the second the task of re-establishing a state. Whole areas of Europe were confronted with the same two problems: they were deprived of any decision-making in the peace; and they faced the terrifying liberties of a land without a state. Thanks in large part to de Gaulle, France solved both problems swiftly: she won her role in the decision-making, and re-established the state. Things did not work out so simply in Eastern Europe, but the case of France does point to a pattern in post-Liberation violence.

For in France as elsewhere, in the margin left by the departing armies, there came, after the purge, a kind of spiritual depression. A series of opinion polls were conducted in late autumn 1944 that indicated a growing indifference to the war. Increasingly aware of this public apathy, French troops in Alsace and Lorraine became demoralized. Resistance organizations, which were nearly all run by the Communists, discovered that they were no longer being treated like heroes; as the cold of winter set in, they were perceived as men of the past who offered no hope for the future. And that winter was the worst of the war. Food supplies in Paris ran out; there was no petrol, no transport; those who did get out to the countryside were roughed up by peasants who refused to hand over their goods. Vigilante bands appeared in the country and the towns. Some of the most violent were bands of American GIs who, exempt from French exchange controls and import duties, made a killing – sometimes literally – on the black market. A heavy trade in drugs developed. The government reacted by closing all dance halls and cabarets (dancing had been prohibited during the occupation). The Minister of Supply, Paul Ramadier, set up control posts around Paris – many manned by the Communist militia that had supposedly been banned in October. By March Parisians were talking of the 'Siege of Paris' and the minister was being called 'Ramadan'. Caffery, the American ambassador, reported to Washington on 20 January: 'There has been snow on the ground for 17 days; previous record 10 days. It is still snowing – water frozen to hydro-electric plants – ice-breakers unable to smash thru 8–12 inch ice on canals to coalfields.'[30]

A *Times* correspondent reported in October that the streets of Paris were empty: 'Except American transport and one or two official cars, there are no vehicles but bicycles, *vélo-taxis*,* and a few fiacres which, with their horses, appear to have emerged from the Second Empire.' *Pace* Sartre, he found something in common with London: 'It is a shabby crowd – as shabby as our own. Where there is a new hat, it is indeed a hat – an Eiffel Tower in miniature.'[31]

'The country is fully aware of what has to be done,' declared de Gaulle on the radio that same month: 'beat the enemy, establish ourselves abroad, and rebuild and renovate at home. First of all we must work.'[32] His programme at home – a planned national economy, a series of nationalizations

---

* Taxis drawn by bicycles.

and a war on 'the trusts' – sounded almost identical to that promoted by the Communist 'National Front', which was indeed the idea. De Gaulle was developing a complicated relationship with the Communists at home and abroad, in Moscow. It was a game of cat and mouse.

Despite the failure of the 'National Insurrection' in August, the French Communist Party did not abandon its attempt to take over the national government after the Liberation. During the first week after taking control of Paris, de Gaulle had ordered the delivery of truckloads of American uniforms and formally incorporated all resistance movements into the French army. Some of the officers joined the army, but the *fifis*, the FFI, could still be seen on the streets of Paris at Christmas time. In October de Gaulle formally dissolved the Communist *milices patriotiques*; in their black berets, they came marching down the Champs Elysées with their rifles and sub-machine guns during the great parade of 11 November – in front of both Churchill and de Gaulle. In the South of France, now that the Germans had gone, there was a veritable explosion in their number. De Gaulle had announced that the Comités de Libération (the CDLs) in the cities and provinces – soviets in all but name – were to be reduced to a 'consultative role'. In the southern half of France the relationship between the formal administrators and the CDLs was reversed. Jacques Duclos who, in the absence of Secretary General Maurice Thorez, acted as head of the Party, declared on 15 November: 'The people of France have created the elements of a new legality; they have set up the organs of Resistance, the local and departmental Committees of Liberation [CDLs] and the CNR [the National Resistance Council]. These are the organs which express the new French legality that is in the process of development.' Georges Cogniot, another Party dignitary, followed the same line in an interview published by the Soviet TASS agency.[33] It was the classic Bolshevik theory of 'dual power'. The Communists took control of most of the major unions, in particular that of the press. They called for further 'purges'. 'Death to the Traitors of Vichy! and Long Live the Republic!' exclaimed Duclos.[34]

But for Communists, as for Resisters in general, the hour of heroics had passed. A rallying speech by de Gaulle on 14 October got an 80 per cent approval rating in a poll taken in Paris at the time. Another poll, taken two weeks later, indicated that only 15 per cent of Parisians would have liked to see more than two Communist ministers in de Gaulle's government. Worst of all, extreme hostility was expressed about the return to France of Maurice Thorez, who had deserted the French army in 1939. The Communists had been clamouring for him. Thorez's host Stalin, in

Moscow, had been watching developments closely. This was de Gaulle's great chance to force Communist hypocrisy into the open and show where legitimate authority in liberated France lay: present a programme that was lifted from the Communist manifestos, make a deal with Stalin, and dump fat Thorez on the Communists' lap. The bargain would be struck before Christmas. But, like Churchill and Roosevelt before him, he would discover that a bargain with the Communist world leadership was a bargain with the devil. For the rest of his long political career, de Gaulle would never be able to shake off that hidden link with the Communists.

De Gaulle had played his game better than any other war leader. From the 1930s he had understood the menace of Hitler; in the critical hour he provided France with an alternative. He knew well that an American-imposed administration, whether under Darlan or Giraud, would never be able to stand up to the 'dual power' then being prepared by the French Communists. He let them play. He held his cards. And finally dealt with devastating effect on both Communists and Americans. Yet he was forced to make a bargain with Moscow, which would cause him much discomfort in the future.

Another of de Gaulle's strengths was his understanding of the chaos that accompanied army movements. Partly this was due to his experience in the First World War, and, most importantly, to the observations he had made in the new state of Poland in 1919–21. France in the Second World War had suffered less than most parts of Europe, but the details were recorded: they give us a first inkling of what happened elsewhere as the Soviet armies moved forward. France was a small-scale experiment which, for the Communists, failed. Ahead of the advancing Allied armies were Tulle, Oradour, the brutality of the Nazis and of Vichy's *milices*. After the passage of the armies came Limoges, Toulouse, Marseilles, the 'Siege of Paris', Alsace: the coldness of the American decision-makers, the demands of Moscow: a war without a political peace settlement.

France acted as a little mirror held up to the West, a tiny reflection on the terrible exactions then being levied in the East. At the time, no Westerner noticed.

Along with the liquidation of several administrators, priests, lawyers, 'bourgeois', 'Fascists', youths on the slightest suspicion, and women for no reason at all, there was the purge of the 'intellectuals'. An administrator can always blame his instructions on others, the soldier says he was following orders; but a writer can never retract what he wrote and published. More writers were executed, imprisoned and otherwise chastised by courts and colleagues than any other profession in France.

The institution chiefly responsible for this was the Comité National des Ecrivains (the CNE) whose clandestine origins could be traced back to 1941, but which made its presence felt in the southern zone only in the spring of 1943 under the energetic guidance of the 'Resistance poet', Louis Aragon. By the end of that year it demanded and got official recognition from de Gaulle's National Committee of French Liberation in Algiers. The main purpose of the CNE and its periodical, *Les Lettres françaises*, was the exclusion and destruction of the careers of writers who had – or were supposed to have – collaborated with the enemy: 'Let us remain united', read its manifesto of 9 September 1944, 'for the resurrection of France and for the just chastisement of impostors and traitors.'[35] This was accompanied by a 'blacklist' of sixty-five names, which was lengthened as time went by. Aragon himself led a particularly vicious attack against André Gide, one of the grandest French authors of the twentieth century, not for any act of collaboration – there was none – but because Aragon could not forgive him for publishing in the 1930s *Retour à l'URSS*, one of the first and most damning criticisms by a former Communist of the Soviet system. René Lalou was excluded from the CNE for including in an anthology of poetry a few poems by Charles Maurras. But the major issue of autumn and winter 1944–5 was over the CNE's demands for imprisonment and death. These sentences all followed regular court hearings under the aegis – and legitimacy – of de Gaulle's Provisional Government; they were not an *épuration sauvage* as practised in the South. Georges Suarez, the Paris collaborationist journalist, was the first to be shot. Trials followed for Paul Chack, Lucien Combelle, Henri Béraud and the historian Jacques Benoist-Méchin. The greatest scandal of the New Year was the trial and execution of Robert Brassillach.

Many of the condemned were authors of hateful, anti-Semitic rubbish. Vercors, famous for his Resistance novel *Silence de la mer*, said that it was wrong to compare an industrialist's collaboration with that of a writer. 'It was like comparing Cain and the devil,' he said. 'Cain's crime ended with Abel, whereas the menace of the devil has no limit.' To which the publisher Jean Paulhan responded: 'You can condemn Cain (even execute him). You can't do anything about Satan.'[36] What is the moral behind shooting a writer? And, relatedly, what was the responsibility of the writer? It was the great problem Sartre took up after 1945; he would speak in the name of a moral '*littérature engagée*'. But in the autumn and winter of 1944–5, as the sentences were passed, he remained as much the individualist as ever; he joined no political party and contributed virtually nothing to the debate. In January, he left for a four-month tour of the land that interested him most – not the Soviet Union but the United States.

The first 'blacklist' was drawn up initially in March 1943 in the Paris flat of the Catholic writer, François Mauriac. During the winter of 1944–5 he would be the most outspoken opponent of the death penalty for writers. But the 'blacklist' had by then been co-opted by the CNE, and there can be no doubt about what party lay behind the CNE. Speaking of its origins in 1943, Aragon and his companion, Elsa Triolet, said: 'One cannot say the committees were organizations of the [Communist] "Front national"; they did however depend on it, while extending beyond it.'[37] This is a very good way of describing how the Communist Party worked during those traumatic years of transition. It gives an insight into what happened in an Eastern European context where there was no de Gaulle, and where the liberating armies were Soviet.

Why exactly did Sartre leave France? While the 'Bulge' was being waged in the Ardennes, as Brassillach stood trial in Paris, the philosopher of Liberation was breakfasting on omelettes, sugar buns and coffee with cream in the Plaza Hotel, New York; in his days and evenings he was wandering among twin rows of great buildings, 'which, like cliffs, bordered the great arteries'. To say Sartre enjoyed New York would be an exaggeration. The instant he arrived he suffered from 'New York sickness' ('*mal de New-York*'), like sea-sickness (*mal de mer*). All European cities protected one from space; they were enclosed, made up of small, identifiable *quartiers*, districts. New York was the exact opposite: it opened itself up to space, its avenues and identical straight streets went on for ever. Moreover, for Sartre, New Yorkers were oblivious of the war: there were bright lights, food, hairdressers still open at eleven at night.[38]

Sickening, yes. Yet, 'I love New York. I learned to love it.' He liked the sky of New York, because New York pushed it upwards. He loved the movement of the city – no *promeneurs* here, everything went fast. Sartre, who had been no real jazz fan, got to listen to Charlie Parker, Art Tatum, Dizzy Gillespie; he visited Jimmy Ryan's, the Three Deuces and heard all the bands. He enjoyed a 'whisky on the rocks' and American cigarettes. What became the popular vision of 'existential Paris' in the late 1940s and 1950s – the café life of Saint-Germain-des-Prés – owed a lot to Sartre's visit to the United States in the last months of the war.

He had been invited, thanks to the intervention of his friend Albert Camus, as part of a group of French writers on a trip financed by the US State Department. 'De Gaulle Foes Paid by US, Paris is Told', ran the headline of the *New York Times* on 25 January. If that had been the purpose of the US State Department, they had made a sorry choice in Sartre. Sartre immediately got into a quarrel with the majority of the French community in New York which had been supporting Cordell Hull's candidate to head a French government, General Henri Giraud, the man slated to replace the assassinated Admiral Darlan and an obvious Vichyite. In his first press conference he came out in open support of the minority Gaullist movement in New York, 'France Forever'. This immediately led to an attack by the French–American columnist, Geneviève Tabouis, who accused Sartre of adopting the same 'anti-Americanism' as de Gaulle. By February the quarrel had become known in New York as the new Dreyfus Affair.[39]

It was calmed by Sartre himself in a letter published in the *New York Times* that emphasized his 'profound affection' and his 'sincere sentiments of friendship' for Americans. On 9 March he shook hands with Roosevelt, who assured him that all the tension between French and Americans was simply the work of the press. Sartre wrote of Roosevelt's 'profound human charm' reflected in his 'long face at once hard and delicate'.[40] The following month, Roosevelt was dead.

Since the Liberation, Sartre had come under a lot of criticism from the French Communists. In the first place, he had produced two plays in occupied Paris that had even been applauded by the Germans; he had also written an article on Melville's *Moby Dick* for the collaborationist paper *Comœdia*. Secondly there was his individualistic, anti-communitarian style – his 'nihilism', the '*misérabilisme*' of his novels, his evocation of the 'most sordid' details of life, his lack of a proper social consciousness. Indeed, the existentialist Sartre, the philosopher of Liberation and choice, was not a Communist. In January 1945 he was a Gaullist.

3 The train to Moscow

Gaullist politics of the 'third way', between the two emerging superpowers, the United States and the Soviet Union, began to take shape the instant Churchill, on his November trip out to the Alsace front with de Gaulle, refused the General's offer of a special 'Anglo-French treaty'. De Gaulle immediately set in motion his plans for a trip to Moscow.

There is some debate over who initiated the idea, the Soviets or the French. De Gaulle had for a long time been ready to play the Russian card; while in England, during his recurrent quarrels with Churchill, he had made discreet contact with Ivan Maisky, the Soviet ambassador to London, and in June 1942, during the Syrian squabble, even considered shifting the whole of Free France to Moscow (Churchill had proposed the Isle of Man instead). In 1943, long before the British and the Americans made so much as a sign of recognition of de Gaulle's Committee in Algeria, the Russians had sent as resident ambassador Aleksandr Bogomolov, a rotund and cheerful participant in the Moscow purges of the 1930s, known among British diplomats as 'Bogo'. De Gaulle had always been suspicious that Bogo was advancing the cause of French Communists at his expense – a suspicion amply confirmed in a report Bogo forwarded to the Soviet Ministry of Foreign Affairs shortly after the Liberation of Paris, in which he spoke of the men surrounding de Gaulle as 'a band of neo-Fascists'. Though he knew the French were seeking a special relationship with Moscow, he thought the best interest of the Soviet Union was to follow the Americans 'in their policy of weakening France'.[41] This was not far from Stalin's own thinking.

De Gaulle claims in his memoirs that it was Bogomolov who insisted on the trip to Moscow. This is possible. Stalin at the time was seeking Western recognition of his puppet Lublin Committee in Poland, the key to his whole programme of expansion into Eastern and Central Europe. A weak France had a useful role to play.

The plan for the trip was ready within a week of Churchill's departure. De Gaulle outlined his policy in a speech made before the Consultative Assembly on 22 November. France, he said, was beginning to play again her role as 'one of the great powers'. She would perform her part in the 'fruitful construction that will lead to the unity of Europe'. It would be a new Europe built on three poles, Moscow, London and Paris. 'Despite the losses, despite the pain, despite the tiredness of men, let us rebuild our power!'[42]

Travelling from Paris to Moscow was no simple task in early winter 1944. De Gaulle took off from Paris on 24 November accompanied by a team of ministers and officials and made a first stop in Cairo. 'We are confident in your future, because we need you,' said the young King Farouk, on receiving the French leader in his palace; Farouk was not happy with Nahas Pasha, whom the British had imposed as Prime Minister. Satisfied that an independent French policy with the Arabs was in the making, de Gaulle flew on to Teheran where he was received by the Shah, Mohammed Reza Pahlavi. The Shah was in a nervous state. 'You see where we are,' he said, noting how much his country was run by the big powers. 'In your opinion what should I do? You, who have taken up the destiny of your own country at the most difficult moment, you are qualified to tell me.' De Gaulle advised him to adopt a stance of 'independence personified'. 'You may be constrained to suffer encroachments, but you must always condemn them,' advised the General. 'Sovereignty may be nothing but a small flame beneath a bush,' he continued; 'but as long as it is kept alight, it will sooner or later catch fire.' He assured the Shah that, when France had recovered her strength and her place in international affairs, she would aid Iran in ridding herself of foreign troops. The Gaullist line in the Middle East was thus set.[43]

His plane took off for the Soviet Union. As 'independence personified' de Gaulle was not going to let a weakened France be used simply as a tool for Stalinist ambitions; France had a role to play in the world, France was going to contribute to the shape of Europe in the years to come – and de Gaulle already had in mind a stage by stage plan by which this would be done. Most pressing was the Communist problem at home. De Gaulle was perfectly aware where the French Communists were getting their orders.

De Gaulle's plane landed at Baku, on the Caspian Sea. Stalin was in no hurry to see this statesman who commanded barely a dozen divisions. The French party was kept waiting in Baku for two days, feasting and visiting theatres, and then was told that the weather was too bad to risk a flight to Moscow. An old train, the one that had been used by the Grand Duke Nicholas before the First World War, was rolled out, and the French party was shunted slowly towards the Volga. Their first stop was amidst the ruins of Stalingrad where Hitler had suffered his first defeat two winters earlier.

Unlike Churchill, who during his flying visits rarely saw anything of the life of the people, de Gaulle did catch glimpses of Stalin's Russia at the end of the war. It has been said that they were still burying the bodies from the battle when de Gaulle arrived in Stalingrad. De Gaulle makes no mention of this, but his memoirs take note – unconsciously – of something much more sinister.

'In the ruins', recorded de Gaulle, 'many labourers were at work; their bosses coaxing them on in a haughty manner with slogans about "national reconstruction".' He was shown a huge tank factory which had been entirely rebuilt and re-equipped. 'On entering the workshops, workers were grouped around us to exchange words of friendship.' Then, as de Gaulle returned to his train, 'we crossed a column of men escorted by armed soldiers. They were, it was explained to us, Russian prisoners, who were on their way to building sites.'[44] De Gaulle thought the 'convicts' looked no better and no worse dressed than the 'free' workers. But he never asked himself who these 'Russian prisoners' were; there had been purges in France, but one never saw French prisoners being marched in columns to building sites in France. What he was witnessing, without knowing it, were scenes of the expanding Soviet Gulag.

★

The slow-moving train journey across the icy plains of Russia made the General impatient. 'It is very interesting, this trip,' he remarked cynically to one of his travelling companions, 'but let us hope a revolution does not occur in France while we are here.'[45] De Gaulle was worried about his Communists.

On Saturday morning, 2 December, the train chugged into Kursk station on the wide, circular boulevard that marked the site of the old 'Earthen Wall' on the east side of Moscow. The building was a modern, Stalinist structure. Molotov, along with his usual retinue of Soviet offi-cials, was there to greet him. De Gaulle made a short speech which, he claims, caused much emotion in the crowd present; Alexander Werth, the Russian-born, London-based reporter, said that nobody had a clue who he was. At any rate, the crowd did not improve de Gaulle's mood. The Soviets had prepared a comfortable suite for him in their official residence on Spiridonovka Street; de Gaulle refused and ordered his Foreign Minister, Georges Bidault, and his assistant to join him in the French embassy, just off Red Square – it had been bombed and had no heating.

The 'Little Father' of All the Russias was unaccustomed to such inso-lence. He summoned de Gaulle to a meeting in the Kremlin the same afternoon. De Gaulle found himself in a lift which carried him up to a long corridor lined by armed guards; Molotov showed him into a large room at the end, furnished with a table and several chairs. After a while, the 'Marshal' – or, as General de Gaulle put it, 'a Communist dressed up as a marshal' – entered. He was, concluded de Gaulle, following a week of conversations and dinners, 'a dictator secluded in his own craftiness, winning others over with an air of good nature which he applied to allay suspicion. But so raw was his passion that it sometimes showed through, though not without a kind of pernicious charm.'

According to the French ambassador, Roger Garreau, the first encounter barely avoided catastrophe. De Gaulle, seated stiff and tall, went into one of his grand monologues on France's position in a world without Germany. Stalin's slanting Asiatic eyes drooped down upon a piece of paper on which he doodled with a pencil an extraordinary pattern of hieroglyphs. But the conversations were continued. 'Your general is an unusually obstinate person, but I like obstinate people,' Stalin said to a French aide when they were over.[46]

The talks were more significant for what they revealed about the two countries as the war drew to a close than for their content. The bilateral Pact signed at their conclusion had little direct impact on the structure of emerging post-war Europe. But it did demonstrate where France and the Soviet Union stood in the world.

Most remarkable was Stalin's singular obsession with securing French recognition of the Lublin Committee – the Russians, after all, had shown more sympathy towards de Gaulle's Algerian Committee of 1943 than either the British or the Americans. Stalin, having 'liberated' Romania and Bulgaria, having agreed with Churchill upon a line across the Balkans, was now set to move his armies across Europe's northern plain. How much of it would be Soviet-controlled? Stalin counted on holding Poland. How much of Germany? What about his influence in France and Italy?

De Gaulle's primary concern, however, remained the intentions of the powerful Communist Party in France; his card was Maurice Thorez in Moscow. Thorez was Stalin's card too. As de Gaulle made his slow journey to Moscow, Stalin let Thorez go to Paris.

On the day before the French Communist leader departed on a Soviet aircraft, he received his instructions from Stalin in an interview at the Kremlin on 19 November. The French Communists, Stalin said frankly, 'are not strong enough to sustain alone the struggle against reaction'. The Leninist 'dual power' strategy could not work now that de Gaulle's Provisional Government had been officially recognized. The French Communists would have to make some temporary political allies. 'The enemy' – Stalin was not thinking of Hitler – 'wishes to isolate the Communist Party,' he said. 'We cannot allow that.'

Thorez thought Stalin was underestimating French Communist strength. He claimed, for instance, that the Communist *milices* had been the principal force of resistance against the Germans and that, though officially banned, they had managed to keep their arms.

'You will have to hide them,' interrupted Stalin. 'The Communist Party [in France] is not strong enough to hit the government on its head.' He came back to his point about the creation of alliances and the use of patience: 'You need to create determined forces grouped around the Communist Party first for defence and, when the situation changes, for the attack.'[47]

So Stalin's aim was to 'attack' the young French state. But not tomorrow. First he had to prove to the world that he possessed Poland, his first step across the northern plain.

De Gaulle was unusually naive in his dealings with Stalin. He seems to have thought that negotiations with Stalin would have a moderating effect on his Communists back home: this was the case in the short term, but, as French Communist discussions with Stalin showed, the Communists' final intention was takeover; the 'anti–Fascist' struggle would continue until this was achieved. De Gaulle was under the same illusions as Churchill and Roosevelt, in regarding Stalin as a normal European head of state, even an ally. He proved neither. Unfortunately this illusion about the nature of Communist heads of state would remain with de Gaulle to the end of his political career in the 1960s.

De Gaulle outlined the basic principle behind his 'negotiations' with Stalin to the American ambassador to Moscow, Averell Harriman. Once Germany was defeated, he explained, France and Russia would be the only two powerful countries in Europe, for Britain would withdraw to her island and her imperial entanglements, while the United States, across the ocean, would be indifferent to the fate of the Continent once the war against Hitler was won – the Americans would simply pull out. The small European nations would thus be totally exposed to the danger of Communist takeover; they would have to rally around France. Harriman told de Gaulle that he doubted the Russians intended to absorb Poland and other neighbouring nations into the Soviet Union; but they would attempt to dominate them, thus ensuring that they would be, as Stalin himself nicely put it, 'friendly neighbours'.[48]

De Gaulle's encounter in Moscow became a tug-of-war over Poland. Greece could be left to the British to deal with, but Russia, insisted Stalin, had just achieved a decisive turning-point with regards to Poland, which had been Russia's 'enemy for centuries'. 'Poland has always served as the corridor through which the Germans have attacked Russia,' he explained. 'This corridor, it has got to be shut, and shut by Poland herself.' Like Churchill, de Gaulle agreed to the Oder–Neisse frontier to the west and the 'Curzon Line' to the east (hoping, it seems, that Russia would consent to French control of the Rhineland). Members of the Lublin Committee were brought in from Galicia to meet the General 'and they repeated the couplets that had been prepared for them'; they performed as the same 'inverted Quislings' they had shown themselves to be before Churchill. All Bolesław Bierut, chairman of the Committee, could talk about was the 'agricultural reform' he was preparing for the liberated land. De Gaulle told Stalin that he could not accept such an 'artificial Poland'; there would have to be elections.

Stalin persisted. When the French drew up the terms of a treaty, the Russians presented the text for a communiqué announcing French recognition of the Lublin Committee, the 'National Committee of Liberation'. Yes, confirmed Stalin, the Poles had lost all faith in the reactionary, émigré government in London – 'those characters' – and all hope of Anders' army down in Italy; London was responsible for the failure of the Warsaw Rising, because they had set it off with the 'worst kind of fickleness'.

Stalin's words were sprinkled with humour. He told de Gaulle not to worry about Thorez. 'I know Thorez,' he said to the grimacing General. 'In my opinion, he's a good Frenchman. If I were in your place I would not put him in gaol – at least not immediately!' 'The French Government', replied de Gaulle coldly, 'treats the French according to the services it expects of them.'

Stalin persisted in his demand for the recognition of the Lublin Committee. In Catherine's Hall within the Kremlin he prepared a grand banquet which resembled the feasts laid on by the eighteenth-century Tsars. Stalin, noted de Gaulle, 'had the air of a peasant', serving himself huge portions of food and gulping down Crimean wine by the glassful. But beneath this debonair appearance, 'the champion of a merciless struggle' could be seen. He spent most of the time talking to Harriman on his left, rather than the very glum de Gaulle on his right. Stalin remarked to Harriman that he found de Gaulle 'an awkward and stubborn man' but that he was determined that the evening would be gay.

About forty Russian officials were seated at the long tables – commissars, diplomats and a large representation of the Red Army – who had been brought in to impress the French General. At the end of the meal, Stalin proposed a polite toast to the French, gulped down another glass of Crimean wine, and then proceeded to toast every Russian hero present, one by one.

As each name was called out, the man concerned would have to stand up, walk the length of the table and respond to the toast: 'Voronov! To your health! Yours was the mission to deploy our system of heavy guns!'; 'Admiral Kuznetzov! Not enough has been said about our fleet. Patience! One day we will dominate the seas!' Thirty such toasts were drunk.

Coffee and brandy were then served in the adjoining room. De Gaulle was seated next to Harriman. Pointing to Marshal N. A. Bulganin, 'Isn't that the man who killed so many Russian generals?' he asked in a loud voice, which the interpreter immediately translated into Russian. Molotov, with his communiqué on Poland ready to hand, was seated next to the French Foreign Minister. Stalin, with a twinkle in his eye, called out to Bulganin: 'Bring the machine-guns! Let's liquidate the diplomats!'

After this fine show of humour, films were put on in Stalin's private theatre. The French had still not signed Stalin's communiqué on Poland. Nikita Khrushchev, Political Commissar of the Ukraine, who had been summoned to Moscow for the meeting, recorded years later that Stalin 'was slightly drunk. In fact, he was more than just slightly drunk. He was swaying from side to side.'[49] The first film presented a brief history of the Soviet Union since 1938, including a futuristic look into the post war world; it showed the treasonous invasion of the Soviet Union by the Germans, the courage of the Russian people and their army, followed by an invasion of Germany and a revolution throughout the country: the Soviet system triumphing over the ruins of Fascism.

Stalin roared with laughter. 'I fear the end of history does not please Monsieur de Gaulle,' he exclaimed, clapping his hands.

'Your victory, at any rate, pleases me,' de Gaulle replied dryly; 'much more so than the true beginning of the war, when things occurred between you and the Germans not quite the way portrayed in this film.' With that little historical point cleared up, the General rose to his feet and retired for the night. The communiqué had still not been signed. Nor had the treaty.

The films continued. Molotov was seen deep in conversation with Stalin. Eventually, in the early hours of the morning, a French messenger was sent round to de Gaulle's unheated rooms bearing tidings that a text was ready for a bilateral treaty along with a simple agreement to send an envoy from Paris, Major Christian Fouchet, to Lublin.

When de Gaulle got back to the Kremlin, however, Stalin handed him the text of an 'accord' recognizing the Lublin Committee – it was the same old text as before. 'France has been insulted,' declared the General, and he got up to go. Stalin calmly turned to Molotov and asked for the new draft.

A bilateral 'Pact' was signed between France and the Soviet Union that Sunday morning, 10 December. It was also agreed that a press announcement would appear on 28 December stating that 'Major Fouchet has arrived at Lublin.' De Gaulle immediately boarded the Grand Duke's old train at Kursk station.

For de Gaulle in his memoirs, and for Gaullists ever since, this day signalled one of France's grand diplomatic victories. The Pact returned a free and sovereign France to the orbit of the Great Powers. In fact, the Pact counted for very little. Neither the United States nor, in particular, the Soviet Union took France seriously; France's real friend, under Churchill's guidance, proved to be Britain. De Gaulle's 'third way, between East and West', which he and Bidault followed as a national policy in 1945, counted for nothing. Nor did de Gaulle's stubbornness over the Lublin Committee add up to much: Stalin's course across Poland into Germany had already been determined. As the film shown in Stalin's private theatre made clear, this was not going to be a mere military operation. Poland, as in Napoleon's day, was once again going to be used as a 'key to the European vault'; Poland, against her own will, would be the key to a Sovietized Europe. Nor did de Gaulle win the peace he desired with his own Communists. As soon as the war in Germany was finished, Thorez, the Party, its unions and its local cells became increasingly aggressive, setting themselves – as during the war – on a course towards 'mass movement', insurrection and, it was their hope, takeover.

De Gaulle arrived in Paris on Saturday, 16 December, just in time to hear the news that Hitler had launched offensive in the Ardennes, thus driving a wedge between British and American forces in North-Western Europe.[50]

4 Silent Moscow

What was life like in Moscow under this jovial dictator, Iosif Vissarionovich Stalin? The truth is that very little is known. One can describe in detail life in London at the end of the war, the streets of Paris and the sentiments of Parisians; we can speak of the excitements and disappointments of booming Washington; we know the scenes and the sense of impending doom felt in Berlin; and, incredibly, we have many details on Warsaw up to the day it was wiped off the map. But a great question mark hangs over Moscow. It is easier to describe the state of Moscow in 1812 than the Moscow of the winter of 1944–5, at the end of the Great Patriotic War. An authentic *Daily Life in Stalin's Moscow* is unlikely ever to be written.

Many serious historians today would argue that this is unimportant – it is a picaresque, literary kind of history that should be of no concern to the scholarly researcher, who should concentrate on the grander matters of diplomacy, administrative structure, economics, class divisions, the general trends, the movement of armies, the command, the commanders, and a summary of the results. That, of course, is what the Soviet authorities said at the time. Later, interest would develop in the Gulag, Stalin's slave labour camps. But no one has yet turned to such ordinary matters as what life was like in the Soviet capital at the end of the Second World War. Such silence is telling.

The Russians have traditionally been a great letter-writing people; diaries and memoirs were abundant in the nineteenth century; the literature was grand. History is also aware of a Russian 'intelligentsia' that survived the Bolshevik *coup d'état* of 1917 and went on to write through the first decades of the Soviet era. Boris Pasternak and Vasili Grossman were silenced; Marina Tsvetaeva committed suicide. Some, like Ilia Ehrenburg, were fêted as Stalin's laureates. Others knew brief fame and were then slipped under the covers of the Soviet oubliettes. This was the fate of Mikhail Bulgakov; he was the victim, wrote his friend Sergei Ermolinski, of 'a veritable conspiracy of silence. As if he were dead. As if he had never existed. He was forgotten, obliterated.' Bulgakov had been a well-known playwright in Moscow during the years of the NEP (in the 1920s), though even then his satires had been savagely attacked in the Soviet press. In 1928, following the introduction of Stalin's First Five Year Plan, Bulgakov's celebrity came to a sudden end. Reduced to poverty, he made a personal appeal to Stalin in 1931, and eighteen months later received a telephone call from him: for a short period he was assistant director to the Theatre of Art and literary counsellor to the Bolshoi Theatre; he lived from his translations and adaptations of other people's work. His friends forsook him – all save his wife Lena, and Sergei Ermolinski, who recorded for posterity the last years of his life.[51]

Bulgakov lived in perpetual struggle with his own fear, 'the worst vice of the soul', as he called it. 'When I was young I was very timid,' he once told Ermolinski, 'and I believe that to the end of my life I will never be able to put aside this fault. I just pretend.' During his last five years he worked, a woollen cap on his head, in his chaotic little study overlooking the Passage Fourmanov, with the sound of the trams rattling by outside. He wrote and wrote in volumes of exercise books a novel which he first called *Notes of a Dead Man* – he knew the work would never be published in his lifetime and suspected that the manuscript would be destroyed on his death. It was a comic Russian fantasia which combined the adventures of Pontius Pilate on his way to Jerusalem to judge Jesus Christ with the travels of the Devil, and a cohort of witches, across contemporary Moscow. By March 1940 he was dying of uraemia. The snow, melting outside, was turning a dirty yellow. He asked his wife to read him passages from his novel, which he patiently corrected. Ten days before he died Fadeyev, of the Union of Writers, came to visit him for the first time. The exchange was bitter. Bulgakov died in agony – he could not prevent himself from screaming – at four o'clock in the afternoon of 10 March: 'I do not know why,' recorded Ermolinski, 'but I always had the impression that he died at dawn.' The following day the telephone rang in Bulgakov's flat; Ermolinski answered. 'This is Stalin's Secretariat,' he heard. 'Is it true that Comrade Bulgakov is dead?' 'Yes it is,' answered Ermolinski. The telephone went silent.

Bulgakov's novel, renamed *The Master and Margarita*, was eventually published in 1966; it is generally regarded as the greatest Russian novel of the twentieth century.

This could of course be considered yet another story of the suffering writing classes, valid anywhere in the world. But in the silence of Stalin's Moscow it probably says more. How many Muscovites suffered from the 'worst vice of the soul'? Housing committees and the systematic surveillance of residences went back to the November *coup* of 1917; in two years the population of the city had halved, city manufacturing was down to one tenth of its pre-war output and the economy was reduced to pre-industrial practices of barter, make-do and robbery; given the climate, whole residential zones simply fell into ruin. 'Everyone cooks in his own pot, hides in his own room, procures food and utensils for his own family,' commented one Muscovite cited in the local press in April 1921. In the 1920s a cooperative movement developed which was responsible for the construction of the great red-brick housing estates that sprang up throughout Moscow over the next couple of decades. But this was not a private enterprise. It was run by the Moscow city and *gubernia* (Soviet regional) federations who could hardly keep up with the demand for housing – and surveillance did not decline with the cooperatives, it increased. With Stalin's collectivization of agriculture after 1930 swarms of landless peasants fled into Moscow. In 1929, as the first rural expulsions began, the population of the city – barely one million in 1920 – had grown to 2,267,000. By 1933 it had reached 3,663,000. In 1941, at the moment of Hitler's invasion, the population of Moscow had reached 4,137,000 – over four times what it had been only twenty years earlier. Dwelling space, of course, went in the other direction. The average Muscovite had 9.5 square metres to live in in 1920. In 1940, the year of Bulgakov's death, he had 4.1 (just twice the amount of 'living space' decreed for inmates of the Gulag). The picture of Bulgakov working in his small room, the sound of the trams outside, the silences and fears within, provides an authentic image of Stalin's Moscow.[52]

A map of daily life in Moscow in the early 1940s would show at the centre the Kremlin, Red Square, the zone to the north where the ambassadors and foreigners resided, and the Arbat (Moscow's Champs Elysées) to the west, along with the southern embankment of the River Moskva, where the *apparatchiki* lived. This was an area frequently described in official histories, Soviet biographies and, most important of all, by foreign observers. Beyond lay *terra incognita*. Few diaries were kept, and survived, from this outer area, few letters, few records. Perhaps a cache of them will be discovered one day buried beneath some old official's dacha, or hidden in Soviet archives that have yet to be revealed. But it is doubtful.

In 1950 the Americans missed the chance of a lifetime. Caught up in the net of migrants and refugees – the human flotsam and jetsam of war – were a number of Soviet citizens, who were still held at that time in camps just outside Munich. Financed by a generous grant from the United States Air Force, the Americans set about interviewing them. The interviews and the long study that resulted (finally published in 1959) was known as the 'Harvard Project on the Soviet Social System' after the famous university which conducted them. Two chapters were devoted to proving that the opinions of these refugees, caught in a maelstrom not of their own making, were representative of opinion within the Soviet Union; this was done by comparing the results with the small amount of information that could be gleaned from the Soviet Union itself. The evidence presented here is most convincing.

Unfortunately, the professors of Harvard University were at the time under the spell of what may be called the Talcott Parsons school of sociology,[53] which cultivated the theme of a universal 'process of modernization', as valid in Birmingham, Bochum and Shanghai as in Kansas City, and ignored the effects of geographic origin. All the respondents from the 'Soviet Union' were batched together and broken down into categories of 'social class'. The results were published, after nearly a decade of study, in the form of statistical tables. Such an approach continued to dominate Soviet studies in the United States, and indeed elsewhere in the West, until the regime collapsed in 1991 from its own internal malignancy and corruption.

The Project offers such gems as: 'In the years 1931 to 1945 . . . because of the rapid industrial expansion, there was a mass upgrading of a large portion of the Soviet population.' Or, on the same period: 'The Soviet Union was experiencing a revolution of "modernization" not too dissimilar in important respects from that which had affected other major countries in Europe and Asia somewhat earlier'; the distinguishing mark of the Soviet Union was 'the mutually linked processes of industrialization and the collectivization of agriculture'. And most notably: 'The size of the industrial labor force more than doubled during the First Five Year Plan.' By 1935 Soviet society had moved 'rapidly toward full-scale social-class differentiation'. Since 'in the Soviet Union there is no private business', it was noted that 'the only substantial opportunity for advancement is within the framework of the Soviet bureaucracy.'[54]

A large majority of those interviewed had two things to praise about the Soviet system: free education and free medical care – here one could find among the people a similar post-war dream to that of Sir William Beveridge. 'In this respect,' said one interviewee, 'the policy of the Bolsheviks is very good.' 'Free education,' said another. 'This must always be. Everybody likes this.'[55]

Some ugly truths, however, did manage to emerge in the report. The section on family cohesion under the 'process of modernization' – a major concern in Parsonian sociology – was particularly revealing. 'Under the Soviet regime we became slaves,' said a former 'middle peasant', 'and it was only natural that at home, we felt secure and safe. At home, we wept, we smiled, we criticized or cursed those who made us poor and hungry.' 'My youngest brother had been killed during the revolution,' commented one fifty-six-year-old former collective farmer who somehow found his way from Moscow to Munich. 'Later a very heavy tax was levied on my father, so heavy that he was not able to pay it. So a younger brother went to Central Asia. My mother and four sisters went to Tiflis, and we all split up in that way, fleeing to different places.'[56]

What the Harvard Project politely called Soviet 'industrialization' ('mutually linked' to collectivization) was – to name a spade a spade – the product of slave labour. Until the rise of Hitler in Germany it had no parallel in the world; the 'process' was unique.

Moscow was, after 1917, swiftly transformed into the capital of this singular economic system: its chief administrators lived there, the first of the slave camp compounds were instituted there. The Soviet Communist Party always claimed to be the party of the working class; in reality, it was, as even the Harvard Project demonstrated, the party of the bureaucrats. Under the Tsars, Moscow was not a city of bureaucrats – the bureaucrats lived in St Petersburg, which later became Leningrad. Moscow had been the commercial capital of Russia; the richest Russian merchants and traders lived there, not in Leningrad; it was their villas and palaces which decorated the landscape of central Moscow, along with many of the outlying estates – the wooden lacework of their 'cake houses', coloured in pastel shades of amber, ochre and rose and built out of the wealth drawn from weavers' mills, is what gave the city the nickname 'Calico Moscow'. As the 'third Rome', Moscow was also the residence since 1328 of the Russian Orthodox Metropolitan, the skyline dominated by ornate churches with their bulbous, gilded towers ('forty times forty,' was the local saying) – which is why, amidst its growing commerce, people still spoke of 'Holy Moscow'.

In March 1918, with the advance of the German armies, the Soviet bureaucrats moved to Moscow and made the city their capital. The capitalist 'parasites' were expelled, their homes converted into offices for the growing army of bureaucrats. By the mid-1920s these were not simply administrators, but Party members within an internal hierarchy selected 'by the list' – *nomenklatura*. Washington may have been a bureaucratic boomtown, but it was not centralized like this; nor, significantly, was Hitler's Berlin. Virtually the whole of central Moscow was, by the 1930s, occupied by the *nomenklatura*. The Kremlin, which was initially intended to be turned into a national museum, was out of bounds to anyone else, though conditions inside its walls were not exactly luxurious; there was no central heating, for example, for the tiny flats of the old Cavalry Guards Barracks and tenants had to carry their food on trays from the distant 'Kremlin Cafeteria'.

From the Kremlin, the bureaucrats spread their tentacles outwards into the neighbouring quarters, taking over the old merchant villas, dividing them up, and building their own ugly looking apartment blocks coated in cinder-grey mastic. The most famous of these was Government House on the south side of the river – the 'House of the Embankment' as it came to be known – which was furnished, unlike most places in Moscow, with telephones, hot water, rubbish disposal units, as well as a department store, a beauty salon and plenty of grim-faced secret servicemen. Upper echelons of the Party bureaucracy also took over whole suburban areas and parts of the surrounding rural hinterland. The 'dacha hamlets' (*dachnye poselki*) had been developed in the years before the First World War to encourage, through major tax incentives, rich Muscovites to move out to the countryside; they had sprung up by railway stations and around major rural landmarks. When the Soviets took over, large zones surrounding them were emptied 'as if a sandstorm had whipped through the dacha settlement'. The wealthy dacha, inhabited by a Communist bigwig, yet surrounded by a rural desert, was one of the permanent features of the environs of Soviet Moscow. Most of the old dacha hamlets, homes of Russia's vanished gentry, were stripped of their valuables and left to ruin. Villages were abandoned. Simone Olivier Wormser, wife of a French ambassador to Moscow, visited in the winter of 1966 the dacha of Zavidovo, reserved as a 'rest place' for foreign diplomatic staff. She managed to slip past the guards and walked on a slippery, muddy road as far as a village, where she found a single shop, 'smelling heavily of lamp oil'. There was nothing in it 'save a few horrible biscuits'. 'I saw only one inhabitant, a poor peasant woman.'[57]

In the city centre the insatiable demand for space by Stalin's *nomenklatura* could not be satisfied by expulsions of 'parasites'. With the advent of Stalin's First Five Year Plan, the churches had to go, the monuments be razed. Ukhtomsky's eighteenth-century Red Gates, with its copper archangel and chiming bells, came down in a day; the seventh-century Church of St Paraskeva on Okhotnyi Riad fell in a night; in the Chudov Monastery in Kitai-Gorod the graceful fourteenth-century Church of the Miracle of the Archangel Michael was dynamited and the cloisters and church of Small Nikolaevsky hacked to pieces by workers over the following weeks. Two of the greatest landmarks of the city, the Simonov Monastery and the Cathedral of Christ, were transformed into piles of rubble, separated from the public by corrugated iron barriers, red flags and the slogan 'In the Place of the Breeding Ground of the Narcotic [Religion] – the Palace of the Soviets': and so it remained throughout the war years. The Soviets destroyed more of Moscow than German bombers.

The Georgian Stalin had hated Moscow just as much as the provincial Hitler despised Berlin. But once these capitals became their seats of power the two dictators competed in their megalomaniac visions of the great metropolis of the future. Hitler had one major plan, a city which he would rename 'Germania'. Stalin had dozens of plans for a city that would be called *Stalinskaya Moskva* ('Stalin's Moscow') or *Veliki Stalingrad* ('Great Stalin City'). Stalin's favourite plan included a Palace of the Soviets, which was to have a building mass six times larger than the Empire State Building and be taller by a hair's breadth thanks to a huge statue of Lenin at its summit. Foundations were completed the year of Hitler's invasion. But they got no further; in the late 1950s Khrushchev had them converted into a vast public swimming pool.

This process of Soviet 'industrialization' had a lot to do with the progress of the war and the way in which it ended. And the case of Moscow is particularly revealing.

'Concentration camps' existed in the First World War. Thus, prisoners of war were often collected in 'concentration camps', as were refugees, foreigners and people of no abode – 'displaced persons' as they would be called in the next war. Conditions were often horrible. Plenty of evidence of this can be found in France, Germany and Russia. Moscow was the first place in Europe where 'concentration camps' became the depots of slave labour. They appeared late in the year of 1918, first in the Novospassky Monastery, then in the Andronikov Monastery and the Ivanovsky Convent – monasteries and convents, with their enclosures hidden from the public eye, were the early preferred sites of such establishments. In August 1919 the presidium of the Moscow City Soviet passed a resolution establishing a general administration of Moscow concentration camps. By October 1921 the seven camps in Moscow and its region held 4,217 inmates. Two years later a list of 'Concentration Camps' was published in the city directory, giving both the addresses and the names of the wardens. Local handbooks also provided names and locations.[58]

According to the Marxist ideology behind the Bolshevik *coup* of 1917, 'prisons' were supposed gradually to vanish in the post-revolutionary world because the cause of crime, the exploitation of the masses, would no longer exist. Indeed, the word 'prison' did disappear from the Soviet Criminal Code of 1926. But, having closed the Constituent Assembly on the first day of its meeting in January 1918, the Bolsheviks had to admit to themselves that as a minority government they needed to put in place certain measures of political control. Over time the 'prisons' in city centres like Moscow became mere points of transit – if not execution – to a new complicated network of camps, kernel of the future Soviet slave labour system.

Moscow, as for many other features of the Soviet system, provided an initial testing ground. The primary motive behind the new camps was the isolation and death of the political enemies of the regime; but very quickly it was realized that, with the abolition of private property and enterprise, the camps offered an easy means of rebuilding the ruined economy. Several camps in the Moscow area and in other major urban centres were closed in 1922. But that was not the result of leniency, it was because of the growth of a far more intensive system of camps to the north in the area around Archangel, beginning with former monasteries on the infamous Solovetsky Islands. The camps then spread to regions of Kemsky and Karelia, where prisoners became official labourers of the state in such sectors as forestry, fishing and agriculture. The system got a boost with the First Five Year Plan and 'dekulakization' or, as the Harvard Project put it, the 'mutually linked processes of industrialization and the collectivization of agriculture'. The term 'kulak' was a misapplication by the Bolsheviks of an old Russian rural term of abuse, meaning a 'fist', used of money-lenders, rentiers, tricksters; for the Bolsheviks it meant, at first, wealthy peasants and, by the late 1920s, any cultivator practising 'capitalist' agriculture.[59] From 1929 onward, over a period of five years, millions of 'kulaks' were robbed of their rural properties. In 1930–1 alone, official figures record 1,803,392 deported in convoys to the northern and eastern extremes of the Soviet Union; others fled, empty-handed, to the cities, and most particularly Moscow. In fact, the whole process of 'collectivization' had its origins in a political *coup* launched by Stalin against Moscow's city government which, under the strongman Nikolai Uglanov and his Agitprop Department of the Moscow Committee (MK), had shown undue sympathy for private business. In 1929, as heads fell, Moscow took an increasingly bullish stand on 'dekulakization'; the new local First Secretary spoke of the 'liquidation of the kulaks as a class' and raised by November 6,600 volunteers for Stalin's 'Twenty-five Thousanders' to 'uproot capitalism in the village'. The southern granary provinces of Russia and the Ukraine were the worst hit. But in the Moscow *oblast* (the Bolshevik 'region') the proportion of rural households 'joining' collective farms, *kolkhozy*, leapt from 0.5 per cent in August 1929, to 3.2 per cent in October, 36.5 per cent in February 1930 and 73 per cent in March. The 'Twenty-five Thousanders' used all means at their disposal to help the process along; the peasants responded with 'medieval forms' of protest, including arson, murder and even crucifixion. Here was the basis of Moscow's 'hyper-urbanization' – along with the growth of the camps.[60]

Stalin's personal commitment to 'industrialization', especially in the heavy industries and showpieces like canals and Moscow's underground, was the driving force behind this. In February 1931, in an address to industrial managers, he said the Soviet Union had ten years in which to catch up with the West or be crushed – Hitler invaded almost on deadline. It was exactly at the moment of Stalin's speech, 15 February 1931, that the 'Chief Administration for Corrective Labour Camps' was set up – *Glavnoe upravlenie lagerei*, the 'GULag', for short.[61]

The drive for slave labour was economic; but the recruitment was selective and ideological. Swiftly on the heels of collectivization followed the Great Purge or, as it was known at the time, the *yezhovschina*, after the head of the NKVD (Commissariat for Internal Affairs), N. I. Yezhov – who himself was replaced in 1938 by Lavrenti Beria, the wartime NKVD chief. Contrary to legend, the Purge was not limited to the elimination of Stalin's rivals at the top of the Communist hierarchy. Out of a total of 690,000 shot between 1937 and 1938, only around 39,000 were from the political and military cadres. To this must be added an uncounted number of the 'disappeared' who went straight into the Gulag and other 'special camps'.[62] The occupation of territories in the west following the Nazi-Soviet Pact increased enormously the number of 'class enemies' and 'suspects' hauled off to camps; there were further 'suspects' caught in the net during the war; and 'liberation' opened up new human seas to trawl. Arrests were underpinned by new Soviet laws. One of the most critical was signed by Stalin in August 1932, making theft of 'state property' punishable by either death or ten years' imprisonment – this was rigorously applied to grain requisitions, which is why peasants called it the 'five stalks law'. A wartime equivalent was GKO Resolution No. 1379 to protect military property. Issued in March 1942 it produced, within two months, 5,973 convictions and 2,679 death sentences – the theft of one kilogramme of army sausage was enough to have a man shot.[63]

Another legend put about in the West by such studies as the Harvard Project, is that phases of stringency were interrupted by phases of leniency. Western visitors to Moscow in the 1920s, for example, witnessed the growth of outside markets as a result of the NEP ('New Economic Policy');

what they did not notice was the centralization of the Communist governing organs and the simultaneous growth of what would become the Gulag. The Second World War corresponded to another 'lenient phase', with markets again appearing in the streets and squares of Moscow – a pleasing sight for visiting Western dignitaries. The number of camps and inmates indeed declined, from an official figure (limited to camps run by the NKVD) of 1,416,000 prisoners in 1941 to only 984,000 in 1942; but this was simply due to the fact that most of the Ukraine and a large part of western Russia was occupied by the Nazis. After 1943 the numbers quickly recovered to reach an all-time high in the early 1950s.

The Moscow underground was one of the showpieces of Soviet public works; the Mayakovskaya station at Gorki Street with its cupola'd ceilings and mosaic panels won a prize at the 1938 World's Fair in New York and was considered a model of socialist 'modernism'. Work had begun six years earlier. Ermolinski could remember skiing in winter down to the River Moskva from the Passage Mansurov with his friend Bulgakov; the winding route took them across temporary, slippery wooden bridges over deep trenches and around snowdrifts that had collected at the metal barriers protecting the construction sites. Responsible for the work was Metrostroi (the Soviet State Trust for Construction Work). Many of its workers were illiterate peasants and nomads brought in from Kazakhstan, Bashkiriya and other non-Slavic territories; there were also the prison labourers brought in – as de Gaulle would later note at Stalingrad – under armed guard. Deep boring was accompanied by collapsing tunnels, timber fires and the agonies of 'the bends' after work in pressurized cabins; the number of casualties remains unknown.[64]

The other major Moscow project of this time, the Moscow–Volga Canal, was started by Mosvodstroi (the Moscow Trust for Waterways Construction) in 1931 and completed six years later almost entirely by slave labour. More earth was displaced than for the Suez Canal; with its weirs, dams, locks and power stations the project astounded visitors by its scale. Yezhov of the NKVD received a huge personal commission to have it finished on time. According to the official figures, 196,000 zeki (prisoners) were working on the project at the beginning of 1935. Some have claimed that as many as half a million died in its construction; dental analysis of corpses found in the area apparently show that many ate bark, roots and grass as a supplement to their meagre rations.[65]

Until late in its history a fortified town, like Vienna and Paris – but unlike Berlin, London and, most of all, Washington – Moscow had been built in concentric circles. This had determined the settlement of the population and the way the town was administered, until the Bolsheviks took over in 1917. It all began, of course, with the Kremlin, a wooden palisade in the twelfth century but, by the end of the fifteenth century, the skewed stone pentagon it remains to this day – the walls were at first painted white but became their natural red in the seventeenth century. Beyond, traders, merchants and vendors gathered in another circle called the Kitai-Gorod, which by the sixteenth century was also surrounded by a thick brick wall; within, a great space was preserved before the red stone Kremlin for parades, festivals and public executions – Red Square. But Tatar cavalry persisted in marauding and burning the wooden-built settlements, so yet another wall was erected in whitewashed stone, creating a further concentric circle, Belgorod, or the White City. The process went on and on, like the construction of a Russian doll. There followed the Zemlyanoi val, the Earthen Wall; then the takeover of the villages and arable land beyond, known as Podmoskovye, 'outer Moscow', which itself naturally formed a circle. So, as circle superseded circle, the roads and boulevards were built. So, after a fashion, was 'Calico Moscow' administered; so the people settled. The threat of fire and high taxes drove handicraftsmen out of Kitai-Gorod to the White City's 'liberties' – this is still reflected in the few street names that have not been changed to those of Soviet heroes. The poor, the exiled, the peasants – who doubled as workers – moved into the outer circles: silent, outer Moscow existed before the Bolshevik bureaucrats moved in from St Petersburg/Petrograd.

The Bolsheviks could not totally erase this physical pattern of settlement. The circles themselves became a means of control, particularly for foreign visitors and observers, who only saw the centre. 'I must get out of this rut,' wrote the reporter Alexander Werth in his diary on 20 July 1941. 'The Narkomindel [Soviet Foreign Office] (or 'Nark' as we call it for short), and the Hotel National, and the Embassy, and the Hotel Metropole, and then back again to the Reuter office, and then the Nark again, with trips to the Central Telegraph thrown in – such is an agency man's daily routine. And to think I was sent out here "to report the Russo-German war".'[66] A native of Russia and foreigner only by passport, Werth would observe a good deal more than most. But the frustration is evident: beyond the inner circle lay *terra incognita*.

What the Bolsheviks did destroy was the natural concord of administrative units with the circular model of settlement. This was no small matter, for it was the demolition of Moscow's local government that set in motion the whole Communist Party machine. In Germany, the Nazi Party developed a perverse means of adapting itself to local government.

In Russia, the Communist Party simply wiped out earlier forms of local government.

At the moment of their takeover, the Bolsheviks introduced *raiony*, or 'districts', that cut through the round city of Moscow like the slices of a cake. The last central circular *raion* of Gorodskoi was partitioned among its outer neighbours in June 1922. The new slices, which had no basis in the geography of the city at all, got names like Leninsky, Dzerzhinsky, Stalinsky and Proletarsky. The Bolshevik slogan in 1917 had been 'All Power to the Soviets'; the gradual suppression of the *raion* soviets during the 'lenient' NEP of the 1920s signalled a major stage in Communist Party centralization. Trotsky, for example, was marginalized and finally ousted by manoeuvring at local government level. Membership of the Muscovite *nomenklatura* was an essential step for a man with ambitions to enter the upper echelons of the Party. Outsiders were brought in to administer the most trivial local functions; Nikita Khrushchev, for example, came in from the Ukraine as a local inspector of apartment superintendents, *koridornye*, and doormen. Molotov and Bulganin both got into the Kremlin through Moscow's *gorkom* (or 'MK' as it was known), which by the late 1920s had total control of the Moscow Soviet of over 1,500 members. No one in the Moscow Soviet would speak out on reports; the members' function was, as one of them put it as early as 1922, 'only to repeat the operation of raising hands'.[67]

As a result, responsibility for essential local chores such as education, health, road maintenance, the railways, and of course the canal and the underground, were gradually abandoned to the central government in the Kremlin. Added to this was the development of a boundless cult of secrecy; local *apparatchiki* spent much of their time arguing over what items should be suppressed from public scrutiny, but none ever questioned the principle of censorship in city government. Consequently, burgeoning 'socialist-planned' Moscow probably had less effective local government than it had had when the Tsars were in St Petersburg. The citizens were reduced to silence.

Alexander Werth found it impossible to buy a map of the town – when he asked at the booksellers' kiosks people looked at him with suspicion. But he was brave enough to take trams out of the normal reporter's circuit – though to ask where one was or where to get off would elicit a grim frown. The new mixture of architecture in Moscow, which he had known before the First World War, astonished him. He travelled down Marx Street: 'it passed through a new quarter with huge and tidy-looking blocks of working men's flats; after that came a mile of nothing but wooden cottages, which looked like a seventeenth-century print of Moscow.' He crossed

Zamoskvoretsky, the *raion* on the south bank. The new scientific institutes impressed him, but then he immediately came upon an area of 'shabby, dilapidated old wooden and stucco houses, with the paint come off, and a derelict and rather indifferent-looking old church with "Kino" in large letters above the entrance'. He climbed the Sparrow Hills, from where Napoleon had first gazed out across Moscow in 1812. 'Large concrete blocks and factory chimneys dominate the skyline of Moscow,' he noted; 'and one can distinguish scarcely more than a dozen churches now, apart from the distant domes of the Kremlin.'[68]

Many of the factories he would have seen were producing weapons – financed, he would have been surprised to learn, by German capital under a Soviet agreement with Weimar Germany made in 1922. To the north, German workers had built the large artillery plant of Podlipki between 1929 and 1932. With Stalin keen to see the aviation industry cooperating with the Germans, Duks – initially an airframe factory – had expanded into the field of interceptors and bombers, and employed a team of German test pilots during the First Five Year Plan. On the west side of town, near the Sparrow Hills, was Fili, which had been built by the famous German aviation group, Junkers. The spirit of the Nazi–Soviet Pact long pre-dated 1939.[69]

5 The man who stayed

In the summer of 1941 Werth had spotted the posters on Moscow's walls: 'Crush the Fascist reptile!' and 'Women go and work on the collective farms!'[70] Hitler's project had been to enslave the Russians; ironically, Stalin's 'planned economy' had much the same aim, the bondage of his own people. Yet they sang to their 'Little Father' and hailed him when he appeared on the granite reviewing stand above Lenin's Mausoleum; they loved him as their sovereign and saviour. Even those who suffered worst could be bewitched by Stalin. Just before his show trial and execution in March 1938, the veteran Bolshevik theorist Nikolai Bukharin, in a personal letter to Stalin, admitted the need for the Purge. 'This is a grand and audacious idea,' he wrote. '*Great* plans, *great* ideas and *great* interests are more important than anything' – certainly more important 'than my miserable person'. His errors were worse 'than original sin, than the sin of Judas', he stated. 'Forgive me, Koba' – as Stalin was known among his most intimate friends.[71] Józef Czapski was a Pole who had been deported in 1939 and, like thousands of his countrymen, released to join Western forces in 1942; he was not the kind of person one would expect to harbour much affection for

Stalin. Yet, he told George Orwell in Paris in March 1945, it was the 'character of Stalin . . . the greatness of Stalin' that saved Russia from the Germans. 'He stayed in Moscow when the Germans nearly took it,' said Czapski. Orwell was convinced. In a new edition of *Animal Farm* he changed a scene in which all the animals, under human attack, fell to the ground; in the revised version, 'all the animals, except Napoleon [Stalin], flung themselves flat on their bellies.' The alteration 'would be fair to Stalin', Orwell explained to his editor, 'as he did stay in Moscow'.[72]

Stalin stayed in Moscow, unlike Prince Kutuzov in 1812: for Russians it was one of the major heroic images of the Great Patriotic War. Hitler had announced 'Operation Typhoon' against Moscow on 2 October 1941. 'Today', he told troops of Army Groups Centre and North, 'is the start of the final, decisive battle of the year'; Jodl proclaimed that it was already the end of the war and the Nazi press chief, Otto Dietrich, formally stated that 'for all military purposes Soviet Russia is done with.' Of course, there were no such announcements in Moscow. Life continued in its normal miserable fashion. Against the air raids the city's defenders devised a unique system of camouflage: the Kremlin's walls were repainted to resemble rows of apartment houses; Lenin's Mausoleum was covered with sandbags and decorated like a country cottage; Mokhovaya Street was zigzagged with lines designed to look like rooftops; canvas over the Bolshoi Theatre was supposed to give the impression of false passageways; the entire façade of the main palace within the Kremlin was covered with green branches. The American reporter, Henry Cassidy, wondered how on earth this was supposed to affect a German bombardier 'flying thousands of feet above the city, blinded by the searchlight rays and shell bursts rising from the well of blackness below him'. The weather was bad; the sleet turned to snow, which formed heaps of yellow slush in the alleys. Central heating was forbidden before 15 October. The house committees were at their most active, organizing fire defences and denouncing anyone who looked suspicious. Most people did not have radios. Over the street loudspeakers there was a stream of martial music, interrupted now and then by an important announcement, frequently in Molotov's voice. Not many bought newspapers; *Izvestia* and *Pravda* were posted behind glass frames in the bus stops.[73]

That was how the panic of October 1941 began. A short communiqué announced on the morning of the 12th that the city of Briansk had fallen to the Germans; though two hundred miles away, Muscovites were quick to realize that this meant the Germans had made a breakthrough. In the afternoon the Germans captured Kaluga, only sixty miles from Red Square; *Pravda* warned of 'terrible danger' facing the capital.

The next day the bulk of the Communist Party, the Stavka (Supreme Command Headquarters) and the civil offices of what remained of Moscow's municipal government were evacuated to Kuibyshev, on the Volga, apparently on Stalin's direct order. Over the next few days almost 500 factories in the Moscow area were disassembled and loaded on to 710 railway vans covered with birch branches and then shipped off to places such as Magnitogorsk, Cheliabinsk and Omutninsk in the east. Behind the vans followed nearly a quarter of a million workers, free and 'slave'. Foreign diplomats were ordered to Kuibyshev on the 15th. Among those who remained, Communist Death Squads were organized; women were platooned into digging deep tank ditches. For those who refused to be evacuated – students were particularly reluctant (Tamara Lisitsin from Tbilisi, Georgia, claimed that she could ride a motorbicycle and fire a rifle and applied to the army) – police provided further motivation: they made 120,000 arrests in four days and shot, according to official statistics, 372.[74]

Some claim that Stalin himself had panicked. Almost as soon as Hitler launched 'Typhoon', Stalin had transferred Marshal Zhukov from Leningrad to Moscow; and thereafter Zhukov was the key commander of Russian military operations. It was during the crisis that Zhukov took one of his staff, General Belov, to discuss plans with Stalin, isolated in the Kremlin. They had to cross a huge bomb crater inside the Kremlin to reach an underground corridor, at the end of which sat the Communist leader at a writing table with a group of telephones in front of him.

Belov had not seen him in eight years. He found 'a smallish man with a tired sunken face', he recalled; 'in eight years he appeared to have aged twenty.' What struck him was the brusque, authoritative way in which Zhukov spoke to him. Stalin continued sitting, taking it all in – such a scene between Hitler and his generals would be unimaginable. Stalin's relationship with his military commanders was established at this moment: Stalin, unlike Hitler, always listened. It was, significantly, Zhukov who persuaded Stalin to remain in Moscow. 'Shall we defend Moscow?' asked Stalin. 'We shall,' answered Zhukov.[75]

The German Panzers, driving through mud and sleet, got as far as a line between the Rivers Nara and Oka – only the Volga Canal, built at such human cost four years before, held them back. Hitler wanted Moscow taken before the celebrations of the 'October Revolution' on 7 November. Stalin was determined not to cancel them: they began on the evening of the festival, in the great Mayakovskaya underground station, another monument created out of the pains of slave labour.

The station was already packed with Party men and officials when the train drew up and Stalin stepped out on to the platform. 'The Germans want a war of extermination against the great Russian nation – the nation of Plekhanov and Lenin, of Belinsky and Chernyshevsky, of Pushkin and Tolstoy . . .' He went on to list poets and men of religion, along with military heroes and Bolsheviks. 'Very well then, if they want a war of extermination they shall have it! Our task now is to destroy every German, to the very last man, who has come to occupy our country. Death to the German invaders!' Stalin had discovered his response to Hitler. A holy war of annihilation. A Patriotic War.

From the balcony of the Lenin Mausoleum the next day, after the first snowstorm of the year, Stalin watched a vast military parade pass by; men from the front and on their way to the front participated; the booming of cannon only forty miles away could be heard. 'The whole world is looking to you as the power capable of destroying the German robber hordes!' proclaimed Stalin. Beria's teenage son, Sergo, speaks of the parade being 'etched in my memory': 'The whole world thought Moscow had fallen, and here was Stalin reviewing his troops!' he records in his memoirs. 'It had a colossal effect.'[76]

That was the turning point, not Stalingrad. The resistance to the invader began to build up; the evacuated factories started to produce; the Partisan war began; the Red Army organized – and 'the man who stayed in Moscow' became a hero. The poet, Vera Inber, remembered hearing those words on the radio while in besieged Leningrad. 'Everything', she said, 'joined for us in one great, shining consolation.' Even among his worst enemies, even for those who were tortured or died at his command, it would be virtually impossible from now on to kill the myth of Stalin.[77]

Born Josef Dzhugashvili – in 1878 or 1879, according to whether you take the parish register or official Party records as your source – Stalin was a native of the frontier territory of Georgia, in the Caucasus, which separated Europe from Asia. Sergo Beria, whose family came from the same region, speaks of Georgia as a 'restless' country under Russian domination. Brigandage and robbery were as well-established trades as grain. Stalin's father, a peasant and a cobbler, was in his own household a tyrant, who roused in his son 'a vengeful feeling against all people standing above him', as his fellow student at the seminary in Tiflis, Gori, put it. It was his mother who wanted Stalin to become a priest, but Stalin preferred reading the radical works of Marx and Plekhanov to the Bible. The inquisitorial monks of Tiflis merely reinforced his childhood aversion to authority; he withdrew into himself and his illicit books.[78]

One book had caught his attention when he was still at church school,

Aleksandr Kazbegi's *The Parricide*. It told the story of a nineteenth-century Caucasian bandit, Koba, who fought for the rights of peasants and looked to avenge the wrongs done to his friends. Stalin called himself 'Koba' before, as an underground Bolshevik, he adopted the name 'Stalin', the 'man of steel'.

As a Marxist, Stalin was already attached to Lenin's movement by the age of twenty, when he was expelled from the seminary for failing to turn up for the exams. An agitator, he organized violent strikes in the oilfields at Batum, May Day parades at Tiflis and even armed robbery of the Tiflis State Bank. He spent several spells in prison or in exile in Siberia. His ability to handle details and organize mass movements caught the eye of the Bolsheviks, and in 1906 he travelled to Stockholm as local delegate to a congress intended to reunite Russian revolutionary factions (but which divided them more than ever). At the same time his talents drew the attention of the Tsarist secret service, the Okhrana, and for the next six years Stalin worked for both the Okhrana and the Bolsheviks. Conspiratorial management was his special field, whilst he remained loyal to no authority but his own.[79]

He was not a ranter like Hitler; one could never imagine Stalin standing on a table, a stool or the pediment of a statue roaring slogans at a crowd, like Lenin or Trotsky. Stalin was always the last to speak at a meeting of Party members; he provided the neat summary, the synthesis, an ideological orthodoxy that somehow always worked in his favour. Like the seminary student he had been at Tiflis, he was quiet and withdrawn; his language invariably moderate, save for the moment of his famous jokes. He was a revolutionary bureaucrat. That is what gave him his staying power.

A professional bandit as well as master bureaucrat, Stalin rose to the top by engineering a process of systematic, ruthless elimination. It was not only individuals who competed for power who were jettisoned, but whole classes, professional groups, races and nations, including his own Georgia. Lenin had created the Party bureaucracy in Moscow that made this possible and was then hoist on his own petard; Stalin had sidelined Lenin before his death. Trotsky had developed a power base in the new Red Army, but it could not rival in strength what the 'man of steel' had acquired as General Secretary of the Communist Party in Moscow: Stalin, by the mid-1920s, had worked his way to the summit of the Muscovite *nomenklatura*, the key to political power in the Soviet Union. To be labelled a 'Trotskyist' by the 1930s was the equivalent of a death sentence. The Red Army was decapitated, a fact that cost Russia dearly in lives and territory when Hitler invaded. The same decade saw the campaign against 'kulaks', Ukrainians,

Cossacks, Georgians and other national minorities expanded. Moscow became Stalin's metropolis, '*Veliki Stalingrad*'. Stalin withdrew to his quarters within the Kremlin.

During the war, Stalin never visited the front; he saw fewer of his soldiers than did Hitler. Only on the occasions of the great international summits, at Teheran in 1943 and Yalta in 1945, did he travel outside Moscow. He had a paranoid fear of assassination. Head of the Soviet state, he lived off the state: for the last twenty-five years of his life he never spent a rouble, never visited a shop, never walked down the streets; he knew nothing of daily life in his own city of Moscow.[80]

There is little to be said about Stalin's private life; his passion was politics, not women, not sport, not luxurious living (his two-roomed home in the Kremlin was a former servant's residence and his dacha at Kuntsevo was notable for its simple furnishings). Svetlana, the daughter of his second wife, Nadezhda Alliluyeva, has described her own growing estrangement from him when she lived in the new family apartment in the Kremlin, where Stalin never slept.[81] His first wife, Yekaterina Svanidze, died of typhus in 1907 after giving birth to a son, Yakov, who died at the age of forty-one, an alcoholic. Yekaterina's brother, Aleksandr, was shot as a spy in 1938, along with several who had known Stalin during his youth; Yekaterina's sister, Maria, died that same year in a prison; Aleksandr's wife and son died in camps. There remains some mystery over his second wife's, Nadezhda's, 'suicide' following an argument at a party held in the Kremlin in November 1932; Stalin's Soviet biographer, Dmitri Volkogonov, cites a letter from her housemaid, Aleksandra Korchagina, who was deported to the camp of Solovki, in which she provides the details of how Stalin himself shot her.[82]

6 Moscow's war and 'liberations'

Stalin played a yet more murderous role in the evacuation and deportation of peoples which accompanied the movement of his armies. The same two margins emerged on the Eastern Front as existed along the line of moving armies in France: before them the fairly narrow zone of effective anti-Nazi resistance; behind them the zone of 'purge' and of minor civil war. But the scale was very different – here the two marginal zones covered several thousand square miles and involved millions of people. In Belorussia, the Ukraine and into Poland there developed before the armies a wide area of Partisan warfare accompanied by 'defection' and 're-defection' campaigns, in which each side attempted to win over the loyalty of enemy troops and inhabitants. Here the line separating 'collaboration' with the Germans from 'resistance' was very hazy indeed. Life was governed by terror and mass murder whatever side one was on. There were cases of whole army units switching from being 'collaborators' with the Germans to Soviet 'Partisans' as the Red Army approached. One of the most famous was the SS Druzhina, made up of defected Russian prisoners of war, which became a Partisan brigade in August 1943; their commander, Gill-Rodionov (who turned out to be a Soviet agent), made a deal, as the Red Army closed in, that his men could 'wipe out their treason' by handing their German commanders over to the Partisans and attacking the Germans in their midst – which they immediately proceeded to do.[83]

The Red Army was always followed by a stream of NKVD agents. Stalin himself contributed to the scenes of devastation in these rear zones. On 14 October 1942 he installed a system by which, in the zone behind the army front, the entire civilian population was to be expelled, without exception, so as 'to prevent enemy agents and spies from infiltrating unit quarters'. 'It is time to understand that inhabited areas that touch the rear are a practical refuge for spies and spying,' he wrote in his own hand – without, evidently, a thought for the civilians who lived there.[84]

In 1943 and through most of 1944 the clearance of the 'liberated' territories was transformed, as Sergo Beria noted in his memoirs, into the 'deportation of some small nations'. I. Serov, Head of the NKVD in the Ukraine, described to Sergo Beria a session of the Politburo in which the decision to deport the Caucasian peoples was made. Beria senior defended his own people, the Georgians, but 'Stalin refused to give the floor to the Georgians who were present. He turned to my father and dryly conveyed the order to carry out the government's decision. "So long as you are Commissar, do as you're told."' So the Georgians, Stalin's own people, were deported along with 'the Chechens and other mountain peoples', though there was not the slightest evidence that they had ever collaborated with the Germans.[85] The pattern was now set for massive deportations as the front moved westwards.

His supposed opposition notwithstanding, it was Beria who personally organized the round-ups and deportations of the Caucasians between November 1943 and May 1944; in contrast to the kulak liquidations of the 1930s they were carried out, he reported, 'with remarkable operational efficiency'. They followed a strict schedule that had been set out hour by hour. The logistics were remarkable: 46 convoys of 60 wagons for the deportation of 93,139 Kalmuks between 27 and 30 December 1943; 194 convoys of 65 wagons for the deportation of 521,247 Chechens and

Ingushi between 23 and 28 February 1944 – for which operation the NKVD had to deploy 119,000 special troops, putting considerable strain on the Red Army as it positioned itself for its last offensive in the Ukraine. Arrests concentrated on 'potentially dangerous elements', between 1 and 2 per cent of the population – many being women, children and the old since most of the men had already been conscripted. The turn of the Tatars in the Crimea – 173,287 of them – came in May. As the Soviet armies advanced, a new system of 'Verification and Filtration Camps' had to be installed behind the front by the NKVD to relieve their heavy task of deportation.[86]

By the end of 1944 the NKVD could proudly claim that their slave labour force was up to about three quarters of its pre-war capacity – and the numbers were growing every month. The quality of the force had changed; most notable was the increase in the proportion of women labourers, from 8 per cent at the outbreak of the war to 24 per cent by its end – the proportion was even higher in the NKVD 'colonies'. Total figures can be misleading and, because – unlike the Nazis' victims exposed immediately after the war – no independent inquiry is possible two generations after the facts, controversy over them is likely to continue.

There were many different types of 'camps' and 'colonies', and they were not all controlled by the NKVD; for example, 'execution camps' (the terminus for all Polish officers) were not under their administration. There were 'special camps' and 'special prisons' – for example, for women or children, sometimes even for ethnic groups. Economic tasks, such as mining, railway building or construction work, were assigned to different administrations. According to the official archival numbers, divulged at the time of the collapse of the Soviet regime in 1991, the total number of forced labourers in the Soviet Union stood at about 4.3 million in 1942 and around 4.0 million in 1945. Deaths, transfers and army recruitment kept up a high rate of inflow and outflow; it has been estimated from the official statistics that 2.42 million passed through the NKVD's camps and colonies during 1943 alone. Death rates have been calculated at 250 per thousand per annum – that is, one in four. Administrative lists suggest that 975,000 men were transferred during the war from the camps to the armed forces. According to official figures, the NKVD contributed during the war 13 per cent of the Soviet Union's nickel, only 2 per cent of its coal and 13 per cent of its mortar shells. But is that the end of the story? One must fear its end will never be told.[87] Like Orwell's old mare, Clover, historians need to be modest, to look down from the knoll and merely wonder at the circumstances men have created. In the Soviet Union, as through much of Eastern and Central Europe, the people 'had come to a time when no one dared speak his mind, when fierce, growling dogs roamed everywhere'.[88]

'I had the feeling of one returned from the dead,' wrote George Kennan in his memoirs of his return to Moscow as American minister-counsellor to Ambassador Averell Harriman in 1944. What struck him, as it did many Western officials, was the isolation of the diplomatic corps from ordinary Muscovites. The secret police considered Westerners, though nominally allies, as 'dangerous enemies' to be kept at arm's length from resident citizens, 'lest we corrupt them, I suppose, with insidious tales of another life'.

This was nothing new to Kennan. Unlike most American Russian specialists and diplomats responsible for Soviet-American relations, Kennan had never been through a 'Marxist phase'. Like his Vice-President, Harry Truman, Kennan was a Midwesterner from a straight line of pioneer farmers; 'the eighteenth-century culture lingered on in these families,' he freely admitted, 'the Puritan culture of Scotland and the north-east of England.' His first mission to Moscow had been as diplomatic secretary to William C. Bullitt at the time the United States had recognized the Soviet Union, in 1934. Bullitt, and most of his staff, had been avid pro-Soviet campaigners since the days of the Russian Revolution; they changed their minds after a few months in Moscow. But the President, Roosevelt, did not; he took the line that the Soviet Union would one day be a great power and his priority was to cultivate its friendship – with little regard 'for the specific issues involved', as Kennan remarked. Bullitt was obliged to resign in 1936 and the State Department's Division of East European Affairs was abolished. Kennan himself was assigned to Prague, then Berlin, then Paris; he had spent most of his war years in Portugal and London.[89]

What made his return to Moscow so ghoulish was not only his isolation from Muscovites; he felt isolated from the people in his own embassy. The streets were the same, the buildings the same – it was he who had chosen, with Bullitt, Spaso House as site of the American embassy. But the personnel was 'a race of people to whom all this past history meant little or nothing. They listened with no more than a bored incredulity when one attempted to speak about these memories, and I soon learned that it was better not to do so.'[90]

In the last months of the war, loudspeakers in the main avenues broadcast piped music, interrupted by propaganda announcements and news of progress on the front. There were firework displays over the Kremlin. Hopes were spread – their source being the re-defection campaigns on the front – that the war would bring the Russian nation together and that with peace a less oppressive Soviet Union would emerge; purges and forced labour would be things of the past. But the seven-day working decree of June 1941 had not been lifted; one could still be arrested for turning up at the workplace twenty-one minutes late. New films were shown in the cinemas (many of these were old converted churches); Eisenstein's *Ivan the Terrible* was particularly popular in 1944. However, by autumn the Party was expressing concern over the development of 'escapism' and 'frivolity' in Moscow, and there were calls for a return to a greater purity of ideology.

But the principal concern of most Muscovites as the war drew to a close was not frivolity, but survival; finding enough to eat. Kennan got a glimpse of this a few days after his return. Like Alexander Werth, his proficiency at the language was such that he could pass himself off as a Russian, so he could board the trams, wander in the parks and boulevards, and take the odd trip into the countryside.

One Sunday he decided to seek out one of the two remaining churches in the Moscow *oblast*, beyond the city. He took the underground to Bryansk station and there noted crowds of people emerging, 'many bearing primitive hoes and other strange implements'. They were making a frantic rush to the suburban ticket offices, pushing and shoving one another. The train was already at the platform, even though the locomotive had not yet been connected. Not a seat was free, the aisles were jammed; people were stationed on the bumpers and the outside platforms, hanging in clusters on to handles and doors. Kennan himself found a bottom step which appeared to have space for one more foot. Immediately a young girl jumped up behind, threw both arms around him in order to grab hold of the guard rails, and cried out, 'Sonya! Sonya! I have found a seat!' Sonya was obviously some way further down the train clinging on to another guard rail.

With a whistle and a puff the train gradually began to roll. A bunch of ragged boys appeared from nowhere and settled themselves on the brake beams. As they picked up speed the skirt of the girl behind Kennan 'flicked each of the switches and signal towers', but this was of no concern to her. Beyond the ridge of the track 'stretched endless victory gardens, chiefly of potatoes', and hunched over them one could see the rounded backs of countless Russian women digging with their hoes.

Kennan found his church. He made a sketch of it while listening to the strains of Gregorian chant which came out of it. His return trip to Moscow repeated the morning's experience in reverse. On the platform was a blind beggar-woman intoning a song, like a priest, about the origins of her suffering; when someone passed her a rouble she would say, 'Thank you, my nice one, my own one; thank you, my good provider. May the Lord grant you great health' – and then return to her song.[91]

The story is reminiscent of Moscow's famous 'bagmen' at the time of the Revolution: desperate townsmen who travelled frequently to the countryside to trade or steal their means of subsistence. Moscow was spoken of then as the 'Big Village', for the majority of its inhabitants were peasants. Stalin's planned economy concentrated on heavy industry; it let the light industries and small trades fall into decay. 'Collectivization' drove more peasants off the land and into the growing outer circles of Moscow; there they lived in barns, closets, dugouts, rickety garages and even mud huts: a crowd of dispossessed urban peasants.[92] Since 1917 the only major change in city life had been the multiplication of numbers, not the quality of life. 'The people of Moscow had lived under martial law and war conditions', stated Kennan in a report on the 'close' of the war in May 1945, 'without respite for thirty-one years.'[93] Moscow's war was unending.

7 Hitler's return

Hitler returned to Berlin on a Tuesday, 16 January 1945, like a thief in the night. The blinds of his train were drawn (as they often were) and he was immediately chauffeured through the blacked-out streets to what was left of the great Reich Chancellery. A recent snowstorm conveniently covered the bombed ruins of the city from the Führer's view. The new Chancellery had only been completed six years earlier to impress fawning diplomats, humbled generals and the conquered; now there were gaping holes in the walls and the windows were boarded up. But miraculously Hitler's own offices on Vossstrasse – the tapestried ante-room and the main conference room carpeted by a heavy handwoven rug leading to the map table, a huge slab of blood-red Austrian marble, by the windows – were untouched.

Two separate stories were now being played out in Berlin. One was the Wagnerian *Götterdämmerung* of the doomed Nazi elite performed in the Chancellery and, by March, in the Führerbunker, fifty feet underground just to the north; the other was the developing catastrophe of Berlin's population, bombed day and night, 'nervous and hysterical' as described by the Minister of Propaganda, Joseph Goebbels, who remained the one tenuous link between the two separate histories. Unlike Moscow, many records exist on the experience of Berlin's population – a clear indication that 'totalitarian' Nazism was not, as is sometimes suggested, a perfect replica of Soviet Communism.

By the second week of January, Hitler had been forced to recognize the failure of the Ardennes offensive. Like Napoleon after Waterloo, he returned to his capital where he hoped to galvanize his people into a new spirit of resistance. The Western Allies remained bogged down in the Ardennes, and there would be no significant movement there until March. But the old military 'yo-yo' pattern was once again at play.

On Friday, 12 January, the Soviets began a massive, staggered offensive across the Vistula. The rubble of Warsaw was 'liberated' by noon, the 17th, though it had been designated by Hitler as a 'fortress', to be defended to the last man. Zhukov's 1st Belorussian Front swept across western Poland and by 29 January was on the Oder, within forty miles of Berlin. To the south, Konev's 1st Ukrainian Front pushed deep into the heart of industrial Silesia. On 20 January Rokossovsky's 2nd Belorussian Front received orders from Moscow to turn north, into East Prussia.

The area was already under attack from the east by Chernykhovsky's 3rd Belorussian Front. Caught between two pincers, this first German territory to be taken by the Russians was exposed to one of the most savage campaigns of the war: villages and towns were razed to the ground, the streets were strewn with bodies, women were raped and then nailed to the wheels of the carts that carried their families.[94]

Albert Speer, Minister of Armaments and War Production, was one of the first to see Hitler on his return to Berlin and – despite a dizzying schedule of trips from one end of what was left of the Reich to the other – was to meet his Führer regularly right up to his very last days. Speer claimed that, as of January 1945, 'it was no longer possible to govern from the capital'; indeed, 'central guidance' was 'more and more meaningless'.

He found a Hitler veering from moods of profound affection (he treated Speer as a son, a fellow artist), to strange fits in the 'grip of euphoria', to white anger, to silence. In January Hitler was arguing with his Chief of General Staff, Guderian, over troop deployment. Guderian wanted to use the navy to evacuate the trapped army group out of Latvia's Courland peninsula and send Sepp Dietrich's Sixth SS Panzer to head off the Russians on the Oder instead of down into Budapest; Hitler, staring with glassy eyes, refused both. On Courland, Guderian was adamant: 'It's high time!' he screamed. 'We must evacuate these soldiers at once.' 'Hitler appeared visibly intimidated by this assault,' recorded Speer: he wondered if such scenes were symptomatic of 'disintegrating authority'. 'Until then, yes even then,' Speer admitted many years later to the journalist Gitta Sereny, 'Germany and Hitler had been synonymous in my mind. But now I saw two entities opposed to each other. A passionate love of one's country could no longer be reconciled with obedience to a leader who seemed to hate his people.' Hitler wanted to destroy his own people. Guderian, reports Speer, was suicidal.[95]

Joseph Goebbels, the Minister of Propaganda, thought differently. Goebbels was the man who had introduced Hitler to Berlin, brought him the crowds, made him a national figure. In the last year of the war, it had been Goebbels who spoke to the nation, not Hitler; it was Goebbels who visited the bomb-sites, never Hitler; Goebbels who encouraged the soldiers at the front, rarely Hitler. And it was Goebbels, the grand showman, who devised, stage-managed and played a principal part in the final, grisly 'twilight of the Gods' fifty feet beneath the Chancellery garden in April 1945. Hitler, it is true, always gave the orders; but they played so well into the stagecraft of the crippled 'little gnome', Goebbels.

Goebbels had been keeping a detailed record of his thoughts, policies and impressions of the Führer in an amazingly prolific diary, which he wrote by hand until June 1941 and from then on dictated to his secretaries in his Ministry, just across the street from the Chancellery. A week passed before he first saw Hitler following his return to Berlin. 'I found him surprisingly fresh and in good health,' Goebbels recorded the next day. 'It is astonishing how a crisis works on the Führer. It doesn't make him weary, but elastic and resistant' – just what the Propaganda Minister wanted to see in him. They talked into the early hours of the morning about the thousands of V-2 rockets they were going to fire on England.[96]

On the map Hitler's Third Reich in January 1945 had the appearance of a long, bent old potato, with sprouts here and there, several bulbous lumps – some of which, like Holland and Courland, had completely separated from the main vegetable – and one long appendix which stretched south-eastwards across Bohemia and Austria in the direction of Budapest in Hungary. This appendix was not only critical in Hitler's own mind; it would have serious repercussions on the outcome of the war and the peace which followed.

The Western Allies were still preoccupied with clearing out the 'Bulge' of the Ardennes. Montgomery was preparing for a large-scale assault in March across the Rhine just north of Wesel. Bradley still pursued the idea of projecting the major part of his forces towards Cologne, so that, together with the British and the Canadians to the north, the whole of the industrial region of the Ruhr would be cut off by a pincer move-ment (in accordance with Montgomery's initial and needlessly delayed plan of the previous August). Patton had, as usual, kept his own pet project to himself: a crossing of the Rhine well to the south and then a single heroic march over the hills of southern Germany, with a final

The day of Paris's Liberation, 25 August 1945, was marked by scenes of jubilation
and violence. The philosopher Sartre compared the atmosphere to that of a bullfight.
Here snipers open fire on celebrators in Place de la Concorde

Above: Miraculously, only one building (the Grand Palais) was seriously damaged during Paris's Liberation. Among the signs in an intact Place de l'Opéra just prior to the German retreat can be read, on the right post, fourth up on its left, in ungrammatical German, *Zur Normandie Front*. *Inset:* On the day of Liberation, a well-dressed Parisian walks off with the same sign

Above: Warsaw, annihilated by the Nazis under the eyes of the Red Army, was 'liberated' by the Red Army on 17 January 1945. Accompanying the army was the Polish photographer, Leonard Sempolinski, who recorded these snow drifts amidst the ruins of the Centre City

Right: The remains of the Augustinian Monastery on Piwna Street, Warsaw – the broken crossbeam resembling a gibbet

Left: Parisians at a street dinner celebrate VE-Day, 8 May 1945. They look more excited at the prospect of a square meal than the dawning of peace

Above: Mothers and children being evacuated from Paddington station as the first v-1 bombs fall in July 1944; such scenes continued in London's railway stations throughout the summer and autumn of 1944

Left: Sporadic bombing went on through the winter and spring. Here rescue-workers arrive on the scene of an attack in the London district of Farringdon where, in March 1945, a v-2 rocket has just killed 380 people

Above right: The crowds come out on VE-Day, 8 May 1945, in Piccadilly

Right: But they were not at the bonfire in Croydon, south of London, that night

Above: Washington, DC, grew from a provincial southern town into a government boom town during the war years. To meet the housing crisis 'tempo' buildings were put up beside the Mall and bridges built across the Reflecting Pond

Left: Fast food became the rage

Right: Despite the conditions, daily life went on in Berlin; people trudged to work in their shattered offices every morning and took the subway back to their ruined homes at night. Here concertgoers in February 1945 return home through rubble and snow after an afternoon out

battle with the Nazis in some mythical Alpine fortress – or perhaps in Bohemia.

For Germany's military and civilian leaders the real threat in late January came from the Eastern Front. Speer made a dangerous trip into the heart of Silesia: the enemy, he reported to Hitler on the 21st, was 'carrying out his supply tasks in close formation, visible from a great distance in the present snowy landscape'. Throw what armoured forces remain immediately into this breach, he urged Hitler.[97] Speer's journey was interrupted when his car collided on ice with an army lorry at Katowice (not far from the Auschwitz death camp), and he had to be rapidly repatriated to Berlin. Goebbels became seriously concerned when the main road from Cracow was cut off by 'the Bolsheviks' on 17 January; he spoke of preparing for a 'life and death struggle in the Polish area' ('Poland', of course, did not exist) and, to his horror, observed that hordes of refugees were advancing on Berlin: 'The Volksdeutsche citizens of the districts of Warsaw and Radom', he noted on 20 January, 'no longer have available means of transportation to safety and now face the arduous task of beating their retreat on foot'[98] – it was worse for the inmates of Auschwitz.

Hitler, however, insisted that one more great offensive could win the war, and he was convinced that his old comrade-in-arms, Sepp Dietrich, was the man to accomplish it. Dietrich's prize Sixth Panzer thus left the Ardennes in early February and slowly made its way across the remains of the Reich, reaching the outskirts of Budapest in the first days of March. On the map, the plan did not appear totally insane. There were oilfields to defend. The approach to Vienna could be cut off. Even more significant was the broad strategy – right across the Eastern Front of Europe – that Moscow seemed so intent on pursuing: like Napoleon, Hitler thought he had found a soft spot through which he could drive forces back into his dream of a German-dominated Ukraine. But the reality was another matter; even Dietrich realized the task was hopeless.

Moscow's strategy was, at this point, decisive to the shape of the emerging new Europe. Militarily, Stalin's halt on the Vistula before Warsaw in August, and his huge flanking movements into the Balkans and northwards into the Baltic states and Finland, made little sense. But Stalin's prime interest was not military; he was pursuing an empire, one modelled after the Soviet state. How far could he go? Hitler, as Speer remarked on several occasions, was not a rational bureaucrat but an artist, whose ambitions went as high as the sky and stretched beyond all horizons. Stalin was the very personification of a bureaucrat; his speeches were wooden and he deferred to the advice of specialists; he rarely, for instance, opposed his General

Staff. Unlike Hitler, Stalin was able to recognize the problem of over-stretch – as the case of Finland proved; but if the power of Soviet arms would have allowed it, he would have been willing to go as far as the Atlantic – as his conversations with the French General Secretary, Thorez, showed. Unlike Hitler, Stalin never got drawn into the detail of oper-ational questions. As Zhukov put it, Stalin concentrated on the 'great strategic questions'. His passion, as in architecture, was for gigantism: the Soviet equivalent of army groups, 'fronts', was Stalin's own innovation, and his favourite manoeuvre was a staggered offensive involving several 'fronts' leading to the encirclement of entire regions. A typical Stalinist offensive would have a breadth of 300 to 500 miles and reach a depth of 200 to 300 miles. In front of the Soviet lines would stretch huge areas of partisan warfare, and 'defection' and 're-defection' campaigns – that was how within a two-week period in August 1943 a unit such as the SS *Druzhina* could be converted into the '1st Anti-Fascist Brigade'. The manichean view of an Eastern Front made up of Communists fighting Nazis does not correspond to the reality of the huge, muddled regional cycles of violence which stretched from the Baltic to the Black Sea in the last year of the war.[99]

Behind Soviet lines was the usual pattern: the NKVD 'filtrated' and a 'National Committee of Liberation' waited to install itself; then came the 'anti-Fascist' purge.

One night in October 1942 Stalin was watching a newsreel which showed, near an area of the front, a half-burnt barn said to be the work of spies; Stalin immediately ordered the entire civilian population in oper-ational zones to be expelled, without exception, 'in order to prevent enemy agents and spies from infiltrating troop encampments'. As the Soviet armies approached the borders of 'capitalist' countries like Romania and Bulgaria, security measures became increasingly severe; expulsions and deportations multiplied. 'Special Camps' or 'Verification and Filtration Centres' were set up behind the lines which gave fresh impetus to the Gulag popula-tion: its rate of growth between 1944 and 1952 was greater than during the 1930s – yet not all former Russian prisoners of war (the *spetskontin-gent*) or foreigners who passed through these camps were counted in formal Gulag statistics. A number of 'execution camps' have been identified in western parts of the Soviet Union; lack of evidence in Siberia and the east suggests that there are still discoveries to be made. Along with the new kind of 'special camps' came special detachments of military counter-intelligence, placed directly under Stalin's control. Their principal occu-pation is neatly summed up in their name, 'Death to Spies', or '*Smert shpionam*': 'Smersh'.[100]

After the deliberate halt of the Red Army outside Warsaw in August 1944 the most rapid advance made by the Soviets was in South-Eastern Europe. Having made contact with Tito's Partisans (now a regular army) in Yugoslavia, they veered north across the southern Carpathians and into the plains of Hungary. Budapest was their obvious aim. Hitler began to think that it was from here that the Soviets would launch their major offensive on Germany itself.

Hitler could not at first believe that the British and the Americans would allow the Soviets to penetrate this far into Central Europe, and to the last days of the Reich he clung to the hope that this unnatural alliance between the Soviet Union and the Anglo-Americans would break down, giving him the chance to manoeuvre. Hence the bitterness of the battle over Budapest: in a classical move of Hitlerite strategy he thought he could achieve not only a breakthrough in the Soviet line, but also the collapse of the anti-German alliance.

The RAF's 'Operation Ratweek' in early September, in aid of Tito's Partisans, should have told him otherwise. Hitler had no way of knowing of Churchill's 'percentage' accord with Stalin in October; but the movements of the Red Army northwards into Hungary show that it was observed to the letter. The effect, to the despair of both Hitler's General Staff and his closest civilian advisers, was to shift the whole emphasis of Hitler's last stand south-eastwards. In the end Hitler was ordering the holdout of two primary 'citadels', Berlin and Prague – which is where the war ended.

Soviet movements also implied a meeting somewhere to the north of Istria of Alexander's essentially British forces and the Soviet Army. With the movement in Central and Eastern Europe of so many millions of prisoners of war, of men of mixed loyalties, of families torn apart, of 'displaced persons' before and behind the lines, this impending encounter of strange 'allies' also hinted at what was to be the final tragedy of the war.

The introduction of new kinds of camps and of a novel repressive personnel laid the way for the exportation of the Soviet system – based on mass incarceration and slave labour – to countries occupied in the west by the Red Army. This corresponded to the tightening up, through the autumn months of 1944, of Communist ideology within the Soviet Party: articles began appearing in the press critical of the 'escapism' present in popular patriotic songs and sentimental plays; 'bourgeois' comedies came in for a lambasting. On 14 October the armed forces' Orgburo ordered a stricter employment of 'ideological-political education' of prospective Party members. A series of Central Committee decrees followed, condemning the 'material' deficiencies of foreign occupied areas, the perversity of property-owning peasants, the dangers of capitalist 'individualism', and of course the ever-present menace of 'Fascism'.

King Michael's *coup* of 23 August 1944 in Bucharest against the Romanian dictator Marshal Ion Antonescu came as a total surprise to Hitler. It led not only to a permanent occupation of the country by the Red Army but opened the way to a rapid German collapse in the whole of South-Eastern Europe. 'Receive with confidence the soldiers of the Soviet Army,' announced King Michael on the radio at ten o'clock that night. 'The United Nations have guaranteed the independence of the country and non-interference in our internal affairs.'[101] Thus began forty-five years of collectivization, mass imprisonment and deportation for this agricultural country on the south-eastern borders of Europe. Within three weeks 165,000 'Fascist' officers and soldiers were arrested and sent to Soviet slave labour camps in Kazakhstan, Siberia and Vorkuta. There were elections in March 1945, but the results (75 per cent non-Communist) were totally ignored. An extermination camp was set up in Valea Neagra. Romania enjoyed also the distinction of special camps: teachers, students, workers and peasants were sent to Gherla; political offenders were locked up in Aiud; Mislea, Miercurea Ciuc and Dumbrăveni were reserved for women. The psychiatric prison of Pitesti has been described by the historian François Furet as 'one of the worst experiments in dehumanization that our era has known'.[102] One of the most famous slave labour sites in all Europe was the Danube–Black Sea Canal; nobody to this day has determined what its function was supposed to be. 'A long time afterwards I had the occasion to pass once more by there,' wrote the novelist Petru Dumitriu: 'all one could see were enormous excavations covered with grass and bramble. There are places where the holes are full of water and wild ducks swim among the reeds. Grass also pushes up between the old rail lines. Everything is dead, as if the canal had been completed but then abandoned over the passage of centuries, like those which linked the Nile to the Red Sea at the time of the Pharaohs.'[103]

Rural Bulgaria had, by a combination of stupidity, location and pure luck, escaped most of the war, even though German troops had been constantly present since the invasion of Greece in spring 1941. After Pearl Harbor she declared war on Great Britain and the United States, but she did not expect anything to come of it. She did not declare war on Russia and never contributed a soldier or a bullet during the German invasion. But after the Red Army had occupied Romania, the Soviet Union, on 5 September 1944, declared war on Bulgaria.

'I don't think the Bulgarian troops will risk engaging the Red Army,' assured the veteran Bulgarian Communist leader, Georgi Dimitrov, in

Moscow.[104] Effectively, not a shot was fired. The Soviets set up a 'Patriotic Front' and Dimitrov was brought in from Moscow. Dimitrov himself initiated the 'purge of the Fascists' in two stages, 'savage' and 'judicial'. As usual, there is disagreement over the number of people arbitrarily massacred over the next twelve months – figures range from 5,000 to 138,000; the few professional historians who have interested themselves in the subject have estimated around 25,000. 'The villages have been well cleared of their Fascists,' reported the Minister of Interior in June 1945; 'in most of the villages we have found 3, 4, 5, or 6' – Bulgaria at the time had 4,419 villages and 237 towns.[105]

By the beginning of October 1944 the Red Army, assisted by Romanians and Bulgarians, had crossed the formidable barrier of the southern Carpathians and was pouring across the Hungarian plain.

On 29 October Stalin telephoned Marshal R. Malinovsky, commander of the 3rd Ukrainian Front, and ordered him to set about the immediate capture of Budapest 'no matter what it costs you'. Malinovsky answered that the assignment could be carried out within five days. 'We cannot consider postponing the offensive for five days,' replied Stalin. 'It is necessary to go over to the offensive for Budapest at once.' This was because of 'political reasons', he explained. Malinovsky continued to make the case for five days. 'You are arguing to no purpose,' said Stalin. 'You do not understand the political necessity of mounting an immediate attack on Budapest.' Malinovsky remained adamant. 'I categorically order you to go over to the offensive for Budapest tomorrow,' concluded Stalin and hung up.[106] The offensive was launched as ordered. What was left of Budapest eventually fell on 13 February 1945, but was still to be subjected to Sepp Dietrich's desperate offensive in March.

After his conversations with Churchill, Stalin was in a hurry to set up the 'Hungarian National Liberation Front' in the capital. Instead he had to settle for a former prisoner-of-war camp in Szeged. In December the 'national committee' and 'national assembly' was moved to the ruined town of Debrecen. A programme was proclaimed for the elimination of all Fascist and 'anti-national' organizations, land reform (collectivization) and the immediate nationalization of major industries. But the Communists of Hungary were forced by Hitler to wait.

The organization of the growing Soviet empire bore a resemblance to the concentric boulevards surrounding Moscow, with each outer peripheral area more secret, and more silent, than the neighbouring one that lay within it. In the centre was the great single-party state, dominated by the image of Stalin, with all orders coming from Moscow, its administration centralized, its industries nationalized, its agriculture collectivized and its economy heavily dependent on slave labour, its policing governed by terror. During the Second World War, first under the Nazi-Soviet Pact, and then with the advance of the Red Army, there grew up a 'community of Socialist states'. In not one single case did the Communist Parties, which seized control of these states, claim in their official histories that they were taking their initiative from Moscow; their stories of 'liberation' were always a story of resistance, mass movement, popular rebellion against 'Fascists' and 'capitalists' (a mix of terms that crept in during the last year of the war), and eventual takeover. Beyond lay an outer periphery of 'brother Parties', which always proclaimed their independence of Moscow, though they were financed by the Soviet Union and their newspapers always followed the Soviet line; their leaders travelled to Moscow and holidayed in Soviet resorts. A guiding point of policy in this outer periphery was the Leninist principle of 'dual power': the 'brother Parties' established local committees and cells; they infiltrated the civil administrations, military administrations and the universities; they were guided and paid by the 'double' system of the Soviet diplomatic corps, one 'legal' and official, the other made up of teams of 'illegal residents', all answerable to Moscow.

The exact extent of this Soviet outer periphery will probably never be known. But revelations made in the 1990s of the Western VENONA decrypts and the handwritten transcriptions of the 'Mitrokhin Archive' – both of which correspond only to a fragment of reality – indicate the existence since the 1930s of clandestine networks working in Western Europe and North America that are astonishing in their size and complexity.

Yet these revelations are known to be incomplete. Not all the Russian archives are yet available; many old KGB files, for example, are kept from public view by Russia's current FSB (Federal Service of Security, *Federalnaya sluzhba bezopasnosti*). As the historian Christopher Andrew notes, 'The originals of some of the most important documents noted or transcribed by Mitrokhin may no longer exist.'[107] Western-based sources such as VENONA have also been edited by Western governments: 'the US Privacy Act . . . protects private citizens not previously identified with espionage or active roles in the Communist Party', while 'the British government [has] demanded some redactions, although the method adopted is more difficult to identify . . . The British . . . seem to have adopted political embarrassment as their principal criterion for eliminating sensitive names.'[108]

The extraordinary feature of this outer network was that Britain was the principal target of Soviet efforts, not Germany, where a major intelligence network was never developed (the Soviets, indeed, relied on British intelligence). Until 1940 Stalin's major concern in international politics was the elimination of Trotsky, not Hitler. As for British and US intelligence in the Soviet Union, until the end of the war it was non-existent. And it may be noted that the greatest prize of Soviet intelligence in the West was the secret of the atom bomb, which was first passed on through British channels in September 1941, and on which Soviet development began in March 1942 – for use not against Germany, but against the West.[109]

Goebbels found himself in a quandary over what to do about the reports of Soviet atrocities. From East Prussia, all through February, descriptions of horrifying deeds had been pouring into his Propaganda Ministry 'with the most appalling realism, such as it would be impossible to exceed'. After publishing some of these reports, along with photographs, he started getting adverse reactions from his readers. For example, 'Special Project Berlin', an inside report on opinion in the capital on 23 February, took note of the population's fear of the 'terrible consequences which a German defeat would have': 'many Berliners take the view that it is not right for the press to carry so many reports of the atrocities by the Bolsheviks. People were already very upset and frightened.'[110] But the dilemma went deeper than that. The Soviets were obviously up to some Nazi tricks, which had themselves been imitated from the Soviets.

Goebbels took his role as propagandist for the National *Socialist* cause most seriously. He always laughed when he heard himself described as a 'Fascist'. 'What a lamentable figure is the Duce, for example, in comparison to Stalin!' he wrote in early March. 'Franco', he said, 'is a veritable turkey.' 'Fascist intellectuals' have 'shown themselves in their true colours, abandoning everything, even their basic principles.' Like Orwell, he noted how the term had become meaningless; the Communists called all their opponents of the day 'Fascist'.

The great revelation in Goebbels's life, it must be remembered, had been his discovery of Lenin; he was still saying, in 1925, that 'no Tsar had understood Russian national instincts so well as Lenin.' His whole early Nazi campaign as Gauleiter in Berlin had been against 'stock-market capitalism', the 'bourgeoisie' – and, of course, 'international Jewry'. Goebbels freely admitted that he felt much more affinity with Stalin's Russia than with the Anglo-Americans, whom he thought very dangerous for National Socialist Germany. This current alliance against Germany was unnatural; he would use Soviet atrocities as propaganda, but only with care.[111]

*

'It is the most appalling weather,' he noted on 5 March 1945:[112] 'snow, rain, cold, and a glacial wind.' That freezing wind was still blowing when the Russians arrived in late April: winter in the *Reichshauptstadt* seemed endless. 'I profited from Sunday to rest a little. But one can't interrupt work, of course.' Unfortunately, there was 'incessant bombardment', but the Ministry of Propaganda, just opposite the Chancellery, was still standing (ten days later its walls blew out and it came crumbling down).

Around midday he plunged himself into Thomas Carlyle's book on Frederick the Great. Poor Thomas! His reputation has never recovered from Dr Goebbels's kind words: 'What an example for us! And what a consolation in these awful days!'

Goebbels also perhaps did a little work on his own new book, *Die Geschichte als Lehrmeisterin* ('The Lessons of History'), which would unfortunately be overtaken by events. It was not until the end of the month that he took up the study of astrology – things would get better in 'the second half of April', then worsen 'around May, June and July' and then 'towards 15 August hostilities ought to end' ('I attach no importance to these astrological predictions; but all the same I intend to use them as anonymous propaganda').[113]

'But to tell the truth the military situation has developed in such a way', Goebbels admitted to himself that Sunday, 'that we have only meagre hopes of realizing something in this domain.' The Western Front was 'seriously deranged'. On that very day the Anglo-Americans reached the Rhine at several points – but, then, the Rhine was a 'remarkable barrier for defence'. On the Eastern Front the situation was 'even worse'. The Soviets were now advancing fast into Pomerania, the coastal province north-east of Berlin; Russian tanks had completely surrounded the port of Kolberg.

Kolberg! In the second half of 1944, as Western and Eastern Fronts approached, Goebbels had spent a fortune and had drafted 187,000 men from the Wehrmacht to produce Veit Harlan's epic colour film about Napoleon's siege of Kolberg in 1807; it premiered on 30 January 1945 when Goebbels had it flown out to the French fortress of La Rochelle, still under siege by the Allies. The German offensive at Lauban had been stopped. There was still some hope in Sepp Dietrich's offensive in Hungary, due to begin the following Tuesday. In the skies, the Anglo-Americans were having a field day. So many bombing raids had been launched that Sunday that the General Staff had lost the means of counting them.

There had to be some sort of political solution, thought the civilian, Dr Goebbels. The best way of ending the war would be for a political crisis to break out within the enemy camp. This was bound to happen soon since Anglo-Americans and Soviets were incompatible – probably it would occur in April when they were due to meet in San Francisco to found a 'United Nations Organization': it would of course be a 'diplomatic farce'. For the present, Germans had to stand their ground, 'whatever the cost'.

In the meantime, the Führer remained in Berlin. Goebbels had told him that his own wife Magda, along with the children, were insisting on staying on. The idea had been inspired by a long conversation he had had five days earlier with one of the multitude of displaced persons thrown up by the jumble of violence in the Eastern borderlands. Only this proved to be a most exceptional person, who had made a great impression on Goebbels: General Andrei Vlasov, commander of the 'Russian Liberation Movement'. Vlasov had been in Moscow in the late autumn of 1941; he told Goebbels that what saved the Russian capital in her hour of crisis was that Stalin stayed in Moscow. To the day of his death, Goebbels never forgot the image of Stalin in Moscow.

The German people, Vlasov had said, would never be able to destroy the Russian people − nor the Russian people the Germans; at some point this would have to be recognized. Goebbels agreed. Vlasov then added that the only thing that could save the Russian people would be their liberation from Communist ideology, but he warned that the ideology had enormous propaganda power − greater, indeed, than Nazism for the Germans. The enormous strength of Stalin was the way in which he had managed to transform the war into a sacred and patriotic cause. Stalin had remained in Moscow and had thus revitalized Russian resistance. 'This is exactly the same sort of crisis that we are facing,' noted Goebbels in his diary that day.[114]

On Sunday evening Goebbels went over to Hitler's underground headquarters, determined to make this point. If the Führer had not come in person to the capital, Goebbels noted in his diary, 'we would perhaps already be on the Elbe today'.

He found the Führer a 'bit depressed' and noted 'with horror' that the trembling of his left hand had become 'much more accentuated'. Hitler's brief visit to the Eastern Front the week before (an afternoon in Lauban) had gone smoothly, but he had refused to have even a communiqué published; as time went by Goebbels noticed that the Führer had developed a total 'fear of microphones' − he would, in fact, never communicate with the German people again.

Among the many notable talents of Joseph Goebbels was his ability to get the Führer to say what he, Dr Goebbels, wanted him to say: he would let the Führer embark on his usual night-time monologue, only interrupting him here and there with a sharp comment, a pertinent question, or simply one of those vast black smiles that would cover half of his gnome-like face – the method invariably worked.

Goebbels began by congratulating the Führer on correctly predicting, contrary to the opinion of the misguided and frequently disloyal General Staff, that the Soviets were going to attack Pomerania rather than drive straight on to Berlin. Such a comment always got Hitler talking. And what a good idea it was to give Himmler, the SS chief, the command of the new Army Group Vistula charged with clearing the Russians out of the province; but what a pity it was he had got this 'infectious malady' and had to direct his armies from his sickbed in Hohenlychen. Well, the SS would prove themselves in Sepp Dietrich's coming offensive in Hungary . . .

Hitler went on about the imbecility of the General Staff, quoting Bismarck's comment that, while he had been able to crush the Danes, the Austrians and the French, he had never been able to overcome the bureaucracy of the Reich. Napoleon had reformed the French army. More recently, Stalin had reformed the Russian armies (that is, murdered all the officers). Yes, Stalin was enjoying some success, but he 'had lost a few feathers'. And his system was quite incompatible with that of the Anglo-Americans – who, with bombing followed by occupation, were intent on executing the Jewish-American Morgenthau Plan.

It was then that Goebbels mentioned the interesting discussion he had had with Vlasov: Stalin was quite untrustworthy; not having a 'public opinion' to worry about, he could change his alliance system overnight. If any of the enemy powers was to show a readiness to talk with Germany, Hitler answered, it would almost certainly be the Soviet Union, because 'they sought war booty, exactly like us'. The San Francisco meeting was bound to be a fiasco. All Germany needed was one military victory, and then Stalin would be ready to talk.

Hitler then launched into one of his strategical flights of fancy. He would reach some sort of settlement with the Soviet Union and then pursue the struggle against England; England had always been the troublemaker in Europe. Once England was knocked out there would be peace. Thus, as late as March 1945, the power of the United States was still absent from Hitler's thoughts.

But what about the propaganda that could be made out of Soviet atrocities? It was a real dilemma. They could not be concealed from the people; indeed, a clear light had to be shed on the true nature of Bolshevism. But, declared Hitler, 'authentic National Socialists should not publish too much about Soviet atrocities because the world would not believe it'. Here lay the end of Hitler's war: an accord between mass murderers, a cover-up, silence. Neither could annihilate the other.

Goebbels was satisfied with himself, Late that night he climbed the concrete staircase, passed through 'Kannenberg-alley' and entered the Chancellery. A 'rather desolate mood' reigned among the personnel here; the Führer alone, down in his bunker, showed the ability to 'remain above this situation'. 'I went directly home late at night and plunged myself into work. That is always the best medicine.'[115]

8 Berlin under bombs

The most perverse thing about Goebbels was that he always had one foot in reality. He may have sought to inspire the troops trapped behind the walls of La Rochelle with dreams of the heroic defence of Kolberg; to the very end he was proclaiming that the war could be turned in Germany's favour. In March he discovered the power of astrology: 'As for me, I attach no importance to these astrological predictions; but all the same I intend to use them as anonymous propaganda'[116] – he even managed to get Hitler and Himmler to believe in the nonsense. But Goebbels had eyes and ears. 'The Reich', he wrote on 2 March, 'is being transformed into a total desert.' That same week he travelled to Himmler's rural command post in Hohenlychen. Berlin, he noted on his way out, had been turned into 'a field of ruins'. The return trip took him across what looked like the land of doom itself 'descending into the night': 'We were constantly overtaking convoys of refugees which struck me almost as the symbol of this gigantic war.'[117]

By the winter of 1944–5 Washington DC, it has been noted, was already living in the post-war world: its plans for the aftermath had been set in concrete and the great American wheel of prosperity was turning – the war was in the news, but it was distant. London was prepared for a drab coexistence with its great ally, for financial belt-tightening, eternal rationing, and for a Socialist landslide that would surprise no one save the Conservative Party – the bombing had virtually ceased. Paris, in the coldest winter of the war, had by now recognized that the Fourth Republic would not be very different from the Third Republic; the political parties had returned, the Communist Party appeared strong, de Gaulle clung on but he was losing some of his popularity – there was no more thought of the war, save for the brief panic during the Ardennes offensive. In Moscow, the Kremlin was confident that it would realize all its imperialist dreams and that it would be little bothered by its Western 'allies' in the conferences scheduled for the months that followed; the population was as silent as always, though increasingly aware that the post-war years would involve a tightening of ideological discipline.

But perhaps most surprising of all was the case of Berlin: Berlin by the winter of 1944–5 was already entering the terrible experience of its immediate post-war years.

'This winter is a good deal colder and a good deal more awful than the last one. And a good deal more hopeless,' wrote Hannelore Holtz in a short story, published in 1947, which ends suddenly in the winter of 1944–5: 'Berlin is a cold, hopeless city in ruins. A city in which the sirens howl, morning, midday, afternoon, evening and night. A city in which food rations are constantly being cut back. A city with no heating. A city which, after the Russian invasion of Upper Silesia, has only a few hours of light and barely any gas . . . It is so cold. I am so tired.'[118]

Inge Deutschkron was, with her mother, among the 6,100 of the 170,000 Jews who lived in Berlin in 1933 who survived the war. One device they employed, late in the war, to acquire false papers was to take a train from Berlin as far east as they could and then join the hordes of refugees travelling in the other direction, claiming to officials that they had lost their suitcases and papers. 'We were looking for chaos.' They did not have to go far. They got on a train crammed with women, children, dogs, crates and trunks; everyone was talking about the Soviet crimes they had just witnessed – rape, pillage, massacre. As the train neared Berlin a new fear arose; everyone had heard of the bombing. Deutschkron and her mother were the most fearful of all; it was already dark and they knew only too well that 'at 7 p.m. the English [bombers] usually arrived', and 'trains were their favourite target.' They pulled into Görlitz station. Sure enough, before they had even come to a halt, the few lights that were shining all went out. In the pitch darkness they tried to find a way out. Loudspeakers announced that the English were approaching Berlin. Sirens wailed. Women screamed. Children yelled, 'Mama! Mama! Where are you?' There was nothing worse than a station shelter. At ten o'clock the curfew began. So the night had to be spent in a soldiers' barracks – men, women, children and dogs all in the same room. Deutschkron and her mother got out early, in time to catch the morning's first tube train, filled, as always, with people going to work: 'people bad-tempered, their eyes still full of sleep; any travellers who joined them, especially if they had cases, were very unwelcome.'[119]

The Canadian historian, Modris Eksteins, recalls the time his family fled their native Latvia from the horrors perpetrated by the Red Army; arriving in Berlin in the winter of 1944–5, they found nothing but a 'moonscape of ruin'. The entries in his father's diary revolved 'around food, lodging, illness, and fear. The acquisition of an apple was celebrated; the theft – from baggage we left in storage at Anhalter train station – of a bit of bacon . . . was lamented at great length.' There was 'the terrible cold'. The family found quarters in central Berlin, near the Anhalter station. 'If only people wouldn't crowd around the entrance so,' noted Eksteins' father. Berliners called British and American bomber crews 'air gangsters' and 'killer pirates'.[120]

The late W. G. Sebald, grand novelist of the effects of war memory, claimed that – though the RAF alone dropped a million tons of bombs on Germany, attacked 131 towns and cities, killing around 600,000 German civilians and leaving another 7.5 million homeless – this devastating bombing 'seems to have left scarcely a trace of pain behind in the collective consciousness, it has been largely obliterated from the retrospective understanding of those affected, and it never played any appreciable part in the discussion of the internal constitution of our country.' A sort of apathy developed; people would go on living in the ruins as if this were a natural part of the landscape. The destruction experienced by the great majority of Germans 'remained under a kind of taboo like a shameful family secret', a 'bleak depression that refuses to lift'. The firestorm created by the raids on Hamburg in July 1943 left one and a quarter million refugees wandering aimlessly across Germany, carrying news of the horror. Tens of thousands of them gathered around the Maximilianplatz in Munich. Many of the women were demented; some arrived in the train from Hamburg with their dead children in their luggage. None 'among the guild of German historians', claimed Sebald, have even attempted to describe the horrors involved.[121]

Soldiers on leave claimed that Berlin under the bombs was more terrifying than the Eastern Front. The huge firestorms created at Hamburg in July 1943 – when flames rose 2,000 metres into the sky, sucking in oxygen so that air currents reached hurricane force and fire rolled down the streets in tidal waves – or at Dresden in February 1945 were exceptional. Casualties during a single raid would normally reach into the hundreds, sometimes thousands, but rarely did they attain the tens of thousands imprinted in popular memory.

Contrary to legend there were, however, firestorms in Berlin. They were experienced, for example, at the opening of the 'Battle of Berlin' in November 1943: a vast area of the centre and central western part of the city was destroyed in less than half an hour; 4,000-pounders blew off roofs; phosphorus canisters created lakes of fire that dribbled down staircases and into the cellars where people were hiding, then set aflame the rows of coal-holes. A German boy working one of the Zoo flak-tower guns (many of Berlin's gunners were teenagers) spoke of the 'whole area round us . . . on fire, getting redder and redder as far as I could see. Then a small hurricane of wind came; it was so fierce that we had to tie ourselves to the rails to avoid being blown over the edge.' Léon Butticaz, a French forced labourer, took shelter in a trench with some Poles: 'A long, slow, gloomy, throbbing noise, like organ crescendos, broke the silence – the engines of the first wave of bombers. It was a sinister sound. Then we saw a multitude of bright lights coming through the cloud, like bunches of grapes of different colours, and our whole area became as bright as day . . . We waited in a perpetual torment of anxiety. All of a sudden there was the sensation of a violent blast of wind blowing the trees, then a crushing sensation . . . Blasts of hot air struck us, whipping our faces, blowing our hair about and going up the legs and sleeves of our clothes . . . We could see that the dark of the night had given way to a bright orange red glow in the distance.' Ellen Slottgo, a student, had her evening at the opera interrupted: 'I hadn't heard the word "firestorm" until then, but that's what it was. I saw masses of sparks and burning particles being carried along in the wind; it made it look as though the air was burning.'[122] It was during these November raids that the Wilhelm Gedächtniskirche was destroyed; the stone matchstick of its remains still stands in West Berlin as a memorial to the bombings and the war.

The flak-tower by the Zoo, a vast chamber of horrors at the time of the Russian attack in April, was already in the autumn of 1944 a centre-piece of terror. Designed as a shelter for 18,000, with seating laid out in pews as in a church, it was housing up to 30,000 during the incessant raids of the last winter of the war. Soldiers made hopeless attempts to control the crowd. The people inside, with little or no light and often forced to stand for hours on end, were described as lifeless, stiffened, petrified.

Beyond, along the shrapnel-peppered street walls, amongst the graffiti, one would often find the scribbled letters 'BU' – '*bleib übrig*', 'keep alive', 'be a survivor' or, more literally, 'keep among the remainder', what is left, the last morsels of life in Hitler's *Reichshauptstadt*. That pretty much described the spirit of Berlin in the winter of 1944–5.

The historian Jörg Friedrich quotes a witness on the Kurfürstendamm – Berlin's Piccadilly – recounting 'one of those indescribable days' of the raids. People swarmed in the street in pitch darkness 'holding their hands out to feel where they were going . . . All over Berlin people wandered as if at sea. Everywhere were the human wrecks of mechanic-ally driven lifeless bodies. The German notion of "emotional paralysis"

(*Emotionslähmung*), found in much post-war literature, was born out of this "intermediate state" – suspended somewhere between death and life. The normal flow of feelings was halted and could not even reach the soul . . . Business continued, survival still counted, one painful step after the other: a batch of essentials would thus be cobbled together. It was useful to have a shawl and a barrow.'[123]

Here amid the ruins were the makings of the psychopathology of post-war Berlin. But why that savage bombing? The British and the Americans dropped more bombs on Berlin alone in the last two years of the war than the Germans dropped on the whole of England in the entire course of the war. During the Blitz, Churchill had warned Germany that the only major arm Britain then possessed was her bomber fleet. As Air Chief Marshal Sir Arthur Harris remarked famously at the time, 'They are sowing the wind and they will reap the whirlwind.'[124] Harris was convinced that he could win the war by vast area bombing alone. With atom bombs, he undoubtedly could have, but not with free-falling bombs of TNT and canisters of phosphorus. What he did succeed in doing was to deliver a blow to morale. There was nothing in Berlin which corresponded to the defiant spirit of London under the Blitz. Harris separated the population of Berlin from the Nazi leadership, and that is precisely what he had intended to do.

Did Berliners in any way merit such bombing? Just under 29 per cent of Berliners had voted Nazi in the violent national elections of July 1932; 25 per cent voted Communist. Thus a majority of Berliners had voted against the parliamentary regime of Weimar. Parliament was dissolved and new elections were held in November. Nationally, support for Hitler declined; but in Berlin it went up. When Hitler was named Chancellor in January 1933, there was a huge celebration in Berlin. Over 50,000 Berliners joined the Nazi Party in the months that followed. The cabarets remained open, the theatres were filled, the concerts were popular; ringroads and autobahns were constructed, all linked to the giant *Funkturm* or radio tower which marked the centre of the city. There was no unemployment. Automobiles were manufactured, and so were armaments; Berlin became the largest and most modern industrial city in Europe. Frau Margarete Fischer (wife of the historian Fritz Fischer) admitted, 'We had *wonderful* years.'[125]

Every major European war since 1860, with the exception of the Russo-Turkish, had been initiated in Berlin: against Denmark in 1864, against Austria in 1866, against France in 1870, and against most of the world in 1914 and again in 1939. Yet, until the last war, not a single battle had been fought with a foreign army inside Germany – which is why Harris argued so vigorously for the need to 'bring the war home to Germany'. In the case of the First World War, Germans argued not only that they had not caused it, but that they had not lost it either: German suffering after 1918 was due to the wicked *Diktat* of Versailles (Germans never spoke of the Paris Peace Conference), the 'stab in the back', and the 'November criminals'. Nearly all Berliners subscribed to this thesis; as Hitler had stated on several occasions in public, there would never again be a 1918 so Germany would never negotiate a surrender.

The development of National Socialist ideology is unimaginable without the experience of 1918. It began as a mutation of Bolshevism, widespread in Germany in the months after the Armistice and the break-up of the Imperial Army; the civil war in Berlin and other cities was fought between the fragments of this army and not between social classes. One of the paradoxes of Nazi development was the refusal to attribute any blame for the First World War and its aftermath to the German army, whilst the Second World War saw the army accused of everything that went wrong.

Under the impact of Allied bombing in 1943–5 Goebbels increased police surveillance, particularly of barracks and troop trains, out of fear of a repetition of a 1918-type rebellion; but Goebbels himself must have known that this was unlikely, given the introduction of 'modern methods' into the army. In his diary he cites the example of the 'modern' Field Marshal Friedrich Schörner of Army Group Centre: his method of dealing with 'stragglers' (*Versprengter*) was 'to hang them from the nearest tree, with a poster tied on them reading: "I am a deserter and I refused to protect German women and children."'[126] Before the end of the war every Berliner had seen bodies of their own soldiers hanging from bridges or lamp-posts.

To this extent, Hitler controlled the population more 'totally' than Bismarck or Kaiser Wilhelm – hence the temptation to compare the Nazi regime with that of the Soviets. Goebbels, too, had been an avid reader of Marx and Lenin. Hitler himself speaks in *Mein Kampf* of the enormous impression made on him, before the First World War, of a Social Democratic mass demonstration in Vienna: 'they marched past four abreast! For nearly two hours I stood there watching with bated breath the gigantic human dragon slowly winding by.'[127] In the first half of 1919 there is evidence that he was a *Vertrauensmann* (an army company representative) working for the short-lived Soviet government in Munich – just the sort of person to be found fighting in the streets during Germany's civil war.[128]

A movement known as 'National Bolshevism' spread widely through Germany in the first months of 1919, becoming particularly popular after the presentation of the Versailles Treaty in May. It was described in March 1919 by Count Harry Kessler, an art connoisseur and occasional diplomat, as a coalition of 'traditional Prussian discipline' with the 'new socialist one' that could 'assume the role of a Rome propagating new brands of civilization at the point of the sword'.[129] At an international level it foresaw an alliance between Germany and the new Bolshevik state against their old enemies of the 'Entente'.

'National Socialism' as it developed under Hitler in the early 1920s was basically Bolshevism with its most essential element, 'class war', replaced by the concept of 'race'. Who was responsible for the war of 1914–18? Not the Germans, of course, but the Slav *Untermenschen*. Who sold out undefeated Germany in 1918? International Jewry. Hitler identified Bolshevism and its class war, which divided the great German nation, with the Jews. Hitler's hatred of Jews ('vermin') and Slavs ('sub-human') was so great that he pointed his machine of war – always intended to effect not simply a revision of 1918 but a total world and racial revolution – eastwards: an alliance with the Soviet Union could only be temporary.

This created permanent tension within the Nazi movement and its supporters. Goebbels, for example, was an Easterner, who would urge peace with Moscow whenever the war seemed to be going badly. It was a sentiment that was widespread among many Prussians and, indeed, many Berliners, who never felt comfortable about the war with Russia. Ironically, it was Goebbels who introduced Hitler to Berlin, thus rendering 'National Socialism' truly national. But Hitler could waver on the matter of peace with Moscow, as Goebbels's conversation with the Führer on Sunday, 4 March 1945, demonstrated.

Hitler still looked *south*-eastwards, across Poland and Czechoslovakia into the Ukraine and the Caucasus. A link-up with Japan around the 'world island'? Incredibly such a link was still being considered in Hitler's quarters late in the winter of 1944–5. That was why Hitler attached such importance to Admiral Dönitz's German navy, and why he held on so desperately to the Latvian peninsula of Courland – for submarine practice in the Baltic.[130]

As for Berliners, the 'wonderful days' did not end with the outbreak of war in 1939. The restaurants remained open, the nightclubs still performed, rationing was minimal – nothing to be compared with the shortages of the First World War. On 6 July 1940 Hitler was welcomed home to his capital as a conquering hero. Looking at the happy crowds the American reporter, William Shirer, wrote: 'I wondered if any of them understood what was going on in Europe, if they had an inkling that their joy, that this victorious parade of the goose-steppers, was based on a great tragedy for millions of others whom these troops and the leaders of these people had enslaved. Not one in a thousand, I wager, gave the matter a thought.'[131]

Berliners were sadly surprised when Hitler's armies failed to take Moscow. The casualty lists lengthened. Stalingrad shocked. Goebbels declared 'total war', closed most of the restaurants, shut the clubs, introduced severe rationing and even forbade dancing. All dreams were turned to cinder by the bombs.

9 German resistance to the Nazis

Effective resistance to the Nazis in Europe, we have seen, only developed ahead of the Allied and Soviet armies as they gradually liberated the German grip on occupied territories. The British hope, and particularly that of the SOE, that they could 'set Europe ablaze' with rebellion had been in vain: the rebellion only came when the armies were in sight.

All Allied army commanders made it clear to their troops that once they crossed German frontiers, they were no longer a liberating force, they were entering enemy territory. Once the troops arrived, the Germans may have hung out home-made white flags of surrender, but there had been no sign of rebellion anywhere prior to that, even under the impact of the guns. How then can one speak of an effective German resistance movement to the Nazis?

Oddly, there is a strong basis for such a claim. The last sixty years have produced almost as many books on the German resistance to the Nazis as on the legendary French resistance; a French specialist on the subject, Gilbert Merlio, has said that nobody in a lifetime could read all the books published on the German resistance to the Nazis. Is it simply a founding myth of the 'good Germans' who eventually set up the German Federal Republic, a model of Western democracy at work?

One thing is clear: there would have been little written on the 'German resistance' had not one brave man, Colonel Claus Count Schenk von Stauffenberg, attempted to blow up Hitler in his East Prussian 'Wolf's Lair' on 20 July 1944; the hut in which the military conference was held that morning was pulverized, but not the Führer, who merely lost his trousers. Stauffenberg was shot that night, along with three other officers, before the headlights of a lorry in the courtyard of the Bendlerblok, headquarters of the Wehrmacht in Berlin. 'Long live holy Germany!' cried out Stauffenberg as the shots rang out – or 'Long live eternal Germany!' according to some accounts. Outside could be heard the thunderous roar of Hitler's supporters, 'Our Führer Adolf Hitler – *Sieg Heil! Sieg Heil! Sieg Heil!*'

'If I speak today, I do so for two special reasons,' said Hitler a few hours later over the radio. 'In the first place, so that you may hear my voice and know that I myself am sound and uninjured; and in the second place, so that you may also hear the particulars about a crime that is unparalleled in German history. A clique – albeit very small – of ambitious, unscrupulous, criminal and stupid officers forged a plot to eliminate me.' 'The clique of usurpers is, as you may expect, very small,' he repeated. There was a general sense of relief throughout Germany and the Führer's popularity rose for a time.[132]

But as Gestapo inquiries showed over the next few weeks, and as historical research has demonstrated over the following decades, Stauffenberg represented no 'small clique'; his network stretched through the officer corps of the army from East to West, among intelligence officers, into the diplomatic corps, through the civilian bureaucracy and into the churches, Protestant as well as Catholic. The number directly or indirectly involved amounted possibly to tens of thousands, and may even have been in excess of a hundred thousand.[133]

Yet this was hardly what one could call a 'resistance movement'; no military force was expected over the horizon and there was no government-in-exile to support it; furthermore, it was seriously divided. 'Don't talk about "resistance [*Widerstand*]",' said one elderly lady to a historian in the late 1970s. 'We did not think of ourselves as being part of a resistance. We merely hoped somehow to survive with dignity.'[134]

The existence in Germany, in the last months of the war, of this element of 'dignity' is perhaps the key. After the war East Germany, the 'German Democratic Republic', nourished the myth, swallowed by many Western academics, that the Communists were at the centre of the resistance struggle in Nazi Germany. It is only a myth. Of course, following the logic of the relationship of resistance to advancing armies this is the way things should have been. The Partisan war, which began in Belorussia in 1942–3, should have spread as the Red Army advanced into Poland and then into Germany. But, unlike France, Italy and South-Eastern Europe, the Communist Partisans were not welcomed in Poland (where they abandoned Warsaw for empty Lublin) and they made no appearance at all in Germany. A few tiny cells had been set up in Berlin and other major cities but, by the outbreak of war, most of these had been broken up and their members sent to Dachau.

The question remains how deep was the division between the German people and the Nazi elite. On Red Army Day, 23 February 1942, Stalin had pronounced, 'It would be ridiculous to confuse the Hitlerite clique with the German people and the German state.'[135] Prime Minister Chamberlain had made a similar statement when declaring war on Germany in September 1939: 'We are not fighting against you, the German people, for whom we have no bitter feelings, but against a tyrannous and forsworn regime which has betrayed not only its own people but the whole of Western civilization.'[136] Chamberlain wasted the next six months attempting to negotiate a peace with the 'German people'; the new prime minister of May 1940, Winston Churchill, put an end to that and instituted a policy of 'absolute silence' to any overtures made by the 'German resistance'.

Stalin's aim in distinguishing 'people' from political 'cliques' was of course not Chamberlain's; he aimed at setting up his own 'people's republic' in Germany. After Stalingrad, in classical manner, he set up a 'National Committee for a Free Germany' and a 'League of German Officers', recruited from German Communists in exile in Moscow and brainwashed prisoners of war. Many of the members of the 'National Committee' did eventually become members of the Soviet puppet state, the German Democratic Republic, set up in 1949. The 'League', on the other hand, turned out to be a bitter disappointment; despite Soviet psychological methods of re-education, several of its members persisted in being anti-Communists. General Walther von Seydlitz-Kurzbach, whose 51st Corps had made a valiant effort to break out of Stalingrad, had the rare honour of being condemned to death twice, first *in absentia* by the Nazi People's Court and then by the Soviet People's Court – Stalin commuted the sentence to twenty-five years' imprisonment; Seydlitz returned to West Germany in 1957 to be greeted by his compatriots as a traitor.

On the walls of shattered Berlin one would occasionally find scribbled, 'The German Communist Party [KPD] lives!' The truth was that the KPD had been killed off in 1933, largely owing to its own inept policy of supporting the Nazis against the Social Democrats (SPD) – 'social Fascists' – in overthrowing the Weimar Republic. In the great Berlin transport strike of November 1932, as a run-up to the elections, Joseph Goebbels and Walter Ulbricht demonstrated together; Nazis and Communists were seen arm in arm in the streets, swastikas and red flags flew together. Hitler became chancellor and turned on the Communists with a vengeance; within six months, by June 1933, Communist membership had been reduced by 60 per cent. By 1937 the Party had virtually disappeared. Stalin did the rest of the work. During the purges he had seven members of the exiled German Politburo murdered, and 41 of the 68 KPD émigrés liquidated; as a sign of good will he deported about five hundred German Communists back to Germany after signing the Nazi-Soviet Pact.

Meanwhile Nazi arrests of Communists had dwindled from 15,000 in 1935, to 11,000 in 1936, 8,000 in 1937 and 3,500 in 1938. With the signing of the Nazi-Soviet Pact in August 1939 the Gestapo registered a return from exile of 4,300 German Communists. The truth is that, by the outbreak of war, all that was left of the German Communist Party inside Germany were a few isolated, ineffectual cells.[137]

The so-called 'Red Orchestra', long trumpeted as the Communist wartime resistance inside Germany, was an invention of the German Gestapo, based on a spy network centred in the Netherlands. The network existed, and was fairly extensive; but few of its members were Communist, and not many were even German. It had branches in France, Belgium and Switzerland and could be more accurately described as the left wing of the famous Kreisau Circle that was eventually linked with the military plot of 20 July 1944. Many of its members were writers, artists, intellectuals, Social Democrats, Catholics and Protestants whose ideas can be traced back to the 'National Bolshevism' advanced by Walther Rathenau and Wichard von Moellendorff at the end of the First World War.[138] Believing in a planned economy and holding the Soviet Union to be the natural ally of a revived Germany, they became very active when Hitler invaded Russia. The leading light of the Circle was Dr Arvid Harnack, who had received his education, and met his wife, in the United States; his PhD thesis had, in the style of American education in those days, been on 'The Marxist Workers' Movement in the United States'. Back in Nazi Germany he created a discussion group, attended by some of the leading intellectuals of the time. One of his chief collaborators was Harro Schulze-Boysen, the grand-nephew of Admiral Tirpitz, founder of the Kaiser's navy. Together they worked on the idea of a 'third way', which would be a synthesis of German nationalism and Socialism. They were behind the attack on the Nazi exhibition, 'The Soviet Paradise', in Berlin's Lustgarten on the night of 17/18 May 1942 – the Gestapo arrested the two men and their families the following December. All in all, about fifty of the so-called 'Red Orchestra' were either hanged, shot or guillotined in the course of 1943; some half a dozen preferred to commit suicide.[139]

The 'White Rose', often presented by the media as the archetype of student rebellion, was made up of six pious Lutheran students and one Catholic who studied medicine at the University of Munich. Led by the brother and sister team of Hans and Sophie Scholl, their principal concerns were religious and philosophical; their main reading consisted of Socrates, St Augustine, Pascal, and the contemporary French Catholic writers Jacques Maritain, Georges Bernanos and Léon Bloy, along with the German Romantic poets. They wrote six tracts condemning the evils of Nazism and distributed thousands of copies through the post. When they were guillotined in February 1943 the Nazi rector of the university announced the glad tidings to the enthusiastic, stamping mass of students before him.[140]

What did these selfless, lonely, brave acts of non-conformity in wartime Nazi Germany really represent? The matter has been muddled by historians who, studying such sources as police reports, have identified areas – such as the Rhineland and Bavaria – of 'silent resistance'. By the same token, most Frenchmen could be considered 'silent resisters' to the Vichy regime, most Russians 'silent resisters' to the Soviet regime. (Indeed, one problem of such studies is that, since they seldom make cross-European comparisons, they are revealed as being more concerned with the postwar search for German national identity.)

German is a language that lends itself to neologisms. In the 1970s a team of researchers under the direction of Professor Martin Broszat, which included Britain's most recent biographer of Hitler, Professor Ian Kershaw, added the German word *Resistenz* to the field of Nazi opposition studies. '*Resistenz*' does not mean what most people have traditionally regarded as 'resistance' – that is an organization prepared to use force against the powers that be – but is, rather, a medical term meaning 'immunity' or an immunological rejection, as when a transplant of the wrong blood-type is placed in the body. This is clearly the wrong image to apply to the case of Nazi Germany where the main body of the people, until well into the war, accepted, and did not reject, their Führer.

The term which corresponds best to the English word 'resistance' – and the one traditionally used in German military manuals – is '*Widerstand*'. The Broszat studies of Bavaria introduced an unending academic debate on how much '*Widerstand*' and how much '*Resistenz*' existed in wartime Germany, a debate that has been a source of much confusion for professors, students, statesmen and historians over the last thirty years.

An issue less discussed but of much greater significance, both during Hitler's war and in the new democratic Germany that emerged after defeat, is the peculiar way in which ancient corporate rights were only partially inserted into the life of the state. Corporations, or 'guilds', had developed in the Middle Ages throughout those parts of Europe which had seen the development of cities, commerce and industry (they were, for the same reason, weak in Russia). In the ancient states of England and France they were early incorporated into the state – one has only to read Keynes on the English Treasury and England's 'old universities' to understand how this was achieved in the case of Britain; in France, the Revolution played a vital role. In German *das alte Reich* of the Habsburgs did not absorb the corporations; on the contrary, it left them largely independent. And so they remained, right through the late unification process under Prussia, through the First World War, the Weimar Republic and into Hitler's Third Reich.

Conversely, Russia had almost no corporate tradition, which is why the term 'totalitarian' cannot be applied indiscriminately to Germany and Soviet Russia alike. The little that did exist in Moscow and southern Russia was wiped out by the Bolsheviks, who introduced a new bureaucracy, centralized in Moscow. Hitler had similar ambitions in Germany, a process which the Nazis called *Gleichschaltung,* or 'synchronization': a shiny, unified piece of state machinery coordinated by Himmler's SS. It never worked.

It was partly Hitler's own fault; he should never have allowed a single man like Himmler, a single ministry, a single state organization to gain so much power, potentially rivalling that of the Führer. Stalin was a bureaucrat at the head of a huge bureaucracy. Hitler was an 'artist', as Speer repeatedly said, an artist of ranting oratory who gained power by convincing a large number of Germans of the Nazi myth of 1918: Germany had never been defeated, Germany had been exploited by foreigners through the *Diktat* of Versailles, Germany had been stabbed in the back, Germany would revive. Nearly all Germans believed this, including all those who participated in the German 'resistance'.

Not one of the many competing branches of Nazi bureaucracy was able physically to control all Germany. The Soviet Union was truly totalitarian; Germany was not. The Nazis lacked the manpower. Hitler presided over organized anarchy, or 'polycracy' as the academics now call it. Most Germans, unlike most Russians, were untouched by state terror; if they had been, the Nazi state would have collapsed early. Nazi terror was selective and, after 1933, concealed.

An American historian, Eric Johnson, has shown in a detailed study of the northern Rhineland, how tiny was the Nazi state apparatus: in 1939, for example, there were only 99 Gestapo officers in Cologne, a city of three quarters of a million; in 1942 they had been reduced to 69. 'Scholars who have studied the Gestapo organizations that operated in other German cities, such as Saarbrücken, Würzburg, Potsdam, Hannover and Leipzig,' notes Johnson, 'arrive at similar estimations of the ratio of the Gestapo to the general population.' Outside Berlin 'there were typically no Gestapo officers operating in the German countryside at all.'[141] No greater contrast could be afforded with Stalin's Soviet system.

The capital of the Reich, Berlin, was a large advanced industrial conurbation, whilst the Soviet capital, Moscow, was an agglomeration of peasants, many of them forcibly removed from their farms. Moscow was much more a product of regime change than Berlin; Hitler may have dreamed of a capital which corresponded to his monolithic ideas, but he had, more or less, to accept what he got, including the bureaucracy, the administrative units, the schools, the separate churches, the arcane local administrations and, most significantly, Germany's army. Hitler had to deal with Germany's inconceivably complex corporate system: its social castes – the nobilities, the guilds, the trade unions; its economic institutions – the old banking networks, the industrial barons, the different peasantries, the old artisanal leagues; its regions – strata upon archaic strata, each with its own frontiers and traditions and dress. All went along with the myth of '1918' – that Germany had not been defeated and required a great national renewal – but each corporate body had its own way of interpreting this. All applauded Hitler, but gradually, and naturally, the tensions developed. This was the origin of the 'German resistance to the Nazis'.

'In other countries suppressed by Hitler's tyranny even the ordinary criminal has a chance of being classified as a martyr,' wrote Count Helmuth James von Moltke in March 1943 in a letter smuggled through to his old English friend Lionel Curtis. 'With us it is different: even the martyr is certain to be classed as an ordinary criminal.' The nobilities of the old Reich sat uncomfortably with the graceless pretenders of the new. Baron Ulrich von Hassell described an embarrassing dinner in September 1940 hosted by the Nazis in Vienna's Hofburg. The reception afterwards at the Rathaus was even worse. The leader of the Hitler Youth 'behaved like a lout with a poor daughter of the "Reich-Drunkard" Hoffman; he was accompanied by an adjutant, heavy with gold braid . . . Later on he took his place, like a petit bourgeois, beside his august wife.' A list of the chief participants in Moltke's secret Kreisau Circle reads like a guest list at the Congress of Vienna. Several members of these old families, like Henning von Tresckow, Fritz-Dietlof von der Schulenburg and even Stauffenberg himself, had played a part in Germany's barbarisms in Russia. But history must recognize the bravery with which they faced their end. Moltke was arrested for 'high treason' in January 1944, six months before Stauffenberg's bomb attempt. He was finally brought before Roland Freisler's People's Court in Berlin in January 1945. Moltke noted that he had not participated in a single act of violence, he had not distributed a single tract; he was being condemned simply for what he 'thought'. The trial, said Moltke, would prove that the Nazis sought 'to annihilate the spirit itself'. The resistance of people like Moltke and the complex network around him was a 'revolt of conscience'. Moltke was hanged; Freisler was killed during the February air raids.[142]

Westerners were puzzled, both during and after the war, by the abstract-ness of thought within this strange German opposition to Hitler; they were repelled by what often seemed to them highly reactionary notions and the fact that every time Hitler successfully conquered territory the 'resistance' appeared to support him. For reactionary thought one simply has to quote the oath Stauffenberg devised for binding together the members of his conspiracy: 'We wish there to be a new order of society, which will make all Germans supporters of the state, guaranteeing them justice and right, but we despise the lie that all men are equal, and accept the natural ranks. We wish to see a people with its roots deep in the soil of its native country, close to the forces of nature, finding happiness and satisfaction in labouring in the status into which it has been called . . . We wish to see leaders from all classes of society, cognizant of the forces of the divine, taking the lead with high-mindedness, virtue and in a spirit of self-sacrifice.'[143] When, early in the war, members of Germany's 'resistance' spelled out their territorial terms for negotiating peace it became quite clear that what they sought was German hegemony in Europe.

But as the war continued, the 'forces of the divine' became an ecumenical Christian movement; the former desire for hegemony was gradually transformed into the notion, espoused particularly within the Kreisau Circle, of a European federation of free nation states. History is not a linear process. Nobody can say today exactly what was the historical significance of the 'German resistance to the Nazis'. Judging from the volume of work published on the subject since the war these people not only helped give the new Germany a national identity, they also forced Germans to face up to their past – a process neatly termed by the Germans *Vergangenheitsbewältigung*, or literally an 'overcoming of the past'.

But perhaps the significance of these courageous acts goes further still. Moltke, Hassell, Stauffenberg and many other isolated individuals did indeed look backwards, but they also stared into an unknown future. Perhaps like Jan Huss and John Wyclif they were harbingers, a hundred years before their time, of a new kind of European Reformation, a novel form of Renaissance. Generations will have to pass before we really know.

But we do have one early sign of what 'German resistance' meant. In the New Year of 1946, the British head of the Allied Control Commission Political Division, Christopher Steel, had lunch with the man the British had just dismissed for 'incompetence' from the mayor's post in Cologne, the seventy-year-old Konrad Adenauer. The old man embarked on a historical monologue, including an overview of the whole Holy Roman Empire, that lasted until seven o'clock in the evening. 'He keeps on insisting that the future must lie with "occidental Christianity",' complained an exhausted Steel to the Foreign Office. 'That's no good for us.'[144] Steel and the British Foreign Office should have paid more attention; Adenauer's two decades of glory were just about to begin.

10 Russian resistance to the Communists

After the relief of Moscow in December 1941 Stalin thought it would be a short affair to push the Germans back from where they came; he was full of confidence and had not yet learnt to listen to his generals – besides, all the old generals had been murdered during the Great Purge and the structure of the new army was still in a state of flux. Early in January 1942 Stalin ordered offensives on all fronts, from the Crimea, across the Ukraine, around the flanks of German Army Group Centre, and north-wards against the enemy forces surrounding Leningrad – around 1,500 miles of war front. So ambitious a strategy spelt total disaster, and prob-ably set the Eastern campaign back at least a year. It gave new courage to the German armies, and – most significantly of all – set the cycles of military-civilian violence swirling; in the 'borderlands', territory and loyalty belonged to no one.

One of Stalin's most painful military losses was the slow annihilation of his Second Shock Army. To relieve Leningrad it had been ordered north through German lines, along the River Volkhov. Naturally, it got cut off at once. Great battles were fought to re-establish a link with the Soviet rear. In spring this was achieved, only to be lost again within a few weeks. On 24 June the Germans dealt their final blow on the surrounded army.

An idea of the vast amount of territory involved in operations like this can be grasped from what happened next: the commander of the defeated army spent more than two weeks wandering alone around the swamps and forests speculating about what to do with himself. Should he take the risk and attempt to cross the lines back into Soviet-held territory? A firing squad or, at best, prison camp awaited a defeated commander there. Like Samsonov and another defeated Second Army in 1914, should he shoot himself? Stalin was hardly worth that honour, he thought. Should he surrender himself to the Germans? He had witnessed their murderous habits and did not find the idea very enticing. Why not just live off the land? After all, tens of thousands of former Russian troops were doing exactly that. He found an abandoned peasant hut in the empty village of Tukhovetchi. On 12 July 1942 a German patrol, led by Captain von Schwedtner of the German 38th Corps; came upon the hut – they suspected

Partisans. The Russian commander appeared at the door with his hands in the air. 'Don't shoot!' he shouted, 'I'm Vlasov!'[145]

There had always been individual opposition to the Soviet system within Russia and even more markedly among the minority nationalities. Every generation produced its clutch of disillusioned idealists just as every generation threw up its new young Communist militants. Instances of rebellion inside the Gulag camps have been noted in memoirs and various other records: hunger strikes among the Poles, work stoppages, a 'cry and clamour' on the long train rides, even prisoners rocking their carriages to the point of derailing the whole train. Most such demonstrations, along with the escapes, were organized by professional criminal bosses who knew the rules of the game and held a gun-barrel on the networks.

Political prisoners were mostly passive; they simply accepted their lot. A major exception was a conspiracy which, as the Germans continued to advance in the autumn of 1941, began in a logging camp, a part of the new Vorkuta complex built in the Arctic tundra of Komi, around 700 miles east of Archangel. The majority were political prisoners, who had already served their terms but had been refused their freedom on account of the war. Their leader, Mark Retiunin, was none other than the chief administrator of the camp. The rebels – around two hundred of them – seized arms and took control of the town of Ust-Uza and then headed for Kozhva, shouting openly anti-Soviet slogans. They attempted to get the local collective farmers to join them. Moscow sent in two military detachments, along with aircraft. Several battles were fought, but by March all the rebels had either been killed or recaptured. Forty-nine were executed in August. News of the rising was, of course, never broadcast. The Soviet administrators regarded Retiunin (who committed suicide on the last battlefield) as a 'Fascist' who sought to establish an alliance with Nazi Germany.[146]

This is the only known case of political armed rebellion within the Soviet Union during the war. There had been no mass political opposition before the war; the last major force to stand up to the Communists had been the 'Workers' Opposition', wiped out by Lenin in 1922 during the months that followed the Civil War. Henceforth, those who opposed the Russian Communist Party had only one of two choices: they could stay and remain silent; or leave the country. Estimates of the number of emigrants from the Soviet Union vary. It is thought that, in the first years following the Soviet takeover, about one million left the country, scattering to neighbouring areas; they were small and isolated communities, with the important exceptions of Berlin and Paris. Collectivization and the purges of the 1930s saw a second wave develop. In 1936 a formal estimate was made that outside the Soviet Union there existed 108 Russian newspapers and 162 journals for a readership of about two million émigrés.

As Stalin was only too well aware, this emigration formed a kernel of Russian opposition to the Soviet system. They were all strongly patriotic and, like the German 'resistance', strongly motivated by their religion of birth. One group, the National Labour Alliance (or NTS), became particularly influential in the 1930s and would provide, during the Second World War, a model programme for the Russian opponents of Communism. Though its members were not prepared to turn the clock back, they argued that a renaissance of Russia could not take place without a consideration of her history. Russia would therefore have to have a strong central government, one however that guaranteed personal liberty, rights to minority nationalities, and most particularly the private ownership of land. Nonetheless, they were critical of 'liberal capitalism', which they considered foreign to Russia, and advocated instead a system of cooperatives for industrial production. Nor could they be considered true democrats: one of the models they admired was Salazar's authoritarian regime in Portugal, which also happened to be favoured by some of the Vichy ministers in France, including Pétain. Indeed, the NTS frequently spoke of its desire in Russia for a 'national revolution'. They would certainly have denied the label 'Fascist' – which is the way the Russian Communists, of course, described them.

Most of them were scientists and technicians, these being the only jobs available to Russian émigrés. During the war this gave them a vast public. Provided with travel permits by reason of their technical expertise, they journeyed the length and breadth of the German-occupied parts of the Soviet Union. In 1943 Germany held territory containing 60 million Soviet citizens; one million Soviet citizens served in the Wehrmacht (wearing the insignia on their German uniforms of the 'Russian Army of Liberation', the Cross of St Andrew on a blue background with a red edge – the national colours of Russia); there were three million Russian forced labourers in the Reich. Most were exposed to the propaganda of the NTS and, later, *Zarya* and *Dobrovolets*, the newspapers of General Vlasov. Thus was born the first Russian anti-Communist mass movement since 1922. Stalin was not entirely wrong to suspect the motives of Russians held in Nazi-occupied Europe.

Russian prisoners in the Reich were isolated. They could not entirely fathom the nature of Nazism, nor could they understand the indifference of the Western Allies to their dilemma.

Lieutenant General Andrei Andreyevich Vlasov was born in 1900 into a peasant family on the east side of the Urals, not far from Tashkent. There was little in his early military career in the Red Army to suggest that he was to become leader of a major anti-Communist movement, save the fact that his brother was executed during the Civil War for anti-Bolshevik activity. Andrei Andreyevich moved up the ranks. He would later be accused by Soviet historians of participating in the military 'Trotskyite' conspiracies which led to the purges of the 1930s, but there is little likelihood of this since he spent most of that time in China giving military advice to General Chiang Kai-shek. He was certainly shocked by the number of officers murdered, and blamed this for Russia's poor performance in the Finnish war of early 1940. Together with General Rokossovsky, who had also escaped with his life from the purges, he was largely responsible for saving Moscow in the winter of 1941. So impressed was Stalin with his performance that he was given command of the Second Shock Army sent to relieve Leningrad — which is what led to his capture in July 1942.

On the front he had seen peasants waiting for the arrival of German troops with flags to greet them and the traditional Russian offering of bread and salt to victorious armies. Since he was on the Russian side of the lines he was not witness to the massacres that then followed; but he had seen the murder and deportation of the kulaks in the 1930s.

Captain von Schwedtner was swift to realize the importance of his prisoner. After a few days Vlasov was transferred to a camp of '*Prominente*' at Vinnitsa, in the Ukraine. He was subject to some mistreatment while being transported, though nothing compared with the brutality meted out to ordinary Russian POWs. At Vinnitsa he received German rations, met other Russian officers and developed with them the idea of forming a Russian National Army, supported by the Germans, that would overthrow Stalin's regime. Naively, he wrote to the authorities in Berlin suggesting a change in German policy.

Vlasov was a powerful personality; he stood six foot five, which, like de Gaulle, made it difficult for him to adopt a disguise — a fact that would eventually prove fatal. With the face of a dark Russian eagle, he had a strong voice that could change the mood of crowds. High-ranking German officers and Nazi diplomats visited him. But in thinking that Nazi Germany was a totalitarian state like the Soviet Union Vlasov misread the situation; he could not conceive that these dignitaries were expressing opinions that differed from those of their chief. The Wehrmacht, the Ostministerium, the Abwehr and the SS were, for him, all cogs in the same machinery of state, not competing sources of power. He believed that the Germans he met were the loyal servants of Hitler and their encouragement suggested to him that Germany was about to change her policy on Russia. In fact many of his interlocutors – like von der Schulenburg, General von Tresckow, Colonel von Freytag-Loringhoven and even Colonel Claus von Stauffenberg – were part of the developing conspiracy to murder Hitler and were all fated to die after the failed attempt of 20 July 1944.

Vlasov was persuaded by his German colleagues to move to Berlin where, in the suburb of Dabendorf, he managed to get permission to set up a Russian training school, along with a Russian press. The following February (1943), and again in May, he made two highly successful speaking tours across the occupied areas of the Soviet Union where he talked about the aims of his 'Russian Liberation Movement' (ROD). Russians themselves must overthrow Stalin, he told a huge audience at Smolensk. The Germans, he emphasized, might be allies, but National Socialism could not be imposed on Russia; 'a foreign coat', he reiterated, 'will not fit a Russian.' He expressed the hope that German policy-makers would help set up a Russian Liberation Army (ROA); Russians and Germans would fight as allies for the destruction of the Soviet system. He spoke on the radio. In the cities of Luga, Volosovo, Siversky, Tomachevo, Krasnog-vardyesk, Pozherevitsy and Dedovichi he was rapturously received. The Germans would help the Russians throw out Stalin just as Russians had aided the Germans to rid themselves of Napoleon. But, asked Vlasov in one auditorium, do they wish to be the slaves of the Germans? The crowd answered in a loud roar, 'No!'[147]

Vlasov showed himself to be a man who was not prepared to compromise, even with the Nazis. During the spring and early summer of 1943 thousands defected from the Red Army to join the German side. Pamphlets were dropped by air. The Communists that summer felt threatened. They developed a new, much more violent 'anti-Fascist' campaign. These were the months during which Jean Moulin was lost in Lyons, Sikorski was killed in Gibraltar, Grot-Rowecki was arrested by the Nazis in Warsaw. The Communists infiltrated the anti-Partisan units in Russia, massacring thousands, but never managed to achieve their objective, to murder Vlasov. However, the Soviet propaganda campaign of 're-defection' worked and, backed up with the important military success at Kursk, many thousands of those who had defected returned to the Red Army.

Thus Russian resistance to the Communists was truer to type than German 'resistance' to the Nazis; it followed the movement of armies. The war on the Eastern Front was as much a Russian civil war as it was a war between Germans and Russians.

★

Vlasov's movement was set back not only by Soviet military successes, but by an evident lack of support from higher Nazi echelons. 'One cannot but be astounded at the lack of political instinct in our Central Berlin Administration,' complained Goebbels in his diary on 29 April 1943. 'If we were pursuing or had pursued a rather more skilful policy in the East, we would certainly be further advanced than we are.'[148]

Vlasov's cause seemed lost for ever when Hitler, during a conference at the Berghof on 8 June, discovered that his army was creating foreign units on the Eastern Front. 'We will never build up a Russian army, that's a phantom of the first order,' he said. He ordered a return to Nazi principles. 'You will not get men for the fight against Russia, but rather an army to proceed against Germany, if the opportunity presents itself.'[149]

Hitler wanted all the Russians sent to labour in the coal mines, but his High Command vigorously opposed this, arguing that it would lead, at this critical moment, to the loss in manpower of between 800,000 and a million soldiers. Eventually Hitler agreed to their transfer to the Western Front, an operation that was completed by the New Year of 1944 – when the Allies landed in June, Soviet troops surrendered in hordes; the Allies found in their POW camps men from the most exotic parts of Eurasia. From that date on, as their number grew from thousands to tens of thousands – and with the entry into Germany, into millions – a poisonous issue weaved its way into the debates of the men who sat at round tables: these prisoners were yet citizens of an 'ally', the Soviet Union. Hitler, with his great understanding of geopolitical affairs, aggravated the problem by sending his own Western POWs to camps in the eastern extremes of the Reich and occupied territories, thus ensuring that they would be 'liberated' by the Red Army.

During those critical summer months of 1944, Vlasov entered a period of profound depression. It seems to have been a trait in the man that could well explain his fortnight's hiding in a peasant cabin before his capture by Captain von Schwedtner. On this occasion, Vlasov began receiving help from an odd quarter, Himmler's SS, which itself was suffering from manpower problems, and had begun recruiting 'Germanic' peoples from every quarter of occupied Europe. Hitler's state of organized anarchy sometimes operated in the most peculiar manner. Vlasov, now considered a prize by Himmler, was sent off to an SS convalescent camp in Ruhpolding, Bavaria, run by a beautiful widow, Frau Heidi Bielenberg. Her mother thought it was the chance of a lifetime: Frau Bielenberg might, within a few months, become the 'first lady' of Russia. Within weeks they were married, though Vlasov spoke no German and Frau Bielenberg no Russian.

Himmler, in the meantime, arranged a meeting in Rastenburg with

Vlasov for, of all dates, the evening of 20 July 1944. The busy events of that day caused the SS Reichsführer to postpone their encounter until 16 September, by which time there was very little of the occupied Soviet Union left. The marriage and convalescent home seems to have worked wonders on Vlasov; he was back to his old outspoken, stubborn self, arguing in front of Himmler for the need for an independent Russian Liberation Army (ROA) run by the Russian Liberation Movement (ROD). Himmler was fascinated by this towering Russian; their meeting lasted for over six hours. But the Reich had its competing fragments and the ROA would always remain a myth, though it is frequently mentioned as a reality by some serious historians. Vlasov in the end got only two Russian infantry divisions, plus an air corps without planes, which began formation on 28 January 1945.

Himmler, who by the previous autumn was beginning to worry about his own political future, did give Vlasov the go-ahead to set up a Committee for the Liberation of the Peoples of Russia (the KONR); at the same time he ordered that corporal punishment no longer be used on Russian prisoners and that the badge '*Ost*' be removed from their clothing.

The Committee was officially set up at a ceremony held on 14 November 1944 in the Hradschin Palace overlooking Prague, the last Slav capital in German hands besides Warsaw, which physically no longer existed (thanks in part to the destructive efforts of troops like the appalling Kaminsky Brigade, soon to be incorporated into Vlasov's two divisions). The 'Prague Manifesto', published the next day, is the clearest outline that exists of Vlasov's political programme for Russia, though it has been argued that it was written under the pressure of German influence. Thus, it identifies the war as being fought by 'the powers of imperialism, led by the plutocrats of England and the USA', the 'powers of internationalism led by Stalin's clique', and by the 'freedom-loving nations, who yearn to live their own way of life'. It makes no mention of Nazi Germany. It accepts the principles of the 'Revolution of 1917' (that is, of February 1917), but it rejects the political party as a source of evil, particularly of course the Bolshevik Party which 'robbed the people of the rights which they had won, and forced them into permanent misery, into lawlessness and exploited them most unscrupulously'. Among the principles the Committee claimed to defend was the 'overthrow of the tyranny created by Stalin', an 'honourable peace with Germany', 'the equality of peoples', the 'abolition of forced labour', the 'inviolability of private property earned by work', the 'freedom of religion, conscience, speech, assembly and the press'. The Manifesto called for the formation of a 'Russian Army of Liberation'.[150]

But as winter approached, members of the KONR had more practical problems to worry about. Victory clearly lay within the grasp of the Red Army. The Anglo-Americans were on the western frontiers of the Reich. Anti-Communist Russians had no doubt about what fate awaited them at the hands of the Red Army. But what would happen to them if they fell within sectors controlled by the British or the Americans? One word became the subject of much discussion and fear after the beginning of December: 'repatriation'.

Several solutions were suggested, most of them preposterous given the military situation. One of them was the idea of fortifying an entire area of Central Europe and waiting for the Americans to come; it was proposed that Central Europeans set up a 'free European Resistance Movement' to defend the zone – an idea supported by Goebbels's favourite 'modern' General Schörner. Vlasov was put in touch with General P. N. Krasnov, Ataman of the Don Cossacks in the war of 1918 and now confined with his Cossack troops to the mountains of northern Yugoslavia where he was involved in the civil war, on General Mihailović's behalf, against Marshal Tito's Partisans. Krasnov's one hope was that, with the advance of the Eighth Army in Italy, he would fall into a British sector. An agreement with Vlasov would perhaps give him negotiating power. But Vlasov, as principled and obstinate as ever, could not abide this old Cossack, and the talks were broken off.

In fact, Vlasov was so convinced of the justice of his cause that he could not see the need to negotiate with the Western Allies at all; weren't they, as they claimed, 'freedom-loving nations'? Didn't they defend the rights of property and the liberty of commerce? KONR's Minister of Foreign Affairs, General Georgi Zhilenkov, an orphan raised in the slums of Lenin's Moscow, followed Vlasov's advice; he did nothing.

This caused much bitterness amongst the older opponents of Bolshevism, members of the 'first' emigration, who had had first-hand experience of Western public opinion – the fickleness of Lloyd George and Wilson, and of leftward-leaning Western intellectuals and politicians. One of the most outspoken was an old émigré from Paris, Yuri Sergeyevich Zherebkov. Do not trust the West, warned Zherebkov; negotiate with them. It was late in the day, but Zherebkov thought he stood a chance of preventing repatriations through the International Red Cross. The Red Cross, he knew, was getting worried – also a little late in the day – that the Germans would commit 'massacres' in their concentration camps before the arrival of the Allies. Zherebkov imagined he could act as a useful intermediary. On 30 April 1945, the day Hitler killed himself, Zherebkov arrived at the Swiss border. But the Swiss would not allow him to cross.

Most realistic was the Czech General Klecanda, a veteran of the Russian Civil War and a witness of the effects of feeble Western diplomacy in 1938. The West, Klecanda told Vlasov, has not the slightest interest in the future of Central Europe and will be as indifferent towards troops of a Russian Liberation Army as it was to Czech officers in 1939. Klecanda recommended that Vlasov collect his army in western Czechoslovakia, so far untouched by the war; but he was not optimistic about the ultimate fate of his Russian friends.

Himmler's SS had its own vague, contradictory plans. One was to collect what units remained outside the combat zones – mostly foreign – in the German Alps; US intelligence wrongly interpreted this as a signal of where the Nazis were going to make their last stand and thus sent Patton's Third Army on a wild goose chase along the southern frontiers of the Reich. Vlasov's Committee, which had its headquarters in the old Czech spa town of Karlovy Vary (or Karlsbad as it had been known to pleasure lovers of the Habsburg Empire), was ordered to transfer to Füssen, on the Austro-Bavarian frontier. In the meantime Vlasov's 1st Division, also in Bavaria, was ordered to join Himmler's forces in Stettin, on the Baltic. The Division's commander, Major General Sergei Kuzmich Buniachenko, refused point blank; he was preparing to march to the Swiss border when Vlasov intervened and told him to obey the German order.

Few documents on this final period of Vlasov's two-division army (of perhaps as many as 60,000 men) have survived; memoirs are contradictory. But it seems that Vlasov was manoeuvring to get his two divisions reunited, as Klecanda had recommended, in western Czechoslovakia. After a brief engagement with the Red Army at Frankfurt-am-Oder (a part of the developing Battle of Berlin), Buniachenko's 1st Division, against all German orders, marched directly south to Dresden and the Czech border, which it crossed on 4 May. On that same day Czech nationalists, on the basis of rumours that Patton's Third Army was approaching, began an uprising in Prague. Buildings in the city centre were festooned with Czech flags, buses were overturned to form barricades, trolley cars crossed Wenceslas Square with the Allied flags flying; a National Committee was set up under the presidency of Professor Albert Prazak. The scene in the streets was very much like that in Paris on 19 August 1944, with this one vital difference: it was the Red Army that was approaching Prague, not the Americans.

'Whoever holds Prague holds Central Europe,' Churchill had said, recalling one of Bismarck's maxims. He had been pushing the new American president, Harry Truman, to get his troops into the Czech capital as quickly as possible. But unknown to Churchill, Eisenhower – contrary to his brief as an Allied commander, which demanded consultation with both the British and the French – had already agreed with Russian High Command that Patton would move no further than Pilsen. When the Czechs learned the truth, they launched a desperate appeal to Vlasov's army, now united in the Czech village of Shukomasty. 'I think we must help our Slavic brothers!' declared Buniachenko. Vlasov turned to the Czech emissaries and said, 'We will support your uprising. Go ahead.'[151]

Thus at midnight, 4 May 1945, free Russians began their march to liberate Prague. By dawn, 5 May, their road was lined with cheering Czechs; peasants offered them bread and salt; young girls strewed their path with flowers.

Vlasov's army liberated Prague that evening. It cleared the streets of the remaining Germans. But the next day, the red flags began to appear, the tanks could be heard; Marshal Konev was entering the city for an official 'liberation'.

'I am hoping that your plan does not inhibit you to advance to Prague,' cabled Churchill to Eisenhower. 'I thought you did not mean to tie yourself down if you had the troops and the country was empty.' Eisenhower, out of fear of a mistaken clash with his Soviet allies, had no intention of moving.

On 7 May Vlasov's forces began their last desperate march south of Prague in the hope of finding the Americans. On Vlasov's own recommendation, they began to break up into smaller units, to seek out either the Americans or the British (coming up from Italy) and negotiate asylum from the Soviets. One group was successful. A helpful academic in Prague, Vladimir Maltsev, and his planeless Air Corps negotiated a surrender to General Kennedy, under the protection of the independent-minded General Patton. Kennedy gave his word that surrendered personnel would not be handed over to the Soviets; the whole of the Air Corps – 8,000 men – managed, in a hazardous night journey down roads broken up by anti-tank obstructions, to cross the line at Bodenwöhr. Kennedy honoured his word, and the lives of 8,000 men were saved – all, that is, save Maltsev who, though he reached the United States, was handed over to the Soviet authorities in May 1946; the Military Collegium of the Supreme Soviet announced his death by hanging shortly after.[152]

Other missions were less successful. General Vasili Malyshkov tried negotiating with General Patch of the American Seventh Army at Nesselwang. Vlasov, before saying farewell to Malyshkov, admitted his doubts. 'I have lost,' he said, 'so I remain a traitor until such time as in Russia freedom comes before bogus Soviet patriotism . . . I do not believe in help from the Americans. We have nothing to offer. We are not a power factor.'[153] Those who surrendered to Patch were repatriated to the Soviets within weeks.

Vlasov, reportedly in a state of apathetic depression, eventually stumbled across the Americans on 11 May at Schlüsselburg; Buniachenko's 1st Division camped in fields nearby. In the castle, Vlasov met a sympathetic Captain Donoghue, of Patton's Third Army. Vlasov burst into an enthusiastic torrent of words explaining his cause and describing his dilemma. 'I thank you, General,' answered Donoghue with admiration in his face. 'What I can do for you I will.' But Eisenhower had negotiated the evacuation of Schlüsselburg that day; the Americans were supposed to be out the next day; the Red Army was advancing.

Buniachenko's 1st Division seems to have got caught up in a wave of panic. They destroyed their papers, their insignia and crowded round their officers asking what to do. Some said go south and join the Americans. Some said it would be better to surrender to the Soviets now. About 10,000 decided on the latter course. The majority, however, slipped into the American zone and handed over their arms; after being moved from one POW camp to another, they were nearly all repatriated to the Soviets.

Vlasov and his fellow officers left Donoghue at his castle early in the afternoon of 12 May. They were driven in a column of eight army lorries with an American scout car at its head in the direction of the American zone. They had not gone a mile when the bushes on the side of the road ahead seemed to move: it was a camouflaged lorry that immediately blocked the road – a large red star could be seen on its side. A battalion commissar of the Red Army stepped out, accompanied by a former captain of Vlasov's army, a man called Kuchinsky; he had decided that the best way to save his own skin was betrayal.

Kuchinsky was frightened for he could see he was under the eye of American authorities. He and the commissar peered into each lorry in turn. On seeing Buniachenko, Kuchinsky grunted. The commissar ordered Buniachenko to get out; Buniachenko shouted that he was an American prisoner and refused. The commissar and his flunkey grimaced and moved on down the line of lorries. In the last one sat General Vlasov. The commissar did not need a grunt from Kuchinsky to know who this giant of a man was. Vlasov got up and simply strode past the two armed Soviets and walked straight to the American commander's car. Through an interpreter Vlasov demanded that the American say they were American prisoners and that the convoy should be allowed to continue on its way unhindered. The American simply stared in silence.

One American lorry managed to start up its engine, turn on the road and race back to Donoghue's castle. Vlasov and others were forced into the Soviet lorry.

In the neighbouring fields Soviet soldiers could be heard greeting the Americans, citizens cheering the victory of the 'Grand Alliance' over Fascism, as the last remnants of Vlasov's army were driven away to captivity.

Little is known of what happened to them next. There is a record that they were interrogated at Smersh headquarters near Dresden. A brief article in *Izvestia* on 2 August 1946 announced that Vlasov and eleven of his accomplices had been tried for treason and hanged. Rumour has it that they were dangled that very day on piano wire, then the supporting butchers' hooks were inserted at the base of their skulls.[154]

But that was not the end of the matter. The drama, and the scale of the tragedy, involved in Europe's transition to peace in 1945 was far greater than the simple extinction of Vlasov's army.

People

People without cities

♈

1 Eight days at Yalta

In the last four months of Europe's war Western and Eastern Fronts approached each other across enemy territory. No such pattern of military events had ever before been witnessed in European history, with the possible exception of the Thirty Years War in the seventeenth century. On both sides, the fronts stretched down the whole width of the European peninsula. And between the two fronts aerial bombing became more intensive. There was no means of escaping the war. A huge human exodus got under way, some of it forced, some of it in flight, much of it in panic. Camps were evacuated – even the extermination camps. The roads were filled with people on foot, fleeing, marching, and dying. But where were they heading? The cities had been flattened.

It was during this period that a conference took place in the old Crimean resort of Yalta. The word 'Yalta' has the same mournful tone as 'Versailles' and 'Vienna'. But 'Versailles' actually refers to the Paris Peace Conference of 1919–20, which founded many international institutions and could – if the West had been blessed with more able statesmen in the 1920s and '30s – have provided the basis of a lasting peace. 'Vienna' was a Peace Conference that gave Europe peace, prosperity and order for a hundred years. 'Yalta' achieved virtually nothing.

Yalta was not a peace congress, so it cannot be compared in scope to the Vienna Congress or the Paris Conference. Like the Treaty of Chaumont, signed between the Allies as they marched on Paris in 1814, or the Allied Supreme War Council which, during the fighting of 1918, drew up the first agenda for a peace conference after the armistice, it was not a peace that ended the war, but it set in motion the diplomatic process that led to its conclusion.

Churchill always expected a Peace Conference after the war and openly expressed his hope for one, particularly during the discussions on Poland. Roosevelt, on the other hand, did not want a Peace Conference, and he was constantly advised by the State Department to avoid any such commitment. Americans had been taught at school that 'Vienna' and 'Versailles' were the products of an old and decadent European aristocracy. Added to this was the general American policy of sidelining Britain and pushing forward the two 'coming' powers in the world, the Soviet Union and China. As for Stalin, he would never have committed himself to a Peace Conference: Marxist historiography showed total contempt for 'Vienna' and 'Versailles'. So Churchill found himself alone. Europe, facing the greatest turmoil in its long history, would have no Peace Conference.

Instead, the 'Crimean Conference' (as 'Yalta' was formally known) produced two concluding documents, a 'Communiqué' and a 'Protocol', which barely filled a printed page. They were signed by the 'Big Three' – France was not invited – on 11 February 1945. All they proved was that the main post-war decisions had already been made the previous year.

In practical terms, the one important article still outstanding of the Dumbarton Oaks plan for a United Nations Organization, on voting rights, was settled by allowing Russia two extra votes in the Assembly (Belorussia and the Ukraine) and accepting the Soviet principle of veto for any one of the five permanent members of the Security Council – a principle which has paralysed United Nations action ever since. The Three Powers agreed to the 'disarmament, demilitarization and the dismemberment of Germany', though the exact lines to be drawn were left for further study; France was granted a zone of occupation, inserted between the already planned British and American zones, and she would have a seat on the Control Commission, which, sitting in Berlin, was supposed to be at the heart of occupied Germany's administration; the frontier of the Soviet zone was still not determined.

The payment of German reparations – far larger in scale than anything imagined in 'Versailles' – came closer to the initial 'Morgenthau Plan', which had been meticulously examined by Soviet economists, than either the Americans or particularly the British wanted: within two years of Germany's surrender, indemnities would be levied in kind ('equipment, machine-tools, ships, rolling stock', etc.) that would be 'chiefly for the purpose of military and economic disarmament'. Over an undetermined period further annual deliveries of products and manual labour would be demanded of Germany. As in the case of the peace of 1919, a Reparations Committee would be set up; but on this occasion it would sit in Moscow, not London. The Committee would take, as a base for study, indemnities and reparations totalling $20 billion, of which 50 per cent would be paid to the Soviet Union. There would be a trial – and not summary executions as Churchill desired – of the major war criminals.

These, in sum, were the basic terms of 'Yalta': not much when compared to Vienna or the Paris Peace Conference.

Included in both documents was a Declaration on an entity called 'Liberated Europe' – imagine what the creative pen of, say, Jean-Paul Sartre could have done with such a piece! But it was neither a Sartre nor a Jefferson that composed the Declaration; one feels, instead, the desperate hand of diplomats in a hurry trying to compose a bland compromise between liberal Allies and Communists. The Declaration foresaw the 'harmonization of the policies of the Three Powers' to assist 'the peoples liberated from the domination of Nazi Germany and . . . the peoples of the States of Europe that were former satellites of the Axis'; the Three promised 'to resolve by democratic means, the most urgent political and economic problems'. The establishment of order in Europe would be realized in a way that would allow the 'liberated peoples to destroy the last vestiges of Nazism and of Fascism, and to create democratic institutions of their choice'.[1]

Yalta was basically a summary of every discussion that had taken place between the Big Three up to 1944. There was little new, little that had not already been ceded to the Soviet Union by force of arms. In the 'Declaration on Liberated Europe' the meaning of the word 'democratic' was left deliberately vague. Poland was the main subject of discussion; the final commitment to early 'free and unfettered elections' left some hope in the West that these might take place. One of the main worries at the time was Stalin's insistence on the 'Oder–Neisse Line' as Poland's western frontier – and by the 'Neisse', he meant the western Neisse.

British officials of the Foreign Office had done a little preliminary calculating: the frontier the Anglo-Americans were seeking (East Prussia, Danzig and Upper Silesia) would involve the transfer of around two and a half million Germans westwards; the Oder frontier without Breslau and Stettin would add a further two and a quarter million; and if the western Neisse were taken as the frontier this would add another three and a quarter million, 'making 8 millions in all'. And that was just the beginning. There was also the problem of Russian citizens picked up in the West.[2]

Hidden from the press was one of the few innovations of Yalta, an accord on 'repatriations' – but even that was only the beginning of the problem of forced transfers, deportations, refugee movements, and the swing of unprecedentedly huge armies in the year 1945. Yalta did not solve anything.

*

399

Since the Quebec Conference the previous September the British had been pushing for a swift Three-Power follow-up in Jerusalem – which the British, in those days, considered the safest spot in the world. But the American President kept on delaying: first there were the elections, then 'a much needed rest' and finally the inauguration of the new Congress and fourth presidential term which, according to the US political clock, was due only on 20 January 1945. In the meantime the Battle of the Bulge had opened, Stalin had been filled with doubts and, in the end, had insisted on the conference taking place in his own back yard, at Yalta. Stalin's offensive had drawn to a virtual halt, just by chance, on the Rivers Oder and Neisse, which he wanted 'democratic' Poland to choose as its western frontier.

Churchill did not like the choice of Yalta one bit. He told Harry Hopkins that 'if we had spent ten years on research we could not have found a worse place in the world than Yalta . . . It is good for typhus and deadly lice which thrive in those parts.' He also warned that the drive across the mountains from the nearest airport, Saki, took six hours, was according to reports from his own people 'frightening and at times impassable', and the health conditions in general wholly unsanitary 'as the Germans had left all buildings infested with vermin'. The American answer to this was to send in an advance party of medical officers aboard the USS *Catoctin* who accomplished 'a very effective job of de-bugging'.[3]

The Soviets did the rest. The Americans were assigned the Tsar's old summer palace of Livadia, Stalin and his party moved into the Yusupov Palace about six miles further south, and the British got the Vorontsov Villa – another six miles further on. One disadvantage was that it took at least three quarters of an hour to get everybody assembled in the same spot – usually the Livadia Palace because of the President's immobility. But the Russians had expended enormous energy and resources to make their guests as comfortable as possible. Hotel staff and secret agents were brought down from Moscow, furniture and furnishings had been carried from every major hotel in the Soviet Union. The meals included plenty of vodka, Crimean wines, caviar, consommé, sturgeon, beef and macaroni; when the daughter of one of the British officers whispered that it would be nice to have a little lemon with her caviar a large lemon tree, covered with fruit, was carried into the orangery next to the dining room. Its perfumed scent was one of the abiding memories of the conference.[4]

Churchill took off on 29 January from Northolt airport in a Skymaster with – as his wife who stayed in London put it – 'a blizzard on his tail'.[5] Like most of Europe, London was under several inches of snow. General

Brooke, in an accompanying plane, noted that 'the little bits of France we saw were covered with snow till we got close to Toulouse.'[6] German V-2 rockets were still bombing London – three of them hit Churchill's own constituency the day after his departure – and there was an acute shortage of coal. The Home Secretary, Herbert Morrison, now the leading campaigner for Labour, repeated dire warnings that Londoners were tired of war and would not stand it for much longer.

They were, however, a good deal more comfortable than most Europeans. In Paris, food and fuel supplies were scarcer than under the German occupation. Snow remained on the ground throughout the month of January. Ice-breakers proved incapable of cutting through the 8 to 12 inches of ice on the canals leading from the coalfields, so deliveries to Paris were cut by a third. Trains were frozen in their tracks. On the Western Front, where an attack towards Düsseldorf was being prepared for mid-February, conditions were grim. Peter White of the 52nd (Lowland) Division, the 'Jocks', described the desolate, winter-gripped landscape between Holland and Germany: 'On 28 January 1945 I climbed, with the rest of the advance party, into a small convoy of trucks in a swirling blizzard, and we threaded our way on sheet-iced roads, wondering towards what?'[7]

The iced roads in Germany were filled with refugees from bombed-out cities heading nowhere. And in late January the great evacuation of the Nazis' eastern concentration and extermination camps began: surviving inmates of Auschwitz, Gross-Rosen and all the other large camp complexes of western Poland and eastern Germany were forced out into the frozen country on what were accurately described as 'death marches' towards camps hundreds of miles to the west, beyond the reach of enemy armies. Many shambled through the snow barefoot, their bodies covered only with rags. Their numbers were to be swollen by the bombing of Dresden on 14 February: a direct result of the military conferences at Yalta.

The first stop for Churchill and his party was the isle of Malta. Though south of Sicily, Brooke complained, 'Weather unpleasantly cold!' On the flight out the Prime Minister's temperature had begun to rise alarmingly; by the time he arrived it was over 102°F – he spent another six hours in bed on his plane and then went out to his cruiser, the HMS Orion, to rest.

Within a day he was back on form. But, as on his trip out to Quebec the previous autumn, he had dismal premonitions about the post-war world and particularly the future for Britain. He had been reading Beverley Nichols' *Verdict on India*. In a letter to his wife on 1 February he recommended the book, though he admitted that 'reading about India has depressed me for I see such ugly storms looming up there which, even in my short flight, may overtake us.' 'We are holding on to this vast Empire,' he went on, 'from which we get nothing, amid the increasing criticism and abuse of the world, and our own people.'

Then there was the matter of Greece. He was sure he was right in suppressing the Communist revolt, yet 'the bitter misunderstandings which have arisen in the United States, and in degenerate circles at home, are only a foretaste of the furies which will be loosed about every stage of the peace settlement.'

And there was Germany. 'I am free to confess to you', wrote Churchill, 'that my heart is saddened by the tales of the masses of German women and children flying along the roads everywhere in 40-mile long columns to the West before the advancing Armies. I am clearly convinced that they deserve it; but that does not remove it from one's gaze. The misery of the whole world appals me and I fear increasingly that new struggles may arise out of those we are successfully ending.' In signing off he wrote, 'Tender Love my darling, I miss you much, I am lonely amid this throng.'[8]

It was Churchill who had insisted on a preliminary meeting between the British and the Americans before they flew together to Yalta. Roosevelt was not keen; he thought it might send a signal to Stalin that the Americans and British were 'ganging up' on him. The facts of Yalta would indicate that it was the Americans and the Soviets who were 'ganging up' on Britain; throughout the conference Churchill was very much alone though, as usual, he proved to be the most articulate and outspoken of the Three.

The encounters at Malta achieved very little. Serious discussion was limited to how to get the Western Front moving again. The British were repeatedly told that they had to understand the 'force of circumstances', that is, that the Americans now had more men in the field and were therefore entitled to lead. 'It had been an unsatisfactory meeting with the Americans,' commented Brooke in a later addendum to his diary, 'which led us nowhere and resulted in the most washy conclusion.'[9] It was certainly not a united Anglo-American party that set out for the 1,400-mile flight to the Crimea.

Reports on Roosevelt's physical appearance at Malta are contradictory. As the USS *Quincy* steamed slowly into port on the morning of 2 February, Churchill, in his peculiar naval uniform, stood on the deck of HMS *Orion*; the two world leaders waved at each other. Two hours later Churchill went over for luncheon on the *Quincy*. 'My friend has arrived in best of health and spirits,' he telegraphed his wife. 'Everything going very well' – a view due more perhaps to Churchill's innate optimism than to the reality of the situation. Marian Holmes, Churchill's secretary, was shocked by the change in Roosevelt since the autumn: 'He seems to have lost so much weight, has dark circles under his eyes, looks altogether frail and as if he is hardly in this world at all.' Eden was also thoroughly shocked: 'he gives the impression of failing powers.' Lord Moran, Churchill's physician, thought he had 'gone to bits'. Admiral Leahy, on the other hand, thought he had lost none of his skills. In the recorded minutes at both Malta and Yalta the President appears coherent and quick – he was receiving prompts from a sick Harry Hopkins, who always sat immediately behind him – but his interventions were in no way 'dominant', as Leahy describes them. In number of words and memorable phrases, Churchill as usual dominated.[10]

The most humiliating moment for Roosevelt was when he landed in the dark hours of the morning, 3 February, in his plane, the 'Sacred Cow', at Saki airport in the Crimea. Churchill, who had arrived earlier, came over to greet the President, accompanied by both Molotov and Vyshinsky. Roosevelt's bodyguard carried a very pale looking president down the gangway and dumped him in a jeep. It moved forward slowly to inspect the assembled Russian guard of honour. Churchill strode at the vehicle's side as in a funeral procession, while newsmen with their cameras walked backwards in front of them to take photographs. Over his shrunken body, Roosevelt held a shawl and looked straight ahead 'with his mouth open, as if he were not taking things in'.[11]

Roosevelt was always the one who opened the daily plenary meetings between the Big Three at Yalta. The line of policy he followed was perfectly consistent with the one he had pursued throughout the war. When Stalin made the point that the three Great Powers, which had borne the brunt of the war, had the 'unanimous right to preserve the peace of the world', Roosevelt agreed – 'the peace should be written by the Three Powers represented at this table.' Churchill was the only one who defended the small powers. 'The eagle', said the Prime Minister, 'should permit the small birds to sing and care not wherefor they sang.' Roosevelt, since his earliest thoughts about the war, never wavered from his general notion of the future distribution of world power, between the United States, the Soviet Union and China. Britain, through her Washington embassy, was long aware of the problem and Churchill was certainly conscious, at least since Quebec, that he was being sidelined. But Churchill was always, with a smile and a cigar, the dominant personality at a conference; his references to 'our long friendship' were perfectly hypocritical – but what other role could this happy warrior play? Roosevelt knew from Churchill's correspondence that the British were not happy; but Roosevelt would never admit, when the two men sat face to face, that there was anything other than an 'old friendship' between them. This was the dishonest base upon which the 'Special Relationship' of the 1950s would be built. The Americans never used the term; the British employed it as a useful diplomatic lie. 'We three . . . have different views because our territories are so very different,' Roosevelt explained to the Big Three during one plenary. 'The British Empire has great populations like Australia, Canada and South Africa. The Soviet Government has great masses of population, like the three areas [Lithuania, Belorussia and the Ukraine] Molotov mentioned. The US is contiguous – no colonies and a constitution that provides for [only] one Foreign Minister.'

There was always at the back of his mind the ejection of the British Empire as a Great Power. It is often said that an ailing Roosevelt proved all too willing to yield to the Soviets; he would willingly cede British, and even more French, areas of strength but he would not budge where US interests were concerned. In a meeting with Stalin and Molotov on the first day of the conference he confided 'something indiscreet' that he would never dare say in front of Churchill: the British for the last two years had 'the idea of artificially building up France into a strong power' so that Britain would always have the time to assemble an army in the case of a crisis along the German frontier. The British, he told Stalin, were 'a peculiar people and wished to have their cake and eat it too'. 'We have had a good deal of trouble with the British,' Roosevelt added.[12]

Roosevelt's understanding of power, territory and frontiers was as abstract as that of his predecessor whom he had so adored, Woodrow Wilson. When Stalin demanded the nullification of the Montreux Convention of 1936, granting Turkey the right to close the Dardanelles Straits – 'It is impossible to accept a situation in which Turkey has a hand on Russia's throat,' protested Stalin – all Roosevelt could think of saying was that 'in the United States we have a frontier of over 3,000 miles with Canada and there are no forts and no armed forces.' Roosevelt felt all frontiers could be like that, including Turkey's. The State Department had been pressing on the President a project of 'territorial trusteeship'; the President jumped at the thought for it fitted in well with his tripartite division of the world. In another of his private interviews with Stalin he said that he had particularly in mind Korea (still in the hands of the Japanese): Korea would become a 'trusteeship' composed of a Soviet, American and Chinese representative. He did not feel 'it was necessary to invite the British to participate'. Stalin interrupted that the British should be invited, otherwise the Prime Minister might 'kill us'. A new world was forming: Churchill was feared, but not the British – Attlee's post-war Britain would count for little. The President persisted in his idea, turning to South-East Asia, which would preoccupy the new superpower America. Indochina ought to be turned into a 'trusteeship', though the British wanted it handed back to the French so that they, the British, could 'keep a hand on Burma'. Stalin nodded: 'Indochina is a very important area,' he told the American. So Roosevelt pursued the point: 'The Indochinese are people of small stature, like the Javanese and Burmese, and are not warlike,' he said, adding, 'France has done nothing to improve the natives since she had the colony.' Roosevelt ended this private conversation by saying that he was convinced the Communists in northern China could cooperate with Chiang Kai-shek's government at Chungking. Stalin again made an understanding nod: Yes, they could make a 'united front against the Japanese'. Such was the kind of foresight Roosevelt had of the world.[13]

One other important matter – which would prove decisive in the way the war ended – brought the Americans and the Soviets together at the conference: the question of military command. It was raised during a meeting of the President with his Joint Chiefs of Staff on Roosevelt's first morning in Yalta. Admiral Leahy, former ambassador to Vichy and now the President's chief adviser, spoke of the need for a direct liaison between Eisenhower and the Soviet General Staff. General Marshall, the Chief of Staff, seconded Leahy, explaining that 'the difficulty had been, not with the Russians but with the British.' He thought the British feared that 'General Eisenhower would become involved in the settlement of matters which would be more appropriate for consideration on a higher level.' At Yalta, the matter was not resolved. Instead, it was Eisenhower himself who, six weeks later, took the initiative unilaterally – with disastrous consequences for the Continent of Europe. Britain, as was a developing habit, was left out of the matter. But Britain, led by a smiling Churchill, again politely said nothing in public.[14]

The main issue of discussion at Yalta was of course Poland. Nobody had a solution for frontierless Poland, Poland of the plain, Poland that had been occupied by both Nazis and Soviets, massacred Poland. Churchill had been able to draw a vague line across the Balkans. He had been able to do nothing for Poland. Roosevelt had not even tried.

'I come from a great distance and therefore have the advantage of a more distant point of view of the problem,' said Roosevelt when he first raised the question on the third day of the conference. One thing the British and the Americans had been able to agree on in Malta was that neither of them would recognize the Lublin government, now installed in the ruins of Warsaw. Roosevelt demanded an 'interim government' that represented all five major political parties, as had existed before the war; then elections. Churchill said that Great Britain had gone to war with Germany for Poland. 'Great Britain had no material interest in Poland,' he commented. 'Her interest is only one of honour because we drew the sword for Poland against Hitler's brutal attack. Never could I be content with any solution that would not leave Poland as a free and independent state.' Stalin asked for a ten-minute break.

When the conference was resumed Stalin began by saying, 'For Russia it is not only a question of honour but also of security.' Poland had always provided the corridor for attack on Russia. What is wrong with the government now installed in Warsaw? he wondered aloud. 'Frankly the Warsaw government has as great a democratic basis in Poland as de Gaulle has in France.' So he returned to the difference, now nine months old, between Paris and Warsaw, the east and the west side of Hitler's Germany. De Gaulle had not held any elections. Why should the Lublin Poles? What was worse was that 'the so-called Underground' had agents who were killing Russians, and attacking Russian supply bases for arms. Roosevelt said it was late and asked for an adjournment.

Churchill demanded a concluding word. He said the British information on Poland did not accord with the Russian. 'Perhaps we are mistaken,' said Churchill, 'but I do not feel that the Lublin government represents even one third of the Polish people.'[15]

The Big Three came to a rough agreement on Poland's frontiers: the 'Curzon Line' to the east and some 'compensation' to the west, though the latter should be left to a 'Peace Conference' after the war. But on the kind of government this Poland should have they encountered a mighty obstacle. They could agree, in fact, on only one word: that it should be 'democratic'.

On the fifth day of the conference Churchill, after listening to a long lecture by Molotov which eventually suggested the possibility of an 'enlargement' of the Lublin government, commented momentously: 'We are at the crucial point of this great conference. This is the question for which the world is waiting. If we accept that each recognize separate governments this will be interpreted all over the world as a sign of cleavage between the Soviet government on the one hand and the US and British governments on the other. The consequences would be most lamentable in the world and would stamp the conference as a failure.' He concluded, 'It is frightfully important that this conference separate on a note of agreement.'[16]

But where to find such a note of agreement? Stalin announced that there would be elections within one month. What of the interim government? They would call it the 'Polish Provisional Government of National Unity'. Who would sit on it? Why not invite members of both sides here to Yalta? Stalin, in his usual beaming way, readily agreed if he could first get the Lublin Poles to make the trip.

Later he announced that none of his staff had been able to contact the Poles; now, it was true that Warsaw in February 1945 was not the easiest town in Europe to telephone. So it was proposed that Molotov, as Soviet Foreign Minister, also responsible for Polish affairs, along with the American ambassador, Averell Harriman, and the British ambassador, Sir Archibald Clark Kerr, invite at an early date an equal number of Lublin Poles and London Poles to Moscow. There they would be asked to form the Provisional Government of National Unity.

But, as Churchill rightly remarked, the conference could not break up without some public 'note of agreement' now on the future of Poland. Churchill insisted: the peace of the world depended on it. On 9 February the Americans[*] drew up a draft note which led to much debate on the actual wording. Molotov kept on referring to the Poles currently living outside Poland as 'émigrés' in contrast to 'those who had stayed'. It was an old Party line consistent with that taken by French Communists of the 'interior' to Charles de Gaulle of the 'exterior'. It went back to Stalin's legendary holding of the fort during the siege of Moscow in 1941. But it was an absurd position to take: most of the Lublin Poles had been émigrés in Moscow, including their leader, Bolesław Bierut, until the Red Army set them up in Lublin in July 1944.

Both Roosevelt and Churchill objected to the term 'émigré'. 'It was applied during the French Revolution to people driven out by their own countrymen, but the Poles were driven out by a brutal enemy,' said Churchill. So it was noted that the new Government of National Unity would be made up of 'all democratic forces in Poland and including democratic leaders from Poland abroad'.

Molotov had a problem with the simple term 'democratic'. What he particularly objected to was the phrase that followed in the American draft, committing the Polish government to 'free and unfettered elections as soon as practicable on the basis of universal suffrage and secret ballot in which all democratic parties would have the right to participate and to put forward candidates'. Molotov asked that 'democratic parties' be replaced by 'all non-Fascist and anti-Fascist democratic parties'. Churchill strongly objected

---

[*] The exact authorship is unknown. Alger Hiss said it was another State Department official, Freeman 'Doc' Matthews; Matthews claimed it was Charles 'Chip' Bohlen. All three were assistants to the Secretary of State, Edward Stettinius, Jr.

to this use of the word 'Fascist'. 'Anybody can call anybody anything,' he said. 'We prefer the terminology democratic parties.'[17]

Molotov suggested the term used by the French Communists during the war, when they were so careful to avoid the word 'Fascist': he proposed 'anti-Hitlerite'. Churchill would not accept that either. The final critical phrase was changed to read: 'In these elections all democratic and *anti-Nazi* parties would have the right to take part and to put forward candidates.' Undoubtedly Churchill would have preferred a reference to 'Nazidom' there, but 'anti-Nazi' was acceptable.

Right to the end of the conference Churchill was complaining how difficult it was to come to an accord over Poland with so little knowledge available about the situation on the ground. He admitted that all his government knew had been gathered by a few agents parachuted into the area. He agreed that there were reports of fighting between former members of the Home Army and the Red Army. 'I am informed that the Lublin government has openly declared its intentions to try as traitors all members of the Polish Home Army,' he added. 'This causes us great anxiety and distress.' Of course, the Red Army should not be hampered in its operations against Germany; but Churchill could never consider the Home Army as either 'Fascist' or 'Hitlerite'.

Roosevelt was pleased with the way the discussion of the Polish problem had turned to a discussion of mere terms. 'I find that it is now largely a question of etymology,' he said, 'of finding the right words.' Historians of a later day can see how wrong he was; what Stalin and Molotov were trying to insert was the classical propaganda language of Communist takeover – it had been reiterated in France and, indeed, in every part of Europe where the Communists played a significant political role in 1945.

Churchill was certainly closer to the problem. 'These are among the most important days that any of us shall live,' Churchill said as they discussed the final draft on the Polish question.[18] He had made a similar comment in a toast he made to Stalin the evening before, 8 February, at a banquet held at the Yusupov Palace. 'We regard Marshal Stalin's life as most precious to the hopes and hearts of all of us,' he said. 'There have been many conquerors in history, but few of them have been statesmen.' No doubt this sort of statement was what drove General Brooke to note in his diary that night, 'The standard of the speeches was remarkably low and most consisted of insincere slimy sort of slush!' But there is something authentic in Churchill's comment that followed: 'I must say that never in this war have I felt the responsibility weigh so heavily on me, even in the darkest hours, as now during this conference. Do not let us underestimate the difficulties.'[19]

Roosevelt, Churchill and Stalin left Yalta making public statements that saluted the success of their encounter. There was the Communiqué, the Protocol and the 'Declaration on Liberated Europe' to prove it. There was also a fourth separately published section devoted entirely to Poland. Pending early 'free and unfettered elections', a 'Provisional Government of National Unity' representing all 'democratic leaders in Poland and abroad' would be set up. The 'Curzon Line' would form the basis of the country's eastern frontier; the western frontier, which would compensate for Poland's eastern territorial losses, was temporarily left open for Poland's representative government to decide. 'We have covered a great amount of ground,' Churchill telegraphed his wife, 'and I am very pleased with the decisions we have gained.'[20] Neither Churchill nor Roosevelt held a crystal ball in their hands. But time would prove that the decisions made at Yalta amounted, in reality, to very little.

2 Hiss

The underlying problem was that both the British and the Americans underestimated Stalin's determination to follow his own autonomous plans of expansion into Europe, projects that were already developing in the young Commissar's mind in 1918. Moreover, through an extraordinary network of 'legal' and 'illegal residents' in Britain and the United States, Stalin knew much more about the United States and Britain than the Western Allies knew of Russia. He knew about the ongoing experiments on an Anglo-American atomic bomb. He was already developing his own Soviet bomb thanks largely to British leaks. He had a constant stream of information on internal foreign policy debates, and who was making the main decisions. The Western Allies had as yet developed no major intelligence network within the Soviet Union; all their efforts went to understanding Nazi Germany – information which they passed on free to the Soviet Union.

However, the critical change in Washington's balance of power between Morgenthau's Treasury and Hull's State Department may well have escaped the Soviet authorities – not because of a lack of information (they had agents at the very top of each department) but because the Soviets, who had already divided the mass of information they received between a civilian agency (the NKGB) and a military agency (the GPU), had never mastered the skills of intelligence analysis. Here the British, working with much less information, were the lords of the planet. Briefly, the Soviets were better informed than either of the other two, but their understanding was often deficient; the British had less information at their disposal than the others, but they had the best understanding of reality; the Americans had not yet even grasped the first elements of the world situation.

With their President so ill, rivalry between and within the major governing departments in Washington had reached a dangerous point for a world power facing the end of a major world war. All the principal post-war international institutions had already been organized by the United States in 1944. Roosevelt had an almost superstitious fear of repeating the same political errors as Woodrow Wilson (who had excluded all Republicans from discussions of the League of Nations) – so, in arrangements for the new United Nations, bipartisan representation on all the American committees involved was essential. A national propaganda campaign was run from the time delegates sat down at Dumbarton Oaks, Washington, to discuss the matter.

But the issue of an American-initiated 'United Nations' went much deeper than that: it exposed some of the most fundamental problems of the American Constitution, designed for an isolated nation but now having to operate in the context of a world superpower. Since the United Nations was a State Department affair this had given the State Department a slight edge over the Treasury, which had concentrated on setting up the world's commercial and banking institutions. The Treasury, moreover, was suffering by the autumn of 1944 from the fallout from the unpopular 'Morgenthau Plan'. The State Department, on the other hand, might have had the upper hand, but it was not in too good a condition itself. Cordell Hull was seriously ill with cancer and had to resign as Secretary of State in November before the Dumbarton Oaks Conference had been completed.

Most were expecting James Byrnes, a man of enormous power and political experience, to step into Cordell Hull's shoes; he was a newspaper owner, a former congressman, senator, justice of the Supreme Court and frequently referred to as 'assistant to the President'. In July 1945 he would, in fact, become Secretary of State under Truman. But during the critical months that covered the end of the war and Roosevelt's death, that role was played by the former Under-Secretary, Edward Stettinius, Jr. At forty-four, Stettinius was the second youngest Secretary of State in American history, though, like Hull, his hair was already marble white. Chairman of US Steel, Stettinius had no experience in international diplomacy. What had made him an attractive candidate to Roosevelt was that he was devoted to pursuing the Wilsonian dream of a new United Nations Organization – one acceptable to the United States.

The British were getting worried about the American obsession with this world organization. Wouldn't it be better first to solve the Polish problem? Eden asked Stettinius at Malta. Eden expressed concern that the United Nations would not amount to much unless the Soviets could be 'persuaded or compelled to treat Poland with some decency'.[21]

It was a typical British, indeed European, approach, working from the particular to the general. American foreign policy always operated the other way round. At any rate, the setting up of the United Nations Organization remained top priority for the American delegation at Yalta, not Poland.

Washington added its own little twist to the problem. Not only was the Treasury at war with the State Department; there were serious political contentions developing within the State Department itself. The former Division of Eastern European Affairs had been absorbed into the Division of European Affairs because Roosevelt did not like the way young American diplomats living in Moscow, like George Kennan or William C. Bullitt, described the frightfulness of life within the Soviet State; after the war Roosevelt's old supporters called them the 'Moscow Mafia' and blamed them in large part for the Cold War.

Roosevelt's absorption of the 'Eastern Europeans' into the Division of European Affairs was, however, not enough to stifle criticism of the Soviet Union. The enlarged Division, particularly under the influence of its director Jimmy Dunn, reckoned that the Soviet Union would be America's chief rival after the war; they warned American policy-makers not to encourage Soviet expansion into Eastern Europe. In total contrast, the Far Eastern Division – which throughout the 1930s had been run by Woodrow Wilson's son-in-law, Francis B. Sayre – considered the Soviet Union a natural partner in post-war affairs. They thought America's chief rival after the war would be Great Britain, because of her hold on Burma and Malaya, while all the US had was the Philippines. Their greatest fear was a revived British Empire. One of their concerns had been that at a critical moment during the European war the King and Queen of England might move out to Australia. They were supported by the Republican Secretary of War, Henry Stimson, and US Fleet Admiral Ernest King.

But here was the crux of the matter: most of the 'UN guys' in the State Department had been promoted through the Far Eastern Division. They followed, like their director, Frank Sayre, the Wilsonite version of history. That is, they thought one of the great mistakes of the Paris Peace Conference of 1919 (which they called 'Versailles') had been its attempt to limit Russia's power in Europe; they saw nothing wrong with the Soviets maintaining 'friendly states' in the Balkans and the eastern half of Europe: the Soviets could feel secure under a kind of Russian 'Monroe Doctrine'.

It was the Western European 'imperialist powers', France and Britain, that had been the initiators of the *cordon sanitaire* – one of the chief causes they thought of the Second World War, because it weakened the states on Germany's eastern flank. Don't let the European 'imperialists' repeat the same mistake this time. In the War Department, Stimson held on to his dossier, the 'Red Plan' – the preparations for war with Great Britain.

For Yalta, Secretary of State Stettinius had initially been allocated the assistance of Jimmy Dunn. Cooperation with the head of the European Division made sense since the subject of the conference was, after all, Europe. But Roosevelt scratched out Dunn's name and in its place put that of Stettinius's favourite assistant, Alger Hiss.

Hiss had entered the State Department through the good graces of Frank Sayre. After serving in the Far Eastern Division he was promoted in spring 1944, at the age of thirty-nine, to the State Department's Office of Special Political Affairs, where within a few months he was named deputy director. The Office had but one objective, the creation of the United Nations Organization. Hiss had became 'Mr UN'.[*]

One could imagine nobody more American than Alger Hiss. In the 1760s the Hiss family had sailed from Holland, Germany or Switzerland – his aunts and uncles could never agree on which – into Baltimore, and there they stayed. The curious first name 'Alger' was part of a good old Southern tradition of adopting the surname of a spouse or close friend as a Christian name for one's offspring; in this case it came from his grand-father's friend, Russell Alexander Alger, who had been a famous general in the Civil War (though after his appalling performance as Secretary of War during the Spanish War, 'Algerism' came to mean 'inefficiency').

Like Washington DC at the turn of the last century, Baltimore and the East Shore farm, where Hiss spent his summers, still had a Southern flavour about them. Manual labour was performed by blacks (ex-slaves or the sons of slaves) while the whites lived in a certain gentility; Hiss would always have a quiet way of speaking. His father had made a mistaken attempt to buy up a cotton mill in South Carolina. 'Leave Baltimore?' said his wife. 'Never!' Hiss's father promptly committed suicide by slitting his throat with a razor. Hiss was only three at the time.

Hiss excelled in Biblical Studies and became a great friend of the local Episcopal priest. At Johns Hopkins, the local university, he was voted the 'most popular man in his class', the Most Prominent in Student Activities,

[*] Until November 1944 the 'United Nations' (the original name of the Allies) was of course officially referred to as the 'World Organization'. A confusion between the two terms continued through the first months of 1945.

winner as Best All-Around Man, runner-up as Most Perfect Gentleman, and came second as Leading Politician. The cult politician at Johns Hopkins was Woodrow Wilson, who had been a graduate student there forty years earlier.[22]

He went on to Harvard Law School and, coming within the top $1\frac{1}{2}$ per cent of his class, was elected to the editorial board of the Harvard Law Review where, with the onset of the Great Depression, he made contributions on labour law. It may not have been the golden age of labourers, but it was the age of opportunity for bright Harvard law students; he became a clerk in Washington DC to Oliver Wendell Holmes, justice of the Supreme Court and hero to this day of all American lawyers.

It was not the happiest time for Hiss; his sister Mary Ann committed suicide while his elder brother, Bosey, died of drink at the age of twenty-six. Holmes became for Hiss the kind of father that he had never had. 'The intellectual excitement of being with him was just extraordinary,' he said. He used to visit Holmes at his summer home and read aloud to him at night. 'He was probably the most handsome man I have ever seen. He had marvelous swirling mustachios, white, plenty of hair, all white, very blue eyes, lovely coloring, lovely ruddy cheeks, and a gorgeous voice. He had this marvelous ringing laugh, as Roosevelt did.'[23]

Hiss liked to admire great men and great causes. The years of the Great Depression moved him. Like many who enjoy plunging into old books, Hiss would regret the way words like 'National Emergency' depreciate so rapidly. But he would repeat as an old man that, on hearing mention of the 'National Emergency' of the 1930s, 'the words stir me.'[24]

Frank Sayre, who introduced him into the State Department, had been one of his former professors. Hiss worked on trade agreements, which naturally put him in contact with Harry Dexter White of the Treasury Department. By 1944 he was working on the United Nations project full-time.

Alger Hiss dominated the Dumbarton Oaks Conference that summer and autumn just as Harry Dexter White had controlled Bretton Woods. It was an entirely American affair. After the conference he and Stettinius went on a speaking tour of the United States to convince their countrymen of the justice of their cause. Hiss was the perfect spokesman. He was a scholar, he knew his history, he was a tall, striking presence in public who could make a complicated problem look simple – like Harry Dexter White. And there was this one other important parallel: just like White, he had been working since the mid-1930s as a Soviet agent.

Thus the world found itself in 1945 at the conclusion of catastrophe, with a whole series of international institutions – ranging from commercial agreements, to exchange rates, to war credits and loans, to the administration of territories without governments, to an ambulating world without citizenship, to the United Nations itself – which had been imposed by the United States. But even more important was the fact that all the 'charters' and constitutions of these world institutions had been composed by America's leading Soviet agents. It is one of the crucial elements of the transition from war to peace in 1945.

Today, there cannot be an atom of doubt about Hiss's role as a Soviet agent, though Hiss himself denied it to the day he died in 1996. The VENONA intercepts are proof to the contrary. Just after the Yalta Conference, with Hiss nominated Secretary General of the United Nations Conference in San Francisco, a message from the Washington 'Resident', Anatoli Borisovich Gromov, of the Soviet Ministry of State Security (MGB) was sent to his Moscow superiors on 30 March 1945. Its contents were recorded by the US Army's secret security organization in Arlington Hall, Virginia:

1. ALES [Hiss] has been working with the NEIGHBORS [Soviet military intelligence, GRU] continuously since 1935.
2. For some years past he has been the leader of a small group of the NEIGHBORS' probationers, for the most part consisting of his relations [probably his wife Priscilla or 'Prossy', and his younger brother Donie].
3. The group and ALES himself work on obtaining military information only. Materials on the BANK [the State Department] allegedly interest NEIGHBORS very little and he does not produce them regularly.
4. All the last few years ALES has been working with POL [probably PAL, Nathan Gregory Silvermaster, head of a network within the US Government], who also meets other members of the group occasionally.
5. Recently ALES and his whole group were awarded Soviet decorations.
6. After the YALTA Conference, when he had gone to Moscow, a Soviet personage in a very responsible position (ALES gave to understand that it was Comrade VYSHINSKY [Deputy Soviet Foreign Minister and Prosecutor during the Purges]) allegedly got in touch with ALES and at the behest of the Military NEIGHBORS passed on to him their gratitude and so on.[25]

The VENONA transcripts were only rendered public in the late 1990s. They were never used in court because, until the collapse of the Soviet Union in 1991, the US Army refused to reveal the existence of its huge code-breaking operation in Virginia.

But one hardly needed VENONA to become suspicious of Hiss's activities. Even without the transcripts, the affair became by 1948 the Hiss Case, with a capital 'C'. It created a sea-change in American politics. It would be America's equivalent of the Dreyfus Affair: just as no one can understand the passions of French politics during the early twentieth century without reference to Captain Alfred Dreyfus, so no one can begin to approach post-war American politics without familiarity with this son of Baltimore, Alger Hiss, chief architect of the United Nations. There was one difference: Dreyfus was innocent, Hiss was not.

The Hiss Case would first gain notoriety through public hearings of the misnamed 'House Un-American Activities Committee' (HUAC), which had been set up in 1938 – the year Republicans gained control of the House of Representatives – to investigate politically extreme groupuscules that seemed to be springing up all over the country. By the 1940s it was concentrating almost exclusively on Communism – and was doing its job very badly, seeking headline-grabbing cases and generally pronouncing the most ridiculous charges. It undoubtedly would have died a natural death from public shame had there not appeared on its benches in 1947 an able young Californian lawyer, turned freshman congressman, called Richard M. Nixon. By 1953 Nixon was Vice-President. In 1968 he was elected thirty-seventh President of the United States.

The Hiss Case made Nixon. Indeed, it followed him right through his long, controversial political career. The Hiss Case moved both reason and unreason in America. Some have even argued that it provided the very dividing line of contemporary American politics and culture.[26]

HUAC was misnamed because, as Hiss's own story proved, there was nothing more American than being a Communist or sympathizing with the Communists in the 1930s and '40s. The Marxist one-dimensional schema of history fitted in well with America's own one-dimensional visions of Manifest Destiny: all roads of civilization led to America, all science, technology and economic progress led to the 'American way of life'. One could hardly blame an American, who had lived through the dark 1930s, for thinking that there was something wrong with 'capitalism', or for hoping that some sort of progressive alternative would emerge from the world war. As W. M. Kiplinger put it in his wartime guide to Washington, 'if the planned economy of war works reasonably well, it undoubtedly will be changed over and adapted for peace.'[27]

Where was the place to look if the future lay in 'planned economy'? For educated Americans it was in the sanitized books they read about the Soviet Union. There was obviously a partnership that could be made between the New Deal of continental America and the New Socialism of the continental Soviet Union. In rising China Communists would co-operate with Nationalists to wipe out the last remnants of Fascist Japan. The only barrier between them were the old-fashioned European 'imperialists' with their failing colonies. So thought Roosevelt. And so thought Alger Hiss.

Hiss's links to Communism first developed during his three years at Harvard Law School – there could be nothing more American than that. His election to the *Law Review* drew his attention to labour law. On a practical level, it brought him into contact with the young rising lawyers and bureaucrats of Henry Wallace's 'Triple A', the Agricultural Adjustment Administration. Many of them had organized small Marxist study groups that sought a definition of the rights of sharecroppers as much as those of industrial labourers. Through his friends in the 'Triple A', Hiss, when he moved to a law firm in New York, joined the International Juridical Association (the IJA) that likewise produced studies on labour and farm problems. That put him just one step away from the 'Movement'.

In 1935 he joined a small Communist network, the 'Ware Group', in which a leading member was a Columbia graduate and journalist, Whittaker Chambers. Chambers was a man haunted by melancholy and doubt. He, too, in effect had no father – his parents were estranged – and his brother's suicide had been one of the major traumas of his youth. Doubt led Chambers to defect from the Party in 1938. For a year he wandered alone, in fear of being murdered. In 1939 he started to provide information to the FBI.

Incredibly, the FBI did nothing with it. It was only in 1942 that a formal report was prepared and passed through the State Department to the President. Roosevelt – who considered the Soviet Union his 'Grand Ally' and who never tolerated Republican charges of being 'soft on Communism' – chucked it away.

That is the chief reason why the trials of Alger Hiss only became the 'Hiss Case' in 1948. But the real turning-point of the affair – the events which determined Hiss's fate – occurred three years earlier, in the last months of the European war, indeed in its last weeks. This was no mere coincidence.

Whittaker Chambers was not a rich man. The chance of his lifetime came when in 1939 he got a job, through one of the men who had persuaded him to quit the Communist Party, at *Time* magazine in New York. *Time* was the bible for news and information for Americans during the war years. In 1944 a special European edition was printed in Paris for distribution among US servicemen.

It covered the whole spectrum of American political opinion – that is, by 1945 its contributors were either pro-Soviet or anti-Soviet. The pro-Soviets easily outweighed the anti-Soviets. The editorial contradictions within this popular magazine in early 1945 are visible at every turn: here is a song of praise to the heroic generals of the Red Army advancing into the heart of Nazi Germany; there an account of Communist violence in the Balkans; here a leading article on the feats of Tito and his Partisans; there a map with half of Europe painted black to indicate Stalin's territorial ambitions.[28] *Time* magazine was as divided as American opinion; the resultant tensions spread like poison gas down its office corridors.

The anti-Soviets came off worst. Calvin Fixx experienced a nervous breakdown, Sam Welles had to take leave of absence and, in the end, finished up working for the State Department (in the 'European Division', of course). Chambers himself was constantly subjected to character smears, rumours that he had spent time in an insane asylum, jokes about his bad teeth and poor health. He lived in constant fear of assassination. His office door was always closed. For lunch (a meal he rarely risked) he would run for the lift, cross the street to the subway, take a fast but devious course through the ground floor of Macy's and quickly munch a bit of ham and bread in the sandwich shop opposite. For most of his career at *Time* he was stuck with the position of editor of the Books Review Section. He did briefly, before his second heart attack, realize his ambition and become editor of Foreign News when its former editor, John Osborne, left for Europe to report on the battle in Normandy. It was a Pyrrhic victory. Osborne returned to New York and set up at *Time* a competing, pro-Soviet 'International Department'.

The director of *Time*, Henry Luce, was a man of exceptional diplomatic ability. He somehow managed to keep the two warring sides working together and produce his magazine once a week. The creation of the 'International Department' was the kind of compromise that he was constantly having to make. But he gave Chambers the support he deserved. 'I have just been told, in a highly confidential manner,' Luce joked at an editorial meeting at the beginning of 1945, 'that Stalin is, after all, a Communist.'[29]

Chambers by now was so ill that he was limited to working from his farmhouse in Westminster, Maryland. Just after the conclusion of the Yalta Conference, as Hiss was preparing for his trip out to San Francisco to open the first United Nations Conference, Chambers composed a feature article called 'The Ghosts of Yalta'. It is as fine a piece of polemical journalism as Zola's '*J'accuse*', which opened the Dreyfus Affair. The shadows of Tsar Nicholas and his murdered family are caught gazing down from the roof of their Yusupov Palace into the hall of the meeting place between the Big Three. With the encouragement of Tsarina Alexandra, Nicholas has become a member of the Soviet Communist Party. He thinks the world of Stalin is the key to the future. Along comes the Muse of History, Clio, to join the imperial ghosts. The great thing about Stalin, explains Nicholas, is 'that he understands how to adapt revolutionary tactics to the whirling spirals of history'. 'Even peace', adds Alexandra, chanting her new Marxist prayer, 'may be only a tactic of struggle.' Nicholas predicts that Britain and America will fall apart with the peace. Clio does not join the ghosts in their human jubilation. 'Two faiths are at issue,' she wisely cautions. If the Big Three below fail to come to a practical accord there will be, says Clio, 'more revolutions, greater proscriptions, bloodshed and human misery'. But, she adds, she never gets involved in human folly 'because I never expect human folly to learn much from history'. Why study the errors of the past? It is of such little use.[30]

At that moment on the stage at Yalta Hiss had greatly angered Churchill with his novel proposition of UN 'trusteeships'. 'The Prime Minister inter-rupted with great vigor', read the Bohlen minutes for the plenary of 9 February, 'to say that he did not agree with one single word of this report on trusteeships. He said that he had not been consulted nor had he heard of the subject up to now. He said that under no circumstances would he ever consent to forty or fifty nations thrusting interfering fingers into the life's existence of the British Empire.' 'I absolutely refuse to engage myself in that [Territorial Trusteeships] without consultation with the domin-ions,' Churchill is quoted as saying in Hiss's own minutes. 'I will not have one scrap of the British Empire [lost]. I will not consent to a representa-tion of the British Empire going to any conference where we will be placed in the dock and asked to defend ourselves. Never, Never, Never.'[31]

Hiss, by now director of the State Department's Office of Special Political Affairs – its UN planning section – wrote back to Washington that 'our British friends were definitely not helpful. The Russians on this, as on almost all other issues, were cooperative and conciliatory.'[32] Hiss was certainly not a man who furthered the Anglo-American 'special relation-ship'. Despite this, it was agreed on the last full day of the Yalta Conference that Hiss would act as Secretary General at the opening meeting of the United Nations on 25 April in San Francisco – the City by the Bay being chosen by Stettinius as a result of a dream he had had the previous evening, so realistic that he could feel the fresh air of the Pacific.[33]

Hiss's troubles began on his return to the United States, with the rapid deterioration of relations between the Western Allies and Russia over

Poland. At the same time the FBI began to get jittery over Hiss's speedy rise within the State Department and decided not only to review the information it had received from Chambers, but also contacted him again for more details. Roosevelt, confident in a Soviet partnership in peace to the end, died in early April and his replacement, Harry S. Truman, was a man of an altogether different mould. In July a new Secretary of State was nominated, James Byrnes, in place of Stettinius, Hiss's patron. A review of the department's chief personnel began.

Hiss, 'chief cook and bottle-washer' of the United Nations, must have had some sense, by the autumn of 1945, that his career had reached its peak. Flying over to London in January 1946 for a second session of the United Nations, he readily accepted the offer, from John Foster Dulles, Republican adviser to the American delegation, to become president of the Carnegie Endowment for International Peace in New York. It was a prestigious post. But it was entirely independent of the State Department. In February, immediately after his return from London, Secretary Byrnes told him: 'You're in trouble. I've just heard that there's some congressman who's going to make a speech on the floor of Congress saying that you're a Red.' America's great Hiss Case was about to explode.[34]

3 Poles without Warsaw

Poland would never be much of an issue in the American press, nor would it be considered significant by historians of the Hiss Case. But Poland was the immediate cause of Hiss's troubles because it rendered the policy of a continued American alliance with the Soviet Union impossible; it made an absurdity of Yalta's 'Declaration on Liberated Europe'.

In March, Churchill's tone on Russian behaviour in Poland turned harsh. Part of this may have been political: following his report to the Commons on 27 February on the 'Crimea Conference' – in which he spoke of the Russian armies being received by the Poles 'with great joy', with 'none of that terrible business of underground armies being shot by both sides' – there was a bitter two-day parliamentary debate that ended with twenty-seven Conservatives (all former appeasers of Nazi Germany) voting against him; Churchill needed Conservative support in the forthcoming elections. But, crucially, what provoked Churchill's anger in March was the international news, and particularly the intelligence reports on Poland. On 6 March, Vyshinsky, acting as Stalin's envoy in Bucharest, brutally imposed a Communist minority government on the Romanian king. Molotov, while remaining Minister of Foreign Affairs, got a similar job in Poland – reports flooded through to London of shootings, arrests and mass deportations.

Though he recognized Romania as lying within a Russian sphere of influence, Churchill was upset by the recent turn of events. He wrote to Roosevelt on 8 March warning that with this Communist government there would be 'an indiscriminate purge of Anti-Communist Romanians, who will be accused of Fascism much on the lines of what has been happening in Bulgaria' which he had also conceded to Russia. Churchill underlined, in his letter, 'the much more important issue of Poland'. He feared the 'well-known Communist technique is being applied behind closed doors in Poland either directly by the Russians or through their Lublin puppets'.[35]

Why should Poland be more important than Romania or Bulgaria? In the first place, Britain had gone to war over Poland. But more significant was the fact that Western Allies were ready to move across the Rhine: the whole German northern plain was opening up to their armies. As in the peace settlement of 1815, a line could now be drawn across the plain and the new Communist Tsar forced to parley. There was no such possibility over Romania.

Nazi repression and round-ups following the Warsaw Rising – under the eyes of the waiting Red Army – had decapitated the Polish Underground State and deprived all Poles of their capital. Under the bleakest circumstances, the Home Army managed to keep going in the western provinces of Poland until the first weeks of 1945, the moment Russian troops crossed the Vistula. One week later, on 19 January, the Home Army dissolved itself and 50,000 Polish soldiers, who had resisted the Germans for more than five years, laid down their arms; they were virtually all arrested by the NKVD, Smersh and their Polish counterparts.

Yet there remained in Poland, largely thanks to a few uncompromising remnants of the Home Army, an Underground 'Council of National Unity', directed by a Polish Socialist, Kazimierz Pużak. On receiving the text of the Yalta communiqué on Poland, the Council passed, on 21 February, a resolution protesting 'in strongest terms the one-sided decisions of the Conference'. All the same, the Council felt 'compelled to submit to these decisions prompted by its desire to see in them the only avenue – under the present circumstances – of salvaging Poland's independence'. So the Council, despite the waves of Communist terror that surrounded it, was ready to talk.

This isolated Council kept up radio contact with the London government-in-exile, which itself was but a windswept sand-bar of the island fortress it had once been under General Sikorski.

Mikołajczyk had hoped he would get support from Roosevelt after his re-election. But Roosevelt remained as silent as ever. Churchill gave no encouragement. On 24 November 1944 Mikołajczyk resigned, pulling out the whole Peasant Party and several other moderate representatives with him. The new London Prime Minister was Tomasz Arciszewski, an old associate of Piłsudski – what remained of the Polish government-in-exile had no intention of either yielding Poland's eastern territories or negoti-ating with Stalin and his toadies.[36]

Churchill would have nothing to do with this new intransigent government-in-exile. But he maintained his contacts with Mikołajczyk in the hope of saving the 'Grand Alliance' – still the essential tool for defeating Hitler.

All that remained of Warsaw in January, when it was 'liberated' by the Soviets, was the poor suburb east of the Vistula, Praga. The Jewish pianist, Władysław Szpilman, who had survived the Ghetto Rising, the Warsaw Rising and the Nazi repressions that followed, was a witness of the city's 'liberation'. He recalled walking down what remained of a once busy main road that was now totally deserted; 'there was not a single intact building as far as the eye could see.' 'I had to clamber over mountains of rubble as if they were scree slopes'; his feet got tangled in 'ripped telephone lines and tramlines, and scraps of fabric that had once decorated flats'. Under a former barricade he found a skeleton – 'it must have been of a girl since long blonde hair could be seen on the skull', and on the bones of the right arm was a red and white armband 'where the letters AK [Home Army] had been shot away'. When Warsaw was liberated, stormy winds rattled the scrap-iron in the ruins and 'snow fell from the darkening leaden sky'.[37] This was the moment the Germans began evacuating, by foot, the inmates of their death camps in the east.

By February 1945 despondency had given way to despair among the London Poles and the Council in Poland. Yet it was the feeble radio signals maintained between them that at last alerted the British Foreign Office to the abominable reality.

'Following is summary of "information received from Poland" trans-mitted to me by the Polish Prime Minister here,' Churchill wired Roosevelt on 10 March. Churchill's list of extortions, political crimes and atrocities fills four pages of the tightly printed collection of correspondence between the two Western leaders: '. . . 24 January 45. Miechow District: A number of members of the Home Army have been shot in Miechow and Slomniki. Radziwill was arrested in Balice, and 40 landowners and farmers in Miechow district for belonging to the Home Army or approving it. The

Polish Workers Party is undertaking the work of denunciation . . . 27 January 45. Piotrkow District: . . . The population is treating the new authorities with great reserve. Soviet paratroops are hunting for leaders of the Home Army. Two have already been shot. Soviet officers have announced that the Home Army is to be exterminated as Fascist . . .' The list went on to cover dozens of such incidents. The Sovietization of Poland was said to be proceeding apace; agrarian reform was being carried out in the territories taken by the Soviet armies. 'In Sandomierz, more Poles have been arrested during the few months of Soviet occupation than during the whole five years of German occupation.' In Lwów province, mass arrests had taken place 'in which 60 per cent of those arrested were Poles, among them 21 university professors, priests and all classes of society . . . In February 1945, 125 cattle trucks from Grodno Province and 242 from Białystok Province, containing arrested Poles, were sent off to Russia. The NKVD are keeping those arrested in cellars, air raid shelters and in every possible place.'[38]

Even today these facts are difficult to accept. Poland, like much of Central and Eastern Europe, remains the great hole in our memory. The poet Czesław Miłosz, master of the phenomenon, has described a temporary prison in medieval Cracow, opposite the place where he was working on his Robinson Crusoe film: 'We saw scores of 'young men behind the barred windows on the ground floor. Some had thrust their faces into the sun in an effort to get a tan. Others were fishing with wire hooks for the bits of paper which had been tossed out on the sand from neighbouring cells. Standing in the window, we observed them in silence.' Miłosz had survived the Rising, escaped from Warsaw and, through his good connections, had been hired by the Communists to make his grand film; that, he explains, is why he became a poet.[39]

In the second week of March the Soviets sent a secret message to members of Pużak's Underground Council inviting them to an 'exploratory meeting' with Colonel Ivanov, who represented the Soviet High Command in Poland. The Council smelt a rat. Nevertheless, after sending an intermediary, who received all the honours the Soviets could dream of, the whole Council set off to a place just outside Warsaw to meet the Russian colonel. They were immediately kidnapped and hauled off to a waiting plane; they ended up in Moscow's Lubyanka gaol.

Churchill, caught in the dilemma between his 'alliance' and the truth, pleaded with Mikołajczyk to keep channels of communication open with Stalin. Eventually – on 15 June – Mikołajczyk complied, bravely flying out to Moscow with a few of his associates for discussions with the Marshal. The day before, the much publicized trial of the sixteen members of the

Underground Council had begun; they were all sent to the Gulag, with sentences ranging from four months to ten years for 'illegal activities, hostility towards the Soviet Union, collaboration with the Germans, sabotage and diversionary activities carried out against the Red Army'.[40]

By March, Churchill was fully aware of the wicked process. 'Poland has lost her frontier,' he cabled Roosevelt on 13 March. 'Is she now to lose her freedom?' He was getting replies from America that were evasive, contradictory or just straight pompous. 'You know, I am sure, that our great desire is to keep in step with you,' he rather desperately wired on 16 March. But he must have wondered in which direction he was stepping.

One rumour going about at the time was that Harry Hopkins was drafting Roosevelt's letters; in fact, Roosevelt's confrère of the New Deal was now in the Mayo Clinic, just outside Washington, dying of cancer. The handwriting of the marginalia points rather to Admiral Leahy, the President's former ambassador to Vichy. Leahy was working with various aides in the State Department: make a 'truce' with the Soviets, they suggested, be patient, no dramatic ultimatums, please – 'I [the novelist's "I"] consider it essential to base ourselves squarely on the Crimea decisions themselves and not allow any other considerations . . . to cloud the issue at this time.'

'Our failure in Poland will result in a set up there on the new Romanian model,' blasted back Churchill. 'In other words, Eastern Europe will be shown to be excluded from the terms of the Declaration of Liberated Europe and you and we shall be excluded from any jot of influence there.'[41]

Roosevelt himself spent March on his estate in Hyde Park. He travelled down to Washington on the 29th, signed a few papers and left that night for Warm Springs, Georgia. There he ate gruel, examined his stamp collection, and sat for a portrait painted by Mrs Elizabeth Shoumatoff, a refugee from revolutionary Russia. By April his health seemed to improve; he even began to write. On 11 April he drafted a presidential cable of his own to Churchill. 'I would minimize the general Soviet problem as much as possible because these problems, in one form or another, seem to arise every day and most of them straighten out . . . We must be firm, however, and our course thus far is correct.'[42] 'Minimize', 'in one form or another', and 'be firm' – it certainly bears his familiar, prevaricating tone.

The next morning, a Thursday, Mrs Shoumatoff was mixing her paints while Roosevelt sat by his card table – the pouch of papers from Washington lay upon it. 'Shoumie', as she was called, noticed how the President's face had regained colour; that awful grey appearance had gone. The butler

423

came in to lay a table for lunch. 'We have fifteen minutes more of work,' declared Roosevelt. Then he lifted his right hand, jerkily moved it across his forehead and, without a word more, collapsed.[43]

One of the cities most affected by the news of Roosevelt's death was London. The inhabitants were just recovering from what many considered the worst winter of the war. Morale was very low; there seemed to be more vandalism in the stations, more litter in the streets, more rudeness on the buses and in the food queues. The announcement about Roosevelt's death came in the same week that the first newsreels of the liberation of the Belsen concentration camp were being shown in the cinemas. It made just too much of a contrast between good and evil in the world – on top of the rigours of everyday life in London. Everybody was crying that Friday over the loss of Britain's 'staunchest friend'. 'Even my old landlady was crying,' recorded the writer C. P. Snow. 'The Underground was full of tearful faces – far more than if Winston had died, I'm sure' – which gives some indication of London's mood as the six-year war drew, haltingly, to its close.[44]

Down in the cellars and bunkers of Berlin's Beelzebub there was brief celebration: 'Mein Führer, I congratulate you! Roosevelt is dead,' Joseph Goebbels telephoned from beneath the rubble of the Propaganda Ministry. It was written in the stars, he said, that this was the turning point. Champagne bottles were opened.

Goebbels had been reading every night to the Führer extracts from Carlyle's *Frederick the Great*; he had been discussing two horoscopes, of 1919 and 1933, found in Himmler's archives. In his diaries Goebbels claimed he never believed in the nonsense, but horoscopes and poor Thomas Carlyle had considerable propaganda effect on the high officials, the bonzes of Nazidom. Perhaps some of it rubbed off on Goebbels himself. As in March, he continued to visit the Eastern Front every week. On Friday, 13 April, he was at Küstrin. He had been lecturing the officers on the main thesis of his 'Historical Necessity and Justice', citing Carlyle's example of the death of Tsarina Elizabeth, an event which had saved the Seven Years War for the Prussian King Frederick. On his way back to Berlin he heard the news of Roosevelt's death. Bombs were raining down upon the city; both the Adlon Hotel and the Chancellery were in flames. As his car drew up to the ruins of the Propaganda Ministry a reporter yelled out, 'Herr Reichsminister, Roosevelt is dead.' One of Goebbels's secretaries remembered the Minister jumping out of his car. 'I shall never forget the look on his face, which we could see in the light of Berlin blazing . . . He was in an ecstasy.'[45]

Parisians were more concerned about the tens of thousands of '*déportés*', who began to appear at their gates, and the rising temper of the French Communist Party; Roosevelt – with reason – had never been considered the guardian of French liberties. Some even had the impression that the Americans would go so far as to send out a special mission to Sigmaringen to retrieve Pétain and set him up again as President.

Moscow, with Stalin retightening his grip to meet the 'imperialist Fascists', delayed the announcement by more than a day. In truth, the Westerners had never been Moscow's allies.

Booming, bureaucratic Washington was in mourning. But here, with the benefit of hindsight, one may note another effect of FDR's death: it pulled the rug from under the feet of the Soviet agents within the American civil service.

4 Repatriating the citizenless

Even as late as April, Hitler and Goebbels held on to the idea that the alliance against them would break up before it was too late. What they could never admit was that the prospect of their own defeat was the only thing that kept their enemies together. As for the Western Allies, they clung to a different dream, that they would work united for ever: they imagined that harmoniously together Britain, the United States and the Soviet Union would construct the post-war peace – such an illusion occurs at the end of many wars. Roosevelt stuck to it to the end of his life; Churchill developed doubts over the last nine months of the war (beginning with the Warsaw Rising). But neither Churchill nor Roosevelt imagined that the 'Grand Alliance' would fall to pieces the instant Germany signed her unconditional surrender.

The Western governments and administrations were even slower than their leaders to adapt to the rapid pace of events at the war's close. They had developed many plans – even institutions for the peace – but did not see the developing reality. The Germans would sign their surrender and somehow the Alliance would go on. As for popular opinion, its faith in 'our heroic Russian friends' was widespread and long-standing. To this was added the British conviction that their 'special relationship' with the United States would endure into the new world order.

The ideal on which these dreams were based – the 'Liberated Europe' declared at Yalta in February – had already lost all meaning by March. In Romania and Poland, as earlier in Bulgaria, Soviet 'popular democracy' demonstrated that it could be no friend of parliamentary democracy in the West.

Less noticed was the developing tension between Britain and her 'staunchest friend', the USA. Most fundamental of all were the declining fortunes of Britain's finances, greatly aggravated by the policies of the US Treasury and State Department which aimed to reduce Britain's liquid assets. Secondly, there was a widening military disagreement on how to defeat Germany. Thirdly, there developed out of the first two facts a difference in approach to the hordes of 'displaced persons' thrown up by the war. This would lead to confusion and tragedy.

In the last twelve months of the war British public finances entered the realm of the unreal. The Treasury was balancing its accounts through a combination of American Lend-Lease and Canadian Mutual Aid, at a rate of about £800 million ($3.2 billion) a year. It was accumulating a debt in the sterling area of £700 million ($2.8 billion) a year. Keynes was forecasting a deficit of £2 billion ($8 billion) over Britain's first three to five years of peace – a serious underestimate as it turned out.

The best financial hope for Britain would be a rapid end to the war in Europe and a prolongation of the war with Japan under the terms of 'Stage II' of Lend-Lease; this would give Britain a chance of simultaneously demobilizing and concentrating on her export trade, while at the same time benefiting from American aid. But if a late 'Victory in Europe' was swiftly followed by a 'Victory in Japan' Britain would be facing, as Keynes called it, 'financial Dunkirk'. The United States in the meantime kept up the pressure for a multilateral convention on trade while remaining completely silent on the future of Lend-Lease at the end of the Japanese war – it was a situation that recalled, from the British point of view, the American silence in 1918–19. In February, at the conclusion of the Yalta Conference, Keynes hoped Roosevelt would have a creative 'brainwave' like that of his Lend-Lease address of 1940. But the gods conspired that it would be otherwise.[46]

There was a fuss over military logistics, not unrelated to Britain's dire financial state. Over the course of March, with the Allies crossing the Rhine while famine spread in German-occupied Holland, the Americans demanded that Montgomery's 21st Army Group replenish its growing requirements from stockpiles in Britain. Current demands, stated Admiral Leahy, 'present most difficult problems of shipping availability and inland transport in the United States'. Churchill angrily replied that existing supplies of meat, sugar, fats and dairy produce came nowhere near meeting the desperate needs of the areas now opening up to the armies. The armies were weakened: but those who really suffered were the citizens whom the armies had 'displaced'.[47]

'Displacement' was the key word in 1945. The squabbles over command boiled down to the fact that Americans in North-Western Europe now outnumbered the British and Canadians by more than three to one.[*]

After Montgomery's recent comments to the press about the realities of the 'Bulge', the Americans were becoming more and more rattled over British command. Field Marshal Alexander withdrew his candidature as Deputy Supreme Commander with Eisenhower and remained with what was left of his armies in Italy. They made up a much diminished force; all they could do now was hold the Rimini–Pisa line, a mountainous area south of the Po valley, and wait for the Reich's inevitable collapse north of the Alps. This, so the American Chiefs of Staff forecast at Yalta, would take place 'at the earliest' on 1 July and 'at the latest' 31 December 1945 – a year or more later than Montgomery had forecast in August 1944. It was not an encouraging thought for the men of the British Treasury.

Britain felt increasingly sidelined. Victory over Germany in the American view would be achieved by the only alliance which really mattered, that between the Americans and the Russians. Admiral Leahy and General Marshall had insisted, on their first day in Yalta, on their 'direct liaison' with Russian command while the British, faithful to the old-fashioned idea of European alliance, wanted to maintain the authority of the Combined Chiefs of Staff – the Second World War's equivalent of the Supreme Allied Council. The Americans were only interested in a bilateral line of communication with the military command of Communist Russia. The British wanted the politicians brought into the settlement; Marshall and Eisenhower thought the defeat of Germany was purely a military affair, between American and Russian commanders.

But there was a catch. During the second plenary session between the Big Three, Roosevelt had said he 'did not believe that American troops would stay in Europe for more than two years'. Naturally Congress and public opinion in America would support any 'reasonable measures designed to safeguard the future peace', but he did not think this would require 'the maintenance of an appreciable American force in Europe'.[48] So the Americans and the Russians would win the European war, and then the Americans would withdraw. Small wonder Churchill made such an enthusiastic case for the role of the French in the occupation of Germany and the peace settlement – Britain and France would have to face the entire Red Army alone. It sounded like the nightmare of 1919 all over again. Yet this kind of ancient political history was of no concern to such modern generals as Eisenhower and Marshall.

[*] At the time of the Yalta Conference there were about 400,000 British and Canadian, 1.5 million American and 100,000 French troops poised to capture the Rhine.

One may well question the wisdom of Churchill's 1944 Italian strategy of pushing into Istria and outmarching, through the 'Ljubljana Gap', the Red Army in its advance towards Austria. But the deliberate winding down of the Italian campaign by the Americans certainly had the opposite effect: the way to Vienna as well as the north-eastern Adriatic was opened to the Red Army and its allies, Tito's Yugoslav Partisans.

There had been a civil war going on in Yugoslavia. All those 'displaced persons' who found themselves on the wrong side of Communism were forced northwards into a trap, their backs up against the Alps. When the British finally advanced into the area in May they encountered scenes more akin to medieval warfare – or Germany's Thirty Years War of the seventeenth century – than the picture normally imagined of Europe at war in the 1940s. Ancient history had its relevance.

The term 'displaced person' (DP) had its origins in the chaotic situation which the Allies had discovered when they set foot in Italy in 1943. The term itself gives an idea of the psychology of the administrators who invented it: a 'displaced' thing, like a vase that a careless maid has stood on the bedside table instead of on the mantelpiece in the drawing room, a pair of boots in the pantry cupboard instead of on the shoe shelf in the cloakroom, a lost bunch of keys – one day, when we eventually get the house in order, these 'displaced' pieces will be returned to where they belong.

UNRRA – the United Nations Relief and Rehabilitation Administration – was created in November 1943 to get wartime 'displaced persons' back to the places where they belonged. The 'United Nations' in this case referred not to the United Nations Organization (which did not yet exist) but to the forty-four 'allies' who had agreed, at least on paper, to overthrow the Nazi tyranny. Ironically, Italy was not among them because nobody had yet been able to decide whether this ruined, ungovernable Mediterranean peninsula was friend or foe. It took another year before UNRRA moved in, by which time the material conditions in 'Italy' were, in places, like Central Africa but more densely populated.

By definition UNRRA's function was temporary. It was dominated by military needs: clear the roads so that the Allied armies can get on with their job; if those 'displaced persons' have nowhere to go then put them into makeshift camps and get them shipped 'home' as quickly as possible. This seemed at least feasible in 1943 when DPs numbered in their tens of thousands. But by late summer 1944 there were millions who were no longer 'at home'. With the entry of the Allies – not wholly united – into the Reich in early 1945, their numbers reached into tens of millions, though the administrators of UNRRA, like policemen with crime statistics, did everything to limit the figure publicized.

With the cessation of hostilities the situation became worse, not better. The equivalent of entire nations were on the move, mostly by foot or in creaking old wooden wagons drawn by mangy horses, donkeys or men; they had no proper clothing, food or healthcare. When the United Nations Organization was finally established in April 1945 its daily business was almost entirely taken up by this nightmare of a problem, for which not even the First World War had prepared it.

A neat remedy was never to be found. It was not a temporary problem. Displaced Persons had no home to go back to. A Europe of nation states could hardly resolve the difficulty. A peace of free, liberated nations was beside the point. Europe, and the world, had entered the 'age of the refugee', the 'migrant'.[49]

'UNRRA, runnrrah!' sang Churchill, to a Gilbert and Sullivan ditty, in his bathtub. Britain – victorious and in sovereign poverty – was caught in a dilemma. It might be summarized by Anthony Eden's cynical but typical response to a plea from the US Secretary of State in 1943 to evacuate 60,000 or 70,000 Bulgarian Jews facing Nazi extermination: 'If we do that,' commented Eden, 'then the Jews of the world will be wanting us to make similar offers in Poland and Germany. Hitler might well take us up on such an offer and there are simply not enough ships and means of transportation in the world to handle them.'[50]

Given the size and the lack of resources of the country, Britain had in fact proved generous to refugees from Nazi-controlled Central Europe. Around 17,000 German Jews and 8,000 Austrian Jews had found shelter in Britain during the war years, a significant part of the total of over 114,000 refugees who remained in Britain throughout the war. Comparative figures with the United States are somewhat misleading; out of a total of around 400,000 Jews who fled Germany, Austria and Czechoslovakia before 1939, the United States took in 63,000, but the fact is that American immigration laws – up to 1950 – were far more stringent than those of any of the small European countries which escaped Nazi invasion. Switzerland, for example, though often criticized for its closed-door policy, accepted around 50,000 Jewish immigrants – not much fewer than the United States.[51]

Such figures, of course, were a drop in the ocean of mass deportations, exterminations and the whole tide of violence, civil war, defections and 're-defections' that swept through Poland, Russia and the borderlands in the early 1940s. By the spring of 1944 Nazi Germany was employing around 8 million foreign workers, who made up 29 per cent of her industrial force and 20 per cent of her total labour force. Almost 6 million Russian prisoners of war were taken by the Germans in the course of hostilities, though about 3.7 million of them died of cold, starvation or murder – Russia, Nazi authorities repeated, had refused to sign the Geneva Convention of 1929. When Hitler's government, for propaganda purposes, asked in 1941 for a Red Cross inspection of Russian POW camps, it also made an appeal to Moscow for a Russian prisoners' postal service. 'There are no Russian prisoners of war,' retorted Stalin. 'The Russian soldier fights to the death. If he chooses to become a prisoner, he is automatically excluded from the Russian community.' That turned out to be a significant point, not fully digested by the administrators of UNRRA.[52]

By May 1945 there were, in the areas of Europe controlled by the Western Allies, about 7 million people on the move, not including the 7.8 million German soldiers who had surrendered in the closing weeks of the war, nor the 12 million ethnic Germans who were about to be expelled from eastern territories no longer considered a part of Germany. There were 1.2 million Frenchmen in Germany.

The influx westwards of Jewish survivors of the Holocaust, the '*She'erit Ha-pletah*' or the 'Spared' as they called themselves, only began in earnest that autumn and turned into a flood in 1946. There were also Balts, Poles, Belorussians and Ukrainians, some of them vicious Nazi collaborators, others escaping the utopian comforts promised by the Communists. Add to these the homeless created by the liberating bombardments of northern France, Germany, Austria and Italy and the figure of those wandering in Western Europe alone is about equivalent to the total population of England and Wales.

'Citizenship is no longer regarded as something immutable,' the future philosopher of 'totalitarianism', Hannah Arendt, remarked in April 1945, 'and nationality is no longer necessarily identified with state and territory.'[53] She was referring to Western Europe, not the East. For many Europeans at the end of the Second World War the notion of the nation state had lost all meaning.

When UNRRA was set up in the autumn of 1943 its administrators were careful to make the distinction between a 'DP' and a 'refugee'. The two Rs in its title, 'Relief and Rehabilitation', defined its aim: to provide aid to those temporarily 'displaced' by the war and expected to return to their national homelands – Europe was still regarded as a neat collection of nation states whose borders were clearly delineated in black lines on a map. Specifically, UNRRA was not authorized to deal with 'refugees' who, 'for any reason, definitely cannot return to their homes, or have no homes to return to, or no longer enjoy the protection of their Governments'.[54]

That certainly kept UNRRA's totals down. Yet, at the end of the war, their camps were bursting with over 6 million DPs. By July 1945 around half of them had returned to their homelands of France, Italy, Belgium and the Netherlands; but the other half came from what was already being called 'Eastern Europe' – Communist Europe – and they showed no intention at all of returning

The Russians, numerous and obstinate, proved a particular embarrassment. The first signs of the problem, in the West, were reported by British Military Intelligence in a secret paper entitled 'Employment of Russian Natives in France'. It noted, on 21 February 1944, that around 200,000 'Russians' – anti-Soviet national minorities, like the Kalmucks, Georgians and the Cossacks, prisoners of war and forced labour battalions – had already arrived in France and that many more were pouring in.[55] What MI3 was picking up was the product of Hitler's order of the previous October – which had caused such a blow to Vlasov and his supporters within the German command – to transfer all Russian forces within the Wehrmacht to German defences in the West. Over one million 'Soviet citizens' by late 1943 had enlisted in the German army. No other belligerent in the world had experienced such a scale of desertion to the enemy. And, obviously, no authority in the Soviet Union was going to admit it. The British passed on their information to the Soviets; the response was a numb, Muscovite silence.

The reports were proved true on D-Day itself, when the first half-dozen Russians were identified in a haul of German prisoners. Within a couple of weeks George Orwell was telling the strange story of the seizure of two German soldiers with Asiatic faces who spoke to each other in a language that nobody could identify. After long interrogation in England it was finally discovered that they were Tibetans who had strayed with their herds into Soviet territory, had been conscripted into the Red Army, captured by the Germans, and ended up defending a beach in Normandy. By the first week of July, 1,200 Russians in German uniforms had been taken. In August special Russian camps were established outside Worthing, Guildford, Durham and on a desolate moor in Yorkshire.

This soon established a pattern – and Britain's dilemma. Whether captured by the Americans or the British, the Russians inevitably ended up on British territory. After operations opened in the South of France, many of the Russians were shipped across the Mediterranean to North

Africa and then passed on to British camps in Egypt and the Middle East. The Soviet authorities remained silent. The Americans did not show much interest in the problem either.

As the number of Russians in Britain doubled and tripled over the summer months, the British Foreign Office groped for a policy line; Moscow was as mute on this issue as on the simultaneous Rising in Warsaw. Legal advice to the Foreign Office came from Patrick Dean. 'In due course,' he proposed, in his lawyer's language, 'those with whom the Soviet author- ities desire to deal must, subject to what is said below, be handed over to them, and we are not concerned with the fact that they may be shot or otherwise more harshly dealt with than they might be under English law.'[56] Dean's concern seems to have been that, if the British did not repatriate the Russians they held, the Germans, who had moved many of the British prisoners of war eastwards, would turn these over to the Russians.

Dean, in the process, set the policy adopted by the Foreign Office over the next two years: send the Russians home so as not to upset the feel- ings of 'our great ally', the Soviets.[*]

After the Liberation of Paris, the new French Provisional Government, which ran a Russian camp north of Paris and one nearer the front at Châlons, started making noises about France's traditional 'right of asylum' to anyone who asked for it. It was virtually the only issue Americans and Frenchmen could agree on in 1944–5 – an old republican right that went back to the revolutionary days of the late eighteenth century. The British felt totally isolated. But the problem, far from going away, loomed ever larger as the war drew to a close – that is, as the armies of East and West approached each other.

On 4 September,[†] the War Cabinet met to discuss the problem. There were by now around 6,000 Russians camped in England, a number that seemed enormous at the time, though it was a tiny fragment of the hordes the British and the Americans would encounter over the next nine months. The Cabinet's decision to approve the Foreign Office line was kept secret, and so it would remain for thirty years. The Soviet authorities, however,

---

[*] Already, that summer, the Foreign Office faced serious opposition from Lord Selborne, Minister of Economic Warfare, who was also responsible for SOE espionage operations on the Continent. This devout Christian received support from the voluble Bishop of Chichester. The Secretary of State for War, Sir James Grigg, joined the chorus; he thought the idea of forced repatriation a 'very unpleasant business'. Churchill himself was haunted by moral scruples though, being the smallest of the Big Three, he did his best to keep them to himself.

[†] A great republican day in France, much discussed in the Paris press of 1944. It commem- orated the collapse of the Second Empire and the establishment of the republican Government of National Defence during the Franco-Prussian War in 1870.

were informed. They showed their gratitude by sending Ambassador Fedor T. Gusev, an old NKVD agent, round to Eden to complain that Soviet citizens under British guard were being 'mistreated'. Eden, always so grandly English, took care not to provoke his visitor.

The first two shiploads, containing 11,000 Russian 'nationals', left Liverpool on 31 October. Another batch of 6,000 left for the Crimea in March 1945 and, two months later, one more shipload set off. Soviet officials oversaw the departures. There were suicides witnessed on the entry gangplank; at least two men cut their own throats, and one hanged himself. One man jumped overboard in the Straits of Gibraltar; several dived into the Dardanelles. Such events were a nasty foretaste of what was to come.[57]

In addition to the issue of asylum, Britain was having two difficulties in achieving a common policy with the United States. One concerned the Geneva Convention which they had both signed in 1929. The Convention clearly established that the nationality of a prisoner of war was determined by the uniform he bore at his moment of capture; belligerents, in other words, should look no deeper than the uniform. All the Russians had to do was to claim their rights under the Convention to prove that their captors were breaking the law. But few Russians knew the law because the Soviet Union had not signed in 1929. The other major problem, which was raised by the American Joint Chiefs of Staff, was that the use of troopships for repatriation would involve a serious diversion from the main war effort. By the winter of 1944–5, with the number of DPs mounting and the battlefronts widening, this was no mean argument.

Gradually, however, the Americans succumbed to political pressures from three sources: from the British government – which sought a coordinated policy; from Eisenhower at SHAEF – who found himself repatriating some prisoners while holding others in camps; and, not least of all, from the Soviet ambassador in Washington, Andrei Gromyko – who, like his colleague in London, was complaining about American 'mistreatment' of Soviet citizens.

Complete confusion reigned at the Allied Forces Head Quarters (AFHQ) at Caserta in Italy. Harold Macmillan, the British Minister Resident, was according to at least one source 'receiving instructions' from the British Foreign Office,[*] while Alexander Kirk, his American counterpart, was getting no directions at all. The new Secretary of State, Stettinius – suddenly very keen on Soviet cooperation with the opening of Hitler's 'Bulge' offensive – finally wired Kirk on 20 December: 'The policy adopted by

---

[*] This was, as will be seen later, probably not the case. Macmillan seems to have been in as much confusion over the issue as Kirk.

the United States Government . . . is that all claimants to Soviet nationality will be released to the Soviet Government irrespective of whether they wish to be so released.' Translated into English, this meant the American go-ahead for forced repatriation.

The first American batch of Russians – 1,100 from Camp Rupert in Idaho – were sent off just after Christmas, including three men who attempted suicide in the process. The cargo of another 2,600 crossed the Pacific for Vladivostok in February. From there they went for a short spell in the Gulag complex around Vorkuta. Manpower needs, however, allowed many of them to participate in the 'liberation' of Berlin before being sentenced to twenty-five years of forced labour for treason.[58]

All the above thus suggests that between D-Day and Yalta a tacit accord developed between the Western Allies, including the French, over the accelerating problem of refugees and prisoners of war in liberated zones. Political leaders and civil servants had been brought up on the belief that Europe was a collection of sovereign nation states, so their instinct was to 'send them all home'. But they could not send them all home. The Russian problem proved particularly sensitive, because they were dealing with a murderous Communist state and the Russians did not want 'to go home'. Yet the Soviet Union had to be treated as an ally. Gradually through 1944–5 a policy of 'forced repatriation' was introduced without any formal accord being made between the Western Allies. An accord was eventually signed at Yalta in the most farcical conditions. Roosevelt and his party were just leaving, on 11 February, when British and American bureaucrats cobbled together a short text that was then presented to the Soviet officials. The wording of this 'secret accord' – quoted by historians as proof that the forcibly repatriated were 'victims of Yalta' – was so vague that it committed nobody to anything like a formal policy. Every decision was left to commanders in the field, camp guards and local administrators to interpret as they saw fit. It was what we would today call a cop-out. Like the whole war the decisions on repatriation, as contradictory as they were cruel, were made by local underlings – and they determined the fate of millions, tens of millions.[59]

5 Haroldo Macmillano, 'Viceroy of the Mediterranean'

On St George's Day, 23 April 1945 – one week before the surrender of the German armies in Italy – Britain's Minister Resident to Allied Headquarters jumped into a jeep with three colleagues and drove from Bologna twenty miles north-west to the small town of Modena, which the Americans were preparing to take. Macmillan and his three friends got there first. As they rode up to the town hall they noticed a crowd of armed men shouting and embracing; they were Italian Partisans.

'The leader of the Partisans', continues the Minister Resident in his diary, 'kissed me on both cheeks on being told that I was the famous Haroldo Macmillano – said by the BBC to be the ruler and father of the Italian people.' There then followed a two-hour battle during which the Partisans began to 'shoot up the Germans in a remarkably professional way'. Apparently, however, it wasn't all fighting. A photograph of the shuffling Macmillan – his swollen lips peeping out from beneath his moustache and rimless spectacles – was taken that day amidst a crowd of pretty, cheering teenagers: Haroldo Macmillano liberating Modena.[60] The shuffling was a result of machine-gun wounds received at Delville Wood, in the Somme, on 15 September 1916; the thick lips were the product of a plane crash in Algiers in February 1943, when he was nearly burnt to death.

When Macmillan describes Italy during the Second World War it always seems to be autumn, whatever the season. The sands are nearing the bottom of the timer, European civilization is running out; the Fates have taken over man's brief moment on the stage. Macmillan certainly recognized the contrast with the First World War: the commanders, like Macmillan himself, were always present on the front – they were young men, driving around in their open jeeps and and thus making an exhibition of their Boy Scout khaki shorts (which today look so ridiculous); these were not the 'château generals' Macmillan remembered from his youth. Yet the Italian war was just 'one mountain ridge after another', a phrase that has the ring of the old Western Front in it. The ruins of Italy are painted in tragic amber. In Florence the Duomo, Baptistery, Giotto's tower, Palazzo Vecchio, Loggia dei Lanzi, Santa Maria Novella are still standing, but 'all the bridges are destroyed, except the Ponte Vecchio'. Rimini turns out to be a ghost town, with barely an inhabitant in it; 'the town is rather badly damaged, but not irreparably; there are some lovely Renaissance buildings as well as some of earlier date [but] it presents a pretty depressing appearance.' When Macmillan meets the Pope, Pius XII, in the Vatican he is less impressed by 'the little saintly man, rather worried, obviously quite selfless and holy' than by the 'unending suites of rooms, the rich furniture and vast store-house of wealth . . . then a sense of time-lessness – time means nothing here.' Macmillan sometimes gets lost in his classical learning, his reading of Gibbon, Aeschylus, Homer and Virgil. Flying down the Gulf of Corinth in January 1945, in the midst of a Greek civil war, he notes the 'splendid view of Mount Parnassos – snow-covered

– and of the great mountains of the Peloponnese on the southern shore. Passing south of Itea, we could see the peaks that dominate Amphissa and Delphi more clearly than usual. It was a bright, frosty day.' Naxos and the 'poor abandoned Ariadne' is a familiar place to the classically trained Harold Macmillan, as are Thebes and Chalcis. At the end of the war, just after 'liberating' Modena, he meets Vittorio Orlando, the Prime Minister of Italy at the end of the First World War and thus a giant for Macmillan: 'Orlando was pessimistic about the immediate future, but confident of the ultimate recovery of Italy.' So thought Macmillan of his classical Mediterranean caught up in a modern war; the present was awful, but it contained deep within it the eternal source of its history.[61]

His family was not at all of the eternal, aristocratic kind that many people thought. No Roosevelt, or even a Churchill, his great-grandparents had been poor crofters in Scotland; it was his grandfather who had set up the publishing firm and his father who made it famous. 'I don't like books about action,' Harold Macmillan told C. P. Snow, 'I like books about what's going on in people's minds.'[62] Like his father, he particularly liked books on economic theory and, most specifically, those of John Maynard Keynes; it was the family's publishing house that had made such a success out of Keynes's *Economic Consequences of the Peace* in 1919. Macmillan was a friend of Keynes and was highly influenced by him. Macmillan himself put about the myth that he solved national economic problems with a box of match-sticks; the record shows otherwise.

Books filled Macmillan's life. He read Dante's *Inferno* to distract himself while recovering from his wounds in 1916, along with Gibbon's *Decline and Fall*. Hardy, Kipling and Yeats were a part of his natural repertoire; Macaulay was his source of history. His American mother's literary salon seems to have had more of a hold on him than his aristocratic wife, Lady Dorothy Cavendish, who enhanced his sense of tragic fate by falling in love with Bob Boothby, one of those bright stars of the Conservative Party who somehow always failed to rise. Macmillan's knowledge of Greek and Latin had been cultivated at Eton and Balliol College, Oxford. But his studies were interrupted by the Great War and, after that, he abandoned them. Oxford, he discovered, was a 'city of ghosts': 'Of our eight scholars and exhibitioners who came up in 1912, Humphrey, Sumner and I alone were alive.' But alive he was. 'I always got the feeling that I shouldn't be killed, I don't know why – absolutely sure of it,' he said of his experience of the First World War. Others knew they would die, and they did.

In Macmillan there always existed, side by side, this sense of survival, long life, and an oppressive susceptibility to the futility of war. 'Mount,

mount, my soul, my seat is up on high,' might have been his motto, 'Whilst my gross flesh sinks downward, here to die.'[63] Macmillan was born with a soul that was as naïve as it was pure; but his body moved in a world that was cruel, where he had to learn the rudimentary lessons of survival. In his private as much as in his public life, there were two Macmillans – one soaring upwards to higher ideals, the other stuck in the ground, calculating.

The job of Minister Resident to Allied Forces Head Quarters (AFHQ) had been created by Churchill shortly after the Allied landings in North Africa, which had led to endless administrative complications. Underlying them was a fundamental disagreement between the Americans and British on how recently liberated territories should be run. The Americans wanted to bring in their trained 'sixty-day marvels' from Virginia and set up their own Allied Military Government for Occupied Territories – 'AMGOT', which in Italy would be later abbreviated to 'AMG' (a kind of prototype for what the Americans had planned for the occupation of Germany). The British, and particularly Churchill, wanted national civil administrations established as soon as possible. For the Americans any such civil administration would have to take its orders from AMGOT.

Many of the most dramatic political events of the end of the war and the immediate post-war period arose from this Anglo–American squabble. America's puppet Vichy candidate for the Algerian government, Admiral Darlan, ready so he said to cooperate with AMGOT, was assassinated on Christmas Eve, 1942. America's second candidate was another Pétain loyalist, General Henri Giraud. He had no hope of survival against the British candidate, Charles de Gaulle and his French Committee of National Liberation.

Churchill called on the Colonial Secretary, Harold Macmillan, to take up the position of Minister Resident in Algiers just after Darlan's assassination.[64] In addition to his ancient Greek and Etonian Latin, Macmillan spoke fluent French. Churchill explained the job: he would report directly to the Prime Minister, he would hold his seat in the House of Commons and would be of Cabinet rank, though not a member of the War Cabinet. He was thus the Prime Minister's direct representative to Allied Command, and not a civil servant.

Churchill repeated this point many times during Macmillan's tenure in the Mediterranean: 'You are not a servant of the Foreign Office,' Churchill would remark. 'You are my servant and colleague and you must do whatever you like.' That is a point missed by some of the recent polemical histories about Macmillan's short career in the Mediterranean – based on

Foreign Office documents deposited in Kew.[65] Macmillan could not give orders to anyone in the army; nor could he receive instructions from the Foreign Office; his job was to represent Churchill before the Allied armies in the Mediterranean theatre, and that was all. His position in North Africa, in Italy and in Greece was always the same, and consistently Churchillian: set up a national civil administration as quickly as possible. When receiving the appointment Macmillan, the fatalist, considered it a mission to 'political Siberia'.[66]

It turned out, of course, to be precisely the opposite. Macmillan persuaded his business friend, Jean Monnet, whom Roosevelt had sent over from Washington to demolish de Gaulle, to join the Gaullist camp. Roosevelt's policy in North Africa was shattered, as was AMGOT. Roosevelt, in declining health, had not fully appreciated the game at play. Monnet was a member of a French managerial class that had grown up under the last decade of the Third Republic – particularly under the influence of André Tardieu, one of Clemenceau's old followers – who wanted to revolutionize entrepreneurial life in France. They were the original French 'technocrats', seeking a complete upheaval in private sector finance, industrial relations, and the heavy-handed manners of the state; they were Thatcherites *avant la lettre*. In the early years of the German occupation some of them had sided with Pétain's abortive 'National Revolution': this was the major reason why, after the war, business management had such a black name in France. Others, like Monnet, ended up in Washington rather than London, because they did not particularly like the stiff, northern Catholic manners of that upstart, uneconomic-minded brigadier general, Charles de Gaulle. It was Macmillan who managed the marriage between Monnet and de Gaulle, an astonishing feat which would mark the whole history of post-war Europe.

A sign of things to come was the setting up – paradoxically, under General Eisenhower before Macmillan's arrival – of a North African Board that was designed to encourage exports from the North African region under Allied control. It played right into Macmillan's hand. Its greatest success was the export of Algerian wines, which would affect the taste of what one finds in a French wine bottle up to our own day.

Macmillan, within six months, would be applying his ideas to Italy and Greece. His greatest success would be his organization of the export of southern Italian hemp for the production of rope, which would help win the war for Western Europe. Underneath it all lay a faith in civil government, the influence of Keynesian planning and Monnet-style management, and an approach that went beyond national frontiers, the black lines drawn on a map.

The vistas this opened for a new, free-trading Europe were radical. But Alexander's armies moved slowly. Such idealistic visions, Macmillan knew himself, hardly corresponded to the violent daily routines of a war floundering across 'one mountain ridge after another'.

In early 1944 there developed, largely thanks again to Churchill, a vague understanding that Greek affairs and the Balkans would lie within the field of action of the armies in Italy. This infuriated the men of the Foreign Office, who regarded the Eastern Mediterranean as the domain of the Minister Resident in Cairo, Lord Moyne (who would be murdered later that year by young Israeli terrorists), and General Paget's forces in the Middle East. Part of the FO's backlash may well have been due to Churchill's growing awareness of Communist agents working within the British civil service in Cairo. In August 1944 he had George Papandreou's Greek government-in-exile moved from Cairo to Italy. This would be of enormous consequence for Macmillan: he now represented Churchill not only in North Africa and Italy, but also in the Balkans and Greece. He became, as many dubbed him at the time, 'Viceroy of the Mediterranean'.

Macmillan made his permanent move from Algiers to Allied Headquarters in the palace of Caserta, just north of Naples, only in July 1944. The palace was an enormous eighteenth-century monument, larger than Versailles, that had seen happier days under the Bourbon kings of the Two Sicilies. Its regal apartments were converted into barracks for thousands of British and American officers, the corridors filled with filing cabinets, and the ballrooms, where courtiers had once performed minuets, became tuck shops and soldiers' messes; small seaplanes landed in the royal ponds. Macmillan expected, in his move to Italy, 'just French politics in 1943 over again'.

The problem was that the Italians could not come up with anyone of the stature of de Gaulle. With the Liberation of Rome on 4 June, two days before D-Day, Ivanoe Bonomi – who had his own Committee of National Liberation – became Head of Government. Signor Bonomi, it must be admitted, faced problems that not even de Gaulle had to solve. There was runaway inflation, the people were starving, and the Allied governments could not decide whether the country was a conquered 'enemy state' (in which case there could be no Lend-Lease or even the benefits of UNRRA), or, as Churchill and Macmillan interpreted the situation in 1944, a 'friendly co-belligerent'. The latter was not the view of the British Foreign Office, and still less that of the US State Department, which simply viewed Italy as the terrain of a military campaign. Macmillan, successfully working with Bonomi, managed to divert some military food supplies to the Italian population, increasing formal rationing above starvation levels and thus partly eradicating the inflationary effect of the black market. But this did nothing to improve his relations with the Foreign Office or the State Department.

Until April 1945 Italy was itself divided into three parts. The northern, most industrialized sector of the country, with a population of 21 million, was still under the control of the German armies and officially run by Mussolini's puppet 'Social Republic'. South of the Rimini–Pisa line was an area of about 5 million inhabitants administered by Allied Military Government (AMG). Further south, with Rome as its capital, was Italy proper governed by Bonomi's own administration, though it faced plenty of interference from the Allied Political Advisory Committee (later called the Allied Control Commission) which, sitting in Caserta, acted as intermediary between AMG and the Italian government. Such a simple administrative description, of course, hides the reality of the daily chaos that both the rulers and the ruled had to endure.

As Churchill's representative, Macmillan became closely involved in the workings of the Allied Military Government, and in early January 1945 was appointed Acting President of the Allied Control Commission. This became the source of enormous friction with the Americans, and especially State Secretary Stettinius who, at the time of the Ardennes offensive in Belgium, accused the British of 'ill will' in Italy. What the Americans had not appreciated at this point, but what the British, and particularly Macmillan, understood from their French experience, was that the Communist Partisans, numerous in the northern German zone, were preparing Italy for a civil war and eventual takeover. Southern Italy, in addition to her own material woes, was already experiencing the joys of *epurazione* – the purge of 'Fascists', as had happened in southern France after the Allied armies had passed. Macmillan on the Allied Control Commission began forward planning for the German collapse in northern Italy. This included infiltration of the Partisan Committees by British officers and their swift integration into the Italian government, whilst most of their members were put into the Italian army – the Gaullist technique. 'Treat the partisans as Allies,' advised Macmillan, 'award them decorations and honours.' This got Macmillan into further trouble with the Foreign Office, hardly soothed by his continued insistence on armed aid to the Partisans up until March. But Macmillan's point was sound. He was fully aware of Allied military weakness in the north and, as he told the Greek Prime Minister, Papandreou, in December, 'We do not wish to start the Third World War against Russia.'[67]

★

Involvement in Greece – a direct result of Churchill's 'percentages agreement' with Stalin in October – taught Macmillan a few more home truths. Once more, Macmillan wanted to establish as soon as possible a non-Communist national civilian government. The King, he advised Churchill, was unacceptable because he was the leader of a party and not a nation, a party moreover that had seriously compromised itself with the German occupiers. Papandreou was weak.

Eventually Macmillan came to focus on the idea of a Regency under Archbishop Damaskinos, the Greek Orthodox Metropolitan, who stood well over six foot tall and in his black robes, with Orthodox hat and silver-topped ebony cane, cut a very impressive figure indeed.

Macmillan began by focusing on economic problems, which were even more severe than in Italy. He called on the Swedish Red Cross to bring in food supplies and, in November, introduced his own version of Bretton Woods: one new drachma for 50 billion old ones; 60 new drachma were tied to the equivalent of £1 sterling.

But his problems did not end with economics. In October the Bulgarians, under Russian encouragement, entered the north and, within two months, Greece, like Yugoslavia, was plunged into civil war. But Churchill would not budge. 'I am sure you will not fail to grasp the opportunity presented,' he wrote to Macmillan, 'remembering always that our maxim is "no peace without victory".'[68]

Macmillan spent almost a month beleaguered in the British embassy in Athens – no water, no electricity, beds in the corridors and bullets flying through the windows; four fifths of the city were in the hands of the Communist-led ELAS Partisans. The government did not have one secure base in the country.

Coinciding with Hitler's Ardennes offensive, the Greek rebellion brought howls from the American press about British 'imperial' intentions in the Balkans. The leftward-leaning British press was growling. Then the US State Department joined in the chorus; Stettinius announced that 'liberated countries' should be allowed 'to work out their problems of government without influence from outside' – hardly a principle the State Department applied; the irony was that the Americans, three years later, found themselves fighting the same war in Greece as the British in December 1944. Meanwhile the Soviet press maintained absolute silence: Stalin was keeping his side of the October bargain with Churchill.

Three whole divisions were released from Italy and soon brought the British campaign to a successful conclusion. A ceasefire was negotiated and Archbishop Damaskinos was installed as Regent. On his return from Yalta, Churchill stopped off at Athens. In an open car, he and Damaskinos rode from the Regent's house to Constitution Square. Tens of thousands filled the streets, the square, the windows, the balconies, they stood on the roofs cheering; for the Greeks, 14 February 1945 was the day the war ended.

But it was not over for Italy. The Greek experience taught Macmillan that Communists were prepared even to fight their former Allies – who had armed them – if they saw power within their grasp. British strength and influence were waning by the month, while the American authorities, military and civilian, showed a detached indifference to the problem. In the Mediterranean, as elsewhere, the 'special relationship' by early 1945 had turned very sour.

Macmillan had always supported Churchill's strategy of a strong thrust through Italy and a north-eastern turn into Istria and the 'Ljubljana Gap' so as to head the Russians off in Austria. Macmillan was as angry as Churchill over the 'Anvil' operation in the French Riviera, which he claimed had 'little or no effect upon the campaign in France'. The movement of the armies certainly encouraged the minor civil war in the southern part of the country and pulled the American forces in Normandy south-eastwards, thus exposing the Ardennes to Hitler's final offensive. 'A break through the Ljubljana Gap and a march into Austria might have altered the whole political destinies of the Balkans and Eastern Europe,' argued Macmillan in his memoirs. He described the American unilateral decision to concentrate on France in June 1944 'as one of the sad turning-points of history'.[69]

Yet, given the terrain and the chaotic conditions in Italy, one cannot help but think that the Americans were right, while Macmillan and Churchill were being unduly optimistic. Even if they had broken through into Istria, it is possible that the Allied forces would have found themselves fighting on two fronts, one of them Russian. Indeed, this very nearly happened in May 1945.

By late winter, the 'Viceroy of the Mediterranean' was in a state of exhaustion. He was still flying between Rome and Athens, pursuing his economic reforms and involving himself in Greek and Roman politics – which contained all the vices of his classical world. He flew up to Salonica, where the entire population lived on barter. He remained Acting Head of the Allied Control Commission in Italy. His closest ally appears to have been Field Marshal Alexander. His greatest quarrels were with the Foreign Office, along with its head, Anthony Eden. Henry Hopkinson, a diplomat on the Control Commission, remembered Macmillan appearing one night, on his return from Athens, 'rather tight and, at the end of a long table,

I can still see him criticizing loudly Anthony's policies – and gesticulating – in the middle of which he suddenly fell over backwards'.[70]

This does not appear to have been a daily occurrence. The eventual opening of the spring offensive in Italy, on 9 April, which advanced much faster than anyone had expected, left little time for drinking. Mrs Clare Boothe Luce turned up in Caserta to give lavish entertainment to the officers, but Macmillan was greatly relieved to begin work again on the Allied Control Commission. His greatest concern was to get the CLNAI – another 'Committee of National Liberation', representing Italian Partisans in the north – incorporated into the Italian government and administration as quickly as possible; he didn't want the CLNAI to turn into another ELAS. He advised Bonomi to organize big victory parades in Milan, Genoa, Turin and Venice, where government members of all the parties should speak; reshuffle the Cabinet so that the left was well represented; and hand out honours to the resistance heroes. Fortunately this worked, with an almost Gaullist efficiency.

But two other major difficulties cropped up that April. First the French proved eager to perform their historic role in northern Italy; in the footsteps of Charles VII and the two Napoleons, they marched an army into the valley of the Po and refused to budge. Eden was infuriated. Macmillan, ever the friend of de Gaulle, thought this was a good idea; both Alexander and General Mark Clark, the American commander of 15th Army Group, who had suffered steady depletion to fulfil Eisenhower's needs, supported Macmillan. The French in Italy were to become an early post-war problem.

But it was the second difficulty that drew Macmillan and a portion of the British armed forces into tragedy – and a controversy that has lasted to this day. Italy's north-eastern frontiers with Yugoslavia and Austria had been contested since the Paris Peace Conference in 1919; Gabriele d'Annunzio's claim for the port of Fiume is often presented as the first sign of the Fascist movement in Italy. As early as March 1945, Tito was demanding that the whole of the two north-eastern provinces of Venezia Tridentina and Venezia Giulia – which had only a minority of Italian inhabitants – be incorporated into his new Communist republic. By April he was making claims on Carinthia, Austria's rural and mountainous south-western province that the Allies had designated as a British occupied zone.

For a year the British and Americans had raged over the merits of the 'Ljubljana Gap' strategy; the Americans had finally prevented the British from attempting an attack on Istria by refusing them landing craft. As in Greece, the Americans believed the British were acting out of pure 'imperial' interests. Suddenly in April they performed a complete volte-face.

The American Joint Chiefs of Staff and the US State Department – joined by the Foreign Office – demanded that Allied Military Government be immediately set up in the whole of the two contested Italian provinces while Carinthia should be held under British control.

Tito's Partisans had, in the meantime, been steadily infiltrating the area, while Marshal Tolbukhin's 3rd Ukrainian Front, having flattened half of Vienna, was heading south-west towards Carinthia. Alexander asked his superiors in London: was he to use force if necessary to clear the area? He never received an answer. Historians may comment on the 'mysterious' disappearance of vital documents. The truth is, they probably never existed. The Allied authorities in Italy were left to act on their own.

On 26 April Alexander reported, at his regular political meeting at Caserta, what he was going to do if he received no instructions. He would seize those parts of Venezia Giulia that were essential for communications with Austria. This would include Trieste and Pola. Tito was simply informed that any Yugoslav troops in the area would come under Alexander's command.

German forces in both Italy and Yugoslavia had, by this time, collapsed – though the formal surrender remained to be signed. Between the collapse and the surrender occurred a race from Yugoslavia to Carinthia – still unoccupied – of the whole of the defeated German Army Group E, including anti-Communist Serbian Chetniks, Croatian Ustachi, anti-Communist Russians, members of the old 'White armies' that had been fighting the Bolsheviks in 1920, Cossacks and other minorities who found themselves on the wrong side as the Second World War drew to a close. None of them wanted to surrender to Tito's Partisans or the Red Army; they all wanted to lay down their arms in the tiny British sector of Carinthia.

It was General Richard McCreery's Eighth Army that got the job of clearing the way into southern Austria. Macmillan thought him 'the most charming man – and a very clever one in addition'. On 2 May the New Zealand Division managed to take Trieste before the Yugoslav Partisans. One of the New Zealand units under General Freyberg seized Gorizia, even though part of the town was by now occupied by Partisans. Finally, during the night of 7/8 May units of the 6th Armoured Division pushed through the Alpine pass of Predil into Austria. At their head was General Keightley's V Corps, made up of tough veterans of the Western Desert, Sicily and Monte Cassino. What they discovered on the other side of the mountain chain were not the empty meadows of the Alps, but frightened crowds the size of cities that had raced in from Yugoslavia.[71]

6 Berlin and the 'Southern Redoubt'

By 1945 army movements in the Mediterranean – along with those of prisoners, refugees and 'displaced persons' – were geared to the greater battle being waged inside Germany. The war had, as Captain Wedemeyer's initial draft of the 'Victory Program' had projected back in 1938, been carried into the continental enemy's heartland. The US Army had accomplished its miracle and, in six years, had increased its effective force from 190,000 to 8.2 million – somewhat under Wedemeyer's estimate! By 1945 two thirds of the world's ships afloat were American, as were 45 per cent of the world's armaments and 50 per cent of the world's goods. America at the end of the Second World War, unlike after the First, had become a military power equal to her commercial power. To the east, the Soviet Union was developing a military power that would always be in excess of her commercial resources. The Italian war, like the Balkan wars, had indeed become 'peripheral'. What determined the future of Europe now was the meeting point, on Europe's northern plain, between the world's two major military powers.

The war had produced its frightful patterns, as 'resistance' movements sprang up in front of the liberating armies while purges and civil wars broke out behind. Because the scale of fighting had been so much greater in the eastern, continental base of Europe, so the accompanying forms of resistance and civil war attained a corresponding level of horror. Inside, around and about the war's firestorms swirled an ugly human pall in movement, migrants who had lost both home and hope. They were the survivors; others had not survived: whole peoples had been massacred; whole peoples were on the move. Europe had never come closer to its Armageddon.

The movement of the great armies influenced everything. By early spring 1945 the 'Grand Alliance' stood poised, ready to enter the enemy's heartland. But where exactly was the heartland of Hitler's Reich?

Even before the annexations of Austria and Bohemia the Reich was a huge territory of over 400,000 square kilometres (156,000 square miles) that dominated Central Europe. The Nazi authorities had no doubts about the heart of their empire; it was Berlin. Well may they have mocked the Berlin of the Weimar Republic when they were a small opposition party in Bavaria; but once Goebbels had introduced Hitler to the capital of Germany the Führer clung to the idea that this was the city that was to rule the world.

The logic behind this was inexorable: even in military defeat Berlin would remain the heart of this defiant, fanatic Nordic Gospel. Their armies may be slaughtered, the leaders dead; but out of the ashes of Berlin, from beneath the ground – like the Barbarossa of legend, beneath his mountain awaiting the rebirth of his Reich – the Nazi spirit would rise again in this northern, urban heart of Germany. There would never again be a 1918! Never again a German surrender!

It was Goebbels who brought Hitler to Berlin. It was Goebbels who wrote the final script. 'The National Socialists will either win together in Berlin,' he said, 'or they will die together in Berlin.'[72] But it was the Führer himself who decided to stay, and die, in Berlin.

Typically, Hitler kept his commanders, ministers and staff guessing right up to the last minute. Plans were even made for his evacuation south to Obersalzberg to which several important administrators and commanders had begun to move in the first weeks of April – not for the final battle but, as Hitler rightly suspected, to plan individually their own escape and, in several cases, to negotiate surrender to the Americans and British. But for Nazi purists this was not a way out; the myth of Nazi defiance had to be maintained to the end: no 1918; win or die. On his fifty-sixth birthday, fifty feet underground, Hitler announced that the Russians were about to meet their bloodiest defeat before Berlin – they had the city almost surrounded. Hitler and his 'magic circle' of subterranean toadies had by now lost all credible link with the average Berlin citizen; the soldiers were mostly outsiders who couldn't find their way about the ruined streets. Hitler spent his last moments in the open air meeting and decorating a few boys from the Hitler Youth (contrary to legend, no photographs or films of this scene survived – the famous footage always shown in documentaries on Hitler's last days was taken in March). A grim birthday party was held in his bunker, followed by a military conference. Convoys of lorries filled with documents and treasure then left for the south, accompanied by a queue of official cars. In one of them was Reichsmarshal Göring. But this was not, as the Reichsmarshal and still formal successor to the Führer had imagined, a signal for the transfer of powers south; in Hitler's eyes, it was the act that betrayed him.

On 21 April Hitler ordered his last major offensive on Russian forces. 'Any commanding officer who keeps men back', ran Hitler's verbal instructions, 'will forfeit his life within five hours.' The attack was to be led by SS General Steiner, who had no organized force under his order. When Hitler heard the following evening that this impossible offensive had not taken place he cried 'Treason!' and announced that the Third Reich was a failure and that he had nothing to do but die. The next day the German radio announced to the world that Berlin and Prague were the twin inviolable citadels of the Reich; that Hitler, Goebbels and the Gauleiter would remain in the capital to the end. 'I will never leave Berlin,' Hitler told Keitel, his new Chief of Staff, and Bormann, the Party's chieftain – '*never!*' That sealed the fate of Hitler and, with Hitler, the fate of the Third Reich.[73]

There was not a Russian who had any doubt about where the heart of the Nazi Reich lay after Stalin's propaganda campaigns of the preceding winter. According to the reporter Alexander Werth, Moscow was revelling in the thoughts of early victory during the New Year celebrations of 1945; the big hotels of the city centre were open all night and, instead of the traditional greeting, people embraced one another with the saying, 'How far to *Berlin?*'[74]

The winter offensive was advanced by several days as a sign of cooperation with the Western Allies, who were still facing trouble in the Ardennes. The word 'Berlin' was slapped in white paint on the tanks that liberated the rubble of Warsaw and then crossed western Poland until they reached the Oder–Neisse line – Poland's western frontier was established by Russian armies even before it was officially declared at Yalta. 'Into the Den of the Fascist Beast'; 'Moscow to Berlin'. The two and a half million men serving in Rokossovsky's 2nd Belorussian Front to the north, Zhukov's 1st Belorussian Front in the centre – thirty-five miles from Berlin – and Konev's 1st Ukrainian Front to the south all knew where they were going. They were delayed partly by politics (Stalin was determined, first, to establish Poland's western frontier), partly by logistics (the build-up of the armies and supporting air forces had first to be assured), and, to an immense degree, by nature. An early thaw had turned what Russians considered the contemptible little Oder into a lake of icebergs. When Marshal Zhukov finally opened his offensive on 16 April, it took him two days and tens of thousands of casualties to take the Seelow Heights opposite – and nearly cost him his prize, Berlin.

Ever since the Normandy landings, with the British-Canadian forces on the left and the Americans on the right, the capture of Berlin, at the heart of the Reich, had been the aim of the Western Allies. The direction of the armies had got disoriented when Patton's Third Army roared southeastwards into the undefended Loire valley, eventually ending up in a three-month stalemate when he came up against the heavily fortified citadel of Metz. Patton gazed eastwards, towards the Rhine and the Saar, as indeed he had in the last months of the First World War. So did his immediate superior, Bradley, with the same old vision of General Pershing guiding him. The fact that the Americans were in the southern sector of the Western Front in both wars pushed them, in both cases from pride and a need to prove their independence of their European allies to the north, south-eastwards, away from Berlin. Pershing's army withered under enemy fire in the Argonne, where he was stuck until the first week of November 1918. Bradley's army met humiliation in the neighbouring Ardennes, the 'Bulge', which cost the Allies three precious months, not counting the stalemate since September caused by too wide a front (and not the legendary lack of petrol, of which Patton had plenty).

It was precisely in September 1944 that Eisenhower's Supreme Headquarters of the Allied Expeditionary Force (SHAEF) in Versailles officially laid down the principle that 'our main object must be the early capture of BERLIN, the most important objective in Germany.'[75] But after the humiliation of the Ardennes – with half the Allied forces falling, out of necessity, under the command of Montgomery to the north – pressure began to build on Eisenhower for a change in direction.

Eisenhower would always claim that his decisions were 'purely military'. But it was not necessary to have read Clausewitz to realize that a commander claiming to make 'purely military' decisions would depend on political decisions being made elsewhere. The problem was that there was no elsewhere; since March 1944 American political decisions had been made by competing Executive Departments because the President could not, by his last winter, work more than two hours a day. By March 1945 his input amounted to nil. On 12 April, four days before the Russian offensive began, he died.

Eisenhower's 'purely military' decisions made no sense at all; they simply aggravated the mayhem in Central Europe. SHAEF was the largest army command Europe had yet seen – far outnumbering the tiny staff that had run the First World War. No centre on the Continent was receiving more military intelligence. But it was incapable of analysing it. Analysis is the human part of military intelligence. It is always subject to wish-fulfilment, is easily influenced by prejudice and, if guided by fear, turns swiftly into paranoia. This is what happened at SHAEF at the time of Roosevelt's death.

Data on preparations for a Nazi last stand in a 'mountain redoubt' were first fed into Washington, in February, by American spies leading their dangerous lives in the hotels and indoor swimming pools of Switzerland. The first movements of Vlasov's unfortunate army collecting, under the guise of 'SS units', near the Austrian frontier may well have been the origin of the Great Fear that then spread through SHAEF's black-and-white tiled offices in Versailles. By late February and early March the reports were being garnished with special visual effects, like underground mountain railways, poison gas supplies and huge munition dumps under the control of 'specially chosen units' (probably poverty-stricken Russian anti-Communists caught in a dilemma, expelled Romanians, and homeless Bulgarians with their families).

Those Nazis in the glacial Alps of western Austria posed a great threat to western freedoms! An American report on 11 March waxed poetical: 'Here [that is, in the frozen Alps], defended by nature and by the most efficient secret weapons yet invented, the powers that have hitherto guided Germany will survive to reorganize her resurrection.' The report at least caught the spirit of an earlier war: man in a struggle with nature: Caspar Friedrich in his mountains in the early nineteenth century.

The head of SHAEF's intelligence department, G-2, was a British general, Kenneth W. D. Strong, who was to admit in late April – when seven American armies were advancing on their mythical target – that 'the redoubt may not be there, but we have to take steps to prevent it being there.'[76]

In addition to the wicked fairy's Alpine 'Redoubt' there was a Red Riding Hood-type tale spreading about 'Werewolves'. The argument being mounted for the total change in direction of America's main forces was that the whole of Germany had to be cleared to prevent the creation of 'fortresses', as still existed in some French ports, and the prolongation of the war by guerrillas, the 'Werewolves'. The rumour of Werewolves ready to rise for the Nazi cause continued long after the war.

Werewolves did exist in two wholly separate forms, but neither conducted guerrilla warfare. The first were a somewhat chaotic paramilitary organization set up by SS Obergruppenführer Hans Prützmann in early 1945 to act behind enemy lines as a force of diversion from the Wehrmacht's main offensives; as Germany's offensives declined so did they. By April they were virtually extinct. Prützmann committed suicide on his capture in Flensburg in May. The second form, entirely independent of Prützmann's organization, was a propaganda station set up on 1 April by Goebbels called 'Radio Werewolf'. It preached Goebbels's message of eternal Nazidom, and a Barbarossa-like resurrection from the soil of the ruined cities; and it became a major source of Allied fears.[77]

As Montgomery had warned his troops on approaching the German frontiers, the rules of war had changed. They could no longer count on being considered by the local population as liberators. The same was true from the German perspective. The invading Western Allied armies could not be viewed as liberators – they were invaders, after all, of German

449

territory, a phenomenon that had never happened since the Napoleonic wars. So there could be no margin in front of the armies constituting 'resistance to the Nazis'. At the most there was just silence (what Martin Broszat later misleadingly called '*Resistenz*'). Hitler had been preaching since 1919 that there would be no repeat of '1918' – German revolution in the homeland and surrender to the army of the Allies. They would fight to the last man. By the time foreign troops appeared on German soil, Hitler had ruled that any civilian caught with a gun (like some of the revolutionaries in 1918) would be hanged: bodies would soon be dangling all over Germany. There would be no irregular militia (as in 1918). Hitler would rely solely on his regular armies. So there would be no guerrilla activity in Germany in 1945. And there would be no 'German resistance to the Nazis'.

The Alpine 'Southern Redoubt' and the 'Werewolves', which many Americans – spurred on by their press – were convinced existed, was a creation of American imagination, American wish-fulfilment: it was a product of the historical accident which placed Americans, once more, in the southern sector of the Western Front, in the dark woodlands of Grimm's fairy tales battling – Hollywood-style – against the final forces of evil in the mountains, vales and hidden grottoes of southern Germany.

A lot of jealousy had developed between Allied commanders, particularly at the time of the 'Bulge', over the way Patton and, to a lesser degree, Montgomery grabbed headlines in the press. Montgomery held the press in total contempt and, in fact, gave few press conferences – his idea of public relations was to travel the front addressing his men from the top of his jeep. Eisenhower's attitude might be considered more modern; he was very much aware of the growing power of the media, gave press conferences at least once a week, and frequently corresponded with Marshall in Washington on questions of public image. Why was it always Patton and Montgomery who got the headlines? Eisenhower felt that General Courtney Hodges of the American First Army deserved more press attention – whenever his men captured something important it was always 'First Army Takes . . .', without any mention of the brave Hodges. The same was true of General William Simpson and his American Ninth Army that had been incorporated into Montgomery's 21st Army Group – the army group that, after skirting the Ruhr, was slated to head for Berlin.

But what upset Eisenhower most of all was the low profile accorded his old West Point classmate, General Omar Bradley of the 12th Army Group. 'I consider Bradley the greatest battle-line commander I have met in this war,' Eisenhower cabled Marshall on 28 March, the day he decided to reorientate the whole Western Allies' campaign.[78] Bradley himself chafed at the fact — kept as secret as possible — that he had lost more than half his army group, including Hodges' First, to Montgomery's command during the debacle of the 'Bulge'. Eisenhower and Marshall worked together to make sure this 'greatest battle-line commander' got the attention he deserved; he was due for retirement at the end of the year and still had only three stars on his cap.

Montgomery, not the world's greatest battle-line diplomat, started the whole business off with a cable sent to Eisenhower on 27 March, the moment he had successfully completed his ambitious 'Operation Plunder', which got most of his 21st Army Group across the Rhine and north of the strategically essential Ruhr region. Montgomery had never changed his general strategy since D-Day: keep the armies together, push round Pas-de-Calais, cross the Rhine to the north, cut off the industrial Ruhr — then 'crack about' the northern plain, and on to Berlin. This had been the gist of his argument, in August, on how to finish the war in 1944: the Russians were still stalling before Warsaw. German generals have testified that there was nothing that could have prevented forty Allied divisions from rushing the Ruhr in the summer of 1944. But that was the moment the Americans split off, and ran south-eastwards, towards their historic hunting grounds in the enchantingly hilly Moselle. That was what had opened the 'Bulge'.

Montgomery's telegram of 27 March to the Supreme Commander announced, in typically grand fashion: 'My intention is to drive hard for the line of the ELBE using Ninth Army and Second Army . . . The operation will be similar in design to those when we crossed the SEINE and drove hard across the rear of the PAS DE CALAIS with Canadian Army mopping up the coastal belt of the PAS DE CALAIS later.' As if that was not enough to grate on the American sensibilities of the Supreme Commander, he added that he was transferring his headquarters — a little caravan convoy — deeper into Germany, at Bonninghardt. From there he would move his caravan on to the Wesel, Münster, Wiedenbrück, Herford, Hanover, 'thence via the Autobahn to BERLIN I hope'.[79] But no, it was not to be, even though Eisenhower had, to date, shown no sign of a change in plan.

Cumbersome, bureaucratic SHAEF had made just one move, from Versailles to Rheims on 24 February once Montgomery's two large operations from the Netherlands into Germany at last got moving. Ostentatiously, Montgomery avoided travelling to this sacred French city of kings; he always expected the Supreme Commander to visit him. Bradley had shifted his huge Army Group Headquarters from his grand hotel in

Luxembourg up to Namur in Belgium at the end of the battle of the 'Bulge', on 28 January. Supposedly this was to be closer to Montgomery, but Bradley proudly recorded in his memoirs that he made every effort not to see the British commander.

Churchill came to watch Montgomery's crossing of the Rhine, and even promenaded on the east bank until German shells started exploding around him. Eisenhower, in the meantime, took a brief holiday in the French Riviera with his personal assistant, Kay Summersby, two staff girls – and his old classmate, Bradley. On the day Montgomery launched his offensive across the Rhine he flew up to Maastricht for a brief visit to Simpson's Ninth Army headquarters and then headed south, first to Bradley's headquarters, and then to Remagen Bridge.

Remagen Bridge, across the Rhine, had been taken by the Americans on 7 March; it was of little strategic importance though it made good copy and got Hitler in a rage (he had nine of the local German commanders hanged). While in Maastricht Eisenhower had received a cable from Marshall in Washington growling about the 'overdose of Montgomery which is now coming into the country'.[80] It was the old story again: too much press coverage of Monty, not enough on Hodges and dear old Brad. Remagen Bridge had been taken by Hodges' First Army, which undoubtedly explained Eisenhower's visit at Montgomery's moment of glory.

Eisenhower then flew back to royal Rheims. But he did not stay there long, for on the night of 26 March he had a secret rendezvous with the attractive Mrs Summersby at the Hôtel Raphaël on the Champs Elysées in Paris. That explains why he was not in Rheims when Montgomery's telegram, announcing he was racing to the Elbe and Berlin, was received. Eisenhower only read it on the morning of the 28th.

This was the day the whole of Western military strategy was changed and the command structure, painfully built up over the last three years between the British and American armies, crumbled. Eisenhower had lunch with Bradley in Rheims that day, and immediately afterwards sent a cable to Stalin.

It was not unusual for the Supreme Commander to communicate with political leaders in the West; he had been close – unusually so – to Charles de Gaulle; he communicated regularly, of course, with Roosevelt; and there is a wealth of correspondence between him and the British Prime Minister. But Stalin was altogether another matter. The tension between Churchill and Stalin over Poland was by now intense. Stalin, at this very moment, was accusing Churchill of making a separate peace with the Germans. Roosevelt was out of the picture.

There had been no discussion at Yalta over military stop-points between Western forces and the Red Army. There had been plenty of talk about the eventual partition of Germany and zones of occupation; in the West, such plans had been in development for at least two years, but for somebody like Eisenhower these plans were 'purely political'. There is no indication, for example, that the European Advisory Commission, which had been set up for this very purpose, had any influence on Eisenhower. There had been, however, some discussion of setting up direct links of communication between SHAEF and the Red Army during meetings preliminary to Yalta, at Marseilles and Malta; the British totally opposed the idea, demanding that all such contacts go through the senior authorities of the alliance, the Combined Chiefs of Staff. Eisenhower's cable to Stalin of 28 March was a signal that the Combined Chiefs of Staff were no longer in charge; henceforth, it was SHAEF and the American Joint Chiefs of Staff that gave the orders. It was an American unilateral declaration of independence which undermined the whole working structure of the Western Alliance.

The contents of Eisenhower's telegram to Stalin were no less extraordinary than its form: 'My immediate operations are designed to encircle and destroy the enemy forces defending the Ruhr.' So it was no longer a question of cutting off Model's Army Group B, in the Ruhr, from the rest of Germany; now Eisenhower intended to destroy it before moving on. 'This will be accomplished by developing offensives around the north of the Ruhr and from Frankfurt through Kassel' – what would be known as the wide 'double envelopment', thus giving Hodges' First Army something major to accomplish. 'I estimate that this phase of operations will terminate in late April or even earlier' – the operation would hold up Allied forces in the west of Germany for yet another month. Field Marshal Walter Model, it might be remembered, was Hitler's 'firefighter', who had stalled the Russians in their assault on Army Group Centre the previous summer, and had then been ordered to France to save German forces after the Falaise battle. He had been the cause of havoc at Arnhem. Now he was defending the Ruhr. Eisenhower's estimated timescale was about right: Model made a final attempt at a breakout on 15 April and then ordered his troops to disperse. On 21 April he shot himself.

'My next task', continued Eisenhower in his note to Stalin, 'will be to divide the enemy's remaining forces by joining hands with your forces' – a 'purely military' proposal that left all political problems to the politicians. 'The best axis on which to effect this junction would be Erfurt–Leipzig–Dresden', well south of Berlin. Why Leipzig and Dresden? As a result of Bomber Command's operations in February, there was nothing left of Leipzig and Dresden; but they did lie opposite Bradley's

12th Army Group. Eisenhower also recommended a secondary junction in 'the Regensburg–Linz area' – southern Germany and Austria – 'thereby preventing the consolidation of German resistance in a redoubt in southern Germany'. So the Allied forces were to be directed southwards. What of Berlin? 'That place', he informed Montgomery three days later, 'has become, so far as I am concerned, nothing but a geographical location, and I have never been interested in these.' European geography was not a matter of concern to the Supreme Commander.[81]

Immediately after drafting his telegram to Stalin, he cabled Montgomery. He told him, in the tones of the commander he was, that he agreed with his plans 'up to the point of gaining contact with Bradley east of the Ruhr'. But thereafter his plans were 'being coordinated with Stalin'. As soon as Montgomery had joined hands with Bradley, 'Ninth United States Army will revert to Bradley's command.' Bradley would then be 'responsible for mopping up and occupying the Ruhr', and only after this would Bradley 'deliver his main thrust on the axis Erfurt–Leipzig–Dresden to join hands with the Russians'. Montgomery's mission was 'to protect Bradley's northern flank'.

So Montgomery's right arm was to be cut off and, instead of directing an operation on to the Elbe and Berlin, he was to play a secondary part somewhere in the north of Germany. On 10 April Bradley informed Montgomery that his forces were no longer needed to protect his left flank and they could go their 'separate ways'. It was a mad move, based officially on the American principle that army command decisions were 'purely military' while politics should be left to the politicians. This was Eisenhower's dogma, soon to be proved vacuous.

Roosevelt died; SHAEF lost its political direction. For days Eisenhower wavered over whether he wanted to abandon Berlin or not. Churchill and Brooke were furious at the way the alliance – and in particular the Combined Chiefs of Staff – had been deliberately overridden. Montgomery rubbed salt into the wounds. With London openly weeping at the loss of Roosevelt, Montgomery cabled Brooke: 'I have even heard it stated that 21 Army Group [now a much diminished force] may have to go up through DENMARK and via SWEDEN into NORWAY and clean up that country.' A week later, when Eisenhower belatedly realized that the Red Army was heading for Denmark, he ordered Montgomery to capture Lübeck, one of the last major operations of the war. In late April, Montgomery's army group was the sole Western military force racing the Soviet forces, bent as ever on their attempt to spread 'popular democracy' throughout Europe. Montgomery at least managed to save Denmark.[82]

★

Eisenhower's determination to send his armies north, south, east, and even west into Holland, had one major side effect that nobody had expected: they revealed to the West the horrors of Nazi concentration camps.

Montgomery's main armed force was, after the withdrawal of the American Ninth, Dempsey's British Second Army, which, instead of heading for the Elbe, now had the job of taking ports, outlying peninsulas, islands and estuaries in the north. But in mid-April with no American support he was nowhere near them; he even warned Brooke, on 15 April, that he might run into difficulty between overwhelming enemy forces and appealed for help from a US Corps. The satisfied American response was that Montgomery was having 'his reputation again menaced by the brilliant tactics of General Bradley'.

But it was not Bradley's brilliant tactics that grabbed the headlines on 15 April. That afternoon Montgomery sent a message to the War Office that his 11th Armoured Division had discovered near Bergen 'two large camps . . . of mostly political prisoners and in both camps were many cases of typhus'. The next evening the picture turned out to be much worse: 'The camps of political prisoners referred to in yesterday's message consist of 25,000 women and 35,000 men and are in an appalling condition, the prisoners being practically starving and they have not even troubled to bury the dead.' Montgomery had travelled the short distance from his headquarters at Soltau to Belsen; he was sickened at the sight before him.[83]

A Jewish girl from Czechoslovakia, Hana Lustig, who had survived one of the death marches from Auschwitz, was one of the witnesses. 'At night, we heard the guns of the advancing armies from Bremen,' she recorded. 'How much longer can it take before they reach us? How much strength will it take to stay alive until then? And then it happened.' A British tank rolled into the camp; an officer announced, in several languages, 'YOU ARE FREE . . . YOU ARE FREE . . . YOU ARE FREE . . .' Thousands however lay dead – among them, the young diarist from Amsterdam, Anne Frank, who had survived the death march from Auschwitz but died of typhus in Belsen three weeks before the arrival of that British tank.

George Campbell was one of the first British officers on the scene. 'Many of our officers and men had witnessed horrors and carnage in the previous ten months but they felt a sense of outrage at what they found. There had been rumours that such camps existed, but this was the first to be discovered in the West.'[84] He was right. There had been even more than just rumours. Photographs had been filling Western newspapers in August 1944 of Majdanek, uncovered by the Red Army the previous month. There had been reports in the London *Times* of horrors being committed in a Polish camp called Oświecim – but curiously enough the Soviets did not say a word about their liberation, the previous January, of Auschwitz until after the Armistice was signed in Berlin on 8 May. The next major Nazi camp to be revealed to the Western press was Dachau, by Patton's forces, on 29 April. The Americans were so nauseated that they offered no quarter to the SS guards running the place; most of them were shot on the spot; one American lieutenant, alone, is reported to have machine-gunned 346 of them.[85]

7 The Holocaust and the Gulag

In the summer of 1938, before the purge of the Jews began in earnest and as Hitler prepared, in readiness for his fiftieth birthday, a little war with Czechoslovakia that never quite came off, there existed in the German Reich six major concentration camps – Dachau (which was the first of its kind), outside Munich; Buchenwald, near Weimar; Flossenburg, near Weiden; Sachsenhausen, which combined with Oranienburg, to the north of Berlin; and Mauthausen, which had been set up that very year near Linz after Austria had been annexed. The number had in fact declined since 1933 when Ernst Röhm's SA, competing in typical Nazi fashion with Himmler's SS, began organizing 'wild camps' and 'beating stations'. After the mass murder in 1934 of Röhm's SA, Himmler and his assistant, Reinhard Heydrich, started organizing a much more covert, streamlined system of camps that they thought, mistakenly, would become the model for a new revolutionary SS state. Hitler would never allow that to happen. To this day – despite massive documentation and whole libraries filled with studies on this grisly subject – nobody knows exactly how decisions were made on camp policy and what command chain existed. There were no files kept on the operations at the very top of the Nazi system; many key documents were destroyed before they could fall into Allied hands. The total number of inmates in these six camps in 1939 was around 21,000, most of whom were non-Jewish German nationals.[86]

In the same summer of 1938, at the height of the 'Great Terror', the number of camps in the Soviet Union were in the range of several thousand, the number of inmates in the millions – anywhere from 1.9 million to 9 million. The problem with counting up the number of camps is that they were made up of huge networks, some, like Kolyma, stretching across the whole north-eastern region of Soviet Siberia. The difficulty in calculating the number of inmates is that the official figures – released only after the collapse of the Communist state – in no way correspond to other estimates, several of which have a reliable basis. Most historians in the West prefer the lower estimates, say 1.9 million prisoners in 1938, declining to 1.2 million around the end of 1942 (with the German occupation of about one third of the Soviet Union), and rising to a peak of approximately 2.5 million in 1952–3. The problem is that these figures take no acount of prison systems existing outside the formal administration of the 'Gulag' (which itself came under different formal names); they ignore movements, death rates, murder and, most of all, what people saw with their own eyes. Multiply these figures by a factor of two or three, and one probably approaches the reality.[87]

Now enter the issue of comparison, Nazi and Soviet. For it must be clear by now to anyone who has followed the story of this book so far – across the northern European plain from Paris to Warsaw, from Berlin to Moscow – that the growth of Nazi and Soviet camps were related to each other: the Nazis and Soviets were neighbours, they were former allies, there was always a temptation to collaborate, the landscape of the camps looked strikingly similar. In fact, Nazis moved into former Soviet camps; the Soviets then took over, and used the old Nazi camps. Worse still, some of these camps would have the same inmates *and* the same administrators. This is the story that has so far not been told.

Alexander Solzhenitsyn, when he first exposed the problem of the Soviet Gulag to the world in 1973, was careful to note its origins and its uniqueness. 'No other regime on earth', he alleged, 'could compare with [the Soviet Union] either in the number of those it had done to death, in hardiness, in the range of its ambitions, or in its thoroughgoing and unmitigated totalitarianism – no, not even the regime *of its pupil Hitler, which at that time blinded Western eyes to all else.*'[88] Western critics, particularly in the United States, were shocked. They had already written their histories of Hitler's camps and of the extermination of the European Jews. Aggravating the reception of Solzhenitsyn's work was the outbreak, in 1973, of a third Israeli-Arab war, which considerably stimulated what is now cynically referred to as the 'Holocaust Industry' – the thousands of books, films, museums and documentary collections devoted to the genocide of the Jews. The Holocaust became the grounds of legitimacy for the new state of Israel; for many Jews, including those who had had no experience and knew little of the Second World War, it became an item of faith. The Holocaust was waved as the standard of a nation state; classic texts on the subject were read as the last book of the Hebrew Bible. The Holocaust was held up as an event without parallel in human history, let alone in the Second World War.[89]

457

In *The Gulag Archipelago*, Solzhenitsyn – who had spent eight years in the Gulag after being arrested in the last months of the war for a minor insult to an officer – took an essentially historical approach; he relied on memoirs, mostly unpublished, and on what he had heard and seen in the camps. His work contains little comparison with the Nazi camps, though a barely concealed parallel runs through most of his text. 'They dumped whole *nations* down the sewer pipes,' he states: isn't that genocide? The Communists in Russia 'burned out whole nests, whole families, from the start', he observes. This was the *first* such experiment – at least in modern history. 'It was subsequently repeated by Hitler with the Jews, and again by Stalin with nationalities which were disloyal to him or suspected by him.' He wonders whether the inhumane conditions, imposed without the support of law and lasting for indeterminate lengths of time (sentences could be repeated and extended at the will of the authorities) were not harsher than death itself. It was a question other memoirs from the Gulag have posed, most notably those of Varlam Shalamov and of Jacques Rossi. Suicide rates – at the camps, not during arrest – appear to have been low in the Gulag, as they were in the Nazi camps. But death was always present. 'According to the estimates of émigré Professor of Statistics Kurganov', states Solzhenitsyn, the Gulag 'cost us, from the beginning of the October Revolution up to 1959, a total of . . . sixty–six million – 66,000,000 – lives.' Aleksandr Yakovlev, who was once a high official in Gorbachev's administration and is now chairman of Russia's Commission for the Rehabilitation of the Victims of Political Repression, places the number at around 35 million. Such figures, though spread over decades, dwarf even the number of Nazi victims.[90]

The Soviets were among the victors of the Second World War – it could even be said they were *the* victors. They made the largest territorial gains, and it was the Red Army which changed the course of the war. The Soviets, moreover – not the British or the Americans – initiated, during Churchill's visit to Moscow in October 1944, the process that led eventually to the Nuremberg Trials of 1945–6. There would be no Nuremberg Trials held on Soviet crimes against humanity, noted Solzhenitsyn, though it was in Russia, he asserted, where the whole modern business of political mass murder started. Vladimir Bukovsky, who spent twelve years in Soviet prisons and psychiatric hospitals and was eventually exchanged against a Chilean Communist in the late 1970s, asks even more pointedly, why were only the Germans judged? Why was there no Nuremberg Trial held in Moscow?[91]

'There was a gap between the Russian and the Western conscience which exists to this day,' noted Solzhenitsyn. 'The West was fighting *only* against Hitler, and for this purpose *all* means and *all* allies were good, the Soviets above all.'[92] Intellectuals, journalists, professors and bureaucrats gave Solzhenitsyn a cool reception in the West. He was considered a crank, a monarchist, a reactionary, an anti-Semite – anything but a hero. Few showed interest in the Gulag. Most Russian victims of the system, who came to the West with their stories, discovered the same phenomenon. After the fall of the Communist regime in Moscow, Bukovsky, then living in Cambridge, England, flew out to Moscow and managed to copy a haul of documents that had been lying secret in the Kremlin. At the time of the collapse the Western press would have paid a fortune for the discoveries he had made. But within two years Western editors and journalists were telling him, 'So what? Who cares?' 'People have got fed up with the tensions of the Cold War,' said one, 'they don't want to hear any more about it. They want only to live, work, and relax . . . and forget this whole bad dream.' Another told him he would have to wait until it all became history.[93] It took almost twenty-five years after the collapse of Nazism before the Jewish Holocaust became a focus of Western concern. Perhaps within twenty years of the collapse of Soviet Communism, the Western world will wake up and take an interest in the Gulag.

But the story is at least now available. The relationship of the Gulag to the Holocaust can be established; it played a major part in how the war developed and, in particular, how it ended. So what actually happened?

The term 'concentration camp' first appeared in the colonial wars of the late nineteenth century. In 1895, when Madrid was desperately trying to keep control of the island of Cuba, the Spanish army of occupation introduced a policy of '*reconcentración*' of isolating the rural population in small agglomerations so as to control them. The policy proved an instant military success, though it led, as expected, to the mass starvation of the '*reconcentrados*'. A hostile American press campaign developed over Spanish cruelties that culminated in the Spanish–American War, ousting Spain from the New World. In South Africa the British had been in a running battle with the original Dutch settlers, the Boers, ever since Britain took control of the colony at the Congress of Vienna in 1815; the chief issue was slavery, which the British opposed. Then it became gold, which the Boers controlled. Finally, in 1899, it became war. Formal military operations came to an end in 1902, but a vicious guerrilla war persisted. In 1900 the British offered to Boer families, who submitted, the protection of 'concentration camps'; there can be no doubt that the idea was borrowed directly from the Spanish example in Cuba. By 1902, when they were dispersed, the camps were overpopulated, their inmates undernourished and subject to appallingly high death rates. The initial intention – to protect families from the effects of war – was probably humane, but the result was the exact opposite. A powerful press campaign against the British was mounted in both America and Europe – the last of these a Nazi campaign mounted in the Munich press, next door to Dachau, in 1940. Nazis and Communists were always keen to claim that the inventors of the 'concentration camp' were British; but the link between what happened in South Africa at the beginning of the century and the great administrative machines of incarceration and death in Central and Eastern Europe seems feeble indeed.[94]

But there is one tender filament. German South-West Africa (annexed as a 'mandate' to South Africa after the First World War) bore evidence of a colonial prototype of what most people today would call a 'concentration camp'. The aim in the German territory, gained by Bismarck, was to transform this virtually deserted, but mineral rich, region into a purely white colony. To the south lived a small tribe of herdsmen, the Herero. They totalled about 80,000 in 1904, when General Lothar von Trotha, commander of German forces in the region, went to battle against them; he slaughtered every one of the 6,000 Herero combatants he encountered and then massacred another 20,000–30,000 civilians. Von Trotha wanted the complete liquidation of the Herero tribe. He was supported by Kaiser Wilhelm II but opposed by the German Chief of Staff, Field Marshal Alfred Count von Schlieffen, and the Chancellor, Bernhard Prince von Bülow. Eventually it was decided that the Herero could be usefully employed as slaves. The survivors were therefore deported on cattle trains northwards to Lüderitzbucht, Swakopmund and Karibib where they were placed in labour camps known as *Konzentrationslagern* – a term borrowed from the British 'concentration camps' in South Africa. The internees were divided into various categories, including *Arbeitsfähige* and *Unfähige* ('Capable of Work' and 'Not Capable'); the same terms were used at Auschwitz. Medical experiments were conducted on the inmates by Professors Theodor Mollisson and Eugen Fischer, the two most influential teachers of Dr Josef Mengele, the famous practitioner at Auschwitz. The Imperial Commissioner of the colony at the time was Dr Heinrich Göring, father of Hermann Göring, the first senior administrator of Hitler's camps. The census of 1911 shows that 15,130 Hereros survived in South-West Africa – 80 per cent of them had been exterminated in seven years.[95]

There was a fundamental change in the world balance of power at this time: the maritime powers gave way to the continental powers, Europe's guns turned inward into Europe, and so did the system of the 'concentration camp'. Solzhenitsyn claimed that the Gulag had nothing to do with war; Primo Levi would say much the same for Auschwitz. But it would be difficult to imagine either the Russian or the German system developing without the two world wars that were centred in Europe.

Germany began to understand, Russia rapidly understood, the United States belatedly understood (thanks largely to Wedemeyer and his studies in Germany), the British never understood (with the exception of dear old Sir Halford Mackinder), that aeroplanes, railways and rockets were shifting power from the maritime to the continental centres. The great battle of the world would henceforth revolve around control of the Euro-Asian 'island'. Who in the future would care about Africa? The First World War turned the tables. Germany lost. But Germany could never admit she had lost. In Russia there was a revolution.

This outcome was to prove a disaster for the European Jews, and a catastrophe for the whole eastern half of Europe.

The pattern of development of 'concentration camps' during the First World War has never been thoroughly analysed. Several were set up in France, largely in the south-western parts of the country, for foreign refugees; the term 'concentration camp' was used widely in the press, with no sinister meaning implied; and though hardly up to the standard of holiday camps, the chief problem for inmates seems to have been boredom, not poor hygiene. Many enemy aliens were held at Alexandra Palace in north London where several complaints about living conditions were made by the inmates.

But much less is known about developments in Germany, Poland, the Baltic states and Russia. Western historians after the First World War, keen to show their pacific intentions towards Germany, claimed that stories of German atrocities in Belgium were pure myth. But this is not what the Belgians reported – several hundred thousand of them were deported by train for forced labour in Germany under the terms of the Hindenburg Plan. This was also the fate of the French in the northern portions of the country occupied by Germany. It is one of those great holes in our memory – speak to the elderly sons and daughters of the survivors of atrocities behind German lines; they will tell of deliberate efforts made by French and British authorities during the inter-war years to stifle the stories so as not to damage German-French peace efforts. Evidence of massive deportations to labour camps in Germany can apparently be found – for those who can afford the trip – in the Red Cross archives in Geneva and the Vatican archives in Rome. The subject was strictly taboo in the politics and newspapers of the inter-war years.[96]

Erich Maria Remarque wrote *All Quiet on the Western Front* at this time. It was hailed in England and France as a great pacifist novel, which of course it was not: it was a novel about the sacrifice of soldiers and the disaster of defeat. 'I know the barracks at the training camp out on the moors,' Remarque writes. 'Next to our barracks is the big POW camp for Russian soldiers. It is separated from us by wire fencing, but the prisoners still manage to get over to us. They behave in a very shy and nervous manner . . . they seem to us like meek and mistreated St Bernard dogs. They creep around our barracks and raid the rubbish bins.' What Remarque is describing is a primitive German concentration camp.[97]

The war ended on the Western Front with the Armistice of 11 November 1918. But that was not the end of the European war: it marched eastwards (with the German Supreme Command keeping in step until it reached Kolberg on the Baltic). There was civil war in Germany between the fragments – soldiers and sailors – of the imperial armed forces. Germans were still fighting Poles in 1920. The Poles' war with the Bolsheviks only ended with the Treaty of Riga in March 1921. Through Central and Eastern Europe there were waged at least two dozen little wars after the Armistice; the peacemakers in Paris were overwhelmed with the problems. Several serious massacres were conducted in the Baltic states between Germans, Bolsheviks and the natives. And then there was of course the Russian Civil War, which gave birth to the Gulag. In Russia and its neighbouring 'Soviet Republics' there was, in effect, no 'inter-war period' of total peace; Russia experienced perpetual wars between 1914 and at least 1945.

Swirling winds of human violence, sometimes an eddy, sometimes a cyclone, were always there throughout the first half of the twentieth century. At times they blew from Russia, at times from Germany or Poland, little gusts over the Baltic, a hurricane across the northern plain. Armies marched, or there would be waves of Partisans, *Einsatzgruppen* (special execution squads), defectors, re-defectors, prisons, camps, exterminations. It all began and spread in the same large region, and followed the same inexorable logic, '*la logique de guerre*' as the French nicely call it. But, unlike the wind, its cause was human, and somebody could have stopped it. But nobody did. Where did the Gulag begin? Where were the very worst Nazi camps? In this region of continual, swirling violence.

The Russian Revolution of 1917 was both a product of the violence and a prime mover of its escalation. There is an interesting coincidence of events between the Western and Eastern Fronts in 1918. The decisive Second Battle of the Marne in France had just begun when Trotsky demanded that the Red Army, on 4 June 1918, lock up a rebel Czech legion (caught in Russia because of the war) in 'a concentration camp'.

The Kaiser's Imperial Army had just suffered on the Somme what Ludendorff called its 'blackest day', when Lenin gave the order on 10 August 1918 'to lock up the kulaks, the priests, the White Guard and other doubtful elements in a concentration camp outside the city'.[98] Within a year, as the German army collapsed and German power receded, Lenin's 'concentration camp' system extended northwards from Moscow towards the White Sea, then eastwards along Russia's Arctic coast; then down into the deserts of Kazakhstan, and northwards up to the Siberian peninsula of Kolyma. In the 1920s and '30s the number of inmates reached the first, and then the second million. The camps of Kolyma eventually covered one tenth of Soviet territory.

Perhaps Lenin had borrowed the term 'concentration camp' from the British imperialists in South Africa. But it would seem much more likely that he had picked it up from the German *Konzentrationslager* developed during the First World War. Some of the very worst had sprung up in East Prussia, Lithuania and the occupied parts of old imperial Russia. They were used to hold civilian hostages who would be shot in reprisal for massacres committed by the enemy. Their wooden barracks, surrounded by barbed wire and guard towers, were barely a hundred miles from where the first camps of the Gulag were built. Russian and German camps breathed death into one another, like the winds of the plain, in an alternating cycle.

The inter-war period made death – that is mass, organized death – ideological, both in Russian Communism and German National Socialism.

Prisons were supposed to disappear from Communist society, as were classes, social distinctions, and the state. But the state never withered and the prisons simply got another name. As for classes and social distinctions, they became greater than ever. The French historian, François Furet, speaks of Stalinism as the 'highest stage of Communism'; that is, after the victory of 1945, Communism became a universal ideal. It was no longer on the defensive. It came as close as it ever would to realizing the 'revolutionary universalism' that it had claimed since the days of Marx. Many Westerners were won round to it, including several people in the highest reaches of power. Decades later, as some of the truth seeped into the West, Marxists would claim that 'Stalinism' was a perversion of Communism. But this was hardly their argument at the triumph of 1945 and its immediate aftermath.[99]

It was something that puzzled people in the eastern half of Europe, who had to live in the Communist utopia for the next forty years. When, in the 1990s, the historian Stéphane Courtois attended conferences in

Eastern Europe on the subject of Communism he was constantly confronted, especially by the young, with the question, 'Why did so many Western intellectuals support Communism?'[100] The answer lay in Stalin's victory, a confirmation of the power of Marxism.

And it was on Marx and Engels that Solzhenitsyn laid the blame for the Gulag: 'Engels discovered that the human being had arisen not through the perception of a moral idea and not through the process of thought, but out of happenstance and meaningless work (an ape picked up a stone – and with this everything began).' Marx, concerning himself with a less remote time (*Critique of the Gotha Programme*), declared with equal conviction that 'the *one and only* means of correcting offenders . . . was not solitary contemplation, not moral soul-searching, not repentance, and not languishing (for all that was superstructure!) – but productive labour.' The Gotha Programme had been an attempt by German Socialists to reform the stony dogma of Marxism. Leninism and Stalinism imposed the practice of putting all 'deviationists' behind barbed wire. 'This means', said Vyshinsky, Stalin's prosecutor and master apprentice of Marxist theory, 'the maximum *strengthening* of corrective-labour institutions.'[101] It took the Communists three decades and more before they arrived at such 'maximum strengthening'.

The remarkable feature about the Nazis was the speed at which they worked. Their regime only lasted twelve years in contrast to the seventy-odd years of Soviet Communism. The Holocaust took place in three. Yet this was also based on an ideology of death. Hitler's conversion to a rabid anti-Semitic racism seems to have been very sudden. As with Goebbels, the basic theme of his ideology was anti-capitalist – 'a grave economic symptom of decay was the slow disappearance of the right of private property, and the gradual transference of the entire economy to the ownership of stock companies,' he stated in *Mein Kampf*. But the cause of the problem was not the 'bourgeois class', but the Jew: 'The deepest and ultimate reason for the decline of the old Reich lay in its failure to recognize the racial problem and its importance for the historical development of peoples'; the Jew 'is and remains the typical parasite, a sponger who like a noxious bacillus keeps spreading as soon as a favourable medium invites him'.[102]

The reason for Hitler's sudden conversion to this vehement racist dogma was the surprise announcement from the outside world in May 1919 – as Germans focused on the great domestic issues of civil war – of the terms of the Versailles Treaty. Like most Germans, Hitler could not believe his country had been defeated in war. The fault, as he explained in *Mein Kampf*, was with 'international Jewry', which had stabbed Germany in the back. 'Never again 1918,' repeated Hitler up until his suicide. Up to the moment of their surrender, the Nazis gave priority not to military defence, but to massacring Jews.

But there exists no written order from the top of the Nazi hierarchy commanding the massacre of the Jews. The Wannsee Protocol of 20 January 1942, often taken as the order, speaks of the Jews being 'evacuated to the East'[103] (a phrase which would give the tiny school of 'Holocaust deniers' the main lever of their perverse argument). Hitler and Himmler had been considering an evacuation of all Jews, first to Madagascar and then east of the Urals. But the loss of any chance for control of these lands and the transformation – much against Hitler's own will – of the military campaign into a total war on all fronts, pushed the Nazis towards massacre, the Holocaust, the 'Final Solution'.

There is much debate about the moment the decision was taken. Preparations for the invasion of Russia as a 'war of annihilation' was without doubt a turning point. 'The Jewish-Bolshevik intelligentsia, the "oppressor" of the people up to now, must be eliminated,' read Jodl's operational guideline of 3 March 1941. The *Einsatzgruppen*, following the armies, put mass murder into practice: 9,012 Jewish men, women and children in Kovno on 29 November; 99,804 civilians (mostly Jews) in the Baltic region of Kovno, Schaulen and Vilna on 1 December 1941. But the executioners themselves were traumatized by the scale of their murders; by autumn 1941 Berlin's hospitals were filling up with executioners suffering from nervous breakdowns – 'I can't do it any more!' they would exclaim, 'I can't do it any more!' Himmler berated his men for 'weakness', but when he himself insisted on attending the execution of just a few hundred Jews in August 1941 he turned white and stared down at his polished boots. The answer was gas chambers in extermination camps – more humane, not for the victims, but for the exterminators.[104]

When was the decision made to build camps for the extermination of all the Jews of Europe? Nobody can give a definite answer to this. The Wannsee Protocol of 20 January 1942* appears to have been less a decision than an affirmation of a policy that had already been determined higher up in the Nazi hierarchy. At the same time, the extermination camps – with their gas chambers – of Chełmno, Treblinka, Sobibór, Majdanek, Bełżec and the extermination zone of Auschwitz-Birkenau were not in operation until 1942. Up until the invasion of Russia in June

---

* Only one copy of the Wannsee Protocol has survived. It was discovered by staff of the US Prosecutor in the 'Ministries Case' at Nuremberg in March 1947, that is after the international war crimes trials of Nuremberg had been conducted and the principal Nazi leaders had been executed. This is one of the facts that has led to so much debate on the meaning of the Protocol – the principal decision-makers were no longer alive.

1941 Hitler was delaying his 'Final Solution' of the Jews until he could see more clearly the outcome of the war. During this time he appears to have wavered between massive deportation and extermination. German economists were predicting that the Reich could not afford to continue the war beyond 1941; Hitler expected world victory to be his by then. But in early autumn his advance into Russia began to slow down; he would never reach Moscow.

Probably the event decisive for the fate of the Jews was initiated not by Hitler, but by Stalin. Between 13 and 15 September 1941 the Volga Germans – who had been in that region since the days of Catherine the Great – were deported to Siberia. Alfred Rosenberg, Minister for the Eastern Territories, told Hitler, correctly, that virtually none of them would survive. It seems that it was between late September and October 1941 that Hitler, not a forgiving man, decided to exterminate the Jews of Europe in return – for the Jews, in Hitler's mind, were the inventors of Communism.[105]

Thus the murderous policies of Nazi Germany suggest a link with the murderous policies of the Soviet Union. The Nazis had no specific plan for a European Holocaust when they came to power in 1933, though the elimination of the Jews by one way or another was certainly crucial to their thinking. The rapid development and execution of the Holocaust after 1941 was a sign not of a deliberate long-thought-out policy, but rather of a war that was getting out of hand, becoming total – exactly what Hitler, since the days of *Mein Kampf*, had wanted to avoid. After 1941 he was obliged to imagine ways in which his Nazi ideology could survive in a world where victory was neither as quick nor as complete as he had at first imagined; it would have to be in a world without Jews. The Jews, all the Jews, would have to be murdered while he still had control, *before* the war was ended.

Again, the speed at which mass murder developed is one of the main contrasts between the Nazi system of concentration camps and the Communists'. The Russian Communist slave labour camps were developed over decades; they permitted the system to survive. Having spread in number across the Eurasian continent between 1917 and 1940, they were precipitated into decline by Hitler's invasion. One cause, beyond the loss of camps and territory to the enemy, was that tens of thousands of *zeki* (inmates) were immediately transferred to the front, where they became the cannon fodder of the Red Army. That was how Hitler was halted, despite the fact that Stalin had already murdered 80 per cent of his generals in the 1930s. As the war began to turn, the number of *zeki* began to creep up again, to heights that had never been known before. Unlike the Holocaust, this was not the sign of approaching defeat, but the symbol of Communist victory; it was the age, as Solzhenitsyn put it, when whole nations were 'dumped down the sewer pipes'. The Volga Germans were the first. There were very few survivors.

Here was the second major difference from the German Holocaust. There *were* a few survivors from the Gulag. Among Jews of the Holocaust there were practically none. Over 99 per cent of those delivered to such specialized German extermination camps as Treblinka, Bełżec, Sobibór or Chełmno – closed, obliterated, and turned into virgin meadows before the end of the war – died.[106] Jews were arrested because they were Jewish, and rarely for any other reason; their chances of survival were tiny.

Most arrests for the Gulag were made on the grounds of Article 58 of the Soviet Criminal Code. It was an administrative matter; judicial courts rarely had any part to play in the imprisonment and sentencing of the 'fifty-eights', as they were known. Many had no idea at all why they were arrested and were surprised when it happened. Formal charges were typed out on a one-page note that the prisoner, after days of interrogation, would always end up signing – the most hardened Communists among them. The administration had invented a number of acronyms, not easily understood by a novice *zek*: ASA for 'Anti-Soviet Agitation', for example; KRD for 'Counter-Revolutionary Activity'; 'KRTD' – a very serious charge that meant almost certain death – for 'Counter-Revolutionary Trotskyite Activity'. There were also the 'Dissemination of Anti-Soviet Sentiments' (VAS), the 'Socially Dangerous Element' (SOE), the 'Socially Harmful Element' (SVE), etc. A colour code was adopted for each category of prisoner that was later imitated by the more efficient administrators of the Nazi camps, 'Stalin's pupils'. The Soviet category ChS stood for 'Member of a Family', which provided the occasion to arrest children. Some specialists of the Jewish Holocaust claim that one of the great contrasts between the Russian Communist system and that of the Nazis was that children were not sent to the Gulag. That is nonsense. They were known as 'the kids' and, in the Gulag, it was wise to keep clear of them for they could be very violent. In addition to being arrested for an accident of family relationship, children could end up in the Gulag for a variety of other reasons – one could get twelve years, for example, for 'carelessness', eight years for 'a pocketful of potatoes', five years for 'a dozen cucumbers'; or three years for the theft of 'socialist property' (which applied to all farm produce).

So the main difference between the two systems was that the Nazis had specific aims whereas the Communists fired in every direction: it was difficult to change one's 'race', whereas anyone could be an 'enemy of the people'.[107]

The great paradox about the Communists' haphazard system of arrest was that it spread terror of the Gulag into all corners of Soviet society – a terror reinforced by the presence of special police and informers in every apartment block in the cities and in every village and hamlet in the country-side. Contrast this with the few dozen Gestapo one might find in a city like Cologne! Most German citizens had nothing to fear from the Nazis. There was still an element of isolated, eighteenth-century provincialism in Hitler's Germany; local guilds still flourished, local identity was still strong, as under *das alte Reich*, the old Reich, the first thousand-year Reich. Germans were very proud of their Führer's victories until the moment the invasion of Russia turned sour. Towards the end of the war their concerns were the daily bombardment and the approach of the front, the sight of refugees, the destruction of their homes; they had lost contact with the Nazi state – their worry was survival. The Russian Communists abolished the old administrative lines, they tore down the ancient hedges and boundaries; they changed the landscape. There had never been guilds in Russia, and the old rural *zemstvos* (communities) had been abolished. There was no local force to protect the Russians; administrative ruling came from on high, the Politburo. The Soviet citizen found every aspect of his life touched in one way or another by the Communist state; each one of them faced the threat of random arrest and confinement in the Gulag. German 'concentration camps' separated certain categories from civilian life and, more often than not, killed them. The Russian Gulag penetrated every aspect of Soviet society. And here was the paradox: it was the Soviet Union – the West's 'grand ally' – that was in strictest terms the totalitarian state, not Hitler's Germany.

8 Final Solution: the finale

But one should never underestimate the Nazi propensity for killing. The priority accorded by Nazi fanatics, at the war's end, to slaughtering Jews – and the incredible speed at which they accomplished this – is illustrated by the case of Hungary. Hungary would become by 1945 Hitler's south-eastern 'appendix', his hope for a last-minute victory, an opening to the Ukraine. But more important than the military operation of shoring up Hungary against the invasion from three sides by the Red Army and its new allies was the great task of murdering Hungary's 800,000 Jews. At this late stage in the war – in the Nazi faith – the only chance their Reich

had to revive itself for a thousand years was through the physical elimination of the traitorous, nationless Jews. Never again 1918! Never again the
stab in the back! About 400,000 Hungarian Jews were gassed at
Auschwitz–Birkenau that spring. A special new railway spur brought
convoy after convoy, day and night, up to the gas chambers. 'Such a smell
of burning flesh wafted towards us,' wrote one rare survivor, 'one not
only smelt the stench but saw the flames rising from the crematoria.'
Another witness was in a train kept for several hours in a siding because
of the heavy traffic: 'We could only hear the shunting of engines, crunch
of people walking outside, and eventually, well into daylight, the door
being pulled open and people being herded out. It was an amazing scene.
It reminded me of what I imagined a lunatic asylum would be like.'[108]

Under its Regent, Admiral Miklós Horthy, Hungary had been as independent an ally of Hitler as it was possible to be; the admiral kept his sea-
less country's involvement in the Russian war to a minimum and, more
remarkably, he refused to hand over the Jews. Even when the Germans
demanded tens of thousands for 'labour required in the war effort', Horthy
insolently replied that he could 'lend' them for a few months, but they
would have to be returned to their homes. As a result, a huge Jewish
community continued to live in Hungary after most of the Jews of Europe
had been slaughtered.

Hitler was worried that Hungary could turn into another Italy, something he could not allow since Hungary was his main gate to the Ukraine.
On 19 March 1944 his troops invaded the country and installed a new
Quisling government under Döme Sztojay, which included several rabid
anti-Semites. Horthy, however, remained Regent. Within less than four
months 437,000 Hungarian Jews were deported to Auschwitz. Sweden and
Switzerland, whose neutrality had become suddenly more 'Western' in
tone after the Allied invasion of Normandy, made representations to
Horthy. The Vatican, too, made an appeal to save the Jews.[109] The convoys
to Auschwitz increased in number, so much so that German military
supplies to their crumbling Army Group Centre in Belorussia were halted.
The defences of Normandy were collapsing at this moment. But the
deportation and mass murder of the Jews were accelerated.

Then, on 7 July, Horthy had the audacity to halt the deportations –
for he, like neutral Switzerland and Sweden, had a sense of the direction
in which the war was going. The last train to Auschwitz shunted out of
Budapest on the morning of 9 July 1944. More than half the Jews of
Hungary were by now dead.

In preparation for this rapid mass murder (committed in Auschwitz
between 15 May and 11 July), the Jews had in the classical Nazi manner

been first collected in city 'ghettoes' in Hungary. The only major ghetto now left was in Budapest, cramped in Pest on the east side of the Danube. It held about 120,000 Jews. The Swiss and the Swedish legations had been active in distributing protective passes, and even setting up special protective houses within the ghetto. One of the most famous diplomats involved was the Swede, Raoul Wallenberg. He had arrived in Budapest on the day the last train left for Auschwitz and remained there until the moment the Red Army stormed the city centre, on 18 January 1945; he was immediately arrested by Soviet authorities and was never seen again. In the previous summer Wallenberg, aided by the Swiss, had taken over a large department store, the 'Glass House', and opened it up for the Jews. Wallenberg and his colleagues saved several thousand lives including those of children, housed in forty children's homes.

For Hitler it was an intolerable situation. Gangs of Nazis and their collaborators ruled the streets of Budapest, attacked the ghetto and murdered men, women and children in broad daylight. On 15 October, while Horthy was negotiating with Stalin in Moscow (during Churchill's visit), Otto Skorzeny made his daring raid on the Citadel of Budapest and established the proto-Nazi regime of Ferencz Szálasi's Arrow Cross. Adolf Eichmann, of Berlin's Department of Jewish Affairs, made his second swift visit to Budapest. 'You see, I am back again,' he told the head of Budapest's *Judenrat* (the Council of Jews which, like most such bodies in Central and Eastern Europe, showed an unexpected willingness to cooperate with the Nazis). 'You forgot Hungary is still in the shadow of the Reich. My arms are long and I can reach the Jews of Budapest as well.' The Soviet pincers were moving in on the city; there was no longer any question of deportation by train. The Jews, said Eichmann, 'will be driven out on foot this time'.[110]

It was a pressing issue – more important for the Nazis than the defence of Budapest itself. Between 20 October and Christmas Day, when the Soviets finally achieved a complete blockade of the city, over 30,000 Jews were driven on foot towards the Austrian border. Thus began a series of death marches, which would prove, over the winter of 1944–5, to be the Nazis' final desperate effort to eliminate all the Jews of Europe – and to save for future generations their own weird National Socialist ideal.

Budapest was surrounded. But despite the shortage of men, weapons and ammunition, the murder of Jews continued in the ghetto. On New Year's Eve Nazis broke into the 'Glass House', ordering Jews out on to the street, where several were shot. The Red Army liberated the Jewish ghetto on 18 January 1945. Elements of the German occupying forces and the Arrow Cross remained in the area until mid-April, thanks again to the indefatigable Colonel Skorzeny, who had returned from disaster in the western 'Bulge'. But he could only hold out for so long. By late April the Soviets were the masters of this ancient Magyar province of the Habsburgs. Having lived through the First World War, an early Communist regime, a royalist-style dictatorship, and Nazi occupation, the Hungarians could look forward to the delights of a new Communist utopia.

9 Last days at Auschwitz

One of Hitler's lasting achievements was to make those few Jews who survived conscious that they were a single people. He also, of course, annihilated whole civilizations. Isaac Bashevis Singer is the scribe of one such civilization wiped out in Central Europe. Born in Poland at the beginning of the last century, he was trained to be a rabbi in old Warsaw but became a journalist instead. In 1935, thank God, he emigrated to New York where he continued to write the stories of his childhood in Yiddish – not exactly a guarantee of bestsellerdom. But he would one day win the Nobel Prize for Literature. 'Yiddish', he explained, being a mixture of old German and Hebrew, 'contains vitamins that other languages don't have.' A '*yid*' means in Yiddish a 'man', but also a 'Jew'. The term is not a slur – though it developed as one among the anti-Semites; the word refers to a civilization that stretched through Poland and into the Russian borderlands. What Isaac Bashevis Singer did for what he called the 'Yiddishists', the Polish Hassidim, can be justly compared to what Homer did for Troy.

They isolated themselves from the Poles because they did not speak the same language. 'Six hundred years in the country', says one of Singer's exasperated Western Jews, Mr Wallenberg, 'and the Jews haven't bothered to learn the language . . . Time passes them by. Mankind progresses, but they remain as static as the Chinese beyond the Great Wall.'[11] They dressed differently, the men in their prayer shawls and skullcaps, their hair falling in long sidelocks, and the women with trains and bonnets, decorated with bows and satin ribbons, and fur-trimmed velvet capes. 'They dressed like Asiatics and believed in *dibbuks* [demons],' says Singer. They had the greatest contempt for those outside their own community – not only the neighbouring Polish peasants, *mischaks*, but also all the other Jews, especially the Lithuanian Jews, who lived in 'The Sands and among the Gentiles'. Sometimes one of their own kind would disappear – usually, in Bashevis Singer's tales, for abandoning a poor adolescent wife. 'The demons had captured him,' the Yiddish would say. 'If the demons capture a man, he is not spotted in Zamość and in Lublin. They drag him behind the black mountains where no people walk, no cattle tread.'[112] Isaac Bashevis Singer has this way of looking forward into doom – or Gehenna, the Jewish hell.

The Yiddish Jews defined themselves by their faith, not their race, nor where they lived. One of Bashevis Singer's greatest novels, *The Manor*, is set in Poland after the great Warsaw Rising of 1863 – like all the Polish risings before 1980 it failed dismally and Imperial Russia continued to hold the reins. But the growth of a tariff war between Imperial Germany and Imperial Russia opened to the Yiddish merchants enormous opportunities for trade, much to the envy of the Polish *mischaks*. The Yiddish began to move from the villages to the neighbouring towns, and from the towns to the suburbs of Warsaw, in particular Wola and Ochota. And they began to lose their faith. Ezriel, for example, leaves for Warsaw to become a doctor and starts asking himself questions – 'Who saw God Give Moses the Torah on Mount Sinai? The Jews have the Torah, and the Christians have something else. If their religion can be false so can ours.' Mr Wallenberg from Paris asked Ezriel one day if he believed that God revealed himself to Moses and gave the Jews the Torah and the Talmud? 'No, I am not that much of a believer,' answered Ezriel. 'If that is so,' retorted Wallenberg, 'then why are you still a Jew?' It was the most terrible of all questions. In the same novel Calman Jacoby becomes very rich and takes over the manor house of a dissipated Polish noble, a participant in the Rising of '63. Calman is miserable; he commits all the sins of the flesh. With age he becomes increasingly depressed. What was his purpose? What was his life? 'It was not death that he wanted, however,' teases the novelist, 'but the life of a Jew.'[113]

The life of the Yiddish, in Poland and the borderlands, is at the core of Bashevis Singer's storytelling – a life that was extinguished by the Nazis. In his stories the clouds that sweep across the Yiddish villages come alive: they would 'resemble a flock of goats', in the purple of evening they would become curly and round, one cloud was 'shaped like a fish', the other 'resembled a hedgehog'; the stars glitter at night. These people had never seen the sea, never looked up at a mountain. But they knew the seasons. In the spring 'there was no death'; 'life existed in every tree and every blade of grass.' Even in winter, when the plains turned into a 'congealed ocean', the snow in the trees lining the roads lay 'like white cats on their branches'. Bashevis Singer is Marc Chagall painting in words. For the Yiddish, everything moved, tempted and terrified; the stars shimmered at night and the Almighty decided all. All. All these people were heading for Gehenna, 'behind the black mountains where no people walk'. At the fall of evening there was invariably a sinister dog barking in the distance.

★

The old town of Auschwitz, near the source of the Vistula, had been flattened by the Germans by the time the Italian, Primo Levi, arrived there in February 1944. The barracks and electrified fences of over forty separate concentration camps stretched as far as the eye could see. Levi's train came in at night, but high powerful projectors made it seem as bright as day. A dozen SS men stood around. At moments they moved into the crowd and, in broken Italian, asked a few, 'How old? Healthy or ill?' Then they pointed in different directions. Of the 650 'pieces' (as the German corporal had called them) deported from the Italian camp of Fossoli di Carpi, 96 men and 29 women were moved into their respective barracks at Monowitz-Buna and Birkenau. The rest, including all the children, were gassed that night. On the platform, at the moment of the selection, 'everything was as silent as an aquarium'. Within moments of their delivery at Monowitz-Buna the men were deprived of everything, clothes, watches, even their hair. They were placed in a row by alphabetical order of names and an official, 'with a sort of pointed tool with a very short needle', rapidly tattooed six numbers on the arm. It was a 'slightly painful' operation. Levi was number 174517.[114]

By his own account Levi only discovered his Judaism after his arrival in Auschwitz. It was what made this chemist a writer. He would live out his life in the same spacious flat on the Corso Re Umberto, Turin, in which he was born in 1919 to the day, in April 1987, when he flung himself, head first, down the three-storey stairwell to his death. The only significant period he spent away from home was the year he was in Auschwitz. Reading had opened his horizons. Before Auschwitz he believed that there was only one Western culture, that of Kant, Galileo and Dante. Levi's home district of Crocetta was the richest part of Turin, with villas and vast parks on the rolling hillside of Moncalieri, and tennis courts overlooking the River Po. It was literally the 'Garden of the Finzi-Contini', whose author, Giorgio Bassani, lived in the same quarter. The story was true. The small wealthy Jewish community of Crocetta did not think of themselves as Jews, save at their bar mitzvahs, their annual visits to the synagogue at Yom Kippur, at their marriages and during the inevitable rites of passage at birth and death.[115]

Levi's father was an electrical engineer who, at the end of the First World War, had worked for a large firm in Budapest. In early 1919 he had witnessed Bela Kun's Communist putsch and ever since had held Communism in horror. His mother could speak an Italian dialect which contained many Hebrew words; this was what led Primo Levi to develop his interest in etymology. But his great passion was mountain climbing. 'Mountains seemed to me', he once said, 'the key to everything. I always wanted to translate the feeling one has when the climber has in front of him a mountain face that closes off the horizon. You climb, you don't see this line . . . and then in an instant, at the top, you discover a new world.'[116] The effort and that sudden discovery was at the base of Levi's fundamental optimism − and it is undoubtedly what saved him at Auschwitz. His father died in his Finzi-Contini world in 1942 without the slightest idea of the disaster that was menacing them. Not even Mussolini's anti-Jewish legislation woke up the Jews of Turin. They had no idea of the slaughter of all the Jews just north of the Alps. They had certainly never even heard of the 'Yids' of Poland.

But when the Allies entered southern Italy and the government of Mussolini fell, long columns of soldiers in field grey marched into the streets of Turin. Levi joined an 'anti-Fascist' brigade and was captured. By February 1944 he was at Auschwitz, *Häftling* (prisoner) no. 174517.

The first months were awful. Life expectancy, even in the outer labour camps, was between three and six months. Sickness and weakness were 'cured' by regular 'selections' − the men selected would be carted off naked in lorries to the gas chambers at Birkenau. But gradually those who survived began to understand the system. Daily rations were carefully calculated in calories to assure that the *Häftlinge* would starve to death within six months, when they would become *Musulmänner*, the slang for those living corpses without flesh that could be seen wandering lost around the camps. It was necessary to steal another man's food in order to live. A complicated hierarchy developed, known as the 'Organization', which nearly always involved some kind of collaboration with the Germans. Throughout German concentration camps political prisoners, usually Communists, got the bureaucratic jobs in the camps, jobs that determined 'selection': these men had the right of life and death over other inmates.[117] As Levi would later explain, all survivors were guilty of some sort of crime, and after the war that guilt was felt, terribly.*

Slowly, Levi became aware of the significance of Auschwitz's numbering system − and it was this that introduced him to the remnants of Yiddish civilization. A number was never replaced, even if the prisoner died. No. 174517 was a 'High Number'; it meant he had arrived late; it even identified him as an Italian Jew. Numbers 30,000 to 80,000 were only represented by a few hundred; they were the Jews from the Polish ghettoes, what remained of 'Yiddishists'. Caution was needed in commercial dealings with numbers 116,000 to 117,000; they were the

---

* This was possibly one of the reasons for the silence of so many witnesses of the Holocaust after the war.

Greek Jews from Salonica; 'so take care they do not pull the wool over your eyes'. High Numbers were the freshmen of the class; they were treated with contempt by the Low Numbers.[118]

Gradually Levi got to know this babbling Germanic tongue of the Low Numbers; German he knew and he could make a link with the dialect his mother spoke. Several months passed before one of the Yiddish Poles taught him the meaning of 'selection'. It happened while he was sick in the camp hospital, '*Ka-Be*' – a common place for 'selections'. One of his neighbours was a Low Number, a Yiddish Pole called Schmulek. 'Show me your number,' he said. 174517? This numbering system began only eighteen months ago, explained the Pole. 'There are now ten thousand of us here at Monowitz-Buna; perhaps thirty thousand between Auschwitz and Birkenau. *Wo sind die Andere?* Where are the others?' 'Perhaps transferred to other camps?' suggested Levi. Schmulek shook his head and turned to another Low Number to say in Yiddish, '*Er will nix verstayen*,' he does not want to understand.[119]

No one felt a man in Auschwitz. No one felt as if they were in a place – it was extraterrestrial. Yet, like Bashevis Singer, Levi tells his story season by season. In the spring the Hungarians arrived and soon the Magyar tongue predominated over Yiddish, despite the high proportion of Hungarian Jews who were gassed on arrival. In the hot summer the Allies bombed the factories of Buna; many survivors have since criticized them for not hitting the gas chambers and the crematoria. All were aware of the Allied landings in Normandy as well as the advance of the Red Army, but none thought they would survive the winter and their liberation. In autumn Levi passed a chemistry exam and thus gained access to an over-heated German chemical laboratory. He could hear the military bands thumping outside as his colleagues were marched out in their striped prison clothes to hard labour; he returned every night to their barracks. 'We fought with all our strength to prevent the arrival of winter.'[120]

But it came. The historian Martin Gilbert notes that the last gassing took place at Auschwitz on 31 October; Levi had the impression that it continued until November. The Germans were frightened by the Red Army offensives to the south; many men were sent to the factory zone at Gleiwitz; women and children were forwarded for extermination at Mauthausen and Gross Rosen. The great labour of winter was the dismantling of the crematoria at Birkenau with the purpose of turning the area into fresh meadows – and thereby creating another of those great holes in our historical memory. But the work was not completed; 'we could hear the distant booming of the Russian guns.' On 11 January 1945 Levi fell ill with scarlet fever; he was sent to the 'Infection Room' of the *Ka-Be*, a closet three yards by five containing thirteen very sick men.[121]

Levi had four peaceful days; it was snowing outside but the room was heated. He became friendly with two Frenchmen, whose language he spoke fluently. They were newcomers and frightened. On the sixth day, 17 January, the barber arrived. Cutting hair and shaving was usually a brutal affair and the worst could be expected in this case: he was a Greek Jew from Salonica who spoke only Spanish and a few words of German. But Levi had started a brisk trade in cigarette-lighter flints – which he made himself – and the Greek got to know about it. Not only did Levi get a gentle shave, he was also given some astonishing news: the Greek barber made a gesture with his chin towards the window and then swept his free hand towards the west. '*Morgen, alle Kamarad weg,*' he said – 'Tomorrow all Comrades go.' The camps were to be evacuated on 18 January.

Levi himself felt no emotion. It was the two sick Frenchmen who, as freshmen at Auschwitz, started asking questions. What was going to happen to the sick? Levi, by now a senior, did not say a word, but he expected to be killed. All those who had the strength would do better to join the march being organized for the next morning. Two in the sickroom left. Levi's old Italian friend Alberto came to the window and waved goodbye – 'he was cheerful and confident, as were all those who were leaving.' But it was the sick who survived. The next day about 20,000 were marched off from the various camps of Auschwitz. Barely any of them would survive. Writing only two years later, Levi remarked: 'Perhaps someone will write their story one day.'[122]

Gradually the story of the death marches has been revealed – a story which lies at the very heart of the massive population movements that characterized the period 1945–6. Numbers are not worth a great deal for this period, for nobody was keeping a register, but it has been estimated that around three quarters of a million concentration camp inmates, all categories mixed, were moved westwards by foot away from the approaching Red Army and towards what remained of the Reich. Between 250,000 and 375,000 died. What the British met at Bergen-Belsen and the Americans at Dachau and Buchenwald were no longer 'concentration camps' in the strict Nazi sense of the word. They were the survivors – the few survivors – of all the camps mixed together. These camps were filled with former inmates of the evacuated camps in the East, people who had been marching for weeks in the snow under the guard of special SS units. It was a chaotic phenomenon, in which neither the prisoners nor their guards knew exactly where they were heading. Those prisoners who could no longer walk were put in wagons, then taken up a side road in the evening and shot in groups. Many others simply fell down in their tracks and died of exhaustion. There was a constant sound of rifle shot at the back of the columns.[123]

Levi and his eleven companions remained in their tiny sickroom. The central heating system had been turned off; outside it was at least 5°F below zero. On the first day, 18 January, there was evidence of a few SS men waiting around: nobody among the sick expected to live more than a day. Then, in the evening, there were a series of bombardments. Windows broke, the barrack shook, spoons rattled; the roar of the explosions was loud enough to break eardrums. The two Frenchmen cowered in a corner. Inmates outside clamoured to be let in, screaming in a dozen languages. But sympathy was not the rule in Auschwitz. The eleven men barricaded their doors.

The next day at dawn, 19 January, there was total silence. The Germans had gone. Levi and his two French friends agreed to go outside in search of food and blankets. What greeted their eyes was a scene out of Dante. There was no electricity, no water; broken windows and doors were banging in the wind; the torn corrugated iron roofs screeched, buildings were burning; skeleton-like men dragged themselves across the frozen ground – some of them able to stand and fight for putrid potatoes, or for a useful tool such as a ladle or an axe, 'cursing in Yiddish between their frozen lips'.

Levi and his friends managed to find food and soiled blankets. They even discovered a battery which would provide them with light at night. Two men in the room died, one a Hungarian chemist, who repeated for hours an obedient '*Jawohl! Jawohl*' and finally, in the middle of the night, fell from his upper bunk to the floor with a thud. Outside, the silence became increasingly eerie; the filth of the dead and the walking skeletons suffering from dysentery invaded every corner of the camp.

On 21 January the silence was broken by the roar of artillery; shells flew over the camp. 'I was thinking life outside was beautiful and would be beautiful again.' But as *Häftling* no. 174517 felt himself transforming back into a man, with his passions, he became increasingly aware that he was sick with scarlet fever. Survival itself had its nightmares. Somogyi, the dead Hungarian, still lay on the floor where he had fallen. On 27 January Levi and Charles – one of the Frenchmen – decided to carry the dead man outside. He was incredibly light. As they tossed his body into the filthy snow, the Russians arrived. 'Charles took off his beret. I regretted not having a beret.'[124]

That, of course, was not the end of Levi's story of his year away from home. In April the Russians evacuated every survivor from Auschwitz; they would not publish a word on the camp until the following month, after the German surrender. Levi found himself in a collecting camp outside Katowice. One day he got a permit to visit the town. There was not a Pole to be seen; the town was filled with Russian troops on the move, some going to the front, others returning to Russia.

He expected the Russians to take him by train to the Crimea, where he would catch a boat to Italy. Instead, he was transported to a camp in Belorussia, where he spent the summer of 1945. In autumn, another train took him, in slow stages, to Austria, then to Munich, then almost back to Auschwitz again. In October he was in Hungary where his convoy was joined by a group of young men and women speaking Yiddish, a language Levi now spoke and loved. Levi had become a European Jew. They were heading, said the Yiddish, for the British mandate of Palestine where they intended to fight the British and establish the independent state of Israel; they had no further interest in Central Europe, the cemetery of the Jews.

Levi, however, eventually returned to Italy. On 19 October 1945, he climbed the winding staircase up the three floors to his apartment on the Corso Re Umberto. He stepped through the door. All the members of his family had been spared. At first they could not recognize this dirty, bearded figure. There were no cries, no tears, when finally they did. 'It's cold,' said his mother. 'Put on a sweater.'

Levi replied, 'No.' Besides, he did not have one. That, presumably, was the day the war ended for Primo Levi.[125]

Endings

ϒ

1 VE-Days

When did it end? Ask the old folk what they were doing on the day the war ended. 'I seem to remember it was terribly cold,' says a French acquaintance of mine. 'I can recall coming out of the theatre: it was *absolutely freezing.*' As a matter of fact, the record shows that it was hot in Paris on Tuesday, 8 May 1945. But it had snowed the previous week, on Tuesday, 1 May, when the Communists were demonstrating in the streets. I personally do not know a single Frenchman who can remember the day the war officially ended in Europe. But they all remember D-Day. And their parents remember – often with tears in their eyes – the day the Great War ended, on 11 November 1918.

Perhaps this is a peculiarly French phenomenon. After all, France had been ingloriously defeated in 1940. Despite all the propaganda, most Frenchmen did not consider 1945 a 'victory'. So ask an elderly Englishman what he was doing on the day the war ended. Outside London, surprisingly few can remember. But they all remember D-Day. And their fathers remember the day the Great War ended, on Monday with the ringing of bells at eleven o'clock in the morning, 11 November 1918.

Some of my elderly friends in California can remember the events of 1945. But none of them have precise memories of what they were up to on 'the day the war ended' in Europe. For them, the main war was in the Pacific. What they remember was the week two atomic bombs were dropped on Japan – and mighty glad they were to hear the news.

After 1942 people talked vaguely, and hopefully, in both America and Europe of a coming 'V-Day', Victory Day. By 1944, because of the two major war theatres, the expression separated into a 'VE-Day', Victory in Europe Day, to which the Allied forces gave first priority, and an eventual 'VJ-Day', Victory in Japan Day, which many thought would come only in 1947. It was hoped by some in Europe that, once the Allies had made their spectacular landing in Normandy, 'VE-Day' would be celebrated before Christmas 1944. Economic calculations were based on this.

The wide gap between 'VE-Day' and 'VJ-Day' was of crucial importance to British national finances. The French had barely entered into economic negotiations with the Americans – and this, along with de Gaulle's under-standable hostility towards the pro-Vichy Roosevelt administration, explains why 'V-Day' remained 'V-Day' in the French press on 8 May 1945.

In Germany, of course, there was no such thing as 'V-Day'. This was true for almost the whole of the rest of Europe, also; people were just waiting for the fighting to end, the bombing to stop, the massacres – industrial and pre-industrial – to cease, and hoping that they would be alive to see it. Stalin had his own special day in Moscow, in celebration of himself and the Red Army to the exclusion of all else, on Wednesday, 9 May.

For the vast majority of Europeans, all this talk about 'VE-Days', 'VJ-Days' and 'V-Days' was a matter of argument for politicians and, later, historians. The 'day the war ended' was the day the bombing stopped, the fighting ended, a loved one came home; or the day one realized the people one most cherished would never be seen again, that the family would never be reunited. In Europe, 'the day the war ended' ranged, according to experience, from the spring of 1944 to the onset of winter in 1945.

Throughout Europe between eastern France and the Soviet Union national borders over the first six months of 1945 were ill-defined; what mattered was the position of the armies. Yet international law – and most significantly the Yalta agreement between the 'Three' on repatriation – was based on nineteenth-century principles of 'national sovereignty' and 'citizenship'. For millions of people, what had previously been their national territory was occupied by foreign troops and they had no papers. 'The day the war ended' for many of them would be the day an arbitrary decision was made by some camp commander on which 'nation' they belonged to. The worst situation was that of the Jews: they belonged to no nation; many came from the Greater German Reich where they had been considered 'enemies of the interior'. None of them had any papers. For months they remained in the concentration camps that the Nazis had set up. Death rates from typhus and dysentery remained high. On 21 July 1945 the World Jewish Congress made an official appeal to the world leaders, meeting in Potsdam, to release concentration camp inmates (almost three months after 'VE-Day') from 'conditions of most abject misery'. There was little consciousness in the world at this time – and indeed for a long time after Nuremberg – of the catastrophic situation still faced by those Jews who survived. Everything was still seen in a 'national' perspec-tive; the word was of 'deportees' and 'displaced persons' – the term 'Holocaust' was as yet unknown.

In fact, anti-Semitism was rife in the Allied armies. One of the worst cases was General Patton himself, who spoke of Jews as 'Yids' and, despite being the liberator of Dachau, made no special effort to relieve the Jews of their misery. The London *Jewish Chronicle* reported at the time of the Potsdam Conference that Patton's Third Army in southern Germany was behaving like Hitler's SS troops. Protests from UNRRA were met with the response from soldiers that 'this was the only way to deal with Jews.' When did the Jews' war end?[1]

Not since the Thirty Years War in the seventeenth century had civilians been so caught up in the horrors and tragedy of war. The Congress of Vienna in 1814 had established the rule of 'sovereignty', embodied in the person of the 'sovereign', be he king, emperor or duke. The nineteenth century had forged the notion of popular national sovereignty, embodied in the people of the 'nation'. 'National sovereignty' governed European political thought in the First World War and, even more, the Paris Peace Conference of 1919. But 'national sovereignty' never corresponded perfectly to reality, especially in Central and Eastern Europe, which was outside the control of the Paris peacemakers.

Nonetheless, the idea of 'national sovereignty' did not go away. Among the Western Allies, the Second World War even reinforced it. They attempted to impose it on the rest of Europe by transferring 'ethnic groups' to national blocs; not only was this inhumane, it had no basis in law, for there was never an international peace settlement. So a terrible legal ambiguity hung over millions of people in Europe. It took more than five years to sort the problem out. Some of the sorting out was brutal in the extreme. The Jews, in the immediate aftermath of the war as throughout the war, suffered the worst: they belonged to no 'nation' and neither the Western Allies nor, in particular, the Soviet Union made much effort to solve the problem. The next major 'ethnic group' by order of suffering was the 'Russians'. In the first place, the Soviet Union could hardly be considered a 'nation state'. Secondly, 'Russians' could in no way be regarded as a uniform 'ethnic group': they were made up of Russians proper, but also of Cossacks, Caucasians, Muslims, Christians, Ukrainians, Lithuanians and even Poles. The administrative confusion this caused was total. The numbers involved were vast. A solution would never be found.

A fascinating case of 'Russian' hardship is to be found in the diary of Elena Skrjabina.[2] Born in St Petersburg in 1906, she was highly educated – one of her uncles was the composer Skriabin – and was something of a beauty, a fact that would contribute to her survival during the Second World War. Like all educated Russians, she spoke fluent French, knew German, but could not speak a word of English. She survived the long

German siege of Leningrad, as St Petersburg became known, witnessed the bombardments and the starvation; the dead were left where they fell in the streets. One and a half million Leningraders died of hunger during the siege. Elena Skrjabina escaped with her two children during the bitter winter of 1942 by the route across the frozen Lake Ladoga, from where she was evacuated by the Russians to Pyatigorsk in the Caucasus. But that was the year of Hitler's rapid advance south-east; she and her children were captured and transported to a Nazi collecting centre at Krivoi Rog in the Ukraine; Elena was separated from her elder son, who became a slave labourer in Lithuania, while Elena and her younger son were deported to a factory in West Germany, the Konkordia works near Bendorf. In the 1930s the factory produced stoves but, under Speer's efficient economy, it had been converted to military production. The *Ostarbeiter*, the Russian slaves, were housed in wooden barracks while the Germans and other workers slept in the cellars of the three-storey building. Though surrounded by wire, the Russian dwellings could not be called a concentration camp; the Russians had access to the town and even made friends with some of the local residents – unthinkable in East Prussia or the occupied Eastern provinces. Elena's charms won her many friends; she and her son were invited to Christmas and other holiday dinners in town.

Bendorf lay on the road to Koblenz, towards which units of the American 9th Armoured Division began to move in the second half of March 1945. Was this the end of the war for Elena Skrjabina? Hardly. As the Americans approached, the Germans began evacuating to Thuringia the numerous French prisoners they had at Konkordia. Elena's charms were again put to work, and she saved several dozen French prisoners from deportation. One prisoner, whom she names Jean in her diary, became the protector of Elena and her son, Yuri, as they waited out the attack in Konkordia's cellars.

The American front-line troops turned out to be a rabble – 'their conduct very much recalls that of the Russians,' recorded Elena on 27 March. In the evening they shared drinks and made efforts to teach the Russians English words and expressions; they left long after midnight. Then came the knocking at the doors. Soldiers could be heard running up and down the stairs, screaming. The disorder went on for days. The French, thankful for being saved from deportation, became the protectors of the Russians, particularly Jean, who spoke fluent English. The Americans, however, having found large supplies of Rhineland wine, 'broke into offices, smashing furniture, typewriters and windows. There is an un- believable roar which terrorizes us all. Involuntarily, I recall the first days of the October revolution in my native land.'[3]

On 6 April the American officers finally arrived and established some semblance of order, what they called 'Allied Military Government'. It did not amount to much. In Bendorf's city square lorries could be seen waiting to take the French, Belgians, Dutch and other Westerners back to their home countries. 'We knew almost all of these prisoners and they greeted us cheerfully.' The lorries were decorated with national emblems, painted signs and flowers. The faces of the young men and women were happy – for them, it was the end of the war. Off went the French singing the *Marseillaise* and songs of the Resistance; then the Belgians and the Dutch, their vehicles decked with flags.

And the Russians? The Americans set up a special camp, behind barbed wire and under guard, in a bleak clearing about twenty kilometres to the north of Bendorf. 'The more clever Russians', recorded Elena, 'do not go to the camp and . . . are riding around on stolen bikes with fluttering red ribbons and Soviet flags. They feed themselves on whatever they chance to come across and spend the nights wherever they can.'[4] They became armed bands of terrorists, over whom the Americans could exert no control.

Jean learned that a French army unit had arrived in Koblenz; he advised Elena to go there and get a job as a secretary. She found herself a bicycle. But the road to Koblenz was hellish. Crowds of impoverished pedestrians could be seen on both sides, while an endless number of vehicles raced along loudly honking their horns. At the end of the road lay the Rhine and French-occupied Koblenz on the other side. The bridge had been blown apart.

The French had not been invited to Yalta, and they had therefore not signed the agreement to repatriate 'Soviet citizens' to the Soviet Union. Most Russians naturally wanted to find themselves in the French sector of occupation. But they were met by this barrier: what remained of the bridge had been connected by narrow boards, 'fastened here and there'; under them 'the Rhine was glistening'. Many were frightened away. On two occasions Elena threw up her hands and decided to 'wait for more peaceful times' before getting employment with the French at Koblenz. She had nightmares about the bridge – 'now I'm falling into the cold waters of the Rhine. I frighten Yuri with my shout.'[5]

Elena's charms worked again. She found a hiding place in the villa of Konkordia's German manager, a man living in fear for his life, constantly threatened by the marauding gangs of Russians as a 'Nazi', a 'Hitlerite'. Elena got her food by bartering with the Germans, while herself being threatened by the Russians. 'How many times during the war have I asked myself the question who are "my people" and who are the "enemies"?

Often, very often, I received more sympathy and understanding from these very enemies than from my own people. Now it's the same story again.'[6]

On 4 May the 'villa' was ransacked by the Russians; the doors were smashed, trunks and suitcases torn open, cupboard doors ripped from their hinges, 'and our countrymen were disappearing down the path with huge sacks on their backs'. The raids went on for almost a week. Elena, her son and the German manager took to hiding behind heavy iron doors in a nearby bunker. The whole of the surrounding countryside was in the grip of Russian looters. There was no sign, as yet, of Allied Military Government. On Wednesday afternoon a meagre dinner was prepared and served on the ground floor of the 'villa', when again a large crowd of camp inmates appeared, coming down the steep slopes of the entry. The villa's inmates decided to stay put; all that was left to take in the building was their own lives.

But 'joyous lads filled up the kitchen and the adjoining rooms and hastened to tell us the joyful news that the war was over.' In her entire diary, which covers the five years to 1950, that is the only point Elena uses the phrase.[7]

The next days were spent barricading the house, for there was now a new group of Russian marauders who had had no difficulty breaking out of a neighbouring 'transit camp' built by the Americans to return these 'Allied' soldiers and prisoners to the Motherland. By 14 May American jeeps began to appear. The Russian bands vanished. The Americans distributed chocolate and chewing gum . . . and at night there came again the knocking at the doors.

After listening to incessant American knocking and screaming for two days Elena decided to go and see the local American commander, whose only advice to her and her son was to return to Leningrad. She nearly took up the offer, but once again her charms began to lead to miracles – not this time on the commander, but his assistant, who lounged silently at the back of the office, his feet on a table. He turned out to be a Pole, named Yankovsky. Yankovsky insisted on driving the mother and child home. 'Have you gone out of your minds?' he asked in broken Russian the moment they got into the car. The whole Soviet operation of 're-patriation' in the area was based on 'endless denunciations'; they would not get back to Russia alive.

Within three days, the 'Allied Military Government' had once again disappeared. The waves of brigandage began again. But one little miracle gave Elena courage: her elder son, Dima, appeared at the front door; he had crossed the whole of Poland and Germany on foot. Elena was now living under the protection of another German family in Bendorf, the

Marxes. The Germans had learnt that their best protection against Allied billeting was to house foreigners; Elena's family got three whole rooms. On 3 June a Belgian unit turned up. 'Obviously,' remarked Elena that day, 'they are now the administrators of our region.' She established 'most friendly relations' with the elderly Belgian commander.

By July she had become an interlocutor between the Germans and the French-speaking Belgians. That was when the most terrifying news arrived: a young friend announced with horror that the French were coming to occupy the region – there would be prolonged pillaging and rape; it would be worse than the Russians. Elena assured the Germans that it would be quite the contrary. And so it proved. Some of the houses were requisitioned. But a smooth-running administration was set up. Local festivals were encouraged. Schools were opened. Elena became an important hostess, inviting both the French and the Germans to her table. In her own small way she re-established trust between this western corner of Germany, which had never much loved Berlin, and France. It was in fact here, in the Rhineland, that a new European community – what would decades later become the European Union – was born out of the fires of war.

Elena by that time had left for the United States where she was to become an accomplished professor of French and comparative literature. Her story of enemies and friends shows that even that most terrible of wars was not entirely Manichean. And it, in a little way, proved that Europe was not simply built of 'nations'. But when did the war end? For Elena, perhaps we can say in July 1945, when the French arrived in Bendorf.

2 Signatures of surrender

There is, of course, an official history of documents, signatures, announcements and ceremonies that should point to 'the day the war ended'. But contact between the American and British Allies had reached an all-time low, the Russians were heading in their own determined directions, and the German armed forces were divided into isolated pockets. The truth is that there is no single moment one can point to as 'the day the war ended'.

There was only one man who could sign the 'unconditional surrender' of the Third Reich, the Führer, Adolf Hitler. And because the myth of the 'stab in the back' of 1918 was so central to Nazi ideology, Hitler would never have done it. Rumours were spread, especially by the Russians, that Hitler had escaped through the British sector. In fact it had been the

Russians who discovered the burnt remains of Hitler's body and that of his newly wed wife in a grave dug in a bomb crater in the Chancellery gardens on 5 May, five days after his suicide. Hitler, Goebbels, their wives and Goebbels's children were buried in unmarked crates in a forest east of Rathenow. Later they were moved to a roadside beyond Magdeburg. In March 1970, on the orders of the KGB director Yuri Andropov, they were dug up and burnt to cinders. But in 1946, three fragments of Hitler's skull were discovered in the ruins of the Chancellery gardens. One of these fragments showed where the bullet had passed out through the top of his head. The pieces were gathered into a box originally used for biro refills, where they have been kept to this day in the State Archive of the Russian Federation on Bolshaya Pirogovskaya Street in Moscow. Hitler, and several of his closest collaborators, chose to die rather than sign an 'unconditional surrender'.[8]

It had been Goebbels's idea to appeal for a truce with the Russians on the very afternoon of Hitler's death (30 April) and to ask for permission to send a delegate to Admiral Karl Dönitz – Hitler's designated successor, who was now in the northern Nazi enclave of Schleswig-Holstein – to ask him to negotiate a formal Russian treaty. Goebbels had always been on the pro-Soviet wing of the Nazi Party; so too was the man he sent out from the Führerbunker at midnight to make contact with Russian command in Berlin, General Hans Krebs. Krebs had been on a military mission to Moscow in March 1941 when Stalin gave him a bear hug in public and said, 'If we stand together like brothers, then nothing can happen to us in the future. You see to it that we remain good friends.' In the dark hours of the morning of 1 May 1945 Krebs, accompanied by an assistant and an interpreter, was met by Russian soldiers who tried to take their pistols away. 'A courageous opponent is allowed to keep his weapons during negotiations,' riposted Krebs, and they were allowed to do so. The three men were taken to an apartment house in Tempelhof where, in a dining room, several Russian senior officers were gathered. None of them made any sign of recognizing the Germans present. Krebs had to open the proceedings himself. He discovered that he was talking to Colonel Vasili Ivanovich Chuikov and his staff. It was the same Chuikov who had fought at Stalingrad and had been suddenly halted on the Vistula from advancing into Warsaw. 'I want you to know that you are the first foreigner to learn that on 30 April Hitler committed suicide.' 'We know that,' replied Chuikov, without batting an eyelid. 'How could you know?' asked Krebs. 'Hitler only committed suicide a few hours ago.' Chuikov, of course, knew nothing. But he was not prepared to negotiate anything. After twelve hours of talks all Krebs could get out of him was immediate unconditional surrender of the city and the personal surrender of all the occupants of the bunker. Krebs and his two companions made the difficult journey back to the bunker – they were fired on several times by SS-troops. 'To that I shall never, never agree!' said Goebbels on hearing the demand for unconditional surrender.[9]

The Battle of Berlin came to an official end when several German officers apeared at Potsdam Bridge at noon, 2 May. Chuikov had already ordered a ceasefire. A raid on the bunker had been conducted that morning. Inside and strewn about the gardens the Russians found the bodies of Krebs, General Wilhelm Burgdorf (an adjutant), Franz Schedle (commander of the SS bodyguard), Goebbels and his family, and around forty other dead.

But that was not the end of the war, for a Nazi government was still functioning in Schleswig-Holstein under the new Reich President, Admiral Dönitz.

The legality of this government was based on Hitler's Last Political Testament, dictated in the bunker to Frau Junge, his secretary, on the night of 29 April, shortly after his marriage to Eva Braun. International Jewry was responsible for the war, he stated, not his government. He would not allow himself to fall into the hands of the enemy and be 'exhibited by the Jews'. 'I have therefore decided to remain in Berlin, and there to choose death voluntarily at the moment when I believe that the residence of the Führer and Chancellor can no longer be held.' He upheld the Navy as a shining example of faithful devotion to duty until death; he spoke of the heroic conduct of the people, and damned the German General Staff. He expelled from the Party his former heir, Hermann Göring, and appointed 'Grand Admiral Dönitz as Reich President and Supreme Commander of the Armed Forces'.[10]

Three copies were made of this critical document, Hitler's last words to the world. Dönitz never received any of them. A copy was found, in the summer of 1945, sewn into the clothing of a certain George Thiers, a Luxembourg journalist who told the British Military Government in Hanover that he had secrets to share on Hitler's last days. Indeed he had. His real name was Heinz Lorenz, a German officer who had been ordered to deliver the Testament to Munich, so that the southern fragment of the Reich would know of Göring's dismissal as Reichsmarshal. In the chaos of the last days of the war, the two other copies got lost. The second copy was found in a trunk that autumn in the Bavarian village of Tegernsee. The third was discovered the following December in a green bottle buried in the back garden of a small house in the Ruhr town of Iserlohn.

The only formal indication Admiral Dönitz had of his promotion was a brief telegram sent by Martin Bormann immediately after Hitler's death, addressed to Dönitz in his baroque Nazi kingdom of Schleswig-Holstein: 'Grand Admiral Dönitz,' it read, 'In place of the former Reichsmarshal Göring the Führer appoints you, Herr Grand Admiral, as his successor. Written authority is on its way. You will immediately take all such measures as the situation requires. Bormann.'[11] Bormann made no mention of Hitler's death because all his power as head of the Party Chancery, leader of the Party, the closest man to the Führer depended on the man now dead. He would prolong his power a few more hours and then make his way out to the new fantasy Reich where he had a chance of re-establishing his honour.

When it became clear the next morning that Krebs's mission to the Russians was not going to work out, Bormann sent a second cryptic telegram to Dönitz: 'Grand Admiral Dönitz, The Testament is in force. I will join you as soon as possible. Till then I recommend that publication be held up. Bormann.'[12] Those are the last words we have of Martin Bormann. There is still no mention of Hitler's death, only the suggestion that he, Bormann, will join Dönitz in Plön, Schleswig-Holstein. For a long time it was thought that he went to live out his Nazi beliefs in Argentina – until a bulldozer uncovered his body in December 1972 by the Lehrter Bahn in central Berlin. He had bitten on a cyanide pill – probably after being surrounded by Russians.

Goebbels – who had already decided to kill himself, his wife and children that night, for the survival and purity of the Nazi 'myth' – no longer had any political ambitions. He was the spirit of the Nazi movement. And it was he who finally sent to Dönitz that afternoon, 1 May, the news that 'The Führer died yesterday at 15.30 hours.' He outlined the government Dönitz was to form in accordance with Hitler's Testament and concluded: 'Bormann intends to go to you today and to inform you of the situation. Time and form of announcement to the press and to the troops is left to you.'[13]

Goebbels died at around 8.30 p.m. and, in true Nazi-Teutonic form, the whole bunker was set aflame with petrol. Few radios worked in Berlin at that time, but if anyone had tuned into Radio Hamburg, they would have heard a voice declaring that a 'grave and important announcement' was about to be made. Extracts of Wagner's operas were performed along with the slow movement of Bruckner's Seventh Symphony. At 10.20 Dönitz announced that the Führer had fallen 'this afternoon', fighting 'at the head of his troops'. Dönitz thus gave Hitler an extra day of life and put him on the battlefront in Berlin. The stories were repeated in *The Times* and the French newspapers the next day – and continued to colour many a rumour in the years since, fed especially by the Soviets, who wanted to keep the fight against 'Fascism' alive.

Heinrich Himmler, head of the SS, director of the Holocaust, and Bormann's great rival, had not given up hope that he could lead a revived Nazi state, despite the fact that Hitler had excluded him from the Party because he had been negotiating with the Western Powers. Being outside Berlin, it was not difficult for him to gain access to Dönitz's new fairy kingdom, which had now moved to Flensburg. There the SS continued to march up and down the streets for the next five days. But Dönitz had decided – in defiance of Hitler's instructions – to exclude all the major Nazis from his government (with the exception of the unexceptional Schwerin von Krosigk, who became his Foreign Minister) and to seek 'unconditional surrender' with the West. This left 'faithful Heinrich' with little to do: he decided on a second escape, southwards into the British sector. He was recognized at the frontier post. His British captors, at their incompetent best, had him stripped naked for a medical examination – at which point Heinrich Himmler, murderer of the Jews, bit into his poisoned pill.

Why Dönitz's fantasy Reich was situated in Schleswig-Holstein, stolen from the Danes in one of Bismarck's wars, may well be asked. It had a lot to do, once more, with the movement of armies. There was complete confusion on the Western Front in the days and weeks that followed Roosevelt's death. The Chiefs of Staff responsible for coordinating Anglo-American command had lost much of their authority since Eisenhower's signal direct to Stalin that he was abandoning Berlin to the Russians; Allied command was essentially being run by personal contact between Eisenhower (SHAEF's Supreme Commander), Bradley (Commander of 12th Army Group) and Hodges (Commander of the US First Army). All three of them were aiming their forces towards the legendary Southern Redoubt – to a point where Bradley even wanted Hodges' army to cross Patton's more southerly army line and head for the mountains. Patton, always the odd man out, had his heart set on Berlin, as did Montgomery.

'I think BERLIN has definite value as an objective,' Montgomery telegraphed Eisenhower on 6 April, 'and I have no doubt whatever that the Russians think the same; but they may well pretend that this is not the case!!'[14] Montgomery was of course right just as Eisenhower was totally wrong. The Russians, delayed on the Oder, were building up all their forces for a battle on Berlin.

The Germans were preparing for it. Dönitz initially set up his head-quarters in the port of Lübeck, to the north-west of Berlin. With canals, lakes, islands and peninsulas in the area he had all the facilities needed to create the kind of military-naval stronghold that had always been his dream. The Americans finally came to a halt at the Elbe and waited for the Russians to move. Their actions in the south, though sometimes involving ferocious battles, had no strategic significance. A large part of the American forces by the second half of April were inactive – for them the war had ended.

The Russian offensive on Berlin finally began on 16 April. The spearhead of Simpson's US Ninth Army (which had formerly been under Montgomery's command) was at Magdeburg, only fifty-three miles from Berlin, with no significant enemy forces in front of them. But the whole of Bradley's Elbe front was now stationary, a holding army, waiting for what the Russians would do. Gradually it began to dawn on SHAEF Headquarters back in Rheims, France, what was happening. The Russians were surrounding Berlin and sending their main secondary force not to shake hands with the Americans on the Elbe, but across the coastal plain towards Schleswig-Holstein and Denmark. Special SS divisions were being moved from Norway down through Denmark to reinforce Dönitz at Lübeck. In the last week of April the truth dawned on Eisenhower: the Southern Redoubt was of no importance at all; the problem was Dönitz's 'Northern Redoubt'.

On 28 April Montgomery received instructions of 'the urgent need to get LUBECK before the Russians'. Of all the Western Allied forces now stationed in Germany, Montgomery's depleted forces were the only ones racing the Russians. The order to take Lübeck was 'adding insult to injury,' Montgomery cabled the War Office.[15]

Amidst fanatical fighting, Montgomery crossed the Elbe at Lauenburg on the night of 29 April – as Hitler was dictating his Testament. 'The refugees are quite appalling in this area,' wrote one of Montgomery's Liaison Officers; 'like a herd of locusts cooking and eating the dead horses by the roadside; pillaging and ransacking all German property.' Along the roads lay crumpled corpses, bloated horses, shattered lorries and tanks, with clothing and human litter hanging from branches as from Christmas trees decorated for death. 'They are hard pressed,' wrote Montgomery of the German troops; they 'had taken a personal oath to Hitler and so long as he is alive they must keep on fighting. Once it is known that he is dead, or has cleared out, there will be a big scale collapse.' On 1 May Lübeck fell to the British 11th Armoured Division, beating the Russians by twelve hours. Dönitz had moved west to Plön, surrounded by lakes, and from there made his announcement of the Führer's death 'at the head of his troops'. Dönitz then moved up to Flensburg, on the Danish frontier, and keeping all leading Nazis out of his government, set to work on a negotiated surrender – to the Western Allies.[16]

There was nothing in twentieth-century warfare that quite resembled Montgomery's nomadic TAC HQ – the Boer laager in the South African wars or the American pioneer wagon circles of the nineteenth century are probably the closest parallels. Montgomery travelled with jeeps and caravans, and later Auster aircraft as the battlefield widened in Germany where his 'gallopers' had to cover ever greater distances. Available landing strips had become a prerequisite in choice of site. So had a suitable position for the radio aerial which had to communicate with London, SHAEF at Rheims, as well as pick up messages from the German armies and headquarters.

At D-Day the whole camp consisted of twenty-seven officers and 150 men. Now it was of regimental size. But it kept moving with the front, for Montgomery insisted on inspecting with his own eyes the point where the battle was at its intensest. In the centre was the radio caravan, an officers' mess, a map room and Montgomery's sleeping quarters, where lights went out at 9.30 sharp, whatever the situation on the horizon. There was a lot of activity going on in the centre. The site was usually under cover of pine trees and a huge amount of camouflage netting served to hide the settlement from unwelcome eyes in the sky. It is amazing, nonetheless, that Montgomery's TAC HQ was never once attacked.

The Lübeck campaign had brought TAC HQ to a bluff on the sandy, windswept heath of Lüneburg. The heather was still brown and crackled underfoot. The weather was freezing. It was here, as a matter of fact, that the Second World War in Europe ended.

On Wednesday evening, 2 May, a message was received that General Blumentritt of the German Parachute Army, facing Montgomery's forces between the Baltic and the River Weser, was coming in the next day at 1100 hours to surrender. Montgomery cabled Brooke that night that he was expecting something bigger.

Sure enough, at eight o'clock the next morning, Montgomery's assistant, Colonel Dawnay, called up to say that a delegation of four German officers were on their way, apparently seeking a compromise surrender, if they could make terms. Montgomery sounded his caravan buzzer, ordered everyone to clear out of the central area and get the Union Jack flying from the central post; when the four Germans arrived they were to stand in a line by the flag, facing his office caravan.

The four Germans entered the small English green in the Pomeranian heath, escorted by military police, who were immediately dismissed. The four officials were, as German officials always were, exceedingly polite and they stood at attention, in a line under the flag, as they had been ordered. Save for the flapping of the flag and the odd threatening roar of a fighter aircraft overhead, there was total silence. The two naval officers wore long black leather greatcoats. The army officers were in grey greatcoats – the one general among them carried a single gay addition, his bright red lapels. (What a grey century these people lived through: compare this to the colours of Fontainebleau in April 1814.) Under the sun, it was getting warm.

Slowly the door of the caravan opposite opened and out came a small, birdlike man in khaki trousers, battledress and a black beret (not regulation) with a Royal Tank Regiment and a Field Marshal badge pinned upon it. He held his hands behind his back. The four Germans immediately saluted, staying in this position until, according to the German rule, the senior officer returned the salute. Montgomery, without as much as a signal, slowly descended the staircase and crossed the twenty-five feet or so that separated them. Then at last he carelessly touched his beret with his right hand. The four Germans dropped their arms. To the first Montgomery shouted out in his high-pitched manner, 'Who are you?' 'General Admiral von Friedeburg, Commander-in-Chief the German Navy, Sir.' 'I have never heard of you,' mumbled Montgomery. It was the same procedure all down the line, until he arrived at the fourth man – Montgomery indeed could not have heard of them since they had only been named by Dönitz that day. 'Who are you?' he asked the fourth. 'Major Friedl.' 'Major!' raged Montgomery, and immediately turned on his heels. 'How dare you bring a major into my Headquarters!' It was a superb act; he had been rehearsing for it all his life.

The sun had got still warmer. The act continued. Montgomery was by now standing in front of the four Germans in their greatcoats: 'What do you want?'

They wanted the Germans fighting the Russians to surrender to the British. What a ridiculous idea, thought Montgomery. If they surrender to anybody, he said, they surrender to the Russians – though, he quietly added, if anybody wandered over to his side 'with his hands up they can surrender to me'. As a matter of fact, he went on, all the armies in front of the British forces – from Holland, through Friesland, the Frisian Islands, and Heligoland, and Schleswig, and Holstein, and Denmark (in other words most of the German forces in northern Germany) 'can surrender to me'.

The four Germans, getting hotter still, did not accept the offer. But they presented a compromise: if they could reach some kind of accord, maybe they could save civilian lives. 'Do you remember a little town in England called Coventry?' remarked Montgomery, 'It no longer exists.' He said he had just visited the camp of Bergen-Belsen; 'you are not the slightest bit interested in civilian lives.' He said he would immediately order heavy bombing – up to ten thousand bombers day and night, with heavy losses of German civilians 'unless they surrendered unconditionally'. He suggested they have some lunch to think about it.

Montgomery laid on the most fantastic lunch in the Visitors' Mess. Bedsheets were used as tablecloths. They were served a grand bottle of wine, coffee and brandy. It was probably out of bedsheets that the mess sergeant's tunic was fabricated; he spoke fluent German. Oh, what a wonderful meal! exclaimed the Germans. We haven't eaten like this for months! 'Our private soldiers won't touch the muck!' the mess sergeant replied curtly.

While the Germans were eating, Montgomery swiftly organized a conference chamber in his map room. On the map the British front line was marked in red, the German in blue. He covered the table with army blankets. He himself would sit at one end of the table, the four Germans would be squeezed together at the other. The Germans, after sipping their last brandy, were swiftly shown into the caravan's 'Conference Chamber' and Montgomery quickly followed – making this time a proud soldierly salute. He briefly pointed at the map. Quite obviously, their situation was hopeless.

'You must surrender to me unconditionally *all* forces,' said Montgomery. They could work out the best occupation procedure. 'If you don't, I will continue fighting and a great many German soldiers and civilians will be killed.' He gave them twenty-four hours to reply and then dismissed them.

'I think they will agree to surrender unconditionally all forces,' he wrote to Brooke that night, 3 May. The European war, he was certain, was at an end.[17]

But it managed to go on, officially, for another five days in the West, and six in the East. Much of this was due to the chaotic conditions at SHAEF back in Rheims, where the Americans were running their own war from their hotel rooms and fine restaurants. Bradley, three hundred miles away in Wiesbaden, nowhere near any front, was still predicting that the war could go on for another year, with the main battle down in the 'Southern Redoubt'. What his source of intelligence was one can only guess. Germany's main forces in Italy had surrendered to Alexander on 29 April. The American 88th Division in the Alps had not heard the news and continued to fight, losing five men on 3 May; it was not until that evening that they tuned into the BBC and heard that the Italian campaign was over. Most American forces in southern Germany had been idle for the previous two weeks. Patton was camped in Pilsen and panting to move on to Prague, but was prevented by Eisenhower. The 19th Canadian Army Field Regiment, Royal Canadian Regiment, was fighting a tough battle outside Oldenburg until 11.40 p.m. on 4 May. At that moment it received a wireless order to 'Stop firing until further orders. Order to Cease Fire will be given at 0800 tomorrow.' 'Soon', reported one witness, 'all was deathly quiet across the entire front.' Alan Moorehead, the war correspondent, reported on 4 May crowds of German soldiers near Lüneburg 'flinging their pistols into a hedge, tearing off their uniforms and getting into tattered civilian clothes stolen from the nearest houses'. Their one hope, he said, 'was to get quickly into a British or American prison camp'. There was some fighting north of Berlin. The Prague Rising broke out on 5 May, with Vlasov's army of anti-Communist resistants, still in German uniforms, fighting a street battle against the local German forces.[18]

Montgomery, as a result of the Lübeck campaign, was already in touch with the Russians and 'everything was very friendly', he told Brooke on the night of the 3rd. The congestion of soldiers and civilians between Russian and British lines was something incredible; the British probably took half a million prisoners that day. Lieutenant Colonel Warren, Montgomery's personal assistant, accompanied the four Germans back to German lines – a route that took them through Hamburg. The city was a pile of burnt rubble; it took them an hour to get through, and Warren an hour to get back; he saw, as he said in a later report, not a living creature, 'not even a cat'. (A British lieutenant, Edward Bramall, who was there on the same day recalled the unforgettable scene: 'The impact of Hamburg was, if anything, worse than that of Hiroshima, which I was to see eight months later.')[19] Schleswig-Holstein, on the other hand, was by now one of the most densely populated provinces in Europe. Four million Russian prisoners of war had been gathered there, and two million civilian refugees had poured in from the east; there remained about ten days of food supplies. The situation could not last. A bitter cold wind wailed across the plain. How perishingly cold it was that spring.

Warren was back at his post north of Hamburg the next morning. No sign of a German parliamentarian. Had Dönitz really decided to continue the war? Finally, at 4.30 p.m. their vehicles were sighted crossing the line. A fifth man accompanied them with a satchel full of German army and naval codes plus a map of minefields stretching from the North Sea to the Baltic. By now there was a driving, freezing rain. Allied fighter planes were droning across the misty sky.

They were all back in Lüneburg shortly after five. The Germans were served hot coffee and brandy. Montgomery asked the head of the group to come to his cabin. General Admiral von Friedeburg looked very dejected. 'Are you going to sign the full surrender terms as demanded?' asked Montgomery. 'Yes,' replied von Friedeburg.

Montgomery told him to wait with the others outside, by the flapping Union Jack. Quickly a trestle table was mounted in the cabin; it was covered with an army blanket, and an inkpot and a twopenny army pen was placed upon it. The Germans were ordered in. Montgomery, in full army dress, read out the surrender terms with his high-pitched lisping accent. Colonel Ewart read the German translation. In a silence, save for a clicking of cameras, the Germans signed in order of seniority. 'Now I will sign on behalf of the Supreme Allied Commander, General Eisenhower.' Montgomery signed at 6.30 p.m., 4 May 1945. From the point of view of army movements, fighting and killing, that was the moment the war ended in Europe.[20]

Messily, the politics followed. Unlike any preceding war in Europe there would be no major treaty, no peace congress, no peace settlement. Clearly the Americans – with a press media that concentrated solely on the progress of American armies – were not going to accept a military surrender offered to Montgomery. No more was the Soviet Union ready to applaud a peace that did not demonstrate the victorious scientific principles of Marxism-Leninism-Stalinism. It was a difficult circle to square.

One of the most astonishing features of the signature in the TAC HQ caravan on Friday evening, 4 May, was that it handed over to Montgomery's command not only the major part of the German armies of North-Western Europe, but also the entire apparatus of the Third Reich: in surrendering unconditionally north Germany, Denmark and Norway to Montgomery, the German delegation surrendered also Flensburg – and all that remained of Hitler's regime according to his own Political Testament of 29 April.

Montgomery cabled Brooke early Saturday, 5 May: 'My general plan is to work through the German military machine and to make use of existing German HQ to get my orders conveyed to German formations and units.' That meant the surrender of every submarine from the Atlantic to the Baltic, every military unit from Holland to Scandinavia to Lübeck. The whole network of German military radio communications henceforth passed through Montgomery's radio units in his caravans on Lüneburg

Heath. The German General Staff had to sit in Schleswig, under the general command of Montgomery, as it set about the surrender to the other Allies. 'When we have no further need of any of them they can be put inside as POWs,' remarked Montgomery.[21]

The surrender worked remarkably smoothly. Montgomery's 21st Army Group sent no forces into Denmark. Within a day or so the Germans themselves organized the delivery to British forces in north Germany of a million and a half armed prisoners, along with two million refugees and half a million people over and above the pre-existing population – leaving the problems to be solved by their new commander, Montgomery. Montgomery, at the top of Europe's plain, stood absolutely victorious. He had his own Liaison Officers working inside the Third Reich at Flensburg – one of them even spied the jobless Himmler strolling down a corridor. Neither the Americans in Rheims nor the Russians, commanded from Moscow, could claim to be in such a position.

With the exception of General Hans Kinsel, Dönitz's Chief of Staff of the German North West Army Command – who was kept on at TAC HQ because he turned out to be 'a very able and highly trained staff officer' – Montgomery put the German surrender delegation on a plane direct for Rheims. They took off on Saturday morning, at 7.30 a.m., while Montgomery cabled Eisenhower, warning him that they would do anything not to surrender to the Russians. He advised Eisenhower to prepare a response to this before their arrival.

But Eisenhower prepared nothing at all. He refused to meet them. Instead, the three German delegates were met in a schoolhouse by two overweight middle-aged men, who were obviously not battle commanders, Lieutenant Commander Walter Bedell Smith ('the Beetle'), Eisenhower's chief of staff, and Major General Kenneth Strong, the man famously in charge of military intelligence at SHAEF. 'Never heard of you,' von Friedeburg might have repeated when introduced to them.

Noting what they had in front of them, the German delegates began negotiating all over again – citing the need to protect civilian lives, the chaotic situation in Eastern Europe, even the limitations on the authority Strong had to sign. Neither Bedell Smith nor Strong were in a position to threaten the flight of ten thousand bombers, day and night, over Germany, and they were far too polite to mention concentration camps and Coventry – none of which they had seen. Eisenhower stayed in his bedroom reading his Western novels.

Negotiations over matters that Montgomery had already cleared up went on all that Saturday and into Sunday morning, 6 May, with von Friedeburg insisting that he had no permission to sign a tripartite surrender with Britain, the USA and Russia. All he was doing was playing for time in order to shift as many German soldiers and citizens out of the hands of the Russians.

But by Sunday Dönitz, officially under Montgomery's command, was getting a little confused about what to do. He asked Montgomery to send one of his Liaison Officers along with Kinsel up to Flensburg. Kinsel told Dönitz that the tripartite unconditional surrender had to be signed at once. Dönitz decided to send immediately down to Montgomery the most authoritive, cruellest and closest strategist to Hitler himself, General Alfred Jodl, Operations Chief of OKW, with full authority to sign everything to everybody. Montgomery told Jodl that it wasn't the Commander of the British 21st Army Group who could sign such an instrument and, like the delegation before him, put him straight on a plane for Rheims, where he arrived at five o'clock that Sunday evening, 6 May. Eisenhower remained in his bedroom reading his Westerns.

In London, Churchill in the meantime was preparing his great victory broadcast which he expected to make that very evening or early the following day. The major press agencies of the world were becoming increasingly vigilant. Washington DC had already celebrated several hours of 'VE-Day' the previous week when jubilant crowds had gathered outside the White House after an Associated Press news flash in San Francisco announced 'Germany has surrendered to the Allied Governments unconditionally' – Hitler was still alive at the time.* But the policy of SHAEF in Rheims was one of strict secrecy.

Jodl seized the opportunity to procrastinate still further by telling Bedell Smith and Strong that he lacked the authority to sign a tripartite surrender – which was a lie. After a couple of hours of such palaver, Eisenhower finally intervened with a warning through Bedell Smith that, unless there was an immediate signature, all Western Allied zones would be closed to German POWs coming in from the East. Jodl went back to his mendacious argument about necessary permission from Flensburg, and thereby gained another forty-eight hours of fumbling: he asked, in a cable, for permission to sign so that 'hostilities will then cease on 9 May 0001 hours our time'. Montgomery's TAC HQ received the message and passed it straight on to Flensburg.

Receiving no answer, Jodl in the early hours of Monday morning, 7 May, started getting worried that he had created an unmanageable situation, and finally admitted that he was authorized to sign the tripartite surrender. Ironically, a few minutes afterwards a two-line answer

* The same kind of false news had led to celebrations in the United States on 7 November 1918, four days before the Armistice.

came in from Flensburg, via Lüneburg of course: 'Full power to sign in accordance with conditions has been given by Grand Admiral Dönitz. Keitel' (Field Marshal Wilhelm Keitel, Jodl's nominal chief of OKH and Hitler's puppet since 1938). So at last, at 2.41, Monday, 7 May, General Alfred Jodl signed the unconditional surrender of all German land, sea and air forces wherever they might be. General Bedell Smith signed for the Allied Expeditionary Force and General Ivan Susloparov, Soviet resident at SHAEF, signed for Soviet High Command; General François Sevez, French resident, signed as the French witness. The official end of hostilities – thanks to Jodl's delaying tactics – was set at one minute before midnight on Tuesday, 8 May 1945. It was only after the signature that Jodl met General Eisenhower in an adjacent room. Eisenhower asked if he thoroughly understood the provisions of the document. Jodl replied, '*Ja.*'

Eisenhower ordered that the whole business be kept secret during the entire two days that preceded the official 'end of hostilities'. So while every newspaper throughout the world was reporting Germany's unconditional surrender on the land, on the seas and in the skies, SHAEF, in its warren of bureaucratic holes, tunnels and bricked hills spread across Rheims, remained as silent as a mole. 'This must be the greatest single Press fiasco of all times,' the *Daily Mirror* reporter, David Walker, telegraphed his editor in London. 'Even in their defeat, the Germans can laugh at us for our confusion.'[22]

It was even worse than Walker imagined. The Americans had not thought of consulting Stalin. General Susloparov had not come to American headquarters – which is all SHAEF basically represented now – to sign a surrender document but to discuss details of the Yalta agreement on Soviet repatriations. It was somehow imagined that an American midnight ceremony, not even attended by the Supreme Commander, Eisenhower, was something acceptable to the whole world.

Stalin's first response was to announce that Monday, 7 May, that the sixteen representatives of the Polish Home Army, made captive on their visit to Warsaw the previous week, were now under lock and key in the Lubyanka gaol for 'diversionary activities against the Soviet State'. Stalin could be pretty certain that Eisenhower, whose limited policy of strict 'military strategy' had led him to abandon Berlin, most of eastern Germany, and the whole of Czechoslovakia, was not going to take any action on behalf the Polish Home Army. SHAEF was, of course, utterly silent on the matter. Eisenhower also had to agree, that Monday morning, that the unconditional surrender be signed again the next day in Russian-occupied Berlin by Field Marshal Keitel, von Friedeburg for the German navy and

General Hans-Jürgen Stumpff for the German air force. The Red Army marshals and generals would turn up, with lines of clinking baubles and decorations at their breast pockets, to prove that it was the Communists who had crushed the Fascists. Representatives of the Allied Expeditionary Force could come along too, if they had the time. Churchill's plans for a national broadcast had to be postponed to Tuesday, 8 May, as did Truman's and de Gaulle's. SHAEF stuck to its unique and incompetent silence as crowds gathered to celebrate in the capitals of the West.

Irony of all ironies, the first official broadcast that the Second World War was over in Europe came not from the Allies but from the Germans in Flensburg – via Montgomery's transmitters on Lüneburg Heath. 'German men and women,' announced Count Schwerin von Krosigk, the Foreign Minister, at 2.21 p.m. on Monday, 'the High Command of the German armed forces, on the orders of Grand Admiral Dönitz, has today declared the unconditional surrender of all German fighting troops.' It was as if the whole initiative had come from Germany. Certainly, there was no sign that the government had been threatened with an ultimatum or had negotiated in any way. Simply, 'after a heroic fight of almost six years of incomparable harshness, Germany has succumbed to the overwhelming power of her enemies. To continue the war would only mean senseless bloodshed and futile disintegration.'[23]

The Soviets informed the British and American governments that they would not be making an official announcement until Wednesday, 9 May, and that would be considered 'VE-Day'. The idea was intolerable for Churchill; people were already celebrating in London's streets on Monday. On Monday evening the BBC announced that Tuesday would be a holiday and was officially declared 'VE-Day'; the Prime Minister would be addressing the nation (with the speech he had prepared for Sunday) at three o'clock, Tuesday afternoon. Immediately the French announced that de Gaulle would be addressing the French nation and the world at exactly the same hour. Truman would speak from the White House at 9 a.m., Eastern Standard Time, which corresponded to 3 p.m. in London and Paris.[*] Thus, in Germany 'Defeat Day' was Monday, 'VE-Day' in the West was Tuesday, and in the Soviet Union it was Wednesday.

Representatives of the Western Allies arrived in Berlin on Tuesday, 8 May, at midday for the third major signing ceremony since Friday. A few junior Russian officers were at the airport to greet them. 'Negotiations' began at 11 p.m. in a former German army engineering college at Karlshorst, one of Berlin's many grey suburbs. Field Marshal Keitel signed

---

[*] Britain was on Double Summer War Time, thus running at the same hour as Paris and six hours ahead of the Eastern United States.

for Germany at 11.30, followed by Marshal Zhukov for the Soviets, and then the three Western Allied representatives.[*]

'I now request the German delegation to leave the room,' said Marshal Zhukov. It was almost midnight when, according to Zhukov, 'incredible commotion broke out in the hall. Everybody was congratulating one another and shaking hands. Many had tears of joy in their eyes.'[24]

3 Celebrations and silences

When Field Marshal Keitel had stepped into the hall at Karlshorst that Tuesday night, 8 May, he spied a French tricolour flying in a corner. He could not contain his anger. 'Ach! The French here, too!' were the first words he exclaimed, 'that's all we needed!'[25] The signing at Karlshorst was, within five days, the fifth anniversary of the German invasion of France. Keitel had stood by Hitler's side when he triumphantly forced the French at Compiègne to sign an Armistice in June 1940 in the same railway carriage that had been used for the Armistice of 1918. No Frenchman – and no British citizen, for that matter – could fail to remember the bitter days of May–June 1940, when Europe 'celebrated' five years later the end of the Second World War.

For both the French and the British the war had been effectively over for six months. Minds had turned to what kind of post-war world they were going to live in, especially in the light of the material shortages both countries had suffered during the preceding severe winter. 'Will we be heated next winter?' was the title of a gloomy article in the *Figaro* on 3 May 1945. Every day the newspaper published details of the place and time of the 'distribution centres' spread throughout Paris. Paul Ramadier was de Gaulle's Minister of Supply, responsible for such matters. Parisians called him 'Ramadan' and his meagre daily rations were known as '*Ramadiète*'. Sir Stafford Cripps, a tall, gaunt Labour politician, would be Chancellor of Exchequer in the Labour government, which ran Britain after July 1945; Sir Stafford could not escape the same jokes: 'Staff the Starver' distributed daily doses of his 'fish 'n' cripps', and managed to keep his mathematics of war rationing in operation until 1951.

By February and March 1945, with ice still in the roads, and in the homes, the old game of partisan politics was restoked. This was, after all, the fuel of democracy, for which the people had supposedly been fighting

---

[*] Air Chief Marshal Sir Arthur Tedder for the Allied Expeditionary Force, General Jean de Lattre de Tassigny, Commander-in-Chief of the First French Army, and General Carl A. Spaatz, commander of the United States Eighth Air Force.

for five years. In Britain, the fires had been burning with fury the previous autumn but died down as German V-2s started landing in London. It was Churchill who revived them at the Conservative Party Conference on 15 March when he equated the Labour Party state welfare programme with 'totalitarianism' and called it unfit for the Free Briton. He followed this up by angering the trade unions by his refusal to amend the Trades Disputes Act of 1927, which Labour claimed was a legislative act of revenge in response to the General Strike of 1926. It became evident that the days of coalition government were numbered.

Churchill would have liked the Coalition to remain in office until the Japanese were defeated. His own party, however, wanted an early election, before people forgot that the man who had led Britain to victory was also head of the Conservative Party. There was indeed a serious problem of popular perception here. Throughout the 1930s the Conservatives had made every effort to exclude Churchill from the leadership. When war eventually came and Churchill appeared to be the only man in the Commons capable of pulling Britain out of a difficult corner, it was the MPs on the Labour benches who cheered at his entry, not the silent Conservatives.

In the Coalition Cabinet, business had worked most smoothly with Clement Attlee – 'Little Clem' – and Ernest Bevin. This was not the case with his fellow Conservatives. A particularly stormy relationship had subsisted between Churchill and his chief Conservative rival, Lord Halifax, which was only solved when Halifax was sent off to Washington as ambassador. 'It was not Churchill who lost us the election,' Harold Macmillan later said of the General Elections of 5 July, 'it was the shadow of Chamberlain.'[26] Many of the commonsensical Great British electorate believed they could vote Labour and still have Churchill as Prime Minister. What they did not want was a Conservative Party that had brought them economic misery in the 1930s and war in 1939.

The British were also filled with the ideas of the 'New Jerusalem' – full employment and high wages; and health, education and housing paid for all. Labour had shifted far to the left during the war. Several of its younger members had been Communists during the 1930s. Harold Laski, chairman of the National Executive, regarded the Second World War as Act II of the Russian Revolution. John Strachey, who would be Minister of Food, had been an active Communist until the Nazi-Soviet Pact. So too had been Major Denis Healey, who expressed his delight, during the 1945 campaign, that the 'Socialist Revolution' was so firmly established in Eastern and Southern Europe. The armed services had been influenced by the creation, in 1941, of the Army Bureau of Current Affairs (ABCA), which organized an hour's lecture to the soldiers given every week by the platoon commander – with the aid of bulletins issued by the bureau. The actor, David Niven, at that time in the Commandos, remembered these lively debates, in which 'the vast majority of men who had been called up to fight for their country held the Conservative Party entirely responsible for the disruption of their lives and in no circumstances would they vote for it next time there was an election – Churchill or no Churchill.' Niven participated in the so-called 'Cairo Parliament', one of the hotbeds of British Communism during the war. Maurice Petherick, MP for Penryn and Falmouth, wrote to Churchill's Parliamentary Secretary in December 1942, 'I am more and more suspicious of the way this lecturing and education of the forces racket is run . . . For the love of Mike do something about it, unless you want to have the creatures coming back all pansy-pink.' Inside and outside the forces the two dominant thoughts in the minds of the electorate were the contents of the Beveridge Report and the heroic acts of the Red Army in turning back the Nazi military machine.[27]

On the other side of the English Channel was another conservative war leader facing an election at the moment Germany fell. In his New Year's radio address of 1945, General Charles de Gaulle, President of the Provisional Government, announced that, after the year which 'history will say was one of the greatest ever lived by France', the people would rediscover 'their right of suffrage': municipal elections would be held throughout the country in the spring.

Municipal elections have always had a special meaning in France.[28] They are at the base of the political machine. They define the local power of the national parties – and often their finances. No deputy in the Chamber has ever had a seat without this local source of support. They determine the political map of France. De Gaulle knew only too well that the Third Republic had been created by the municipal elections of the 1870s and '80s. It would be a test of what kind of France would be created after the Second World War.

De Gaulle was totally unclear in his mind about what kind of France this should be. Up until now he had been preoccupied by France's 'rank' in the world, France's 'place at the table' as he put it. But what France? During the war he had made it very clear that he did not want a return of the Third Republic and its manoeuvring parties: they had failed to stand up to Hitler. Ideally it would have to be a France of the Resistance, of 'the one hundred and six million men and women who populate France and her Empire, united in their confidence, loyalty, fraternity'.[29] The last phrase, 'France and her Empire united', was no mean point. De Gaulle wanted to underline that there would be no distinction – as the Communists made – between a 'Resistance of the Interior' and of the 'Exterior'. In September de Gaulle had dressed the 'Interior Resistance' in American uniforms and sent them off to fight in Germany because they were all under the influence of the French Communists. In early spring 1945 he had spoken at length in praise of the French colonies and their contribution to the French war – his words were to have an immediate impact on the post-war world. At the same time he embarked on a series of radical reforms that corresponded to the French version of a 'New Jerusalem'. At the rhythm of one major nationalization a month, de Gaulle set about the state takeover of coal, gas, electricity and public transport. Five of the great banks were nationalized, starting with the Bank of France. These activities seemed to please national opinion, as expressed in the press; they were also identical to the French Communist plan as it had evolved in the post-Moulin National Council of Resistance (the CNR). Now there would be municipal elections, which emphasized the local base of the French state – a basic Communist tenet. Was this Northern Catholic conservative, General Charles de Gaulle, a Communist in disguise?

De Gaulle himself would have denied it, but his subsequent political career was full of ambiguities towards the Communists; sometimes he made war on them, even on the streets; sometimes he used them as allies. Basically, as long as he could exert authority over them, they could serve as 'useful idiots' against the 'regime of parties'. It was a serious miscalculation. He could never admit that this was what he was doing. He remained perplexed. 'We are in an unprecedented situation,' the General, obviously distressed, remarked to two of his advisers at Neuilly. 'In earlier revolutions there was always another regime ready to replace it. Here, it is not just a question of one regime collapsing, but two [the Third Republic and Vichy]!'[30] Worse for de Gaulle, there were at least two regimes waiting to replace them: the Communist Resistance and an ideal Gaullist assembly (*ralliement*) of the people; there were also the old parliamentarians waiting in the wings (the 'regime of parties').

The series of nationalizations were a sign of support to the 'Resistance movements' (now dominated by the Communists) – but only a sign. He talked to the old parliamentarians of the Third Republic, but he was not going to hand power to them. All the same, de Gaulle appears to have had no plans for a new constitution. He certainly did nothing to prevent the return of the old political parties. They were all invited to participate in his Cabinet. They sat together in the Consultative Assembly, in the same proportion as under the Third Republic.

Perhaps de Gaulle intended to use the municipal elections – the first round was on 30 April, the second on 14 May – as an indicator of popular intent. They were nothing of the kind. Not even the best journalists could make any sense out of them.

Women voted for the first time in French history. The elections' most novel feature was the introduction of a new party, the Mouvement Républicain Populaire (or MRP), which *Le Monde* described as 'democratic and Christian', and 'of Gaullist doctrine, such as can be drawn from a reading of the speeches of General de Gaulle'. 'Christian Democratic' would be its clearest equivalent in a European context – and that would be the trend that would govern Europe for the next forty years.

Nationwide the MRP won about a quarter of the vote. But it had not been openly supported by the General himself, and within months he would begin spurning it. High scores by the SFIO, the old Socialist party, suggested that the country was turning left. But then what of the Communists? The problem was that the elections were presented in the form of lists. The Communists ran several front parties, such as the 'Patriotic Union of Republicans and Anti-Fascists' or the 'Republican Anti-Fascist Resistance Alliance',[31] which in several constituencies were in competition with one another. It was a typical Communist distraction, a political mask, covering what they really represented.

The day after the preliminary round was the First of May, a great day for the left. The Communists made as large a demonstration as they could, their red banners swirling in the wind, declaring slogans such as 'No pity for the Traitors and Fascists!' – 'Fascist' and 'Anti-Fascist' had made a notable return to French Communist vocabulary since the end of the war. With the return of the *déportés* and first reports about the nature of Auschwitz – 'one enters by the gate and leaves by the chimney'[32] – there was even an upsurge in 'wild purging' (political murder) in the Paris region. But the demonstration was not a great success. It snowed in Paris on 1 May.

Such was the state of radical ferment – as it was described at the time – in the two great democracies of Western Europe just before their two conservative leaders, Churchill and de Gaulle, formally announced, to the surprise of no one, that the war was over.

The language of the three Western leaders, as they spoke simultaneously on the radio, was in their best of styles: Churchill was Churchillian, de Gaulle was at his most Gaullist, and Truman spoke with the simple Midwestern phrases that Americans were only just getting to know.

Each paid tribute to the other Allies. When Churchill pronounced slowly the words, 'Finally almost the whole world was combined against the evil-doers – who are now prostrate before us,' the crowd listening to the address on loudspeakers in Parliament Square apparently 'gasped'. He reminded his huge audience across Europe that there still remained Japan. 'Advance, Britannia!' he ended, his voice breaking with emotion. 'Long live the cause of freedom! God save the King!' There were British prisoners of war in Germany for whom this address was the first time they had heard the Prime Minister's voice since his 'blood sweat and tears' in 1940. Clearly it had not changed.

'The war is won!' began de Gaulle. 'This is victory! It is the victory of the United Nations and it is the victory of France!' Like a drummer he beat out, adagio, 'Germany is conquered and she has signed the deed of defeat!' At the end, he took up his lyre: 'Honour! Honour for always! To our armies and to their commanders! Honour to our people . . . ! Honour to the United Nations which mixed their blood with our blood, their suffering with our suffering, their hope with our hope . . . ! Ah! Vive la France!'

'This is a solemn but glorious hour,' said Truman. 'I only wish that Franklin D. Roosevelt had lived to witness this day.' 'We must work to finish the war,' he concluded, reflecting on Japan. 'Our victory is but half won.'[33]

London, Paris and New York had already been celebrating 'VE-Day' for twenty-four hours. But Moscow Radio and the Soviet press remained silent through all this. It was not until Wednesday, 9 May, that the news was announced. At ten o'clock that evening Stalin made two addresses, one to the armed forces, the other to the people. Neither contained any reference to the Allies. To the armed forces he said: 'The Great Patriotic War, which has been waged by the Soviet people against the Germano-Fascist invaders, ends with the victory of our arms. Germany is irremediably beaten.' To the people he said: 'The historic day of the victory of our people over German imperialism has come . . . Henceforth the flag of free peoples, which is also the flag of peace, will float over Europe.' If this was meant to be a reference to Allied flags as well, it was a curious way of phrasing it; some Allies could have interpreted it as a threat. 'Eternal glory to the heroes who have fallen in the struggle, and who have sacrificed their lives for the freedom and happiness of our people,' he concluded. Stalin's style was classical Stalinist.[34]

The greatest celebration of 'VE-Day' was outside Europe, in New York City. There had already been wild jubilation with the false report of 27 April; that was just the preliminary. For three days, Monday, Tuesday and

Wednesday, 7–9 May, New York went mad. Not a bomb had fallen in the streets, not a plane been shot down; a few Germans, who had wandered from their U-boat on to a beach near Ocean City, had been picked up in 1943 and were immediately shot – but that was the extent of New York's experience of war.

New Yorkers, and many Americans besides, thought they were invulnerable in 1945. They thought it was their troops and their money that had won the war; they were the genuine emissaries of human rights and freedom. And they were unbeatable. One journalist, Louis Sobol, described the wild scenes around Times Square, where an amateurish papier-mâché copy of the Statue of Liberty had been set up – 'There were shouts, and tears, and people kissing each other and banging each other on the back.' But most notable was the way he explained this joy: 'The German soldier loses his place in history as a valiant, fearless, unbeatable foe . . . [Now] we know them for what they are, whiners and crumble-uppers when the going gets tough. As for the Yanks, I leave it to you. When have they ever been licked?'[35] A profound optimism swept through America. Americans had never felt so confident in their history.

In Washington it was raining. Truman was celebrating his sixty-first birthday the day he made his radio address. 'I call upon every American to stick to his post until the last battle is won,' he had said – that was his usual way of celebrating a birthday. The city was in fact fairly calm. It was no holiday. The most important event was the arrival of an army truck at Blair House to pick up Harry and Bess Truman's few belongings and move them into the White House; it took twenty trucks to move Mrs Roosevelt out.[36]

Quite a crowd had gathered outside the White House. Major Keith Wakefield of the Australian Military Mission tried driving through it. As he and his comrades crept forward, yard by cheering yard, they lost their caps and then the Australian mudguard flag. 'This was a forerunner of the manifestation of a universal desire of Washingtonians to strip us of our uniforms,' continued Major Wakefield. 'Lasses of all shapes and sizes invaded our car and made interesting suggestions.' In the fountain pool outside Union Station naked girls and boys cavorted about in pagan ritual.[37]

The weather in London and Paris turned out to be unexpectedly hot – during the war there were no weather forecasts on the radio or in the press (one of the major reasons why the Allies won D-Day). In London 'VE-Day' was essentially Churchill's day; the greatest crowds in Britain were around where he stood, followed him where he drove, listened to him where the loudspeakers were placed, such as in Trafalgar Square or Victoria Station. On his way over to Buckingham Palace for lunch with the King the Prime Minister was espied, by an excited schoolboy, as he emerged from his wartime quarters at Storey's Gate. The schoolboy ran across the street and tried to touch him. The police pushed him back. 'Leave the boy alone,' shouted Churchill and waved to him a V-sign. 'What a moment that was for a schoolboy,' said Lord Wolfson of St Marylebone, that schoolboy, fifty years later. 'My dear friends,' said the Prime Minister from a balcony overlooking Parliament Square, 'this is your hour. This is not a victory of any party or of any class' – there were thousands standing before him. 'It is a victory of the great British nation as a whole.' Maybe. But for the thousands below it was Churchill they wanted to see and hear.

Churchill had been late arriving at Parliament that afternoon because of all the crowds surrounding his car. And the star in the House was of course Churchill. The House of Commons, he said, had proved itself 'the strongest foundation for waging war that has ever been seen in the whole of our long history'. Then, recalling Armistice Day more than twenty-five years earlier, he moved 'That this House do now attend at the Church of St Margaret, Westminster, to give humble and reverend thanks to Almighty God for our deliverance from the threat of German domination.' 'This', said Churchill, 'is the identical Motion which was moved in former times.' So the whole House – Protestant, Catholic, Nonconformist and Jew – filed out to St Margaret's to give thanks to the Almighty for their deliverance.

And for whom was it that the tens of thousands were waiting outside Buckingham Palace late that afternoon? The King? The Queen? Their two young daughters? It was, naturally enough, Churchill. When Churchill appeared beside royalty and waved his V-sign, a roar came up from below.[38]

Because it was so warm, lunches and dinners were organized in several streets. People danced the hokey-cokey and the Lambeth walk; they sang 'Land of Hope and Glory', 'God Save the King', and 'For He's a Jolly Good Fellow'. The chairs in Green Park were torn to pieces for victory bonfires; wood from bombed houses was added to the flames. The streets had lighting again. Many of the monuments were floodlit.

But the skies on the evening of VE-Day in London, brightened red by all the bonfires, reminded many of the Blitz. The East End lay flattened in ruins. So too did much of the South Bank. Here there was silence, or the sound of an odd radio. In fact, beyond the main gathering points, there was a certain eerie quietness. Even some points of the West End were no more busy than normal for that late stage of the war. London's celebration of 'the day the war ended' was conducted with a certain sobriety.

That was true also of Paris. On Monday evening it was clear that Paris was getting 'very excited', as one American serviceman wrote home to his parents in Baltimore. But the streets did not start getting packed with people until late afternoon on Tuesday, after de Gaulle's address. An American Mitchell bomber managed the feat of flying *under* the Eiffel Tower, American jeeps drove about with twenty or more people clinging on to each one of them. A lot of the old songs of the First World War, particularly 'Madelon', were chanted. The monuments were illuminated, the Opéra in red, white and blue – as it had been on 11 November 1918. But this was not Armistice Day, nor was it the Liberation. Pierre Brisson, director of *Le Figaro*, best captured the mood when he wrote in his paper, 'For us it is a climb out of the abyss. Our country has climbed out of a chasm where the world might have taken us for lost . . . This evening is a very different one from Foch's victorious return at the head of his armies. The hour is solemn. We have known the worst adversity . . . Let us be content tonight that we are survivors.' On Wednesday, even the richest quarters seemed deserted – a typical Parisian day in that year of severe rationing, 1945.[39]

Though Moscow remained silent on the matter of German capitulation, it delighted the world with the news, that Monday, of what had happened to the sixteen non-Communist emissaries sent in March by Kazimierz Pużak's Underground Council to Warsaw – where they had disappeared. They had been flown to Moscow and locked up in Lubyanka gaol, where they were awaiting trial for 'high treason' directed against 'the reborn Polish State'. On Wednesday morning – Moscow's VE-Day – Beria, the NKVD chief, handed Stalin a decree for the celebration of the people's victory: all Soviet soldiers taken prisoner by the Germans and all Soviet citizens liberated and repatriated, under the terms of the Yalta agreement, were to be placed in camps. These camps were now ready to receive them, each one designed to hold 10,000 people. There were over a hundred camps, some in 'Polish territory' (was this not an independent nation?) which would serve to house a million people. A million new prisoners for the Gulag! What a victory! Stalin signed without hesitation.[40]

Just after 1 a.m. Moscow time, the blast of Russian music on Radio Moscow was turned down and Yuri Levitan, the senior announcer, came on the air to pronounce the news the rest of the world had known for four days. 'Attention, this is Moscow,' he said in a grave tone. 'Germany has capitulated. This day, in honour of the victorious Great Patriotic War, is to be a national holiday, a festival of victory.'

Within minutes central Moscow was filled with people, some still in their nightclothes, crying, 'Victory! Victory!' – what happened in the rest of Moscow remains as secret as its whole history during the war. Red Square and its surroundings, right down to the river's edge, were packed with people, cheering, sobbing, praying. It had been cool in the morning but by midday the sun picked out the bright colours of the women's kerchiefs. *Pravda* contained a long poem 'To our own Stalin – glory and praise!' Hugh Lunghi of the British Military Mission and his men got caught by a mob of revellers in the History Museum Passage, which led into Red Square. Noticing their uniforms they bear-hugged and kissed them until they were drawn into the square 'where we were lifted on to shoulders then tossed in the air'. The same happened to members of both the American and British embassies – though Mrs Churchill, who was present, was apparently spared the experience. In the evening a salvo of a thousand guns was fired before Marshal Stalin made his inspiring address to the people. Searchlights scanned the night sky. The greatest firework display of the war was then launched into the air: most impressive was the fiery picture of Stalin which hung for a few minutes over the roofs of old Moscow.

In Lubyanka gaol the inmates – who included the sixteen emissaries of Poland's Underground 'Council of National Unity' along with a former Red Army captain, Alexander Solzhenitsyn, arrested in East Prussia for 'conducting anti-Soviet propaganda' – were wondering what was going on. The blackout shades on the cell windows were taken down before 1 May, so obviously the threat of air attack was fading. During the following days there was a thirty-gun salute. That meant a national capital had fallen to the Red Army, and since there remained only Prague and Berlin it must have been one or the other. Then all the interrogators disappeared, which left the building in a terrible silence; you could hear the sound of each isolated prisoner in his cell and, for the first time, sense where each cell was located. One inmate started complaining. He was taken out of his cell and placed in a 'box'. Because the doors of the box were left open, in the 'suspended silence every blow on his soft and choking mouth could be heard clearly'. On 9 May they were brought dinner along with their lunch – which usually happened only on the First of May and Revolution Day, 7 November. In the evening there was another thirty-gun salute, so no national capitals were left. This was followed by a huge salvo – 'and that was the end of all the ends'. 'Above the muzzle of our window, and from all the other cells of the Lubyanka, and from all the windows of all the Moscow prisons, we, too, former prisoners of war and former front-line soldiers, watched the Moscow heavens patterned with fireworks and crisscrossed by the beams of searchlights.' Some of the prisoners still wore the overcoats which had been torn to tatters by German shell fragments. But, as Solzhenitsyn noted, the victory of 9 May was 'not for us. And that spring was not for us either.'[41]

One of the notable phenomena of Armistice Day 1918 had been the eruption of celebrations in the large towns and, in particular, the capital cities, whilst on the Western Front, except for a small part of the American sector in the south, there had been silence. Soldiers were dazed. Others continued their work, clearing rubble, building roads, mending the wires – it must be remembered that even in the First World War soldiers did not spend the majority of their time fighting.

A similar phenomenon occurred at the end of the Second World War, except that there was no clear 'Front' this time, just a lot of rubble, from the English Channel, right across Germany, Poland and Russia, and up through the Italian peninsula. The celebrations were confined almost exclusively to London, Paris and Moscow. Even in England, though victory bonfires may have been lit in various village squares, these were, by all accounts, pretty tame affairs.

Thousands of British POWs were flown into Britain from Germany by Lancaster bombers in the first weeks of May 1945. One of them, Roger Peacock, had been captive since 1940 and arrived home on VE-Day. 'I cannot speak for my friends,' he recalled, 'but for myself the capacity to react to events was overloaded. I could not feel.' He was not the least bit interested in the 'Victory junketing', as he called it, merely that *I'd made it.* He spoke like a First World War survivor. An American GI in Bavaria, Benjamin Ferencz, had been inactive for three weeks. As he walked past the day-room he heard on the radio that the war was over: 'I just listened silently and seriously, and it's still hard for me to believe,' he wrote to his fiancée. 'The other fellows seemed to feel the same way.' British XXX Corps was preparing to move into Denmark when the news came. 'Apart from the festive consumption of much alcohol,' said Captain Vivian Herzog, 'I do not recall anything special.' A Polish Jew, George Topas, liberated by the Americans, found himself in the neutral zone that constituted the Czech 'border' at that time: 'I began to feel a sense of anxiety that displaced the mood of hopeful expectation. I was not yet fully aware that the world I once knew existed no more.'[42]

Paul Fussell, the writer, is best known for a book he wrote about English literature of the First World War. He was seriously wounded during a German offensive in March 1945. His closest friend was killed beside him. On Western VE-Day he was in a hospital in Epinal when the news came through: 'I was seized with an unstoppable fit of crying, motivated, I think, both by shock and guilt.' He was not the only man that day to suffer from 'survivor's guilt'. Today Fussell is a famous staunch pacifist.[43]

Between Moscow and Paris there were the roads. They were filled with pedestrians, and a few people on carts, the odd rumbling lorry – prisoners of war who had been abandoned by their guards, concentration camp survivors, death marchers, German soldiers seeking refuge from the Russians, refugees who had no idea where they were heading. On Lüneburg Heath a British intelligence officer, Lieutenant Frank Green, was studying aerial pictures when the news of VE-Day came through on the radio. 'I went outside,' he remembered, 'and stood with a few of my friends from where we could at first hear, and then see, the beginning of a column of grey men in grey uniforms. The sound of their boots and the beaten look on their faces told the whole story. The column continued past us for hours, thousands of them. We could not hate them.' An American corporal near Schwerin spent his day with a drunken Ukrainian and a group of German citizens digging a mass grave for the dead outside the local town hall. One heavy German was helped by his daughter to dig a special grave for a thin desiccated corpse. In the liberated concentration camps thoughts were on survival. Bergen-Belsen after three weeks of liberation had already lost three thousand of its inmates. One of them recorded that, though they heard the bells of Big Ben and Chopin on the radio when the news of the capitulation came through, 'we were more afraid of death and the victory did not sink in as fast as it should have done'. For another, '8 May left just a ripple in my memory.' Another remembered his first night in a clean, white bed. Was it 8 May? 'I heard from very far the sound of bells,' said yet another, lying in a hospital with spotted typhus, 'somebody said to me "the war is over" but I felt no joy. I knew that my whole family was wiped out. I felt miserable and thought I was dying.'[44]

American and British troops had a strange feeling after passing through the devastated areas of Padua into Venice on 8 May. The gondolas were still waiting for clients. St Mark's Square was almost completely empty; some of the statues were encased in timber. North, at Treviso airport, squadrons were performing aerobatics as they waited for a Victory Dinner to be flown in. Captain Anthony Crosland, later a Labour politician, was with the 6th Armoured Division in northern Italy where he saw Italians returning from slave labour: 'a sad never-ending procession, huge packs or cases on their backs, bent double beneath the weight . . . Their release is costing them something near the limit of physical suffering.' Sergeant Paul Kavon was in western Czechoslovakia with Patton's forces when they liberated a crowd of 'Russians': 'they cried for joy, cheered us, shook hands, saluted and tried to show us in every way possible how much they welcomed the sight of the American Army.'[45]

4 Britain repatriates the Cossacks

Within three weeks these Russians would be in Beria's new camps – or dead. The full details of post-war repatriations to Russia and her new Eastern European satellite states are still not known today. This is notably the case of the American-controlled southern sector of occupied Germany, where so many of Vlasov's army made an attempt to escape. Here again one encounters another great gap in the historical memory.

The forced repatriations of Russians, against their will, is part of the much larger story of how the Eastern and Western Fronts eventually met up once Nazi Germany had been defeated. It is an episode that, in recent years, has been distorted by historians seeking a spectacular story from recently released documents purporting to demonstrate evil deeds committed by people of authority who are still alive – though very old. In France the main subject of polemic and 'historical' court cases has been, over the last thirty years, Vichy administrators and their treatment of the Jews; in Germany, it is the mix of business with past Nazi crimes; in Italy and Spain it is the 'cover-up' of past membership of far-right wartime organizations (never the extreme left). In Britain, court cases revolve around 'Holocaust denial' (but never 'Gulag denial') and in particular one record libel case concerning the repatriation of Cossacks and Yugoslavs from British-occupied Austria to the Red Army and Tito's Communist Partisans: a case whose only real historical value was that it revealed details, in one small corner, about what happened when East met West at the end of the Second World War. In May 1945, the West still insisted on the myth that the Soviet Union was its 'ally', while this was quite obviously not the attitude (and never had been) of the Soviet Union and its growing Communist empire.

In December 1989, the plaintiff, Lord Aldington, deputy chairman of the Conservative Party and formerly Brigadier Toby Low of V Corps, Eighth Army, in occupied Austria, was awarded £1.5 million in libel damages against the defendants, the historian Count Nikolai Tolstoy, one of the many descendants of the famous writer, and a property developer from Tunbridge Wells, Nigel Watts. The court case was of ludicrous origin. Watts had a grievance over a claim he had made to an insurance company chaired by Aldington; discovering to his delight that Aldington had been accused of commanding some highly questionable activity involving repatriations in Austria at the end of the war, he struck up a partnership with Nikolai Tolstoy, who had long been furious about Western treatment of the Russian 'ethnic group' and had become the expert historian on the subject; together (in fact, the author was Tolstoy) they wrote a widely distributed pamphlet in which Aldington was accused of being a 'war criminal': the source of the libel writ. Tolstoy himself had the opportunity of remaining outside the case, but volunteered to be tried in court in the hope that he could use the court as a forum to present his life's work. This work centred on the British army's activities in southern Austria in May 1945. The chief man in Tolstoy's sights, however, was already three years dead: Harold Macmillan, British Minister Resident in Italy and, according to Tolstoy, chief conspirator in the repatriation of anti-Communist Yugoslavs and Cossacks.

To his surprise, the case went badly for Tolstoy. If the jury decided that damages were to be awarded, the presiding judge said in summing up the case, they should not be influenced by their estimation of the financial means of the parties involved: 'You do not deal in Mickey Mouse money, just reeling off noughts because they sound good.' He recommended that the sum of damages be calculated in terms of the price of a house, or the principal of an investment that would yield a decent living. The jury made their calculation. They found Tolstoy guilty of libel and set damages and court costs at a record £1.5 million.*[46]

'Historical' court cases like this usually confuse the issue because of the unending appeals and bitterness they engender; they kill common memory and hence the general interest in history. The *Tolstoy v. Aldington* case has been no exception. The details it revealed on repatriation, important as they are, now need to be extracted from the legal battle and placed in the wider historical context out of which they arose.

The first factor to consider – as always in the case of 1945 – is the general movement of the armies and the political geography they created. The shape of the Eastern and Western Fronts resembled an ill-made glass ampoule closed cack-handedly at both ends. At the north end was its narrow neck where – across the northern plain – the two fronts had been brought closely together: Montgomery had sealed the top with the capture of Lübeck, thereby preventing the Red Army access to Scandinavia; the Americans in the meantime had advanced in some places more than 150 miles inside the area that had been agreed to be the Soviet sector of Germany; the Americans had also taken a substantial amount of Czech territory. But at the approaches to the Alpine system of Austria and northern Yugoslavia the ampoule opened up to such an extent that,

---

* Not a penny of this was paid by Tolstoy. In fact, it was Aldington who was ruined by legal costs. The case went on like *Jarndyce v. Jarndyce* in Dickens's *Bleak House*. In 1995 the European Court of Human Rights ruled that the libel award was excessive and violated Tolstoy's freedom of expression.

at some points, the two fronts were two hundred miles or more apart. Right at the bottom, in the Adriatic peninsula of Istria – and specifically at the contested port of Trieste – it was Alexander's Eighth Army that closed up the bottom of the ampoule, by making contact with Tito's Communist Partisans.

All population movements in Europe over the next twelve months were shaped by these two military fronts, pinched shut at top and bottom, but widely separated by 'neutral territory' in the hills and mountains of southern Central Europe. The 'scum' of Europe – as the author Arthur Koestler had once expressed it – gathered here in this closed ampoule: the stateless, the homeless, Jews who had escaped the Nazi net, survivors of Communist massacre, those who had fought for their country and not their dictators, vagabonds caught up in the lawless human tornado of violence that had swept across the Russian borderlands and into the Balkans.

Europe's 'scum', shut up in a bottle, may have appeared alien to a Western eye. But were they any odder than the West's odd mix of Eastern 'allies'? Marshal Tito had in fact been negotiating with the Germans in 1943 – not Mihailović and his royalist Chetniks, as the NKGB agent of SOE Cairo, James Klugmann, had maliciously reported. As for Stalin, he had always been ready to negotiate with Hitler – after Stalingrad, after Kursk. Only in late 1943, when he saw he could realize his expansionist aims without Hitler, did he stop talks with the Nazis in Stockholm. In the meantime, through civil war and massacre – and thanks to British aid – Tito had managed to create the only Partisan force in Europe that constituted a national army. What did loyalty mean in this lawless Eastern European world, where the only rule of survival was to join the enemy of one's enemy? How could any Western court of justice ever judge them? How were the victorious armies, which even after the German surrender continued to press forward, supposed to treat that 'scum' they found, closed up in that bottle?

The United States had a new president. 'At this moment I have in my heart a prayer,' concluded Harry Truman in his address to Congress four days after Roosevelt's death. 'As I have assumed my duties I humbly pray Almighty God, in the words of King Solomon, "Give therefore Thy servant an understanding heart to judge Thy people, that I may discern between good and bad: for who is able to judge this Thy so great a people?"'[47] No professional speechwriter had composed that. It was pure Truman, straight from his Midwestern soul. And a tough soul it was. Truman was quick to show this to the world.

But at the moment of his succession, he knew nothing about foreign policy. He would prove a quick learner – Truman would soon have the reputation of the fastest decision-maker the White House had yet known (in contrast to Roosevelt). Yet, in the critical month when the war in Europe ended – Truman's first month in office – he had to depend on whatever advisers he could find.

One of them was, of course, Churchill. Churchill had not attended Roosevelt's funeral, which a lot of people thought curious for this travelling old lion. Many took it as a sign of Churchill's growing frustration with America, and particularly America's failure to stand up to the Russians. Poland remained a sore issue. Recent Russian behaviour in the Balkans – Romania and Bulgaria – had made a mockery of Yalta's Declaration on Liberated Europe. Because he had not been at the funeral, he had not met Harry Truman. Instead, in the typical Churchillian manner, he wrote long letters of advice to the new president. Truman of Missouri was not accustomed to these flourishes of the pen.

'An iron curtain is drawn down upon their front,' said Churchill, using the phrase for the first time concerning the Russian lines, in a cable to Truman on 12 May. 'We do not know what is going on behind.' Churchill had been urging for a week that the Western Allies not retreat from their advanced positions. Truman answered that it would be a mistake not to adhere to the Yalta agreement. Churchill became seriously alarmed – the Russians were evidently not keeping their side of the accord. With Russia now taking control of Poland, eastern Germany, the Baltic provinces and Hungary with no response from the West, it was like 'witnessing an event in the history of Europe to which there has been no parallel'. Yet the Americans were already pulling out their forces from Europe as fast as they could. Half the American air force had gone by the time Churchill wrote on 12 May. 'I am profoundly concerned about the European situation,' he cabled.[48]

In his private correspondence, as well as in the personal diary he kept, Truman admitted that he felt unsure of himself: he was confronted with decisions on atom bombs; the situation in Europe; on 9 May he signed an order, presented by the State Department, cutting back Lend-Lease to Russia, Britain and France – he later admitted he had not read it and had to countermand the order. But ships had already been turned back to America. 'I can't understand it,' he wrote in his diary, 'except to attribute it to God. He guides me, I think.'[49]

Truman pulled Harry Hopkins from his death bed in the Mayo Clinic and sent him on a special mission to Moscow. Churchill sent Anthony Eden on a special mission to Washington. Eden was very impressed with the new president – he showed none of his doubts in public. Yet the rapid pull-out of forces from Europe continued. It was agreed that a summit of the Big Three, Churchill, Truman and Stalin, should be arranged as soon as possible.

On 12 June Eisenhower made his triumphal visit to the nation's capital. He was entertained to a White House dinner that night. 'He's a nice fellow and a good man,' Truman reported to his wife, Bess. 'He's done a whale of a job.' Everybody was speaking about what a good president he would make. Truman confided, in his letter to Bess, what a nice idea this would be: 'I'd turn it over to him now if I could.'[50]

Hopkins came back from his Russian mission the same day. Stalin had shown himself at his jovial best. Both Eisenhower and Hopkins emphatically assured Truman that it would be wrong not to withdraw to the lines agreed at Yalta. Truman immediately informed Churchill that the Americans were going to let the Russians have their 'Soviet Sector' in Germany. The Russians, Truman wrote in his diary, had 'always been our friends and I can't see why they shouldn't always be'.[51] For the moment it seemed as though it was Roosevelt's men who were setting American foreign policy. And the primary aim of Roosevelt's policy had been friendship with Russia.

British strategy, with centuries of history behind it, had always had as one of its aims that of keeping the Russians out of Central Europe. That had been the purpose of the Italian campaign, the swift advance with forty divisions from Normandy on to the Ruhr and then Berlin, and ultimately the idea behind Montgomery's lightning campaign on Lübeck. American strategy had only developed during the First World War – and it showed their inexperience in Europe. Their central military aim had been to push south of the Ardennes, across the middle Rhine, into Bavaria and on to the 'Southern Redoubt'. Their course south of the Ardennes had given Hitler his chance at 'the Bulge', thus delaying the end of the war by several months. Their wanderings across southern Germany had caused large sections of their army to lie idle; apart from Patton in Czechoslovakia, the southern sector made no contact with the Russians. And the 'Southern Redoubt' proved to be the wild fantasy that it was.

Meanwhile the Italian campaign, run by Field Marshal Alexander from Allied Forces Head Quarters (AFHQ) in palatial Caserta, had been run down. Seven divisions had been pulled out in summer 1944 for 'Operation Dragoon' in the French Riviera. The withdrawals continued, morale sank; in winter the advance of Alexander's polyglot army came to a complete halt: the Italian campaign had become the 'forgotten war'. The last battles of spring 1945 were fought around Ravenna and thence across the Po valley to Venice, which British and American troops entered just before the formal surrender of all German forces in Italy and southern Austria. It might have been the first major German capitulation on the Western Front, but Alexander's eighteen divisions – of which only four were now British – were as war-weary as the enemy.

Austria had, like Germany, been divided into 'occupied zones' on the recommendation of the European Advisory Commission, whose proposals had been adopted finally at Yalta. Britain would occupy the South-West, America the North-West, and the Soviet Union the East. Vienna, like Berlin, was also to be split into sectors. The whole point of the Italian campaign had been, as Churchill had so vigorously argued in 1944, the double aim of defeating the Nazis and cutting off the Communist armies before they reached Hungary and Austria. He had been bitterly disappointed, and held the Americans responsible.

In spring 1945 he came in for another nasty surprise. Marshal Tito, the grand strategist that he was, had taken note of the dispersal of Western Allied forces in Germany. He had also observed the West's apparent lack of interest in Berlin and Prague, which Hitler had not called the 'twin citadels' for nothing. No Central European could fail to recognize their importance. Encouraged by Stalin, he began developing his Marxist-Leninist theory of a 'Greater Yugoslavia', which would include Italy's two north-eastern provinces of Venezia Giulia and the southern Austrian province of Carinthia.

His original military plan had been, after the fall of Belgrade, to provide a flanking attack to the left of the Russians as they crossed the Hungarian plain into Austria. By late winter the task was virtually complete. So Tito turned to his theory. He split his forces in two, sending the Yugoslav Fourth and Third Armies up the Dalmatian coast towards the northern province of Slovenia, into Ljubljana – where the anti-Communist Yugoslavs, in retreat, had assembled a 'National Committee' – then on to Istria and the port of Trieste, and northwards, into the southern Austrian province of Carinthia. The British in Italy watched these movements with increasing horror.

The Americans, in late April, urged the British to move into Venezia Giulia as well as their designated southern Austrian sector of Carinthia. At the same time they still refused to get bogged down in the 'Balkan arena'. It sounded like Roosevelt all over again. America in late April was living through a political interlude, as her new president learnt his trade. But by mid-May a Truman policy was cautiously emerging. Just as Churchill was pushing the President for a forward policy on the northern neck of Europe's unoccupied bottle, so did Truman press the British forward at its southern tip. It was a critical interlude that was to affect the lives of millions of Europeans: it seemed to be falling to Britain, at the moment Lend-Lease was reduced and Americans were pulling out of Germany, to assume the task of facing up to the Communists with their Eighth Army in Italy. The atmosphere at Caserta was permeated with unease. In June Truman's policy became clearer and distinctly more anti-Communist; he began by promising aid from the north of Austria: Patton's forces were to move south. The problem was that in those intervening six weeks a large part of the 'scum' of Europe, gathered at the bottom of the bottle, had been 'repatriated' in order to clear the field for action – and one of the worst post-war massacres had already taken place.

Alexander knew he did not have the forces to occupy effectively both Venezia Giulia and Carinthia. His first move was to place Eighth Army Headquarters, under General Richard McCreery, in Udine, some sixty miles north of Venice. McCreery, in turn, ordered the best of his three corps – V Corps, commanded by General Charles Keightley – to move carefully northwards towards Austrian Carinthia, hidden behind the precipitous Carnian and Karawanken Alps.

On 3 May Tito announced that the British were advancing into areas 'already liberated' from the Fascists and declared his intention not to withdraw any of his Partisans they might run into. Harold Macmillan, the Minister Resident, was spending more and more of his time at Caserta, giving advice to the military. But he was as perplexed by the situation as Alexander. They seemed to be moving straight out of one war and into another. 'I am very tired – and very worried about this Tito affair,' he divulged in his diary on 9 May, as Moscow celebrated 'VE-Day'. 'Neither British nor American troops will care for a new campaign in order to save Trieste for the "Eyeties". On the other hand to give in completely may be a sort of Slav Munich.'[52] A 'Slav Munich' was the last thing that this devoted follower of Churchill – and de Gaulle – would have wanted to be accused of.

V Corps had started filing its way across the mountains the previous day, as London celebrated 'VE-Day'. They were divided into two major groups. The main force, headed by General Horatio Murray's 6th Armoured Division, lumbered up through the Predil Pass and on to Carinthia's provincial capital of Klagenfurt. In the meantime Major General Robert Arbuthnott's 78th Infantry Division clambered through the Plockenpass, seventy miles to the west, to reach an area between the small towns of Lienz and Spittal. The mountain routes they took were ancient winding tracks and from a distance they must have appeared like Hannibal's army crossing the Alps or Pizarro's sixteenth-century army climbing the Andes.

They did not move much faster – with the exception of Colonel Peter Wilkinson's 6th Special Forces, SOE, which raced forward in a Ford station wagon and Land Rovers to reach Klagenfurt that evening, 8 May

It took three days to get the full forces in position in Austria. Soldiers crossing the mountain barrier got the surprise of their lives as they came over the summit. They had been fighting in the Western Desert, in Sicily, in the olive groves of Monte Cassino, and the vineyards of Florence. Before them lay a lush green valley, 100 miles long and around 50 miles wide, with pine trees and Alpine meadows in flower – the weather in those first weeks in Austria was heavenly. Down the centre of the valley, from one end to the other, flowed the River Drau (or Drava, as it entered Yugoslavia at its eastern end); the whole valley was interspersed with long, sparkling mountain lakes.[53]

But that was not all. The valley was crowded with human beings. From high on the mountains the soldiers could see not just the picturesque little mountain villages, but also camps, shanty towns, temporary settlements of all kinds. As they descended into the valley they began to feel as if they were entering another age. A *Times* reporter described tens of thousands of Cossack men, women and children near Lienz 'no different in any major detail from what an artist might have painted in the Napoleonic wars'. There were peasants, their faces tired and bewildered, with horses and wooden wagons 'like a convoy of prairie schooners trekking onwards'. There was the odd camel. A Croatian general recalled that 'so thickly packed together were wagons, tanks, oxcarts, carriages, motor cars, trucks and vans of all descriptions that at many points no ground could be discerned between them.' It was 'a mass migration like that of the Ostrogoths some 1,500 years earlier'.

The 'forgotten war' had found the 'forgotten peoples', the dregs at the bottom of the bottle. Their dress was outlandish. Many were in torn and dirty German uniforms, though they could not speak a word of German; others wore Cossack fur hats and the traditional Cossack long coats, the cherkess. Some were in Tsarist uniforms that had not been seen in forty years.

The vast majority were Slav. There were the Domobranci, a militia formed to save Slovenia from Tito's Partisans; there were 'Serbian Volunteers', or 'Chetniks', who claimed to be still defending Mihailović's royalist cause; the German-named *Schutzkorps* turned out to be made up largely of anti-Communist Russians, a number of them having emigrated from Russia since the civil war of 1919–21. But there were many other nationalities present, too. Around the capital of Klagenfurt there were collections of French, Belgian, British and South African prisoners of war;

Italian, Spanish and Ukrainian refugees; and many Germans, a lot of them seriously wounded – whole areas, for example, had been converted into foul 'convalescent camps' for untreated amputees. Worst of all were the 'hideous-looking' Partisans of Tito who had already taken over the centre of Klagenfurt and were tearing down Allied Military Government signs almost as fast as the British were getting them up. In battered old lorries they roamed around country roads with semi-automatic weapons hanging over their shoulders, robbing, raping and murdering the other temporary inhabitants.

What was the British V Corps supposed to do in this Alpine inferno? Most of the British had been fighting a nationalist war against Germans, with Poles, Dutch and the French on their side, Russians and Yugoslavs as 'allies', and Italians on everybody's side. The British expected that everybody would be in a rush to go home, return to their 'nation state', once the war was over. In the Drau valley they were confronted, for the first time, with the absurdity of this nationalist view of war. They also came up against the unreality of those great ideologies that everybody was supposed to be fighting for or against – 'democracy', 'Nazism', 'Fascism', 'Communism'. Nothing made any more sense in Alpine Carinthia. Even the inhabitants spoke a German that nobody could understand – which often enough turned out to be Slovenian. To add to the confusion was a basic misunderstanding by British 'other ranks' of the situation in Yugoslavia, which they considered an ally, even if it now appeared a threat to their commanders. What the British, especially in the field, could not grasp was that Yugoslavia had not only been fighting the Second World War; a vicious civil war had also been going on which still had not ended.[*]

What then was V Corps' task? The administration of refugee camps, made up of a majority who had been fighting for the German enemy? Or preparing for action against the Yugoslav 'ally'? The soldiers were confused, the commanders of V Corps puzzled. Which explains the muddle of orders which went up and down the chain of command, from the Corps commanders to Army Headquarters in Udine and on to AFHQ in Caserta: a rich spaghetti and alphabet soup of orders that would delight polemical researchers when all these documents were released to the public thirty years later.

---

[*] An important exception to the British view was the ambassador to Belgrade, Sir Ralph Stevenson, who since April had been arguing that refugees from Yugoslavia, though certainly 'collaborators' with the Germans, were more the product of an internal civil war and therefore ought to be granted 'the traditional right of asylum' and not be repatriated. Churchill appears to have been sympathetic to this view. The refugees, however, ended up in Carinthia, from where most of them, as shall be seen, were forcibly repatriated.

At the centre of the later scandal was a decision to repatriate, with the shortest possible delay, all these refugees and prisoners to their 'home countries', even if against their will. The British Foreign Office had been arguing for forced repatriation since D-Day. Anthony Eden, the Foreign Secretary, had been hammering out the case since summer 1944. Churchill had had his moments of doubt and so had the Americans. But the Americans, the British and the Soviets had all signed the Repatriations Agreement at Yalta on the final day of the conference, 11 February – a confirmation of acts already committed, for the British had been forcibly repatriating Russians since the summer, and the Americans since late autumn 1944. What was disturbing about the particular case of Carinthia was the mix of ethnic groups, which made nonsense of the idea of 'nationality'; and the reckless, indiscriminate haste in which 'repatriation' was carried out.

Only a minority of V Corps were ordered to carry out the actions of late May and early June. But the scenes witnessed, many recounted by V Corps soldiers themselves, were awful. There seems to have been little truth to later claims that the war-weary British had no sympathy for the people – many of whom had fought alongside the Germans – that they were now deporting by force. As the General Election of 5 July demonstrated, there was a strong leftward bias in the British armed services and continuing faith in 'our brave Soviet ally' – a power, it can hardly be denied, that had done much to destroy the Nazis. But that did not mean that British soldiers enjoyed sending Croats, Slovenes, Cossacks and anti-Communist Russians – including many women and children – into the arms of their enemy. Most of V Corps never saw anything: they enjoyed those sunny days on the side of the lakes, fishing, water-skiing with battalion motor boats, playing football and hiking in the mountains.

But the soldiers who were ordered to repatriate the unarmed masses were disgusted by their duties (one thinks of the psychological damage done to many Germans in carrying out their more murderous 'duties' on the Eastern Front in 1941). A young Russian woman, Ariana Delanich, is reported by Tolstoy to have witnessed many horrors at the camp of Viktring, just south of Klagenfurt, on 30 May, including British troops laughing as they shot a cripple trying to escape on crutches. Christopher Booker, a journalist who has spent several decades researching and disputing Tolstoy's account, claims that 'there is not the slightest indication that any such incidents occurred' – on the basis that other Yugoslav eyewitnesses who appeared at the libel trial forty-four years later never mentioned them. But what does this prove?

Most British witnesses who had the miserable task assigned to them do not seem to have had much fun. Captain Anthony Crosland (many years later a Labour Foreign Secretary) recorded in his diary at the time that there was almost civil war in the British army. He confirmed the horror in a letter written to a friend, saying that repatriation was 'the most nause-ating and cold-blooded act of war I have ever taken part in'. Captain Nigel Nicolson, who was a witness in favour of Tolstoy at the libel trial, recorded in his log on 18 May 1945, the day before his brigade was set to deport 2,000 Croats to Yugoslavia, that 'the whole business is most unsavoury, and British troops have the utmost distaste in carrying out their orders.' Brigadier Musson of the 36th Infantry Brigade – whose situation report offers one of the key records of the horrors involved – told his men before they set about deporting Cossacks to the Red Army, 'You have a very big task and a very unpleasant one', and that if they had to resort to force, 'do so promptly and without fear.' The weather had changed. The skies had turned a stormy grey and as men were loaded on to the lorries it was raining.

Most sources agree – as do both parties to the libel trial – that the deportation of 25,000 Cossacks was the most 'unpleasant' task of all. Some had to be carried in lorries over a hundred miles from camps in the west of Carinthia to the point of handover at Peggetz. The Cossacks, though never formally told what their destination was, became desperate. From the lorries, they hung out black flags and signs reading 'We will die or starve rather than return to the USSR.' They chanted hymns and wailed.

Recent debate centres not on whether British forces killed some of these Cossacks, including women and children, but on the number they killed and the number who committed suicide. Some of the Cossacks begged to be shot. As the lorryloads crossed the bridge at handover point, men, women and children are reported to have thrown themselves into the raging torrent of the River Drau far below. The problem here is that there are two bridges at Peggetz, one of them high, and one of them low. Tolstoy claims it was the high bridge they were taken across; his oppo-nents say it was the low one.

There is no disagreement that the repatriated Yugoslavs faced massacre, and that the repatriated Soviets (in fact some of them had left the 'Soviet Union' before it was created in 1922) faced the Gulag. The disagreement concerns the number of Yugoslavs who were massacred, and where. It is absolutely proven that several thousands were machine-gunned to death in the infamous Kocevje Pit, a rocky cleft in the midst of a forest not far from the Austrian border; after the shooting the rocks were dynamited to cover the victims. But some of them lived to tell the tale.

There is no disagreement that all repatriated 'Russians' were sent to the

Gulag – save those accused of treason who were put in the Lubyanka gaol and eventually executed. The point of contention is how long they were in the Gulag and how many of them died. Christopher Booker has claimed that the vast majority were released after a year and that few of them died. A one-year sentence in the Gulag, under Stalin's tightened post-war rule, must be one of the great exceptions in Soviet history.

There can be little doubt that something very ugly happened in the Austrian province of Carinthia during the month that followed the collapse of Nazi Germany. It was a sad end to what was supposed to be the British campaign of the war, the Italian campaign that would take the Allies into Istria, Hungary and Austria – the campaign that was supposed to limit the influence of the Communists, not hand further victims over to them. Who exactly was responsible for this disaster? Count Tolstoy believes that the chief villain was the Minister Resident, Harold Macmillan.

As Tolstoy's accusations accumulated in the 1980s Macmillan, then in his nineties, became increasingly baffled. He could not remember any of this. He said little about the affair in public. But how could he be accused of being a major 'war criminal' and not even remember what precisely he had done? Or was he simply putting on an act? His official biographer, Alistair Horne, claims that it was no act.

Tolstoy's book of new findings on Macmillan's 'war crimes' was eventually published in 1986. Macmillan read the book with incomprehension. Six months later he was dead at the age of ninety-two. According to Horne those last six months, thanks to Tolstoy's allegations, were months of total, paralysing hell.

There are, it has to be said, certain points that lean in Tolstoy's favour. Typical of the British at the time and particularly those of Macmillan's own educational background (Eton and Balliol College, Oxford), the Minister Resident did show a certain naivety where the Soviets were concerned. In Algiers he made great friends with Bogomolov and Vyshinsky, who may be counted among the worst criminals of the Soviet administration. 'Ah!' declared Bogomolov, organizer of the Italian Communist Partisans, 'Eton, a splendid school – a fine tradition – a splendid school' – and he continued repeating this as he and Macmillan travelled one day across the Algerian capital. Macmillan found Bogomolov 'gracious – a little royal even'. With Vyshinsky, chief prosecutor during the purges, and 'Bogo' Macmillan used to enjoy fantastic luncheons in wartime Algiers: caviar, smoked salmon, Russian bacon, tunny and sturgeon washed down with vodka 'like water from carafes'. Macmillan also took a liking to Vyshinsky, with his 'red fat face and white hair, the image of every Conservative mayor or constituency chairman', and found it difficult to visualize in him the cruel prosecutor of the Russian terror.[54]

The graduates of Oxford and Cambridge, who then entered government service, had been very much in awe of the Soviet Union. In 1941 another Oxford graduate, William Emrys Williams, an educationalist and director of Penguin Books (thus a publisher, like Macmillan), had founded the Army Bureau of Current Affairs, designed to improve the minds of soldiers. It was, as previously mentioned, enormously popular. Pamphlets of the ABCA read today like crude pieces of pro-Soviet propaganda.[55]

As Orwell bravely pointed out at the time, that is the way the British Establishment, educators, publishers, journalists and soldiers thought in those days. The Communists of Eastern Europe were their friends and allies; it was inconceivable to them that they could also be mass murderers. Tolstoy perhaps goes a little far when he claims that Macmillan was working under the influence of the NKVD. But the idea is not as far-fetched as his opponents have suggested.

What is preposterous is the notion that Macmillan and Keightley, in a single meeting at Klagenfurt on Sunday, 13 May, somehow managed to concoct the whole programme of forced repatriations in Carinthia, against the will of Allied command in Caserta. Macmillan was a civilian. He was in no position to give orders to Keightley. The purpose of his visit was the growing crisis with Tito. He had flown up to the main headquarters of the Eighth Army as an intermediary from an increasingly anguished AFHQ in Caserta – to find out exactly what was going on on the ground and communicate thinking at AFHQ. Macmillan, eloquent and cool-headed – as Churchill had learned – was the ideal man for the job.

Though it is true that in campaigns the initiative of exactly where and when to attack, or retreat, is often left to local commanders, there is no way such an enormous programme of forced repatriation, lasting over four weeks, could not have been approved by high command. A conspiracy between the civilian Macmillan, even if he was 'Viceroy of the Mediterranean', and the Corps commander Keightley over such an enormous project would have been impossible without high command being involved. When Allied Military Government (AMG) was set up in an occupied area, the army was in complete control. Repatriation in the Austrian context was just not in Macmillan's charge; it was the responsibility, ultimately, of General Alexander (who Tolstoy claims was trying to prevent it).

There was the problem. And there is the lesson of the Carinthian affair. The whole problem of Germany from the nineteenth century derived from the army's complete independence of civilian, parliamentary control. Independent armies get out of hand. That is what happened in Carinthia. And we only know this because of the great historical polemic and subsequent court case that erupted in the 1970s and '80s. But it is not difficult to imagine that such horrors were committed elsewhere. The situation in the immediate post-war period in areas occupied by Allied armies invited them: for weeks, even months, their civilian governments exerted little or no control over their armies.

Independent armies are dangerous. Millions of Eastern Europeans were forcibly repatriated to their 'home countries' in the months that followed 'VE-Day'. It would be interesting to know, for example, how exactly Vlasov's army was repatriated by the Americans from south-eastern Germany. We know that the 'Russians' were placed in camps controlled by Patton's Third Army. We also know from a few comments quoted earlier that Patton's soldiers were not too kind in their treatment of Jewish survivors – many of whom were still held in their former Nazi concentration camps. Somewhere in the US National Archives there are probably piles of documents on how Patton's army treated the remnants of Vlasov's army. They had been forced 'to surrender' and we know that within weeks they were no longer in south-eastern Germany. What happened? Why have no Americans studied this problem? A repatriations scandal here would rather spoil the heroic aura that surrounds Patton's Third Army – which, in truth, had not achieved much since it had rushed off south down the empty Loire valley after the Battle of Normandy. Indeed, Patton is at the centre of the whole mythology about 'how the Americans won the war for Europe'. That is why the story of the American role in repatriations has never been told. But it certainly happened. Repatriations were going on all the way up the line. In northern Germany the British were repatriating 'Russians'. Repatriations were probably most violent in southern Austria because V Corps was faced with the prospect of war with Tito's Partisans and they were clearing the field for battle. But nowhere in that area of Europe which separated the Western Allies from the Communist bloc do we know the full story of repatriations. One thing is certain, the 'Russians' are unlikely to have been received with open arms in the Soviet Union. How many of them ended up in the Gulag and how many of them were executed is unknown, and probably never will be known.

That is the problem with the end of the Second World War: there remains a great hole in our memory, and no amount of research into extant documents will fill it. All we get are fragments and, of course, the odd over-focused scandal.

5 'Starvation Corner' and the General Election

After his two-hour encounter on 13 May with Keightley, during which Macmillan's 'war crime' conspiracy was supposedly hatched, the Minister Resident returned to Caserta to confer once more with Alexander. Alexander was getting increasingly doubtful about the support he would get in northern Italy and Austria from the Americans, despite the tough tone Truman had adopted over Yugoslavian forces in the area. Macmillan reported to London that 'if the Americans are undecided and get cold feet they will naturally try to cover themselves.' They would put the blame on Alexander or Macmillan. 'The President says he cannot make war against the Yugoslavs unless they "attack" our troops,' explained Macmillan. The problem was that southern Austria and northern Italy were swarming with Yugoslav soldiers and Partisans; they had no need to attack British troops since they had already installed themselves – 'unless we can push them out by force, there is no way of ejecting them.'[56] In the meantime, within two weeks of VE-Day, the Americans were pulling their forces out of Germany (most of them in the southern part of the country and not even in contact with the Russians) as fast as they could. Most of them left for America where they were put into intensive training for the invasion of Japan; but the invasion never happened. In Europe, West and East, the armies were still on the move, in the weeks, and months, that followed Hitler's death and the Nazis' unconditional surrender.

On Friday, 18 May, Macmillan was sitting in his office in Caserta when an unexpected telegram arrived from Churchill summoning him immediately to get on board a plane for London. He was to spend the three-day Whitsun weekend in the Prime Minister's official rural residence at Chequers. Macmillan was flown back home on a B-52 bomber.

Churchill was in a tired, yet angry mood. Jock Colville, his private secretary, was complaining that the Prime Minister was not getting through his papers in his normally efficient way; they were in fact in chaos. Instead, the Premier was spending most of his day in bed, ruminating on the 'disastrous situation in Europe' and on a gloomy future for Britain. He was even lunching alone. In his own account of this period of 'victory', Churchill admitted that after Cabinet meetings beneath the Annexe a couple of marines would have to carry him upstairs in a chair. It would seem that, as during his Atlantic crossing in September 1944 – when the same dark thoughts dominated his mood – the Prime Minister was once more ill. Churchill's only social hours, at any rate, were in the night – late into the night. To prepare Macmillan for what promised to be a gruelling encounter, Colville took him straight from the airport to Beacon Hill in Buckinghamshire, not far from Chequers, for a view of England's green and peaceful land in spring.

Macmillan discovered that the larger part of Churchill's conversation consisted of domestic politics, and particularly Macmillan's future position. That Friday, when Macmillan received the telegram at Caserta, Clement Attlee, the Labour Party leader, had returned from the United Nations meeting in San Francisco. He had told Churchill that he and his Labour colleagues would be willing to continue the Coalition Government until the defeat of Japan, on condition that the government would begin instituting Labour's plans for social security and full employment. Attlee immediately left for Blackpool, where the annual Labour Party Conference was in full swing. Churchill did not like the sound of this at all.

The electoral fever of the previous autumn was returning with the flowers of the spring. In mid-March, at the Conservative Party Conference, Churchill had spoken of Socialism as a first step to totalitarianism. This would become the mainstay of his campaign. Political parties were fine; they fostered honourable bonds and were not incompatible with the national tradition of freedom – in private, Churchill often referred to himself as an old Liberal, not a Conservative. But there was a great ideological gulf between the British Liberalism of Gladstone, Rosebery and Lloyd George and the foreign dogma of Socialism, 'which in its more violent form [was] Communism'.[57]

What so infuriated Churchill was this rise in partisan tempers, this passion for a domestic 'New Jerusalem', when the whole of Europe was facing chaos, starvation, and what Montgomery was calling the coming 'Battle of Winter' – a lack of coal.

Britain herself was confronted with bankruptcy; Truman seemed ready to back out of the agreements made only the previous autumn over 'Stage II' of Lend-Lease. Macmillan provided a sympathetic ear; he admits in his memoirs that, after four years in the Mediterranean theatre, he found Britain in 1945, with her petty politics, a foreign place – or 'flat' as he described it.

How could one afford the energy for an electoral campaign now while, as Churchill saw it, the gravest problems in the history of the world had to be resolved within a matter of weeks? At least the French had managed to stave off elections until November. Polish borders, the freedoms of Central Europe, the advance of the Red Army, tens of millions of 'Displaced Persons' on the roads, and increasingly violent Communist voices to be heard in France and Italy – all this had to be solved, and quickly. Stalin would entrench himself in his military positions. Time was on his side. All Central and Eastern Europe risked being lost. It was a European situation without historical precedent, Churchill repeated. The British, in northern Italy and Carinthia, seemed to be the only people willing to take a stand.

If Labour and the Liberals insisted on elections now – 'yielding to the tactical temptation to acquire more seats'[58] – Churchill thought he could win. But he wanted Macmillan on his side. On the evening of Whit Monday, 21 May, Attlee telegrammed Churchill that Labour was pulling out of the government. So Attlee was going back on his word. Churchill was certain that Attlee was acting under the orders of Labour's National Executive Committee, chaired by the dogmatic Professor Harold Laski. 'Winston was hurt at the unnecessarily waspish and even offensive tone of Attlee's reply. It arrived during dinner,' recorded Macmillan in his diary.[59]

So there would be an election, probably in early July – just as the next, crucial Big Three conference was supposed to take place. If the Conservatives were returned to power, would Macmillan accept the Air Ministry? or the Ministry of Labour? Certainly not the latter, replied Macmillan, he had been out of the country for too long. Then take the Air Ministry *now*, answered Churchill. Macmillan flew back to Caserta the following day, a Tuesday, and left Italy for good on Saturday, 26 May. Britain's historic Coalition Government had resigned three days earlier. It is difficult to imagine how Macmillan could have organized his 'war crimes' conspiracy in Austria in so short and so dramatic a time.

'I suggest we use the code word TERMINAL for the forthcoming Berlin conference,' Churchill cabled Truman three weeks later, with the British election campaign fully under way.[60] Truman accepted. Did Churchill really believe this was the end?

A major colloquium of British economists was held at King's College, Cambridge, during the same Whitsun weekend when Attlee pulled the rug from under the Coalition Government. The colloquium was dominated, of course, by John Maynard Keynes. The occasion was a visit by a Canadian delegation – Canada was then Britain's second major creditor within the Commonwealth (India was the first).

Without the support of the American Lend-Lease programme of 1941 – with its complex wartime formula for exchanging arms against trade – British Treasury officials had calculated that their country would have, by June 1945, a balance of payments deficit of £2.1 billion, or a little over $8 billion. Optimistically it was thought that exports would, over the next five years, begin to fill the gap. Indeed, this is what did happen, up to the year 1946, because Britain had no competitors in Europe. But her productive capacity was based on a nineteenth-century technology fuelled almost uniquely by coal. Giant steamships were still loaded and unloaded by muscular brown-capped dockers, while black smoke belched out of tall bricked chimneys that appeared to have been built when Dickens was a child. On Britain's recently asphalted Anglo-Saxon cowpaths, little green diesel lorries travelled at 20 mph, holding up road traffic throughout the nation. And nobody – including Churchill's friends – had as yet come to terms with Labour's stunning underestimate of the costs of the New Jerusalem.[61]

But concern there was about Britain's growing dependence on the United States. After Keynes's negotiations in Washington in late autumn 1944 a National Debt Enquiry was set up by the government with the purpose of planning Britain's financial future. 'Stage II' – which provided a modified form of American Lend-Lease between the defeat of Germany and that of Japan – had been exhaustively negotiated by Keynes in the autumn. 'Stage III' – a further extension of Lend-Lease after the final defeat of Japan – had been discussed, but the details had not been worked out. In the autumn of 1944 everybody had expected Germany to be defeated by December, while the war with Japan was forecast to go on until 1946 or 1947. In the autumn of 1944, Britain's crucial financial needs were thought to be covered by 'Stage II' of Lend-Lease.

But the financial prophets had to modify their plans with the New Year of 1945. Clearly the war with Germany was going to last several more months, while the Japanese were now retreating before MacArthur's 'isle-hopping' in the Pacific theatre. Thus 'Stage II' could not be expected to last nearly as long as calculated in the autumn, while 'Stage III' could be but months, if not weeks away. Britain faced a potentially desperate financial situation.

Once again it was Keynes who seemed, from Britain's point of view, to come up with the best solution. In March 1945 he produced a policy paper with the exciting title, 'Overseas Financial Arrangements in Stage III'.[62] It had a totally unexpected effect on the thinking of Winston Churchill and his colleagues. In April, just before Roosevelt's death, Churchill had a dinner in London with FDR's old financial adviser from South Carolina, Bernard Baruch. Churchill invited Keynes to join them. Keynes was his usual eloquent self. Baruch and, more importantly Churchill, were enormously impressed. In May Keynes's project for Stage III was formally presented to the Coalition Government a few days before Labour's walk-out.

A closeness developed between Churchill and Keynes. For the first time in his life Churchill became interested in the arcane subject of national finance. If only time had allowed a marriage of these two great minds –

Churchill's understanding of European geopolitics with Keynes's liberal economics – Britain, immediately after the war, might well have been a more comfortable place to live in.

There was, it was true, something inevitable about the decline of Britain's influence in the world. We have seen how the geographer, Sir Halford Mackinder – with his insight into the new technologies of land as against maritime travel – had forecast a decline of maritime as against continental power. Dr Karl Haushofer, Rudolf Hess's favourite geographer in Munich, had transformed Mackinder's ideas into the German theory of *Lebensraum*; Hitler, in his turn, had made it a base of Nazi ideology. And then along came the young American officer, Albert Wedemeyer, for a short spell of education at the Deutsche Kriegsakademie. Dr Haushofer's continental principles, borrowed from Mackinder, were carried by Wedemeyer across the Atlantic to become the American theory of 'heart-lands', the basis of Wedemeyer's 'Victory Program', and the ideological driving force behind American plans for 'D-Day' and the defeat of Germany. All of this posited a new continental style of power, equipped with railways, autoroutes and air power, that would gradually marginalize maritime powers like Britain.

A gradual marginalization. But Britain did not have to suffer the precipitate decline she actually experienced between 1945 and 1950 in the cloistered drabness of Sir Stafford Cripps's planned and rationed economy.

Keynes's paper on 'Stage III' – a revised version of which he read at the Whitsun colloquium at King's College – contained the traditional Keynesian mix of rigorous economic analysis and Edwardian morality. The analysis grew out of his 1936 magnum opus, the *General Theory of Employment, Interest, and Money*. The morality was inherited from his Nonconformist father and developed from his exposure at Cambridge to the ethical philosophy of G. E. Moore – which translated into a Keynesian mathematical economics of probabilities and choices. A more unlikely partnership with the war leader and historian, Winston Churchill, one can hardly imagine. But it happened. And it happened because both men were faced with the demise of their brilliant, elegant Edwardian civilization.

Keynes's influence on Churchill is to be found in the multiple appeals for financial talks the Prime Minister began to make to Truman in May. It is also present in the language he used during the electoral campaign of June – where he has often been condemned by Labour-voting histor-ians as being reactionary and incompetent. In the light of sixty years of history, one must conclude that he was neither. Churchill's campaign was old Liberal, and has more to say to our own times than the 'revolutionary' language of Attlee or Morrison.

What, asked Keynes, were the alternatives open to Britain if America proved hostile to an extension of Lend-Lease as he had outlined in 'Stage III'? The moralist soul of the Cambridge professor provided the answer. Britain could respond in three ways: through 'Austerity' (which, as the electoral campaign developed, he renamed 'Starvation Corner'), 'Temptation' and 'Justice'.

'Starvation Corner' would be the worst choice, in Keynes's view. It was the option favoured by economic nationalists, imperialists and the Socialists. One could hear it among many of the corporate bodies of the Bank of England and the Treasury, and also in the senior ranks of the Labour Party. It was the argument against free trade, the argument for controls. Keynes himself had defended British interests against the famous Article VII of the Lend-Lease Act, which had called for an almost immediate liberalization of world trade. But he had never taken the position that this should not be the ultimate aim of trade talks, the best route to a more prosperous world. In the early 1930s he had argued for a self-sufficient Britain; Britain would dictate her terms by choosing her trading partners one by one in 'bilateral' talks; to some of her partners she would offer the status of 'favoured nations'. But Britain would ultimately control all the trade that passed through her ports. This was the way the Nazi economy had been run by Dr Hjalmar Schacht. This was why all those who defended protectionism, 'imperial preference' and limited 'bilateral' trade talks came to be known as 'Schachtians'. This was 'Starvation Corner', as Keynes described it.

Keynes admitted that it was a brilliant way of running a war economy. It had been practised by the Nazis to the point of reducing their own people to starvation – that is how they held out for so long. The Russian Communists practised an identical trade system, choosing their partners one by one in bilateral talks. But the sacrifice the Russian people had had to make was incalculable. This was not an ideal for a world at peace to follow. Barriers would ultimately have to be pulled down; 'multilateral' trade talks, involving all the nations together, would have to be held. That was the final aim of the International Monetary Fund, founded at Bretton Woods the previous summer.

It was the speed at which reform in world trade could be achieved, not the reform itself, that Keynes questioned. Britain at the end of the war was facing bankruptcy. So was most of Europe. And the Americans were proving as tight-fisted as they had been at the end of the First World War. But 'Starvation Corner' – unilateral protectionism – was not a way of answering the Americans, as so many in Britain thought at the time. How would Britain feed herself? The 'Schachtian' practices of Nazi

Germany finally ruined her. The 'Schachtian' methods of the Soviet Union proved that she could be no long-lasting peaceful ally. If Britain, in her turn, adopted such protectionist measures she would break up what had been the Western 'liberal front' against Germany. That was Keynes's message to Britain at Whitsun: a planned economy, based on single 'bilateral' trade agreements, would lead at one point or another to withdrawal to a Stalinist island fortress, because multilateral, international dialogue would be stifled.

'We would have to retire, as Russia did between the wars, to starve and reconstruct,' Keynes wrote. 'We might, like Russia, emerge in good health half a generation later, but *nothing much less than Russian methods* would have served our turn meanwhile.' (My emphasis.) As his biographer Robert Skidelsky has demonstrated, Keynes was defending a liberal idea of Britain that would shun a policy that was the 'antithesis of free enterprise'. Here was the essential theme of Churchill's short campaign in June: Britain must remain within the liberal front.[63]

Keynes's dismissal of 'Starvation Corner' pushed him to support the two alternative policy choices that Britain could consider when faced with the accounting mentality of the US Congress and the new banker President who had grown out of it. 'Temptation' and 'Justice' soon merged in Keynes's mind as part of the same policy – the demand for an American gift or, at the very least, a low-interest loan. Unlike 'monetarist' economists of our own day, Keynes did not believe that interest rates had much influence on the growth and the wealth of an economy. What was important was the breaking down of national trade barriers. It would be in America's own national interest to make such a gift. Keynes's paper on 'Stage III' recommended that the United States make an outright gift of $5 billion in return for a liberalization of British trade controls. He also asked of his sterling creditors (Canada and India) a cancellation of wartime debts and a new funding agreement. This led directly to his third policy point, 'Justice'.

'Temptation' was to use the threat of 'Starvation Corner' as a bluff to elicit from America the $5 billion Britain needed for the freedom to adapt and manoeuvre as she gradually enacted the free-trade reforms demanded in Article VII of the initial Lend-Lease Act. America, thought Keynes, should be willing to offer Britain this in the form of a commercial loan as low as 2 per cent, with repayment postponed for ten years.

'Justice' was to be Britain's counter-argument, if America refused such easy terms. If America refused, so went the argument, Britain would be forced to begin the peace with debts – to the Commonwealth as well as to the United States – of $20 billion. This was exactly the sum the Big Three had agreed at Yalta would be Germany's total reparations bill. Such a situation would be an outrageous affront to the enormous sacrifice Britain had made for the cause of freedom over the previous six years.

Once more, Churchill took his lead from Keynes. His letters to Truman between May and July, as well as the arguments he and his Chiefs of Staff presented to the Americans at Potsdam, were founded on Keynes's theme of 'Justice'. When Labour took over after the election results were announced and then rapidly began to set up their 'New Jerusalem' in Britain, it was the same argument of 'Justice' that Keynes himself employed when he flew to Washington later that summer to negotiate a way out of British bankruptcy, Britain's 'economic Dunkirk'.

Labour pulled out of the Coalition Government at precisely the moment Keynes made his presentation to the Canadians at King's College. So did the Liberals. The government dissolved itself on 23 May. At a reception held at Downing Street for his former ministers Churchill showed the same generosity to the resigned party members which he had demonstrated throughout the war. 'The light of history will shine on all your helmets,' he said, tears running down his cheeks.[64]

At the same time, Keynes was showing the Canadian delegation around the sites of Cambridge. A concert was held at the Arts Theatre. Keynes took them on a walk down the Backs to the banks of the River Cam. 'How beautiful it is,' exclaimed one of the Canadians. 'Yes, it is beautiful, isn't it,' replied Keynes. 'And we want to keep it, you know. That's why you're here.'

For a successful academic like Keynes, the Backs of Cambridge was England, and everything England had fought for. It was his undergraduate life, it was his loyalty to his college, it was his membership of the exclusive society of the Apostles (several of whom became Soviet spies), it was his friendship with the Bloomsbury Group (most of whom were pacifists of the extreme kind), it was his position as a 'conscientious objector' during the First World War, it was his exalted entry into the Treasury, it was his struggle against 'Versailles', it was the reason for his propaganda booklet, *The Economic Consequences of the Peace*; and it was the ground upon which he established his deserved reputation as the greatest economist of the twentieth century.

But the Backs of Cambridge was not why the Canadians were there. They had sacrificed themselves at Vimy, Cambrai, Ypres, Passchendaele and Valenciennes; they were a major reason for Britain's victory in 1918. In the Second World War they had been the spine of the British army as it worked its way up the coast from Caen, to Le Havre, to Amsterdam, across the Rhine and into the Ruhr. They were Britain's creditors and they lived on the plains of Saskatchewan and Alberta, not the Backs of Cambridge.

Keynes could explain the cost of full employment in the Western world, the operation of the multiplier effect on prices, and the advantages – and disadvantages – of multilateral trade. But Keynes was always a Cambridge man, a provincial, not an internationalist. Even when travelling in Europe he was a Cambridge man. In Washington, Bretton Woods and Toronto – where he spent most of his time shut up in a hotel room – Cambridge was in his soul. He needed someone with eyes that saw beyond the horizons of the Cam. That person was the 'old Liberal', Churchill.

By early June the campaign was under way. It was a campaign unlike any that he had ever fought. Most of it was conducted on the radio – or the 'wireless' as one said at the time. The BBC temporarily stopped programmes like *The Brains Trust*, which could prove to be controversial, and concentrated on special political broadcasts. Unlike today, these attracted enormous audiences. People would stand out in the streets and listen to them on public speakers.

Churchill opened the debate with a radio speech on Monday evening, 4 June, that has never been forgotten in the ranks of Labour. As Socialists conducting the entire life and industry of the country – forecast Churchill in his growling tone – 'they would have to fall back on some form of *Gestapo*.' Clementine had pleaded that he leave the phrase out. It caused an outrage and set the whole tone of the campaign.

Where did he pick up the phrase? His mind was preoccupied with the situation in Europe and what he was now repeatedly referring to as the 'iron curtain'. The Americans seemed weak and showed no gesture of credit – quite the opposite. Their media was claiming that they exclusively had won the war, had pulled Europe out of its own violent mess; there was no thought of Justice to Britain. They had allowed the Soviets to advance to the centre of Germany. The situation was critical. A few days of negotiation could make the difference. How could Labour dare force an election now?

Britain, if not tied down with New Jerusalem talk, could perhaps make the difference. He had been battering the new president with the idea through a series of letters. Britain could make the difference provided she had the money. Europe was in more than a difficult position, he explained to the veteran New Dealer, Joseph E. Davies, whom Truman had sent over to London on special mission. 'A desperate situation confronted Europe at the hands of the Soviets if American forces were withdrawn from Europe,' said Churchill. 'If need be, England would stand alone, if she had to.' He had said the same thing in the Commons a fortnight earlier: 'We have had to hold out from time to time all alone, or to be the mainspring of coalitions, against a continental tyrant or dictator . . . In all these world wars our island *kept the lead of Europe or else held out alone.*' (The italics are Churchill's own.)[65]

Churchill went on in his first broadcast of the campaign to emphasize how much he regretted that elections were being held now. He wanted to keep the Coalition together until the war with Japan was over. 'We should go on to the end and finish the job.' But the Socialist Party had been eager to set out on the 'political warpath', promising the kingdom of Heaven while Europe faced Pandemonium. In this context, he particularly regretted the departure of the Liberal Party for 'there is scarcely a Liberal sentiment which animated the great Liberal leaders of the past which we do not inherit and defend'. On the other hand, 'between us and the orthodox Socialists there is a great doctrinal gulf, which yawns and gapes'; its 'principles are the absolute denial of traditional Liberalism'. 'My friends, I must tell you that a Socialist policy is abhorrent to the British ideas of freedom,' he went on. 'Socialism is, in its essence, an attack not only upon British enterprise but upon the right of an ordinary man or woman to breathe freely without having harsh, clumsy, tyrannical hands clapped across the mouth and nostrils.' Then came his 'Gestapo' warning: 'I declare it to you, from the bottom of my heart, that no Socialist system can be established without a political police.'[66]

This was not very far from Keynes's vision of Starvation Corner, which he had personally presented to Churchill only a few weeks earlier: 'nothing much less than Russian methods' would have to be used. With the Soviet presence in Central Europe and finances foremost in his mind, it is not impossible to imagine that the 'Gestapo' phrase was inspired by Keynes.

Attlee the next day did nothing to close the gulf. 'The Conservative Party believe that the basis of our economic activities must be what they call private enterprise, inspired by the motive of private profit,' he announced. 'They would reduce direction, by and for the nation, to the minimum. They seem to hold that, if every individual seeks his own interest, somehow or other the interests of all would be served.' 'Our industries', he concluded, 'are ripe for state service.'[67] Britain in June 1945 was entering the most ideologically fought election campaign of her history, just as the British, the Americans and the Soviets were preparing to sit down in Berlin to discuss peace.

Keynes might well have had indirect responsibility for another major theme that was spreading fast through British government circles as they prepared for the talks in Berlin, the idea of a Western European Community. It made a definite mark on Churchill.

There had been considerable scepticism within various sections of the Treasury over Keynes's views of Temptation and Justice. So sure was he of American generosity and his own powers of persuasion that, in spring, he was telling colleagues that the Americans were bound to make the gift of $5 billion he was requesting in his Stage III project. But first he had to contend with Sir Wilfred Eady, Joint Second Secretary at the Treasury. He was a pure Schachtian, pessimistic about Britain's ability to build up her exports and expecting no kindness from the Americans; if the Americans tried to negotiate anything less than what Britain demanded it was his opinion that Britain should hold out in Starvation Corner. Eady was supported by the British financial experts in Washington, the so-called 'American Whitehall'. Americans had nothing but contempt for British efforts during the war. The newspapers never carried a story of a British campaign. Montgomery was hated. The moment the Japanese war was ended, Congress would cut off Lend-Lease, and that would be it. 'American Whitehall' proved to be correct.

The leading figure in Washington was Robert Brand, whose friendship with Keynes went back to the Paris Peace Conference in 1919. He advised that Britain cut down food imports from America and instead begin bi-lateral trade talks with non-dollar countries. Richard 'Otto' Clarke, in the Overseas Financial Division in London, went further. He foresaw, correctly, British export deficits persisting into the 1950s, largely due to Britain's inefficient, unambitious business managers. Clarke did not think Justice would work with the Americans and he thought that Temptation – an American loan – would land Britain in even greater debt and dependence. The only solution would be to expand the sterling area into non-dollar countries. Eady joined him in this. They began to speak at the Treasury of a 'non-dollar bloc' – in other words, a Western European Community and its empires.

Keynes rejected the idea out of hand. All it would mean was a club of war-torn nations, each one of them in debt to America. But events were overtaking Keynes.

The idea of a European Community went back decades, even centuries. The French Prime Minister, Aristide Briand, had tried in the 1920s to string it up to Weimar Germany but that turned out to be a very weak knot. Nazi Germany had itself propagated the idea in its western puppet states; most Frenchmen were not Nazis, but the Nazi link tainted the thought in the popular mind for generations. The Communists always opposed it because it competed with their own idea of the Great Community. It was precisely this fact that got the British Foreign Office interested – in particular Eden and Macmillan.

A series of Foreign Office papers were written on the subject just after D-Day; it became a matter of diligent study after the Bretton Woods and Dumbarton Oaks conferences in America. Jan Smuts, the South African premier and a veteran internationalist, had made a famous speech in November 1943 advocating a Western European bloc under British leadership that would counter both Soviet and American encroachments on Europe. The idea was discussed at length in *The Times* and *The Economist*. The embryonic 'World Organization' actively encouraged the formation of 'regional associations'; this would be incorporated into Chapter VIII of the United Nations Charter signed in San Francisco in May 1945.

Since 1944, the Foreign Office's idea was to make an Anglo–French alliance the kernel of the 'Western Group'. Churchill at the time distanced himself from the scheme, largely because of his differences with de Gaulle – he had turned down de Gaulle's offer for just such a treaty when he went over to France for the Armistice Day celebrations in 1944. De Gaulle immediately set out on his long excursion to Moscow. This was enough to make Churchill change his mind: he offered de Gaulle a trilateral treaty with Paris and Moscow – it presented a marvellous opportunity to de Gaulle, in his turn, to snub Churchill: the Moscow Pact remained bilateral, and empty of meaning. The Foreign Office kept on pressing the Prime Minister for a treaty with France and the formation of a 'Western Group'. On 6 July 1945, the day after the British elections, an embassy official had dinner with de Gaulle's Minister of Justice, Pierre-Henri Teitgen. Forget the pinprick policy of General de Gaulle, said Teitgen, 'with the world as it is, in which there exists an Eastern and an American bloc, England cannot stand by herself and must unite with France and the other Western Powers, but of course on a basis of friendship with the other two blocs.'[68]

France, of course, would have liked nothing better than to have discussed the matter over the table at Berlin with the Big Three; it was Stalin who vetoed the idea. At any rate, France became caught up in a major judicial affair. Embarrassingly for de Gaulle, in April his old patron Marshal Pétain crossed the frontier into France from Switzerland, where de Gaulle would have preferred him to stay, and demanded his own trial. It opened in July and lasted throughout the month. The French could talk of nothing else. Pétain was eventually sentenced to death. De Gaulle, in an unusual act of clemency, commuted the sentence to life imprisonment.

But, with the great financial debate intensifying in the Treasury, the

British Foreign Office could not let go of its own idea of a 'Western Group'. On 12 July it produced a long brief on the subject, in the expectation that it might come up at Berlin. 'Public opinion in the United Kingdom and France appears generally in favour of a Franco–British Treaty, and also of a wider association,' noted the brief, 'although opinion in neither country would accept the leadership being vested exclusively in the other.' No progress towards such an association could be made without the Franco–British treaty set up at its core. Its principal purpose would be to guard against 'the renewal of German aggression' and it would draw on the lessons of the last war 'where the Continental countries were destroyed "one by one"'. At the same time the paper noted that 'we must on no account antagonize Russia by giving the appearance of building up the Western European bloc against her.' The first purpose of the 'Western Group' would be common security against renewed German aggression. But the paper also noted that the Group 'has its advocates on purely economic grounds. There would undoubtedly be very great advantages in close economic association between the countries of Western Europe.' The French, it said, were 'hankering after a treaty'. Other potential members were Belgium, Holland, Luxembourg, Denmark, Norway and Iceland. Even Portugal was showing an interest. Most active, since the autumn of 1944, was the Belgian Foreign Minister, Paul-Henri Spaak – who would be a figure to watch over the next few years.

Communist organizations throughout these countries had shown the greatest hostility, but Stalin himself, in preliminary discussions, had been encouraging. As for the Prime Minister's current attitude, he was said to have 'expressed misgivings about the burdens which a Western association would impose on the United Kingdom, but has said that the matter should be discussed in Cabinet at the proper time'.[69] Clearly, despite Keynes's reservations, the non-dollar 'Western Group' could prove an alternative to Starvation Corner if the Americans – as they appeared at the moment – proved to be as tight-fisted as they had been at the close of the First World War.

Along with his controversial broadcasts, Churchill did some traditional campaigning in an open car, crowds lining the roadsides as he passed and huge assemblies applauding him in city squares at night. Attlee travelled around the country in a saloon car driven by his wife to the odd civic meeting where a few dozen auditors would listen to his schoolmasterly lessons on the 'Labour programme'. Churchill even travelled into enemy territory: Central Wandsworth was where Ernest Bevin held his seat, Herbert Morrison was the candidate for East Lewisham. Churchill did get booed in East London, and at Tooting Bec a firework was thrown at him, narrowly missing his face. But as he said to the crowds of Central Wandsworth, 'We are going to win – I feel it in my bones.'[70]

The weather was glorious on election day, 5 July, and thousands turned out. 'In all my experience I have never known so heavy a poll,' said one government candidate in Sussex. All the parties were whipped up to full strength, most especially Labour. But few imagined that the Lion of Britain could be defeated.

There then followed a three-week wait for all the service votes overseas to be counted. Churchill set off for a fortnight's holiday and painting at Hendaye in the Basque Country in preparation for the meeting of the Big Three in Berlin.

Churchill had advised Truman at the outset of the electoral campaign that, at Berlin, it will 'be necessary to bring with me Mr Attlee, the leader of the Socialist Party in Great Britain'.[71] During a party political broadcast Professor Laski, the chairman of Labour's National Executive Committee – which Churchill dubbed the 'Politburo' – said Attlee could only act as an 'observer'. It suggested, as Churchill pointed out, that Attlee had no authority at all.

6 The smile of Truman

One would have to go back to the year 1814 when Englishmen, for the first time since the brief Peace of Amiens in 1802, crossed the Channel to 'foreign' Europe, to find anything like a parallel to the exoticism of the voyage made by tens of thousands of Europeans to America in 1945 and the years that followed. It was exhilarating, it was fearful; it was discovery, it was disenchantment; above all, it was alien. The cross-Channel trip of 1814 exposed Englishmen to unimaginable poverty, to grand rural vistas and colours they had never seen in their own provincial towns and capital. The transatlantic voyage opened a curtain for Europeans on night lights, music, bustling commerce and above all a richness that was nowhere to be seen in rationed, rubble-strewn Europe. Among the voyagers was a high proportion of Europe's educated elites who had found themselves among the 'people without cities'. There were also those who were invited. A few were famous. Jean-Paul Sartre was profoundly influenced by what he saw in New York in the first months of 1945; he carried his experiences back to liberated Paris, installing in the cafés of Saint-Germain-des-Prés a culture of philosophy, cigarettes and jazz that changed the way we look at the world. Like the painter Benjamin Haydon in Paris in 1814,

Warsaw's poet Czesław Miłosz in 1946 'walked the streets of Chicago and Los Angeles as if I were an anthropologist privileged to visit the civilizations of Incas or Aztecs'. These strange people seemed to believe that their society 'had arisen from the very order of nature' and pitied the rest of humanity for having strayed from the norm; they had lost all 'sense of history' and had no 'sense of the tragic', which could only be born from history. He visited Albert Einstein in his little white house on Mercer Street, Princeton. 'You had better stick to your country,' advised Einstein, his voice quivering with emotion. Miłosz did – temporarily – return to 'his country'. 'When I embarked in New York my teeth were chattering.' Meanwhile the university faculties in America filled with the flow of Europeans. The polymath literary critic, George Steiner, also at Princeton, was wondering a decade later what would happen to American universities – so isolated from the rest of American life – as the flow of European talent dried up.[72]

In Europe in 1945 one gave thanks for survival. In America one celebrated victory. Halifax, the British ambassador, spoke of a wave of optimism sweeping the country. 'Wherever the average American looks,' he reported on 8 July, 'he perceives favourable omens: President Truman's popularity is immense . . . The new Cabinet equally appears to satisfy everyone: the [United Nations] Charter is universally approved . . . Distrust of the Soviet Union has been muffled. Other problems seem on the way to solution. *Time* magazine wonders what the Big Three will find to discuss.' The government might have expressed some concern about feeding Europe in the coming winter, but this did not 'disturb the prevailing buoyantly optimistic mood'.[73]

Morgenthau had resigned from the Treasury, which would almost certainly lead to the 'retirement or diminution in influence of Dr Harry White'. There was 'dancing in the corridors' of the State Department, where the Treasury's incursions into foreign policy had been deeply resented. The State Department had a new Secretary, James Byrnes, and that meant the demise of Alger Hiss.

The Americans showed complete indifference to the future of Poland. The Randolph Hearst and Robert McCormick newspapers – chief among them the *Morning Journal* in New York and the *New York American* – continued their anti-Russian campaign. But this was countered by the liberal Chicago publisher, Marshall Field, who told one British official that 'he was horrified to discover that his normally Anglophile east coast friends were bitterly complaining that Britain intended to manoeuvre the United States of America into war with the Soviet Union.'

★

Truman was part of this bright new optimism in America. He made a sharp contrast to the 'Knickerbocker', aristocratic Roosevelt.

Roosevelt's mother had been so certain that her son would become President that she kept detailed notes on his childhood development, so that they could be lovingly perused by future historians. Truman's mother did no such thing. Virtually nothing is known about his rural childhood in Lamar, Missouri, apart from the odd anecdote, such as the beating he received after driving the cart of his father, an animal dealer, into a pond. He lived on the poor side of town when his family moved to Independence. Apart from work, one of the major pastimes of the Truman family was singing hymns around the piano: Truman, unlike Roosevelt, was a talented musician. As President, he would entertain the troops with ragtime. But he would entertain Stalin with Paderewski's Minuet in G – when the Polish pianist had given a concert in Kansas City in the 1920s, the young Truman had gone backstage and learnt from the master how to perform the difficult thematic turn at the beginning of the piece.[74]

Truman's family did not have the money to send him to college or university. He made his name as an honest banker in Kansas City – and it was this that brought him into contact with the far from honest political machine of Thomas Pendergast, one of the last of the great 'city bosses' of nineteenth-century America. It was Pendergast who got him into the US Senate, and it was his knowledge of the Pendergast machine that may well have brought about his nomination as chairman of a committee to investigate corruption in the growing Roosevelt bureaucracy of the 1930s and '40s. Truman developed a healthy dislike for bureaucrats and could never be regarded as a manipulator, as Roosevelt had been. He is said never to have stolen so much as a stamp from the White House. He was a man of the people, and an honest man to boot.

But in foreign affairs, during his first months in office, he was naive. He trusted the Russians. He did not trust Churchill, whom he took as another kind of Roosevelt, an aristocrat, a manipulator; like the people, he thought Britain was trying to manoeuvre the US into war with the Russians. He thus saw his role at the coming conference as a 'mediator', one who would 'prevent collisions between Great Britain and the Soviet Union', a man who would 'promote toleration and avoid major crises'. The key to the peace, he thought, was Unity.[75]

'Terminal' was designed to be the last of the wartime conferences between the Big Three. Following the centuries-old custom of European peace-making, this was to be followed by a Peace Conference, which would draw up the treaties between the former belligerents, set the boundaries, and then establish the principles upon which the peace was to be founded.

The Americans had upset the order of things in 1919 when they insisted on establishing the principles first, in the form of Wilson's League of Nations (from which the Americans promptly withdrew). This time, the principles had already been set – at least in theory – by the signing of the Charter of the 'United Nations'. With a Congressman like Truman in the White House it was expected that the US Senate would ratify the Charter in early August, thus avoiding the absurd situation that had developed under the isolated President Woodrow Wilson in 1919.

But there was much 'principle' still to be discussed – the Soviet interpretation of the Yalta 'Declaration on Liberated Europe' seemed completely at odds with the Anglo-American interpretation – and the treaties still had to be signed. Churchill had complete confidence in a forthcoming Peace Conference. Stalin paid lip-service to the idea; it helped him delay decisions, and, as Churchill repeatedly pointed out to the Americans, time was on Stalin's side. The Americans did not want a Peace Conference.

Stettinius, in his last act as Secretary of State, had represented the United States at the UN Conference in San Francisco. While there he and his aides wrote a memorandum urging the Americans 'to avoid the convocation of a full-fledged peace conference'. It would be 'slow and unwieldy'. The memo recommended liquidating the European Advisory Commission – whose representatives, in London, of the Big Three plus France had dealt almost solely with German problems – and creating a regular 'Council of Foreign Ministers', composed of the Big Three, plus France and China, that would meet in, say, Brussels or Vienna. They could deal with treaties and other problems on an 'ad hoc basis'. It had already been agreed that the Reparations Committee would sit in Moscow. And a Control Commission, made up of the Allied commanders of Germany's occupied zones, would somehow manage to govern Germany as a single economic unit.[76]

This became US State Department policy. There would be no Peace Conference such as had humiliated Woodrow Wilson in 1919. Europe's great problems would be solved by a scattering of special organizations, all dominated by the Big Three. One can see why Americans saw the 'Unity of the Big Three' as their central objective. Britain agreed to the creation of the 'Council of Foreign Ministers', but insisted that it meet in London and hold its first conference before 1 September 1945. But Britain also wanted a fully-fledged Peace Conference. The Russians committed themselves to the Council of Foreign Ministers and, throughout the meeting of the Big Three in Berlin, seemed to agree in principle to a Peace Conference.

The second major initiative of Truman's new government was the US recognition of the Polish Government in Warsaw – a somewhat expanded version of the Lublin Committee set up by the Soviets one year before. Truman announced the recognition on 5 July, that is the day of the British elections. There had been no consultations with the British. But Britain, in such great financial debt to America, followed along like a trained poodle and just after midnight announced its own recognition of the Warsaw Poles. Within twelve hours the London Poles were thrown out of their embassy and government buildings in the British capital. Three days later a delegation of Warsaw Poles arrived in London to lay claim to their 'assets'. It was one of the most shameful acts of British diplomacy in the post-war era – committed at the same time as the forced repatriations in Austria. When Churchill, the day after the election, left for his painting holiday in the French Basque Country he was in dismal mood.

Shortly before departure he wrote to Halifax in Washington, 'I have the impression that the Americans take a rosier view of European prospects than we do. They seem to think that, given the settlement of a few outstanding problems, and the enunciation of general political principles and desiderata, Europe can safely be left to look after itself.' But the supply of food was dangerously low. The normal surplus areas of South and South-Eastern Europe were barely self-sufficient. How could one expect a 'Control Commission' in Berlin, made up of four different commands, to administer the ruins of Germany? As for the Warsaw government, 'the most influential figures . . . are Communists and fellow-travellers'.[77]

Churchill's hand had been forced on the Polish recognition. The Americans seemed unaware that this prejudiced a whole series of issues that were supposed to be discussed by the Big Three in Berlin. The formal decision on Poland's western frontier had not yet been made; yet recognition made the Oder–Neisse line, imposed by the Red Army that winter, almost a foregone conclusion. A large portion of pre-war Germany had been 'lopped off' unilaterally by the Soviets and handed to the Communist Poles. Did that mean that the commanders of each occupied zone could 'lop off' bits of Germany in favour of their own friends? Linked to this was the pressing issue of reparations. Russia was to have 50 per cent of the $20 billion to be paid by Germany – but that was calculated on a Germany that had existed in 1937. How was Berlin to be heated in the coming winter without the mines of Silesia? Marshal Zhukov told the other Allied commanders that this was not his problem, since Silesia was now a part of Poland. So Russia's half slice of German reparations was to be taken out of an already truncated Germany? American withdrawal from all lands east of the Elbe completely engulfed Poland with Russian armies and the NKVD. Recognition had left the British and the Americans with just one Polish issue to discuss at Berlin: the involvement of democratic parties in the promised 'free and unfettered elections'. American withdrawal from Czechoslovakia had the same implications in Central Europe.

In May, Churchill had demanded early discussions with the Americans on these points. Truman answered that he was tied up with 'domestic affairs' and could not get away until the end of America's fiscal year, 30 June. It was a rather lame excuse to a Prime Minister who was facing General Elections on 5 July; and it became positively insulting when American recognition of the Warsaw Poles was announced on that very day.

American military authorities added scorn to insult when the Joint Chiefs of Staff, under Admiral Leahy (former ambassador to Vichy and Roosevelt's closest foreign policy adviser), decided not to meet the Combined Chiefs of Staff – chief organ of the Anglo-American alliance – 'prior to the meeting of the Heads of State' in Berlin. The favourite phrase in American governing circles was that they would be perceived by Stalin as 'ganging up' against the Russians. The Combined Chiefs of Staff had not met since the 'Bulge' the previous winter. The Anglo-American military alliance in effect no longer existed.[78]

Montgomery, commander of the British zone in Germany, sent a warning to Eden on the desperate situation that was developing in his part of Germany two months after the Nazi surrender. He had 20 million German citizens to feed in the forthcoming 'Battle of Winter'. In addition there were uncounted Displaced Persons and at least two million German veterans of war. Every town was in a state of ruin. Country roads were regularly cut off by road blocks. There were no signs of resistance to the British, but many identity papers were proving false. There was a law banning 'fraternization' between British troops and Germans. Montgomery thought this should be lifted at once: 'we cannot re-educate twenty million people if we are never to speak to them.' In the Russian zone there was apparently plenty of mixing, thus encouraging the spread of Communist propaganda. The Allies, Montgomery said, would soon have to decide whether they wanted 'two Germanies' or 'one': free circulation existed between the three Western zones, but the Allies could not enter the Russian zone. 'There is in fact', reported Montgomery, 'a complete "wall" between the Russian Zone and the Zones of the western Allies.'[79]

'We have very little precise evidence', confirmed a SHAEF intelligence report at the same time, 'from which to assess Russian policy towards the part of Germany which they occupy.' There were some signs of a few 'preliminary purges' being conducted and it was known that large numbers of young Germans were being deported to Russia as cheap labour. 'Practically no young and robust males are to be seen in Berlin,' added the report, 'and labour is requisitioned by tens of thousands to perform any task the Russians desire.' The inhabitants of Magdeburg were 'extremely depressed at seeing the American troops depart'.[80]

But nothing would hurry Truman. His 'domestic duties' came first. He had before him, it must be admitted, the precedent of Wilson, who had spent too much time abroad. Truman wanted to take care of his Congress. And that he did very well. Smiling Truman had an approval rating in the national polls of over 80 per cent – the highest ever recorded.

Why Truman chose Joseph E. Davies, one of Roosevelt's old cronies, as a substitute for the meeting Churchill demanded with Truman before 'Terminal' remains a mystery. Davies had been US ambassador to Moscow during the Vyshinsky–Stalin purges of 1936–8. He succeeded the controversial William C. Bullitt, a former enthusiast for the Russian Revolution whose two-year experience as first US ambassador had transformed him into a staunch anti-Communist – not the sort of conversion Roosevelt appreciated. George Kennan, the fluent Russian-speaking aide at the embassy, describes in his memoirs 'the degree of dismay, bewilderment and discouragement' the embassy staff felt on the appointment of the politically correct Davies; the majority of them, including Kennan, thought of resigning in a body, but changed their minds. Kennan acted as interpreter for Davies at the Purge trials that were then going on. Davies's official reports lent considerable credence to the 'fantastic charges' Vyshinsky levelled at his victims, all of whom were subsequently executed. After returning to America Davies wrote *Mission to Moscow*, turned almost simultaneously into a film, that 'seemed in many ways to palliate the Soviet system', as Churchill put it in his own memoirs.[81]

A less generous prime minister might have taken the Davies mission to London as a snub from the new president. But Davies was invited down to Chequers for a whole weekend; on Monday, 28 May, he had a private interview with Eden; and on Tuesday got another interview at 10 Downing Street with Churchill again.

On their first encounter Davies repeated all the old Roosevelt lines about the need for 'unity' in peace and the appearance of not 'ganging up' against Stalin. Churchill, 'vehement and even violent', riposted that a 'steel curtain' – according to Davies's notes – was being clamped down on the eastern half of 'liberated Europe'. Communist propagandists and leaders, Churchill went on, were being sent in 'like locusts' and were imposing their powers with 'Secret Police and Gestapo methods'. If the Americans continued to withdraw their forces from Europe, Communism would become a threat even in the western half of the Continent.

All this was very troubling to an East Coast liberal like Davies, and he told Churchill so: 'I told him frankly that I had been shocked beyond words to find so violent and bitter an attitude, and to find what appeared to me so violent a change in his attitude toward the Soviets. It staggered me with the fear that there could be no peace.' Now was not the time to revive the classic Bolshevik fear that they were surrounded by hostile nations. The poor old Soviets would remember 'the Prime Minister's historic hostility towards them in '18 and '19'. The Soviet Union would naturally take steps to protect themselves, said Davies. Davies ended his little speech by comparing Churchill's ideas to the 'doctrine of Hitler and Goebbels'.

Churchill obviously realized what he was up against. It was by now 4.30 in the morning. He took Davies to his bedroom door and said good-night 'with cordiality and fine hospitality'. Churchill, on parting, said only how much he had enjoyed talking with a person 'so familiar with European problems during these years'. Davies, apparently not a master of irony, took this as a compliment and recorded that Churchill was one of the greatest statesmen of the world.[82]

Through the rest of May and June Churchill exchanged cables with Truman on the need for an early meeting of the Big Three, reiterating that time was on Stalin's side. Truman continued to urge his 'domestic duties'. Churchill insisted that even General Elections in Britain would make no difference. At some point a muddle developed over whether the 'victory meeting' would take place on '15 June' or '15 July'; '15 July, after June, much too late,' telegrammed Churchill, 'I propose 15 June, before July.' Stalin intervened, delighted to confirm '15 July'. Churchill reluctantly accepted, expressing his 'profound misgivings' over American military withdrawals, 'thus bringing Soviet power into the heart of Western Europe and the descent of an iron curtain between us and everything to the eastward'.[83]

There was the question of venue. Churchill did not want to be in Soviet-controlled territory once again. Truman, half-heartedly, suggested some point in Alaska. Churchill thought some 'unshattered town' in western Germany would be better. Stalin once again intervened: Berlin. 'I shall be very glad', cabled Churchill, with habitual irony, to the Soviet Marshal, 'to meet you and President Truman in what is left of Berlin.'[84]

7 'Terminal' at Potsdam

The 'victory meeting', as a humorous Churchill had dubbed the Potsdam Conference, would not be met by the kind of crowds that had cheered the 'victorious sovereigns' in London and Vienna in 1814 nor by the huge celebrations that greeted the return of King Louis XVIII to Paris after Napoleon's disastrous little venture in 1815. There would be no popular promenades such as had welcomed Wilson, Lloyd George and King George V to Paris at the opening of the Peace Conference in 1918–19. Truman, Churchill and Stalin encountered each other in the south-western suburbs of Babelsberg (how suitable a name!) and Potsdam on the very edge of Berlin's ruins – amid the stench of death.

The Americans and British arrived on Sunday, 15 July, with Berlin's first stifling heatwave of the year. Truman and most of his party were housed in a yellow stucco villa; a 'nightmare' of a house, thought the President, with a couple of tombstone chimneys that made 'the place look like hell but purely German'. There were, unlike in Washington or Independence, no screens on the windows, so that the rooms were constantly filled with mosquitoes and blueflies. The lavatories were 'wholly inadequate'.

All the Americans knew was that the Babelsberg villas had housed Goebbels's movie industry. What they did not know at the time was that their residence, No. 2 Kaiserstrasse, had been the home of a famous publisher, Gustav Müller-Grote, who had received many scientists, writers and artists before and during the war. The whole family moved in there with the outbreak of the Battle of Berlin because they thought it safe, which it was not. The daughters were raped in front of their elderly parents, the furniture was smashed, and late in May the Russians ordered them all out at an hour's notice. The building was refurnished with booty – old Teutonic chairs and oriental carpets totally out of keeping with the building – the Russians had picked up elsewhere.[85]

Churchill's party had a group of villas, somewhat more comfortable, on the edge of a lake. The CIGS, Alan Brooke, was delighted at the prospect of a little fishing, though he does not seem to have had much luck.[86]

During the three weeks of the conference, which was supposed – at least in Churchill's view – to decide the fate of the world, the weather became heavier, the storm clouds moved in and at the end of the first week a minor tornado swept across the ruins of Berlin, tearing off the metal roof of a Russian hangar and killing one of its occupants. Despite his holiday, Churchill showed signs of exhaustion. Eden was suffering from a duodenal ulcer.

And for the first twenty-four hours there was no sign of Stalin. Green-capped Russian soldiers were to be seen in every street and along the lake-front. But not a word was said about their missing Great Leader. The opening of the conference had to be postponed. Churchill called up Truman and said he would be delighted to meet him. Truman, an early riser, set an appointment for 9 a.m., Monday morning. Churchill turned up at the 'Little White House' at eleven. His daughter, Mary, dressed in the uniform of the Auxiliary Territorials, chauffeured him to the President's villa; she wrote to her mother that she had never, in the last ten years, seen 'Papa' get up so early in the morning.

Churchill was impressed by the new President; his straight talk and decisive manner attracted him most. 'I want peace and I'm willing to fight for it,' said Truman. Churchill was convinced. 'He takes no notice of deli-cate ground,' he told his doctor, Lord Moran, that night on going to bed, 'he just plants his foot down firmly upon it'; to illustrate this Churchill, in his pyjamas, jumped into the air and crashed back to earth on his bare feet.

Truman's first impression of Churchill was exactly the opposite. The banker from Missouri was not swayed by flattery and Churchill, he felt, had tried to 'soft soap' him. 'He gave me a lot of hooey about how great my country is and how he loved Roosevelt and he intended to love me, etc., etc.,' Truman wrote to his wife Bess that night. 'Well, I gave him as cordial a reception as I could – being naturally (I hope) a polite and agree-able person.' The main ingredient of soap, he remembered from his rural days in Lamar, was a substance called lye.

Churchill's long interventions about the 'mighty Republic' and the 'Grand Alliance' during the conference generally bored Truman, but he always listened because Churchill would occasionally let loose 'a pearl'. Gradually he began to appreciate the 'old man', which he never would Eden or Attlee – 'Oxford graduates', as he called them, whose English he could not understand. So remained the relationship between the British and the Americans until near the end of the conference when it dawned on Truman that Churchill had several valid points to make. Churchill himself thought the Americans had organized the conference far too late to make any deal with the Russians, and that when they began to realize that a deal was needed it was again too late.[87]

Adding tension to Anglo-American relations at Potsdam was the lament-able state of British finances. Truman had started placing restrictions on

A Russian soldier attempts to seize a bicycle from a German woman in the streets of Berlin, August 1945

The worst way out. Every soldier of the Axis powers sought to avoid capture by the Russians. Here German prisoners of war are marched down one of the main arteries of Moscow to the railway stations where they will be transported to camps in the East

German prisoners of war are kicked and spat at by French citizens in Normandy

The best way out – German prisoners of war are marched westwards along an autobahn north of Frankfurt. Their only onlookers are Allied tanks headed in the opposite direction

German prisoners of war marching to internment through a suburban English street

Above: Field Marshal Montgomery accepts the German surrender in his forward Headquarters at Lüneburg Heath, 4 May 1945. Montgomery had been preparing this scenario since the beginning of the war

Left: A German soldier returns to his home in Frankfurt, in 1946

Above right: German civilians search a bombed broom factory for fuel, Mönchengladbach, April 1945

Right: The potato handout: a rite that seemed all too infrequent to Berliners in the summer of 1945

Left: Teenagers
consult a noticeboard
in search of missing
persons, somewhere
in Normandy, July
1944

Right: Refugees
aboard a train
westward-bound
for a still undefined
'Germany', 1945
or 1946

Below: British Nissen
huts for the homeless
dominate the
landscape of a Berlin
district, 1946

In autumn 1945 in a vast rubbish dump, where scavenging children are visible to the horizon, a skinny German boy discovers a mouldy loaf: he seems to accept it as bread from heaven, the sign of a new life

Lend-Lease on 11 May, three days after VE-Day; it affected the Russians as much as the British and seemed to disregard all the negotiations that had been conducted between Keynes and Morgenthau the previous autumn – with its 'Stage II' and 'Stage III'. Morgenthau had been fired from his post as Treasury Secretary on 3 July. Then, in the middle of the conference, came the announcement that the Japanese were probably going to be defeated within a few weeks, and not in a year's time. Britain was faced with the prospect of entering 'Stage III' without the Americans even having fulfilled their promises for 'Stage II'. It was left to the British Chiefs of Staff to negotiate a temporary financial solution – yet another sign that the Anglo-American alliance had collapsed.

That Monday was broiling hot. With still no sign of Stalin, several members of the British and American delegations decided, after lunch, to visit the 'sites' of Berlin. Anne O'Hare McCormack of the *New York Times* imagined the missing Stalin was also secretly wandering around the ruins of the German capital he had insisted on destroying. She conjured up the picture of 'three men walking in a graveyard; they are the men who hold in their hands most of the power of the world.'[88]

Stalin was in fact still in Moscow, perhaps negotiating an attempted Japanese offer for peace, but more likely sick. He would be indisposed again during the conference. But the scene was ghoulish even without Stalin stalking about the wastelands. Half-crumbled houses, with gutters hanging senseless in mid-air, bedrooms and bathrooms exposed to the sun, torn, dusty relics of furniture lying in the piles of rubble; it seemed that not a window had not been blown out in the apartment houses that remained. The Soviets had bulldozed a clearing through the main streets, leaving monstrous hills of broken stone and dust on either side. Lines of ragged civilians hauled wood in prams and wheelbarrows; they seemed totally indifferent to the passing convoy of American cars, including the open Lincoln that carried the President – Berliners did not even recognize him. The cars stopped at what remained of the Chancellery. Truman stood up in his Lincoln. 'It is a terrible thing,' he said briefly, 'but they brought it on themselves.'[89]

Among the purposes of Allied occupation one finds, listed in an American briefing book drawn up a month earlier: 'to convince the German people that they have suffered a total military defeat and that they cannot escape responsibility for what they have brought upon themselves.'[90] Contrary to legend, the same principle of national responsibility – that all Germans bore a liability for the war and chaos they had brought upon the world – governed Western Allied policy in the months and years after the Second World War as had been contained in the Treaty of Versailles at the end of the First.

Churchill arrived at the Chancellery about an hour after Truman. Quite a crowd had gathered outside; Berliners knew who Churchill was. He got out of his car and walked among them; they began to cheer 'except for one old man who shook his head disapprovingly'. He entered the building and walked through its 'shattered galleries and halls'. A guide took him down the 'Kannenberg-alley' into the Führerbunker, or what Churchill called 'Hitler's air-raid shelter'. 'A sordid and unromantic spot,' wrote Alan Brooke when he was there three days later. The Russians in charge explained that Hitler himself had escaped to Spain or Argentina – a story confirmed by Stalin at the conference, even though he knew perfectly well that Hitler's charred remains, along with those of his new wife, now lay buried in the suburb of Ratenow. Brooke reports visiting the 'Gestapo HQ' opposite the Chancellery (he surely means Goebbels's Ministry). In one part, there lay masses of Iron Crosses with ribbons on the floor. 'On the way up', continues the British CIGS in his diary, 'I was handed a German decoration in its box by a Russian private soldier!!' The whole afternoon, touring ruined Berlin, 'seemed like a dream'. It should have been a celebration of the end of the war. Instead, Brooke later added to his diary, 'I remember only too well those feelings of unaccountable flatness that hung over me'.[91] There were Allied military reviews, march pasts along Hitler's Victory Alley in the remains of the Tiergarten, and there was the silence of Berliners – disturbed only occasionally by the rumble, in the bulldozed streets, of a Soviet lorry or an American jeep, or the roar of a plane overhead. Otherwise everything was silent and hot – stiflingly hot.

Eight thousand miles away, at precisely the moment Churchill and Truman were touring Berlin, a bomb exploded at Alamogordo in the desert of New Mexico. It was supposed to go off in the middle of the night, but bad weather postponed the experiment to 5.30 a.m., and the first light of dawn. The bomb had been placed on the top of a hundred-foot pylon. Nobody had any idea of what its power would be, not even the most specialized scientists who had been working on the atomic bomb project since 1941. That is important, because many historians have said that Churchill and Truman went to Potsdam in full knowledge that they possessed the atomic bomb; they may have known they had a new bomb, but they had not the first idea what it represented. Some scientists had calculated that the device at the top of the pylon would be the equivalent of about 2,000 tons of TNT, some said 10,000 tons, a few spoke of

15,000 tons; there were even a few who predicted it would be a total failure. The effect of the blast exceeded all expectations: it was the equivalent of 20,000 tons of TNT.

At first there was a huge ball of fire, with a radius of twenty miles and the light equivalent, according to the official report, of 'several suns at midday'. The fireball, linked to the earth 'by a grey stem', lasted several seconds and was clearly visible from Albuquerque, Santa Fe and El Paso – 180 miles away. The sound was picked up more than 100 miles away and windows were shattered at 125 miles. A dark massive cloud billowed upwards reaching the sub-stratosphere at 41,000 feet, where scientists expected temperature inversion to stop it, in five minutes. But at that moment there were two additional explosions, so the clouds continued upwards and outwards creating for distant observers the appearance of a mushroom, and for the scientific observers on the ground the fire and darkness of doomsday. The iron pylon had evaporated. The crater was over a thousand feet in diameter. A huge 220-ton test cylinder, 70 feet high and half a mile from the explosion site, was so twisted and torn that it lay flat on the ground. In the control centre, the leading scientists embraced each other with a sense of glee mixed with awe at the realization that that dawn in New Mexico had seen the 'birth of a new age'.[92]

The news – in the form of a simple telegram to the Secretary of War, Stimson – arrived in Babelsberg just as Truman and Churchill got back from their trip through the remains of Berlin. Truman shared his information with Churchill at a lunch two days later, on Wednesday, 18 July.[93] But up to that moment all that was known was that the experiment had been 'successful' while 'full diagnosis' was still being made. The complete report arrived by air on Wednesday evening. By the end of the first week of the conference it had been fully analysed by both American and British military staff. It was thus only during the weekend of 21–22 July that the Western Allies knew what they had, which left little time for Churchill: he had just three more days at the conference before flying home to hear the results of the General Elections.

The first draft of what was to be known as the Potsdam Declaration was presented by the Americans to the British that weekend. It pointed out the fact of 'futile and senseless German resistance to the might of the aroused free peoples of the world', adding that 'the might that now converges on Japan is immeasurably greater.' Freedom of speech, of religion and of thought were guaranteed, but the Government of Japan was called upon to proclaim the unconditional surrender of all Japanese armed forces: 'The alternative for Japan is prompt and utter destruction.'[94]

The use of the bomb against Japan was, as Churchill called it, 'a decision that was not a decision'. The only real problem was finding a target. The main islands of Japan were now being subjected to round-the-clock Allied bombing that would prove more devastating than the atom bomb. One napalm attack on Tokyo in April had created a firestorm exceeding 1800° Fahrenheit and levelled 15.8 square miles; over 70,000 died. In May, a further 80,000 were killed in Tokyo, including those who had jumped into the boiling water of the rivers. Sea-to-shore bombardment was, in addition, being carried out by American destroyers which, in turn, suffered no more opposition from Japan's now non-existent fleet. But Japan would not surrender. So an invasion force was being organized for November, either on Kyushu or the plain of Tokyo. 'Ultra' intelligence revealed that 600,000 Japanese troops had assembled in Kyushu by mid-June, all prepared to fight to their deaths (it was later revealed that there were in fact 900,000). The Americans knew what to expect after the battles for the small islands of Iwo Jima and Okinawa: it would be a bloodbath. And nobody could expect the Tokyo operation to be finished before autumn 1946.

By the end of July it had been calculated that the United States would possess three atomic bombs. Truman made his decision on Tuesday, 24 July – Churchill's last full day at the conference. The first atomic bomb would be dropped on an undamaged Japanese city not before 1 August, and no later than 10 August.[95]

Both Churchill and Truman were aware that, by the time the Americans had dropped their third terrible bomb, the war with Japan would be over. This was Truman's principal concern. But it was not Churchill's. Churchill was worried about what he was now constantly referring to as the 'desperate situation in Europe', both economic and political. On Monday, the 23rd, Brooke with two other Chiefs of Staff and Foreign Secretary Eden, went round for a lunch with Churchill. 'I was completely shattered by the PM's outlook!' wrote Brooke in his diary. 'He had seen the reports of the American results of the new TA [Tube Alloys] secret explosive experiments which had just been carried out in the States. He had absorbed all the minor American exaggerations, and as a result was completely carried away! It was now no longer necessary for the Russians to come into the Japanese war, the new explosive alone was sufficient to settle the matter. Furthermore we now had something in our hands which would redress the balance with the Russians! The secret of this explosive, and the power to use it, would completely alter the diplomatic equilibrium which was adrift since the defeat of Germany . . . Now we could say if you insist on doing this or that, well we can just blot out Moscow, then Stalingrad, then Kiev . . . And now where are the Russians!!!'[96]

But if, in Churchill's mind, the atomic bomb settled the Russian political problem, it at the same time aggravated Europe's, and most particularly Britain's, financial situation. The Americans had already gone back on their agreements on 'Stage II'. With the defeat of Japan possibly just days away, 'Stage III' was imminent. Perhaps the Soviets would be successfully pushed back. But was Europe going to starve with the approaching 'Battle of Winter'? At the very same lunch at which Truman brought news of the atom bomb experiment, Churchill reported that 'I spoke of the melancholy position of Great Britain, who had spent more than one-half her foreign investments in the time when we were all alone for the common cause, and now emerged from the War the only nation with a great external debt of £3,000 millions.' It was an appeal to Keynes's sense of Justice. For once Truman responded, speaking of 'the immense debt owed by the United States to Great Britain for having held the fort at the beginning. If you had gone down like France, we might well be fighting the Germans on the American coast at the present time.' But Churchill never heard that message from Truman again.[97]

The five thousand or so pages of minutes, memoranda and other diplomatic papers that the British and Americans collected on the Potsdam Conference make dull reading. One has read it all before – on Teheran, Moscow and Yalta. The agendas were the same, the decisions had all been made. Potsdam added virtually nothing to what had already been agreed between the Three. And it solved nothing that had not been agreed. But there was drama. And the documents provide as clear a picture as one can get of Europe – the whole of Europe – two months after the Germans laid down their arms.

There was first the difficult question of procedure, which had scuttled more than a few efforts at peace in the past. The traditional European procedure, with a Peace Conference following a formal surrender, was still on the books. The Americans were secretly against the idea, but Truman did not hesitate to appeal to the 'Peace Conference' as the right place to discuss any question he was not prepared to talk about now; this was particularly the case with European frontier issues. Stalin had openly proclaimed his support for a Peace Conference – treaties would be drawn up between all the former belligerents, frontiers would be formally agreed upon, Europe would be reconstituted into a collection of 'sovereign nations'. It would give Stalin an aura of legitimacy, for Stalin would always refer to his new satellite states as 'sovereign nations'; and, like Truman, he could use a future 'Peace Conference' as a delaying tactic. This was certainly not Churchill's motive. He, if anything, wanted to use the 'Peace Conference' as a way of forcing the major issues through and speeding things up. In his rare moments of optimism at Potsdam he imagined he would win a working majority at home and would be named President of the Peace Conference – the crowning achievement of his career, like Clemenceau at the end of the First World War.

Potsdam was a royal village of eighteenth-century châteaux and summer residences that had, at least in outward appearance, been untouched by the cauldron of violence next door, in Berlin. The hub of the conference was the Cecilienhof, former home of the Hohenzollern Crown Prince, a nineteenth-century ivy-covered 'neo-Tudor' building that some compared to a large English country estate; its gardens extended from the lakeside up to a central court. Inside there was a dingy, oak-panelled reception hall with wrought-iron chandeliers hanging from the high ceiling; the only redeeming feature of the room were the tall windows looking out on the gardens and lake. A large round table, about twelve feet in diameter, had been placed in the centre of the room, and fifteen chairs had been placed around it – five for each of the three delegations.

Every morning the Foreign Ministers would meet at about eleven and prepare the agenda of the day. Lunches were a protracted affair. Often generals, marshals, presidents and prime ministers found themselves attending two or even three lunches in a day, lunches that could last well into the afternoon – a far cry from the simple *déjeuners à la fourchette* that the delegates in Vienna attended in 1814–15; but they, in their turn, rarely went to bed at night. Another contrast was that, as in Paris in 1919, few women were present. Peacemaking in the murderous twentieth century had become a seriously male affair. At 5 p.m. the 'plenary session' of prime ministers and presidents would get under way. Evening banquets would not start until nine or ten and could continue until the early hours of the morning. Again, these were strictly reserved for men. The whole business was upsetting for Truman, an early riser; but they pleased the customs of Churchill and Stalin, neither of whom left their beds until after midday.

By the second day of the conference an agreed procedure for the 'peace settlement' of Europe seemed to be making progress. To content the Americans, Churchill agreed to the formation of a Council of Foreign Ministers, which would meet every three months in London, beginning no later than 1 September 1945. This would avoid, as Churchill put it, the 'laborious process' of getting the entire UN to draw up European treaties. But it was Europe that Churchill was interested in; the Council would be made up of the ministers of Britain, the United States and the Soviet Union. France would later be included, but China would not be represented, as the Americans desired. The Council would make its recommendations to the United Nations and that would, in turn, lead to the 'Peace Conference'.

All occupied former enemy powers were to be governed, as agreed in earlier wartime conferences, by military 'Control Commissions', made up of the military commanders of the occupying forces. But Churchill made a case for Italy's early inclusion in the United Nations. It had been the first of the Axis nations to sign an armistice with the Allies and it was making swift progress towards a liberal democracy. This became a point of contention. Stalin asked why Romania, Bulgaria and Hungary, referred to as former 'satellites' of Germany, should not likewise be admitted into the United Nations. After all, he argued, they were 'sovereign nations' that were also making swift progress towards 'democracy'. Stalin had his own special way of defining 'democracy', as mentioned in the Yalta 'Declaration on Liberated Europe'. During the unusual morning plenary of 25 July – Churchill had to fly back to London that afternoon – Stalin described 'democracy' as being 'not Fascist'. Thus the 'former satellites', Bulgaria, Romania and Hungary, were 'democratic'. Indeed, he argued, they were more 'democratic' than Argentina, which had just been admitted into the United Nations even though it was 'Fascist'.[98]

Truman got very tired of arguments about the Balkan states and Greece, and at one point agreed with Stalin that these were but 'trifling matters'. But Churchill persisted. He persisted, in the first place, because he felt Stalin was letting him down on the so-called 'percentage agreement' of the previous October; and, secondly, because he realized the bearing Stalin's 'not Fascist' argument had on the future of Poland where he had failed to draw any lines.

The Potsdam Conference stood or fell over the issue of Poland's western frontier – created by the Red Army as it prepared for its offensive on Berlin between January and April 1945. It stood and fell, in other words, on the same issue that was the cause of the Second World War, Germany's incursion across Poland's western frontier in September 1939 – made possible by the Nazi-Soviet Pact one week earlier, in late August 1939. It fell.

The Pact was no anomaly. Two of Europe's most anti-democratic, anti-liberal regimes were dividing up the world – to be joined by Italy and Japan and a few 'satellite states'. Soviet Russia had been arming Germany since the 1920s. It was odd that Stalin should make such a fuss about former German allies. After all, he had been one of them – and one of the keenest, supplying Germany with all her needs, maintaining special relations with Berlin, and – for which he forfeited a good deal – never developing an intelligence network in Germany. Stalin's 'alliance' with the West was forced on him by Hitler. Even his atomic bomb project, begun in 1942 before Stalingrad, was designed for use against the Western 'imperialists', not Hitler. By 1945 his armies had advanced further than his wildest dreams – with the exception of one area, the Turkish Straits, which he had demanded from Hitler and which he had the gall to demand at the Potsdam Conference, along with Soviet fortifications in the area.

Why did the Allies never remind Stalin that he had been an ally of Hitler? It would, after all, have strengthened their case in Central and South-Eastern Europe. Because the Americans – Truman following in the steps of Roosevelt – wanted to make friendship with the Soviet Union, and then China, the basis of a world continental peace. They saw as their main rival maritime Britain and did everything to weaken her influence. The Americans had a vision of a totally new world that would replace the old European-dominated system.

By July 1945 the American withdrawal from Europe was accelerating while their hope grew that there would be an early Japanese surrender – thus permitting the rise of a new continental power, China. America, the Soviet Union and China would govern world peace. American interest in Europe was diminishing by the day: they were even reneging on the financial aid earlier promised to this war-torn corner of the world.

Truman was bored by talk about frontier problems in Italy, Greece and Yugoslavia. He saw no dangers there. The Middle East was a British problem and, as he pointed out to Stalin during the conference, the British had 'enough troops' in the area to maintain order. He was a little surprised when Stalin started to demand Soviet 'trusteeships' in Italy's former colonies, and put the issue off for the 'Peace Conference'. The emphasis of Truman's remarks was that the United States had no interest at all in the Middle East and North Africa. In one interesting exchange with Churchill, Truman remarked that the United States already had enough 'poor Italians' (from Africa). 'And poor Jews?' asked Churchill. Truman was saved from embarrassment by Stalin's astonishing new claim to African trusteeships.[99]

Truman was – as Churchill had been – enchanted by Stalin when the Soviet dictator finally turned up at the President's villa on Tuesday, 17 July. They talked for a while in Truman's study; Truman even tried out Roosevelt's former joke about 'Uncle Joe' – Roosevelt's and Churchill's private name for the Russian Generalissimo – which predictably did not go down very well. Then Truman invited Stalin to an informal American lunch of liver and bacon. 'I felt hopeful', Truman told his private secretary afterwards, 'that we could reach an agreement satisfactory to the world and to ourselves.' He liked Stalin's brevity, the way he stuck to the point.

On the other hand, Churchill's interventions during the plenary sessions about European borders and the freedom of the press in Eastern Europe struck Truman as unending prattle. 'I'm getting sick of the whole business,' he wrote to his wife, Bess, after the Third Plenary. 'I'm not going to stay around this terrible place all summer just to listen to speeches.' By the end of the week he simply shrugged his shoulders: 'Some things we won't and can't agree on,' he wrote again to Bess, 'but I already have what I came for.' Stalin had promised to enter the war against Japan, a pledge he had already made to Roosevelt at Yalta. Truman, even at this point in time, was still not certain what the effect of a couple of atomic bombs on Japan would be.[100]

But everything fell to pieces when it came to Poland. It took nearly a week before the two Western delegations realized what was happening. At a preliminary meeting in Berlin on 10 July designed to set up the Control Commission for Germany, Marshal Zhukov, commander of the Russian zone, stated that Silesian coal could not be taken into consideration because 'territory east of the Oder–Neisse line was not within his jurisdiction'. He explained that Silesia was now part of the sovereign state of Poland. Before the war the Silesian coal mines, a part of the German Reich, had provided 40 per cent of Berlin's coal needs.[101] Both British and American authorities considered that one of the principal purposes of the Control Commission in Berlin was to treat Germany as a single economic unit, coordinating the free flow of fuel, food and manufactured items throughout the four occupied zones. The basic frontiers of the zones had been drawn up by the London-based European Advisory Commission, which now occupied itself almost entirely in solving German problems. The EAC's recommendations on the four zonal frontiers – Russian, American, British and French – had been adopted at the Yalta Conference. Eisenhower's vast withdrawal behind the Elbe in June, pulling back in some places more than a hundred miles, was legally based on this decision. Churchill had been furious because it deprived the West of a vital negotiating asset. He was very soon proved right. Russia in July changed the shape of her zone.

Since the Teheran Conference of 1943 it had been agreed between the Big Three that Poland would be moved westwards. Her eastern frontier would correspond roughly to what Westerners agreed to call the 'Curzon Line' (a British recommendation of 1919 that had never been legally established) and to what Stalin gleefully recognized as the Ribbentrop–Molotov line of the 1939 Pact. Stalin created this as a *de facto* frontier by the movement of his troops in the winter of 1943–4. At Saturday's plenary of 21 July Stalin explained at length to Truman the 'Russian fashion of fighting during war'. The army, he said, 'required a quiet rear area since an army cannot wage war both on its front and on its lines of communication' – basically this was where the NKVD worked and established its 'clearing camps', ensuring that the Red Army's front line was a Soviet frontier line. That was how Poland's new eastern frontier was established. The same was true of Poland's western frontier, secured by Red Army manoeuvres in the late winter of 1944–5 prior to the attack on Berlin. Stalin was blithely indifferent to conference agreements and recommendations from the European Advisory Commission. What mattered, in the last months of the war, was the way he stalled, set up his frontiers, and then moved on. Quite unlike the Western army movements, directed by Eisenhower, Stalin's manoeuvres had become purely political – whatever the human toll.

During the same weekend at Potsdam – as American and British delegations were absorbing the report on the atomic bomb experiment at Alamogordo – the Soviet Union submitted a brief draft to her 'allies' outlining the frontiers of the Lithuanian SSR (annexed by the Soviet Union at the time of the Nazi-Soviet Pact) and the Polish Republic in the area of 'former East Prussia'. The British delegation shot back on Monday morning, 23 July, that the draft was 'not acceptable'. The Soviet draft, pointed out the British brief, announced that 'East Prussia no longer existed'; it denied any authority of the 'Allied Control Council in Germany' in this area; it recognized 'the incorporation of Lithuania in the USSR'. The British brief noted that, according to the European Advisory Commission, the 'Province of East Prussia was mentioned as forming part of the Soviet Zone within the 1937 frontiers of Germany'.[102] To put it bluntly, the Soviet Union was unilaterally abolishing a state that had played a major, and often dominant, part in Europe's northern plain since the seventeenth century. There was no historical precedent for this. The closest parallel was the Partition of Poland in the late eighteenth century; but Poland could hardly be considered at that time a major power. One may also call to mind Tsar Alexander's attempt to diminish Prussia at the Congress of Vienna in 1814 – but he did not destroy Prussia. Stalin did.

One can understand why many Westerners applauded this at the end of six years of war. Prussia, not Germany, was considered by large numbers as the enemy of Europe. Churchill had said as much during the years of the war. But in July 1945 he foresaw a dangerous imbalance developing between what was left of a genuinely democratic Europe in the West, and Stalin's totalitarian Communism that now stretched into the heart of the Continent. At the plenary of Sunday evening, the 22nd, President Truman said that he 'could not understand the urgency of the matter'. Surely it could be finally settled at the 'Peace Conference'. It had been a helpful discussion, but enough had been said. 'Moderator' Truman believed in delay. Churchill, who was leaving for the General Election results three days later, emphasized 'with great respect to the President's views' the urgency of the matter: 'The Poles, who had assigned themselves, or had been assigned this area, would be digging themselves in and making themselves masters.' Churchill's list of points included the rupture of the economic unity of Germany, the transfer of eight or nine million Germans out of the new western parts of Poland against the transfer of two to three million Poles from east of the 'Curzon Line'. Stalin insisted that there were no Germans left in the new western Poland; they had all 'fled' with the approach of the Red Army. Churchill replied that 'great numbers, running into millions, were still there' – though 'we, of course, had not had the opportunity of checking these figures on the spot'. Over the next three days the debate became increasingly vicious. Stalin dismissed Churchill as telling 'fairy tales'. Truman thought it could all be put off to the 'Peace Conference'.[103]

But, unfortunately for Truman, the 'Polish Question' – so boring for his predecessor, Roosevelt – had implications beyond those of wicked European geopolitics. It had a direct impact on the issue of German reparations. During the First World War, reparations from Germany had never been – in terms of pounds, shillings and pence – a major issue until the Americans introduced the problem of Allied 'war debts' in November 1918. The same was true of the Second World War. The United States abandoned its commitment to Lend-Lease in June 1945, under Truman's signature, which he later admitted to be the most serious blunder of his life.[104]

More pressing still was what to do with the millions of Displaced Persons the new Oder–Neisse line had created. There had not been such movements of peoples since the invasions of the barbarians at the end of the Roman Empire – and even then the actual numbers involved had been comparatively small. Where was all the food and fuel needed for these new millions introduced so suddenly into a reduced Germany? 'If enough food could not be found to feed this population,' said Churchill, 'we should be faced with conditions in our zone of occupation such as had existed in the German concentration camps, only on a scale a thousand times greater.' Stalin responded that they would have to import their food and fuel from Poland. So the frontiers would be open to such movement, would they? For the present it was clear they were not.[105]

The atmosphere at Potsdam had been reasonably calm during the earlier sessions, even when the Foreign Ministers' report on the authority of the

Control Council for Germany was first raised. At the Second Plenary, of Wednesday, 18 July, Churchill, with the odour of his Berlin tour still in his nostrils, asked, 'What is meant by "Germany" in this report?' If pre-war Germany was meant, then he was in general agreement; the frontiers of the zones had already been agreed upon. America, he thought, had mistakenly withdrawn to her zone. He just hoped Russia would keep to hers – which included East Prussia. 'Germany was what she had become *after* the war,' retorted Stalin. 'There was no other Germany. The term "Germany" certainly did not include Austria.' 'Germany of 1937 [which excluded Austria] should be taken as a basis,' interjected the 'moderator', Truman. 'It is impossible to get away from the results of the war,' replied Stalin. 'Final frontiers must be decided at the Peace Conference,' said Truman. Stalin replied that he wanted a decision on Poland's western frontier right now. 'No,' retorted Truman, 'the right plan would be to take 1937 Germany as a starting point.' Churchill leapt at the chance, 'I agree.' It was two against one, what Churchill had always wanted. 'That was a starting point, or hypothesis,' replied an unusually conciliatory Stalin – he accepted the 1937 frontiers of Germany as a basis of discussion.

The mood was kept cheerful by the night-time banquets. On Thursday the Americans offered a party on the back porch of the 'Little White House' overlooking the lake and Berlin's lingering northern lights of summer. A grand piano had been moved out to the porch for the occasion and two of America's finest musicians had been flown in from Paris – Sergeant Eugene List played the piano, accompanied by Stuart Canin on the violin. Stalin was enchanted. Churchill was bored stiff. The President himself performed Paderewski's Minuet in G. 'Ah yes,' commented Stalin after the performance, 'music's an excellent thing – it drives out the beast in man.' Churchill remained silent, puffing away at an eight-inch cigar. As if to make a point, Truman then requested a piece by another Pole, Chopin's Waltz in A Minor, Opus 42. List did not know the work and asked if someone could turn the pages of the score for him. Up got the President again. 'Just imagine!' List wrote to his wife. 'Well you could have knocked me over with a toothpick. Thank goodness I was able to get through the waltz in creditable, if not sensational manner.' Stalin was delighted. 'The old man loves music,' Truman wrote to Bess.[106]

Churchill had his revenge the next evening at the British banquet; he ordered an RAF band to play throughout the meal.

The Russian turn came on Saturday night, a 'wow' as one American soldier described it. Stalin had brought in the best musicians from Moscow, a pianist and two women opera singers. 'The gals were rather fat,' wrote Truman to his mother.

The next day the Soviet delegation circulated its plan to abolish Prussia.

The unilateral declarations of the Soviet Union on the frontiers of Lithuania, Poland and Germany – thus reshaping the whole eastern half of Europe's strategic northern plain – affected every other subject under discussion at Potsdam. Britain's refusal to accept the initial draft on 'former East Prussia' got a swift response the same Monday morning in the form of a reparations bill. In accordance with Yalta, Germany was to pay $20 billion in reparations. Half of the sum was due to the Soviet Union, first of all in the form of 'once and for all removals' from the national wealth of Germany within two years after the capitulation. Primo Levi, after his liberation from Auschwitz, had spent several months in the southern Polish town of Katowice. Evidently the process of 'once and for all removals' was already under way in March and intensified after VE-Day. Levi was free to walk around what was left of the town – a place of 'desolation, poverty and chaos'. There were no Poles to be seen; in their place was a multitude of Russian soldiers returning from Germany. The stations were crowded. Huge train convoys passed through, carrying German POWs, every kind of merchandise imaginable, 'livestock, furniture, machinery, armaments and food'.[107] For the British delegation on the Reparations Committee one of the main problems was making a distinction between 'war booty' and 'reparations'. It was not something that seemed to worry the Russians too much.

But in their bill of 23 July the Russians detailed under the first category 'war and chemical industries, iron and steel, non-ferrous metals . . . building industry, textiles, food industry . . . foreign investments . . . shares of the German enterprises . . . miscellaneous' – all with a price attached. The second category of payments was 'by the way of the annual deliveries in kind within nineteen years after the capitulation': 'coal brickets, chemicals, machinery, tools, cement, building materials, sugar, cattle, agricultural produce', etc. Sir Walter Monckton of the British delegation, after consulting with the Americans, drafted a memorandum on 24 July saying that it would be impossible to check Russian assessments 'even if she allowed us to make inspections in her Zone'. That would result in 'competing claims' which 'would lead to a series of squabbles'. In fact, it would lead to the Cold War.[108]

What, anyway, was this 'Russian Zone'? They could not arbitrarily claim that East Prussia no longer existed and that the western area taken over by 'sovereign' Poland did not fall in what had been collectively defined as the Russian zone. A private meeting on the 23rd of American and British Foreign Ministers and staff decided that '50 per cent of Germany's industrial wealth is in the Russian Zone' so that Russia had already managed to take, or was in the process of taking, the 50 per cent to which she laid claim. That same Monday evening British and American members of the Reparations Committee concluded that a 'bargain could be made' and that 'now was the time to make it.' By bargaining they were not simply referring to economics; now was the time to push for the 'free and unfettered elections' in the new Poland that the Russians had pledged at Yalta.

Andrei Vyshinsky, Stalin's old prosecutor, spoke for Polish affairs. Contradicting the Yalta communiqué, he had begun arguing the previous weekend that the Russians had 'agreed', not 'pledged', elections in Poland. It was all anyway now a matter of 'bilateral discussion' between 'sovereign' Poland and the Western Allies – Russia of course could not interfere with the internal affairs of this independent state; the elections were 'purely a domestic matter for the Polish Provisional Government'.

The matter came up at Saturday's plenary. All the delegations had agreed that the 1937 frontiers of Germany should be used as a starting point for discussions. They had also agreed on the zones of occupation. Were the Russians now giving a part of their own zone to the Poles? Truman said he would 'raise no objection if the Soviet Government wanted to use a Polish administration in its own zone of occupation in Germany'. After all, Britain and the United States had given a part of their zones to France. Stalin realized that this could have immense consequences on his reparations account. All the Germans had fled, he insisted. Poland's frontiers now defined independent Poland. There were no Germans left there.

Truman was willing to put this whole problem off for the 'Peace Conference'. Churchill had been given the advice to 'bargain'. With knowledge of the atomic bomb behind him, he bargained. On Sunday, he argued that what the Russians were claiming would 'rupture the economic unity of Germany'. Furthermore, the 'British Government believed that great numbers, running into millions' of Germans were still in what the Russians claimed to be western Poland. Stalin refused to admit it. But to calm Churchill he suggested that 'representatives of the Polish Provisional Government' be invited to Berlin to express their views. Truman said he could not understand the urgency of the matter – it could all be settled at the 'final Peace Conference'. Churchill said there was great urgency and it was eventually decided to invite President Bolesław Bierut, a former Lublin Pole, and the Deputy Prime Minister, Stanisław Mikołajczyk, the famous Prime Minister of the London Poles whom the British had imposed on the new Warsaw government. Mikołajczyk would be able to bear witness to all that had been going on in Poland since his arrival there in spring.

An unbreachable gulf now opened between the Western Allies on the one hand, and the Soviets on the other. Had Stalin committed a colossal error, or did he provoke it? One has a feeling it was the latter. Stalin, after all, held all the cards. The Americans were still pulling out of Europe in vast numbers. The Red Army was not going to pull back one foot. Germany, Italy and France were unstable. Britain had just held a General Election, in which members of the Opposition had expressed great sympathy for the 'Soviet model'. Stalin could even move forward.

Churchill stepped into the breach, calling into question the way the Soviet Union was administering all the occupied areas of Eastern Europe. On Tuesday, the 24th, the evening before Churchill left for London, Truman started the meeting by explaining that the United States could not recognize the 'satellite states' of Bulgaria, Romania and Hungary because they were not 'responsible and democratic'. Stalin replied that this was a slur on those states. 'If they were not Fascist, then they must be democratic,' was his strange way of reasoning. Churchill said it was impossible to know anything that was going on in any of the areas occupied by the Soviets. Everywhere British representatives went they were supervised. In Bucharest, he said, one could not even take out one's private car without being followed. Great delays were being imposed on British aircraft. As for the so-called 'Control Commissions', these were supposed to be made up of three members, 'but nearly always the meetings consisted of two members': that was to say that the Soviet member sometimes saw the United States member and sometimes the British member, but rarely saw them both together. The Russians were welcomed, on the other hand, in Italy, and were free to travel wherever they liked. Between the Western zones and the Soviet zone 'an iron curtain had been rung down.' 'Fairy tales!' retorted Stalin.[109]

Churchill got up early the next morning to meet President Bierut, before going to a special plenary at 11 a.m. Bierut was in a cheerful mood. Churchill was not. 'War', said Bierut, 'provided an opportunity for new social developments.' 'Does that mean that in the chaos caused by war, Poland is to plunge into Communism?' Bierut tried to assure Churchill that Poland would be far from Communist. Churchill turned to the planned 'free and unfettered elections'. 'Was for instance the NKVD leaving the country?' asked Churchill. Bierut replied, again reassuringly, that the Russian army was leaving and 'the NKVD had no role in Poland at present.' On parting, Bierut said, 'Poland would be one of the most democratic countries in Europe.' Churchill commented, 'I hope you are getting on well with Mr Mikołajczyk.'[110]

Meanwhile Mikołajczyk was having a very different style of conversation with Eden and his colleagues. Eden had to leave after one hour for the special plenary. The report that Mikołajczyk gave – supported by reports that were coming in from the new British embassy in Warsaw – was devastating. Bierut was claiming that there were twenty-three political parties in Poland. This, said Mikołajczyk, 'was nonsense'. His own Peasant Party was being filled with Communist stooges; he had no right to nominate his own members in the puppet parliament, the National Home Council (which did all its voting by the raising of hands); he was not permitted to publish his party's programme, and his party's newspaper had been outlawed. The plight of the other parties was worse; Bierut was 'aiming at setting up the one-party system'. A few weeks ago, if elections had been held, the Communists would have got some 20 per cent of the vote; now they were so hated they would not get more than 1 per cent in a free election. After Eden left he talked about general conditions in the country. The NKVD was 'tolerable in Central Poland and the Cracow district and in the south'. But they were particularly active in the west – Poznań and the Pomeranian areas – and at their worst in the Lublin district. Arrests, usually made at night, were nothing out of the ordinary. Most of their victims were local officials. The way the Red Army was withdrawing did not make them loved. In the Jarocin district, for example, the Germans had left about 80 per cent of the livestock and material. Now only 8 per cent remained. As for the famous new lands to the west, only about 100,000 Poles had so far been transferred there. The lands stood empty. Violence, rape, arbitrary requisitioning were going on; there were 'shooting affrays between the Soviet Army' and Poles. As for the 'Polish Army', it was now mainly made up of Russians in Polish uniforms, most of whom spoke no Polish. There could be no free elections. The 1921 Constitution was supposed to be the law of the land, but Bierut did not intend to use it. Mikołajczyk was very much opposed to Truman's desire to delay everything until the 'Peace Conference'. 'I say Poland will be independent if we have speedy elections; the elections in turn are dependent on the fixing of the frontiers and the removal of Soviet troops from Polish territory,' he declared. The Russians were taking everything and, at the same time, conducting a fearful propaganda campaign. He appealed to British aid – for example a British-sponsored newspaper in Polish. But, after the American withdrawal to the Elbe, Britain was not in a strong position to provide help.[111]

At Wednesday's morning plenary, Churchill again made the claim that there were at least 1.5 million Germans still in the western parts of Poland. He said the area should still be considered a part of Russia's zone in

Germany, under the authority of the Control Commission in Berlin. All this, he warned, would be considered in the final account of reparations, and the Russians had a duty to supply food and fuel to keep Germans alive. Churchill was particularly incensed that the Poles were now apparently selling Silesian coal to Sweden; this coal did not belong to them.[112]

That afternoon he boarded his Skymaster for London. He looked out once more on the ruins of Berlin, and upon one shattered town after another.

Churchill had a family dinner that night in the small wartime Downing Street Annexe and was in bed by 1.15 a.m., an unusually early hour for him. Most of the world had expected the grand wartime leader to win the elections of three weeks earlier. Churchill himself had spoken of gaining a working majority of 80 seats; but several anxious calls he made from Potsdam to London suggested that in his heart he felt otherwise. Nonetheless he had told both Truman and Stalin that he would be back for the Friday plenary. Lord Moran, his doctor, was so confident that he left his luggage behind.

On Thursday, 26 July, just before dawn, Churchill tells how he woke 'with a sharp stab of almost physical pain'. He felt he had been beaten. 'All the pressures of great events, on and against which I had mentally so long maintained my "flying speed", would cease and I should fall.'[113] He eventually got up at nine, spent an hour in his bathtub, and then went to the Map Room where results were being shown as they came in. It was clear by noon that the Socialists had won.

It was a crushing loss. The Conservative Party and its allies were 201 seats behind Labour and its allies – Labour alone had 393 seats against the Conservatives' 198 (358 seats in the old Parliament). Thirty-two members of the government had lost their seats. Harold Macmillan was one of the first to learn of his loss. The Liberals, divided at the end of the First World War, now disappeared as a significant political power; they lost all their major leaders, including the father of the Welfare State, Sir William Beveridge – he lost to a Conservative. Over a quiet family lunch Clementine announced to Churchill that it could be a blessing in disguise. 'At the moment it is certainly very well disguised,' replied her husband.[114]

'We intend to conquer and overcome all difficulties,' said the victorious Mr Attlee. 'Think of our comrades, too, all the world over, for we are a great international movement. Its principles are plain, based on the brotherhood of man.' 'We have won a great victory for Socialism,' said Harold Laski. Attlee in a press conference that night stated that 'we are on the eve of a great advance of the human race.'[115]

Churchill made a farewell statement: 'The decision of the British people has been recorded in the votes . . . It only remains for me to express to the British people, for whom I have acted in these perilous years, my profound gratitude for the unflinching, unswerving support which they have given me during my task.'[116]

Churchill could have returned to Potsdam and waited for Parliament to dismiss him. But the vote was overwhelming. At seven o'clock the same evening he was chauffeured to Buckingham Palace and presented his resignation to the King. Half an hour later Mr Attlee arrived in his car, driven by his wife, and was appointed Prime Minister.

On 1 August the new House of Commons assembled. Churchill appeared for the first time as Leader of the Opposition; his party sang a rousing, 'For He's a Jolly Good Fellow' – a song that had accompanied the British armies as they had struggled across Africa and up the boot of Italy. The Labour Party then stood up in response and gave an example of what Orwell might have called 'misplaced patriotism': they sang 'The Red Flag'.

'What a ghastly mistake to start elections at this period in the World's History!' wrote Brooke in his diary the day the results came in. 'May God forgive England for it!'[117]

Attlee was no match for Stalin. He had only spoken once during the previous nine plenaries at Potsdam. He arrived at Babelsberg with his new Foreign Secretary, Ernest Bevin, on Saturday night, 28 July. Truman was sincerely upset over the loss of Churchill, despite his complaints during the first week of the conference. Clearly Truman was moving towards a more Churchillian attitude to the Soviets. He wrote to his daughter that the two new leaders of the British delegation were 'sourpusses'. 'Attlee is an Oxford graduate and talks with that deep throated swallowing enunciation same as Eden does,' he went on. 'Bevin is a tough guy. He doesn't know of course that your dad has been dealing with that sort all his life, from building trades to coal mines. So he won't be new.'[118]

The list of incomplete business at the conference, presented to Attlee that Saturday, was longer than the original agenda and was proof enough that the discussions were getting nowhere. Leading civil servants, however, were told that 'Mr Attlee wishes to return to London as soon as possible and does not expect resumed discussion to last more than two or three days.' The Polish question dominated the last days and made every other problem insoluble, reparations in particular. The Control Commission in Berlin was looking increasingly impotent. On the Balkan 'satellite states', Cadogan admitted, 'we have caught nothing.'[119] Stalin, on meeting Attlee on his return, congratulated him on his success and – referring to Churchill's famous opening sally of the campaign – asked him if he had yet organized his Gestapo.[120]

As before, Attlee said very little at the plenaries. It was Bevin who took up the cudgels. He took a particularly strong position in favour of the Berlin Control Commission's authority in the 'Russian Zone', which he implied included those parts annexed to Poland. He gave, however, indications that his government would be more generous over reparations than Churchill, who considered that Russia had already had its 50 per cent.

The final four plenaries were devoted almost entirely to the drafting of a long Protocol and Communiqué which managed to put off all major issues to the future 'Peace Conference'. A very nasty incident occurred during the plenary of 1 August. Truman made an effort to get one of his pet projects approved – the opening of European waterways and canals to international traffic. 'I agree,' said Attlee. 'I have accepted a number of compromises during this conference to conform with your views,' Truman added in addressing Stalin, 'and I make a personal request now that you yield on this point.' The interpreter did not even have time to finish translating. 'Nyet!' exclaimed Stalin, and then added in English, 'No, I say no!' That night Truman wrote to his mother; the Stalinist regime, he said, was a 'police government pure and simple: a few top hands just take clubs, pistols and concentration camps and rule the people on the lower levels.'[121] Truman's attitude towards the Soviet Union was now set; it was not the same as Roosevelt's.

'The Conference is ending tonight in good atmosphere,' Attlee telegraphed Churchill just after this meeting. But 'Uncle Joe was not in a good mood at the start caused I think by an indisposition which kept him in bed for two days.'[122]

The final plenary took place late that night and was not over until the early hours of the morning. The Protocol and Communiqué were approved and the delegates then said goodbye in a hurry. Stalin had wanted the next meeting to take place in Tokyo. Parting in disagreement, Truman shook hands with Stalin and expressed the hope that the next meeting would be in Washington. 'God willing!' exclaimed the atheist dictator. Truman would never see Stalin again.[123]

Europe, Europe

♈

1 Truman's Europe

The idea of 'Truman's Europe' seems almost comic. On leaving Potsdam the President vowed to an aide that he never wanted to live in Europe and never wanted to go back. True to his word he never did.

Truman's paradise on earth was right in the centre of the United States, Missouri (which he pronounced, like the southern farmers of the state, 'Mizzoorer'). His idea for inaugurating the political season of autumn 1945 was to go to the south-state country fair in Curuthersville. In his first years in office he proved no public speaker; after being exposed to twelve years of Roosevelt's Harvard accent, Truman's Missouri twang started to grate on the East Coast press. Editorial criticism began to heap up. Budget Director Smith entered the Oval Office one day in September 1945 and found the President fingering through a pile of newspaper clippings: 'Just looking at the day's poison,' Truman commented. He cheerfully admitted that his potted speeches did not add up to much. The press would come into his office – television cameras and all – for information on some vital piece of legislation, and he would order them straight back out: 'Fellows, please get somebody else to do it. Those cameras frighten me, and I just can't do it. I can't make a speech.' For friends and enemies alike, Truman's succession to Roosevelt came to be known as the 'Missouri Compromise'.[1]

Peace fell on Truman's shoulders in the twinkling of a Midwestern eye. Hostilities with Germany were over within his first month of office; in less than three months, to the astonishment of all (including the nuclear scientists) the war with Japan was done. Two atomic bombs put an end to the Pacific fighting. Truman was at sea having lunch on Monday, 6 August, when the telegram announcing the Hiroshima bombing, four hours earlier, came through. 'Results clear-cut successful in all respects,' it read: 'Visible effects greater than in any test.' 'This is the greatest thing in history,' responded Truman, grabbing the ship captain's hand. Thrilled, he ordered the crew to assemble. 'We have just dropped a new bomb on

Japan which has more power than twenty thousand tons of TNT,' he announced, then added with a smile, 'We won the gamble!' Everybody began cheering.

The immediate death toll at Hiroshima was well over 100,000. But one can understand the jubilant sailors. Quite obviously the Second World War was finished for good. And the United States was producing more than half the world's wealth: America was an unchallenged superpower.[2]

Truman was spending the first day at his desk in the White House, on Thursday, 9 August, when news came through that a second bomb had gone off at the central port of Nagasaki. Around 70,000 were killed in an instant. Film footage taken by the bomber's crew shows that the bomb missed target; it exploded some way up a steep valley, a fair distance from the city centre – otherwise, tens of thousands more would have died. Within twenty-four hours Emperor Hirohito, against the advice of his soldiers, decided to 'bear the unbearable' and surrender. The formal signature was made on Tuesday, 14 August 1945. But there was the same diplomatic mess that followed the German surrender: VJ-Day was actually celebrated on 2 September. Americans danced the conga. There was a ticker-tape parade in New York. Barely anyone noticed in ruined Europe.

For most Americans, including the President, that – they imagined – was the end of their country's major military and financial commitments overseas. Roosevelt himself had told his allies at Yalta that American troops would stay in Europe 'no more than two years'. Lend–Lease to Russia and to Britain was cancelled. Now it was time to concentrate on domestic problems, of which there were plenty. In September, as Truman's popularity began to plummet, the wives of servicemen organized Bring Back Daddy clubs across the country. By December, thousands of letters were pouring into Washington stamped 'No Boats, No Votes'. In the year 1946 occurred one of those rare historical mid-term elections, involving issues that went beyond the usual obsession with road funds, railways and teacher employment. The 1946 elections could be justly compared with 1866, after the Civil War, and 1918, which came just one week before the Armistice of 1918: each marked a turning point in American history, and in each case the incumbent came out very badly. Truman in November 1946 lost his majority in both houses of Congress and had to face for two years an aggressive Republican Party, which had every expectation of winning the presidential elections in 1948. The Republicans developed their interest in the effects of Communism, at home and abroad.

Like his predecessor, Truman feigned to ignore this. Indeed, until 1947 Truman and his Cabinet were totally preoccupied by domestic politics.

The army and the navy disintegrated over the winter of 1945–6 – faster indeed than they had grown up in 1939–44.[3] The only conventional military force that the United States possessed in 1946 was a carrier task force made up of four aircraft carriers that the Secretary of the Navy, James V. Forrestal, secretly kept to one side just in case – as the diplomatic corps at Moscow and throughout Europe were warning – Stalin did decide to go to war. Yes, the United States possessed a nuclear monopoly; it consisted of nine bombs with no reliable delivery system. Truman's concern at the time was not at all the developing 'Cold War', as that inveterate political critic in the *Washington Post*, Walter Lippmann, called it in a book; the Truman Administration was totally preoccupied with price and wage controls, the hostility of businessmen, and the government's constant battle with the unions. Housing the millions of returned servicemen was another headache, solved – like the Washington wartime bureaucracy problem – by the building of 'tempos' throughout the country.

For all that, the history of Europe and the world did not come to an end. There was even a 'Paris Peace Conference' in this year of America's abstention, 1946. But it was not at all comparable to the great conference of 1919; it could in no way be considered a peace settlement. Nonetheless, it lasted most of the year. The US Secretary of State, James Byrnes, would occasionally put in an appearance. All the conference achieved was a series of bilateral treaties recognizing certain frontiers. Its most important 'achievement' was the recognition of Stalin's East European governments, thus granting *de facto* assent to Communist domination of over half of Europe – not exactly, for the West, a victory fanfare for the close of the war. But most remarkable was the great non-event: the lack of any treaty with Germany – centrepiece of the Paris Peace Conference in 1919, utterly ignored in that of 1946. The question of 'Germany' remained as unsettled as it had been at the close of the Potsdam Conference; the country had no legal existence at all. The situation continued until the collapse of the Soviet bloc and the signature of a treaty (of all places, at Versailles) in October 1990 between the former four occupying powers and a newly united German Federal Republic. The Conference on Security and Cooperation in Europe which met in Paris in November 1990 signalled the legal end of the Second World War.

During America's year of absence, 1946, the armies might have stopped moving, but the crowds of refugees – people without cities – did not. 'Displaced Persons' camps' were still to be found in Germany and France in 1954, almost ten years after the end of hostilities. The United States was the last country in the western world to open its gates to the DPs, in the year 1951.

In 1946 Truman still lived with the basic precepts of his predecessor's policy. He thought world peace could be maintained without great armament and expenditure by the 'Four Policemen', the United States, Russia, China and Britain. It was to work throughout the world like the two-hundred-year-old American Constitution – a tick-tocking machinelike affair, without need of interference and set in motion by a hidden clockmaker God.

Despite Stalin's insidious behaviour at Potsdam, especially over Poland and the American proposal on inland waterways, Truman was still able on his return to assure Henry Wallace, the Communist sympathizer now demoted to Secretary of Commerce, that 'Stalin was a fine man who wanted to do the right thing.' He told his private secretary, Jonathan Daniels, that 'Stalin is as near like Tom Pendergast [the Kansas City boss] as any man I know' – a greater compliment from Truman one cannot imagine. Truman, like most Americans, had no interest in Poland and he was certainly not going to make a fuss about what boats sailed down the Danube. Right through 1946 Russia remained one of the world's crucial 'policemen'.[4]

As under Roosevelt, Chiang Kai-shek's Nationalist China was to be treated as a superpower and thus another of the world's policemen. China's poor performance in 1944 – the only ally to be overrun by the enemy in the last year of the war – was assiduously ignored. So, amazingly, was the civil war that broke out between Nationalists and Communists in 1946. By late 1949 Mao Tse-tung had proclaimed the People's Republic of China and America's ally, Chiang Kai-shek, was marooned on the island of Formosa (Taiwan).

There remained Great Britain. Neither Roosevelt nor Truman ever spoke of a 'special relationship' with the British. On the contrary, of the four policemen Britain was the one which the two American presidents held in highest suspicion. Britain was 'imperialist' and 'colonialist' – and if there was one label the Americans wanted to avoid it was that. They were on the progressive side of history, they fought for human liberty – that was not merely a policy in America, it was a cult, and stood beside the slogan printed on their money, 'In God We Trust'. Americans would have nothing to do with Britain's 'imperialist' ambitions in the Middle East and the Balkans; they would prefer to be seen siding with the Soviet Union than getting mixed up in that sort of thing. Such thinking would mark – dramatically so – the policy of Truman's successor, General Eisenhower.

But Truman at Potsdam had developed a real affection for the old man, Churchill, even if he could never grasp the wonders of his language.

When Churchill was holidaying in Florida in the winter of early 1946 Truman offered him what the President considered the greatest of all honours, the chance to speak at a small college in Fulton, Missouri. Churchill leapt at the chance. The two men travelled together in Roosevelt's old train, the *Ferdinand Magellan*. On 5 March Churchill pronounced at Fulton the speech that made his expression 'iron curtain' famous. 'From Stettin in the Baltic to Trieste in the Adriatic,' he said, 'an iron curtain has descended across the Continent. Behind that line lie all the capitals of the ancient states of Central and Eastern Europe.' They were all now 'subject in one form or another, not only to Soviet influence but to a very high and, in many cases, increasing measure of control from Moscow'. Perhaps the Soviets did not want war, he went on, but they sought the fruits of war 'and the indefinite expansion of their power and doctrine'. Military weakness, he warned, was the Western democracies' greatest danger: they would have to unite against this threat.

America's East Coast press went into a furore. Churchill was accused – and Truman along with him – of being 'remarkably inept'. America did not need Allies, said the *Wall Street Journal*; all Churchill was doing was stirring up poison. The *Nation* considered it a 'call for war' while all the Americans wanted was a harmonious, non-colonial peace. Truman swiftly backed off from his association with Churchill. As he said to Henry Wallace, Churchill had 'put me on the spot'.[5] Six years later, in January 1952, Truman was at the airport in Washington to greet Churchill, recently renominated Prime Minister. Churchill pulled out some notes from his pocket and walked over to the waiting microphones. But he had barely pronounced a phrase when Truman – one can watch this on a newsreel – put his hand on a shoulder of the astonished Churchill and led him away. Not only was the world deprived of a great Churchillian speech, it also has on film an apt record of the nature of the 'special relationship'.

But for all her immense idealism, America after 1945 could no longer hide from a world she had done so much to create. The world of 1945 would last several decades, and America was inexorably drawn into it. At its centre was Europe, not because of its power but because of its position: all world wars – which one can trace back to the sixteenth century – had their origin here; all subsequent world crises had their base in Europe. No world power could afford to ignore Europe. After the defeat of Hitler, its most fundamental fact was its division, the 'iron curtain'.

What was the origin of the 'Cold War'? Not 1948, nor 1945. It lay in the Nazi-Soviet Pact of 1939. Stalin and his successors never abandoned the world vision the Pact had opened up to them: the fortified Black Sea straits, the opening into the Mediterranean, a hand in the Middle East, control of the 'world island' of Euro-Asia, even – as expressed at Potsdam – colonies in Africa. Stalin's policy through the last years of the war and into the peace was an extension of the Nazi-Soviet Pact, with the Nazis conveniently excluded. This was never a subject of genuine negotiation: it was based on the positions the Red Army had been able to take up in 1945 in Europe and, by Truman's invitation, its invasion of Manchuria in preparation for an attack on Japan – a position that put the Red Army right alongside Mao Tse-tung's Communist Partisans as they prepared for war with the Chinese nationalists.

By an irony, as Truman wound down his forces in 1946, Stalin, that February, made a speech in Moscow declaring Communism and Capitalism incompatible. Another war was inevitable, he said. He announced a new Five Year Plan to increase production in preparation for that war, which he predicted would come in the 1950s when America would slide into another depression.

One week after the speech, on 16 February, the Canadian government in Ottawa revealed the existence of a huge Soviet spy ring, operating throughout North America, that had been passing the secrets of the atomic weapons on to the Russians. Belatedly, the American FBI began investigations in earnest, drawing up secret 'loyalty files' – and it discovered that security, especially within the Treasury and the State Department, had throughout the war been very lax.

Truman, during this important mid-term election year, played down the significance of the Stalin speech and the Ottawa revelations. He said not a word on a long telegram which George Kennan, the embassy aide in Moscow, had sent to the State Department that same February. Yet this 8,000-word document would set a pattern for American foreign policy for the next four decades. Kennan warned the American government of the fanatical nature of Russian Communism; that 'peaceful coexistence' between the two powers would not be possible; that the Russians would push 'their country on to ever newer heights of military power in order to guarantee external security for their internally weak regime'; but that, at the same time, they were highly sensitive 'to the logic of force' and would usually back off when faced with strength.[6]

For the sake of the electorate, the American government could – as it had so often in the past, even during world war – stand back for six months, even twelve months, without taking any major initiative on foreign policy. Truman's hand was indeed forced; there was talk, in 1946, of impeachment if the boys were not brought home. And he lost the elections that year, to be faced with what he called the Republican 'good-for-nothing, do-nothing Eightieth Congress'.

But no American government could ignore for long the realities of power that had been established in 1945 – in large part due to American military action, and dithering. After his unwelcome speech on the 'Iron Curtain' in Fulton, in March 1946, Churchill became the leading spokesman of a European Movement. In September, before a vast crowd in Zurich he advocated the establishment of a United States of Europe. 'We must begin now.' Then, 'This may astonish you a bit,' he added – the new union would have to be based on a partnership between France and Germany. 'In this way only can France', he said, 'recover the moral and cultural leadership of Europe,' while 'There can be no revival of Europe without a spiritually great Germany. We must recreate the European family in a regional structure called, as it may be, the United States of Europe.' In war, defiance; in victory, magnanimity. The authority of Churchill lay in the authenticity of his words.[7]

Europe and the world was moving on. The Iron Curtain was a fact. Like a wounded cat, which the westward-pointing peninsula resembled, Europe inhaled all the problems of the world, then exhaled them all out again. It was a physical fact that had been repeating itself for centuries – pull in all the armies, then expel them all throughout the world: 'European civil war' followed by 'colonial' or 'imperialist war' – call it what you will. The Second World War and its aftermath did not stop the process: inhale all the armies, then spew them all out again. That second, outward movement of the armies in the post-war period has been identified with a process of 'decolonization' and European 'imperialist' reaction to it. But it is more closely related to the unnatural division of Europe into two blocs, one free, one Communist. The Americans, being an 'anti-colonial' power, and hoping to maintain their 'alliance' with the Soviet Union, would have preferred to have stayed out of the violence of 'decolonization', but they could not – because the whole analysis was wrong. They showed no interest in the initial 'European Movement' in the heart of the Continent; but they could not ignore it because, after the Second World War, they were a part of it. Indeed, within two years they were actively encouraging it. Because of the tendency to study Communism, decolonization, the development of the European Community and the origins of the Cold War as separate subjects – with little reference, what is more, to the way in which the Second World War ended – a lot of misunderstanding has developed.

In the light of 1945, it is interesting to note the process as it developed over the next decade or so. As in 1919, the United States turned her back on Europe in 1946. Save for a few humiliating loans, financial aid was cut off and military forces were drastically reduced. The Russian Communists and their European confrères kept up their aggression. Free Europeans were the first to react. The Americans had a vast surplus to sell, but nobody to buy it; they were faced with a choice of boom or bust. By 1947, after Europe had suffered one of the worst winters in its history, the writing was on the wall: the Americans had to create a market. The Marshall Plan (or European Recovery Program, ERP) was announced in June 1947 when the new Secretary of State, George Marshall, the former Chief of General Staff, made a vague speech on the subject at Harvard University. It contained no commitments at all. Indeed, the whole point was to avoid another UNRRA, where the United States had paid out money to the local foreign administrators of 'Displaced Persons'. Marshall spoke of European 'self-help'. Even then it took almost a year to push through Congress. So the first grants were not received in Europe until early summer 1948, or more than three years after the conclusion of the war. The Marshall Plan could hardly be considered an act of philanthropy.

The details of the Plan were worked out after the speech. Under the guidance of the American economist, Paul Nitze, the US State Department presented Europe with four conditions, or 'essentials', designed to create a 'workable self-sustaining European economy, independent of special outside aid'. The first was to 'reactivate the most efficient existing productive facilities' with the idea of inducing rapid expansion – these existed on the borders of France, Germany and the Benelux countries. The second was to enforce currency stability under the terms of Harry Dexter White's Bretton Woods agreement of summer 1944. The third was to create a European free-trade zone so as to foster 'multilateral intra-European trade'. The fourth was to set up an organization that would review the progress of each of the participating European countries on a continuous basis. The former President Herbert Hoover, who as an influential businessman had played a major role in the direction of the Paris Peace Conference in 1919, remarked, as the debate developed around the Plan, that 'we should *insist* upon certain principles in operations of gifts and loans.' It was the opinion of most Americans.[8]

Thus the United States, major belligerent in the war and by force of post-war circumstances, laid the foundations of a new Europe.[9] The sums involved were not large when compared with Europe's national budgets, and the programme was terminated in 1952. But Europe was not booming in 1952 – it was another five years before the 'post-war boom' took off. In strict financial terms it is not at all sure that the Marshall Plan directly contributed to Europe's later economic growth.

But that is beside the main point. A certain 'idea of Europe' was born – today's Eurosceptics would give it a capital 'I'. A permanent organization was created, the OEEC or 'Organization for European Economic Cooperation' (today's OECD or 'Organization for Economic Cooperation and Development'). It was a compromise between the two main organizers of the programme in Europe, Britain's Foreign Secretary, the West Country yokel and trade unionist, Ernest Bevin (who hated everything about 'Europe'), and the French Foreign Minister, none other than the Resistance leader and rebel within the Gaullist movement, Georges Bidault (for whom an organized European federation of some sort was the best guarantee against another devastating war). Daggers drawn, the conflict between Bevin and Bidault was the beginning of an Anglo-French squabble over Europe that remains with us to this day. But the 'idea of Europe' would never go away. Here lies the origin of the European Union.

'Truman's Europe' exerted an influence way beyond the term of Truman's presidency. Truman, despite his enchantingly modest self, provided the material drive behind the European Movement. There was a generational factor involved – which in politics is always an overlapping factor. Most of the people with whom Truman's Administration dealt were leaders during the war. By the time of Eisenhower's two terms in the presidency in the 1950s the United States was dealing no longer with the leaders, but with the fighters – the passionate side of the 'European idea'. They had made up the armies that had fought across Europe, the refugees who had walked across Europe, the crowds that had occupied the streets of liberated Paris, that stretched out their hands in starving Holland, the miserable youth of defeated Germany, the applauding audience when Winston Churchill stood before a microphone at Zurich on 19 September 1946. Michael Palliser was an example of the new, passionate generation. 'Simply taking a train journey from Berlin through the Ruhr and up to the Hook of Holland, you saw a place that was absolutely flattened,' he later recorded. 'I came out feeling this was something one simply can't allow to happen again. It hit you like a kick in the stomach.' Palliser later married the daughter of the Belgian Prime Minister, Paul-Henri Spaak, one of the 'founding fathers' of Europe, and became himself a leading 'Eurocrat'.[10] Palliser's generation was followed by one that had never experienced war, had caught a mere glimpse of the rubble, overgrown with grass and hidden behind tall glass buildings; a generation in revolt in the 1960s and living off the privileges of the boom which people like Palliser had created. 'Euroscepticism' was born, national arrogance revived, old hatreds returned. Only one thing remains certain: they will be followed by another generation that will reject their values.

Other points emerge from this developing European story, first of all in connection with 'Truman's Europe'. Stalin's speech, Churchill's warnings and Kennan's telegram – which would be turned into a longer report – all had an effect on Truman. Moreover, the Ottawa revelations were transformed; with the new Republican Congress, scandal was turned into political hysteria. Hiss was tried and justly condemned to a gaol sentence; the evidence that he was a Soviet spy is, today, irrefutable. Harry Dexter White died of a heart attack the night before he was due to give evidence to the House Committee on Un-American Activities (such a death, especially for such an energetic, centrally important man as Dr White, inevitably carries a sinister undertone). The madman, Senator Joseph McCarthy of Wisconsin, with his fictitious list of '57 Communists who are in the State Department at present' did not appear until February 1950. Truman was undoubtedly right when he told a reporter later that year, 'I think the greatest asset that the Kremlin has is Senator McCarthy.'[11] 'McCarthyism' was the greatest propaganda gift ever made to Communist apologists, who responded with their own hysteria, especially in the streets of Paris and Rome. The affair has to be seen in an international perspective. McCarthyism killed only two people, Julius and Ethel Rosenberg, who were electrocuted in 1953; Ethel Rosenberg's death was particularly gruesome. Communism killed many more. The Rosenbergs were certainly guilty, as evidence from both VENONA and KGB files proves. They were central figures in the passing of atomic secrets to the Soviet Union. Whether people should be executed in a civilized country is of course another issue.

'McCarthyism' is often accused of 'witch-hunting'. Curiously, genuine witch-hunting grew up in the aftermath of religious wars in the sixteenth and seventeenth centuries – and the 'witches' were put to a horrible death. McCarthyism had no such parallel. Yet it was a sign of popular hysteria, on the left as well as the right, in Europe as well as in America. Popular hysteria (one need only reflect on Germany, or America for that matter, just after the First World War) is a common phenomenon in the aftermath of a great war.

The growing mood of anti-Communism in America provided a popular base for an about-turn in Truman's foreign policy, openly expressed with the announcement on 12 March 1947 of what came to be known as the Truman Doctrine. With a better knowledge of the war and the ambiguous nature of the Soviet 'alliance' one is tempted to say today that it was about time. Half of Europe had already been condemned to Communist government. The Truman Doctrine, however, made the opposition to Communism not a strategic or geographical issue but one of abstract principle: as in the case of Roosevelt, the language of Woodrow Wilson can be found in Harry Truman. He turned the fight into a struggle of two ways of life: 'One way of life is based upon the will of the majority, and is distinguished by free institutions . . . The second way of life is based upon the will of a minority forcibly imposed upon the majority. It relies upon terror and oppression.'[12] True as this might have been, it was not the problem of the post-war struggle between the West and the Communist bloc. The key to the problem – and what would eventually determine the ultimate success of the liberal West – was the division of Europe into two unnatural, unhistorical halves. This had been created solely by the movement of the armies up until the moment of the formal end of hostilities in May 1945. Central to this was the fact that the 'formal end' was never made formal. There was no peace settlement. In the hostile Soviet mind, their totalitarian revolution simply went marching onwards, an extension of the Nazi-Soviet Pact with the Nazis eliminated.

The Truman Doctrine was an answer to this. But in rendering the struggle so abstract Truman handed the choice of battlefield to the Soviet Union, which then dominated the Eurasian 'world island'. America had taken on a commitment that she would be materially unable to keep; instead of committing herself to Europe she had declared that she was ready to combat Communism anywhere in the world. Anywhere in the world: it was another gift to the Russian Communists. Wherever they detected an American weakness – in the Pacific, in the Indian Ocean, in Central Africa – they could pick their fight.

It just so happened that Europe was at that moment exhaling her wartime armies into the world to combat the so-called process of 'decolonization'. Decolonization it most certainly was not. In the majority of cases, independence from Europe was exchanged for Communist dictatorship governed from either Moscow or later Peking, both of which proved calamitous for the economies of the developing world. Gaps were created. Small pockets emptied of political power appeared. Little nooks and crannies, gasping for aid, developed throughout the globe, its population multiplying at an unprecedented rate. Chaotic black holes. Thus was 'anti-colonial' America drawn into distant, meaningless battles. All was a product of the great event which had never occurred: the European peace settlement of 1945.

One of the greatest ironies, from the perspective of the war, was America's involvement in a new Greek civil war. Roosevelt had ruled out American involvement in 'the Balkans', which for the Americans stretched from Austria to Crete. He had promised no aid at all to British involvement in the area, which he regarded as the product of their 'imperialist' interests. The US Treasury, under the influence of Harry Dexter White, in the meantime made strenuous efforts to undermine the sterling area. They were only too successful. Britain, already in debt and yet committed to Labour's 'New Jerusalem' at home, suffered worse than any other European country from the harsh winter of 1946–7. Coal supplies were brought to a standstill. Offices in London worked by candlelight. Hundreds of small towns were isolated. Late in February 1947 the British ambassador to Washington delivered a formal note to the Secretary of State, George Marshall: it announced that Britain was withdrawing 40,000 troops from Greece and that all economic aid to Greece and Turkey would be cut off. Dean Acheson, a man with a strong sense of geopolitics, was at that time Marshall's Under-Secretary; he would step into Marshall's shoes the following year. Acheson warned that the British move could signal their withdrawal from the whole Middle East; he added that the 'complete disintegration of Greece' was only weeks away. Truman, just back from a trip to Mexico, characteristically made a decision on the spot. 'It means', he told his Cabinet on 7 March, 'that the United States is going into European politics.'[13]

But it would take the United States yet another two years before she went into European politics and, under European pressure, signed up to the North Atlantic Treaty Organization (NATO) to defend Western Europe from Communist aggression – the first peacetime treaty the United States had been involved in in her history. The initiative came entirely from a frightened and impoverished Europe, and most particularly from that continually sparring couple, Ernest Bevin and Georges Bidault. In another famous compromise they managed, in April 1948, to patch together the Pact of Brussels, which bound Britain, France and the three Benelux countries – Belgium, the Netherlands and Luxembourg – in defensive union. 'The time is right for consolidation,' announced Bevin.[14]

Indeed it was. The term 'Fascism' was once again in style among Europe's Communists, though there was no Fascist party to be seen in East or West, while the Nazis had completely collapsed. The source was Moscow. In September 1947 Andrei Zhdanov, at that moment Stalin's chief member of the Politburo and his closest foreign policy adviser,[*] had set up a new form of the Comintern, called the 'Cominform', to bring together all Communist Parties of the world around the core 'Popular Democracies' – the Soviet satellites. Cominform's aim was, according to Zhdanov, to form an 'anti-Fascist front': 'The imperialist and anti-democratic camp', declared Zhdanov at the opening meeting in Szklarska Poręba in Poland,

[*] 'After Kirov, Stalin liked Zhdanov best,' the Soviet Foreign Minister, V. M. Molotov, recalled.

'has as its basic aim the establishment of world domination of American imperialism and the smashing of democracy, while the anti-imperialist and democratic camp has as its basic aim the undermining of imperialism, the consolidation of democracy and the eradication of the remnants of Fascism.'[15] That autumn Communists in France broke their alliance with the Fourth Republic and instigated a series of strikes so violent that leading reporters in the press began talking about civil war. Ominously Czechoslovakia and Finland had been added to Zhdanov's September list of Popular Democracies. Finland, with every minister surveyed by a Soviet 'aide', managed to maintain a degree of independence. But in Czechoslovakia the Communists carried out a *coup d'état* the following February, 1948. Among its victims was Jan Masaryk, son of the Republic's founder, who slipped from a top-floor window to his death – no witness reported quite how he managed this feat over a high metal balcony.

For another year Bevin and Bidault urged the Americans to join their Pact, for they knew Europe could not stand up to the forces of Stalin's Red Army. Finally, in a Washington hotel on 4 April 1949, twelve nations signed their adherence to the North Atlantic Treaty Organization. 'It is a simple document,' said Truman at the ceremony, 'but if it had existed in 1914 and 1939, supported by the nations who are represented here today, I believe it would have prevented the acts of aggression which led to two world wars.' Article 5 stated that an armed attack on any member was to be regarded as an attack upon them all.[16]

It was indeed a simple treaty – and almost unique in Western history. One power maintained command of all the armed forces assembled by the twelve nations; one power was responsible for the organization of the command. The US State Department, which had arranged the treaty, argued before the Senate that, in conformity to the highest Wilsonian principles, it was not designed 'to influence any shifting "balance of power"', which Wilson had considered to be the chief cause of the First World War. Acheson himself argued that it was not even designed to counter any nation in particular, and he quoted from the Bible to prove his point. Indeed it was not even a military alliance, but 'an alliance against war itself'.[17] So it was an alliance against the principles of the 'balance of power', it denied the existence of an enemy, and it was not military, it did not stand for the status quo (which must have surprised Bevin and Bidault), and it proposed to abolish all war: there was just one parallel in Western history, Tsar Alexander I's original pencilled draft for a 'Holy Alliance' in 1815.

Like the Holy Alliance, it was the eventual reality that mattered, not the ideal. NATO brought together such a huge military force in Europe

that it prevented war on that dangerous peninsula for over two generations. The Russian Communists were obliged to seek their chances elsewhere.

2 Stalin's Europe

Shortly after his return from Potsdam Stalin suffered a major physical
collapse. It was either a heart attack or a stroke – the documentation is
of course scanty, not least because Stalin was becoming increasingly suspicious about the loyalty of doctors to the Soviet State. Through his last
eight years he spent an increasing amount of time on holiday in the Crimea
or at one or other of his two dachas outside Moscow. Blizhnaya, closest
to the capital, became his favourite. Some, like his daughter Svetlana, have
put forward his poor health as a reason for his increasing paranoia and
taste for vengeance. His voice became more hollow. He would occasionally burst out in rages – which, sucking on his pipe, he had managed to
control in earlier times. He developed an almost obsessive fear of death
(he was sixty-six in 1945). But all this made him only more determined
to maintain absolute power. Stalin was not like Hitler, he delayed his
actions, waiting for the most opportune moment for attack. He would
never spontaneously lash out at his enemies; everything was rehearsed,
contrived, prearranged; he applied cruelty with caution, never wrote
anything down and developed his plots with detached inhumanity, like a
mathematician. Anastas Mikoyan, who kept a secret diary at Blizhnaya,
told how one December evening in 1948, on returning from one of his
holidays, Stalin invited Poskrebyshev, his private secretary, along with a
few important members of the Politburo. Poskrebyshev's presence was most
unusual, but this of course was part of the plan. 'A typically pleasant
conversation took place for such an occasion,' noted Mikoyan. Then, right
in the middle of the meal, Poskrebyshev got up and said, 'Comrade Stalin,
while you have been relaxing in the south Molotov and Mikoyan in
Moscow have prepared a conspiracy against you.' Mikoyan immediately
shouted out, 'Bastard!' and threw a chair at him. Molotov turned pale.
Stalin took Mikoyan calmly by the hand and said, 'Why do you shout
here, you're my guest, he's a Central Committee member.' Stalin was not
in the least bit agitated. Gradually he turned the conversation to another
theme. Molotov was not demoted for another two years.[18]

Soldiers and citizens throughout the great Socialist paradise – with the
exception of Solzhenitsyn and several million others in the Gulag and the
overcrowded city gaols – had never been happier than that night of 9 May

1945, when victory over the Fascists and Hitlerites was finally declared. The celebrations lasted all night; the night which followed lasted eight long years, the 'Black Years' as they were known by those who remembered them. America enshrined in its history books the years of 'McCarthyism', during which two major Soviet spies suffered rather unpleasant deaths and a few university professors and film directors temporarily lost their jobs, then returned to write their books. Post-war hysteria went somewhat further with America's ally, the Soviet Union. The victims can be counted in millions.

Soviet hysteria began with the 'anti-cosmopolitan campaign' of 1946. It was a year of famine. Khrushchev, commissar of the Ukraine, speaks in his memoirs of witnessing cannibalism. Zhdanov was the chief spokesman of 'anti-cosmopolitanism' – Stalin was always careful never to identify his name with such a plot. Its origin can be traced back to the Great Patriotic War, which witnessed an increase in Soviet Communist Party membership from 2,300,000 in 1939 to 5,760,000 in 1945. Many of the new members were Jews who had seen their families and villages wiped out by the Nazis. A 'Jewish Anti-Fascist Committee' had been founded in Moscow in August 1941. The Central Committee welcomed it into the anti-Fascist struggle by having its two directors, Henryk Erlich and Viktor Alter, thrown into the Lubyanka gaol; Erlich committed suicide in May 1942, Alter was shot in February 1943. The great actor from Lithuania, Solomon Mikhoels, picked up what was left of the JAC and made an extraordinarily successful theatrical tour of the United States in 1943 on behalf of Stalin's suffering Russia; the painter Marc Chagall provided stage scenery. Stalin could not miss this opportunity for Soviet propaganda and for a few years Mikhoels was the hero of his country – until Stalin ordered an automobile 'accident' to be arranged in Minsk in January 1948. The obituary in *Pravda* was full of praise for the dead actor, but the JAC was on its way out.

Zhdanov, who himself had some literary pretensions (it was he who condemned the works of Boris Pasternak and Anna Akhmatova), began his campaign with attacks on 'Occidental decadism', 'anti-Russian particularism' and that inevitable little fleuron of Communist spite, 'petit-bourgeois individualism'. Russian Communists did not like being referred to as 'anti-Semitic', which had been the 'Fascist' scourge, a feature of the last stage of capitalism. Zhdanov and his colleagues were rather combating 'Zionism', a 'very serious danger these last years'; it 'has become an important instrument of American and British imperialism'. Like anti-Semitism for the Nazis, anti-Zionism for the Russian Communists – and through them for Communist Parties throughout the world, including the small

Israeli Communist Party — was a theoretical link to other political crimes mercilessly prosecuted in the Soviet Union. Just as the Great Purge of the 1930s came to be known after the NKVD boss as the *yezhovchina*, so did the mass murders and deportations of Stalin's last years earn the name *zhdanovchina*.[19]

The *zhdanovchina* was prosecuted under much greater secrecy than the *yezhovchina*. Inside the Soviet Union there were few show trials; these were reserved for the new Popular Democracies in Europe, as an encouragement for lagging popular support. Russian Communists were concerned to avoid the inevitable charge in the Western capitalist press of anti-Semitism. Members of the Jewish Anti-Fascist Committee did not help by refusing, even under torture, to confess to the charges brought against them. Stalin, through Zhdanov, applied his typical tactic of silence and delay. Since the war one of the major projects of the JAC had been a compilation of Nazi atrocities against the Jews in the Nazi-occupied areas of the Soviet Union. At first it seemed an excellent idea to the Soviet authorities — until it turned out that a large proportion of the malefactors had been Soviet citizens, especially Ukrainians (who had also formed the main death squads during the Warsaw Rising of 1944). Publication of the JAC's *Black Book* was at first delayed and finally, in a 1947 ruling, forbidden outright: 'It is indispensable', read one of the charges against the JAC, 'to revise with greatest care all documents and accounts, especially those concerning the Ukraine . . . so that no one can imagine that local anti-Soviet elements played a central role in the destruction of the Jews.'[20] Leading members of the JAC were arrested in January 1949; they were executed, in conditions of the utmost secrecy, only on 12 August 1952.

'Rootless cosmopolitanism and anti-patriotism' became standard charges for a term in the Gulag in the late 1940s and early 1950s, despite the paradox that the Soviet net now spread as far as the Elbe, beyond the Danube and as far as the Balkans. The presence of foreigners in the 'Gulag' — the term itself was in official use for only a year and covered whole networks of different, chaotic administrations, some run by the local mafia — went back to Stalin's liquidation of Communists and fellow-travellers who had arrived voluntarily in the Soviet Union in the 1930s. By the war — both during the alliance with Hitler and after the invasion of 1941 — mass deportations had become a common phenomenon throughout the whole state. Few of the victims were ever put on trial. The NKVD proved to be just as efficient as the Gestapo in their task: in May 1944 31,000 of them managed to evacuate 200,000 Tatars from the Crimea in three days, using 100 US jeeps, 250 lorries and 67 sealed trains. The fact that their victims were given only fifteen minutes to pack their belongings helps explain the greater speed of the operation than the deportation of 13,000 Parisian Jews to the Vel' d'Hiv' in July 1942 – which indeed seems almost a minor event in comparison.[21] The camps to which the deportees were transported were barely organized; many of the trains' contents were dumped in isolated Siberian villages or in the middle of frozen forests. Women and children were among them. 'Mommy', runs one child's account, 'took a rope, a little bread and went into the woods. I held my Mommy back in her grief but she hit me with the rope and went away. A few hours later they found Mommy on a spruce tree, Mommy had a rope around her neck . . .' The Russian commandant then cut down the spruce with an axe, the child's story continues, and 'Mommy', still miraculously alive, managed to grab the axe and kill the commandant by striking him in the back.[22]

Westerners always want to know how many died in the Gulag during these years and those that followed. Their number will almost certainly never be known. Nothing was known about these events at the time. Some of the West's most educated, most privileged researchers – victims of 'McCarthyism' – showed total indifference to the problem for the two generations that followed. The long-awaited 'opening of the Soviet archives' lasted only a short period. Many of these archives have probably been destroyed; the fact that the current Russian president is a former chief of the KGB suggests that little further light will ever be shed on the matter. 'We never, of course, lost hope that our story *would* be told: since sooner or later the truth is told about all that has happened in history,' explained Solzhenitsyn in a concluding section of his *Gulag Archipelago*. 'But in our imagining this would come in the rather distant future – after most of us were dead.'[23] Then, like Tolstoy, Solzhenitsyn follows this passage with a long analysis of the nature of history. Yet it is difficult not to conclude that one of the major chapters of the Second World War and its immediate aftermath will remain a black hole for ever.

There are, however, the official statistics, which have been known since the collapse of the Communist bloc. They were compiled by the NKVD which, to complicate matters still further, was split in early 1946 into two organizations, the MGB (or Ministry of State Security, headed by Zhdanov) and the MVD (or Ministry of Internal Affairs). Since the NKVD and its successors only controlled a part of the Gulag these figures are a gross underestimate of the numbers held in the so-called 'Gulag'; foreigners, in particular, found themselves assigned to special camps. The official figures were compiled on 1 January each year and indicate that there were 179,000 prisoners in 1930. With the Great Purges the figures passed a million in 1936; by 1941, before the Nazi invasion, they had reached almost 2 million.

During the war they rapidly declined, only to pick up again in 1943. By 1950 they had surpassed 2.5 million. The official figures thus show that between the last year of the war and 1950 the Gulag population had more than doubled. This suggests – but can only suggest – that Stalin's post-war purges were the worst on record.[24]

These figures do not include, either, the extension of the Soviet system across half of Europe. As the Red Army advanced into Central Europe, so did the NKVD, setting up first its 'Verification and Filtration Camps'. But that was only the beginning. By 1946 a process of consolidation, or 'Sovietization', was begun in the new Popular Democracies. Here, in contrast to the Soviet Union itself, there was no fear of using show trials as a means of convincing the people that their brave new world was both popular and democratic. The main targets of these show trials were members of foreign Communist Parties (which thus confirms Soviet domestic policy during the post-war years); they were accused of not being genuine Communists but, instead, bourgeois cosmopolitans working secretly for American imperialist agents. These open, media-covered scandals coincided exactly with the rise of 'McCarthyism' in the United States, though their outcome was a good deal more horrifying. Lázló Rajk, a militant Hungarian Communist of the Bela Kun school, had spent most of the war years in Nazi concentration camps. In 1946 he became Minister of Foreign Affairs in the Communist government of Mátyás Rákosi; but Rajk proved far too popular for the likes of Stalin. Linked on the most dubious grounds with the arrest of an American fellow-traveller, Noel Field, who had set up home in Prague, Rajk, along with several colleagues on the Hungarian party's Central Committee, was put on public trial. It proved a great success: Rajk and his colleagues confessed to being traitors and spies, and within days of their trial were hanged. The connection with Prague led to one of the biggest Communist show trials of the post-war era. Around sixty Czech names were drawn up out of the Communist Party that had seized power in Prague in 1948. Through torture, Communist authorities in 1951 were able to reveal to the Czech people a vast 'Zionist' plot, led by no less a person than the Secretary General of the Czechoslovak Communist Party. Again Stalin's silence and delaying tactics lay behind this: Moscow had been preparing the show trial for several years. On 20 November 1952 the 'trial of the leading members of a conspiracy against the State, with Rudolf Slánský at its head' began in Prague. On 27 November Slánský and ten of his 'collaborators' were condemned to death, three others were given life sentences. The eleven condemned men were hanged in Prague's Pankrac gaol in the early hours of 3 December. It was at exactly the same period that Ana Pauker, one of the most notorious

Romanian Communists of the war era, was deprived of her function as Foreign Minister in Bucharest. As during the Great Purge in Russia in the 1930s these show trials were merely the tip of an iceberg of murder, torture and inhumane isolation which lay submerged in the dark waters of Eastern European popular democracy. The Cold War may have been at its height in the early 1950s, but little was said of the deep currents of terror flowing through Eastern Europe at the time. Indeed, many Western Europeans joined in the Soviet-organized demonstrations – throughout Europe and North America – of the 'Partisans for Peace', culminating in the Stockholm Peace Appeal of 1950, to coincide with the Korean War, which had been fostered by the Communists. Some of the West's greatest artists and intellectuals got caught up in the movement. Pablo Picasso devoted much of his art at this time to the Communist cause; it was then that he designed his dove of peace – for a Party that was murdering its own members and plunging half of Europe into tyranny. Bertrand Russell, the philosopher, organized conferences and seminars in the name of 'anti-Fascism', though not a Fascist existed any more. Sartre began his slide into the unreason of the *raison dialectique*. The intellectuals of the West had committed themselves to politics of the worst kind. Unlike Animal Farm, Stalin's post-war Europe stretched into every part of the Continent.[25]

Petru Dumitriu's grand novel, *Incognito*, after following its anti-hero Sebastien Ionesco through war, through the camps, through political re-education courses given by Ana Pauker, through torture, through isolation cells, through the inevitable, humiliating acceptance of Communist Party membership, ends with a great parade in Bucharest celebrating the achievements of scientific Socialism. There are salvos of cannon, ten thousand doves of peace are released into the air, a 'swarm of little girls and little boys in white shirts with red ties streams towards the stage of Politburo members to offer flowers to the great bureaucrats'. Beside them are foreign visitors, among them a certain Mr Martin. His 'name is perfectly Western; he could be English, French, German, Spanish   "more Catalan," says Mr Martin.' His patron saint is rational philanthropy, which he shares with a strong sympathy for the 'working class'. Sebastien and two of his friends approach him and tell him their story. 'Look, admit it!' exclaims Mr Martin in English. 'Come on, come on, my young friends, you are the future of the world, even if you ought to be punished for your scepticism!' Like many of his countrymen, Mr Martin 'thinks he knows more than others about the East, even when addressing three sons of the East'. Mr Martin is overjoyed by the colourful spectacle in Bucharest. 'How fantastic,' he cries out. 'Ah! these Romanians! How enchanting! What an enchanting country!'[26]

There were not enough camps in this artificial entity of 'Eastern Europe' to hold all the prisoners that the post-war era produced, despite all the construction the Nazis had contributed during their twelve years of rule. Stalin, one must never forget, rarely expressed himself and never wrote anything down; it made such a contrast to Hitler's night-time meanderings over tea and Bavarian cake – monologues all recorded, reliably so in the case of Goebbels. No one knew the thoughts of the '*Vozhd*', or 'Boss', as he was known in the dangerous inner circle of the Central Committee; nobody knew and nobody dared ask at the risk of their own lives; life at the top was conducted by means of innuendo, delay and interminable silence. But the Foreign Minister Molotov did catch Stalin saying shortly after Potsdam that 'we must expand the limits of our Motherland as far as possible.' At the same time Stalin's adviser on Germany, Daniel Melnikov, distinctly picked up the phrase, puffed out from the *Vozhd*'s pipe, 'We need all of Germany, not part of Germany, all of Germany.'[27] The capitalist powers of Western Europe and America would not hold together; their collective will was weak. Wait. That was the byword of Stalin's policy. Wait, he told the French chief of the PCF, Maurice Thorez, when he arrived in Moscow – in the midst of the most violent post-war strikes in Western Europe – for Stalin's advice in November 1947. Wait, all Europe will one day be Communist.[28]

But such a vast empire required financing, and the only kind of growth Communism knew was instituted by Five Year Plans and executed by slave labour. The first post-war Five Year Plan was announced by Stalin in his warmongering speech of February 1946; the Americans had turned their back on Europe; the British Labour government was still under the illusion of a 'Soviet alliance'.

The Gulag and its Eastern European imitators were expanding at an exponential rate in 1946. Czechoslovakia was lagging because it still had bourgeois elements in its government. Hungary, Romania and Bulgaria had camps and prison systems dotted throughout their countryside. Poland's camps were so overcrowded that the inmates – including masses of foreigners – had to be deported to Siberia, or the Western DP camps. But the worst case of all was what was left of the Soviet zone of Germany.

The Soviet Union had a double policy in this area. The first was to strip as much of the wealth as they could before Allied armies arrived in the small section they claimed in the western parts of Berlin. This city lay one hundred miles east of the line to which Eisenhower had withdrawn because, in the illegal note he had written directly to Stalin in March 1945, Berlin was 'of no strategic significance': he spent almost half of his two-term presidency defending the rights of West Berliners; it was worse for his successor John Kennedy. Once the Russians had destroyed a good part of the city in the unnecessary battle of April 1945 they spent two months stripping it of currency and industrial goods; the great treasures were burned, looted or melted down; factories were pulled to pieces; rail wagons were shipped to the east; raped women (there were few men) were forced into the dismantling crews. German Communists – those who had survived the purges – were shipped in from their refuges in Moscow to become 'Obleute' or supervisors, copied from the Nazi block system. At the head was Obleute Walter Ulbricht, who would become first president of the 'German Democratic Republic' in 1949.[*] Political parties were revived just before the arrival of the Allied armies in West Berlin, but only those authorized by the Soviet Union, essentially the SPD (Social Democrats) and the KPD (the Communists). In October 1945 these two parties were united into the SED (Socialist Unity Party); the symbol of the one-party government of the German Democratic Republic was the shaking of two hands, which should have been manacled. The Communist philosophy was that the German working class – many of whom, like Ulbricht, had never touched a screwdriver – was not responsible for the Fascist Nazis, who simply represented the last stage of capitalism.

Those who disagreed, or who proved not 'socially useful', were shipped out to the concentration camps, or *Spetzläger* as they were renamed in the Communist tongue. The main shiploads were deported in 1946 – America's absentee year – to Sachsenhausen, Buchenwald, Hohenshonhausen, Jamlitz, Forst, Roitsch-Bitterfeld, Mühlberg, Bautzen, Altenhain, Stern-Buchholz, Ketschendorf and Neubrandenburg (yes, the former Nazi camps). But the Nazi camps were not sufficient and about a dozen new ones had to be set up. Witnesses record the skeleton-like appearance of the inmates. Of the 13,000 prisoners initially taken to Neubrandenburg, only 6,000 were still living after six months. Bautzen was an execution camp; the Communist method was arms tied behind the back and a bullet in the back of the head. About a million people were killed by the Communists in the People's Democracies in the first five post-war years – French specialists reckon the figure was higher, but there is no science about the matter. Mass graves were uncovered at Ravensbrück after the fall of the Berlin Wall; they are, today, the site of a new supermarket.[29]

---

[*] Stalin never gave the GDR full diplomatic recognition, since he was hoping it would be united with the rest of Germany – 'neutral' but Communist. It was only after the Geneva Conference in 1955 – a repeat performance of the Locarno Conference thirty years earlier, where the West found itself offering peace to an interlocutor who had no intention of maintaining it – that Nikita Khrushchev, returning to Moscow, gave full recognition to Ulbricht's GDR.

Ghost-town Berlin had been filled with refugees. It was largely the Soviets who removed them. West Berlin was marred by Soviet kidnapping and murder; frequently Communist thugs were murdered in their turn. The year 1946 witnessed scenes of street warfare. Many of the refugees fled, that year, to the DP camps of the Western German zones. Poverty-stricken Jewish refugees, for example, only began arriving in the West in the early months of 1946.

This whole story of how the Soviets established themselves in their sector of Berlin is a small-scale example of what was going on elsewhere in Eastern Europe. But the Soviets made one fatal error here. In most of Eastern Europe they could keep their activities secret. In Berlin they acted under the eyes of the West. For those who wanted to see Communism in action – and unfortunately, even here, many Westerners remained deliberately blind to the facts (maintaining the wartime mythology of an 'alliance') – they could see. For a few with eyes it was becoming obvious that Eastern Europe was being systematically destroyed. Berlin provided a peep-hole into the future, for Europe has to live with the legacy of that post-war destruction to this day.

An unusual proportion of Politburo members died from heart attacks, even when compared to the vodka-drinking Russian population in general. It was for this reason that the hearts, and other organs, of deceased Politburo members were preserved in jars in a secret gallery of the Kremlin.[30]

On the evening that Moscow celebrated the victory over Hitler – being a Soviet celebration it was, naturally, not on the same day as the rest – the forty-four-year-old First Secretary of the Moscow *oblast* (or region) and candidate for the Politburo, A. S. Shcherbakov, spent a cheerful few hours watching the fireworks in Red Square. The next day he was in a Kremlin hospital bed, dead. The diagnosis of the doctors at the time was that he had died of a heart attack. One of the staff consulted, but by no means central to the case, was Dr Yakov Etinger. Etinger was a Jew. Shcherbakov was infamous for his anti-Semitic opinions. Yet Etinger had been quite friendly with Shcherbakov; they frequently, for example, drank together. Shcherbakov had been ill for some time. The person responsible for undertaking Shcherbakov's electrocardiograms was Dr Sophia Karpai; she also happened to be a Jew. Being a man of some importance, Shcherbakov had his heart preserved in the Kremlin's secret gallery. When it was re-examined again seven years later the doctors came to the conclusion that Shcherbakov 'had died of an infarct' – the same conclusion as the doctors in 1945. But by that time Dr Etinger had been tortured to death in the infamous Lefortovo gaol. And Dr Karpai had been arrested by the special T- (Terror) Department of the MGB. Tens of thousands of other Soviet Jews were also languishing in Soviet gaols and camps, if they had not already been shot. As the most recent historians of the 'Doctors' Plot', Jonathan Brent and Vladimir Naumov, have put it, Soviet society at large was, by late autumn 1952, experiencing a kind of anti-Semitic 'hallucination'[31] at exactly the same time as 'McCarthyism' reached its height in the USA. But there was this difference: McCarthy was conducting his campaign in the heart of the American Congress, as a Western parliamentarian, inarticulate and mentally disturbed as he was. The 'Doctors' Plot' had been developed slowly and deliberately by a man who was far from insane, the great Dictator, Stalin himself.

No disappearance in the inner circle of the Kremlin could be considered innocent. Since the Second World War major war leaders had become marginal. One would have expected Molotov, for example, Foreign Minister and the Politburo member in charge of foreign affairs, to have become a major figure; perhaps even heir to Stalin. But he turned out to be nothing of the kind; he kept his titles, he did not keep his prestige. Beria and Mikoyan and Malenkov were known to Western observers during the war; but in a couple of years they were no longer in control of government. This left some gaping holes.

Leningrad had been cut off from Moscow during a large part of the war. From the very start of the Bolshevik *coup d'état* there had been rivalry between the two Soviet cities. But with the departure of Stalin's Moscow cronies, the Leningrad party had their chance, with people the outside world did not know. This was particularly the case of the tough Leningrad hero, A. A. Zhdanov. He and Stalin had the same sense of humour. They both considered themselves men of high culture. And neither showed the slightest qualm when ordering a thousand men to their deaths. Yet Zhdanov showed just a little too much confidence. Hard-worked Zhdanov had a heart problem. On 9 July 1948 he passed out on a street on his return from his office. 'Take a little rest at Valdai,' suggested Stalin. It was a special health care centre for the bonzes just outside the city. Zhdanov knew exactly what this meant: at least his demotion, at most his 'unexpected death'. It would be the latter, on the night of 31 August 1948. A rushed autopsy was carried out, under the eye of two MGB officers, in his own bathtub, before the heart was carried to the secret gallery of the Kremlin. Was Zhdanov murdered?

His son Yuri, a doctor, had had the gall to criticize the theories of Dr T. D. Lysenko, a crackpot Marxist-Leninist geneticist who claimed to have uncovered the fraud of Mendel's capitalist genetics. On the day his father was sent by Stalin to Valdai, Yuri published a profusely apologetic letter in *Pravda*: 'I consider it my duty to assure You, comrade Stalin, and in Your person the Central Committee of the Party that I was and remain an ardent Michurinist [a supporter of Lysenko's Marxist-Leninist biological theory]. My errors flowed from the fact that I insufficiently analysed the history of the issue, incorrectly established the front of the struggle for Michurinist doctrine. All of this is the outcome of inexperience and immaturity.'[32] It was a most unusual kind of confession for *Pravda* to publish. Later research has proved that the letter was edited in Stalin's own hand. In Communist Russia one was guilty by association with the man accused. Zhdanov's career had come to a sudden end. The doctors, who all read *Pravda*, realized this. One never took direct orders high in the Communist hierarchy – action was taken in silent assumption of what was required. Nothing was done to prolong the life of Andrei Zhdanov.

One of the consulting doctors, though he never left Moscow, was Dr Etinger, the Jew involved in Shcherbakov's case of May 1945. Oddly enough the first person to perform an electrocardiogram on Zhdanov was Dr Sophia Karpai, the cardiographologist in Shcherbakov's case. According to one story published only in 1988 Stalin was enjoying one of his prolonged winter holidays at Sochi on the Black Sea in the winter of 1949 when he was visited by Yefim Smirnov, the Minister of Public Health. They took a stroll around Stalin's private orchard of lemon and orange trees, with Stalin flaunting his Georgian proficiency in fruit and flowers. Then suddenly he stopped in mid-track and asked who had treated Zhdanov and the Bulgarian Georgi Dimitrov, former head of the Comintern, who had succumbed a few months later. 'Isn't it strange?' commented Stalin. 'One doctor treated them and they both died.' In fact, all of the doctors who had treated Zhdanov had also treated Dimitrov.[33]

Smirnov must have taken the cue. That was the way orders came from the top: an informal question, a hint, a fleeting parallel drawn by the *Vozhd*. If the important state servant to whom it was addressed did not pick it up then he would disappear in a few months, or perhaps years, for Stalin was never in a hurry. The dignitary, having got the hint, was then supposed to return to Moscow and spread rumour – but never the whole truth – within the inner circle which, in its turn, would perform the same task down through the whole Soviet bureaucracy. The same procedure would operate in reverse, from the base upwards. In 1951 Semyon Ignatiev, charged with internal intelligence within the Ministry of State Security (until his own fall that year), administered over ten million informants; though 'administered' is not quite the right word. Informants 'denounced' their colleagues, in medicine, in law, in teaching, in the kolkhozes of the countryside and the block committees of the towns, to save their own lives. The Nazis, with their comparatively modest Gestapo and groups of informants, had nothing approaching this kind of system. Soviet informants never knew the entire story. It was, as Brent and Naumov have pointed out, Western liberal democracy stood on its head where the individual counted for nothing, was cut off from fellow citizens and lived in perpetual, isolated terror. Both Bulgakov and Vasili Aksionov have written about this in their novels. Stalin used to refer to the 'tens of millions of simple, ordinary, modest people' as '*vintiki*', literally 'little screws' or 'cogs' of the great Soviet machine, 'the people who maintain us as the base maintains the summit'.[34]

From base to summit, from summit to base, each '*vintik*' remained ignorant of and isolated from the other. Stalin, in effect, had fulfilled Marx's prediction of the 'withering away of the state'. Far from being Hobbes's *Leviathan*, Stalin had created a state to which nobody belonged. The 'Soviets' had disappeared as a genuine power and all genuine power had been invested in the Party, the Politburo and the Central Committee. But, with the purges of the 1930s, their own power became severely limited. Nobody knew entirely what was going on. Stalin muttered vague Olympian statements from his pipe, but rarely wrote anything down. Nobody was responsible for anything; everybody acted under the threat of death. This cannot be described as a state.

As the late French historian, François Furet, pointed out, the Stalinist system was 'the supreme stage of Communism'. Talent could not be recognized; individuality did not exist; the human being disappeared into the system, unknowingly, inexorably. Western Communist apologists would call the system 'Stalinist' because they did not want to be identified with it. Yet they supported it. And every time the Communists seized power, the system became 'Stalinist'. Nobody, even within the 'inner circle', could identify with it. It was, since 1917 up to its collapse in 1991, a system of perpetual *coups d'état* – a vicious circle which not even Boris Yeltsin or Vladimir Putin have managed to break. A system, such as that of the United States, already isolated from the more realistic state system of Western Europe, was incapable of understanding what was going on in the Soviet Union; Americans remained convinced that maintenance of the wartime alliance was possible. Stalin, in his speech of February 1946, as America slept, announced that war was inevitable. Hitler had not even been dead a year. But Stalin had been at war with the West even during the war; the idea of a 'wartime alliance' had been the West's great illusion.

Stalin in his citrus orchard set off the process of the 'Doctors' Plot'. The details are of no concern here. The consequences are. By the autumn of 1952 there is evidence – always slim, never direct – that Stalin had 'ordered' the building of extra camps for arrested Soviet Jews. The 'Plot' was officially announced in *Pravda* on 13 June 1953. The round-up of Jews was possibly being prepared for March. But Stalin died on 5 March 1953. No autopsy has ever been discovered – most curious in the case of the 'Presidential Archives' of the Kremlin.

Many accounts of Stalin's death have been published; none of them are in accord. The only fact that can be verified is that the trouble apparently began at a dinner party on 28 February attended by several of Stalin's would-be successors. Stalin only drank a small amount of light Crimean wine. He appears to have fallen ill the next day; Stalin would never have called a doctor – he had arrested his own physician, Dr V. N. Vinogradov, for suggesting his resignation one year before (he was released after Stalin's death). All that is known is that he was found in a comatose state on the floor of his dacha at 3 a.m., 2 March, by his guards who had been too afraid to enter earlier. The death agony lasted until the evening of 5 March, with Beria, Malenkov and other top Politburo members tearfully at his bedside – knowing that if he lived their lives were under threat. The cause of death was ascribed by the press to a 'cerebral haemorrhage'.

'They've killed my father, the bastards!' screamed his son Vasili to the few reporters allowed to approach the dacha. Vasili may have been correct. A popular poison in the Soviet Union at the time was Warfarin, a rat poison made up of transparent crystals that are tasteless. Was it Beria who placed them in Stalin's glass with Khrushchev's knowledge? Stalin's symptoms correspond alarmingly to that of a man poisoned by Warfarin. But the timing between the party and the death creates some problems with the theory.[*]

Beria, who succeeded Stalin, was arrested on 26 July 1953, tried in secret and shot on 23 December. There followed a five-year period of extreme instability; Khrushchev only managed to establish full authority in 1958. But even then, his policies, especially his foreign policy, were contested.

---

[*] Jonathan Brent and Vladimir P. Naumov, *Stalin's Last Crime* (London, 2003), 312–29 make the case, cautiously, for such a murder. *Pravda* reported that Stalin suffered a stroke in the Kremlin, which was false. Khrushchev in his memoirs, *Khrushchev Remembers* (Boston, 1974), II, 340–1, is accused by Brent and Naumov of a cover-up. The memoirs are certainly full of distortions. Dmitri Volkogonov, *Staline* (Paris, 1991), 571, gets the hours of death drastically wrong. Stalin's daughter invents a fantastically romantic tale, with Stalin, at his very last breath, raising his hand and damning all those about him. But do all these contradictions amount to a conspiracy, even if the number of murders, executions and plots around Stalin in the early 1950s may well provide a motive for his colleagues to slip Warfarin into the *Vozhd*'s Crimean wine glass?

The Gulag gradually declined in size after Stalin's death, not on account of a more humane policy in the Kremlin, but because slave labour proved so inefficient in the nuclear age. There were a series of strikes within the Gulag, starting in 1954, which paralysed the system, though elements of it survived into the age of Gorbachev. What replaced it – preposterously in the light of the 'Doctors' Plot' – was a system of hospitals and insane asylums, designed for punishment, not cure. This would be the experience of the younger generation of 'Dissidents'; they did not know the classic features of the Gulag, though their sufferings were, for all that, not much less.

This stateless totalitarian regime pursued a foreign policy as obscure as its domestic politics. Nobody in the West, accustomed to national policies, really understood it. Churchill came closest, though he made egregious errors.

After reviewing the war, and most particularly its conclusion, the clearest explanation that seems to emerge is that Stalin was intent upon continuing the war against his supposed Western Allies, the imperialists. He had never asked them to be allies. What he sought was their wealth and war material which he could then turn on them. The only power in Europe that he had treated as a genuine ally was Nazi Germany which, in his analysis, was the most advanced capitalist power and so came closest to the Socialist order of the Soviet Union. With all imperialists locked in perpetual war, as Lenin had forecast, the Nazis seemed the most natural allies of the Soviet Union. They could divide the world together, with Fascist Italy counting as a distant third partner. The Nazi-Soviet Pact drove these three advanced states southwards, into the colonial territories of the less advanced imperialists.

But, against all principles of good Marxist-Leninist theory, the Nazis invaded the Soviet Union. At Stalingrad and Kursk they paid for their heresy. The Pact, however, did not cease at that time because – as far as Stalin was concerned – it was a pact against imperialists, and the war against imperialists continued. The odd wartime peace conference may, with its bear hugs and toasts, have obscured the fact from many Western observers. Churchill even thought he had made a friend out of Stalin. Yet he realized, before Roosevelt, that Stalin was no friend.

The wartime peace conferences set the frontiers on paper, but not in iron. Stalin had no intention of submitting to a peace settlement, not like the Americans out of moral squeamishness, but because he intended to march on against the imperialists. This was the point he made in his famous speech of 9 February 1946: war between Socialists and imperialists was inevitable. Churchill's 'Iron Curtain' speech did nothing to move the Americans away from their commitment to the Soviet alliance. The speech irritated Stalin, too. Stalin had no intention of stopping at an iron curtain. He intended to pass straight through it. He was not too impressed with the American monopoly of atom bombs; thanks to his team of spies in the West he would explode his own in 1949.

He did not, in fact, believe in atomic strategy. Steeped in the teaching of Lenin that imperialists could only make war on themselves, Stalin had no faith in the joint will of the West to defend itself – what a lesson on Western discord Hitler had been! What he did believe in was big armies. 'How many divisions does the Pope have?' he is supposed to have said at Potsdam, though the story appears to be apocryphal. Nonetheless, Truman liked it and kept on repeating it. Truman and his colleagues did believe that good moral politics always won in the end, and that Stalin's Soviet Union could be converted – like one of those evil characters in a Hollywood movie who sees the light of goodness in the last five minutes of the film.

There was an element of this belief in Churchill. In the 1950 general election campaign he promised an attempt at an international conference with the Soviet Union included; it would provide a formal and happy end to the Second World War. Churchill lost the election. But he was returned in the election of October 1951. By now the United States had a new president, General Eisenhower, and one of the most idealistic Secretaries of State the country had ever had: John Foster Dulles, a former lawyer who had first made his mark in politics with Woodrow Wilson at the Paris Peace Conference of 1919. Now that they had set up NATO and a Western German Federal Republic friendly to the West, neither Eisenhower nor Dulles wanted to open up the European question again. Eisenhower and Dulles would show themselves capable of self-contradiction. But for the next few decades the Second World War did not get its happy ending.

Churchill's idea of a peaceful Europe – to judge by his speeches while in opposition in the 1940s – seems to have been based on a Franco-German alliance that could face up to the Soviet challenge, a withdrawal of the four occupying forces from Germany, free German elections which would somehow manage to maintain neutrality between the two super-powers, while the Soviet satellites would be turned into buffer states on the model of Finland, friendly to, but independent of the Soviet Union. One detects the European in Churchill here: his plans of 'bringing forward' this power, 'pushing back' that, show familiarity with the politics of Lord Castlereagh and Prince Talleyrand at the Congress of Vienna.

This was the kind of language Stalin could understand. Indeed, he sent a Peace Note to the Western powers in March 1952 – just as his purges at home were gathering momentum – that seemed to follow Churchill's lines. It was a game of European chess in its most classical form. Churchill – not for the first time in his life in total disagreement with the perpetually smiling Eisenhower – would have been willing at least to put forward one of his own pawns. It was not only the smiling Eisenhower who avoided committing America to a Peace Conference. The austere Catholic German Chancellor, Konrad Adenauer, did not want one either; it could have committed Europe to, horror of horrors, a treaty with Germany – a united Germany – which Adenauer wanted to avoid at all costs. Adenauer, as shrewd a player as Churchill, had his reasons. Churchill went along with his Western colleagues, as he always did in the end. He could sense what was happening. As he had remarked in 1946, as America turned her back on Europe, Stalin seemed to want all the fruits of war while actually being unwilling to wage war.[35]

Stalin's underlying belief, as it was of his successors, was that the Western imperialists would never fight. But, though placed in the centre of the Continent, Stalin had already by the early 1950s suffered serious setbacks in Europe. He seriously underestimated his enemy.

One of his first concerns, before marching forward through the Iron Curtain to the Atlantic, had been to mend the holes that already existed within that first barrier. There was one yawning hole in particular he wanted removed: Berlin. One hundred miles inside the Soviet occupied zone it represented a dangerous leak within the normally watertight Soviet system. Surely the three Western penetrators – the US, Britain and France – could be forced out and the hole closed.

Hitler had created a number of autobahns, all leading to Berlin. General Lucius Clay, representing Eisenhower shortly after the surrender, accepted just one of these for Western access to the capital. He did add a railway line and two air corridors. On 1 July 1945, when the Americans and the British tried to approach Berlin they were stopped at Soviet checkpoints, harassed by Soviet troops at the point of guns; the British were told that Magdeburg Bridge had been closed. It took the Western Allies several weeks, not a day as planned, to reach Berlin. For two years the harassment continued. The years 1945–8 are remembered as the 'Hunger Years' in Berlin; the Soviets would not feed the citizens, and the Allies lacked access. Refugees continued to pour in from Soviet-controlled Europe. In Berlin they could see what Westerners enjoyed; over 80 per cent of Berlin's population, including the suburbs, listened to RIAS (Radio In the American Sector), not the Soviet pronouncements. Already this was a disaster for Stalin; he had lost German popular opinion. But the opinion of 'vintiki' was not Stalin's central concern. In January 1947 the American and British zones were merged into 'Bizonia' and one year later they introduced the Deutschmark to replace the valueless old Reichmark; it became legal currency even in Berlin, with the exception of the Soviet zone where it was declared a crime to possess it. Yet, despite Soviet rulings, there could be no doubt that the imperialist economy was making serious inroads into the Socialist world. Stalin maintained absolute faith in the superiority of the Communist system. But he had to stop the spread of this capitalist rot.

As in the war – the war with no end – it was military might that mattered most in the Kremlin's mind. The Pope, having no divisions, may have had no consideration behind the Iron Curtain – a fact that would prove a great error in the 1980s. But for Westerners the problem was that the Americans, too, were rapidly losing their standing. General Clay had 6,500 troops in Berlin and, by 1947, there were only 60,000 in the whole of Europe. Stalin had over 400,000 within striking distance of Berlin.

During all this period, the Council of Foreign Ministers was still regularly held, as stipulated at the Potsdam Conference. It never achieved much. Molotov and his delegation would abandon their seats in a huff every now and then. The Four-Power Allied Control Commission still met in Berlin. But Potsdam became a mere historical memory when in early March 1947 the Western Foreign Ministers met in London to discuss the possibility of setting up an independent West German government. On 20 March Soviet Marshal Vasili Sokolovsky complained that the Foreign Ministers' meeting in London had not been approved by the Soviet authorities. General Sir Brian Robertson replied that there had been no need, in this case, for Soviet 'approval'. Marshal Sokolovsky read out a long wooden speech, concluding, 'I see no sense in continuing this meeting and declare it adjourned.'[36] Off walked the Soviets. There was never an Allied Control Commission held in Berlin again. All the wartime preparation for a formal peace following the Second World War thereby came to a halt. The much despised system of the Paris Peace Conference following the First World War survived ten full years. The wartime preparations for peace during the Second World War had not survived two years beyond the war. Whatever the claim of national mythologies, no one could seriously describe the peace of 1945 as a success, even when compared to 1919: Europe was divided on an unhistorical, ungeographical basis; Eastern Europeans were driven into slavery, their pre-war economies destroyed; Western Europeans faced dire poverty – it was still another year before the Marshall Plan came into operation; there were fewer Americans present than after the First World War.

Stalin started turning the screws on Berlin, unannounced, and as usual by delayed action. At first, Western forces were unaware of what was going on. There were 'traffic delays' on the one autobahn open to Berlin; bridges had to be repaired. Ernest Bevin admitted in the Commons that 'the regulations for travel to and from Berlin are not so clearly specified.' That was before he and his Allies realized that they were only weeks from the outbreak of what could have turned into World War III. The barricades went up. All ground traffic in and out of Berlin was halted.

Then the US Army called in Lieutenant General Albert Wedemeyer, the man who had masterminded D-Day. He had saved Chiang Kai-shek's regime from certain ruin by flying in American- and Chinese-equipped troops across the Himalayas. Wedemeyer devised an even greater 'air bridge' into Berlin – the world has never before or since seen anything like it. The first Allied planes landed at Tempelhof Airport on 26 June 1948. By August aircraft were landing, unloading and taking off in twenty minutes. The pilots were the best trained the West could find – Freddie Laker, who later created Laker Airlines, was one of them. A new airport was built at Tegel in the French sector. The Russians built a radio tower in front of it. General Jean Ganéval ordered it blown up. General Kotikov came storming into his office: 'How could you do such a thing?' 'With the help of dynamite and French sappers, *mon général*.'[37]

By January 1949, when Stalin had estimated that Berliners would be starved into submission, the Allies were actually stockpiling food and fuel, to the envy of every frozen Soviet soldier stationed in the capital. Lieutenant Gail S. Halversen came in with a US bomber at that time – an atom bomb? two hundred pounds of TNT? Lyons and Hershey chocolate bombs appeared in the streets of Berlin. Children gathered in crowds to collect the parachuted goodies in the sheets they held out. This was only four years after the Anglo-American carpet bombing of Berlin. Halversen came to be known as the 'chocolate bomber'. His name would live on for decades. Old men and women would turn out in crowds to welcome him when he revisited Berlin after the fall of the Communist wall.

In August 1948 the three Western ambassadors to Moscow had a meeting with Stalin, who showed himself at his moderate, jovial best. He was convinced at that time that he was going to win. 'We are still allies,' he said to the ambassadors.[38] Just like in the war days. The same old lies.

But Stalin lost seriously over Berlin. He had lost whatever sympathy was left among the Germans and NATO, unexpectedly for Stalin, held together. The new currency became the strongest in Europe. The Western sectors of occupation showed astonishing coordination for competing imperialists. With the Western Federal Republic of Germany established,

Stalin abandoned his battle over Berlin. The Iron Curtain proved to be of steel. It did not move from where the Red Army had managed to place it – as they hoped, temporarily – in May 1945. There would be no further movement in Europe.

What happened next is the unknown chapter of European 'decolonization'. Without movement in Europe, the Communists had to look elsewhere. The Truman Doctrine, combined with Kennan's doctrine of 'containment', encouraged this. Americans were now obliged to face Russian aggression anywhere in the world. The Russians, stationed in North Korea because of their agreement in 1945 to attack Japan, were responsible for persuading the North Koreans to attack across the line on 25 June 1950. The Russians, sensibly, pulled out, leaving the newly installed Chinese Communist regime to help the Koreans, who were hopelessly outnumbered and out-equipped. This would lead to serious tensions between Russian and Chinese Communists. The Americans, with the help of a few UN troops, most notably from Britain, did manage after two years to re-establish the former frontier line between Northern and Southern Korea, but at a cost of 150,000 men or the equivalent of one third of their losses during the entire Second World War.[39]

The French were barely present in Korea, being busy defending their colony in Indochina, Vietnam, against another Soviet ally. The doctrine of 'National Liberation Fronts' had been pronounced by Stalin in his speech of February 1946 (though it dated back to the Comintern's 'Popular Front' war against 'Fascists' in the 1930s). Its purpose was to encourage division among the imperialists – the old Leninist doctrine.

Division, however, did not occur between capitalist imperialists in Vietnam. By 1952, under Dulles and Eisenhower, the United States was already supplying the French with over half of their war materials and at least half of their war expenses. For the Americans, Vietnam was a logical extension of 'containment' theory, and so it remained for the next twenty-five years – disastrously so. As Kennan, its author, already noted in revising his doctrine in 1951, it contained no sense of geography and strategy. But for most Americans this was of no importance. The essence of war and peace was moral, not geographical.

Stalin, like his successors, had his own ideological reasons for moving beyond Europe. He may have been disappointed in Europe, but he still had in mind the old idea of his ally, Hitler. Members of the Pact would move southwards to meet in the southern portions of the Eurasian 'world island' and deprive the Western Allies of their colonies – this was the reason why Stalin could not believe that Hitler would make war on the

Soviet Union, it countered Marxist–Leninist principles. Stalin had revived the idea within a year of Hitler's death.

Stalin's opportunity came as in a dream. He had certainly not planned it. But in its early stages it seemed to fit in well with the purges which in 1948 were not yet fully formulated in his mind: the creation of the state of Israel. Contrary to myth, the United States did not create independent Israel; this was achieved by the Soviet Union. With the old European cat once again spewing forth her armies into the four corners of the earth, Stalin moved in to counter them, in the Far East and the Middle East. In truth, it was merely a continuation of the unfinished Second World War; a fulfilment of the Pact's promise to move south and cut off the West from its wealth and colonies. Stalin carried on the policy independently after the Nazi defeat at Stalingrad. His first step towards the Mediterranean was in Cairo, where he set up a mission in 1943 and a highly successful spy ring. His object, like Hitler's, was to undermine British power and influence which he was certain was going to crack shortly after the war. In the years 1943–5 he set up several other missions in the Middle East with the initial aim of stirring up a popular Arab 'Liberation Front' movement against the French and the British, but he judged their leaders feudal and ultra-reactionary. Far more promising were reports coming in from Palestine – both from Arabs and Jews – that a Socialist state could be formed there with friendly links with the Soviet Union.[40]

America at the time wanted to show its anti-colonial credentials and would have nothing to do with an area it considered imperialist and British. Churchill himself noted at both Yalta and Potsdam that he found the task most 'ungratifying'. When Stalin asked for a mandate over former Italian colonies, Churchill showed no opposition; it was the Americans who stopped the project. On the other hand, Stalin's attempt to set up fortifications on the Turkish Straits failed dismally. So all Stalin had as a possible base in the area was Palestine. The Soviet Union became the most enthusiastic supporter of an independent Israel.

What is remarkable is what little initial support Israel got from American Jews and their powerful organizations. Even prominent Jews in the American press regarded the creation of Israel as an imperialist project made at the expense of the Arabs.[41]

The 'anti-cosmopolitan' campaign did not seem to encourage a friendly policy with Israel, until seen in association with immediate post-war Soviet emigration policy. Despite the Nazi atrocities in the occupied zones, the Jewish population in the Soviet Union increased from 3,020,000 in 1939 to 4,800,000 in 1945 – largely due to the annexation of the Baltic states. The number was a good deal higher in the satellite states. In July 1946 an accord was drawn up between Warsaw and Moscow promising repatriation of all Polish citizens to Poland – most of them were Jews. Over the next year, up to 1 August 1946 when the programme was suddenly stopped, over 200,000 Polish Jews left the Soviet Union for Poland. What is slightly terrifying in these figures is that they did not stop there – and were not encouraged by the Polish Communist authorities to stop there: 150,000 Jews left Poland in the year 1946 for the Western zones of Germany and Austria. The result was a sudden and unexpected swelling in numbers in the Western DP camps. Many others of these forced Jewish migrants from Poland made the forbidden (by the British) journey to Palestine. It was no holiday trip. Stalin in fact encouraged Jewish emigration from all the Popular Democracies. Between the creation of Israel in 1948 and 1951, when the Communist gates were violently closed, officially around 300,000 Jews left Eastern Europe for Israel. The largest contributors were Poland and Romania. But like all official statistics for this period they must not be taken too seriously. Indirect routes, especially via the Western DP camps, had a distorting effect. The true number was probably much higher. Israel was first populated by Eastern European Jews. Many sympathized with the Communists. Thus one finds Primo Levi, on his long return journey from Auschwitz, encountering a new wagon attached to his long train convoy filled with young Jews. They were all very combative. Against the Germans? Against the Austrians? No. 'We are going to Palestine to fight the British and create the Jewish State.' Primo Levi found their enthusiasm – in their flight from the cemetery of European Judaism – life-inspiring.[42]

The British, in their attempt to control migration to Palestine, were represented by Soviet propaganda as 'private pirates', 'Fascists' and of course 'acquisitive imperialists'. The Americans had no kind words for the British either.

Andrei Gromyko, Soviet apparatchik incarnate, then Assistant Minister of Foreign Affairs, made on 14 May 1947 the decisive speech at the United Nations for a partition of Palestine into two states, Jewish and Arab. The Kremlin, it appears, only arrived at its policy a few weeks earlier in April on account of its failure to find a solid footing in any other part of the Middle East – it had failed in Turkey, it had failed in Iran, it had failed with the Arabs. Jews in Palestine of every class showed sympathy for the Soviet Union. Moreover, Israeli terrorist groups openly announced themselves as representing 'workers' and embracing 'anti-imperialism'. Most of all, it was an effective way of undermining Britain's position in the Middle East. Gromyko underlined the suffering of 'the Jewish people in Europe' – a phrase hardly expected from the Soviet Union; those few who did survive, he went on, were 'without country, without shelter and without means of subsistence'. 'None of the countries in Western Europe', he stressed, 'had been ready to accord the Jewish people necessary aid for their defence.'[43]

The speech had an astonishing effect on the Assembly. Jews the world over could not believe their ears. Here, right in the midst of the Soviets' 'anti-cosmopolitan' campaign, was a high-ranking Soviet minister advocating an independent Israeli state. 'The taking of such a position was for us an unimagined godsend,' said the Zionist leader Abba Eban: 'in an instant all our plans and calculations over the United Nations debate were overturned.'[44]

On 14 May 1948 the independent state of Israel was proclaimed and four days later Egypt invaded its narrow borders, thus starting the first Arab Israeli war. Moscow had officially recognized the state the day before; it took the Americans more than a year to grant legal recognition. Truman's government placed an arms embargo on Israel. All of Israel's arms and munitions came from the Soviet bloc, especially the newly Communist Czechoslovakia. The Czechs even attempted to send an International Brigade, similar to that dispatched to the Spanish Civil War; it was not particularly effective since the Israelis immediately split it up among Israeli army units.

It was about this time that Soviet-Israeli relations began to get tense. Golda Meir, the first Israeli ambassador to Moscow, became openly critical of the way the Soviet Union was treating its Jews. But the real problem, as always for the Soviet Union, was military. Britain tried to hold on to her military bases in Egypt as a means of protecting the Suez Canal; nostalgia for the first great victories over the Nazis could not be discounted as a factor, too. The United States suffered from no such nostalgia and remained determined to demonstrate that it was not an imperialist power – which for the Europeans, including secretly the Soviets, was a negation of power itself. The Americans proposed in 1951 the creation of a local system of defence, the Middle East Command (or MEC), which had for the Soviets the alarming appearance of a Mediterranean NATO. One year later young officers of the Egyptian army, furious over their humiliating defeat by Israel in 1948–9, staged a *coup d'état* under the charismatic leadership of Gamal Abdel Nasser. MEC never saw the light of day. Nasser started on a spectacular international career which promised to unite all Arabs in a single anti-imperialist movement. Another window of opportunity opened itself to the Soviet Union. As in Asia, 'National Liberation Fronts' sprang up right across North Africa and the Middle East. The alliance with Israel was ended for ever.

There is some parallel between the development of the Israeli alliance and later NLFs, and the 1939 German Pact and the later Partisan war that the Soviets promoted after Hitler's invasion. Both show the opportunistic nature of Soviet foreign policy. Nobody could make a science of it. Soviet foreign policy drifted with the wind, often running completely at odds with its ideological pronouncements. Its one constant feature was its aim of complete domination, in the Second World War, of Europe; and in the post-war era of the entire world. This second version of expansion was due to the West's success in reinforcing the Iron Curtain with thick steel rods, and America's belated policy of 'containment' (which in the tradition of American foreign policy contained no sense of geography). The United States, under the impulsion of Europe (the Brussels Pact), had created a North Atlantic Treaty Organization which stopped Soviet military (but not political) expansion in Europe in its tracks: Czechoslovakia was the last formally democratic state to fall under the military force of the Soviets. In Berlin they never succeeded in expelling Western freedoms. But 'containment' went beyond Europe. It involved the entire world in an ideological war. Or, to put it more realistically, it handed the Soviet Union the choice of where to hit out from its Eurasian 'world island'. The Soviet Union naturally looked for the weakest points, north, south, east and west. Westwards did not work, so they pushed south into the Middle East and Africa – this did not prove very promising and (if one follows the logic closely) is what led to an anti-Semitic campaign, clothed in the jargon of 'Fascist, imperialist cosmopolitanism'. Pushing south, it must be recalled, was a part of the Nazi-Soviet Pact. They could go north, but an inter-ballistic missile system was required for that, which strained an economy based on slave labour to its limits. So all that was left was the East; and this proved the West's weak point.

The NLFs were modelled on the wartime Partisans: they were divided into cells; they set up both political and military 'fronts' which were careful to avoid the label 'Communist'. Their enemies were not merely imperialists; they were 'Fascist imperialists'. They appealed, like the Partisans, to all political parties of the left. They were a good deal more successful in the process of alliance, rupture, insurrection and takeover than they had been in Western Europe at the end of the Second World War. In the process of 'decolonization' one newly 'independent' nation after another was taken over by a Marxist dictatorship. This gave each newly independent nation the same exciting prospects of political freedom and economic growth as existed inside the Soviet Union. The one exception was India, largely because India was granted independence in 1947, too early for any NLF to form. But, generally speaking, 'decolonization' was not decolonization at all.

Stalin's Europe was at the heart of the war that never ended, the failure to find a genuine peace settlement in 1945. Stalin's Europe was based on the visions of the Nazi-Soviet Pact of 1939, the origin of the Second World War. Stalin's Europe appealed to the 'have-nots': those who had no influence in the world. In Western Europe and America this referred not so much to various working classes – which had other problems to worry about – as to frustrated intellectuals. Stalin's Europe represented the continuation of the Second World War.

3 Adenauer's Europe

For forty years Europe was frozen into two unnatural armed blocs because of a failure to reach a peace settlement, and particularly an international treaty with Germany. Europe stopped where the armies stopped in the spring of 1945, right in the middle of Germany. A Europe organized into nation states – a very recent phenomenon anyway – quite obviously did not exist in 1945. Nor was it certain that this should be the aim of reconstruction: the nineteenth-century construction of nations east of the Rhine had brought war, not peace. Since the devastation of the first war a lot of idealists had dreamt of a 'rule of law to be established throughout the world' – that had once been the vision of Clement Attlee and many others on the new Labour government benches of the House of Commons.

But a world order was perhaps beyond the energies of man. Why not start with Europe? After all, the area had a culture in common and for half a millennium all world wars (going back to the sixteenth-century colonial wars) had started there. The United Nations Charter included a chapter that encouraged the creation of regional zones of collective defence and economic harmony. Furthermore, the 'European idea' was as old as the nation state: it paralleled and preceded it. Victor Hugo is generally considered the inventor of the 'United States of Europe'. The word 'Europe' itself went back to the Greeks; they used it to distinguish between the civilization of their own city states and the land of 'barbarians' – people who spoke with an incomprehensible 'bar-bar' tongue – which lay on the other side of the seas and the mountains. The Habsburg Emperor Charles V in the early sixteenth century genuinely sought a united Christendom; he died in a monastery, not in island exile or in a concrete bunker like later conquerors. The ideal of a united Europe was as old as European writing.

The real novelty occurred when it was realized, in the twentieth century, that Europe could not be politically organized – as had been attempted at the end of the First World War – solely on the principle of nation states. In 1945 tens of millions belonged to no nation. With no peace settlement, frontiers had not even been decided. Poland, the 'key to the vault', had been annexed into a Soviet empire. Germany had been cut up into occupied zones, and a huge iron curtain had been slammed by armies across the centre of Europe. Nobody could talk realistically in 1945 of a 'Europe of nation states'.

The idealists – like the French businessman, Jean Monnet, who produced plan after plan for a new supranational Europe – and the political realists, who had lived through three generations of democratic nationalist enthusiasm, and war; these two groups, idealists and realists, had to meet on a common ground. Europe had no alternative in 1945.

The story of the construction of Europe after the Second World War had no precedent. The hegemonic conquerors of the Napoleonic, Wilhelmine and Hitlerite genre had failed once and for all. For many, the years that immediately followed the war were even worse than those of the war. After the winter of 1946–7 Britain, for example, was living on more stringent food and fuel rations than at any time during the war. Denmark, Sweden and Switzerland had escaped relatively unscathed (Denmark even had a popular election during the Nazi occupation) – which perhaps explains why a 'European consciousness' did not develop in these countries as strongly as elsewhere. In the rest of Europe it was a good deal worse. The DP camps were overwhelmed by a new wave of migrants from the east as Stalin's new purges took hold. The United States passed out a few meagre loans, but the country was still, in 1946, isolated from the realities of Europe.

The idealists and their plans played, it is true, an important role in the rebuilding of Europe in the immediate aftermath of the war. They were a source of ideas. Many of the leading planners were profoundly Christian in their faith, such as Jean Monnet and Robert Schuman, the latter rising to French Foreign Minister and Prime Minister, and a man, like Charles V, who was familiar with monastic life. But several of the statesmen who laid the first bricks of Europe's post-war institutions were far from the regular image of a European idealist. It was Winston Churchill – through the power of his name and his oratory – who got the movement going at Zurich in September 1946: Europe must be built now, he had said, and the only solid foundations would be a partnership between France and Germany. Macmillan, who like Churchill had the Union Jack and its Empire printed on his heart, was in the crowd. It was British Churchill who encouraged the creation of a 'Council of Europe'. It never got very far, but it did act as a sounding board between the idealists and the statesmen. Churchill recommended that a number of empty seats be arranged around the table to represent the Eastern European countries unable to be present.

The extraordinary feature of post-war Europe is that it was constructed – it is hard, in the context, to speak of it being 'reconstructed' or 'reborn' – not by the idealists, but by statesmen whom one would consider the embodiment of nationalist pride: Winston Churchill, Harold Macmillan, Konrad Adenauer and Charles de Gaulle. They were of the war generation; they were frequently in bitter conflict. Nonetheless they built a new type of world peace. The idealists could have done nothing alone.

The story began with the incorporation of Adenauer's shattered western half of Germany – the enemy of all – into Europe. France, as Churchill foresaw, would be the first and foremost partner. Then the peripheral powers joined. The last pages of this book will attempt to indicate the first major steps in the process. It is, one is tempted to say, the final happy chapter of the Second World War, its miracle even – the birth of the present, the emergence of an unprecedentedly prosperous Europe that took on a political shape never before known.

But there is polemic even in this. Has the thousand-year diplomatic game of hegemony and balance disappeared from Europe for ever? Or is this some slow transition back to a golden age of a 'Europe of nation states', which has never in fact existed? All one can say is that the new Europe has been with us for sixty years and has recently spread into the former Communist bloc.

There has never been, in European history, a dominant power so swiftly and utterly defeated in war as Germany in 1945. France in 1815 perhaps is the closest example. But the France of the time had citizens fighting on both sides, Bourbon and Napoleonic, so the defeat could never be considered as total as it was for Germany in 1945. Germany lay in a dazed silence. There were not even enough ambulances to carry the sick and the dead; they had to be transported in carts and wagons, as in pre-industrial days. Many of the cities lay in ruins in the heat of summer without a sound to be heard. The Germans called it *Stunde Null*, Zero Hour. This state tempted Adenauer to remark before his first federal Cabinet in September 1949, 'In view of the confused times behind us a general *tabula rasa* is called for.'[45] That was not at all the intention of Germany's former enemies and victims. Nor was it even the goal of many Germans, Adenauer included. After all, Germany had a very long history that had given much that was good and grand to Europe. The real issue before Germans immediately after the war became what was to be known, in typically Teutonic fashion, as that of '*Vergangenheitsbewältigung*' – literally, 'consciousness of the past', or more closely, the 'overcoming' or 'mastering of the past'. The Germans did attempt this, though one may question the way many did it. (By comparison, Russians after the fall of Communism – or their many apologists in the West – have not yet come to terms with their past; but then, they were never actually defeated.)[46]

No victors in war have ever been faced with such a situation as 1945. Between them they could decide anything. There was no negotiation. The only opposition was among themselves. Frontiers were drawn, food was distributed and justice was administered by the armies.

Churchill had written on many occasions throughout the last year of the war that he wanted no trial of the leading Nazi war criminals. Their guilt was obvious and the idea of being ensnared in long-drawn-out legal proceedings was abhorrent to him; they should, he argued, be identified in front of drumhead courts martial as the armies entered Germany and shot within six hours. The number involved – party heads, military commanders and ministers – would, in Churchill's estimate, be between fifty and a hundred men. What arguments for human justice had they listened to? It was the Soviets who demanded a trial. The International Military Tribunal, which sat in Nuremberg between November 1945 and October 1946 (local and minor cases dragged on until 1949), was organized to avoid a Soviet-style show trial; the Americans organized another tribunal for those accused in their own zone at the concentration camp of Dachau.

In the end, twenty-two German civilian and military leaders were charged with conspiracy to wage aggressive war, crimes against peace, war crimes and crimes against humanity. The major 'general cases' (those not applying to one region) were tried in Nuremberg. The American prosecution experts, in particular, demonstrated special thoroughness in the preparation of their legal dossiers – an expertise that derived, in most cases, from decades of experience in the investigation of American stock fraud. The prosecuted had their own choice of defence lawyers, picked from among the finest in Germany. Reichsmarshal Hermann Göring was an especially impressive witness – this was, in its perverse way, his hour of glory; he managed to maintain his Nazi sense of honour by committing suicide just hours before his execution. The ten other condemned men were hanged from a beam in a Nuremberg gymnasium at dawn on 16 October 1946 – their corpses photographed to prove they were dead. Four were acquitted, and the other seven were sentenced to long prison terms, including Rudolf Hess, whom court psychiatrists had proved to be insane at the time.[47]

What was the effect of hanging ten men from a beam in a city more than half destroyed by Allied bombing, leaving a quarter of a million homeless? The town was on the north-eastern hills of Bavaria and Bohemia, not exactly a central location. The films of the Nazi camps had become daily fare in London cinemas in March and April; Germans had been watching them since June, while citizens had been forced to assist in mass burials. Nobody began to talk openly about the horrors of the Holocaust until the 1970s, during the Arab-Israeli wars.[48]

Students of law could learn a good deal from the Nuremberg procedure of trying war criminals, of whom there are plenty in our own world. Nuremberg undoubtedly set major precedents; but it was not the sole legal precedent for the conviction of war criminals. The first procedure for trying war criminals was set up by a special committee in the Paris Peace Conference of 1919. Subsequent analysis has shown that German belligerents were responsible for more major war crimes – such as the massacre of civilians in occupied areas and their deportation in tens of thousands for slave labour – in the First World War than any of the other belligerents. Those responsible were, however, tried in Germany itself; it was not a great success.

In addition, Nuremberg cannot be considered a practical precedent because it was a *military* tribunal representing armies that had totally defeated their enemy. Such a situation is never likely to occur again. In 1993 a civil War Crimes Tribunal was set up in The Hague; and over time one may expect it to have an effect on atrocities committed throughout the world, particularly in Europe. Yet the most powerful country in the world has yet to adhere to it: up to now, if you are the victim of an American war crime, you will have to go through American courts to prove it – like victims of the Germans after the First World War.

One of the scandals of Nuremberg was the presence of Soviet prosecutors, though this was politically unavoidable. Once more, the Soviets proved themselves not to be allies of the West, or of humanity. Every effort was made to avoid reference to the Nazi-Soviet Pact; the Soviets accused the Nazis of the murder of 11,000 Polish officers assassinated by the Russians in cold blood at Katyn and elsewhere, and no reference was made to the millions of Poles deported to Siberia. John McCloy, America's High Commissioner after the setting up of West Germany's Federal Republic in 1949, formally argued with German citizens who considered the trials unjust that 'the Nuremberg system' was a healthy alternative to the 'Morgenthau Plan' envisaged by the Soviet agent Harry Dexter White – that is, the 'pastoralization' of Germany, which would have led to the suffering of millions. The Morgenthau Plan was eventually executed by the Soviets in their zone. It made the matter of calculating German reparations virtually impossible.

The 'Nuremberg system' also began the process of 'denazification' that had been an Allied war aim since the Casablanca Conference of 1943. Again, in the Soviet zone, this was hardly an issue: one was arrested on the grounds of social class, not actual deed. The number of 'Fascists' thus rounded up and placed in former Nazi camps has never been accurately estimated; many were deported to Siberia, never to be seen again. The 'working class', on the other hand, was not considered guilty of 'Fascist' excesses.

'Collective guilt' had never been an issue in the Allied Western courts or in the specially set-up German *Spruchgerichte* (denazification courts) – which of the 24,000 held throughout the Western zones found over two thirds of the cases guilty. In German law the distinction began to emerge between '*Haftung*', or 'civil responsibility', which incurred a liability to reparations or damages, and '*Schuld*', or 'guilt', which attracted the penal law and punishment. Curiously enough, it was on this basis that the German nationalists launched their great propaganda campaign against the Versailles Treaty in May 1919 – indeed, the campaign went back to the 'psychological methods' of Prince Max of Baden in 1916: the issue of German 'war guilt'. Nowhere in the Versailles Treaty was there any mention of 'war guilt'. But at the head of the chapter on German reparations there was a reference to the principle of 'national responsibility'. The Western zones of Germany accepted the idea of 'responsibility' for the war. The reparations that the democratic German Federal Republic has paid since its creation in 1949 are incalculable, and they have no time limit. In the First World War the time limit of 1960 was set – forty-two years after the war. Today, in 2004, the Federal Republic is still paying reparations for the Second World War, sixty years after the war. Most impressive of all were the huge reparations – constituting over half Germany's receipts from the tardily paid Marshall Plan – which the Federal Republic agreed to pay to Western Jewish survivors of the Holocaust. Adenauer, sensibly, conducted these negotiations in secret.[49]

'Collective responsibility' of course requires the existence of a nation state, and that is, of course, exactly what was missing from Germany in 1945. The same is the case wherever the principle is applied. The Paris Peace Conference rested on the idea that Europe was made up of nation states. In 1945, this was obviously no longer the case. The Americans, easily the most powerful of the victors, simply turned their backs on the problem: there was no peace settlement. But Europe, and most especially Germany, which was no longer a nation state, desperately needed peace.

One did not need to be an idealist of the Monnet variety to realize that a European solution had to be found.

For as long as he was winning the war the Germans loved their Führer, but from 1943 they became indifferent to politics and even to the outcome of the war. German opinion surveys, such as they existed in 1945–6, indicate a generally positive view of the main Nuremberg trials. Naturally all media were under the control of the occupying forces. But even in 1950, with a free press and a new federal government, only a third of those surveyed regarded Nuremberg and the subsequent trials as unjust.[50] But it was a well-organized third.

The slowly developing legitimacy of the Federal Republic and its institutions, along with the growing crisis of the Cold War, brought the 'struggle to free the war criminals' to the fore. In Heidelberg a 'jurists' circle' had been formed, consisting mainly of former defence lawyers at Nuremberg. Academics and churchmen, of all denominations, joined in the chorus. Political parties of the right, most notably the German Party, made it their main campaign topic. Adenauer's ruling coalition, the CDU–CSU (the Christian Democrats from the British zone and the Christian Social Union of Bavaria), attempted on the face of it to maintain a neutral line. But even some of the Western Allies, as the years passed, began to recognize that more leniency was required in the denazification programme. Linked to this was a recognition among the occupying powers of a need to integrate their zones into a single West German state because of deteriorating relations with the Communists.

'Denazification' had been expressed as a Western Allied aim at the Casablanca Conference back in January 1943. But it was never very well defined. No effort to lay down a legal definition was ever made by either the Western Allies or the local German authorities. The Communists faced no such problem: 'Nazism' was the ideology of the 'bourgeoisie' in the late stage of capitalism, an offshoot of 'Fascism' as defined by the Popular Front politicologues of the 1930s Comintern. But in the Western zone, what of the primary school teacher, the petty bureaucrat, the local policeman? The Americans in 1946 established five categories of 'Nazi' that were adopted soon after in the French and British zones. They were based on questionnaires distributed to every member of the population over eighteen years old: '*Hauptschuldige*' were the principal guilty Nazis; '*Belastete*' were those who faced major charges; '*Minderbelastete*', those with proven minor charges in their dossiers; '*Mitläufer*', 'fellow-travellers' who were not subject to any specific penalties; and '*Entlastete*', those who were pardoned but were not considered innocent. Every zone and every region had its own way of applying these categories. 'Persil' certificates, nicknamed after the detergent, were issued to those who paid the right price. And, just as in Nazi Germany there had been 'economically useful Jews', so in occupied Germany there were 'economically useful Nazis'. The Americans made a special case of scientists – the most famous being Dr Werner von Braun, who had designed the V-2 and went on to become one of the founding fathers of American space research.[51]

The level of corruption was just as great, if not more so, in the Soviet zone. It did not need the German Party to point out that 'denazification' by 1950 had descended into a pure fiasco. The central issue of debate in the Federal Republic's first Bundestag was amnesty. A partial amnesty was passed by the house in December 1949; it went through the upper house, the Bundesrat, the same month and on 20 December Adenauer's government presented the bill to the Allied High Commissioners, who sat in a luxury hotel on a high hill overlooking Bonn, the Petersberg. The High Commissioners, to prove that they still had control over Federal legislation, neither rejected nor corrected the law. Adenauer signed and the law took effect on the last day of the year 1949: Adenauer's New Year's present to the German people. As a result, over the next two years 792,176 persons were, in the term of the day, 'privileged' – that is, amnestied from Nazi crimes. Full amnesty was granted to those not falling under the military tribunals' judgement by a General Treaty negotiated between the Republic and the three occupying powers between 1951 and 1952. By then West Germany was already integrated into the new and growing form of European community.[52]

As for military law, it was beginning to lose its effect. The institutions set up during the war and at Potsdam – the Four-Power Control Commission and the 'regular' Council of Foreign Ministers – had lost all significance by 1948 in the face of Soviet intransigence. In fact, the Control Commission in Berlin passed only one law of importance, the abolition of the state of Prussia in February 1946. Thus, with a stroke of a pen, disappeared a state that had been a major power in Europe since the Thirty Years War of the seventeenth century, and the dominant power of Europe since the mid-nineteenth century. The Federal Republic did not, in fact, formally consent to the ruling until, with the unification of Germany and the Paris Conference of 1990, it recognized Poland's Oder–Neisse line – a frontier in fact formed by the manoeuvres of the Red Army in the first months of 1945. Thus was Prussia wiped off the map.

Adenauer had never liked Prussia, though – born in Cologne in 1876 – he was, by virtue of Castlereagh's insistence at the Congress of Vienna in 1814 on 'bringing Prussia forward' to the Rhineland provinces, a Prussian citizen. He was a year older than Churchill, whom he thought on his first encounter 'looked very old', and he was two years younger than the Weimar Republic's famous Foreign Minister, Gustav Stresemann, who died in 1929. Adenauer had already been mayor of Cologne for over twelve years. His wrinkled, mummified face, with high cheekbones and Mongolian eyes, had been disfigured by a serious automobile accident in March 1917, six months before he was elected mayor.

Adenauer had been dismissed from his post by the Nazis in March 1933. Retiring to the nearby monastery of Maria Laach in the Eifel mountains, he separated himself from his family for their own security. At the monastery he took up gardening and the study of flowers. But, most of all, he deepened his Roman Catholic faith. This never left him. During the war years, already well in his sixties, he left his monastery and returned to his small home and family in Rhöndorf, not far from Cologne. There he maintained a strict programme of reading and gardening.

When the American armies freed a bombed Cologne in March 1945 they reinstalled Adenauer as mayor to educate, as Adenauer himself claimed, 'the German people from the ground up to the idea of peace'. The British, on taking over the zone, promptly sacked him for 'incompetence'; Adenauer always thought this was the work of the new British Socialist government. The decision was not, in fact, made at a high level; British command in Berlin once more reinstated him in December. It was at that moment that the Christian Democratic Union, or CDU, was founded. Adenauer became its natural leader.

His first major act as leader was to make a long speech in March 1946 in the main hall of the University of Cologne, its columns still damaged by bombardment, cold draughts gusting down the aisles. The place was packed. 'How was it possible', he asked, 'that the German Republic we established in 1918 only lasted fifteen years?' How was the Third Reich possible? How could the country embark again on war? He then made an analysis of the 'Prussian view of the state', its materialism, its militarism. This kind of nationalism had found its strongest resistance in those parts of Germany, Catholic and Protestant, which 'had fallen least under the spell of the teaching of Karl Marx – of Socialism! That is absolutely certain!' Adenauer was careful not to mention Catholic Bavaria, which provided support for his coalition in the form of the CSU. The only way forward, said Adenauer, was a 'return to the values and sense of justice of Western Christendom'. Here was, and would remain for his next seventeen years as leader of West Germany, the main plank of his platform. Christianity was always put in the forefront; atheistic Socialism and Communism were always the main enemy; economic liberalism, administered by Ludwig

Erhard, Adenauer's future Economics Minister from Bavaria, was the main material feature of the programme. For the next quarter century West Germany would be the most economically liberal and, by the 1950s, the most prosperous country of Europe.[53]

Adenauer owed his political power to his presence in the British zone, the most populous and heavily industrialized of the four zones. West Berlin was quickly marginalized – too Prussian in Adenauer's view. Adenauer frequently paid lip-service to German unification, but in fact it was the last thing he wanted. Present at Zurich during Churchill's rallying call for a European Movement, Adenauer already had his eyes on France as a means of reincorporating Germany into Europe. He wanted his federal capital as far west as possible. Frankfurt had been under consideration, but the Americans, always more concerned about local control than the British (who had, in their Empire, left the natives to themselves), were unwilling to grant the Federal Republic control over the city; the British offered the Republic Bonn. Adenauer noticed the proximity of the French zone.

As early as 1946, three years before the formation of the Republic, Adenauer, unknown to the British, was travelling regularly to the French zone to discuss with French military representatives the possibility of cooperation between the French and the Germans in the Rhineland. From the time of their occupation, the British had begun dismantling industrial plants in the Ruhr as part of wartime agreements on German reparations in kind. Indeed, much of the plant equipment found itself en route to the Soviet Union. For the purpose, the British set about organizing a 'Ruhr authority'. 'The Versailles Treaty is a bed of roses by comparison,' remarked Adenauer. Britain's dismantling policy, Adenauer was quick to point out, ran at complete odds to the proposed Marshall Plan as it developed in late 1947. In place of a 'Ruhr authority', he suggested to his nearby French friends, one could perhaps set up some sort of Franco-German authority in the same area.

The French could not have been more delighted. Adenauer continued to make his secret trips to the French sector in a large car, wrapping himself up in a blanket and cramming his homburg hat – Adenauer's equivalent of Churchill's cigar – hard down on his head so that it would not be noticed by the prying eyes of British guards. That winter he met Robert Schuman, then French Foreign Minister, for the first time. Schuman had spent his childhood in Lorraine before the First World War when it was under German rule. His mother tongue was German, which he spoke with a Rhinelander accent, like Adenauer. His faith was as Catholic as that of Adenauer; he had, in fact, spent part of the last war, when he was active in the French Resistance, living in a monastery and deepening his faith. He may not have had Adenauer's cool, calculating character, but he had visions of a European-wide peace that made the German Chancellor's politicking in West Germany look provincial. Harold Macmillan described him as a 'strange quixotic figure, half politician, half priest'.[54] Adenauer's winter travels also took him to Luxembourg and Switzerland, where he met the Italian Prime Minister, Alcide de Gasperi. Plans were produced galore, most of them by that master of European blueprints, Jean Monnet. By 1950 one plan under discussion was for an international administration – a so-called High Authority – that would govern not only the Ruhr area, but also coal- and steel-producing areas in the three Benelux countries, West Germany, France and Italy.

On 9 May 1950 Schuman held a press conference in Paris announcing the plans for a High Authority for a European Coal and Steel Community. The Americans were encouraging. Britain's Foreign Office, under a then ailing Ernest Bevin, was taken by complete surprise. But on 11 May Britain was invited to join. The Labour government, having recently nationalized the coal industry, felt this would be impossible. So Britain stayed out, while Germany entered a new European community of six members. The European Coal and Steel Community was created by a Treaty of Paris on 18 April 1951. Monnet became president of the High Authority. But it was Adenauer's politics which had created it. The new Germany was now part of a new European community.[55]

4 De Gaulle's Europe

Had it been presented to General Charles de Gaulle, who saw himself as St Joan of Arc, he would never have signed the Treaty of Rome, which created the European Economic Community of the 'Six'. But the Treaty came into operation on 1 January 1958. The General returned to power four months later: it was too late. So, like Adenauer, here was another case of a wartime statesman – the most nationalistic of them all – leading Europe into a community that hardly corresponded to his intentions. Such is the relationship of the individual, even one of de Gaulle's stature, to history.

One cannot escape the peculiar nature of his character, which was to make a unique contribution to the Community as it continued to develop. Pierre Mendès-France, certainly the most imaginative statesman of the post-war Fourth Republic, made the mistake of disliking de Gaulle; Mendès-France was the lesser for it. Yet he picked out those features familiar to anyone who crossed the path of 'France's policeman'. 'De

Gaulle', said Mendès–France, 'is a solitary figure. There was his height, his intelligence, and his shyness: he overcame the lot, and then overcame France. 'You have to understand there is a madnees at the root of de Gaulle,' said Mendès–France.[56]

For a man who considered himself the personification of 'France', the internationalism of the European Common Market must have been a definition of hell. Yet he could not abandon the alliance he had made with Adenauer, another 'founding father' out of tune with the Common Market. Despite every effort, he was unable to destroy it (he had kept up a remorseless campaign against Schuman's European projects and had stated publicly that the Treaty of Rome implied the loss of French national sovereignty). But the Common Market, which came into operation in January 1958, was a product of a war that had demolished many a nation state east of the Rhine, and had made the birth of others impossible. De Gaulle simply had to live with that change.

As he did with his change in physique since the days of the war. The alteration in his appearance, it is true, added to his grandeur and made his embodiment of France more convincing than ever. His stomach had expanded to royal dimensions. His neck had disappeared under a ruffle of Bourbon double chins. His nose now had the sharpness of a Napoleonic eagle. His eyes were as eager and as Gallican as they ever had been, now surrounded by Saturnine rings. The top of his head was no larger than it had been when Churchill's civil servants played with his little kepi in the waiting room at Downing Street. He was no longer Saint-Cyr's 'asparagus' or Alexander's 'ramrod'; he was Obelisk, without the smile.

Resistance leaders, who had made the highly dangerous trip to London during the war, were astonished by his stiff manners, his lack of welcoming warmth. So it was when Dean Acheson – Truman's former Secretary of State – met Charles de Gaulle in the Elysée Palace on 22 October 1962. American U-2 spy planes had just confirmed French intelligence reports that the Soviets were building nuclear missiles in Cuba. Acheson noted in his secret account: 'I crossed the room and he extended his hand: "Your President has done me a great honour sending me such a distinguished emissary."' Acheson was totally taken aback; according to his account, he was stunned into silence. 'Then he returned to his desk,' Acheson continues his report. 'He pointed to an armchair, crossed his hands, and looked at me. He did not say "I hope your President is well," or "Did you have a pleasant voyage?", no, nothing of that sort. I had asked to see him, I had a message for him, then let us get down to business.'[57] It was the same man, Charles de Gaulle of France.

Resistance leaders twenty years before had been surprised how little this gangling man sitting opposite them was concerned with events inside France. That was because, quite unpretentiously (it was a position he had been forced into), 'France' depended not on geography, but on where de Gaulle was. *La Résistance de l'intérieur* was obviously an ally of France. But it was not France. *La Résistance de l'extérieur* was made up of what France ought to have been before she was betrayed by the *politiciens de l'intérieur*, the men of the Third Republic who had been mere provincials, white serviettes tucked under their collars during long hours of lunch, who simply never knew and never wanted to know anything of the world beyond their restaurant, their office chairs, their petty honours; they could not comprehend the 'idea' of France.

De Gaulle had resigned the Presidency of the Republic in January 1946 because the Constitution of the Fourth Republic no longer corresponded to his 'idea' of France; it was the Third Republic all over again, a 'Republic of parties'. There would be a musical chairs of ministries, de Gaulle predicted, and the President would exert no authority; France would descend into the same irresponsible chaos that had made her so weak in the 1930s. The prognosis was correct. De Gaulle left.

In the meantime the world moved on, while the provincial-minded politicians continued to manoeuvre and chatter in their delightful provincial restaurants. The Iron Curtain was slammed across half Europe. The Americans adopted their creed of 'containment', as Truman expressed it in his new policy statement – a policy that failed to take into account the enormity of the area 'contained'. The Soviets – who for so nationally minded a man as Charles de Gaulle, always remained 'the Russians' – continually jumped the line, keeping up the expansionist policy they had first put in motion in alliance with the Nazis in 1939. Their first forays across the 'containment' line were into the Asian sphere, where the Americans were ill-prepared; 'the Russians' had tried Berlin and dismally failed. In 1950 they moved on Korea and Indochina. The propaganda was Leninist, anti-imperialist, anti-Fascist. It was most effective because the Americans themselves pretended to be 'anti-colonialist'. When they started to defend the French in Indochina, they did not have a leg to stand on. 'Containment' was much too sophisticated, too strategic an idea for the average American to comprehend. Many Americans, like many Europeans, joined the 'Peace Movement' that had been set up by the Cominform in 1950 at Stockholm. Western members of the Peace Movement marched in the streets of London, Paris and Rome against the military activities of their nations against 'National Liberation Fronts' in Asia and Africa, thousands of miles away; they said not a word about the military occupation then terrorizing the eastern half of Europe, in some places barely three hundred miles away.

America continued to pose as the 'anti-colonial' power, although this became increasingly problematic as she came up against the 'National Liberation Fronts' of her old Communist ally. In her European sphere of influence it was not so difficult: there, it was basically an argument, corresponding to the truth, of the 'free world' against the 'Communist world'. But how could America, in the rest of the world, support 'colonialists' in the name of the 'free world'? The Communists had the upper hand as far as propaganda was concerned.

La République est morte à Dien Bien Phu was the title of a wonderful film documentary which showed how the French Fourth Republic descended into chaos after the devastating – and horrifying – defeat of the American-supported French army at Dien Bien Phu in 1954 at the hands of Ho Chi Minh's National Liberation Front. After that, Eisenhower began to engage Americans in the eastern part of Indochina, Vietnam. The switch from American 'anti-colonialism' to 'defence of the free world' was a gradual process in South-East Asia. In the meantime, Communist hopping of the 'containment' line spread to other parts of the world. George Kennan, the inventor of 'containment', but nonetheless a realist who could see that the developing local wars throughout the world had no limit, began advocating a new policy of 'disengagement'; it corresponded better to America's vast, but limited, material power; however it was not appreciated by all the powers-that-be in Washington. Eisenhower's politics as President were identical to his strategy as Second World War commander-in-chief: a combination of withdrawal and stand-fast – he had no politics at all.

De Gaulle, at that time, remained shut up in his isolated farmhouse in Champagne, at Colombey-les-Deux-Eglises. He wrote his war memoirs, which are to this day among the best of this genre. The personification of France as he considered himself, legitimate authority was – for him – not the vote, the compromise of a constitution, the arguments in parliament, the perpetual turnover of governments made up of essentially the same people; it lay in his 'certain idea' of France: a constitution that gave him, Joan of Arc, the authority to govern. His first attempt to create a constitution to his own taste, with the formation of the Rassemblement du Peuple Français (RPF) after a rallying call in 1946 at Bayeux (the first town to be liberated in 1944), was a fiasco. Gangs of the RPF fought street battles with gangs of the French Communist Party in 1947. At least this showed that both groups were militants outside the political status quo.

De Gaulle always had an ambivalent feeling towards his domestic enemies, and it cannot be denied that, as during the war, there existed in de Gaulle's grand heart a soft spot for the Communists. But time was moving on. In March 1958, as the Fourth Republic lurched from one major crisis to another, he told the British ambassador to Paris, Gladwyn Jebb – like himself a believer in national sovereignty – that, before this corrupt regime collapsed, he himself would be dead. Jebb noticed tears pouring down his round Gallic cheeks.[58]

Yet the Second World War, and its failure to find a peace settlement, caught up with him. Behind the Nazi-Soviet Pact of 1939 lay a plan of directing the Axis forces, including the Soviets, southwards in a way that would guarantee dominion of the Eurasian 'world island'. Stalin never expected the Nazis, in the final throes of bourgeois capitalism, to hold on to their imperial share; while Hitler was already planning his invasion of Russia, of the Caucasus, and an eventual link-up with Japan in the Indian Ocean.

After Stalingrad and Kursk Stalin realized he would be able to achieve his own expressed aims in the Pact without his Fascist imperialist ally. These aims emerged again, in full clarity, at Potsdam: fortifications in the Turkish Straits and Soviet mandates in North Africa. At the same time, Stalin had nothing but contempt for the military strength of his temporary 'Western Allies'. Marxist doctrine taught him that they would be forever locked in imperialist, capitalist combat. Stalin joined first the Americans, the strongest among them, to knock out the weakest of the 'Three', Britain, in the area that mattered most to the British, the Middle East. For the first decade after Potsdam, Truman and then Eisenhower formed a peculiar alliance with the Soviets on this one issue: to oust the British from the Middle East. The 'anti-colonialist' Americans were equally determined to get the French out of North Africa. These policies not only failed to win favour among the Arabs but also ran counter to the American project of containment. It was a fatal flaw in American strategic and political thought – already apparent during the Second World War – which haunts America's position in the Middle East to this day.

Stalin's first move south was made in that critical year of changing fortunes, 1943. In his classic manner, he set up official residents and 'illegals' in Cairo, which at the time still served as British headquarters for their Mediterranean operations. Stalin scored some brilliant successes. Cairo became one of the chief beehives of British Soviet agents. They persuaded Churchill to switch his allegiance from Mihailović to Tito in Yugoslavia and also spread the propaganda message to the Americans that the British were simply pursuing their 'imperial' interests in the Mediterranean. When the British first went bankrupt in 1947 it was the Americans who had to send forces into Greece and Turkey. It was a pattern that would repeat itself again and again in the eastern Mediterranean.

Moscow, since 1943, had been considering an alliance with Arab nationalists. But even after the death of Stalin problems of Marxist-Leninist principle troubled competing schools within the Politburo: Arab leaders were not even capitalists, they were still trapped in the feudal stage of history, while the Arab 'masses' were ignorant of their historical interests. It would require a more progressive, modernist state – an independent Israel – to impel the Arabs into modernity and thus develop the means, with the help of Soviet 'National Liberation Fronts', to throw off the British imperialist yoke. The French, mere pawns in Stalin's game, would be thrown out, too. This was the reasoning behind the Soviet Union's initial backing of an independent Israel – which not even the World Congress of Jews in the United States supported.

Stalin's double aim was to undermine the British position in the Middle East and, at the same time, to push the Arabs, with the help of the Israeli challenge, into modernity. A minority in the Politburo even believed that Israel, with its system of *kibbutzim* communities, could be gradually turned into a Communist state. Stalin's own 'anti-cosmopolitan' and 'anti-Zionist' campaigns, much more in line with Nazi policy, demonstrated that this was not a majority view. For Stalin and his successors support for Israel was simply a first step southwards.

The first surprise incursion across America's world 'containment' line, in Korea, was not an enormous success. Moreover the French, in Vietnam, proved much more resilient than expected, even though their defeat did finally bring despair to the French army – an army much in need of success so soon after the European war. Both Korea and Vietnam ended with partition, not at all what the Soviets wanted.

While the French army may have been approaching despair in a world that was not at peace, an element of despondency crept into the Kremlin in the early 1950s. In the final year of his life Stalin sent a peace note to the British, French and the Americans in which he called for a Peace Conference that would finally settle the Second World War and would include a treaty with a unified, 'neutral' Germany. Adenauer, who had by now committed himself to a Western European community, smelt a rat. The three occupying Western Powers complied with Adenauer's wishes and never answered. Given the appalling domestic situation in the Soviet Union – the growth of the slave camps and the spread of the police state – this did indeed look very much like one of Hitler's 'peace proposals'. But the 'Peace Movement' in the West thought the world had lost its chance for a final peace settlement.

That same year, 1952, a group of frustrated young Egyptian officers, under Gamal Abdel Nasser, overthrew the regime of King Farouk in Cairo. It looked as if Soviet strategy was working. But Stalin died – or was murdered – a few months later. Khrushchev had Beria shot six months after that. Then began the war of the long knives inside the Politburo. It put Khrushchev in a predicament: too expansionist a foreign policy threatened his limited powers; too pacifist a policy invited attack from the hawks among his murderous colleagues. So Khrushchev – in keeping with his temperament – wavered between a policy of 'peaceful coexistence' and war with the Fascist imperialists of the West. The new group of colonels in Cairo seemed, furthermore, dubious allies to the Marxist Ukrainian peasant that was Khrushchev; after all, several of them had been educated in English imperialist schools; and nearly all of them had supported the Nazis during the war, including Nasser's faithful assistant, and later President of Egypt, Anwar Sadat.

Yet gradually the stakes began to mount in the Middle East. Anti-colonialist America and anti-imperialist Russia began competing for the favour of the colonels; it was Khrushchev's larger bribes for the Aswan Dam – 365 feet high and three miles long, and intended to regulate irrigation throughout the Lower Nile – that handed the prize of Egypt to the Soviets. In 1955 the Soviets initiated a great Peace Conference at Geneva, a sure sign, as Adenauer pointed out, that the Soviets were preparing some sort of *coup* along the line of 'containment'. It came on 26 July 1956 when Nasser announced he was nationalizing the Suez Canal, one of Britain's last strongholds in the Middle East.

'This, O citizens, is the battle in which we are now involved,' said Nasser in a radio address to all Arabs. 'It is a battle against imperialism . . . and a battle against Israel, the vanguard of imperialism.' As a warning to the French he mentioned Ferdinand de Lesseps, the French engineer who had built the canal, and noted that he was not just looking eastwards: 'We can never say that the battle of Algeria is not our battle.'[59]

It was the perpetual threat of Communist aggression, combined with the Algerian war and Nasser's nationalization of the Suez Canal, that eventually opened the door to de Gaulle's post-war Europe.

In the world of European imperialism, Algeria had always been something of a curiosity. It had been established for the French back in the reign of Charles X, through the private negotiations of a couple of wealthy Jewish merchants. King Charles was the most reactionary of post-Revolutionary kings and he was thrown out of France in a classic Parisian revolution in 1830. The new 'King of the French', Louis-Philippe, set up

Algeria in the name of the French. But Louis-Philippe also lost his job in an even more violent revolution, in 1848, which led to the establishment of the French Second Republic. There is no republic that so swells the democratic social heart of the left – *démoc-soc* as it called itself at the time – in France than the Second Republic of 1848. The Constitution of the Second Republic incorporated Algeria into metropolitan France, and divided it up into three metropolitan departments.

The workers of Paris were famously poor during the years of the Second Republic. Lafayette and his poetic colleagues in the government set up 'national workshops' to fulfil their promise to the brave artisan fighters of their 'right to work'. The workshops were a total fiasco. So government turned to another outlet: Algeria. The first *colons* of Algeria were the radical workers of Paris. They were Parisians who not only thought they stood for France, but, like de Gaulle, thought they *were* France. Algeria was divided into plots and Algeria *became* France – not a colony.

That was why French Socialists, for generations, had such powerful ties with French Algeria; it was a part of France, a part of the *patrie*, an integral part of the French Socialist movement. This was still true in the 1950s. Among the most fanatical supporters of keeping Algeria a part of France were the French Socialists. Not of course the Communists, who took their orders from the 'anti-imperialist' Cominform; but the Communists had left the government in 1947 and were now pursuing an insurgency stage of political action which they expected would lead eventually to takeover. There was also an extreme right that had developed in the post-war years, the Poujadists, made up largely of artisans. The post-war Fourth Republic began looking most unstable.

Ironically, the first major Arab revolts against the French *colons* took place in Algiers on 8 May 1945, VE-Day, as Europeans, in their despondent manner, celebrated their victory over Hitler. Twenty-seven *colons* were hacked to death that day, and the next day another twenty-five met the same fate. The French army, based in Constantine, reacted out of all proportion to the crimes, shooting down mothers and children in front of their families and wiping out whole villages with cannon and machine-guns. German and Italian prisoners of war were employed to help in the massacre. So, with the official announcement of peace in Europe, Europe's war spilt over into Africa. By 1956 the Algerian rebellion had developed into a full-scale war. On the French side was an embittered army that had not forgotten 1940 and, in addition, had suffered under horrifying conditions a defeat in 1954 at Dien Bien Phu, an isolated peninsula in North Vietnam. On the other was one of those 'National Liberation Fronts' that would do as much for the liberation of peoples as the Communist Partisans had done for the Eastern Europeans. Ironic indeed was the fact that this new war would take place in the one area in North Africa that had represented de Gaulle's growing power base for a Free France. It was this that created all the passion that went into the war and the determination of whole sections of the new French army to keep Algeria French. '*Algérie française!*' cried the French army and its supporters: it would be a mistake to imagine that those who proclaimed this were simply reactionary 'imperialists'; many indeed had their origins in the left. Georges Bidault, the former Resistance leader, was among them. So were several members of the SFIO, the French Socialist party of the day.

In 1956 the French Prime Minister was Guy Mollet, a former professor of English literature. Though a Marxist Socialist, he would have nothing to do with the Communists, primarily because of their unyielding position on 'imperialism'. Mollet was just as uncompromising on the other side: Algeria was a part of the Republic, he claimed in the fashion typical of the French left, and would stay so for ever. His hardline position explained why he remained the longest-serving prime minister of the Fourth Republic; his government lasted seventeen whole months. Beyond the defence of Republican institutions, he had one great passion: he wanted the British, the true liberators of France, to become part of the developing new Europe.

One year before Mollet entered office the Foreign Ministers of the six members of the Coal and Steel Community met in the Sicilian town of Messina ostensibly to coordinate the ongoing activities of the Community. It turned, however, into a marathon of a meeting that led eventually to the creation of the European Economic Community, or the 'Common Market'. A committee had been set up under the Belgian Foreign Minister, Paul-Henri Spaak, which over the coming months developed a whole programme of economic integration, including a levelling of tariff barriers within the Community and a common customs policy with the outside world. Whitehall dismissed Spaak's work as a piece of 'mysticism' that would get nowhere; a country like protectionist France, it believed, would never surrender its sovereignty to the kind of Court, Commission and Council that Spaak was proposing.[60] But Whitehall's prognoses on Europe were always 100 per cent wrong: France and the other five members did eventually sign up to the Treaty of Rome, which created the Common Market, in March 1957.

Mollet had been very keen on British membership; in fact he could not imagine the Community operating without British participation. He thought this could be achieved through a military cooperation that would solve both the Suez crisis and the Algerian war in one go. What he did not count on was the hostility of Eisenhower's 'anti-colonial' America.

Khrushchev, detecting a split in the Western Alliance, poured arms into Egypt, part of which went into the Egyptian army while an enormous portion was shipped off to the National Liberation Front in Algeria. With both the Soviets and the Americans against them, it seemed most unlikely that Britain and France would get support in the United Nations Security Council, though in October 1956 both European countries made immense efforts at negotiating a maritime conference that would place the canal under an international authority. On 29 October, encouraged by the French, Israel invaded the Sinai. Further desperate negotiations were attempted. Khrushchev threatened to atom bomb Britain and, in a further show of bravado, sent tanks into Hungary to crush an anti-Communist rebellion that had developed there. The link between Soviet actions in Eastern Europe and Soviet-supported 'decolonization' in North Africa became all too obvious. On 4 November British and French forces entered the Sinai.

But since the Second World War the Americans had engineered – through the good offices of the late Dr Harry Dexter White and his peculiar administration, within the US Treasury, of the Lend-Lease programme – control over British sterling reserves. When the British and French entered the Sinai there was, quite miraculously, a run on the pound. Within a period of twenty-four hours, Britain faced complete bankruptcy. The Americans stood aside. Eden, who had only replaced Churchill as Prime Minister one year before, threw in the towel. Eden was a sick man and he was no Churchill. British and French forces were withdrawn after less than forty-eight hours on the ground.

It was the end of the British presence in the Middle East – a fact applauded by both Khrushchev and Eisenhower. The parallel between Eisenhower's behaviour over Suez and his abandonment of Central Europe in the last months of the Second World War showed the world that he was still absolutely blind to his own country's interests. In less than two years American marines had landed in Lebanon: America now had to defend not just Greece and Turkey, but the whole Middle East from Khrushchev's incursions. There remained partitioned Korea and partitioned Vietnam in the Far East. The over-extension of American forces began to look alarming.

Britain had been humiliated by her American ally. But in France the situation was much worse. The army conducted a *coup d'état* in Algeria and set up a 'Committee of Public Safety', reminiscent of the French Revolution. The outbreak of the Algerian war led to the collapse of the

Fourth Republic and the advent of de Gaulle's Fifth Republic – a collapse brought about by an extreme left in France cooperating with an extreme right: a combination of Socialism with the forces of French nationalism. (One had witnessed such a combination earlier in Europe – in Hitler's Germany.) The movement of rebellion spread to Corsica. Mollet's government collapsed in May 1957 and then began a year of total governmental instability, an 'absurd ballet' as de Gaulle called it. The last government of the Fourth Republic under Pierre Pfimlin was no government at all. As André Siegfried, the great politicologue, noted, 'France was administered rather than governed.' The reporter, Alexander Werth, put it much more starkly: 'The police in Corsica had failed completely to deal with the *putsch* there. The Paris police were an uncertain factor. M. Pfimlin's Minister of War had no army; his Minister of the Interior had no police; and his Minister for Algeria could not even go there, since he would have been arrested on the spot.'[61] The hour of de Gaulle – patriot, *dirigiste*, the man of the French state and no friend of such international European creations as the Common Market – had arrived.

De Gaulle was certainly created by the army. Or to put it more crudely, it was the military *coup d'état* in Algiers of May 1958 that launched de Gaulle's return to power. Gaullists had been preparing the stage for the *coup*, most particularly Jacques Soustelle, Jacques Chaban-Delmas and Léon Delbecq, after it became evident that France no longer had a government. It is also interesting to note how, after he had eventually manoeuvred his way into the Elysée, de Gaulle insisted on being addressed as '*Mon Général*' and not '*Monsieur le Président*' – though he only had two stars on his kepi, the result of a last-minute promotion just before the fall of France in 1940. But de Gaulle had never been a great fan of the army, nor had the reverse been the case. 'Committees of Public Safety' were quite out of keeping with de Gaulle's high idea of national sovereignty and it was clear that they were to be dismissed with the same thoroughness as the partisans of the Resistance in August 1944. '*Moi, la France,*' was a philosophy he understood, but an Algeria – however radical its origins – that did not bow to the authority of the President of the Republic would never be tolerated. Even more pressing was the loyalty of the army to the civil institutions in Paris. This was de Gaulle's entire preoccupation during the first four years of the Fifth Republic, from 1958 to 1962. De Gaulle pulled out of Algeria because he realized that he could never subject Algeria to French authority in Paris, and most particularly because he would not be able to enforce obedience on a French army in Algeria. He knew the situation very well. After all, it was through Algeria that he himself had been able to undermine the authority of Vichy. For the first four years after de Gaulle's accession to power he had to fight a war to re-establish the French state; it was not a war for Algeria, not a war against the Communists, not a war against extremist parties of the left and the right; it was a war against his own French army, and to win it he was prepared to kill – and be killed. It has been estimated that there were, during those four years, at least thirty attempts on de Gaulle's life, mostly by officers of the army who considered themselves defenders of freedom. De Gaulle correctly believed that only the civil state, backed up by the law, could defend freedom; for an army to run the state was the swiftest route to tyranny. The army officers who shot at de Gaulle were not evil men. But they were not statesmen either. De Gaulle responded to their attacks in kind. The most famous assassination attempt was on the evening of 22 August 1962 when twelve men, armed with automatic weapons, fired on the General's car as it passed the crossroads at Petit-Clamart. The car was riddled with bullets. One bullet missed the General's head by less than an inch. But the only casualty was the chicken in the boot which Madame la Générale (popularly known as 'Tante Yvonne') was transporting home for dinner. Colonel Jean-Marie Bastien-Thiry, the leader of the commandos and a saint of a man by disposition, who truly believed he was fighting for the cause of freedom, was shot at the Fort d'Ivry on 11 March 1963 as he turned his prayer beads in his fingers. 'The French need martyrs,' commented de Gaulle. 'I have given them Bastien-Thiry. That fellow, he had the makings of a martyr . . . He merited it.' It is said to have been one of the most melancholy affairs of de Gaulle's life.[62]

'Why on earth do you imagine a man of sixty-seven would want to set off on a career as a dictator?' commented de Gaulle with a shrug of his huge shoulders at a tense press conference on 19 May 1958. It was the first time he had spoken in public since the army rebellion in Algeria had broken out a month earlier. He insisted that, far from being a threat to civil liberties, he was their defender.[63]

During his first four years de Gaulle had little to say about the Common Market; his concern was with re-establishing civil authority in Paris, which had totally crumbled during the last miserable year of the Fourth Republic, and the national sovereignty of France. But there was a new Realpolitik at play here which explained – much more than the federalist dreams and plans of the idealists – why the momentum of the European Community kept moving forward. Specifically, France alone did not have the power to pursue the sovereign policies that de Gaulle had in his sights. Suez had been a disaster for France. It completely undermined her hopes of holding on to a French Algeria; it weakened her position vis-à-vis the Soviet Union (which had been exactly Khrushchev's aim); and it destroyed her confidence in the United States. Following his wartime experience, de Gaulle had never trusted the USA, which had since 1940 attempted to undermine de Gaulle's Free French movement. Until the end of 1942 the United States had even tried to negotiate with Vichy, in the hope that she would switch sides and become the pliant ally of America's Europe. De Gaulle had nothing but contempt for Eisenhower: he had observed how Eisenhower had abandoned the whole of Central Europe to the Soviets by insisting on withdrawal from Eastern Germany; he considered Eisenhower's betrayal over Suez as a second withdrawal in the face of Soviet pressure. De Gaulle was certain it would happen again. And indeed it did. Eisenhower showed willingness to talk again with the Soviets about the creation of a united 'neutral' Germany. This may have represented a long-sought peace settlement of the Second World War, but it was not the peace settlement de Gaulle wanted – it would have meant a Europe dominated by the Communists. That was also Adenauer's view. De Gaulle and Adenauer became inseparable allies. But the legitimacy of Adenauer's Federal Republic depended upon the institutions of the European Community. De Gaulle, in his ongoing battle with American hegemony, may have been ready to pull out of NATO; but he could never, because of his dependence on Adenauer, pull out of the European Community.

De Gaulle, with his impressive memory, would – like Marcel Proust – base his principal ideas and policies on events that went far back in his life. A small image, established in his mind decades gone by, could become a centrepiece of his work – the work of sustaining the national sovereignty of France. Thus: 'How is it possible to govern a country with 328 types of cheese?' The phrase comes from one of his childhood schoolbooks. It stuck in his mind and remained a fundamental belief at the moment he founded the Fifth Republic: France was anarchic and basically ungovernable; only Charles de Gaulle could save the Republic, as he had done, alone, in 1940. Or again: 'Europe is a Continent that stretches from the Atlantic to the Urals.' The phrase is from the same childhood schoolbook. But that was de Gaulle's Europe, which he could not reject because of his necessary alliance with Adenauer.

It got Adenauer very worried when he received an invitation to de Gaulle's isolated home at Colombey-les-Deux-Eglises for September 1958. It was a singular honour, assured the Fifth Republic's first Foreign Minister, Maurice Couve de Murville. Adenauer continued to be anxious as he drove in his grand Mercedes-Benz across the flat plains of Champagne where the bodies of so many Germans and Frenchmen lay buried. Was de Gaulle's Europe going to include the Soviet Union? One of the most regular visitors to Colombey during de Gaulle's wilderness years of the Fourth Republic had been the Soviet ambassador to Paris. The Soviet Union would always remain one of de Gaulle's cards in his game with the European Community – but only as the Ottoman Turks had been for Francis I in the early sixteenth century. De Gaulle fought Communists at home by flirting with Communist powers abroad. His Communist enemies were a card, but not the end-game. There remained Adenauer, the pillar of de Gaulle's Europe.

There was another schoolboy phrase that stuck in his mind, a mind that pre-dated the First World War – '*L'Europe des Etats*'. Even in 1910 the 'Europe of States' did not include all Europe. It was the Europe of 'sovereign states', that is, the ones that dominated all the others. To Adenauer's dismay, de Gaulle confirmed this idea only one month after his luncheon with the German Chancellor at Colombey, when de Gaulle gave a speech at Grenoble announcing that the only reality in Europe was that of the nation state. For Adenauer this was pure myth, blown to pieces under his own eyes during the last months of the war. But '*L'Europe des Etats*' had its appeal in those western parts of Europe that clung to the myth of national victory and total national sovereignty; those parts of Europe that had been through the least upheaval and had their school-book maps of Europe and the world brightly coloured and divided up with clear black national frontiers. Nobody east of the Rhine after 1945 lived in such a Europe. But chaotic France and declining Britain wanted to believe that it was so.

The Suez crisis had ousted Eden and brought in a new Conservative Prime Minister, Harold Macmillan, the former 'Viceroy of the Mediterranean', who had swum naked on the shores of Algeria while his friend, Charles de Gaulle, sat stiffly on the rocks in his brigadier general's uniform. Macmillan had saved the General from Roosevelt's determination to destroy him. Macmillan had protected de Gaulle from Churchill's wrath. In fact it was Macmillan, while Minister Resident in Algeria, who had set de Gaulle on his fantastic political career.

Macmillan, like many of his leading countrymen, also believed in a Europe of 'nation states' – basically Britain and France. But when de Gaulle spoke of '*L'Europe des Etats*' the British press got troubled. A 'Europe of States' sounded dangerously like a 'United States of Europe'. So they deliberately mistranslated him and quoted him as saying: the '*Europe des Patries*'. De Gaulle went out of his way to explain that he had never used such a phrase; it was not the *patrie* that was important to de Gaulle (this was a *démoc-soc* idea of 1848 and the source of all anarchy as far as the General was concerned); what mattered was the State – *et l'Etat, c' est moi*.

In the early 1960s Macmillan, about as enthusiastic about the idea of 'Community' as de Gaulle, found himself pulled into the new game of post-war Europe. Like de Gaulle, he could not avoid it. Like de Gaulle and like Adenauer, he turned out to be one of the founding fathers, despite himself. But that is where the war had led him.

5 Macmillan's Europe

Algeria dominated all colonial affairs by 1960, despite more troubles in the Middle East, a new civil war in the Belgian Congo, demands for independence in Nyasaland, Northern and Southern Rhodesia, and murderous events in South Africa, which was still a member of the Commonwealth. For Macmillan it was the 'multi-racial Commonwealth' – the name 'Empire' was dropped in the early 1950s – that would provide the main wall against the challenge of Communism. 'Though we may be able to reduce tensions here and there from time to time,' he told the Australian Prime Minister, Robert Menzies, before a huge audience in Sydney in February 1958, 'the great struggle and conflict of ideas will continue. We must "lean up against them" – steadily and firmly.'[64]

The great surge in movements for independence throughout the world after the Second World War was due to a number of factors. The belief in London was that the process was inevitable and that this indeed was the purpose of the Commonwealth: to make the transition manageable and avoid bloodshed. There was nothing like Algeria, an officially integrated part of the mother country, in the Commonwealth. But Macmillan, as much as de Gaulle, was aware that 'National Liberation Fronts' were not innocent parties. 'Anti-colonial' America would be confronted with the same challenge. But if the Americans were not willing to support the Europeans, the Europeans would have to decide, particularly after the Suez affair, whether it was wise to stay on in their old colonies or not. De Gaulle seems to have had a clearer picture of reality than Macmillan. Both before and after he came to power in May 1958, he was sending the same message through to Macmillan. At one point de Gaulle's Prime Minister, Michel Debré, told Macmillan's son-in-law, Julian Amery, in the bluntest manner that the French and the British, as the chief colonial powers, would have to decide *jointly* to stay in Africa or *both* clear out.[65] Events would suggest that some informal coordination between the two countries was in fact operating in the late 1950s and early '60s. Thus, in 1959, when de Gaulle shocked the French army with an offer of self-determination to the Algerians, Macmillan decided to follow suit. It was no accident that

British negotiations for entry into the Common Market started up at the same time.

As part of the plan to set up an economically viable and peacefully independent British Africa, Clement Attlee's government had planned a Central African Federation (CAF) between Nyasaland, Northern Rhodesia and Southern Rhodesia. It was set up in 1953 by Churchill's Conservative government. The idea was to create a purely economic federation that would combine Northern Rhodesia's copper belt with Nyasaland's labour resources and Southern Rhodesia's rich agriculture. The scheme obviously had been partly inspired by the European Coal and Steel Community, and, in turn, was at the root of the British attempt to counter the more politically oriented European Economic Community (EEC) with a purely European Free Trade Area (EFTA).

The CAF proved a disaster. By 1959 Nyasaland was demonstrating, violently, for independence; Dr Kenneth Kaunda had taken over the northern half of Northern Rhodesia with a 'National Liberation Front'.

In the first weeks of 1960 – as French whites killed French whites in the streets of Algiers – Macmillan made a second trip through British Africa, culminating in Cape Town, the capital of apartheid South Africa. The whole purpose of this voyage appears to have been to prepare British Africa for the kind of shock de Gaulle had delivered to Algeria six months earlier. He would do it in a carefully prepared speech he delivered to the South African Parliament on 3 February 1960. Macmillan was in a high state of nerves. Both reporters and the public at large were aware that something major was about to happen. Shortly before he made his speech the Prime Minister was led to a lavatory, where he vomited. But the speech itself is generally considered the grandest of his lifetime. It was, in a Churchillian vein, broadly historical in style. 'Ever since the break-up of the Roman Empire,' he said, 'one of the constant facts of political life in Europe has been the emergence of independent nations.' 'Today', he went on, 'the same thing is happening in Africa.' Throughout his six-week trip he had noted a rise in 'African national consciousness'. Then he pronounced the most famous phrase of all, said to be borrowed from Stanley Baldwin: 'The wind of change is blowing through this continent, and, whether we like it or not, this growth of national consciousness is a political fact. We must all accept it as a fact, and our national policies must take account of it.'[66]

The growth of the nation state: Harold Macmillan's whole Edwardian education had been built on this historical premise; so had de Gaulle's. It was not conceivable to him that the world, Africa included, could go in any other direction. After the Second World War it was clear that a 'wind of change' was blowing through the world. But it was not clear that the globe was going to be divided up into neatly independent, sovereign nation states. With the hindsight of fifty years it would appear that this would not be the future for Africa. And, despite its present-day enthusiasts, the sovereign nation state has been losing its focus in Europe since the perpetration of the Second World War's horrors – tens of millions of 'Displaced Persons', refugees, hundreds, if not thousands, of concentration camps spread across Eastern Europe and onwards into Siberia, frontiers established solely by force of arms, and no peace settlement.

The two proudest defenders of a Europe built on sovereign nation states were the two oldest, Britain and France. After Suez, the two went in opposite directions. France went enthusiastically 'into Europe', with the idea, as it eventually emerged under de Gaulle, that it would be sovereign France that led Europe against both the expansive Soviet Union and the untrustworthy United States. Britain under Macmillan turned to the 'Special Relationship' she had with the United States. In January 1957, on taking office, he listed his six main aims: restoring the people's confidence in the government; clearing up the Middle East after the Suez mess; restoring the alliance with the United States; solving the perpetual nightmare of Britain's trade imbalance; cutting the costs of defence; and providing a future for the Commonwealth. There was no mention of Europe. The signing of the Treaty of Rome in March 1957 got no mention in his diaries and when the Common Market came into force he was travelling the Commonwealth.

The term 'Special Relationship' with the United States only came into political currency with the Suez crisis – that is, the very moment Eisenhower jilted Britain. This is indeed the sort of thing that sometimes occurs between lovers, and it demonstrates how much emotion, rather than reason, lay in the phrase. 'We are still a great power,' Macmillan said on television when he became Prime Minister. That could only be due to the 'Special Relationship'.

It was spoken in Britain with a piety that resembled some dogma of the Anglican Church, or a bewigged magistrate's introductory phrase on entering court – as if it were an age-old maxim of the British constitution. But no nineteenth-century British statesman would have ever employed it; one cannot imagine it dropping from the lips of Lloyd George during the First World War; most politicians of the inter-war period only spoke of the United States with contempt; and though Roosevelt was a hero in Britain during the Second World War it is rare to find the phrase in Churchill's language – though the phrase is obviously modelled on the supposed wartime friendship that existed between Roosevelt and Churchill.

But why did Macmillan use it on assuming power? It was Britain's substitute for de Gaulle's 'Europe'. Britain could not pretend to be a Great Power after 1956 without the support of the United States, any more than France could make the pretension without Europe. 'Poodle Policy' would have been a more honest description of the price Macmillan paid for American friendship after 1956 – but that would not have been very popular with the electorate. As for the Americans, they only spoke of the 'Special Relationship' at diplomatic receptions.

Roosevelt's policy of undermining the British Empire proved a startling success; his efforts at destroying the sterling area were more effective than anyone in the early 1940s had dared to imagine. France was also reduced to the bankruptcy and helplessness that Roosevelt had worked so hard to achieve. The only major post-war problem that developed out of Roosevelt's wartime strategy was that of his alliance with the Soviet Union: for three generations the United States had to face it alone, not only in Europe, but, owing to the policy of 'containment', at every point in the globe that the Soviet Union chose. And she had to do this without allies.

There was of course NATO. But the United States basically ran NATO – no other ally, as de Gaulle correctly pointed out, held any initiative within it. There was the 'Special Relationship' with Britain. Britain got cheap access to bombers, missiles and nuclear weapons. But it was the United States that held the trigger, not Britain. For the 'Special Relationship' Britain sacrificed more of her national sovereignty than any other nation in Europe.

But 'Super-Mac', as he came to be known as his popularity at home rose, was well aware that he could never sell the idea of a European Community to Britain in the way this had been achieved on the Continent. He put about the idea that Britain had the Commonwealth from which she could buy cheap food. This was true. The Commonwealth steadfastly refused to buy Britain's inefficient industrial produce; nor did the United States; the growing market for Britain's still sluggish output was Europe, which herself was slowly recovering from the destruction of war. By 1960 it became clear to Macmillan, the most Churchillian of the post-war prime ministers, that Britain would not only have to encourage a 'European Movement'; she would have to negotiate her own way into it. But opposite her now stood Gaullist France. De Gaulle, so determined to be Europe's leader, gave Britain two sound '*Nons*', in 1963 and again in 1967. It was only after de Gaulle's death that Britain was able to negotiate an entry into the European Community, in 1973.

★

The last time Harold Macmillan met his old wartime companion, General Charles de Gaulle, whose political position he had done so much to promote, was at an Anglo-French summit at the Château de Rambouillet in December 1962. Macmillan had come to argue that Britain, as a Great Power like France, could do more to preserve national sovereignty within the EEC than outside it; Macmillan was perfectly aware of the General's discomfort with the European Community. De Gaulle was preparing his first 'Non'. 'There cannot be two cocks on the dung-hill' – whether the phrase was the General's or not cannot be proven, but it made the round of the diplomatic chancelleries at the time.[67]

The château was a significant setting. It was where General Leclerc had gathered his 2nd Armoured Division, the *Deuxième DB*, as he awaited de Gaulle's order to march on to liberate Paris; where de Gaulle turned up on 24 August 1944, after disappearing for two days; where the waitress in the local tavern dropped her cocktail tray on the floor when espying the tall figure strolling down the pavement opposite – 'It's de Gaulle! it's de Gaulle! it's de Gaulle!' It was at his bedroom desk in the Château de Rambouillet that de Gaulle wrote his speech that night, '*Paris libérée*.' It was at the Château de Rambouillet that de Gaulle met Macmillan for the last time some eighteen years later.

Their meeting began in a manner reminiscent of the Algerian beaches, although on this occasion Macmillan did not go swimming; he set out on a pheasant shoot. De Gaulle did not participate. He stood stiffly behind his guests and called out loudly every time they missed a bird. No exact record was kept of the discussions. According to Macmillan, de Gaulle repeated the old charges that the Commonwealth and the British people were not ready for entry into the EEC. Macmillan answered that the last six months had proved absolutely the contrary. There were perpetual problems of under-standing. Macmillan's French was perfect but he 'did talk elliptically'. De Gaulle, out of pride, refused to have an interpreter. On the second day de Gaulle became frankly disagreeable. He declared that at the moment France could say 'no' against even the Germans; she could stop policies with which she disagreed. But 'once Britain and all the rest joined the organization things would be different.' According to Macmillan's diary, the Prime Minister indig-nantly retorted that 'If that was really the French view, it ought to have been made clear at the start. It was not fair to have a year's negotiation and then bring forward an objection of principle. De Gaulle seemed rather shaken.' The two men got up and 'on this depressing note our conference ended'. Macmillan recorded that 'we returned to London on 16 December with rather heavy hearts.' De Gaulle's quarrels over *les anglo-saxons* and Europe would never go away. They were in his Gallic blood.

According to de Gaulle himself the scenes at Rambouillet were even more dramatic. Macmillan insisted that Britain had not been reduced to making a choice between America and Europe; Britain was still a Great Power and as such shared interests with France, which he also considered a Great Power. It was an emotionally charged moment that must have brought Macmillan back to his days of collaboration with de Gaulle's Committee in Algiers in 1943 – back even to London in June 1940 and the project to merge France and the United Kingdom into one sovereign nation at war with the Nazis. According to de Gaulle, Macmillan was on the point of tears. 'This poor man,' he later said, 'to whom I had nothing to give, seemed so sad, so beaten that I wanted to put my hand on his shoulder and say to him, as in the Edith Piaf song, "*Ne pleurez pas, milord.*"'[68]

The Second World War had shaken such notions as citizenship, national sovereignty, the nation state and Great Powers to their roots. Assumptions accepted in 1930 had been swept away by 1945. Those who survived the horrors of the war still clung desperately to a world that had gone. As for the horrors, they continued to spill over into distant corners of the globe. There was no peace settlement. There was no treaty with 'Germany' until 1990 as the Communist bloc collapsed. The Second World War was the war that never ended.

Chronology

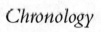

1943	Washington, London, Western Front	Berlin and Central Europe	Moscow and Eastern Front
15–24 Jan	Casablanca Conference – Roosevelt announces war aim of 'unconditional surrender'		
16 Feb	*Service du Travail Obligatoire* (STO, or Forced Labour) introduced by France's Vichy regime Rapid growth of French Resistance, particularly Communist Partisans		
19 April–10 May		Warsaw: Jewish Ghetto Rising and annihilation	
27 May	Paris: CNR (National Council of Resistance) holds inaugural meeting, chaired by Jean Moulin		
30 May	Algiers: CFLN (French Council of National Liberation) established by de Gaulle at the moment of his arrival		
21 June	Lyons: Jean Moulin arrested by Gestapo		
30 June		Warsaw: General Grot-Rowecki, commander of Polish Home Army, arrested by Gestapo	
4 July	Gibraltar: General Sikorski killed in air crash		

4–13 July		Battle of Kursk
11 July	Invasion of Sicily	
14 July	Algiers: de Gaulle completes tour of Algiers with famous speech, 'Let us lift up our heads', which establishes his authority as leader of 'Fighting France'	
17 Aug	Peenemünde, Baltic: RAF raid sets V-2 rocket programme back a year	
13 Oct	Italy declares war on Germany	
19–30 Oct		Moscow Conference of Foreign Ministers
26–29 Nov		Teheran Conference
1944		
1 Jan	Warsaw: Polish Workers' Party (PPR) sets up the Communist 'National Homeland Council' (KRN)	
19 March	Hungary: Germans begin occupation of Hungary Deportation of Hungarian Jews to Auschwitz begins	
28 March	Warm Springs, Georgia: Roosevelt suffers serious heart attack	

1944 cont.	Washington, London, Western Front	Berlin and Central Europe	Moscow and Eastern Front
April			Civil war in the Ukraine
13 April		German press forecasts 'D-Day'	
17 April	Allied Supreme Command orders shift from German 'area bombing' to tactical air support in France in anticipation of D-Day		
21 April	Algiers: by decree, de Gaulle defines local government in France, thereby forestalling both Americans and Communists		
26 April	Marshal Pétain's first and last wartime visit to Paris		
4 June	Liberation of Rome		
6 June	D-Day		
16 June	London: first V-1 ('doodlebug') raids		
22 June			'Operation Bagration' begins in Belorussia: destruction of German Army Group Centre
26 June	Cherbourg captured		
5–19 July	Bretton Woods Conference: creation of International Monetary Fund and World Bank		

20 July		'Wolf's Lair', Rastenburg, East Prussia: attempted assassination of Hitler Berlin: repression of German officers begins	
23 July			Lublin, first Polish town taken by Red Army (Chuikov's Eighth Guards); Stalin sends Polish Committee of National Liberation (PKWN) to administrate
26 July	London: Polish prime minister Mikołajczyk leaves for Moscow	Warsaw: temporary evacuation of Germans halted	
27 July		Warsaw: citizens ordered to 'fortification work' – most refuse	Brest-Litovsk falls to Red Army; Russian forces enter Polish eastern territories
29 July			Chuikov's Eighth Guards reach Magnuszew, 20 miles from Warsaw; confused instructions from Moscow
30 July	Avranches: US breakthrough on western Normandy front		Red Army stalemate before Warsaw
1 Aug	Leclerc's 2e DB lands in Normandy; Polish 1st Armoured Division lands in Normandy	Warsaw: outbreak of Rising (codenamed 'Tempest')	
2 Aug	Hitler orders destruction of Warsaw Hitler orders 'Operation Lüttich' designed to close American corridor at Avranches		

1944 cont.	Washington, London, Western Front	Berlin and Central Europe	Moscow and Eastern Front
4 Aug		Warsaw: Bach-Zelewski launches first attack on city – insurgents lose initiative	
7 Aug	Caen: Canadians break through and head for Falaise Paris: arrival of General von Choltitz, last German military governor		
8 Aug		Warsaw: Monter's appeal to Rokossovsky for 'speedy relief'	
9 Aug		Warsaw: bombing of Old Town begins	Moscow: Polish prime minister Mikołajczyk 'negotiates' with Stalin
10 Aug	Paris: Communists order 'General Strike' (most of Paris already on holiday) Paris: Laval attempts to recall parliamentary chambers of 1940 London: Churchill and Brooke (CIGS) leave for a two-week survey of Italian theatre – no leading commanders in London for next fortnight		
11 Aug	Hitler's final Norman offensive, 'Operation Lüttich', draws to conclusion at Mortain		

15 Aug	Assumption Day: holiday in Paris Paris at midnight: last train of deportees leaves Paris; Pierre Laval leaves for Germany Riviera: American and French troops land ('Operation Anvil', renamed 'Dragoon')
16 Aug	Paris: German military staff, non-combatants and Gestapo withdrawn
18 Aug	Warsaw: all communications, including radio, cut with rest of world
19 Aug	Warsaw: siege of Old Town begins – some citizens escape by sewers Paris: insurrection begins Maupertuis, Normandy: de Gaulle lands in France Granville, Normandy: stormy encounter between de Gaulle and Eisenhower; de Gaulle begins 4-day speaking tour of liberated areas of France Condé, Normandy: Bradley announces decision to separate American forces from British forces in Normandy: for the remainder of war they head in different directions – one of the most decisive strategic decisions of the war
19–21 Aug	2nd Polish Armoured Regiment defends 'Maczuga', closing 'Falaise Pocket' Road opened to Paris
19–22 Aug	Moscow: two Stalin telegrams to Churchill and Roosevelt referring to

1944 cont.	Washington, London, Western Front	Berlin and Central Europe	Moscow and Eastern Front
19–22 Aug cont.			'reckless Warsaw adventure' and 'power-seeking criminals' of Warsaw
20 Aug	Paris: 'ceasefire' between Gaullist Provisional Government and German authorities – never recognized by Communists; Vichy: German authorities order Pétain to leave for Germany		Romania: Russian invasion begins
21 Aug	Paris: Day of the Barricades		
23 Aug	Ecouché: Leclerc's *2e DB* begins (unauthorized) march on Paris	Warsaw: Home Army 'Radio Lightning' opens	Bucharest: palace *coup* topples Antonescu
24 Aug	Paris, 9.23 p.m.: Liberation		
25 Aug	Paris: von Choltitz formally surrenders city; de Gaulle takes second surrender at Gare Montparnasse; Paris, evening: de Gaulle's most famous speech at Hôtel de Ville – '*Paris libéré!*'		
26 Aug	Paris: de Gaulle's procession to Notre Dame	Warsaw: remnants of Underground State and Home Army Command escape to Centre City	
28 Aug		Warsaw: John Ward's morse messages over 'Lightning' received by the BBC. First reports in Western press	

29 Aug–11 Nov	Washington: Dumbarton Oaks Conference – proposals for United Nations Organization drawn up
31 Aug	Warsaw: Monter and remaining troops abandon Old Town
3 Sept	British and Canadians at Antwerp, and isolated to north of city
5 Sept	Soviet Union declares war on Bulgaria
8 Sept	London: first rocket V-2s explode in city / Red Army occupies Bulgaria
9 Sept	Eastern Front: Soviet airfields finally opened to Allied aircraft flying aid to Warsaw
10 Sept	Patton's US Third Army reaches the fortress of Metz, and stalls all autumn, into winter / Hodges' US First Army reaches Aachen fortress lines, and stalls all autumn–winter
11–14 Sept	Second Quebec Conference, 'Octagon'
17 Sept	Arnhem, Netherlands: 'Market-Garden' operation begins
20 Sept	Berlin: Goebbels recommends Hitler to make peace with Moscow
24 Sept	Budapest: Admiral Horthy telegrams Stalin, requesting talks
27 Sept	London: Churchill's return from Quebec

1944 cont.	Washington, London, Western Front	Berlin and Central Europe	Moscow and Eastern Front
2 Oct		Warsaw: surrender and evacuation of remaining population; demolition of entire city begins	
7 Oct	London: Churchill leaves for Moscow		
9–19 Oct			Moscow Conference ('Tolstoy'): Churchill and Stalin
10 Oct		German evacuation of Greece and Balkans begins	
12 Oct			Moscow: Mikołajczyk and London Poles arrive; London Poles forced by Churchill and Stalin to yield half their lands
13 Oct		Athens: Germans evacuate	
15 Oct		Budapest: German SS stages *coup*, ousting Horthy and installing Ferencz Szálasi	Moscow: Admiral Horthy of Hungary signs an armistice dictated by Molotov
19 Oct–22 Nov	Washington: Keynes negotiates 'Stage II' of US-British Lend-Lease		
21 Oct	New York: Roosevelt's greatest campaign day – falls seriously ill	Rastenburg, East Prussia: final plans adopted for Hitler's Ardennes offensive	
22 Oct	London recognizes French Provisional Government		

23 Oct	Washington recognizes French Provisional Government	Moscow recognizes French Provisional Government
29 Oct		Moscow: Stalin orders, against local commanders' advice, offensive on Budapest – campaign lasts four months
31 Oct	Auschwitz: last gassing of prisoners	
2 Nov	US elections: Roosevelt fourth-term victory	
14 Nov	Prague: Committee for the Liberation of the Peoples of Russia (KONR) formally opened; General Vlasov's *Prague Manifesto* issued next day	
22 Nov	Leclerc's *2e DB* liberates Alsace	
24 Nov	Paris: de Gaulle leaves for Moscow	
2–10 Dec		Moscow: de Gaulle and Stalin in conference
16 Dec	Ardennes: Hitler's final major offensive in West begins, 'The Bulge'; German offensive lasts until New Year; 'clearing up' lasts all January. Paris: de Gaulle's return from Moscow	
Dec–Jan		Greece: civil war – Communists cleared from Athens and Attica by General Scobie

1945	Washington, London, Western Front	Berlin and Central Europe	Moscow and Eastern Front
1 Jan		Hitler's last radio address Hitler launches 'Operation North Wind' against Alsace: first use of fighter jets in history	
2 Jan	Versailles: de Gaulle's representative threatens withdrawal from Alliance if Strasbourg abandoned		
12 Jan		Hitler leaves Western Front for Berlin	Soviet staggered offensive across River Vistula
16 Jan		Berlin: Hitler's return	
17 Jan		Warsaw: Red Army 'liberates' the rubble	
18 Jan		Auschwitz and other eastern camps evacuated; 'death marches' begin	
20 Jan			Rokossovsky's 2nd Belorussian Front invades East Prussia
21 Jan		Russians liberate what remains of Auschwitz (Soviet press announces this only on 8 May, 'VE-Day')	
28 Jan		Eastern Front: Russian Liberation Army (ROA) created under command of General Vlasov	

28 Jan		Eastern Front: Russian Liberation Army (ROA) created under command of General Vlasov
29 Jan		Zhukov's 1st Belorussian Front reaches River Oder
2–3 Feb	Malta Conference: Churchill, Roosevelt and the Chiefs of Staff	
4–11 Feb		Yalta Conference
11 Feb		Yalta: 'secret accord' on forced repatriations between US, Britain and Soviet Union
13 Feb		Budapest: Germans surrender
13/14 Feb		Dresden fire-bombed
March	Tito's Partisans infiltrate southern Austria and north-eastern Italy; Yugoslavia makes territorial claims on provinces of Venezia Tridentina and Venezia Giulia	
7 March	Hodges' US First Army takes Remagen Bridge	
27 March	Last V-2 explodes in Britain	
28 March	Rheims: Eisenhower cables Stalin that Berlin is not his military objective	
29 March	Last V-1 explodes in Britain	

1945 cont.	Washington, London, Western Front	Berlin and Central Europe	Moscow and Eastern Front
April	Yugoslavia claims Carinthia province in southern Austria		
15 April	Ruhr pocket surrounded. British 11th Armoured Division enters the camp of Bergen–Belsen		
16 April			Zhukov launches offensive across River Oder for Berlin
25 April	San Francisco: United Nations Organization inaugurated		
30 April		Hitler's suicide. Red Army takes Reichstag	
30 April–14 May	France: municipal elections		
1 May	British 11th Armoured Division takes Lübeck, thus preventing Russian access to Denmark		
2 May	Units of British Eighth Army take Trieste		
4 May	Lüneburg Heath: first German surrender – to Montgomery		Belgrade: Tito warns off British advancing into areas of northern Adriatic 'already liberated from the Fascists' by Yugoslav Partisans

4 May	1st Division (Buniachenko) of Vlasov's Russian Liberation Army (ROA) enters Czechoslovakia	
5 May	Liberation of Prague by ROA	
6 May	'Liberation' of Prague by Red Army (Konev)	
7 May	SHAEF, Rheims, France: second German surrender	
7/8 May	Units of British Eighth Army (6th Armoured Division) cross passes into Carinthia, Austria	
8 May	VE (Victory in Europe) Day	
9 May		Soviet VE-Day
14 June		Moscow: sixteen members of Polish Underground Council, kidnapped in March, sentenced to internment in Gulag
6 July	British General Elections (results delayed for three weeks because of 'Service vote')	
15 July	Alamogordo, New Mexico: successful atom bomb experiment	
15 July–1 Aug	Potsdam Conference	
23 July–15 Aug	Paris: Marshal Pétain on trial for high treason (de Gaulle commutes death sentence to life imprisonment)	

1945 cont.	Washington, London, Western Front	Berlin and Central Europe	Moscow and Eastern Front
21 July		Potsdam: Soviet paper unilaterally announces (a) abolition of the state of Prussia, and (b) western Oder–Neisse frontier for Poland	
26 July	British election results: landslide for Clement Attlee's Labour Party; Churchill resigns that evening		
6 Aug	Hiroshima bombing		
9 Aug	Washington: Truman's return Nagasaki bombing		
14 Aug	Japanese surrender		
2 Sept	VJ (Victory in Japan) Day		
4–9 Oct	Paris: Pierre Laval tried		
15 Oct	Fresnes, near Paris: Laval executed		
21 Oct	French elections confirm de Gaulle as President (resigns 20 January 1946)		
20 Nov		Nuremberg Trials opened against leading Nazis	

Glossary of names
℣

Note: Well-known figures, such as Churchill, Montgomery, de Gaulle, Stalin, etc., are not listed.

Abetz, Otto. A cultivated man, who had encouraged cultural exchanges between the youth of France and Germany before the war – including in 1933 young *Jean-Paul Sartre* on a year-long visit to Berlin (where he did not even notice the Nazi takeover). In 1940 Abetz was named Nazi Germany's ambassador to Paris. Through Abetz's good name many an atrocity, including the shipment of Jews to their deaths, was organized by the occupying authorities with the cooperation and even on the initiative of the French government in Vichy.

Aldington, Brigadier Toby Law, Lord. As a young brigadier in British V Corps, when it entered Austria in May 1945, Toby Law oversaw many of the 'forced repatriations' of Eastern Europeans to Communist Yugoslavia and the Soviet Union. At the time V Corps was facing possible war – armed conflict had occurred – with Yugoslavia. In the post-war years he became deputy chairman of the Conservative Party, after which he chaired a life insurance company. This last situation led to a bizarre court case initiated by *Nigel Watts*, who had a grievance over an indemnity claim. The case brought in the historian *Count Nikolai Tolstoy*, who had devoted his life to revealing the injustices of forced repatriations. The legal claims and counter-claims have gone on now for thirty years. The story demonstrates that history lessons are best given in classrooms, not courtrooms.

Alexander, Field Marshal Sir Harold. Churchill's favourite commander, undoubtedly due to his easy-going manner combined with a strong, hard-working discipline. He made a total contrast to the rough manners of the outspoken Montgomery. He should have been senior British commander, but it was in fact Montgomery who pulled in all the honours once Churchill belatedly named him to field command in North Africa. Alexander did not have Montgomery's drive, nor Montgomery's common touch with the soldiers in the field. After the Italian campaign got under way he installed himself in *AFHQ* at Caserta. But he was, unlike Eisenhower, no château general; he was frequently on the front and present at many an unpleasant campaign. His main weakness was not of his own making: the winding-down of the Italian campaign following D-Day.

Antonescu, Marshal Ion. First Prime Minister and later dictator of Romania – a small-time dictator caught up in the great wars of his region. Romanians certainly preferred Antonescu's regime to the spectacularly repressive Communist governments imposed by the Soviet Union after the country's 'liberation'. He negotiated with Mussolini, negotiated with Hitler, negotiated with the Allies and negotiated with Stalin. King Michael of Romania dismissed him on 23 August 1944 during the first days of the Soviet invasion, or 'liberation'. The Soviets had him put on a show trial, after which he was executed.

Bach-Zelewski, SS-Obergruppenführer Erich. Directly under Reichsführer Heinrich Himmler, Bach-Zelewski was given the order to destroy completely the city of Warsaw after the outbreak of the Rising on 1 August 1944. A major portion of his troops were not German, but were drawn from the Eastern borderlands, where ethnic hatreds were deep and widespread. Some of the worst atrocities were committed by Ukrainians.

Beria, Lavrenty. Head of the *NKVD*, Soviet security, during the Second World War, he was not actually highly placed within the Communist Party hierarchy at the time. But he became an intimate colleague of Stalin, seeing him almost on a daily basis. His position as head of the NKVD made him one of the central figures of the Partisan war as it developed after 1942; this also made him a key figure in Soviet terror as the Red Army marched into Eastern and Central Europe. After Stalin's death in 1953 he was briefly a member of the triumvirate governing the Soviet Union. But his enthusiasm for reform did not please the hierarchy of the Party. Within months of taking office he was arrested, tried in secret, and shot.

Bidault, Georges. The president of the *National Resistance Council (CNR)*, following *Jean Moulin's* arrest and death in summer 1943. His politics were moderate. By no means a weak man, he was, however, unable to prevent the French Communists from taking over control of the Resistance by the end of 1943. This earned him de Gaulle's distrust, which would last into the post-war years. Under the Fourth Republic he founded the centrist *Mouvement républicain populaire (MRP)*. Several times Minister of Foreign Affairs, he was a fervent supporter of the idea of a 'European Union'. With the development of the Arab revolt in Algeria in the mid-1950s he became a supporter of *Algérie française* (the maintenance of Algeria's status as a part of metropolitan France). A bitter opponent of de Gaulle during the General's second presidency, Bidault went into exile with the French recognition of Algerian independence in 1963. Though he eventually returned to France, Bidault's political career was in tatters. Never a man of extremes, Bidault's life indicates the appallingly difficult political choices France faced both during and after the Second World War.

Bogomolov, Aleksandr. Moscow's ambassador to de Gaulle's Committee of National Liberation in Algiers, where he befriended Harold Macmillan.

Bonomi, Ivanoe. Liberated Italy's first Head of Government. He had effective control only of the southern half of the country, which was violent, corrupt and starving. During his year in office he became a great friend of Harold Macmillan, Britain's influential Minister Resident.

Bór-Komorowski, General Tadeusz. Commander of the Polish Home Army after Grot's arrest by the Gestapo in June 1943. A stubborn leader who quarrelled with everyone, including the London government-in-exile and the civilian Delegacy in Warsaw. Considering himself the authentic leader of liberated Poland, he was the one who instigated the Warsaw Rising of 1 August 1944. His decision was not without reason: after the Soviets' appalling treatment, as the Red Army advanced through eastern Poland, of soldiers of the Home Army – all ended up in the Gulag – Bór realized there was no alternative to the Rising in Warsaw.

Bousquet, René. Pierre Laval's chief of police, who negotiated with the SS in Paris the round-up of Jews in 1942. Laval and Bousquet were so concerned with maintaining 'police sovereignty' in France that they offered more Jews for deportation than the Germans were demanding or even ready to receive in their as yet unprepared extermination camps. It was in these negotiations that Laval and Bousquet managed to link Nazi terror (hostage shooting) to an extermination programme that had not even been fully developed by the Nazis themselves. Thus the Vichy authorities actually anticipated and encouraged German thinking on the Jewish Holocaust and did not simply follow plans laid down by the occupier. After the war Bousquet followed a successful career as a businessman and became a close friend of

President François Mitterrand. He was unfortunately assassinated by a madman in 1993 before facing a court trial which could have been most revealing.

Bradley, General Omar. An intimate friend of General Dwight D. Eisenhower since West Point days. As commander of the US First Army he directed US landings in Normandy on D-Day. Later as commander of the US 12th Army Group he led the major US offensives into Nazi Germany. More a man of tactics than strategy, he shared responsibility with *General Patton* for the widening of the Western Front and the chance this gave Hitler for his surprise Ardennes offensive, the Battle of the Bulge, in December 1944.

Brooke, Field Marshal Sir Alan. After a series of British disasters, Brooke was named Chief of Imperial General Staff (CIGS) in 1941. Unlike Montgomery he was never, even as a commander in the field, a man of the front line. He got into vicious arguments with the Americans over the conduct of the war – and specifically never approved of the D-Day operation 'Overlord'. His wicked but always trenchant comments about his contemporaries, including Churchill, have been preserved in a now famous diary.

Catroux, General Georges. The only colonial governor (Indochina) to respond to de Gaulle's call of 18 June 1940 to combat Nazi Germany. After Vichy France abandoned Indochina to the Japanese, he moved to Lebanon and became Delegate General of the Free French in the Middle East. He did much to calm Anglo-French tensions in Syria and Lebanon. After the war he was briefly French ambassador to Moscow.

Chaban-Delmas, Jacques. Parachuted into occupied France after D-Day and entering Paris under disguise, he was de Gaulle's military representative in the French capital in the weeks preceding the Liberation. He set up his own network within the Paris police ('Honneur et Patrie') and decided, with the collaboration of *Alexandre Parodi*, to organize an insurrection that would begin a few hours before the Communist-planned insurrection in Paris. Chaban-Delmas remained a loyal Gaullist throughout his life. He was mayor of Bordeaux for several decades.

Chambers, Whittaker. A witty correspondent for *Time* magazine during the war, he had also been a member of the American Communist Party, which he left in 1938. Haunted by the very real threat of assassination, he was a wary informer to the FBI, America's chief intelligence agency. It was only after the war that the US Government began to take his mass of information on Communist agents within the Federal Government seriously. His chief revelation was a long-time intimate link between *Alger Hiss* of the US State Department and the Soviet Union.

Cherwell, Lord. Oxford physics professor. He acted as personal adviser to Churchill on the atom bomb project, though he is not usually regarded as being qualified for such a role.

Choltitz, General Dietrich von. Last German military commander of 'Greater Paris'.

Chuikov, General Vasili. One of the heroes of Stalingrad. As commander of the Second Tank Army he was given the responsibility of cutting off German reinforcements to Belorussia by crossing the River Vistula south of Warsaw in summer 1944. He was stunned by Stavka's order, on 3 August, to stop his operation, just as the Rising in Warsaw began. The halt effectively sealed the fate of Warsaw. Chuikov's Eighth Guards Army played a major role in the Battle of Berlin in April 1945. He became commander of Russian occupation forces in Germany after the war and later Deputy Minister of Defence.

Colville, Sir John, 'Jock'. Churchill's favourite private secretary, whom the wartime Prime

Minister had adopted from his predecessor. Colville appears to have been at Churchill's side on all occasions, including moments in the great Churchillian bathtub. Many a famous anecdote about Churchill has its origin in Colville's lively chronicle.

Cripps, Sir Richard Stafford. A gaunt, severe man who, as Chancellor of the Exchequer (1947–50), gave Clement Attlee's post-war Labour government a bad name by introducing an austerity programme that included further rationing of foodstuffs and other essentials. During the war he had served as ambassador to Moscow during the first year of Hitler's invasion. In 1942, Churchill brought him into the War Cabinet where a very strained relationship between the two men developed. On his departure from the Coalition Government in 1945, Churchill remarked, 'There, but for the grace of God, goes God.' An isolated man, a highly qualified lawyer, a planner, Cripps remained to the end of his not very long life totally hostile to private enterprise.

Cunningham, Admiral Sir Andrew. A fighting admiral, who achieved more than any other British military commander during the dismal period of 1940–1: he established British naval superiority, by a margin, in the Mediterranean. It was this that made American military intervention in Europe possible – beginning with the Anglo-American landings in Algeria in November 1942. Cunningham was almost certainly involved in the assassination of Admiral Darlan, America's Vichy governor of Algeria, that December. In October 1943 he was transferred to London to become First Sea Lord. In that capacity, he became a major strategic adviser to Churchill.

Dietrich, General Sepp. Hitler had enormous affection for this man until the very last week of his life. Dietrich had served as bodyguard to Hitler before he came to power. In the last six months of the war, after service in the East, he commanded the Sixth (SS) Panzer Army in the West. During the Ardennes offensive in December, Dietrich and his forces fought with notable courage. Dietrich's army was then transferred to Hungary where, in Hitler's strategic logic, lay the hope of the whole Reich. On his last birthday, 20 April 1945, Hitler raged that even Dietrich was 'leaving him in the lurch'. Captured by the Americans, Dietrich provided under interrogation valuable information on German army movements during the last days of the Reich.

Dimitrov, Georgi. Head of the minority Bulgarian Communist Party before the war, he exiled himself to Moscow, survived the purges and was ultimately named Secretary General of Comintern. He became a close friend of Stalin's. In 1944 he set up the first Bulgarian Communist government, following the Russian invasion of September. Communist leadership was divided and, after numerous purges, he again fled to Moscow, where he died in 1949.

Dönitz, Admiral Karl. An advocate of the policy that U-boats alone could win the war for Germany, he replaced Admiral Erich Raeder, who had placed more faith in battleships. Dönitz never gave up hope that new U-boat technology could bring victory to Germany, even in spring 1945 – it was the reason why the Germans held out with a pocket of troops on the Courland peninsula. Hitler admired Dönitz's stamina and loyalty, and named him his successor as Head of State, after dismissing Göring as Reichsmarshal. Dönitz set up a small Nazi state first in Lübeck and, after Montgomery captured that city, in Flensburg, in Schleswig-Holstein, from where he negotiated Germany's unconditional surrender in early May 1945. He was condemned to ten years in prison for war crimes at the Nuremberg Trials.

Frank, Hans. The Nazi lawyer who became Governor of the General-Gouvernement, as the Germans termed occupied Poland. The Governor lived in the luxurious Wawel Castle, above Cracow. The diary he kept is among the most chilling documents of the war. Tried at Nuremberg in 1945–6, Frank was hanged in a gymnasium there on 16 October 1946.

Guderian, Colonel General Heinz. Already established as a tank strategist before the war, he was one of the main architects of France's defeat in 1940. Hitler dismissed him along with many Eastern commanders in 1942, then recalled him the following February. He became Chief of Staff after the Officers' Bomb Plot in July 1944. But Hitler never listened to his advice, and eventually dismissed him on 21 March 1945, a fact that probably saved his life. He died a natural death in 1953.

Harriman, Averell. US ambassador to Moscow during the war. He understood, unlike the ailing Roosevelt and his government colleagues in Washington, that the Soviets were not really 'Allies' of the West. But his views were less acute than those of his junior assistant, the fluent Russian speaker, George Kennan.

Hiss, Alger. A leading civil servant within the State Department, he played a major role in the Dumbarton Oaks Conference at Washington in 1944, which laid the foundations of the United Nations Organization. He became Secretary General of the UN on its formal establishment in San Francisco in April 1945. But his career came to an end within a year following revelations that he had, since the 1930s, been a Soviet agent. He was imprisoned for two years for 'contempt of court'. In the 1960s he became a hero of the American left, and gave well-paid lectures at the country's most prestigious universities along with many television interviews. His guilt was proven by the publication of the VENONA transcripts in the 1990s, shortly after his death.

Hull, Cordell. Secretary of State from 1933 and close to Roosevelt until sickness overcame him in the last year of the war. He was utterly determined that Allied policy should follow the line of the State Department. One of his main policies was that Vichy France was the legitimate government of France and, if it could serve the Germans so well, then it could surely, with sufficient persuasion, be induced to serve the interests of the United States. Hull developed a visceral hatred of de Gaulle after forces of the latter seized two tiny French islands off Newfoundland, Saint-Pierre and Miquelon. But de Gaulle proved popular with the Americans at large, and particularly the East Coast press. This only further angered Hull and his boss, Roosevelt. Hull's policy towards France completely backfired and remained a cause of bitterness for generations. He was an active promoter of the United Nations Organization.

Ismay, General Sir Hastings, 'Pug'. Churchill's Chief of Staff. His diplomatic skills were universally admired and he probably did more than anyone to soothe relations between Churchill and both British and American General Staffs. He was a liaison man, always hovering in the background of the major international wartime conferences. *The Memoirs of Lord Ismay* (London, 1960) are a brief but vital source on Allied politics during the war.

Jodl, General Alfred. A former Bavarian artillery officer, by 1944 he was head of the operations staff of *OKW* (High Command of the Armed Forces) and thus officially deputy to *Field Marshal Keitel*. But in reality Jodl was the commander, attending every one of Hitler's two daily military conferences. Jodl signed Germany's military surrender at Rheims on 7 May 1945. Tried for war crimes at Nuremberg, he was hanged in a gymnasium there on 16 October 1946.

Keightley, General Charles. Commander of British V Corps, the first British army unit to enter Austria. There he faced the daunting task of ousting Tito's Partisans from the province of Carinthia. This was linked to a most inhumane episode, in May and June 1945, of 'forced repatriations' of Eastern Europeans who had taken refuge in the area. Keightley may have been responsible for serious errors of judgement but the charge, by some historians, of 'genocide' seems misplaced.

Keitel, Field Marshal Wilhelm. Generally considered a man of feeble abilities, he was named commander of *OKW* in 1938. No single strategic initiative has been traced to his name; he was entirely under Hitler's control. *Jodl*, his deputy, also dominated him. In 1945–6 he was tried at Nuremberg and subsequently hanged for war crimes.

Keynes, John Maynard. One of the greatest economist of all times. A professor at Cambridge, a member of the Treasury and adviser to the governments of both Churchill and Attlee until his death in 1946. Ultimately his policies for keeping Britain solvent failed, though this can hardly be blamed on Keynes. *Harry Dexter White*, the US Treasury assistant, did much to undermine Keynes's work of foresight. Clement Attlee's fiscally irresponsible post-war government did the rest.

Koenig, General Marie Pierre. Commander of the Free French Army, he held out against Rommel's Panzers at the fort of Bir Hakeim with French recruits from Syria between May and June 1942. Though only a stalling action, it is generally considered one of the major factors contributing to eventual Allied success in the area – in particular, Montgomery's October victory at El Alamein. Koenig was later named by de Gaulle commander of the *French Forces of the Interior (FFI)*; with this force of the Resistance integrated into the French army, French Communist ambitions to take over government offices were thereby obstructed.

Laval, Pierre. One of the most complicated and controversial politicians of contemporary French history. Like many politicians of the Third Republic, he began his career on the left and ended on the right (though a right peculiar to France). He was a leading pacifist in the First World War, calling for a negotiated peace in 1917. His wish to avoid war with Germany a second time in a generation pushed him down the path to collaboration. Deputy Prime Minister in 1940 and Prime Minister from 1942 until the Liberation he found himself increasingly a mere instrument of the Nazis. After a trial in Paris for high treason, which lasted less than a week, he was shot on 15 October 1945 (having taken cyanide that was pumped seventeen times out of his stomach before he was led to the stake). Despite this horrible end and the touching portrait left in private notes by his daughter, it is difficult to sympathize with the politics of Pierre Laval.

Leahy, Admiral William. It was undoubtedly Roosevelt's old links with the US Navy that attracted the President to this most reactionary of figures. After William C. Bullitt's brief and ineffectual tenure as US ambassador to Pétain's regime (Bullitt at least had the courage to remain in Paris), Leahy took over the post at Vichy. He remained a supporter of the Vichy regime until the day of his death (1959) and did much to influence American policy in this direction. On his return to the United States in 1942 – when it was simply no longer feasible to maintain diplomatic ties with this collaborationist regime – he became Roosevelt's personal representative to the US Joint Chiefs of Staff. But his influence went far beyond his official post, especially after the President's debilitating illness in 1944. His effect on American foreign policy was enormous. Present at most wartime international conferences, his main aim was to set up *Allied Military Government*, that is American military government, in all areas occupied by the Allies. His support for Vichy derived from a belief that Pétain and his colleagues could be turned into pliant clients of the American government. He remained a supporter of Vichy during the Liberation of Paris, and was still publicly supporting the defunct regime at the Quebec Conference of September 1944. This rude and unpleasant man was no friend of democratic Europe.

Leclerc (*pseud.*), General Philippe de Hauteclocq. Practically every town and village in northern France has a street or avenue named after General Leclerc. He was commander of the *2e DB (Deuxième Division Blindée* or 2nd Armoured Division) which landed in Normandy on 1 August 1944 and liberated Paris on 24/25 August. Leclerc's force had marched all the way from French Equatorial Africa across the Sahara and first joined the Allies in North Africa. On the day of Leclerc's death in an air accident in 1947, de Gaulle stopped smoking. The movements of Leclerc's 2e DB need to be watched against the movements of the Polish 1st Armoured Division, which landed in France on the same day, 1 August 1944, the day the Warsaw Rising broke out. Paris was liberated, Warsaw was annihilated. In this context, the parallel movements of the two divisions on the Western Front – both initially recruited from Nazi-occupied Europe – becomes uncanny.

McCreery, General Richard. Commander of Eighth Army Headquarters at Udine (near Venice) when this was established at the end of the war. McCreery was given the charge of moving British troops into the north-eastern Italian province of Venezia Giulia and the southern Austrian province of Carinthia, zones also claimed – and occupied – by Tito's Yugoslav Partisans. Faced with a thoroughly chaotic situation, McCreery has been accused of responsibility for the violent 'repatriations' of Eastern Europeans in southern Austria in May and June 1945.

Marty, André. A leading French Communist. He returned from exile in Moscow in 1943 to join de Gaulle's Consultative Assembly in Algiers. He remained a Communist deputy during the Fourth Republic until his exclusion from the Party following Stalin's death in 1953.

Mikołajczyk, Stanisław. Polish Prime Minister of the Government-in-exile in London following Sikorski's death in July 1943. He was the only London Pole to return to join the Soviet puppet government in Warsaw after the 'Liberation', but he was soon purged.

Miłosz, Czesław. Theodor Adorno, though an accomplished musician as well as a famous German sociologist, once said that 'After Auschwitz there will be no more art.' Miłosz, who lived and fought in the Warsaw Rising of 1944, came to exactly the opposite conclusion, believing that the only possible truth that can be expressed after such human atrocities is through poetry. He also provides an interesting contrast to *Sartre*, of the Paris Liberation, who found truth in philosophy. Miłosz's poetry, as well as his prose, concentrates on the individual and the detail. In contrast to commentary on historical processes, which he believes to be the lie in both Nazism and Communism, the detail and the date is what Miłosz regards as the truth of history. 'The words are written down, the deed, the date,' he warned Poland's Communist rulers. He received the Nobel Prize for Literature in 1980 and is undoubtedly one of the greatest poets of the twentieth century. Even translated into English his poetry, when read aloud, causes wonder – and a respect for this true man of history.

Model, Field Marshal Walther. The kind of pure Nazi that was rare within German High Command, he won a reputation for ruthlessness on the Eastern Front, where, however, he rarely won a battle. By summer 1944 he had earned the nickname 'Hitler's firefighter' through his energetic efforts at saving what he could of Army Group Centre after Stalin's 'Operation Bagration'. As the Battle of Normandy reached its disastrous conclusion at Falaise, he was named, on 17 August, Commander-in-Chief in the West. Finding the situation hopeless he withdrew, unbeknown to Hitler, as many troops as he could to eastern France and Benelux in preparation for the autumn defence of Germany (thus saving Paris from a bitter battle). In command of Army Group B, he contributed to the British setback at Arnhem in September 1944. Surrounded in the Ruhr pocket in April 1945, he disbanded his army group and, on 21 April, shot himself.

Molotov, Viacheslav M. One of the early Bolsheviks who managed to survive Stalin's purges and even get named in 1939 Minister of Foreign Affairs. It was he who negotiated with von Ribbentrop, Hitler's Foreign Minister, the Nazi-Soviet Pact of 1939. By 1941 he was, as formal deputy to Stalin as well as Foreign Minister, the most powerful man in the Soviet Union.

Throughout the war he played a major part in the wartime conferences with the Western Allies. But in 1949 he was suddenly demoted from his posts and replaced by his rival, *Andrei Vyshinsky*. For a brief time after the death of Stalin he returned to the Ministry of Foreign Affairs. But Khrushchev, once in power, accused him of 'Stalinist tendencies' and 'anti-Party activities'. In 1957 he was named ambassador to Mongolia.

Moltke, Count Helmuth James von. Descendant of the famous Prussian military family, he organized after 1941 on his east Prussian estate at Kreisau discussions among various notables on how to overcome Nazism and create a better Germany. Many have half-jokingly said that he was paying for the sins of his destructive ancestors. He has also been dismissed as being impractical. Moltke's writings, including letters to his wife, are of a high literary quality and, after 1941, become increasingly religious. He was arrested in January 1944 for developing a relationship with the Jesuits, outlawed in Hitler's Germany. He could therefore have had no connection with the Stauffenberg plot to assassinate Hitler the following July. He was tried and hanged in January 1945, officially for 'high treason'; Moltke said for 'thought'. Moltke's Christian beliefs as developed in the Kreisau Circle probably had more influence on post-war Germany than any other 'German resistance' movement. Its themes can be found in the programme of the Christian Democratic Party, and they were frequently repeated in the speech of that party's leader, Konrad Adenauer. Moltke should be viewed as a martyr.

Monnet, Jean. Monnet made his fortune out of the sale of his home-town liqueur, Cognac. He made his name as an economic planner. In the First World War, with the encouragement of the politicians André Tardieu and Georges Clemenceau he travelled to the United States to participate in projects for financing the Allied war effort. There he established lifetime friendships with leading American statesmen and industrialists. In the early 1920s he was Secretary General of the League of Nations. But it was American methods of business that led him to go into private management and, again in close association with Tardieu, organize France's first 'technocrats' in the 1930s. In 1940 he drafted a programme that would unite Britain and France in a single nation against Nazi Germany. It was approved by both Churchill and de Gaulle, but rejected with violence by the Vichy authorities. Monnet returned to the United States to organize war finances. Roosevelt greatly appreciated him and sent him to Algiers in 1943 in the hope that he would act in American interests against de Gaulle. Instead, the two men became the greatest of friends. Following the war he drafted plan after plan to foster not only peace in Europe but a united political and economic Europe. Every single major European project of the 1940s and '50s bears the stamp of Jean Monnet, which is why he is known as 'the father of Europe'. But the plans would never have got very far without the support of Europe's leading post-war statesmen. The European Movement, which led ultimately to the formation of the European Union, owed as much to the Realpolitik of Adenauer, de Gaulle, de Gaspieri and Macmillan as it did to the plans of Jean Monnet.

Monter-Chruściel, Colonel Antoni. Warsaw District Commander of the Home Army. He played a central part in the decision to launch the Rising on 1 August 1944.

Moran, Sir Charles Wilson, Lord. Churchill's private physician, which could never have been an easy task. Churchill's attitude towards his health swung from complete indifference to obsession. He frequently required Moran to be by his side to take his pulse; at the same time he ignored most of Moran's recommendations. Moran's memoir, *Winston Churchill: The Struggle for Survival* (London, 1966), is as much about Moran's own mental survival as it is about his patient's incredible but at times insufferable stamina. As a result, it is not an entirely reliable source.

Morgenthau, Henry. US Secretary of the Treasury, he frequently came into conflict with the Secretary of State, *Cordell Hull*, though they were both old friends of Roosevelt. Formerly a wealthy apple-grower and neighbour of Roosevelt, he never really mastered the art of government finance and economics. Much of this he left to his brilliant assistant, *Harry Dexter White*.

Morrison, Herbert. A British Labour MP who played a decisive role in ousting Neville Chamberlain from the premiership in May 1940. Churchill, Chamberlain's successor, named Morrison Home Secretary, a role he played heroically under the strains of war. Morrison was the chief organizer of Britain's civil defence. By early 1945 he was programming Labour's most socialist campaign of the twentieth century. Following Churchill's defeat he was a leading figure in the British government's programmes of nationalization, education and national health – which had disastrous effects on the British economy.

Moulin, Jean. The youngest prefect in France before the war (Chartres, Eure-et-Loir), he was closely associated with politicians of the leftward-leaning Popular Front of 1936. His switch in loyalty during the war to the Gaullists raised many an eyebrow, even at the time. It has been argued that Moulin manoeuvred himself into the role of de Gaulle's representative in the various interior French Resistance movements. He founded the *French National Resistance Council (CNR)* in May 1943 and, within a month, was arrested by the Gestapo. Who betrayed Jean Moulin remains one of the great unresolved mysteries of the war. Possibly there was no betrayal at all, but it cannot be denied that the French Communists profited from his disappearance.

Nordling, Raoul. Swedish Consul General at Paris during the German occupation. His role, in August 1944, in saving Paris from destruction by German military commander General von Choltitz has become the subject of some controversy. The affair demonstrates many of the dilemmas facing the German occupiers of France, the occupied, and the Western Allies in France during that summer of Liberation.

Orwell, George (*pen-name for* **Blair, Eric**). If *Sartre* is Paris's man of 1945 and Miłosz Warsaw's man of 1945, George Orwell is London's man of 1945. He was not in any sense a philosopher and he did not live long enough to become a poet. But he was an accomplished, even visionary polemicist – in the tradition of Jonathan Swift. Many of Orwell's insights into the weaknesses of Britain's left-wing establishment have been proven correct. Yet he himself remained a Socialist until the day of his early death, in 1950. The odd result is that, today, his thinking has been co-opted by both the political left and right in Britain and America. His most important contribution – from the point of view of the end of the Second World War – was his exposure of the West's hypocritical attitude towards its supposed 'ally' in the war, the genocidal Soviet Union. Posing as a man of the country, he was in fact a man of the city, like most of his countrymen. His ideas of 'Englishness' went no deeper than urban Sartre's notions of 'Frenchness' – which were in no way profound. Sartre was a philosopher. Orwell was an extremely good urban polemicist, who represented his era with nobility and honour.

Palewski, Gaston. A close aide to de Gaulle throughout the General's life. The relationship dated from de Gaulle's military service in Poland in 1920 and symbolized France's 'special relationship' with Poland. Of an old Polish aristocratic family, Palewski, significantly, has written a major account of Talleyrand and the Napoleonic era, upon which the Palewski family left a major mark.

Parodi, Alexandre. De Gaulle's General Delegate in Paris. He was in the French capital weeks before the Liberation organizing an administration, on behalf of de Gaulle, which would take over all local and national ministries the instant the Liberation began. Thus de Gaulle's Provisional Government pre-empted the actions of both the Americans (who would have imposed AMGOT) and the French Communists. He followed an important diplomatic career during the post-war period.

Patton, General George. A man who was very much influenced by his experience in the American Tank Corps in 1918. Commanding the newly formed US Third Army he led a major part of the US forces in Normandy at speed along a south-eastern route across the empty plains of central France until they came up against the Germans at Metz. Patton's arguments in favour of a 'wide front' allowed Hitler to open his last offensive in the Ardennes, the Battle of the Bulge. Patton's line of advance into Germany closely resembled General Pershing's plans for an American victory over Germany in 1919. Without it, the war might have ended in 1944 rather than 1945. Made a hero by the American press, Patton died in a car accident shortly after the war, in 1945.

Piłsudski, Marshal Józef. A great Polish patriot whose Polish Legions fought with the Austro-Hungarian armies against the Russians during the First World War. This led to accusations, especially by the British, that the Poles were not friends of the Allies – Lloyd George called them Central European 'Irishmen'. But Piłsudski was manoeuvring for an independent Poland, which he won, almost despite the Paris Peace Conference, in 1919–22 – a period that included a war with Lenin's Bolsheviks. Piłsudski established in the 1920s the increasingly dictatorial *Sanacja* regime; in the 1930s it resorted to the violent repression of minorities. He died in 1935, but his regime survived until the war. All the members of the wartime Polish government-in-exile had been part of the growing resistance to the *Sanacja* regime; they established a base in Switzerland long before the war. The Soviets would accuse the London government-in-exile of being of 'Fascist' *Sanacja* origin and, illogically, of being long-time exiles at the same time. 'Exile' for the Soviets carried the pejorative sense of reactionary *émigré* at the time of the French Revolution (an interpretation they did not of course apply to Polish Communist exiles in Moscow).

Rokossovsky, Marshal Konstantin. A survivor of Stalin's 1938 army purges, he was released from prison to lead the first major tank offensives in the Ukraine against the Germans in 1941. Further north, that winter, he was at the centre of the successful Russian defence of Moscow. He was master of one of the major breakthroughs to the west of Stalingrad in December 1942, thus surrounding the German Sixth Army. He played a central role at Kursk in 1943. In July 1944 he was one of the chief architects of the German collapse in Belorussia, and it was his 1st Belorussian Front which stopped short of Warsaw at the moment of the Rising (see *Chuikov*) that August. Having played a major role in the Battle of Berlin, he became commander, because of his Polish ancestry, of the Russian forces in Poland – not a happy conclusion to his career.

Rol-Tanguy, Colonel Henri. One of the leading figures during the week of the Liberation of Paris. He was at that time Commander of the 'FFI–Ile-de-France'. As a close collaborator of both Charles Tillon's Communist Resistance movement, the Francs-Tireurs et Partisans, and André Tollet's Parisian Committee of Liberation, this spiky little Breton represented not only a major source of opposition to the German occupation, but also to the more democratically oriented Gaullist movement. Rol-Tanguy had his headquarters in the underground Catacombs, near Place Denfert-Rochereau, from where he maintained a secret telephone communications network throughout Paris. The story of how de Gaulle outmanoeuvred Rol-Tanguy's Communist Resistance in the days of Paris's Liberation is one of the great dramas of contemporary French history. Rol-Tanguy would remain a lifetime member of the French Communist Party, even after the collapse of the Eastern European Communist bloc. His politics were foolish. But nobody can deny him his courage.

Sartre, Jean-Paul. The most versatile novelist, playwright and philosopher of the twentieth century. The man of the Liberation and of 1945. Sadly he gradually slid into politics, for which his creative mind was not suited, thereby making a fool of himself in the last two decades of his life. Asked why he took no action against Sartre's destructive stupidities, de Gaulle blandly answered, 'One does not imprison Socrates.'

Sauckel, Gauleiter Fritz. The Reich's Commissar-General for Labour. He played a major part in the Reich's slave-labour programme. Of particular note were his negotiations with Vichy France, represented by *Laval* and *Bousquet*.

Schacht, Dr Hjalmar. Inventor of the 'Schachtian' system of bilateral barter designed to provide a nation with total economic autonomy. It proved a brilliant success for Nazi Germany and was imitated by the Soviet Union. Many Western economists in the inter-war years fell under its influence, including, for a brief period, *John Maynard Keynes*. Schacht himself first drew international attention when he was appointed special commissioner to control German hyperinflation in 1923. The Nazis were attracted to his plans for economic autonomy and he was appointed by Hitler to be President of the Reichsbank and Economics Minister. But Schacht, a conservative businessman, was never a member of the Nazi Party. He deplored high military expenditure and, though hardly a part of the 'German Resistance to the Nazis', found himself in prison after the Bomb Plot of July 1944. He was tried for war crimes at the Nuremberg Trials and acquitted.

Sikorski, General Władisław. A Polish de Gaulle. He had been a leading opponent of the pre-war dictator Józef Piłsudski and the succeeding regime – which is why he was in Paris when Germany invaded Poland in September 1939. After Poland's defeat Sikorski was the natural choice for Prime Minister of the Polish government-in-exile, which was set up in Paris and then moved to London after the French defeat. One of the most charismatic war leaders, he and most of his General Staff died in an air crash at Gibraltar on 4 July 1943. Was it an accident? Sikorski's death was a disaster for martyred Poland.

Sosnkowski, General Kazimierz. London Commander-in-Chief of all Polish armed forces. Thanks largely to Soviet propaganda, he has been widely represented as a right-wing extremist. He was utterly intransigent over the question of eastern Polish territories and refused all co-operation with the Communists. For Sosnkowski, the Second World War was a two-front war waged against both the Soviets and the Nazis. Given what is now known about Soviet behaviour, one has to admit he had a point.

Spaak, Paul-Henri Charles. If *Jean Monnet* is to be considered the planner of the European Economic Community – what would become the European Union – it was the Belgian Foreign Minister Paul-Henri Spaak who created it, at a meeting of European foreign ministers in Messina, Sicily, in June 1955. It was here that the project that would lead to the Treaty of Rome (March 1957) and the 'Common Market' was born under Spaak's dynamic chairmanship. Spaak had held several ministerial posts in Belgium in the 1930s, before leaving for London to be Foreign Minister of the Belgian government-in-exile. It was in wartime London that the idea of some sort of European union, which would include Britain, became his passion. Spaak was far too energetic a man, in the view of the British Foreign Office, to stand between the traditional representatives of nation states; Britain vetoed his candidature for the presidency of the *Organization for European Economic Co-operation (OEEC)* in 1948. But Britain had lost control of Spaak, and his European project, by 1955.

Speer, Albert. He would probably have been one of the world's great architects had he not got caught up in Hitler's inner circle. Instead he spent most of his life in gaol, and was lucky not to have been executed after the Nuremberg Trials. He showed his talents as an administrator when he became Armaments Minister in 1942 – and showed no qualms either in using slave labour or over working people to death. His memoirs are revealing, as are the interviews he granted, in old age, to the journalist Gitta Sireny.

Stauffenberg, Colonel Claus von. A German combat officer in Poland in 1939, in France in 1940 and later in North Africa, where in 1943 he was seriously wounded by enemy aircraft gunfire. While in hospital he dreamed up his mission to kill the Führer. His opportunity came when he was promoted Chief of Staff of the Reserve Army, a post which demanded sessions with Hitler and his staff at Rastenburg. Huge numbers were involved in the plot, especially German officers in France who enjoyed notably more freedom of action than elsewhere in Nazi-occupied Europe. Stauffenberg himself was a mystic and his programme reactionary: he sought to re-establish a German Reich along pre-1914 lines – as did many who followed him. He was no democrat. He was no organizer. Indeed, his conspiracy serves as a model of how not to plan a plot. His bomb did not kill Hitler on 20 July 1944; it simply blew off his trousers. Stauffenberg, believing Hitler dead, flew off to Berlin where he was shot that night in the courtyard of the War Ministry on the orders of a fellow conspirator, who was trying to hide the traces of his own guilt.

Stroop, SS Brigadeführer Jürgen. German commander responsible for suppressing the Warsaw Ghetto Rising of 19 April–10 May 1943.

Thorez, Maurice. General Secretary of the French Communist Party. Called up for military service after the signature of the Nazi-Soviet Pact of 1939, he deserted when in Belgium and fled to Moscow, where he spent most of the war. Completely under the control of Stalin though Thorez was, de Gaulle thought he could use him as a moderating force on the French Communists. De Gaulle negotiated with Stalin his return to France in 1944. For about a year Thorez fulfilled his role, but by 1947, when the Communists withdrew from the French government, he had become the source of much turbulence.

Vendroux, Yvonne. De Gaulle's lifelong wife from Lille. The marriage was arranged by his family after de Gaulle, on service in Poland in 1920, started showing an interest in a married Polish princess. Popularly known as Tante Yvonne, not a single recording of her voice has been preserved.

Vlasov, General Andrei. Originator of the movement, the *Committee for the Liberation of the Peoples of Russia (KONR)*, and the anti-Soviet army, the *Russian Liberation Army (ROA)*, Vlasov must be considered one of the most complicated personalities of the Second World War. Not that he himself was complicated: he was, until his capture by the Germans on the Volkhov Front to the south of Leningrad in May 1942, a patriot, a soldier, a man who fought courageously for his country. But Communist, and Communist-apologist, historians have made him complicated. Because he represented Russian resistance to the Communists – a far more authentic movement than German resistance to the Nazis – he has been classified in East and West as a 'Fascist'. He was subject to immense bouts of depression, but this is understandable given his circumstances. His enemy was Communism and murderous fanaticism; he had no hope of support in the West which considered the Soviet Union an 'ally'. 'I have lost, so I remain a traitor until such time as in Russia freedom comes before bogus Soviet patriotism,' he told one of his colleagues before his capture by the Red Army in Czechoslovakia.

Vyshinsky, Andrei. Chief prosecutor during the Soviet purges of the 1930s. Deputy Foreign Minister during the war. In 1943 he was Soviet Representative to the Advisory Council for Italy, which oversaw Italian political affairs in the early years of the Allied occupation of Italy. A man of distinct personal charm, he had no scruple in ordering the murder of tens of thousands. After the war he organized mass purges in 'liberated' Romania.

White, Harry Dexter. The son of a poor Lithuanian Jewish immigrant family that settled in Boston, White built his career on his brilliant academic performance. In 1938 he became the Treasury Department's Director of Monetary Research. Many of the plans attributed to *Morgenthau* were actually of his own pen. Most notable was his management of Lend-Lease, a complicated aid programme to the Allies. White was convinced that the days of British power were over and that the true future partner of the United States would be the Soviet Union. Intent on helping the process along, he devised a mechanism that would undermine British liquidity and destroy the sterling area – long before the British, including *John Maynard Keynes*, became aware of the fact. White founded almost single-handedly the International Monetary Fund, Keynes merely invented the name. White died of a supposed heart attack on the eve of appearing before a Senate Committee, in 1948, on charges of passing secrets to the Soviet Union. Transcripts released in the 1990s prove he was central to a network of Soviet agents within the Treasury Department throughout the war years.

Zhdanov, Andrei. For a short time Zhdanov was Stalin's favourite member of the Politburo, the Minister of State Security and Stalin's closest foreign policy adviser. He was responsible for the creation of Cominform, a replacement of the pre-war Comintern, in February 1948. The Soviet 'anti-cosmopolitan' and 'anti-Zionist' campaigns were organized by him. But in July Zhdanov had a heart attack – always something that carried a grain of suspicion if suffered by a member of the Politburo. Stalin sent him to the Valdai clinic, designed for senior Party members. A little over a month later he was dead. In 1952 Stalin used Zhdanov's death as the grounds for the 'Doctors' Plot', which led, in its turn, to the last great purge of Stalin's life. Stalin died – or was possibly murdered – in the midst of the affair, in March 1953.

Zhukov, Marshal Georgi. Deputy Supreme Commander in Chief of the Red Army for almost the entire war. He was both responsible for general strategy decisions and also commanded some of the most important Russian offensives. After signing the German surrender in Berlin on 8 May 1945, Zhukov, most illustrious of the Russian commanders, was gradually pushed by Stalin into obscurity.

Glossary of organizations

℣

AFHQ (Allied Forces Head Quarters). This was the first Western Allied command organization of the Second World War. It was established in 1942 during the North African campaign with permanent headquarters finally set up in Algiers after the 'Torch' landings of November. In April 1944 it moved to the luxurious palace of Caserta, outside Naples. It became a vast administration with both military and political sections. Mediterranean policy was run from here. As American divisions withdrew to North-Western Europe, AFHQ increasingly assumed a British character under the leadership of *Field Marshal Alexander*. By the summer of 1944 the Western Alliance was dominated by two competing top command posts: *SHAEF* in North-Western Europe was essentially American, *AFHQ* was British. This naturally led to much tension between the Allies.

AMGOT (Allied Military Government for Occupied Territories) – simplified to **AMG (Allied Military Government).** It was, in the beginning, a purely American plan for military government that would be installed behind Allied lines. Administrative training for its administrators ('the sixty-day wonders') was conducted in Charlottesville, Virginia. AMGOT included the imposition of its own printed currency. The Charlottesville administrators turned out to be no wonders at all: in southern Italy in 1942–3 they were a source of corruption and encouraged the development of the black market, particularly in Naples. De Gaulle refused to allow the Americans to treat liberated France as 'occupied territory' and, shortly after D-Day, pre-empted American efforts by swiftly installing his own administrators – often, it is true, drawn from the Vichy authorities (with whom the Americans had been flirting). A form of AMG was developed as the British took over administration in northern Italy and southern Austria (in competition with Communist Partisans). AMG was also introduced as a preliminary form of government by all Western Allies in conquered Germany. No civilians in Europe enjoyed administration under 'AMGOT'/'AMG'. As Macmillan, and many other British administrators pointed out, it was basically a form of gangsterism and deep-seated corruption.

BCRA (Bureau Central de Renseignements et d'Action). De Gaulle's ineffective intelligence bureau set up in Duke Street, London. Its director, Colonel Passy (André Dewavrin), has described in his memoirs an almost comic history – though that was not its purpose – of the BCRA. The main problem was a lack of personnel. Passy himself had no experience in intelligence. Anti-Gaullists have claimed that torture chambers were set up in its cellars: difficult to imagine for an organization which could not even operate its own telephones. The rumour was put about by Communist sympathizers in London, both French (particularly André Labarthe's France Libre – nothing to do with de Gaulle's 'Free French') and British (particularly the *Guardian*).

Bomber Command. The origin of this branch of the Royal Air Force went back to the 1930s as the prospect of a new war developed with Germany. Behind it lay the idea of the bomber as a strategic weapon, not a tactical weapon that would merely be an aide to the movement of ground armies. The British army never felt comfortable with the notion and, as a result, Bomber Command developed only slowly. Its principal proponent was Marshal Arthur Harris, who was named Chief of Bomber Command in February 1942. Harris was one of the first air commanders to develop what became known as the 'bomber dream' – the idea that wars could be won by bombing only. In the age of free-falling bombs, it was not an idea that could be defended easily. The fact is, his 'area bombing' of Germany achieved far less militarily than expected, while it caused immeasurable civilian distress. His reputation suffered accordingly. But to consider him a 'war criminal' is an absurdity. It was not he who began the war, while he did at least 'bring the war home to Germany', which manifestly was not achieved in the First World War. A precursor of much strategic thinking about war today, Harris and his Bomber Command will always remain the subject of immense controversy, not unlike the First World War generals who developed strategies that would win the war for the Allies in 1945.

Coal and Steel Community (CSC). The CSC was initiated by the French Foreign Minister, *Robert Schuman*, in a surprise announcement made in Paris in 1949. The institution was to pool all resources of coal and steel of member states in a single community run by a High Authority. Britain was invited to join, but the Labour government rejected the offer on the grounds that these two industries had already been nationalized. Shuman already knew, through a series of secret meetings with Adenauer in the French zone, that he would have the support of the German Chancellor. Alcide de Gaspieri, the Italian Prime Minister, was also a keen supporter of the project. The Benelux countries, Belgium, the Netherlands and Luxembourg, were at the geographic heart of the Community. Thus were born 'the Six', who in 1957 would go on to form the *European Economic Community (EEC).*

Comité Français de la Libération Nationale (French Committee of National Liberation, CFLN). Established by de Gaulle at the moment of his arrival in Algiers, on 30 May 1943. To all intents and purposes this was the French government, not even in exile since it was on French territory. Vichy by this time had lost all credibility in French eyes. Within weeks, all the London governments-in-exile had recognized the Committee as the French government. Moscow sent a high-ranking diplomat to Algiers as ambassador, though the Soviet Union was bound not to recognize the Committee without the accord of the two other members of the 'Big Three'. Neither the Americans nor the British would recognize it – basically because of Roosevelt's personal hatred of de Gaulle. Just before D-Day, de Gaulle renamed the Committee the Provisional Government of the French Republic (GPRF). Within hours of the Allied landing in Normandy it was setting up its local administrations within France, thus forestalling American attempts to install *AMGOT* – their own military admin- istration – in the country; French Communist 'Liberation Committees', on the Soviet model, were likewise paralysed. The Gaullist Provisional Government had all ministries in Paris under its control before the Americans arrived, and before the Communists could take over. Allied recognition was belatedly made on 23 October 1944. De Gaulle's bitterness over America's ineffectual delaying tactics remained with him until his death in 1970; to this day the affair scars Franco-American relations.

Conseil National de la Résistance (CNR). The French National Resistance Council was organized by *Jean Moulin*, de Gaulle's representative in France, and held its first meeting in Lyons on 27 May 1943. It was designed as an umbrella organization for all Resistance move- ments and political parties in Northern (occupied) and Southern (unoccupied) France. Within less than a month Jean Moulin was arrested by the Gestapo and died in incarceration. After that the National Resistance Council rapidly lost its independent authority to Communist front organizations.

Control Commission, Allied. Set up in Berlin by the four occupying powers, the United

States, Britain, France and the Soviet Union, it was supposed to act as Allied central consultative council for a united, yet occupied Germany. But the Soviet Union never cooperated with the Western Allies. The Control Commission was eventually wound down in 1949 with the formation of the German Federal Republic in the West, and the German Democratic Republic in the former Soviet zone. Since 1946, however, it had achieved nothing.

Council of Foreign Ministers. Established at the Potsdam Conference in July 1945, the Council of Foreign Ministers (the United States, Britain, the Soviet Union and France) was supposed to meet every three months in London, beginning 1 September 1945, as a means of coordinating problems of peace – principally in Europe – and maintaining the wartime 'alliance'. Since the Soviet Union had never been a genuine ally, the institution turned out to be a fiasco. By December 1945 it was already effectively dead, though meetings did continue, on an irregular basis, until 1948.

Council of National Unity (RJN). Secret Polish Parliament set up in Warsaw in early 1944. The Council did not officially approve of the Warsaw Rising of 1 August and, like the *Delegacy*, disappeared during the tragic course of the Rising.

Delegacy (Delegatura). The Polish Government Delegacy (or 'Delegation' as it is sometimes known in English) was the interior executive civilian branch of Poland's Underground State. It lived in secrecy in Warsaw through the support of the London government-in-exile along with services of communication and supply provided by Britain's SOE. Official histories of the Delegacy are somewhat misleading: the conditions in which it worked were worse than intolerable. The first two Warsaw Delegates (the chiefs of the Delegacy) died under Gestapo torture, the third survived a short while and in 1943 managed to set up eight ministries. The fourth, J. S. Jankowski, lived to witness Soviet 'liberation'. In July 1944, just before the Warsaw Rising, a Council of Home Ministers was set up. The Delegacy never formally approved of the Rising, which was started on 1 August 1944 by the Home Army in Warsaw. But the Delegacy did manage to maintain primitive services – such as health, justice and communications – until September 1944, by which time nothing was left of this brave, isolated organization.

EAM/ELAS. EAM was the Communist Resistance Movement in Greece, named after the Greek initials of the organization. ELAS made up its armed forces. Neither were of much significance until after the sudden withdrawal of German forces in late 1944. They thereupon attempted to take over the government in Athens, leading to a major civil war at Christmastime. British forces, against systematic opposition from the American government and press, served to shore up the civilian Greek government. Ironically, the Americans were obliged to play the same role as the British after 1947.

European Advisory Commission (EAC). In 1943 the EAC was set up in London, under the initiative of the Foreign Office, to provide coordinated plans between the Allies, including the Soviet Union and France, on the future of Central Europe, particularly Germany. Often dismissed as an ineffective body, it in fact produced many reports employed in discussions at Yalta in February 1945 and Potsdam in July 1945. After the latter conference it was dissolved. Yet it proved a significant precursor to a multitude of post-war European institutions – most of which, it is argued in this book, were born out of the failure to arrive at a peace settlement on Central Europe.

European Economic Community (EEC). The origins of the EEC go back to a meeting of Foreign Ministers in Messina, Sicily, in June 1955, to discuss the future of the *Coal and Steel Community (CSC)*. Britain was invited to participate as an observer but declined the offer. The Belgian Foreign Minister, *Paul-Henri Spaak*, as chairman of the CSC made a surprise presentation of the programme to 'the Six' present. So passionate and dynamic was Spaak that a whole treaty, the Treaty of Rome, was ready for signing in March 1957. Its preamble famously called for 'an ever closer union of European states'. Thus was born a European Community, with a political dimension, that – with the abolition of all customs barriers – would become the European Union (EU).

European Free Trade Association (EFTA). An institution formed in 1960 under British initiative, it was designed to correspond more closely to Britain's view of Europe as a strictly economic community of free trading nation states. Its purpose, as the Prime Minister, Harold Macmillan, repeatedly pointed out, was not to compete with the EEC, but on the contrary, to expand the influence of the latter by dealing with countries outside the EEC. Its first members were, besides Britain, six peripheral states to the north of the EEC. EFTA never exercised the influence that the British had hoped. But the institution has never been formally abolished either. In 1994 it was renamed the European Economic Area (EEA) and it is quite possible that, with the collapse of the Communist bloc, the institution will provide a critical means of relating former Communist states to the heart of Europe. One of the weaknesses of EFTA is its insistence that Europe is made up of independent 'nation states' which, since 1945, is obviously a false perception.

European Recovery Program (ERP). The official name of what is more popularly known as the *Marshall Plan*. The programme was announced in general terms by George Marshall – wartime Chief of General Staff and now Secretary of State – at a Harvard commencement address in June 1947. It contained no commitments at all; Marshall at the time spoke of European 'self-help'. It took a year to push through Congress. The first grants were not received in Europe until summer 1948. Between that year and 1952, when the programme was wound down, $13 billion were distributed to sixteen Western European nations (the Communist bloc refused to participate). But Western Europe was not booming in 1952; the 'post-war boom' in Europe took place in the second half of that decade. Its most important effect was the creation of trust between the United States and Europe, which would gradually lead to the growth of international trade. Most significant also was the establishment of the *Organization for European Economic Co-operation (OEEC)*, a prerequisite for the receipt of funds and a major step in the direction of a European Community.

Forces Françaises de l'Intérieur (French Forces of the Interior, FFI). After the formal unification under Jean Moulin of the various movements of the French Resistance into the *National Resistance Council (CNR)* in May 1943 an effort was made to unite the various para-military forces that had developed – all calling themselves the 'French Resistance'. Histories of these efforts tend to give the development a much greater sense of order than in fact existed. The French Forces of the Interior (FFI) was set up in December 1943 as an organization that fused all military groups. The history of the next twelve months – both before and after the Liberation – proved that national unity was still far from being achieved. Most military units of the Resistance by the end of 1943 were Communist front organizations. As the Allies approached in spring 1944 the French Communists hoped that they would be able to fuse the French army into the FFI, which they effectively controlled. With the Liberation of Paris in August 1944, de Gaulle achieved the exact opposite: he placed all units of the FFI under the command of *General Koenig* and fused them into the army. The Americans helped de Gaulle by supplying him with truckloads of American army uniforms – which became the uniforms of the French army. For several months, however, Communist elements of the FFI (*fifis* as they were known) continued to spread terror and civil war throughout southern France.

Gulag. The term is generally applied to the Soviet slave labour camps that go back to the origin of the regime and were gradually abandoned during the 1950s after a series of riots and the realization that slave labour did not work economically. The term itself has its origin in the establishment, in February 1931, of the 'Chief Administration for Corrective Labour Camps' – in Russian, *Glavnoe upravlenie lagerei*, or 'GULag'. This administration officially existed for two years. But, typical of Soviet nomenclature, even official documents continued to refer to 'GULag' for many years afterwards. Alexander Solzhenitsyn in *The Gulag Archipelago* (1973) was the first to reveal the extent of its horrors to an ignorant West. But full knowledge about its victims is unlikely ever to be achieved. This is one of the great black holes of history.

Home Army (Armia Krajowa, AK). The Polish Home Army was organized at the surrender of Warsaw to the Germans in October 1939. Since the Soviet Union had also invaded Poland it became a force of Resistance against both powers. No other Resistance movement in Europe resembled in size and organization the Home Army and its related Underground State. Much tension existed between these two organizations as well as with the Polish government-in-exile in London. The Home Army has been blamed for setting off the fatal Warsaw Rising prematurely, on 1 August 1944.

Komsomols. The Komsomols (members of the Communist Youth League) were organized in 1919 in the early months of the Russian Civil War. For the Bolsheviks they were regarded as a central channel for transforming human behaviour to fit the new Communist society. Under Lenin, they became a major unit of repression in the countryside. They were employed as execution squads at the time of the Kronstadt revolt of 1921. Stalin used them for a similar purpose. During the war, they were the spearheads of Soviet terror during Red Army offensives.

KONR (Committee for the Liberation of the Peoples of Russia). Founded by *General Vlasov* and officially inaugurated on 14 November 1944 in Prague in the presence of Nazi dignitaries. The direct product of the opening ceremony was the *Prague Manifesto*, outlining Vlasov's political programme.

Lend-Lease. A programme of US defence aid – first to Britain and later extended to the Soviet Union and, later still, the Provisional Government of France – which had its origins in the Lend-Lease Act of January 1941. It was not a gift. Attached to the supply of war materials were several stringent conditions concerning the receiving country's trade practices. Article VII's requirement of 'free trade', at a time of war, was to cause much friction between Britain and the United States. Under the influence of *Harry Dexter White* the Treasury Department, charged with administering the programme, devised a system of undermining Britain's sterling area through a mechanism deliberately designed to reduce British cash reserves and increase her dependence on the United States. Britain remained for long unaware of this. In autumn 1944 a gradual system of dissolving Lend-Lease – 'Stage I', 'Stage II' and 'Stage III' – was negotiated between Britain and the United States. But this complex system, designed to help increase Britain's export sector, was abandoned when President Truman unilaterally cancelled Lend-Lease at the end of the war. Britain's new Labour government was forced to negotiate, in August 1945, a prohibitively expensive loan.

Marshall Plan. See **European Recovery Program (ERP)**.

National Homeland Council (KRN). Set up in Warsaw in January 1944 by the minority Polish Communists (PPR or Polish Workers' Party) to form an alternative to the London government-in-exile. At its head were two veteran Polish Communists, Bolesław Bierut and Władysław Gomułka, who had escaped Stalin's purges in Moscow in the 1930s and, evidently, found Nazi Warsaw a safer place to live. Policy statements were dictated from Moscow.

NKVD (*Narodnyi komissariat vnutrennikh del*). The NKVD or 'People's Commissariat for

Internal Affairs' was officially set up in 1922 as the Commissariat presiding over all Soviet internal security matters. However, like much Soviet nomenclature the term was used indis criminately (even in official documents) in reference to several different security organiza- tions, which evolved over time. The NKGB (*Narodnyi komissariat gosudarstvennoi bezopasnost*), the Soviet security and intelligence service, was through most of the war a part of the NKVD. Immediately after the war the NKGB was transformed into a separate MGB, forerunner of the KGB (established in 1954). GRU, the Soviet military intelligence service, was a separate organization altogether. It was GRU that was subject to the American VENONA deciphers from 1943 on. Revealed to the public only in the 1990s, VENONA provided documentary evidence of the widespread network of Soviet agents working both in the United States and the West in general; names are still only being gradually revealed. The Mitrokhin Archives, again only revealed in the 1990s, have provided valuable documentary evidence on the Western network of Soviet agents working for the KGB. These networks are now known to be far wider than ever before imagined.

During the Red Army's advance into Eastern Europe in 1944–5, the NKVD moved in behind the army and rounded up all foreigners within the occupied territory, including all Russian prisoners, and placed them in 'Special Camps' or 'Verification and Filtration Centres'. Often these were former Nazi concentration and even extermination camps. The inmates were then sent to the Russian interior or to Siberia. Many were never seen again. German POWs were officially returned in 1954. But several prisoners – French, Italians, Scandinavians – were still returning in the 1990s. The most famous case of a late returning prisoner is that of the Frenchman, Jacques Rossi, who eventually made his way back in the 1990s, aged over ninety. He continues to appear on French television though aged over a hundred.

North Atlantic Treaty Organization (NATO). Grew out of the Brussels Pact, an entirely European initiative to create a Western European alliance of defence against growing Communist aggression. The three Benelux countries (Belgium, the Netherlands and Luxembourg), France and Britain were the first members of this Pact, signed in April 1948. Attempts to involve the United States were at first unsuccessful. But NATO was eventually signed in Washington on 4 April 1949 with the most stringent American conditions attached, including complete American control of military command. Its most important clause was Article 5, which confirmed the principle that an armed attack on any one of its members would be regarded as an attack on them all. NATO, for the next four decades, provided sufficient deterrence to further Soviet military aggression within Europe.

OKH (Oberkommando des Heeres). German High Command of the Army.

OKW (Oberkommando der Wehrmacht). German High Command of the Armed Forces. OKH and OKW frequently found themselves in conflict, like many 'centralized' organiza- tions of the Nazi state. This was a deliberate policy – of divide and rule – set by Hitler so that he might hold supreme power. Germany consequently had a highly complex military command structure. Hitler mistrusted his commanders and rarely listened to them. He envied Stalin for his 1938 Purge. Hitler was more involved in day-to-day strategic questions than any other war leader. As a result he was exhausted.

Organization for European Economic Co-operation (OEEC). Initially an American idea born out of the Marshall Plan's requirement for a free-trade association to be created in Europe before American funds were made available. It rapidly developed in 1947–8 into an intergovernmental body, forming the basis of what Marshall himself termed a 'closer integration of Western Europe'.

Orgburo. Directorate of political commissars placed within the Red Army after its advance into Eastern and Central Europe.

OSS (Office of Strategic Services). The American equivalent of Britain's *SOE*, and about as effective. No single revolt in Europe against the Nazis was inspired by the OSS. Its most notable achievement was to set up a Vichy regime under Admiral Darlan in Algiers after the Allied landings in October 1942. Darlan was assassinated the following December – almost undoubtedly through the actions, arms and training of the British SOE.

People's Army (Armia Ludowa, AL). The Polish Communist interior armed forces whose activities consisted mainly of assassination and sabotage of Nazis and other 'Fascist' nuisances to the Communist cause. In late 1943 they numbered about 10,000, in contrast to the 400,000 members of the Polish *Home Army (AK)*.

Polish Committee of National Liberation (PKWN). Set up in Moscow during the Bagration Offensive of July 1944 as a Soviet puppet government in Poland. It was flown out to empty Lublin, the first town taken in Poland, on 27 July. The Polish Committee immediately started arresting soldiers of the Home Army and imprisoned them in Majdanek, a nearby former Nazi extermination camp.

PPR (Polish Workers' Party). The new Polish Communist Party set up in 1942, probably spontaneously, by Polish fellow-travellers after a prolonged Soviet propaganda campaign. Its actions – assassination and sabotage – were coordinated with Russian Partisans. Leaders of the previous Polish Communist Party had been liquidated by Stalin while in Russian exile in the 1930s. The new Party remained marginal until Russian 'liberation' in 1944.

ROA (Russian Liberation Army). Himmler was in favour of granting *General Vlasov* his own independent army in 1944, but Hitler refused authorization. It eventually began to constitute itself into two purely Russian divisions on 28 January 1945 – rather late in the day.

RPZ (Council for Assistance to Jews). A branch of the Polish Home Army that organized the delivery of arms via Warsaw's sewers to the Jewish Ghetto prior to the Ghetto Rising of spring 1943.

RSHA (Reichssicherheitshauptamt). The Reich Security Head Office, which was directed by Reinhard Heydrich until his assassination in Czechoslovakia in 1943 in an SOE operation. He was succeeded by Ernst Kaltenbrunner. It was the Nazis' main police arm against rebellion and resistance within occupied territories. Contrary to the terms of the 1940 Armistice, which forbade the presence of German police in France, it was secretly installed in the country where it became popularly but mistakenly known as the 'Gestapo' (the Gestapo was only one part of the RSHA). The French were supposed to do their own policing. After the extremely unpopular deportation of Jews in the Vel' d'Hiv' operation of 16 July 1942 – a sentiment that included the French police – this became impossible. Indeed, the French police developed into a force of resistance, a fact overlooked by many early post-war historians. The RSHA, on the other hand, played an increasingly important policing role in France and elsewhere in occupied Europe.

Supreme Headquarters of the Allied Expeditionary Force (SHAEF). Established in early 1944 to act as an umbrella command of all Allied operations in North-Western Europe. General Dwight D. Eisenhower was named its commander, because Roosevelt wanted to keep General George Marshall in Washington. SHAEF remained in England until August 1944, when it transferred to Granville in Normandy. It moved to Versailles in the autumn and, by the end of the war, it had got as far east as Rheims, in French Champagne. A vast, chaotic military bureaucracy, SHAEF, in its distance between command and the Front, made the famous 'château generals' of the First World War look minor offenders when compared to the administrative puppetry exercised by SHAEF during the Second World War. General Bernard Montgomery was the exception – undoubtedly because of his first-hand experience of soldiers' suffering in the First World War. His caravan command followed the front line of the armies into the heart of Germany. SHAEF not only prolonged the war unnecessarily; its armies of bureaucrats were the source of much material corruption in liberated areas, especially around Paris.

Smersh (*Smert shpionam*). Or, in English, 'Death to Spies'. Established by the Red Army to aid the *NKVD*, in 'liberated' regions, in its burdensome task of filtrating enemy aliens, suspected Russians and all those millions suspected of being enemies of the Soviet state. It became, essentially, a terrorist organization and long outlived its usefulness, even for James Bond.

SOE (Special Operations Executive). Set up at Churchill's orders in August 1940 to 'set Europe ablaze' with anti-Nazi rebellion. It has been the subject of many romantic stories and films about Lysanders landing in moonlit French fields, but its real effectiveness has often been questioned. Unfortunately for democracy, it was a flea in comparison to the Soviet Partisan movements.

Stavka. Supreme military command of the Red Army. Stavka often met secretly in one of Stalin's dachas outside Moscow. Its members, save Stalin himself, were not permanent, but were called from the Front as the situation warranted. While Stalin undeniably held complete control over Stavka's general strategy, he listened to his generals, took their advice and even allowed them to argue with him without having them subsequently murdered. This was one of the major contrasts between Hitler and Stalin.

STO (Service du Travail Obligatoire). As *Gauleiter Sauckel* tightened the screw on Vichy France's supply of labour to Germany, *Laval* and *Bousquet* continued to negotiate. By autumn 1942 Sauckel's demands had become so excessive that it was no longer possible to rely on volunteers. Laval's law setting up the *Service du Travail Obligatoire* was eventually put into execution in February 1943. No single measure did more to swell the number of Resisters, and particularly Communists, in France. A *déporté* henceforth denoted a worker in Germany, not a Jew. This led to the plight of Jews being overlooked, in contrast to the earlier sympathy felt for them in 1942.

SVR (*Sluzhba vneshnei razvedki*). The current Russian Foreign Intelligence Service and heir to the KGB. After a brief period in the 1990s, it would appear that much sensitive material on Russia's Communist past has been closed to the public and has possibly been destroyed. Nobody can hope for a complete history of what happened over the seventy years of Communist rule in Russia and its neighbouring countries.

UNRRA (United Nations Relief and Rehabilitation Administration). The organization was set up in November 1943 to deal with the swarms of refugees first encountered by Western Allies when they entered Italy. UNRRA was an army organization – hence 'United Nations', which stood for the sixty or so Allies involved in the war against Hitler (the United Nations Organization did not at that time exist). The United States was the chief contributor of funds, which became a contentious issue after the war when Congress imposed a self-help system on what was to become the Marshall Fund in 1948. UNRRA's first task was to clear the roads for army movements; refugees were placed in temporary camps from which it was assumed that they would soon return 'home'. But as the war developed, with refugees numbering in tens of millions, it became evident that many had no 'home' to return to. Immigration programmes had to be organized and the programme was only slowly phased out in the early 1950s. The whole drama called into question traditional notions of 'citizenship' and whether one could consider Europe simply a collection of 'nation states'. Those post-war questions remain with us to this day.

War Production Board (WPB). Established immediately after Pearl Harbor (December 1941) to oversee the planning of US war production. It was directed by Donald Nelson, a Sears Roebuck executive. Thus began the growth of 'dollar-a-year men' in Washington – businessmen who would work for the burgeoning war administration for a dollar a year. A deep, abiding hatred developed between the 'dollar-a-year men' and the preceding generation of Washington bureaucrats, the New Dealers.

Notes

℣

One flag, one shot

1. 'Stalins Rede' in Peter Gosztony (ed.), *Der Kampf um Berlin 1945 in Augenzeugenberichten* (Dusseldorf, 1970), 17–19; Alexandra Richie, *Faust's Metropolis* (New York, 1998), 561.
2. Cornelius Ryan, *The Last Battle* (New York, 1967), 290.
3. S. N. Perewjorkin, *Dönto csapas* [Magyar: 'The Decisive Battle'] (Budapest, 1950) in Gosztony (ed.), *Der Kampf*, 341.
4. Details of the fighting around the Reichstag can be found in the works of two military veterans who served in Berlin after the war, Tony Le Tissier, *Race for the Reichstag* (London, 1999), 141–6, 158–9, 166–9; and Pierre Rocolle, *Le Sac de Berlin, avril–mai 1945* (Paris, 1992), 141–55.
5. Should one take seriously the existence of a certain Alexander Kvapishevski, or 'Sasha Kvap', a Soviet agent who worked his way up the Gestapo hierarchy to the point of becoming an aide to General Wilhelm Burgdorf, Hitler's chief military adjutant? Ivan Paderin, who was charged with the 'political affairs of the regiment' that stormed the Reich Chancellery on 2 May, claimed in an interview made in the 1990s that Kvap 'became Hitler's messenger in the Bunker'. He seems to have been an inefficient spy. Whatever information he passed on had no influence on Soviet military operations in Berlin, which continued to concentrate on taking the burnt-out Reichstag. After the fall of the city, the Soviet government was obliged to set up at least two investigative commissions to discover what actually did happen in the Bunker during Hitler's last days. See Ada Petrova and Peter Watson, *The Death of Hitler* (London, 1995), 133–9.
6. Le Tissier, *Race*, 167–8.
7. Perevertkin suggests that the sailors had landed on the narrow strip that had been opened on the east–west axis in the Tiergarten but, given the size of their aircraft, it seems more likely that they arrived at Gatow Airport before the Russians seized it on the 28th.
8. Perevertkin, *Dönto csapas*, 343.
9. Le Tissier says '70 minutes before midnight', *Race*, 169, but contradicts himself in the following paragraph; Richie says 'seventy minutes before the dawn', *Faust's Metropolis*, 596.
10. The official photographs by the Ukrainian photographer, Yevgeni Khaldei, were taken on 2 May. They show Yegorov and Kantaria in a most improbable battle position as they purportedly hoist a huge flag over the back pediment of the Reichstag, a precipice directly overlooking Hermann-Göring-Strasse and, just visible in the background, the Brandenburg Gate. Khaldei admitted shortly before his death in 1997 that the man with the flag 'was called Aleksei Kovalyov'. The soldier hanging on to his legs to prevent him from falling 'was a guy from Dagestan whose name I never got'. Yegorov and Kantaria were made 'Heroes of the Soviet Union'. The men who beat them to the roof were rewarded with a lesser decoration, the Order of the Red Banner. See ibid., n. 101, p. 1039; and Le Tissier, *Race*, 169.
11. Only two municipal services remained in operation throughout the Battle of Berlin:

the manufacture of beer (the city's seventeen breweries were kept open by government decree), and the Reich's meteorological station out in Potsdam. See Ryan, *Last Battle*, 425. Several Berliners, in their rooms with glassless windows, noted the cold winds of 30 April. Ivan Paderin, deputy commander of the 220th regiment in the Russian 8th Guards Army noticed the wind veer from east to west on 30 April, permitting a smoke cover during the crossing of the Landwehr Canal: see Petrova and Watson, *Death*, 134.

12. Anonymous, *A Woman in Berlin*, trans J. Stern (London, 1955), 84, 99; Ryan, *Last Battle*, 396; Paul David, *Am Königsplatz* (Zurich, 1948), in Gosztony (ed.), *Der Kampf*, 345.

13. Anonymous, *A Woman*, 61.

14. Ryan, *Last Battle*, 334.

15. Anonymous, *A Woman*, 75–6, 87, 95; Margret Boveri, *Tage des Überlebens: Berlin 1945* (Munich, 1968), 91, 99.

16. Rocolle, *Le Sac*, 102–4; Vassili Chuikov, *Das Ende des Dritten Reiches* (Munich, 1966), in Gosztony (ed.), *Der Kampf*, 344.

17. On the extent of devastation in Berlin, often overestimated, see Brian Ladd, *The Ghosts of Berlin* (Chicago, 1997), 175–8.

18. These narrow, airless closets did not, however, provide perfect security against rampaging Russians: the anonymous diarist describes the case of a neighbouring teenage refugee from Königsberg gang-raped under her roof. Anonymous, *A Woman*, 74.

19. Boveri, *Tage*, 76–89.

20. Anonymous, *A Woman*, 55–6.

21. Ibid., 90–1; Boveri, *Tage*, 78; Richie, *Faust's Metropolis*, 564.

22. Although see interviews conducted by Ryan, *Last Battle*, 432–3, 455.

23. Anonymous, *A Woman*, 77–8.

24. Richie, *Faust's Metropolis*, 563–4; Rocolle, *Le Sac*, 80.

25. Boveri, *Tage*, 101; see also Anonymous, *A Woman*, 76.

26. Boveri, *Tage*, 76, 82–3.

27. Ibid., 74, 89; Anonymous, *A Woman*, 35.

28. Rocolle, *Le Sac*, 149; Heribert Schwan and Rolf Steininger, *Besiegt, besetzt, geteilt von der Invasion bis zur Spaltung Deutschlands* (Oldenburg, 1979), 149–59 (text accompanied by colour photographs taken by the Allies on their arrival in June).

29. Rocolle, *Le Sac*, 18.

30. Ibid., 117–18.

31. Ryan, *Last Battle*, 398–9.

32. Rocolle, *Le Sac*, 149. In scenes like this, the men were not heroes. The anonymous diarist was told by a woman queuing for water how, as she was being dragged away by Russians, a man in her cellar had cried out, 'Go along, for God's sake! You're getting us all into trouble!' Anonymous, *A Woman*, 91.

33. The anonymous diarist met a neighbour on 24 April who had got through to a friend in Wedding by telephone. 'The people', she heard, 'are massing on the pavement, laughing and waving, holding up their children': ibid., 42. Le Tissier's well-researched account of the taking of Moabit and Wedding is a good deal more gruesome and contains no hint of welcome: see *Race*, 87–91, 131–2, 141–5; also Ryan, *Last Battle*, 449.

34. Ibid., 454; Rocolle, *Le Sac*, 149.

35. Ryan, *Last Battle*, 250–2, 423. This contrasts with the impression of most visitors immediately after the war when the main rooms of the Führerbunker had been burnt and the furniture destroyed; they found it 'ghostly and bleak', the rooms 'cramped', and imagined that the atmosphere inside during the last days of the Reich must have been like 'working in a public urinal'. See Petrova and Watson, *Death*, 29, 103.

36. Hugh Trevor-Roper, *The Last Days of Hitler* (Chicago, 1992), 148–50, 231; Ryan, *Last Battle*, 423.

37. Ibid., 252.

38. Ian Kershaw, *Hitler* (London, 2000), II, 813–15.

39. See my *1815: The Roads to Waterloo* (London, 1996), 127–32.
40. Ernst Jünger, *The Storm of Steel* (London, tr. 1929), 46–7, 318–19.
41. Adolf Hitler, *Mein Kampf* (London, tr. 1992), 150, 152.
42. Kershaw, *Hitler*, I, 93; II, 742, 746; Hitler, *Mein Kampf*, 183–7; Hitler to Field Marshal Wilhelm Keitel, 'Valediction to the German Armed Forces', quoted in Trevor-Roper, *Last Days*, 224.
43. Kershaw, *Hitler*, II, 802.
44. Ibid., 819.
45. Trevor-Roper, *Last Days*, 213.
46. Kershaw, *Hitler*, II, 745.
47. Trudl Junge, Hitler's secretary, quoted in Petrova and Watson, *Death*, 65. Several witnesses of Linge's panic, including Linge himself, are quoted in James O'Donnell, *The Berlin Bunker* (London, 1979), 251–3.
48. Ibid., 256.
49. Anonymous, *A Woman*, 127; Boveri, *Tage*, 94; Rocolle, *Le Sac*, 181.
50. J. Stalin, *Discours et ordres du jour, 1941–1945* (Paris, 1945), 116–18.

ARMIES

Beginnings

1. The newsreel is included in Romain Goupil's 'Paris, août 1944: une libération exemplaire', BDIC audiovisuels KV 616/6.
2. *Combat*, 26 August 1944.
3. *L'Humanité*, 26–27 August 1944.
4. Charles de Gaulle, *Mémoires de guerre* (Paris, 1999), I, 78, 87–9. For some insights into de Gaulle's world view of the war, see Daniel J. Mahoney, *De Gaulle: Statesmanship, Grandeur, and Modern Democracy* (New Brunswick, NJ, 2000), 71–87.
5. Régis Debray, *A demain, de Gaulle* (Paris, 1990), 79.
6. Jean Lacouture, *De Gaulle* (Paris, 1984), I, 336; de Gaulle, *Mémoires*, I, 62; Winston Churchill, *The Second World War* (London, 1948–54), II, 162.
7. 'Appel aux Français', 18 June 1940, in de Gaulle, *Mémoires*, I, 329–30.
8. There is, in fact, some confusion over what time de Gaulle actually went on the air. The administrators of the BBC recorded Churchill's address, but did not record de Gaulle. The recording we have was made at a later date. The famous slogan 'France has lost a battle! But France has not lost the war!' appeared on posters in the streets of London in July; it does not appear in de Gaulle's initial appeal. It is often said that few in France heard de Gaulle's speech. This is true. But it was fairly widely reported in the French press – which had not yet censored de Gaulle – and got good coverage in the British. Thus it can be said that de Gaulle's address was read, widely read, rather than heard. See Lacouture, *De Gaulle*, I, 368–72.
9. Churchill, *Second World War*, II, 197–9.
10. As one historian has recently noted, the 'Allies did not have victory handed to them on a plate; they had to fight for it': Richard Overy, *Why the Allies Won* (London, 1995), xii.
11. Gerhard L. Weinberg, *A World at Arms* (Cambridge, 1994), 142, 145; Martin Gilbert, *Winston Churchill* (London, 1983), VI, 357.
12. For the American disdain for maps both in war and peace see my *1918: War and Peace* (London, 2000), especially pp. 60–3, 357–69.
13. Richard M. Leighton and Robert W. Coakley, *Global Logistics and Strategy* (Washington, DC, 1955), I, 133–4.
14. Sir Halford Mackinder, *The World War and After* (London, 1924), 270.
15. Albert C. Wedemeyer, *Wedemeyer Reports!* (New York, 1958), 61–301; John Keegan, *Six Armies in Normandy* (London, 1992), 31–4.

16. Albrecht Haushofer, *Zur Problematik des Raumbegriffs* (Heidelberg and Berlin, 1935), 14. This is in fact quoting from Karl Haushofer's son. Father and son worked very closely together, and even conspired to get Rudolf Hess to England during the war. Neither were members of the Nazi Party, a fact which cost them both their lives.

17. The strategic significance of the Indian Ocean was acknowledged in the Japanese war plans of August–September 1941. See Weinberg, *World at Arms*, 256–7.

18. Leighton and Coakley, *Global Logistics*, I, 119.

19. Ibid., 126–38.

20. The US Army actually reached its peak of 8.2 million men in 1945, half a million short of Wedemeyer's 1943 requirement: ibid., 131.

21. Ibid., 133–4.

22. Churchill, *Second World War*, II, 198.

23. I have discussed at some length the peace settlement of 1919 in my *1918: War and Peace*.

24. Ibid., 467.

25. Quoted by Henry Kissinger, *Diplomacy* (London, 1994), 304–5.

26. Churchill, *Second World War*, II, 161.

27. Adolf Hitler, *Mein Kampf* (London, 1992), 323.

28. Ibid., 421.

29. Ibid., 305.

30. Ibid., 330.

31. Ibid., 362, 493–5, 577.

32. Ibid., 603.

33. Ibid., 147.

34. Dallas, *1918*, 476–7.

35. Hitler, *Mein Kampf*, 317.

36. Norman Davies, *God's Playground* (Oxford, 1981), II, 435.

37. Karl Haushofer and his wife committed suicide in Nuremberg in January 1946 during the Military Trials. Their son, Albrecht, had been arrested by the Gestapo after the Bomb Plot of July 1944. He was murdered by SS Kommandos at Moabit gaol, in Berlin, on 24 April 1945. See the relevant entries in *Neue Deutsche Biographie* (Berlin, 1969).

38. Many Hitler specialists still argue, like A. J. P. Taylor as reviewed below, that *Mein Kampf* contained no blueprint for his foreign policy of the 1930s and '40s – that he was an opportunist. This is true in the detail, in the alliances he contracted, in the isolated strikes he undertook, in the short-term priorities he set himself. But it seems to me that there is a general logic and sense of direction in *Mein Kampf* that too many historians continue to overlook. Consider, for example, the following passages from the book: 'The new Reich must again set itself on the march along the road of the Teutonic Knights of old, to obtain by the German sword [land] for the German plough and daily bread for the nation . . . Only an adequately large space on this earth assures a nation freedom of existence . . . We National Socialists must hold unflinchingly to our aim in foreign policy, namely, to secure for the German people the land and soil to which they are entitled on this earth . . . We take up where we broke off six hundred years ago. We stop the endless German movement to the south and west, and turn our gaze towards the land in the east . . . If we speak of soil in Europe today, we can primarily have in mind only *Russia* and her vassal border states.' Hitler, *Mein Kampf*, 128–9, 587, 596, 598.

39. A. J. P. Taylor, *The Origins of the Second World War* (Greenwich, Conn., 1968).

40. Hitler, *Mein Kampf*, 597.

41. Ian Ousby, *Occupation* (London, 1997), 62

42. Antony Beevor, *Stalingrad* (London, 1999), 404; Overy, *Why the Allies Won*, 84.

43. Weinberg, *World at Arms*, 239.

44. Churchill, *Second World War*, III, 347, 352.

45. François Furet, *Le Passé d'une illusion* (Paris, 1995), 372.

46. Tony Judt, 'Preface' to Istvan Deak, Jan T. Gross and Tony Judt (eds.), *The Politics of Retribution in Europe: World War II and Its Aftermath* (Princeton, NJ, 2000), xi.

47. Patrick Marnham, *The Death of Jean Moulin* (London, 2000), 193–5, 263.

48. Julian Jackson, *France, The Dark Years, 1940–1944* (Oxford, 2001), 459–60, which still places the blame on Hardy. Hardy was acquitted in two separate treason trials in 1947 and 1950: see Marnham, *Death*, 223–32. Aubrac defended himself before a panel of historians in 1997: see *L'Evénement du jeudi*, 3 April 1997.

49. Marnham, *Death*, 179, 184, 190

50. His inefficiency both as a smuggler on behalf of the Republicans in the Spanish Civil War and as a producer of aircraft won him the reputation as 'the gravedigger of French aviation': ibid., 78.

51. Cot was identified in his correspondence with the Soviets as 'Daedalus', Labarthe as 'Jerome'. See Nigel West, *VENONA* (London, 1999), 59, 88–92. In 1994, at the request of Cot's family, a historical commission was set up in France to investigate Cot's relationship with the Soviets. It concluded that the claim that Pierre Cot was a Soviet agent – 'knowingly and deliberately transmitting information to a foreign power' – rested on 'no serious historical basis and cannot be held as valid'. See Serge Berstein, Robert Frank, Sabine Jansen and Nicolas Werth, *Rapport de la commission d'historiens constituée pour examiner la nature des relations de Pierre Cot avec les autorités soviétiques* (Paris, 1995), 4, 70. That conclusion was contested at the time by Stéphane Courtois, *Remarques sur un rapport* (Paris, 1995). The VENONA documents prove beyond doubt that Cot was, while in New York during the war, passing information on to the Soviet NKVD.

52. Jan Nowak, *Courier from Warsaw* (Detroit, 1982), 105, 163–4.

53. Jan M. Ciechanowski, *The Warsaw Rising of 1944* (Cambridge, 1974), 82, 97.

54. Nowak, *Courier*, 62.

55. Julian Eugeniusz Kulski, *Dying We Live* (New York, 1979), 146–7.

56. On the break in Russo-Polish diplomatic relations, see Ciechanowski, *Warsaw Rising*, 5. On Stalin's ordered massacre of the Poles, Dmitri Volkogonov, *Stalin: Triumph and Tragedy* (New York, 1991); 360; Andrzej Pacskowski, 'Pologne, la "nation-ennemi"', in Stéphane Courtois et al., *Le Livre noir du communisme* (Paris, 1998), 428–34; Jean-François Revel, *La Grande Parade* (Paris, 2000), 126–31. At a lunch in April 1943 Sikorski told Churchill that he had proofs the Russians had murdered '15,000 Polish officers and other prisoners'. Churchill replied, 'If they are dead nothing you can do will bring them back.' In Churchill, *Second World War*, IV, 679.

57. *The Times*, 6 July 1943.

58. Nowak, *Courier*, 447.

59. Ciechanowski, *Warsaw Rising*, 6.

60. John Erickson, *The Road to Berlin* (London, 1999), 65–6, 97–113.

61. *The Times*, 23 June 1943.

62. Alan Moorehead, *Eclipse* (London, 2000), 5–7.

63. *The Times*, 16 June 1943.

64. Erickson, *Road*, 93–4.

65. Ciechanowski, *Warsaw Rising*, 87–115; Davies, *God's Playground*, II, 447–52.

66. John Keegan is particularly good on Sikorski's tourists: *Six Armies*, 261–4.

67. Joanna K. M. Hanson, *The Civilian Population and the Warsaw Uprising of 1944* (Cambridge, 1982), 14; Davies, *God's Playground*, 441–6, 463.

68. Hanson, *Civilian Population*, 16–18.

69. Paul Johnson, *A History of the Jews* (London, 1987), 234–8.

70. Hanson, *Civilian Population*, 7–8, 16–18; Davies, *God's Playground*, 441, 456–64, Nowak, *Courier*, 105–6; Kulski, *Dying We Live*, 26, 43–9, 56–8, 62–4, 88, 110–15, 130–46.

71. Nuremberg Document no. 2325 and Frank's diary quoted in Hanson, *Civilian Population*, 13.

72. Professor Jan T. Gross finds that Polish 'historiography of the war could not grapple with fundamental subjects', and that 'important synthetic studies are yet to be written on the period.' To help correct the problem he has proposed, with modesty, to 'take one thread – the history of Polish-Jewish relations in this fateful decade – in order to confront the stereotyped thinking prevailing on this subject in Polish historiography.' Gross's work ('A Tangled Web' in Deak, Gross, Judt (eds.), *Politics of Retribution*, 74–129; and *Neighbors: The Destruction of the Jewish Community in Jedwabne, Poland* [Princeton, 2000]) has led to brawling rather than cool confrontation. The ensuing 'debate' on Polish-Jewish relations honours neither the victims of the war, nor the academic bruisers who currently pursue it. See, in particular, correspondence in the *Times Literary Supplement* under the title 'The Massacre at Jedwabne', January–June 2001.

73. Ousby, *Occupation*, 102; Jackson, *France*, 128.

74. Ousby, *Occupation*, 41.

75. Ibid., 85–6; David Pryce-Jones, *Paris in the Third Reich* (London, 1981), 234; Robert O. Paxton, *Vichy France* (New York, 1972), 74–7.

76. Jackson, *France*, 233–5.

77. National opinion polls were taken on several critical issues in France after the founding of IFOP, the Institut Français d'Opinion Publique, in 1938. However, unlike in the United States where, from 1939 onwards, President Roosevelt regularly studied the results of opinion polls, politicians in France totally ignored them. Crowds may have welcomed the Munich accords in September 1938, but only 57 per cent of the French polled in October approved of them, 37 per cent opposed them, and 70 per cent answered that, if Hitler were to make any further demands, France and Britain should resist him by force. Thus, a serious gap had developed between public opinion in the last months of peace and the politicians who had been elected in 1936. See Christel Peyrefitte, 'Les premiers sondages d'opinion', in René Rémond and Janine Bourdin (eds.), *Edouard Daladier, Chef de Gouvernement, avril 1938–septembre 1939* (Paris, 1977), 265–78.

78. See Jackson's review of the literature, *France*, 274–8.

79. For an evocative description of Vichy, see Adam Nossiter, *The Algeria Hotel* (New York, 2001), 97–218.

80. Geoffrey Warner, *Pierre Laval and the Eclipse of France* (London, 1968), 299–311.

81. Ousby, *Occupation*, 81.

82. Paxton, *Vichy France*, 86.

83. Announced by the Prime Minister, Raymond Barre, in the Chamber of Deputies in February 1979. For this and other French statistics see Michael R. Marrus and Robert O. Paxton, *Vichy France and the Jews* (New York, 1981), 343–4; Jackson, *France*, 362. On Poland, see Davies, *God's Playground*, 265–6, 488–9.

84. Paul Webster, *Pétain's Crime* (London, 1990), 94; Marrus and Paxton, *Vichy France*, 226–7.

85. Ibid., 224.

86. For a clear, first-hand account of how the administrative machinery of Vichy was set up in Paris see the memorandum prepared by senior civil servants of the regime reproduced in Pryce-Jones, *Paris*, 233–5.

87. Jackson, *France*, 215; Jean Galtier-Boissière records, in his diary on 20 July (four days after the 'Grande Rafle' in Paris), hearing Laval say *'Je crois à la victoire allemande et j'ajoute que je la souhaite'*, *Journal 1940–1950* (Paris, 1992), 107.

88. Interview of Albrecht Krause, in Pryce-Jones, *Paris*, 238.

89. Marrus and Paxton, *Vichy France*, 233–4.

90. George Wellers, 'A propos d'un crime oublié', *Le Monde juif*, No. 138, April–June 1990, 92–3.

91. Maurice Rajsfus, *Jeudi noir* (Paris, 1992), 28–30; Blanche Finger and William Karel (eds.), *Opération 'Vent printanier'* (Paris, 1992), 153–4.

92. Ibid., 38–9, 72–3, 155; Claude Lévy and Paul Tillard, *La Grande Rafle du Vel d'Hiv* (Paris, 1967, 1992), 64.

93. Aron and Wellers quoted in Jackson, *France*, 366.
94. The documentation is very clear on this point, though it is often forgotten today. See Lévy and Tillard, *Grande Rafle*, 188–97. The question of Catholic 'silence' may be raised with regard to the Vatican and the French Catholic hierarchy before July 1942; it rapidly loses its relevance after that date.
95. Finger and Karel (eds.), *'Vent printanier'*, 99, 120, 141, 154; Wellers, 'A propos', 94–5.
96. For exceptions, see Lévy and Tillard, *Grande Rafle*, 46.
97. Ibid., 40–3.
98. For example, ibid., 69. A poignant account has been left by Annette Muller, who was nine at the time. Forty years later she remembered a five-hour lorry drive from the Vel' d'Hiv' to the French camp at Beaune-la-Rolande where, in August, children under twelve were separated from their mothers. 'The gendarmes hit out with the butts of their rifles and their truncheons or sprayed us with firehoses full of ice-cold water to force the children to leave their mothers . . . The gendarmes tore off the women's clothing looking for jewels or money . . .' The children were shipped to Drancy in cattle trucks. Some of them, including the Muller children, were later moved not to Poland, but to a huge refugee camp in Paris because they were considered French. In the police van that transferred them, the children started singing and shouting. 'At a certain moment,' continued Annette Muller, 'I turned towards the policemen sitting behind us. They were listening to us in silence, crying. I realized we weren't going home, so I cried too.' In Webster, *Pétain's Crime*, 118–19.
99. Annie Kriegel, *Ce que j'ai cru comprendre* (Paris, 1991), 153–4.
100. Wellers, 'A propos', 93.
101. Finger and Karel (eds.), *'Vent printanier'*, 98, 119, 139, 165. The best account of the early French Communist resistance groups remains Stéphane Courtois, *Le PCF dans la guerre* (Paris, 1980), especially 249–95.
102. *L'Humanité*, 20 January 1943.
103. Pryce-Jones, *Paris*, 179.
104. *L'Humanité*, 18 February 1944.
105. Ibid.
106. For a portrait of Piłsudski, see my *1918*, 149–52.
107. Hanson, *Civilian Population*, 17.
108. Nowak, *Courier*, 171.
109. Kulski, *Dying We Live*, 82–3.
110. Nowak, *Courier*, 216, 221.
111. Ciechanowski, *Warsaw Rising*, 7.
112. Ibid., 26.
113. Ibid., 56.

Movements

1. Robin Neillands, *The Bomber War* (London, 2001), 268–9, 283.
2. Ibid., 309.
3. *Aujourd'hui*, 19 April 1944; *Les Nouveaux Temps*, 19 April 1944.
4. Newsreel: 'Le Maréchal Pétain à Paris', *France actualités*, 28 April 1944.
5. Philippe Henriot, *26 avril 1944: le Maréchal à Paris* (Montrouge, 1944).
6. Alain Peyrefitte, *C'était de Gaulle* (Paris, 1994), I, 14; II, 327.
7. Colonel Passy, *2e Bureau, Londres* (Monte Carlo, 1947), 33.
8. Christian Pineau, *La Simple Vérité* (Geneva, 1972), I, 158.
9. Charles de Gaulle, *Mémoires de guerre* (Paris, 1999), I, 7–8; Marcel Proust, *A la recherche du temps perdu* (Paris, 1987), I, 25–33.
10. Charles Williams, *The Last Great Frenchman* (London, 1993), 37, 165, 346.
11. De Gaulle, *Mémoires de guerre*, II, 43–4. The British transcript of Churchill's acerbic conversation with de Gaulle at Downing Street on 30 September 1942 is quoted in full

in François Kersaudy, *Churchill and De Gaulle* (London, 1981), 203–9.

12. De Gaulle, *Mémoires de guerre*, I, 8.

13. Ibid., 8–9.

14. Jean Lacouture, *De Gaulle* (Paris, 1984), I, 139.

15. Ibid., 170. For a description of the lectures see Williams, *Last Great Frenchman*, 66–7.

16. Lacouture, *De Gaulle*, I, 174.

17. Gregor Dallas, *At the Heart of a Tiger* (London, 1993), 592.

18. Lacouture, *De Gaulle*, I, 144–6.

19. Ibid., 136.

20. Ibid., 105.

21. Charles de Gaulle, 'Conférences prononcées à l'Ecole de Guerre', in *Lettres, Notes et Carnets (1919–juin 1940)* (Paris, 1980), II, 219.

22. Quoted in Denis Mack Smith, *Modern Italy: A Political History* (New Haven, Conn., 1997), 405.

23. Alistair Horne, *Harold Macmillan* (London, 1988), I, 202.

24. Alan Moorehead, *Eclipse* (London, 2000), 66, 78.

25. Williams, *Last Great Frenchman*, 178, 201, 218.

26. Charles de Gaulle, Broadcast of 19 June 1940, in *Discours et messages* (Paris, 1970), I, 14.

27. *The Times*, 15 July 1940.

28. Ibid., 15–16 July 1942.

29. *New York Times*, 9–14 July 1942.

30. Williams, *Last Great Frenchman*, 232.

31. Stéphane Courtois, *Le PCF dans la guerre* (Paris, 1980), 435–8.

32. Joseph Stalin, 'Rapport . . . , 6 novembre 1943', in *Discours et ordres du jour, 1941–1945* (Paris, 1945), 98–109.

33. Communist ideology, said François Furet, a master commentator on the phenomenon, was a 'string of tautologies that supplanted the uncertainties of the "bourgeois" democratic form of political representation: the working class was the liberator of the people, the Communist Party was at the head of the working class, Lenin was at the head of the Party.' Furet was writing about Communism in the early 1920s, but substitute 'Stalin' for 'Lenin' and the formula applies equally well to European Communism during the Second World War. François Furet, *Le Passé d'une illusion* (Paris, 1995), 124.

34. Courtois, *PCF*, 355.

35. *Vie Ouvrière*, 3 July 1943, in ibid., 393.

36. *L'Humanité,* 16 May 1940.

37. Henri Amouroux, *La Grande Histoire des Français sous l'Occupation* (Paris, 1999), III, 115.

38. Horne, *Macmillan*, I, 187.

39. Ibid., *157*.

40. Ibid., 186.

41. Ibid., 188–9; Williams, *Last Great Frenchman*, 347.

42. *L'Humanité*, 1 January 1944.

43. Courtois, *PCF*, 428.

44. Horne, *Macmillan*, I, 209.

45. Williams, *Last Great Frenchman*, 246.

46. *L'Humanité*, 16 June 1944. H. W. Henderson, writing in September 1944, traces the term 'émigré government' to an article written by a certain N. Battinsky, appearing in the Soviet journal *War and the Working Class*, in early 1944. It was, he claimed, relayed to the world press. Extracts appeared in the British press and the article was reprinted in its entirety in the British Soviet journal of the *Russia Today Society*. 'The émigré government is restraining not only rebellion, but all forms of struggle against the German invaders,' it was claimed. Stalin repeated the same words in several diplomatic discussions

in the first half of 1944. See Henderson, *The Glory and the Shame of Warsaw* (Perth, 1944), 15.

47. Petru Dumitriu, *Incognito* (Paris, 1962), 302–16.
48. John Erickson, *The Road to Berlin* (London, 1999), 198.
49. Czesław Miłosz, *To Begin Where I Am* (New York, 2001), 123
50. Jan M. Ciechanowski, *The Warsaw Rising of 1944* (Cambridge, 1974), 113–14.
51. Julian Eugeniusz Kulski, *Dying, We Live* (New York, 1979), 182.
52. Czesław Miłosz, 'A Legend', in *New and Collected Poems 1931–2001* (London, 2001), 99.
53. Czesław Miłosz, 'The Prioress', in *To Begin Where I Am* (New York, 2001), 85–101
54. *What the Nation Is Fighting For*, reproduced in Joanna Hanson, *The Civilian Population and the Warsaw Uprising of 1944* (Cambridge, 1982), 60–1.
55. 'Letter to Jerzy Andrzejewski' in Miłosz, *To Begin*, 189. For Miłosz's portrait of Andrzejewski, including the quotation in this paragraph, see 'Alpha the Moralist', in ibid., 116–41.
56. Czesław Miłosz, *The Seizure of Power* (London, 1955), 42–3.
57. 'You Who Wronged', in Miłosz, *Collected Poems*, 103.
58. 'Songs of Adrian Zielinski' in ibid., 69.
59. Miłosz, *To Begin*, 98, 189–201.
60. 'A Song on the End of the World', in Miłosz, *Collected Poems*, 56.
61. The second half of a verse by Verlaine. See Alexander McKee, *Caen: Anvil of Victory* (London, 1964), 32.
62. '*Quand Saint-Etienne croulera / La monarchie anglaise disparaîtra*' in André Gosset and Paul Lecomte, *Caen pendant la bataille* (Caen, 1946), 27.
63. Field Marshal Lord Alanbrooke, *War Diaries 1939–1945* (London, 2002), 555.
64. On Harris's unchanging position, see Henry Probert, *Bomber Harris: His Life and Times* (London, 2001), 289–96
65. Cornelius Ryan, *The Longest Day* (New York, 1959), 62.
66. Doug Halloway, *A Soldier's Memories 1944–1945* (London, 1998), 15.
67. Quoted in McKee, *Caen*, 9.
68. Moorehead, *Eclipse*, 100–2.
69. McKee, *Caen*, 53, 72.
70. Nigel Hamilton, *The Full Monty* (London, 2001), I, 406, 525, 533–4.
71. Ibid., 504.
72. Moorehead, *Eclipse*, 87–8.
73. Hamilton, *Full Monty*, I, 384.
74. McKee, *Caen*, 206.
75. Erickson, *Road to Berlin*, 218.
76. Richard Woff, 'Rokossovsky', in Harold Shukman (ed.), *Stalin's Generals* (London, 1997), 177–96.
77. Erickson, *Road to Berlin*, 245.
78. Woff, 'Rokossovsky', 191.

SEASONS

Paris and Warsaw in summer

1. J. V. Stalin to W. Churchill, Moscow, 23 July 1944, in Jan M. Ciechanowski, *The Warsaw Rising of 1944* (Cambridge, 1974), 61.
2. Norman Davies, *God's Playground* (Oxford, 1981), II, 472.
3. Jan Nowak, *Courier from Warsaw* (Detroit, 1982), 334.
4. Joanna Hanson, *The Civilian Population and the Warsaw Uprising of 1944* (Cambridge, 1982), 65.
5. Ibid., 68.
6. Nowak, *Courier*, 326.

7. Ibid., 329.

8. On variations in the 'historical' stages of Communist propaganda, see Z. Nagorski, *Warsaw Fights Alone* (London, 1944), 10; and H. W. Henderson, *The Glory and the Shame of Warsaw* (Perth, 1944), 15–16.

9. George Bruce, *The Warsaw Uprising* (London, 1972), 83.

10. Nowak, *Courier*, 337–8.

11. Hanson, *Civilian Population*, 205.

12. Ibid., 208.

13. Witnesses quoted from Anna Bogusławska, *Food for the Children* (London, 1975), 1–30; Nowak, *Courier*, 342–63; Hanson, *Civilian Population*, 75–92.

14. Erickson, *Road to Berlin*, 268, 275–80.

15. Konstantin Rokossovsky, *A Soldier's Duty* (Moscow, 1970), 256.

16. John Keegan, *Six Armies in Normandy* (London, 1992), 235.

17. Nigel Hamilton, *Monty* (London, 1985), II, 773.

18. Hanson, *Civilian Population*, 83–5.

19. Walter Warlimont, *Inside Hitler's Headquarters* (New York, 1964), 449.

20. Hanson, *Civilian Population*, 106.

21. Nagorski, *Warsaw Fights Alone*, 22.

22. Stephen Ambrose, *The Supreme Commander* (London, 1971), 473.

23. Hamilton, *Monty*, II, 792.

24. Ibid., 794–5; Ambrose, *Supreme Commander*, 476.

25. Eddy Florentin, *Stalingrad en Normandie* (Paris, 1994), 577.

26. Hamilton, *Monty*, II, 780, 782.

27. Florentin, *Normandie*, 581–2, 594–5.

28. Ibid., 426–8, 477–614; James Lucas, *Das Reich: The Military Role of the 2nd SS Division* (London, 1991), 143–50.

29. Simone de Beauvoir, *La Force de l'âge* (Paris, 1960), 677.

30. Jean-Paul Sartre, 'The Liberation of Paris', in Sartre, *Modern Times* (London, 2000), 141 (first published in *Clarté*, 24 August 1945).

31. Czesław Miłosz, *To Begin Where I Am* (New York, 2001), 74, 364.

32. Jean-Paul Sartre, *Situations, III* (Paris, 1949), 24, 33, 38.

33. De Beauvoir, *La Force*, 604.

34. 'Un promeneur dans Paris insurgé', *Combat*, 28 August–4 September 1944.

35. Bogusławska, *Food*, 102, 134.

36. Nowak, *Courier*, 356–7.

37. Hanson, *Civilian Population*, 107.

38. Ibid., 108, 113.

39. Ibid., 114; Nowak, *Courier*, 372.

40. Bogusławska, *Food*, 134.

41. Hanson, *Civilian Population*, 200–1.

42. Jean Galtier-Boissière, *Journal 1940–1950* (Paris, 1992), 182, 185; Alfred Fabre-Luce, *Journal de la France, 1939–1944* (Paris, 1969), 653.

43. Dominique Lapierre and Larry Collins, *Paris brûle-t-il?* (Paris, 1964), 114–41, 183–4.

44. Quoted in David Pryce-Jones, *Paris in the Third Reich* (Paris, 1981), 197.

45. Raoul Nordling, *Sauver Paris: Mémoires du consul de Suède (1905–1944)* (Brussels, 2002), 79.

46. Ibid., 92.

47. Ibid., 63–4.

48. Ibid., 95–6.

49. Dietrich von Choltitz, *Un soldat parmi les soldats* (Paris, 1969), 193.

50. Lapierre and Collins, *Paris*, 166.

51. Ibid., 167.

52. Nordling, *Sauver Paris*, 112–16, 141–2.

53. Eric Roussel, *Charles de Gaulle* (Paris, 2002), 446.
54. *Vie Ouvrière*, 11 April 1944, quoted in Stéphane Courtois, *Le PCF dans la guerre* (Paris, 1980), 433–4.
55. *L'Humanité*, 9, 16 June 1944.
56. See Courtois, *PCF*, 438–40.
57. *L'Humanité*, 30 June 1944.
58. A comparison of Communist plans for the Paris insurrection with their projects for the 'German Revolution' during the aftermath of the First World War is most instructive. See my *1918: War and Peace* (London, 2000).
59. Lapierre and Collins, *Paris*, 393.
60. De Gaulle, *Mémoires de guerre*, II, 353.
61. Reproduced in ibid., 491–4.
62. Lacouture, *De Gaulle*, I, 827.
63. C. M. de Talleyrand Périgord, *Mémoires* (Paris, 1982), 632.
64. De Gaulle, *Mémoires de guerre*, II, 342; Bourdet and 'Directive' in Lacouture, *De Gaulle*, I, 805, 808.
65. Roussel, *De Gaulle*, 445–6; De Gaulle, *Mémoires de guerre*, II, 373–6.
66. Nordling, *Sauver Paris*, 94; Yves Pourcher, *Pierre Laval vu par sa fille* (Paris, 2002), 326–7.
67. De Gaulle, *Mémoires de guerre*, II, 350.
68. Full text in Lacouture, *De Gaulle*, I, 821–2.
69. Henri Amouroux, *La Grande Histoire des Français sous l'Occupation* (Paris, 1999), IV, 914.
70. Lapierre and Collins, *Paris*, 301–3.
71. De Gaulle to Eisenhower, Rennes, 21 August 1944, in de Gaulle, *Mémoires de guerre*, II, 491.
72. De Gaulle to Charles Luizet, Rambouillet, 23 August 1944, in ibid., 494–5.
73. Quoted in Lacouture, *De Gaulle*, I, 827.
74. Hamilton, *Monty*, II, 822.
75. Lapierre and Collins, *Paris*, 453.
76. Ibid., 482–3. Some historians insist on placing Speidel in Saint-Germain-en-Laye, which had been evacuated by Model immediately upon his arrival in France.
77. In de Gaulle, *Mémoires de guerre*, II, 495–6.
78. Lacouture, *De Gaulle*, I, 825–6.
79. Philip Mansel, *Paris Between Empires* (London, 2001), 198.
80. On Barrès, Péguy and Charles de Gaulle's entry, see Maurice Agulhon, *De Gaulle: Histoire, symbole, mythe* (Paris, 2000), 66–8.
81. *Front national*, 27 August 1944; see also *Ce Soir*, 28 August.
82. 'The Liberation of Paris', in Sartre, *Modern Times*, 141–5.
83. 'Alpha the moralist' and 'Speaking of a mammal', in Miłosz, *To Begin*, 127, 202–17.

London and Washington in autumn

1. Churchill, in a speech of 30 July 1934 warning the House of Commons of the danger of the German Luftwaffe, referred to London as 'the greatest target in the world, a kind of tremendous, fat, valuable cow tied up to attract the beast of prey'. 'We cannot move London,' he noted four months later. Roy Jenkins, *Churchill* (London, 2001), 476.
2. Gerhard L. Weinberg, *A World at Arms* (Cambridge, 1994), 560–6.
3. Quoted in Angus Calder, *The People's War* (London, 1969), 559.
4. Quoted in Philip Ziegler, *London at War* (London, 1997), 288, 291.
5. Jan Nowak, *Courier from Warsaw* (Detroit, 1982), 238, 251–2; *The Times*, 1 September 1944, 4 October 1944.
6. Ibid., 16 September 1944.
7. Ibid., 11 September 1944.
8. Richard Lamb, *Churchill as War Leader* (London, 1991), 308–10.
9. Ziegler, *London*, 293–4.

10. Lord Ismay, *Memoirs* (London, 1960), 359.

11. Lamb, *Churchill*, 308–9.

12. For statistics and details on the protective barrier around London, see reports appearing in *The Times*, September–October 1944.

13. Ibid., 8 September, 11 November 1944; Calder, *People's War*, 562; Ziegler, *London*, 297.

14. *The Times*, 14 September 1944.

15. James Sterling Young, 'The Washington Community, 1800–28' in Paul Kramer and Frederick L. Holborn (eds.), *The City in American Life* (New York, 1971), 58–66.

16. W. M. Kiplinger, *Washington is Like That* (New York, 1942), 64.

17. Jonathan Daniels, *Frontier on the Potomac* (New York, 1946), 5; Kiplinger, *Washington*, 66–9.

18. Quoted in James MacGregor Burns and Susan Dunn, *The Three Roosevelts* (London, 2001), 369.

19. For White, David Rees, *Harry Dexter White: A Study in Paradox* (London, 1973); Robert Skidelsky, *John Maynard Keynes* (London, 2000), III, 233–63, presents an excellent synthesis.

20. See my *1918: War and Peace* (London, 2000), 47–52, 58–63, 77–9, 98–100, 104–8, 120–1.

21. Weinberg, *World at Arms*, 238; Ian Kershaw, *Hitler* (London, 2000), II, 442–6.

22. David Brinkley, *Washington Goes to War* (New York, 1989), 61.

23. Kiplinger, *Washington*, 10.

24. Constance McLaughlin Green, *Washington: Capital City, 1879–1950* (Princeton, 1963), 468–9.

25. Daniels, *Frontier*, 211.

26. Green, *Washington*, 471; Brinkley, *Washington*, 108.

27. Kiplinger, *Washington*, 2, 44, 500; Daniels, *Frontier*, 13; Brinkley, *Washington*, xii.

28. Ibid., 228.

29. Montgomery to General Kennedy, ACIGS, 20 August 1944, in Nigel Hamilton, *Monty* (London, 1983), II, 806.

30. Montgomery to General Nye, 26 August 1944, in ibid., 815–16.

31. Marshall to Eisenhower, 17 August 1944, in Richard Lamb, *Montgomery in Europe 1943–1945* (London, 1983), 181–2.

32. Quoted in Hamilton, *Monty*, II, 801–2.

33. Ibid.

34. Doug Halloway, *A Soldier's Memories* (London, 1998), 73.

35. Lamb, *Montgomery*, 210.

36. Ibid., 251.

37. Cornelius Ryan's *A Bridge Too Far* (New York, 1974) still rings true. Richard Attenborough used it as a base for his wonderfully inaccurate film, well worth seeing on a wide screen for its authentic reconstructions of Holland in battle.

38. Peter White, *With the Jocks* (London, 2001), 1–27.

39. Weinberg, *World at Arms*, 758.

40. Churchill to Roosevelt, 8 December 1940, in Kimball, I, 311.

41. *The Times*, 28 September 1944.

42. Ibid., 22 September, 4 November 1944.

43. Calder, *People's War*, 364–6; George Orwell, 'As I Please', *Tribune*, 16 June 1944, in Orwell, *The Collected Essays, Journalism and Letters* (New York, 1968), III, 170–2.

44. Correlli Barnett, *The Lost Victory: British Dreams, British Realities 1945–1950* (London, 1995), 419.

45. *The Times*, 4 September 1944.

46. Ibid., 29 September 1944. Jock Colville, of Churchill's private office, recorded that the 'day of prayer' did not go well: 'Lunched at the Churchill Club, where I found Hinch [Viscount Hinchbrooke, MP for Dorset], in a high state of indignation about the inadequacy of the morning service at Westminster Abbey today, a day of National Prayer. Leslie Rowan and I went at 3.00 p.m. to Evensong and formed the same opinion. A

small male choir of ten monopolized the singing and the character of the service was very unsuitable. The vast congregation took little part and can hardly have been inspired. Only the sermon, by Canon Don, was good.' In John Colville, *The Fringes of Power* (London, 1985), 3 September 1944, 508.

47. Correlli Barnett, *The Audit of War* (London, 2001), 15.
48. Peter Davison (ed.), *Orwell and Politics* (London, 2001), 180.
49. Orwell, 'As I Please', *Tribune*, 21 July 1944, in Orwell, *Essays*, III, 188.
50. *Partisan Review*, Fall 1944 (written 24 July), in ibid., 195.
51. Orwell, 'A Hanging', *The Adelphi*, August 1931, in Davison (ed.), *Orwell and Politics*, 11-13.
52. Orwell, 'Shooting an Elephant', *New Writing*, Autumn 1936, in ibid., 23-5.
53. Orwell, 'As I Please', *Tribune*, 4 February 1944, in Orwell, *Essays*, III, 87-9.
54. Orwell's preface to the Ukrainian edition of *Animal Farm*, 21 March 1947, in Davison (ed.), *Orwell and Politics*, 319.
55. Orwell to Gleb Struve, 17 February 1944, in Orwell, *Essays*, III, 95-6.
56. Smollett's anonymous letter is reproduced in Davison (ed.), *Orwell and Politics*, 306. Proof of Smollett's career as a Soviet spy, which included the organization of pro-Soviet propaganda in Britain (such as a mass Albert Hall rally with readings by John Gielgud and Laurence Olivier in February 1943), is in Christopher Andrew and Vasili Mitrokhin, *The Mitrokhin Archive* (London, 2000), 158.
57. Orwell to Dwight Macdonald, 5 December 1946, in Davison (ed.), *Orwell and Politics*, 230.
58. A new edition of *Animal Farm* is reproduced in ibid., 234-305.
59. Orwell, 'As I Please', *Tribune*, 24 March 1944, in Orwell, *Essays*, III, 111-14.
60. Orwell review of Arthur Koestler's work, *Focus*, no. 2, 1946, written in September 1944, in ibid., 234-5.
61. Orwell, 'Why I Join the ILP', *New Leader*, 24 June 1938, in Davison (ed.), *Orwell in Politics*, 37.
62. The idea of a 'Popular Front', allying Social Democrats with Communists, was actually developed by the then French Communist, Jacques Doriot, who, early in 1934, had ambitions of becoming General Secretary of his Party. Moscow rejected his line and Doriot was expelled from the Party, ironically, just before Moscow, in June 1934, adopted the 'Popular Front', 'anti-Fascist' line. Doriot went on to found the extreme-right Parti Populaire Français which, during the German occupation of France, supported the Nazis. See Andrew and Mitrokhin, *Archive*, 91.
63. François Furet, *Le Passé d'une illusion* (Paris, 1995), 262-3.
64. Orwell, 'The English People', written in May 1944, published by Collins in August 1947, in Davison (ed.), *Orwell in Politics*, 36.
65. Orwell, Preface to *Animal Farm*, in ibid., 310, 314.
66. Orwell, Review of books by E. W. Horning and by James Hadley Chase, *Horizon*, October 1944 and *Politics*, November 1944, in Orwell, *Essays*, III, 212-24.
67. Martin Gilbert, *Winston Churchill*, VII, 1017.
68. Ibid., 911.
69. House of Commons speech, 5 March 1905, made just before quitting the protectionist Conservative Party, in Jenkins, *Churchill*, 97.
70. Ibid., 322.
71. The 'bullfight' analogy was made before John Colville on 1 September 1944. The 'waiting till the bull's head was down' was Churchill's way of explaining why no cross-Channel invasion was attempted in 1943. He added that the operation launched by the Americans and French in the South of France on 15 August 'had been a pure waste'. In Colville, *Fringes*, 507. Churchill letter to Roosevelt, Naples, 29 August 1944 (though in fact Churchill was flying back to London that day and was extremely ill), in Warren Kimball (ed.), *Churchill and Roosevelt: The Complete Correspondence* (Princeton, 1984), III, 299.

72. Revelation 21:2. A Board of Trade report published in October 1944 noted that British exports for the twelve months up to the end of 1943 were half the sterling value of 1938, but in real terms, represented only 27 per cent of the export volume of 1938, cf. *The Times*, 21 October 1944. Correlli Barnett, master historian of British economic decline, is careful to avoid these sorts of statistics: he simply repeats that British exports had hit 'rock bottom', cf. Barnett, *Audit*, 38–62. In September 1941, J. M. Keynes forecast a prospective deficit for Britain of between 50 and 100 per cent of her pre-war exports, in Skidelsky, *Keynes*, III, 205.

73. Gilbert, *Churchill*, VII, 937.

74. Colville, *Fringes*, 510.

75. Even then his comments were confined to American servicemen in Britain: see 'As I Please', *Tribune*, 3, 17 December 1943, 26 May, 11 August 1944; *Partisan Review*, 15 January 1944, in Orwell, *Essays*, III, 54–5, 58–9, 76–7, 153–4, 204–6.

76. Winston to Clementine Churchill, Naples, 17 August 1944, in W. and C. Churchill, *Speaking for Themselves* (London, 1998), 501.

77. Field Marshal Lord Alanbrooke, *War Diaries* (London, 2002), 5 September 1944, 587.

78. Ibid., 7–10 September 1944, 588–90; Colville, *Fringes*, 8 September 1944, 511; Ismay, *Memoirs*, 373.

79. Clementine to Winston, 7 September 1944, in W. and C. Churchill, *Speaking*, 504.

80. Colville, *Fringes*, 6–7 September 1944, 510.

81. Quoted in Skidelsky, *Keynes*, III, 358; *The Times*, 5 October 1944.

82. Colville, *Fringes*, 9 September 1944, 511.

83. Ibid., 5–6 September 1944, 509.

84. Gilbert, *Churchill*, VII, 942.

85. Alanbrooke, *War Diaries*, 590.

86. Ismay, *Memoirs*, 367–8; John Charmley, *Churchill: The End of Glory* (London, 1993), 566–7.

87. Andrew and Mitrokhin, *Archive*, 167; see Veronica Maclean–Richard Lamb correspondence, *Spectator*, 28 August–1 September 1999.

88. Weinberg, *World at Arms*, 524–5.

89. Gilbert, *Churchill*, VII, 948.

90. Colville, *Fringes*, 511.

91. Doris Kearns Goodwin, *No Ordinary Time* (New York, 1994), 543.

92. *New York Times*, 16 September 1944.

93. Ibid., 15 September 1944.

94. Ibid.

95. Keith Sainsbury, *Churchill and Roosevelt at War* (London, 1994), 4–5; Burns and Dunn, *Three Roosevelts*, 15–19, 81.

96. Ibid., 79.

97. Ibid., 368–9.

98. Kiplinger, *Washington*, 31.

99. Robert H. Ferrell, *The Dying President* (Columbia, MI, 1998), 141–3.

100. Truman to his administrative assistant, August 1944, in ibid., 89.

101. Ibid., 78–9, 86–8; Goodwin, *No Ordinary Time*, 534.

102. Ferrell, *Dying President*, 86–8.

103. Roosevelt to Churchill, 3 and 5 September 1944, in Kimball (ed.), *Correspondence*, III, 309, 313; Andrew and Mitrokhin, *Archive*, 143, 782.

104. Gregor Dallas, *1918* (London, 2000), 200.

105. Hugo Young, *This Blessed Plot* (London, 1998), 104.

106. Skidelsky, *Keynes*, III, 126–31.

107. Ibid., 203–8.

108. Duggan left the State Department in June 1944 to become 'diplomatic adviser' to the newly set-up United Nations Relief and Rehabilitation Administration (UNRRA),

which catered to 'displaced persons' in Europe. See Andrew and Mitrokhin, *Archive*, 144, 783.

109. Skidelsky, *Keynes*, III, 251.

110. Ibid., 325, 339.

111. *The Times*, 10 October 1944.

112. *New York Times*, 10 October 1944.

113. On Chambers' initial revelations in 1939, see Andrew and Mitrokhin, *Archive*, 141–2.

114. Stepan Apresyan, New York, 4–5 August 1944, VENONA decrypt in Nigel West, *VENONA* (London, 1999), 310–12.

115. Andrew and Mitrokhin, *Archive*, 137.

116. Rees, *White*, 239–51; Skidelsky, *Keynes*, III, 362–3; Kimball commentary in Kimball (ed.), *Correspondence*, III, 316–17.

117. Kurt Keppler, *Tod über Deutschland: Der Morgenthauplan* (Tübingen, 1971), 82–7.

118. West, *VENONA*, Apresyan transcript, New York, 4–5 August 1944, 311.

119. Ismay, *Memoirs*, 373; Gilbert, *Churchill*, VII, 965; Ferrell, *Dying President*, 84–5; Colville, *Fringes*, 513–14.

120. Ibid. According to Ferrell there are no records showing that Roosevelt had had a check-up in June 1944: *Dying President*, 85.

121. Gilbert, *Churchill*, VII, 968.

122. Kimball (ed.), *Correspondence*, III, 316; Keppler, *Tod*, 130.

123. Churchill, *Second World War*, VI, 129; Alanbrooke, *War Diaries*, 593.

124. Colville, *Fringes*, 513.

125. Gilbert, *Churchill*, VII, 963; Kimball (ed.), *Correspondence*, III, 322–3.

126. Gilbert, *Churchill*, VII, 961.

127. Keppler, *Tod*, 131; Goodwin, *No Ordinary Time*, 543–5.

128. Ismay, *Memoirs*, 374; Brooke, *War Diaries*, 592; Gilbert, *Churchill*, VII, 964–5; Colville, *Fringes*, 515.

129. Goodwin, *No Ordinary Time*, 544; Keppler, *Tod*, 131.

130. Ibid., 82–90.

131. Ibid., 134–5.

132. Details of the zone agreement in Churchill, *Second World War*, VI, 141–2.

133. *Stimson Diaries*, 16–17 September 1944, 3, in Keppler, *Tod*, 156–7.

134. Ibid., 141–8; *New York Times*, 24 September 1944.

135. Ibid., 30 September 1944.

136. *Stimson Diaries*, 5 October 1944, 5, in Keppler, *Tod*, 166–7.

137. Skidelsky, *Keynes*, III, 365.

138. Ibid., 366–72.

139. *The Times*, 27 September 1944.

140. Quoted in Gilbert, *Churchill*, VII, 969–70.

141. Ibid., 976–8; Harold Nicolson, *Diaries and Letters* (London, 1967), II, 402; Colville, *Fringes*, 520 Colville frequently gets his dates wrong. His diary entry for the speech is 'Wednesday, September 27th'; the speech was on Thursday.

142. Text of speech in *The Times*, 29 September 1944.

143. Ibid., 2–5 October 1944; Gilbert, *Churchill*, VII, 978–84.

144. Kimball (ed.), *Correspondence*, III, 343–4.

145. Churchill to Jan Smuts, 9 October 1944, in Gilbert, *Churchill*, VII, 975.

146. Alanbrooke, *War Diaries*, 598–9.

147. Churchill to Brigadier Whitby, n.d., in Gilbert, *Churchill*, VII, 972.

148. For a summary of London's devastation, see Stephen Inwood, *A History of London* (London, 1998), 809–11; on Beveridge's White Paper, *The Times*, 26 September 1944.

149. Ferrell, *Dying President*, 82–3; Goodwin, *No Ordinary Time*, 546–9.

150. *New York Times*, 6 October 1944.

151. Ibid., 22 October 1944; on Eleanor's apartment, Goodwin, *No Ordinary Time*, 551.

152. Text of speech in *New York Times*, 22 October 1944.
153. Ibid., 2 November 1944.
154. W Averell Harriman and Elie Abel, *Special Envoy to Churchill and Stalin 1941–1946* (London, 1976), 354–6.
155. Churchill, *Second World War*, VI, 429.
156. Joan Bright Astley, *The Inner Circle* (London, 1971), quoted in Gilbert, *Churchill*, VII, 989.
157. A detailed presentation of the dialogue that follows is in ibid., 990–6.
158. In a telegram to Roosevelt on 18 October Churchill stated that it was Molotov's claim that 'you had expressed agreement with the Curzon Line at Teheran,' adding that 'neither I nor Eden could confirm this statement.' Stalin confirmed that it had been during a private conversation he had had with Roosevelt, 'though you had expressed a hope about Lvov being retained by the Poles'. Churchill to Roosevelt, Moscow, 18 October 1944, in Kimball (ed.), *Correspondence*, III, 359.
159. Churchill to Roosevelt, Quebec, 17 September 1944, in ibid., 329–40.
160. 'Major war criminals. UJ ["Uncle Joe"] took an unexpectedly ultra-respectable line. There must be no executions without trial otherwise the world would say we were afraid to try them. I pointed out the difficulties in International law, but he replied if there were no trials there must be no death sentences, but only life-long confinements.' Churchill to Roosevelt, en route London, 22 October 1944, in ibid., 364.
161. Alanbrooke, *War Diaries*, 604.
162. Harriman and Abel, *Special Envoy*, 357.
163. 'Proceedings of the Moscow Conference on Polish Affairs', 13 October 1944, in Gilbert, *Churchill*, VII, 1007–9.
164. Churchill to Attlee, Moscow, 17 October 1944, in ibid., 1023.
165. Ibid., 1012, 1020.
166. Ibid., 1025.
167. Ibid., 1027.
168. Quoted in François Kersaudy, *Churchill and de Gaulle* (London, 1981), 368.
169. Churchill to Roosevelt, Moscow, 14 October 1944; Roosevelt to Churchill, Washington, 19 October 1944, in Kimball (ed.), *Correspondence*, III, 355, 362.
170. Jean Lacouture, *De Gaulle* (Paris, 1985), II, 78.
171. Ibid., 80.
172. Ismay, *Memoirs*, 381; Alanbrooke, *War Diaries*, 621.
173. Kersaudy, *Churchill and de Gaulle*, 377–8.
174. Alanbrooke, *War Diaries*, 623–4.
175. Charles de Gaulle, *Mémoires de guerre* (Paris, 1999), III, 67–70.
176. Alanbrooke, *War Diaries*, 624.

Berlin and Moscow in winter

1. Charles B. MacDonald, *The Battle of the Bulge* (London, 1984), 102–6.
2. Ibid., 97.
3. Ibid., 129.
4. Though the first person to use the term 'Battle of the Bulge' was actually Churchill. See Charles Whiting, *The Battle of the Bulge* (London, 2003), 37.
5. Nigel Hamilton, *Monty* (London, 1986), III, 141.
6. Ibid., 210–11.
7. Diary of Lieutenant-Colonel T. S. Bigland, in ibid., 190.
8. Whiting, *Bulge*, 26.
9. Otto Skorzeny, *Special Mission* (London, n.d.), 32.
10. Gerhard Weinberg, *A World at Arms* (Cambridge, 1994), 1102.
11. This was going too far for Montgomery. He announced to London the same day: 'I am sending Horrocks back to England for a few days. He has gone mad . . .' Diary of William C. Sylvan, 27 December 1944, in Hamilton, *Monty*, III, 255.

12. Josef Goebbels, *Tagebücher* (Munich, 1991), 20–1 September 1944, V, 524–5.
13. Danny S. Parker (ed.), *Hitler's Ardennes Offensive* (London, 1997), 233.
14. Ibid., 15.
15. Ibid., 23–7.
16. MacDonald, *Bulge*, 222.
17. Ann Tusa and John Tusa, *The Nuremberg Trial* (London, 1995), 30.
18. Parker (ed.), *Ardennes*, 238.
19. Hamilton, *Monty*, III, 236, 242.
20. Ibid., 285, 300–13.
21. Ian Kershaw, *Hitler* (London, 2000), II, 744.
22. Parker (ed.), *Ardennes*, 26–7.
23. Charles de Gaulle, *Mémoires de guerre* (Paris, 1999), III, 159–60, 173–4.
24. Ibid., 175–81; Jean Lacouture, *De Gaulle* (Paris, 1985), II, 70–5; Eric Roussel, *De Gaulle* (Paris, 2002), 479–81.
25. The most even-handed survey – which includes comparative tables drawn from several sources – is in Henri Amouroux, *La Grande Histoire des Français après l'Occupation* (Paris, 1999), IX, 63–99. Julian Jackson, *France: The Dark Years 1940–1944* (Oxford, 2001), 577–85, emphasizes the lower estimate, and manages to omit any mention of the Communist role in his account. De Gaulle, *Mémoires de guerre*, III, 50.
26. Philippe Buton, *Les Lendemains qui déchantent* (Paris, 1993), 141–2, 173.
27. Amouroux, *Grande Histoire*, IX, 103; de Gaulle, *Mémoires de guerre*, III, 209.
28. Patrick Marnham, *The Death of Jean Moulin* (London, 2000), 212–17.
29. J. P. Sartre, 'Paris sous l'occupation', *La France Libre*, 1945, in J. P. Sartre, *Situations* (Paris, 1949), III, 15–17.
30. Buton, *Lendemains*, 179; Antony Beevor and Artemis Cooper, *Paris after the Liberation: 1944–1949* (London, 1995), 115–16, 140–3.
31. *The Times*, 3 October 1944.
32. Ibid., 16 October 1944.
33. Jacques Duclos, *Le Communisme et l'ordre* (1944) in Buton, *Lendemains*, 147–8.
34. Ibid., 122.
35. Quoted in Gisèle Sapiro, *La Guerre des écrivains* (Paris, 1999), 567–8.
36. In ibid., 616.
37. Ibid., 474.
38. Sartre, 'New-York, ville coloniale', *Town and Country*, 1946, in *Situations*, III, 113–24.
39. Annie Cohen-Solal, *Sartre* (Paris, 1985), 382–400.
40. Ibid., 409.
41. Roussel, *De Gaulle*, 466–7.
42. De Gaulle, *Mémoires de guerre*, III, 71–3.
43. Ibid., 74–5.
44. Ibid., 76–7.
45. Quoted in Lacouture, *De Gaulle*, II, 86.
46. Ibid., 87; Roussel, *De Gaulle*, 468, 476–7; de Gaulle, *Mémoires de guerre*, III, 78–9.
47. Philippe Buton (ed.), 'L'entretien entre Maurice Thorez et Joseph Staline du 19 novembre 1944', *Communisme*, No. 45–46 (1996), 7–30. See also Stalin's revealing comments to Thorez two years later, in Mikhail Narinski (ed.), 'L'entretien entre Maurice Thorez et Joseph Staline du 18 novembre 1947', *Communisme*, No. 45–46 (1996), 31–54. Thorez, now much more confident, told Stalin that de Gaulle had shown his true face as 'a reactionary, a Fascist'. Stalin assured Thorez that if Churchill had delayed D-Day any longer the Red Army would have entered Paris. 'The French people would have welcomed the Red Army with enthusiasm,' replied Thorez. Stalin asked and Thorez confirmed that 'camouflaged warehouses of arms' had been stored in France by the Communist Party. Clandestine radio contact with Moscow was being maintained via Sofia, Bulgaria.

48. W. Averell Harriman and Elie Abel, *Special Envoy to Churchill and Stalin 1941–1946* (London, 1976), 231, 376.

49. Nikita Khrushchev, *Khrushchev Remembers* (New York, 1974), II, 348–9.

50. For the de Gaulle–Stalin encounter, de Gaulle, *Mémoires de guerre*, III, 79–100; Harriman and Abel, *Special Envoy*, 375–8; Alexander Werth, *De Gaulle* (New York, 1965), 181–6.

51. Sergueï Ermolinski, 'Introduction' in Mikhail Boulgakov, *Le Maître et Marguerite* (Paris, 1968), 7–43.

52. Timothy J. Colton, *Moscow: Governing the Socialist Metropolis* (Cambridge, Mass., 1995), 123–4, 757–8, 795–8.

53. Talcott Parsons and Merle Fainsod were major figures behind the Harvard Project; see the report, Alex Inkeles and Raymond A. Bauer, *The Soviet Citizen* (Cambridge, Mass., 1959), 9.

54. Ibid., 70, 132, 193–4, 196.

55. Ibid., 132–3. J. Arch Getty reproduces exactly the same apology for Soviet Communism – free education and free health – in his recent article, 'The Future Did Not Work', *Atlantic Monthly* (March 2000), 113–16. One merely wonders what progress in health and education Russia may have made in the twentieth century without such enlightened help from the Communists.

56. Inkeles and Bauer, *Soviet Citizen*, 212, 215.

57. Colton, *Moscow*, 127; Simone Olivier Wormser, *Deux années à Moscou* (Paris, 1985), 81.

58. Colton, *Moscow*, 90, 177; Edwin Bacon, *The Gulag at War* (London, 1994), 43; Anne Applebaum, *Gulag* (London, 2003), 27–39.

59. Orlando Figes, *A People's Tragedy* (London, 1996), 91.

60. Nicolas Werth, 'Collectivisation forcée et dékoulakisation', in Stéphane Courtois et al., *Le Livre noir sur le communisme* (Paris, 1997), 171–85; Colton, *Moscow*, 204–9.

61. Bacon, *Gulag*, 55–6. Officially the 'Gulag' was only in operation between February 1931 and June 1934. Names were henceforth changed and administrations altered (chiefly with the aim of keeping the camps out of view of foreign observers). But even administrative documents continued up until the 1950s to call the main camp system, under the NKVD (the People's Commissariat for Internal Affairs), the 'Gulag'.

62. Stéphane Courtois, 'Du passé faisons table rase!' (a title borrowed from the 'Internationale'), in Courtois et al., *Du passé faisons table rase!* (Paris, 2002), 105–8.

63. Bacon, *Gulag*, 108–10.

64. Colton, *Moscow*, 254–7, 327; Ermolinski, 'Introduction', in Boulgakov, *Le Maître*, 31.

65. Colton, *Moscow*, 257–9, 835–6.

66. Alexander Werth, *Moscow War Diary* (New York, 1942), 78.

67. Colton, *Moscow*, 181.

68. Werth, *War Diary*, 106, 135–6.

69. Colton, *Moscow*, 212.

70. Ibid., 31.

71. Quoted in Courtois, 'Du passé', 109–11.

72. George Orwell, *Orwell and Politics* (Harmondsworth, Middlesex, 2001), 233, 285.

73. Cathy Porter and Mark Jones, *Moscow in World War II* (London, 1987), 95–139; Alan Bullock, *Hitler and Stalin* (London, 1998), 800; Henry C. Cassidy, *Moscow Dateline, 1941–1943* (Boston, 1943), 84–5.

74. David M. Glantz and Jonathan House, *When Titans Clashed* (Lawrence, Ka., 1995), 81; Porter and Jones, *Moscow*, 193–12; Colton, *Moscow*, 250.

75. Bullock, *Hitler and Stalin*, 801–2; Porter and Jones, *Moscow*, 117.

76. Sergo Beria, *Beria, My Father* (London, 2001), 76.

77. Porter and Jones, *Moscow*, 127–9.

78. Bullock, *Hitler and Stalin*, 3–16, 28–45.

79. Stalin's work as a double agent before the First World War had been known to the Bolshevik secret services since at least 1926, and was revealed to the Americans in 1946.

It has been argued that one of Stalin's principal motives in purging the Party in the 1930s was to cover up his own pre-war activities. This was undoubtedly a part of the story, but only a part; Stalin's main drive was his inability to work with any competing authority. See Roman Brackman, *The Secret File of Joseph Stalin* (London, 2001).

80. Dimitri Volkogonov, *Staline* (Paris, 1991), 369–70, 441, 465.
81. Svetlana Alliluyeva, *Twenty Letters to a Friend* (London, 1967).
82. Volkogonov, *Staline*, 437–8.
83. John Erickson, *The Road to Berlin* (London, 1999), 95 6.
84. Volkogonov, *Staline*, 398.
85. Beria, *Beria*, 95–6.
86. Nicolas Werth, 'L'envers d'une victoire' in Courtois et al., *Livre noir*, 257–8.
87. Bacon, *Gulag*, 24, 29–36, 115, 122, 144–55.
88. George Orwell, *Animal Farm*, in Orwell, *Orwell and Politics*, 277.
89. George F Kennan, *Memoirs* (New York, 1969), 4–6, 84–90, 198–200.
90. Ibid., 199–200.
91. Ibid., 201–5.
92. See, for example, Colton, *Moscow*, 344.
93. Kennan, 'Russia's International Position at the Close of the War with Germany (May 1945)', in Kennan, *Memoirs*, 565.
94. Erickson, *Road to Berlin*, 466–7.
95. Albert Speer, *Inside the Third Reich* (New York, 1970), 496–9; Gitta Sereny, *Albert Speer* (London, 1995), 472, 483.
96. Several editions of Goebbels's diaries have been published. The edition used here includes several additions and corrections revealed recently in the Russian archives. Goebbels's dating is always one day following the events described. Joseph Goebbels, *Die Tagebücher* (Munich, 1995), II:XV, 192 (23 January 1945).
97. Speer, *Inside*, 500.
98. Goebbels, *Tagebücher*, II:XV, 138, 160 (17, 20 January 1945).
99. See Volkogonov, *Staline*, 369–71, 394–401.
100. Ibid., 398; Bacon, *Gulag*, 31, 37, 62, 119, Christopher Andrew and Vasili Mitrokhin, *The Mitrokhin Archive* (London, 2000), 177.
101. Romulus Rusan et al., 'Le système répressif communiste de Roumanie', in Courtois et al., *Du passé*, 375.
102. Ibid., 412.
103. Petru Dumitriu, *Incognito* (Paris, 1962), 539 – required reading for anyone who wants to know what happened in South-Eastern Europe in the last years of the war, and the long, painful aftermath.
104. Erickson, *Road to Berlin*, 371.
105. Diniou Charlanov et al., 'La Bulgarie sous le joug communiste', in Courtois et al. (ed.), *Du passé*, 323–4.
106. Erickson, *Road to Berlin*, 396.
107. Andrew and Mitrokhin, *Mitrokhin Archive*, 29.
108. Nigel West, *VENONA* (London, 1999), xv.
109. Andrew and Mitrokhin, *Mitrokhin Archive*, 150–1.
110. 'Special Project Berlin', 23 February 1945, in Jeremy Noakes (ed.), *Nazism 1919–1945* (Exeter, 1998), IV, 649–50.
111. Goebbels, *Tagebücher*, II:XV, 392, 398 (1 March 1945); Ralf Georg Reuth, *Goebbels* (Munich, 1990), 93–5.
112. Since Goebbels's diary entries are always dated on the day after the events, the following describes his Sunday, 4 March 1945. In *Tagebücher*, II:XV, 419–27.
113. Ibid., 638–9 (30 March 1945).
114. Ibid., 185–6, 391 (23 January, 1 March 1945).
115. Ibid., 427 (5 March 1945).

116. Ibid., 639 (30 March 1945).

117. Ibid., 399, 451 (2, 8 March 1945).

118. Hannelore Holtz, *Wir lebten in Berlin* (Berlin, 1947), 78, 82.

119. Inge Deutschkron, *Ich trug den gelben Stern* (Berlin, 1978), 193–8.

120. Modris Eksteins, *Walking Since Daybreak* (London, 2000), 197–9.

121. W. G. Sebald, *On the Natural History of Destruction* (London, 2003), 3–5, 10–11, 88–9. Sebald's text is based on lectures he delivered in Zurich in 1997. The answer to the complaint on the lack of study on the effects of bombardment is Jörg Friedrich's German bestseller *Der Brand* (Munich, 2002), which can be usefully compared to Robin Neillands's *The Bomber War* (London, 2001).

122. Martin Middlebrook, *The Berlin Raids* (London, 1988), 154–7.

123. Friedrich, *Der Brand*, 370.

124. Neillands, *Bomber War*, 283, 392.

125. Alexandra Richie, *Faust's Metropolis* (New York, 1998), 473.

126. Goebbels, *Tagebücher*, II:XV, 459 (9 March 1945).

127. Adolf Hitler, *Mein Kampf* (London, 1992), 38. For Hitler's commentary on Social Democracy and Marxism, which immediately precedes his analysis of Jews, see pp. 35–47.

128. Kershaw, *Hitler*, I, 116–21.

129. In Gregor Dallas, *1918* (London, 2000), 435.

130. On the issue of the relationship of Bolshevism to Nazism, see Ernst Nolte, *La Guerre civile européenne 1917–1945* (Paris, 2000), esp. 133–50.

131. In Richie, *Faust's Metropolis*, 493.

132. Stauffenberg's last words may even have been 'Long live secret Germany!', ibid., 1029, n. 189; Hans B. Gisevius (one of the few survivors of the plot), *To the Bitter End* (New York, 1998), 572.

133. Gilbert Merlio, *Les Résistances allemandes à Hitler* (Paris, 2001), 299–300.

134. Marie-Louise Sarre, quoted in Klemens von Klemperer, *German Resistance against Hitler* (Oxford, 1992), 1.

135. Merlio, *Résistances*, 275.

136. Klemperer, *German Resistance*, 154.

137. Richie, *Faust's Metropolis*, 404; Merlio, *Résistances*, 43; Michael Burleigh, *The Third Reich* (London, 2000), 666–9.

138. Dallas, *1918*, 428–30.

139. Merlio, *Résistances*, 191–8.

140. Ibid., 166–82.

141. Eric A. Johnson, *Nazi Terror* (London, 1999), 47.

142. Klemperer, *German Resistance*, 4–5; Burleigh, *Third Reich*, 688, 709–11; Merlio, *Résistances*, 135.

143. Peter Hoffmann, *The History of the German Resistance 1933–1945* (London, 1977), 241, 321.

144. Charles Williams, *Adenauer* (London, 2000), 306.

145. Catherine Andreyev, *Vlasov and the Russian Liberation Movement* (Cambridge, 1987), 37–40. See also Sergei Fröhlich, *General Wlassow* (Cologne, 1987).

146. Anne Applebaum, *Gulag* (London, 2003), 356–70; Bacon, *Gulag*, 155.

147. Andreyev, *Vlasov*, 46–50.

148. Ibid., 48.

149. John Toland, *The Last Hundred Days* (London, 1965), 567.

150. 'The Prague Manifesto', in Andreyev, *Vlasov*, 216–23.

151. Toland, *Hundred Days*, 564–9. In Nikolai Tolstoy's account, Vlasov did not approve of aid to the Czech nationalist rising. Since an encounter in Nuremberg on 19 March, when Vlasov had discovered 'General Buniachenko and his Chief of Staff hopelessly drunk and lolling in their chairs before a table covered with vodka bottles and half-filled

glasses – their only companions [being] two junior officers and a couple of half-dressed girls of unmilitary appearance', relations between the two men had been poisonous. See Tolstoy, *Victims of Yalta* (London, 1978), 286, 293–5.

152. Ibid., 288–91.
153. Ibid., 292.
154. Andreyev, *Vlasov*, 79.

PEOPLE

People without cities

1. 'Declaration' and 'Protocol' in Foreign Relations of the United States (FRUS), *The Conferences at Malta and Yalta 1945* (Washington, 1955), 968–84. Some useful commentary on these documents can be found in Jean Gilles Malliarakis, *Yalta et la naissance des blocs* (Paris, 1982), 30–64.
2. British calculations on German transfers in 'Conversations [between Eden and] Mr Stettinius', Malta, 1 February 1945, in FRUS, *Malta and Yalta*, 509.
3. 'The President's Log', in ibid., 460.
4. General Lord Ismay, *Memoirs* (London, 1960), 387.
5. Clementine to Winston Churchill, London, 30 January 1945, in *Speaking for Themselves* (London, 1998), 510.
6. Field Marshal Lord Alanbrooke, *War Diaries* (London, 2002), 651.
7. Peter White, *With the Jocks* (London, 2001), 130.
8. Winston to Clementine Churchill, Malta, 1 February 1945, in *Speaking*, 512–13.
9. Alanbrooke, *War Diaries*, 653.
10. Martin Gilbert, *Winston Churchill* (London, 1986), VII, 1167; Robert H. Ferrell, *The Dying President* (Columbia, Mi., 1998), 105–6.
11. Lord Cadogan, quoted in Gilbert, *Churchill*, VII, 1171.
12. FRUS, *Malta and Yalta*, 572–3, 589–90, 722.
13. Ibid., 770–1, 903–4.
14. Ibid., 565.
15. Ibid., 677–81.
16. Ibid., 787–8.
17. Ibid., 815, 850, 853.
18. Ibid., 850.
19. Gilbert, *Churchill*, VII, 1194; Alanbrooke, *War Diaries*, 660.
20. Winston to Clementine Churchill, Yalta, 12 February 1945, in *Speaking*, 515.
21. John Toland, *The Last Hundred Days* (London, 1966), 43.
22. Tony Hiss, *Laughing Last* (Boston, 1977), 37–9.
23. Ibid., 54–6.
24. Ibid., 66.
25. John Earl Haynes and Harvey Klehr, *VENONA* (New Haven, Conn., 1999), 270–3; Allen Weinstein, *Perjury* (New York, 1997), 325–6.
26. See, for example, Kenneth O'Reilly, 'Liberal Values, the Cold War, and American Intellectuals: The Trauma of the Alger Hiss Case, 1950–1978', in Athan G. Theoharis (ed.), *Beyond the Hiss Case* (Philadelphia, 1982), 309–40.
27. W. M. Kiplinger, *Washington is Like That* (New York, 1942), 31.
28. Original copies of the 1945 Paris editions of *Time* are to be found in the BDIC, Nanterre, carton 4° P 2 664.
29. Weinstein, *Perjury*, 305.
30. Ibid., 306; *Time*, 14 March 1945.
31. FRUS, *Malta and Yalta*, 844, 856.
32. Weinstein, *Perjury*, 314–15.
33. Toland, *Hundred Days*, 112; FRUS, *Malta and Yalta*, 925.

34. T. Hiss, *Laughing Last*, 105, 122.
35. Churchill to Roosevelt, 8 March 1944, in Warren F. Kimball (ed.), *Churchill and Roosevelt: The Complete Correspondence* (Princeton, 1984), III, 547–8.
36. Jan Karski, *The Great Powers and Poland* (Lanham, Md., 1985), 564–8, 619–21; Andrzev Paczkowski, 'Pologne, la "nation-ennemi"', in Stéphane Courtois et al. (eds.), *Le Livre noir du communisme* (Paris, 1997), 434–9.
37. Władysław Szpilman, *The Pianist* (London, 2000), 186–7.
38. Churchill to Roosevelt, 10 March 1945, in Kimball (ed.), *Churchill and Roosevelt*, III, 553–9.
39. Czesław Miłosz, 'Alpha the Moralist', in Miłosz, *To Begin Where I Am* (New York, 2001), 132–3.
40. Karski, *Great Powers*, 622.
41. Churchill to Roosevelt, 'Roosevelt' to Churchill, 13, 27, 29 March 1945, in Kimball (ed.), *Churchill and Roosevelt*, III, 565, 588, 593.
42. Roosevelt to Churchill, 11 April 1945, in ibid., 630; Winston Churchill dates the same text 12 April, in *The Second World War* (London, 1954), VI, 398.
43. Ferrell, *Dying President*, 118. Heart sounds continued for another three hours. Roosevelt, aged sixty-three, was pronounced dead at 3.35 p.m., 12 April.
44. Philip Ziegler, *London at War* (London, 1998), 310.
45. Hugh Trevor-Roper, *The Last Days of Hitler* (Chicago, Ill., 1992), 140–2.
46. Robert Skidelsky, *John Maynard Keynes* (London, 2000), III, 375, 378–86.
47. Churchill to Roosevelt, 'Roosevelt' to Churchill, 13 February, 1, 2, 10, 16, 21, 23 March 1945, in Kimball (ed.), *Churchill and Roosevelt*, III, 535–6, 540–1, 559–60, 570, 578–9, 584.
48. 'Second Plenary Meeting', 5 February 1945, in FRUS, *Yalta and Malta*, 617.
49. See the collection of essays, good though obviously written before the total collapse of the Communist bloc, in Göran Rystad (ed.), *The Uprooted* (Lund, Sweden, 1990).
50. Quoted in Nikolai Tolstoy, *Victims of Yalta* (London, 1978), 60.
51. Mark Wyman, *DP* (Philadelphia, 1989), 20–1.
52. Ibid., 22; Tolstoy, *Victims*, 34–9.
53. Quoted in Wyman, *DP*, 35–6.
54. Quoted in Guy S. Goodwin-Gill, 'Different Types of Forced Migration Movements as an International and National Problem', in Rystad (ed.) *Uprooted*, 22.
55. Tolstoy, *Victims*, 42–3.
56. Ibid., 51–2; Nikolas Bethell, *The Last Secret* (London, 1974), 7.
57. Wyman, *DP*, 65.
58. Tolstoy, *Victims*, 88–9.
59. For the text of the agreement, see FRUS, *Yalta and Malta*, 985–6; earlier drafts and exchanges between British and Americans in ibid., 691–6, 754–7, 864–6.
60. Harold Macmillan, *The Blast of War* (London, 1967), 702–3.
61. Ibid., 540, 549–50, 556, 644–9, 704.
62. Alistair Horne, *Harold Macmillan* (London, 1988), I, 63.
63. Ibid., 43–9; Shakespeare, *Richard II*.
64. On which many a question can be posed. See Gregor Dallas, 'Who Killed the Admiral?', in *BBC History Magazine* (December 2002), 42–3.
65. Nikolai Tolstoy, *The Minister and the Massacres* (London, 1986) – if you can get hold of it – provides a somewhat biased account of Macmillan's involvement in Austrian repatriations in May and June 1945. But no other historian has ever spent so much of his life, or gone into so much detail, on the problem of repatriations. Tolstoy's *Victims of Yalta* must be considered a classic on the subject. After *Minister*, Tolstoy distributed 10,000 copies of a pamphlet, which led to a libel suit, a lost trial and a record fine of £1.5 million. The sordid details of the trial, along with a re-examination of Tolstoy's documents, can be found in Christopher Booker, *A Looking-Glass Tragedy* (London,

1997). The Tolstoy trial seems to have set the precedent for a genre of polemical history in the 1990s and afterwards that has been guided by trial by judiciary and intellectual terror. It has to be said that this tendency, if good for publicity, has added little to our knowledge and has been detrimental to the writing and study of good history. Work on the Second World War has been particularly damaged by the development – in regard, for example, to the German occupation of France, the Vichy government, the situation of the Jews in Europe, the history of Poland, the Holocaust, the Gulag, the history of Communism, etc.

66. Horne, *Macmillan*, I, 151.
67. Macmillan, *Blast*, 619, 684.
68. Ibid., 606.
69. Ibid., 510–11.
70. Horne, *Macmillan*, I, 247–8.
71. Macmillan, *Blast*, 690–5, 699; Booker, *Looking-Glass*, 143–51.
72. Antony Beevor, *Berlin: The Downfall 1945* (London, 2002), 139.
73. Trevor-Roper, *Last Days*, 157–60.
74. Alexander Werth, *Russia at War* (London, 1964), 246.
75. Memorandum by Planning Staff, SHAEF, 24 September 1944, quoted in Nigel Hamilton, *Monty* (London, 1986), III, 449.
76. Stephen E. Ambrose, *Eisenhower and Berlin* (New York, 2000), 74–9.
77. Trevor-Roper, *Last Days*, 93–7.
78. Ambrose, *Eisenhower and Berlin*, 68.
79. Hamilton, *Monty*, III, 440.
80. Ibid., 423.
81. Eisenhower to Stalin, 28 March 1945, and Eisenhower to Montgomery, 31 March, in ibid., 445; Ambrose, *Eisenhower and Berlin*, 48–9, 60; Toland, *Hundred Days*, 308.
82. Hamilton, *Monty*, III, 442–3, 474, 479.
83. Ibid., 484, 496.
84. Martin Gilbert, *The Day the War Ended* (London, 1995), 15–16.
85. Ibid., 37–8.
86. Joël Kotek and Pierre Rigoulot, *Le Siècle des camps* (Paris, 2000), 298–314, 339; Mark Roseman, *The Villa, the Lake, the Meeting* (London, 2002), 1–6.
87. The bibliography on this subject is enormous. Of particular note, for a basis of discussion, is Edwin Bacon, *The Gulag at War* (London, 1994), 10, 24, 107–22; and Anne Applebaum, *Gulag* (London, 2003), esp. 515–22.
88. Alexander Solzhenitsyn, *The Gulag Archipelago* (New York, 2002), 342 (my emphasis).
89. See Norman G. Finkelstein, *The Holocaust Industry* (London, 2001) – which, though close to the polemic, is a generally fair account.
90. Solzhenitsyn, *Gulag*, 19, 26, 129, 178, 300–1; Yakovlev's estimate in Edward E. Ericson's 'Introduction' in ibid., xvii. Western historians, such as Anne Applebaum, no longer dare make overall estimates, which indeed seems the most respectable position to take. A new, complete collection of Varlam Shalamov's ('Chalamov' in French) *Récits de la Kolyma* has recently been published (Paris, 2003); they leave one in no doubt of the horror involved. Essential reading also includes the memoirs of Jacques Rossi, *Qu'elle était belle cette utopie!* (Paris, 2000). Rossi, a former French Communist, participated in the Spanish Civil War, worked for Comintern, was summoned to Moscow in 1937, when he was arrested. He eventually returned to France in 1985. In his late nineties, he lives today in a convent in Paris.
91. Solzhenitsyn, *Gulag*, 313; Vladimir Boukovsky, *Jugement à Moscou* (Paris, 1995), 57–9.
92. Solzhenitsyn, *Gulag*, 103.
93. Boukovsky, *Jugement*, 13.
94. Kotek and Rigoulot, *Siècle des camps*, 47–79.
95. Ibid., 81–107.

96. See Helen McPhail, *The Long Silence: Civilian Life under the German Occupation of Northern France 1914–18* (London, 2002); and John Horne and Alan Kramer, *German Atrocities, 1914: A History of Denial* (New Haven, Conn., 2001).

97. Erich Maria Remarque, *All Quiet on the Western Front* (London, 1995), 133–4.

98. Kotek and Rigoulot, *Siècle des camps*, 145.

99. François Furet, *Le Passé d'une illusion* (Paris, 1995), 432, 438.

100. Stéphane Courtois, *Du passé faisons table rase!* (Paris, 2002), 151.

101. Solzhenitsyn, *Gulag*, 210, 215.

102. Adolf Hitler, *Mein Kampf* (London, 1992), 214, 257, 277.

103. Reproduced in Roseman, *Villa*, 108–18.

104. Ian Kershaw, *Hitler* (London, 2000), II, 353–4; Alexandra Richie, *Faust's Metropolis* (London, 1998), 510; Raul Hilberg, *The Destruction of the European Jews* (New York, 1985), 125–44.

105. Roseman, *Villa*, 40–2.

106. Kotek and Rigoulot, *Siècle des camps*, 465.

107. Solzhenitsyn, *Gulag*, 115–19, 265–78; Applebaum, *Gulag*, 127–47.

108. Martin Gilbert, *The Holocaust* (London, 1985), 675, 677. Gilbert, unlike the majority of historians who cite figures of over 800,000, estimates the total number of Jews in Hungary at 750,000. The difference could be due to the fact that many thousands of Jews, long before, had converted to Christianity. This, of course, made no difference to the Nazis.

109. See the Preface of Randolph L. Braham and Scott Miller (eds.), *The Nazis' Last Victims* (Detroit, Mich., 1998), 17–22; and Robert Rozett, 'International Intervention: The Role of Diplomats in Attempts to Rescue Jews in Hungary', in ibid., 137–52. Many Holocaust historians claim the Vatican could have done more.

110. Gilbert, *Holocaust*, 752.

111. Isaac Bashevis Singer, *The Manor* (London, 1975), 41.

112. Isaac Bashevis Singer, 'Disguised', in *The Death of Methuselah and Other Stories* (London, 1988), 50.

113. Singer, *Manor*, 147, 189.

114. Primo Levi, *If This is a Man* (London, 2000), 31–44.

115. Myriam Anissimov, *Primo Levi ou la tragédie d'un optimiste* (Paris, 1996), 32–50.

116. Quoted in ibid., 62.

117. Jorge Semprun, a Spanish-French Communist at the time, tells how at Buchenwald a similar system operated in *La Mort qu'il faut* (Paris, 2001).

118. Levi, *Man*, 44.

119. Ibid., 72.

120. Ibid., 151.

121. Gilbert, *Holocaust*, 760; Levi, *Man*, 168–9, 182.

122. Ibid., 182–7.

123. Daniel Jonah Goldhagen, *Hitler's Willing Executioners* (London, 1996), 327–71.

124. Levi, *Man*, 187–207.

125. Anissimov, *Levi*, 339–404.

Endings

1. Mark Wyman, *DP: Europe's Displaced Persons* (Philadelphia, 1989), 134–5.

2. Elena Skrjabina, *The Allies on the Rhine 1945–1950* (Carbondale, Ill., 1980).

3. Ibid., 28 March 1945, 12.

4. Ibid., 11 April 1945, 21.

5. 13–18 April 1945, 22–4.

6. 1 May 1945, 28.

7. 9 May 1945, 31.

8. Ada Petrova and Peter Watson, *The Death of Hitler* (London, 1995), 75–6, 87–9.

9. Hugh Trevor-Roper, *The Last Days of Hitler* (Chicago, Ill., 1992), 236–9; Cornelius

Ryan, *The Last Battle* (New York, 1967), 460–71; Antony Beevor, *Berlin: The Downfall* (London, 2003), 366–9.

10. Trevor-Roper, *Last Days*, 209–11.
11. Ibid., 236.
12. Ibid., 239.
13. Ibid., 240.
14. Nigel Hamilton, *Monty* (London, 1986), III, 471.
15. Ibid., 492.
16. Ibid., 498.
17. Ibid., 501–8.
18. Martin Gilbert, *The Day the War Ended* (London, 1995), 53, 62–4.
19. Ibid., 67.
20. Hamilton, *Monty*, III, 509–16.
21. Ibid., 521.
22. Gilbert, *Day*, 137.
23. Ibid., 91.
24. Ibid., 267.
25. Erich Roussel, *Charles de Gaulle* (Paris, 2002), 498.
26. Alistair Horne, *Macmillan* (London, 1988), I, 281.
27. Quotations in Paul Addison, *Now the War is Over* (London, 1985), 13–14.
28. *Le Monde*, 2 January 1945.
29. Ibid.
30. Roussel, *De Gaulle*, 518.
31. *Le Figaro* reported on 15 May these two 'independent' parties 'competing' with one another in the workers' suburb of Levallois. Thus Levallois became one of the many Communist suburban fiefs of Paris.
32. *Le Monde*, 21 April 1945. *Pravda* first reported the Red Army's liberation, the previous January, of the camps of Auschwitz on 7 May. See *Le Monde*, 9 May 1945; Gilbert, *Day*, 148–9.
33. Ibid., 173–5; Charles de Gaulle, *Mémoires de guerre* (Paris, 1999), III, 455–6; David McCullough, *Truman* (New York, 1992), 381–2.
34. Quoted in *Le Monde*, 11 May 1945.
35. Quoted in Gilbert, *Day*, 294.
36. McCullough, *Truman*, 382.
37. Gilbert, *Day*, 295.
38. Ibid., 155, 198, 200–1, 209–10.
39. Ibid., 122; Antony Beevor and Artemis Cooper, *Paris after the Liberation* (London, 1995), 238–40; *Figaro*, 8 May 1945.
40. Cathy Porter and Mark Jones, *Moscow in World War II* (London, 1987), 210.
41. Alexander Solzhenitsyn, *The Gulag Archipelago* (New York, 2002), 94–5.
42. Gilbert, *Day*, 107, 208–9, 256, 269–70.
43. Ibid., 217.
44. Ibid., 109, 245–6, 254–5.
45. Ibid., 125, 229–30, 280.
46. Christopher Booker, *A Looking-Glass Tragedy* (London, 1997), 396; *Sunday Times*, 30 July 2000.
47. McCullough, *Truman*, 360.
48. Winston Churchill, *The Second World War* (London, 1948–54), VI, 480–4.
49. McCullough, *Truman*, 390.
50. Ibid., 398.
51. Ibid., 399.
52. Quoted in Horne, *Macmillan*, I, 247.
53. Essential reading for this sad epic are Nicholas Bethell, *The Last Secret* (London, 1974),

which contains many good descriptions; Nikolai Tolstoy, *The Minister and the Massacres* (London, 1986), if you can find it (a court ordered Century-Hutchinson to pay Lord Aldington [Brigadier Toby Low] £30,000 in damages and court costs and were ordered 'to remove every copy of the book from shops and libraries all over Britain' – and this seems to have been applied with equal efficiency in France); Nikolai Tolstoy, *Victims of Yalta* (London, 1978), which rehearses many of the arguments later presented in a more accusatory tone in *Minister*. Among those books already cited in this chapter: Christopher Booker, *Looking-Glass Tragedy*, which provides a 500-page summary of the massive research conducted by the self-styled 'Cowgill Committee', designed to prove distortions in Count Tolstoy's work; Alistair Horne's relevant chapter in *Macmillan*, I, well-written and balanced; and some interesting general comments and independent witnesses interviewed by Mark Wyman, *DP*. Press commentary has been more or less pro-Tolstoy, and thus dismissive of Macmillan and top British commanders. The same can be said of several TV documentaries made on the subject. The whole subject has been seriously distorted by bitter 'scientific' polemic over documents found in the PRO, focusing primarily on events within the Drau Valley. As Booker argues, one should at least consider the context of the Tito crisis in northern Italy and Carinthia. But even this view is too narrow. The major crisis of the time was not, as Booker claims, Venezia Giulia, but the future of all Europe – as demonstrated by the exactly contemporary correspondence between Truman and Churchill. The Americans were pulling out of Germany as fast as they could, just as the crisis in Carinthia came to a head. Unless otherwise indicated, the above cited sources are those used in the following paragraphs.

54.   Harold Macmillan, *The Blast of War* (London, 1967), 414, 468–9.
55.   Quotations in Addison, *War is Over*, 12–15.
56.   Horne, *Macmillan*, I, 268.
57.   *The Times*, 5 June 1945.
58.   Ibid.
59.   Horne, *Macmillan*, I, 268.
60.   Churchill to Truman, London, 15 June 1945, in Foreign Relations of the United States (FRUS), *The Conference of Berlin (The Potsdam Conference)* (Washington, 1960), I, 98.
61.   Correlli Barnett, *The Lost Victory* (London, 1996), 194–211.
62.   John Maynard Keynes, 'Overseas Financial Arrangements in Stage III', in J. M. Keynes, *Collected Works* (London, 1979), XXIV, 249–92.
63.   Robert Skidelsky, *John Maynard Keynes* (London, 2000), III, 378–86.
64.   Roy Jenkins, *Churchill* (London, 2001), 791.
65.   'The Chairman of the President's War Relief Control Board (J. E. Davies) to the President', 'Supplementary Report', Washington, 12 June 1945, in FRUS, *Berlin*, I, 69.
66.   *The Times*, 5 June 1945.
67.   Ibid., 6 June 1945.
68.   As reported in Holman to Eden, Paris, 7 July 1945, in *Documents on British Foreign Policy Overseas (DBFPO)* (London, 1984), 1:1 (*The Conference at Potsdam*), 30–1.
69.   Foreign Office, 'Franco-British Treaty and Policy in Western Europe', London, 12 July 1945, accompanied with annexes, in ibid., 234–51.
70.   *The Times*, 5 July 1945.
71.   FRUS, *Berlin*, I, 92.
72.   Jean-Paul Sartre, 'Villes d'Amérique', 'New-York, ville coloniale', 'Présentation' in *Situations* (Paris, 1949), III, 93–132; Czesław Miłosz, 'Tiger', in Miłosz, *To Begin Where I Am* (New York, 2001), 147, 166–8; George Steiner, *Real Presences* (London, 1989).
73.   Earl of Halifax to Eden, Washington, 8 July 1945, in *DBFPO*, 1:1, 61–8.
74.   Robert H. Ferrell, *Harry S. Truman* (Columbia, Mi., 1994), 16.
75.   Halifax to Eden, 8 July 1945, in *DBFPO*, 1:1, 64.
76.   Stettinius to Grew, San Francisco, 19 June 1945, in FRUS, *Berlin*, I, 283–7.
77.   Churchill to Halifax, London, 6 July, in ibid., 3–7.

78. Leahy to Wilson, Britain Joint Staff Mission, Washington, 15 June 1945, in ibid., 99.
79. Montgomery to Eden, Bad Oeynhausen, 8 July 1945, in *DBFPO*, 1:1, 69–72.
80. JIC, SHAEF, 'Political Intelligence Report', 9 July 1945, in ibid., 92–8.
81. George F. Kennan, *Memoirs* (New York, 1969), 85–7; Churchill, *Second World War*, VI, 501–5.
82. 'The Davies Mission to London', in FRUS, *Berlin*, I, 63–78.
83. Churchill to Truman, London, 4 June 1945, in ibid., 92.
84. Churchill to Stalin, London, 29 May 1945, in ibid., 87.
85. McCullough, *Truman*, 407–8.
86. Alanbrooke, *War Diaries* (London, 2002), 15 July 1945, 705.
87. McCullough, *Truman*, 410–12; Ferrell, *Truman*, 204.
88. *New York Times*, 18 July 1945.
89. McCullough, *Truman*, 414.
90. 'Principles to Govern the Treatment of Germany in the Initial Control Period', undated (c. June 1945), in FRUS, *Berlin*, I, 444.
91. Churchill, *Second World War*, VI, 545–6; Petrova and Watson, *Death of Hitler*; Alanbrooke, *War Diaries*, 16 and 19 July 1945, and later reflections, 705, 707, 711.
92. McCullough, *Truman*, 430–1; Richard Overy, *Why the Allies Won* (London, 1945), 241–2.
93. *DBFPO*, *Berlin*, 367.
94. 'Draft Proclamation by the Heads of Government', 23 July 1945, in ibid., 550–3.
95. Ferrell, *Truman*, 210–15.
96. Alanbrooke, *War Diaries*, 23 July 1945, 709.
97. *DBFPO*, *Berlin*, 368.
98. Ninth Plenary, 25 July 1945, in ibid., 648.
99. Sixth and Seventh Plenaries, 22–23 July 1945, in ibid., 541, 589.
100. McCullough, *Truman*, 426–7, 434.
101. Sir W. Strang to Sir J. Grigg, Lübeck, 10 July 1945, in *DBFPO*, *Berlin*, 122.
102. 'Draft Submitted by the Soviet Delegation, Berlin', 22 July 1945, and 'Brief by the United Kingdom Delegation, Berlin', 23 July 1945, in ibid., 549–50.
103. Sixth Plenary, 22 July 1945, in ibid., 535–6. The final sentence of this paragraph refers to a debate over the following two days concerning the 'Satellite States' of the Balkans, which did not, at the time, appear to worry Truman. For Churchill, on the other hand, it represented a betrayal of the 'Percentage Agreement', the line drawn at Moscow in October 1944. For the Americans the drawing of lines was a wicked European habit. What mattered was, as with Woodrow Wilson in 1919, the essential principle of 'democracy'. Unfortunately, this was not a principle easily 'moderated' through the good offices of Stalin.
104. McCullough, *Truman*, 382.
105. Fifth Plenary, 21 July 1945, in *DBFPO*, *Berlin*, 510.
106. McCullough, *Truman*, 427–8; Ferrell, *Truman*, 208.
107. Myriam Anissimov, *Primo Levi* (Paris, 1996), 351–6.
108. 'Memorandum Submitted by the Soviet Delegation: Plan of Reparations', Berlin, 23 July 1945; 'Memorandum by Sir W. Monckton', Berlin, 24 July 1945, in *DBFPO*, *Berlin*, 594–5, 616–18.
109. Eighth Plenary, 24 July 1945, in ibid., 648–51.
110. 'Record of Meeting between Mr Churchill and Mr Bierut', Prime Minister's house, 25 July 1945, 10 a.m., in ibid., 678–80.
111. 'Record of Conversation', Secretary of State's house, 25 July 1945, in ibid., 681–9.
112. Ninth Plenary, 25 July 1945, in ibid., 690–4.
113. Churchill, *Second World War*, VI, 584.
114. Ibid.
115. *The Times*, 27 July 1945.
116. Ibid.

117. Alanbrooke, *War Diaries*, 26 July 1945, 712.
118. McCullough, *Truman*, 447–8.
119. Bridges and Dixon to Cadogan and Brooke, 27 July 1945, Cadogan to Eden, 27 July, in *DBFPO, Berlin*, 919, 939.
120. Molotov, at a luncheon he gave at Potsdam on 31 July, even seemed to take this seriously and proposed that the Labour Party consult the Russians, an offer that was politely refused. Luncheon Party, Potsdam, 31 July 1945, in ibid., 1063.
121. McCullough, *Truman*, 451.
122. Attlee to Churchill, Berlin, 1 August 1945, in *DBFPO, Berlin*, 1143–4.
123. McCullough, *Truman*, 452.

EUROPE, EUROPE

1. Robert H. Ferrell, *Harry S. Truman* (Columbia, Mi., 1994), 217–22.
2. David McCullough, *Truman* (New York, 1992), 454–9.
3. Total US expenses for the military during the Second World War had been $176 billion – 'the sum still staggers the imagination,' wrote an official US Army historian in the 1950s. The Army's manpower peaked at 8,290,000 in May 1945. In September 1945, just after VJ-Day, the Army's budget was slashed by 60 per cent. Many US military theatres – not unlike America's staunchest Allies – suddenly found all aid withdrawn and were forced to rely on loans. See Walter Rundell, *Military Money* (College Station, Texas, 1980), xii, 3, 75–6.
4. McCullough, *Truman*, 451–2.
5. Ibid., 486–90.
6. Ibid., 490–1. The complete text of Stalin's speech of 9 February 1946 can be found in *Documentation française* (1952), XLVII, 47–51.
7. Hugo Young, *This Blessed Plot* (London, 1998), 16–17.
8. Imanuel Wexler, *The Marshall Plan Revisited* (Westport, Conn., 1983), 19–20, 29.
9. Christopher Booker and Richard North, *The Great Deception* (London, 2003), insist on the importance of America's liberal (in the American sense) Council of Foreign Relations that had been set up in 1920, after the United States had pulled out of the League of Nations and the State Department abandoned its earlier policies on Europe. During the Second World War, under the influence of several European refugees, including the financier Jean Monnet, it began lobbying for a European 'federation' and European 'self-help'. At any rate, the subsequent Marshall Plan certainly acted as a detonator for European notions of 'an ever closer union'.
10. Young, *Blessed Plot*, 102–3.
11. Robert J. Donovan, *The Presidency of Harry S. Truman* (New York, 1982), II, 170.
12. Henry Kissinger, *Diplomacy* (New York, 1994), 452.
13. McCullough, *Truman*, 545.
14. Young, *Blessed Plot*, 32–3.
15. V. M. Molotov, *Molotov Remembers* (Chicago, 1993), 222; Alan Bullock, *Hitler and Stalin* (London, 1998), 1018–19.
16. Donovan, *Presidency*, II, 44.
17. Kissinger, *Diplomacy*, 458–9.
18. Jonathan Brent and Vladimir P. Naumov, *Stalin's Last Crime* (London, 2003), 69–70.
19. Laurent Rucker, *Staline, Israël et les Juifs* (Paris, 2001), 247–74. Rucker presents a first-rate analysis of the century-long tension between Marxism and Zionism (or 'Jewish nationalism' and its search for a home state) – a tension that was well appreciated by Goebbels in his early years as he worked on the theoretical foundations of Germany's National Socialism.
20. Ibid., 255.
21. Anne Applebaum, *Gulag* (London, 2003), 387–8.

22. Ibid., 385.
23. Alexander Solzhenitsyn, *The Gulag Archipelago, 1918–1957* (New York, 2002), 451.
24. Statistics in Edwin Bacon, *The Gulag at War* (London, 1994), 24, 144–55; Applebaum, *Gulag*, 515–16.
25. Karel Bartosek, 'Europe centrale et du Sud', in Stéphane Courtois et al., *Le Livre noir du communisme* (Paris, 1997), 493–506; François Furet, *Le Passé d'une illusion* (Paris, 1995), 482–4.
26. Petru Dumitriu, *Incognito* (Paris, 1962), 678–96.
27. Alexandra Richie, *Faust's Metropolis* (New York, 1998), 619.
28. Philippe Buton (ed.), 'L'Entretien entre Maurice Thorez et Joseph Staline du 26 novembre 1947', *Communisme*, No. 45–46 (1996), 30–9.
29. Richie, *Faust's Metropolis*, 633–57.
30. Brent and Naumov, *Stalin's Last Crime*, 193.
31. Ibid., 283.
32. Ibid., 83.
33. Ibid., 167–8.
34. Ibid., 5, Bullock, *Hitler and Stalin*, 998.
35. Kissinger, *Diplomacy*, 505.
36. Richie, *Faust's Metropolis*, 659.
37. Ibid., 667.
38. Bullock, *Hitler and Stalin*, 1027.
39. Statistics in Kissinger, *Diplomacy*, 491.
40. Rucker, *Staline, Israël*, 73–5.
41. Norman G. Finkelstein, *The Holocaust Industry* (London, 2001), 16–19.
42. Rucker, *Staline, Israël*, 90; Uri Bialer, *Between East and West* (Cambridge, 1990), 62; Primo Levi quoted in Myriam Anissimov, *Primo Levi* (Paris, 1996), 397.
43. Rucker, *Staline, Israël*, 98–101.
44. Ibid.
45. Norbert Frei, *Adenauer's Germany and the Nazi Past* (New York, 2002), 6–7.
46. This is the major point made by Vladimir Bukovsky, *Jugement à Moscou* (Paris, 1995). Why, asks Bukovsky, have the Communists never been forced to face up to their past?
47. The best, most readable account of the Nuremberg Trial – which includes a fair but not over-theoretical account of the legal history behind the setting up of the International Military Tribunal – is Ann and John Tusa, *The Nuremberg Trial* (London, 1995).
48. The point is famously made, justifiably in this author's view, by Norman Finkelstein, *The Holocaust Industry* (London, 2001).
49. This incredible story, amounting to reparations of over $70 billion, is known to all citizens of Israel and all Western Jewish survivors. It is told in detail in Ronald W. Zweig, *German Reparations and the Jewish World* (London, 1987). Those in receipt certainly deserved the sum; it never made up for their suffering. But the demand, in the 1990s, by private jet-travelling lawyers in New York for yet *further* reparations – for those who never even lived in the war – is obscene, especially when it is considered that few Eastern European Jews, under Communist governments, received any reparations. Nor have any of the victims of Communism received reparations.
50. Frei, *Adenauer's Germany*, 98.
51. Alfred Grosser, *L'Allemagne en Occident* (Paris, 1985), 33–5.
52. Frei, *Adenauer's Germany*, 1–23, 177–201.
53. Charles Williams, *Adenauer* (London, 2000), 314.
54. Quoted in ibid., 338. The Catholic Church took note. In 2003 Pope John-Paul II formally proposed that he be named *le Bienheureux* Robert Schuman, a step below sainthood.
55. Young, *Blessed Plot*, 44–70; Booker and North, *Deception*, 47–57.
56. Quoted in Vincent Jauvert, *L'Amérique contre de Gaulle* (Paris, 2000), 15.

57. Ibid., 78.
58. Charles Williams, *The Last Great Frenchman* (London, 1995), 364.
59. Kissinger, *Diplomacy*, 530.
60. Young, *Blessed Plot*, 78–94.
61. Alexander Werth, *De Gaulle* (New York, 1965), 235–6.
62. Jean Lacouture, *De Gaulle* (Paris, 1986), III, 270–82.
63. Eric Roussel, *Charles de Gaulle* (Paris, 2002), 591.
64. Alistair Horne, *Macmillan* (London, 1989), II, 87.
65. Ibid., 177.
66. Ibid., 195.
67. Young, *Blessed Plot*, 134.
68. Ibid., 136–7; Horne, *Macmillan*, II, 429–32.

Bibliography

ᵡ

Printed works cited

Acheson, Dean. *Present at the Creation: My Years in the State Department.* New York: W. W. Norton, 1969.

Addison, Paul. *Now the War is Over: A Social History of Britain 1945 51.* London: Pimlico, 1985.

Adlon, Hedda. *Hotel Adlon. Das Haus in dem die Welt zu Gast war.* Munich: Kindler, 1955.

Agulhon, Maurice. *De Gaulle: Histoire, symbole, mythe.* Paris: Plon, 2000.

Alanbrooke, Field Marshal Lord. *War Diaries 1939–1945,* ed. Alex Danchev and Daniel Todman. London: Phoenix, 2002.

Alliluyeva, Svetlana. *Twenty Letters to a Friend.* London: Hutchinson, 1967.

Ambrose, Stephen E. *The Supreme Commander: The War Years of General Dwight D. Eisenhower.* London: Cassell, 1971.

—— *Eisenhower and Berlin 1945: The Decision to Halt at the Elbe.* New York: Norton, 2000.

Amouroux, Henri. *La Grande Histoire des Français sous l'Occupation.* Vols. VII–VIII: *Un Printemps de mort et d'espoir, Joies et douleurs du peuple libéré.* Paris: Laffont, 1999

—— *La Grande Histoire des Français après l'Occupation.* Vol. IX. *Les Règlements de comptes, Septembre 1944–Janvier 1945.* Paris: Laffont, 1999.

Andrew, Christopher, and Mitrokhin, Vasili. *The Mitrokhin Archive: The KGB in Europe and the West.* London: Penguin, 2000.

Andreyev, Catherine. *Vlasov and the Russian Liberation Movement: Soviet Reality and Emigré Theory.* Cambridge: Cambridge University Press, 1987.

Anissimov, Myriam. *Primo Levi, ou la tragédie d'un optimiste.* Paris: Lattès, 1996.

Annan, Noel. *Changing Enemies: The Defeat and Regeneration of Germany.* London: HarperCollins, 1995

Anonymous. *Le Drame de Caen, juin–juillet 1944,* pref. Jean Léon-Jean. Rouen: Imprimerie Rouennaise, 1945.

Anonymous. *A Woman in Berlin,* trans. James Stern. London: Secker & Warburg, 1955.

Applebaum, Anne. *Gulag: A History of the Soviet Camps.* London: Allen Lane, 2003.

Ardagh, John. *Germany and the Germans: After Unification.* London: Penguin, 1991.

Astier, Emmanuel d'. *De la chute à la libération de Paris, 25 août 1945.* Paris: Gallimard, 1965.

Axionov, Vassili. *Une saga muscovite,* trans. Lily Denis. 3 vols. in one. Paris: Gallimard, 1995.

Bacon, Edwin. *The Gulag at War: Stalin's Forced Labour System in the Light of the Archives.* London: Macmillan, 1994.

Barnett, Correlli. *The Audit of War: The Illusion and Reality of Britain as a Great Nation.* London: Pan, 2001.

—— *The Lost Victory: British Dreams, British Realities 1945–50.* London: Pan, 1996.

—— *The Collapse of British Power.* London: Pan, 2002.

Bartosek, Karel. 'Europe centrale et du Sud', in Courtois et al., *Livre noir,* 456–529.

Beauvais, Daniel. *La Pologne.* Paris: La Marinière, 2004.

Beauvoir, Simone de. *La Force de l'âge.* Paris: Gallimard, 1960.

Beevor, Antony. *Stalingrad*. London: Penguin, 1999.

—— *Berlin: The Downfall 1945*. London: Penguin, 2003.

—— and Cooper, Artemis. *Paris after the Liberation: 1944–1949*. London: Penguin, 1995.

Beria, Sergo. *Beria, My Father: Inside Stalin's Kremlin*, ed. Françoise Thom, trans. Brian Pearce. London: Duckworth, 2001.

Berstein, Serge, Frank, Robert, Jansen, Sabine, Werth, Nicolas. *Rapport de la commission d'historiens constituée pour examiner la nature des relations de Pierre Cot avec les autorités soviétiques*. Paris: B & Cie., 1995.

Bethell, Nicholas. *The Last Secret: Forcible Repatriation to Russia 1944–7*. London: André Deutsch, 1974.

Bialer, Yuri. *Between East and West: Israel's Foreign Policy Orientation 1948–1956*. Cambridge, Cambridge University Press, 1990.

Bogusławska, Anna. *Food for the Children: A Diary of the Warsaw Rising, Summer 1944*, trans. Ewa Barker. London: Leo Cooper, 1975.

Booker, Christopher. *A Looking-Glass Tragedy: The Controversy over the Repatriations from Austria in 1945*. London: Duckworth, 1997.

—— and North, Richard. *The Great Deception: A Secret History of the European Union*. London: Continuum, 2003.

Bór-Komorowski, T. *The Secret Army*. London: Gollancz, 1950.

Boukovsky, Vladimir. *Jugement à Moscou: un dissident dans les archives du Kremlin*, trans. Louis Martinez. Paris: Laffont, 1995

Boulgakov, Mikhaïl. *Le Maître et Marguerite*. Paris: Laffont, 1968.

Boveri, Margret. *Tage des Überlebens: Berlin 1945*. Munich: Piper, 1968.

Brackman, Roman. *The Secret File of Joseph Stalin: A Hidden Life*. London: Cass, 2001.

Braham, Randolph L. and Miller, Scott (eds.). *The Nazis' Last Victims: The Holocaust in Hungary*. Detroit, Mich.: Wayne State University, 1998.

Brent, Jonathan, and Naumov, Vladimir P. *Stalin's Last Crime: The Doctors' Plot*. London: John Murray, 2003.

Brett-James, Antony. *Conversations with Montgomery*. London: W. Kimber, 1984.

Brinkley, David. *Washington Goes to War*. New York: Ballantine, 1989.

Bruce, George. *The Warsaw Uprising*. London: Hart-Davis, 1972.

Bullock, Alan. *Hitler and Stalin: Parallel Lives*. London: HarperCollins, 1998.

Burleigh, Michael. *The Third Reich: A New History*. London: Macmillan, 2000.

—— *Death and Deliverance: Euthanasia in Germany 1900–1945*. Cambridge: Cambridge University Press, 1994.

Burns, James MacGregor, and Dunn, Susan. *The Three Roosevelts: The Leaders Who Transformed America*. London: Atlantic Books, 2001.

Buton, Philippe. *Les Lendemains qui déchantent: Le parti communiste français à la Libération*. Paris: Presses de la Fondation nationale des sciences politiques, 1993.

—— (ed.). 'L'entretien entre Maurice Thorez et Joseph Staline du 19 novembre 1944', *Communisme*, No. 45–46 (1996), 7–29.

Caen, Ville de. *Témoignages: Récits de la vie caennaise, 6 juin – 19 juillet 1944*. Caen: Imprimérie de Caen, 1984.

Calder, Angus. *The People's War: Britain 1939–1945*. London: Jonathan Cape, 1969.

Chalamov, Varlam. *Récits de la Kolyma*. Paris: Verdier-Slava, 2003.

Charlanov, Diniou et al. 'La Bulgarie sous le joug communiste. Crimes, résistances et répressions', in Courtois et al. (eds.), *Du passé faisons table rase!*, 313–68.

Charmley, John. *Churchill: The End of Glory*. London: Hodder & Stoughton, 1993.

Choltitz, General Dietrich von. *Brennt Paris? Adolf Hitler, Tatsachenbericht des letzten deutschen Befehlshabers in Paris*. Mannheim: Weltücherei, 1950.

—— *Un soldat parmi les soldats*, trans A. M. Becourt, Martin Briem, Klaus Diel, Pierre Michel. Paris: J'ai lu, 1969.

Chuikov, Vassili. *Das Ende des Dritten Reiches* (Munich, 1966), in Gosztony (ed.), *Der Kampf*, 342–4, 346–7, 351–5.

Churchill, Winston S. *The Second World War*. 6 vols. London: Cassell, 1948–54.

—— and Clementine. *Speaking for Themselves: The Personal Letters of Winston and Clementine Churchill*, ed. Mary Soames. London: Doubleday, 1998.

Ciechanowski, Jan M. *The Warsaw Rising of 1944*. Cambridge: Cambridge University Press, 1974.

Cocteau, Jean. *Journal 1942–1945*. Paris: Gallimard, 1989.

Colton, Timothy J. *Moscow: Governing the Socialist Metropolis*. Cambridge, Mass.: Belknap, 1995

Colville, John. *The Fringes of Power: Downing Street Diaries, 1939–1955*. London: Hodder & Stoughton, 1985.

Conquest, Robert. *Kolyma: The Arctic Death Camps*. New York: Penguin USA, 1978.

—— *The Nation Killers: The Soviet Deportation of Nationalities*. New York: Sphere, 1972.

—— *Stalin: Breaker of Nations*. London: Weidenfeld & Nicolson, 2000.

Conte, Arthur. *Yalta ou le partage du monde*. Paris: Laffont, 1975.

Cordier, Daniel. *Jean Moulin: l'inconnu du Panthéon*. 3 vols. Paris: Lattès, 1989–93.

Courtois, Stéphane. *Le PCF dans la guerre. De Gaulle, la Résistance, Staline* . . . Paris: Ramsay, 1980.

—— *Remarques sur un rapport*. Paris: S. Courtois, 1995.

—— et al. *Le Livre noir du communisme: crimes, terreur, répression*. Paris: Laffont, 1997.

—— et al. *Du passé faisons table rase! Histoire et mémoire du communisme en Europe*. Paris: Laffont, 2002.

Dallas, Gregor. *1918: War and Peace*. London: John Murray, 2000.

—— *1815: The Roads to Waterloo*. London: Cohen, 1996.

—— *At the Heart of a Tiger: Clemenceau and His World, 1841–1929*. London: Macmillan, 1993.

—— 'Who Killed the Admiral?' *BBC History Magazine* (December 2002), 42–3.

Dallin, Alexander. *German Rule in Russia 1941–1945: A Study of Occupation Politics*. London: Macmillan, 1986.

—— *Political Terror in Communist Systems*. London: Macmillan, 1970.

Daniels, Jonathan. *Frontier on the Potomac*. New York: Macmillan, 1946.

Dansette, Adrien. *Histoire de la libération de Paris*. Paris: Perrin, 1994.

David, Paul. *Am Königsplatz: Die letzen Tage der Schweizerischen Gesandtschaft in Berlin*. Zurich: Thomas, 1948.

Davies, Norman. *God's Playground: A History of Poland*. Vol. II: *1795 to the Present*. Oxford: Oxford University Press, 1981.

—— *Rising '44: The Battle for Warsaw*. London: Macmillan, 2003.

Davis, Kenneth S. *FDR: The War President, 1940–1943*. New York: Random House, 2000.

De Gaulle, see Gaulle, Charles de.

Deak, Istvan, Gross, Jan T., and Judt, Tony (eds.). *The Politics of Retribution in Europe: World War II and Its Aftermath*. Princeton, NJ: Princeton University Press, 2000.

Debray, Régis. *A demain, de Gaulle*. Paris: Gallimard, 1990.

Degrelle, Léon. *La Campagne de Russie 1941–1945*. Paris: La Diffusion du Livre, 1949.

Desnos, Robert. *Chantefables et Chantefleurs*. Paris: Gründ, 2003.

Deutschkron, Inge. *Ich trug den gelben Stern*. Cologne: Berend und Nottbeck, 1978.

DeZayas, Alfred M. *Nemesis at Potsdam: The Expulsion of the Germans from the East*. London: Routledge & Kegan Paul, 1977.

Documents on British Foreign Policy Overseas (DBFPO), ed. Rohan Butler, M. E. Pelly, H. J. Yasamee. Series 1, Volume I: *The Conference at Potsdam, July–August 1945*. London: Her Majesty's Stationery Office, 1984.

Donovan, Robert J. *The Presidency of Harry S. Truman*. 2 vols. New York: Norton, 1977–82.

Dronne, Raymond. *La Libération de Paris*. Paris: Presses de la Cité, 1970.

Dumitriu, Petru. *Incognito*. Paris: Seuil, 1962.

Eisenberg, Carolyn. *Drawing the Line: The American Decision to Divide Germany, 1944–1949.* Cambridge: Cambridge University Press, 1996.

Eksteins, Modris. *Walking Since Daybreak: A Story of Eastern Europe, World War II and the Heart of the Twentieth Century.* London: Macmillan, 2000.

Erickson, John. *The Road to Berlin: Stalin's War with Germany.* London: Cassell, 1999.

Fabre-Luce, Alfred. *Journal de la France, 1939–1944.* Paris: Fayard, 1969.

Ferrell, Robert H. *The Dying President: Franklin D. Roosevelt.* Columbia, Mi.: University of Missouri Press, 1998.

—— *Harry S. Truman: A Life.* Columbia, Mi.: University of Missouri Press, 1994.

Ferro, Marc. *Pétain.* Paris: Fayard, 1987.

Figes, Orlando. *A People's Tragedy: The Russian Revolution 1891–1924.* London: Pimlico, 1996.

Finger, Blanche, and Karel, William (eds.). *Opération 'Vent printanier': 16–17 juillet 1942: la rafle du Vel' d'Hiv'.* Paris: La Découverte, 1992.

Finkelstein, Norman G. *The Holocaust Industry: Reflections on the Exploitation of Jewish Suffering.* London: Verso, 2001.

Fleming, Gerald. *Hitler and the Final Solution.* London: Hamish Hamilton, 1985.

Florentin, Eddy. *Stalingrad en Normandie: la destruction de la VIIe armée allemande, 30 juillet – 22 août 1944.* Paris: Presses de la Cité, 1994.

Foreign Relations of the United States (FRUS). *The Conferences at Malta and Yalta 1945.* Washington: Government Printing Office, 1955.

—— *The Conference of Berlin (The Postdam Conference) 1945.* 2 vols. Washington: Government Printing Office, 1960.

Frei, Norbert. *Adenauer's Germany and the Nazi Past: The Politics of Amnesty and Integration,* trans. Joel Golb. New York: Columbia University Press, 2002.

Frenay, Henri. *La Nuit finira.* Paris: Laffont, 1973.

Friedrich, Jörg. *Der Brand: Deutschland im Bombenkrieg 1940–1945.* Munich: Ullstein Heyne, 2003.

Fröhlich, Sergei. *General Wlassow.* Cologne: Markus, 1987.

Furet, François. *Le Passé d'une illusion: essai sur l'idée communiste au XXe siècle.* Paris: Laffont, 1995.

Galtier-Boissière, Jean. *Journal 1940–1950.* Paris: Quai Voltaire, 1992.

Gaulle, Charles de. *Discours et messages, juin 1940–janvier 1946.* Paris: Club français des bibliophiles, 1971.

—— *Lettres, Notes et Carnets.* 12 vols. Paris: Plon, 1980–97.

—— *Mémoires de guerre.* 3 vols. Paris: Pocket, 1999.

Getty, J. Arch. 'The Future Did Not Work'. *Atlantic Monthly* (March 2000), 113–16.

Gilbert, Martin. *Winston Churchill.* Vols. VI–VIII. London: Heinemann, 1983–8.

—— *The Day the War Ended: VE-Day in 1945 in Europe and Around the World.* London: HarperCollins, 1995.

—— *The Holocaust: The Jewish Tragedy.* London: Fontana, 1987.

Gildea, Robert. *Marianne in Chains: In Search of the German Occupation 1940–45.* Oxford: Oxford University Press, 2002.

Gisevius, Hans B. *To the Bitter End: An Insider's Account of the Plot to Kill Hitler 1933–1944,* trans. Richard and Clara Winston. New York: Da Capo, 1998.

Glantz, David M., and House, Jonathan. *When Titans Clashed: How the Red Army Stopped Hitler.* Lawrence: University of Kansas Press, 1995.

Goebbels, Joseph. *Die Tagebücher,* ed. Elke Fröhlich. Part II: *Diktate 1941–1945.* 15 vols. Munich: K. G. Sauer, 1995.

Goldhagen, Daniel Jonah. *Hitler's Willing Executioners: Ordinary Germans and the Holocaust.* London: Abacus, 1996.

Goodwin, Doris Kearns. *No Ordinary Time: Franklin and Eleanor Roosevelt: The Home Front in World War II*. New York: Touchstone, 1994.

Goodwin-Gill, Guy S. 'Different Types of Forced Migration Movements as an International and National Problem', in Rystad (ed.), *Uprooted*, 15–46.

Gosset, André, and Lecomte, Paul. *Caen pendant la bataille*. Caen: Ozanne, 1946.

Gosztony, Peter (ed.). *Der Kampf um Berlin 1945 in Augenzeugenberichten*. Dusseldorf: Karl Rauch, 1970.

Green, Constance McLaughlin. *Washington: Capital City, 1879–1950*. Princeton, NJ: Princeton University Press, 1963.

Grenkevich, Leonid D. *The Soviet Partisan Movement 1941–44*. London: Frank Cass, 1999.

Gross, Jan T. 'A Tangled Web: Confronting Stereotypes Concerning Relations between Poles, Germans, Jews, and Communists', in Deak, Gross and Judt (eds.), *Politics of Retribution*.

—— *Neighbors: Community in Jedwabne, Poland*. Princeton, NJ: Princeton University Press, 2000.

Grosser, Alfred. *L'Allemagne en Occident*. Paris: Fayard, 1985.

Halloway, Doug. *A Soldier's Memories 1944–1945: Fifty Years On*. London: Minerva, 1998.

Hamilton, Nigel. *The Full Monty*. Vol. I. *Montgomery of Alamein, 1887–1942*. London: Allen Lane, 2001.

—— *Monty*. 3 vols. London: Hamish Hamilton, 1981–6.

Hanson, Joanna K. M. *The Civilian Population and the Warsaw Uprising of 1944*. Cambridge: Cambridge University Press, 1982.

Harriman, W. Averell, and Abel, Elie. *Special Envoy to Churchill and Stalin 1941–1946*. London: Hutchinson, 1976.

Haushofer, Albrecht. *Zur Problematik des Raumbegriffs*. Heidelberg and Berlin: Kurt Vowinckel, 1935.

Haushofer, Karl. *Wehr-Geopolitik*. Berlin: Junker und Dünnhaupt, 1941.

Haynes, John Earl, and Klehr, Harvey. *VENONA: Decoding Soviet Espionage*. New Haven, Conn.: Yale University Press, 1999.

Henderson, H. W. *The Glory and Shame of Warsaw*. Perth: Munro Press, 1944.

Henriot, Philippe. *26 avril 1944: le Maréchal à Paris*. Montrouge: Information de l'Etat Français, 1944.

Herman, Arthur. *Joseph McCarthy: Reexamining the Life and Legacy of America's Most Hated Senator*. New York: Simon & Schuster, 2000.

Hilberg, Raul. *The Destruction of the European Jews*. New York: Holmes & Meier, 1985.

Hiss, Tony. *Laughing Last: Alger Hiss*. Boston: Houghton Mifflin, 1977.

Hitler, Adolf. *Mein Kampf*, trans. Ralph Manheim. London: Pimlico, 1992.

Hoffmann, Peter. *The History of the German Resistance, 1933–1945*, trans. Richard Barry. London: Macdonald & Jane's, 1977.

Holliday, Laurel (ed.). *Children's Wartime Diaries: Secret Writings from the Holocaust and World War II*. London: Piatkus, 1995.

Holtz, Hannelore. *Wir lebten in Berlin*. Berlin: J. H. W. Dietz, 1947.

Horne, Alistair. *Macmillan: The Official Biography*. 2 vols. London: Macmillan, 1988–9.

Horne, John, and Kramer, Alan. *German Atrocities 1914: A Human History of Denial*. New Haven, Conn.: Yale University Press, 2001.

Inkeles, Alex, and Bauer, Raymond A. *The Soviet Citizen: Daily Life in a Totalitarian Society*. Cambridge, Mass.: Harvard University Press, 1959.

Inwood, Stephen. *A History of London*. London: Macmillan, 1998.

Ismay, General the Lord. *The Memoirs of Lord Ismay*. London: Heinemann, 1960.

Jäckel, Eberhard, and Rohwer, Jurgen (eds.). *Keine Kameraden: die Wehrmacht und die sowjetischen Kriegsgefangenen 1941–1945*. Bonn: J. H. W. Dietz Nachf, 1991.

Jackson, Julian. *France: The Dark Years, 1940–1944*. Oxford: Oxford University Press, 2001.
Jauvert, Vincent. *L'Amérique contre de Gaulle: histoire secrète 1961–1969*. Paris: Seuil, 2000.
Jenkins, Roy. *Churchill*. London: Macmillan, 2001.
Johnson, Eric A. *Nazi Terror: The Gestapo, Jews, and Ordinary Germans*. London: John Murray, 1999.
Johnson, Paul. *A History of the Jews*. London: Weidenfeld & Nicolson, 1987.
Jucker, Ninette. *Curfew in Paris: A Record of the German Occupation*. London: Hogarth Press, 1960.

Karski, Jan. *The Great Powers and Poland 1919–1945: From Versailes to Yalta*. Lanham, Md.: University Press of America, 1985.
Keegan, John. *Six Armies in Normandy: From D-Day to the Liberation of Paris*. London: Pimlico, 1992.
Kennan, George F. *Memoirs*. New York: Bantam, 1969.
Keppler, Kurt. *Tod über Deutschland: Der Morgenthauplan: Vorgeschichte, Geschichte, Wesen, Hintergründe*. Tübingen: Verlag der Deutschen Hochschullehrer, Zeitung Grabert Verlag, 1971.
Kersaudy, François. *Churchill and De Gaulle*. London: Collins, 1981.
Kershaw, Ian. *Hitler*. 2 vols. London: Allen Lane, 1998–2000.
Keynes, John Maynard. *Collected Works*, ed. Donald Moggridge. Vol. XXIV: *Activities 1944–1946: The Transition to Peace*. Cambridge: Cambridge University Press, 1979.
Khrushchev, Nikita. *Khrushchev Remembers*, trans. and ed. Strobe Talbott. 2 vols. Boston: Little, Brown & Co., 1971–4.
Kimball, Warren F. *Churchill and Roosevelt: The Complete Correspondence*. 3 vols. Princeton, NJ: Princeton University Press, 1984.
Kiplinger, W. M. *Washington is Like That*. New York: Harper & Bros., 1942.
Kissinger, Henry. *Diplomacy*. London: Simon & Schuster, 1994.
Klemperer, Klemens von. *German Resistance against Hitler: The Search for Allies Abroad, 1938–1945*. Oxford: Clarendon, 1992.
Korbonski, Stefan. *Fighting Warsaw: The Story of the Polish Underground State 1939–1945*, trans. F. B. Czarnomski. London: Allen & Unwin, 1956.
Kotek, Joël, and Rigoulot, Pierre. *Le Siècle des camps*; Paris: Lattès, 2000.
Kramer, Paul, and Holborn, Frederick L. (eds.). *The City in American Life: From Colonial Times to the Present*. New York: Capricorn, 1970.
Kriegel, Annie. *Ce que j'ai cru comprendre*. Paris: Laffont, 1991.
Kulischer, Eugene M. *Europe on the Move: War and Population Changes 1917–1947*. New York: Columbia University Press, 1948.
Kulski, Julian Eugeniusz. *Dying We Live: The Personal Chronicle of a Young Freedom Fighter in Warsaw (1939–1945)*. New York: Holt, Rinehart & Winston, 1979.
Kurowski, Franz. *Hitler's Last Bastion: The Final Battles for the Reich 1944–1945*. Atgen, Pa.: Schiffer, 1998.

Lacouture, Jean. *De Gaulle*. 3 vols. Paris: Le Seuil, 1984–6.
Lamb, Richard. *Churchill as War Leader: Right or Wrong?* London: Bloomsbury, 1991.
—— *Montgomery in Europe 1943–1945: Success or Failure?* London: Buchan & Enright, 1983.
Ladd, Brian. *The Ghosts of Berlin: Confronting German History in the Urban Landscape*. Chicago: University of Chicago Press, 1997.
Lapierre, Dominique, and Collins, Larry. *Paris brûle-t-il? L'épopée de la libération de Paris*. Paris: Laffont, 1964.
Laqueur, Walter. *The Terrible Secret: Suppression of the Truth about Hitler's 'Final Solution'*. Boston: Little, Brown, 1981.
Leahy, Admiral William D. *I Was There: The Personal Story of the Chief of Staff to Presidents Roosevelt and Truman Based on His Notes and Diaries Made at the Time*. London: Gollancz, 1950.
Lechevrel, Jean. *Les Dès sont sur les tapis: Caen et les environs, été 1944*. Caen: SOGISS, 1984.

Lee, Sabine. *Victory in Europe: Britain and Germany since 1945*. Harlow, Ex.: Pearson, 2001.

Leighton, Richard M., and Coakley, Robert W. *Global Logistics and Strategy, 1940–1943, 1943–45*. 2 vols. Washington, DC: Office of the Chief of Military History, 1955–65.

Le Tissier, Tony *Zhukov at the Oder*, Westport, Conn.; Praeger, 1996.

—— *Race for the Reichstag: The 1945 Battle for Berlin*. London: Frank Cass, 1999

Levi, Primo. *If This is a Man*, trans. Stuart Woolf. London: Folio, 2000.

—— *The Periodic Table*, trans. Raymond Rosenthal. Harmondsworth, Middlesex: Penguin, 2001.

—— *The Truce*, trans. Stuart Woolf. London: Abacus, 1987.

Lévy, Claude, et Tillard, Paul. *La Grande Rafle du Vél d'Hiv*. Paris: Robert Laffont, 1967, 1992.

Lucas, James. *War on the Eastern Front 1941–1945*. London: Sydney & June, 1979.

—— *Das Reich: The Military Role of the 2nd SS Division*. London: Cassell, 1991.

McCullough, David. *Truman*. New York: Simon & Schuster, 1992.

MacDonald, Charles B. *The Battle of the Bulge*. London: Weidenfeld & Nicolson, 1984.

MacDonogh, Giles. *Berlin*. London: Sinclair Stevenson, 1997.

Mack Smith, Denis. *Modern Italy: A Political History*. New Haven: Yale University Press, 1997.

—— *Mussolini*. London: Weidenfeld & Nicolson, 1981.

McKee, Alexander. *Caen: Anvil of Victory*. London: Souvenir Press, 1964.

Mackinder, Sir Halford. *The World War and After: A Concise Narrative and Some Tentative Ideas*. London: George Philip, 1924.

Macmillan, Harold. *The Blast of War 1939–1945*. London: Macmillan, 1967.

—— *War Diaries: Politics and War in the Mediterranean, January 1943–May 1945*. London: Macmillan, 1984.

McMillan, Richard. *Miracle Before Berlin*. London: Jarrolds, 1946.

McPhael, Helen. *The Long Silence: Civilian Life under the German Occupation of Northern France 1914–1918*. London: I. B. Tauris, 2002.

Malliarakis, Jean Gilles. *Yalta et la naissance des blocs*. Paris: Albatross, 1982.

Mansel, Philip. *Paris Between Empires, 1814–1852*. London: John Murray, 2001.

Marabini, Jean. *La Vie quotidienne à Berlin sous Hitler*. Paris: Hachette, 1985.

Marnham, Patrick. *The Death of Jean Moulin: Biography of a Ghost*. London: John Murray, 2000.

Marrus, Michael R., and Paxton, Robert O. *Vichy France and the Jews*. New York: Basic Books, 1981.

Merlio, Gilbert. *Les Résistances allemandes à Hitler*. Paris: Tallandier, 2001.

Middlebrook, Martin. *The Berlin Raids: RAF Bomber Command, Winter 1943–44*. London: Viking, 1988.

Mikołajczyk, S. *The Rape of Poland: The Pattern of Soviet Aggression* [British title: *The Pattern of Soviet Domination*]. New York: Whittlesey House, 1948.

Miłosz, Czesław. *The Seizure of Power*. London: Faber & Faber, 1955.

—— *To Begin Where I Am: Selected Essays*. New York: Farrar, Straus & Giroux, 2001.

—— *New and Collected Poems 1931–2001*. London: Allen Lane, 2001.

Molotov, I. V. *Molotov Remembers: Inside Kremlin Politics*, ed. Alber Resis. Chicago: Ivan Occ, 1993.

Moorehead, Alan. *Eclipse*. London: Granta, 2000.

—— *Montgomery: A Biography*. London: Hamilton, 1947.

Mosse, George L. *The Fascist Revolution: Toward a General Theory of Fascism*. New York: Fertig, 1999.

Nagorski, Z. *Warsaw Fights Alone*. London: Maxwell, Love & Co., 1944.

Narinsky, Mikhaïl (ed.). 'L'entretien entre Maurice Thorez et Joseph Staline du 18 novembre 1947', *Communisme*, No. 45–46 (1996), 31–54.

Navasky, Victor. 'Weinstein, Hiss and the Transformation of Historical Ambiguity into Cold War Verity', in Theoharis (ed.), *Hiss Case*, 215–45.

Neillands, Robin. *The Bomber War: Arthur Harris and the Allied Bomber Offensive 1939–1945*. London: John Murray, 2001.

Nicolson, Harold. *Diaries and Letters, 1939–45*, ed. Nigel Nicolson. London: Weidenfeld & Nicolson, 1967.

Noakes, Jeremy (ed.). *Nazism 1919–1945: A Documentary Reader*. 4 vols. Exeter: Exeter University Press, 1998.

Nolte, Ernst. *La Guerre civile européenne 1917–1945: national-socialisme et bolchevisme*, trans. from German Jean-Marie Argelès. Paris: Syrtes, 2000.

Nordling, Raoul. *Sauver Paris: Mémoires du consul de Suède (1905–1944)*, ed. Fabrice Virgili. Brussels: Editions Complexes, 2002.

Nossiter, Adam. *The Algeria Hotel: France, Memory and the Second World War*. New York: Houghton Mifflin, 2001.

Nowak, Jan (pseud. Zdzisław Jeziorański). *Courier from Warsaw*. Detroit: Wayne State University Press, 1982.

O'Donnell, James P. *The Berlin Bunker*. London: Arrow Books, 1979.

O'Reilly, Kenneth. 'Liberal Values, the Cold War, and American Intellectuals: The Trauma of the Alger Hiss Case, 1950–1978', in Theoharis (ed.), *Hiss Case*, 309–40.

Orska, Irena. *Silent is the Vistula: The Story of the Warsaw Uprising*, trans. Marta Erdman. New York: Longmans, Green, 1946.

Orwell, George. *The Collected Essays, Journalism and Letters*, ed. Sonia Orwell and Ian Angus. 4 vols. New York: Harcourt, Brace & World, 1968.

—— *Orwell and Politics*, ed. Peter Davison. Harmondsworth, Middlesex: Penguin, 2001.

—— *Orwell's England*, ed. Peter Davison. Harmondsworth, Middlesex: Penguin, 2001.

Ousby, Ian. *Occupation: The Ordeal of France, 1940–1944*. London: John Murray, 1997.

Overy, Richard. *Why the Allies Won*. London: Pimlico, 1995.

Pacskowski, Andrzej. 'La Pologne, la "nation-ennemi"', in Stéphane Courtois et al., *Le Livre noir du communisme* (Paris, 1998), 423–55.

Parker, Danny S. *Hitler's Ardennes Offensive: The German View of the Battle of the Bulge*. London: Greenhill, 1997.

Passy, Colonel [André Dewavrin]. *2e Bureau, Londres*. Monte Carlo: Raoul Solar, 1947.

Paxton, Robert O. *Vichy France: Old Guard and New Order, 1940–1944*. New York: W. W. Norton, 1972.

Perrier, Jean-Claude. *De Gaulle vu par les écrivains: d'Aragon à Zagdanski*. Paris: Table Ronde, 2000.

Peyrefitte, Alain. *C'était de Gaulle*. 2 vols. Paris: Fayard, 1994.

Peyrefitte, Christel. 'Les premiers sondages d'opinion', in Rémond and Bourdin (eds.), *Edouard Daladier*, 265–78.

Pineau, Christian. *La simple vérité: Histoire vécue de la Résistance*. 2 vols. Geneva: Crémille, 1972.

Pipet, Albert. *Mourir à Caen*. Paris: Presses de la Cité, 1974.

Pomian, Krysztof. *L'Europe et ses nations: le débat*. Paris: Gallimard, 1990.

Porter, Cathy, and Jones, Mark. *Moscow in World War II*. London: Chatto & Windus, 1987.

Pourcher, Yves. *Pierre Laval vu par sa fille, d'après ses carnets intimes*. Paris: Le Cherche Midi, 2002.

Probert, Air Commodore Henry. *Bomber Harris: His Life and Times*. London: Greenhill, 2001.

Proust, Marcel. *A la recherche du temps perdu*. 3 vols. Paris: Laffont, 1987.

Pryce-Jones, David. *Paris in the Third Reich: A History of the German Occupation, 1940–1944*. London: Collins, 1981.

Quétel, Claude. *Caen, 1940–1944: La guerre, l'occupation, la libération*. Rennes: Editions Ouest-France, 1994.

Raack, R. C. *Stalin's Drive to the West 1938–1945: The Origins of the Cold War.* Stanford, Ca.: Stanford University Press, 1995.

Radzinsky, Edward. *Stalin.* New York: Doubleday, 1996.

Rajsfus, Maurice. *Jeudi noir: la rafle du 16 Juillet 1942.* Paris: Manya, 1992

Rees, David. *Harry Dexter White: A Study in Paradox.* London: Macmillan, 1973.

Remarque, Erich Maria. *All Quiet on the Western Front,* trans. Brian Murdoch. London: Vintage, 1996.

Rémond, René, and Bourdin, Janine (eds.). *Edouard Daladier, Chef de Gouvernement, avril 1938–septembre 1939.* Paris: Fondation Nationale des Sciences Politiques, 1977.

Reuth, Ralf Georg. *Goebbels.* Munich: Piper, 1990.

Revel, Jean-François. *La Grande Parade: essai sur la survie de l'utopie socialiste.* Paris: Plon, 2000.

Richie, Alexandra. *Faust's Metropolis: A History of Berlin.* New York: Carroll & Graf, 1998.

Rocolle, Pierre. *Le Sac de Berlin, avril–mai 1945.* Paris: Armand Colin, 1992.

Rokossovsky, Konstantin K. *A Soldier's Duty.* Moscow: Progress Publishers, 1970.

Rossi, Jacques. *Le Manuel du Goulag.* Paris: Cherche Midi, 1997.

—— *Qu'elle était belle cette utopie: chronique du Goulag,* Paris: Cherche Midi, 2000.

Roussel, Eric. *Charles de Gaulle.* Paris: Gallimard, 2002.

Rucker, Laurent. *Staline, Israël et les Juifs.* Paris: Presses Universitaires de France, 2001.

Rundell, Walter. *Military Money: A Fiscal History of the US Army Overseas in World War II.* College Station, Texas: Texas A&M University Press, 1980.

Rusan, Romulus, et al. 'Le système répressif communiste de Roumanie', in Stéphane Courtois et al. (eds.), *Du passé faisons table rase!,* 369–444.

Ryan, Cornelius. *The Longest Day.* New York: Simon & Schuster, 1959.

—— *A Bridge Too Far.* New York: Simon & Schuster, 1974.

—— *The Last Battle.* New York: Pocket Books, 1967.

Rystad, Göran (ed.). *The Uprooted: Forced Migration as an International Problem in the Post-War Era.* Lund, Sweden: Lund University Press, 1990

Sainsbury, Keith. *Churchill and Roosevelt at War: The War They Fought and the Peace They Hoped to Make.* London: Macmillan, 1994.

Sampson, Anthony. *Macmillan: A Study in Ambiguity.* London: Allen Lane, 1967.

Sapiro, Gisèle. *La Guerre des écrivains, 1940–1953.* Paris: Fayard, 1999.

Sartre, Jean-Paul. *Modern Times: Selected Non-Fiction,* ed. Geoffrey Wall, trans. Robin Buss. London: Penguin, 2000.

—— *Situations, III: lendemains de guerre.* Paris: Gallimard, 1949.

Schäfer, Hans Dieter. *Berlin in Zweiten Weltkrieg.* Munich: Piper, 1991.

Schenk, Ernst-Günther. *Ich sah Berlin sterben.* Herford: Nicolaische Verlagsbuchhandlung, 1970.

Schramm, Wilhelm von. *Aufstand der Generale: Der 20. Juli in Paris.* Munich: Kindler, 1964.

Schukman, Harold (ed.). *Stalin's Generals.* London: Phoenix, 1997.

Seaton, Colonel Albert. *The Battle for Moscow.* New York: Sarpedon, 1971.

Sebald, W. G. *On the Natural History of Destruction,* trans. Anthea Bell. London: Hamish Hamilton, 2003.

Semprun, Jorge. *La Mort qu'il faut.* Paris: Gallimard, 2001.

Sereny, Gitta. *Albert Speer: His Battle with Truth.* London: Macmillan, 1995.

Shalamov, Varlam, see Chalamov, Varlam.

Singer, Isaac Bashevis. *The Manor,* trans. Joseph Singer and Elaine Gottlieb. Harmondsworth, Middlesex: Penguin, 1975.

—— *The Death of Methuselah and Other Stories.* London: Cape, 1988.

Skidelsky, Robert. *John Maynard Keynes.* Vol. III: *Fighting for Britain 1937–1946.* London: Macmillan, 2000.

Skorzeny, Otto. *Special Mission.* London: Futura, n.d.

Skrjabina, Elena. *The Allies on the Rhine 1945–1950,* trans. Norman Luxenburg. Carbondale, Ill.: Southern Illinois University Press, 1980.

Solzhenitsyn, Alexander I. *The Gulag Archipelago 1918–1956*, trans. Thomas P. Whitney and Harry Willetts, ed. Edward E. Ericson. New York: HarperCollins, 2002.

Speer, Albert. *Inside the Third Reich: Memoirs*, trans. Richard and Clara Winston. New York: Macmillan Company, 1970.

Stalin, Joseph. *Discours et ordres du jour, 1941–1945*. Paris: Editions France-URSS, 1945.

—— *Speech delivered . . . at meeting of voters, 9 February 1946*. Washington: Information Bulletin of the Embassy of the USSR, March 1946.

Steiner, George. *Real Presences*. London: Faber & Faber, 1989.

Steinhoff, Johannes, Pechel, Peter, and Showalter, Dennis. *Voices from the Third Reich: An Oral History*. Washington DC: Regnery Gateway, 1989.

Szpilman, Władysław. *The Pianist*. London: Phoenix, 2000.

Talleyrand-Périgord, C. M. de. *Mémoires*. Paris: Plon, 1982.

Taylor, A. J. P. *The Origins of the Second World War*. Greenwich, Conn.: Fawcett, 1968.

Terry, Sarah Meiklejohn. *Poland's Place in Europe*. Princeton, NJ: Princeton University Press, 1983.

Thalmann, Rita. *Etre Femme sous la Troisième Reich*. Paris: Robert Laffont, 1981.

Theoharis, Athan G. (ed.). *Beyond the Hiss Case: The FBI, Congress, and the Cold War*. Philadelphia: Temple University Press, 1982.

Thorwald, Jürgen (pseud. Heinz Bongartz). *Das Ende an der Elbe*. Stuttgart: Steingrüben, 1950.

—— *Flight in Winter*, trans. Fred Wieck. London: Hutchinson, 1953

Toland, John. *Battle: The Story of the Bulge*. New York: Random House, 1959.

—— *The Last Hundred Days*. London: Phoenix, 1966.

Tolstoy, Nikolai. *Victims of Yalta*. London: Hodder & Stoughton, 1978.

—— *The Minister and the Massacres*. London: Hutchinson, 1986.

Tournoux, J-R. *Pétain et de Gaulle*. Paris: Plon, 1954.

Trevor-Roper, Hugh. *The Last Days of Hitler*. Chicago, Ill.: University of Chicago Press, 1992.

Tribouillard, Edouard. *Caen après la bataille: la survie dans les ruines*. Rennes: Editions Ouest-France, 1993.

Tucker, Robert C. *Stalin in Power*. New York: W. W. Norton, 1990.

Tusa, Ann, and Tusa, John. *The Nuremberg Trial*. London: BBC, 1995.

Ulam, Adam B. *Stalin: The Man and His Era*. New York: Viking, 1973.

Vidal, Gore. *The Golden Age*. New York: Abacus, 2001.

Volkogonov, Dmitri. *Staline: Triomphe et tragédie*, trans. Yvan Mignot. Paris: Flammarion, 1991.

Warlimont, Walter. *Inside Hitler's Headquarters 1939–45*, trans. R. H. Barry. New York: Praeger, 1964.

Warner, Geoffrey. *Pierre Laval and the Eclipse of France*. London: Eyre & Spottiswoode, 1968.

Webster, Paul. *Pétain's Crime: The Full Story of French Collaboration in the Holocaust*. London: Macmillan, 1990.

Wedemeyer, Albert C. *Wedemeyer Reports!* New York: Henry Holt, 1958.

Weinberg, Gerhard L. *A World at Arms: A Global History of World War II*. Cambridge: Cambridge University Press, 1994.

Weinstein, Allen. *Perjury: The Hiss–Chambers Case*. New York: Random House, 1997.

Wellers, Georges. 'A propos d'un crime oublié'. *Le Monde juif*, no. 138, April–June 1990, 84–103.

Werth, Alexander. *De Gaulle: A Political Biography*. New York: Simon & Schuster, 1965.

—— *Moscow War Diary*. New York: Knopf, 1942.

—— *Poland Today*. New York: Polish Research and Information Service, 1948.

—— *Russia at War 1941–1945*. London: Barrie & Rockliff, 1964.

—— *Russia: The Postwar Years*. London: Robert Hale, 1971.

Werth, Nicolas. 'Collectivisation forcée et dékoulakisation', in Courtois et al., *Le Livre noir sur le communisme*.

West, Nigel, *VENONA: The Greatest Secret of the Cold War*. London: HarperCollins, 1999.

Wexler, Imanuel. *The Marshall Plan Revisited: The European Recovery Program in Economic Perspective*. Westport, Conn.: Greenwood Press, 1983.

White, Peter. *With the Jocks: A Soldier's Struggle for Europe 1944–45*. London: Sutton, 2001.

Whiting, Charles. *The Battle of the Bulge: Britain's Untold Story*. London: Sutton, 2003.

Williams, Charles. *The Last Great Frenchman: A Life of General de Gaulle*. London: Abacus, 1995.

—— *Adenauer: The Father of the New Germany*. London: Little, Brown, 2000.

Wistrich, Robert. *Who's Who in Nazi Germany*. London, Weidenfeld & Nicolson, 1982.

Woodward, Sir Llewellyn. *British Foreign Policy in the Second World War*. London: HMSO, 1962.

Wormser, Simone Olivier. *Deux années à Moscou*. Paris: Julliard, 1985.

Wyman, Mark. *DP: Europe's Displaced Persons*. Philadelphia: Balch Institute Press, 1989.

Young, Hugo. *This Blessed Plot: Britain and Europe from Churchill to Blair*. London: Macmillan, 1998.

Young, James Sterling. 'The Washington Comunity, 1800–28', in Kramer and Holborn (eds.), *The City in American Life*, 57–73.

Zaremba, Zygmunt. *La Commune de Varsovie: Le nouvel impérialisme russe*. Paris: Spartacus, 1982.

Zawodny, J. K. *Nothing But Honour: The Story of the Warsaw Uprising, 1944*. London: Macmillan, 1978.

Ziegler, Philip. *London at War 1939–1945*. London: Arrow, 1998.

Zweig, Ronald W. *German Reparations and the Jewish World: A History of the Claims Conference*. London: Frank Cass, 2001.

Index

𝜰

Note: Ranks and titles are generally the highest mentioned in the text.

716